Mediation and Negotiation: Reaching Agreement in Law and Business

Second Edition

Mediation and Negotiation: Reaching Agreement in Law and Business

Second Edition

E. WENDY TRACHTE-HUBER
Principal
Trachte-Huber Consulting

STEPHEN K. HUBER
Foundation Professor of Law
University of Houston Law Center

Library of Congress Cataloging-in-Publication Data

Trachte-Huber, E. Wendy

Mediation and negotiation : reaching agreement in law and business / E. Wendy Trachte-Huber, Stephen K. Huber. — 2nd ed.

   p. cm.

Includes index.

ISBN 9781422421376 (hardbound)

1. Dispute resolution (Law) — United States. 2. Negotiation — United States. 3. Mediation — United States Huber, Stephen K. II. Title.

KF9084.T73 2007

347.73'9 — dc22   2007005722

NOTE TO USERS

To ensure that you are using the latest materials available in this area, please be sure to periodically check the LexisNexis Law School web site for downloadable updates and supplements at www.lexisnexis.com/ lawschool

---

Editorial Offices
744 Broad Street, Newark, NJ 07102 (973) 820-2000
201 Mission St., San Francisco, CA 94105-1831 (415) 908-3200
701 East Water Street, Charlottesville, VA 22902-7587 (804) 972-7600
www.lexis.com

(Pub.3557)

DEDICATION

To Our Children: Jennifer and Robert

In Memory of: Penelope Daniels Pearson

PREFACE

The best thing about the second edition of any book is that there is sufficient felt need and demand for the work to warrant a second, and updated, version thereof. When we started work on the first edition, many scoffed that there was little to write about in this "emerging" field. As many others have recognized in the decade since our last edition, there is much to write and think about in the dispute resolution field. The changes since the turn of the century are extensive, as nearly all courts of larger metropolitan areas have adopted one or more forms of dispute resolution in their case management activities. We also see more recognition that the most important business skill one can possess today is the ability to negotiate effectively. Even though this skill is recognized as a core competency, we see course offerings as spotty at best in our business and law curricula. The root word for negotiation is to carry on business and those who speak Spanish recognize the similarity for the word for business: *negocio*.

Our perspective is one of an academic-practitioner and a practitioner-academic. We bring practical lessons to intense theoretical concepts. We consider business and legal education. We believe that excellence in dispute resolution requires a thorough grounding in both theory and practice, with each deepening an understanding of the other. In terms of course structure, the theory is found largely in the readings, while most classes are devoted to practice — and how it is informed by theory.

The subject matter of these teaching materials is consensual dispute resolution processes, predominantly mediation and negotiation. We examine most of the processes and issues associated with what is commonly called alternative dispute resolution (ADR). The major omission from the ADR canon is arbitration, although we do provide brief consideration of binding private arbitration (in Chapter 11) and court-annexed arbitration (in Chapter Ten). Arbitration has become such an important topic that it has become a separate course. See Stephen K. Huber & Maureen A. Weston, ARBITRATION: CASES AND MATERIALS (2d. ed. 2006).

These materials focus on business transactions, defined broadly to include employment and consumer disputes. The only important exceptions are two forays into criminal law. Plea bargaining is examined in Chapter Six as an important example of negotiation, and victim-offender mediation (VOM) is discussed in Chapter Nine as an interesting use of mediation. Criminal matters present uniquely difficult challenges, and thus present an excellent basis for thinking about negotiation and mediation. The central omission, compared to other books about dispute resolution, is the total exclusion of family matters, notably divorce and child custody.

This book can be used for a variety of courses including Introduction to ADR, Negotiation, Mediation, Mediation Advocacy, and Mediation & Negotiation.

We combine negotiation and mediation in a single book because mediation is simply, albeit importantly, facilitated negotiation. These materials are designed for use in graduate level courses in law schools, business schools, and the social sciences. However, we have also used these materials to teach dispute resolution to undergraduate students at Rice University, which leads us to conclude that strong college students are capable of handling this challenging subject matter. Our thoughts and specific suggestions for using these materials for teaching each of these different audiences are found in the accompanying Teacher's Manual.

These materials include a relatively large number of cases compared to other ADR materials, but fewer cases than are typical for law school courses (and also law courses taught elsewhere in a graduate school setting). There are ample cases for teachers who want to undertake serious case analysis, although this is not recommended for law school courses due to the extensive focuses on judicial decisions in other courses.

Many of the authors whose works appear in this book have strong views on dispute resolution issues, and no effort is made to hide them. Indeed, many of the pieces presented here were selected precisely because they represent diverse points of view. We have exercised due diligence and "best efforts" to present works that are serious and accurate, but the reader must also remember that the authors often are advocates for particular positions.

This book is divided into five Parts and sixteen Chapters, which we briefly outline here. Further detail is found in the opening section of each chapter. Part I (Chapters One to Three) introduces the subject matter of the course, and examines dispute resolution generally. The focus of these chapters is alternative dispute resolution (ADR), but it is important to recognize that judicial trials are one of the many alternative ways to resolve disputes. In Chapter One we introduce the array of approaches to disputes. Then we turn to the modern ADR movement, and offer several different perspectives on public and private approaches to addressing disputes.

Chapter Two is devoted to communications, both the theory and the practice. Effective communication is a core competence for effective interactions with others, and particularly for reaching agreements and resolving disputes. Our experience is that while a few students learned quite a bit about communications theory and psychology in college, many other students learned almost nothing about this topic. The readings provide the theory, and "hands on" exercises provide the practice.

Chapter Three explores the contributions of various social sciences to thinking about disputes and disputing processes. These include rational choice (economics), game theory, psychology, agency theory and anthropology. Particular attention is given to two important models of behavior: the Tragedy of the Commons and the Prisoner's Dilemma.

Part II (Chapters Four to Six) introduces negotiation, the core dispute resolution process. Chapter Four offers several models of negotiation, followed by a
consideration of strategies for successful negotiation and important factors that
impact the negotiation process. The theory is presented in the readings, and
should be supplemented with negotiation exercises that allow for the practical
application of negotiation principles. Chapter Five is devoted to trans-national
and cross-cultural considerations in negotiation. At the trans-national level,
we focus on negotiation in Japan, and examine the clash of American and
Japanese attitudes and approaches to negotiation. There are also many cultures
within a nation, and cultural factors have an important impact on negotiations
among people from the same culture or community.

Chapter Six is devoted to negotiation applications. Two major areas are considered in depth: commercial (including consumer) transactions, and plea bargaining in criminal cases. Business transactions are the central focus of these
materials, while plea bargaining might be regarded as the single most important negotiation context because nothing less than the liberty of the subject is
at issue. The legislation process is considered here because the dance of legislation can be viewed as a collection of negotiations. Finally, we examine negotiation conduct of questionable integrity — a category that ranges from lying,
through dishonesty to misrepresentation are commonly employed. We consider
concerns about fairness in negotiation when the endowments of the parties,
measured by power, wealth, education and similar factors, are significantly
different. Of course, these factors are also applicable, *mutatis mutandis*, to
other disputing processes.

Part III is composed of three chapters devoted to mediation — facilitated
negotiation. Chapter Seven commences with mediation theory and then turns
to mediation practice. Once again, the use of participatory exercises is essential
to understanding the mediation process. In Chapter Eight, we consider several
important mediation topics. The first is the law of mediation — and, ironically,
there turns out to be a considerable amount of relevant law. Perhaps the defining characteristic of mediated processes is that the parties disclose information
in confidence to the mediator (or other third party neutral). Confidentiality is
much discussed in legislation, notably the Uniform Mediation Act, academic
commentary, and case law. The next major topic is mediation advocacy — what
it is and when advocacy is appropriate in mediation. Good faith participation in
mediation is considered in Chapter Eleven, because the good faith participation
most commonly arises in the context of court-connected mediation.

Chapter Nine is devoted to mediation applications. From the many possibilities, we selected three arenas where mediation plays an important role. Mediation in the medical setting encompasses a variety to topics, from insurance
coverage disputes to bioethics issues to malpractice claims. Huge sums of money
are involved, and the number of disputes is vast, so mediation will continue to
have a central role in the resolution of medical care disputes. The next topic is
Victim Offender Mediation (VOM). Attempting to reconcile victims and offend-

ers of criminal action offers an extremely difficult challenge for mediation and mediators, which makes an examination of VOM particularly interesting and important. The final topic, mediators as business deal makers, is more speculative than those just mentioned, because mediators are not commonly retained to facilitate business transactions. However, if mediation really can bring value to parties in disputes with one another, it seems they should be able to add value in assisting willing parties in reaching mutually beneficial deals.

Chapters One to Nine constitute the core of the course, because they thoroughly cover negotiation and mediation. Much of what follows might be regarded as variants on already established themes. In Part IV (Chapters Ten to Fourteen), we examine additional ADR processes and procedures that involve the use of a third party neutral. Chapter Ten considers court-connected ADR processes. Absent contrary agreement by the parties, these processes are necessarily consensual. While courts cannot require litigants to reach an agreement, they generally can require parties to participate in (and pay for) mediation or some other settlement process. Although mediation is the most common court-connected settlement process, we here focus our attention on three other approaches: early neutral evaluation (ENE), summary jury trial (SJT), and (non-binding) arbitration.

Assuming that a court can require parties to participate in an ADR process, there remains the question of what level of participation may be required — sometimes referred to as a requirement of good faith participation. Put another way, can a party be required to do any more than show up and listen? — while adopting a settlement position of millions for defense but not one cent for tribute? Special considerations may apply when the party is the government rather than a private party. We close the chapter with mediation at the appellate court level. Because the parameters of the dispute have been defined and narrowed by the trial court decision, mediation at the behest of an appellate tribunal is often successful.

In Chapter Eleven we turn to private ADR processes other than mediation. We start with the mini-trial, which calls for the participation of senior executives in business disputes. Then we turn to an extensive examination of private binding arbitration. Arbitration is sweeping the American legal landscape as a form of binding dispute resolution, but that subject is largely beyond the scope of this course. Collaborative law, in which settlement counsel agree in advance not to serve as litigation counsel if the dispute cannot be settled, is the newest star in the dispute resolution firmament. Heretofore, collaborative law has been largely limited to family law disputes, but this approach could readily be extended to other types of disputes. The Ombudsman originally was a Swedish official who assisted persons who had problems in their who had dealings with the government. In America, ombuds have spread from the public to the private sector, and this approach is now widely used in businesses and universities. Partnering and dispute review boards are widely used for large dollar construction projects.

Chapter Twelve considers the many ways in which ADR is employed by the government, which means the Executive Branch (which executes the laws enacted by the legislature). The Administrative Dispute Resolution Act (1990, as amended in 1996) committed the executive branch, under the leadership of the Department of Justice, to comprehensive reliance on ADR in addressing present and potential disputes. Today the federal government is a leader in using ADR for all manner of disputes, both large and small. There are also numerous initiatives at the state and local government level, but it is difficult to generalize about them. A useful exercise is to have students search for and report on local examples of government ADR.

Specific examples of government use of ADR are numerous, and we limit our discussion to a few examples. One instance is the process used by the Department of Justice to address claims arising under the Federal Tort Claims Act (FTCA). Farmer-Lender mediation illustrates the joint dispute resolution activities of federal and state agencies. The Internal Revenue Service has utilized ADR for many decades — long before anyone used the term ADR. Finally, we consider Negotiated Rulemaking — popularly known as "Reg-Neg" — a process in which all the groups interested in a federal rulemaking seek to negotiate an agreement that all can live with. The agency is not required to adopt the result of a reg-neg proceeding, but agencies usually do so, and that result commonly is not subject to judicial challenge.

Chapter Thirteen examines the law, policy, and practice related to the settlement of disputes. This might seem to be a strange topic in the midst of a book devoted to the settlement of disputes. The central goal is to critically examine the values of settlement, and whether compromise is always the best approach. We also examine contemporary settlement practices. Although trials (often with the use of a jury) are central to the law school experience and television shows about law, in fact most cases settle (and most disputes settle without ever becoming cases). We close the chapter with an examination of the quite considerable body of law related to the enforcement of purported settlement agreements.

Chapter Fourteen considers the impact of the technology revolution on the nature of disputing, and the manner in which disputes are processed in our brave new world of instant communication. Both of your authors are over 40, and we are less comfortable making use of the modern tools for exchanging information than are our children, but it is clear that the manner in which disputing parties interact with one another will change dramatically over time, and ever fewer interactions will take the form of a single face-to-face, in person meeting. We are confident that dispute resolution, and the lives of dispute resolution professionals, will change dramatically during the 21st century, even if we are presently unable to predict the nature and extent of these changes in any detail.

In Part V (Chapters Fifteen and Sixteen), the focus shifts from disputing processes to dispute resolution professionals. Chapter Fifteen considers qualifications for dispute resolution professionals, as well as potential errors and omissions liability ("malpractice" is such an ugly word). Fortunately for mediators, professional liability is an entirely theoretical concern, and even if a basis for liability was found the measure of damages would be modest. With the increasing importance of mediation, and more persons devoting a considerable portion of their professional careers to mediating, there has arisen a movement for credentialing (mandatory or voluntary) of mediators. There is considerable fear regarding this approach by many dispute resolution practitioners, who regard credentialing as a strategy by attorneys to exclude others from (paying) mediation practice.

Chapter Sixteen addresses planning for and avoiding disputes, a process that often goes by the name of systems design. Good business and commercial planners think about potential disputes before they happen, and make plans so that they never happen — or, if a dispute does arise, its impact will be minimal. Such planning, accompanied by staff training, is an attractive option in the workplace because employers and employees are engaged in a common enterprise on a long term basis. We offer several examples of dispute resolution planning in several employment contexts. Finally, we offer three examples of planning for and managing conflict: construction bid protest processes; implementing ADR in the Coast Guard; and health care.

The Teacher's Manual presents exercises, problems, and role plays, along with suggestions about their use to further pedagogical goals. It also includes further guidance on the use of these materials, confidential facts for participants in role plays, and additional "hands on" exercises and problems. Most of the textual material can be understood by graduate students without extensive classroom discussion; in teaching these materials we devote much class time to dispute resolution exercises, followed by debriefing and discussion.

ACKNOWLEDGMENTS

We are indebted to the authors of the articles and judicial opinions whose work we have used in this book. In many instances, we know these writers only by the excellence of their work product; in others they are also friends. We also are in the debt of our students — notably at the University of Houston (Law and MBA), Rice University, and Pepperdine Law School — who have taught us so much about disputes and disputing.

Much assistance was provided to us by the good people at LexisNexis, notably Jennifer Beszley, Christopher Sollog, and Sean Caldwell. The librarians at the University of Houston Law Library, notably Peter Egler, provided considerable assistance in locating both legal and other materials. This book could not have been completed without considerable help from Michelle Ozuna and Debora Rebollar. Our law student daughter Jennifer Trachte provided able research assistance. A research grant from the University of Houston Law Foundation was important, and is hereby gratefully acknowledged.

Few observations are truly original, and most of what we know represents the ideas of others, or at least is based on what we hear and read. We cannot do better than to borrow from Rudyard Kipling, who limned the class acknowledgment of the obligation of authors to the work of others.

When 'Omer Smote 'is Bloomin Lyre

When 'Omer smote 'is bloomin lyre,
He'd 'eard men sing by land an' sea;
An' what he thought 'e might require,
'E went an' took — the same as me!

The market girls an' fisherman,
The shepards an' the sailors too,
They 'eard old songs turn up again,
But kept it quiet — same as you!

They knew 'e stole; 'e knew they knowed.
They didn't tell, or make a fuss,
But winked at 'Omer down the road,
An' 'e winked back — the same as us!

Strikingly, Kipling chose this poem, rather than his much more famous *Recessional*, as the final piece in his collected poems.

Abramson, Harold, *Problem-Solving Advocacy in Mediations: A Model of Client Representation,* 10 HARV. NEGOT. L. REV. 103 (2005). Copyright © 2005. Reprinted with permission.

Adler, Robert S., *Flawed Thinking: Addressing Decision Biases in Negotiation,* 20 OHIO ST. J. ON DISP. RESOL. 683 (2005). Copyright © 2005. Reprinted with permission.

Alfini, James J., *Trashing, Bashing, and Hashing It Out: Is this the End of "Good Mediation"?,* 19 FLA. ST. U. L. REV. 47 (1991). Copyright © 1991. Originally published in the *Florida State University Law Review.* Reprinted with permission.

Armstrong, Phillip M., *Georgia-Pacific's ADR Program: A Critical Review After 10 Years,* 60-JUL DISP. RESOL. J. 19 (2005). Copyright © 2005. Reprinted with permission.

Arnold, Tom, *Twenty Common Errors In Mediation Advocacy,* ADR TODAY, Spring 1995, at 2. Copyright © 1995. Reprinted with permission.

ATWATER, EASTWOOD, I HEAR YOU 1-3, 165-74 (1992). Copyright © 1992. Reprinted with permission.

Bald, Ronald J. & Ungar, Evette E., *An Alternative Dispute Resolution Systems Design for the United States Coast Guard,* 3 J. AM. ARB. 111 (2004). Copyright © 2004. Reprinted with permission.

BEDMAN, WILLIAM L., ADR: THE HALLIBURTON EXPERIENCE, *available at* Mediate.com (2002). Copyright © 2002. Reprinted with permission.

Bernard, Phyllis E., *Mediating with an 800-Pound Gorilla,* 60 WASH. & LEE L. REV. 1417 (2004). Copyright © 2004. Reprinted with permission.

Bibas, Stephanos, *Plea Bargaining Outside the Shadow of Trial,* 117 HARV. L. REV. 2463 (2004). Copyright © 2004. Reprinted with permission.

BINDER, DAVID A., BERGMAN, PAUL & PRICE, SUSAN C., LAWYERS AS COUNSELORS 69-81, 237-50 (1991). Copyright © 1991 West Publishing Company. All rights reserved. Reprinted by permission.

Blumberg, Abraham S., *The Practice of Law as a Confidence Game,* 1 LAW & SOC'Y REV. 15 (1967). Copyright © 1967. Reprinted with permission.

Braeutigam, Andrea, *Fusses that Fit Online: Online Mediation in Non-Commercial Contexts,* 5 APPALACHIAN L.J. 275 (2006). Copyright © 2006. Reprinted with permission.

Brazil, Wayne D., *Should Court-Sponsored ADR Survive?,* 21 OHIO ST. J. ON DISP. RESOL. 241, 242-44, 252-258 (2006). Copyright © 2006. Reprinted with permission.

Brown, Jennifer Gerarda, *Creativity and Problem-Solving,* 87 MARQ. L. REV. 697 (2004). Copyright © 2004. Reprinted with permission.

Brown, Jennifer Gerarda, *The Use of Mediation to Resolve Criminal Cases: A Procedural Critique*, 43 EMORY L.J. 1247 (1994). Copyright © 2004. Reprinted with permission.

BUSH, ROBERT BARUCH & FOLGER, JOSEPH P., THE PROMISE OF MEDIATION: RESPONDING TO CONFLICT THROUGH EMPOWERMENT AND RECOGNITION 15-27 (1994). Copyright © 1994. Reprinted with permission.

Coben, James R. & Thompson, Peter N., *Disputing Irony: A Systematic Look at Litigation About Mediation*, 11 HARV. NEGOT. L. REV. 43 (2006). Copyright © 2005. Reprinted with permission.

Cole, Sarah Rudolph, *Mediator Certification: Has the Time Come?*, 11-3 DISP. RESOL. MAG. 7 (Spring 2005). Copyright © 2005. Reprinted with permission.

CONSTANTINO, CATHY A. & MERCHANT, CHRISTINA SICKLES, DESIGNING CONFLICT MANAGEMENT SYSTEMS — A GUIDE TO CREATING PRODUCTIVE AND HEALTHY ORGANIZATIONS 19-32, 117-33 (1995). Copyright © 1995. Reprinted with permission of John Wiley & Sons, Inc.

Cooley, John W., *Defining the Ethical Limits of Acceptable Deception in Mediation*, 4 PEPP. DISP. RESOL. L.J. 263 (2004). Copyright © 2004. Reprinted with permission.

Craver, Charles B., *Negotiation Ethics: How to Be Deceptive Without Being Dishonest; How to Be Assertive Without Being Offensive*, 38 S. TEX. L. REV. 713 (1997). Copyright © 1997. Reprinted with permission.

Craver, Charles B., *The Negotiation Process*, 27 AM. J. TRIAL ADVOC. 271 (2003). Copyright © 2003. Reprinted with permission.

Craver, Charles B., *Negotiation Styles: The Impact on Bargaining Transactions*, 58-APR DISP. RESOL. J. 48 (2003). Copyright © 2003 American Arbitration Association. Reprinted with permission.

Crowne, Caroline Harris, *The Alternative Dispute Resolution Act of 1998: Implementing a New Paradigm of Justice*, 76 N.Y.U. L. REV. 1768 (2001). Copyright © 2001. Reprinted with permission.

Delgado, Richard; Dunn, Chris; Brown, Pamela; Lee, Helena & Hubbert, David, *Fairness and Formality: Minimizing the Risk of Prejudice in Alternative Dispute Resolution*, 1985 WIS. L. REV. 1359. Copyright © 1985. Reprinted with permission.

DEMENTE, BOYE LAFAYETTE, HOW TO DO BUSINESS WITH THE JAPANESE: A COMPLETE GUIDE TO JAPANESE CUSTOMS AND BUSINESS PRACTICES (1993). Copyright © 1993. Reprinted with permission of the McGraw-Hill Companies.

Docherty, Jayne Seminare, *Culture and Negotiation: Symmetrical Anthropology for Negotiators*, 87 MARQ. L. REV. 711 (2004). Copyright © 2004 Reprinted with permission.

Girardi, Debra, *The Culture of Health Care: How Professional and Organizational Cultures Impact Conflict Management*, 21 GA. ST. U. L. REV. 857, 884-890 (2005). Copyright © 2005. Reprinted with permission.

Gordon, Daniel I., *Constructing a Bid Protest Process: The Choices that Every Procuremen Challenge System Must Make*, 35 PUB. CONT. L.J. 427 (2006). Copyright © 2006 by the American Bar Association. Reprinted with permission.

Hadfield, Gillian K., *Delivering Legality on the Internet: Developing Principles for the Private Provision of Commercial Law*, 6 AM. L. & ECON. REV. 154 (2004). Copyright © 2004. Reprinted with permission.

Harmon, Kathleen M. J., *Construction Conflicts and Dispute Review Boards: Attitudes and Opinions of Construction Industry Members*, 58-JAN DISP. RESOL. J. 66 (2004). Copyright © 2004. Reprinted with permission.

Harter, Philip J., *Ombuds: A Voice for the People*, 11 DISP. RESOL. MAG. 5 (Winter 2005). Copyright © 2005. Reprinted with permission.

Hodgson, James Day, Sano, Yoshihiro & Graham, John L., DOING BUSINESS WITH THE NEW JAPAN 33-46 (2000). Copyright © 2000 by Rowman & Littlefield Publishing Group. Reprinted with permission.

Jolls, Christine, Sunstein, Cass R. & Thaler, Richard A., *Behavioral Approach to Law and Economics*, 50 STAN. L. REV. 1471 (1998). Copyright © 1998. Reprinted with permission.

Korobkin, Russell, Moffitt, Michael & Welsh, Nancy, *The Law of Bargaining*, 87 MARQ. L. REV. 839 (2004). Copyright © 2004. Reprinted with permission.

Lande, John, *Using Dispute System Design Methods to Promote Good Faith Participation in Court-Connected Mediation Programs*, 50 UCLA L. REV. 69 (2002). Copyright © 2002. Reprinted with permission.

Larson, David Allen, *Technology Mediated Dispute Resolution (TMDR): A New Paradigm for ADR*, 21 OHIO ST. J. ON DISP. RESOL. 629 (2006). Copyright © 2006. Reprinted with permission.

Lawrence, James K.L., *Mediation Advocacy: Partnering with the Mediator*, 15 OHIO ST. J. ON DISP. RESOL. 425 (2000). Copyright © 2000. Reprinted with permission.

Lax, David A. & Sebenius, James K., *Interests: The Measure of Negotiation*, 2 NEGOT. J. 73 (1986). Copyright © 1986. Reprinted with permission.

Lebed, Marc R. & McCauley, John J., *Mediation Within the Health Care Industry: Hurdles and Opportunities*, 21 GA. ST. U. L. REV. 911 (2005). Copyright © 2005. Reprinted with permission.

LeResche, Diane, *A Comparison of the American Mediation Process with a Korean-American Harmony Restoration Process*, 9 MEDIATION Q. 323 (1992). Copyright © 1992. Reprinted with permission.

Libbey, Colleen A., *Working Together While Waltzing in a Mine Field: Successful Government Construction Contract Dispute Resolution with Partnering and Dispute Review Boards*, 15 OHIO ST. J. ON DISP. RESOL. 825 (2000). Copyright © 2000. Reprinted with permission.

Lieberman, Jethro K. & Henry, James F., *Lessons from the Alternative Dispute Resolution Movement*, 53 U. CHI. L. REV. 424, 427-29, 432-35 (1986). Copyright © 1986. Reprinted with permission.

Lodder, Arno R. & Zeleznikow, John, *Developing an Online Dispute Resolution Environment: Dialogue Tools and Negotiation Support Systems in a Three-Step Model*, 10 HARV. NEGOT. L. REV. 287 (2005). Copyright © 2005. Reprinted with permission.

Louthan, Thomas Carter, *Building a User-Friendly Internal Revenue Service: ADR Programs are Set for Taxpayer Use*, 18 ALTERNATIVES TO HIGH COST LITIG. 1 (Jan. 2000). Copyright © 2000. Reprinted with permission of John Wiley & Sons, Inc.

MARCH, ROBERT M., THE JAPANESE NEGOTIATOR 15-17 (1990). Copyright © 1990 Kodansha International Ltd. Reprinted with permission.

Mathews, Gregory P., *Using Negotiation, Mediation and Arbitration to Resolve IRS-Taxpayer Disputes*, 19 OHIO ST. J. ON DISP. RESOL. 709 (2004). Copyright © 2004. Reprinted with permission.

McEwen, Craig, *Giving Meaning to Mediator Professionalism*, 11-3 DISP. RESOL. MAG. 3 (Spring 2005). Copyright © 2005. Reprinted with permission.

McMillan, Daniel D. & Rubin, Robert A., *Dispute Review Boards: Key Issues, Recent Case Law, And Standard Agreements*, 25-SPG CONSTRUCTION LAW. 14 (2005). Copyright © 2005. Reprinted with permission.

McThenia, Andrew W. & Shaffer, Thomas L., *For Reconciliation*, 94 YALE L.J. 1660 (1985). Copyright © 1985. Reprinted by permission of the Yale Law Journal Company.

Meister, Jonathan D., *The Administrative Dispute Resolution Act of 1996: Will the New Era of ADR in Federal Administrative Agencies Occur at the Expense of Public Accountability?*, 13 OHIO ST. J. ON DISP. RESOL. 167 (1997). Copyright © 1997. Reprinted with permission.

Melling, Tom, *Dispute Resolution Within Legislative Institutions*, 46 STAN. L. REV. 1677 (1994). Copyright © 1994. Reprinted with permission.

Menkel-Meadow, Carrie, *Toward Another View of Legal Negotiation: The Structure of Problem Solving*, 31 UCLA L. REV. 754, 760-762 (1984). Copyright © 1984. Reprinted with permission.

Mentschikoff, Soia, *Commercial Arbitration*, 61 COLUM. L. REV. 846 (1961). Copyright © 1961. Reprinted with permission.

Moffitt, Michael, *Suing Mediators*, 83 B.U. L. REV. 147 (2003). Copyright © 2003. Reprinted with permission.

Moffitt, Michael L., *Schmediation and the Dimensions of Definition*, 10 HARV. NEGOT. L. REV. 69 (2005). Copyright © 2005. Reprinted with permission.

Nadler, Janice, *Rapport in Legal Negotiation: How Small Talk Can Facilitate E-Mail Dealmaking*, 9 HARV. NEGOT. L. REV. 223 (2004). Copyright © 2004. Reprinted with permission.

NAIPAUL, SHIVA, NORTH OF SOUTH: AN AFRICAN JOURNEY 47-52 (1978). Copyright © 1978 by Shiva Naipaul. Reprinted with the permission of Simon & Schuster Adult Publishing Group.

Peppet, Scott R., *Contract Formation in Imperfect Markets: Should We Use Mediators in Deals?*, 19 OHIO ST. J. ON DISP. RESOL. 283 (2004). Copyright © 2004. Reprinted with permission.

Pou, Jr., Charles, *Assuring Excellence or Merely Reassuring? Policy and Practice in Promoting Mediator Quality*, 2005 J. DISP. RESOL. 303. Copyright © 2005. Reprinted with permission of the author and the *Journal of Dispute Resolution*, University of Missouri-Columbia, Center for the Study of Dispute Resolution, 206 Hulston Hall, Columbia, MO 65211.

Raines, Susan R., *Mediating in Your Pajamas: The Benefits and Challenges for ODR Practitioners*, 23 CONFLICT RESOL. Q. 359 (2006). Copyright © 2006. Reprinted with permission of John Wiley & Sons, Inc.

Ramasastry, Anita, *Government-to-Citizen Online Dispute Resolution: A Preliminary Inquiry*, 79 WASH. L. REV. 159 (2004). Copyright © 2004. Reprinted with permission.

Read, Daniel Shane, *The Courts' Difficult Balancing Act to be Fair to Both Plaintiff and Government Under the FTCA's Administrative Claims Process*, 57 BAYLOR L. REV. 785 (2005). Copyright © 2005 Baylor University School of Law. All rights reserved. Reprinted by permission.

REARDON, KATHLEEN KELLY, THEY DON'T GET IT, DO THEY? COMMUNICATION IN THE WORKPLACE — LOSING THE GAP BETWEEN MEN AND WOMEN 40-45 (1995). Copyright © 1995. Reprinted with permission.

Resnik, Judith, *Many Doors? Closing Doors? Alternative Dispute Resolution and Adjudication*, 10 OHIO ST. J. ON DISP. RESOL. 211 (1995). Copyright © 1995. Reprinted with permission.

Riskin, Leonard L., *Two Concepts of Mediation in the FmHA's Farmer-Lender Mediation Program*, 45 ADMIN. L. REV. 21 (1993). Copyright © 1993. Reprinted with permission.

Robinson, Peter, *Contending with Wolves in Sheep's Clothing: A Cautiously Cooperative Approach to Mediation Advocacy*, 50 BAYLOR L. REV. 963 (1998). Copyright © 1998. Reprinted with permission.

Sternlight, Jean R., *Lawyers' Representation of Clients in Mediation: Using Economics and Psychology to Structure Advocacy in a Nonadversarial Setting*, 14 OHIO ST. J. ON DISP. RESOL. 269 (1999). Copyright © 1999. Reprinted with permission.

Stuntz, William J., *Plea Bargaining and Criminal Law's Disappearing Shadow*, 117 HARV. L. REV. 2548 (2004). Copyright © 2004. Reprinted with permission.

Suchman, Mark C. & Cahill, Mia L., *The Hired Gun as Facilitator: Lawyers and the Suppression of Business Disputes*, 21 LAW & SOC. INQUIRY 679 (1996). Copyright © 1996. Reprinted with permission.

Sylvester, Lynn & Lobel, Ira B., *The Perfect Storm: Anatomy of a Failed Regulatory Negotiation*, 59-JUL DISP. RESOL. J. 44 (2004). Copyright © 2004 American Arbitration Association. Reprinted with permission.

Taylor, Melissa Conley & Bornstein, Jackie, *Accreditation of On-Line Dispute Resolution Professionals*, 23 CONFLICT RESOL. Q. 383 (2006). Copyright © 2006. Reprinted with permission of John Wiley & Sons, Inc.

Tidmarsh, Jay, *Pound's Century and Ours*, 81 NOTRE DAME L. REV. 513 (2006). Copyright © 2006. Reprinted with permission by *Notre Dame Law Review*, University of Notre Dame.

TRACHTE-HUBER, E. WENDY, ADR SYSTEM DESIGN (1993). Copyright © 1993. Reprinted with permission.

Twining, William, *Alternatives to What? Theories of Litigation, Procedure and Dispute Settlement in Anglo-American Jurisprudence: Some Neglected Classics*, 56 MOD. L. REV. 380, 380-83, 385-87 (1993). Copyright © 1993. Reprinted with permission.

Umbreit, Mark S.; Vos, Betty; Coates, Robert B. & Lightfoot, Elizabeth, *Restorative Justice in the Twenty-First Century: A Social Movement Full of Opportunities and Pitfalls*, 89 MARQ. L. REV. 251 (2005). Copyright © 2005. Reprinted with permission.

Vidmar, Neil & Rice, *Jeffrey, Jury Determined Settlements and Summary Jury Trials*, 19 FLA. ST. U. L. REV. 89, 95-103 (1991). Copyright © 1991. Reprinted with permission.

Welsh, Nancy A., *Perceptions of Fairness in Negotiation*, 87 MARQ. L. REV. 753 (2004). Copyright © 2004. Reprinted with permission.

White, James J., *Machiavelli and the Bar: Ethical Limitations on Lying in Negotiation*, 1980 AM. B. FOUND. RES. J. 921. Copyright © 1980. Reprinted with permission.

White, James J., *Review Essay: The Pros and Cons of "Getting to YES" by Roger Fisher & William Ury*, 31 J. LEGAL EDUC. 115 (1981). Copyright © 1981. Reprinted with permission.

Young, Paula M., *Rejoice! Rejoice!, Rejoice, Give Thanks and Sing: ABA, ACR, and AAA Adopt Revised Model Standards of Conduct For Mediators*, 5 APPALACHIAN J.L. 195 (2006). Copyright © 2005. Reprinted with permission.

Young, Paula M., *Take It or Leave It, Lump It or Grieve It: Designing Mediator Complaint Systems That Protect Mediators, Unhappy Parties, Attorneys, Courts, The Process, and the Field*, 21 OHIO ST. J. ON DISP. RESOL. 721, 731-741 (2006). Copyright © 2006. Reprinted with permission.

TABLE OF CONTENTS

Part II
NEGOTIATION

Part III
MEDIATION

Part IV

ADDITIONAL PROCESSES AND APPROACHES

**Part V
DISPUTE RESOLUTION PROFESSIONALS**

Part I
ADDRESSING DISPUTES: GENERAL CONSIDERATIONS

Chapter 1

AN OVERVIEW OF DISPUTE RESOLUTION

A. INTRODUCTION

This chapter presents an overview of the multiple ways that disputes arise and are resolved. Since the central focus of this book is alternative dispute resolution (ADR) — predominantly mediation and negotiation — it is necessary to address the question, alternative to what? A large part of the answer is judicial trials, but that response is both over-inclusive and under-inclusive.

Today, ADR is commonly considered as a species of modern reform agenda. While the expanded use of ADR in recent decades has been impressive indeed, resorting to ADR was a feature of pre-Independence America. Indeed, what we call ADR was all that was available to settle disputes in early societies without formal government. To offer just one ancient instance, we all know the story of King Solomon and how he determined which of two claimants was the real mother of a baby. These materials are largely limited to recent uses of ADR, with the main emphasis being on law and practice in the United States.

The various dispute resolution options considered in this book are largely dealt with on an instrumental basis, with much attention given to the advantages and disadvantages of various ADR processes. You should not, however, lose sight of the broader implication for a society of choices about disputes and disputing.

> The varieties of dispute settlement, and the socially sanctioned choices in any culture, communicate the ideals people cherish, their perceptions of themselves, and the quality of their relationships with others. They indicate whether people wish to avoid or encourage conflict, suppress it, or resolve it amicably. Ultimately the most basic values of a society are revealed in its dispute settlement procedures. Although every society provides institutions for dispute settlement, by no means are these necessarily, or exclusively, legal institutions. Conceptions of the role of law change, and assessments of the advantages and disadvantages of submitting disputes to its processes not only shift, but exist in perpetual tension.

JEROLD AUERBACH, JUSTICE WITHOUT LAW 1 (1981).

ADR is not simply a set of options. For many, ADR is a "movement," with true believers in the cause, zealous advocates, and specialized vocabulary. There is a vast body of literature about ADR and a number of journals devoted exclusively to ADR. The existence of a common set of classifying terms does not mean that participants in the ADR movement agree on what "it" is or about how

3

ADR ought to evolve. Indeed, some of the most acrimonious disputes are between insiders who want to shape the contours and direction of the movement. These debates will be examined throughout the course. The ADR Movement is commonly said to have some combination of four objectives:

1) reduce court congestion, as well as the associated cost and delay;

2) expand and enhance community involvement in the dispute resolution process;

3) expand and facilitate access to justice; and

4) offer more and better approaches to dispute resolution.

It is important to recognize that these goals can, and often do, overlap and conflict with one another. Consider, for example, the problem of "excessive" access. If society is too ready to provide access for all kinds of disputes, this will lengthen the queue and aggravate the congestion problem. Measures designed to relieve court congestion would take a very different form from measures designed to enhance community control over dispute settlement.

Section B introduces the array of dispute resolution processes. Section C considers the origins and development of the modern alternative dispute resolution movement and asks to what ADR is the alternative. Section D considers the choice among potential ADR processes when a dispute has arisen. Section E presents some critiques of ADR developments. Our central goal here is to introduce important topics and questions that will be reconsidered throughout the course.

B. THE ARRAY OF DISPUTE RESOLUTION PROCESSES

1. The Dispute Resolution Continuum

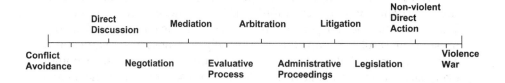

2. Core Consensual Dispute Resolution Processes: Negotiation and Mediation

The central focus of this course is negotiation — both directly and with the assistance of a third party mediator. Outcomes are based on the consent of the parties to the negotiation. Where a third person participates in the process, she assists the parties in reaching consensus, but the parties determine the contours of any agreement. The consensual processes discussed below all include elements of negotiation and the assistance of some (usually neutral) third party. Processes that produce a binding decision — binding arbitration and judicial decisions — also make use of a third party neutral but one who imposes an outcome on the disputants. A full three chapters are devoted to both Negotiation (Chapters 4 to 6) and Mediation (Chapters 5 to 7), so nothing further is said about them here.

3. Dispute Resolution Processes

There are a wide array of responses to problems or disputes that can be arranged along a continuum based on numerous factors, including:

a. from the least to the most intrusive;

b. from voluntary to involuntary; and

c. from non-binding to binding.

The listing of processes that follows, which does not fully take account of all three factors, is offered as an introductory aid for readers; the placement of the listed dispute resolution options should be regarded as an approximation.

DEFAULT POSITION

Conflict Avoidance

Deny Conflict Exists

DIRECT COMMUNICATION

Collaborative Law

Discussion Between Principals

Discussion Through Agents

Negotiation

INTERVENTION BY THIRD PARTY

Conciliation

Early Neutral Evaluation

Mediation

Mini-Trial

Moderated Settlement Conference

Negotiated Rulemaking (Reg-Neg)

Non-Binding Arbitration

Ombudsman

Shuttle Diplomacy

Summary Jury Trial

BINDING PROCESSES

Administrative Adjudication

Binding Arbitration

Judicial Trial

Mass Claims Facilities

Justice of the Peace/Small Claims Courts

EXTRA-LEGAL PROCESSES
Non-Violent Direct Action
Violence/War

Our purpose here is simply to indicate the broad range of dispute resolution processes that often are encompassed under the ADR rubric. Many of the listed processes will be discussed at greater length later in this course. Also considered will be hybrids that combine features of various ADR processes. Indeed, a major advantage of private ADR is that dispute resolution processes can be customized to fit particular situations and needs. Government-provided dispute resolution processes tend to be much less flexible — indeed, uniformity of treatment is regarded as an important value. Private processes are more amenable to adjustment to meet the needs and desires of the parties to a dispute. Parties often make use of multiple processes — in succession, or even simultaneously.

C. THE MODERN ADR MOVEMENT: ALTERNATIVE TO WHAT?

1. Modern Origins: The 1976 Pound Conference

The origin of the modern ADR movement is commonly traced to the Pound Conference sponsored by the American Bar Association in 1976, the bicentennial of the Declaration of Independence. *See, e.g.*, Laura Nader, *Controlling Processes in the Practice of Law: Hierarchy and Pacification in the Movement to Re-Form Dispute Ideology*, 9 OHIO ST. J. ON DISP. RESOL. 1 (1993) ("For my research, the turning point was 1976, the year of . . . the Roscoe Pound Conference. . . .") The conference was named after Dean Roscoe Pound in recognition of the 70th anniversary of his famous speech to the ABA: *The Causes of Popular Dissatisfaction with the Administration of Justice*, 29 A.B.A.J. 295 (1906). As long as one recognizes that tracing the origin of a movement to a particular event or date is arbitrary, dating the modern ADR movement from the Pound Conference is convenient and useful. While the expanded use of ADR since 1976 has been impressive indeed, resorting to ADR has a long history in America. Earlier ADR developments are mentioned in several places in the ensuing chapters.

If a single document evidences the founding of the modern ADR movement, it is the paper presented at the Pound Conference by Harvard Law School Professor Frank Sander. Excerpts from that paper follow after an explanation of the importance of Roscoe Pound's 1906 speech.

2. Jay Tidmarsh, *Pound's Century and Ours*, 81 NOTRE DAME L. REV. 513 (2006)

On August 29, 1906, a little known Nebraska lawyer climbed to the podium at the twenty-ninth American Bar Association convention in St. Paul, Minnesota, and commenced the most thoroughly successful revolution in American law. The success of the revolution has been so complete that it swept clean lawyers' collective memory of what it had replaced, obliterated a system that had taken centuries to construct, killed off an entire vocabulary, and inverted the way in which every lawyer — every person, really — thinks about the law. In the words of John Henry Wigmore, who was present, the speech was "the spark that kindled the white flame of progress." The lawyer was Roscoe Pound, and the title of his address was *The Causes of Popular Dissatisfaction with the Administration of Justice*, 29 Rep. A.B.A. 395 (1906), reprinted at 35 F.R.D. 273 (1964). . . .

Pound's insight was to make procedure and substance work in an integrated fashion. In England (and eventually America), procedure had dominated substance for much of the time since the eleventh century. The question often was not "What substantive right has the defendant violated?" but rather "What legal form, with what procedural attributes, must the plaintiff use to assert the claim?" As Maine famously observed, "[s]o great is the ascendancy of the Law of Actions [i.e., common law procedure] . . . that substantive law has at first the look of being gradually secreted in the interstices of procedure." SIR HENRY SUMNER MAINE, DISSERTATIONS ON EARLY LAW AND CUSTOMS 389 (Arno Press 1975) (1886); *see also* S.F.C. MILSOM, HISTORICAL FOUNDATIONS OF THE COMMON LAW 59 (2d ed. 1981) ("There was no substantive law to which pleading was adjective. These were the terms in which the law existed and in which lawyers thought.") The energy devoted to constructing a procedural system yielded dozens of technical terms — such as the praecipe quod reddat, the capias ad respondendum, the demurrer, the general issue, the plea in avoidance, the traverse, and the wager of law — whose meanings would have been clear to lawyers one hundred years ago, and whose intricacies often determined the outcome of cases.

The system for which Pound advocated was based on the classic model of equity, in which procedure (in theory) never got in the way of deciding cases on the merits. It was, as Pound said, "justice without law." Procedural rules should be general, discretionary guidelines placed into the hands of judges whose scientific administration would lead to the just determination of each case. Increased judicial involvement would constrain the excesses of the adversarial system. The substantive merits would determine the outcome. The procedural system we developed in the twentieth century clung closely to the specifics of Pound's proposals. But we never fully integrated procedure and substance. Instead, we now have a system in which the importance of substance and procedure has been inverted. Substance now dominates procedure.

3. Frank E.A. Sander, *Varieties of Dispute Processing*, 70 F.R.D. 111 (1975)

[One] way of reducing the judicial caseload is to explore alternative ways of resolving disputes outside the courts, and it is to this topic that I wish to devote my primary attention. By and large we lawyers . . . have been far too single-minded when it comes to dispute resolution. In point of fact there is a rich variety of different processes which, singly or in combination, may provide far more effective dispute resolution. Let me turn now to the two questions with which I wish to concern myself:

1) What are the significant characteristics of various alternative dispute resolution mechanisms (such as adjudication by courts, arbitration, mediation, negotiation, and various blends of these and other devices)?

2) How can these characteristics be utilized so that, given the variety of disputes that presently arise, we can begin to develop some rational criteria for allocating various types of disputes to different dispute resolution processes?

One consequence of an answer to these questions is that we will have a better sense of what cases ought to be left in the courts for resolution, and which should be "processed" in some other way. . . .

What I am advocating is a flexible and diverse panoply of dispute resolution processes, with particular types of cases being assigned to differing processes (or combinations of processes), according to . . . criteria [such as]: nature of dispute, relationship between disputants, amount at issue, cost, and speed. . . . One might envision by the year 2000 not simply a court house but a Dispute Resolution Center, where the grievant would first be channeled through a screening clerk who would then direct him to the process (or sequence of processes) most appropriate to his type of case. The room directory in the lobby of such a Center might look as follows: Screening Clerk — Room 1; Mediation — Room 2; Arbitration — Room 3; Fact Finding — Room 4; Malpractice Screening Panel — Room 5; Superior Court — Room 6; Ombudsman — Room 7.

Of one thing we can be certain: once such an eclectic method of dispute resolution is accepted there will be ample opportunity for everyone to play a part. Thus a court might decide on its own to refer a matter to a more suitable tribunal. Or a legislature might, in framing certain substantive rights, build in an appropriate dispute resolution process. Institutions such as prisons, schools, or mental hospitals also could get in the act by establishing indigenous dispute resolution processes. Here the grievance mechanism contained in the typical collective bargaining agreement (CBA) stands as an enduring example of a successful mode. Finally, once these patterns start to take hold, the law schools, too, should shift from their preoccupation with the judicial process and begin to expose students to the broad range of dispute resolution processes. . . .

It seems appropriate to end this fragmentary appraisal on a modest note. There are no panaceas; only promising avenues to explore. . . . We need more evaluation of the comparative efficacy and cost of different dispute resolution mechanisms. And we need more data on the role played by some of the key individuals in the process (e.g., lawyers). Do they exacerbate the adversary aspects of the case and drag out the proceedings (as many clients believe), or do they serve to control otherwise overly litigious clients (as trial lawyers often assert)? What is the optimal state of a country's grievance machinery so that festering grievances can be readily ventilated without unduly flooding the system and creating unreasonable expectations of relief?

Above all, we need to accumulate and disseminate the presently available learning concerning promising alternative dispute resolution mechanisms, and encourage continuing experimentation and research. In this connection we must continue to forge links with those from other disciplines who share our concerns. Their differing orientation and background often give them a novel perspective on the legal system.

4. To What Is ADR the Alternative?

a. The implicit answer to the "alternative to what?" question is alternative to formal legal process, but that response is both over-inclusive and under-inclusive. Indeed, the very approach is grounded in a legal perspective. An anthropologist would say that the topic is dealing with disputes, and that the judicial process merely represent one of the alternatives. How would you respond to the "alternative to what" question? You should revisit this question after you have learned more about ADR processes.

b. The standard answer to the "alternative to what?" question is negotiation, mediation, and arbitration, together with a variety of more specialized processes. Defining something by what it is not inevitably produces an answer that is uncertain, and lacking in internal coherence. Why, for example, is arbitration included in the ADR pantheon? Private (as opposed to court annexed) arbitration produces a (nearly always) binding decision rendered by a third neutral called an arbitrator. Arbitration strikes many observers as much closer to litigation than to consensual dispute resolution processes, because the central feature of both processes is that a third party renders a decision that binds the parties — instead of helping the parties to work out their own solution.

c. Arbitration has become such an important dispute resolution process, and has generated such a large body of applicable legal principles, that it is commonly the subject of a separate course. *See* STEPHEN K. HUBER & MAUREEN WESTON, ARBITRATION: CASES AND MATERIALS (2d ed. 2006). While there will be references to arbitration and the topic is discussed in Chapter Eleven, arbitration is not a central topic of this course.

d. The next two articles consider the nature and purpose of ADR. Jethro Lieberman is a journalist turned law professor; James Henry was for many years the President of the Center for Public Resources (CPR), a leading ADR organization. William Twining, a distinguished English law professor and a close observer of the American legal scene, seeks to place the ADR movement in a jurisprudential context. Writings by several of the American legal thinkers discussed by Twining appear later in these materials: Karl Llewellyn in Chapter Three, Lon Fuller in Chapter Seven, and Owen Fiss in Chapter Thirteen.

5. Jethro K. Lieberman & James F. Henry, *Lessons from the Alternative Dispute Resolution Movement,* 53 U. Chi. L. Rev. 424 (1986)

The ADR roster includes such well-known processes as arbitration, mediation, and negotiation. These processes can be used to settle existing disputes or to prevent disputes from developing. There are also new hybrid devices that borrow from courtroom procedure — including, most prominently, the mini-trial. The roster may also be expanded to include the roles played by certain officials and quasi-officials (such as court-appointed masters, special masters, and neutral experts), by private persons retained as neutrals, by ombudsmen, and by private judges. Changes in procedural rules to provide incentives to the parties to settle (for example, further penalizing parties who turn down reasonable settlement offers), and the greater use of partial summary judgment might also be viewed as ADR techniques.

It is easier to point to discrete practices than to discern the entire direction of the new movement. ADR has no generally accepted abstract or theoretical definition. But it does have a fundamental premise: it is worthwhile both to reduce the costs of resolving disputes, however this can be accomplished, and to improve the quality of the final outcome. We offer a working definition of ADR as a starting point for analysis: ADR is a set of practices and techniques that aim (1) to permit legal disputes to be resolved outside the courts for the benefit of all disputants; (2) to reduce the cost of conventional litigation and the delays to which it is ordinarily subject; or (3) to prevent legal disputes that would otherwise likely be brought to the courts.

The "disputes" with which ADR is centrally concerned should be distinguished from "problems," "grievances," or "claims." Problems are the troubles that affect the human lot, such as damage from storms or sudden illness. Grievances are those problems that affect a particular person, but which may or may not have a particular person or group as the cause of the distress. When the sufferer asks the person thought to be causing the grievance to forbear, the grievance has become a claim or complaint. A dispute arises only when the one against whom the complaint is lodged fails to respond satisfactorily to the aggrieved party, and a "legal" dispute arises only when the claim is grounded in a legal entitlement. ADR, then, should be viewed as a set of practices that are truly alternatives to the courts for the resolution of disputes that could legitimately be disposed of by judicial decree.

Finally, ADR can be "alternative" in one of two senses: because the parties privately choose to avoid litigation (or to terminate it short of judgment), or because legal rules require or permit the courts to send the dispute elsewhere (as in court-annexed arbitration). The analysis that follows largely takes the perspective of parties who have privately and voluntarily chosen to resolve their disputes outside the formal procedures of adjudication.

What often prevents disputes from being resolved is a failure to communicate stemming from a lack of trust between the parties. ADR is premised on the hypothesis that if the parties could overcome this distrust, they could voluntarily reach a settlement as just as the result a court would impose. The adversary process — the engine of the adjudicatory system — operates on a theory of fundamental distrust: never put faith in the adversary. Litigation thus becomes formal, tricky, divisive, time-consuming, and distorting. These characteristics are reflected in the common image of discovery in large-scale-commercial cases that takes years to conduct, in the careful coaching and preparation of witnesses, and in the skillful impeachment of sound witnesses during cross-examination.

In contrast, the creation of trust is central to the design of many ADR processes. Mediation leads to the building of trust . . . [by permitting] a neutral to learn intimate facts from both sides that they would never have shared with each other in the course of trial preparation. By building on the parties' trust in the mediator, the process thus allows the parties to explore workable options. With the knowledge that he gains, the mediator can learn how far apart the parties are and devise ways of bridging the gap.

One lesson that ADR teaches, then, is that processes designed to restore and build trust can overcome the suspicion and mutual hostility fostered by the adversary system and can lead the parties to settle their differences. When the substantive outcome is compared to the likely result in court — and the costs of continued litigation are weighed in the balance — both parties generally benefit from ADR. A working hypothesis of ADR is that the results of ADR are often superior to court judgments — and even more clearly superior to conventional settlements. Although the hypothesis is difficult to test, it is supported by several considerations.

First, adjudication is characterized by a "winner-take-all" outcome. This cannot be wholly true, for jury damage awards can work compromises, and the parties can shape consent decrees through bargaining. Nevertheless, in many cases, the fundamental issue of liability can be resolved only by holding for the plaintiff or the defendant. ADR, by contrast, is not bound by the zero-sum game of adjudication. While we have defined ADR as concerned with "legal disputes," participants in ADR are free to go beyond the legal definition of the scope of their dispute. They can search for creative solutions to the problem that gave rise to the dispute, and those solutions may be far more novel than any remedy a court has the power to provide.

Second, in classes of cases involving complex institutions, negotiations conducted by executives are likely to yield results superior to those conducted by the lawyers. The executives are far more familiar than their lawyers with the nuances of their business and can respond more quickly and creatively to proposals raised by their counterparts. We do not mean to diminish the role or responsibilities of lawyers in the negotiations; their legal knowledge will often be crucial to successful settlements and good lawyer-negotiators may be more skillful than poorly trained executive-negotiators. Nevertheless, the business executive may be presumed to be less distracted by the shadow the law casts over the dispute; the executive will look at the complete business picture, unconstrained by the narrow parameters imposed by legal doctrine.

Third, direct involvement by the client can obviate or minimize difficulties arising from the self-interest of lawyers. This point may be particularly instructive for judges. By requiring clients to attend pretrial conferences, judges can be sure that the clients know and approve of the propositions their lawyers will assert in court on their behalf.

Fourth, ADR techniques and processes can be far more systematic than the horse trading of conventional settlement negotiations. Settlement negotiations are often perceived as consisting of sharp tactics and bluff. "Unprincipled" negotiations occur in large part because the parties lack a means of communicating with each other. ADR processes permit realistic assessments of whether offers and counteroffers are in good faith.

Fifth, properly designed ADR processes make it more likely that settlement decisions will be based on the merits of disputes. Various factors may contribute to more or less settlement. Delay in the judicial system tends to increase the likelihood of settlement by reducing the stakes in the case in part because delay diminishes the present value of the ultimate award. Other factors include rules governing prejudgment interest and the availability of pretrial discovery. This analysis could lead the courts to advocate policies that would increase delay (or other costs of litigation) in order to prompt settlement. The resulting settlements would not necessarily be just, however, because they would not have taken account of power disparities. The party with the more meritorious claim might not prevail, because he is too poor to amass the requisite evidence through the discovery process. Society may have the power to foster higher settlement rates by manipulating the factors that induce people to stay out of court, but many proponents of ADR would not view such policies as consonant with the ADR philosophy. A dispute should not merely be settled; it should be settled justly.

Finally, a sixth reason to think that ADR leads to "better" outcomes is that the use of private neutrals permits the parties to submit their dispute to one with greater expertise in their particular subject than does the luck of the draw in the courtroom. Many complex disputes involve data and concepts that lie beyond the knowledge of generalist judges (and of all juries). The ADR neutral can be selected for a particular expertise, thus saving the parties the cost of educating the fact-finder (and the risk of failing to do so). Moreover, if the parties have personally participated in selecting the neutral, they may be psychologically disposed to accept his statement of the case, whether it is a binding decision (as in arbitration) or an advisory opinion (as in a mini-trial).

6. William Twining, *Alternatives to What? Theories of Litigation, Procedure and Dispute Settlement in Anglo-American Jurisprudence: Some Neglected Classics,* 56 MOD. L. REV. 380, 380-83 (1993)

Concern with different institutions and methods of dispute settlement has a long history. But the rapid growth in lawyers' interest in "alternative dispute resolution" (ADR) is widely perceived to have gathered momentum in the late

1960s in the United States. [Since then] there has indeed been a remarkable growth in the "ADR industry" exemplified by the development of organizations, courses within law schools, continuing legal education and an extensive literature. The main stimuli appear to have been largely pragmatic and political rather than theoretical or "scientific." Three particular concerns seem to have predominated: a feeling on the part of the American legal establishment that the court system was becoming intolerably overloaded by an increased volume of civil claims and criminal prosecutions; a felt need, on the part of professionals and others, for specialized private fora to serve particular interests; and a view that over and above the concomitant increase in congestion, delay and expense, the system was incapable in more fundamental ways of living up to the ideals of "access to justice" for all.

When a "movement" relating to law develops in the United States, one outcome is almost invariably a massive, confusing and largely unsystematic body of literature of variable quality. The ADR movement is no exception. In so far as any general patterns can be discerned from the American ADR literature, perhaps three main strands can be differentiated: first, a body of writing that is concerned with institutional design, in which the central questions relate to the appropriateness of different methods of dispute resolution to various types of dispute. The pioneering work of Lon Fuller in the latter phases of his career is a prominent example.

Second, there has been a series of essentially political debates about the desirability and necessity of encouraging and developing ADR on a large scale. The diagnosis, prescriptions and the motives of the enthusiasts were challenged by skeptics of varying political persuasions: for example, radical critics, . . . while doubting that "justice" was routinely achieved in litigation, argued that the alternatives prescribed by advocates of ADR were no more likely to enhance either access to or delivery of justice in practice and that the net effect of the movement would be to discourage the disadvantaged from trying to assert their legal rights. From a rather different perspective, Owen Fiss argued forcefully "against settlement" not only on the grounds that negotiation and mediation tend to favor the powerful, but also because the development of alternatives would undermine the creative role of the courts in developing public policy and inventing new solutions — an optimistic (and perhaps prototypically American) conception of the political role and importance of courts.

A third strand of literature is specifically educational. While some of the most prominent educational works deal with broad issues of institutional design and its political implications, the main thrust is to prepare lawyers for participation in these alternative modes by developing "skills" in respect of such matters as counseling, interviewing, negotiation, mediation and non-curial advocacy.

The vast bulk of these three bodies of literature is atheoretical. By and large it represents a series of pragmatic and ad hoc reactions to some specific perceived problems in the American legal system at a particular period in history. There are two main exceptions to this broad generalization: first, quite extensive reference is made to the specialized and generally excellent literature of legal anthropology exemplified by such writers as Malinowski, Llewellyn and

Hoebel, Gluckman, Gulliver, and [Laura] Nader. Second, a substantial body of detailed empirical research has been done on criminal process, civil litigation and some alternative processes. Most of this research has been informed by contemporary social science methodology and fits within the kind of theoretical framework that is associated with "the process school" in American jurisprudence — that is to say, a perspective that views litigation and other legal processes as a largely linear and discrete series of decisions and events involving a variety of participants, arenas, procedures, discourses and outcomes.

This characterization of a vast and complex body of American literature is, of course, a great simplification. However, in so far as it is broadly correct, it suggests that this heritage has two characteristics that need to be borne in mind by outsiders. First, it focuses on concerns, institutions and phenomena that are specifically American, despite the de-parochializing influence of anthropology. Second, it is largely divorced from what is widely perceived to be "mainstream" Anglo-American jurisprudence as exemplified, on the one hand, by English positivists in the tradition of Bentham, Austin, Hart and Raz, and by their, largely American, critics such as Rawls and Dworkin. The two main exceptions are . . . Lon Fuller and Karl Llewellyn. However, there is, or at least there is generally thought to be, a disjuncture between these two jurists' "sociological" writings about dispute settlement and their most memorable contributions to mainstream jurisprudence. Only a tenuous connection is perceived between Fuller's writings on mediation and adjudication and his attacks on positivism; similarly, Llewellyn's reputation as the spokesman and interpreter of Legal Realism, the architect of the Uniform Commercial Code, and the author of *The Common Law Tradition* is generally treated as separate from *The Cheyenne Way* and his "law jobs" theory. . . .

In so far as there is a perceived disjuncture between the literature on ADR and mainstream Anglo-American jurisprudence, this is puzzling because one of the most persistent concerns of our legal theorists has been about the nature of appellate jurisdiction. Twentieth-century Anglo-American jurisprudence has been extraordinarily court-centered, with many of the main debates focusing on the role of judges and reasoning about questions of law in hard cases. If *alternative* dispute resolution is mainly concerned with alternatives to civil adjudication, it seems strange that mainstream theories of adjudication do not feature prominently in discussions of ADR.

Two related factors may help to explain this disjuncture. First, Anglo-American legal scholarship and legal education have tended to focus on analysis, exposition and argumentation about legal doctrine. In respect of this, the most visible and interesting tend to surface in atypical arenas, notably appellate courts. This sometimes obscures the obvious point that in only a tiny percentage of litigated cases is an adjudicative decision required; only a small percentage of adjudicative decisions involve disputed questions of law rather than of fact or disposition; and the percentage of cases that are appealed is strikingly small. The vast majority of civil cases are settled or abandoned before trial; and an even greater percentage of criminal cases involves a guilty plea that precludes an adjudicative decision on either the facts or the law. Accordingly, in so far as a great deal of Anglo-American jurisprudence focuses on the roles and reasoning of appellate judges, . . . it treats statistically insignificant and atypical decisions as central.

The phrase "alternative dispute resolution" is revealing. The word "alternative" implies exceptional or secondary or even deviant in contrast to something that is normal or standard or ordinary. But, alternative to what? To litigation? Hardly, for some of the standard alternatives such as negotiation, compromise and mediation regularly feature such phases *within* litigation. To adjudication? If so, it is not just our theorists who are obsessed with the atypical; rather, court centered thinking and discourse are deeply ingrained in our legal culture.

For closely related reasons, those enclaves of legal theory which have focused most directly on non-curial legal activities and phenomena — sociology of law, legal anthropology, and its precursor historical jurisprudence — have generally been marginalized in our legal culture. Thus the main parts of our theoretical heritage that are seen as relevant to dispute resolution are largely outside the mainstream of Anglo-American jurisprudence. . . .

D. MAKING USE OF ADR: PICKING A PROCESS

1. Comments and Questions

a. Much can be said about the costs and benefits of various dispute resolution processes, and how to weigh the relevant factors, but when disputes arise people need to make decisions — and to do so on the basis of incomplete information. In this section, we present two approaches to making a (provisional) choice about dispute resolution. Sander and Rozdeiczer present a model for making this decision. Their approach is paired with an article by the general counsel of Georgia Pacific Corporation, Phillip Armstrong, about a decade of experience using ADR as an important part of the firm's approach to dispute resolution.

b. Frank Sander's paper at the Pound Conference in 1976 was just one among many writings about ADR and related matters. The article that follows presents his latest thinking on how to select an appropriate ADR process — to fit the forum to the fuss. Note Professor Sander's bottom line conclusion: mediation should be the default position, and usually is the best choice.

2. Frank E.A. Sander & Lukasz Rozdeiczer, *Matching Cases and Dispute Resolution Procedures: Detailed Analysis Leading to a Mediation-Centered Approach*, 11 HARV. NEGOT. L. REV. 1 (2006)

One of the most challenging problems in the field of alternative methods of dispute resolution (ADR) is deciding which process or processes (e.g., arbitration, mediation, trial, or some hybrid of these primary processes) are most appropriate for a particular dispute. This question may be asked by a lawyer, a client, or a court official. Indeed its reach extends to any setting where disputes are pending. We will begin by looking at the context in which this problem commonly arises. Then, in Part II, we will analyze the various responses given in the literature and offer our conclusions, as well as a modified approach derived partly from the work of our predecessors. Finally, in Part III, we will suggest a simplified, user-friendly solution — namely, to begin with mediation in all cases except a limited group of situations in which mediation is inappropriate.

The key question is what process or processes can best satisfy the interests of the party that is seeking guidance on what dispute resolution method to use. This party could be either the client or her lawyer. Although choosing the process remains art rather than science, we believe that there are both theoretical and practical indications to guide this process choice. Although . . . we focus on the choice of process that would best satisfy the interests of one party, it should be noted that "the most appropriate process" could also be defined as one that best satisfies the interests of both parties. The highest payoff for both parties is a Pareto efficient outcome, which can often be achieved by a problem-solving process like mediation. The most appropriate process can also mean a procedure that best satisfies the goals of a court, society, or the state. . . .

Probably the most important process choice takes place when the parties first choose their dispute resolution process. That original choice, however, may not continue to be optimal. Due to possible changes of conditions throughout the dispute and gains in understanding of the dispute pending its resolution, the parties could profit from changing their dispute resolution procedure during the processing of the dispute. Thus, they should continually question their choice of procedure throughout the process and keep a flexible mind attuned to possibly changing or modifying the selected procedure. For example, during a pre-agreed mediation of a family dispute, the parties may decide that it will be more beneficial for them to use arbitration instead, perhaps because they need a definitive third-party expert opinion. In a commercial dispute, a mediator and two mid-level managers may conclude that their goals may be better achieved through the participation of more senior company officials with broader perspectives. Therefore, the parties may decide that a mini-trial will be more appropriate to resolve their dispute than mediation.

One of the key problems in selecting the most appropriate procedure for a case involves the choice between court-related and out-of-court processes. Although public and private processes can share an identical name (e.g., court-annexed "mediation" and private divorce "mediation"), they may produce very different results. For example, even if the party knows that she prefers mediation, she can choose not only from an array (continuum) of forms of mediation, but she can also decide whether she wants some court connection and assistance, such as help in choosing a mediator, more formal discovery, or enforcement. A similar relationship exists between court adjudication and private judging, private arbitration and court-annexed arbitration, and early neutral evaluation (ENE) and case evaluation. Another approach to this problem is to look at critical differences in court-related and out-of-court processes in general and not with regard to particular processes.

Considerations in assessing the options include finding out the dispute resolution climate in the place of dispute and deciding whether to select a third party neutral. Different state and federal courts offer a variety of ADR procedures to choose from. A party can only make an informed choice between a court-related process and a private process when that party knows which processes are available in court. In addition, if a party wants to retain the choice of the neutral, she should decide on a private process. Sometimes parties have such great confidence in a particular neutral that they leave the choice of process to her, but often the choice of a neutral comes after the procedure is already chosen.

Private and public processes are not mutually exclusive, and it is possible to combine them. For example, particularly where a factual issue needs to be established, a party may file a claim in order to go through discovery and later settle the dispute through a more facilitative and creative process like mediation. This raises the strategic question of how best to sequence private and public procedures. Should parties sue first and then settle, or is it better to start with the friendlier private procedure? Or, should the public and private processes proceed on parallel tracks? . . .

The problem of matching the case to the process can be looked at from two ends: the fuss and the forum. . . . The first method assumes that the dispute resolution procedures are somewhat fixed, and therefore, prior to knowing the case, one can predict what kind of case should be matched to a certain procedure. To some extent this is true, and such predictions are possible. However, since disputes usually include a great number of elements that can influence and determine the most appropriate procedure, the latter approach of fitting the forum to a described fuss seems more efficient. Beginning the analysis from the parties' goals and case characteristics, which are hard to change, and then fitting (tailoring) the most appropriate forum for such a case seems a more reasonable approach. Moreover, since one procedure can have a variety of forms, knowing the case allows one not only to match it to one of the known procedures, but also to adapt a procedure to best fit the given dispute. Although the latter approach seems to be superior in most circumstances, in this Article we combine both perspectives. In the first step of the process of matching cases with procedures, we focus on examining the fuss through the lens of the goals of the parties. In the second step, we analyze the facilitating features of both cases and procedures. Finally, in the third step, which deals with how particular procedures can overcome impediments to an effective resolution, we focus mainly on the features of the forum. . . .

We believe that three lenses are key to focusing the analysis: goals, facilitating features, and impediments.

Goals. The first question regarding the choice of the most appropriate process relates to the kind of objectives the party would like to achieve during, or at the end of, this process. In other words, this future-oriented approach asks what should happen as a result of the choice of the particular dispute resolution process. As a party will usually have more than one objective, she should also prioritize her various goals.

Facilitating Features. When the party determines the desired (future) outcome, she should reflect on her present resources, i.e., the attributes of the case that make it particularly suitable or unsuitable to solving the case. We therefore propose that the party should focus next on the attributes of the process, the case, and the parties that are likely to facilitate reaching effective resolution. For example, if the dispute involves lower-level representatives of the parties, but requires a broader view of the problem from the perspective of the whole company, this might suggest the use of a mini-trial, which involves high-level officials.

Impediments. In the third step of the analysis, we suggest that one should focus on the ability of various procedures to overcome impediments to effective resolution. This is a focus on the forum.

In this three-part analysis we apply our mixed forum and fuss approach. In the first two steps above, (Goals and Facilitating Features), we emphasize analysis of the case and the parties (the fuss). In the last step (Impediments), we direct our main focus to the procedures (Forum) and the effect they may have on the dispute in question. Our analysis has one more dimension — time. While the first step of the analysis is future-oriented (what should happen), the latter two ask about the present situation and resources: What is available now?

A. The Goals of the Parties

One of the most basic aspects of finding the appropriate dispute resolution procedure is to look to the goals of the parties and how they can be satisfied by various processes. . . . The determination of the goals leads to the particular process or processes that will achieve those goals. One of the most essential tasks of a party and her counsel is assessing appropriate goals. . . . The benefits of mediation are also salient in the context of commercial contracts: fifty-nine percent of attorneys in the Cornell Survey stated that an important reason for choosing mediation over adjudication was "preserving good relationship." *See* David B. Lipsky & Ronald L. Seeber, *The Appropriate Resolution of Corporate Disputes: A Report on the Growing Use of ADR by U.S. Corporations* 17 (2003). Research shows a higher compliance rate with consensual agreements than with decrees that are forced upon the parties. Therefore, particularly when the parties desire continued cooperation in the future, they may prefer voluntary agreements to court decisions.

A particular challenge arises when the dispute is one of a group of disputes or centers on one event in a series. Not only does the party have to consider the future relationship with the other side, but the party must also determine how this case relates to other cases, which may completely change the goals of the party. For example, a party may care less about the outcome of a particular case than about such factors as precedent, future claims, economies of scale, chronology of the cases, or relationships with other parties (repeat players). Thus, when the perspective of the party widens from one specific case to a few linked cases, her goals, and hence the analysis of the most appropriate procedure, will shift as well. . . .

After deciding which goals the party wants to achieve, . . . she must determine which process best satisfies her goals. Such an approach, however, assumes that all of these concerns are of equal value to the party, which may not be true. A better approach would consist of both ranking and weighting the goals. Therefore, a party could assign a weight, in points, to each of her concerns, and then multiply them by the measure by which such procedure satisfies these goals. . . . Assigning weights to these different goals should then be followed by multiplying the assigned weight by the effectiveness of each procedure in satisfying this goal. . . .

Although this example and proposed method involves a lot of counting and weighing, we still think that this method is more art than science. It is very important to remember that the outcomes of these calculations should not be taken literally, but rather that they only provide guidance for evaluating the parties' goals. Sometimes the primary benefit will be the exercise of going through this process rather than the numerical result reached.

Parties who have consistent goals probably can be convinced easily to use one process. However, what if the goals of the other party are inconsistent and would suggest another process? One option might be that they would agree to start from mediation, which seems to be a "safe" procedure (no commitment) for both parties, unless the case is one when even mediation is not appropriate. Another approach is suggested by the New Hampshire court rules. When the parties' ADR preferences are incompatible, the court will utilize the least binding process (e.g., mediation over arbitration). . . .

B. Features of the Process, the Case, and the Parties that Facilitate Effective Resolution

Certain features of the case and the parties can facilitate reaching effective resolution. However, only with an appropriate dispute resolution procedure will they be triggered. For example, a good relationship and trust between the parties' attorneys can facilitate communication and lead to a better settlement. These facilitating features would not be maximally utilized if the parties selected litigation. Moreover, litigation could quickly destroy both a good pre-existing relationship and trust, creating an impediment to settlement later. Therefore, it is crucial for the parties to recognize the attributes of the case that may facilitate effective resolution, and to match these attributes with the process (e.g., mediation) that may trigger them.

Generally speaking, every procedure is capable of activating some of the facilitating features of the case or the parties. For example, mediation and mini-trial can facilitate communication and maximize the parties' chances for a value-creating resolution. Summary jury trial and early neutral evaluation may provide an opportunity to make an early assessment of the strengths and weaknesses of the case, allowing the parties to make a more informed decision about a possible settlement. Adjudication (and binding arbitration) provides certain procedural tools that can serve parties' needs, including court enforcement during the dispute resolution process and at the implementation stage.

In our mixed approach of fitting the forum to the fuss and the fuss to the forum, we think it is crucial not only to analyze the features of the case and the parties, but also to recognize the individual features of each procedure that can benefit the party. For example, if discovering assets of the defendant is important, or if a third party needs to appear at the proceedings, a party may prefer litigation, which offers ways of achieving these objectives, such as through discovery or impleader. In cases where the specific expertise of a neutral is needed, litigation may not be the best option. Other procedures like mediation, mini-trial, or case evaluation, where parties can choose an expert-neutral, will be more advantageous. Each procedure may have many strengths.

C. Capacity of a Procedure to Overcome Impediments to Effective Resolution

The vast majority of cases ultimately settle. At least, most parties try to settle, for they often perceive settlement as more beneficial than the binding decision of a third party. Therefore, in considering impediments to resolution, parties and their counsel should mainly focus on impediments to settlement and particularly on the capacity of different procedures to overcome such impediments.

There are cases in which impediments can be better overcome by some adjudicative procedure (e.g., important principle, "jackpot" syndrome, or different view of facts). For that reason, and in order to give the parties the full spectrum of procedures from which to choose, adjudicative procedures are added to the table below. There are other instances where settlement is not an appropriate resolution of a case. This problem is described in Part III.B of this Article dealing with cases where mediation is not appropriate because of private or public perspectives. . . .

[The potential impediments to resolution include Poor Communication; Need to Express Emotions; Different View of Facts; Different View of Law; Important Principle; Constituent Pressure; Linkage to Other Disputes; Multiple Parties; Different Lawyer-Client Interests; Jackpot Syndrome; Fear of Disclosing True Interests (Negotiator's Dilemma); Psychological Barriers; Inability to Negotiate Effectively; Unrealistic Expectations; and Power Imbalance.] This list of impediments is not exhaustive. Parties should be encouraged to look for other impediments in their particular case. . . . Two of the most challenging impediments are discussed below.

1. Power Imbalance. Disputes can be resolved based either on (1) rights of the parties, as through litigation, or (2) parties' interests, often through facilitative mediation because the more evaluative the mediation, the more rights-based it usually is, or (3) power, such as through coercion or war. The implications of power imbalances for process selection represent one of the most difficult and unsettled subjects of dispute resolution. Generally speaking, an interest-based approach is preferable, because it is usually cheaper and faster, and because it has the potential of providing mutual benefits. However, the interest-based approach also provides an opportunity for exploitation by the more powerful party. This may suggest the use of a rights-based approach, like adjudication, in situations where there is disproportionate power and a higher probability of such abuse. One must also keep in mind the alternative to using a particular process. For example, power imbalances pose a difficult challenge for mediation, but often the alternative to mediation is negotiation rather than litigation, and, arguably, power imbalances are aggravated in negotiation.

There is a serious discussion in the dispute resolution literature of not only whether mediation could mitigate power imbalances but, more importantly, whether it ought to do so. Some authors believe that mediation is not capable of mitigating these power imbalances and that mediation should not attempt to mitigate such imbalances, as this would be against the principle of neutrality. Other commentators think that sometimes mediators can mitigate such imbalances but believe that the parties should be warned in advance about the mediator's inclination to do so.

Disproportionate power may be the result of various differences between the parties, such as financial resources, legal arguments and representation, negotiation skills, emotional dependence, etc. Depending on the source of power, the parties may have different strengths in different forums. Knowing her sources of power, the weaker party should strategically select a forum where her powers are relatively strongest. For example, in a case that requires extensive discovery, a poor party may prefer to "forget the past" and focus on the future, proposing to mediate or to use ENE instead of going through a long and costly discovery. Litigation could also be beneficial if a party can withstand long delays and significant risk. If the party knows that her case is strong on law, and that in negotiation she would be intimidated by powerful and sophisticated lawyers on the other side, she may prefer to go to court with a lawyer instead of engaging in face-to-face negotiation or mediation. Moreover, as many mediators do not believe that power balancing is a part of their role, a weaker party (particularly an unrepresented party) may be better protected in court than in mediation. With respect to the success rate of mediation, according to research, mediation is more likely to end with a settlement where there is disproportionate power between the parties. This, however, does not answer the question of the fairness, and thus appropriateness, of the procedure.

2. Questions of Law, of Fact, or Both. Facilitative processes, such as mediation, are less appropriate in cases where facts need to be determined. This is particularly true where a case depends on a witness's credibility or complex discovery. On the other hand, even when facts are uncertain but relevant for the case, a facilitative method might direct the solution away from the past and toward some future-oriented resolutions. Another situation where parties might decide not to dispute all the facts might be when this would inflict great costs on them. In such a case, instead of resorting to costly and time-consuming expert witnesses, parties may prefer a creative solution based on some other criteria. The parties can also agree to start with an evaluative process determining the facts, and based on such findings to follow with a facilitative, problem-solving process like mediation. Depending on the agreement of the parties, the fact determination can be either binding (such as through adjudication and arbitration) or non-binding (such as through non-binding fact-finding or non-binding arbitration). When, however, the sole issue in the case is a legal one, a court proceeding may be the most efficient approach. Parties may resolve the dispute by filing motions to dismiss or motions for summary judgment. When legal issues are in question, there is often a need for precedent, and thus, adjudication would be the most appropriate procedure.

III. A User-Friendly, Mediation-Centered Approach

A. Step One: Assume Mediation

The combination of the theoretical examination presented above and the empirical data suggests that mediation is almost always a superior starting process.

We roughly divide advantages of mediation into two categories — ones generically present in any mediation (which we call "macrobenefits") and ones applicable to particular cases and parties (which we call "microbenefits").

1. Macrobenefits. In most cases, mediation is capable of resolving disputes. Even if mediation does not produce a settlement, it becomes a route leading to other processes. Trying to resolve disputes through mediation can result in three possible outcomes, each usually making a party better off than if she had gone straight to litigation: (i) The case can settle; (ii) In case of failure, the mediator may be able to give an informed recommendation for another procedure; (iii) Mediation can assist in settling some of the issues, leaving others for another possibly more coercive procedure. This approach is consistent with writings on dispute resolution system design where less invasive and less expensive methods are usually preferred and should precede the more expensive and invasive ones. Mediation is very flexible. It can be fitted to many different contexts and made to accommodate different party needs and case characteristics.

Mediation is most likely to overcome impediments to settlement. Since mediation is more likely to produce a Pareto efficient result than adjudication, it is more likely to be responsive to the needs of both parties to the dispute, often by avoiding the need to resolve disputed questions of fact and focusing instead on a forward-looking solution. Mediation is most likely to trigger facilitating features of the case and the parties and thus facilitate efficient resolution of the dispute. Even where one or both parties believe they will win in litigation, mediation will still be useful by quantifying the likelihood of victory and exploring more attractive alternative solutions. A settlement obtained through mediation is more likely to be complied with. According to empirical research, mediation is preferred by practitioners and parties. Mediation has a higher participant satisfaction rate than any other procedure.

2. Microbenefits. In addition to the above macrobenefits of mediation, there are a number of potential microbenefits that argue for resort to mediation in most cases: (a) Clarifying the issues in dispute; (b) Helping channel or control anger or other negative emotions; (c) Giving one or both parties an opportunity to tell their stories and to be fully heard by the other side; (d) Providing an opportunity for an apology; (e) Providing a "reality check" from a knowledgeable intermediary of their positions or expectations; (f) Providing a confidential setting in which to explore each other's interests and needs; (g) Helping to explore the possibility for trade-offs or creative solutions; (h) Helping to educate the decision-makers on either side; (i) Providing an intermediary who could make offers and counteroffers more acceptable by presenting them as his or her own; and (j) Providing an intermediary who can reframe proposals, inject her own ideas as appropriate, and take blame, if necessary.

Finally, if "the most appropriate process for dispute" is defined as the one that best satisfies the interests of both parties and creates the largest possible pie (has the largest probability of producing a Pareto efficient outcome), mediation, having the highest value-creating potential, should be the process of first choice. Since mediation is the most often used, and often the most useful, process of dispute resolution, a simpler, more efficient approach to matching cases with procedures is to regard mediation as a point of departure, unless there are contraindications to its use. . . .

3. Mediation and Adjudication: Opposite Sides of the Same Coin? At the outset, it should be noted that . . . there is a complementary relationship between the capacities of mediation and adjudication to achieve particular goals. Goals such as improving the relationship or minimizing costs that are highly likely to be attained through mediation are highly unlikely to be achieved through adjudication. Similarly, goals such as obtaining a precedent are highly likely to be achieved by adjudication but very unlikely to be achieved through mediation. Thus, many of the cases that are inappropriate for mediation are those cases that require adjudication. Note that when a procedure does not satisfy a particular goal, such a goal may later become an impediment to efficient resolution of the dispute through this procedure.

We notice that: (1) since mediation and adjudication satisfy or do not satisfy opposite goals, and (2) the goals that are not satisfied by a certain procedure become contraindications to this procedure, certain conclusions follow. Mediation's goals are contraindications to satisfactory adjudication, and adjudication's goals are contraindications to mediation. Therefore, in the great majority of cases, either mediation or adjudication will satisfy the goals of the parties and will overcome impediments to resolution. Finally, in cases where goals of the parties are not satisfied by litigation, mediation should be employed.

B. Step Two: When Is Mediation Not Appropriate?

1. Party's Perspective. As a matter of party choice, mediation may be inappropriate or insufficient for certain kinds of disputes. Some of the indications for such a situation might be the following features: (1) A party's need to attain a goal that only a court or an arbitrator can provide, such as a precedent valid beyond immediate parties, maximizing or minimizing the recovery, or public vindication; (2) The case turns on a matter of principle; (3) There is a wholly frivolous claim — if so, the client may have standard policy for handling such claims; (4) The jackpot syndrome. Besides these examples, parties may have other specific reasons why mediation would not be appropriate.

In other circumstances, mediation is simply less likely to be successful (partial contraindication), and other procedures may be more appropriate. The first category of partial contraindications is where there are different views of the law. There are a variety of ways to clarify legal uncertainty in other processes, ranging from evaluative mediation to early neutral evaluation or arbitration and court adjudication. A second category of partial contraindications to mediation is where the parties anticipate needing judicial enforcement. This is not a contraindication to mediation itself. For example, a specific case where court enforcement is particularly important is where there is a need for a "structural injunction" — a case in which an outcome is an order that will govern the parties for a certain period of time and under which there will be repeated occasions for new disputes to arise. In some other situations where enforcement issues are anticipated but the case basically needs the problem-solving feature of mediation, the resulting agreement could be embodied in a court decree. Third, mediation may be partially contraindicated where there are different views of key facts that need to be established. Even in these cases, mediation may still be helpful after the facts have been established (e.g., by a neutral third party or a panel of experts). Mediation might not be appropriate where there is a significant imbalance of power. Finally, parties may not want to use mediation when they have full information and only seek a neutral opinion on the extent of damages and other limited issues, or they believe they have all relevant information and they are positive that they will prevail in court or arbitration.

If such contraindications exist, the case may be inappropriate for mediation. These impediments, however, do not exclude mediation but simply should be weighed against the goals of the parties, strengths of the parties and the case, and other factors that may result in mediation still being superior to its alternatives. If this analysis results in a 50-50 case for mediation, then mediation should still be utilized, because it is a hospitable procedure. It is always easier, if necessary, to go from mediation to adjudication than to take the reverse course. Moreover, frequently, the case may lend itself to fragmentation. One or more issues could be resolved by mediation, while the remainder are resolved by some other approach that is likely to suggest itself in the course of the mediation proceeding.

2. Public Perspective. The public concern about process selection may arise in a number of ways. Sometimes, for public policy reasons, the legislature provides specific procedures for particular transactions or bars them for others. Where courts have the power to assign cases to various ADR procedures, they may take account of the public interest when making such an assignment. For example, a court might conclude that a garden-variety tort case posing no novel issues should be settled, and therefore, referred to mediation or ENE. However, unless that referral is only a step preliminary to litigation, it could be challenged on the ground of denial of access to court. Conversely, a court may decide that a case raises novel issues of statutory or constitutional interpretation and may insist that the case be litigated. With the exception of specialized cases requiring court approval for settlement, however, there is no way for a court to prevent the parties from settling the case and dismissing the lawsuit.

Aside from specific statutory directives of the kind mentioned, the most salient cases against settlement from a public policy perspective resemble, in some respects, those listed from a party perspective, namely: cases presenting "a genuine social need for an authoritative interpretation of law;" cases involving serious power imbalances; cases that may involve issues of judicial enforcement; cases involving a need for public sanctioning (e.g., serious health code violations by a landlord); and recurring violations (e.g., of consumer protection laws).

C. Step Three A: If Mediation, What Type?

Although the implication of having mediation as a presumed process may sound simplistic, there is, in fact, a whole range of mediation processes that may be applied in each case. Mediation is not a simple, pre-determined single process, but a range of processes. The most important kinds of mediation are: facilitative/elicitive; evaluative/directive; transformative/problem-solving; and court-related/out-of-court. These approaches are not exclusive; there is a continuum of mediator behaviors that can be both evaluative and facilitative — on the same issue, on different issues, simultaneously, or at different times. It is also possible to be facilitative on substance, yet directive on process.

Other choices for the design of mediation include: with/without caucuses, with/without lawyers, length of the process, etc. There are at least two ways of deciding what kind of mediation a party needs. Some disputants have a clear view of the kind of mediation they want. For example, in a commercial case where the parties are far apart, a more evaluative form of mediation may be preferred. . . . In other instances, where parties do not quite know what they need, they may look for a certain kind of mediator and let her take the lead on deciding about the type of process.

D. Step Three B: If Not Mediation, Then What?

Where mediation is not appropriate, . . . parties must resort to the three-step analysis in Part II of this article in an effort to fit the forum to the fuss, including the possibility of designing a custom-made process that responds to the needs of the parties and the characteristics of the case. We believe that the case where mediation is inappropriate will be relatively rare. According to data from the federal courts, ninety-eight percent of all civil cases and ninety-five percent of criminal cases settle through agreement of the parties or are withdrawn from the court without a final court decision. Hence, our thesis is that one should begin the search for the most appropriate process with automatic resort to mediation, leaving open the question of the type of mediation that is most suitable for the particular case.

E. Summary and Conclusions

Selecting an appropriate dispute resolution procedure for the effective resolution of a particular dispute is a challenging task — more art than science. It may involve a number of intangible factors, such as the ADR culture in the venue in question and the power dynamics between the parties. In this Article, we have examined the theoretical issues presented by some of the leading scholars and organizations who have looked at the problem. . . . There are no ironclad, definitive answers. However, in this Article we tried to present several reasons for our suggested approach of normally beginning with mediation (a revealing and flexible process that readily opens the way to other processes as needed). The only exception to this approach comes in the limited situations where there are contraindications to mediation. In all other situations, using some form of mediation at the outset is likely to be most productive.

3. Phillip M. Armstrong, *Georgia-Pacific's ADR Program: A Critical Review After 10 Years*, 60-JUL DISP. RESOL. J. 19 (2005)

Georgia-Pacific Corporation is a Fortune 500 consumer and wood products company headquartered in Atlanta, Georgia. Georgia-Pacific was one of the first Fortune 500 companies to establish a formal ADR program. After a decade of ADR experience (January 2005 marked the 10th anniversary of Georgia-Pacific's program), it seems appropriate to critically review that program to determine how it has fared over this period, how it changed (if at all), what improvements were made (if any), and what have we learned and can impart to other institutions from our experience. In short, as the person responsible for developing Georgia-Pacific's ADR program, I felt the need to take stock, to stand back and ask where we are after nearly a decade of experience using ADR. The assessment below reviews costs and other aspects of having an ADR program for 10 years, including the need for management support and training of Law Department personnel.

1. Cost Savings. The cost savings, which were significant in the beginning of the ADR program, remain so today. The ADR program started small in 1995, the first full year of operation. Cases handled in the program increased significantly from 1997 through 2000, leveled off during 2001-2003, and then showed a significant bump in 2004. [During this ten year period, ADR was used in about 600 cases, with a total estimated savings of $33 million, or $55,000 per case. These aggregate numbers hide considerable differences among cases, both with respect to the amount at issue and the amount saved.] In brief, . . . the ADR program has saved Georgia Pacific many million dollars since its inception.

2. Need for Top Management Support. Georgia-Pacific obtained the support of top management for the ADR program at the beginning. Indeed, the program could not have gotten off the ground without it. Although the support was there at the beginning, and the ADR program has been successful from a financial point of view, it is still necessary to keep that support and have top management "buy in" to the program. Why? Management changes. New business managers must be regularly educated on the benefits of ADR, and existing managers must be periodically reminded of why ADR works and why it is good for the company.

3. Training. Likewise, new lawyers in the law department must be trained on both the process and benefits of ADR. True, most law schools now offer ADR courses, but they are seldom part of the required curriculum. ADR practitioners routinely express surprise at how often they face an opposing counsel with little or no ADR experience.

4. Contract Clauses. Ten years of ADR experience has changed the way Georgia-Pacific addresses dispute resolution in its commercial contracts. In 1998, the company used three multi-step clauses, all of which included arbitration. Today we often use a simpler three-step clause that ends in mediation. With some exceptions, the company's current view is that if it cannot reach a settlement with an adversary using the steps provided in the ADR clause, it prefers to keep its options open.

Georgia-Pacific does not always have a choice. The abundance of arbitration clauses in commercial contracts often forces the parties into arbitration. Even though there is an arbitration clause, parties could always agree to mediate first. Fortunately, most large U.S. corporations generally find mediation to be their preferred dispute resolution method. Georgia-Pacific is no different. On occasion, Georgia-Pacific will enter into voluntary arbitration based on the facts and circumstances of a given case.

5. Litigate When Necessary. Since its inception, Georgia-Pacific's ADR program has focused on legitimate claims, i.e., bona fide disputes where both parties have a genuine, good-faith belief in the rightness of their position. Conversely, the program did not apply to bogus claims and lawsuits: (1) naming Georgia-Pacific only because it has a deep pocket, (2) where the company's product, even if in the chain of distribution, had no role in the liability or damages alleged, (3) where an overriding principle or precedent is at stake, or (4) where the company believes that the case will open the floodgates to frivolous claims. In short, Georgia-Pacific prefers to defend against these kinds of cases in court, rather than settle, notwithstanding ADR's economic benefits. It also litigates cases where the business manager who is the "client" strongly believes in the rightness of Georgia Pacific's position, despite the fact that an economic benefit analysis suggests it could be cheaper to settle. Despite its commitment to ADR, Georgia Pacific still litigates more cases than it mediates or arbitrates, a clear indication to potential claimants that the company litigates when appropriate.

6. Settlement Mentality. A concern often expressed by management when starting an ADR program is how such an initiative might be perceived in the marketplace. Thus, when Georgia-Pacific started its ADR program, there was a concern that the company's problem-solving approach, both as to claims it brought as well as defends against, might result in lawsuits "coming out of the woodwork." In fact, Georgia-Pacific's experience was just the opposite. The program did not invite a host of new lawsuits. The company . . . has not identified any pattern of lawsuits or repeat cases brought with the hope that it will settle. The fact that Georgia-Pacific litigates the majority of lawsuits against it warns prospective plaintiffs that it will not "roll over" just because a suit is filed.

7. Types of Cases. In the early stages of Georgia-Pacific's ADR program, certain types of claims (notably personal injury actions) were presumed to be poor candidates for ADR. The assumption was that only commercial or contract cases were appropriate for mediation or arbitration. Over the past several years we have learned that ADR is suitable for almost any type case and that no claim should be summarily rejected as unsuitable for ADR. At present, virtually all lawsuits or claims undergo an early case assessment and ADR analysis . . ..

8. Types of ADR Processes Used. When Georgia-Pacific started its ADR program, it assumed it would use a wide variety of ADR processes. That turned out to be an erroneous assumption. Georgia-Pacific has tended to use mediation most often, with arbitration a distant second. This is consistent with most Fortune 500 companies. We have used other types of ADR (e.g., summary jury trial, mini-trial, med-arb) very sparingly. This reflects Georgia-Pacific's confidence in the mediation process (a confidence other Fortune 500 companies also seem to share). Though we are not averse to hybrid forms of ADR, we have not yet felt the need to expand in that direction.

9. Selection of a Neutral. In the early stages of Georgia-Pacific's ADR program, the company typically selected neutrals from nationally known service providers (e.g., American Arbitration Association, JAMS, the CPR Institute for Conflict Resolution). While the company occasionally will draw from these national service providers, particularly where a contract clause requires that the rules of a specific organization be used, it tends to rely more heavily on recommendations from outside counsel with whom it has forged long-standing relationships. If, for example, the company would like to mediate a case in California, it would seek a recommendation from the outside counsel it uses in Los Angeles or San Francisco and, in most cases, would follow that recommendation. Though it may seem counter-intuitive, Georgia-Pacific has found that agreeing to the other side's choice of a mediator often leads to a successful resolution of the dispute. That decision tends to establish instant credibility with both the mediator as well as the other side.

Georgia-Pacific is not willing to accept the other side's choice of an arbitrator. . . . In an arbitration proceeding, Georgia-Pacific conducts the usual background checks and satisfies itself that the arbitrator candidate has the requisite experience, knowledge, impartiality, and independence to serve as the decision maker in the case.

Conclusion

Years of experience has reinforced Georgia-Pacific's commitment to ADR. It now considers virtually every case a candidate for early case assessment or ADR, not just commercial disputes with other large companies. Over the last 10 years, the ADR program has undergone some modification, but overall, it has largely remained intact. The greatest change is that increasingly more cases are reviewed with ADR in mind and ultimately mediated. We have found that all of the oft-quoted benefits of mediation — cost savings, confidentiality, preservation of business relationships, finality and more satisfying results — are real. Our 10-year reassessment indicates that these benefits have all been part of the Georgia-Pacific experience.

One recommendation is essential to establishing a successful ADR program. From its inception, Georgia-Pacific appointed one person in charge of managing, promoting and advancing the cause of the ADR program within the company. In corporations as well as other institutions, ADR needs someone responsible for encouraging and promoting its use and helping to overcome any lingering bias in favor of litigating every case that comes through the door. The "win at all costs" mind-set will always be found in some members of management and among lawyers as well. Combating this mind-set is a challenge that must be met time and time again.

Sample Dispute Resolution Clause Used by Georgia-Pacific

The parties will attempt in good faith to resolve any controversy or claim arising out of or relating to this Agreement promptly by negotiations between representatives and Senior Executives of the parties who have authority to settle the controversy.

If a controversy or claim should arise, appropriate representatives of each party ("Managers") will meet at least once and will attempt to resolve the matter. The Managers will make every effort to meet as soon as reasonably possible at a mutually agreed time and place. If the matter has not been resolved within twenty days of their first meeting, the Managers shall refer the matter to Senior Executives who do not have direct responsibility for administration of this Agreement.

Thereupon, the Managers shall promptly prepare and exchange memoranda stating (a) the issues in dispute and their respective position, summarizing the evidence and arguments supporting their positions, and the negotiations which have taken place, and attaching relevant documents, and (b) the name and title of the Senior Executive who will represent that party. The Senior Executives shall meet for negotiations at a mutually agreed time and place within fourteen days of the end of the twenty-day period referred to above and thereafter as often as they deem reasonably necessary to exchange relevant information and to attempt to resolve the dispute.

If the matter has not been resolved within thirty days of the meeting of the Senior Executives, or if either party will not meet within thirty days of the end of the twenty-day period referred to in the preceding paragraph, the parties will attempt in good faith to resolve the controversy or claim by mediation in accordance with the current model procedural rules of the [CPR Institute for Dispute Resolution] [American Arbitration Association]. If the matter has not been resolved pursuant to the aforesaid mediation procedure within thirty days of the commencement of such procedure, or if either party will not participate in a mediation, either party may initiate litigation or otherwise pursue whatever remedies may be available to such party.

The procedures specified in this section shall be the sole and exclusive procedures for the resolution of disputes between the parties arising out of or relating to this Agreement. Provided, however, that a party may seek a preliminary injunction or other preliminary judicial relief if in its judgment such action is necessary to avoid irreparable damage. Despite such action, the parties will continue to participate in good faith in the procedures specified in this section. All applicable statutes of limitation shall be tolled while the procedures specified in this section are pending. . . . All deadlines may be extended by mutual agreement.

E. THINKING ABOUT THE ALTERNATIVES

1. Comments and Questions

a. The two articles in this section provide an introduction to many of the big questions about disputes and disputing; we will return to these themes throughout the course. The issues raised here are ones you should keep thinking about as you read the ensuing chapters.

b. The authors of the two articles in this section are both leading thinkers about the uses of, and potential problems with, various dispute resolution processes. Judge Harry Edwards taught at the University of Michigan Law School (Negotiation and Labor Law, among other subjects) prior to his appointment to the United States Court of Appeals for the District of Columbia. Judith Resnik is the leading commentator on the role of courts and judges, as well as the alternatives to judicial dispute resolution, and a Professor at Yale Law School.

2. Harry T. Edwards, *Alternative Dispute Resolution: Panacea or Anathema?*, 99 HARV. L. REV. 668 (1986)

If alternative dispute resolution mechanisms are most significant as substitutes for traditional litigation, then it is important to assess the specific problems facing our judicial system that ADR seeks to address. Fortunately, the literature on this subject is so extensive that it is unnecessary here to rehash the issues or to resolve the ongoing debate as to whether we are truly an overly litigious society. It is enough to note that, in recent years, the cost of litigation has substantially increased and the number of cases filed in state and federal courts has mushroomed.

Given the inadequacy of traditional responses to the manifold problems with our court systems, it is not surprising that many commentators believe that we must develop new approaches for dispute resolution in lieu of litigation. Generally I concur, but I think that there are two critical threshold inquires that we must make before we leap to embrace any system of ADR. First, we should consider whether an ADR mechanism is being proposed to facilitate existing court procedures, or as an alternative wholly separate from the established system. Second, we must consider whether the disputes that will be resolved pursuant to an ADR system will involve significant public rights and duties. In other words, we must determine whether ADR will result in an abandonment of our constitutional system in which the "rule of law" is created and principally enforced by legitimate branches of government and whether rights and duties will be delimited by those the law selects to regulate.

Many disputes cannot be easily classified as solely private disputes that implicate no constitutional or public law. Many commentators have tried to distinguish "public" and "private" disputes; but, in my view, no one has been fully successful in this effort. The problem is that hidden in many seemingly private disputes are often difficult issues of public law. In this Commentary, I offer no easy solution to the definitional problem of public/private disputes. I do suggest, however, that there are a number of public law cases that are easily identifiable as such. These include constitutional issues surrounding existing government regulation and issues of great public concern. The latter category might include, for example, the development of a legal standard of strict liability in products liability cases. Although less easily identifiable than constitutional and regulatory issues, such issues of great public concern can be accommodated so long as ADR mechanisms are created as adjuncts to existing judicial or regulatory systems, or if these issues can be re-litigated in court after initial resolution pursuant to ADR.

One way to deal with the caseload problem is simply to divert cases from litigation by limiting the jurisdiction of the courts. There are two difficulties with such a "demand-side" approach. First, limiting the jurisdiction of courts may result in diminished rights for minorities and other groups, whose cases in areas like civil rights, prisoner suits, and equal employment are likely to be the first removed from the courts. Second, the jurisdiction-limiting solution fails to recognize the potential role of ADR within the traditional court systems. If we rush to limit the substantive jurisdiction of our courts, we may lose our best opportunity to experiment with the promise of ADR.

Implicitly recognizing these two difficulties, many ADR advocates have suggested the use of ADR as an adjunct to federal and state court systems. ADR would not replace litigation, but instead would be used to make our traditional court systems work more efficiently and effectively. Because the vast majority of all court cases are settled rather than adjudicated, many commentators believe that ADR has an enormous potential for reducing caseloads by enhancing the effectiveness of settlement; at the same time, because ADR would be under the careful supervision of courts, there is far less danger that ADR would become a nefarious scheme for diminishing the rights of the underprivileged in our society.

There are several ways in which the enormous settlement-enhancing potential of ADR can be tapped. Many lawyers insist that a neutral, penetrating, and analytical assessment of a case greatly enhances the prospects of a successful negotiation by offering a realistic view of what could transpire if a case goes to full-blown adjudication. Furthermore, because too many lawyers view the suggestion of compromise as an admission of weakness, mechanisms that place the onus of suggesting settlement negotiations on neither party have tremendous potential for initiating settlement at much earlier stages in the litigation.

Indeed, many private litigants and courts already use ADR because it offers such a neutral assessment and requires parties to think about compromise at earlier stages in the litigation. For example, several corporations have pioneered the resolution of large and complicated business disputes by mini-trials. Although the result is non-binding, mini-trials have been tremendously successful in settling cases quickly. Business litigants frequently find the opinion of a third party invaluable in deciding how best to settle many quite complicated cases. The mini-trials also have the virtue of forcing corporate litigants to confront the weaknesses in their cases. However, mini-trials are a realistic option only for the wealthy, and the success of mini-trials may result from the fact that they are initiated by the parties, who thereby show their predisposition to settle.

Court-annexed arbitration (CAA), quickly being adopted in many state and federal courts, may offer a "poor man's mini-trial." Many jurisdictions have compulsory non-binding arbitration for particular classes of cases — primarily tort and contract disputes with potential damage awards below an established dollar ceiling. Critically, therefore, CAA is most often used to resolve private disputes rather than difficult public law issues. Indeed, by diverting private disputes to arbitration, federal and state courts may be able to expend more time and energy resolving difficult public law problems.

The experience in most state court-annexed arbitration programs is very encouraging. A large percentage of the disputants accept the arbitrated settlements and express satisfaction with the arbitration process. In Pittsburgh, for example, court-annexed arbitration ends three-quarters of all cases without appeal, and the median time to a hearing is three months, in marked contrast to an eighteen-month wait for trial. In Michigan, although disputants accept the arbitration award in less than half of the cases, only seven percent of all cases in which the arbitration award is rejected actually go to trial.

Of course, in the excitement over the docket-clearing potential of CAA, we must not make the mistake of ignoring the quality of arbitration outcomes. The Seventh Amendment right to a jury trial requires that arbitrated settlements be non-binding (unless the parties agree otherwise). In cases seen to be very important to the litigants — whether for monetary reasons or otherwise — losing parties are rarely willing to accept the result of arbitration as long as a trial de novo remains available and they have so little to lose by resorting to full-blown litigation. Only if parties agree beforehand to waive their jury rights can arbitration be fully effective.

Even with this problem of finality, CAA has increased the ease with which cases are settled. Most parties that reject arbitration decisions eventually settle — often earlier than they would have in the absence of arbitration. Even if parties do not accept the outcome of arbitration, the arbitrator's decision forces both parties to focus on a neutral third party's realistic assessment of the case.

As our experience with court-annexed arbitration demonstrates, federal and state courts are striving mightily to accommodate and encourage the development of demonstrably effective dispute resolution mechanisms, especially in cases involving private disputes. At the same time, because these alternatives allow for careful supervision by the judiciary, there is less danger that the poor will find no room on the docket. Most importantly, under these ADR mechanisms, which function as adjuncts to existing court systems, there is little likelihood that we will see the creation or development of public law by private parties. By focusing on [disputes] offering the least concern — the resolution of mostly private disputes by ADR systems that act as adjuncts to courts — programs such as CAA may diminish the pressure on courts to reduce substantive rights in response to perceived or actual excessive case-loads.

It is clear, however, that a number of ADR proponents have a far more ambitious vision of ADR than that set forth so far. Some, such as Jerold Auerbach, seem to favor community resolution of disputes using community values instead of the rule of law. Others, such as Chief Justice Burger, complain that "there is some form of mass neurosis that leads many people to think courts were created to solve all the problems of mankind," and believe that ADR must be used to curb the "flood of new kinds of conflicts" . . . that have purportedly overwhelmed the judicial system. In either case, these ADR advocates propose a truly revolutionary step — the resolution of cases through ADR mechanisms free from any judicial monitoring or control.

If we can assume that it is possible to finance and administer truly efficient systems of dispute resolution, then there would appear to be no significant objections to the use of even wholly independent ADR mechanisms to resolve private disputes that do not implicate important public values. For instance, settling minor grievances between neighbors according to local mores or resolving simple contract disputes by commercial norms may lead to the disposition of more disputes and the greater satisfaction of the participants. In strictly private disputes, ADR mechanisms such as arbitration often are superior to adjudication. Disputes can be resolved by neutrals with substantive expertise, preferably chosen by the parties, and the substance of disputes can be examined without issue-obscuring procedural rules. Tens of thousands of cases are resolved this way each year by labor and commercial arbitration, and even more private disputes undoubtedly could be better resolved through ADR than by adjudication.

However, if ADR is extended to resolve difficult issues of constitutional or public law — making use of nonlegal values to resolve important social issues or allowing those the law seeks to regulate to delimit public rights and duties — there is real reason for concern. An oft-forgotten virtue of adjudication is that it ensures the proper resolution and application of public values. In our rush to embrace alternatives to litigation, we must be careful not to endanger what law has accomplished or to destroy this important function of formal adjudication.

The concern here is that ADR will replace the rule of law with nonlegal values. . . . For example, many environmental disputes are now settled by negotiation and mediation instead of adjudication. Indeed, as my colleague Judge Wald recently observed, there is little hope that Superfund legislation can solve our nation's toxic waste problem unless the vast bulk of toxic waste disputes are resolved through negotiation, rather than litigation. Yet, as necessary as environmental negotiation may be, it is still troubling. When Congress or a government agency has enacted strict environmental protection standards, negotiations that compromise these strict standards with weaker standards result in the application of values that are simply inconsistent with the rule of law. Furthermore, environmental mediation and negotiation present the danger that environmental standards will be set by private groups without the democratic checks of governmental institutions.

A subtle variation on this problem of private application of public standards is the acceptance by many ADR advocates of the "broken-telephone" theory of dispute resolution that suggests that disputes are simply "failures to communicate" and will therefore yield to "repair service" by the expert "facilitator." . . . Mutual understanding and good feeling among disputants obviously facilitates intelligent dispute resolution, but there are some disputes that cannot be resolved simply by mutual agreement and good faith. It is a fact of political life that many disputes reflect sharply contrasting views about fundamental public values that can never be eliminated by techniques that encourage disputants to "understand" each other. Indeed, many disputants understand their opponents all too well. One essential function of law is to reflect the public resolution of such irreconcilable differences; lawmakers are forced to choose among these differing visions of the public good. A potential danger of ADR is that disputants who seek only understanding and reconciliation may treat as irrelevant the choices made by our lawmakers and may, as a result, ignore public values reflected in rules of law.

We must also be concerned lest ADR becomes a tool for diminishing the judicial development of legal rights for the disadvantaged. . . . ADR may result in the reduction of possibilities for legal redress of wrongs suffered by the poor and underprivileged, "in the name of increased access to justice and judicial efficiency." Inexpensive, expeditious, and informal adjudication is not always synonymous with fair and just adjudication. The decision makers may not understand the values at stake and parties to disputes do not always possess equal power and resources. Sometimes because of this inequality and sometimes because of deficiencies in informal processes, lacking procedural protections, the use of alternative mechanisms will produce nothing more than inexpensive and ill-informed decisions. And these decisions may merely legitimize decisions made by the existing power structure within society. Additionally, by diverting particular types of cases away from adjudication, we may stifle the development of law in certain disfavored areas of law. Imagine, for example, the impoverished nature of civil rights law that would have resulted had all race discrimination cases in the sixties and seventies been mediated rather than adjudicated. The wholesale diversion of cases involving the legal rights of the poor may result in the definition of these rights by the powerful in our society rather than by the application of fundamental societal values reflected in the rule of law. . . .

Even with these concerns, however, there are a number of promising areas in which we might employ ADR in lieu of traditional litigation. Once a body of law is well developed, . . . ADR mechanisms can be structured in such a way that public rights and duties would not be defined and delimited by private groups. The recent experience of labor arbitrators in the federal sector, who are required to police compliance with laws, rules, and regulations, suggests that the interpretation and application of law may not lie outside the competence of arbitrators. So long as we restrict arbitrators to the application of clearly defined rules of law and strictly confine the articulation of public law to our courts, ADR can be an effective means of reducing mushrooming caseloads. Employment discrimination cases offer a promising example. Many employment discrimination cases are highly fact-bound and can be resolved by applying established principles of law. Others, however, present novel questions that should be resolved by a court. If the more routine cases could be certified to an effective alternative dispute resolution system that would have the authority to make some final determinations, the courts could devote greater attention to novel legal questions, and the overall efficiency of an anti-discrimination law might be enhanced. . . .

Finally, there are some disputes in which community values — coupled with the rule of law — may be a rich source of justice. Mediation of disputes between parents and schools about special education programs for handicapped children has been very successful. A majority of disputes have been settled by mediation, and parents are generally positive about both the outcome and the process. At issue in these mediations is the appropriate education for a child, a matter best resolved by parents and educators — not courts. Similarly, many landlord–tenant disputes can ultimately be resolved only by negotiation. Most tenant "rights" are merely procedural rather than substantive. Yet tenants desire substantive improvement in housing conditions or assurances that they will not be evicted. Mediation of landlord-tenant disputes, therefore, can often be more successful than adjudication — both parties have much to gain by agreement.

In both of these examples, however, the option of ultimate resort to adjudication is essential. It is only because handicapped children have a statutory right to education that parent-school mediation is successful. It is only because tenants have procedural rights that landlords will bargain at all. ADR can thus play a vital role in constructing a judicial system that is both more manageable and more responsive to the needs of our citizens. It is essential — as the foregoing examples illustrate — that this role of ADR be strictly limited to prevent the resolution of important constitutional and public law issues by ADR mechanisms that are independent of our courts. Fortunately, few ADR programs have attempted to remove public law issues from the courts. Although this may merely reflect the relative youth of the ADR movement, it may also manifest an awareness of the danger of public law resolution in nonjudicial fora.

Apart from the issues concerning the appropriate application of ADR mechanisms, two additional overriding considerations should affect the employment of ADR. One has to do with research and appraisal, the other with the training and expertise of those who will serve as neutrals in ADR systems. There are a number of ADR proponents who appear to believe that a good neutral can resolve any issue without regard to substantive expertise. Our experience with arbitrators and mediators in collective bargaining proves the folly of this notion. The best neutrals are those who understand the field in which they work. Yet, the ADR movement often seeks to replace issue-oriented dispute resolution mechanisms with more generic mechanisms without considering the importance of substantive expertise.

Some would respond that judges are generalists and yet we trust our state and federal judiciary to resolve a broad range of disputes. This argument, however, is deceptive because judges are specialists in resolving issues of law. Law aims to resolve disputes on the basis of rules, whereas alternative dispute resolution mechanisms turn to non-legal values. If disputes are to be resolved by rules of law, the legal experts designated by our state and federal constitutions — that is, the judges — should resolve them. If non-legal values are to resolve disputes, we should recognize the need for substantive expertise.

3. Judith Resnik, *Many Doors? Closing Doors? Alternative Dispute Resolution and Adjudication,* 10 OHIO ST. J. ON DISP. RESOL. 211 (1995)

As the title for this lecture forecasts, my review prompts me to be less optimistic than others about the array of options that are and will be available to litigants seeking decision making from the state. The assumption of many proponents, that ADR will increase the options available to litigants within the publicly financed system, may not be borne out. As the state makes alternative dispute resolution its own, both ADR and adjudication are being reconceptualized. In this interaction, we may soon find ourselves with a narrower, not a richer, range of forms of dispute resolution.

* * *

II. THE CALL FOR MANY DOORS

I turn back to the Pound Conference, . . . at which Professor Frank Sander called for a "multi-doored" courthouse. . . . Professor Sander took as his burden the need to explain the "significant characteristics of various alternative dispute resolution mechanisms." He took as his task to educate his readers on what else there was [besides litigation] and then to persuade his readers of the desirability and utility of those "alternative dispute resolution forms." His purpose was to suggest "promising avenues to explore." Professor Sander's key move was to focus the discussion not on substantive areas . . . but rather on process. He urged that across a wide variety of disputes, the process should be elaborated, and a mediation, conciliation, or alternative phase be incorporated into it. Professor Sander pointed to some experiments with these processes, labeled "alternative dispute resolution," as evidence of the plausibility of his proposals.

Pause to consider the metaphor that has come to encapsulate his ideas: a "multi-doored courthouse." The image has a good deal of appeal, stemming in part from its implicit reliance on the phrase "access to justice" to posit a structure with several doors of entry. In his reprinted speech, Frank Sander actually described a "lobby" in which a litigant could be "channeled through a screening cleric" to one of six doors, comprising "a diverse panoply of dispute resolution processes." Specifically, one might be sent to "mediation, arbitration, fact finding, malpractice screening panel, superior court, or an ombudsperson."

While "flexible," this model also assumed something presumably stable: the courthouse was a known, readily conjured-up entity. In fact, one of the doors in the Sander lobby was to something called the "superior court." Moreover, one of Professor Sander's goals was to "reserve the courts for those activities for which they are best suited and to avoid swamping and paralyzing them with cases that do not require their unique abilities." Whatever the number of doors, the call was for access to and preservation of the courthouse.

It is fair to say that, within a very short time period, Frank Sander's call has been heard. It is worth mapping that shift, from disinterest and some hostility toward ADR to the embrace of it as a mode of responding to disputes. Before detailing the shift, both in practice and in ideology, to show the markers in law and doctrine that delineate the state's endorsement of ADR, a definitional framework for alternative dispute resolution is needed. Thus far, my shorthand phrase "ADR" has assumed a uniformity of activity unfair to the complexity and richness of the ADR arena. I will not detail all its array here, but I do not want to be heard as blurring distinctive aspects of the many modes of dispute resolution under the ADR umbrella. . . . I will group the various methods into modes that are delineated by the nature of the work of that third party.

A first mode is quasi-adjudicatory; this form of ADR offers a truncated, abbreviated fact-finding process that yields an outcome, decided by a third party, in the hopes that with that result, the parties will conclude their dispute. Both private contractual and court-annexed arbitration fit this mode. The difference is that under contractual arbitration, individuals or entities have an agreement to arbitrate, and that agreement also specifies the mechanism for selection of arbitrators. In contrast, under many court-annexed arbitration programs, litigants are sent to arbitration without such prior agreements and have varying amounts of control over the selection of arbitrators. Court-annexed arbitration typically permits parties to reject the arbitrator's decision and litigate, albeit sometimes with penalties and disincentives. However, if the parties do not object, the judgment of the arbitrator functions as a judgment of the court.

Under both court-annexed and contractual arbitration, the assumption is that information, provided to an outsider, will enable that outsider to render a fair outcome. What makes this process not adjudication is that the proceeding is not conducted by a state-employed individual who bears the title "judge," formal evidentiary rules do not apply, and opinions are often not written. It is, however, important to keep in mind that this process shares with adjudication a commitment to a case-specific outcome made by a third party and predicated upon an inquiry into the claims of fact made by disputants.

A second mode of ADR also relies upon some third party intervention but for a different purpose. A third party is introduced not to make a decision, but rather to inform the disputants of how outsiders view the dispute and how these outsiders would decide, were they asked to do so. The hope is that with such information, the disputants themselves will obviate the need for third party intervention by settling their differences. That settlement, however, is presumed to have been shaped in light of the views of the outsiders. The views of those outsiders, in turn, are presumed to have been shaped by the information that the parties provided in a format akin to adjudication. In both "summary jury trials" and "mini-trials," information comes either from witnesses or with arguments by lawyers or litigants.

A third form of ADR moves farther away from formal modes of information development. Conversation (sometimes called mediation, sometimes called a conference, sometimes called evaluation) is employed to elicit agreement by the parties. Judge-run settlement conferences are an example of this genre of ADR, as are "early neutral evaluations" ("ENE"). In this form of ADR, the relationship between information and outcome may be obscure, in part by virtue of the absence of formal articulation by the third party of its views of the respective positions of the disputants. Reaching agreement is one goal, as is the narrowing of the dispute, should further proceedings or adjudication be needed. When settlements take place, it is because of parties' consent, which may or may not track their legal rights.

Some commentators have attempted to limit the use of the term ADR and resist its application. For some, settlement programs or judicial management are not properly classified as ADR. A vivid example of a settlement expressly detached from legal right comes from Judge Jack Weinstein's work in the Agent Orange litigation. His efforts produced a $180 million settlement for the class, which he then approved. Thereafter, Judge Weinstein dismissed the claims of those who had "opted out" — on the grounds that these individuals had no legal claim, that as far as he could then tell, dioxin did not cause their injury.

For others, criteria are imposed to qualify a program as ADR. The impulse to constrain the vocabulary stems from a variety of concerns, including that too much is being packaged as ADR, confusing the analysis, and that certain forms of intervention, such as judicial engagement with the parties to search for settlement, would be better described as "creative judicial management" ("CJM") or settlement efforts, and separately considered, rather than subsumed within the ADR framework.

The effort to peel settlement programs away from ADR is, in my view, hard to sustain. Settlement remains a central purpose of many forms of ADR, including those not styled "settlement conferences." Even those forms of ADR closely resembling adjudication, such as court-annexed arbitration, rely on parties' acceptance of the outcomes (a form of settlement) rather than parties' insistence on adjudication. Moreover, many within the legal community include settlement efforts as part of their own descriptions of the reasons for ADR, or link various forms of ADR to court management and settlement. Hence, the discussion that follows considers settlement programs as a species of ADR.

The concern about the way in which an overflowing "ADR basket" can make mushy an analysis is a different kind of criticism, one well taken in many contexts. Were this essay an inquiry into the quality of outcomes or processes of ADR, it would be necessary to consider each form individually and not to speak of ADR as a "generic." However, my interest here is in the relationship between ADR in its generic form, as an idea of an alternative regime (much as Professor Sander sought) to state-based adjudication. Because the legal establishment's promotion of the variety of forms of ADR has generally been as a package, it is appropriate within the confines of this lecture to consider ADR as an undifferentiated set of processes. . . .

Congressional Promotion of ADR and ADR's Use in Administrative Agencies. The Federal Rules of Civil Procedure are largely the work product of the judiciary, acting through its special committees. These rules come into being by virtue of congressional inaction. But Congress has not been silent in the ADR conversation. Over the past few years, many members of Congress have also voiced enthusiasm for ADR, and some of their views have become part of legislation. The Civil Justice Reform Act of 1990 reiterated by statute the aspiration that district courts use ADR. This legislation is the major statement by Congress on civil processes of the last decade. Its stated purposes are to reduce delay and expense, and alternatives to trial and adjudication are important aspects of the legislation.

A related piece of legislation is the Administrative Dispute Resolution Act of 1990 (ADRA) which requires each federal agency to "adopt a policy that addresses the use of alternative means of dispute resolution and case management." The act instructs agencies to consider using ADR at all phases of their work, from rulemaking and enforcement actions to agency adjudication. The ADRA is predicated upon congressional "findings" of ADR's desirability. Congress believed ADR to be "faster, less expensive, and less contentious," and that ADR could generate "more creative, efficient, and sensible outcomes" than does "litigation in the Federal courts." This legislation represents a "government-wide emphasis" on ADR. Like ADR in the federal courts, programs existed in agencies before legislation authorized their use. Like ADR in the courts, commentators report uneven implementation, but the aspiration for expansive use remains strong. . . .

The Legalization and Institutionalization of ADR. Let me pause to summarize. In 1976, Frank Sander called for more modalities of dispute resolution — based in the courts. His call has been more than heard; it has become law via legislation, national and local rule making, and executive proclamation. Every branch of the federal government has signaled its support of ADR. While the pattern of implementation is varied, and the discussion of it encompasses a range of procedures, approval in theory of ADR has become commonplace. The current legal issues are not whether ADR is a desirable mode for courts and agencies to adopt or whether courts should play a role in encouraging parties to settle and to explore a variety of procedures to help them achieve an agreement. Rather, today's issues are what forms of ADR should be adopted, what kinds of settlement programs are acceptable, what kinds of disputes are appropriate to which forms of ADR, whether ADR providers are (like judges) immune from suits and the reach of their jurisdiction, and how to increase the use of ADR procedures. Discussion centers about the permissible and impermissible incentives to settle.

V. CLAIMS MADE FOR ADR AND VIEWS OF ADJUDICATION

The discussion below maps differing kinds of benefit perceived to be conferred by ADR and the relationship between that benefit and what adjudication is supposed to afford. Because ADR's success is often marked by distinguishing ADR from adjudication, attitudes about what adjudication does and does not do can be found, explicitly or implicitly, in discussions of ADR. One could read the rules and statutes on ADR as a national referendum, standing for the proposition that the conclusions reached by ADR in general and by settlement in particular are either equal to or better than those achieved by adjudication by either judge or jury. What is particularly interesting is that some of the prominent proponents of this claim are themselves judges, whom we might have thought would be adjudication loyalists. What are the elements for the stature of ADR? . . .

1. ADR as a Default Position. A major premise of one strand of ADR advocacy is that current adjudicatory procedures are simply inadequate to the task. ADR functions not so much as a good, in and of itself, but rather as a good because the system is in "crisis" and something is needed to fix it. ADR is one of many techniques of managing this crisis and might be on an equal footing with other proposed curative measures, such as curtailing discovery rights or controlling abusive attorneys. When ADR is proposed on these grounds, it is seen as a useful alternative because of the claim that ADR is cheaper and quicker than trial, which is the baseline often used in the discussion.

The claim that ADR is less expensive than adjudication may also entail the claim that litigation is unnecessarily expensive and wasteful. Sometimes an ADR form is preferable because it provides a quicker, cheaper quasi-adjudication (i.e. court-annexed arbitration), and sometimes an ADR form is preferable because it eschews adjudication altogether. Under this view, ADR moves out from under; ADR is no longer a default position but a practice preferred to adjudication, for it is a way to make the world "better."

2. ADR as More Congenial than Adjudication. A second form of praise for ADR is about its potential for kindness as contrasted (sometimes explicitly) with nastiness, which is associated with adjudication. ADR is perceived to be friendly, flexible, and nicer than the uncivil exchanges that characterize litigation. This congenial theme contains a bundle of claims, which is worth sorting through.

One means by which ADR is believed to achieve a congenial tone is because some forms of ADR have the potential to reduce the role of attorneys. Less lawyering is not only a way to minimize fees and thus make the process less expensive and speedier. A world with fewer lawyers is imagined to be less rigid and more inventive. The assumption is that, without lawyers, the disputants are empowered to act, and with that empowerment, can shape solutions more responsive to their needs than third parties, in role as adjudicators, would impose.

The ADR-as-congenial set of claims is not wholly dependent upon the elimination of lawyers. Rather, ADR is also seen as beneficial when lawyers are present — to educate and civilize lawyers by focusing them on the needs of their clients. Some forms of ADR aspire to teach lawyers that initiating settlement negotiations and engaging in various forms of compromise are not signs of weakness. Other forms of ADR hope to provide clients with information directly, enabling clients to better monitor their lawyers who may not always be loyal agents. While adjudicatory modes increase parties' dependence on lawyers, ADR may under this view, both lessen parties' dependence on lawyers and focus lawyers' attention more directly on parties' needs and interests.

The vision of ADR as communicative and congenial comes with a frank critique of many of the attributes of adjudication. The formality of adjudication is perceived as undermining open communication. The procedural requirements of adjudication are described as roadblocks to communication and to fairness. The rights of public access and information are seen as intrusive on private parties, who might otherwise respond to the state in its role as facilitator of agreements. Adjudication is seen as a process that often brings out the worst in its participants, either because it distorts their abilities to pursue self-interest or because it defines self-interest in such a fashion that requires inflicting losses, rather than maximizing gains.

3. ADR as More Efficient than Adjudication. For those forms of ADR that are focused on settlement, three assumptions result in efficiency: first, settlements by parties are voluntary; second, the parties have better information than adjudicators; third, with information and volition, parties have the control to achieve outcomes that are better than those imposed by adjudicators. Settlement-oriented ADR thus becomes a more efficient way to resolve disputes than adjudication.

Efficiency claims on behalf of ADR forms that are quasi-adjudicatory rest not on consent as much as on speed, accessibility and on the quantum of procedure provided. Court-annexed arbitration is described as a quicker, shorter, less formal trial. Because efficiency is not simply equated with economy but also entails accuracy (or sufficient accuracy in light of reduced costs), claims made for scaled-down adjudication embody a serious critique of adjudication. The point made is that the outcomes are just as good, or good enough, with less process, less cost, less delay.

4. ADR as Fairer than Adjudication. The efficiency arguments for ADR are sometimes turned into or related to arguments about fairness. Both arguments share a view that parties have superior access to and actual possession of infor-

mation than do third party decision makers. From this vantage point, adjudication is seen as a technique that can both distract and confuse. Legal rules operate to frame debates in a fashion that obscures parties' goals and that results in either wins or losses, rather than a richer set of possible resolutions. In contrast, ADR is seen as focusing on issues, relaxing the law, and thus providing more "just" results.

The perceived fairness of ADR may, like the other claims detailed above, vary with the kind of program used. For example, proponents of ADR as more fair may cite litigant reports of more satisfaction with court-annexed ADR than with judicially run settlement conferences at which they are not present, and argue for court-annexed arbitration but not other forms of ADR. Moreover, not only may proponents argue on behalf of a particular form of ADR (such as mediation), they may also believe that those processes are inappropriate for particular kinds of cases.

VI. CONCLUSION: CHANGES TO BE WELCOMED?

Before concluding, I want to be sure that I am not heard as putting forth too pat a story; our legal culture is not unitary or without nuance. . . . My task here is not to elaborate a structural analysis of why procedural forms have been transformed over the last three decades. Rather, I have considered the changes in the ways in which adjudication and ADR have been framed and discussed by members of the legal establishment. I turn now toward the future. I believe we are approaching a time when many a civil trial will be characterized as a "pathological event." One possibility is that this development is to be welcomed as an appropriate correction to what John Langbein calls the "too trial-centered" Anglo-American tradition. From this perspective, one must recall that a strong source of pressure for ADR comes from the judiciary. Judicial endorsement of ADR is a demonstration from individuals with firsthand knowledge of the weakness of adjudication, its failures and limitations. To the extent judicial support of ADR affects our understanding of the value of adjudication, judges may wisely be participating in a societal shove that will result in the demise of civil adjudication as it is currently understood. Further, the decline of civil adjudication in law courts, and its shift to governmental agencies, claims facilities, and private dispute resolution centers may be the appropriate denouement of this cycle of procedural reform.

Alternatively, anxiety about the triumph of ADR can come from across the spectrum, from those perceived to be proponents of ADR as well as from those styled proponents of adjudication. Proponents of ADR have succeeded in making it "an integral part of our federal judicial system." In the process, they have helped to change both "our federal judicial system" and ADR. For those who envisioned ADR as the blossoming of something different and generative, they should worry . . . about its institutionalization and its transformation into the very adversarial processes that they had hoped to avoid. As courts make ADR their own, that formalization may well undermine the very attributes of ADR that prompted its praise. Further, as courts compel ADR, the relationship between ADR and volition weakens, pushing it ever closer to a state-imposed mode of resolution. On the other hand, when ADR mimes adjudication, the critique of ADR as a lawless or factless process loses strength.

Similarly, those who think adjudication has something to offer had better start explaining why one would aspire to a preserve for adjudication, and why relatively highly paid government officials (to wit federal and state judges) should be empowered to do some of it. If there is an important and affirmative, if not a cheerful, story to be told for the preservation of adjudicatory forms, with judges in distinctive roles, and why a culture would value, cherish, fund, encourage, and sometimes insist on adjudication, then those who believe so had better speak up soon, for it is becoming increasingly hard to hear those claims. . . .

Chapter 2

COMMUNICATIONS: THEORY AND PRACTICE

A. INTRODUCTION

This chapter addresses the theory and practice of communication. Law school largely presents facts as a given, and where facts are changed, this typically happens by assumption. Those who live in the world of business and law know that facts are things that need to be discovered, and often the state of the world is difficult to determine with certainty. Even when full information is potentially available, obtaining that information often is cost-prohibitive. Determining the actual or probable facts of a situation often is difficult, and individuals (even clients and associates) frequently are less than fully forthcoming with information.

Communication is integral to the settlement of disputes, but it is integral to much else in life as well. So, the reader might reasonably ask, why a chapter on communication in a set of materials on ADR that is addressed to graduate students? Formal education spends much time on the tools of communication (vocabulary, grammar) and on writing skills, but little attention is given to two-way communication. Those who participate in forensics learn to argue effectively, which requires skills of persuasion, but not an exchange of information. One can obtain an excellent college education without ever being required to collect information from another individual, let alone one who is a participant in a serious and upsetting dispute. In addition, even people who have excellent communications skills can learn more. The focus here is on matters that are not commonly taught, so written communication is largely ignored, while particular attention is given to oral and nonverbal communication.

This chapter divides the discussion of communication into three sections: (1) effective communication and eliciting information through questions, (2) the context of communication, and (3) the management of impressions. Section E considers negotiation by women, and whether there are systematic differences between the manner in which women and men negotiate.

The material on effective communication reviews the stages and processes of communication. The essence of any communication is the exchange between encoder and decoder. The encoder and the decoder send messages back and forth across various channels, all of which are prone to incomplete or inaccurate communication. It is incumbent on the encoder to provide as strong and clear a signal as possible for the encoder to avoid noise or confusion. Likewise, the encoder must also use acceptable cues to complement the message. Finally, the decoder must make a reasonable attempt at receiving and comprehending the message for it to be fully understood. Understanding the stages and processes of communication allows the negotiator to be better prepared to adapt when necessary to changing situations.

The process of eliciting information through questions provides the negotiator with the ability to ask goal-directed questions, and at the same time provides an opportunity for exploration of new ideas and directions. Additionally, using questions properly allows the questioner to assist the client in developing their own ideas and thoughts in new directions. Both open-ended and closed-ended questions have merit, yet also entail risks. Open-ended questions provide the questioner with a rich array of information, some of which may be new, yet prevent the questioner from dictating the desired objective. Closed-ended questions result in specific and pointed answers, yet they are only as revealing as the framing of the question. A generous use of both types of questions is the best way to elicit information from clients.

The context of the communication is critically important for the informed negotiator. Without sufficient context, the meaning of the communication or message is lost. Personality variables, personal history, and heuristics all serve to affect the interpretation and understanding of the message. Being aware of these factors allows a skilled negotiator to go beyond the surface meaning of the message, and also to place the message in a different context to evaluate its veracity.

All the world is a stage, and we are all actors thereon in our interactions with others. The management of impressions serves to regulate the presentation of information to others in order to influence them in some manner. This regulation allows the encoder to present an image consistent with the information being presented. The audience, as a result, develops an understanding of the presenter's expectations. Coupled with heuristics, this image or role frames the presenter for the audience and allows for less noise in the transmission of the communication. It is reasonable to assume that if the audience has a preconceived (and at least moderately accurate) notion of what is being presented, then the audience will understand and comprehend the message faster than if there had been no initial cues.

The final section addresses women as negotiators. Do men and women, as a class, differ in their approach to negotiation? Or, to borrow Carol Gilligan's famous phrase, do women negotiate "in a different voice"? To the extent that systematic differences between women and men with respect to negotiation can be identified, do these differences lead to different negotiation outcomes? We focus the discussion on educated and sophisticated negotiators, such as attorneys and business officials.

B. LISTENING SKILLS AND EFFECTIVE COMMUNICATIONS

1. Communication as an Interactive Process

Effective communication is a two-way path flowing from one person to another and back again through the process of feedback. The difficulty in this process lies at various stages beginning with the individual who sends the information (the encoder) as well as how the information is encoded, and the channel through which it is transferred. The receipt and evaluation of information by the decoder provide an additional opportunity for misunderstanding. Apart from the parties, there may be problems with "noise" (anything that interferes with effective communication) during any stage of the process.

When encoding a message, the sender must determine how it is to be framed. Having encoded the message, the next step is to transmit it, directly or through agents, to the desired recipients. The recipient could be a single individual or a group of people, and the method of communication may vary (face-to-face, over the telephone, etc.). The number of people for whom the message is intended also may affect the content of the communication.

The decoder must then evaluate the message sent via the transmission from the encoder and decipher it, while accurately filtering out "noise." For the decoder, the deciphering process includes not only attending to the specific verbiage, but also to any and all accompanying tonality, language style, and nonverbal communication. Additionally, the decoder will have to take into account any other information potentially relevant to the message, such as relationship to the sender, subject matter expertise, and personality factors. The meaning of a communication may be affected by prior interactions between the parties and their relationship to one another.

Feedback from the decoder is the final stage of communication. Without feedback directed from the decoder to the encoder, the communication becomes unidirectional. Unidirectional communication represents more of a command or directive than a dyadic interaction. If the encoder does not seek feedback and the decoder does not offer it, there is no assurance or validity check that the message was properly received. We can all think of instances when we have given unidirectional commands, directives, or requests and received something quite unexpected due to an absence of clarification. Too much feedback, however, can cause information overload, and creates unneeded noise that can disrupt the flow of the interaction. Consequently, it is important during the negotiation process to generate an appropriate amount of feedback to ensure effective communication.

As elaborate as this process may seem, we engage in it frequently on a day-to-day basis, with some results being more effective than others. Think of instances when you have attempted to effectively communicate with other people. Give consideration to where the process may have broken down. What steps, if any, could you have taken to change the results? How could you have enhanced the effectiveness of the message?

2. EASTWOOD ATWATER, I HEAR YOU 1-3, 165-74 (1992)

Whatever Happened to Listening? Despite the amount of time spent in listening, the average person does not listen very well. Immediately after hearing someone talk, we generally understand and remember only about half of what was said. Within the next forty-eight hours, we forget half of that again, so that we retain only 25 percent of what we originally heard. . . .

How Well Do You Listen? To find out how well or poorly you listen, you might try this: The next time someone initiates a conversation with you, ask yourself, "Am I really listening or am I thinking of what I want to say next?". . . . Use this simple exercise to become more aware of your listening habits, especially the difficulty of listening well. . . . How would you rate yourself as a listener? How do you think others would rate you? Ask a friend, someone at work, or your spouse or child for their opinions.

Faulty Listening Habits. Often, we fail to listen well for some rather obvious reasons. Many times we are too busy talking to listen, or we may be preoccupied or distracted. Sometimes, we are simply too tired or too lazy to listen. After all, listening is hard work, because it requires concentration. But most often, it's because of our faulty listening habits.

Think of the worst listeners you know, and describe their listening habits. . . . The poor listener commonly: interrupts; jumps to conclusions; finishes the speaker's sentences; is inattentive; changes the subject; writes everything down; doesn't give any responses; is impatient; loses his or her temper; and fidgets nervously. Sound familiar? Probably so, because each of us has engaged in some of these practices at one time or another. However, when we exhibit any of these at least 40 percent of the time, others tend to see them as habitual or characteristic of us.

Vocal Expressions. A good listener . . . hears more than the speaker's words. He also hears the speaker's pitch, tone of voice, and rate of speech. He notices the variations of speech, like failing to complete a sentence and/or pausing frequently. . . . Tone of voice is an especially valuable clue to feelings. Rollo May, a famous psychotherapist, often asks himself "What does the voice say when I stop listening to the words and listen only to the tone?" . . . From the listener's standpoint, anger and sadness are usually the easiest to recognize, while nervousness and jealousy are among the most difficult. The volume and pitch of the speaker's voice, how high or low, or how loud or soft it sounds, are also helpful in decoding the speaker's message. . . . The rate of speech also tells us something about the speaker's feelings. People talk faster when they are excited or anxious, or when they are speaking about a personal problem or something that is threatening to them. People are also apt to speak faster when they are trying to persuade us or sell us something. People usually talk more slowly when they are depressed, grief-stricken, disgusted, contemptuous, or tired.

3. DAVID A. BINDER, PAUL BERGMAN & SUSAN C. PRICE, LAWYERS AS COUNSELORS (1991)

INHIBITORS TO COMMUNICATION

The seven inhibitors described below are common in lawyer-client dialogues. While other phenomena may also inhibit active client participation, these seven operate across a wide range of client personality types. Though the discussion treats each inhibitor as a separate phenomenon, in practice each often intertwines with others. Of the seven inhibitors, the first two — ego threat and case threat — probably play the most pervasive role in blocking full communication.

A. Ego Threat. Clients tend to withhold information which they perceive as threatening to their self-esteem. The requested information may relate either to past or anticipated behavior, and the feelings that a question may arouse can range from mild embarrassment to a strong sense of guilt or shame. If a client believes that a truthful response will lead you to evaluate the client negatively, such a response threatens the client's self-esteem; the response is "ego threatening." Rather than risk your negative evaluation, the client may answer . . . [inaccurately or incompletely]. Ego threat may at times arise not because a client fears your personal negative evaluation but because a client fears that certain information may become public. [A] client may fear that disclosing information may lead friends, relatives or others to think ill of the client. In such a situation, a client may admit damaging information as long as the client believes that you will keep the information confidential.

B. Case Threat. A second major factor tending to inhibit client communication is "case threat." A client may believe that revealing information will "hurt my case." For example, an innocent criminal defendant may not want to reveal to you that she was near the scene of a crime because she fears that if the judge and jurors find it out she will lose. Alternatively, the client may fear that revealing the information will cause you to believe that the case is a loser and to fail to pursue it zealously. (In such situations, ego threat may be present as well. If the client believes that revealing that she was at the scene of the crime will cause the lawyer to disbelieve her claim of innocence, the potential loss of self-esteem may well inhibit a truthful response.)

"Case threat" may also inhibit clients who have transactional matters. Assume that Jean consults you in connection with a proposal to lease space in an office building. During a conversation about negotiation strategy, you inquire about the maximum length lease that Jean will accept. Jean is willing to accept a ten-year lease, but she hopes the owner will agree to a five-year term. Jean may be unwilling to reveal her willingness to accept a ten-year deal, feeling that once you know her "bottom line," you will not press as hard as you otherwise might for a shorter lease term.

C. Role Expectations. Most of us have sets of beliefs about what kind of behavior is appropriate within the confines of particular relationships. For example, most people think there are certain ways that one should (or should not) behave when interacting with parents. Similarly, most people have beliefs about how employers should relate to employees. We may each have different sets of beliefs, but most of us do approach many relationships with preset expectations. . . . Role expectations develop from a variety of sources, from both actual and vicarious experiences. Family, friends, associates, news media, institutions and the like constantly deliver messages about what constitutes appropriate behavior when one assumes a particular position. In short, role expectations are learned and shaped by life experiences.

What does this phenomenon have to do with lawyers and clients? Clients will frequently enter your office with a set of expectations about what constitutes appropriate "client behavior." The expectations will vary from client to client; not all clients will have acquired their expectations from the same learning sources. In many instances, however, clients think of their lawyers as occupying positions of authority. Such clients may be somewhat reluctant to communicate fully in the belief that you know what subjects are deserving of inquiry. Thus, if you fail to broach a topic which a client feels is important, the client may assume (again, either consciously or intuitively) that the topic is not a significant one. Interestingly, many clients have an opposite set of beliefs. This second group of clients tends to believe that a lawyer's role is limited to carrying out their wishes and that it is their privilege to speak their minds about any and all topics. In short, these clients see themselves in a dominant position vis-a-vis their counsel, and they are often not interested in fully responding to inquiries they perceive as unimportant. The closer a client's expectations come to either extreme of the dominant-subordinate spectrum, the more difficulties you may expect to encounter in developing full information. . . .

D. Etiquette Barrier. A fourth inhibitor is the "etiquette barrier." Often, an individual has information that he or she will freely provide to some persons but not to others. For example, there are things that women tell women but not men; that blacks tell blacks, but not whites; that students tell students, but not teachers; that doctors tell doctors, but not patients. Information is perceived to be appropriate for peers but not for those in other groups or roles. The etiquette barrier arises from people's desires not to shock, embarrass, offend, or discomfort. It reflects a person's thinking about the effect of information on a listener, not a person's thinking about how the listener will view him or her. Hence, loss of self-esteem is not a component of the etiquette barrier. . . .

E. Trauma. This phenomenon occurs when you ask a client to recall an experience which evokes unpleasant feelings. Many events cause people to experience such negative feelings as fear, anger, humiliation, and sadness. When you ask clients to recall such events, they may re-experience the negative feelings. . . . Likewise, an estate planning client who is considering disinheriting a close relative may, for similar reasons, be reluctant to talk about the reasons he or she wants to disinherit the person.

F. Perceived Irrelevancy. This inhibitor is often more difficult to recognize, as it does not involve any feelings of discomfort or threat. The feeling involved here is one of "no reason to provide that data." A client feels that nothing will be gained by providing the information you request and so is reluctant to provide it. . . . Assume you represent a partnership which has asked you to negotiate the purchase of a building. You may ask the partners for information about why the owner wants to sell, so that in problem-solving fashion, you can structure the deal in such a way that it meets both your clients' and the seller's needs. But the clients, perhaps seeing little importance in exploring the seller's needs, may provide only perfunctory information.

G. Greater Need. The last inhibitor is "greater need." This situation is characterized by a client's need or desire to talk about a subject other than that which is of immediate interest to you. As a consequence, the client cannot concentrate on your question, and full and accurate information is not forthcoming. For example, an incarcerated defendant concerned primarily with bail or O.R. [own recognizance] release will often be unable to turn full attention to questions relating to the underlying charge. Similarly, a tenant threatened with eviction may be more concerned with when and where he can move than with inquiries related to a potential "habitability defense." In such situations, your questions are not perceived as irrelevant or threatening. Rather, the client is simply concerned with a subject which, while perhaps secondary to you, is primary to the client.

FACILITATORS OF COMMUNICATION

The five facilitators described below encourage clients to participate fully in counseling dialogues. . . . Note that you typically may employ facilitators without waiting for client reluctance to rear its annoying head. That is, you routinely incorporate the facilitation into all dialogues, whether the clients are enthusiastic or reluctant participants.

A. Empathic Understanding. Empathic understanding typically gives clients feelings of trust and confidence in an attorney-client relationship and thereby motivates clients to participate fully in conversations. Despite the motivational power of empathic understanding, lawyers commonly fail to utilize it when talking with clients. People have limited opportunities in our society to express their thoughts and feelings to someone who is willing to (1) listen, (2) understand, and (3) at the same time, not judge. . . . Almost without realizing it, people will tend to provide an ever-increasing amount of information [self-propelling effect]. . . .

The opportunities for you to utilize empathic understanding are endless. Clients almost always are emotionally involved in their problems and, thus, repeatedly express feelings about what has occurred or is likely to occur. Their recitals of information are likely to be accompanied by and intertwined with feelings about such diverse matters as: (1) how they felt at the time an event occurred; (2) how they feel about people or institutions involved in their problem; (3) why events have unfolded, and why people have behaved as they have; (4) how they feel about an event at present; and (5) how they feel about what is likely to happen in the future. . . .

B. Fulfilling Expectations. The phenomenon of "fulfilling expectations" refers to people's tendencies to want to satisfy the perceived expectations of those with whom they interact. Your simply communicating, verbally or nonverbally, your expectations will often be the catalyst that motivates a client to undertake a particular discussion. This facilitator is especially useful when you sense that certain inhibitors are making a client reluctant to provide information. On sensing the reluctance, you can verbally convey a strong expectation that the sought data should be revealed. The client's need to conform to your expectations may well be stronger than whatever needs have given rise to the reluctance to respond. In such situations, the inhibitors will be overcome and the information revealed.

Note two additional points about fulfilling expectations. First, the phenomenon can be useful in overcoming memory difficulties as well as inhibitors. Second, the phenomenon can be inadvertently employed to create an expectation that the sought data need not be revealed. The following example will help you consider both points. Assume that a client has indicated that she cannot remember much of what occurred at a meeting held two years earlier. You may convey your expectation that by probing her memory further, the client will be able to recollect more information:

> I understand how hard it is to recall; I've often had that difficulty myself. Often I find, however, that if I concentrate for a while things start to come back. Why don't you think about it a little more?

This statement employs two facilitators. First, you empathize; you articulate your understanding of the difficulty. Additionally, you convey your expectation that with more effort, the client will be able to provide more information. Your message is, "though the task may be difficult, I expect that you will attempt it." Unfortunately, you may inadvertently convey an expectation that a client need make no further effort to recall information. For example, assume that in the example above you had said: "I understand that it is difficult to remember the details of an event that happened so long ago." This statement does nothing more than empathize with the client's difficulty, and standing alone it may be counterproductive. While you convey understanding of the client's dilemma, you also convey the idea that you do not expect an answer.

C. Recognition. Human beings often need attention and recognition from people outside their close circle of family and friends. They enjoy feeling important and seek the attention and esteem of outsiders. Thus, giving an interviewee "recognition" motivates the interviewee to be more open and cooperative. Assuming you are not a client's close friend or relative, you may supply "recognition" simply by sincerely praising a client's cooperation or help: "Your giving me that information is very helpful." "That was very important information you just gave me." "You're really doing a good job of setting out the consequences of not demanding an option to renew at this time."

D. Altruistic Appeals. People often need to identify with a high value or cause that is beyond their immediate self-interest — [often] identification with the objectives of a large social group. A person's performance of altruistic deeds usually increases the person's self-esteem. Thus, clients are often motivated to participate fully when doing so makes them feel altruistic.

E. Extrinsic Reward. Realizing that certain behavior is in their self-interest usually motivates people to engage in that behavior. Thus, a person with the mindset, "what's in it for me?" at times is reluctant to provide information. Hence, you may facilitate disclosure of information that a client seems reluctant to discuss by pointing out why the sought data may aid in resolving the client's problem. You thereby indicate that providing the information is in the client's best interest.

As the term "extrinsic" may suggest, this facilitator differs in an important way from those previously discussed. The earlier phenomena drew their motivational strength from satisfying clients' psychological needs within the counseling interaction itself. Use of extrinsic reward, on the other hand, achieves motivational force from a client's realizing how participation in the interview will satisfy needs external to the interview — i.e., a favorable resolution of a client's matter. A client's reward comes from outside the interview: "Mr. Edwards, if you will tell me a bit more about your investments, I'll be able to draft the trust in a way that minimizes taxes." . . .

PERSONALITY CONFLICTS

Though this chapter has described a number of psychological phenomena, . . . it has not mentioned one factor that all would recognize as important to the interaction of any two people — their personalities. All of us are more comfortable with some people than with others. Lawyer-client communications are often inhibited by some degree of personality conflict. If a client . . . perceives you as someone with whom he or she is not comfortable, or someone who is too aggressive or too passive to handle a matter effectively, the client may feel reluctant to participate fully. By the same token, you may, for one reason or another, perceive a client as too aggressive, passive, unscrupulous, or disorganized; and such perceptions may inhibit your interaction with the client. . . .

ELICITING INFORMATION: QUESTIONS

The information you get from clients, their motivation to speak and their attitudes towards you are all influenced to some degree by the kinds of questions that you ask. Of course, human behavior is too complex to conclude that a particular form of question will always generate the same type of client response. Nonetheless, research and experience demonstrate that different forms of questions are likely to alter the amount, nature and quality of information that you receive. By understanding the forms of questions, and the typical consequences each is likely to produce, you can make explicit questioning choices tailored to your goals, the type of information you are seeking and the particular client with whom you are dealing.

FORMS OF QUESTIONS

A. Generally. Questions come in a variety of forms, ranging from open to leading. No hard and fast line separates one form from another. But the principal touchstone that distinguishes forms of questions is the degree of freedom a question allows in a response. . . . The freer a client is to choose the scope of a response, the more "open" a question is. And the more a question restricts a response, the more "closed" it is. Neither form of question is necessarily more effective than the other. Given how clients typically react to open and closed questions, each has its purposes.

B. Open Questions. Open questions allow clients substantial latitude to select the content and wording of a response. Open questions indicate your expectation that a client respond at some length and allow a client to respond in his or her own words. At their broadest, open questions even allow a client to choose the subject matter of a response. Examine the following questions:

1. "Tell me what brought you in here."

2. "Tell me about your family."

3. "What happened after the meeting?"

4. "What took place during the conversation?"

5. "How will your employees react if you move the business to a new location?"

Each question is open. Each invites a lengthy response, on a variety of potential topics, and in words of the clients' own choosing. Even within the open question category, you find distinctions. No. 1 imposes no subject matter restriction at all. . . . No. 2 imposes some subject matter limitation — the client is limited to a discussion of "family." . . . No. 3 imposes a chronological limitation — the client is limited to talking about what took place "after the meeting." . . . No. 4 imposes a different sort of limitation — the client's response is limited to a single conversation. Yet, this question too is open. The client may talk about the parties to the conversation, what they said, and/or what activities took place during the conversation. Lastly, No. 5 asks the client to discuss possible consequences of a proposed decision on a group of employees. . . .

C. Closed Questions. Closed (narrow) questions select the subject matter of a client's response and also limit the scope of a reply. Closed questions seek specific data. Examples include:

1. "In which hand was she holding the gun?"

2. "How fast was the blue car going?"

3. "Just where did the chicken cross the road?"

4. "How many employees are likely to quit if you move the business to a new location?"

D. Yes-No Questions. "Yes-No" questions are a commonly employed form of closed question. Yes-No questions even more severely limit the scope of a client's response by including in the question all the information you select and asking the client only to confirm or deny it. All closed questions can be restated in Yes-No form. The Yes-No versions of the questions above are:

1. "Was she holding the gun in her left hand?"

2. "Was the blue car exceeding the speed limit?"

3. "Did the chicken cross the road at the crosswalk?"

4. "Will some employees quit if you move the business to a new location?"

E. Leading Questions. Leading questions not only provide all the information that you select but also suggest the desired answer. Leading questions are little more than outright assertions accompanied either by a tone of voice or language clue that you desire a particular answer. They are closed questions in assertive form. In leading form, the closed questions from subsection C are:

1. "She was holding the gun in her left hand?"

2. "The blue car was going over 65, correct?"

3. "The chicken crossed the road at the crosswalk, didn't it?"

4. "I take it you'll lose some employees if you move the business to a new location?"

The rather dramatic "Isn't it true . . ." phrase that cross-examiners tend to use during trial is certainly not a necessary characteristic of leading questions.

Questions two and three have other and less dramatic verbal clues, while the first and fourth rely on voice intonation.

ADVANTAGES AND DISADVANTAGES OF DIFFERENT FORMS OF QUESTIONS

A. Open Questions.

1. Open Questions Often Motivate Full Client Participation. Because they allow clients to decide what information is significant, open questions provide "recognition." You show confidence in their ability to know what information is significant. Both the recognition and the fact that they are talking about what they see as important tend to provide motivation.

Open questions typically avoid potential inhibitors. The primary inhibitors that open questions avoid are ego threat, case threat, and the etiquette barrier. Often, clients are uncomfortable about certain aspects of their problems and are, therefore, reluctant to talk about those aspects. A closed question seeking information about an uncomfortable topic may, therefore, harm rapport by forcing a client either to talk about an uncomfortable topic or consciously avoid it. Open questions leave clients free to avoid talking about threatening subjects.

As a lawyer, you often have to ask clients about sensitive subjects. When planning a client's estate, for example, you may raise the possibility that a client's child may predecease the client. Talking to a business client, you may ask about the integrity of the client's partner or office manager. As a criminal defense lawyer, you may ask about a client's mental state and past criminal record. Clients may be uncomfortable and reluctant to talk if, with a closed question, you directly seek such sensitive information. Open questions allow clients to discuss sensitive information in their own way and when they are ready to do so. . . .

2. Open Questions Often Facilitate Your Gaining Complete Data. Because both problems and clients' experiences are unique, you almost never will be able to think of everything that might be important to achieving a satisfactory solution. . . . Qualitative answers — feelings, reasons, other experiences — can only come when the question is open-ended, not closed, and when the answer must be a paragraph, not a word. . . . Psychological research has shown that answers to open questions are more accurate than answers to closed questions. . . . However, be warned that a number of disadvantages are associated with open questions.

3. Open Questions Sometimes Inhibit Full Client Participation. Open questions put much of the burden for recalling and describing information on a client. Many people are not comfortable in the conversational limelight and will prefer you to carry the load. In such situations, open questions may elicit only short, minimal responses.

4. Open Questions Are Not Sufficient for Gaining Complete Data. Open questions do little to stimulate memory. . . . Compared to other forms of report, narrative reports tend to be less complete. A narrative produces much higher accuracy but much lower quantity. . . . Thus, to get complete data you typically have to ask a combination of open and closed questions. Because of the ability to call specific data to a client's attention, closed questions are generally more successful than open ones at stimulating a client's recall.

Open questions may also fail to elicit information that clients do remember, but which they do not recognize as being legally salient. When a client is mistaken about or unaware of legal requirements, the client may well omit information from a narrative response in the belief that the information is without legal significance.

5. Open Questions Are Sometimes Inefficient. Open questions may not be effective with clients who ramble or are extremely verbose. Certain clients may regard a question such as, "What happened since our last meeting?" as an invitation to describe irrelevant events in great detail, and to vilify all with whom they disagree. Asking open questions of such clients may be the equivalent of pouring gasoline on a fire.

B. Closed Questions

1. Closed Questions Elicit Details. The most important advantage of closed questions is that they allow you to elicit details. . . .

2. Closed Questions Sometimes Motivate Clients. Some clients may be uncertain of how to respond to an open question. For example, a question such as, "What consequences do you see if we reject the proposal?" may confuse some clients. Does the question call for every possible consequence, or only for the most significant ones? How much elaboration do you expect? Does the question somehow "test" the client to see how many consequences the client can identify? Clients for whom open questions create such thoughts will probably be reluctant to answer fully and openly. Such clients may find closed questions "easier" to answer: their topics are readily identifiable, their scope is readily apparent, and a client has only to produce a limited amount of information. Therefore, for such clients, closed questions may provide greater motivation to answer.

Closed questions may provide greater motivation than open questions in other contexts as well. Recall the suggestion that open questions often motivate clients by allowing them to postpone mention of sensitive topics until the client feels comfortable doing so. You may employ closed questions to delay discussion of sensitive matters as well. Closed questions allow you to "tippy toe" either into or around sensitive topics. When you know or strongly suspect that a client will be reluctant to discuss a particular topic, through closed questions you can pursue the topic a small bit at a time, and stop at the point that a client becomes obviously reluctant to proceed further. Alas, as you undoubtedly suspect, closed questions also have disadvantages:

3. Too Many Closed Questions May Harm Rapport. Over-reliance on closed questions may result in clients leaving meetings feeling that they never had a chance to say what was really on their minds. The more you ask questions which limit the scope of a response, the less likely are you to learn everything that a client thinks is important. In turn, a client is likely to be less engaged in identifying a problem and actively participating in its resolution.

4. Closed Questions Often Prevent You from Learning Important Information. Asking numerous closed questions is likely to cause you to miss both trees and the forest. You miss trees, because in any matter, there are too many for you to find with closed questions. Moreover, clients tend not to volunteer information when faced with a plethora of closed questions, figuring that if a bit of data is important, surely you will seek it out. At the same time, your focus on individual trees is likely to obscure your view of the forest. The immersion in bits of detail frustrates your learning a client's overall story. . . .

5. Closed Questions Can Create Inaccurate Responses. Closed questions tend to produce more erroneous information than open questions. One potential reason may be a combination of the motivational factor, "fulfilling expectations," and the "filling" phenomenon. When you ask closed questions seeking details, clients usually try to fulfill your expectations by supplying such details. But because of the "filling" phenomenon, the answers may come not from clients' recollection of actual events, but from clients' past experiences. Therefore, clients who are asked for details may well respond with what their schemas tell them probably occurred, not what actually did occur.

Closed questions may distort responses in another way. Because closed questions define the topics for clients to a greater extent than do open questions, closed questions usually reflect a lawyer's choice of vocabulary, not a client's. For instance, compare the open question, "Describe his behavior" with the closed question, "Was he angry?" The closed question not only identifies a specific emotion, it also attaches a label to it. And closed questions' verbal labels often distort responses. In one study, changing a word in a question from "frequently" to "occasionally" produced markedly different results. In this study, which has been replicated often, one group of random respondents was asked, "Do you get headaches frequently and, if so, how often?" Another group was asked, "Do you get headaches occasionally, and, if so, how often?" The first group reported an average of 2.2 headaches per week; the second group only 0.7 headaches per week. . . .

C. Leading Questions

Although the term "leading question" is often accompanied by or greeted with sneers, such questions are sometimes proper and necessary for eliciting a full picture of a client's problem.

1. Leading Questions Sometimes Overcome Potential Inhibitors. Leading questions sometimes help you to overcome the inhibitors of ego threat, case threat and the etiquette barrier. These inhibitors sometimes make clients reluctant to disclose matters they perceive as sensitive. Hence, when a discussion may touch on a sensitive matter, use of leading questions suggests that you already know about the troublesome data, that the client need not fear letting the cat out of the bag, and that you are prepared to talk about it in a forthright manner. . . . The examples below illustrate how leading questions may overcome embarrassment in two typical legal situations. Compare the following sets of questions:

1. "Have you ever been arrested before?"

2. "I guess you've had some problems with the police before?"

3. "Do you see any problems in letting them look at your books?"

4. 'The acquiring company's examination of your books will bring to light things like allowing employees to use company cars for personal use. How should we talk to them about these matters?"

Assuming that you strongly suspect that the troublesome conduct has in fact occurred, the use of leading questions may overcome these clients' fear and embarrassment, and consequent reluctance to talk openly and honestly. However, as the sneer that often accompanies the term "leading" suggest, leading questions are not without their disadvantages.

2. Leading Questions Sometimes Prevent You from Learning Important Data. A leading question often reflects your ardent desire to have facts come out in a way favorable to a client. . . . You may thereby introduce inaccuracy into a discussion. When you later discover the inaccuracy (or have it pointed out to you by another party), it may be too late to seek solutions which you and a client might have pursued if the true data were known earlier.

3. Leading Questions May Be Ethically Improper. Use of leading questions in your office sometimes is even more improper than it may be at trial. Generally, you cannot ethically suggest "correct" answers to clients. . . .

D. Conclusion

Motivating clients to participate fully and gathering complete data usually requires you to employ each form of question. However, even employing the "correct" form of question at the "correct" time is no guarantee that motivation and complete, accurate data will result. Because no single client is typical in all respects, a question that motivates one client may inhibit another. Moreover, some clients will treat a yes-no question as little different from an open one, while others will respond quite literally. Lastly, any one client may respond to the same form of question differently at different times. Thus, you need to adapt the forms of questions to the dynamics of individual conversations.

4. Comments and Questions

a. The choice of language can have a major impact on a settlement process. For example, family mediators avoid judgmental language such as speaking of "failed marriage, broken home, custody, and visitation. They prefer nonjudgmental terms such as ending the relationship, mom's house and dad's house, parenting, access, and residence." JOHN M. HAYNES, THE FUNDAMENTALS OF FAMILY MEDIATION 185-186 (1994).

b. It is often helpful for a party to a negotiation to restate positions or views expressed by the other party. This ensures that the hearer has not misunderstood what she heard and also evidences careful listening.

c. Mediators frequently restate or reframe party statements to edit out incendiary language or to subtly change the focus of remarks. Sometimes, the mediator asks a party to explain a position in words that are more likely to appeal to the other party. While "restate" and "reframe" are commonly used as synonyms, some authors make a distinction between the two terms.

Restate connotes stating a few sentences in a way that reflects what the speaker said, but with a slight change of focus or removing offensive language. *Reframing* connotes a statement about the problem or issues and is used to help the parties to view the problem or concern in a different light.

KIMBERLEE K. KOVACH, MEDIATION: PRINCIPLES AND PRACTICE 181 (2004).

C. CONTEXT OF COMMUNICATIONS

1. Comments and Questions

a. How much is one ton? Is a ton exclusively a measure of weight, or can it be a measure of volume? The answer depends on which unit of weight or volume is under consideration, and there are more options than you might have imagined:

1. long ton or metric ton (2,240 pounds);

2. short ton (2,000 pounds);

3. register ton (100 cubic feet of cargo space in a ship);

4. freight ton (40 cubic feet); or

5. long ton of seawater (35 cubic feet).

The related concept of tonnage, meaning the carrying capacity of a ship, also varies. In England, tonnage is measured in the actual tons that the vessel can safely transport; in the U.S., tonnage is based on the cubic capacity of the hold. Tonnage as a measure of weight is sometimes measured in hundredweights, which is 100 pounds for a short ton but 112 pounds for a long ton.

b. Words take their meaning from the context in which they are used. This illustration, and the two items that follow, are designed to show the difficulties of clear and precise communication.

c. Similar issues are addressed by writers about meaning in literature and in law. *See, e.g.,* STANLEY E. FISH, IS THERE A TEXT IN THIS CLASS? (1980); RICHARD POSNER, LAW AND LITERATURE (1988).

2. FRANZ LIEBER, LEGAL AND POLITICAL HERMENEUTICS 17-19 (3d ed. 1880)

Let us take an instance of the simplest kind, to show in what degree we are continually obliged to resort to interpretation. Suppose a housekeeper says to a domestic: fetch some soup meat, accompanying the act with giving some money to the latter. Common sense and good faith will tell the domestic:

1. That he should go immediately, or as soon as his other occupations are finished;

2. That the money handed him by the housekeeper is intended to pay for the meat thus ordered, and not as a present to him;

3. That he should buy such meat and of such parts of the animal as has commonly been used at the house for making soup;

4. That he should go to the butcher that normally provides the family, or to some convenient stall, and not to an unnecessarily distant place;

5. That he return the rest of the money;

6. That he bring the meat home without adding anything injurious or disagreeable; and

7. That he fetch the meat for the use of the family and not for himself.

(Many more instructions might be added.) We are constrained, then, always to leave a large part of our meaning to be discovered by interpretation, which in many cases must necessarily cause some obscurity with regard to the exact meaning which our words were intended to convey (and which they in fact convey) to the other party.

3. *Frigaliment Importing Co., Ltd. v. B.N.S. Int'l Sales Corp.*, 190 F. Supp. 116 (1960)

FRIENDLY, Circuit Judge.

The issue is, what is chicken? Plaintiff says "chicken" means a young chicken, suitable for broiling and frying. Defendant says "chicken" means any bird of that genus that meets contract specifications on weight and quality, including what it calls "stewing chicken" and plaintiff pejoratively terms "fowl." Dictionaries give both meanings, as well as some others not relevant here. To support its position, plaintiff sends a number of volleys over the net; defendant essays to return them and adds a few serves of its own. Assuming that both parties were acting in good faith, the case nicely illustrates Holmes' remark "that the making of a contract depends not on the agreement of two minds in one intention, but on the agreement of two sets of external signs — not on the parties' having meant the same thing but on their having said the same thing." I have concluded that plaintiff has not sustained its burden of persuasion that the contract used "chicken" in the narrower sense.

The action is for breach of the warranty that goods sold shall correspond to the description. Two contracts are in suit. In the first, dated May 2, 1957, defendant, a New York sales corporation, confirmed the sale to plaintiff, a Swiss corporation, of "US Fresh Frozen Chicken, Grade A, Government Inspected, Eviscerated 2½-3 lbs. and 1½-2 lbs. each, all chicken individually wrapped in cryovac, packed in secured fiber cartons or wooden boxes, suitable for export."

The second contract, also dated May 2, 1957, was identical save that only 50,000 lbs. of the heavier "chicken" were called for, the price of the smaller birds was $37 per 100 lbs., and shipment was scheduled for May 30. When the initial shipment arrived in Switzerland, plaintiff found that the 2½-3 lbs. birds were not young chicken suitable for broiling and frying but stewing chicken or fowl; indeed, many of the cartons and bags plainly so indicated. Protests ensued. Nevertheless, shipment under the second contract was made on May 29, the 2½-3 lbs. birds again being stewing chicken. Defendant stopped the transportation of these at Rotterdam. This action followed.

Since the word "chicken" standing alone is ambiguous, I turn first to see whether the contract itself offers any aid to its interpretation. Plaintiff says the 1½-2 lbs. birds necessarily had to be young chicken, since the older birds do not come in that size, hence the 2½-3 lbs. birds must likewise be young. This is unpersuasive — a contract for "apples" of two different sizes could be filled with different kinds of apples even though only one species came in both sizes. Defendant notes that the contract called not simply for chicken but for "US Fresh Frozen Chicken, Grade A, Government Inspected." It says the contract thereby incorporated by reference the Department of Agriculture's regulations, which favor its interpretation; I shall return to this after reviewing plaintiff's other contentions.

The first hinges on an exchange of cablegrams which preceded execution of the formal contracts. The negotiations leading up to the contracts were conducted in New York between defendant's secretary, Ernest R. Bauer, and a Mr. Stovicek, who was in New York for the Czechoslovak government at the World Trade Fair. A few days after meeting Bauer at the fair, Stovicek telephoned and inquired whether defendant would be interested in exporting poultry to Switzerland. Bauer then met with Stovicek, who showed him a cable from plaintiff dated April 26, 1957, announcing that they "are buyer" of 25,000 lbs. of chicken 2½-3 lbs. weight, Cryovac packed, Grade A Government inspected, at a price up to 33¢ per pound, for shipment on May 10, to be confirmed by the following morning, and were interested in further offerings. After testing the market for price, Bauer accepted, and Stovicek sent a confirmation that evening.

Plaintiff stresses that, although these and subsequent cables between plaintiff and defendant, which laid the basis for the additional quantities under the first and for all of the second contract, were predominantly in German, they used the English word "chicken"; it claims this was done because it understood "chicken" meant young chicken whereas the German word, "Huhn," included both "Brathuhn" (broilers) and "Suppenhuhn" (stewing chicken), and that defendant, whose officers were thoroughly conversant with German, should have realized this. Whatever force this argument might otherwise have is largely drained away by Bauer's testimony that he asked Stovicek what kind of chickens were wanted, received the answer "any kind of chickens," and then, in German, asked whether the cable meant "Huhn" and received an affirmative response.

Plaintiff attacks this as contrary to what Bauer testified on his deposition in March, 1959, and also on the ground that Stovicek had no authority to interpret the meaning of the cable. The first contention would be persuasive if sustained by the record, since Bauer was free at the trial from the threat of contradiction by Stovicek, as he was not at the time of the deposition; however, review of the deposition does not convince me of the claimed inconsistency. As to the second contention, it may well be that Stovicek lacked authority to commit plaintiff for prices or delivery dates other than those specified in the cable; but plaintiff cannot at the same time rely on its cable to Stovicek as its dictionary to the meaning of the contract and repudiate the interpretation given the dictionary by the man in whose hands it was put. Plaintiff's reliance on the fact that the contract forms contain the words "through the intermediary of," with the blank not filled, as negating agency, is wholly unpersuasive; the purpose of this clause was to permit filling in the name of an intermediary to whom a commission would be payable, not to blot out what had been the fact.

Plaintiff's next contention is that there was a definite trade usage that chicken meant young chicken. Defendant showed that it was only beginning in the poultry trade in 1957, thereby bringing itself within the principle that when one of the parties is not a member of the trade, his acceptance of the standard must be made to appear by proving either that he had actual knowledge of the usage or that the usage is so generally known in the community that his actual individual knowledge of it may be inferred. Here, there was no proof of actual knowledge of the alleged usage; indeed, it is quite plain that defendant's belief was to the contrary. In order to meet the alternative requirement, the law of New York demands a showing that the usage is of so long continuance, so well established, so notorious, so universal, and so reasonable in itself, as that the presumption is violent that the parties contracted with reference to it, and made it a part of their agreement.

Plaintiff endeavored to establish such a usage by the testimony of three witnesses and certain other evidence. Strasser, resident buyer in New York for a large chain of Swiss cooperatives, testified that "on chicken I would definitely understand a broiler." However, the force of this testimony was considerably weakened by the fact that, in his own transactions, the witness, a careful businessman, protected himself by using "broiler" when that was what he wanted and "fowl" when he wished older birds. . . . A witness' consistent failure to rely on the alleged usage deprives his opinion testimony of much of its effect. Niesielowski, an officer of one of the companies that had furnished the stewing chicken to defendant, testified that "chicken" meant the male species of the poultry industry. That could be a broiler, a fryer or a roaster, but not a stewing chicken; however, he also testified that upon receiving defendant's inquiry for "chickens" he asked whether the desire was for "fowl or frying chickens" and, in fact, supplied fowl, although taking the precaution of asking defendant, a day or two after plaintiff's acceptance of the contracts in suit, to change its confirmation of its order from "chickens" as defendant had originally prepared it, to "stewing chickens." Dates, an employee of Urner-Barry Company, which publishes a daily market report on the poultry trade, gave it as his view that the trade meaning of "chicken" was "broilers and fryers." In addition to this opinion testimony, plaintiff relied on the fact that the Urner-Barry service, the Journal of Commerce, and Weinberg Bros. & Co. of Chicago, a large supplier of poultry, published quotations in a manner which, in one way or another, distinguish between "chicken," comprising broilers, fryers and certain other categories, and "fowl," which, Bauer acknowledged, included stewing chickens. This material would be impressive if there were nothing to the contrary. However, there was, as will now be seen.

Defendant's witness Weininger, who operates a chicken eviscerating plant in New Jersey, testified, "Chicken is everything except a goose, a duck, and a turkey. Everything is a chicken, but then you have to say, you have to specify which category you want or that you are talking about." Its witness Fox said that in the trade "chicken" would encompass all the various classifications. Sadina, who conducts a food inspection service, testified that he would consider any bird coming within the classes of "chicken" in the Department of Agriculture's regulations to be a chicken. The specifications approved by the General Services Administration include fowl as well as broilers and fryers under the classification "chickens." Statistics of the Institute of American Poultry Industries use the phrases "Young chickens" and "Mature chickens," under the general heading "Total chickens." The Department of Agriculture's daily and weekly price reports avoid use of the word "chicken" without specification.

Defendant advances several other points which it claims affirmatively support its construction. Primary among these is the regulation of the Department of Agriculture, 7 C.F.R. § 70.300-70.370, entitled, 'Grading and Inspection of Poultry and Edible Products Thereof' and in particular § 70.301, which recited the following classes of chickens: broiler or fryer, roaster, capon, stag, hen or stewing chicken or fowl, and cock or old rooster.

Defendant argues that the contract incorporated these regulations by reference. Plaintiff answers that the contract provision related simply to grade and Government inspection and did not incorporate the Government definition of "chicken," and also that the definition in the Regulations is ignored in the trade. However, the latter contention was contradicted by Weininger and Sadina; and there is force in defendant's argument that the contract made the regulations a dictionary, particularly since the reference to Government grading was in plaintiff's initial cable to Stovicek.

Defendant makes a further argument based on the impossibility of its obtaining broilers and fryers at the 33¢ price offered by plaintiff for the 2½-3 lbs. birds. There is no substantial dispute that, in late April, 1957, the price for 2½-3 lbs. broilers was between 35 and 37¢ per pound, and that when defendant entered into the contracts, it was well aware of this and intended to fill them by supplying fowl in these weights. It claims that plaintiff must likewise have known the market, since plaintiff had reserved shipping space on April 23, three days before plaintiff's cable to Stovicek, or, at least, that Stovicek was chargeable with such knowledge. It is scarcely an answer to say, as plaintiff does in its brief, that the 33¢ price offered by the 2½-3 lbs. "chickens" was closer to the prevailing 35¢ price for broilers than to the 30¢ at which defendant procured fowl. Plaintiff must have expected defendant to make some profit — certainly it could not have expected defendant deliberately to incur a loss.

When all the evidence is reviewed, it is clear that defendant believed it could comply with the contracts by delivering stewing chicken in the 2½-3 lbs. size. Defendant's subjective intent would not be significant if this did not coincide with an objective meaning of "chicken." Here it did coincide with one of the dictionary meanings, with the definition in the Department of Agriculture Regulations to which the contract made at least oblique reference, with at least some usage in the trade, with the realities of the market, and with what plaintiff's spokesman had said. Plaintiff asserts it to be equally plain that plaintiff's own subjective intent was to obtain broilers and fryers; the only evidence against this is the material as to market prices and this may not have been sufficiently brought home. In any event, it is unnecessary to determine that issue. For plaintiff has the burden of showing that "chicken" was used in the narrower rather than in the broader sense, and this it has not sustained.

4. Comments and Questions

a. Arthur L. Corbin's view of the *Frigaliment* decision was based on his rural upbringing. "For ten years on a Kansas farm it had been a regular job to 'feed the chickens' with no suggestion that the old hens and roosters were to be excluded." CORBIN ON CONTRACTS, 543B (1960). This was written a short time before Corbin's death. Corbin objected to the search for an "objective" meaning of "chicken."

b. It seems, however, that Friendly — apart from being unable to resist the opportunity to show off his extraordinary judicial virtuosity — was looking for objective sources that might have been used by the parties as the basis of their bargain. Friendly sought (without success) to determine what these sophisticated merchants meant by the word "chicken" by examining possible sources of trade usage, course of dealing, and course of performance. There is an objective approach that is more useful and realistic than to identify the meaning of chicken by reference to words, usage, or interpretation — and that is to apply economic criteria to this contract between organizations experienced in international chicken transactions. Did Friendly adopt this approach?

c. *Frigaliment* could not be disposed of solely on the basis of burden of proof; because the first shipment was accepted and used, the buyer clearly owed some money to the seller. Assume that the first shipment was not paid for, seller sues for payment, and buyer (plaintiff in *Frigaliment*) raises the defense of breach of contract by seller. What result and why?

D. THE MANAGEMENT OF IMPRESSIONS: "ALL THE WORLD'S A STAGE"

1. Comments and Questions

a. William Shakespeare famously observed: "All the world's a stage, and all the men and women are mere players." As You Like It, Act II, Scene VII. Many others have compared life to a theatrical performance, with individuals presenting themselves to others as they want to be seen. This is done by words, deeds, dress, and through all the other devices known to actors.

b. Is it useful to think of a judicial trial as a play presented just once for a very small audience, in a jury trial, or even an audience of one, in a bench trial? Members of the general public may view the performance, but their views and judgment are of no consequence. In some instances, a lawyer may pack the audience with family members or crime victims as part of the court presentation.

c. To what extent do the parties, counsel, or third party neutrals participating in a dispute resolution process engage in ceremonies?

d. Consider Sartre's description of the waiter, in the excerpt below. Can you create an analogous description of the role of mediator or judge? What of the role of the district attorney and defense lawyer in the process of plea bargaining? Ask yourself the same question again after reading the plea bargaining materials in Chapter 6, particularly the Blumberg article.

e. How people present themselves will have an impact on how others perceive them. At the same time, the recipient of impressions knows that the other person may be putting on a show for her benefit, and she may respond in kind. In the next piece, sociologist Erving Goffman examines the dynamic of generating and observing impressions.

2. ERVING GOFFMAN, THE PRESENTATION OF SELF IN EVERYDAY LIFE 1-8 (1959)

When an individual enters the presence of others, they commonly seek to acquire information about him or to bring into play information about him already possessed. Information about the individual helps to define the situation, enabling others to know in advance what he will expect of them and what they may expect of him. Informed in these ways, the others will know how best to act in order to call forth a desired response from him. . . . If unacquainted with the individual, observers can glean clues from his appearance and conduct which allow them to apply their previous experience with individuals roughly similar to the one before them or, more important, to apply untested stereotypes to him. They can also assume from past experience that only individuals of a particular kind are likely to be found in a given social setting.

However, during the period in which the individual is in the immediate presence of the others, few events may occur which directly provide the others with the conclusive information they will need if they are to direct wisely their own activity. Many crucial facts lie beyond the time and place of interaction or lie concealed within it. For example, the "true" or "real" attitudes, beliefs, and emotions of the individual can be ascertained only indirectly, through his avowals or through what appears to be involuntary expressive behavior. Similarly, if the individual offers the others a product or service, they will often find that during the interaction there will be no time and place immediately available for eating the pudding that the proof can be found in. They will be forced to accept some events as conventional or natural signs of something not directly available to the senses.

Let us now turn from the others to the point of view of the individual who presents himself before them. He may wish them to think highly of him or to think that he thinks highly of them, or to perceive how in fact he feels toward them, or to obtain no clear-cut impression; he may wish to ensure sufficient har-

mony so that the interaction can be sustained, or to confuse, mislead, antagonize, or insult them. Regardless of the particular objective which the individual
has in mind and of his motive for having this objective, it will be in his interest
to control the conduct of the others, especially their responsive treatment of
him. This control is achieved largely by influencing the definition of the situation which the others come to formulate, and he can influence this definition by
expressing himself in such a way as to give them the kind of impression that
will lead them to act voluntarily in accordance with his own plan. Thus, when
an individual appears in the presence of others, there will usually be some reason for him to mobilize his activity so that it will convey an impression to others which it is in his interests to convey. . . .

The others, of course, may sense that the individual is manipulating the
apparently spontaneous aspects of his behavior, and seek in this very act of
manipulation some shading of conduct that the individual has not managed to
control. This again provides a check upon an individual's behavior, thus reestab-
lishing the asymmetry of the communication process. Here I would only add
that the arts of piercing an individual's effort at calculating unintentionality
seems better developed than our capacity to manipulate our own behavior, so
that regardless of how many steps have occurred in the information game, the
witness is likely to have the advantage over the actor. . . .

3. JEAN PAUL SARTRE, BEING AND NOTHINGNESS 59 (1956) [The Waiter]

Let us consider this waiter in the café. His movement is quick and forward,
a little too precise, a little too rapid. He comes toward the patrons with a step
a little too quick. He bends forward a little too eagerly; his voice, his eyes
express an interest a little too solicitous for the order of the customer. Finally
there he returns, trying to imitate in his walk the inflexible stiffness of some
kind of automaton while carrying his tray with the recklessness of a tightrope-
walker by putting it in a perpetually unstable, perpetually broken equilibrium
which he perpetually reestablishes by a light movement of the arm and hand.
All his behavior seems to us a game. He applies himself to chaining his movements as if they were mechanisms, the one regulating the other; his gestures
and even his voice seem to be mechanisms; be gives himself the quickness and
pitiless rapidity of things. He is playing, he is amusing himself. But what is he
playing? We need not watch long before we can explain it: he is playing at being
a waiter in a café. There is nothing there to surprise us. The game is a kind of
marking out and investigation. . . . The waiter in the café plays with his condition in order to realize it. This obligation is not different from that which is
imposed on all tradesmen. Their condition is wholly one of ceremony. The public demands of them that they realize it as a ceremony; there is the dance of the
grocer, of the tailor, of the auctioneer, by which they endeavor to persuade
their clientele that they are nothing but a grocer, an auctioneer, a tailor. A grocer who dreams is offensive to the buyer, because such a grocer is not wholly a
grocer. Society demands that he limit himself to his function as a grocer. . . .

4. WILLIAM SANSOM, A CONTEST OF LADIES 230-32 (1956)

[Preedy is an Englishman, on summer holiday in Spain. Sansom describes Preedy making his first appearance on the beach of his hotel.] But in any case he took care to avoid catching anyone's eye. First of all, he had to make it clear to those potential companions of his holiday that they were of no concern to him whatsoever. He stared through them, round them, over them — eyes lost in space. The beach might have been empty. If by chance a ball was thrown his way, he looked surprised; then let a smile of amusement lighten his face (Kindly Preedy), looked round dazed to see that there were people on the beach, tossed it back with a smile to himself and not a smile at the people, and then resumed carelessly his nonchalant survey of space.

But it was time to institute a little parade, the parade of the Ideal Preedy. By devious handling he gave any who wanted to look a chance to see the title of his book — a Spanish translation of Homer, classic thus, but not daring, cosmopolitan too — and then gathered together his beach-wrap and bag into a neat sand-resistant pile (Methodical and Sensible Preedy), rose slowly to stretch at ease his huge frame (Big-Cat Preedy), and tossed aside his sandals (Carefree Preedy, after all).

The marriage of Preedy and the sea! There were alternative rituals. The first involved the stroll that turns into a run and a dive straight into the water, thereafter smoothing into a strong, splashless crawl towards the horizon. But of course not really to the horizon. Quite suddenly he would turn on to his back and thrash great white splashes with his legs, somehow thus showing that he could have swum farther had he wanted to, and then would stand up a quarter out of water for all to see who it was.

The alternative course was simpler, it avoided the cold-water shock and it avoided the risk of appearing too high-spirited. The point was to appear to be so used to the sea, the Mediterranean, and this particular beach, that one might as well be in the sea as out of it. It involved a slow stroll down and into the edge of the water — not even noticing his toes were wet, land and water all the same to him — with his eyes up at the sky gravely surveying portents, invisible to others, of the weather (Local Fisherman Preedy).

5. Comments and Questions

a. This passage is striking for its careful depiction of the impressions that a person is seeking to make about himself. Preedy does not come off well from this description. What we learn is that Preedy is vain, perhaps foolish, and unduly concerned about appearances.

b. In what situations have you noticed similar behaviors such as alternating between two separate identities or roles on demand? For example, consider the stereotypic situation of a young man bringing home his new love to meet the parents. In one sense, the young man must play the role of the dutiful son, yet at the time must also play the role of the loving and tender partner to his new love. These roles may not oppose one another so much as with Preedy, but the essential duality still is present.

c. Consider also the process of negotiation. In one situation, the negotiator may attempt to "play hardball" while a few minutes later the same negotiator may want to "become friends." While incongruent, these behaviors are understood to be part of the negotiation — something accepted by both parties, because they acknowledge that this is how the game is played. There are negative ramifications to that type of performance, though. Some people prefer consistency in behavior and demand one type of role all the time. Attempts to take on multiple roles with a person who has preferences for one role may cause negotiations to quickly fall apart.

d. People engaged in dispute resolution procedures commonly pay considerable attention to appearances. Defense lawyers tell their clients to be well dressed when they appear in court, and may even help with the selection of an appropriate outfit. It is common to have families of parties seated in the courtroom. Many an unpresupposing physical specimen of a judge is impressive indeed when wearing robes (in England, a wig as well), and sitting above the proceedings below — after all have risen, at the order of the bailiff for the entry of the judge. (Would it be far fetched to suggest an analogy to the Wizard of Oz?) Similarly, the animal kingdom offers many examples of creatures offering enhanced or altered versions of themselves to scare off enemies, court potential mates, or appear as less of a threat in the face of danger.

e. In a negotiation, both parties go to considerable efforts to present themselves as being in a strong position, and unlikely to offer much by way of concessions. Their position is likely to include claims or requests that they are quite prepared to bargain away, and may even have been included for that purpose. Perhaps we were a bit too hasty in judging Preedy so harshly.

f. To what extent do attorneys participating in a dispute resolution process engage in ceremonies? Does the practiced trial lawyer or mediator know what is "real" and what is role? In this regard, consider the following observation by the distinguished philosopher, George Santayana.

6. George Santayana, Soliloquies in England and Later Soliloquies 131-32 (1992)

Masks are arrested expressions and admirable echoes of feeling, at once faithful, discreet, and superlative. Living things in contact with the air must acquire a cuticle, and it is not urged against cuticles that they are not hearts; yet some philosophers seem to be angry with images for not being things, and with words for not being feelings. Words and images are like shells, no less integral parts of nature than are the substances they cover, but better addressed to the eye and more open to observation. I would not say that substance exists for the sake of appearance, or faces for the sake of masks, or the passions for the sake of poetry and virtue. Nothing arises in nature for the sake of anything else; all these phases and products are involved equally in the round of existence.

E. WOMEN AS NEGOTIATORS

1. KATHLEEN KELLEY REARDON, THEY DON'T GET IT, DO THEY? COMMUNICATION IN THE WORKPLACE — CLOSING THE GAP BETWEEN MEN AND WOMEN 40-45 (1995)

Turning Around Dysfunctional Communication Patterns. Dysfunctional communication patterns (DCP) cannot be eradicated unless women are willing to risk altering them. When an interaction emanates from an outmoded stereotype, speaking up and exiting are two approaches women can take to improve the communication cultures in which they work. Speaking up has gotten an undeserved bad reputation, especially for women. . . . A wide range of communication strategies exists between demure and abrasive. Clinging to either end of the range is a recipe for failure. The following scenario demonstrates what to look for and how to change a negative interaction:

Michael: You came on a bit strong in that meeting.

Jessica: I was just trying to make a point.

Michael: Well, you sure did that.

Jessica: Do you think I overdid it?

Michael: It isn't what I think that counts.

Jessica: Did Al say anything to you about what I said?

Michael: He didn't have to. Didn't you see his eyes?

In this DCP, Jessica gave that power to Michael. When she said, "I was just trying to make a point," her defensive stance signaled to Michael that she was willing to participate in the DCP he had started. When she later said, "Do you think I overdid it?" she confirmed his control over the definition of her actions and reinforced the direction of the DCP. She prolonged the process by adding, "Did Al say anything about it?" This interaction would have been quite different had Jessica been unwilling to let Michael's definition of her actions survive unscathed. Consider this possibility:

Michael: You came on a bit strong in that meeting.

Jessica: Somebody had to. The project is too important to worry about making everyone feel cozy.

In the above example, Jessica's response is swift, short, and unexpected. It pulls the two communicators out of the scripted DCP and into new territory — one more positive and professional. It also conveys that Jessica is confident and that she has a persuasive, legitimate, work-related reason for her actions. Her conviction signals to Michael that she won't yield to his definition of her actions at the meeting. People often retry initiating a DCP when others have refused to cooperate. Despite Jessica's assertive reply, Michael might try to throw her off track with this statement:

Michael: Well, you sure made your point.

Again, Jessica has a choice. She can participate in a negative DCP or respond in a way that is unexpected, positive, and likely to bring the interaction to a close. The following is an example:

Michael: Well, you sure made your point.

Jessica: Thank you.

Jessica has refused to participate in the DCP. Even if Jessica is concerned about the reactions others at the meeting might have had to her assertive comments, she needn't convey the message that she is worried. It just encourages people to continue emphasizing differences in a negative manner.

2. Comments and Questions

a. Do women in general negotiate as well as (or better than) men? Do specific subsets of women, such as law students, negotiate as effectively (judged by bottom line results) as similarly situated men? Is there cause for concern about women being able to participate effectively in the myriad personal and business negotiations that are part of daily life?

b. To the extent that there are substantial differences between men and women in negotiation behavior, what (if anything) should government, or society at large, do about the situation?

c. There is a vast literature on differences (and similarities) between women and men in how they interact with others. Books devoted to women and negotiation that will provide a helpful introduction to the subject (and a wealth of additional citations) include LINDA BABCOCK & SARA LASCHEVER, WOMEN DON'T ASK: NEGOTIATION AND THE GENDER DIVIDE (2003); CAROL GILLIGAN, IN A DIFFERENT VOICE (1982); DEBORAH M. KOLB & JUDITH WILLIAMS, THE SHADOW NEGOTIATION: HOW WOMEN CAN MASTER THE HIDDEN AGENDAS THAT DETERMINE BARGAINING SUCCESS (2000); LEE E. MILLER & JESSICA MILLER, A WOMAN'S GUIDE TO SUCCESSFUL NEGOTIATING (2002); DEBORAH TANNEN, TALKING FROM 9 TO 5: HOW WOMEN'S AND MEN'S CONVERSATIONAL STYLES AFFECT WHO GETS HEARD, WHO GETS CREDIT AND WHAT GETS DONE AT WORK (1994). *See also* Trina Grillo, *The Mediation Alternative: Process Dangers for Women*, 100 YALE L.J. 1541 (1991).

d. Where there are systemic differences in the manner that men and women negotiate, they commonly are subtle ones. To borrow Carol Gilligan's title, *Women Negotiate "In a Different Voice" from Men*. Avoid books that suggest that men and women communicate as if they came from different planets, or make similarly broad assertions. *See, e.g.*, John Gray, MEN ARE FROM MARS, WOMEN ARE FROM VENUS (1992).

3. Professor Charles Craver's Research on Gender Differences in Negotiation

Professor Craver has long maintained that, in the aggregate, there is no material difference between the negotiation results achieved by male and female law students — and he supports this conclusion with empirical data from his legal negotiation classes. *See* Charles B. Craver, *If Women Don't Ask: Implications for Bargaining Encounters, The Equal Pay Act, and Title VII*, 102 MICH. L. REV. 1104 (2004); Charles B. Craver & David W. Barnes, *Gender, Risk Taking, and Negotiation Performance*, 5 MICH. J. GENDER & L. 299, 331-33 (1999); Charles B. Craver, *The Impact of Gender on Clinical Negotiating Achievement*, 6 OHIO ST. J. ON DISP. RESOL. 1 (1990).

Craver's comparison of negotiation results by gender examines two critical components: the average results obtained by male and female students, and whether results were skewed within either group. Even if the average results were materially identical, male negotiators might employ a more competitive negotiating style with more divergent results in both directions that would not be shown by averaging results. In view of the absence of any statistical difference in negotiating results based on gender, Craver concludes (102 MICH. L. REV. at 1110-11):

> This finding should induce students, teachers, and practitioners to reassess the validity of stereotypical beliefs concerning the behavior of men and women attorneys in competitive interactions. This indicates that well-educated and specially trained students should be able to overcome any differences one might expect to find due to gender-based role expectations. There is simply no reason to suspect that female lawyers cannot attain outcomes as beneficial as those obtained by their male counterparts in any bargaining setting.

It bears reiteration that only a small and select subset of women and men attend law school, and they may be atypical in numerous ways. Accordingly, Craver's conclusions about gender and negotiation may or may not be true of men and women generally.

Chapter 3
THEORETICAL APPROACHES TO DISPUTES AND DISPUTING

A. INTRODUCTION

The purpose of this chapter is to provide an introduction to social science methodology and research (without the accompanying mathematics) that offers helpful insights into the processes of disputing and dispute resolution. These disciplines include anthropology, economics, game theory, psychology, and sociology. Needless to say, the coverage is selective.

The material in this chapter can be thought of as taking the form of theme and variation. The theme is that most people (both individual and legal) most of the time know what is best for them, given their economic and other circumstances, and that their actions accurately reflect their values and preferences. In a phrase, people are "rational maximizers"; a fancier term is "rational choice theory." The term "homo economicus" sometimes is used, although some of the values that people seek to maximize are not economic in any normal sense of that word. (Economists, of course, cast their web far beyond economic behavior.)

Indeed, there is a field of inquiry, known to some as "behavioral economics," that examines the ways in which people's behavior differs in systematic ways from the behavior predicted by the classic model of economic behavior. Others regard the economists as presumptuous by claiming to swallow up other social sciences that have the temerity to claim — and to prove — that people often do not act as predicted by standard economic theory.

Much of the work on negotiating and decision behavior considered in this chapter is based on or influenced by the work of *psychologists* Daniel Kahneman and Amos Tversky. Kahneman was awarded the Nobel Prize in Economics for this work. [Nobel Prizes are awarded only to living persons; but for Tversky's untimely death, he likely would have shared the award with Kahneman.] Economics is the only social science for which there is a Nobel Prize, so the economists may succeed in their entrepreneurial aggression to annex major parts of other social sciences.

We turn next to game theory, and a behavioral conundrum known as the Prisoner's Dilemma. Then we look at a set of problems subsumed under the rubric the "Tragedy of the Commons." Each of these "stories" has been widely influential in both the natural and social sciences, far beyond the dispute resolution context. Section E examines agency theory, notably through an article that demonstrates the power of the prisoner's dilemma as an analytical model.

Section F introduces the valuable insights offered by the field of anthropology to thinking about disputes and disputing.

B. RATIONAL CHOICE THEORY AND ITS CRITICS

1. ADAM SMITH, AN INQUIRY INTO THE NATURE AND CAUSES OF THE WEALTH OF NATIONS 118-19 (1776) (Penguin 1986)

The division of labour, from which so many advantages are derived, is not originally the effect of any human wisdom, which foresees and intends that general opulence to which it gives occasion. It is the necessary, though very slow and gradual, consequence of a certain propensity in human nature . . . to truck, barter, and exchange one thing for another. Whether this propensity be one of those original principles in human nature of which no account can be given; or whether, as seems more probable, it be the necessary consequence of the faculties of reason and speech, it belongs not to our present subject to inquire. It is common to all men, and to be found in no other race of animals, which seem to know neither this nor any other species of contracts. . . .

Two grey-hounds, in running down the same hare, have sometimes the appearance of acting in some sort of concert. Each turns her towards his companion, or endeavors to intercept her when his companion turns her toward himself. This, however, is not the effect of any contract, but of the accidental concurrence of their passions in the same object at that particular time. Nobody ever saw a dog make a fair and deliberate exchange of one bone for another with another dog. Nobody ever saw one animal by its gestures and natural cries signify to another, this is mine, that yours; I am willing to give this for that. When an animal wants to obtain something either of a man or of another animal, it has no other means of persuasion but to gain the favour of those whose service it requires. A puppy fawns upon its dam, and a spaniel endeavors by a thousand attractions to engage the attention of its master who is at dinner, when it wants to be fed by him.

Man sometimes uses the same arts with his brethren, and when he has no other means of engaging them to act according to his inclinations, endeavors by every servile and fawning attention to obtain their good will. He has not time, however, to do this upon every occasion. In civilized society he stands at all times in need of the cooperation and assistance of great multitudes, while his whole life is scarce sufficient to gain the friendship of a few persons. . . . Man has almost constant occasion for the help of his brethren, and it is in vain for him to expect it from their benevolence only. He will be more likely to prevail if he can interest their self-love in his favour, and show them that it is for their own advantage to do for him what he requires of them. Whoever offers to another a bargain of any kind, proposes to do this. Give me that which I want, and you shall have this which you want, is the meaning of every such offer; and it is in this manner that we obtain from one another the far greater part of those good offices which we stand in need of. It is not from the benevolence of the butcher, the brewer or the baker that we expect our dinner, but from their regard to their own interest. We address ourselves, not to their humanity but to their self-love, and never talk to them of our own necessities but of their advantages. Nobody but a beggar chooses to depend chiefly upon the benevolence of his fellow-citizens.

2. Comments and Questions

a. Before Smith, exchange transactions were regarded as sterile, because no net benefit resulted; one person's gain equaled the other person's loss. In modern terminology, exchange was seen as a "zero sum game." It was Smith's great accomplishment to demonstrate to the world that exchanges benefitted both parties (else they would not occur). Value was personal to individuals, and often related to one's stock of resources, so both parties to an exchange could benefit.

b. In a competitive economy, individuals acting in their own self-interest will produce an economically efficient system. In Smith's memorable phrase, this will occur as if people's conduct was guided by "an invisible hand." Smith, trained in moral philosophy, worried about the paradox that selfish behavior, while a private vice, is a public virtue.

c. Adam Smith's work in the sphere of economic activity suggests that the solutions parties agree upon to resolve disputes will be for the best, both in terms of the individuals and the society — and this is often the case. In other instances, however, the result of action based on individual self-interest may be dreadful for the larger society — and even bad for the individuals involved.

d. The Jolls, Sunstein, and Thaler (JST) article that follows sets forth the market model, as well as beginning our consideration of the behavioral critique of the pure economic model. The article by Robert Adler continues the consideration of decisional biases that produce results at variance with the rational maximizer model, with a particular focus on negotiation. Adler places greater emphasis on biology/evolution (echoing Adam Smith) than on instrumental values as determining the basis for human conduct.

3. Christine Jolls, Cass R. Sunstein & Richard Thaler, *A Behavioral Approach to Law and Economics*, 50 STAN. L. REV. 1471 (1998)

I. Foundations: What Is "Behavioral Law and Economics"?

In order to identify, in a general way, the defining features of behavioral law and economics, it is useful first to understand the defining features of law and economics. [T]his approach to the law posits that legal rules are best analyzed and understood in light of standard economic principles. Gary Becker offers a typical account of those principles: "All human behavior can be viewed as involving participants who [1] maximize their utility [2] form a stable set of preferences and [3] accumulate an optimal amount of information and other inputs in a variety of markets." The task of law and economics is to determine the implications of such rational maximizing behavior in and out of markets, and its legal implications for markets and other institutions. What then is the task of behavioral law and economics? How does it differ from standard law and economics? . . .

A. *Homo Economicus and Real People.* The task of behavioral law and economics, simply stated, is to explore the implications of actual (not hypothesized) human behavior for the law. How do "real people" differ from homo economicus? We will describe the differences by stressing three important "bounds" on human behavior, bounds that draw into question the central ideas of utility maximization, stable preferences, rational expectations, and optimal processing of information. People can be said to display bounded rationality, bounded willpower, and bounded self-interest. All three bounds are well documented in the literature of other social sciences. . . . Each of these bounds represents a significant way in which most people depart from the standard economic model. . . .

1. *Bounded Rationality.* Bounded rationality refers to the obvious fact that human cognitive abilities are not infinite. We have limited computational skills and seriously flawed memories. People can respond sensibly to these failings; thus it might be said that people sometimes respond rationally to their own cognitive limitations, minimizing the sum of decision costs and error costs. To deal with limited memories we make lists. To deal with limited brain power and time we use mental shortcuts and rules of thumb. But even with these remedies, and in some cases because of these remedies, human behavior differs in systematic ways from that predicted by the standard economic model of unbounded rationality. Even when the use of mental shortcuts is rational, it can produce predictable mistakes. The departures from the standard model can be divided into two categories: judgment and decisions. Actual judgments show systematic departures from models of unbiased forecasts, and actual decisions often violate the axioms of expected utility theory.

A major source of differences between actual judgments and unbiased forecasts is the use of rules of thumb. As stressed in the pathbreaking work of Daniel Kahneman and Amos Tversky, rules of thumb such as the availability heuristic — in which the frequency of some event is estimated by judging how easy it is to recall other instances of this type (how "available" such instances are) — lead us to erroneous conclusions. People tend to conclude, for example, that the probability of an event (such as a car accident) is greater if they have recently witnessed an occurrence of that event than if they have not. What is especially important in the work of Kahneman and Tversky is that it shows that shortcuts and rules of thumb are predictable. While the heuristics are useful on average (which explains how they become adopted), they lead to errors in particular circumstances. This means that someone using such a rule of thumb may be behaving rationally in the sense of economizing on thinking time, but such a person will nonetheless make forecasts that are different from those that emerge from the standard rational-choice model. Just as unbiased forecasting is not a good description of actual human behavior, expected utility theory is not a good description of actual decisionmaking. . . .

2. *Bounded Willpower.* This term refers to the fact that human beings often take actions that they know to be in conflict with their own long-term interests.

Most smokers say they would prefer not to smoke, and many pay money to join a program or obtain a drug that will help them quit. As with bounded rationality, many people recognize that they have bounded willpower and take steps to mitigate its effects. They join a pension plan or "Christmas Club" (a special savings arrangement under which funds can be withdrawn only around the holidays) to prevent undersaving, and they don't keep tempting desserts around the house when trying to diet. In some cases they may vote for or support governmental policies, such as social security, to eliminate any temptation to succumb to the desire for immediate rewards. Thus, the demand for and supply of law may reflect people's understanding of their own (or others') bounded willpower; consider "cooling off" periods for certain sales, and programs that facilitate or even require saving.

3. Bounded Self-Interest. We use the term bounded self-interest to refer to an important fact about the utility function of most people: They care, or act as if they care, about others, even strangers, in some circumstances. (We are not questioning here the idea of utility maximization, but rather the common assumptions about what that entails.) Our notion is distinct from simple altruism, which conventional economics has emphasized in areas such as bequest decisions. Self-interest is bounded in a much broader range of settings than conventional economics assumes, and the bound operates in ways different from what the conventional understanding suggests. In many market and bargaining settings (as opposed to nonmarket settings such as bequest decisions), people care about being treated fairly and want to treat others fairly if those others are themselves behaving fairly. As a result of these concerns, the agents in a behavioral economic model are both nicer and (when they are not treated fairly) more spiteful than the agents postulated by neoclassical theory. . . .

B. Testable Predictions. Behavioral and conventional law and economics do not differ solely in their assumptions about human behavior. They also differ, in testable ways, in their predictions about how law (as well as other forces) affects behavior. To make these differences more concrete, consider the three "fundamental principles of economics" set forth by Richard Posner in his Economic Analysis of Law, in a discussion that is, on these points, quite conventional. (Posner's discussion represents an application of the basic economic methodology set forth by Becker above.) To what extent would an account based on behavioral law and economics offer different "fundamental principles?"

The first fundamental principle for the conventional approach is downward-sloping demand: Total demand for a good falls when its price rises. This prediction is, of course, valid. . . . However, confirmation of the prediction of downward-sloping demand does not suggest that people are optimizing. [E]ven people choosing at random (rather than in a way designed to serve their preferences) will tend to consume less of a good when its price goes up as long as they have limited resources. This behavior has also been demonstrated with laboratory rats. Thus, evidence of downward-sloping demand is not evidence in support of optimizing models.

The second fundamental principle of conventional law and economics concerns the nature of costs: Cost to the economist is "opportunity cost," and "sunk" (incurred) costs do not affect decisions on prices and quantity. Thus, according to traditional analysis, decisionmakers will equate opportunity costs to out-of-pocket costs, and they will ignore sunk costs. But each of these propositions is a frequent source of predictive failures. The equality of opportunity costs and out-of-pocket costs implies that, in the absence of important wealth effects, buying prices will be roughly equal to selling prices. This is frequently violated, as is well known. Many people holding tickets to a popular sporting event such as the Super Bowl would be unwilling to buy tickets at the market price (say $1,000), yet would also be unwilling to sell at this price. Indeed, estimates of the ratio of selling prices to buying prices are often at least two to one, yet the size of the transaction makes it implausible in these studies to conclude that wealth effects explain the difference. . . .

The traditional assumption about sunk costs also generates invalid predictions. Here is one: A theater patron who ignores sunk costs would not take into account the cost of a prepaid season pass in deciding whether to rouse himself. . . . to go out on the evening of a particular performance; the decision would be made purely on the basis of the benefits and costs from that moment forward. However, in a study of theater patrons, some of whom were randomly assigned to receive discounted prices on prepaid passes, the patrons who received discounts were found to attend significantly fewer performances than those who did not receive discounts, despite the fact that the benefit-cost ratio that should have mattered — benefits and costs going forward — was the same on average in the two groups. In short, sunk costs mattered; again, the standard prediction proved invalid.

The third fundamental principle of conventional law and economics is that "resources tend to gravitate toward their most valuable uses" as markets drive out unexploited profit opportunities. When combined with the notion that opportunity and out-of-pocket costs are equated (see fundamental principle two), this yields the Coase theorem — the idea that initial assignments of entitlements will not affect the ultimate allocation of resources so long as transaction costs are zero. Many economists and economically oriented lawyers think of the Coase theorem as a tautology; if there were really no transaction costs (and no wealth effects), and if an alternative allocation of resources would make some agents better off and none worse off, then of course the agents would move to that allocation. Careful empirical study, however, shows that the Coase theorem . . . can lead to inaccurate predictions. Even when transaction costs and wealth effects are known to be zero, initial entitlements alter the final allocation of resources. These results are predicted by behavioral economics, which emphasizes the difference between opportunity and out-of-pocket costs.

Consider the following experiment conducted to test the Coase theorem. . . . The subjects were forty-four students taking an advanced undergraduate course in law and economics at Cornell University. . . . Half the students were given Cornell coffee mugs. . . . Here behavioral analysis generates a prediction distinct from standard economic analysis: Because people do not equate opportunity and out-of-pocket costs for goods whose values are not solely exogenously defined, those endowed with mugs should be reluctant to part with them even at prices they would not have considered paying to acquire a mug had they not received one.

Markets were conducted and mugs bought and sold. The assignment of property rights had a pronounced effect on the final allocation of mugs. The students who were assigned mugs had a strong tendency to keep them. Whereas the Coase theorem would have predicted that about half the mugs would trade (since transaction costs were essentially zero, and mugs were randomly distributed), instead only fifteen percent of the mugs traded. And those who were endowed with mugs asked more than twice as much to give up a mug as those who didn't get a mug were willing to pay. . . . This effect is generally referred to as the "endowment effect"; it is a manifestation of the broader phenomenon of "loss aversion" — the idea that losses are weighted more heavily than gains. . . .

II. Behavior of Agents

A. The Ultimatum Game. We begin with bounded self-interest, the third bound described above. A useful first example of this bound is agents' behavior in a very simple bargaining game called the ultimatum game. In this game, one player, the Proposer, is asked to propose an allocation of a sum of money between herself and the other player, the Responder. The Responder then has a choice. He can either accept the amount offered to him by the Proposer, leaving the rest to the Proposer, or he can reject the offer, in which case both players get nothing. Neither player knows the identity of his or her counterpart, and the players will play against each other only once, so reputations and future retaliation are eliminated as factors.

Economic theory has a simple prediction about this game. The Proposer will offer the smallest unit of currency available, say a penny, and the Responder will accept, since a penny is better than nothing. This turns out to be a very bad prediction about how the game is actually played. Responders typically reject offers of less than twenty percent of the total amount available; the average minimum amount that Responders say they would accept is between twenty and thirty percent of that sum. Responders are thus willing to punish unfair behavior, even at a financial cost to themselves. This is a form of bounded self-interest. And this response seems to be expected and anticipated by Proposers; they typically offer a substantial portion of the sum to be divided — ordinarily forty to fifty percent. . . .

What would happen if the stakes were raised substantially, or the game was repeated several times to allow learning? In this case, we know the answer. To a first approximation, neither of these factors changes the results in any important way. Raising the stakes from $10 per pair to $100, or even to more than a week's income (in a poor country) has little effect; the same is true of repeating the game ten times with different partners. . . . We do not see behavior moving toward the prediction of standard economic theory. . . .

The fairness results obtained in various experimental settings, such as the ultimatum game, cannot be explained on grounds of reputation. The parties are interacting anonymously and in a one-shot fashion. Of course, many real-world situations may reflect a combination of reputational and fairness factors. Thus, for example, firms that violate the norms of an industry are ostracized, presumably at some cost to the remaining firms, partly because of a rational fear that the offending party might be untrustworthy, and partly because of a spiteful tendency to punish unmannerly behavior, even when the punishment is costly to administer. . . . Often it is impossible to disentangle the two effects. The value of the experimental method is precisely that situations can be created in which the reputational factor is absent (because the transactions are anonymous and one-shot), allowing one to test directly for fairness. The ultimatum game results show that we find it: People will often behave in accordance with fairness considerations even when it is against their financial self-interest and no one will know. . . . Most people leave tips in out-of-town restaurants that they never plan to visit again. . . .

B. *Self-Serving Bias.* Even among the well-mannered, fair-minded agents that populate behavioral economics, self-interest is very much alive and well. For often there will be room for disagreement about what is fair (or, equivalently, what is the appropriate reference transaction) — and thus there will be the opportunity for manipulation by self-interested parties. These parties may tend to see things in the light most favorable to them; while people care about fairness, their assessments of fairness are distorted by their own self-interest. This is a form of bounded rationality; specifically, a judgment error. People's perceptions are distorted by self-serving bias.

This form of bias can help to explain the frequency of failed negotiations. It is quite common, even in cases involving . . . commercial disputes, to see protracted litigation in circumstances in which it might be expected that the parties would be able to reach negotiated solutions (although it of course remains the case that most suits settle). On the standard account, the existence of such protracted litigation is somewhat of a puzzle. With a good sense of the expected value of a suit, parties should settle more than they do. It may be possible to explain some of the observed behavior in terms of asymmetric information and signaling, which may interfere with settlement prospects. However, this account is difficult to test.

By contrast, the effects of self-serving bias in negotiations have been tested empirically. . . . Researchers have conducted experimental studies on the role of self-serving bias in preventing negotiated agreements. The studies involved a tort case based on real litigation in Texas. Subjects — college and law students — were randomly assigned to the role of plaintiff or defendant; in this role they were asked to negotiate a settlement. They received a short summary of the case and also twenty-seven pages of materials from the original case. Subjects were told that the same case materials had been given to a judge in Texas, who had reached a judgment between $0 and $100,000. Before beginning to negotiate, subjects were asked to write down their guesses about what the judge awarded. They were also asked to say what they considered a fair amount for the plaintiff to receive in a settlement. The authors found quite substantial self-serving biases in subjects' assessments of the judge's award. The subjects acting as the plaintiffs guessed an average $14,527 higher than the defendants', and the plaintiffs' fair settlement values averaged $17,709 higher than those of the defendants. Nonsettlement was strongly connected to the discrepancy in predictions about the judge's likely award. Note that the hypothetical, role-playing nature of this study in some ways strengthens the interpretation of the result.

In the short time that it took to read all the materials, subjects adopted the point of view of their roles and the bias that comes with it. . . .

C. Hindsight Bias. Frequently, juries are called upon to determine the probability of an event that ended up occurring; a prominent example is the negligence standard, which (in the formulation favored by the economic analysis of law) requires jurors to assess the costs and benefits of the defendant's course of action from an ex ante perspective, and thus to determine the probability that harm would end up coming of that action. These determinations are made with the "benefit" of hindsight; jurors know at the time they make their decision that the event in question did in fact occur. Jurors' determinations are, thus, likely to be afflicted by "hindsight bias" — the tendency of decisionmakers to attach an excessively high probability to an event, simply because it ended up occurring. Hindsight bias has been observed in a large number of studies, including studies of "expert" actors such as physicians, who, when asked to assess the probabilities of alternative diagnoses, given a set of symptoms, offer significantly different estimates depending on what they are told the actual diagnosis turned out to be. Hindsight bias also appears to occur in the specific context of negligence determinations. Hindsight bias will lead juries making negligence determinations to find defendants liable more frequently than if cost-benefit analysis were done correctly — that is, on an ex ante basis. Thus, plaintiffs will win cases they deserve to lose. . . .

4. Robert S. Adler, *Flawed Thinking: Addressing Decision Biases in Negotiation*, 20 OHIO ST. J. ON DISP. RESOL. 683 (2005)

As negotiators, . . . we typically aspire to reach thoughtful, rational agreements. Of course, what constitutes a "rational" agreement is not always obvious, but for most people, it means, at a minimum, that they have maximized the possibilities for reaching their goals. Unfortunately, if recent studies are to be believed, people often negotiate irrationally rather than as calm, deliberate, utility maximizers. To say that negotiators do not bargain rationally is not to suggest that they do so arbitrarily or randomly. To the contrary, the errors that people make are often quite predictable, reflecting what appear to be certain "hard-wired" mental predispositions. Examples abound of behavior that seems difficult to justify on purely rational grounds. . . .

[H]umans analyze situations according to deep-inborn impulses outside the boundaries of classical rationality models. Why do people stray so far from the classic models of rationality? First, and not surprisingly, we all face limits on our capabilities imposed by shortfalls in intelligence, data, energy, memory, perceptions, patience, and time that prevent full processing of critical information. Second, and less well-recognized, people typically rely on mental "rules of thumb," often called "heuristics," in reading situations and making decisions that, while generally quite useful, can sometimes produce sub-optimal approaches and decisions.

To organize the analysis, I propose to divide biases into those that result from illogical or poor thinking (cognitive biases) and those that result from egocentric thinking (egocentric biases). Stating the distinction in a simplified way, the former errors result from failing to reason logically, while the latter result from excessive self-absorption that clouds good judgment. Beyond these two categories, however, lies a third that defies easy categorization. In it, I have placed a variety of miscellaneous negotiation biases that do not easily fit into either of the categories just named. In some cases, they relate to neither category; in others, they seem to fit within both, but with no logical basis for choosing between the two.

III. COGNITIVE BIASES ASSOCIATED WITH HEURISTICS

A. *Availability Heuristic.* The availability heuristic organizes and retrieves human memories as a guide to future action. People use the availability heuristic whenever they take action or reach conclusions about the world based on how easily they can recall or imagine instances of what they are thinking about. This heuristic guarantees that events that are more vividly and emotionally implanted in our minds will leap to our consciousness when we face a decision. . . . The survival benefit of the availability heuristic seems clear. If we are confronted with dangers similar to those previously encountered, the ability to recognize and react to them quickly is valuable. . . . Everyday decisions rely on this heuristic as well. If we had to process all potentially relevant information each time we drove our cars or took a walk, we would be frozen in indecision while we processed our voluminous memory data banks. . . . For example, . . . if we remember how dissatisfied we were in our last negotiation when our first offer was immediately accepted, strongly suggesting that the offer was too low, we might quietly determine to make our first offer more aggressive next time. . . .

1. *Biased Reasoning.* Biased reasoning can result from the misapplication of the availability heuristic. For example, . . . estimates of disease frequency by doctors vary depending on whether they had recently treated a similar case (or had read about it in a recent medical journal). . . .

2. *Recall Errors.* The easier something is to recall, the more likely that people will include it in their decision making. This often makes sense, but does not when the event involved is vivid, but rare. For example, when asked whether motor vehicle accidents or stomach cancer cause more deaths per year, most respondents reply motor vehicles. Yet, stomach cancer kills at roughly twice the rate of motor vehicle accidents. What skews most people's thinking in this case is that the media constantly report motor vehicle accidents and deaths, but rarely do so for stomach cancer. . . .

3. *"False Consensus" Effect.* This effect refers to the fact that most people think that others agree with them more than is actually warranted. For example, smokers estimate that a much higher percentage of the population smokes than do nonsmokers. . . . In many cases, these attitudes reflect only that one associates with those who share common views; in others, they only reflect that one notices those who agree and ignore those who disagree.

B. Representativeness Heuristic. This heuristic applies when people make judgments about persons or events based on the similarities that they have with previous persons or events in their experience. That is, if a person or thing appears similar to members of a known category, we assume that they belong in that category (and that the category is homogeneous). The benefits of this characteristic are obvious — quite similar to availability. Representativeness provides a classification scheme that enables rapid reactions to outside stimuli that can be life-saving. . . .

1. Stereotypes and Illusory Correlations. Perhaps the most common example of the representativeness heuristic is stereotypes. Virtually every group, whether ethnic or professional, produces an image in the public's mind of the type of personality they project and the kind of behavior in which they engage. . . . Stereotypes, of course, do not spring from sterile soil. Typically, there is an element of truth or insight in the stereotype. . . . People tend to remember facts that fit in with their ideas about groups and to ignore evidence that contradicts their ideas [illusory causation]. This operates in a particularly strong way when the information is vivid, in either a good or a bad sense.

Negotiators . . . need to focus on the benefits and drawbacks of the representativeness heuristic when they bargain with someone from a different culture or of a different gender. To ignore obvious differences could prove fatal to a high-stakes negotiation, but to leap to an automatic reliance on broad stereotypes could prove equally troublesome. In fact, flexibility is the key to avoiding this potential trap.

2. "Base Rate" Fallacy. The representativeness heuristic can generate bias in calculating probabilities. Given the frequency with which negotiators rely on probabilities in making points in bargaining sessions, one can see the potential for harm in misreading them. . . . A "base rate" is the frequency with which something occurs in the general population. When one extrapolates from one or two data points, ignoring broader and more valid data, one commits this fallacy. . . .

3. "Halo" and Contrast Effects. Two psychological effects of an ostensibly opposing nature illustrate the reach of the representativeness heuristic. The so-called "halo" effect operates when we extrapolate specific positive (or negative) features to people (or things) based on our general impressions of them. For example, study after study confirms that observers rate physically attractive people positively on numerous dimensions, such as trustworthiness or intelligence, even in the absence of meaningful confirming data. Advertisers often use the halo effect to promote sales. One of the most effective ways of doing this is for a company to sponsor an event viewed as promoting a worthy cause. Potential customers will then attribute the good image of the event to the sponsor and be more inclined to trust the company and to purchase its products or services. . . .

The flip side of the halo effect is what social scientists refer to as the "contrast" effect. Where the halo effect leads to attitudes consistent with our general impressions, the contrast effect leads to exaggerated notions of differences based on recent impressions we have of people or experiences. That is, we tend to see people or things as more different than they actually are if we encounter differences close in time or vividness. For example, if we lift a light object before lifting a heavy object, we will estimate the second object to be heavier than we would have had we lifted it without first lifting the light object. . . .

Unfortunately, the contrast effect can be used to great advantage by sales agents and negotiation opponents. Consider that retailers invariably seek to peddle expensive items first and then move the customers to lesser items (often overpriced) as part of a sales pitch. The marketers know that, rather than showing reluctance to make additional purchases after spending a huge sum on the first item, customers will often be more willing to make additional purchases because the next items, even expensive ones, will seem cheap compared to the first purchase. This same psychology obviously operates in many bargaining situations.

4. Gambler's Fallacy. This bias occurs when a person assumes that what occurs on average will take place next or immediately, or that which occurs in the long term will be "corrected" in the short term. The simplest illustration is tossing a coin. If one takes an evenly balanced coin and flips it many times, one can reliably predict that it will land on heads roughly half the time and tails half the time. Yet, one who predicts that a coin that landed on heads the last five times will land on tails the next time because tails is "due" commits the gambler's fallacy. In fact, the previous tosses have no relevance at all to the sixth toss. The odds remain 50/50. . . .

C. Anchoring Heuristic. When people are presented with a possible answer and then given an opportunity to reach their own answer, their answer tends to be close to the answer they were previously shown — irrespective of any relevance of the initial answer. In a famous experiment by Tversky and Kahneman, subjects were asked to give an estimate of the percentage of African countries in the United Nations (UN). Before making their estimates, subjects watched as experimenters spun a giant wheel which they believed generated random numbers between 1 and 100 (actually the wheel was rigged to stop at 10 half of the time and 65 half of the time). After they saw the "random" number, subjects were asked if they thought the actual percentage of African Countries was higher or lower. They were then asked to give their own estimate. Interestingly, subjects who saw the number 10 estimated the percentage of African nations in the UN to be 25%, on average, and subjects who saw the number 65 estimated it to be 45%. Even though they thought the numbers were random and had nothing to do with the question, subjects were evidently still influenced by seeing the numbers. As Tversky and Kahneman observed, the subjects "anchored" their estimates to the provided numbers. Providing a number through the spinning wheel made it available, thus estimates tended to cluster around it.

Negotiators particularly need to know about and appreciate the anchoring phenomenon. When negotiators bargain about the price of an item, they need to be wary of first offers advanced by their opponents who may use these offers to "anchor" the negotiation around their number, thus subtly limiting the range of bargaining. Anchoring operates especially well when there are few market indicators to help establish an appropriate price or where one has little relevant experience or knowledge. Unfortunately, even when one brings considerable experience to the table, he or she can still fall prey to anchoring.

Anchoring occurs not just with numbers. Negotiators also need to worry generally about "impression management" from their opponents. Research suggests that parties typically establish the entire tone of a negotiation through the first array of moves and gestures. Thus, the first impression that one projects in a negotiation will often carry through the entire bargaining sequence. Psychology professor Solomon Asch describes this as the "primacy effect," and it means that negotiators involved in high stakes deals need to be concerned from the very start of a negotiation about how they come across to the other side. At a minimum, negotiators need to present an image of strength and confidence. This does not necessarily mean that one needs to attack or display hostility. It does mean, however, that one should present an image indicating that one is prepared for all eventualities and that one is able to cope with the pressures of bargaining.

IV. EGOCENTRIC BIAS

People focus on matters that concern themselves, often to the exclusion of others. As with other human traits, this can be explained, at least in part, by evolution. Without a healthy devotion to one's self-interest, one is unlikely to survive for long. Sometimes, unfortunately, our built-in absorption with ourselves produces a world view that is biased, because it neglects the reality outside of ourselves. When that occurs, we find ourselves misled about others' motives, thoughts, and plans. Our drive to pursue our own agendas leads us to view those who stand as obstacles as uncaring or evil. This is especially so in negotiations, which present a high potential for conflict, high anxiety, and tension. The focus in this section is on egocentric biases and how they skew our thinking about the world — and how we negotiate.

A. Confirmation Traps and Self-Fulfilling Prophecies. When one tests a hypothesis, especially one that he or she wishes to be true, there is a natural instinct to look for evidence that supports it and to ignore that which contradicts it. This bias arises from the extraordinary ability that humans have to see logical connections in the world rather than to view life's events as a series of random bits of data. One applauds, for example, when the famous fictional detective Sherlock Holmes sees the connection between a dog's failure to bark and the theft of an expensive race horse. This talent for seeing obscure connections serves Holmes and humanity well most of the time. Yet, the very control of events and life that we enjoy because of our connection-drawing skills sometimes entices us to reach unsupported conclusions. . . .

If one enters a negotiation with an assumption about his or her opponent's behavior, one is likely to find confirming examples of this behavior even when evidence for it may be skimpy. This can have either a positive or a negative effect. When one's opening impression is favorable, a "Pygmalion" effect will result, leading to easy acceptance and approval; if one's mindset is negative, then the exchange will become unfavorable, often leading to unnecessarily conflict-laden exchanges.

B. Egocentric Interpretations of Fairness. The exquisite attention that most people devote to fairness faces at least two major confounds that can stymie good decision making and effective negotiating. First, there are many situations in which what is fair is highly debatable. . . . Second, most people unwittingly perceive matters of fairness through their own eyes. That is, we tend to filter what we see and what we think in terms of our self-interest. This tendency produces what researchers describe as a "self-serving" bias and dramatically affects our perceptions of what is fair. A study by Professors David Messick and Keith Sentis demonstrates this effect. In that study, the professors asked subjects to specify a fair rate of pay when they had worked 10 hours and another person had worked 7 hours, or where they had worked 7 hours and the other person had worked 10 hours. When the subjects were told that they had worked 10 hours and the other participants had worked 7 hours and had been paid $25, the subjects claimed that they should be paid on average $35.24 for their 10 hours. When, however, the subjects were told that they had received $25 for 7 hours of work, they thought that their colleagues who had worked 10 hours should earn only an average of $30.29 — a $5 difference explainable only by egocentric bias. Clearly, the subjects' views of fairness changed according to which role they assumed.

1. Imputations of Evil. Egocentric concerns lead us not only to think selfishly, but also to attribute ulterior and sometimes evil motives to those who disagree with us. . . . When these feelings emerge, negotiated settlements of disputes rapidly become difficult, because the atmosphere becomes charged with "score-settling" or "evil-eradicating" and not with reaching a reasonable accommodation or splitting the difference.

2. Reactive Devaluation. Reactive devaluation arises from the tendency that negotiators have to see less value in concessions made by opponents than those arising from more neutral parties. In one revealing study, researchers asked subjects about whether an arms control proposal favored the United States or the Soviet Union. In the group that was told that Soviet leader Mikhail Gorbachev had developed the proposal, 56% felt that it favored the Russians, 16% thought it favored the U.S., and 16% concluded that it favored neither side. In contrast, when a second group was told that President Ronald Reagan had crafted the proposal, 45% felt that it favored both sides equally, 27% thought that the proposal benefitted the Soviet Union, and 27% thought the proposal favored the United States. . . .

Reactive devaluation also leads to perceptions that concessions that are actually offered are rated lower than concessions that have been withheld, and that a compromise is rated less highly after it has been put on the table by the other side than it was before the other side offered it. Needless to say, reactive devaluation can make almost any negotiated settlement difficult to achieve.

C. Fundamental Attribution Error. Fundamental attribution error is the tendency to jump the inferential gun and to draw conclusions about the characters of others, even when there are plausible alternative explanations for their conduct. . . . Egocentric bias, however, is often implicated in the fundamental attribution error. This occurs when one attributes one's success to one's positive personal traits while simultaneously pointing to external forces to explain failures. Accepting blame without attributing failure or fault to others (or to external forces) surely must rank as one of mankind's least enjoyable tasks — which means that we do not easily do it. . . . Fundamental attribution errors can easily undermine negotiations. Fundamental attribution errors invariably play a major confounding role, because each side, when asked to name the cause of the dispute, will attribute the negative aspects of the conflict to the dispositions and evil motives of the other party.

D. Illusion of Control. The "illusion of control" bias arises when one overestimates his or her ability to affect outcomes that are really determined by factors outside of one's control. . . . In fact, so strong is this drive that even factors as small as touching a physical object can give people a sense that they control events when they do not. For example, in a study of securities analysts, individuals were divided into two groups. Each was asked to pay $1 to participate in a game where, if they picked the correct card out of a pack of 52 cards, they would win $100. The first group was shown the card while the second group was allowed to see it and touch it. Analysts who had only been shown the card asked for an average of $1.89 in return for relinquishing their opportunity to win the $100, but those who had touched the card demanded an average of $8.96 before they would give up their opportunity to win the prize. Interestingly, those analysts with MBA degrees who had touched the card, despite their higher education, demanded even more — an average of $11.19 — for surrendering their chance to win the $100. . . . Participants in a lottery who choose their own tickets demand a substantially higher price to relinquish them than those who have been assigned tickets.

Negotiators . . . confront illusion of control issues every time they bargain. They should be particularly aware of this tendency when confronting matters that involve future events or that present high degrees of risk. The inability to make precise determinations obviously presents a major source of anxiety and concern. Rather than inflating one's predictive powers, however, one would be far better off seeking ways to protect one's interests against unforeseen contingencies, say, by incorporating provisions that explicitly condition the terms of the deal according to future outcomes.

E. Overconfidence. . . . Most people, when asked how they will do in an upcoming negotiation, strongly predict that they will do better than average. . . . Perhaps the clearest example of this is a study by Professors Max Bazerman and Margaret Neale, in which they asked negotiators in a "final-offer" arbitration exercise (i.e., in which an arbitrator, without the authority to "split the difference," must select one side's final offer depending on which the arbitrator feels is fairer) to estimate their likelihood of prevailing. Invariably, the negotiators estimated a greater than 50% chance of having their offer chosen. . . . Similarly, despite extensive research demonstrating that most new businesses fail within a few years, generation after generation of entrepreneurs has ignored this grim statistic and plunged into the market. . . .

F. Self-Enhancement Bias. Given that people tend to be overconfident, it should come as no surprise that they also think of themselves in a particularly positive light compared to how they think of others. . . . Most people think that they are more intelligent and fair-minded than average. [M]ost negotiators believe themselves to be more flexible, more purposeful, more fair, more competent, more honest, and more cooperative than their counterparts. . . .

V. "MIXED" AND MISCELLANEOUS BIASES

A. Avoidance of Loss/Risk Aversion. Classic economics holds that people should treat equal risks equally, but they do not. To the contrary, study after study confirms that humans react far more negatively to the risk of loss than to the potential for gain. This is a well-known phenomenon called "risk aversion," i.e., the notion that most people will take a sure thing over a gamble, even where the gamble may have a somewhat higher expected payoff. There seems to be a feeling of humiliation associated with losses that makes them so unacceptable. This explains why gamblers, when losing money, will often take enormous risks to break even rather than leave the table with a loss — thus the popularity of long shots on the last race of the day. Similarly, loss aversion explains why investors are two-and-a-half times more likely to sell stocks that have increased in value than those with price declines.

The aversion to loss carries special importance in negotiations, because bargaining almost always involves trading gains and losses — opening up numerous pitfalls leading to thwarted deals. Loss aversion strongly suggests that negotiators will be much less likely to strike deals that include unavoidable losses than to include the promise of extra gains. . . . Risk aversion can easily lead defendants to fight lawsuits that they would be better off settling. In addition, to avoid the losses, defendants often undertake long-shot strategies that have little chance of succeeding.

B. Endowment Effect and Status Quo Bias. [P]eople demand more to give up an object than they would be willing to pay to acquire it. . . . The endowment effect reflects a preference for the status quo, a well-known human trait that most people exhibit for, other things being equal, leaving things as they are. This reflects the common observation that people would prefer to make sins of omission rather than commission. . . .

C. Cultural Biases. Researchers have long recognized that culture affects one's values and beliefs. Americans, for example, tend to value freedom of religion and speech, while other cultures recoil from the notion that people should be free to say what they want or to follow any religious system that appeals to them. Recent research suggests that culture's influence extends beyond these patterns — evidently culture affects both whether and how people reason. According to this research, Americans favor logical approaches that reject contradictions, while Chinese prefer dialectical approaches that accept contradictions. . . . The broad lesson to be learned . . . is the need for greater awareness of cultural differences. . . .

D. Excessive Commitment to a Previous Course of Action/Escalation of Conflict. [This topic is examined at length below, in the article by Barry Staw.]

E. Sunk Cost Bias. . . . Sunk costs are those that, once expended, cannot be retrieved. In the abstract, most people understand that one cannot justify future investments on the basis of previous expenditures, however large. . . . For example, other things being equal, a rational actor faced with two competing projects — one that requires $50 in future investment versus one that requires $100 — that promise to return $1,000 in profit should choose the $50 option irrespective of the costs that he or she has already incurred. Yet, it is highly likely that one who has already sunk $200 in the more expensive alternative . . . will persist in pursuing that scheme. Sunk costs lead people astray for many of the same reasons that people escalate their commitments to previously selected courses of action. Their perceptions become biased towards seeking confirmatory data in support of their original plan and their fear of appearing foolish drives them to stay the course. . . .

F. "Fixed-Pie" Bias. . . . As numerous researchers have pointed out, assuming that one's interests directly conflict with one's opponents is both common — and often wrong. . . . One of the great sources of error behind the "fixed-pie" bias is the belief that the issues most important to oneself are also the most important to one's opponents. . . . The "fixed-pie" bias is particularly difficult to address, because it tends to persist even after negotiators are presented with accurate information about their counterparts' interests.

G. Framing Bias. Sales people have long known that how one characterizes a deal may well determine its acceptability to the other side. The more favorably one "frames" the terms for a customer, the more likely he or she is to reach an agreement. Framing a deal is to be distinguished from "sweetening" the terms of a deal. The latter concerns providing better terms, e.g., lowering the price of an item; the former addresses how one paints a picture of the deal without necessarily improving its terms. For example, clothiers will invariably try to sell a customer the costly item first and then move to the less expensive item. As Professor Cialdini explains:

> Common sense might suggest the reverse: If a man has just spent a lot of money to purchase a suit, he may be reluctant to spend very much on the purchase of a sweater. But the clothiers know better. . . . Sell the suit first, because when it comes time to look at sweaters, even expensive ones, their prices will not seem as high in comparison. A man might balk at the idea of spending $95 for a sweater, but if he has just bought a $495 suit, a $95 sweater does not seem excessive.

Framing becomes . . . critical when the issue becomes one of losses avoided versus gains made [because] . . . people are moved more to avoid losses than to acquire gains — roughly speaking, they are twice as unhappy with losses as they are happy with equivalent gains. Accordingly, how one views a transaction may very well determine whether he or she is willing to enter into a deal. One who purchased a house for $120,000 and who has listed it for $200,000 may well receive an offer of $190,000 favorably or not depending on whether one views it as a $70,000 gain or a $10,000 loss. This will likely depend on the reference point that one has in mind for what a fair offer for the house should be. This, in turn, may be influenced by how effectively either or both sides "anchor" their first offers. That is, when one has staked out an initial position, that may influence the point around which negotiations revolve even when there is little market justification for the anchor.

Knowing how frames affect the attractiveness of offers to negotiators can help in bargaining situations. . . . So, for example, rather than argue, "Look, Joe, I'm only asking you to lower the price by $10,000 to $40,000," one might do better by defining an effective anchor point and then pointing to the benefits that the other side will realize from there: "Joe, I was only prepared to pay $30,000, but you've convinced me to up my offer to $40,000 because you're a tough bargainer and because your product is so good." . . .

H. Hindsight Bias. Hindsight bias occurs when people make . . . a particular prediction about an event. If, in the meantime, they discover the correct judgment, their memory of their own judgment changes to accord with the new information. Revising one's past estimate typically occurs unconsciously. . . . [P]hysicians asked to assess the probabilities of alternative diagnoses, given a set of symptoms, offer significantly different estimates depending on what they are told the ultimate diagnosis turned out to be. Similarly, studies suggest that juries apply hindsight bias in negligence cases, likely leading to more findings of negligence than may, in fact, actually occur. . . .

C. GAMES PEOPLE PLAY: REAL AND THEORETICAL

1. The Theory of Games and the Game of Negotiation

Game theory is about games of strategy. The word "game" is not used in the sense of amusement or entertainment. Many "games" that people play are not "games" as defined by game theory. Conversely, such serious matters as business and even war can be usefully analyzed as games. (The field might better have been named "strategy theory.") Games involve interactive situations where a choice by one person will have an impact on another person, who may respond in a manner which promotes the second person's interests. Game theory and economics have common intellectual roots, together with an emphasis on formal assumptions and structured (usually mathematical) modes of analysis. Both focus on questions of distribution that are important for dispute resolution.

The approach of game theory is to seek insight about complex interactions by examining structured, abstracted, and simplified versions of decisions that include a strategic component. The prototype situation is a two-person, one-issue game. (The introduction of even a single additional party or issue makes the analysis far more complex.) Two players (often, a buyer and a seller) seek to assign a value of some continuous variable (money but not a child) that they can mutually adjust. The value reflects the thing being bargained about, but the measurement is in money.

The seminal work on game theory is JOHN VON NEUMANN & OSCAR MORGENSTERN, THEORY OF GAMES AND ECONOMIC BEHAVIOR (1944). The seminal work on the application of game theory to negotiation is HOWARD RAIFFA, THE ART AND SCIENCE OF NEGOTIATION (1982). Game theory is characterized by high levels of abstraction, and the leading work is a branch of advanced mathematics. Von Neumann & Morgenstern begin by telling us, in the first sentence of their preface, that they are presenting an exposition of "a mathematical theory of games."

(p. v). Raiffa became interested in the theory of games while a graduate student in mathematics.

SCOTT BIERMAN & LUIS FERNANDEZ, GAME THEORY WITH ECONOMIC APPLICATIONS 68-70 (1993) state the following requirements for a properly defined game:

> (1) a set of players; (2) an order of play; (3) a description of the information available to any player at any point during the game; (4) the set of actions available to each player whenever called upon to make a decision; (5) the outcome that results from every possible sequence of actions by the players; and (6) a utility ranking for every player over the set of outcomes.

Game theory assumes that all players know the rules just described, and that each player behaves rationally. Accordingly, the behavior of each player is pre-ordained (defined) by the rules of the game, which are analogous to a computer algorithm.

The basic description of a simple two-party game must be detailed and specific — in effect, mathematical relationships are being stated in words. To address a simple two-party situation, game theory requires strict assumptions (rules of the game). For the game of negotiation, these rules include the following:

1. There are only two parties to the negotiation;

2. There is no neutral third party (mediator);

3. A continuous variable (money but not a child);

4. Each bargainer is monolithic (able to make a binding decision);

5. The bargainers are concerned about this deal only, thus eliminating such factors as:

   a. linkage to other transactions;

   b. linkage to other outstanding problems;

   c. consideration of past or future dealings; and

   d. setting of a precedent;

6. Time is not a factor;

7. Contracts are inviolable and enforceable;

8. A single threat environment (terminate negotiations);

9. Each bargainer knows her reservation price, but has only a probabilistic knowledge of the other party's reservation price; and

10. The setting, language, and individual variables are all irrelevant.

This model assumes that bargaining is done directly by the parties, and not through agents. The introduction of action through agents raises a whole new set of problems, which are addressed in the section of this chapter on agency theory. (See particularly the Gilson & Mnookin article, which makes extensive use of the Prisoner's Dilemma as a heuristic device.) Finally, note that the tenth item assumes away most of disciplines such as anthropology, sociology, and psychology.

Such highly abstract models are judged not by their correspondence with the "real" world, but by their usefulness. It requires only the most elementary programming skills to "teach" a computer to play tic-tac-toe so well that it never loses. At a more sophisticated level, computers have been created that can play chess better than all (or nearly all) of the best human chess players in the world. However, similar success has not been achieved for less difficult games whose rules and alternatives cannot be fully described — e.g., the "game" of negotiation.

The rules of a game, such as the sentencing options in the Prisoner's Dilemma, may not be "adjusted" any more than the rules of chess may be "adjusted" by permitting pawns to jump over other pieces in specified circumstances. To pursue the chess analogy, the only objective statement to be made about a game in which pawns jump over other pieces is that this game is not chess, because the game is defined by its rules. If one was inclined toward normative judgments, one might conclude that the new game is "better" than chess, but that game is not chess.

In repeated two-player games, studies have demonstrated that "tit-for-tat" is the most effective strategy: cooperate the first time, and then do whatever the other person did in the prior iteration of the game. With multiple players, however, this strategy often will not produce optimum results.

2. The Prisoner's Dilemma

The most widely known aspect of game theory is that under proper circumstances it can lead to poor results (from the perspective of the participants) in joint decision situations. The popular name of this problem comes from the standard example, the prisoner's dilemma. The easiest way to introduce the Prisoner's Dilemma is to begin with a concrete example. There are many versions of the prisoner's dilemma story, but the version offered here is representative of the genre.

Two persons (A and B) commit a bank robbery. They are subsequently arrested, and are immediately placed in two different locations in order to prevent communication between them. The District Attorney (DA) knows that A and B committed the bank robbery, but she lacks adequate evidence to convict them of this crime. The DA does, however, have sufficient evidence to convict both A and B of a lesser offense, illegal possession of a firearm, for which the sentence is one year.

The DA makes identical offers to both A and B, in an attempt to induce confessions. This strategy is disclosed to both prisoners, so each fully understands the situation. The following are the exclusive sentencing options (rules of the game):

1. If A and B both decline to confess, then neither will be convicted of bank robbery, but each will receive a sentence of one year imprisonment for the lesser firearms offense.

2. If A confesses and B does not confess, then A goes free and B will receive a sentence of ten years imprisonment.

3. If A does not confess and B confesses, than B goes free and A will receive a sentence of ten years imprisonment.

4. If A and B both confess, then each will receive a sentence of seven years imprisonment.

Now we are ready for each prisoner to make a rational and self-interested response to the choices offered by the DA. The options for both A and B are simple, and two in number: confess ("defect") or remain silent ("cooperate"). In order for each prisoner to make a sensible decision, account must also be taken of what the other prisoner will do. The analysis is identical for both prisoners, so we will limit ourselves to the analysis for Prisoner A. Let us consider the outcome for A under each option — cooperate and defect — assuming first that B confesses and then that B remains silent:

1. *B Confesses.* If A remains silent, then A goes to jail for ten years. If A also confesses, then A goes to jail for seven years. So, A is better off by confessing than by remaining silent.

2. *B is Silent.* If A confesses, then A is set free, If A also remains silent, then A goes to jail for one year (the lesser charge). So, A is better off by confessing than by remaining silent.

Under either possible response by B, Prisoner A is better off by confessing. Prisoner B, applying the same analysis, will also decide to confess. Put the two results together, and we have the "solution" to the Prisoner's Dilemma. Both parties confess, and each goes to jail for seven years. The reader will observe that maximizing behavior on the part of A and B does not produce an optimum result for A and B taken together, or even for A and B taken individually. Indeed, measured in terms of total years of imprisonment for A and B jointly, the Prisoner's Dilemma produces the worst possible result for them — 14 years in prison.

Instances of Prisoner's Dilemma situations are surprisingly common, You should be able to find several examples from books, movies, TV shows, and other courses. The Gilson and Mnookin article, excerpted below, demonstrates the sophisticated use that can be made of the Prisoner's Dilemma as an analytic model.

3. The Tragedy of the Commons

Periodically, an idea has an impact on thinking in fields far removed from the specific topic being considered. A short article by Garret Hardin, *The Tragedy of the Commons*, 162 SCIENCE 1243 (1968), offers a prime example. The expression "tragedy of the commons" is widely used in many areas of intellectual inquiry.

A recent Westlaw legal articles search produced over 1,200 citations to "tragedy of the commons" (often but not always accompanied by a citation to Hardin). Hardin was a population biologist and a professor at the University of California at San Diego. As indicated by the publication in Science, this article was addressed to the scientific community.

A commons is property that can be freely used by everyone, such as a pasture. Since use of the pasture is free, rational maximizers (as ever, other things being equal) prefer to graze their cattle on the public land rather than their own land. If an owner of cattle does not own land, the commons is the alternative to renting pasture land. So long as people and cattle are within the carrying capacity of the commons, the regime of free use can survive. (Relevant variables include war, poaching, disease, other readily available land, and similar factors.) At some point, however, the day (or decade) of reckoning arrives. At this point, Hardin tells us, "the inherent logic of the commons remorselessly generates tragedy." The Commons becomes overgrazed, and is destroyed.

It should be noted that there are simple solutions (at least conceptually) to many commons problems, notably those that are subject to negotiation with limited transaction costs. [This situation is similar to the problem addressed by the Coase Theory, considered above by JST.] Where private resolution is impractical, other approaches are available of two fundamental sorts: privatizing of the common, or government regulation thereof.

4. Comments and Questions

a. The idea of a commons provides a useful model for thinking about all manner of problems. What examples of a commons can you think of? Standard examples are the oceans, and schools of fish outside territorial waters. Air pollution is usefully conceived of as a commons problem.

b. Imagine that you are having dinner with several friends, and there is a shared (unspoken) agreement that the bill will be shared equally. The individual, by ordering a sumptuous feast, can benefit from a "free rider" effect, while the "responsible" member of the group who orders an inexpensive meal will incur increased costs. This situation represents an everyday example of the idea that what is in the interest of the individual at a particular time is not necessarily in the best interest of the group, and may not even be in the long-run best interest of the individual.

c. Once the number of individuals in the group and their meal options are specified, a mathematical model of the Restaurant "game" can be mapped. If the game is played only once, the rational participant in the Restaurant will "defect" and maximize individual good rather than group benefit. But, since everyone faces the same calculus, all will eat expensively and all will face a higher bill than any of them individually or as a group would desire. Even with repetitions expected, defections are likely to occur in the absence of group action.

d. If one were so inclined, this situation might be called the Tragedy of the Restaurant. Make this a two-person game, and we have a variant that might be called the Diner's Dilemma.

e. Now, let us suppose that our diners, after several high-dollar dinners seek to find a less costly solution, without giving up the "all-for-one and one-for-all" conviviality associated with sharing the dinner check. That is, the group does not want to abandon the dinner game by adopting a pay your own bill approach. What suggestions can you offer? Play the options you generate as new iterations of the Restaurant game.

f. Suppose the group wants to play a modified version of the game, by splitting into two (adjoining) tables, with separate group bills for the persons at each table. How might the groups be configured to achieve maximum fairness? These and related issues are discussed in Natalie S. Glance & Bernardo A. Huberman, The Dynamics of Social Dilemmas, SCIENTIFIC AMERICAN, March 1994, at 75.

D. MAKING CONCESSIONS AND ADJUSTING TO CHANGE

1. LEON FESTINGER, A THEORY OF COGNITIVE DISSONANCE 1-6, 261-67 (1957)

The individual strives toward consistency within himself. His opinions and attitudes tend to exist in clusters that are internally consistent. . . . Granting that consistency is the usual thing, perhaps overwhelmingly so, what about these exceptions which come to mind so readily? Only rarely, if ever are they accepted psychologically as inconsistencies by the person involved. Usually more or less successful attempts are made to rationalize them.

But persons are not always successful in explaining away or in rationalizing inconsistencies to themselves. For one reason or another, attempts to achieve consistency may fail. The inconsistency then simply continues to exist. Under such circumstances, there is psychological discomfort [dissonance]. The core of the theory of dissonance is rather simple. It holds that:

1. The existence of dissonance, being psychologically uncomfortable, will motivate the person to try to reduce the dissonance and achieve consonance.

2. When dissonance is present, in addition to trying to reduce it, the person will actively avoid situations and information which would likely increase the dissonance.

3. Manifestations of the operation of these pressures include behavior changes, changes of cognition, and new opinions.

In short, I am proposing that dissonance . . . is a motivating factor in its own right. Cognitive dissonance can be seen as an antecedent condition which leads to activity oriented toward dissonance reduction just as hunger leads to activity oriented toward hunger reduction. Although the core of the theory is simple, it has rather wide implications and applications to a variety of situations which on the surface look very different.

Although psychologists have paid a great deal of attention to the decision-making process, there has only been occasional recognition of the problems that ensue when a decision has been made. One of the major consequences of having made a decision is the existence of dissonance. A number of situations have been denoted as implying the existence of cognitive dissonance.

1. Dissonance almost always exists after a decision has been made between two or more alternatives. The cognitive elements corresponding to positive characteristics of the rejected alternatives, and those corresponding to negative characteristics of the chosen alternative, are dissonant with the knowledge of the action that has been taken. Those cognitive elements corresponding to positive characteristics of the chosen alternative and negative characteristics of the rejected alternative are consonant with the cognitive elements corresponding to the action which has been taken.

2. Dissonance almost always exists after an attempt has been made, by offering rewards or threatening punishment, to elicit overt behavior that is at variance with private opinion. If the overt behavior is successfully elicited, the person's private opinion is dissonant with his knowledge concerning his behavior; his knowledge of the reward obtained or of the punishment avoided is consonant with his knowledge concerning his behavior. If the overt behavior is not successfully elicited, then his private opinion is consonant with his knowledge of what he has done, but the knowledge of the reward not obtained or of the punishment to be suffered is dissonant with his knowledge of what he has done.

3. New information may create cognitive elements that are dissonant with existing cognition.

If dissonance is to be reduced or eliminated by changing one or more cognitive elements, it is necessary to consider how resistant these cognitive elements are to change. . . . What, then, are the circumstances that make it difficult for the person to change his actions? [Reasons include:] . . . the change may be painful or avoid loss; the present behavior may he otherwise satisfying; and making the change may simply not be possible. . . . Some behavior, especially emotional reactions, may not be under the voluntary control of the person.

2. Comments and Questions

a. Festinger's work is a classic in psychology. In other parts of the book, he discusses how people learn to rationalize discordant information. People who keep using tobacco, despite its devastating and well-known health hazards, offer an obvious example, and it is striking that Festinger was already employing this example in 1957.

b. What does the theory of cognitive dissonance have to do with dispute resolution? How might it be applied before, during, and after a negotiation?

c. Individual responses to dissonance vary among individuals, with the range of responses approximating a normal curve. Just as some persons are more "risk adverse" than others, it is reasonable to suppose that some persons are more or less tolerant of dissonance than others. Thus, different people will respond in varying ways to the same change in dissonance, risk, and most other types of change.

d. In the ensuing article, Professor Staw examines the consequences of commitment to a position, which then can serve as an impediment to considering new evidence and changing course. This is an important matter, because major decisions are commonly arrived at over a period of time and may be composed of many sub-decisions. How is Staw's analysis related to cognitive dissonance?

3. Barry M. Staw, *The Escalation of Commitment to a Course of Action*, ACAD. MGMT. REV., October 1981, at 577

Many of the most difficult decisions an individual must make are choices not about what to do in an isolated instance but about the fate of an entire course of action. This is especially true when the decision is whether to cease a questionable line of behavior or to commit more effort and resources into making that course of action pay off. Do individuals in such cases cut their losses or escalate their commitment to the course of action? Consider the following examples:

1. An individual has spent three years working on an advanced degree in a field with minimal job prospects. The individual chooses to . . . finish the degree rather than switching to an entirely new field of study. Having obtained the degree, the individual is faced with the options of unemployment, working under dissatisfying conditions, such as part time or temporary status, or starting anew in a completely unrelated field.

2. An individual purchased a stock at $50 a share, but the price has gone down to $20. Still convinced about the merit of the stock, he buys more shares at this lower price. Soon the price declines further and the individual is again faced with the decision to buy more, hold what he already has, or sell out entirely.

3. A city spends a large amount of money to improve its sewer and drainage system [that] involves digging 131 miles of tunnel shafts, reservoirs, and pumping stations. The excavation is only 10 percent completed and is useless until it is totally finished. The project will take 20 years to complete and will cost $11 billion. . . . The deeper the tunnels go, the more money they cost, and the greater are the questions about the wisdom of the entire venture.

As evidenced in the above examples, many of the most injurious personal decisions and most glaring policy disasters can come in the shape of sequential and escalating commitments. Judging by popular press accounts and the observation of everyday events, it appears that individuals may have a tendency to become locked in to a course of action, throwing good money after bad or committing new resources to a losing course of action. The critical question from an analytical point of view is whether these everyday examples denote a syndrome of decisional errors or are just a post hoc reconstruction of events. That is, do decisions about commitment to a course of action inherently lead individuals to errors of escalation or are we, as observers, simply labeling a subset of decisions whose outcomes turned out to be negative?

In the psychological literature, there have been two primary ways of explaining decisional errors. One is to point to individual limitations in information processing. Individuals are limited in their ability and desire to search for alternatives and input information, recall information from memory, and to compare alternatives on multiple criteria. Because of the limitations to individual ability at each phase of cognitive information processing, the end product of individual decisions may optimize neither personal utility nor collective welfare. A second way to explain decisional errors is to attribute a breakdown in rationality to interpersonal elements, such as social power or group dynamics. . . . Cohesive groups . . . may suppress dissent, censor information, create illusions of invulnerability, and stereotype enemies. Any of these byproducts of social interaction may, of course, hinder rational decision making and lead individuals or groups to decisional errors.

The limitations to rationality posed by the group dynamics and information processing literatures . . . do not seem to capture the central element of the commitment dilemma. A salient feature of the preceding case examples is that a series of decisions is associated with a course of action, rather than an isolated choice. The consequences of any single decision, therefore, can have implications about the utility of previous choices as well as determine future events or outcomes. This means that sunk costs may not be sunk psychologically but may enter into future decisions.

Under traditional models of economic rationality, resources should be allocated and decisions entered into when future benefits are greater than future costs. Losses or costs that may have been experienced in the past but that are not expected to recur should not enter into decision calculations. However, individuals may be motivated to rectify past losses as well as to seek future gain. One source of this motivation may be a desire on the part of individuals to appear rational in their decision making. The literature on self-justification processes [e.g., Festinger, 1957] supports this proposition and some of the tendency to escalate commitment may be explained by self-justification motives.

The largest and most systematic source of data on the justification of behavior is provided by the social psychological literature on forced compliance. Typically, in forced compliance studies, an individual is induced to perform an unpleasant or dissatisfying act when no compensating external rewards are present. It is generally predicted that individuals will bias their attitudes on the experimental task in a positive direction so as to justify their previous behavior. . . .

Although research on commitment has emphasized the role of justification, these studies have chiefly tapped what could be labeled an internal justification process. When justification is considered primarily as an intra-individual process, individuals are posited to attend to events and to act in ways to protect their own self-images. But within most social settings, justification may also be directed externally. When faced with an external threat or evaluation, individuals may be motivated to prove to others that they were not wrong in an earlier decision and the force for such external justification could well be stronger than the protection of self-esteem.

In addition to the internal and external forms of justification, norms for consistency in action may be another major source of commitment. A lay theory may exist in our society, or at least within many organizational settings, that administrators who are consistent in their actions are better leaders than those who switch from one line of behavior to another. Survey and anecdotal data point to the possibility of an implicit theory of leadership, according to which effective administrators are fully committed to and steadfast in a course of action.

In order to test for the existence of such a lay theory, Ross and I conducted an experiment on the reactions of individuals to selected forms of administrative behavior. Subjects included practicing managers, undergraduates in business, and undergraduates in a psychology course. Results showed that administrators were rated highest when they followed a consistent course of action and were ultimately successful. . . . This supported a predicted "hero effect" for the administrator who remained committed through two apparent failures of a course of action, only to succeed in the end. Finally, the effect of consistency on ratings of the administrator was shown to vary by subject group, being strongest among practicing administrators, next strongest among business students, and weakest among psychology undergraduates. These results suggest not only that consistency in action is perceived to be part of effective leadership, but that this perception may be acquired through socialization in business and governmental roles.

Motivation to justify decisions can be seen as a function of responsibility for negative consequences, as well as both internal and external demands for competence. Responsibility for negative consequences leads to a motivation to justify previous decisions, if there is a need to demonstrate competence to oneself or others. . . . The traditional literature on dissonance and self-justification considers only the desire of individuals to be correct or accurate in decision making for reasons of self-esteem, but the need to demonstrate competence to external parties may also be a potent force.

Such predictions may be culture-bound; but emphases on individual rationality and competence are so strong in Western societies that they are likely to foster concomitant needs for rationalizing one's actions. Likewise, because norms for rationality are so dominant in business and governmental organizations, decision makers in these settings may also find it necessary to justify their actions to constituents within and outside the organization. In sum, it is ironic that both internal and external needs to demonstrate competence can lead to justification, because justification is exactly what may detract from the rational or competent decision making that both individuals and organizations seek to achieve.

Forces for justification can lead to a form of "retrospective rationality." The individual, when motivated by a need to justify, seeks to appear competent in previous as opposed to future actions. In contrast, SEU (subjective expected utility) models of behavior posit that the individual is prospectively rational, seeking to maximize future utility. What adds to the complexity of decision making is the fact that both forces may operate in commitment decisions.

As determinants of prospective rationality, some set of perceived probabilities and values should affect resource allocation decisions. Already within commitment situations, we have validated the effects of the efficacy of resources and the causal persistence of a setback. However, it is possible that individual perceptions of the likelihood and value of various outcomes are also influenced by non-objective factors. . . . As shown in an experiment by Fox, individuals make more use of information that exonerates them for an earlier error than information that is implicating. Thus, it can be expected that motivation to justify decisions will affect the search for and storage of information by individuals. Likewise, having been responsible for negative consequences may make the achievement of future outcomes all the more important. The value of future returns may intensify if they are needed to cover past losses.

In addition to the confluence of retrospective and prospective rationality, there is probably a third force of major importance to commitment decisions. Individuals can become committed to a course of action, simply because they believe consistency in action is an appropriate form of behavior. Individuals sometimes model their own behavior on those they see as successful within organizations and society in general. These effects may be time-dependent inasmuch as high-level administrators model their behavior on leadership stereotypes that exist in the culture at a given time in history. These effects can also be non-cognitive, since behavior may be modeled without a direct calculation of costs and benefits. . . . Likewise, norms for consistency can be viewed as an outgrowth of individual needs for cognitive consistency [Festinger] or socialization for consistency within the general society.

This article began with a series of examples and an inquiry into whether commitment situations can inherently lead individuals into errors of escalation. The examples were tilted in the direction of an escalation of commitment, and in each case, the escalation seemed to lead to further problems or losses. Obviously, it is also possible that escalation of commitment can bring a turnaround of results and positive, as well as negative, consequences. But this is not the point. The crucial issue is whether there is a tendency to escalate commitment above and beyond what would be warranted by the "objective" facts of the situation. From our research, the answer to this question must be a qualified Yes. . . .

If we accept the conclusion that there is a tendency to escalate on the part of individuals, what are its implications? Perhaps the most likely victims of an escalation tendency will be behaviors that are perceptually associated as parts of a single course of action. In such sequences of behavior, both justification and consistency influences have been found to override more objective elements of the situation. Prime candidates for escalation, therefore, include resource allocation or investment decisions that are identified by an entering and exit value, life choices that are linked together with the label of a career, and policy decisions for which administrators are held accountable by others in an organization or by the general public. In these situations, one must be especially wary of escalation tendencies and, perhaps, take counteractions to restore balance to decision making.

In counterbalancing an escalation tendency, individuals should seek and follow the advice of outsiders who can assess the relevant issues of a decision situation without being responsible for previous losses or subject to internal or external needs to justify past actions. Likewise, organizations that have experienced losses from a given investment or course of action should rotate or change those in charge of allocating resources. One applied instance of such a counterbalancing strategy was recently uncovered . . . in a comparative case study of procedures in two banks for coping with the problem of delinquent loans. The more financially aggressive bank, which had issued loans with greater risk, utilized separate departments for lending and "workout," the latter department being in charge of efforts to recover the bank's investment from problem accounts. In contrast, the more conservative bank which had fewer delinquent loans, had developed no formal procedure for separating responsibility for lending and workout, the original loan officer being charged with all phases of the loan relationship.

[In summary,] . . . our research has shown that administrators sometimes become trapped in a course of action by external demands for success, and administrative experimentation is often viewed as an inappropriate form of leadership behavior. Thus, it may be important to revamp performance evaluation systems facing administrators so that the motivation for action will shift from the defense of past actions to attainment of future gain (e.g., from a retrospective to a prospective basis). It may also be necessary to re-train administrators and re-socialize students that enter governmental and business organizations about the merits of experimentation versus consistency. In each of these ways, the actions of decision makers can perhaps be directed away from the tendency to escalate.

E. AGENCY THEORY

1. Comments and Questions

a. When a principal has to act through an agent, as happens constantly in an industrialized society, the actions of the agent may be at variance with the desires of the principal. That is, the interests of the agent may be less than completely congruent with those of the principal, and the action of the agent may vary accordingly. Employment of lawyers is an important principal-agent situation, and the ensuing article examines agency theory in this context.

b. A distinct message to be taken from the Gilson & Mnookin article relates to their use of the Prisoner's Dilemma as a heuristic tool. In the classic version, as presented earlier in the Chapter, the Prisoner's Dilemma no doubt struck the reader as cleverly illustrating a fairly simple idea about human behavior. This article demonstrates advanced use of the Prisoner's Dilemma.

c. There is a voluminous literature on principal-agent problems. For useful examples that focus on negotiation, *see, e.g.*, Jayne Seminare Docherty & Marcia Caton Campbell, *Teaching Negotiators to Analyze Conflict Structure and Anticipate the Consequences of Principal-Agent Relationships*, 87 MARQ. L. REV. 655 (2004); James K. Sebenius, *When a Contract Isn't Enough: How to Be Sure Your Agent Gets You the Best Deal*, HARV. BUS. REV., July 2004, at 3.

d. Students of politics have long been interested in agency theory, because it reflects a fundamental concern about representative government. Public choice theory argues that legislators and bureaucrats often will act in their own interests, which may not be identical with those of the public. So too do interest groups, which obtain benefits through the intervention of government.

e. A certain similarity to agency theory is found in the concept of "moral hazard" that is a central concern for vendors of insurance. The problem is that people who purchase insurance will behave less carefully than those who are not insured, with attendant costs to the insurer. There is a vast amount of evidence that demonstrates the "moral hazard" phenomenon, quite apart from instances of fraudulent claims or intentional activity such as arson. (For this reason, the word "moral" might be regarded as a misnomer.)

f. Examples of principal-agent problems abound. Collect several examples from the daily newspapers and from materials covered in other courses. The agency issues faced by defense lawyers in the context of plea bargaining are considered at length in Chapter Six.

g. During the reign of Saddam Hussein in Iraq, Nicholas Kristof of the New York Times was menacingly questioned by two government officials about an article he had written.

> Neither man could speak English and they hadn't actually read the offending column. My government minder took my column and translated it for them. I saw my life flash before my eyes. But my minder's job was to spy on me, and he worried that my tough column would reflect badly on his spying. Plus, he was charging me $100 a day, and he would lose a fortune if I was expelled, or worse. So he translated my column very selectively. There was no mention of burning beards or nails in heads. He left out whole paragraphs. When he finished, the two senior officials shrugged and let me off scot-free.

The minder was not a faithful agent for the government, due to the economic (and perhaps other) incentives to inaccurately report about Kristof's writings.

2. Ronald J. Gilson & Robert H. Mnookin, *Disputing Through Agents: Cooperation and Conflict Between Lawyers in Litigation*, 94 COLUM. L. REV. 509 (1994)

Do lawyers facilitate dispute resolution or do they instead exacerbate conflict and pose a barrier to the efficient resolution of disputes? A distinctive characteristic of our formal mechanisms of conflict resolution is that clients carry on their disputes through lawyers. Yet, at a time when the role of lawyers in dispute resolution has captured not only public but political attention, social scientists have remained largely uninterested in the influence of lawyers on the disputing process. Economists have developed an extensive literature that models one or another aspect of the litigation and settlement process. But the economic literature, with rare exceptions, shares a troublesome feature. Almost by convention, litigation is modeled as a two-person game between principals, thereby abstracting away the legal system's central institutional characteristic — litigation is carried out by agents.

While any model must make concessions to tractability, this simplifying assumption is especially troublesome because lawyers have long been considered to have a special influence on how litigation is conducted, even if there has been no consensus on whether lawyers dampen or exacerbate conflict in litigation. Today, the dominant popular view is that lawyers magnify the inherent divisiveness of dispute resolution. According to this vision, litigators rarely cooperate to resolve disputes efficiently. Instead, shielded by a professional ideology that is said to require zealous advocacy, they endlessly and wastefully fight in ways that enrich themselves but rarely advantage the clients. Many within the legal profession share this pessimistic view. . . .

Purveyor of needless conflict need not be the only vision of the lawyer's role in litigation. Over a century ago, Abraham Lincoln suggested that lawyers can play an extraordinarily constructive role in disputes — as peacemakers who facilitate efficient and fair resolution of conflict when their clients could not do so for themselves. ABRAHAM LINCOLN, NOTES FOR A LAW LECTURE, IN THE LIFE AND WRITINGS OF ABRAHAM LINCOLN 328-330 (Philip V. Stern, ed. 1940). From this perspective, a central characteristic of the formal legal system — that clients carry on their dispute through lawyers who are their agents — has the potential for damping rather than exacerbating the conflictual character of litigation. In this Article we offer a conceptual foundation for this alternative perspective — a foundation that rests on the idea that lawyers may allow clients to cooperate in circumstances when their clients could not do so on their own. We construct this foundation using basic notions drawn from game theory and agency theory.

We begin by using the prisoner's dilemma as a heuristic to understand better the circumstances of disputants locked in a legal conflict in an abstract world in which there are no lawyers — only the parties themselves and a judge. In Part I, we describe a litigation game in which each disputant faces a single choice: she can either cooperate by volunteering all relevant information to the other side or defect by using the discovery process in an adversarial manner to hide unfavorable information. We analyze litigation initially in the form of this one-round, two-person prisoner's dilemma, in which the inability of parties to commit effectively to cooperation results in dominant strategies that yield suboptimal results. Because a single lawsuit has a number of strategic interactions, we then analyze litigation as a finite number of repeated games, each of which is structured as a prisoner's dilemma. Our primary message in Part I is that in many legal conflicts each disputant may feel compelled to make a contentious move in order to avoid being exploited by, and to take advantage of any weakness in, the other side. Nevertheless, the net result of contentious moves by both may be an outcome that is less efficient than if the disputants had cooperated.

In Part II, we explore the role that lawyers might play in overcoming the prisoner's dilemma. Our analysis in this Part, unlike most game theoretic models of the litigation process, acknowledges the central institutional characteristic of the legal system — litigation is carried out by lawyers on behalf of their clients. We suggest that, in contrast to clients who are unlikely to litigate against one another ever again, lawyers are repeat players who have the opportunity to establish reputations. At the core of our story is the potential for disputing parties to avoid the prisoner's dilemma inherent in much litigation by selecting cooperative lawyers whose reputations credibly commit each party to a cooperative strategy.

At this point, we introduce a dialectical tension between game theory and agency theory. On the one hand, we suggest that the possibility for commitment to cooperation exists because the incentives for a cooperative lawyer, who is a repeat player concerned with maintaining her reputation over time, differ from those of her client, who as a one-shot litigant may be tempted to defect. On the other hand, we suggest that because the interests of the client (as principal) and the interests of her lawyer (as agent) diverge in some respects, cooperation may be undermined in two very different ways. One danger is that the agents may "collude" to exacerbate conflict when that behavior serves their own interests. Alternatively, a principal may persuade a previously cooperative agent to defect in order to increase the principal's payoff.

We expose these dangers and the difficulties of establishing and maintaining an equilibrium in the market for cooperative lawyers first by exploring the problem in a world in which all lawyers are sole practitioners. Next, we examine whether law firms might be more effective repositories of reputation than individual lawyers. Through this analysis we show that the firm can ameliorate some principal-agent conflicts that may undermine cooperation. But, like the introduction of individual lawyers to the basic prisoner's dilemma game, the introduction of law firms adds a new level of agency conflict, now between the firm and the individual lawyers who compose it. . . .

I. Litigation as a Prisoner's Dilemma

The prisoner's dilemma provides a useful heuristic to illuminate a common characteristic of dispute settlement through litigation. In many disputes, each litigant may feel compelled to make a contentious move either to exploit, or to avoid exploitation by, the other side. Yet, the combination of contentious moves by both results in a less efficient outcome than if the litigants had been able to cooperate.

A. The Litigation Game: A One-Round Prisoner's Dilemma. Consider the following "litigation game," a highly abstracted model of litigation possessing the attributes of a one-round prisoner's dilemma. Able and Baker dispute the proper division of $100 according to some legal standard. For the moment, assume that litigation does not involve lawyers, but only the two parties and a judge. Each party holds information not known by the other side. Some of this information is favorable and some of it is unfavorable. Before the judge decides the case, there is a one-stage simultaneous disclosure process in which each party hands to the judge and the opposing party a sealed envelope containing information. Only two moves are possible, and neither player can know in advance what the other will do. One move is cooperation: a player voluntarily (and at no cost to the other side) discloses to the other side and to the judge all material information in her possession. The second option, defection, involves the adversarial use of the disclosure process to hide unfavorable information. As a consequence, the other side must spend $15 to force disclosure of some but not all of the information withheld. After the envelope exchange and the "purchase" of some of the withheld information, the judge resolves the dispute based on the information disclosed.

With the payoff structure indicated in the following matrix, this game poses a prisoner's dilemma. If both players cooperate, there are no discovery expenses for either side and we will assume the Judge awards $50 to Able and $50 to Baker. If both players defect, each must spend $15 to pry out some but not all of the unfavorable information possessed by the other side. Although the judge lacks complete information, we assume that she divides the $100 in the same ratio; the net recovery to the parties is now $35 to Able and $35 to Baker. The third scenario, in which one player defects while the other cooperates, provides the defector with a higher payoff ($70) and hurts the "sucker" in two ways. First, because the cooperating player has disclosed all of its unfavorable information while the defecting party has only disclosed some of the information unfavorable to it, the judge awards the sucker a gross recovery of only $30. Second, the sucker has spent $15 to get less than all of the information unfavorable to the other side before the judge (without which his recovery would be even lower). Thus, the sucker's net recovery is only $15.

In this litigation game, Able's best response to whatever strategy Baker chooses is to defect. In other words, defection is Able's dominant strategy. The same, of course, is true for Baker. Defect-Defect, therefore, is a "dominant strategy equilibrium," even though this result guarantees each party only $35, rather than the $50 produced by a strategy of mutual cooperation. If there is no way for the disputants to bind each other to make a cooperative move, rational actors end up with less than "fools" who simply cooperate.

B. Is the Prisoner's Dilemma an Appropriate Model for Litigation? To what extent does the prisoner's dilemma represent an appropriate, albeit highly simplified, model of the litigation process? Focus first on the payoff structure. In a prisoner's dilemma, the best payoff for a player occurs when that player defects and the other player cooperates. The worst payoff results when a player cooperates while the other player defects. The other two outcomes fall between these extremes, with the reward for mutual cooperation better than the payoff for mutual defection. This means that a prisoner's dilemma cannot be a zero sum or purely distributive game: the total combined payoff from mutual cooperation must exceed the total combined payoff from mutual defection. Indeed, in a symmetric prisoner's dilemma, each player's payoff from mutual cooperation must be greater than each player's payoff from mutual defection.

How realistic is it to assume that in litigation the payoff structure takes this form? In many disputes, the assumption that mutual cooperation might benefit both sides seems entirely plausible. Mutual cooperation involves lower total litigation costs than mutual defection. Moreover, when parties share information, reveal their true underlying interests, and engage in collaborative problem-solving, they may sometimes develop new options that "create value" or "expand the pie" for both disputants in comparison to the result flowing from mutual defections. Both parties may sometimes gain from a negotiated resolution that takes a form a judge could not impose. . . .

The rules of the game for a prisoner's dilemma also require that each player remains ignorant of what the other player will do before making a move: enforceable commitments or contracts are not possible and thus the parties cannot credibly bind themselves to cooperate. At first glance, this restrictive assumption seems entirely inappropriate. Disputants in litigation can enter into enforceable agreements with respect to future conduct. The prisoner's dilemma disappears if the parties can, at reasonable cost, spell out the terms of an enforceable agreement to cooperate in the litigation, and thereby bind each other to exchange all relevant information so as to decrease litigation costs.

Agreements with respect to certain aspects of litigation — for example, limiting the number of depositions, or adopting a particular discovery schedule — may be easy to write and enforce, but it may be very difficult or expensive to specify fully a contract to "conduct a lawsuit cooperatively" or "to disclose all material information." Moreover, even if the terms can be specified, it may be very difficult to determine whether a defection has occurred. Even where a breach of such a contract is observable by the parties, a violation may be difficult to verify to a judge, thus making enforcement problematic.

Discovery disputes in contentious cases reveal the severity of these problems. If one party claims that the other party has breached an agreement by engaging in abusive discovery practices, a judge often faces substantial evidentiary difficulties. Typically, the judge knows little about the information available to either the responding or the requesting party. As Judge Frank Easterbrook has stated, *Discovery as Abuse*, 69 B.U.L. REV. 635, 638-39 (1989):

> Judges can do little about impositional discovery . . . . The judicial officer always knows less than the parties. . . . A magistrate supervising discovery does not know the expected productivity of a given request, because the nature of the requester's claim and the content of the files (or head) of the adverse party are unknown. Judicial officers cannot measure the costs and benefits to the requester and so cannot isolate impositional requests. . . . We cannot prevent what we cannot detect; we cannot detect what we cannot define; we cannot define "abusive" discovery except in theory, because in practice we lack essential information.

If the responding party were to produce fully the information sought and display it to the judge, the responding party would already have incurred all the costs that [she] was trying to avoid. In the absence of such production, the responding party has some leeway with which to exaggerate the burden of response, and a wise judge will thus to some extent discount the protestations of that responding party. The requesting party provides no more reliable guidance, as that party possesses the incentive to exaggerate, in a complimentary fashion, the ease with which the responding party can produce the information. . . .

In sum, the payoff structure specified for a prisoner's dilemma seems appropriate for many disputes. Moreover, verification problems make the adequate enforcement of binding general commitments to cooperate in litigation (whether imposed by contract or rule) highly problematic. Therefore, despite its restrictive assumptions about payoffs and blind action, the prisoner's dilemma game is a powerful heuristic for understanding the barriers to cooperation in litigation.

C. Litigation as a Multi-Round Prisoner's Dilemma Game. At first glance, litigation between principals who are unlikely to sue each other again appears to be a one-round game. However, one can view a single lawsuit as consisting of a number of strategic encounters: each discovery request, the scheduling of depositions, and each motion might be seen as a separate game between the same parties. If each of these many tactical encounters during a lawsuit has the structure of a prisoner's dilemma, does the fact that the same parties play each other on multiple occasions over the course of a single lawsuit provide an opportunity for cooperation that is not available to players in a one-round game?

The answer seems to be no, although the explanation is more complicated than it once appeared. There is a rich theoretical literature analyzing "repeated games," which explores how rational players might behave in the context of a long-term relationship. Duncan Luce and Howard Raiffa demonstrated some time ago that, so long as the prisoner's dilemma game is played a known finite number of times, rational players still have no incentive to cooperate. The reasoning is straightforward. In the last round, both players recognize that there is no incentive to cooperate, because the final game is identical to the one-round game described above. Now consider the next-to-last round. Because the players know that both will defect in the last round, the next-to-last round is no different from the last. Reasoning backwards round by round, the multi-round game unravels all the way back to the first round.

More recent research, however, suggests that cooperative behavior can develop in a multi-round prisoner's dilemma under certain conditions. Suppose that, instead of a known finite number of rounds, there is only a known probability that the game will end before infinite time has passed. If there is a high enough probability in each round that the parties will play an additional round, the prospect of future dealings can induce cooperation, depending upon the payoff function. Robert Axelrod studied the question of what would be a good strategy if players were confronted with an iterated prisoner's dilemma. Axelrod invited game theorists to participate in a computer tournament in which each submitted a strategy that was paired off with every other submission. Amazingly enough, the winner was the simplest of all strategies submitted. "This was TIT FOR TAT, the strategy which cooperates on the first move and then does whatever the other player did on the previous move." Other theoretical research suggests that cooperation may be sustained even in games of a known number of rounds, provided the number of rounds is large enough and the players believe there are at least a few players in the population who will always play cooperatively.

Together, this work indicates that there may be circumstances under which the parties can escape the prisoner's dilemma if there are significantly high prospects that they will have a large number of future dealings with each other and that they care enough about the outcomes of those future dealings. Unfortunately, the conditions necessary for cooperation in the course of a single lawsuit, even when broken down into a series of subgames, are sufficiently rigorous that the one-shot prisoner's dilemma remains the correct heuristic with which to explore the potential for lawyers to facilitate cooperation.

First, unlike the multi-round games considered in the theoretical literature, the aggregate payoff to the subgames of the decomposed litigation remains reasonably fixed. Also, the number of subgames in litigation, while perhaps unspecifiable ex ante, has predictable finite limits. To be more precise, because players can locate with reasonable precision the final round of a lawsuit, unraveling may begin. In this sense, a lawsuit is unlike a repeated game in which there is simply a finite probability that the game may end after any given round. Finally, the strategies that induce cooperation in repeated games require that each party know after each round whether an opponent cooperated or defected. In litigation, where even cooperative behavior occurs in the context of a competitive environment, the risk of misunderstanding an opponent's move is significant. In the prisoner's dilemma, each player has only two basic moves: cooperation or defection. In litigation, there are many gray tones between the black and white of these two pure moves. The opposing party often takes an action that must be evaluated by degree: Was the action too competitive and therefore a defection? Mistakes and misunderstandings can lead to conflictual outcomes even when both parties seek to follow a cooperative strategy.

II. The Role Lawyers Might Play in Overcoming the Prisoner's Dilemma

We are now ready to introduce individual lawyers into the clients' prisoner's dilemma model of litigation. Assuming the particular litigation game has the payoff structure of a prisoner's dilemma, each client would prefer mutual cooperation to mutual defection. However, each lacks the means credibly to commit to her good intentions. In this Part, we show how disputing through lawyers may provide a means to make such a commitment: Lawyers, acting as agents, have the potential to solve the game theoretic problem of mutual defection. We then consider the first level of the game theory agency theory dialectic: how use of an agent to pre-commit to cooperate creates its own set of agency problems. Initially, we consider a world of sole practitioners — all lawyers practice alone. Later, we consider representation by firms of lawyers.

A. The Pre-Litigation Game: Choosing Lawyers. Assume that both clients must litigate through a lawyer (an assumption that, for a change, is descriptively accurate). Further suppose that there exists a class of sole practitioners who have reputations for cooperation which assure that, once retained, they will conduct the litigation in a cooperative fashion. Three final assumptions define our "pre-litigation game." First, clients disclose their choice of lawyer — and thus, whether they have chosen a cooperative lawyer — prior to the beginning of the litigation game. Second, if one client chooses a cooperative lawyer and her opponent does not, the client choosing a cooperative lawyer can change her mind without cost before the litigation game begins. Third, after the litigation game begins, clients cannot change lawyers.

Under these assumptions, disputing through lawyers provides an escape from the prisoner's dilemma. As we have defined the pre-litigation game, each client's dominant strategy is to choose a cooperative lawyer, because the choice of a cooperative lawyer binds each client to a cooperative strategy. If client A chooses a cooperative lawyer, and client B also chooses a cooperative lawyer, both clients receive the higher cooperative payoff. Alternatively, if client B does not choose a cooperative lawyer, client A is no worse off having initially chosen to cooperate. In that event, client A replaces her cooperative lawyer with a gladiator and is in the same position as if she had chosen a gladiator in the first instance. Thus, her dominant strategy is to choose a cooperative lawyer and to switch if her opponent does not adopt a parallel strategy. Of course, client B confronts the same choices and has the same dominant strategy. The result is a cooperative equilibrium because the introduction of lawyers has transformed the prisoner's dilemma payoff structure into a game in which the only choices are mutual cooperation or mutual defection. Mutual cooperation obviously has the higher payoff for each party.

This is the easy part. Designing a game in which the players can credibly commit is not difficult, if one assumes the availability of commitment techniques. What makes the game interesting from a policy perspective is the extent to which its assumptions are consistent with institutional patterns. This consistency is what interests us about lawyers as sources of credible commitments: We believe the assumptions that define the pre-litigation game are roughly consistent with the way litigation occurs.

In the pre-litigation game, we first required clients to disclose their choice of lawyer before the game began. In real litigation, plaintiffs must typically disclose their choice of lawyer at the outset of litigation: the lawyer's name is, quite literally, the first thing that appears on the complaint. Similarly, the defendant must have a lawyer to respond to the complaint, and even to request an extension of the time in which to file an answer to the complaint. Again, this discloses the identity of the lawyer chosen. We next assumed that a plaintiff choosing a cooperative lawyer could costlessly switch to a gladiator upon learning that her opponent had chosen a gladiator. In the real world, there are costs in switching lawyers, but these costs are likely to be low at the outset. The third assumption, that clients cannot change lawyers during the litigation game, is more problematic. At first glance, the assumption seems patently false; a client may discharge counsel at any time. On closer examination, the presence of substantial switching costs may provide a reasonable proxy for a prohibition against discharging cooperative counsel once the litigation is well underway. Indeed, the longer the litigation continues, the more switching will cost.

Thus, the special assumptions underlying our pre-litigation game are not implausible. What remains, however, is the most critical of the assumptions on which lawyers' potential to facilitate cooperation depends: the existence of lawyers with reputations for cooperation. How and why are such reputations created and sustained? How do clients learn which lawyers are cooperative?

B. A Reputation Market for Cooperative Lawyers. The preceding discussion suggests why there might be a demand for cooperative lawyers. Both parties to a lawsuit with a prisoner's dilemma payoff schedule would like to hire cooperative lawyers, because that allows them to commit to a cooperative strategy. Clients should, therefore, be willing to pay a premium for such lawyers, reflecting a portion of the amount by which the cooperative payoff exceeds the non-cooperative payoff.

Establishing the supply side is also straightforward. Lawyers would be willing to invest in achieving a reputation for cooperation, because they would receive a return on that investment by virtue of the premium fees clients would be willing to pay. As in standard reputation models, the lawyer's investment in reputation serves two functions. First, it identifies the lawyer as one who possesses the desired, but otherwise unobservable, attribute; the client must be able to find a cooperative lawyer. Second, it represents the penalty that the market will impose if the lawyer treats his reputation as bait rather than as bond by turning into a gladiator at the request of an opportunistic client. Non-cooperative behavior would forfeit the lawyer's investment in a cooperative reputation. Thus, so long as the lawyer's possible loss of investment in reputation exceeds the size of the bribe an opportunistic client would be willing to pay, cooperative lawyers will not be suborned, and a market for cooperative lawyers should be available. . . .

C. Agency Problems that May Subvert Cooperation. The employment of lawyers with identifiable reputations does have the potential to facilitate cooperation between clients in litigation. However, the use of agents to make credible the commitment to cooperate itself poses two potential agency problems. First, the two lawyer-agents may "conspire" to maximize their incomes at the expense of their clients through non-cooperative behavior that prolongs the litigation and increases legal fees. When each lawyer stands as gatekeeper against the other lawyer's individual non-cooperative misconduct, what protects both clients from the lawyers' joint determination to behave non-cooperatively? Second, a client may subvert a lawyer with a reputation for cooperation. This second problem represents the converse of the first. . . .

1. A Conspiracy of Agents. While we proffer lawyers as a means to allow clients to pre-commit to cooperation, it is only fair to acknowledge that this idea stands current conventional wisdom on its head. The public typically views lawyers as the source of the problem, not its cure. . . . [The] problem is not simply that an individual litigator takes advantage of his client, but that opposing lawyers implicitly conspire to take advantage of both clients. Most cases are settled, but not until years of contention run up large legal fees, because lawyers, who benefit most from litigation, are in control — not the clients who pay the bill.

Our model leaves room for this type of collusive behavior. While opposing clients who thought that they were each retaining cooperative lawyers would certainly discharge both lawyers if they discovered that the lawyers were conspiring to make lucrative trouble, our story relies heavily on a client's own lawyer to detect misconduct by opposing counsel. During both the pre-litigation game and the litigation itself, a client's lawyer is the first line of defense against non-cooperative behavior, because many instances of non-cooperative conduct will be more easily observed by the lawyer than by the client. Non-cooperative conduct that might otherwise be observable to the client may be obscured when the client's lawyer actively participates in its camouflage. Lawyer collusion thus reduces the observability of misconduct and thereby threatens the structure of lawyer-mediated cooperation between clients.

2. Giving in to Client Threats. The second potential problem with using sole practitioners to allow clients to pre-commit to cooperate results not from the lawyers' collusion against their clients, but from an individual lawyer's willingness to collude with the client. Here the concern is that the very circumstance that creates the potential for cooperation also creates the risk of defection. An individual practitioner can represent only a limited number of clients in ongoing litigation. The larger and more complex the matter, presumably the greater is the opportunity that exists for gain through cooperation. However, the larger and more complex the matter, the greater the percentage of a lawyer's practice it represents, and the more intimidating is a client's threat to change counsel unless the lawyer breaches his reputation. Because the opposing client would anticipate the risk of defection, in this situation the pre-litigation game might not allow for a cooperative result.

D. Law Firms and Reputational Commitments. Problems of self-interest and client pressure hinder the use of sole practitioners as cooperative agents. Using law firms as reputational repositories has the potential to mitigate these problems. But, as with sole practitioners, the game theory-agency theory dialectic also plagues the use of law firms to overcome the problem of credible commitment. Solving the cooperation problem through the use of an organization as primary agent simply exposes a different set of agency problems that arise between the organization and its own agents — the individual lawyers composing the firm.

1. How the Law Firm Might Bond Cooperation When an Individual Lawyer Cannot. Because a firm may provide a larger repository of reputational capital — at a minimum composed of the aggregate reputational capital of its component lawyers — using a law firm instead of a sole practitioner has the potential to mitigate the problem of collusion between opposing counsel. In effect, the firm pledges its reputation behind the cooperative commitment of each of its lawyers. Defection by any single lawyer in any single case may damage the entire firm's reputation for cooperation. The size of the penalty imposed on the firm for non-cooperation in any single case may, therefore, be larger than the penalty that can be imposed against a sole practitioner for a similar defection. In this way, the difficulties of detection discussed earlier are balanced by an increase in the penalty if the misconduct is observed.

Additionally, using a law firm in lieu of an individual can directly reduce the potential for collusion. Precisely because the firm allows each lawyer to invoke its entire reputation, the firm has a substantial incentive to monitor the behavior of its own lawyers. Thus, in addition to relying on an individual firm lawyer to detect misconduct on the part of opposing counsel, the client can rely on the firm, acting in its own interest, to monitor the conduct of the particular lawyer actually doing the client's work. . . .

Using a law firm also mitigates the danger that an individual lawyer will be susceptible to economic pressure by his large clients to risk his reputation by behaving non-cooperatively. Large law firms often have a diversified client base, with no single client or matter representing a material percentage of total firm revenues. As a result, the size and credibility of the threat posed by a client even in a large matter is reduced and so, correspondingly, is this danger to a cooperative outcome in the pre-litigation game.

2. Agency Problems with Precommitting to Cooperation through Law Firms. . . . While reliance upon a firm may mitigate the agency conflicts between lawyer and client, it creates new agency conflicts between the law firm and its agents — the lawyers acting on behalf of the firm. . . . These conflicts threaten the effectiveness of using lawyers to solve the prisoner's dilemma game. This can happen in two ways.

First, law firm income-sharing rules may increase the size of the client's threat. While a law firm's diversified client base diminishes a client's ability to subvert a lawyer with a reputation for cooperation by threatening to withdraw its work, the incentives created by the way a firm splits its income among its lawyers may alter this happy outcome. It has become commonplace for a law firm to divide its profits among its lawyers based on some measure of the productivity of individual lawyers. . . . Productivity-based profit splitting increases the incentives for collusion between opposing counsel. If the lawyers on both sides of a case are members of firms that split profits in this way, each has an interest in increasing the total billable hours of work required by the dispute.

A final manifestation of this phenomenon yields the same result. Firms pay young lawyers in two ways: current compensation in cash and deferred compensation through the promise of a performance-dependent probability of becoming a partner. Suppose that the probability of becoming a partner depends in important part on the number of hours a young lawyer bills. In many large firms, lawyers who will soon be considered for partnership — senior associates — have substantial authority to influence the extent and intensity of discovery, which is commonly a major source of litigation conflict. In this setting, the senior associate has an incentive to risk the firm's reputation for cooperation by creating conflict; conflict generates additional work and, therefore, an increased probability of making partner.

The scenarios described here share a common core. In each, the individual lawyer is in a position to gain — whether through an increased share of current profits or an increased probability of a chance to share in future profits — from actions that risk the firm's reputational capital. And in each, the lawyer gets the bulk of the return from risking the firm's reputation, but bears only part of the loss if that risk is realized. The conflict of interest between the law firm and its lawyers, an agency cost of disputing through a multiple agent entity, threatens the potential for a firm-mediated solution to the prisoner's dilemma game.

Second, client preferences may deconstruct the law firm, thereby reversing the increased investment in reputation that supported any single lawyer's commitment to cooperation. The catch phrase for large clients has become that they "hire lawyers, not law firms." Their goal is to maintain competition among firms for their work. . . . Shifting the search for reputation back to the individual from the firm potentially offsets the increase in the size of the reputational capital achieved by moving from individual to firm representation. If it is only the individual lawyer's reputation upon which the client relies, then the aggregate of the reputational capital of the lawyers in the firms does not bond the conduct of the individual lawyers.

That precommitting to cooperate through use of a law firm rather than an individual lawyer evokes its own set of agency problems is not to say that law firms may not be more efficient repositories of reputation than individual lawyers. It merely reflects the operation of the game theory-agency theory dialectic. Any solution to the problem of assuring cooperation in a competitive game that relies on agents generates agency costs. Like friction, we may reduce these costs but we cannot eliminate them. But understanding the ways in which agency incentives can plague cooperative solutions does allow the analysis to take both a positive and a normative turn.

IV. Facilitating Cooperation

We now take up some of the normative implications of our analysis: What institutional reforms hold promise for reducing the barriers to lawyers facilitating cooperation between their clients? We consider three levels of reform proposals. First, we survey norms of professional conduct to determine whether the governing rules create space for cooperative practice — can a reputation for cooperation be established and maintained if litigation requires zealous advocacy? Next, we consider strategies for overcoming the barriers law firms face in developing reputations for providing cooperative services. Here, the hope is to provide a counterweight to the increasingly adversarial nature of commercial litigation. Finally, we consider how professional organizations can facilitate the development of more efficient cooperative reputational markets: by clarifying what constitutes cooperation and defection; by developing a sense of community and shared norms; and by developing through certification a means to increase repeat play and sanction defection. . . .

Our analysis suggests two strategies through which law firms might develop reputations for cooperation, each of which involves noise reduction through specialization. One strategy envisions creating a boutique that only furnishes cooperative representation. The second contemplates a specialized cooperative department within a large firm. The two strategies have different advantages and drawbacks; in the end, each may be best suited to different segments of the profession. The boutique strategy is designed for lawyers forming new firms; the specialized department strategy is directed at existing large firms. . . .

A professional organization might facilitate cooperation among its members and have a dramatic effect on the development of a reputational market. Imagine an organization that limited its membership to attorneys who specialized in cooperative representation. Such an organization might promulgate standards defining cooperative conduct and defection in various contexts. The organization might then certify an attorney as cooperative, but only after intensive screening and review: a number of existing members might have to vouch for the fact that the nominee had consistently behaved appropriately over an extended period of time and had never defected. The organization might also stand ready to impose sanctions — including suspension or expulsion — in order to maintain cooperative norms. . . . [N]o such organization presently exists. . . .

CONCLUSION

Our story weaves together three principal ideas: (a) the prisoner's dilemma offers a suggestive and powerful metaphor for some aspects of litigation; (b) a lawyer's reputation may serve to bond a client's cooperation in the litigation process, thereby resolving the prisoner's dilemma; and (c) principal-agent conflicts (whether between lawyers and clients, or between lawyers and their firms) create incentives that sometimes facilitate cooperation in litigation but that, at other times, undermine cooperation. Our message is that the relationship between opposing lawyers and their capacity to establish credible reputations for cooperation have profound implications for dispute resolution: if the payoff structure establishes cooperation as the most desirable strategy and supportive institutional structures exist, lawyers may be able to damp conflict, reduce transaction costs, and facilitate dispute resolution. Our story rests fundamentally on the idea that lawyers develop reputations and that the reputation for being a cooperative problem-solver may be a valuable asset. When opposing lawyers know and trust each other, we believe there often will be substantial opportunities for both parties to benefit by reducing transaction costs. . . .

3. Collaborative Law: An Answer to the Risks of Cooperation

Suppose that two parties to a dispute agree to attempt a cooperative approach to resolving their dispute, and to that end they agree to hire "cooperative" lawyers. In order to protect against the possibility of defection by agents or clients, the contracts of employment provide that settlement counsel (whether a solo practitioner or a firm) for both parties are prohibited from serving as litigation counsel in the event that settlement efforts fail. [The approach should be carefully explained to the clients, to ensure their informed consent, and the agreement should call for each attorney to assist litigation counsel in "getting up to speed" in order to limit client costs.] Does this approach appear to solve the agency issues considered by Gilson and Mnookin?

The approach just described is called collaborative law (CL), and participating lawyers often think, speak, and write of CL as a movement — and it has achieved considerable prominence in the family law area. CL counsel advocate for their clients; they are not neutrals. There are CL practice groups, and legislation in several states expressly authorize and support the CL approach. *See, e.g.*, the Texas dispute resolution legislation, set forth in the Appendix. Collaborative law is examined in Chapter Eleven, Section D.

F. ANTHROPOLOGY AND SOCIOLOGY

1. Sally Engle Merry, *Disputing Without Culture: Review of Stephen B. Goldberg, Eric D. Green & Frank E.A. Sander, Dispute Resolution* (1985), 100 HARV. L. REV. 2057 (1987)

Legal anthropology turns the legal paradigm upside down: instead of looking at the different ways law handles conflicts, anthropologists examine the various ways conflicts are resolved, with law representing only one possible approach. Thus, anthropologists view law as an alternative mode of settling disputes, not the other way around. . . . In general, anthropological studies indicate that when disputants are bound together by multi-stranded social relationships, they will seek to compromise their differences, but when they have only single-stranded social ties, they will seek victory in adversarial contests rather than attempt to reach compromise.

In their enthusiasm over the discovery that law is only one mode among many for dealing with disputes, proponents of ADR tend to ignore the important role that law and legal consciousness play in American culture and the social differences between American society and small-scale societies in which processes like mediation exist naturally. For example, many of these societies either do not have a state at all, or if one exists, it is remote from day-to-day village life. In contrast, the state plays a central role in ordering details of neighborhood, family, and community life in modern America and in structuring the shape of the economy and society. Small-scale societies also do not usually have a highly developed cultural awareness of legal rights, equality, or the rights to legal participation that are characteristic of American society. . . .

2. Jayne Seminare Docherty, *Culture and Negotiation: Symmetrical Anthropology for Negotiators*, 87 MARQ. L. REV. 711 (2004)

One commonly used heuristic device for thinking about culture is the iceberg. This model begins with the empirical observation that cultures differ in terms of normative behaviors and other traits, but assumes that these are like the tip of an iceberg. There is much more to culture under the surface of what we can readily observe. Above the surface we find behaviors, artifacts and institutions. Just below the surface we find norms, beliefs, values and attitudes. A sensitive observer can "uncover" these and become more knowledgeable about a culture. The deepest level is all but invisible even to members of a cultural group. It contains the deepest assumptions about the world, the sense-making and meaning-making schemas and symbols, the beliefs about what is real in the world, and beliefs about how individuals experience the world. This is a useful model, but it is also misleading. It does not reflect the dynamic quality of cultures, which are far from frozen. . . .

Unfortunately, some negotiation texts — particularly, but not exclusively, popular books on negotiation — focus almost entirely on the part of the iceberg visible above the surface. . . . Lists of do's and don'ts — do not offer your left hand to an Arab; learn how to deeply bow to a Japanese negotiator — treat culture as a superficial overlay that covers a universal human nature or perhaps a universal human culture. Deep down, where it counts, all persons are fundamentally the same when it comes to reasoning, emotionality, needs, and desires. . . . There is a generic human culture, a species-specific attribute of Homo sapiens, an adaptive feature of our kind on this planet for at least a million years or so. But there are also local cultures — those complex systems of meanings created, shared, and transmitted (socially inherited) by individuals in particular social groups. It is local cultures that can create problems in a negotiation.

A more sophisticated approach to culture in negotiation involves identifying patterns or types of cultures by studying a large group of cultures. Instead of getting inside of a specific culture to understand it, this approach stands outside of cultures and looks for patterns or cultural styles. These are often presented as a list of dichotomous characteristics including: high context/low context; individualism/collectivism; and egalitarian/hierarchical. A high-context culture often relies on indirect communication, because the participants are expected to understand the complex meaning of relatively small non-verbal gestures. A low-context culture will tend to rely on direct statements and formal, clear ratification of written negotiated agreements. Negotiators from individualist cultures may worry less about preserving relationships than negotiators from collectivist cultures. And, negotiators from egalitarian cultures are likely to be less concerned about issues of rank and privilege than negotiators from hierarchical cultures.

Some authors have tried to develop fairly rigid cultural profiles. Taken to its extreme, this approach leads to arguments such as Samuel Huntington's claim, in THE CLASH OF CIVILIZATIONS AND THE REMAKING OF THE WORLD ORDER (1998), that the world is reorganizing around a "clash of civilizations." Huntington offers little hope of negotiating across cultures, but others do not assume that patterns of cultural differences foreclose the possibility of negotiation. For example, RAYMOND COHEN, NEGOTIATING ACROSS CULTURES (1991), describes "eastern" and "western" cultures and their approaches to negotiation, and he illustrates ways that eastern and western negotiators can achieve success despite their differences.

The goal in identifying types of cultures or developing cultural profiles is to alert negotiators to communication patterns and to provide cautionary advice about how to communicate in a particular cultural context or with someone from a particular culture. This way of thinking about culture is more useful for negotiators than lists of traits as long as they recognize the following: these dichotomies are actually continua; within cultures, changes in context (e.g., family versus business setting) will lead people to locate in different places along the continua; there are subcultural variations within any culture; and not all individuals carry their culture in exactly the same way.

At least this approach to culture alerts people to the fact that they have a culture too! The issue is not what is wrong with that person from another culture, but where the mismatches are between our cultures. On the other hand, describing cultures as a collection of styles or preferences that impact communication and therefore negotiation still does not get us to the deepest part of the iceberg. Many people who talk about culture this way miss the point that conflict as a domain of social interaction and negotiation as a mechanism for communicating about conflict are both culturally constructed. All cultures have conflict, but not all cultures see the same problems as conflicts, nor do they make the same assumptions about how human beings should respond to conflict. All cultures have processes we can identify as negotiation, but they do not all negotiate the same way.

The most complete and sophisticated way of thinking about culture and negotiation requires that we greatly enrich our definition of culture. Kevin Avruch offers the following definition: "For our purposes, culture refers to the socially transmitted values, beliefs and symbols that are more or less shared by members of a social group, and by means of which members interpret and make meaningful their experience and behavior (including the behavior of others)." He also points out that this definition includes a number of assumptions. First, individuals belong to multiple groups and, therefore, carry multiple cultures. The implication is that an encounter between two individuals is likely to be a multicultural encounter, since each participant can draw on more than one culture to make sense of the situation. This includes negotiation encounters. Second, it is important to understand the institutions and mechanisms that transmit culture. Third, culture is almost never perfectly shared by all members of a community or group. Individuals have the capacity to selectively adopt and adapt their multiple cultures, so you cannot assume that a person from culture X will do Y. Each party can draw from, adapt, and modify a multifaceted set of cultural norms and rules; therefore, every intercultural encounter is a complex improvisational experience.

It is critically important to remember that our own cultures are largely invisible to us; they are simply our "common sense" understandings of the world. Hence, "conflict" is, at essence, the construction of a special type of reality. . . . Culture frames our responses to conflict by giving us cognitive and affective frameworks for interpreting the behavior and motives of others and ourselves. Most negotiation models assume that each individual human being pursues his or her personal values and self-interest, typically in the context of — and against others — rationally pursuing their own self-interest and their personal values. But this is not the only way to think about human beings and their motives. Some cultures may assume that human beings are inherently relational beings who seek to preserve their relationships even if it "costs" them something. Or a culture may assert that protecting traditions is the most important imperative for all members of the community. . . .

3. Comments and Questions

a. Professor Docherty observes that many books about negotiation "contain little or no reference to culture." Among the examples she cites is the single best known and most widely read book about negotiation: ROGER FISHER & WILLIAM URY, GETTING TO YES: NEGOTIATING AGREEMENTS WITHOUT GIVING IN (2d ed. 1991).

b. Cultural factors are a pervasive factor in planning for and conducting negotiations. The topic of cross-cultural influences in negotiation and disputing is the focus of Chapter Five.

c. Such limited knowledge as American lawyers have about "law ways" among indigenous American communities is likely to come from KARL N. LLEWELLYN AND E. ADAMSON HOEBEL, THE CHEYENNE WAY (1941). Hoebel was a distinguished anthropologist. The two came to work together because Llewellyn recognized a central truth, well known to anthropologists and sociologists: reasonable success in addressing disputes is a central task for any culture, group or society — else it will cease to exist. Llewellyn's general theory of law ways is summarized in the following piece by Llewellyn's biographer, William Twining. The excerpt from The Cheyenne Way that follows is vintage Llewellyn — there is no mistaking his uniquely fractured prose.

d. Llewellyn's views about the role of disputes and disputing was stated succinctly in a famous set of lectures to first semester law students:

> What, then, is this law business about? It is about the fact that our society is honeycombed with disputes. Disputes actual and potential; disputes to be settled and disputes to be prevented; both appealing to law, both making up the business of law. But obviously those which most violently call for attention are the actual disputes. . . . Actual disputes call for somebody to do something about them. First, so that there may be peace for the disputants; for other persons whose ears and toes disputants are disturbing. And secondly, so that the dispute may really be put to rest, which means, so that a solution may be achieved which, at least in the main, is bearable to the parties, and not disgusting to the lookers-on. This doing something about disputes, this doing it reasonably, is the business of the law.

KARL LLEWELLYN, THE BRAMBLE BUSH: ON OUR LAW AND ITS STUDY 12 (1931). Note the absence of any mention of a sovereign power, a constabulary to enforce rules, or written laws.

4. William Twining, *Alternative to What?: Theories of Litigation, Procedure and Dispute Settlement in Anglo-American Jurisprudence: Some Neglected Classics,* 56 MOD. L. REV. 380, 385-87 (1993)

Karl Llewellyn's "law-jobs" theory . . . represents a relatively neglected part of his thought. [*See especially* Karl Llewellyn, *The Normative, the Legal and the Law-Jobs,* 49 YALE L.J. 1355 (1940).] It is relevant in the present context because it places dispute prevention and dispute settlement at the centre of a general sociological theory of law-government. The outline of the theory can be summarized as follows: All of us are members of groups, such as a family, a club, a teenage gang, a school or commercial organization, a trade union, a political party, a nation state, the world community. In order to survive and to achieve its aims, in so far as it has aims, any human group has to meet certain needs or ensure that certain jobs are done. The first, perhaps the most important, of these jobs is to channel behavior and expectations of members of the group in order to avoid conflicts or disputes within it. Second, when disputes arise, they have to be resolved or, at least, be kept at a tolerably low level, or else the group will disintegrate or its objectives will be frustrated or impaired. Third, as the circumstances of the group change, so the behavior and expectations of members of the group have to be adjusted to such changes in order to avoid conflicts and disappointments. Fourth, decision-making in the group needs to be regulated both in respect of who has power and authority to participate in decisions and in respect of the procedures by which decisions are arrived at. This allocation of authority and power is typically the primary function of a "constitution" of, for example, a club or a nation state. Fifth, in any group, but especially in complex groups, techniques, practices, skills and devices need to be developed for satisfactorily meeting the first four needs. Channeling behavior, settling disputes, making smooth adjustments to change and providing for acceptable ways of reaching decisions can often be difficult tasks, involving high levels of skill or quite refined or sophisticated devices and institutions.

First, the theory boldly claims to apply to all human groups, from a two-person unit . . . to the world community. It includes submarines, prisons, clubs, tribes, villages, and multinational corporations, and regional groupings as well as nation states. Controversy has surrounded how useful it is to treat all human groups as comparable, but in so far as one can ask certain standard questions about how disputes are avoided and handled in any group, its claim to comprehensiveness is particularly significant. For example, it helps to free legal theory from focusing exclusively on the nation state, and it thus provides a starting point for theories of legal pluralism and "non-state law."

Second, the theory provides one escape route from obsessive concern with the definition of law. For Llewellyn, "the institution of law-government" was the main, but not the only, institution specialized to performing the law jobs in those groups we choose to call societies; conversely, the law jobs are the main, but not the only, functions of that institution. In specific contexts for particular purposes, it may be useful to distinguish between the "legal" and "non-legal," but these are merely secondary issues of taxonomy. From this perspective, it matters little whether, for example, the Kpelle moot, a university disciplinary committee, an Ifugao "go-between," a marriage guidance bureau, or a "rent-a-judge trial" are labeled as "legal" or not — they are all institutionalized dispute-processing mechanisms that can be compared and contrasted within a single framework.

Third, Llewellyn claimed that all of the law-jobs are essential to group survival and successful achievement of collective goals. But any particular task can be done by a variety of means, singly or in combination. Dispute prevention in most societies, for example, is served by a complex mixture of formal and informal norms, education, rewards and incentives, hedges, barbed wire, physical force, and other means of social control. Similarly, in any group, one should expect dispute settlement to be achieved by a variety of means. In a famous passage, Llewellyn summed up the basic insight, which he credited to Max Weber:

> The jobs to be done are jobs to be done: modern complexity of institution serves merely to highlight processes which require to be gone through, in some fashion, in any group. The jobs, therefore, get themselves done after some fashion always — or the group simply is no more. Hence if the officially announced imperatives fail to put themselves over, one must look elsewhere for the doing of the jobs. . . . Hence to see a legal regulation which is not working is promptly to face a problem of further inquiry: What is working and how?

Finally, as this passage suggests, the law-jobs theory is a contextual theory which requires that any particular institution, device, "case," or other phenomenon should be viewed in the context of a larger whole. Any decision or event in a process such as litigation should be viewed in the context of the process as a whole. Thinking in terms of total pictures and total processes was part of the basic methodology of Llewellyn's realism. This leads naturally to one of the basic insights and truisms of modern dispute settlement theory: that in any given society, only a tiny proportion of all disputes are likely ever to reach those institutions we . . . call courts, or even those processes which might be included within the sphere of litigation. A natural starting point for the consideration of any particular dispute settlement method or institution is a realistic demographic total picture of all disputes in the society or group and how they are presently being resolved.

5. KARL N. LLEWELLYN & E. ADAMSON HOEBEL, THE CHEYENNE WAY 20-22 (1941)

Law has as one of its main purposes to make men go around in more or less clear ways; law does in fact to some extent make men go round in more or less clear ways. Law purposes to channel behavior in such manner as to prevent or avoid conflict; and law does in important degree so channel behavior. Without the purpose attribute, law is unthinkable; without the effect attribute, law cannot be said to "prevail" in a culture, to have "being" in it. But there is more to law than intended and largely effective regulation and prevention. Law has the peculiar job of cleaning up social messes when they have been made. Law thus exists also for the event of breach of law and has a major portion of its essence in the doing of something about such a breach.

What has been said lays out three roads into exploration of the law-stuff of a culture. The one road is ideological and goes to "rules" which are felt as proper for channeling and controlling behavior. Students of ethics and legal philosophers are likely to call these felt standards for proper behavior "norms." . . . The second road is descriptive; it deals with practice. It explores the patterns according to which behavior actually occurs. The third road is a search for instances of hitch, dispute, grievance, trouble, and inquiry into what the trouble was and what was done about it. . . .

The three approaches are related; indeed they flow each into the other. For it is rare in a simple group or society that "norms" which are felt or known as the proper ones to control behavior are not made in the image of at least some of the actually prevalent behavior; and it is rare, on the other hand, that they do not to some extent become active in their turn and aid in patterning behavior further. The three approaches are thus related; nor can any of them be understood without the others.

Norms for conduct differ in quality and in power according as they do or do not coincide with the clearer practices of life. Practices, in turn, have variant meaning not only according to the degree, range, and sharpness of their existence, but according to the kind and power of norms which sustain or oppose them. Further, norms and practices alike take flavor from the frequency of breach and from the nature and regularity of what is done in case of trouble. . . . Even as what is done in trouble-cases draws inspiration, in its nature and in its extent, from what are known as practices or are felt as norms, so also what has been done in trouble-cases shapes later living in its image. The three, then, are intimately related.

Part II
NEGOTIATION

Chapter 4
THE NEGOTIATION PROCESS

A. INTRODUCTION

Just as we have been speaking prose most of our lives, we have been negotiating since we were small children. Much of our interaction with other people, whether face-to-face or through some other medium of communication, can be characterized as negotiation. Even if the scope of negotiation is limited to disputes and planning, this still covers much activity. The purpose of this chapter is to provide a framework for reflecting upon a form of activity with which you already have considerable experience, and to raise some of the issues and problems that arise in negotiation. Attention also is given to negotiation strategy. The objective is to improve both your understanding of negotiation, and your ability to put that knowledge to use.

The most fundamental concepts are the hardest to define, but a brief effort may be helpful. To negotiate means to discuss or meet about a present or potential question or problem. There are three essential elements:

1. Two (or more) parties;

2. The matter(s) under consideration; and

3. Interaction between the parties about the matter.

A broader term, such as negotiation activity or behavior, includes related activities like preparation for a negotiation and taking action with respect to the matter under consideration.

Negotiation is the primary activity engaged in by attorneys (and everyone else). Negotiation is the primary method used by managers, and even by lawyers, to address issues and solve problems. Except in television shows, lawyers spend little time in court. Even full-time litigators spend 95 percent of their time in preparation for trials or appeals.

Section B introduces negotiation by presenting several conceptual models of the negotiation process. These models, like the economist's model of a competitive market, are an "ideal type"; they do not purport to offer an operative description of any particular interaction. Such models are useful in thinking about human behavior precisely because they filter out "noise," the variables of specific instances that can get in the way of thinking clearly about the process.

Section C introduces the law of bargaining, which law consists of the legal constraints on bargaining behavior. In addition, negotiating conduct is strongly influenced by the substantive legal norms that would govern a situation if reviewed by a court. Particularly where parties are attempting to settle an existing dispute, they bargain "in the shadow of the law."

Section D examines the negotiation process from several perspectives, with an emphasis on strategies for success in negotiation. We introduce the leading book about negotiation, Getting to YES, and the strongest critique thereof. This sets the stage for section E, which considers several approaches to improving the negotiation process and attaining better negotiated outcomes.

B. MODELS OF NEGOTIATION

1. Observing and Thinking About Negotiation in Daily Life

All of us engage in multiple negotiations every day; you should apply the theoretical learning about negotiation in the ensuing materials to your own negotiations. We offer a list of questions for use in thinking about specific negotiations.

a. Getting Started: Who spoke first? Effective start to process?

b. Initial discussion, small talk. How handled?

c. Effective transition into substantive matters?

d. Clear break between "social" and "business" talk, or period of both?

e. Did parties listen carefully? Interrupt each other? Talk past each other?

f. Who made the first offer? How introduced? Partial or Comprehensive?

g. What was the counter-offer? Was it made immediately?

h. Note key events or actions that promoted/hindered movement toward settlement.

i. Questioning skills: what type of questions used, and when in negotiation process?

j. Throughout process, look for non-verbal cues and messages.

k. What were the apparent strategies of each party for managing the negotiation?

l. Did anyone bluff or threaten during the course of the negotiation?

m. What was the outcome? How satisfied were the parties?

n. What else did you notice that is useful for thinking about this negotiation?

Identify and think about the last three negotiations in which you participated. What were the outcomes? Did the participants find or create a high quality solution? How, if at all, did you prepare for each of them? What is your next negotiation opportunity? How will you apply knowledge about the process and theory of negotiation in preparing for future negotiations?

2. P. H. Gulliver, NEGOTIATIONS: A CROSS-CULTURAL PERSPECTIVE 79-80 (1979)

Professor Gulliver, a Canadian anthropologist who has studied dispute settlement among many groups, notably the Warusha tribe in Tanzania, has developed a multiple-phase model of the negotiation process. Gulliver assumes the existence of a dispute; one might add one or more phases for gaining acknowledgment from both parties of the existence of a dispute that requires their joint attention. Of course, the phases of a negotiation do not always take place in the suggested order; there is commonly overlap between phases, and sometimes parties retreat from a later to an earlier phase. "Phase" is a better term than "step" precisely because the latter is more suggestive of separation, while "phase" suggests imprecision at the edges, and overlap.

1. *The search for an arena.* A forum where negotiations can occur needs to be accepted. Addressing problems that are not easily resolved commonly involves one or more in-person meetings, but the forum could be the telephone or even the Internet.

2. *Composition of agenda and definition of issues.* While the parties have acknowledged the existence of a dispute, and are prepared to do something about it, there commonly is disagreement (or at least a lack of clarity) about the agenda and issues.

3. *Establishing maximal limits to issues in dispute.* In this phase, the parties limit issues and stake out their positions. Gulliver makes a point of rejecting the proposition that this is the beginning of "real" negotiations, because negotiation over substance often takes place during the negotiation over ground rules for the negotiation.

4. *Narrowing the differences.* In this phase, the parties come together, and differences are narrowed. The emphasis, and often the tone, shifts from differences and antagonism to coordination and even cooperation. The transition to this phase may be gradual or abrupt (as when one party makes a significant concession or the first realistic offer). Several strategies are commonly employed to narrow differences where multiple issues are outstanding:

   (a) the simple agenda method;

   (b) focus on the one or two most important issues;

   (c) reduce issues to the attributes of a single objective;

   (d) solve the less difficult issues; and

   (e) trading and package deals.

The very act of selecting one of these approaches will result in simplifying the issues and providing a focus to the negotiation.

5. *Preliminaries to final bargaining.* With the issues defined in scope and limited in number, the differences between the parties are more starkly revealed. This focusing process is a necessary predicate for serious bargaining. Such a sharpening of the issues sometimes will make the ultimate solution clear to the parties, whereupon they can proceed with relative ease to a final disposition. The opposite can occur as well, and the parties may for the first time truly appreciate the full extent of their disagreement.

This stage encompasses other matters that must be addressed before a final bargain can be made. Much needed information is exchanged, and sub-issues are addressed. In a labor-management negotiation, for example, even if the basic wage rate has been agreed upon, there may still be issues about adjustments for different types of work, skill level, seniority, various types of overtime, holiday pay, productivity bonuses, etc. Formulas may be devised and tradeoffs made that bring the parties closer to agreement.

6. *Final bargaining.* This is when the parties close the deal, disposing of the few issues or problems that remain unsettled. In a listing of negotiating steps, final bargaining seems to lead inevitably to a bargain, but it is well to remember the wisdom of that great American philosopher Lawrence G. (Yogi) Berra: "It ain't over till it's over."

7. *Ritual affirmation.* Rituals are grist for the mill of anthropologists, while they are a legal irrelevance if not a distraction to lawyers. (In earlier days, rituals were of legal consequence, because the ritual was evidence of agreement.) The rituals best known in modern America are hand-shaking after a deal has been made, and kissing by spouses after the person presiding has declared them to be married. Ceremonies and parties are common, and in some instances gifts are given to commemorate the event. More dramatically, an agreement between warring parties to end hostilities may be accompanied by the exchange of prisoners.

3. John S. Murray, *Understanding Competing Theories of Negotiation*, 1986 NEGOT. J. 179

Negotiation theorists appear to be deeply divided between proponents of competitive and problem-solving theories. . . . Many teachers — and most students — of negotiation are confused by the often polemical dialogue between opposing theorists. Adding to this confusion is the lack of precision with which theorists and practitioners use terms like theory, strategy and style. Commentators . . . have referred to many different negotiation theories and models:

1. competitive and coordinative.
2. competitive and cooperative.
3. adversarial and problem-solving.
4. hard, soft and principled.
5. distributive and integrative.
6. functional and developmental.

Although these multiple references appear to sift naturally into the two competing camps that I am calling competitive and problem-solving, the confusion remains. Are there really two competing theories that explain realities in the negotiating setting? Should there be just one? If there are two, do the strategies that each favors necessarily conflict? What behavioral characteristics does each explain, and what are the downside risks that are hidden within each? . . .

The stereotypical competitive negotiator is a zealous advocate: tough, clever, thorough, articulate, unemotional, demanding, aggressive, and unapproachable, . . . the type who achieves victory by defeating his opponent. The problem-solver is also thorough and articulate, but in addition: personable, cooperative, firm, principled, concerned about the other side's interests, and committed to fairness and efficiency. . . . Even terminology reflects the distance between the patterns. A competitive bargainer . . . negotiates against an opponent; a problem-solver negotiates with the other side. . . . Each of these views has a significant and distinct impact on the behavior of negotiators who accept it.

The competitive negotiator appears to have a narrow perspective on the negotiation as a whole, but broad and flexible standards for selecting strategies and manipulating the process. The problem-solving negotiator, on the other hand, holds a broad perspective on the negotiation as a whole, combined with more rigid limits on strategy and conduct.

4. Comments and Questions

a. The focus on winning and losing that is common to competitive negotiating is badly misplaced, according to those who prefer a predominantly problem-solving approach. Roger Fisher and William Ury conclude:

> In most instances, to ask a negotiator "Who's winning?" is as inappropriate as to ask who's winning a marriage. If you ask that question about your marriage, you have already lost the most important negotiation — the one about what kind of game to play, about the way you deal with each other, and your shared and differing interests.

GETTING TO YES 154 (1981).

Are you persuaded by the analogy of negotiation to a marriage? What are the major factors you considered in arriving at an answer?

b. Based on Murray's explanation of the two forms of negotiating behavior, which do you think he favors? Here is the final paragraph of the article (page 186):

> The conclusion may be unavoidable that only the problem-solving theory satisfies all three quality standards for a general theory: it describes negotiation realities with reasonable accuracy, is useful in developing strategies, and provides consistently good outcomes for the competent negotiator. The recognizable competitive variant may just reflect different negotiator personality and style characteristics, and the quality and consistency of outcomes may depend partly on the relative levels of negotiator competence.

A statement that employs the qualifier "may" three times in two sentences probably is too hedged for evaluation. Absent those qualifiers, do you agree with Murray's conclusion, and why?

5. Carrie Menkel-Meadow, *Toward Another View of Legal Negotiation: The Structure of Problem Solving*, 31 UCLA L. REV. 754, 760-62 (1984)

The primary, but not exclusive, criterion for evaluation of a negotiation model is the quality of the solution produced. That includes the extent to which the process utilized contributes to or hinders the search for "quality" solutions. In elaborating on approaches to negotiation, I consider the following criteria of evaluation:

1. Does the solution reflect the client's total set of "real" needs, goals and objectives, in both the short and long term?

2. Does the solution reflect the other party's full set of "real" needs, goals and objectives, in both the short and long term?

3. Does the solution promote the relationship the client desires with the other party?

4. Have the parties explored all the possible solutions that might either make each better off or one party better off with no adverse consequences to the other party?

5. Has the solution been achieved at the lowest possible transaction costs relative to the desirability of the result?

6. Is the solution achievable, or has it only raised more problems that need to be solved? Are the parties committed to the solution so it can be enforced without regret?

7. Has the solution been achieved in a manner congruent with the client's desire to participate in and affect the negotiation?

8. Is the solution "fair" or "just?" Have the parties considered the legitimacy of each other's claims and made any adjustments they feel are humanely or morally indicated?

Criteria one through seven are all based on a utilitarian justification of negotiation. By satisfying these criteria, a negotiation may produce results which are more satisfactory to the parties, thus enhancing commitment to and enforcement of the agreement. The final criterion is applicable to those negotiators who wish to consider the effects of their solution on the other party from a humanitarian or ethical perspective.

6. Charles B. Craver, *The Negotiation Process*, 27 Am. J. Trial Advoc. 271 (2003)

This Article explores the six stages of the negotiation process and explains the purposes of each. It begins with the importance of thorough preparation, recognizing that knowledge is power when people negotiate. The Article then discusses the preliminary stage during which bargaining parties establish their identities and the tone for their substantive talks. The information exchange is evaluated to be certain that individuals know the best ways to obtain relevant information from others and the most effective way to disclose their own critical information. This stage allows the participants to articulate their respective needs and interests to let each side know which items are more or less important.

Once the information exchange is finished, the distributive bargaining commences, as the participants seek to claim for their respective sides what is available for division. If the distributive portion of the process functions well, the parties will move toward an agreement and enter the closing part of their interaction. Once parties achieve an agreement, many negotiators part company to allow someone else to draft the terms of the agreement. They omit the cooperative phase in which they should work to expand the overall pie and maximize their joint returns.

It does not matter whether lawyers negotiate to resolve disputes or to structure business transactions. A more thorough understanding of the bargaining process will improve their ability to obtain optimal terms for their clients. It will also diminish the anxiety lawyers experience when negotiating, which is often caused by lack of understanding of the overall process. Attorneys will begin to enjoy bargaining interactions as they move through the various stages from preparation to efficient final agreements.

I. The Preparation Stage: Establishing Limits and Objectives

"If you know the enemy and know yourself, you need not fear the result of a hundred battles. If you know yourself but not the enemy, for every victory gained you will also suffer a defeat. If you know neither the enemy nor yourself, you will succumb in every battle." Sun Tzu, The Art of War 43 (J. Clavell ed., 1983). Persons who thoroughly prepare for bargaining encounters generally achieve more beneficial results than those who do not, because knowledge constitutes power at the bargaining table. Well prepared negotiators possess the knowledge they need to value their impending interactions, and exude a greater confidence in their positions than their adversaries. Their confidence undermines the conviction of less prepared opponents and causes those persons to question their own positions. As less prepared advocates subconsciously defer to the greater certainty exhibited by their more knowledgeable adversaries, they tend to make more frequent and greater concessions. . . .

Negotiating lawyers should not be constrained by judicial authority or usual business practices. Negotiators can agree to any terms that are legal. Clients often prefer results that could not be achieved through adjudication (e.g., retractions in defamation actions or apologies in harassment cases) or which might not be consistent with usual business arrangements (e.g., in-kind payments). Lawyers should not ignore these possibilities merely because courts could not award them or because many business leaders would not approve them. As long as client interests are maximized, such considerations should be irrelevant. . . .

After attorneys become familiar with the relevant factual and legal matters affecting their own side, they must determine their bottom line — that is, their Best Alternative to a Negotiated Agreement (BATNA). What are the best results they could realistically hope to obtain through other channels? It is critical for negotiators to have a set bottom line to be certain they will not enter into agreements that would be worse than if no accords were obtained.

Negotiators who are initially unable to evaluate the results of non-settlements must take the time to develop alternatives. This is especially important for transactional experts. Their client may be seeking a buy-sell agreement with a single firm or a licensing arrangement with one party. Are there other potential purchasers or sellers they should contact, or other potential license partners? As alternatives become more numerous, lawyers may wish to create decision trees that graphically depict the strengths and weaknesses associated with each option. Each limb represents a different alternative, with the advantages and disadvantages of each option being listed with the likelihood of obtaining those results. This visual approach makes it easier for many individuals to appreciate the comparative values of the different options. . . .

Once attorneys have determined their own side's expected value, they often think they have completed this part of the evaluative process. Many lawyers who come to this conclusion ignore an equally important part of the preliminary equation: their opponent's expected value. . . .

II. The Preliminary Stage: Establishing Negotiator Identities and Tone for the Interaction

As lawyers begin the Preliminary Stage, they should take the time to develop some rapport with the opposing counsel. Through warm eye contact and a pleasant demeanor, they can establish a mutually supportable environment. This reduces the unproductive anxiety created by adversarial conduct. Negotiators should recognize that they can be forceful advocates without resorting to disagreeable tactics. . . .

The preliminary portion of bargaining encounters is critical, because the participants create the atmosphere that affects their entire bargaining transaction. Studies have found that people who commence interactions in positive moods negotiate more cooperatively and are more likely to use problem-solving efforts designed to maximize the joint returns achieved by the participants. . . . It is thus beneficial for individuals beginning bargaining encounters to take a few minutes to create supportive environments designed to create positive moods that should make their interactions more pleasant and enhance the probability the parties will interact cooperatively and maximize their joint returns. . . .

III. The Information Stage: Value Creation

Once the negotiators establish their identities and the tone for their interaction, the first substantive stage of the process begins. Lawyers can easily observe the commencement of the Information Stage, because this point coincides with a shift from small talk to questions regarding the other side's needs and interests. During this part of the process, the participants work to determine the items available for joint distribution. They hope to discern the underlying interests and objectives of the other party. Proficient bargainers also look for ways to expand the overall pie to be divided, recognizing that in most situations the parties do not value each of the items identically and oppositely. The more effectively the participants can expand the pie, the more efficiently they should be able to conclude their interaction. . . .

Skilled negotiators actively listen and carefully observe opponents during the Information Stage. . . . Since negotiators cannot impose their will on opponents, they must ascertain the underlying needs and interests of their opponents and seek to at least minimally satisfy the basic goals of those participants. Through patient and strategically planned questioning, they can try to learn as much as possible about their opponent's interests, objectives, and relative preferences. What issues would the other side like to have addressed, and which terms are essential, important, and desirable? Which items do both sides consider essential or important, and which are complementary terms that can be exchanged in ways that simultaneously advance the goals of both parties? . . .

IV. The Distributive Stage: Value Claiming

The transition from the Information Stage to the Distributive Stage is usually visible. The participants cease asking each other what they want and why they want it, and begin to talk about what they have to have or are willing to give up. During the Information Stage, the focus is primarily upon opponents, as the negotiators try to ascertain what is available for distribution and determine the degree to which the other party values the items to be exchanged. During the Distributive Stage, the focus is on our own sides as we (and our adversaries) begin to claim the items we discovered during the previous stage. No matter how much altruistic negotiators try to create win-win bargaining environments, there will always be items both sides wish to obtain. . . . Throughout the Distributive Stage, the parties compete for these mutually desired terms. . . .

As the Distributive Stage develops, the parties frequently encounter temporary impasses. The participants are attempting to obtain optimal terms for their respective clients, and each is hoping to induce the other to make the next position change. Individuals who have viable external options should not hesitate to disclose (at least minimally) this critical fact. The more that their adversaries know about these alternatives, the more likely the adversaries are to appreciate the need for more accommodating behavior. It is usually more effective to convey information about viable external options in a calm and non-confrontational manner. Bargainers who refuse to divulge the scope of their non-settlement options at critical points often fail to achieve accords that otherwise may have been attainable had their adversaries been fully aware of the bargainers' actual circumstances. . . .

No matter how effectively negotiators have been interacting, they occasionally find themselves moving toward an impasse. Before negotiators permit an impending stalemate to preclude further talks, negotiators should consider other options that may enable them to keep the process moving. They may rephrase extremely emotional issues in an effort to find more neutral language that may be more acceptable to both sides. They may also temporarily change the focus of their discussions by moving to other issues that may regenerate stalled discussions. They may briefly talk about recent political events, sports, weather, mutual acquaintances, or similar topics, helping to relieve the bargaining tension. It can be helpful to recount a humorous story that will humanize the participants and remind them not to take the current circumstances too seriously. . . .

Parties encountering bargaining difficulties may request the assistance of a mediator. A neutral facilitator can often reopen blocked communication channels and induce the negotiators to rephrase emotional issues and to refocus their efforts on less controverted items that they may have ignored. If the mediator can get the parties to explore areas for joint gains, the parties' temporary impasse may be broken. When the parties later return to more controversial issues, both sides may be less contentious because of the progress they have made on other less conflicted terms. . . .

V. The Closing Stage: Value Solidifying

Near the end of the Distributive Stage, the participants realize that a mutual accord is likely to be achieved. They feel a sense of relief, because the anxiety generated by the uncertainty of the negotiation process is about to be alleviated by the attainment of a definitive agreement. Careful observers can often see signs of relief around the mouths of the negotiators, who may exhibit more relaxed postures. . . . By the conclusion of the Distributive Stage and as the Closing Stage begins, both sides have become psychologically committed to a joint resolution. Neither wants prior bargaining efforts to culminate in failure. . . .

When negotiators reach the Closing Stage, they should recognize that the time is ripe for settlement. It is imperative that they keep the process moving inexorably toward a satisfactory conclusion. Although negotiators should continue to use the techniques that got them this far, they should eschew the use of disruptive tactics such as walking out or hanging up the telephone. If someone breaks off discussions at this crucial point, it may take days or even weeks for the parties to again achieve auspicious settlement conditions. Instead of employing negative threats or warnings, negotiators should use affirmative promises that permit joint movement in a face-saving manner. Temporary impasses can be easily overcome through the promise of concurrent position changes that allow the parties to move together. . . .

The Closing Stage can be a highly competitive portion of the negotiation process. It often involves a substantial number of position changes and a significant amount of participant movement. Negotiators who think that this part of the interaction consists primarily of cooperative behavior are likely to obtain less beneficial results than strategic opponents who use this stage to induce naive adversaries to close most of the outstanding distance between the two sides. . . .

VI. The Cooperative Stage: Value Maximizing

Once the Closing Stage has been successfully completed through the attainment of a mutually acceptable agreement, many persons [mistakenly] consider the negotiation process finished. . . . Once a tentative accord has been reached through the Distributive Process, the negotiators should contemplate alternative trade-offs that might concurrently enhance the interests of both parties. The bargainers may be mentally, and even physically, exhausted from their prior discussions, but they should at least briefly explore alternative formulations that may prove to be mutually advantageous. During the Information Stage, the parties often overstate (or understate) the actual value of different items for strategic reasons. During the Distributive and Closing Stages, parties tend to be cautious and opportunistic. Both sides are likely to employ power bargaining tactics designed to achieve results favorable to their own circumstances. Because of the tension created by these distributive techniques, [optimal] arrangements are rarely attained by this point in the negotiation process. The participants are likely to have only achieved acceptable terms, and if they conclude their interaction at this point, they may leave a substantial amount of untapped joint satisfaction on the bargaining table.

If the Cooperative Stage is to develop successfully, several prerequisites must be established. First, the parties must achieve a tentative accord. Second, at the conclusion of the Closing Stage, one or both parties should suggest movement into the Cooperative Stage. If one side is concerned that the other will be reluctant to progress in this direction until a provisional agreement has been attained, the concerned side can suggest that both parties initial the terms they have already agreed upon. Although proficient negotiators may occasionally merge the latter part of the Closing Stage with the introductory portion of the Cooperative Stage, most bargainers only move into the Cooperative Stage after having reached a mutually acceptable distribution of the pertinent items.

It is crucial that both sides recognize their movement from the Closing to the Cooperative Stage. If one party attempts to move into the Cooperative Stage without the understanding of the other, problems may arise. The alternative proposals articulated may be less advantageous to the other participant than the prior offers. If the recipient of these new positions does not view them as incipient cooperative overtures, she might suspect disingenuous competitive tactics. It is thus imperative that a party contemplating movement toward cooperative bargaining be sure her opponent understands the intended transition. When such a move might not be apparent, this should be explicitly communicated. . . .

Both sides must be quite open during the Cooperative Stage if the process is to function effectively. Through the use of objective and relatively neutral inquiries, the participants should explore their respective needs. Parties should use brainstorming techniques to develop options not previously considered. They should not be constrained by traditional legal doctrines or conventional business practices, thus recognizing that they can agree to anything that is lawful. They should not hesitate to think outside the box. When one side asks the other if another resolution would be more beneficial than a prior agreement, the respondent must be forthright. Only where the parties have effectively explored all possible alternatives can the parties truly determine whether their initial agreement optimally satisfies their fundamental needs. . . .

When the Cooperative Stage is finished, the participants almost always have a final agreement. It is helpful for negotiators to leave their opponents with the feeling that they got a good deal. If their opponents have this impression, they are more likely to honor the accord and behave cooperatively when the same people have to negotiate in the future. Some advocates work to accomplish this objective by making the final concession on a matter not highly valued by their own side. Even a minimal position change at this critical point is likely to be appreciated. Others try to accomplish the same goal by congratulating their adversaries on the mutually beneficial agreement achieved. Bargainers must be careful, however, not to be too effusive. When negotiators lavish praise on their opponents at the conclusion of interactions, those individuals may become suspicious and think they got poor deals. . . .

Before concluding their interaction, participants should briefly review the specific terms they think have been agreed upon. They may occasionally find misunderstandings. Since participants are psychologically committed to agreements, they are likely to resolve their disagreements amicably. If the parties did not discover the misunderstandings until one side drafted the accord, there might be claims of dishonesty. Thus, it is preferable to confirm the basic terms before concluding the encounter. . . . [Often the parties write and sign a skeletal agreement on the spot, with a fully drafted agreement to follow.]

C. THE UNDERLYING LEGAL CONTEXT

1. "Bargaining in the Shadow of the Law"

The expression "bargaining in the shadow of the law" is commonly used by lawyers, and in the academic literature. The origin of this expression is Robert H. Mnookin & Lewis Kornhauser, *Bargaining in the Shadow of the Law: The Case of Divorce*, 88 YALE L.J. 950 (1979). The fundamental idea is that negotiation behavior is shaped in important part by existing legal rules, and expectations about how a matter would be treated if brought to a court. Private ordering does not take place in a vacuum, but is significantly shaped by the framework of applicable law. Legal norms are a centrally important factor (but not the only one) in most (not all) negotiations that are of sufficient importance to involve lawyers, and many others as well.

2. Russell Korobkin, Michael Moffitt & Nancy Welsh, *The Law of Bargaining*, 87 MARQ. L. REV. 839 (2004)

Negotiation is often compared to poker. This analogy is apt in two related respects. First, poker players and negotiators both sometimes perceive opportunities to deceive or exploit their counterparts in ways that produce a distributive advantage. Indeed, lies, bluffs, false signals, and manipulation occupy a significant place in the repertoires of some negotiators. Second, the ability of both negotiators and poker players to deceive and exploit is constrained by rules governing behavior. This essay surveys the ways in which law constrains such behavior on the part of negotiators.

At least three categories of rules comprise the law of bargaining. First, common law limitations govern virtually all negotiators: the doctrines of fraud and misrepresentation limit the extent to which negotiators may deceive, and the doctrine of duress limits the extent to which bargainers can use superior bargaining power to coerce agreement. Second, context-specific laws sometimes circumscribe negotiating behavior in specific settings when general rules are less restrictive. Third, the conduct of certain negotiators is constrained by professional or organizational regulations inapplicable to the general public. These categories are discussed in turn. The final section of this essay reflects on constraints on negotiator behavior in the absence of law.

I. Common Law Limits on Bargaining Behavior

When a negotiated agreement results from false statements made during the bargaining process, the common law of tort and contract sometimes holds negotiators liable for damages or makes their resulting agreements subject to rescission. The common law does not, however, amount to a blanket prohibition of all lying. Instead, the common law principles are subject to the caveats that false statements must be material, the opposing negotiator must rely on the false statements, and such reliance must be justified. Whether reliance is justified depends on the type of statement at issue and the statement's specificity. A seller's specific false claim ("this car gets eighty miles per gallon gas mileage") is actionable, but his more general claim ("this car gets good gas mileage") is probably not, because the latter statement is acknowledged as the type of "puffing" or "sales talk" on which no reasonable buyer would rely.

While it is often said that misrepresentations of fact are actionable, but misrepresentations of opinion are not, this statement is not strictly accurate. Statements of opinions can be false, either because the speaker does not actually have the claimed opinion ("I think this Hyundai is the best car built in the world today") or because the statement implies facts that are untrue ("I think this Hyundai gets the best gas mileage of any car"). However, statements of opinion are less likely to induce justified reliance than are statements of specific facts, especially when they are very general, such as a claim that an item is one of "good quality."

Whether reliance on a statement of fact or opinion is justified depends significantly on the context of the negotiation and whether the speaker has access to information that the recipient does not. A seller "aggressively" promoting his product whose stated opinions imply facts that are not true is less likely to find himself in legal difficulty if the veracity of his claims are easily investigated by an equally knowledgeable buyer than if his customer is a consumer unable to evaluate the factual basis of the claims. The case for liability is stronger still when the negotiator holds himself out as being particularly knowledgeable about the subject matter that the expressed opinion concerns. Whether a false statement can be insulated from liability by a subsequent disclaimer depends on the strength and clarity of the disclaimer, as well as on the nature of the false statement. Again, the standard is whether the reasonable recipient of the information in total would rely on the statement at issue when deciding whether to enter into an agreement.

It is universally recognized that a negotiator's false statements concerning how valuable an agreement is to her or the maximum she is willing to give up or exchange in order to seal an agreement (the negotiator's "reservation point," or "bottom line") are not actionable, again on the ground that such false statements are common and no reasonable negotiator would rely upon them. So an insurance adjuster who claimed that $900 was "all he could pay" to settle a claim is not liable for fraud, even if the statement was false. The law is less settled regarding the status of false statements concerning the existence of outside alternatives for a negotiator. A false claim of an offer from a third party is relevant, because it implies a strong reservation point, so a negotiator might logically argue that such a claim is no more actionable than a claim as to the reservation point itself. But courts have occasionally ruled that false claims of a specific outside offer are actionable, on the ground that they are material to the negotiation and that the speaker has access to information that cannot be easily verified by the listener's independent investigation.

The most inscrutable area of the law of deception concerns when a negotiator may be held legally liable for failing to disclose information that might weaken his bargaining position (rather than affirmatively asserting a false claim). The traditional laissez-faire rule of caveat emptor eroded in the twentieth century, with courts placing greater disclosure responsibility on negotiators. It is clear that any affirmative action taken to conceal a fact, including the statement of a "half-truth" that implies a false fact, will be treated as if it were an affirmative false statement. Beyond this point, however, the law becomes murky. Although the general rule is probably still that negotiators have no general disclosure obligation, some courts require bargainers (especially sellers) to disclose known material facts not easily discovered by the other party.

Just as the law places some limits on the use of deceptive behavior to seal a bargain, so too does it place some limits upon negotiators' ability to use superior bargaining power to coerce acquiescence with their demands. In general, negotiators may threaten to withhold their goods and services from those who will not agree to their terms. Courts can invoke the doctrine of duress, however, to protect parties who are the victims of a threat that is "improper" and have "no reasonable alternative" but to acquiesce to the other party's demand, such as when one party procures an agreement through the threat of violence, or through the threat to breach a prior agreement after using the relationship created by that agreement to place the victim in a position in which breach would cause non-compensable damage. Judicial intervention is most likely when the bargaining parties' relationship was not arms-length. For example, the common law provides the defense of undue influence to negotiators who can show that they were dependent upon and thus vulnerable to the other, dominant negotiator.

II. Context-Specific Regulation of Negotiators' Behavior

Beyond the general common law constraints on negotiators' behavior, the law imposes particularized parameters on bargainers engaged in negotiations in some specific contexts. For example, labor law places a number of procedural restrictions on negotiating behavior. Compared with their counterparts in non-unionized settings, employers, employees, and their representatives involved in collective bargaining all have considerable limits on their ability to adopt certain approaches to negotiating the terms and conditions of employment. . . . The most vivid encapsulation of these requirements is the duty imposed on both sides by the National Labor Relations Act to bargain in "good faith." The concept of "good faith" bargaining lacks clear parameters, but a "totality of conduct" standard has given way to a list of proscribed behaviors, such as disengaging from the negotiations and presenting take-it-or-leave-it offers.

In other contexts, the law imposes affirmative duties of disclosure rather than attempting to define the parameters of negotiation behavior. For example, in residential real estate transactions in many states, sellers have a legal obligation to disclose a range of information, even if the buyer does not request it. Supplanting the baseline principle of caveat emptor, many states have judged that real estate transactions require different foundational principles.

Finally, in certain bargaining contexts that seem unusually prone to exploitation, the law provides paternalistic protection for potential victims. For example, certain legal disputes involving seamen on the high seas and their employers require judicial approval, because of the perceived power imbalance between seamen and ship owners. Similarly, most jurisdictions require court ratification of divorce agreements. To protect principal parties with little ability to monitor their agents, settlements of class action and shareholder derivative suits also require a judicial finding of fairness. Rather than judicial oversight, many jurisdictions give consumers in certain vulnerable contexts the self-help remedy of unilaterally rescinding an agreement within several days of acceptance, such as when they accept a bargain proposed by telemarketers or door-to-door salespersons. Finally, the law sometimes establishes alternative dispute resolution mechanisms for contexts frequently characterized by dissatisfaction with negotiated agreements. For example, lemon laws anticipate that some percentage of negotiations over car purchases will result in unhappy consumers. In states with lemon laws, consumers who are dissatisfied with their purchase need not establish one of the traditional bases for rescinding a contract or ceasing performance (for example fraud, duress, or material breach). Instead, consumers have a streamlined system for demonstrating eligibility for the law's protections after the fact.

III. Professional and Organizational Constraints on Bargaining Behavior

Some negotiators operate not only within the legal constraints applicable to the general public, but also within the parameters of professional or organizational codes of conduct. These parameters can provide another layer of substantive constraints on negotiating behavior (in addition to those provided by generally applicable law), additional or enhanced enforcement mechanisms, or both. As an example, attorneys are subject not only to generally applicable legal constraints on negotiating behavior but also to the administrative regulations of their state bar associations, which generally reflect the American

Bar Association's Model Rules of Professional Conduct. Model Rule 4.1(a) provides that "[i]n the course of representing a client a lawyer shall not knowingly . . . make a false statement of material fact or law to a third person." The commentary to the rule suggests that the scope of the rule roughly parallels the common law. For example, estimates of "price or value" are not considered material, thus permitting lawyers in general to "puff" as well as lie outright about their reservation prices.

One important difference, however, between the administrative law governing lawyer-negotiators and the common law governing all bargainers is the absence of the requirements of reliance and damages in the regulatory context. To sustain a tort or contract action, the victim must actually suffer harm. Although punishment for transgressions in bargaining outside of the doors of the courthouse is a relatively rare occurrence, lawyers can face disciplinary action for making material misrepresentations, even if no legally cognizable damage results.

IV. Negotiations Beyond Law's Reach

Not all negotiations take place in a context in which legal structures can constrain the behavior of negotiators. Some negotiations are conducted in such a private forum that law serves at most a minimal function. Spouses' negotiations about the division of household tasks, child rearing philosophies, and appropriate toilet seat protocols may take place largely beyond the reach of the law. The law has only minimal impact on other negotiations because of unlikely enforcement prospects. The black market thrives on the wings of vibrant negotiation, yet the law provides few behavioral boundaries in those negotiations. Similarly, the law of nations includes an expectation that parties will negotiate terms of treaties. No consistent, enforceable legal structure exists, however, to give force to any constraints on the negotiating behavior of those states. Finally, in some negotiations, the product of the bargain precludes any obvious remedies — even in cases when one of the parties exceeded expected boundaries of behavior. If two businesses deceive each other in crafting the terms of a joint venture, the law informs how the damage from their conduct may be remedied. If, however, two legislators deceive each other in negotiations over the terms of a new piece of legislation, no obvious bases for legal rescission or damages exist.

In these contexts, the threat of extra-legal penalties (in addition, of course, to personal ethical commitments) may constrain negotiators' behavior. For example, in many of the circumstances described above, an aggrieved negotiator may impose a reputational sanction on the transgressor by revealing the allegedly inappropriate behavior. Many parties will behave differently in a bargaining session they believe to be entirely private than in negotiations that take place within the shadow of a threat to disclose. Although the prospect of publicity is different in structure from legal sanction, it nevertheless holds some promise of altering the negotiating behavior of those who are beyond the reach of the formal law of bargaining.

D. THE NEGOTIATION PROCESS: STRATEGIES FOR SUCCESS

1. WILLIAM R. POTAPCHUK ET AL., GETTING TO THE TABLE: A GUIDE FOR SENIOR MANAGERS (1990), U.S. Army Corps of Engineers Working Paper No. 3 [IWR Working Paper 90-ADR-WP-3]

When you are involved in a difficult situation, ongoing assessment of the actors, issues, and other dynamics is essential to developing effective strategy and making wise choices. Broad participation in an analysis and assessment process by all the parties will help build a shared perspective on the problem and the steps necessary to move forward. Indeed, joint analysis is often a key step in bringing parties to the table. The following guide offers a series of questions to help you identify useful information. The commentary is specifically focused on data from the analysis that will impact the building of a forum and the getting-to-the-table stage of disputes. Assessment also is useful for developing and clarifying your interests in preparation for negotiations. While this task is not emphasized here, we encourage you to be well prepared as you enter negotiations.

A. Who Are The Parties? Who is responsible for making the decision? Who may be affected by potential solutions? Who may be able to block or ensure a particular decision? Understanding the broad set of stakeholders can help you begin to assess how many persons or organizations will need to be involved, and how much narrowing can be accomplished.

B. How Is Each Party Organized? Are the parties primarily organizational entities? What is their structure — hierarchical? collective? Does each organization have identified leadership? What is the relationship between the leadership and others? If each party is well organized and will vest responsibility in its leadership, ascertaining representatives will be easier.

C. What Is The Power Base Of Each Of The Parties? Of the parties who do not have formal authority for the decision, but seek to influence the decision: Does any party have the capacity to block decisions they do not approve? Does any party have an incentive to escalate the conflict? What is the capacity of each party to sustain its involvement over time? Does any party need another party in order to accomplish its goals? Does interdependence exist between these parties and the decision makers? Does any party have past experience with joint decision-making processes? Would any party need specific assistance to effectively participate in a joint decision-making process?

If some parties have the capacity to block decisions, they will certainly need to be involved in the process. If parties have the capacity to sustain activities, they may be able to effectively participate in a joint decision-making process, and staffing by decision makers will not be effective. If the parties need each other to accomplish their objectives, joint decision-making may be appropriate. Of the parties who do have formal authority for the decision: Can the parties make and implement any decision they please? Can the parties protect their essential interests in the decision no matter how the decision is made? How? Are the parties constrained by previous decisions or decisions made by others (e.g., legislative bodies, precedent)? Can the parties sustain their involvement over time in any kind of process (e.g., legal, negotiated)? Do the parties need other parties to accomplish their goals? Do the parties have any experience with joint decision-making processes? . . .

D. How Has Power Been Used In The Situation? Have any of the parties used their power such that other parties have felt it has been to prevent them from reaching their goals? Have any of the parties used their power to help other parties? If one of the parties has systematically used its power in a direct attempt to injure other parties, those parties will be distrustful and be very wary of joint decision-making processes.

E. What Do Each Of The Parties Want? What are the stated positions of each party? What are the stated goals of each party? What are the underlying interests of each party? What are the dominant values that appear to guide the actions of each party? Are they mutually exclusive? Do any of the positions, goals, interests, values, or issues of any party challenge the identity of other parties? Does this situation represent high stakes for any party? Are there common interests which might provide the basis for an agreement? Knowing what motivates each of the parties and whether there are overlapping interests can help predict whether the parties will see any value in coming to the table. Parties involved in identity or high stakes conflicts will need a table where each party believes their essential interests are protected.

F. Past Relationships. Do any of the parties have a history of relationships with other parties? Has that history been productive or conflictual? Were the relationships characterized by trust and respect? Have any of the parties avoided other parties because they believed working relationships would be difficult? Past relationships that worked well can be the basis for developing joint decision-making efforts. Difficult relationships, especially those characterized by distrust, may need to be addressed directly for joint decision-making to be productive.

G. Current Status Of Relationships. Has the nature of the relationships between the parties changed over time? Are there existing working relationships? How are the parties communicating with each other? If they are not communicating directly, are there any trusted intermediaries? Do the parties accept each other's role in developing a joint agreement? If the current relationships are healthy, joint decision-making will help maintain strong relationships. If current relationships are contentious or characterized by lack of trust, a strong past relationship, a desire for a future relationship, or high levels of interdependence can mitigate current difficulties.

H. Desire For Future Relationships. Do any of the parties desire a future working relationship with other parties? Will the parties need to work together on implementing an agreement? Are the parties forced to interact regularly because of the nature of their work or networks? A desire for a future working relationship can be a strong impetus for using joint decision-making processes.

I. Who Are The Main Stakeholders? Who are the primary stakeholders? Why? Who are the secondary stakeholders? Primary stakeholders will probably need to be directly involved in joint decision-making. Secondary stakeholders may need to be kept informed or participate only at key points in the process.

J. What Is The History Of The Situation? Have there been several stages (e.g., latent, emerging, litigation)? Have external events influenced the situation? How? Will they affect a decision-making process or the outcomes? The history of the situation may be a guide to future action for disputants and the third party.

K. Are There Any Parameters Set Externally That Must Be Followed? Are there any statutes or regulations that govern action in this situation? Is there any legal liability? Have there been any similar situations whose outcome will influence what happens here? The external context may limit what is possible or what the parties believe is possible.

L. Is There A Formal Process Typically Used For Resolving These Issues? Can all the stakeholders use the formal process? Is the formal process adjudicative, administrative, consensual, or legislative in nature? The formal process often helps define the informal process. Joint decision-making processes may only be able to produce advisory outcomes if formal legislative or judicial action is needed. If all of the primary stakeholders cannot participate in the formal process, they may seek to sabotage the formal process or engage in alternatives.

M. Are There Any Likely Existing Forums For Resolving The Issues? Are there any forums which have been used to resolve similar situations in the past? Have they been perceived as productive? Do some of the issues require a certain kind of forum (i.e., constitutional issues may require court involvement)? The existence of several forums may allow some parties to go forum shopping. Sometimes the choice of forum is limited by the issues.

N. How Does Each Party See Its Alternatives? How does each party see its best alternative to a negotiated agreement? Its worst alternative? Its most likely alternative? Do any of the forums lack credibility from the perspective of any party? If the parties have superior strategic alternatives to a joint process, they may pursue those alternatives. Some forums may be particularly difficult to "sell" to some of the parties.

O. What Are The Issues? How does each party describe its own central issues? Do the issues differ between those who have authority for the decision and those who seek to influence the decision? Can all the issues be addressed in a joint decision-making process? Is resolution of the issues likely to be precedential? Are there secondary issues that may have an impact on the process or the outcome? Is there a framing of the issues that will address the concerns of all the parties? Once the issues are clear, some determination can be made about how they can be approached. Some issues may be addressed only through one approach. Others may be addressed through a range of approaches. Putting some issues on the table or taking others off may be a prerequisite for some parties agreeing to come to the table.

P. Are The Issues Framed As Integrative, Distributive, Or Redistributive? Are the issues either-or? Can distributive or redistributive issues be reframed as integrative? Can the resources be increased? Integrative issues — which by definition are those that can be resolved by meeting everyone's needs — are the easiest to negotiate and promote cooperative approaches. Distributive issues, such as how shall this new money be allocated, often produce competitive orientations. Redistributive issues, such as how shall the city's agencies respond to a 10 percent budget cut, promote adversarial approaches. Either-or issues, such as do we build the highway or not, also promote adversarial approaches. Reframing the issues or increasing the resources available can help promote cooperative approaches.

Q. How Does Each Party See The Available Options For Each Issue? Have options been developed for each central issue? For secondary issues? Are the options well defined? Have all the potential options been explored by all the parties? Do any of the options seem to meet the needs of all the parties? Does any party feel that none of the options meets its needs? If new options are generated, will extensive or expensive further study be required? If all the potential options have been generated and none seems to meet the needs of the parties, joint decision-making may be difficult. If new options can be created that better meet the needs of the parties, joint decision-making processes may be appropriate. If new options require extensive or expensive study, pre-negotiation protocols should address the group's ability to generate new options.

R. What Are The Data And Information Needs? Do each of the parties believe sufficient data is available? Are the data and their analysis considered trustworthy by the parties? Will each party feel comfortable working with a common body of data? Developing a common understanding of the problem may require further data collection or additional analysis. Each party must feel comfortable with the data.

2. Implicit Negotiations Ancillary to the Main Negotiation

In any moderately complex negotiation situation, where parties are represented by agents, there are (at least) three negotiations going on at once: the explicit negotiation between the actual participants, and implicit negotiations between the representative of each party and her colleagues at the organization being represented. [Issues associated with a misalignment of interests between principal and agent were considered in Chapter Three.] Can you identify examples of such multiple negotiations from your personal experience or topics that you have studied in school?

Consider the position of an agent for a seller who is negotiating to obtain a large order from a potential buyer, with attendant benefits to both the company and the sales agent. The primary negotiation here is between the agents for seller and buyer, but at the same time, the agent must take account of ancillary actual and potential negotiations. There are ancillary negotiations. One might think that a seller — which, after all, is in the business of selling — would be thrilled to receive a large order at a favorable price. However, the matter may not be so simple. The credit department may be concerned about the buyer's ability to pay. The legal department may be concerned about the generous warranty provisions promised by the sales person. Production prefers long, constant production runs rather than large orders for quick delivery. Human resources may be faced with the problem of quickly finding and hiring several additional skilled workers — without paying more than the compensation level for current employees. Maintenance may have planned to service production equipment that has to be postponed if this new order is to be filled in a timely manner. Even the sales department may be concerned if another agent has also produced a new order, or a rush order was received from a valuable existing customer. This array of problems for the seller is far from exhaustive, and a variety of similar problems might arise on the buyer's side of the transaction.

The negotiations within an organization can take place prior to agreement about the business relationship, or a deal can precede the internal negotiations. Of course, these two approaches are not mutually exclusive, but the approaches are fundamentally different. As we will see in the materials on negotiation between Japanese and American businesses, the Japanese tend to employ the former approach, while Americans follow the latter approach. See Chapter Five.

3. David A. Lax & James K. Sebenius, *Interests: The Measure of Negotiation*, 2 NEGOT. J. 73 (1986)

People negotiate to further their interests. And negotiation advisors urge attention to interests. . . . Yet the classic admonition to "know thyself" surely scoops any late twentieth century advice of this sort. . . . [N]egotiators often focus on interests, but conceive of them too narrowly; we will argue for a more expansive conception. Interests often conflict, so negotiators need ways to assess the relative importance of their various interests.

GENERAL LESSONS FOR ASSESSING INTERESTS

As hard as it may be to sort out one's own interests, understanding how others see theirs — their subjective scheme of values are perceived through their peculiar psychological filters — can be extraordinarily difficult. Obviously, suggesting a stretch "in the other person's shoes" is good advice; equally obvious, it is only a starting point. In contrast to the apparent crispness of the issues, interests are often vaguer. There may be no apparent scale with which to measure — say, precedent or organizational status. Yet the same logic that is useful for making issue tradeoffs can apply to assessing the relative impact of interests. The generic steps are as follows:

- Identify the interests that may be at stake.

- For each interest, imagine the possible packages that serve it best and worst; for example, imagine the range of precedents that might follow from the negotiation. This roughly defines the increment of value associated with each interest.

- The importance of each interest depends on the relative importance of its increment compared to those of the other interests; for example, how does the gain from the worst to the best possible precedent compare with the gain from the worst to the best possible monetary outcome?

The currency of negotiation generally involves positions on issues, but the results are measured by how well underlying interests are furthered. As such, it is helpful constantly to shuttle back and forth between abstract interests and more specific issues, both to check for consistency and to keep real concerns uppermost in mind. Finally, . . . a negotiator should constantly assess his counterparts' interests and preferences. Beyond various ways of trying to put oneself in the other's shoes, assessment of another's interests may be improved by investigating:

- Past behavior in related settings, both in style and substance.

- Training and professional affiliation: engineers and financial analysts will often have quite different modes of perception and approaches to potential conflict from, say, lawyers and insurance adjusters.

- Organizational position and affiliation. Those in the production department will often see long, predictable manufacturing runs as the company's dominant interest, while marketers will opt for individual tailoring to customer specs and deep inventories for rapid deliveries. This is another example of the old and wise expression "where you stand depends on where you sit."

- Whom they admire, whose advice carries weight, and to whom they tend to defer on the kind of issues at stake. In the end, interests are bound up with psychology and culture.

- Beyond the obvious tangible interests that may be affected by issues to be discussed, consider subtler interests in reputation, precedent, relationships, strategy, fairness, and the like.

- Distinguish underlying interests from the issues under discussion and the positions taken on them.

- Distinguish between intrinsic and instrumental reasons for valuing interests, especially some of the subtler ones.

- In seeking to understand others' interests, remember that interests depend on perceptions, that perceptions are subjective, and thus, that to assess interests is to probe psyches. This process can be aided by clear communication, the advice of third parties, role playing, and taking into account past behavior, training, professional affiliation, organizational position, as well as those to whom the others defer.

- Keep in mind that interests and issues can change on purpose or accidentally as the parties learn, events occur, or certain tactics are employed.

ASSESSING TRADEOFFS

- Tradeoffs are as important to interests as proportions are to recipes.

- To assess tradeoffs among intangible interests, it is sometimes helpful to imagine services one could buy otherwise to satisfy the same interests.

- To assess tradeoffs among issues: Specify the worst and best possible outcomes on each issue to define the possible increments.

    a. Compare increments by thinking hard about underlying interests and how each is valued.

    b. Break increments into smaller pieces and similarly compare their relative valuation.

    c. Change assessments as more is learned about how positions on issues affect interests.

    d. Assess interest tradeoffs using the same logic.

Negotiation is a process of potentially opportunistic interaction in which two or more parties with some apparently conflicting interests seek to do better by jointly decided action than they could otherwise. For evaluating alternatives and creating agreements, interests are the measure and raw material. The alternatives to negotiated agreement or what the parties could each do alone define the threshold of value that any agreement must exceed. The potential of negotiation is bounded only by the quality of the agreements that can be devised. The processes of negotiation are creating and claiming value.

4. Donald G. Gifford, *A Context-Based Theory of Strategy Selection in Legal Negotiation*, 46 OHIO ST. L.J. 41, 45-58 (1985)

The type of negotiation strategy likely to yield the most favorable outcome for a client is an important question, because the attorney is professionally obligated to seek an advantageous result for her client in all negotiations. . . . This section defines the characteristics of three primary negotiation strategies and suggests that the negotiator's view of his relationship with the other party is the primary determinant that identifies each theory and distinguishes it from the others. The competitive negotiator seeks to force the opposing party to a settlement favorable to the negotiator by convincing the opponent that his case is not as strong as previously thought and that he should settle the case. The cooperative strategy mandates that the negotiator make concessions to build trust in the other party and encourage further concessions on his part. The third strategy, integrative bargaining, seeks to find solutions to the conflict which satisfy the interests of both parties. . . .

A negotiation strategy is a separate and distinct concept from the negotiator's personal characteristics; a strategy is the negotiator's planned and systematic attempt to move the negotiation process toward a resolution favorable to his client's interests. Negotiation strategy consists of the decisions made regarding the opening bid and the subsequent modifications of proposals. Admittedly, strategy and personal style are frequently intertwined. A negotiator who has a "forceful, aggressive, and attacking" personal style frequently will succeed in causing an opponent to lose confidence in himself or his case, thereby inducing substantial unilateral concessions, a goal of the competitive strategy. In another instance, however, a negotiator who is "courteous, personable and friendly" may, through competitive strategic moves such as high opening demands and infrequent concessions, be even more successful in destroying the opponent's confidence in his case and inducing unilateral concessions from the opponent. Usually, a negotiator's personal characteristics positively correlate with his preferred negotiating strategy. Separating personal style and negotiation strategies, however, yields new flexibility for the negotiator. It is possible for negotiators with cooperative personal characteristics to adopt a competitive strategy when it would be advantageous, and naturally competitive individuals can adopt a cooperative strategy. Further, a negotiator should often make competitive, cooperative, and integrative moves within a single negotiation. If negotiation strategies are recognized as something distinct from the personal style of negotiators, then the essential elements of each strategy can be disseminated in writing and taught to prospective negotiators. . . .

A. The Competitive Strategy

The competitive negotiator tries to maximize the benefits for his client by convincing his opponent to settle for less than she otherwise would have at the outset of the negotiation process. The basic premise underlying the competitive strategy is that all gains for one's own client are obtained at the expense of the opposing party. The strategy aims to convince the opposing party that her settlement alternative is not as advantageous as she previously thought. Competitive tactics are designed to lessen the opponent's confidence in her case, thereby inducing her to settle for less than she originally asked. The competitive negotiator moves psychologically against the other person, with behavior designed to unnerve the opponent. Competitive negotiators expect similar behavior from their opponents, and therefore, mistrust them. In undermining their opponents' confidence, competitive negotiators employ a strategy which often includes the following tactics:

1. a high initial demand;

2. limited disclosure of information regarding facts and one's own preferences;

3. few and small concessions;

4. threats and arguments; and

5. apparent commitment to positions during the negotiating process.

A negotiator who utilizes the competitive strategy begins with a high initial demand. Empirical research repeatedly demonstrates a significant positive relationship between a negotiator's original demand and his payoff. A high initial demand conceals the negotiator's minimum settlement point and allows the negotiator to grant concessions during the negotiating process and still achieve a favorable result. The negotiator's opening position may also include a false issue — a demand that the negotiator does not really care about, but one that can be traded for concessions from the opponent during the negotiation. Generally, the more that the negotiator insists upon a particular demand early in the negotiation, the larger the concession that ultimately will be obtained from the opponent in exchange for dropping that demand. In addition, the opponent may have evaluated the negotiator's case more favorably than the negotiator has; a high demand protects the negotiator from quickly agreeing to a less favorable settlement than one which he might later obtain. If the demand is high but credible, the opponent's response to the demand may also educate the negotiator about how the opponent evaluates her own case.

The competitive negotiator selectively and strategically shares information with his opponent. . . . The competitive negotiator carefully hides not only his reservation point, but also any information which would allow the opponent to determine his true reservation point. For example, in a criminal case, the prosecutor might conceal from the defense attorney information regarding her caseload, her familiarity with the case, her own vacation plans, and the attitude of the victim toward the case. Conversely, the competitive negotiator selectively discloses information which strengthens his case and which undermines the opponent's case. The competitive negotiator should pursue tactics that glean information about his opponent's reservation price, his opponent's attitude toward the case, and specific facts about the case.

The competitive strategy of negotiation mandates that the party make as few concessions as possible. If a concession must be made, it should be as small as possible. The competitive negotiator makes concessions reluctantly, because concessions may weaken one's position through both "position loss" and "image loss." Position loss occurs because, in most negotiations, a norm exists against withdrawing a concession. Further, an early concession results in an opportunity loss for something that might have been extracted in exchange for the concession later in the negotiation process. Image loss occurs because, after a concession, the opponent perceives that the negotiator is flexible; in the opponent's mind, this may suggest that further concessions can be obtained. Obviously, however, concessions are generally an inevitable part of the negotiating process. Concessions made by a negotiator build an expectation of reciprocity and lead to further concessions by the opponent, which bring the parties closer to agreement. Granting concessions prevents premature deadlock and impasse and maintains goodwill with the adversary. This may be necessary to complete the negotiations or to foster a continued cooperative venture in the future. When possible, the competitive negotiator seeks to create the illusion in his opponent's eye that he is making a concession without diminishing his own satisfaction. This is done by conceding on an issue the negotiator does not care about, or appearing to make a concession without really making one.

The competitive negotiator obviously strives to force his opponent into making as many and as large concessions as possible while he makes few concessions, small in degree. To force concessions from his opponent, he employs both arguments and threats. In negotiations, arguments are communications intended to persuade the opponent to draw logical inferences from known data. For example, a plaintiff's attorney might describe a favorable eyewitness account of a collision and ask the defense counsel to infer the probability that her client will be found liable. Arguments should suggest to the opponent that her case is weaker than she previously thought and, therefore, that she should make new concessions. A threat, on the other hand, is a communication intended to inform the opponent that, unless she agrees to a settlement acceptable to the negotiator, the negotiator or his client will act to the opponent's detriment. For example, a union negotiator might threaten that the union will strike if management refuses to make wage concessions.

The competitive negotiator not only uses offensive tactics to force concessions from his opponent, but he also makes as few concessions as possible. The competitive negotiator ignores both arguments and threats, believing that this is the best response. When the negotiator must make a concession, the competitive strategist suggests that the negotiator give the opponent a "positional commitment," a reason why he is not conceding more. Without such a positional commitment, according to the competitive strategist, the opponent will perceive the grant of a concession as a weakness and will expect further concessions. The negotiator's resolve to concede nothing more can be substantiated by linking the concession to a principle, to the negotiator's personal reputation, or to a threat of ending negotiations.

To the extent that the success of a negotiation strategy is measured by the payoff in a single negotiation involving the division of limited resources between two parties, studies of simulated negotiations suggest that the competitive strategy yields better results than other strategies for the negotiator. However, the competitive strategy suffers severe disadvantages. The likelihood of impasse is much greater for negotiators who employ the competitive strategy than for those who use other approaches. Competitive tactics engender tension and mistrust, . . . which can give the appearance that the parties are farther apart than they really are. These negative attitudes may carry over into matters other than the current negotiation and may make continuing relationships difficult.

B. The Cooperative Strategy

A view of human nature different than that upon which the competitive strategy is premised, with its emphasis on undermining the confidence of opposing counsel, underlies most collaborative interaction. In everyday events, even when they are deciding how to divide a limited resource between them, two negotiators often seek to reach an agreement which is fair and equitable to both parties and seek to build an interpersonal relationship based on trust. This approach to negotiation can be designated the cooperative strategy. The cooperative negotiator initiates granting concessions in order to create both a moral obligation to reciprocate and a relationship built on trust that is conducive to achieving a fair agreement.

The cooperative negotiator does not view making concessions as a necessity resulting from a weak bargaining position or a loss of confidence in the value of her case. Rather, she values concessions as an affirmative negotiating technique designed to capitalize on the opponent's desire to reach a fair and just agreement and to maintain an accommodative working relationship. Proponents of the cooperative strategy believe that negotiators are motivated not only by individualistic or competitive desires to maximize their own utilities, but also by collectivistic desires to reach a fair solution. Cooperative negotiators assert that the competitive strategy often leads to resentment between the parties and a breakdown of negotiations.

According to Professor Otomar Bartos, an originator of the cooperative strategy, the negotiator should begin negotiations not with a minimalist position, but rather with a more moderate opening bid that is both favorable to him and barely acceptable to the opponent. Once two such opening bids are on the table, the negotiators should determine the midpoint between the two opening bids and regard it as a fair and suitable outcome. External facts, such as how large a responsive concession the negotiator expects from the opponent, whether she is representing a tough constituency that would view large concessions unfavorably, and whether she is under a tight time deadline and wants to expedite the process by making a large concession, affect the size of the negotiator's first concession. According to Professor Bartos, the negotiator should then expect the opponent to reciprocate with a concession of similar size so that the midpoint between the parties' positions remains the same as it was after the realistic opening bids were made. The concessions by the parties are fair, according to Bartos, as long as the parties do not need to revise their initial expectations about the substance of the agreement.

The term cooperative strategy embraces a larger variety of negotiation tactics than Bartos' detailed model. Cooperative strategies include any strategies that aim to develop trust between the parties and that focus on the expectation that the opponent will match concessions ungrudgingly. Endemic to all cooperative strategies is the question of how the negotiator should respond if the opponent does not match her concessions and does not reciprocate her goodwill. The major weakness of the cooperative approach is its vulnerability to exploitation by the competitive negotiator. The cooperative negotiator is severely disadvantaged if her opponent fails to reciprocate her concessions. Cooperative negotiation theorists suggest a variety of responses when concessions are not matched. Professor Bartos recommends that the negotiator "stop making further concessions until the opponent catches up."

Because of its vulnerability to exploitation, the cooperative theory may not initially appear to be a viable alternative to the competitive strategy. As mentioned previously, in tightly controlled experiments with simulated negotiations, the competitive strategy generally produces better results. However, in actual practice, the competitive approach results in more impasses and greater distrust between the parties. Furthermore, most people tend to be cooperative in orientation and trusting of others. Professor Gerald Williams found that sixty-five percent of the attorneys he surveyed used a cooperative approach. This, of course, means that in a majority of cases, the cooperative negotiator will not be exploited by her opponent, because the opponent also uses a cooperative approach. Most cooperative negotiators probably would not feel comfortable using the competitive negotiators' aggressive tactics, which are designed to undermine the opponent and his case. Nor would they relish living and working in the mistrustful milieu which may result from the use of the competitive strategy.

C. The Integrative Strategy

Both the competitive and cooperative strategies focus on the opposing positions of the negotiators — negotiator attempts to achieve as many concessions from the other as possible. These concessions move the negotiations closer to an outcome favorable to the negotiator; however, each concession diminishes the opponent's satisfaction with the potential agreement. Integrative bargaining, on the other hand, attempts to reconcile the parties' interests and thus provides high benefits to both. Integrative bargaining is usually associated with a situation in which the parties' interests are not directly opposed, and the benefit of one widget for one party does not necessarily result in the loss of one widget for the opponent. Instead, the parties use a problem-solving approach to invent a solution which satisfies the interests of both parties.

Integrative bargaining recently has received widespread attention as the result of the publication of Professors Roger Fisher and William Ury's popular text, Getting to YES: Negotiating Agreement Without Giving In. Professors Fisher and Ury's negotiation strategy is largely based on integrative bargaining theory, although it goes beyond integrative theory in important ways. The authors call their strategy principled negotiation and identify four basic points to this approach:

People: Separate the people from the problem.

Interests: Focus on interests, not positions.

Options: Generate a variety of possibilities before deciding what to do.

Criteria: Insist that the result be based on some objective standard.

The first point distinguishes integrative bargaining from both cooperative bargaining and competitive bargaining, according to Professors Fisher and Ury. The competitive bargainer believes that his relationship with the opponent is important, because he seeks to change the opponent's position through sheer willpower. The cooperative negotiator builds trust in order to reach a fair agreement. In contrast, Professors Fisher and Ury's principled negotiator attempts to separate the interpersonal relationship between the negotiators from the merits of the problem or conflict.

Fisher and Ury's second and third points are the standard components of integrative bargaining theory. The negotiation dance of concession matching or positioning, which is a part of both competitive and cooperative behavior, often obscures the parties' real interests. A major component of integrative bargaining is the free exchange of information between the negotiators so that each party's motives, goals, and values are understood and appreciated.

Integrative bargaining attempts to locate a solution that satisfies both parties' respective interests. Professor Dean Pruitt, a social psychologist, identifies several types of integrative agreements. The most dramatic integrative solution emerges when the parties "brainstorm" and develop a new option that satisfies the significant needs of both parties. The second type of integrative bargaining is often referred to as "logrolling." In logrolling, each negotiator agrees to make concessions on some issues, while his counterpart concedes on other issues; the agreement reconciles the parties' interests to the extent that the parties have different priorities on the issues. For example, a plea bargaining agreement might provide that the defendant will plead guilty to a felony, and the prosecutor will recommend that the defendant receive probation. Defendants are often most concerned with the possibility of imprisonment; the prosecutor in a particular case, may care more about securing a felony conviction than she does about the defendant's sentence.

Another form of integrative bargaining is described by Professor Pruitt as "cost cutting." A negotiator, in order to reach an agreement, may find ways to diminish the tangible or intangible costs to the opponent when the opponent accepts an agreement that satisfies the negotiator. For example, a management attorney who agrees to the wage demands of a certain type of worker might be concerned that, in the future, the union will expect similarly generous agreements for other workers. The union negotiator may reassure management that she understands that this wage agreement for certain employees stems from special circumstances, such as historical inequities, and that similar wage concessions should not be expected for other employees.

Several procedures can facilitate reaching an integrative agreement. The free exchange of information and brainstorming efforts to invent options for mutual gains were discussed previously. In addition, the possibility of logrolling suggests that disputed issues should be considered simultaneously rather than sequentially. The negotiator should also develop a set of goals and other requirements in order to generate and screen alternative proposals. To the extent that the parties exchange negotiating proposals, the integrative negotiator should try to incorporate into his proposal some element of an opponent's previously suggested solution. Finally, the negotiator should continually alter his own proposal incrementally, so he only gradually reduces the level of benefit to be realized by his client. This behavior is referred to by Professor Pruitt as "heuristic trial and error."

Traditional integrative bargaining strategy does not have universal applicability. The strategy is utilized most easily when the parties share a problem-solving orientation, and either an identifiable mutual gain option is available, or multiple issues which can be traded off against one another exist. It is less useful when the parties disagree on only a single issue and the parties' interests are inherently opposed. Examples of situations that present direct conflicts include personal injury litigation and plea bargaining.

Professors Fisher and Ury urge the "principled negotiator" to insist upon a result based on objective criteria when the parties' interests seem to directly conflict and no mutually advantageous solution appears to be available. In this situation, they recommend the following steps:

1. Frame each issue as a joint search for objective criteria.

2. Reason and be open to reason as to which standards are most appropriate.

3. Never yield to pressure, only to principle.

By stressing the desirability of reaching a fair decision, Professors Fisher and Ury appear to be borrowing from the principles of the cooperative strategists, especially from Professor Otomar Bartos. With this addition to traditional integrative bargaining, Professors Fisher and Ury claim to have found an "all-purpose strategy" that can be used in any negotiation, regardless of the number of issues, the nature of the issues, or the orientation of the opposing party. . . .

D. The Strategic Choice Model

The three negotiation strategies outlined above are not mutually exclusive; frequently, a negotiator will use more than one strategy in a single negotiation. Some issues in a negotiation may lend themselves to an integrative approach, while others must be resolved through competitive or cooperative bargaining. Furthermore, most negotiations that begin with competitive approaches will culminate prior to agreement with either cooperative or integrative bargaining. . . . The strategic choice model suggests that the negotiator must choose between engaging in competitive behavior, making a unilateral concession, and suggesting an integrative proposal at every point in the negotiation process. These alternative tactics correspond closely with the competitive, cooperative, and integrative strategies previously outlined. . . .

5. Comments and Questions

a. With this background, we are ready to consider the ideas embodied in the best known and best selling book about negotiation: ROGER FISHER & WILLIAM URY, GETTING TO YES: NEGOTIATING AGREEMENT WITHOUT GIVING IN (1981). (A second, and expanded, edition was published in 1991, with Bruce Patton added as a co-author).

b. Professor Gifford's discussion of strategy selection in the previous section provides a summary of Getting to YES, so we turn directly to the most critical review received by the book, by Professor James J. White, and the response by Roger Fisher. Whatever one thinks of the tone of White's review, his views are entitled to serious consideration. White is a leading commercial law scholar and a serious thinker about negotiation.

c. Make a list of the areas of disagreement between White and Fisher & Ury. In each instance, who do you think has the better of the arguments, and why?

6. James J. White, *Review Essay: The Pros and Cons of "Getting to YES" by Roger Fisher & William Ury,* 31 J. LEGAL EDUC. 115 (1981)

Getting to YES is a puzzling book. On the one hand, it offers a forceful and persuasive criticism of much traditional negotiating behavior. It suggests a variety of negotiating techniques that are both clever and likely to facilitate effective negotiation. On the other hand, the authors seem to deny the existence of a significant part of the negotiation process, and to oversimplify or explain away many of the most troublesome problems inherent in the art and practice of negotiation. The book is frequently naive, occasionally self-righteous, but often helpful.

Initially, one should understand what the book is and what it is not. It is not a scholarly work on negotiation. The book is not rigorous and analytical, rather it is anecdotal and informative. It does not add fundamentally to our under-standing of the negotiation process. Rather it points to a need for change in our general conception of negotiation, and points out errors of emphasis that exist in much of the thinking about negotiation. The book's thesis is well [stated at page 43]:

> Behind opposed positions lie shared and compatible interests, as well as conflicting ones. We tend to assume that because the other side's posi-tions are opposed to ours, their interests must also be opposed. If we have an interest in defending ourselves, then they must want to attack us. If we have an interest in minimizing the rent, then their interest must be to maximize it. In many negotiations, however, a close exami-nation of the underlying interests will reveal the existence of many more interests that are shared or compatible than ones that are opposed.

This point is useful for all who teach or think about negotiation. The tendency of those deeply involved in negotiation or its teaching is probably to exaggerate the importance of negotiation on issues where the parties are diametrically opposed and to ignore situations where the parties' interests are compatible. By emphasizing that fact, and by making a clear articulation of the importance of cooperation, imagination, and the search for alternative solutions, the authors teach helpful lessons. The book therefore provides worthwhile reading for every professional negotiator and will make sound instruction for every tyro.

Unfortunately the book's emphasis upon mutually profitable adjustment, on the "problem solving" aspect of bargaining, is also the book's weakness. It is a weakness because emphasis of this aspect of bargaining is done to almost total exclusion of the other aspect of bargaining, "distributional bargaining," where one for me is minus one for you. Students of negotiation have long distin-guished between that aspect of bargaining in which modification of the parties' positions can produce benefits for one without significant cost to the other, and on the other hand, cases where benefits to one come only at significant cost to the other. They have variously described the former as exploring for mutual prof-itable adjustments, the efficiency aspect of bargaining, or problem solving. The latter has been characterized as distributional bargaining or share bargain-ing. Thus some would describe a typical negotiation as one in which the parties initially begin by cooperative or efficiency bargaining, in which each gains something with each new adjustment without the other losing any significant benefit.

Eventually, however, one comes to bargaining in which added benefits to one impose corresponding significant costs on the other. . . . One can concede the authors' thesis (that too many negotiators are incapable of engaging in problem solving or in finding adequate options for mutual gain), yet still maintain that the most demanding aspect of nearly every negotiation is the distributional one in which one seeks more at the expense of the other. My principal criticism of the book is that it seems to overlook the ultimate hard bargaining. Had the authors stated that they were dividing the negotiation process in two and were dealing with only part of it, that omission would be excusable. That is not what they have done. Rather they seem to assume that a clever negotiator can make any negotiation into problem solving. . . . To my mind this is naive. By so distorting reality, they detract from their powerful and central thesis.

Chapter 5, entitled "Insist on Objective Criteria," is a particularly naive misperception or rejection of the guts of distributive negotiation. Here, as elsewhere, the authors draw a stark distinction between a negotiator who simply takes a position without explanation and sticks to it as a matter of "will," and the negotiator who is reasonable and insists upon "objective criteria." Of course the world is hardly as simple as the authors suggest. Every party who takes a position will have some rationale for that position; every able negotiator rationalizes every position that he takes. Rarely will an effective negotiator simply assert his price and insist that the other party meet it.

The suggestion that one can find objective criteria (as opposed to persuasive rationalizations) seems quite inaccurate. . . . The distributive aspect of the negotiation often turns on the relative power of the parties. One who could sell his automobile to a particular person for $6,000 could not necessarily sell it for more than $5,000 to another person, not because of principle, but because of the need of the seller to sell and the different need of the two buyers to buy. To say that there are objective criteria that call for a $5,000 or $6,000 price, or in the case of a personal injury suit for a million dollars or an $800,000 judgment, is to ignore the true dynamics of the situation and to exaggerate the power of objective criteria.

Any lawyer who has been involved in a personal injury suit will marvel at the capacity of an effective plaintiffs lawyer to appear to do what the authors seem to think impossible, namely to give the superficial appearance of certainty and objectivity to questions that are inherently imponderable. For example, an effective plaintiffs lawyer will sometimes fix a certain dollar amount per week for the pain and suffering which one might suffer. He will then multiply that amount by the number of weeks per year and the number of years in the party's life expectancy. Thus he produces a series of tables and columns full of "hard" numbers. These have the appearance of objectivity but in fact they are subjective, based (if on anything) on a judgment about how a jury would react to the case. Every lawyer who has ever been involved in a lawsuit in which experts have been hired by each side will have a deep skepticism about the authors' appeal to scientific merit as a guide in determining a fair outcome in the negotiation of any hotly disputed problem.

In short, the authors' suggestion that one can avoid "contests of will" and thereby eliminate the exercise of raw power is at best naive and at worst misleading. Their suggestion that the parties look to objective criteria to strengthen their cases is a useful technique used by every able negotiator. Occasionally it may do what they suggest: give an obvious answer on which all can agree. Most of the time it will do no more than give the superficial appearance of reasonableness and honesty to one party's position.

The authors' consideration of "dirty tricks" in negotiation suffers from more of the same faults found in their treatment of objective criteria. At a superficial level I find their treatment of dirty tricks to be distasteful because it is so thoroughly self-righteous. The chapter is written as though there were one and only one definition of appropriate negotiating behavior handed down by the authors. Apart from the rather trivial concern about their self-righteousness, their discussion is troublesome because it discloses an ignorance of, or a disregard for, the subtleties involved in distinguishing between appropriate and inappropriate conduct in negotiation. . . . There is no recognition that the setting, participants, or substance may impose a set of rules. Rather a whole host of things labeled "dirty tricks, deliberate deception, psychological warfare, and positional pressure" are out of bounds. Consider their treatment of threats [at page 143]:

> Good negotiators rarely resort to threats. They do not need to; there are other ways to communicate the same information. . . . Warnings are much more legitimate than threats and are not vulnerable to counter threats: "Should we fail to reach agreement, it seems highly probable to me that the news media would insist on publishing the whole sordid story. In a matter of this much public interest I don't see how we could legitimately suppress information. Do you?"

The statement which they approve (and label as a "warning" and not a "threat") would likely be construed as a threat. One who wishes to threaten his opponent in a negotiation is not likely to say, "If we do not reach agreement I will see to it that the information concerning your client becomes public." Rather he is likely to say what the authors suggest. . . . In fact the authors have suggested merely a more subtle and more Machiavellian form of threat.

The question of deception is dealt with in the same facile way: Less than full disclosure is not the same as deception. Deliberate deception as to facts or one's intentions is quite different from not fully disclosing one's present thinking. Good faith negotiation does not require total disclosure. The authors seem not to perceive that between "full disclosure" and "deliberate deception" lies a continuum, not a yawning chasm. They seem to ignore the fact that in one sense the negotiator's role is, at least passively, to mislead his opponent about his settling point while at the same time to engage in ethical behavior. Most who have engaged in significant negotiation will concede the tension between those two responsibilities. . . .

Marvin Mindes identifies three prominent images of lawyers: hero, helper, and trickster. From Machiavelli onward much classical negotiating behavior could certainly be classified as trickster behavior, yet the trickster is the most pejorative of the various lawyer models. In a sense Getting to YES may be regarded as a plea for the recognition that a lawyer can be a good negotiator without deviating at all from his role as "helper." I believe that the authors are fundamentally mistaken about that. Anyone who would maximize his potential as a negotiator must occasionally do things that would cause others to classify him as a "trickster," whether he so classifies himself or not. To suggest that the world is otherwise is to mislead the reader.

7. Roger Fisher, *Comment on James White's Review of "Getting to YES,"* 31 J. LEGAL EDUC. 128 (1981)

The editor has kindly invited me not to "respond" to Jim White's review, but rather to clarify areas of disagreement between us, and to suggest where my own thinking has changed since Bill and I wrote Getting to YES. But for the editor's fortunate prohibition, there would be a tendency to react to a review that describes oneself or one's book as distasteful, self-righteous, not rigorous, not scholarly, distorting, and naive. Although I do not agree with those adjectives, I, too, see some inadequacies in the book. . . .

Although clearer, I believe, than most books on negotiation, concepts such as "position" and "power" are not presented as precisely as they might be, nor is it made sufficiently clear how using objective criteria to talk about fairness can be combined with being an advocate. Getting to YES, however, is beyond recall. With twelve foreign editions and a third of a million copies in print, the book will have to take care of itself. Far more important is jointly working to improve our collective analysis and understanding of the negotiation process.

1. Different Purposes? To some extent, I believe, White is more concerned with the way the world is, and I am more concerned with what intelligent people ought to do. One task is to teach the truth — to tell students the unpleasant facts of life, including how people typically negotiate. But I want a student to negotiate better than his or her father. I see my task as to give the best possible prescriptive advice, taking into account the way other human beings are likely to behave as well as one's own emotions and psychological state. . . .

The world is a rough place. It is also a place where, taken collectively, we are incompetent at resolving our differences in ways that efficiently and amicably serve our mutual interests. It is important that students learn about bluffing and hard bargaining, because they will certainly encounter it. It is also important that our students become more skillful and wise than most people in dealing with differences. Thus, to some extent, White and I are emphasizing different aspects of what needs to be taught.

Are distributional issues amenable to joint problem solving? The most fundamental difference between White's way of thinking and mine seems to concern the negotiation of distributional issues "where one for me is minus one for you." We agree on the importance of cooperation, imagination, and the search for creative options where the task is to reconcile substantive interests that are compatible. White, however, sees the joint problem-solving approach as limited to that area. In his view, the most demanding aspect of nearly every negotiation is the distributional one in which one seeks more at the expense of the other. Distributional matters, in his view, must be settled by the ultimate hard bargaining. He regards it as a distortion of reality to suggest that problem solving is relevant to distributional negotiation.

Here we differ. By focusing on the substantive issues (where the parties' interests may be directly opposed), White overlooks the shared interest that the parties continue to have in the process for resolving that substantive difference. How to resolve the substantive difference is a shared problem. Both parties have an interest in identifying quickly and amicably a result acceptable to each, if one is possible. How to do so is a problem. A good solution . . . requires joint action.

The guts of the negotiation problem, in my view, is not who gets the last dollar, but what is the best process for resolving that issue. It is certainly a mistake to assume that the only process available for resolving distributional questions is hard bargaining over positions. In my judgment it is also a mistake to assume that such hard bargaining is the best process for resolving differences efficiently and in the long-term interest of either side. . . .

2. Objective criteria. It is precisely in deciding such distributional issues that objective criteria can play their most useful role. Here is a second area of significant disagreement. White finds it useful to deny the existence of objective standards: "The suggestion that one can find objective criteria (as opposed to persuasive rationalizations) seems quite inaccurate." To his way of thinking the only approach is for a negotiator first to adopt a position and later to develop rationalizations for it: "every able negotiator rationalizes every position that he takes."

No one has suggested that in most negotiations there is a single objective criterion that both parties will quickly accept as determinative. The question is rather what should be treated as the essence of the negotiation, and what attitude should be taken toward arguments advanced in the discussion. White thinks it better to treat positions of the parties as the essence of the negotiation, and objective standards advanced by either party as mere rationalizations. That is one approach. A different approach is possible and, I believe, preferable. . . .

What we are suggesting is that, in general, a negotiator should select to persuade by coming up with better arguments on the merits rather than by simply trying to convince the other side that he is the more stubborn. A good guideline is for a negotiator to advance arguments as though presenting them to an impartial arbitrator, to press favorable bases for decision, but none so extreme as to damage credibility. (On the receiving side, a good guideline is for a negotiator to listen to arguments as though he were an impartial arbitrator, remaining open to persuasion despite self-interest and preconceptions.) My experience suggests that this method is often more efficient and amicable than hard positional bargaining and more often leads to satisfactory results for both parties.

3. Power. White seems to find the concept of "raw power" useful for a negotiator. I do not. For a negotiator, the critical questions of power are (1) how to enhance one's ability to influence favorably a negotiator on the other side, and (2) how to use such ability as one has. My ability to exert influence depends upon the cumulative impact of several factors: skill and knowledge, the state of our relationship, the legitimacy of our respective interests, the elegance of a proposed solution, my willingness and ability to commit myself, and the relative attractiveness to each side of its best alternative. In advance of a negotiation, I can work to enhance each of those elements. During a negotiation, I can orchestrate my use of these factors so that they reenforce and augment each other, or I can use some elements in ways that undermine others. Unless I am careful, a threat to use "raw power" will weaken rather than enhance my total ability to influence the other side, since it is likely to deprive me of knowledge, damage a relationship, and undercut my legitimacy.

Incidentally, I consider warnings (of what it will be in my interest to do, or of what will happen independent of my action) to be not simply a more Machiavellian form of threat. Being more legitimate than a threat (of harm I could cause you), a warning tends to exert more influence.

4. Deception. White correctly calls attention to the difficult issue of ethical behavior, where disclosure of what a negotiator would be willing to do if he or she had to in order to reach agreement would be damaging to self-interest. The problem is particularly acute if the substance of the negotiation is haggling over positions — over statements of what one is willing or unwilling to do. With such positional bargaining in mind, White sees the negotiator's role as being "to mislead his opponent about his settling point while at the same time to engage in ethical behavior."

I believe White fails to appreciate the extent to which the ethical problem is reduced if instead of negotiating by making a series of offers and counteroffers (each often intended to deceive the other as to what one is really willing to do), one treats negotiation as a joint search for an appropriate objective basis for decision, taking into account legitimate interest. If one tries to persuade the other side on the merits, as one would by to persuade an arbitrator, the rewards for — and need for — misleading are far less.

5. Changed thinking. Getting to YES says "Don't Bargain Over Positions." There are categories of negotiations where positional bargaining is the best way to proceed. On single-issue negotiations among strangers where the transaction costs of exploring interests would be high and where each side is protected by competitive opportunities, haggling over positions may work better than joint problem solving. An example is negotiating a sale on the New York Stock Exchange.

Another chapter heading, "Separate the People from the Problem," also puts the matter too broadly. In some cases, the people are the problem; negotiating a good relationship with them may be more important than the substantive outcome of any one negotiation. And good relations can ease future substantive negotiations. I still think that relationship issues and substantive issues should be separated to the following extent: One should not threaten a relationship as a means of trying to coerce a substantive concession; nor should one make an otherwise unjustified concession in hopes of buying a good relationship.

Getting to YES as a whole, I believe, blurs a desirable distinction between descriptive analysis and prescriptive advice. Descriptively, it sorts facts into useful categories: positions vs. interests; people issues vs. substantive ones; inventing vs. deciding; discussing what negotiators will or will not do vs. discussing what they ought to do. Those distinctions, like distinctions between reptiles and mammals, or between short snakes and long snakes, are objectively true and, despite possible difficulties in drawing lines, exist as facts in the real world. Whether or not they are useful is another question.

We go beyond suggesting these descriptive categories by advancing some prescriptive rules of thumb, indicated by the chapter headings in the book. These are not advanced as guidelines that will in every case produce the desired result. No such guidelines can exist, since negotiators who deal with each other often desire different results. The rules of thumb we advanced are the best we could come up with. Without knowing the particular subject matter of a negotiation or the identity of the people on the other side, what is the best advice one can give to a negotiator? People may prefer to ask different questions, but I have not yet heard better answers to the question on which we were and are working.

E. FACTORS AFFECTING NEGOTIATION

1. Comments and Questions

a. This section examines a variety of factors that can have a significant impact on the negotiation process and the quality of settlements achieved by the parties thereto. The topics covered include the impact of negotiation styles on bargaining transactions; creativity and problem-solving as aids to successful negotiation; the impact of perceptions of fairness; and the affect of (high) aspirations on negotiation results.

b. Unlike the prior readings, Schweitzer and Kerr consider a factor that is extrinsic to the negotiation process itself: the role of alcohol in negotiation. Alcohol loosens inhibitions, which can result in diminished bargaining success. However, the social setting and trust associated with letting down one's guard can enhance a bargaining process, particularly where the parties are more concerned about creating or repairing a longer term relationship than just settling a dispute or consummating a one-time transaction. While the discussion here focuses on alcohol consumption, it is generally applicable to social interactions that have an impact on business negotiations.

2. Charles B. Craver, *Negotiation Styles: The Impact on Bargaining Transactions*, 58-APR DISP. RESOL. J. 48 (2003)

[W]hat makes a negotiator effective? This article looks at the characteristics of cooperative problem-solvers and competitive adversarial bargainers and discusses how they interact. It reports on the effectiveness of these two negotiation styles, as well as a hybrid style that employs qualities of both. Perhaps the most effective negotiators are competitive problem-solvers who hope to obtain good deals for themselves, while simultaneously trying to improve the results for opponents. . . . Negotiator styles significantly affect bargaining interactions.

In the early 1980s, Gerald Williams conducted a study among attorneys in Phoenix and Denver to determine how their colleagues behave. GERALD R. WILLIAMS, LEGAL NEGOTIATION AND SETTLEMENT (1983). He asked the respondents to indicate what percentage of the individuals with whom they had recently interacted were cooperative problem-solvers and what percentage were competitive adversarials. He found that the respondents considered 65% of their colleagues to be cooperative problem-solvers, 24% to be competitive adversarials, and 11% to be unclassifiable.

I often ask attorneys who attend my legal negotiation courses the same question. They usually suggest a 50-50 split, and they are surprised when I tell them about Professor Williams' empirical findings. What would account for this discrepancy? When we interact with others, we tend to remember the negative experiences better. Thus, if we interact with 20 people today, 15 of whom are pleasant and cooperative, and five of whom are aggressive and rude, we remember the unpleasant experiences and, therefore, over-estimate the number of competitive adversarial opponents we have encountered. But when we see a list of the names of the 20 people with whom we interacted, we recognize that most were cooperative problem-solvers. . . .

How we react in a negotiation often depends on how we are approached. How would you react if a legal adversary came to your office and told you that he is going to take you to the cleaners in this negotiation and then insulted you?. . . It is surprising how quickly people change their demeanor to avoid exploitation. When this hypothetical was presented to my negotiation class, their responses were classic. Most said they would respond in a competitive adversarial manner. For example, they said they would not disclose critical information, lest this opponent take advantage of their openness. They also said they would employ strategic tactics designed to neutralize the competitive behavior of their adversary. For example, they would begin with less generous opening positions and seek better terms for themselves.

What if, instead, a legal adversary visited your office and politely showed interest in achieving a mutually acceptable agreement that would satisfy the underlying interests of both sides? Most likely you would respond in kind, in an open and cooperative manner designed to maximize the joint results achieved. My students would. They begin to appreciate how much easier it is to obtain beneficial results when the negotiators cooperate with each other to reach their goals. They also recognize how much more difficult it is for openly competitive adversarial bargainers to achieve their one-sided objectives.

Prof. Williams asked the respondents in his study to classify opponents as "effective," "average," and "ineffective" negotiators. The respondents classified 59% of cooperative negotiators, and 25% of competitive negotiators, as effective. They considered 3% of the cooperative problem-solvers and 33% of competitive adversarial bargainers to be ineffective negotiators.

In the late 1990s, Andrea Kupfer Schneider replicated Prof. Williams' study using attorneys in Milwaukee and Chicago. Andrea Kupfer Schneider, *"Shattering Negotiation Myths: Empirical Evidence on the Effectiveness of Negotiation Style,"* 7 HARV. NEGOT. L. REV.143 (2002). Her findings reflect changes that have affected our society in general and the legal profession in particular. People are less pleasant to one another today than they were two decades ago. It seems that many more people are impatient and less courteous. Prof. Schneider observed that "the competitive negotiator described by Williams in the 1980s was not nearly as unpleasant and negative" as the contemporary competitive bargainer.

I would have expected the competitive adversarial negotiators described in Prof. Schneider's study to be even less effective than the competitive adversarial bargainers described in the Williams study, and this is exactly what Prof. Schneider found. She found only 9% of contemporary competitive adversarials to be effective, compared to 25% in the Williams study. There was only a relatively slight decline in the effectiveness of cooperative problem-solvers: Schneider's respondents found 54% of them to be effective negotiators (compared to 59% effective in the Williams study).

The findings with respect to negotiators who were considered to be ineffective are even starker. While there was barely any change in the percentage of cooperative problem-solvers considered to be ineffective bargainers (3% in the Williams study and 3.5% in the Schneider study), she found a profound change with respect to the percentage of ineffective competitive adversarials. In the Williams study, the respondents considered 33% of competitive negotiators to be ineffective. Schneider's respondents found 53% to be ineffective. The increase in perceived ineptitude among competitive adversarial negotiators is most likely attributable to their bad manners and unpleasant demeanor. Since they are more irritating, stubborn and arrogant, they provoke negative feelings in their opponents, who would likely consider them to be less effective bargainers.

The notion that one must be uncooperative, selfish, manipulative and even abrasive to be successful is erroneous. To achieve beneficial results in a negotiation, negotiators must only possess the ability to say "no" forcefully and credibly to convince opponents that they must enhance the offer to achieve agreement. This objective can be accomplished courteously and quietly, and as effectively as those who behave more demonstrably.

In my legal negotiation course exercises, I have noticed only three significant differences with respect to the outcomes achieved by different styles of negotiators. First, if a truly extreme agreement is reached, the prevailing party is usually a competitive adversarial negotiator. Since cooperative problem-solving bargainers tend to be more fair-minded, they generally refuse to take unconscionable advantage of inept or weak opponents. Second, competitive adversarial bargainers generate more "nonsettlements" than their cooperative cohorts. The extreme positions taken by competitive bargainers and their frequent use of manipulative and disruptive tactics (rudeness, threats) make it easy for their opponents to accept the consequences associated with nonsettlements.

Third, cooperative problem-solvers tend to achieve more efficient combined results than their competitive adversarial colleagues — i.e., they tend to maximize the benefits to all parties. Because they are willing to work cooperatively, they share information and try to see the problem from more than one side.

Thus, they are more likely to attain higher joint values than bargainers who are primarily interested in getting the most for themselves. Advocates who hope to achieve mutually efficient agreements that benefit both sides must be willing to cooperate sufficiently to permit the participants to explore areas of possible joint gain. While these people may simultaneously act in their own interests to achieve their own goals, their attention to opponents' interests increases the likelihood of agreement and the probability of mutually efficient terms. In addition, the more the participants can expand the pie, the more likely each side will obtain more satisfactory results. . . .

Prof. Williams found that certain traits are shared by effective bargainers of both types. Successful negotiators are thoroughly prepared, behave in an honest and ethical manner, are perceptive readers of others, and are analytical, realistic and convincing. Both endeavor to maximize their own client's return. Prof. Schneider's study also made this finding. Maximizing client returns is the quintessential characteristic of competitive adversarial negotiators. The fact that it is common to both groups suggests that many effective negotiators who are identified by their peers as cooperative problem-solvers are really wolves in sheepskin. They adopt a cooperative style, but seek competitive objectives.

Most successful negotiators are able to combine the most salient traits associated with the cooperative problem-solving and the competitive adversarial styles. They seek to accomplish their business objectives in a congenial and seemingly ingenuous manner. Unlike less proficient negotiators who view bargaining encounters as "fixed pie" endeavors in which one side's gain is the other side's corresponding loss, effective bargainers realize that the parties generally value various terms differently. So, while they may attempt to claim more of the distributive items desired by both sides, they will both look for shared values, which are more likely to lead to agreement and increase the potential for settlements. They seek . . . "win-win" results — optimal deals for themselves, while providing opponents with the best terms possible given what they have achieved for themselves.

3. Jennifer Gerarda Brown, *Creativity and Problem-Solving*, 87 MARQ. L. REV. 697 (2004)

Negotiation experts seem to agree that creative solutions are often the key to reaching value-maximizing outcomes in integrative, interest based bargaining. Sticking to the problem as it is initially framed and considering only the solutions that most readily present themselves will sometimes yield the optimal result, but more often, the situation will require the parties and their representatives to think more expansively. This process of thinking more expansively — thinking that ventures out from the accustomed way of considering a problem, to find something else that might work — is often referred to as creativity or creative thinking. . . . On the theory that both creativity and creative thinking can be enhanced with some training and work, this essay will use the terms interchangeably.

I. Beyond Brainstorming

Brainstorming is a somewhat formalized process in which participants work together to generate ideas. I say that it is formalized because it proceeds according to two important ground rules: participants agree not to evaluate the ideas while they are brainstorming, and they agree not to take "ownership" of the ideas. They strive to generate options and put them on the table, no matter how wacky or far-fetched they may seem. The "no evaluation" rule encourages participants to suspend their natural urge to criticize, edit, or censor the ideas. Evaluation can come later, but the notion here is that solutions will flow more easily if people are not assessing even as they articulate them. The "no ownership" rule also facilitates innovation, because participants are encouraged to feel free to propose an idea or solution without endorsing it — no one can later attribute the idea to the person who proposed it, or try to hold it against that person. People can therefore propose ideas that might actually disadvantage them and benefit their counterparts without conceding that they would actually agree to such proposals in the final analysis. The ground rules for brainstorming constrain the natural inclination to criticize, so that participants are free to imagine, envision, and play with ideas, even though these processes come less easily to them.

Why is brainstorming so popular, both in practice and in negotiation training? Perhaps the answer lies not so much in what it activates, but in what it disables. . . . It may be easier to teach people what not to do — rather than what to do affirmatively — in order to enhance their creative thinking. We may not know much about how to unleash new sources of creativity for negotiators, but we are pretty sure about some things that impede creative thinking. Theory and practice suggest that creative thinking is difficult when people jump to conclusions, close off discussion, or seize upon an answer prematurely. Indeed, the very heuristics that make decision-making possible — those pathways that permit people to make positive and sometimes normative judgments — also lead people astray. One of the ways they may be led astray is that the heuristic prompts them to decide too quickly what something is or should be. Once judgement has occurred, it is tough to justify the expenditure of additional energy that creative thinking would require. Creativity could be considered the "anti-heuristic"; it keeps multiple pathways of perception and decision-making open, even when people are tempted to choose a single, one-way route to a solution. If we do nothing else, we can attempt to delay this kind of judgment until negotiators have considered multiple options. Brainstorming provides the structure for this kind of delay.

But is brainstorming the only technique for enhancing creativity? The answer would seem to be an easy "no." . . . This section will summarize these suggestions.

A. Wordplay. Once an issue or problem is articulated, it is possible to play with the words expressing that problem in order to improve understanding and sometimes to yield new solutions. [Techniques include shifting emphasis from one word to another; changing a word; deleting a word; and adding a word.] . . .

B. Mind-Mapping / Word Clustering. Participants write the problem out and then write down words that come to mind, randomly, as related to the problem. The words are written without any particular order all over a paper, and once that aspect is completed, lines are drawn connecting the words as connections come to mind. This technique . . . can help participants discover the inner pathways by which their brains are connecting aspects of the problem in hidden ways. These connections can then lead parties to creative ideas about the problem.

C. De Bono's "Six Hats" Technique. Edward de Bono has proposed a technique he calls "Six Thinking Hats," in which six aspects of a problem are assessed independently. As problem solvers symbolically don each of six differently colored hats, they focus on an aspect of the problem associated with each color: red for emotions, white for facts, yellow for positive aspects of the situation, green for future implications, black for critique, and blue for process. . . . The technique of isolating the black/critique hat may be especially important for lawyers, whose tendency to move quickly into a critical mode may prevent them from seeing other important aspects of a problem. If the black hat is worn at or near the end of the process, the Six Hats technique displays a characteristic shared by brainstorming: it delays critique and judgment until other approaches can be tried. And shutting down judgment may enable creativity, as suggested above. By forcing themselves to address separately the emotional, factual, and process issues at stake in a problem, parties may discover room for creative solutions. Similarly, creative solutions are sometimes found in the terms of a future relationship between the parties. Wearing the green hat may force participants to come to terms with a future they would rather ignore.

The prospect of changing hats, even (perhaps especially) if it is done symbolically, could make some participants uncomfortable. Negotiators and neutrals should bear in mind that age, sex, ethnicity, and other cultural specifics may create dignitary interests for some participants that would be threatened or compromised by some techniques for boosting creative thought. Some people would feel embarrassed or humiliated if they were asked to engage in the theatrics required by some of these exercises. For others, the chance to pretend or play might be just the prod they need to open new avenues of thought. In a spirit of flexibility (surely a necessary condition for creativity), therefore, one should be thinking of ways to modify these techniques to fit other needs of the parties.

D. Atlas of Approaches. Another technique for stimulating creative ideas about a problem from a variety of perspectives is called the "Atlas of Approaches." . . . [P]articipants adopt the perspectives of professionals from a variety of fields. By asking themselves, for example, "What would a journalist do?", "What would an economist do?", "How would a psychologist view this?", and so on, negotiators are able to form a more interdisciplinary view of their problem. With this more complete picture of the issues and potential outcomes, they might be able to connect disciplines in ways that give rise to creative solutions.

E. Visualization. When parties use the visualization technique, they take time to imagine the situation they desire, one in which their problem is solved. What do they see? What specific conditions exist, and how might each of those conditions be achieved? . . . [P]arties can engage in visualization simply by closing their eyes and thinking about the problem in terms that are visual rather than abstract. Another approach is to "look at the problem from above, and see things otherwise invisible." The goal is to deploy a variety of the brain's cognitive pathways (verbal, visual, spatial, and abstract), the better to make connections that give rise to creative solutions.

F. "WWCD": What Would Croeses Do? This process requires a participant to take the perspective of an unconstrained actor. What solutions suggest themselves if we assume no limit to available money, time, talent, technology, or effort? In some ways, one could think of the WWCD method as a more specific application of brainstorming. As the proponents of brainstorming are quick to point out, creativity and the free flow of ideas can be impeded by criticism or assessment. WWCD takes off the table any assessment based on constraints — financial, technological, etc. If we assume that we can afford and operationalize any solution we can come up with, what might we discover? A second phase of this approach requires participants to think about the extent to which their unconstrained solution might be modified to make it workable, given the existing constraints.

G. "Feel My Pain." There can be great payoffs to asking whether you're feeling other people's pain, because ignoring others' interests leads to inefficient decisions. Solutions to this call for the parties to design incentives so that all parties more fully feel the impacts that their decisions have on each other.

H. Flipping or Reversal. With this technique, one asks whether flipping or reversing a given situation will work. . . . In the reversal method, one takes things as they are and then turns them round, inside out, upside down, back to front. Then one sees what happens — one is not looking for the right answer but for a different arrangement of information which will provoke a different way of looking at the situation.

Chris Honeyman sometimes uses this technique in his work as a neutral when he asks the parties to put forward some really bad ideas for resolving the conflict. When people offer ideas in response to a call for "bad" ideas, they may free themselves to offer the ideas they partially or secretly support; again, as in brainstorming, they disclaim ownership of the ideas. It is also possible that the instruction to offer bad ideas stimulates creative thinking, because it can seem funny to people. Humor is a good stimulant for creativity. The theory is that bad ideas are easy to come by (they can often be found in abundance), and in many bad ideas there resides the kernel of a good idea. Framing them as "bad" ideas effects a sort of reversal or flipping. . . . Most conflicts are multidimensional, giving rise to multiple sites at which elements could be reversed. Once the parties have broken down the situation into component parts, they can try reversing or flipping some elements to see whether this yields superior solutions.

I. Idea Arbitrage. With idea arbitrage, parties see an existing solution in one context and ask themselves where else it might work. A great example of this from the field of consumer products design is the electric toothbrush with rotating bristles. . . . [T]his terrific invention actually grew out of a much more trivial discovery — the rotating lollipop! The inventors of the lollipop knew they had a good thing, so they looked for new places to put it to use. Similar stories can be told about velcro or polycarbonate wheels. This building upon prior discovery is the root of creativity in art and science. With idea arbitrage, the creativity stems from solutions — that is, expanding the problems to which an existing solution may be applied, rather than from a focus on the problems themselves. This approach assumes that there are solutions in search of problems, rather than the other way around.

J. Toys. A final technique for stimulating creativity would be a no-brainer for anyone under 16 (and for some of us who are considerably older than that): Toys! One former colleague of mine used to bring a Nerf basketball hoop to class occasionally to permit students to take a shot after a particularly insightful answer. . . . Barry Orton uses "Nerf weaponry" when facilitating negotiation of complex telecommunications disputes. He argues that the toys give people a harmless and humorous way to blow off steam and sometimes introduce an element of levity into tense situations. . . .

II. Creative Thinking in Negotiation

[C]an the techniques summarized here all find specific application in negotiation? Surely some of them will be less useful than others. WWCD, for example, may have limited use in most conflict situations. Suspending critique during brainstorming is one thing, but many negotiators will be reluctant to assume away all constraints. Or they may fear that WWCD discussions will be a waste of time, because once the constraints are again taken into account, the solution will go away entirely.

Idea Arbitrage might also seem to have limited applicability to most negotiations, because the very genesis of the negotiation is a problem to be solved, not a solution in search of a problem. On the other hand, Idea Arbitrage may be helpful as a persuasive tool — one that supports creativity. Suppose that a negotiator has come up with a creative solution to a problem and knows that the solution has been used successfully in another context. Presenting the new, creative solution as an old idea rather than a new one may make it more acceptable to the other side. Lawyers, as we know, love precedent. Idea Arbitrage gives a creative solution a kind of pedigree or set of credentials it might otherwise lack if presented as a brand new idea.

Perhaps persuasion is part of creativity — we need tools not only to generate creative thinking, but also to make the results of creative thinking more acceptable to our fellow problem solvers. Thus, all of these techniques belong in the negotiator's toolbox, even if some will have more specialized applicability. It also seems clear that the nature of the negotiation will strongly determine the kinds of creativity-enhancing techniques that are useful.

4. Nancy A. Welsh, *Perceptions of Fairness in Negotiation*, 87 MARQ. L. REV. 753 (2004)

Often, when people negotiate, their goal is to win. At the very least, people work to achieve outcomes (or allocations of value) that they can call fair, and particularly "fair enough to me!" We all know people (including ourselves) who have offered more than was necessary in negotiation sessions or rejected offers even though they made economic sense. These behaviors, which have been replicated by researchers in experiments involving "ultimatum games," seem irrational but can be explained by examining fairness perceptions. Negotiators rely upon their perceptions of distributive and procedural fairness in making offers and demands, reacting to the offers and demands of others, and deciding whether to reach an agreement or end negotiations.

The concept of distributive fairness focuses on the criteria that lead people to feel that they have received their fair share of available benefits — i.e., that the outcome of a negotiation or other decision making process is fair. . . . The definition of distributive fairness is inevitably subjective. This realization leads to the following questions: What criteria do people, including negotiators, use to guide their judgments regarding distributive fairness? What variables influence people's selection among different criteria, and why do people find it difficult to reach agreement even when they share a commitment to achieving an equitable outcome?

The various criteria for judging the fairness of outcomes can be distilled into four basic, competing principles or rules — equality, need, generosity, and equity. The equality principle provides that everyone in a group should share its benefits equally. According to the need principle, "those who need more of a benefit should get more than those who need it less." The generosity principle decrees that one person's outcome should not exceed the outcomes achieved by others. Finally, the equity principle ties the distribution of benefits to people's relative contribution. Those who have contributed more should receive more than those who have contributed less. The closer that the actual outcome of a negotiation is to the outcome a negotiator anticipated based on the application of these principles, the greater the likelihood that the negotiator will perceive the outcome as fair.

Imagine the application of the four principles to a negotiation between two individuals who are establishing a joint venture and negotiating the distribution of income. The first negotiator, who has little capital, is contributing the idea and the time and energy to implement the idea. The other negotiator is supplying the needed funds for the development and marketing of the idea. If these individuals are guided by the equality principle, they will distribute the income from the joint venture equally. If they use the need principle, the poorer negotiator who is contributing "sweat equity" will receive a greater share of the income. Under the generosity principle, neither negotiator would want his income to exceed the income of the other. Perhaps most difficult, is the application of the equity principle. Both contributions are needed. Whose is more valuable? The negotiators' assessments regarding the relative value of their contributions are likely to be affected by many factors [including self-interest, relationships between negotiators, situational needs, and cultural norms]. . . .

Even when negotiators express a desire to be fair and to allocate resources in a manner that is equitable, their definitions of "equitable outcomes" are almost inevitably affected by self-interest or an "egocentric bias." People value their own contributions much more highly than they value the identical contributions of others. In one research project, for example, when people were asked to determine what amount should be paid for accomplishing a particular task, they expected to be paid substantially more for their own work than they were willing to pay to someone else.

Another interesting study simulated the impact of the egocentric bias in the litigation context. The subjects in the research project learned all the facts involved in a personal injury accident in which a motorcyclist was hit by a car and injured. They then determined what they thought would be a fair settlement to compensate the motorcyclist for his injuries. After this, the researchers assigned the subjects to play the role of either the motorcyclist or the driver of the car and to negotiate a settlement. Settlements were reached in nearly every case. The researchers then worked with another set of subjects but, this time, began by assigning them to the roles of the motorcyclist and the driver. While playing their roles, the subjects learned the facts, calculated a "fair" settlement, and tried to negotiate a settlement. These subjects had a very difficult time reaching a settlement. Their perceptions of fairness were affected by the roles they were playing. The motorcyclists' pre-negotiation judgments of a fair settlement generally involved a large damage award, while the drivers were much more likely to assess a small damage award. Not coincidentally, these assessments worked to their own favor. The farther apart the pre-negotiation judgments regarding fair outcomes, the more likely the negotiations were to end in impasse. Equitable distribution, it seems, is in the eyes of the self-interested beholder.

5. Andrea Kupfer Schneider, *Aspirations in Negotiation*, 87 MARQ. L. REV. 675 (2004)

Aspirations are the specific goals in a negotiation that a negotiator wishes to achieve as part of an agreement. Aspirations can be monetary . . . or non-monetary. . . . Aspirations are based on the underlying needs and interests of the negotiator, and they are conceptually independent of the negotiator's bottom line. For example, a negotiator might be willing to sell her house for $150,000 if that is the best offer she can solicit, while aspiring to receive a sale price of $300,000. . . .

Negotiators should establish optimistic aspirations, because empirical evidence has shown that negotiators with higher aspirations tend to achieve better bargaining results. The classic study demonstrating this proposition was run by psychologists Sidney Siegel and Lawrence Fouraker in 1960. One set of negotiators were given a modest goal of $2.10 profit in a buy-sell negotiation and the other set were given the "high aspirations" of $6.10. Both sets were told that they could keep any profits they made and could qualify for a second, "double-their-money" round if they met or exceeded their specified bargaining goals. The negotiators with the more ambitious $6.10 goal achieved a mean profit of $6.25, far outperforming the median profit of $3.35 achieved by those with the modest $2.10 goal. More recently, Sally Blount White and Margaret Neale set up an experiment in house buying where buyers and sellers were each given reservation prices in addition to aspirational goals for the house price. Again, those buyers with high aspirations (to buy the house at a low price) did better than those buyers with low aspirations (as did the sellers with high aspirations).

There are different explanations for this effect. First, a negotiator's aspirations help to determine the outer limit of what she will request. Because a negotiator will almost never achieve more than what she asks for, setting relatively high goals is important so that the negotiator makes suitably aggressive demands.

Second, optimistic aspirations can cause negotiators to work harder at bargaining than they otherwise might, increasing the likelihood of achieving a desirable outcome. Professor Jennifer Brown hypothesizes that when negotiators set an aspiration level, they gain more utility as offers increase toward that level versus the utility gained as offers proceed beyond that level. In other words, the marginal utility associated with each improvement beyond one's aspirations is less than the marginal utility associated with movement toward the aspirations. This theory implies that negotiators will care relatively more about achieving their aspirations than exceeding them.

[O]ne effect of negotiators working harder is that negotiators with high aspirations will also exhibit more patience at the bargaining table than those with low aspirations. Rather than getting frustrated and either walking away or giving in, the negotiator with high aspirations will be more willing to tolerate a longer give-and-take in order to reach her aspirations. As more patient negotiators achieve a greater share of the gains of negotiation than less patient negotiators, high aspirations can lead to better outcomes. Aspirations should be specific. A general goal of "doing well" or "let's see what they say" is insufficient to trigger the positive behavioral benefits of setting aspirations discussed earlier. Much in the same way that negotiators learn to define their BATNA and then use it to determine their bottom line, negotiators should take vague aspirations and turn them into specific goals for the negotiation — either monetary or actions or both.

In addition, specific goals for the negotiation can keep the negotiator more focused on his or her interests than on the game of negotiation. If a negotiator enters the negotiation with an ambiguous "let's see what happens" agenda, it is far easier to become entangled in debilitating negotiation mistakes such as getting anchored on the counterpart's numbers, assuming a fixed pie, or getting one's ego trapped in a game of chicken.

While negotiators should set relatively aggressive aspirations, those aspirations should be reasonable enough to be justifiable for several important reasons. First, aspirations should be consistent with other aspects of effective negotiation behavior. Assuming that demands are based on aspirations, negotiators will be more likely to succeed in convincing their adversary to reach an agreement based on their aspiration level if they can argue that such an outcome is derived from objective criteria. These objective criteria include what a court would decide. . . .

The availability of objective criteria makes it easier for the negotiator to justify a refusal to make concessions. Demands that are not objectively grounded are harder to hold onto during the bargaining process. Imagine a scenario where a seller would like to get $500,000 for her house, because it is a nice round number and she could use it to buy another house, versus a scenario in which the seller lists her house for $500,000, based on the fair market value of the house in comparison to other houses in the neighborhood. In the latter case, the seller has fair and convincing arguments for why she will not accept less. Demands that lack an objective justification also encourage the opposing negotiator to make unprincipled counter demands.

An additional reason that aspirations should be modest enough to be justifiable is that overly aggressive aspirations can lead to negotiation impasse when mutually beneficial agreements are possible. Negotiators often fail to follow the "optimistic but justifiable" approach to setting aspirations, instead setting vague goals such as "achieving a good deal" or aspiring to relatively low, easy-to-achieve results. Why? One reason is that specific, optimistic aspirations can result in disappointment when they are not achieved. Setting low or non-specific goals — what Richard Shell calls a "wimp-win" approach — maximizes the likelihood of success and protects self-esteem. . . .

Another circumstance in which negotiators set low aspirations is when the negotiator feels that she lacks enough information about the other side's interests and bottom line to confidently predict what results are possible. A negotiator may assume that she needs the deal more than her counterpart or may not understand why reaching a settlement is important to the other side. Without this information, she may set her goals lower than the goals should be from an objective perspective. For example, if a house seller receives an offer that is $20,000 below the listed price after the house has been on the market for several weeks without any interest, the seller's response depends, to a great extent, on the information the seller has about the buyer. Without any information, the seller might be so excited to get an offer that she accepts the offer immediately. On the other hand, if the seller learns that the buyer needs to move next month or has told his realtor that this was his favorite house, the seller may be more willing to hold onto high aspirations. Just as setting aspirations takes preparation and the appropriate criteria, it also requires preparation about the other side.

Finally, a negotiator may set low goals when she is relatively uninterested in the result or wants to avoid conflict with another person who seems more concerned than she is about the money, power, or other issues at stake. These low goals may be appropriate as long as the negotiator makes a rational decision about this. . . .

6. Maurice E. Schweitzer & Jeffrey L. Kerr, *Bargaining Under the Influence: The Role of Alcohol in Negotiations*, 14 ACAD. MGMT. EXEC. AT 47 (May 2000)

This article describes the advantages and disadvantages of mixing alcohol with business, and offers advice regarding the use of alcohol for managers and negotiators making decisions or setting policy. Rather than drinking out of habit or social pressure, managers should make the decision to drink carefully and rationally. We begin by identifying the role alcohol can play in building relationships. We then identify the harmful consequences of mixing alcohol with business, with particular emphasis on the potential harm alcohol can cause in negotiations. We report new evidence linking alcohol to aggressive negotiator behavior and to inefficient negotiation outcomes. We then offer prescriptive advice for when it makes sense to mix or avoid mixing alcohol with business. For situations in which managers prefer to avoid or limit their alcohol consumption, we suggest methods for avoiding social pressures to drink.

Alcohol Can Facilitate Relationship Building. Alcohol has traditionally played a role in developing business relationships. As one commentator remarked, "When you wanted to meet another company you invited its managers to your smoke-filled dining room and drank yourself into a partnership." Alcohol facilitates relationship building in several ways. Drinking can relieve stress and create a social routine that is comforting and familiar. In fact, the mere presence of alcohol can cue an entire set of expected social behaviors, signal commitment to the relationship, and change an atmosphere to enable participants to engage each other on a more cordial and personal level. Although formal routines reassert themselves as the group returns to its primary business, lingering effects from this positive bonding experience remain. . . .

Alcohol's potential relationship benefits are particularly relevant to negotiations. Building relationships is an essential element for successful negotiations, and alcohol can play a role in enabling negotiators to recognize common interests. Because alcohol lowers inhibitions and encourages a sense of camaraderie, people tend to exchange information more freely. In Japan, for example, information about upcoming projects and office politics is most likely to be discussed during drinking sessions.

Alcohol can also help parties reach an agreement. After consuming a few drinks, negotiators may become more receptive to new ideas and more likely to make concessions. In fact, one commentator suggests, "At drinking parties, go for business concessions on your contract. If they are available, this is the setting in which you'll win them." Alcohol can also facilitate negotiations by influencing mood and affect. Although reactions to alcohol depend on the individual and the context, alcohol generally decreases anxiety and promotes a positive mood. Recent research has linked affect with negotiator behavior, and found that negotiators in good moods tended to be more cooperative, creative, and effective in achieving joint gains. . . .

Cross-Cultural Drinking Norms. Drinking norms vary widely across cultures. This is true even within the United States, where substantial variation in alcohol liability laws and prosecution rates exists across regions. From an international perspective, these disparities are even greater. Long-established traditions influence cultural norms concerning drinking in general and business drinking in particular. While customs dictate strict abstinence in Islamic countries such as Saudi Arabia (though not Egypt), copious drinking is common in many parts of Japan, where the refusal to drink may be interpreted as a sign of mistrust. . . . Even the type of alcoholic beverage, such as maotai in China or makkolli in Korea, can carry deep cultural significance.

U.S. managers working abroad are likely to find that alcohol is a more common aspect of business meetings than they are accustomed to in the United States. In fact, decreasing public tolerance of DWI (Driving While Intoxicated) violations, coupled with increasing corporate and personal liability, has resulted in heightened sensitivity within the U.S. to consumption of alcohol in business settings. Most foreigners are less sensitive to individual preferences for abstinence and are less concerned with corporate liability for inebriated behavior. Consequently, U.S. managers may be surprised by the drinking norms and expectations they encounter abroad.

While Western managers are generally accustomed to the idea of celebratory drinks at the conclusion of a negotiation, in Russian, Asian, and many other cultures, drinking may be used to initiate proceedings and to symbolize each party's commitment to a mutually satisfying outcome. Easterners often strive for successful business outcomes after personal relationships have been established, while Westerners develop social relationships after business interests have been addressed. . . .

For centuries, Japanese business dealings of all kinds have been accompanied by drinking parties where drinking is viewed more as a ritual duty than a social pleasure. These drinking sessions can occur in large groups, as they often do in China, or in groups as small as two people. In Japan, important business meetings are often held after hours with the expectation that participants will become extremely intoxicated. In fact, many Japanese managers believe it is impossible to truly know someone without drinking heavily with them, and may feel uncomfortable with anyone who refuses to drink at a party or celebration. The discomfort a Japanese or German businessperson might experience with a non-drinking American counterpart derives from their unequal gestures of vulnerability. In many cultures, drinking is equated with openness and candor. Thus, a refusal to drink could signal an unwillingness to let down one's guard. . . .

The symbolic candor and vulnerability associated with alcohol can also work across hierarchical levels, both in U.S. organizations and abroad, by allowing astute managers to open channels of communication with subordinates that might otherwise seem awkward. By joining subordinates for drinks, the boss sends a signal . . . that in this setting he or she is like others, dependent on the community. He or she can be approached, issues can be raised, and the strictures of protocol and hierarchy can be at least temporarily de-emphasized.

The cross-level communication effects of alcohol are perhaps most clearly seen in Japanese organizations. Hierarchical relationships and protocols are especially formal, except during tsukiai, when superiors are free to give candid feedback to their subordinates. These are lengthy, after-hours events typically involving large quantities of scotch. The obvious inebriation of the boss (whether actual or feigned) permits him to discuss a subordinate's performance and shortcomings without the painful loss of face such direct feedback would entail under sober conditions. Since the exchange occurred under the influence of alcohol, both parties can come to work the next day free of the embarrassment such candor would normally produce in a Japanese organization. A subordinate, such as a teetotaling American manager who forgoes *tsukiai* sessions, . . . misses an important opportunity to establish a more complete relationship with his superiors.

It is important to note that attitudes toward overt drunkenness vary across cultures almost as much as attitudes toward drinking itself. An obvious state of inebriation may elicit little or no negative reaction among Russian business associates and may even be considered a symbol of camaraderie and cohesion by Japanese or Korean hosts. In Germany, however, while alcohol consumption is high among males of all social strata, the ability to hold one's drink is considered an important aspect of masculine comportment among professional and managerial classes. Similarly, obvious signs of inebriation are considered unseemly and unacceptable in Mexico, Malaysia, Indonesia, and the Philippines. There are also important cross-cultural differences with respect to accountability for the things you say while inebriated. For example, Koreans are more likely to hold you accountable for things you promise while drinking than are Japanese. . . .

The usefulness of alcohol in negotiations depends on the degree to which feelings of cooperation and common interest are lacking yet necessary in the relationship. For example, in a stalled negotiation in which the parties are having difficulty understanding and accepting each other's positions, a social interlude that includes alcohol can diffuse tension and enable negotiators to recognize areas of agreement. Of course, this same relaxation of boundaries may also produce dangerous ambiguity regarding acceptable behavior. In an era of heightened sensitivity to sexual harassment and political correctness, behavior that seems acceptable in a context containing alcohol may be deemed unacceptable upon the next day's sober reflection. . . .

Hazards of Consuming Alcohol During Negotiations. Drinking can harm the negotiation process in a number of important ways. The link between alcohol and aggressive behavior is well established. Prior work has documented a stable relationship between alcohol use and aggressive, and even violent, behavior. While assertiveness may aid a negotiator in specific circumstances, excessive aggression can escalate a conflict.

A recent experiment investigated the influence of a moderate amount of alcohol on the bargaining process. Negotiators were randomly assigned to either a sober or an inebriated treatment condition. Inebriated negotiators consumed a moderate amount of alcohol to reach a blood alcohol level of about 0.05. This amount of alcohol is well below the legal intoxication limit for driving in all states, and translates to the consumption of about two and a half beers within an hour by a person weighing 180 pounds. Negotiations were tape recorded and independently coded for specific negotiator behaviors. Negotiated outcomes were also measured, and since the negotiation contained opportunities for joint gains, some dyads reached more efficient agreement than others. Inebriated negotiators used significantly more aggressive tactics than sober negotiators. Inebriated negotiators were more likely to insult, mislead, and threaten their negotiation partner. . . . In some cases these tactics can strengthen a negotiator's bargaining position, but there are costs to their use. They may escalate conflict and lead to less integrative outcomes. Alcohol also impairs cognition. This impairment can harm work performance and increase the likelihood that managers will make mistakes. In negotiations, alcohol's influence on cognition may contribute to less integrative outcomes as negotiators miss opportunities for realizing joint gains.

Alcohol reduces the amount of information people can process, impairs short-term memory, and causes decision makers to become myopic. As a result of these disadvantages, inebriated negotiators have difficulty reaching efficient solutions and tend to use simplified strategies for resolving their differences. Results from the alcohol and negotiation experiment revealed that sober dyads were able to reach significantly more efficient agreements than inebriated dyads. Sober dyads were more likely to logroll (trade-off issues of different value) and realize opportunities for joint gains. Sober dyads also reached more efficient agreements than dyads where one sober negotiator was paired with an inebriated negotiator. In these cases, the inebriated negotiators were more aggressive than the sober negotiators and, as expected, the inebriated negotiators claimed a larger share of the smaller pie. That is, sober negotiators did particularly poorly when negotiating against someone who was drinking. These results suggest that managers should take particular care in bargaining with someone who has consumed even a moderate amount of alcohol.

Inebriated negotiators are also more likely to make mistakes. Even moderate amounts of alcohol impair a manager's ability to handle complex situations and solve problems. Inebriated negotiators are likely to perform especially poorly in situations requiring mathematical agility. Inebriated negotiators are more apt to focus on irrelevant information or to miss key components of a problem. Because drinkers must exert greater mental effort to focus on core issues, they are likely to neglect subtle aspects of a negotiation. For example, inebriated negotiators are less likely to grasp the underlying implications of an argument and thus more likely to misinterpret the key concerns of their counterparts. . . .

Studies have also found that alcohol consumption inflates positive self-perceptions. This can lead to overconfidence, especially since inebriated people frequently fail to notice nonverbal cues and negative feedback. In a quote attributed to Elizabeth Johnson, wife of the 18th century lexicographer and essayist Samuel Johnson, "Alcohol does not improve conversation. It only alters the mind so you are more pleased with any conversation." In a negotiation, inebriated managers may perceive that they are more convincing or more agreeable than they really are. Exaggerated self-perceptions may also explain the finding that people are willing to assume greater business risk under the influence of alcohol than they would when sober. . . .

Guarding Against the Strategic Use of Alcohol by a Negotiation Partner. Although alcohol is often not introduced for strategic aims, careful managers should be aware of several negotiation tactics that involve alcohol. One obvious tactic derives from differences in inebriation levels. Individual reactions to alcohol vary considerably, and differences in body weight, age, consumption history, and even genetics make one individual more susceptible than another to alcohol's effects. While many factors affect blood alcohol levels, such as time elapsed since drinking and an individual's metabolism, there is an approximate relationship between the number of drinks consumed, body weight, and blood alcohol level. . . .Task practice will also make a difference. We know from the literature on drunk driving that the driving performance of intoxicated drivers who routinely drive under the influence of alcohol suffers less than the performance of inexperienced drunk drivers. Analogously, negotiating over drinks may confer a relative advantage to negotiators who routinely negotiate over drinks.

Since drinking increases self-disclosure, an inebriated negotiator is more likely to disclose confidential business information or personal problems that provide a negotiating advantage to his or her counterpart. Such revelations are more likely when a negotiator perceives his or her counterpart to be inebriated and therefore equally vulnerable. At times, actual levels of inebriation can be difficult to discern; Japanese, for example, may pretend to be more drunk than they really are. Japanese are also more comfortable with silence. The combination of alcohol, simple questions, and long periods of silence can prompt accidental disclosures by unwary Westerners. As one American executive warns, "Americans are prone to very modestly launch into lectures of valuable technical information — in some cases the very asset which they are hoping to sell."

The psychological effects of alcohol can also lend themselves to manipulation. Under the influence of alcohol, for example, arguments based on emotional appeal may appear more convincing and salient than they would otherwise. Appeals based on nostalgia (old times) or guilt (past favors or perceived wrongs) are likely to have greater impact when the target has been properly prepared. While alcohol's influence on physical and intellectual functioning is well known, its effect on emotional states is generally less recognized. . . .

Although alcohol is often introduced without strategic aims in mind, the fact remains that alcohol's capacity to undermine a manager's negotiating abilities provides his or her counterpart with a tempting opportunity to manipulate the context within which their business is transacted. Managers who negotiate frequently are likely at some point to encounter a situation in which alcohol is used as a tool to obtain information or concessions. Reasonable prudence suggests that managers need to think carefully and realistically about the setting in which negotiations are to take place, the probability that alcoholic beverages will be present and their own tolerance for drinking. Whether the effect is intentional or not, there is no doubt that alcohol can seriously interfere with a manager's ability to achieve his or her objectives.

Chapter 5
TRANS-NATIONAL AND CROSS-CULTURAL PERSPECTIVES

A. INTRODUCTION

This chapter examines trans-national and cross-cultural negotiation. The term culture is used broadly to encompass a set of values, norms, and standard practices commonly (not universally) used by a group. Generalizations about groups are just that — general statements. A pejorative label for such classification is stereotyping. Max Weber used the term "ideal type" (with "ideal" meaning "archetype" rather than expressing a value judgment). Group membership neither defines nor limits a person, but it often provides a convenient way to identify information about a person with whom one interacts. Even if additional information is available, acquisition thereof is costly and may be precluded by time constraints.

If you want to create a business relationship or resolve a problem, it helps to understand the values, background, and aspirations of the party with which you are dealing. This is true whether the parties reside in different countries or different cities. Of course, geography and language are just a few of the many variables that are found in particular subcultures. It has become common in the business world to talk about "corporate culture." Understanding the culture of the business or individual you are working with often is helpful in reaching a desired goal.

Different cultures are found all around us; one need not look to distant lands, or even different racial or ethnic groups. What do most educated adults know about the world of letters of credit (both commercial and standby), bills of lading (both straight and negotiable), holders of security interests (perfected and unperfected), conditions (precedent, concurrent, and subsequent, not to mention those that are precedent in fact but subsequent in form and vice-versa), bulk sales, CIF and FAS terms (acronyms too well known to require explication), the midnight deadline, the battle of the forms, or the perfect tender rule? These are aspects of American commercial culture about which nearly all newly minted college graduates (even most business majors) are blissfully ignorant — much more so than about discrimination against ethnic minorities, the oppression of women, and the beleaguered white male.

We have previously considered a variety of critiques and concerns about private settlement of disputes. In Section B, Richard Delgado raises a different and distinctly more ominous cultural concern about ADR processes, which is that the informality of ADR can provide an environment in which prejudice can thrive, thereby undermining the value and legitimacy of ADR for the poor and minorities. The context of his comments largely is ADR procedures with third party intervention, rather than direct negotiation. [Concerns about the private settlement of disputes with a public dimension are discussed in Chapter Thirteen.] Delgado argues that the public aspect of judicial process provides protection for cultural and economic minorities against bias that can more easily come to the fore in private dispute resolution processes.

By way of juxtaposition to the concerns raised by Delgado, leading ADR scholar Carrie Menkel-Meadow discusses one of the classic law review articles of recent decades: Marc Galanter, *Why the "Haves" Come Out Ahead*. After considering Galanter's explanation and analysis of why "have-nots" do not fare well in the judicial system, Professor Menkel-Meadow then considers whether the same problems are likely to arise in the ADR context.

Section C provides an introduction to the Korean-American harmony restoration process, and compares it to the typical approach taken by an American mediation center. Section D examines business negotiations by Americans overseas. International negotiation is too important to ignore, but far too large a topic for even cursory coverage. Accordingly, discussion is limited to negotiating in a single important country: Japan. Readers will not become experts on Japan, but should get a sense of major differences in negotiating practices from those that are standard in the United States. Some consideration is also given to Japanese firms doing business in this country.

The cross-cultural readings in this Chapter are not designed to make you an expert on harmony restoration among Korean-Americans or negotiation in Japan, although you will learn a good bit about each of these matters. Rather, the purpose is to sensitize you to cultural differences, and to offer some ideas about how to adjust to such differences. While the differences between the examples just cited and ordinary everyday negotiations in familiar surroundings is large, different cultures are all around us.

B. HOW DO MINORITIES AND "HAVE-NOTS" FARE IN ADR?

1. Richard Delgado, Chris Dunn, Pamela Brown, Helena Lee & David Hubbert, *Fairness and Formality: Minimizing the Risk of Prejudice in Alternative Dispute Resolution*, 1985 WIS. L. REV. 1359

Alternative Dispute Resolution (ADR) has been heralded as one of the most vital and far-reaching procedural reforms of our time. Writers have praised this loose collection of deformalized, decentralized procedures — including negotiation, mediation, arbitration, neighborhood justice centers, and consumer complaint panels — as offering speedy, non-intimidating, flexible justice for the common person, the litigant of modest means or one whose claim is so small that it cannot be processed economically in court. . . .

Except for a small group of leftist critics, the movement has few detractors. This Article raises a concern that has seemingly been overlooked in the rush to deformalize — the concern that deformalization may increase the risk of class-based prejudice. ADR has been promoted, in large part, with the rhetoric of egalitarianism. Moreover, it is aimed at serving many groups whose members are particularly vulnerable to prejudice. Thus, if our criticism is correct — if the rhetoric is untrue or if ADR injures some of those it is designed to help — society should proceed cautiously in channeling disputes to alternative mechanisms. . . .

III. THEORIES OF PREJUDICE AND ADR

This part examines theories of prejudice and their relation to ADR. Though based primarily on studies of prejudice among whites toward blacks, many of the findings are also applicable to prejudice against Hispanics, Indians, women, and other groups, as well as inter-ethnic group prejudice. After surveying the leading theories of how prejudice develops and is expressed, we examine prejudice in relation to the "American Creed." According to a leading school of thought, many persons suffer from a "moral dilemma" which arises from a conflict between socially espoused precepts of both equality and humanitarianism, and personal attitudes that are less egalitarian.

The manner in which these conflicts are resolved depends largely on situational factors. Certain settings tend to foster prejudiced behavior, while others tend to discourage it. We apply these findings to the formalism-informalism dichotomy and find that formal dispute resolution is better at deterring prejudice than informal adjudication. A number of theories seek to explain racial or ethnic prejudice. Because of the complexity of the behavior, it seems likely that no one theory can account for all forms of it. Several theories — psychodynamic, social-psychological, and economic — all play a part.

1. Psychodynamic Theories. Psychodynamic theories of prejudice look to personality traits and tendencies to explain why some individuals react with hostility to certain groups. The dynamics of prejudice became a focus of study after World War II as researchers sought to explain the horror of the Holocaust. Since then, theorists have sought to identify cognitive or emotional processes common to prejudiced persons and to determine whether prejudice is part of a larger "syndrome."

In a landmark study, ADORNO, FRENKEL-BRUNSWIK, LEVINSON AND SANFORD, THE AUTHORITATIVE PERSONALITY (1969), identified a personality structure which they believed particularly susceptible to ethnic prejudice. According to the authors, highly prejudiced persons tend to have an "authoritarian personality," characterized by rigidity, conventionality, difficulty in accepting impulses they consider deviant (for example fear, weakness, aggression, and sex) as part of the self, a tendency to externalize these impulses by projecting them on others, and a need for status and power in personal relationships.

According to psychoanalytic theory, the authoritarian personality develops through a process of displaced hostility. Hostility arises when frustrations or deprivations are imposed on an individual by harsh authority figures, such as parents, to whom the individual is closely tied by bonds of affection. The individual represses the hostility he or she feels, directing it not against the source of the frustration, but against a substitute target, or scapegoat — often an individual or group who cannot easily respond.

Experimental studies confirm Adorno's theory. Berkowitz found that highly anti-Semitic college students experienced increased hostility toward other persons when subjected to frustration. Tolerant subjects, by contrast, became friendlier. Prejudiced persons were also more susceptible to frustration than were tolerant persons. For example, in a study of war soldiers, Bettleheim and Janowitz found that prejudiced soldiers were more frustrated than tolerant servicemen, although they served under similar conditions.

Authoritarian personalities are dogmatic and dichotomous; they are unable to differentiate flexibly or change their mental sets. They want definiteness, finality and authority in human relationships and reject groups less familiar and safe than their own. Because ethnic minorities possess characteristics that seem different from those of the dominant group, they become ready targets for rejection and displaced hostility.

Researchers posit two requirements for a group to become a target of displaced hostility — high visibility and little power to retaliate. Many ethnic groups have both characteristics. In addition, groups may become objects of especially intense hostility, if they are in competition with the authoritarian individual or symbolize traits (e.g., nonconformity, irresponsibility, urbanism) which he or she dislikes. Some theorists assert that the differences most disliked by the prejudiced person are those he unconsciously recognizes as potential characteristics of himself. This is particularly true of "sins of the flesh" — lechery, laziness, aggression, and slovenliness — traits prejudiced individuals often ascribe to the Black. Similarly, the sins of pride, deceit, unsocialized egotism, and grasping ambition are often ascribed to the Jew. The traits ascribed to blacks reflect our "id" impulses; the traits ascribed to Jews, violations of our "superego," or conscience. Thus, "our accusations and feelings of revulsion against both groups symbolize our dissatisfaction with the evil in our own nature."

Psychodynamic theory cannot provide a complete explanation for prejudicial attitudes — for example, it cannot explain selective prejudice against one ethnic group rather than another. Although personality attributes may determine susceptibility, a full understanding of prejudice also requires a historical and sociocultural analysis.

2. Historical Approaches: Socioeconomic and Political Causes of Prejudice. Many historians insist that one must have in mind the experiences of oppressed groups in this country in order to understand the causes of prejudice in the United States. . . . Psychological studies are enlightening only within narrow limits. For personality is itself conditioned by social forces; in the last analysis, the search for understanding must reach into the broad social context within which personality is shaped. Just as persons, with their particular desires and ambitions make history, so too history makes people.

Some writers in the sociohistorical school see racism as a means by which society purifies itself of rage, anxiety, and guilt resulting from rapid social change and economic disruption. Like members of the psychodynamic school, these writers use the concept of a scapegoat to explain the operation of prejudice, although the scapegoat serves slightly different functions for each school. For members of the sociohistorical school, the driving force behind racism is social and economic dislocation, which generates widespread anxiety. This anxiety causes a search for victims on whom the anxiety can be discharged. These scapegoats — often members of minority groups — are assigned traits of personal inadequacy to defend the prevailing belief that the American system is fair and just. Scapegoating also channels aggression into acceptable directions and insures social loyalty.

Scapegoating of racial minorities is especially easy, because many of them are visibly poor. Black Americans were originally owned as property, and even after slavery disappeared, a caste system remained. Their oppressed status and resulting poverty, in turn, confirmed the beliefs of some whites that blacks are inferior. Class prejudice becomes a proxy for race prejudice: "Some white people do not like blacks, not because of racial differences, but because they are poor."

Some blacks manage to escape poverty, however, and many try. Upward mobility, an ideal enshrined in the American ethic, leads to economic competition. A group of scholars within the historical school considers this competition to be a key source of prejudice. They point out that as blacks and other groups have demanded a larger share of the good life, the dominant majority has reacted with hostility. For example, northern whites' enthusiasm for civil rights decreased markedly when the movement moved north. The threat of competition causes greatest alarm to members of society who live in fear of a downward slide. Studies have shown that persons dissatisfied with their jobs (one indicator of downward mobility) were more prone to prejudice than those secure in their jobs. In the United States, it is principally members of the most favored economic groups who can afford to fight vigorously for equality, since others are threatened by it.

3. Social-Psychological Theories of Prejudice. A final approach to prejudice emphasizes social-psychological factors, especially the role of group influence and socialization. . . . For most social psychologists, there are no innate antipathies toward the members of different social, national, religious, or other groups. Rather, we learn whom to dislike, just as we learn other group values. Prejudiced attitudes generally emerge in early childhood as the child develops an awareness of skin color and its social significance. A study by Goodman of black and white nursery school children found well developed awareness of racial characteristics and the social implications of racial membership in children as young as three. As they become older, "children shift from describing themselves . . . and the people around them by reference to their own names or names of specific individuals to the use of ethnic designations." The level of prejudice stabilized when the children reached late adolescence and rarely changed after that.

Children acquired attitudes toward different groups by observing the behavior and attitudes of persons around them, particularly parents. Some of the learning is coercive; it is made plain to the children that they were expected to adopt the attitudes and designations of members of their group. The pressures toward conformity, although often subtle, are very real, especially if the individual deviates from the established ethnic norms of his own group. Once acquired, prejudiced attitudes tend to persist: "Realistic threats may come and go, but the solid core of prejudice remains, no matter how anachronistic it may become."

Many social-psychological theorists explain this persistence in terms of in-group/out-group categories. Humans have a natural propensity to categorize arising from the general need to organize and simplify experience. "A million events befall us every day. We cannot handle so many events. If we think of them at all, we type them . . . we cannot handle each event freshly in its own right." Some of the categories are rational — they have a close and immediate tie to first-hand experience. But irrational categories may also be formed through error, the need to oversimplify experience, or social pressures. Thereafter, these categorizations assume a life of their own: "What enables people to reject members of other races is the supportive (unconscious and automatic) bias elicited by categorization."

Ethnic categories not only simplify experience; they satisfy a basic psychological need by strengthening ties of group membership. At an early age, children are capable of understanding that they are members of various groups, including family, neighborhood, religion, and race. All such groups have "characteristic codes and beliefs, standards and 'enemies' to suit their own adaptive needs," and apply continual pressure to insure that their members adopt them. Loyalties to the in-group are often accompanied by dislike of out-groups. Dislike is accommodated by barriers to communication and by oversimplified, undifferentiated categorizations according to which all members of the out-group are the same. Thus, factors that cause individuals to form prejudiced attitudes are functionally related to an individual's membership in a group — "to adopting the group and its values (norms) as the main anchorage in regulating experience and behavior."

Authorities disagree on what characteristics of racial minorities cause them to be seen as out-groups. Some believe it is skin color and other physical differences. Others assert that prejudice is based less on physical characteristics than on lack of belief congruence — by the view that the beliefs and values of members of other races are inconsistent with one's own. Members of this latter school assume that most people will accept minorities who hold beliefs similar to their own and argue that prejudice can be reduced by simply showing, through contact, that most minorities do so. The manner in which this "social contact" theory can be used to promote fairness in dispute resolution is discussed later. At this point, however, it is worth noting that social contact theorists do not assert that all social contact reduces prejudice; the nature and quality of the contact are also important. For Allport, the type of contact that best dispels prejudice is "equal status contact . . . in the pursuit of common goals." Moreover, the effect is greatly enhanced if this contact is sanctioned by institutional supports (i.e., by law, custom or local atmosphere), and if it is of a sort that leads to the perception of common interests and common humanity. . . .

B. The American Ideal — An Ideal Imperfectly Realized

As we have seen, many factors — personal dynamics, scapegoating, economic dislocation, power disparities, socialization, and in-group/out-group cognitive categories — contribute to the development of prejudice. Their effect is widely felt — many Americans harbor some degree of prejudiced attitudes, values, and behavior. Many individuals harbor some degree of prejudice, but the expression of that prejudice is called up and magnified by features in the environment. However, running parallel, but in stark contrast to these attitudes are the public values of equality and humanitarianism known as the "American Creed." [This term was coined by Gunnar Myrdal.] . . .

American culture has been described as highly concerned with fair and ethical treatment of all human beings. The American Creed emphasizes liberty, equality, and human worth — values that arise from the basic tenets of democratic and Judeo-Christian teachings. The Creed represents a collective national conscience, commanding high respect; according to Myrdal, "no other norm could compete in authority over people's minds." The authority of the Creed is reinforced by the Constitution and maintained by institutional structures, such as churches, schools, and courts. Although these institutions also accommodate local interests and prejudices, they direct individuals to show more fairness and justice than many would otherwise be inclined to display.

The contradiction between the principles of the American Creed and the reality of class and race-based prejudice exists on a societal level, where it affects the behavior of groups and institutions. This contradiction also exists in the consciences of particular individuals, so that the average American experiences moral uneasiness and individual and collective guilt. Allport demonstrated this conflict in a well-known study in which college students were asked to write about their experiences with members of minority groups. Only about 10% of the students who admitted experiencing prejudice did so without expressing feelings of guilt or conflict. Behavior became a series of difficult-to-predict moral and prudential compromises. While some students rejected prejudice on an intellectual plane, it lingered on an emotional level and shaped behavior. A typical response in Allport's college essay study was as follows: "Although prejudice is unethical, I know I shall always have prejudices. I believe in goodwill toward the Negro, but I shall never invite him to my house for dinner. Yes, I know I'm a hypocrite."

C. Resolution of the Conflict

Persons afflicted by prejudice resolve this inner conflict in different ways. According to a leading theorist, the main methods are: (1) repression (denial); (2) defense (rationalization); (3) compromise (partial resolution); and (4) integration (true resolution). Repression denies that a problem exists in order to avoid the turmoil of inner conflict. Most persons do not want to be at odds with their consciences. Thus, they react by denying the existence of their prejudices or by citing nonracial explanations. An employer, for example, might explain the failure to hire a black worker by saying the worker dressed peculiarly.

Another straightforward way of resolving one's prejudices is to disparage the victim; a form of rationalization. Devaluing the target of prejudice decreases moral discomfort — if the victim receives shoddy treatment, that is what he or she deserves. Prejudice may also be rationalized by selectively perceiving or interpreting reality. For example, whites may rationalize their opposition to integration by stating that black children would be frustrated in academic competition with whites.

A larger group of persons "attempt to conceal the conflict between their different valuations of what is desirable and undesirable, right or wrong, by keeping away some valuations from awareness and focusing attention on others." This concealment results in ambivalence, a tendency to hold extremely positive (i.e., friendly, accepting, sympathetic) as well as extremely negative (i.e., rejecting, denigrating, hostile) attitudes toward certain ethnic groups. In the U.S., where prejudicial attitudes conflict with a humane creed, many resolve this conflict by varying the expression of these beliefs to conform to particular circumstances, a response known as "situational specificity." Ambivalence and situational specificity explain why many persons behave in egalitarian ways in some situations and in discriminatory ways in others. An example of a situationally determined reaction is when an individual uses racial slurs within his or her own home or other intimate setting, but avoids using that same language in a public forum.

Finally, a few individuals resolve their inner conflicts by effectively ridding themselves of prejudice. These persons "face the whole issue and get it settled so that their daily conduct will be under the dominance of a wholly consistent philosophy of human relationships." . . .

E. The Optimal Setting for Reduction of Prejudice: Formal vs. Informal Dispute Resolution

With the etiology of prejudice in mind, we now turn to theories of how to reduce prejudice, and we apply those theories to the problem of minimizing prejudice in dispute resolution. . . . The selection of one mode or another of dispute resolution can do little, at least in the short run, to counter prejudice that stems from authoritarian personalities or historical currents. Prejudice that results from social-psychological factors is, however, relatively controllable. Much prejudice is environmental — people express it because the setting encourages or tolerates it. In some settings, people feel free to vent hostile or denigrating attitudes toward members of minority groups; in others, they do not.

Our review of social-psychological theories of prejudice indicates that prejudiced persons are least likely to act on their beliefs if the immediate environment confronts them with the discrepancy between their professed ideals and their personal hostilities against out-groups. According to social psychologists, once most persons realize that their attitudes and behavior deviate from what is expected, they will change or suppress them.

Given this human tendency to conform, American institutions have structured and defined situations to encourage appropriate behavior. Our judicial system, in particular, has incorporated societal norms of fairness and even-handedness into institutional expectations and rules of procedure at many points. These norms create a "public conscience and a standard for expected behavior that check overt signs of prejudice." They do this in a variety of ways. First, the formalities of a court trial — the flag, the black robes, the ritual — remind those present that the occasion calls for the higher, "public" values, rather than the lesser values embraced during moments of informality and intimacy. In a courtroom trial, the American Creed, with its emphasis on fairness, equality, and respect for personhood, governs. Equality of status, or something approaching it, is preserved — each party is represented by an attorney and has a prescribed time and manner for speaking, putting on evidence, and questioning the other side. Equally important, formal adjudication avoids the unstructured, intimate interactions that, according to social scientists, foster prejudice. The rules of procedure maintain distance between the parties. Counsel for the parties do not address one another, but present the issue to the trier of fact. The rules preserve the formality of the setting by dictating in detail how this confrontation is to be conducted. . . . Formality and adversarial procedures thus counteract bias among legal decision makers and disputants. But it seems likely that those factors increase fairness in yet a third way — by strengthening the resolve of minority disputants to pursue their legal rights.

F. Dispute Resolution and the Minority Disputant

Early in life, minority children become aware of themselves as different, especially with respect to skin color. This awareness is often not merely neutral, but associated with feelings of inferiority. Separate studies by psychologists Kenneth Clark and Mary Goodman in which minority children were presented with dolls of various colors illustrate this graphically. For example, when asked to make a choice between a white and black doll, "the doll that looks like you," most black children chose the white doll. A black child justified his choice of the white doll over the black doll as a friend because "his feet, hands, ears, elbows, knees, and hair are clean." In another experiment, a black child hated her skin color so much that she "vigorously lathered her arms and face with soap in an effort to wash away the dirt." As minority children grow, they are "likely to experience a long series of events, from exclusion from play groups and cliques to violence and threats of violence, that are far less likely to be experienced by the average member of the majority group." Against a background of "slights, rebuffs, forbidden opportunities, restraints, and often violence . . . the minority group member shapes that fundamental aspect of personality — a sense of oneself and one's place in the total scheme of things."

Discriminatory treatment can trigger a variety of responses. Writers identify three main reactions: avoidance, aggression, and acceptance. A minority group member may display one or more of these responses, depending on the setting. In some situations, victims of discrimination are likely to respond with apathy or defeatism; in others, the same individuals may forthrightly and effectively assert their interests. In general, when a person feels "he is the master of his fate, that he can control to some extent his own destiny, that if he works hard things will go better for him, he is then likely to achieve more. . . ." That is, minority group members are more apt to participate in processes which they believe will respond to reasonable efforts. They are understandably less likely to participate in proceedings where the results are random and unpredictable.

Thus, it is not surprising that a favored forum for redress of race-based wrongs has been the traditional adjudicatory setting. Minorities recognize that public institutions, with their defined rules and formal structure, are more subject to rational control than private or informal structures. Informal settings allow wider scope for the participants' emotional and behavioral idiosyncrasies; in these settings, majority group members are most likely to exhibit prejudicial behavior. Thus, a formal adjudicative forum increases the minority group member's sense of control and, therefore, may be seen as the fairer forum. This perception becomes self-fulfilling: minority persons are encouraged to pursue their legal rights as though prejudice were unlikely, and thus, the possibility of prejudice is in fact lessened. . . .

V. PREJUDICE IN ADR — ASSESSING AND BALANCING THE RISKS

ADR increases the risk of prejudice toward vulnerable disputants. Our review of social science writings on prejudice reveals that the rules and structures of formal justice tend to suppress bias, whereas informality tends to increase it. The social science findings are reinforced, on a sociopolitical level, by ADR's left-wing critics, who see ADR as increasing the power of authoritarian social institutions over individuals, extending state coercive power into new areas of citizens' lives, and discouraging collective action.

This Part assumes that the social-science and left-wing critiques are at least partly valid — that ADR does indeed increase the risk of unfair treatment for minority disputants, women and the poor. From this, it proceeds to address two final questions: (i) How much weight should be assigned to such a risk? and (ii) Can the risk be minimized without forfeiting the benefits and advantages of ADR?

If ADR increases the risk of prejudice or bias in adjudication, it does not follow immediately that ADR should be curtailed. Equity concerns are only one value among many; conceivably, the gains in flexibility, speed, and economy that ADR's proponents cite could override moderate losses in fairness. A survey of the role of the ideal of fairness in American procedural law suggests, however, that the balance should be struck on the side of fairness.

American procedural law's history evidences a strong and steady evolution toward fairness, an evolution that has at times overshadowed the impulse toward economy and efficiency. Over a century ago, the Field code simplified pleading rules, largely to eliminate traps for the unwary and to render legal paper work intelligible to ordinary persons. The great procedural reforms of this century, civil discovery and long-arm jurisdiction, were likewise intended to equalize power and opportunity among litigants. Discovery enables litigants of modest means to learn facts about the dispute that might otherwise remain in the exclusive possession of the more powerful party. Long-arm jurisdiction enables citizens injured by corporations and other powerful entities to bring them to account where the injury occurred, instead of being forced to sue where the defendant is found.

Civil and criminal reforms have made access to court cheaper and more readily available to all. Public defenders and legal aid attorneys represent individuals who cannot afford the costs of a private lawyer. Transcripts on appeal in some cases have been held a defendant's constitutional right. A panoply of rules and procedures, reviewed earlier, have developed to assure fairness, despite the added costs they impose. Many of these are minor, such as the rule permitting modification of time rules for good cause. Others are broader, cutting across areas and stages of litigation, such as the requirement of trial by jury. Although efficiency and fairness are often in tension, our jurisprudence regards fairness in litigation as an important ideal not to be discarded lightly — and certainly not in broadbased, systemic fashion. The next section addresses the question of how best to preserve that value in informal proceedings without sacrificing the benefits of informality.

ADR offers a number of clear-cut benefits. It can shape a decree flexibly so as to protect a continuing relationship between the parties. It is low-cost, speedy, and, for some at least, not intimidating. Yet there is little benefit for a minority disputant in a quick, painless hearing that renders an adverse decision tainted by prejudice.

Part III showed that the risk of prejudice is greatest when a member of an in-group confronts a member of an out-group; when that confrontation is direct, rather than through intermediaries; when there are few rules to constrain conduct; when the setting is closed and does not make clear that "public" values are to preponderate; and when the controversy concerns an intimate, personal matter rather than some impersonal question. Our review also indicated that many minority participants will press their claims most vigorously when they believe that what they do and say will make a difference, that the structure will respond, and that the outcome is predictable and related to effort and merit.

It follows that ADR is most apt to incorporate prejudice when a person of low status and power confronts a person or institution of high status and power. In such situations, the party of high status is more likely than in other situations to attempt to call up prejudiced responses; at the same time, the individual of low status is less likely to press his or her claim energetically. The dangers increase when the mediator or other third party is a member of the superior group or class. Examples of ADR settings that may contain these characteristics are prison and other institutional review boards, consumer complaint panels, and certain types of cases referred to an ombudsman. In these situations, minorities and members of other out-groups should opt for formal in-court adjudication, and the justice system ought to avoid pressuring them to accept an alternate procedure. ADR should be reserved for cases in which parties of comparable power and status confront each other.

ADR also poses heightened risks of prejudice when the issue to be adjudicated touches a sensitive or intimate area of life, for example, housing or culture-based conduct. Thus, many landlord-tenant, inter-neighbor, and intra familial disputes are poor candidates for ADR. When the parties are of unequal status, and the question litigated concerns a sensitive, intimate area, the risks of an outcome colored by prejudice are especially great. If, for reasons of economy or efficiency, ADR must be resorted to in these situations, the likelihood of bias can be reduced by providing rules that clearly specify the scope of the proceedings and forbid irrelevant or intrusive inquiries, by requiring open proceedings, and by providing some form of higher review. The third-party facilitator or decision maker should be a professional and be acceptable to both parties. Any party desiring one should be provided with an advocate, ideally an attorney, experienced with representation before the forum in question. To avoid atomization and lost opportunities to aggregate claims and inject public values into dispute resolution, ADR mechanisms should not be used in cases that have a broad societal dimension, but forward them to court for appropriate treatment.

Would measures like these destroy the very advantages of economy, simplicity, speed, and flexibility that make ADR attractive? Would such measures render ADR proceedings as expensive, time-consuming, formalistic, and inflexible as trials? These measures do increase the costs, but on balance, those costs seem worth incurring. The ideal of equality before the law is too insistent a value to be compromised in the name of more mundane advantages. Continued growth of ADR, consistent with goals of basic fairness, will require two essential adjustments: (1) It will be necessary to identify those areas and types of ADR in which the dangers of prejudice are greatest and to direct those grievances to formal court adjudication; (2) In those areas in which the risk of prejudice exists, but is not so great as to require an absolute ban, checks and formalities must be built into ADR to ameliorate these risks as much as possible. With both inquiries, the preliminary investigations and tentative identifications of troublesome areas made in this Article may prove useful starting points.

2. Carrie Menkel-Meadow, *Do the "Haves" Come Out Ahead in Alternative Judicial Systems? Repeat Players in ADR*, 15 OHIO ST. J. ON DISP. RESOL. 19 (1999)

Marc Galanter's essay, *Why the "Haves" Come Out Ahead: Speculations on the Limits of Legal Change*, 9 Law & SOC'Y REV. 95 (1974), set an important agenda for those who care about the distributive effects of legal processes. . . . A seminal work in the socio-legal studies canon, Galanter's article demonstrates the complex patterns of how law and legal institutions actually work, beyond descriptions of legal doctrines and assumed efficacy and "penetration" of law. In some senses, it is a continuation of legal realism, reminding us of the importance of studying the legal institutions in which the law is embedded and suggesting . . . how we might reform or "adjust" those institutions to produce optimal social change (in this case, redistribution of resources and delivery of justice).

Yet, it is also . . . one of the significant pieces of work associated with critical legal studies, for it provides the theoretical analysis for operationalization and empirical testing of the proposition that "the basic architecture of the legal system creates and limits the possibilities of using the system as a means of redistributive (that is, systemically equalizing) change." In this, the piece recognizes the limits of law, legal institutions, and perhaps of rights strategies, so essential to much of the critical scholarship on the legal system written in the 1970s and 1980s.

In this landscape-shaping work, Galanter reminds us that legal institutions and social change are structurally marked. The components of the legal system, parties, lawyers, institutions, rules, and alternatives to the official system, in their social, economic, and political variations and interactions, shape the outputs of courts, litigation, and disputes. Galanter criticizes the political dysfunction of a system that allows certain advantaged participants (the "repeat players") to maximize their long-term gains over those "one-shotters" who may seek justice, but participate with fewer resources. Galanter thus uses a sociology of law to uncover the "myths" or fictions of a faith in law, doctrine, and legal institutions that appear to promote "equal justice" but, in reality, deliver power instead. Law, embedded in society, produces not universalistic truths but variable outcomes that are effected by the endowments of the players who are, in turn, embedded in social structures that shape and transcend what law itself can do.

The intellectual problem that Galanter set for himself was to consider, sociologically, "under what conditions can litigation be redistributive?," implicitly assuming, of course, that redistribution (or equalization) efforts in the system are normatively desirable. Within the frame of a social scientific perspective, Galanter began his piece with a series of propositions-hypotheses about how the constituent elements of a legal system produce outputs (rules, adjudications, and enforcements) that may be less than optimal for those seeking such normatively desirable ends (of redistribution).

Aside from Galanter's many astute observations about the patterning of the legal system and its players, his article is prescient in its acknowledgment of "court-like agencies" and "alternatives to the official system" that will comprise this Article's basic concern — why the "Haves" are still coming out ahead in current alternatives to the official systems of adjudication. The continued relevance of *Why the "Haves" Come Out Ahead* in a time of somewhat diminished interest in litigation is evidenced by Galanter's own recognition that not all cases would make it to high-level or "peak" institutions. Thus, even twenty-five years ago, Galanter recognized that much law would be made, developed, and enforced either in "field level" agencies or in "alternatives to official systems" such as those which were "appended" to formal institutions (e.g., routine case processing, plea bargaining, court-oriented settlement, and even negotiation between the parties) or those which were "private remedy systems" (religious courts, arbitration tribunals, institutional grievance mechanisms, ombuds, mediation, conciliation, trade associations, unions, complaint bureaus, and even public opinion).

While the bulk of *Why the "Haves" Come Out Ahead* is devoted to resource mobilization and advantage of certain parties in litigation, the end of the piece traces the effects of "Haves" advantage in these less official arenas and thus, is most timely for revisiting in this era of increased use of "alternatives to official systems," or as it is currently termed, ADR. . . . Galanter accurately notes that what processes parties might use for their disputes, conflicts, and transactions would depend on the "density" of their relationships — that is, how often they interacted with each other. He predicted that parties who often interact with each other (repeat players with repeat players) would be less likely to use the official litigation system and would be more likely to employ the less official systems of private remedies. Thus, it is particularly useful for us now to look at how repeat players and one-shotters are faring in environments of increased use of less "official" dispute resolution systems.

II. THE ARGUMENT AND SOME TERMS OF DEFINITION

Galanter's basic argument in *Why the "Haves" Come Out Ahead* was that certain classes of litigants (repeat players) are more able to mobilize legal and other resources to maximize long-term gain in litigation (formal adjudication of disputes in courts). Galanter began by decomposing the constituent elements of litigation into parties (divided into repeat players or one-shotters), lawyers, institutions (different layers of courts and court-like agencies), and rules and alternatives. He then theorized that, in most cases, repeat players could use the litigation system to their advantage and, to successfully repel serious efforts to use the courts for legal rule change, to achieve power and economic equalization or social redistributive effects. With many cases in the system, repeat players have low stakes in any one case and thus can maximize long-term gain by resisting settlements, developing advance intelligence, and being able to plan for future engagement. Further, repeat players can cultivate a "bargaining or litigation reputation" to accomplish particular goals or simply to develop trust and legitimacy with court personnel, developing long-term relationships with institutional incumbents, by participating actively in procedural as well as substantive rule construction and adoption. Thus, winning any one case may not matter as much as being a player in the system who can manipulate rules, decision makers, and court personnel to deliver, over the long-term, optimal and reliable outcomes. Lawyers, as representatives of some repeat players, likewise develop substantive expertise; their knowledge of institutional incumbents, reliable business-getting strategies, and reputations allow them to serve as brokers or gatekeepers to the larger system.

Institutions, such as overloaded courts, also serve to advantage repeat players, because with the deflection of cases away from full scale litigation, currently existing rules will be less likely to be challenged, and knowledge of the system will add to the bargaining endowments that occur in the shadow of the law and courts. With large case loads and great delay, Galanter posited, powerful repeat players (especially when defending against plaintiffs seeking rule changes) will benefit from a lack of rulings and the inability of one-shotters to enforce or monitor rule changes. Possessors (landlords, creditors, and employers) will be more likely to be able to hold on to what they have when the system works slowly. In an ironic twist, Galanter suggested that the more process there is (remember, this was written at the time of the procedural due process revolution), the more delay and status quo protection there will be for the "possessors" (the "Haves"). Given the expense of mobilizing lawyers who know and can use the system and its rules, the one-shot litigant, especially one who seeks to challenge the status quo, will often, but not always, be overwhelmed and unsuccessful. Thus, rule change for the one-shot "Have-not" will be expensive, incremental, and largely symbolic. In Galanter's words, "litigation then is unlikely to shape decisively the distribution of power in society."

In the final portion of his paper, Galanter urged social structural changes so that litigation could be made more effective; thus, he did not abandon litigation as a site of social change activity. He sought instead to offer reforms to alter power relations between the parties. He suggested that one-shotters need to become more like repeat players. For this, he offered a variety of suggestions which have been utilized in the last twenty-five years, particularly by those who seek social change through law. Class actions and aggregations of claimants can make some one-shotters more like repeat players, as can organizational client groups and organizational litigation strategies (like those of the NAACP, Inc. Fund) which also focus on long-term gain, perhaps sometimes sacrificing an individual case. Use of repeat player lawyers (such as legal services lawyers and other public interest or cause lawyers committed to particular social change objectives and not just to professional roles) to bring well-planned and strategized test cases are all ways of converting one-shotters into repeat players in the system. To the extent that such strategies were successful, Galanter reminded us of the resistance to such equalization of power. In defense of then Governor Ronald Reagan's veto of the California Rural Legal Assistance (CRLA) program, the head of the California Office of Economic Opportunity's legal services program said, "[w]hat we created in CRLA is an economic leverage equal to that of a large corporation. Clearly that should not be." Such lawyer leverage was successful in both substantive and procedural rule changes, notably, for example, with respect to attorneys fees statutes and the "due process revolution," as well as in consumer rights, civil rights, and employment discrimination cases.

On the other hand, Galanter's focus on changing the social structure of litigation to maximize its effects for rule change was missing one very important component — politics. By calling for increased mobilization of legal resources to turn one-shotters into repeat players, Galanter assumed that courts and official decision makers would be responsive to substantive equalization goals. This has proved to be less than true, even with all of the successful public interest and other class mobilization of repeat, but "Have-not," claimants. . . . To the extent that Galanter's repeat player advice has worked for "Have-nots," it has been most successfully deployed by personal injury plaintiffs' lawyers who, in some cases, have moved rapidly from trying difficult-to-prove cases to maintaining hugely successful mass tort practices. This has converted the lawyers, if not the clients, into very successful repeat players.

Galanter's analysis also suggested that, as interaction increases between repeat players themselves, there will be increased privatization, decentralization, and legal pluralism, and less public norm enforcement. In this, he was prescient as well, because so many repeat player interactions, even pre-dispute, have been converted to more informal, bilateral forms of dispute resolution in the pluralistic, particularistic, and decentralized forms of ADR that are so common now. . . . [W]ith increased use of both public and private dispute resolution processes, and with increased public imprimaturs applied to private disputing forms, the question of whether the "Haves" come out ahead in ADR is manifest. . . . Recent efforts to consider fairness, justice, and redistributive standards in ADR have attempted to confront questions regarding who are repeat players in ADR and what difference repeat playing makes for the individuals involved, as well as for the larger justice system.

Note the many ways in which there may be repeat players in the use of alternative justice systems. The corporation, employer, health care provider, bank, educational institution, securities broker, or other repeat play institution using a clause in a form contract to provide or offer services and requiring as a condition of service, employment, or sale of product that the customer, consumer, employee, or client submit to mandatory arbitration or other dispute resolution is a repeat player, in choice of forum as well as form, with implications for choice of law, convenience, cost, and stake in litigation. These clauses often eliminate choices with respect to decision maker, rules of evidence and procedure, or substantive law to be applied. They also set limits on appeals, define the standard of review to be applied if there is an appeal, and determine whether or not there will even be a written decision elaborating the reasons or basis for a decision (in arbitration).

To the extent that ADR systems designers are hired specifically to institutionalize forms of disputing in labor relations, corporations, hospitals, government agencies, universities, and the like, individuals contracting with large organizations will have virtually no ability to choose, let alone to mobilize legal or other resources needed to defend, as well as claim, in certain contexts. The obvious placement of such cases in Galanter's Type II or III — RP (repeat player) vs. OS (one-shotter) or OS vs. RP — makes clear the various advantages that will flow to the repeat player who controls virtually all aspects of the disputing process.

Even in mid-dispute or post-dispute use of ADR, some of the same effects may occur. Repeat players such as large corporations, who expect repetitive litigation, may not be able to contract in advance for a particular form of dispute resolution in all cases, but once a case is ripe or is filed, they may be able to control some aspects of the disputing process. For example, one large law firm which specializes in employment cases uses the same ADR firm repeatedly to mediate its cases when it is able to persuade employment claimants to use "voluntary" mediation. Thus, some disputants may be repeat players in the use and choice of particular third party neutrals, who may, in turn, have repeat play expertise, either in substance or with respect to the parties (mediators, arbitrators, private judges, or evaluators) or particular processes (some repeat players prefer the finality of decisions in arbitration and others prefer the flexibility of mediation). In some cases, as in labor-management arbitrations, where collective bargaining has institutionalized the selection processes to include partisan arbitrators in repeat play labor contract grievances, the disputes may fall more fairly into Box IV of Galanter's taxonomy (RP vs. RP).

Third party neutrals may themselves become repeat players, either through specification in predispute contracts or assignment to court rosters, or by developing specialized expertise. It is common in some areas of law, for example, for the parties to seek "wise elders" who understand the substance of the dispute or the community in which it is embedded, such as in intellectual property cases. Lawsuits already have (thus far unsuccessfully) challenged the bias of presumed repeat players who are thought to represent the repeat player interest of securities brokers or the securities industry or who are too homogeneous demographically and not sufficiently representative of the claimants. And, courts may select repeat players by maintenance of court rosters of mediators and arbitrators or by selection of mediators or arbitrators during litigation. Disputants also may choose from private rosters of repeat play third party neutrals when they turn to the lists of such organizations as the American Arbitration Association (AAA), the Center for Public Resources (CPR), the National Academy of Arbitrators (NAA), Resolve, JAMS-Endispute, or . . . lists maintained by government agencies, often "sorted" for subject matter expertise.

Finally, the lawyers themselves who routinely appear in ADR proceedings may be repeat players in all of the ways originally documented by Galanter. Just as repeat play plea bargainers may bargain away the cases of their individual clients for long-term credibility or long-term goals, union lawyers, repeat play lawyers in mass torts hearings, and repeat play representatives in ongoing ADR proceedings may enable repeat play "Have" disputants to get their way — not only in system design of the whole process, but in the concrete results achieved in each case. Increasingly, lawyers and law firms are seeking training in "mediation advocacy" to enable them to learn how to "win in ADR."

To the extent that many forms of ADR do not permit class actions, reasoned or even written opinions, punitive damages, or other remedial possibilities, the very individuation of claims in ADR processing potentially eliminates all of the reforms suggested by Galanter to counter the advantages of repeat players against the "Have-not" one-shotter. So what is the currently existing evidence of dangers to justice or other equalization goals in the use of ADR by repeat players? And, what is the possibility of reform if what Galanter suggested is not feasible?

III. DO THE "HAVES" OF ADR DO BETTER?

With the increased use of ADR for a variety of different reasons, one of the greatest ironies of the "movement" for better disputing has been its recent adoption as a "mandatory" process in both private, contractual contexts (usually involving mandatory predispute arbitration clauses) as well as in-court referrals to ADR in the public sector (either through some mandatory assignment or in "optional" application of ADR menus or choices). To the extent that courts, employers, banks, health care providers, the securities industry, franchisors, manufacturers, and now even educational institutions are insisting on mandatory arbitration clauses in their contracts and relationships with customers, clients, and patients, it must be that such repeat players who deal with large volumes of customers and clients believe there is some advantage to insisting on such processes. To date, there has been little empirical testing of whether such mandatory ADR processes in fact redound to the benefit of repeat players, but it is quite clear that representatives of consumers, patients, employees, and other individual claimants clearly believe that such mandated processes are problematic. . . .

As "Haves" increasingly push the "Have-nots" into privatized justice systems, what will be left in the courts? Will Galanter's study of the "Haves" and "Have-nots" in litigation simply be of historical interest as employees, consumers, students, patients, investors, and all potential litigants are pushed into private arbitration systems? Even when such parties perceive themselves

as injured and try to litigate, they will find they are increasingly being channeled into various ADR proceedings within the courts themselves. . . . Though
there are differences of views within the judiciary, as well as the bar, about the
advantages and disadvantages of adding ADR to more traditional court functions, we still do not have good data on outcome differences or usage patterns
of ADR with which to evaluate the strident claims made about ADR in the
courts. More importantly, we do not really know how the availability of ADR in
courts (and in the private sector) affects choices about claiming behavior —
whether more will claim in the first place (the increased "access" argument) or
whether the choice of how or where to claim will change (whether claimants will
resist ADR and pursue litigation, pursue both, or whether more litigants are
"lumping it" after "losing" in ADR).

IV. DO THE "HAVES" COME OUT AHEAD? WHAT
WE NEED TO KNOW

We have little empirical verification of the claims made both for and against
arbitration and ADR, including positive assertions made about reduced cost,
speed, and access to dispute mechanisms, as we really do not have much data
about whether one-shotters . . . do worse in institutionally established ADR. . . .
More problematically, we know even less about a wide variety of private uses of
ADR, both within organizations and in the millions of private disputes that use
some form of ADR, with or without contracts. We are beginning to see some
important studies of micro-behavior within some private forms of ADR, like
mediation, which demonstrate some concerns about other kinds of "power
imbalances" within ADR, including linguistic, race, class, and gender endowments, that may empower some other forms of "Haves" over "Have-nots," but
this research has just begun and often suggests more questions than it provides
clear answers.

So, what do we need to know? [What are the] patterns of outcomes in relation
to particular processes? Do claimants do better or worse (as a percentage of what
they demand) in arbitration or mediation than in other fora? Do they claim
more often? Less often? Does it make a difference if they are represented or not?
By a lawyer or nonlawyer? How do we measure outcomes if nonmonetary solutions (like job transfers, promotions, new or exchanged products) are achieved?
Do different processes have varying impacts on outcomes? Do repeat players
have the same advantages in mediation as they might have in arbitration?
What is gained by the use of particular processes? For example, the repeat
player mediator or arbitrator who is expert in a particular field (like discrimination law) actually may provide not only "better" quality resolutions, but more
efficient and claimant-sensitive services. These measurement questions are
not new, but remain problematic for operationalization of studies about ADR.
What are the "newer" problems associated with repeat play providers? Conflicts
of interests, monopolization of services, quality control, barriers to entry in
the field? Privatization and accountability?

[W]e think we know that the "Haves" come out ahead in ADR, as they do in
litigation, but they may come out ahead in different ways or for different reasons. Therefore, . . . it behooves the legal and social empiricists and reformers
among us to collect the data we need so we can be more certain that the solu-

tions we suggest will solve the problems that actually exist and not the ones we simply think exist. If the "Haves" come out ahead in both litigation and ADR, then where will we go next to achieve social justice in disputing?

3. Comments and Questions

a. Do you believe, as Professor Delgado asserts, that "the adversary system introduces a systematic evidentiary bias in favor of the weaker party"? Note that Delgado does not simply argue the clearly true proposition that the legal system sometimes favors the weak, but that the adversary system introduces a "systematic bias" in favor of weaker parties. What sort of evidence, either current or historical, might be raised to support Delgado's assertion?

b. Professor Menkel-Meadow has dubbed this position "litigation romanticism," and asks this question: How often has the "little consumer" really had an empowering democratic encounter in a courtroom with one of the three major car companies? Carrie Menkel-Meadow, *The Many Ways of Mediation: The Transformation of Traditions, Ideologies, Paradigms, and Practices*, 1995 NEGOT. J. 217, 233. Are there good answers to her question? There is considerable evidence that the "game" of litigation is a "lose-lose" situation, compared to negotiated settlements.

c. Suppose Delgado's views about prejudice in ADR are substantially correct. What then? What does Delgado suggest? What do you think? Even if ADR was suboptimal for minorities, it would not follow that they would be better off in judicial proceedings.

d. The conventional wisdom among scholars from all over the ideological spectrum is that the legal system reflects power relationships, notably economic interests, within the society. Lawrence Friedman in his much acclaimed A HISTORY OF AMERICAN LAW 14 (1973) put the matter this way: "The basic premise of this book is that, despite a strong dash of history and idiosyncracy, the strongest ingredient in American law, at any given time, is the present: current emotions, real economic interests, concrete political groups." This conclusion is sometimes known as "the Golden Rule" — them that have the gold make the rules.

e. Delgado observes that: "ADR is most apt to incorporate prejudice when a person of low status and power confronts a person or institution of high status and power." Do you agree? Now substitute litigation for ADR. Is your answer the same? Is it likely that, whatever the regime of rules, and whatever the arena, persons of "high status and power" will generally prevail in contests with persons of "low status and power"?

f. In evaluating ADR, it is important to consider the "compared to what" question. For most people, the alternative to an ADR process is not a full-blown due process trial with a team of the finest lawyers in the land. For them, the choices often are to do nothing, or to go into debt to hire a relatively inexpensive attorney. Judge Wayne Brazil makes a similar point, in defending court-annexed ADR. See discussion in Chapter Ten.

g. Some of the criticism of ADR cited by Delgado is based on the success (and not the failure) of ADR in settling disputes. For example, "informalism" is criticized "for draining energy from collective action" by the settlement of individual grievances, which if unsettled would lead to collective action "that would be of greater benefit to disadvantaged groups." That is a fair enough point from the perspective of a political organizer, but it hardly follows that, therefore, the informal process is defective. Rather, the complaint is that, by resolving individual disputes more effectively, opposition to the system is reduced.

h. Even if one succeeded in showing that ADR is no worse than litigation or other options in terms of the prejudice faced by minorities, immigrants, or other disfavored classes, this is hardly a large compliment. Professor Delgado's title states a goal that clearly is desirable: "minimizing the risk of prejudice in ADR." Seriously addressing that objective requires a deeper understanding of ADR procedures and the differences between them. Achieving such an understanding is a central goal of this course.

i. Legal literature is replete with references to "repeat players," as well as the concern that they are systematically favored in their dealings with "one-shot players." Galanter's terminology has become part of the standard vocabulary of legal discourse.

C. DISPUTE SETTLEMENT WITHIN CLOSELY KNIT COMMUNITIES

1. Comments and Questions

a. It is commonly observed that closely knit communities, of which immigrant ethnic groups are a notable example, are particularly likely to favor nonlegal dispute resolution. Professor Auerbach cites examples going back through American history.

b. Dr. Diane LeReche examines a contemporary immigrant group, Korean-Americans, and how traditional processes of dispute settlement are retained in a new country. Casual observation, common sense, and empirical research all show a strong tendency of immigrant groups in this country to make modified use of the customs from which their family emigrated, including those for dealing with discord, which usually diminishes over time.

c. One impact of mass media (notably radio and television), along with institutions such as the public schools, is to speed the acculturation of immigrants, and the pace of absorption of at least the second generation into the dominant culture. Before one becomes too nostalgic for the fine traditions of the old country it should be observed that there are costs as well as benefits to the preservation of "traditional norms" and an absence of "outside scrutiny" on members of immigrant communities — particularly for the least skilled, least educated, and women (of course, these are not mutually exclusive categories).

2. JEROLD AUERBACH, JUSTICE WITHOUT LAW? 3 (1981)

From the Dutch in New Amsterdam [the early name for New York City] to the Jews of the Lower East Side, in a wide geographical arc that encompassed Scandinavians in the Midwest and the Chinese on the West Coast, some newcomers from other cultures and traditions tried to place their disputes as far beyond the reach of American law as possible. Aliens in a hostile land, they encountered a society whose legal institutions were overtly biased against them or, at best, indifferent to their distinctive values. Their own indigenous method of dispute settlement, centuries old in some instances, shielded them from outside scrutiny and enabled them to inculcate and preserve their traditional norms.

3. Diane LeResche, *A Comparison of the American Mediation Process with a Korean-American Harmony Restoration Process*, 9 MEDIATION Q. 323 (1992)

The basic assumption of the American mediation centers is that conflict is a natural phenomenon. It is neither positive nor negative; it simply exists. Although conflicts can be disruptive, they are not considered totally bad. They may even be viewed as good, insofar as they can result in circumstances changing from unhealthy to healthy ones. The Koreans in America, on the other hand, tend to perceive conflicts as negative situations that represent a shameful inability to maintain harmonious relationships with others. A conflict is not an acceptable condition; hence, careful attention must be paid to avoidance of any activity that may cause discord. Prevention and an emphasis on minimizing attention to frictions are the first action and reaction to any disruption in harmony. . . .

In general, mediation centers see interpersonal conflicts as problems in communication between people. Poor communication leads to misunderstandings, both between persons who have known each other for long periods and between persons known to one another solely in the immediate situation. Conflicts are considered to be ubiquitous. Korean-Americans, by contrast, posit that conflicts occur when at least one person does not behave in the proper manner toward another. When someone is selfish or insults another person, a conflict is created. Insults are actions that reflect that one is not showing the respect another is entitled to receive. Insults are offensive attacks. Conflicts occur between persons within a familial or social network. Because Korean-Americans rarely interact with people they consider to be outside their networks, they do not realize conflicts with those with whom they have no connections. These distinct variations in the values attached to interpersonal conflicts and their causes lead to some contrasting views of the purpose of resolving conflicts, as well as how to do so.

There are similarities also in the objectives and goals of the two resolution processes. The ultimate goal of an American mediation center process is to obtain a formal agreement that specifies which of the parties will take what future actions where and when to remedy the issues discerned during the mediation sessions. The written agreement is to have been created by the parties so that it will be mutually acceptable and beneficial and therefore endure. There are competing demands that the goal be relationship centered or agreement centered. Both are deemed desirable and sometimes possible to achieve, but the nurturance of the relationship between the parties is usually the ultimate goal. Secondary goals are to show the parties a method of focusing on their interests and needs in the generation and selection of solutions to conflicts and to teach effective communication skills in order to prevent conflicts in the future. Objectives linked to the goals are to intervene quickly in conflicts before they escalate to violence, to provide an efficient means of resolving conflicts (that is, low cost, time saving, and convenient for the parties), and to offer a confidential and private process. By advocating the use of a rational, collaborative process, the centers also attempt to empower people to resolve their own conflicts now and in the future.

The centers do not aim to determine who is at fault, to assess blame, or to punish. The process used by Korean-Americans is similar in not seeking to assign blame, although it expects apologies to be made. However, since all persons involved in the conflict are seen to have contributed to it in some way, each one acknowledges and offers apologies for mistakes made during the course of the unharmonious state.

The supreme goal for Korean-Americans is to have harmonious relations among all persons within one's network of family, friends, and colleagues. Hence, the main purpose of a conflict resolution procedure is to restore harmony where it does not exist. This purpose entails the reconciliation of people through helping them understand their relationships. The Korean-American process is centered on future relationships between those directly, and less directly, involved in the conflict more than on details of a contract. An objective of the process is to find a solution that does not engender bitterness for the long term, helps all to save face, and preserves customary proper conduct between people in defined role relationships. A concomitant objective is for the intermediary to convince the conflicting persons to accept a reasonable solution, which means making necessary adjustments in their behavior, coping with a difficult situation, accommodating to others in the short term, and compromising, especially for the good of the whole group, even to the neglect of self. These are the objectives of making *hwa hae* (harmony).

How the Process Is Initiated. There are virtually no commonalities in how the two procedures are initiated. . . . The chief distinction is that the focus of the American center is on how to get the parties to come to the mediation table; for Korean-Americans, it is on how a suffering person can find the most suitable intermediary.

Efforts are made by people affiliated with the American mediation center to inform people of their services . . . through impersonal outreach, advertising, education, and public relations. Social service agencies are appealed to for referrals to the center. When a conflict is manifested, persons may refer themselves to the center or make contact on the advice of someone else. A request for information or an appointment for help may be initiated by one or more of the actual parties in conflict. A staff person at the center questions the "complainant" and initiates contact with the other party in an effort to get everyone to come into the center for a meeting with mediators. The intake worker makes an official appointment at a time convenient to all concerned and informs the parties about the mediation process, the fees for the service, and the need to sign a contract agreeing to participate in mediation.

A Korean-American generally launches a semiformal resolution process when all patience and attempts at handling the situation have been exhausted. He or she probably considers the potential ramifications of asking various persons to assist as an intermediary, narrows the choice to the most appropriate person, and then carefully approaches that person, politely and submissively requesting guidance. The person asked to assist may be reluctant to do so and will not be unduly pressured to perform this role. Unspoken responsibilities to assist one another in times of need are understood by all involved.

The persons at the heart of the conflict have different roles to play and different responsibilities in each of these processes. When taking part in American community-based mediation, the parties are expected to generate potential solutions, make their own decisions about acceptable outcomes, and act on their own behalf. They are to be rational, control their emotions, and behave in an orderly, restrained manner, separating mind, body, and spirit. The parties are to take turns telling their views of the conflict situation and their interests and needs in relation to it. They are urged to be direct and verbal, disclosing themselves fully and acting in good faith. Thoughts are to be conveyed in a relatively formal, businesslike manner. The focus of discussion is to be on those aspects of one's life that are central to the immediate conflict; in other words, one's personal, political, social, and economic realms are to be kept separate. Parties are expected to work at finding a solution. Parties are to agree to and abide by ground rules established by the mediators. It is considered a virtue to be assertive and to claim one's rights with regard to terms of the agreement. One may demand and be aggressive for what one believes is a fair and just outcome, but one is to conform to the process managed by the mediators.

Similar conformity and assertiveness are also evidenced by Koreans in America. Koreans in America are more passive, however, in generating potential solutions to the conflict at this stage (for they have already made extensive attempts before enlisting the intermediary's help). They are expected to listen carefully to the intermediary, consider seriously the advice offered, consult with others in their network about proposed solutions, taking the *kibun* (similar to the English concepts of morale, face, self-esteem, state of mind) and wishes of others into account before acquiescing to the intermediary. Feelings and intuitions are as fundamental to their actions, as is information. . . . One remembers that the social, personal, political, and economic aspects of life are interrelated, so that decisions made and actions taken have many far-reaching effects. A person is not expected to interact in the same way with everyone. Though there is some reciprocity, there are basic inequalities and differences in how persons relate to one another. The hierarchical, paternalistic design of Confucius for relationship behaviors is adhered to, sometimes subconsciously. Hence role behaviors depend on the relationship and context of each conflict. Loyalty, trust, and deference to intermediaries is probably consistently the norm.

The Korean-Americans follow the lead of their intermediaries, waiting for the solution offered, the reasons for selecting it, and the persuasive comments about embracing what is necessary to make *hwa hae*. Those participating in the American mediation centers are very actively involved in creating and choosing the solutions relevant to their personal needs; they attend only to their mediators' directions about the steps to follow in the process.

Characteristics, Roles, and Responsibilities of Third Party. The Korean-American intermediary takes an active part in almost all dimensions of the lives of those he or she is working with in order to restore harmony. The intermediary's responsibilities are many and taken quite seriously, for the harmony of the larger groups to which they all belong is at stake. It is a temporary role, which he or she has felt an obligation to perform for persons in some way personally related. The intermediary has an informal relationship with the conflicting persons, having been personally known to each of them, in fact often interacting with them in other situations.

The ideal intermediary is wise, intelligent, experienced, and fair. He or she has the ability to use *nunch'i* ("eyeing the situation," an ability to pick up the subtle cues that reveal how someone is feeling; being perceptive about the emotions and attitudes of another person and knowing how to respond sensitively to that person), does not disturb anyone's *kibun*, and is respectful of people. These abilities are all informally learned. The intermediary has had no formal training in being a third party, but has demonstrated in some way a capacity to fill the roles of fact finder, planner, thinker, diplomat, persuader, adviser, generator of reasonable solutions, go-between, and arranger of social events.

In contrast, mediators in the American conflict resolution center have been trained specifically to fill the role of process manager, facilitator of communication, and advocate for a collaborative process. They have received some training in listening effectively, guiding the parties sequentially through their tasks, keeping them attuned to the ground rules and focused on reaching an agreement. The relationship between mediators and the parties is a contractual one, for they are operating in a professional, official capacity as third parties and do not interact with the parties in other contexts. They are frequently part-time volunteers at the mediation center. They are required to be able to demonstrate empathy, neutrality, and impartiality and to advocate and use a collaborative process for resolving conflicts.

The dominant parallels between the two types of dispute resolvers are, first, the third parties are respected and trusted by those in conflict (with Korean-Americans, they are also highly respected by the broader community) and, second, the third parties exhibit respect for the people, acting to minimize anxieties, fears, and uneasiness. In both cases, they are responsible for the comfort of the parties and the atmosphere in which the conflict and solutions are discussed. Both act as "agents of reality," helping parties to assess costs and benefits of an ongoing conflict, versus a swift resolution, and to evaluate the viability of solutions. On the surface, these features appear to be very similar. However, the ways in which they are displayed vary. The traits that make a third party respected and trusted are not the same for each group. Methods of alleviating anxieties differ.

Differences between the two third parties are even more numerous. Korean-Americans prefer intermediaries who are personally known to them, have substantial knowledge of their life circumstances, and who can encourage people to do good and behave properly. It is important that they give advice — sound advice. Mediators in American conflict resolution centers are trained not to offer solutions or any other type of advice. The third party in the mediation center is seen as a resource person for the parties, someone knowledgeable and skilled about a process for resolving conflicts. Korean-Americans consult the third party for his or her knowledge about proper actions to take in troubled situations, for substantive guidance to the best decisions.

Third-Party Preparation. In general, preparation by mediators in the community-based centers is concentrated in their formal training for the position of mediator. That preparation is considered to be adequate for any type of conflict case they may mediate. A Korean-American intermediary does fresh, extensive personal preparation during each phase of every actual conflict situation.

American mediation centers emphasize the adequacy of mediator training as preparation for all types of conflict cases, because they believe in treating all persons equally, in individuals' responsibility for their own resolutions. The mediator's role is to manage the general process rather than to be intimately involved in the substantive issues. Training in communication skills and the sequential aspects of the mediation process is considered the foundation that will carry the mediator through each case. Mediators do not need to be experts on the issues of concern to the parties. They do spend some time just before the mediation session reviewing very basic information about each of the parties and a synopsis of the conflict issues, as presented on the intake form. . . . There is a strong belief that by plugging into the general process and techniques learned in the training workshops, the mediators can handle any conflict case efficiently.

It is not essential for the Korean-American intermediary to be efficient. Rather, thorough and thoughtful preparation is highly valued. The ideal intermediary is planning throughout the process, which begins with fact-finding about the wider relationships between or among the groups of which the conflicting persons are members (historical, current, and potential future interactions), the opinions of others about the conflict, and the characters of those involved. Preparation includes seeking a profound understanding of the conditions of the parties involved, their expected behaviors, their characters, and the social context in which they live and will live. They draw on the teachings of others, their own experiences, what the sages have said about proper conduct in society, and other relevant material. The Korean-American process considers contemplation to find optimal solutions, the best presentation of a solution, and the most persuasive arguments for appropriate behavior. Preparation also comprises making arrangements for meeting with people at various locations and times, such as for the concluding social occasion in which harmony is restored.

Third-Party Meetings with Conflicting Parties. Contrasts are apparent in the pattern of activities when the third party and those central to the conflict convene. An important area of difference is in structural features, for example, where they meet (in an office or an informal setting), who is present (third party and conflicting parties; face-to-face or separate meetings with the go-between; only the immediate parties present or extended family and friends also permitted), and the duration and pace of the meetings (relatively few lively meetings or numerous meetings and gradual progress over a period of time).

The degree of structure and the atmosphere of the meetings are different. The gathering in the mediation center is very structured and businesslike, with a stress on hard work and confidentiality regarding all that is said. The tone is serious; light humor is used primarily to ease tensions. Displays of emotions by all are controlled and limited by the mediator. A definite sequence is followed: the announcement of ground rules, uninterrupted story telling, the generation of optional solutions, discussion and negotiation of the final terms of agreement, the joint signing of a written contractual agreement. All is done through what is usually designated as a collaborative problem-solving approach. The process used in the mediation center is very action oriented, that is, the pace is deliberately kept active and little time is allowed for contemplation by anyone.

The Korean-American process allows more time for thoughtful discussion and individual contemplation by the third patty as well as by those considered to be suffering the conflict. The structure is less formal, partly because the go-between meets separately with each person when their *kibuns* are most likely to be receptive to the type of discussion he or she wants to have with them, initially to gather information, later to give advice and encourage them to accept a solution. Neither the process as a whole nor the individual meetings have a clear time frame. Each meeting may last for minutes or for several hours. It may take several weeks or months until understanding occurs and *hwa hae* is achieved. There are no set days of the week, hours, or locations in which the meetings may take place. The process is fluid and flexible.

The mediation center's process is virtually always a face-to-face interaction of the parties, in which they do most of the talking directly to each other. The mediators direct them to address certain topics and move the discussion from stage to stage. The Korean-American intermediary, meeting individually with each of the persons in the conflict, probably talks more than they do: describing the solution and reasons for recommending it, trying to convince each person of the benefits of accommodating or compromising, and relaying the thoughts of the other persons with whom he or she has been conferring. Emotional outbursts by those in conflict tend to be accepted and left to run their own course.

In both processes, effective communication is valued. The emphasis for the center's mediators is on listening skill. Although being a good listener is also considered important for both the Korean-American intermediaries and the persons they are speaking to, effective speaking skills (primarily connoting the sensitive phrasing of ideas) are emphasized more. In the mediation center, direct communication among all present is the modus operandi, whereas among Korean-Americans, use of indirect communication is more prevalent and is the accepted norm. One of the ways in which Yam (1988) differentiates between these two communication styles is by noting that, for East Asians, communication cannot be compartmentalized; it is an ongoing, infinite process of interpretation between people. The North American orientation, on the other hand, is to perceive communication as the transfer of messages during a short-term, discontinuous relationship.

The mediation centers emphasize the importance of giving all parties the opportunity for full and open expression of their views of the conflict and what they want to do about it. Korean-Americans interviewed did not mention this goal at all. The content of the discussions is also different in each procedure. The Korean-Americans are more likely to talk of the moral dilemmas involved, proper conduct, the rights and wrongs of individual behaviors, duties and considerations for other people, and one's obligations to the harmonious functioning of society. Deliberations can be lengthy and philosophical. The mediators in the community-based centers keep the discussions on a more matter-of-fact level, [largely limited to] the immediate situations of the parties and the conflict. In both processes, all parties try to discover what ingredients are necessary to end the conflict and accept that the ultimate responsibility for making the final decisions belongs to those engaged in the conflict, not to the third party.

Generation of Options and Selection of Solutions. The Korean-Americans interviewed stressed that they want the advice of an intermediary about the best way for each of them to handle the conflict. They believe that if they need help, it is because their emotions are inhibiting their abilities to make good decisions, and that the intermediary is the objective analyst they require. Although they may contribute ideas to the intermediary, they rely on his or her thoughtful guidance to generate viable solutions.

The philosophy of the American mediation center is that people need to create their own solutions, because they know better than the third party what is feasible for resolving the conflict, and because solutions generated by the parties are more likely to be sustained than those generated by someone else: the parties must "own" the agreement. The self-generation approach follows from the American accent on self-reliance. The plan of the mediation center process is for the parties to the conflict to define the issues clearly and identify their respective needs and underlying interests, before seeking potential solutions. The mediator leads the parties through the steps: brainstorming potential options, establishing criteria for selecting the best ones, negotiating something for each person, and then narrowing the list of possibilities to the final selection and refinements. Mediators may suggest ideas if the parties seem unable to produce any acceptable to both sides. They may also query the parties to do some reality checking about the solutions proposed. . . .

The Korean-American intermediary gathers ideas from the parties in order to generate possible solutions. The intermediary's own experiences and the words of respected sages are also considered in the search for solutions appropriate to a particular configuration of symbiotic relationships. Thus, no one's allegiance to a group is questioned, face-saving is maintained or restored, and the persons in the dispute can find ways to come together ideologically. The intermediary contemplates and composes one or more solutions to propose to each person, along with reasons why they should be seriously considered. In effect, he or she negotiates with each person and, as go-between, refines and builds an understanding acceptable to both. The solution need not be innovative; it may be patterned on precedents, and it may mean learning to cope with an existing situation.

There is very likely more emphasis on conformity in the Korean-American process than in solutions generated by the mediation center process. Final understandings will be those that make the persons concerned feel best, feel most in harmony with one another. Restoration of harmony is more important than resolution of material issues. Complementary relations mean that no one loses, for each person has some type of protracted obligation to the other that may not be evidenced in the immediate situation or even in this generation. The binding understanding is based on a long-term perspective of the common good. For the short term, self-interests may be subordinated to the honor and well-being of one's family and other relevant groups. People neither owe nor own anything by themselves. . . .

Concluding the Process. The find phases of the Korean-American process are not events that explicitly announce the conclusion or the definitive resolution of the conflict. They incorporate a more intuitive recognition that an understanding has been reached and harmony has been restored. There is a social occasion in which the reestablishment of harmonious relationships is unofficially observed. The Korean-American understanding is oral. Apologies are important components. The celebration of restored harmony takes place in a relaxed social atmosphere, with gaiety, refreshments, and probably the ritual of sharing a glass.

On the other hand, the conclusion of the conflict resolution procedure used by the American mediation centers is solemnized in at least three undisguised steps: the writing and signing of an agreement, closing statements, and a follow-up with the parties by a center staff person to determine the status of the agreement. The formal agreement (usually on a special form) specifies in detail who will do what, when, and how. Copies are given to each party, and one is kept in the center's files. A relatively cursory evaluation of the case may also be done by the mediator.

In both processes, the third party acknowledges in some fashion the positive aspects of what has occurred: for example, the mediator congratulates the parties on reaching an agreement and for working hard to do so; the Korean-American intermediary affirms the fine character of each person as shown by what each has done for the good of the larger group. . . .

D. NEGOTIATING IN JAPAN: A PRIMER FOR AMERICANS

1. Comments and Questions

a. There are a vast number of recent books that purport to teach Americans about how to do business around the world, not to mention innumerable articles and Internet sources. One book about doing business internationally, after some general discussion, proceeds through the continents (not countries) seriatim, with Asia being dispatched in nine pages!

b. Any acceptably concise discussion of international negotiation, and the negotiating style of people from other nations, runs the risk of being inaccurate, shallow, naive, and racist (anyway, ethnocentric). Our response to this quandary is to provide a series of short readings on doing business and negotiating in a single country. Japan was selected because of its homogeneity and stability; the importance of the political and economic ties between the United States and Japan; the difficulties in trade negotiations between Americans and Japanese at the individual, firm, and national level; and the availability of abundant high quality publications.

c. One thing that is clear from even a cursory consideration of business negotiations in Japan is that attorneys play little, if any, role. Bringing counsel to a meeting will be treated as evidence of distrust and is far more likely to derail negotiations than to move them forward.

d. There is a discussion in Chapter Six by Professor Richard Shell of the negotiations (in the United States) at the highest levels between MCA/Universal and Sony.

2. GLEN FISHER, INTERNATIONAL NEGOTIATION: A CROSS-CULTURAL PERSPECTIVE (1980)

Americans see negotiating sessions as problem-solving exercises, and "problems" are precisely the dragons that Americans take joy in slaying. Westerners who negotiate with Japanese feel that the very idea of holding a formal session specifically to negotiate is somewhat foreign to many Japanese. Americans are frustrated when their counterparts do not enter into an expected give-and-take. . . .

There is little in Japanese culture to make Japanese feel comfortable with articulate advocacy in polite company, most especially in formal settings. They see such meetings as the occasion to ceremonially adopt what has already been worked out in a patient, consensus-generating process. To openly disagree at a formal stage is distasteful and embarrassing, like enduring a husband and wife spat at a dinner party. Certainly, the Japanese are not prepared to change their position in such a setting. . . . Harmony is important to Japanese. They still use go-betweens to assure smoothness in social relations in all kinds of dealings. . . .

In Japan, the progression to leadership and status is by professional competence, but also very much by seniority and experience. Hence, the team leader might be only marginally competent in the specific subject matter under negotiation, but still be the obvious head. He holds his position by being the representative of a consensus process through which the negotiating position has been derived. The Japanese system disallows flexibility at the negotiating table and requires long periods of time to consider new proposals. . . . It is a decision-making process where ideas and supporting decisions tend to come from the bottom up, or at least from mid-level up, rather than from the top down. The negotiator speaks from the authority of a consensus, something that cannot be easily changed in the give-and-take of negotiation.

In Japan, new initiatives depend heavily on middle-level technical experts, and their superiors tend to accept their judgements. Their accumulation of data and information serves both the deliberation process and implementation. Top managers serve as prestigious representatives of the structure over which they preside, avoiding the stance of the dynamic decision-making executive. . . . In any case, to the Japanese, a negotiated agreement is seen as an indication of the direction to be taken, with adjustments and modifications to be made according to conditions and consensus among the parties. Thus, a U.S. expectation of contractual finality is uncongenial to Japanese culture. And the Japanese inclination to suggest "sensible" changes after a contract is signed is seen from the U.S. side as devious.

3. Dean Allen Foster, BARGAINING ACROSS BORDERS: HOW TO NEGOTIATE BUSINESS ANYWHERE IN THE WORLD 264-93 (1992)

The very definition of negotiating can vary culture to culture. Many cultures view negotiation primarily as an opportunity to build a relationship; resolving a particular issue is simply not the first goal. Such cultures often view the initial meeting as the beginning of a larger negotiation encompassing many meetings. . . . The Japanese view the negotiation as a collaborative process of "mind-meeting," which can mandate several meetings before substantive issues are even discussed. Americans who have traveled halfway around the world to meet their Japanese counterparts for the first time in Tokyo on Monday and expect to be back in their office in Detroit on Friday with a signed deal will surely be disappointed.

Americans tend to view negotiating as a competitive process of offers and counteroffers, while the Japanese tend to view the negotiation as an opportunity for information sharing. . . . At the beginning of a business relationship between an American and a Japanese, the immediate substantive issue is simply not on the table as far as the Japanese are concerned. . . . For the Japanese, bargaining too soon can be a sign of untrustworthiness. It is for this reason that Americans in the now classic Japanese-American cross-cultural business scenario lose the deal by bargaining about price just because they are made anxious by Japanese silence.

Cultures such as Japan . . . view conflict at the table as dysfunctional. Correspondingly, these cultures seek to avoid conflict and are indirect, as opposed to confrontational, in their response to it. The maintenance of *wa*, or harmony, in Japan is such a basic and critical value that it significantly affects much of the behavior during negotiation, as well as determines attitudes toward it. In their effort to maintain harmony, to avoid conflict at the table, the Japanese will employ indirect and avoidant behavior. They will also place priority on face-saving, status acknowledgment, and the establishment of an ongoing system of mutual obligation, expectation, and fulfillment, as symbolized by their often elaborate (and expensive) gift-giving and hosting customs.

Because the Japanese choose their chief negotiators on the basis of status and seniority, these people may not be the ones most informed about the details necessary to make a decision. In fact, their assistants may be better equipped with the facts to respond to your question. However, assistants are not usually empowered to approve decisions.

In Japan, cards are exchanged upon meeting in order for the individuals to learn many things about each other, not the least being status. In Japan, cards are received with two hands, lovingly examined, and carefully arranged in front of you on the table, in an order that represents the seating of your opposite numbers. They must never be mishandled, written upon, folded, or put in one's back pocket to be sat upon. . . . Many hotels in Japan will translate your business card for you, for a small fee, if you send it to them in advance of your trip.

In Japan, "the nail that sticks up gets hammered down" — that is, the individual who brings attention to himself or herself will be sharply put back in his or her place. Group or individual orientation affects the negotiation process in a number of ways. In group-oriented societies, the other side will probably be a team, as opposed to an individual or a few individuals. Decisions will probably not be made at the table, but rather will be discussed among the group members after the meeting is over.

The time the Japanese take to make their decisions may seem interminable to the Americans awaiting a decision, but the information exchanged at the table must be taken back to all parties concerned and decided upon in many mini-meetings among themselves. This Japanese decision-making system is known as *ringi seido*, or "reverential inquiry about superior's intentions from below.". . . The Japanese retain today the need to have the entire group in agreement (harmony, again) on an issue before it is implemented. . . . Traditionally (and this is changing, too, depending on the industry), lower levels "inquire" about the intentions of the next level up. Ideas and decisions move from the bottom up, with each level seeking approval from the next higher level. At each step upward, consensus must be reached by the players before the issue is "recommended" upward again. The final form reaches the decision makers at the top, who then put their stamp of approval (often literally) on it.

By this time, of course, all players have discussed the issue at length and have "bought in." Therefore, although the decision-making time in Japan may seem extremely long to the impatient American, once the decision is made, implementation is usually quite rapid, since all concerned with the project are already intimately familiar with it. And it is at this point that the Japanese get their turn to complain about how slowly the Americans move. For Americans may make decisions more quickly, may even decide them directly at the table, but then the project, once decided upon by the top, must move back down through the organization, getting everyone's "buy-in," understanding, and compliance along the way — usually after the decision is made.

4. ROBERT M. MARCH, THE JAPANESE NEGOTIATOR: SUBTLETY AND STRATEGY BEYOND WESTERN LOGIC 15-17 (1990)

Among themselves, the truth is that the Japanese do not like negotiation. It has disagreeable connotations of confrontation, to be avoided whenever possible. The Japanese instinct is for agreements worked out behind the scenes on the basis of give and take, harmony and long-term interest. . . . Very few Japanese even know how to negotiate in the Western sense. In everyday life in Japan, there is little experience of bargaining to buy household goods at lower prices, or even of using arguments in a debating fashion to win points. The common Western ideal of a persuasive communicator — one who is highly skilled in argumentation, who overcomes objections with verbal flair, who is an energetic extrovert — would be regarded by most Japanese as superficial, insincere, and . . . a little vulgar. What the Japanese learn in their culture is that vagueness in discussion is a virtue. They learn to involve others, to listen to their views, and, when no strongly dissenting views remain, a decision is made. It is noteworthy that nobody seems to make the actual decision, rather it just seems to "happen." As for individual involvement, as a Japanese everyone knows that as long as you remain silent, you project a favorable impression and are assumed to be thinking deeply about the problem.

The culturally approved use of ambiguity in Japan extends even to the business setting, where it is linked in the Japanese mind to the issue of personal trust. Whereas . . . American negotiators may develop bargaining ranges and strategic options as a matter of course in their pre-negotiation planning, this is still rare among the Japanese. This is especially true when the foreigner adopts a bargaining or "horse trading" approach. . . . [A]n invitation to "horse trade" provokes in many Japanese a certain aristocratic disdain for the merchant mind.

It is still commonly accepted that if two parties trust each other, money and other details need not be discussed. Thus, in many industries in Japan, neither contracts nor invoices or even product catalogs are used. On occasions when contracts are used, a point will be made of not reading the fine print, for to do so would imply a lack of trust.

Despite this, the Japanese employ an array of means to influence others and achieve their goals, means that if not completely unknown in the West, are often carried to extremes that seem bizarre or undignified to Westerners. The reason behind such behavior is that they are doing everything they can to avoid appearing either self-centered (as they fear they would were they to speak about the merits or superiority of their company or their products) or coldly rational (as they also fear they would were they to concentrate only on economic or business issues, without relating sympathetically to the other side). There are powerful injunctions in Japanese society against both of these attitudes, and their behavior will make better sense if this is understood.

5. SANJYOT P. DUNUNG, DOING BUSINESS IN ASIA: THE COMPLETE GUIDE (1995)

The Japanese place a very high importance on personal interactions and spend a great deal of their time building relationships and developing trust. Accordingly, there is very little cold calling in Japan. All new contacts are developed via introductions by third parties. You will find that having a strong personal connection with a highly respected third party who acts as your introducer, will give you a better chance of achieving business success, especially if the person you want to meet has a sense of obligation to your introducer. The introducer (*shokaisha*) can also function as a trusted and respected go-between and may be called upon later to advise both sides or act as a mediator during a difficult negotiation. . . .

Most Japanese are not accustomed to dealing with women in business situations. As international business has increased, the frequency of business interactions involving Japanese men and non-Japanese women has increased, but not significantly. If you are a foreign woman with patience and gentle persistence, you will be able to gradually win their respect and business, but do not expect close relationships with them. . . . Some, particularly younger, Japanese will be able to deal with you better than their older colleagues.

In Japan, age is synonymous with wisdom and experience. Consequently, the Japanese often have a difficult time negotiating or conducting business with foreigners who appear substantially younger and inexperienced. In Japanese business, a man's marital status may influence his career path. Traditionally, while it is acceptable for a man to remain a bachelor until his late twenties, he faces distinct social and professional pressure to find a wife soon after turning thirty. An unmarried man over thirty may be bypassed for promotion and suffer poor postings or assignments, because the Japanese view marriage and family as symbols of stability and maturity.

No matter how hard you work at building your relationship, remember that you, as a non-Japanese, will always be perceived as a . . . foreigner to the Japanese. . . . Foreigners should not let this reality obstruct business relationships, but simply recognize that the concept of close business relationships will take on a new and more formal dimension in Japan. . . .

One Japanese concept that is particularly difficult for non-Japanese to comprehend is *honne* and *tatemae*. *Honne* refers to the substance or real or inner truth of an issue, and *tatemae* is the public, diplomatic truth or official position. This important concept helps the Japanese to maintain harmony. The Japanese will avoid voicing their true feelings or *honne* in order to preserve harmony. The best way to counter this problem is to ask more questions to get a better sense of an issue. Remember to keep the questions inoffensive and somewhat indirect to avoid causing any embarrassment to your Japanese counterpart.

The Japanese often avoid sustained eye contact, as it can be considered intimidating. Junior people are less likely to make eye contact and will keep their visual focus low out of respect for the speaker. Westerners should not assume that this posture implies a lack of trust, honesty, or sincerity. Do not try to fill up the silent gaps during a conversation. Silence usually means the Japanese are seriously contemplating the issue. The Japanese rarely ever say "No" outright. A blunt "No" is considered rude, almost like an opinion on a person rather than on his idea. Other expressions that can mean "No" include . . . it is difficult, I am not sure, I will think about it, and [apparent affirmations followed by "but"].

If you need to say "No," do so in a similarly roundabout manner to avoid a confrontation and offending your counterpart. Never say "No" outright, as it may cause your counterpart to lose face. The Japanese routinely engage in a verbal and physical gesture that is best described as a guttural moan with the tilt of the head. This is usually done in a situation in which they feel uncomfortable. . . . The nervous laugh or smile can also indicate difficulty. The Japanese also indicate "No" by placing their hand perpendicular to their face and waiving it rapidly back and forth.

6. BOYE LAFAYETTE DEMENTE, HOW TO DO BUSINESS WITH THE JAPANESE: A COMPLETE GUIDE TO JAPANESE CUSTOMS AND BUSINESS PRACTICES (1993)

There are three basic principles to business success in Japan. You must have a product or service that the Japanese want to buy; you must have an extensive network of contacts in Japan that you can orchestrate to achieve your goals; and you must have sufficient cross-cultural skills to gain the confidence and goodwill of the Japanese and make them comfortable dealing with you.

It helps tremendously if you are starting out with a product that has been successful in the American market. Often, the first criterion the Japanese apply to any foreign-made product is how successful it has been in its own home market. In Japan, even more so than in the United States, every product has a distinctive identity, image, acceptable role, and what Japan marketing specialist Earle Okumura calls its "contact infrastructure." . . . One of the major differences between the Japanese market and the American market is that the contact infrastructure in Japan tends to be far more deeply entrenched and more influential in the marketing of any product. . . . Once you have established your network, it is also necessary to spend more time nurturing it to keep it working smoothly.

The first characteristic of business in Japan is its personal nature. The second characteristic is its competitiveness — fierce competition that drives the engine of the economy domestically as well as internationally. . . . The obsession for exquisite design, high quality, an almost unlimited amount of aftermarket service, and a steady stream of new product makes the Japanese marketplace the most competitive in the world.

Cultural insensitivity and casual-to-arrogant attitudes remain the greatest handicaps afflicting many foreigners . . . interested in the Japanese market — Americans in particular. Americans generally rank at or near the bottom in sensitivity to other cultures. We continue to downplay the importance or ignore the importance of speaking the language of people we want to do business with. We do not give sufficient value to the life-styles, habits, likes and dislikes of Japanese consumers.

The guiding principle of most Westerners is that profit must be made. This standard pervades virtually all our endeavors and actions. We give only secondary consideration to the needs of our employees. We tend to look upon society at large and our government as separate entities and we often think of government as an adversary.

Leading Japanese businessmen, on the other hand, automatically identify themselves as Japanese first and entrepreneurs second. Their guiding principles are (1) their overall responsibility to Japan, (2) their responsibilities to their employees, and (3) the need to be successful in business to fulfill the first two obligations. This is not to suggest . . . that the Japanese do not try to make a profit. But time and again, in situations in which the Westerner's behavior is determined entirely by profit, the Japanese businessman's behavior is determined largely by other considerations. He will strive to maintain harmony in the company, in the market, or in the country; avoid laying off employees; or enhancing his reputation. [Japanese businesses] consider their interests and those of the government to be essentially the same, and they expect the government to exercise significant control over their industry. Where the government has not taken a direct hand in the conduct of business, the businessmen have formed associations and cartels with others in the same industry and then sought government approval and guidance. . . .

Japanese businessmen do not like to sign detailed, restrictive contracts. To them, no agreement is final for the simple reason that circumstances change, and they want to be able to change with them. They prefer a loose arrangement based on sincerity and goodwill. . . . The flexibility provided by this type of contractual arrangement gives the Japanese a tremendous advantage over those who are bound by tightly limiting contracts. If they do sign American contracts with lots of fine print, they will usually abide by the terms until conditions change; then they renegotiate. The Japanese do not use lawyers in their negotiations and seldom consult them in case of disputes (there are only some 16,000 attorneys in the country). . . . Disliking the legalistic approach to contracts or business, they have taken a very strong position against foreign legal firms operating in Japan.

7. PHILIP R. HARRIS & ROBERT I. MORAN, MANAGING CULTURAL DIFFERENCE (1991)

Tips for Business Interactions with the Japanese

1. Saving face and achieving harmony are more important factors in business dealings for the Japanese than achieving higher sales and profits.

2. Third party introductions are important. They prefer this indirect approach whereby you use a go-between or arbitrator who may be involved until the conclusion of the negotiation.

3. Whomever you approach in the organization, do so at the highest level; the first person contacted is also involved throughout the negotiation.

4. Avoid direct communication on money; leave this to the go-between or lower echelon staff.

5. Never put a Japanese in a position where he must admit failure or impotency.

6. Avoid praise of your product or services; let your literature or go-between do that.

7. Use business cards with your titles, preferably both in Japanese and English.

8. The logical, cognitive, or intellectual approach is insufficient; the emotional level of communications is considered important.

9. Wait patiently for meetings to move beyond preliminary tea and inconsequential talk.

8. JAMES DAY HODGSON, YOSHIHIRO SANO & JOHN L. GRAHAM, DOING BUSINESS WITH THE NEW JAPAN 33-46 (2000)

Chapter 4. THE JAPANESE NEGOTIATION STYLE

The Japanese negotiation style is perhaps the most distinctive in the world. Moreover, contrary to what one might expect, the Japanese style is far different from negotiation styles in Taiwan and Korea, Japan's closest neighbors. Compared to the aggressive haggling more typical of Korean and Chinese businesspeople, the subtle, low-key bargaining of Japanese executives appears foreign indeed. The historical and cultural roots of the Japanese negotiation style run far deeper than those of the American style. Their history is much longer and relatively uninfluenced from the outside. Another characteristic that sets the Japanese style apart from all others is the suitability of the Japanese style for international use. An important aspect of the Japanese style of business negotiations includes adapting bargaining behaviors to those of the host country or firm.

The Roots of the Japanese Style of Business Negotiation

The natural environment of Japan has had a pervasive influence on the character of social systems, personal relationships, and yes, even the process of business negotiations. Three environmental factors are salient: (1) the insular and mountainous geography, (2) the dense population, and (3) the importance of rice as the basic food crop.

Throughout its history, Japan has been an isolated country. Until the fifteenth century, the surrounding seas formed a substantial barrier preventing invasions and limiting influence from the Asian continent. Even with the dramatic changes throughout the rest of the world brought about by Western Euro-

pean maritime power in the sixteenth century, the political policies of the Toku-
gawa Shogunate kept foreigners out of the country: Indeed, Japan was the
country least influenced by Western European culture through the mid-nine-
teenth century. And not only did the maritime barriers keep foreigners out, but
they also kept the Japanese from leaving. Thus, social systems and personal
relationships developed in a concentrated environment where geography dictated that cooperation was essential. Ethnicity, cultural values, and behavioral
norms are, therefore, uniquely consistent and homogeneous.

The mountains in Japan have always made travel within the country difficult,
adding further to the isolation of social groups. Because of the mountains, only
about 10 percent of the land can be cultivated. Japan is the most densely pop-
ulated of all countries in the world with respect to people per square mile of
arable land. This crowding has fostered a tightly organized society that highly
values obedience and cooperation. Crowding does not permit the aggressive
independence and equality so characteristic in the United States.

The final environmental factor influencing values and behaviors in Japan is
the historical importance of rice cultivation. Until 100 years ago, five-sixths of
the population of Japan was employed in rice cultivation. Rice production
requires community effort and cooperation. Irrigation, planting and harvesting
are most efficiently accomplished with the participation of groups of families.
Thus, the small group has evolved as the salient social unit in Japan. Individual needs and desires are de-emphasized in favor of one's social unit. In the historical agrarian society, the family and village were key. Now in Japan, one's
family and one's work group are central. Loyalty and consensus decision making are key elements that bind such groups together.

Because of this unique combination of environmental influences, a social
system has evolved in Japan that avoids conflict and promotes harmony. And,
as in America, classroom behavior is influenced by and tends to reinforce these
cultural values and behavioral norms. Lively case discussions are not part of the
educational experience in Japan. Rather, professors present lectures with no
questions and feedback allowed from students. Listening skills and obedience,
rather than debating skills and independent thinking, are rewarded in the
Japanese educational system. It should be understood that the Japanese negotiation style characterized in the paragraphs to follow is deeply influenced by
and reflects these salient environmental factors and the values and social structures associated with them.

Tate Shakai (Living and Working in a Vertical Society)

Perhaps the most important difference between the Japanese negotiation
style and other styles, particularly the American, concerns status relationships.
At an interpersonal level, the bases for the status distinction might be age,
sex, education, or occupation. The power position in business relationships has
more to do with size and prestige of the company, industry structure (e.g., number of competitors), and very often, which company is the buyer. There are
cases when sellers are more powerful — large manufacturers versus small
retailers — but most often Japanese buyers expect and receive deference from
Japanese sellers. Indeed, in Japan, the buyer is said to be "kinger." A pam-

phlet provided by the Manufactured Imports Promotion Organization of Japan states:

> In Japan, as in other countries, the "buyer is king," only here he or she is "kinger." Here, the seller, beyond meeting pricing, delivery special specifications, and other usual conditions, must do as much as possible to meet a buyers wishes. . . . Many companies doing business in Japan make it a practice to deliver more than called for under the terms of their contracts.

The key point here is that the roles of the buyer and seller are very different in Japan. Status relations dictate what is said and what bargaining strategies may be used during Japanese business negotiations. The norms of behavior for the seller are very different from those for the buyer.

In America, the way in which status distinctions affect how we behave is almost the opposite of that in Japan. In Japan, people at all levels feel uncomfortable if status distinctions do not exist or are not understood. But in our egalitarian American society, we often go out of our way to establish an interpersonal equality. There is little distinction between roles and relatively few rules for adjusting behavior. Americans expect (and do) affect business outcomes at the negotiation table. For Japanese, negotiation is more of a ritual, with actions predetermined and pre-specified by status relations.

Amae (Indulgent Dependency)

Hierarchical personal and business relationships are difficult for Americans to understand. "Doesn't the lower-status seller get taken advantage of? That's what would happen in the United States." However, understanding an additional aspect of Japanese hierarchical relationships is essential for full appreciation of the Japanese business system. It is true that Japanese buyers have the freedom to choose the deal they want. They will get little argument from the Japanese sellers. But along with this freedom goes an implicit responsibility to consider the needs of the sellers. Japanese sellers can trust the buyers not to take advantage of them. This theme of *amae* is woven into every aspect of Japanese society: Consider, for example, the relationship between management and labor. Management has much more control over labor in Japan than in the United States. But with that control comes a large measure of responsibility for the welfare of the labor force, exceeding that in America. In Japan, buyers take care of sellers. Buyers consider the needs of sellers before making demands that sellers defer to. In America, conversely, we all take care of ourselves. If buyers make unreasonable demands, they will most likely hear an argument.

Nagai Tsukiai (Long-Term Relationships)

Another aspect of business relationships in Japan that influences negotiation behavior regards the importance and expectation of long-term relationships. The fact that Japanese managers are more predisposed than American managers to take a long view of business affairs has been given much attention. The importance of establishing long-term relations is grounded in the cultural heritage of being isolated and having no other place to go. Personal and group relationships are for life and therefore entered into slowly, carefully, and in a socially prescribed way: The same is true for business relationships.

Perhaps no society values reliability and trust in relationships more than the Japanese. These are ingredients on which they have built their sturdy culture. The intricate web of interdependence between persons and institutions in that society both creates and depends on a foundation of trust. So in Japan, trust must not be merely sought, it must be won. But once won, a legacy of trust between the parties can become their most valuable joint asset, an asset worth preserving.

This aspect of Japanese values has two important implications for business negotiations with Japanese dents or partners. First, the Japanese side will want to spend more time getting to know prospective American associates. They will be more willing to invest time and money in negotiation preliminaries and rituals. The second, and perhaps the more important, implication has to do with the structure and presentation of the business deal itself. Japanese bargainers will be looking for long-term commitments. Short-run profits are important but secondary to a long-run business association benefitting both sides.

Shinyo (Gut Feeling)

[There are] four stages of the negotiation process: non-task sounding, task-related information exchange, persuasion, and concessions and agreement. . . . From the American point of view, the persuasion stage is the heart of the matter. It is different in Japan. Compared to Americans, Japanese spend a considerable amount of time in non-task sounding activities. The Japanese view the time and money spent in the initial stages of bargaining as an important investment. The typical Japanese negotiation involves a series of non-task interactions and even ceremonial gift giving. . . . To the American critic, this may seem a waste of time. However, the Japanese place great importance on establishing a harmonious relationship. This helps them avoid expensive litigation if things go wrong, which seems more and more common in the United States.

Naniwabushi (A Seller's Approach)

In Japan, information exchange during the second stage of negotiations is generally unidirectional. Sellers describe in great detail what they need, and buyers consider this information and make a decision. Sellers do not object to or question the decision, because they can trust the buyers to take care of them. Thus, the information flows principally from sellers to buyers. Robert March, author of two excellent books on Japan, explains that the seller's agenda is often ordered like a Japanese narrative chant dating back to the fifteenth century: A *naniwabushi* (both the chant and the negotiation approach) consists of three phases: "The opening, which is called *kikkake*, gives the general background of the story and tells what the people involved are thinking or feeling. Following this is the *seme*, an account of critical events. Finally, there is the *urei*, which expresses pathos and sorrow at what has happened or what is being requested." The request comes last, after a long explanation of the reasons why it is being made.

Alternatively, the American style of information exchange . . . starts with the request (without the sorrow), and the explanation is provided only if necessary: American persuasive appeals are couched in terms of "you should" rather than the Japanese, "my company needs." To the American mind, the *naniwabusi* seems melodramatic and a waste of time. However, this is the kind of behavior higher-status buyers expect from lower-status sellers. It is the kind of behavior that makes Japanese negotiators feel comfortable. . . .

Banana *No Tataki Uri* (The Banana Sale Approach)

In the days of street vendors in Japan, banana sellers were notorious for asking outrageous prices and quickly lowering the prices when faced with buyers' objections. The term banana no *tataki uri* is now used in Japan to describe a similar approach often taken by Japanese businesspeople. But instead of bananas, factories, distribution chains, even banks are sometimes bargained for using the "banana sale" approach. Japanese executives are more likely to use such a tactic during international negotiations, because they do not know what to expect from foreign buyers, and they feel that it is safer to leave much room to maneuver.

Wa (Maintaining Harmony)

Western negotiators universally complain about the difficulties of getting feedback from Japanese negotiators. There are three explanations for this complaint. First, the Japanese value interpersonal harmony, or *wa*, over frankness. Second, the Japanese perhaps have not come to a consensus regarding the offer or counteroffer. Third, Westerners tend to miss the subtle but clear signals given by the Japanese.

Wa, like *amae,* is one of the central values of the Japanese culture. Negative responses to negotiation proposals are principally nonexistent, and when they are given, they are given very subtly. We have all heard the classic story about the Japanese response of, "We'll think it over," to an American's request. A simple response like this usually means no in American terms, for if the Japanese really wanted to think it over, he or she would explain the details of the decision-making process and the reason for the delay. A Japanese negotiator would be loathe, however, to use the word "no." Indeed, Japanese scholar Keiko Ueda has described sixteen ways to avoid saying no in Japan. Moreover, we have found that Japanese negotiators tend to use the word "no" less than two times per half-hour in bargaining simulations, while Americans use "no" five times per half-hour, Koreans seven times, and Brazilian executives forty-two times. And we must add a couple of other options to Ueda-san's list: (17) changing the topic, and (18) letting lower-level negotiators say "no" in informal settings.

Regarding ambiguous responses, Japanese negotiators follow the cultural double standard of *tatemae* and *honne. Tatemae* can be translated as "truthful" (or "official stance") and *honne* "true mind" (or "real intentions"). It is important for the Japanese to be polite and to communicate the *tatemae* while reserving the possibly offending, but also informative, *honne*. Additionally, this difference in the Japanese value system manifests itself in statements by Japanese negotiators in retrospective interviews. The Japanese often describe Americans as honest and frank, but to the point of discomfort for the Japanese. . . . To the American point of view, this distinction between *tatemae* and *honne* seems hypocritical. However, the discrepancy is borne by the Japanese in good conscience and in the interest of the all-important *wa*.

Ringi Kessai (Decision Making by Consensus)

Because of the importance of *wa,* it is very difficult to get a "no" from a Japanese client. But because of group decision making by consensus, it may also be difficult to get a "yes." Often, the Japanese side simply has not made up its mind. In the voluminous comparative management literature, much has been made of the bottom-up approach to decision making typical in Japanese organizations. It has the disadvantage of slowing down the decision making, but the advantage of quick and orchestrated implementation. Moreover, this approach to decision making has proved very successful in coordinating group efforts in modern companies as well as in the traditional rice-growing agricultural communities. However, it has also been a substantial stumbling block and source of frustration for executives of American companies dealing with Japanese firms.

In business schools in the United States, we teach the importance of identifying the key decision makers in an organization. In marketing terms, we look for the key buying influences. Generally, these key executives are located higher up in the organization. Once the key decision makers have been identified, special persuasive efforts are directed toward them. We try to determine the special interests (commercial and personal) of these key individuals, and communications are tailored accordingly.

Such an approach is not likely to work in Japan. The decision-making power is not centralized in key or high positions. Rather, the decision-making power is spread throughout the organization, and all executives involved in or influenced by the deal are important. All of them will have to be convinced that your proposal is the best before anything happens. The key buying influence in Japan is the executive who says no. Thus, the typical business negotiation in Japan will include talking to more people and will require repetition of the same information and persuasive appeals — much to the frustration of impatient Americans.

For American bargainers, perhaps the greatest source of frustration associated with the consensus style of decision making has to do with the difficulty of getting feedback. American bargainers asking, "What do you think of our proposal (or our counteroffer)?" often receive no answer. The Japanese are not being cagey, or coy, or dishonest; more often than not, a consensus has not been reached, and Japanese negotiators (even senior people) are simply unwilling and unable to speak for the group.

Ishin-Denshin (Communication without Words)

The third reason foreigners complain about little feedback from Japanese negotiators has to do with the importance of nonverbal communication and subtlety in Japanese history, society, and business talk. Japan's ethnic homogeneity, isolation, and tradition of lifetime personal relationships with daily contact all permit the use of very subtle forms of communications. Subtlety is not only possible in such a fixed social system but is also required from the standpoint of *wa*.

America's tradition as a melting pot and the general transience of our personal relations make explicit communication necessary. Words are considered to be the most important vehicle of communication. In Japan, much more is communicated nonverbally — through tone of voice, eye contact, silence, body movements, and the like. It is difficult for Americans to appreciate this difference in communication style and the importance of nonverbal channels in Japan. Takeo Doi, at the University of Tokyo, explains that in Japan the most important information, the content of the communication, is transmitted via nonverbal channels. The verbal communication provides a context for the central information. The opposite is true in the United States, where communications researchers think of nonverbal signals as providing a context for the words spoken, the content of communication.

From the American point of view, the Japanese mode of communication is incomprehensible. We know that nonverbal communication is very important, but how can a delivery date or a purchase price be communicated nonverbally? The explanation goes back to the concept of *shinyo* (gut feeling). To the Japanese, the key information in a negotiation concerns the qualities of the long-term, personal relationships that exist in the context of the business deal. The long discussion of minute details so prevalent in Japanese negotiations provides a context for development of comfortable personal relationships and a positive *shinyo*, and this is what makes the business deal go or not. Information about *shinyo* is communicated nonverbally and subtly. Delivery dates and purchase prices, which must be communicated verbally, are important; but these details are not the critical information in a Japanese business deal. So, Americans bargaining with Japanese are not only looking for the less important information but are also focusing on the wrong channel of communication. Thus, we have another explanation for the difficulty Americans have in getting feedback from Japanese clients and partners.

Kazuma Uyeno further explains the importance of nonverbal communication in his definition of *hara-gei*. Anatomically, *hara* is the abdomen or stomach. Used in figures of speech, the word can mean the heart or the mind of a man (but not of a woman). *Hara* appears in a large number of expressions. It is presumptuous to try to explain in just a few lines the Japanese problem-solving technique of *hara-gei* (stomach art), but for our purposes here, *hara-gei* may be explained as a technique for solving a problem through negotiation between two individuals without the use of direct words. You do not reveal to the other party what is in your *hara*, but you unmistakably and effectively communicate your purpose, desire, demand, intention, advice, or whatever. . . . To do this, you bring into play psychology, intuition, and your knowledge of the other party's personality, background, ambitions, personal connections, and so forth and also what the other party knows about you. Only people with plenty of experience and cool nerves can make it succeed, but a lot of communication between Japanese in high positions is through *hara-gei*.

Nemawashi (Preparing the Roots)

"Care to prepare the roots and the tree grows tall and strong" is an old Japanese saying. Its traditional wisdom holds critical importance for Americans bargaining with Japanese executives. The idea is that, in Japan, what goes on at the negotiation table is really a ritual approval of what has already been decided before, through numerous individual conversations in restaurants, bath houses, and offices. In Japan, the negotiation table is not a place for changing minds. Persuasive appeals are not appropriate or effectual. If an impasse is reached, typical Japanese responses are silence, a change of subject, a request to consult the home office, or any of the several options for avoiding saying no. All members of the group must be consulted before new concessions or commitments are made. . . .

Americans do expect minds to change at the negotiation table. Why else have the meeting? When an impasse arises, we use our best arguments and persuasive appeals to change the other side's point of view. Although the *nemawashi* approach is often used in the United States — we sometimes call it lobbying — and it may often be the smart strategy, it is not the norm.

Shokai-Sha (introducer), *Chukai-Sha* (Mediator)

Boye DeMente, in his book The Japanese Way of Doing Business, mentions the importance of friendly and neutral third parties in establishing relationships and settling disputes between Japanese firms. This is not a new idea in the West, but in Japan, the functions of *shokai-sha* and *chukai-sha* are institutionalized. Generally, business relationships in Japan are established only through the proper connections and associated introductions. "Cold calls" are simply not made. Instead, a third party (often a bank or trading company executive) familiar with both parties arranges and attends the initial meeting. This third party is called *shokai-sha* in Japan. At later stages in the negotiation, if things go wrong, another outside party or *chukai-sha* may be asked to mediate the conflicts. However, the *shokai-sha* will usually act in both capacities. Only in rare instances will the *shokai-sha* feel it necessary to call in another person to act as *chukai-sha*. . . .

The Special Problem for American Sellers

A special point of conflict exists when American sellers call on Japanese buyers. Given the horizontal relationship between American negotiators and the vertical relationship between Japanese negotiators, what happens in cross-cultural negotiations? It is our belief that a Japanese seller and an American buyer will get along fine, while the American seller and Japanese buyer will have great problems. We believe this consideration to be a key factor in our trade difficulties with Japan.

When Japanese sellers come to America to market their products, they naturally assume the lower-status position, act accordingly (showing great deference for the American buyer), and a sale is made. Initially, Japanese sellers are taken advantage of. After all, they expect American buyers to respect their needs. But in any case, a relationship is established between firms. The door is open, and the Japanese sellers have the opportunity to learn the American way, to adjust their behavior, and to establish a more viable long-term relationship.

Such a conception of the Japanese experience in America is supported by both field interviews and experiences and by our laboratory observations. Universally,

Japanese executives in the United States report that their companies "took a beating" when entering the American market, but they also report adjusting their business and negotiation practices to fit the American system. Moreover, in our management laboratory, the Japanese were more likely to adjust their behavior. In cross-cultural interactions, Japanese executives dramatically increased eye contact, increased the number of smiles, and decreased the number of aggressive persuasive tactics. Also, there were fewer silent periods in cross-cultural negotiations, but this is apparently not due to Japanese adjustments as much as to Americans filling potential silent periods with new arguments.

There is an important implication underlying this apparent adjustment made by the Japanese but not by the American negotiators. Anthropologists tell us that power relations usually determine who adapts their behavior in a cross-cultural setting. Japanese executives in an American business setting are likely to be the ones to modify their behavior. Moreover, in American negotiations, status relations are less defined and less important. Japanese sellers can apparently fit into such a situation without offending American buyers.

However, if American sellers take their normative set of bargaining behaviors to Japan, negotiations are apt to end abruptly. American sellers expect to be treated as equals and act accordingly. Japanese buyers are likely to view this rather brash behavior in lower-status sellers as inappropriate and disrespectful. Japanese buyers are made to feel uncomfortable and thus, without explanation, politely shut the door to trade. American sellers do not make the first sale and hence, do not learn the Japanese system.

Chapter 6

NEGOTIATION APPLICATIONS

A. INTRODUCTION

This chapter considers negotiation in three specific contexts: the settlement of business disputes, the adoption of legislation, and plea bargaining in criminal cases. In the final section, we examine the integrity of negotiation conduct, both in the abstract and in specific bargaining situations.

Section B presents three quite different examples of business negotiations. For another example, see Judge Friendly's *Frigaliment* decision, found in Chapter Two. Additional examples are as close at hand as your other classes, and any major Sunday newspaper.

Section C offers up a case study of the legislative process as an exquisite, albeit often unsightly, process of many negotiations and compromise. As Otto von Bismarck famously observed, there are two things you do not want to watch being made: sausage and legislation. The result may be fine, but the process is less than edifying. The making of deals in the executive and judicial branches of government are considered at numerous places in this book, so it seemed appropriate to also give some attention to the branch of government that makes the laws. Court-connected ADR is the subject of Chapter Ten, while Chapter Twelve is devoted to the use of ADR by the executive branch of government.

Section D discusses the processing of persons who are accused of crimes and decide to settle the case, through a process known as plea bargaining, rather than have resort to the trial (by jury, if desired) guaranteed by the United States and state constitutions. The vast majority of criminal cases (over 90 percent) are settled out of the public eye in a process that has nothing to do with the full due process trial that is the subject of criminal law courses and a staple of television trials. As with legislation, the process is not always edifying. The settlement of civil cases is the subject of Chapter Thirteen.

Section E considers the vexed topic of integrity in negotiation, both by principals and by their agents (often attorneys). Reasonable people do not expect complete candor in all circumstances from other parties to contested negotiations, but both the law and common practice demand some level of basic integrity. Alas, general principles do not decide hard questions, and they do not tell us where along the continuum from mere puffing to impermissible dissimulation to draw the line.

B. COMMERCIAL (INCLUDING CONSUMER) TRANSACTIONS

1. Arthur Allen Leff, *Injury, Ignorance and Spite: The Dynamics of Coercive Collection*, 80 YALE L.J. 1, 25-26 (1970)

The "solution" to many of the diverse disputes between businessmen takes the form of some variation on one of the following scenarios. The scene of each is simple: split screen, two telephones:

Buyer: Hello, Morris? Those widgets you sent us. They're breaking every minute. You want me to pay for such junk?

Seller: Look, if your men don't know how to use widgets right, what do you want from me? They're just what you ordered, Grade A-2 stainless steel widgets.

Buyer: Stainless steel they're not. Swiss cheese maybe, orange-crate wood, but not steel.

Seller: Look, Kevin, maybe we've been having a little quality control problem — just temporary. Do the best you can and we'll make it up next time.

Buyer: OK, but don't forget. The noise of popping widgets my partner doesn't like to hear.

Seller: Hello, Kevin? So — what's with our last bill?

Buyer: My bookkeeper's been sick.

Seller: Uh huh. Your hand cramps when you pick up a pen?

Buyer: Soon, Morris.

Seller: How soon? Tomorrow?

Buyer: Come on, Morris; did I make such a stink when you were shipping out those cardboard widgets?

Seller: OK, OK. Maybe I'll give you a couple of weeks more. You're not really in trouble are you?

Buyer: Absolutely not. I got plenty of orders. Go check with some of the other guys.

Seller: Don't worry. I already did. OK, take a couple of weeks.

Seller: So Kevin. Where's the money?

Buyer:	Soon.
Seller:	It's been soon a long time. Now it's now.
Buyer:	Look Morris, I could have gotten the stuff from Acme or Nadir cheaper. I gave you the trade.
Seller:	Now you're giving me the business. Now! Or there'll be trouble.
Buyer:	Tell you what I'll do. I'll pay you today, right now, what I could've got the merchandise for from Acme.
Seller:	Tell you what I'll do. I'll break your head is what I'll do. We got a goddam contract Kevin, and you pay the goddam contract price.
Buyer:	Morris, you don't like my deal, sue me with your contract.
Seller:	I may and I may not. But one thing I know I'll do; anyone asks me if you pay your bills the answer is no. [The last clause is delivered in a shriek of absolute credibility.]
Buyer:	Morris? Half today, the rest at the end of the month?
Seller:	O.K.

2. Comments and Questions

a. The three brief negotiations described by Professor Leff teach us much about relations between commercial sellers and buyers. The disputes portrayed are the most serious problems faced by each type of party. The fundamental concern of sellers is that buyers will not make full and timely payment, with total nonpayment being the ultimate horrible. The range of potential problems for buyers is greater, but defective goods (breach of warranty) is unquestionably the most significant.

b. Buyers and sellers are merchants: parties who deal in goods of the kind in the transaction at issue. Merchants are experienced and expert with regard to whatever product is the subject of a transaction. Merchants are experts about two related aspects of the thing being bought or sold: the product itself and the market for that product.

c. Merchants are "repeat players," frequently engaging in particular types of transactions. This has two consequences in terms of knowledge about the type of transaction, including the sorts of things that can go awry. First, the merchant becomes expert simply by repetition. Even the least skilled person or firm learns a good bit from doing something twenty or fifty times, be it riding a bicycle, mediating a dispute, or purchasing a truckload of widgets. Second, the per transaction cost of investing in information drops as the number of instances increases, making it rational for a merchant to pay (whether in money or in time) to acquire further information about commonly engaged in transactions.

d. Businesses that deal regularly with a product (be it finished goods, semi-finished, or raw materials) become experts in addressing problems that arise commonly. Imperfect widgets usually are not a calamity — a zero defect approach makes sense only for the space shuttle and a few other special situations. Where parties deal regularly with one another, as commonly occurs, the possibility for trade-offs arise, as Leff's examples illustrate. The buyer makes do with less than perfect widgets, the seller is patient about receiving payment.

e. One aspect of expertise is the ability to distinguish between minor or temporary problems and serious ones. A buyer can find out from other buyers about their experience with the quality of seller's goods, responsiveness when problems arise, willingness to be flexible in accommodating buyer's needs, etc. Similarly, a seller that is not being paid can find out if a buyer has serious problems, or just temporary difficulty. Recall from Leff's second negotiation: The seller asks whether the buyer is really in trouble, and the buyer responds no, you can check with others in the trade. The seller's answer is, "Don't worry. I already did."

f. Expertise about problems means that fewer arise, and those that do often can be solved more easily — particularly when the parties have dealt with one another before and plan to do so again. An established business relationship is not to be severed casually. This supplier or customer may be imperfect, but the alternative could be worse — and uncertainty is itself a cost. Even if the alternative is not "worse," there are costs associated with making a change and adjusting to a new situation.

g. Merchants often do not need the assistance of third parties to resolve disputes, because they have access to very effective informal sanctions. In Leff's third dialogue, when the buyer suggests that the seller is welcome to file a lawsuit, seller's response is to threaten the far more effective sanction of telling others in the trade that buyer does not pay his debts. (There are often more formal mechanisms for broadcasting credit information, ranging from credit bureaus to trade organizations.) Of course, the ultimate informal sanction for seller is to decline to sell to buyer, or do so only on a cash basis, but that "solution" carries costs in lost business.

Where buyer is the aggrieved party, its informal sanction is both simple and highly effective: take its business elsewhere. In unusual instances, the alternatives may be few or inconvenient, but normally there will be several other sellers who are willing and able — nay, eager — to serve the buyer's needs. The rational strategy for buyer is to switch rather than to fight.

h. The matters at issue in business disputes are largely about economic relationships. It is a mistake to think matters like ego and friendship are irrelevant, but compared to divorce and child custody problems, the non-economic aspects of the dispute usually are minor. The importance of the matter negotiated about also is modest in most instances. The worst case scenario for the wronged party just is not terribly bad — the occasional bad debt or defective goods are a normal (if unwelcome) incident of doing business.

i. Of course, not all business negotiations are as easily dispatched as those in Leff's dialogues. A small debt is a problem primarily for the debtor. A large debt is a problem for the creditor. Small firms with limited capital lack the leverage available to a large firm. No firm wants to be dependent on a single customer. A sound rule for long time survival of a firm (and a lot less worry for its senior managers) is to avoid having any customer represent more than five percent of its business. From the perspective of the customer, being the dominant customer of a supplier has the benefit of leverage over the supplier and excellent service, but this approach also raises the risk of dislocation in the event the supplier goes out of business or has severe quality problems. In this circumstance, litigation is unlikely to be helpful, because the most likely consequence is to drive the supplier to file for bankruptcy. Even if the customer was awarded a substantial money judgment, it almost certainly would be uncollectible. A judgment creditor is a species of unsecured creditor, and such claims get paid last and very late — if at all.

j. Business contracts often provide for resort to ADR mechanisms if attempts at informal settlement do not work. Solutions short of litigation nearly always suffice because of the situational characteristics described above. Disputes between merchants and consumers, who are "one shot players," do not settle so easily. In what fundamental ways is the consumer transaction different from the transactions between merchants, and how do these differences impact potential settlement of buyer-seller disputes? How should these differences influence the design of a dispute settlement regime for consumer purchases of "big ticket" items?

3. G. RICHARD SHELL, BARGAINING FOR ADVANTAGE 138-44 (1999)

AKIO MORITA GETS A VISIT

In September 1976, Sidney Sheinberg, president of both Universal Pictures and its parent company, MCA, had a problem. Sony was launching a new electronic device called Betamax. The forerunner of what we now call the VCR, the Betamax permitted television viewers to copy and replay TV programs. Sheinberg was upset with this development.

Universal's business was licensing networks and television stations to show its copyrighted motion pictures and television productions. A substantial portion of those revenues came from reruns of programs, including movies. In addition, MCA had invested millions in developing a technology called a "videodisk" that would permit consumers to watch prerecorded movies at home. Unlike the VCR, the videodisk was a playback-only system.

As Sheinberg saw it, the Betamax was a threat to his basic business strategy. It would enable consumers to tape Universal's movies and TV shows free of charge and replay them as often as they liked. If the audience already had an original show on tape, what station would pay for a rerun? Who would buy the videodisk?

"It's [the Betamax] a copyright violation. It's got to be," said Sheinberg when he heard about the Sony machine. "I'd be crazy to let them [market it]."

To complicate matters, MCA and Sony were engaged in a number of joint projects. In particular, MCA was hoping that Sony would become a key manufacturer of playback machines to run MCA's videodisks. The two firms had also cooperated before on several deals. The name Sony, as Akio Morita had hoped years before, was rapidly becoming a household name in high-quality electronics, and Morita had gained a reputation as one of the smartest Japanese businessmen in America. He had no reason to suspect that Sheinberg had a problem with anything he or Sony was doing.

So, from Sony's point of view, the two firms were in a collaborative relationship. But from Sheinberg's point of view, the stakes had just risen sharply. It was a ticklish situation.

As it happened, Sheinberg and MCA's chairman, Lew Wasserman, had a dinner meeting with Morita scheduled for the following week in New York to discuss Sony's participation in the videodisk project. They hoped the informal setting of a dinner conversation following a cooperative, brainstorming session about the videodisk project would be an effective way to raise the Betamax issue without threatening the overall Sony-MCA relationship.

In preparation for the meeting, Sheinberg had his law firm research and prepare a legal memorandum regarding the legality of the Betamax. Reading the memo, Sheinberg became even more convinced that he could and should stop the advance of this technology. His positioning theme was straightforward: The Betamax was an illegal machine. His job was to get that point across to Morita.

Sheinberg decided to make his point by giving Morita an ultimatum: Either Morita would have to address MCA's concerns — preferably by dropping the Betamax — or Sheinberg would stop the technology in its tracks by suing Sony for copyright law violation.

FRIENDS DON'T SUE

On the afternoon of the appointed day, Sheinberg and Wasserman met as planned with Morita and Sony's top U.S. executive, Harvey Schein, at Sony's U.S. corporate headquarters. The four men then engaged in a lengthy, animated discussion of the videodisk project. There was no mention of the Betamax.

They then moved to a catered dinner in Sony's main boardroom. As the dinner came to a close, Sheinberg reached into his coat pocket and pulled out the memorandum from MCA's lawyers supporting his argument that the Betamax violated U.S. copyright law. To his astonished audience, Sheinberg explained his view that the Betamax was illegal and that Universal would be forced to sue unless Sony either dropped the product or made some other type of accommodation. Morita would later recall that Wasserman said, "We may have to do this, because if the Betamax is successful the videodisk will never get off the ground."

Morita reacted with surprise and confusion. Hadn't the parties just finished discussing a major cooperative deal? What was all this about lawsuits?

As a business matter, Morita rejected MCA's analysis regarding the conflict between the Betamax and the videodisk. "I totally disagree with that argument" he said, "because in the future the videodisk and the video recorder will coexist, just as the record and tape recorder coexist in the audio field."

Morita then went on to express his confusion about what the dispute would mean for the MCA-Sony business partnership. It was hard, Morita said, to see how two business partners such as Universal and Sony could be talking about a joint project such as the videodisk one minute and about suing each other the next.

He tried to make his point with an image that any Japanese would understand. "When we shake hands [with one hand]," he told Sheinberg, "we will not hit you with the other hand." That was a basic principle of Japanese business, Morita told his guests, and a personal principle that he intended to live by — even in America.

Sheinberg and Wasserman were not prepared to listen or argue. They had come with their lawyer's opinion, and they had not heard anything from Morita to shake their faith in it. Case closed.

After Sheinberg and Wasserman had departed, Morita assured Harvey Schein that MCA could not really be serious about a lawsuit. "We've done a number of things over the years, and we're talking about the videodisk," Morita said. "Friends don't sue."

Sheinberg and Wasserman were equally confident that they had delivered their message: Negotiate or we sue you with everything we've got. From their point of view, it was Morita's turn to make a move.

But Morita did not make a move. Instead, he returned to Japan. Within a month, Universal had formed a coalition with Walt Disney and other entertainment producers and began drafting its lawsuit. Private investigators were gathering evidence to prove that the Betamax was being used to copy legally protected television shows. Finally, on November 11, 1976, still not having heard from Morita, Universal and Disney filed their lawsuit against Sony.

Morita was getting ready to play golf in Japan when he heard the news. As a colleague later recalled it, "He let out a kind of death cry" when he was told about the lawsuit.

But once he was sued, he accepted the challenge. And Sony eventually won the case. Eleven years and millions of dollars in legal fees later, the United States Supreme Court put an end to the dispute by upholding Sony's right to make and sell the videocassette recorder.

By the time the lawsuit was over, everyone involved in the case — from Disney and Universal to Sony — was making millions of dollars selling a new product, videotapes, through an entirely new type of convenience outlet, the video store. Contrary to Sheinberg's fears, TV stations were still paying top dollar for reruns. And everyone was still going to theaters to watch movies — even to see films they could rent and watch on videotape. Morita, meanwhile, had written and given a talk at Harvard University entitled "The Role of Lawyers in Handicapping Entrepreneurial Efforts in the United States."

DON'T BE A "BLABBERMOUTH" NEGOTIATOR: ASK QUESTIONS

What can we learn about effective information exchange from the failed Sheinberg-Morita negotiation over the future of the VCR? Sheinberg made three classic mistakes: He thought he could gain advantage by surprising an unprepared opponent, he focused on delivering information instead of asking questions and listening, and he ignored a potential cross-cultural difference. For his part, Morita failed to get beyond his own relational frame of reference and into his opponent's shoes. He did not listen to what the other side was telling him. Let's look at each of these mistakes in turn.

First, what did Sheinberg gain by surprising Morita with the Betamax issue? It would have cost Sheinberg nothing to have told Morita in advance about his Betamax concerns and then staged a discussion between equals. Morita could do nothing to take away MCA's lawsuit. But for reasons that are not clear (perhaps Sheinberg was afraid a well-prepared Morita might talk him out of his position), Sheinberg preferred to launch a surprise attack.

People who approach negotiation as if it were a game or sport often think they can gain an advantage by tricking or surprising the other side. They think they can score a bargaining point by faking one way and moving in another. But this is usually a mistake in important negotiations. You actually do better when the other side is prepared to deal with the real issues.

A professional labor mediator and I were once called in by management to help facilitate a union-management labor negotiation. The company viewed the union as stubborn and disrespectful. The union leaders, disorganized and new to their jobs, assumed the company was out to take advantage of the workers. Relations at the plant were terrible. What did we do? We spent the first three months of the engagement helping the union become better organized. Why? Because it had not had a real meeting in over a year and the leaders were both inexperienced and out of touch with the real issues. To make progress, management needed an organized and informed opponent at the bargaining table.

Sheinberg's critical mistake came from his lack of curiosity about Morita's interests, issues, and perceptions. By framing the problem as a matter of legal rights on which there could be no debate, he shut down communication regarding business interests. He obtained Morita's views on the possible synergies between videodisk and videotape technologies almost by accident. The lawsuit was a "showstopper" in terms of communication.

Finally, Sheinberg failed to consider Morita's Asian frame of reference for business relationships. Human differences such as culture, gender, and personal style must be considered for the signaling part of information exchange to work. Morita was Japanese; Sheinberg was American. Was there a cultural issue to worry about in this encounter?

Yes. The Japanese have a significantly different way of viewing legal disputes than Americans do. Virtually all Japanese contracts contain a clause stating that the parties will work in good faith to resolve future differences through negotiation. American contracts assume that litigation may be needed and feature clauses stating where and by what set of legal rules disputes will be resolved.

Americans file literally millions of court cases each year. In America, litigation is not a last resort; it is a normal part of being in business. In Japan, very few disputes go to court. To the Japanese, a lawsuit is a burial service for a productive business relationship.

On Sony's side of the table, Morita showed a cultural blindness of his own. His emphasis on relationships was rooted in the Japanese approach to business, but he was in New York, not Japan. He did not understand the importance of the stakes as seen from his opponent's perspective. Nor did he listen to what his opponent was telling him.

4. SHIVA NAIPAUL, NORTH OF SOUTH: AN AFRICAN JOURNEY 47-52 (1978)

[The author, brother of the far better known V. S. Naipaul, was of Indian descent. He was born and raised in Trinidad, spent many years in England

and traveled extensively throughout Africa. The title refers to parts of Africa north of the country of South Africa. The Kikuyu are the largest tribal group in Kenya. Kenyatta Avenue is a main thoroughfare in Nairobi, the capital and largest city in Kenya.]

A certain embarrassment had so far prevented me from making use of the service offered by the shoeshine boys who line Kenyatta Avenue. The occupation had too many unpleasant associations. But observation had shown that my reservations were not shared by many people. My scruples were rapidly eroded. My chosen shoeshine "boy" was not a boy at all — though, I should add, many of the fraternity literally are. He was a gray-headed, rheumy-eyed Kikuyu. He wagged his head and clucked his tongue when he saw the state of my shoes.

"Expensive," he said, kneading the leather and nodding appreciatively. "Not very," I said cautiously. "I am first-class shoeshine boy. I will make them be like new for you. They will shine just like mirror. I am best shoeshine boy in the whole of Nairobi. Many years' experience." He began loosening the laces.

"What's your charge?" "Charge?" "How much will I have to pay you? How many shillings?" He waived his arms airily. "Don't worry about charge." "But I do worry." He sighed. It was as though I had caused him profound spiritual pain. "Worries no good for the heart, I ask reasonable price. No need to worry." He produced a bottle containing a yellowish liquid. . . . This he applied liberally, rubbing it in with vigor. "Is that polish?" "Special ingredient," he said, switching his attention from one shoe to the other. "Secret formula. Highly secret formula."

I started to feel uneasy. It occurred to me that I had behaved extremely foolishly. I should have insisted on settling what the price would be before allowing him to start. He explained that the treatment he was giving me would make any further polishing unnecessary for one whole year. "You just take a soft cloth and wipe it over. It will shine just like mirror. I give you full guarantee." "Nonsense." "Not nonsense," he replied equably. "True. This is Deluxe Special I give you. Not nonsense." I withdrew my foot completely.

"Look." He took a crumpled sheet of paper from his shirt pocket and handed it to me. "Read what it says there." It was a typewritten testimonial. "This is to certify that I did not need to have my shoes polished for one year after receiving the Deluxe Special. During all that time my shoes shone like a mirror." The scrawled signature was impossible to decipher. "Do you expect me to believe this rubbish?" I examined my shoes. The kerosene-soaked leather had gone dull and blotchy.

He watched me composedly. "You cannot meet your friends with your shoes looking like that." I saw his point: I was trapped. I surrendered my feet to him. "Remember — no more secret ingredients and formulas. Just polish." "Just polish," he repeated. "You are hard man to please, bwana." With swift dispatch he polished and shined, coaxing out an indifferent gleam from the damaged leather. It would have to do.

I held out five shillings, thinking myself more than generous in the circumstances. I did not want to create a scene. He looked at the money; he looked at me. "What is that for?" "For your labor." He laughed the way one laughs at an obvious absurdity. "Bwana, bwana." "Are you trying to tell me that you expect to be paid more than five shillings for destroying my shoes?" He nodded. "How much?" "Sixty shillings, bwana." He folded his arms across his chest. He showed me a neatly typewritten card that listed the various services he claimed to provide and their cost.

Super Deluxe Special:	100 shillings
Deluxe Special:	80 shillings
Deluxe Ordinary:	50 shillings
Special:	35 shillings
Ordinary:	20 shillings
Quick polish:	5 shillings
Quick brush:	3 shillings

"Which one of these am I supposed to have had?" "You had the Deluxe Special for eighty shillings. But — he looked furtively at my shoes — I give you discount price." I returned the card. "Five shillings or nothing." "The card, bwana. Read what the card says." "I don't care what it says. Five shillings or nothing."

He ran to the neighboring shoeshine boy. The Kikuyu, gabbing now in his native tongue, pointed at the card, then at me, then at my shoes. He was the very picture of outraged virtue. His ally glowered at me. I went over to them. "What is he saying?" "He is saying," the ally replied, "that you are refusing to pay him. He is saying he will call the police for you." He was grim; unfriendly.

I looked up and down the avenue. There was not a policeman in sight. The Kikuyu was gabbing again, pointing at the card and at me. I too now sought an ally. I approached one of the passers by and asked what he normally paid to have his shoes shined. He shrugged and continued on his way. I asked another. He was no more helpful. An absurd panic gripped me. I offered ten shillings. The Kikuyu refused, folding his arms across his chest. I offered fifteen. He refused that too. I flung the fifteen shillings on his stand and walked away with as much resolution as I could summon. The Kikuyu pursued me down the avenue.

"I call the police for you. They throw you in jail. They beat you up. They kill you. I myself kill you." I fled into the safety of the first hotel I came to.

6. Comments and Questions

a. How much should Naipaul pay for the shoeshine? Whether the theory is contract or restitution, he received a service that had value and was rendered at his request. When price is not agreed upon, the vendor is entitled to receive the "fair market value" for the goods or services in question. That, of course, is a difficult matter to determine. What about warranty issues?

b. How is the shoeshine problem different from the dispute that can (and often does) occur when a person uses an unlicensed taxi in any major city (in America or elsewhere), and does not determine the price prior to commencing the ride?

c. One of the authors (a former resident of East Africa) has used this situation for some years in teaching Contracts, as a device to drive home the importance for buyers of prior agreement on the price term. The exotic (to American students) setting for the shoeshine problem, and the diverse backgrounds of the parties, has never been a barrier to the contract law analysis.

C. NEGOTIATION IN LEGISLATIVE BODIES

1. Tom Melling, *Dispute Resolution within Legislative Institutions*, 46 STAN. L. REV. 1677 (1994)

While legal literature abounds with dispute resolution techniques for our court system, scholars have neglected to analyze their importance for the legislative process. Instead, scholars study the content of statutes, their application, and legislative history, but ignore the process that produced the legislation. Similarly, practicing lawyers clamor to learn about ADR techniques that substitute for litigation, yet they know little about how the legislative process affects the formation of statutes.

This failure to evaluate the legislative process from the perspective of dispute resolution is surprising; given the modern importance of statutory law and the role that lawyers, lobbyists, and legislators play in drafting and passing statutes. Lawyers can better advance their clients' interests if they understand the barriers to collaborative legislative decision-making. By understanding different dispute resolution techniques, legislators can build consensus among competing interest groups and achieve more favorable results. Judges can also interpret statutes better by studying the legislative process. Moreover, cooperative approaches to legislative decision-making are increasingly important as competing interest groups have nearly mired the federal government in gridlock. Because the legislative process is naturally flexible and receptive to innovation, legislative dispute resolution techniques deserve study.

This note applies dispute resolution theory to legislative conflict. The focal point of the analysis is a case study of the Central Utah Project Completion Act (CUP), a monumental legislative settlement that revolutionizes water management in Utah. Western water policy is particularly apt for the study of dispute resolution, because Western farmers, environmentalists, and cities are continually fighting over this vital but finite resource. Although this conflict continues, Utah's environmentalists and water users worked together to craft novel solutions, making the CUP the "reform model" for future water planning.

[There are] . . . three barriers to the cooperative resolution of conflict within legislative institutions: strategic voting and institutional structure, bargaining through the mass media, and bargaining through elected representatives. Understanding these barriers can do more than just explain why negotiations fail; it can help us devise strategies to overcome the barriers. [During the CUP negotiations], the legislators and disputing parties used three dispute resolution techniques to overcome these barriers. The techniques used were a unanimous decision rule, negotiation in private, and mediation by a politician. A unanimous decision rule eliminates the instability and chaos of cyclical voting by compelling the parties to develop a mutually beneficial solution through cooperative bargaining. Negotiation in private eliminates the politician's dilemma by eliminating the use of the media as a bargaining weapon. Mediation by a politician or a group of politicians encourages interest groups to come to the bargaining table and to resolve their disputes face to face.

A. The CUP: A Case Study of Water Policy Reform

For Utahns, the CUP Completion Act is perhaps the most important legislation enacted by the United States Congress in the last decade. It authorizes the expenditure of nearly $1 billion to complete a water project that will deliver water to urban areas along the Wasatch Front and to farmers in Central Utah. Despite Utah's position as the second most arid state, the CUP will allow the state's economy to grow well into the twenty-first century.

The CUP was originally designed to solve a difficult predicament in Utah. If past trends continue, virtually all population and economic growth will occur in the Salt Lake Valley corridor of North-Central Utah. Yet Utah's most abundant water resource, the Colorado River, lies on the state's eastern border, shielded by a mountain range that rises to 12,000 feet. Thus, in 1956, Congress approved the CUP. It was designed to divert water from fifteen tributaries of the Colorado River through the range of separating mountains to the state's population and agricultural centers. The massive scale of the project nearly caused its demise. By 1987, twenty-one years after construction began, cost overruns approached $500 million. In addition, the environmental impacts were profound. The CUP de-watered or seriously degraded approximately 245 miles of streams, riparian areas, and associated wetlands, destroying thousands of acres of wildlife habitat. The Bureau of Reclamation added to the problem by delaying the project's environmental mitigation far behind project construction.

In 1988, the funds authorized by Congress to complete the project ran out. The CUP was less than 50 percent complete; yet it had not delivered one drop of water from the Colorado River tributaries. Realizing that the CUP was in danger of becoming a white elephant, Utah's congressional delegation tried to obtain additional funds. They introduced a one-paragraph reauthorization bill requesting an additional $750 million. The leadership of the House Interior Committee, however, refused to move the bill, because it lacked genuine fiscal and environmental reforms. The Committee's rejection set the stage for four years of difficult negotiations.

The legislative dispute concerned two broad issues: fiscal and environmental reform. The substantive issues were complex, but the parties fell into several identifiable groups. Environmental organizations led the demand for fiscal and environmental reform. On the other side, agricultural interests and water users fought these reforms, arguing that Congress should keep its commitment to complete the project. At the political level, Utah's congressional delegation split along party lines. The Republicans supported agricultural interests and opposed environmental reforms. Utah's Republicans, however, could not move the bill through the Democratically controlled House without the support of Representative Wayne Owens, the sole Democrat in Utah's congressional delegation.

Representative Owens supported the environmentalists' call for fiscal and environmental reform; nevertheless, he needed the project completed for his own political survival.

Round One: 1988-1990. For over two years. Utah's politicians tried to redesign the project themselves. The negotiations were combative and bitter, spearheaded primarily by Utah Senator Jake Garn and Representative Owens. Both sides played political hardball. Representative Owens enlisted the General Accounting Office to investigate past expenditures sponsored by Senator Garn, undermining the Senator's credibility in the eyes of the House and Senate committee chairmen. Senator Garn enlisted the Utah Republican Party to file an ethics complaint against Representative Owens alleging improper congressional behavior. In early 1990, Utah's congressional delegation finally reached a compromise and again submitted legislation to the Interior Committee. Despite several fiscal and environmental improvements, national environmental organizations remained opposed to the bill, claiming it had "serious problems." Because of this opposition, the chairman of the Interior Committee once again refused to move the bill.

Round Two: 1990-1991. Water users still desperately wanted to get the CUP reauthorized. Environmentalists were equally eager to remedy the damage caused by $1 billion of unfinished construction. Given this glimmer of mutual interest, Representative Owens used his influence with national environmental organizations and with Utah's water community to bring these traditional foes together. In this new round of negotiations, the politicians took a back seat. With Representative Owens acting as a mediator, the groups discovered many common interests. Two and a half months later, the parties signed an agreement that became the blueprint for the CUP Completion Act.

The redesigned CUP contains unprecedented reforms that make it the most fiscally responsible and environmentally progressive federal water project in the West. The CUP's water conservation program significantly increases state cost-sharing requirements and thus sets the standard for future reclamation financing. To address the environmental damage caused by the project's construction, the CUP removes the lackluster Bureau of Reclamation from the task of environmental mitigation and replaces it with a new environmental commission that oversees all mitigation and habitat restoration. In short, by working together, the parties found ways to deliver the water and to protect the environment in a way that made all the parties better off. This agreement, forged during the second round of negotiations, was not fortuitous; it was the result of a specific process that created a cooperative negotiating environment. The three procedural strategies identified earlier helped the parties to overcome legislative barriers and to bargain cooperatively.

1. A Unanimous Decision Rule. When the Utah congressional delegation initially requested additional funds to complete the CUP in 1988, the House Interior Committee chairman stipulated that all affected parties must support the legislation before he would move it out of the committee. This meant the entire Utah congressional delegation, national and local environmental organizations, the governor of Utah, public power interests, and the North Ute Indian Tribe all had to support the bill.

In multiparty negotiations, parties must manage the decision-making process, either explicitly or implicitly, by adopting decision rules. Although a majority decision rule generally governs in our democratic processes, the CUP experience suggests that the use of a consensus process can help overcome the barrier of strategic voting and institutional structure. A unanimous decision rule was critical to the negotiation process for several reasons. First, it encouraged reluctant parties to come to the bargaining table. Although the environmentalists might have blocked a reauthorization of the project, either by lobbying Congress or by challenging the project in court, the chairman's requirement of unanimous agreement eliminated any concern that they would lose their leverage or be ignored if they entered negotiations. As a result, they were able to devote their energies to resolving problems rather than to fighting reauthorization.

In addition to fostering greater participation, a unanimous decision rule eliminated the instability associated with shifting coalitions and strategic voting. Rather than seeking proposals to create a majority coalition, the parties sought solutions that everyone could support. Therefore, the negotiation environment fostered brainstorming and compromise, not strategic behavior and splintered coalitions. Ultimately, the parties discovered subtle alternatives that "enlarged the pig." As dispute resolution scholars have asserted: Consensus, defined and developed by the stakeholders, is more likely to resolve a dispute than a vote of a legislative body, a decision by an administrative agency, or a court decree, because it is likely to meet more of their interests.

Finally, the unanimous decision rule helped create a more stable and lasting agreement. Since all parties participated in crafting the solution, they all worked for its passage. Significantly, the parties agreed not to sabotage the bill with floor amendments, eliminating a fear that often clouds legislative negotiations. In addition, because the parties left the process satisfied with their result, they have continued to consult each other, identifying and solving potential problems before they arise.

Recent empirical studies of group negotiation explain why a unanimous decision rule can overcome the barrier of strategic voting and institutional structure. One study found that groups using a unanimous decision rule were more likely to achieve higher joint outcomes, to integrate the interests of group members, and to distribute resources more equitably than groups using a majority decision rule. A majority decision rule creates fewer opportunities for the parties to discover the priorities of others, which can impede problem-solving activities that maximize the combined utility of group members. A majority decision rule can also be vulnerable to paradoxes of voting that result in inefficient outcomes. Under a unanimous decision rule, the parties have more control over the process and feel more satisfied with and committed to the group's decision. . . .

Several factors must be present for a unanimous decision rule to be practical. Most important, the prospect of no agreement must be worse for all parties than a negotiated settlement. This was critical to the CUP negotiations. If the parties had not reached an agreement, the water users would have wasted millions of dollars and would still not have received any water. For the environmentalists, an unfinished project would have made permanent over $1 billion of construction scars and degradation. The Northern Ute Indian Tribe would have lost its water rights without receiving any compensation. Public power groups would have undermined their relationship with a politically valuable ally, agricultural interests. Finally, an unfinished project would have jeopardized the careers of Utah politicians. Thus, all parties had strong incentives to reach an agreement.

A great risk of requiring unanimity is that each party receives veto power. This increases the bargaining power of weaker parties, who may be tempted to prevent resolution. For example, studies have shown that juries operating under a unanimous decision rule "hang" more often. Because of this possibility, some researchers believe that, in a zero-sum negotiation, a majority decision rule may work better than a requirement of unanimity.

Under a unanimous decision rule, parties may also threaten to veto to gain strategic advantage. During the CUP negotiations, a couple of parties threatened to oppose the bill if others did not acquiesce to their demands. While these threats initially caused great concern, other parties exercised strong group pressure that encouraged the threatening parties to back down. While the effectiveness of group pressure has never been studied with juries, there are several reasons why group pressure in the political arena may be highly effective at decreasing the danger of threats. First, most government officials are repeat players; therefore, wielding veto power against other parties has long-term reputational consequences. Second, if a party actually carries out a veto threat, the public will blame that party for creating gridlock. In the case of the CUP, no party wanted to be targeted as responsible for killing the project.

Other concerns may also make a unanimous decision quite impractical. As the number of negotiating parties increases, a majority decision rule becomes more efficient. Jury studies have shown that impasse becomes more frequent, and deliberations take longer, in larger groups. All parties that can realistically block an agreement must participate in the negotiation process. If an important group is left out, especially a powerful party, any agreement may be meaningless. In the first round of CUP negotiations, Utah's politicians did not include the national environmental groups. Although the Utah political delegation reached a consensus, the environmental groups blocked the agreement and another round of negotiations began. On the other hand, the parties excluded the Bureau of Reclamation, the original architects and builders of the project. Making an "end run" around the Bureau allowed the parties to craft historic reforms to complete the project. The Bureau opposed the second agreement, because it was not a party involved in the development of the [new bill] but could not stop its passage. Excluding the Bureau was possible only because Senator Garn had considerable clout with the Bush administration. Ultimately, he had to appeal to President Bush's Chief of Staff John Sununu to fend off the Bureau's attempt to sabotage the reauthorization bill.

2. Negotiation In Private. The bargaining atmosphere during the two rounds of CUP negotiations demonstrates how the politician's dilemma creates a barrier to the cooperative resolution of conflict. During the first round of negotiations, parties used the press to stake out positions, to make threats, and to attack other parties. Tensions escalated, and the parties overlooked many mutually beneficial solutions. For example, when Senator Garn publicly opposed

Representative Owens' proposal to create a fund for future environmental repairs, he took a rigid bargaining position, making future negotiation more difficult. The press focused on this single issue, causing the parties to ignore other relevant considerations. For Senator Garn and Representative Owens, going to the press became the dominant strategy, since each felt compelled to protect his position and to take advantage of any exploitable weakness. This approach wasted time and resources that could have been used to research or discuss alternatives.

When the second round of negotiations began, the CUP parties agreed to a truce. They no longer relied on the press to influence the negotiation; they bargained in private. When they reached closure on an issue, the parties would address the press together. Removing the press from the decision-making process helped to "smooth out the playing field," making a search for joint solutions possible. It eliminated the temptation to use outside strategies and, hence, eliminated the politician's dilemma.

Some may contend that, although the media hinder cooperative bargaining, it is better for society to involve the press in every step of the legislative process, because the press squares government policies with popular opinion and discourages unethical or disingenuous behavior by elected officials. This argument should not prevent private political negotiation. First, if the parties operate under a unanimous decision rule, and if all of the affected parties are included in the negotiation, a watchdog like the press is not needed. Even if a party is left out of the bargaining process, the proposed bill must pass through Congress. During congressional debate, there is more than ample time for the press to scrutinize a bill and to alert the public to problems in the legislative process. For example, Congress took over thirty months to enact the CUP Completion Act after the parties reached the agreement they made public.

3. Mediation By A Politician. The CUP experience suggests an unorthodox role for politicians: the mediation of disputes between conflicting interest groups. When the CUP conflict began in 1988, Representative Owens played the role of an active advocate. Motivated by the need to move the bill out of the House Subcommittee on Water, Power, and Offshore Energy Resources, he spearheaded environmental reform efforts. After two years of protracted, frustrating, and disappointing bargaining, Representative Owens had achieved significant environmental reforms. Nevertheless, environmental organizations refused to support the result. They sought greater environmental protections, as well as slightly different objectives. In other words, the water users and environmentalists failed to reach an agreement because of the elected representative barrier.

In the second round of negotiations, the water users and environmentalists eliminated this problem by negotiating directly, with Representative Owens acting as a mediator. Because Representative Owens enjoyed the respect of all the parties, he was able to persuade them to begin a new round of negotiations. Once the environmentalists became directly involved in the negotiation process, they could express and achieve their objectives directly.

By stepping into the role of mediator, Representative Owens not only eliminated the elected representative barrier but also assisted the dispute resolution process. During the negotiations, he helped create viable alternatives and guided the parties towards agreement. Sometimes he acted as a facilitator, helping to sustain the bargaining process. He organized meetings, facilitated communication, and kept notes during the negotiations. . . . At other times, he was an "activist mediator." When the parties could not agree on several issues, they "looked to somebody who would resolve those issues." Because both sides respected his judgment, they accepted Representative Owens' position as the final settlement. On more than one occasion, both sides nearly walked out. Without Representative Owens acting as a mediator, the process probably would have failed. Each time, he succeeded in persuading the frustrated party to stay and resolve the problem.

There are several good reasons for politicians to remove themselves from the traditional role of an agent and step into the role of mediator. Many of the typical characteristics of politicians make them effective mediators. Mediators must have intelligence, stamina, energy, patience, a sense of humor, persuasiveness, credibility, and impartiality. Except perhaps for impartiality, these are valuable skills for anyone who hopes to win a grueling campaign for elected office. Without these skills, Representative Owens would not have been nearly as successful in bringing the groups together and mediating the dispute. For example, his sense of humor often kept disagreements from escalating out of control.

In addition to possessing traits needed to play the role of mediator, politicians bring a special advantage to the position of mediator: their stature gives them influence over the parties. For example, the parties to the CUP dispute valued their relationship with Representative Owens and, consequently, were willing to work with him and to accept his position as the mediated solution to an impasse when necessary. Jacob Bercovitch refers to the mediator's ability to influence the outcome as "leverage." Elected officials tend automatically to have a certain amount of leverage, making them well-positioned to mediate disputes. Bercovitch, a critic of the traditional emphasis on impartial mediation, argues that mediators need leverage to achieve their primary tasks of reframing and persuasion.

On the other hand, some politicians may not be well-suited to the role of mediator. Usually, politicians define themselves to their constituents as advocates for specific policies or popular legislation. Many politicians believe the only thing in the middle of the road is yellow paint and dead chickens. [The Texas version of this adage is, yellow stripes and dead armadillos.] Thus, politicians may develop such strong reputations for their positions that they lose their ability to act as neutral third parties. Often, a politician's outsized personality cannot fit into the mediator's "ego container, an imaginary box to constrain one's self-importance." Politicians may also try to take advantage of their power to unfairly mediate a dispute. But credibility may be the greatest barrier to mediation by politicians. To be effective, a mediator must build trust and maintain the respect of the parties. In the world of politics, past voting records, well-publicized opinions, and affiliation with political parties shape political credibility. Although Representative Owens was clearly not entirely neutral in the CUP dispute, both the water users and the environmentalists trusted him to set aside his substantive goals and to devote his attention to helping the parties resolve the dispute.

2. Comments and Questions

a. Melling certainly is correct that the ADR literature has largely ignored legislatures, perhaps following the injunction that there are two things that one does not want to see made — sausage and legislation. Political scientists have long been interested in the legislative process although, like so much of the social sciences, recent writings are so full of specialized vocabulary and mathematics as to be incomprehensible to the uninitiated.

b. Many people think that the best single work on how the legislative process works at the federal level still is ERIC REDMAN, THE DANCE OF LEGISLATION (1973). Redman takes his title from the writing of a distinguished political science professor, Woodrow Wilson: "Once you begin the dance of legislation, you must struggle through its mazes as best you can to the breathless end — if any end there be."

c. It is striking that the metaphor of legislation as dance can be traced back at least as far as Wilson, because settlement negotiations, both facilitated and directly between parties, are commonly spoken of as a "dance" toward an agreed solution.

d. A unanimity rule is standard in Negotiated Rulemaking (reg-neg). This topic is discussed in Chapter Twelve. This parallel is not surprising, because rulemaking by administrative agencies is a legislative process. [The English use the expression "subordinate legislation" for rules.]

e. Note how Representative Owen moved from being a partisan participant to becoming a mediator, without ever giving up his legislative position. Would similar behavior be acceptable for a conventional mediator? Is party consent an essential consideration?

f. Melling suggests that the need for legislators to frequently make compromises, and to view issues from multiple perspectives, is good training for mediation. Many mediators are former judges, notably among the ranks of those charging the highest fees. Judges serve as umpires and decide disputes, rather than brokering compromises. Might political experience provide a better training ground for mediators than being a judge?

D. PEOPLE ACCUSED OF CRIMES: PLEA BARGAINING

1. Comments and Questions

a. Nearly all persons convicted of crimes never receive a trial. Instead, the accused pleads guilty to an agreed upon offense — almost always a lesser offense than would be charged at trial. The sentence that the prosecutor will recommend to the judge is also agreed upon. Judges are not bound by sentencing deals struck between the prosecutor and the accused, but the recommendation of the prosecutor is nearly always followed. A different approach would undermine the ability of the prosecutor to obtain plea bargains and result in an enormous number of trials. (If 95 percent of the accused enter pleas, a reduction to 90 percent pleas would double the number of trials.) Few judges find that an attractive prospect.

b. Counsel for defendants are part of the assembly line process that constitutes our criminal law system. The pervasive reliance on plea bargaining is widely regarded as an abomination, but it is much easier to critique the status quo than to produce a suitable alternative.

c. Professor Blumberg, who was initially trained as a sociologist, characterizes the usual resort to plea bargaining as a confidence game, in which the accused is the victim, and his attorney is one of the victimizers. Professors Stuntz and Bibas provide updated critiques of plea bargaining, with an emphasis on the settlement incentives faced by the players. Both conclude that the model of bargaining "in the shadow of the law," discussed in Chapter Three, has limited application in the context of plea bargaining.

d. Professor Gifford discusses negotiation strategies for plea bargaining, from the perspective of both the prosecutor and defense attorney. To what extent are the same considerations and strategies applicable in other negotiation situations, and to what extent are they special to the criminal law context?

e. The related topic of victim-offender mediation is considered in Chapter Nine.

2. Abraham S. Blumberg, *The Practice of Law as a Confidence Game*, 1 LAW & SOC'Y REV. 15 (1967)

The overwhelming majority of convictions in criminal cases (usually over 90 percent) are not the product of a combative, trial-by-jury process at all, but instead merely involve the sentencing of the individual after a negotiated, bargained-for plea of guilty has been entered. [S]cant attention has been paid to the organizational structure and personnel of the criminal court itself. Indeed, the extremely high conviction rate produced without the features of an adversary trial in our courts would tend to suggest that the "trial" becomes a perfunctory reiteration and validation of the pretrial interrogation and investigation.

The institutional setting of the court defines a role for the defense counsel in a criminal case radically different from the one traditionally depicted. It is grounded in pragmatic values, bureaucratic priorities, and administrative instruments. These exalt maximum production and the particularistic career designs of organizational incumbents, whose occupational and career commitments tend to generate a set of priorities. These priorities exert a higher claim than the stated ideological goals of "due process of law" and are often inconsistent with them.

Organizational goals and discipline impose a set of demands and conditions of practice on the respective professions in the criminal court, to which they respond by abandoning their ideological and professional commitments to the accused client, in the service of these higher claims of the court organization. All court personnel, including the accused's own lawyer, tend to be coopted to become agent-mediators who help the accused redefine his situation and restructure his perceptions concomitant with a plea of guilty. . . . [Defense] lawyers, whether privately retained or of the legal-aid, public defender variety, have close and continuing relations with the prosecuting office and the court itself through discreet relations with the judges via their law secretaries or "confidential" assistants. Indeed, lines of communication, influence and contact with those offices, as well as with the Office of the Clerk of the Court, Probation Division, and with the press, are essential to present and prospective requirements of criminal law practice.

Accused persons come and go in the court system schema, but the structure and its occupational incumbents remain to carry on their respective career, occupational and organizational enterprises. The individual stridencies, tensions, and conflicts a given accused person's case may present to all the participants are overcome, because the formal and informal relations of all the groups in the court setting require it. The probability of continued future relations and interaction must be preserved at all costs.

This is particularly true of the "lawyer regulars," i.e., those defense lawyers, who by virtue of their continuous appearances in behalf of defendants, tend to represent the bulk of a criminal court's non-indigent case workload. . . . Some of the "lawyer regulars" are highly visible as one moves about the major urban centers of the nation; their offices line the back streets of the courthouses, at times sharing space with bondsmen. Their political "visibility" in terms of local club house ties, reaching into the judge's chambers and prosecutor's office, are also deemed essential to successful practitioners. Previous research has indicated that the "lawyer regulars" make no effort to conceal their dependence upon police, bondsmen, and jail personnel. Nor do they conceal the necessity for maintaining intimate relations with all levels of personnel in the court setting as a means of obtaining, maintaining, and building their practice. These informal relations are the sine qua non not only of retaining a practice, but also in the negotiation of pleas and sentences.

The client, then, is a secondary figure in the court system, as in certain other bureaucratic settings. He becomes a means to other ends of the organization's incumbents. He may present doubts, contingencies, and pressures which challenge existing, informal arrangements or disrupt them; but these tend to be resolved in favor of the continuance of the organization and its relations as before. There is a greater community of interest among all the principal organizational structures and their incumbents than exists elsewhere in other settings. The accused's lawyer has far greater professional, economic, intellectual, and other ties to the various elements of the court system than he does to his own client. In short, the court is a closed community.

This is more than just the case of the usual "secrets" of bureaucracy, which are fanatically defended from an outside view. Even all elements of the press are zealously determined to report on that which will not offend the board of judges, the prosecutor, probation, legal-aid, or other officials, in return for privileges and courtesies granted in the past and to be granted in the future. Rather than any view of the matter in terms of some variation of a "conspiracy" hypothesis, the simple explanation is one of an ongoing system handling delicate tensions, managing the trauma produced by law enforcement and administration, and requiring almost pathological distrust of "outsiders" bordering on group paranoia.

The hostile attitude toward "outsiders" is, in large measure, engendered by a defensiveness itself produced by the inherent deficiencies of assembly line justice, so characteristic of our major criminal courts. Intolerably large caseloads . . . [that] must be disposed of in an organizational context of limited resources and personnel, potentially subject the participants in the court community to harsh scrutiny from appellate courts, and other public and private sources of condemnation. As a consequence, an almost irreconcilable conflict is posed in terms of intense pressures to process huge numbers of cases on the one hand, and the stringent ideological and legal requirements of "due process of law" on the other hand. A rather tenuous resolution of the dilemma has emerged in the shape of a large variety of bureaucratically ordained and controlled short cuts, deviations, and outright rule violations adopted as court practice in order to meet production norms. Fearfully anticipating criticism on ethical as well as legal grounds, all the significant participants in the court's social structure are bound into an organized system of complicity. This consists of a work arrangement in which the patterned, covert, informal breaches, and evasions of "due process" are institutionalized, but are, nevertheless, denied to exist. . . .

A wide variety of coercive devices are employed against an accused-client, couched in a depersonalized, instrumental, bureaucratic version of due process of law and which are, in reality, a perfunctory obeisance to the ideology of due process. These include some very explicit pressures which are exerted in some measure by all court personnel, including judges, to plead guilty and avoid trial. In many instances, the sanction of a potentially harsh sentence is utilized as the visible alternative to pleading guilty. . . . Too often, the discretionary power as to bail is part of the arsenal of weapons available to collapse the resistance of an accused person.

The defense attorneys, therefore, whether of the legal-aid, public defender variety, or privately retained, although operating in terms of pressures specific to their respective role and organizational obligations, ultimately are concerned with strategies which tend to lead to a plea. It is the rational, impersonal elements involving economies of time, labor, expense, and a superior commitment of the defense counsel to these rationalistic values of maximum production of court organization that prevail in his relationship with a client. The "lawyer regulars" are frequently former staff members of the prosecutor's office and utilize the prestige, know-how and contacts of their former affiliation as part of their stock in trade. Close and continuing relations between the "lawyer regular" and his former colleagues in the prosecutor's office generally overshadow the relationship between the regular and his client. The continuing colleagueship of supposedly adversary counsel rests on real professional and organizational needs of a quid pro quo, which goes beyond the limits of an accommodation or modus vivendi one might ordinarily expect under the circumstances of an otherwise seemingly adversary relationship. Indeed, the adversary features which are manifest are, for the most part, muted and exist even in their attenuated form largely for external consumption. The principals, lawyer and assistant district attorney, rely upon one another's cooperation for their continued professional existence, and so the bargaining between them tends usually to be "reasonable" rather than fierce.

Defense lawyers condition even the most obtuse clients to recognize that there is a fine interconnection between fee payment and the zealous exercise of professional expertise, secret knowledge, and organizational "connections" in their behalf. Lawyers, therefore, seek to keep their clients in a proper state of tension, and to arouse in them the precise edge of anxiety which is calculated to encourage prompt fee payment. Consequently, the client attitude in the relationship between defense counsel and an accused is, in many instances, a precarious admixture of hostility, mistrust, dependence, and sycophancy. By keeping his client's anxieties aroused to the proper pitch, and establishing a seemingly causal relationship between a requested fee and the accused's ultimate extrication from his onerous difficulties, the lawyer will have established the necessary preliminary groundwork to assure a minimum of haggling over the fee and its eventual payment. . . . [B]ecause there are great risks of non-payment of the fee, due to the impecuniousness of his clients, and the fact that a man who is sentenced to jail may be a singularly unappreciative client, the criminal lawyer collects his fee in advance. . . .

The criminal lawyer must serve three major functions, or stated another way, he must solve three problems. First, he must arrange for his fee; second, he must prepare and then, if necessary, "cool out" his client in case of defeat (a highly likely contingency); third, he must satisfy the court organization that he has performed adequately in the process of negotiating the plea, so as to preclude the possibility of any sort of embarrassing incident which may serve to invite "outside" scrutiny.

In assuring the attainment of one of his primary objectives, his fee, the criminal lawyer will very often enter into negotiations with the accused's kin, including collateral relatives. In many instances, the accused himself is unable to pay any sort of fee or anything more than a token fee. It then becomes important to involve as many of the accused's kin as possible in the situation. This is especially so if the attorney hopes to collect a significant part of a proposed substantial fee. It is not uncommon for several relatives to contribute toward the fee: the larger the group, the greater the possibility that the lawyer will collect a sizable fee by getting contributions from each.

But the larger the fee the lawyer wishes to exact, the more impressive his performance must be, in terms of his stage managed image as a personage of great influence and power in the court organization. Court personnel are keenly aware of the extent to which a lawyer's stock in trade involves the precarious stage management of an image which goes beyond the usual professional flamboyance, and for this reason alone the lawyer is "bound in" to the authority system of the court's organizational discipline. Therefore, to some extent, court personnel will aid the lawyer in the creation and maintenance of that impression. There is a tacit commitment to the lawyer by the court organization, apart from formal etiquette, to aid him in this. Such augmentation of the lawyer's stage managed image as this affords, is the partial basis for the quid pro quo which exists between the lawyer and the court organization. It tends to serve as the continuing basis for the higher loyalty of the lawyer to the organization; his relationship with his client, in contrast, is transient, ephemeral and often superficial.

The lawyer has often been accused of stirring up unnecessary litigation, especially in the field of negligence. The strong incentive of possible fees motivates the lawyer to promote litigation which would otherwise never have developed. However, the criminal lawyer develops a vested interest of an entirely different nature in his client's case: to limit its scope and duration rather than do battle. Only in this way can a case be "profitable." Thus, he enlists the aid of relatives not only to assure payment of his fee, but he will also rely on these persons to help him in his agent-mediator role of convincing the accused to plead guilty, and ultimately to help in "cooling out" the accused if necessary.

It is at this point that an accused defendant may experience his first sense of "betrayal." While he had perhaps perceived the police and prosecutor to be adversaries, or possibly even the judge, the accused is wholly unprepared for his counsel's role performance as an agent-mediator. In the same vein, it is even less likely to occur to an accused that members of his own family or other kin may become agents, albeit at the behest and urging of other agents or mediators, acting on the principle that they are in reality helping an accused negotiate the best possible plea arrangement under the circumstances. Usually, it will be the lawyer who will activate next of kin in this role . . . with entreaties to the accused's next of kin, to appeal to the accused to "help himself" by pleading.

In effect, in his role as double agent, the criminal lawyer performs an extremely vital and delicate mission for the court organization and the accused. Both principals are anxious to terminate the litigation with a minimum of expense and damage to each other. There is no other personage or role incumbent in the total court structure more strategically located, who by training and in terms of his own requirements, is more ideally suited to do so than the lawyer. In recognition of this, judges will cooperate with attorneys in many important ways. For example, they will adjourn the case of an accused in jail awaiting plea or sentence if the attorney requests such action. While explicitly this may be done for some innocuous and seemingly valid reason, the tacit purpose is that pressure is being applied by the attorney for the collection of his fee, which he knows will probably not be forthcoming if the case is concluded. Judges are aware of this tactic on the part of lawyers, who, by requesting an adjournment, keep an accused incarcerated awhile longer as a not too subtle method of dunning a client for payment.

The judge will help an accused's lawyer in still another way. He will lend the official aura of his office and courtroom so that a lawyer can stage manage an impression of an "all out" performance for the accused in justification of his fee. The judge and other court personnel will serve as a backdrop for a scene charged with dramatic fire in which the accused's lawyer makes a stirring appeal in his behalf. With a show of restrained passion, the lawyer will intone the virtues of the accused and recite the social deprivations which have reduced him to his present state. The speech varies somewhat, depending on whether the accused has been convicted after trial or has pleaded guilty. In the main, however, the incongruity, superficiality, and ritualistic character of the total performance is underscored by a visibly impassive, almost bored reaction on the part of the judge and other members of the court retinue.

Afterward, there is a hearty exchange of pleasantries between the lawyer and district attorney, wholly out of context in terms of the supposed adversary nature of the preceding events. The fiery passion in defense of his client is gone, and the lawyers for both sides resume their offstage relations, chatting amiably and perhaps including the judge in their restrained banter. No other aspect of their visible conduct so effectively serves to put even a casual observer on notice, that these individuals have claims upon each other. These seemingly innocuous actions are indicative of continuing organizational and informal relations, which, in their intricacy and depth, range far beyond any priorities or claims a particular defendant may have.

The "cop-out" ceremony, in which the court process culminates, is not only invaluable for redefining the accused's perspectives of himself, but also in reiterating publicly in a formally structured ritual the accused person's guilt for the benefit of significant "others" who are observing. The accused not only is made to assert publicly his guilt of a specific crime, but also a complete recital of its details. He is further made to indicate that he is entering his plea of guilty freely, willingly, and voluntarily, and that he is not doing so because of any promises or in consideration of any commitments that may have been made to him by anyone. This last is intended as a blanket statement to shield the participants from any possible charges of "coercion" or undue influence that may have been exerted in violation of due process requirements. Its function is to preclude any later review by an appellate court on these grounds, and also to obviate any second thoughts an accused may develop in connection with his plea.

However, for the accused, the conception of self as a guilty person is in large measure a temporary role adaptation. His career socialization as an accused, if it is successful, eventuates in his acceptance and redefinition of himself as a guilty person. However, the transformation is ephemeral, in that he will, in private, quickly reassert his innocence. Of importance is that he accept his defeat, publicly proclaim it, and find some measure of pacification in it. Almost immediately after his plea, a defendant will generally be interviewed by a representative of the probation division in connection with a pre-sentence report which is to be prepared. The very first question to be asked of him by the probation officer is: "Are you guilty of the crime to which you pleaded?" This is by way of double affirmation of the defendant's guilt. Should the defendant now begin to make bold assertions of his innocence, despite his plea of guilty, he will be asked to withdraw his plea and stand trial on the criminal charges. Such a threatened possibility is, in most instances, sufficient to cause an accused to let the plea stand and to request the probation officer to overlook his exclamations of innocence.

It is popularly assumed that the police, through forced confessions, and the district attorney, employing still other pressures, are most instrumental in the inducement of an accused to plead guilty. It is actually the defendant's own counsel who is most effective in this role. Further, this phenomenon tends to reinforce the extremely rational nature of criminal law administration, for an organization could not rely upon the sort of idiosyncratic measures employed by the police to induce confessions and maintain its efficiency, high production and overall rational-legal character. The defense counsel becomes the ideal agent-mediator since, as "officer of the court" and confidant of the accused and his kin, he lives astride both worlds and can serve the ends of the two as well as his own. . . .

3. Donald G. Gifford, *A Context-Based Theory of Strategy Selection*, 46 OHIO ST. L.J. 41, 73-82 (1985)

It is possible to recommend a plea bargaining strategy likely to be effective in most cases, because the plea bargaining process generally exhibits certain characteristics that determine which strategy is likely to succeed, even though the specific mechanics of plea bargaining and behavior patterns of prosecutors and defense attorneys vary from one locality to another and from one case to another. The defense attorney's negotiation strategy is construed broadly here to include not only formal plea discussions, but also tactical considerations in deciding whether to file particular motions, how to handle discovery and the exchange of information in plea bargaining, the timing of the guilty plea, and all informal discussions with the prosecutor.

The first factor a defense attorney should consider in choosing a negotiation strategy is the strategy of the opponent — the prosecutor. Although few prosecutors consciously design a purposeful negotiation strategy, an identifiable pattern exists in most prosecutors' opening demands and concessions. . . . The prosecutor's overall strategy, in most cases, is substantially defined by certain characteristics of the criminal justice system and the prosecutor's role in it.

The charges initially filed against the defendant, together with the probable sentence after conviction, determine the prosecutor's opening demand in plea bargaining negotiations. In almost all cases, the prosecutor's opening demand mirrors what would be expected from a negotiator who follows the competitive strategy: a high, but credible, demand. The initial charge is usually a high demand both because the prosecutor has overcharged and because legislatively defined criminal sentences are generally unrealistically lengthy. Overcharging allows the prosecutor to make concessions, in the form of reduced charges, to the defendant in order to encourage him to plead guilty. The initial charge also is a threat to the defendant: if he does not enter into an agreement, then he might be convicted on more serious charges and serve a longer sentence.

Although the prosecutor's strategy may include both competitive and cooperative tactics as plea bargaining proceeds, her strategy will probably become predominantly cooperative. The primary factor accounting for the frequency of a cooperative strategy among prosecutors in the later stages of plea bargaining is the prosecutor's unique role as a "minister of justice." The prosecutor's goal is not to maximize the length of the defendant's sentence or even the severity of the crime to which the defendant pleads. Empirical studies suggest that a prosecutor's attempt to individualize justice by considering equitable factors about the circumstances of the offense and the characteristics of the offender, such as the youth of the defendant, the lack of a prior criminal record, and provocation by the victim, provides the primary motivation for a prosecutor to make bargaining concessions. The prosecutor's orientation in bargaining, therefore, parallels that of the cooperative negotiator, who attempts to achieve a fair solution.

Other factors contribute to the prosecutor's cooperative orientation. These factors include her continuing relationship with defense attorneys, pressures from judges to reach agreement, large caseloads, and the prevailing cooperative norms of plea bargaining. Finally, in most cases the prosecutor can afford to adopt a noncompetitive rather than a competitive strategy, because she is not highly accountable to a constituent. Unlike the defense attorney, whose concessions in plea bargaining must be ratified by his client, the prosecutor makes independent decisions about bargaining concessions. In any particular case, specific circumstances may influence the prosecutor to adopt a competitive strategy. However, the pattern of prosecutorial conduct discussed above is prevalent enough to strongly influence the defense attorney's selection of a negotiation strategy.

The second factor a defense attorney should consider in choosing a negotiation strategy is the relative bargaining power of the defense attorney compared to that of the prosecutor. In most cases, the prosecutor possesses much greater power in plea bargaining than does the defense attorney. The consequences for the defendant of failing to achieve an agreement with the prosecutor, that is, the defendant's "best alternative to a negotiated agreement," are not attractive. Most defendants have little chance of being acquitted if they proceed to trial. . . . If convicted after trial, most defendants will receive a sentence considerably longer than if they had pleaded guilty.

The defense attorney's plea bargaining strategy frequently will be affected by his desire to maintain good working relationships with the prosecutor and the judge. . . . The necessity of disposing of a large number of cases leads to symbiotic relationships among the prosecutor, defense attorney, and judge. Professors Arthur Rosett and Donald Cressey describe the group comprised of these three actors as the "committee on criminal justice," and they develop an accommodative working relationship: "Day by day, judges, prosecutors, defenders, and probation officers encounter the same basic types of cases. . . . In time, courthouse workers develop a group sense of justice. They come to understand each other and learn to take each other's views into account." . . .

Although many of the described factors may suggest the adoption of a noncompetitive strategy, the defense attorney's need to maintain good rapport with a client who is hostile toward the prosecutor may lead him to employ a different approach. A competitive strategy is probably advantageous to convince the client that the attorney is "on his side." Defendants are very critical of plea bargaining, usually because they perceive that their attorneys are insufficiently adversarial in representing their interests and are too inclined to sell-out their interests. . . . This attitude may be exacerbated if the defense attorney adopts a noncompetitive strategy.

Finally, in choosing between a competitive and a noncompetitive strategy, the defense attorney should consider the norms that govern the tenor of the relationship between the prosecutor and the defense attorney in plea bargaining. Generally, prosecutors expect that defense attorneys will be cooperative in plea bargaining; they punish attorneys who are too adversarial in representing their clients by refusing to grant the typical plea bargaining concessions to these attorneys' clients.

The issues negotiated in plea bargaining are predominantly zero-sum issues, but some opportunities for integrative bargaining may exist. . . . The prosecutor and the defendant prioritize the issues at stake differently. Prosecutors are most interested in gaining a conviction, while defendants are most interested in minimizing the length of the sentence. Guilty plea agreements that allow the prosecutor to convict a defendant on a charge which accurately reflects the seriousness of the crime but that provides for a comparatively light sentence may serve the interests of both the prosecutor and the defendant. The parties may also want to avoid the expense, anxiety, and time consumed by litigation. Finally, an inventive defense attorney can use the integrative techniques of brainstorming to generate non-incarceration sanctions, such as restitution. . . .

In the early phases of the negotiation, the defense attorney should begin with a competitive strategy, but in a cooperative style. Even though several practice manuals suggest that defense attorneys should be extremely cooperative and seek to achieve a guilty plea agreement early in plea bargaining, negotiation theory establishes at least four reasons that the defense attorney's early tactics should be competitive. First, the government's opening demand, usually characterized by overcharging and [lengthy] prison sentences, is very competitive. . . . A negotiator who uses a cooperative strategy against a competitive negotiator is severely disadvantaged. Thus, a defense attorney risks exploitation if he begins negotiations with a cooperative strategy. Second, the defendant usually has low bargaining power; some social scientists recommend that the less powerful negotiator begin competitively and become more cooperative later in the negotiation. Third, it may be necessary to adopt a competitive strategy initially to communicate to the prosecutor that the attorney intends to zealously represent the client and that he will not "cave in" because of his caseload or other personal or institutional pressures. Finally, early competitive moves often convince the client that his attorney intends to represent him vigorously; this improves client relations. . . .

Following the initial stages of plea bargaining, virtually all the factors discussed previously suggest adopting a noncompetitive strategy for plea bargaining. Usually, the cooperative strategy will be more effective than the integrative strategy, although some opportunities for integrative solutions may exist. The following factors suggest the adoption of a noncompetitive strategy: (1) the prosecutor will probably use a cooperative strategy; (2) the prosecutor has greater bargaining power; (3) an amicable continuing relationship between the defense attorney and the prosecutor should be maintained; (4) various pressures to reach agreement fast; and (5) the prevailing norms in plea bargaining mandate the use of cooperative tactics. . . .

It is important to reiterate the distinction between negotiation strategy and negotiation style. If an attorney hopes to appeal to the prosecutor's equitable discretion later in the negotiation, his personal style should be accommodative, not antagonistic. The defense attorney should attempt to argue defenses and other legal issues vigorously, while maintaining cordial personal relationships. An attorney with an accommodative personal style can often switch from a competitive to a cooperative strategy during a negotiation. It is more difficult for an antagonistic attorney to build a relationship on trust and seek discretionary favors from a prosecutor later in a negotiation. . . .

4. William J. Stuntz, *Plea Bargaining and Criminal Law's Disappearing Shadow*, 117 HARV. L. REV. 2548 (2004)

Most bodies of substantive law define citizens' obligations. Criminal law is different. Its primary role is not to define obligations, but to create a menu of options for prosecutors. If the menu is long enough, and it usually is, prosecutors can dictate the terms of plea bargains. When that is so, litigants in criminal cases do not bargain in the shadow of the law. Rather, they bargain in the shadow of prosecutors' preferences, budget constraints, and political trends. Law's shadow disappears.

A quarter-century ago, Mnookin and Kornhauser wrote a brilliant article explaining that litigants in civil cases bargain "in the shadow of the law." Robert H. Mnookin & Lewis Kornhauser, *Bargaining in the Shadow of the Law: The Case of Divorce*, 88 YALE L.J. 950 (1979). What that wonderful phrase means for any particular class of cases is a very complicated matter, but the basic point is simple: there is a market for settlements in civil cases, and that market internalizes the governing law. Criminal litigation likewise has a working settlement market. So one might suppose that the Mnookin-Kornhauser thesis applies to criminal settlements. . . . [T]hat is not so: in a variety of ways and for a variety of reasons, criminal settlements do not efficiently internalize the law.

There is, though, a deeper problem with plea bargains, one that goes squarely to the relationship between those bargains and the bodies of law that define crimes and sentences. The problem is that law's effect on plea bargaining is much smaller than conventional wisdom would have it. For some crimes, the law may have no effect at the margin. That is quite different from the world of civil settlements. In employment discrimination or products liability cases, a change in the governing legal rules (either liability rules or remedies) is certain to have some effect on settlements, and the effects are, at least in rough measure, predictable. In criminal cases, by contrast, the definition of the relevant crime or the applicable sentence can change dramatically yet leave plea bargains unaffected.

This difference between civil and criminal settlements stems from a difference between the bodies of law that govern civil and criminal cases. Civil laws define obligations; those obligations in turn define litigation outcomes. Parties bargain in the shadow of those outcomes, hence in the law's shadow. Some of criminal law works like that. But for the most part, criminal law and the law of sentencing define prosecutors' options, not litigation outcomes. They are not rules in the shadow of which litigants must bargain. Rather, they are items on a

menu from which the prosecutor may order as she wishes. She has no incentive
to order the biggest meal possible. Instead, her incentive is to get whatever
meal she wants, as long as the menu offers it. The menu does not define the
meal; the diner does. The law-on-the-street, the law that determines who goes
to prison and for how long, is chiefly written by prosecutors, not by legislators
or judges.

Law's Shadow on Civil and Criminal Settlements

Suppose a state legislature decides that pain and suffering are not adequately compensated in its courts. Suppose further that, on average, juries
have been awarding pain and suffering damages equal to the plaintiff's out-of-
pocket loss. The legislature therefore passes a statute saying that, in the future,
pain and suffering damages should be equal to three times the plaintiff's out-
of-pocket loss. What effect will the new statute have on settlements in personal injury cases? A precise answer would require a great deal more
information, but this much is clear: the settlement value of personal injury
claims will rise. Some claims that were not worth settling before will be worth
settling now, and some claims that settled for small amounts before will produce
larger payouts now. The point holds true for changes in liability rules as well. . . .

A lot of criminal litigation does not fit this straightforward pattern. Imagine
a jurisdiction where the legally mandated sentence for robbery with a firearm
is ten years in prison, meaning that judges must impose that sentence for that
crime. Prosecutors remain free to charge a variety of different crimes, each of
which carries its own mandatory sentence. Imagine further that prosecutors in
this jurisdiction believe that defendants who are guilty of robbery with a firearm
deserve five years in prison. Conveniently enough, simple robbery carries a
sentence of five years. In order to preserve their bargaining power, prosecutors
are willing to impose the ten-year sentence on robbery-with-a-gun defendants
who go to trial and lose, but they believe the right sentence is five years. Finally,
imagine that prosecutors in this jurisdiction operate under severe resource constraints. They lack the time to prosecute all the winnable cases they have. Consequently, prosecutors only prosecute when they have at least a 75% chance of
winning at trial. Weaker cases are dismissed. . . .

Though it has some artificial assumptions, I believe the hypothetical is realistic. It has three key features. First, prosecutors do not try to maximize total
prison time. Second, due to docket pressure, prosecutors lack the time to pursue even some winnable cases. And third, the legally authorized sentence is
harsher than the sentence prosecutors want to impose. While these conditions
do not all hold true for all criminal cases, each one does hold true for a large fraction of criminal cases, and there are many cases in which all three conditions
are satisfied. When that is so, the law — both substantive criminal law and the
law of sentencing — casts a very small shadow on plea bargaining.

Take these three conditions one at a time. The first is the most important.
Prosecutors are not like civil plaintiffs: they are not paid by the conviction,
with bonuses for each additional month the defendant spends in prison. That
proposition leads to another: extra months in prison are not like marginal dollars in civil cases. Once the defendant's sentence has reached the level the pros-

ecutor prefers — or, if you like, the level that the local voters who elect her boss demand — adding more time offers no benefit to the prosecutor. Indeed, prosecutors may actually value "extra" prison time negatively. Plea bargains do not always, maybe not even usually, involve haggling over a surplus as in negotiated settlements in civil cases. A civil plaintiff has the incentive to take every dollar he can, just as the defendant wishes to pay as little as possible. In criminal cases, one of the two parties is like that: the defendant almost always prefers freedom to incarceration and less incarceration to more. The prosecutor's utility function, though, is much more complicated. Voters' preferences, courthouse customs, the prosecutor's reputation as a tough or lenient bargainer, her own views about what is a proper sentence for the crime in question — all these things play a role in defining the sentences that prosecutors are likely to seek in plea bargains. The law may play a role too: rule-of-thumb discounts — a given district attorney may think that half or two-thirds of the legally authorized sentence is appropriate for defendants who plead guilty — are one plausible strategy prosecutors may follow. . . .

The second condition, extreme docket pressure, is more the rule than the exception in America's underfunded criminal justice system. Most criminal cases are brought by local district attorneys' offices. Giving localities responsibility for law enforcement guarantees that law enforcement will be stretched for dollars. Poor counties have more crime, and less money to spend fighting it, than rich ones. Even if the money is there, local governments are loath to tax it to support law enforcement. Policing and prosecution are redistributive services; they disproportionately benefit residents of poor neighborhoods but are mostly paid for by wealthier citizens. Rich taxpayers can flee the jurisdiction if taxes get too high. It is only natural that high-crime cities and counties would tend to be a little stingy with law enforcement agencies — even when they can (in theory) afford to be more generous.

One result of that stinginess is docket pressure, which is likely to be especially acute during periods of high crime that require large investments in law enforcement. The number of state-court felony prosecutions more than doubled between 1978 and 1990; the number of prosecutors grew by less than twenty percent. Though crime has fallen since 1990, dockets haven't. And prosecutorial budgets have never caught up with the earlier increase in caseloads. All of which means that prosecutors in most jurisdictions have more cases than they have time to handle them. Another indication is to compare the number of arrests with the number of criminal convictions; the second figure is roughly one-fifth of the first.

The third condition — that prosecutors want to impose lower sentences than the law allows, sometimes lower than the law mandates — involves more guesswork; we lack the data necessary to establish how often this condition is satisfied. Still, the likely answer is very often indeed. . . .

Ask how a rational legislator will vote on a piece of criminal legislation that, in the legislator's view, authorizes a level of punishment that is appropriate in a few very bad cases but excessive in a great many other cases. The smart move is to vote "yes." A contrary vote risks blame when one of those few awful cases comes along, and a prosecutor points the finger at the legislature that failed to provide her with the legal tools necessary to do justice. As for the many cases in which lesser punishment or none at all seems right, prosecutors will likely share the legislator's preferences — and if they don't, they, not the legislator, will take the political hit. It sounds odd, but legislators' incentive is to vote for rules that even the legislators themselves think are too harsh. So the legal rules that define crimes and sentences tend to err on the harsh side — not because of anyone's ideological stance, but because of the way the lawmaking process works. . . .

And where law does not reign, the district attorney's office generally does. This is one point on which I differ with Professor Bibas. In his view, defense attorneys are the linchpins of the plea-bargaining system: improve the quality of the advice defendants get from their lawyers, and bargains will improve too. There is some merit to that position. But given the array of weapons the law provides, prosecutors are often in a position to dictate outcomes, and almost always have much more to say about those outcomes than do defense attorneys. The key to the system is the prosecutor's incentive: to achieve the results that forces other than the law — her own preferences, her boss's electoral ambitions, local voters' priorities, and the like — suggest. The law serves only to define her opportunities. And she generally has more opportunities than she needs. . . .

None of this is to say that sentencing rules are irrelevant. On the contrary, the nature and size of the menu matter a lot. It is only to say that the structure of sentencing law probably matters less than the substance. Political incentives being what they are, the substance generally gives prosecutors a great deal of power over post-trial sentences and, therefore, over plea-bargained sentences as well.

5. Stephanos Bibas, *Plea Bargaining Outside the Shadow of Trial*, 117 HARV. L. REV. 2463 (2004)

Plea-bargaining literature predicts that parties strike plea bargains in the shadow of expected trial outcomes. In other words, parties forecast the expected sentence after trial, discount it by the probability of acquittal, and offer some proportional discount. This oversimplified model ignores how structural distortions skew bargaining outcomes. Agency costs; attorney competence, compensation, and workloads; resources; sentencing and bail rules; and information deficits all skew bargaining. In addition, psychological biases and heuristics warp judgments: overconfidence, denial, discounting, risk preferences, loss aversion, framing, and anchoring all affect bargaining decisions. Skilled lawyers can partly counteract some of these problems but sometimes overcompensate. The oversimplified shadow-of-trial model of plea bargaining must thus be supplemented by a structural-psychological perspective. In this perspective, uncertainty, money, self-interest, and demographic variation greatly influence plea bargains. Some of these influences can be ameliorated, others are difficult to correct, but each casts light on how civil and criminal bargaining differ in important respects. . . .

Plea bargains do not simply reflect expected trial outcomes minus some proportional discount. Many other structural factors influence bargains. Sometimes these factors help or hurt certain classes of defendants; in other cases, the effects are more idiosyncratic. Either way, bargains reflect much more than just the merits. These structural distortions produce inequities, overpunishing some defendants and underpunishing others based on wealth and other legally irrelevant characteristics.

1. Prosecutors' Pressures and Incentives. The ideal of the adversary system presumes that prosecutors will decide whom to prosecute based on the evidence, the equities, and the justifications for punishment. In other words, prosecutors should decide to prosecute based on the likelihood of conviction and the need to deter, incapacitate, rehabilitate, reform, and inflict retribution. Of course, prosecutors are supposed to pursue justice, not just convictions. In some cases, doing so means pursuing lower sentences if the equities warrant them, or it may mean not prosecuting at all. While justice should temper the pursuit of punishment, self-interest should not. To be sure, prosecutors may be merciful to sympathetic defendants. In addition, they may not insist on a higher sentence for one defendant when they have recently given a lower sentence to a similarly situated defendant. They may also drive hard bargains on particular crimes to send messages, teach lessons, and deter especially harmful or prevalent crimes. Apart from these considerations, plea bargains should depend only on the severity of the crime, the strength of the evidence, and the defendant's record and need for punishment. This ideal asks prosecutors to be perfectly selfless, perfectly faithful agents of the public interest.

The reality is much more complex. The strength of the prosecution's case is the most important factor, but other considerations come into play. Trials are much more time consuming than plea bargains, so prosecutors have incentives to negotiate deals instead of trying cases. Prosecutors have personal incentives to reduce their workloads so that they can leave work early enough to dine with their families. Additionally, prosecutors are paid salaries, not by case or by outcome, so they have no direct financial stake in the outcome. The only countervailing financial incentive is that prosecutors might jeopardize their jobs by losing a string of trials and so drawing supervisors' or voters' wrath. Self-interest, in short, may discourage prosecutors from investing enough work in plea-bargained cases, in which more work might lead to heavier sentences. Some of this plea bargaining serves the public interest by freeing up prosecutors to pursue many more cases. Even if the public might prefer the extra work needed for trial, however, prosecutors have personal incentives to strike plea bargains.

In addition to lightening their workloads, prosecutors want to ensure convictions. They may further their careers by racking up good win-loss records, in which every plea bargain counts as a win but trials risk being losses. The statistic of conviction, in other words, matters much more than the sentence. Favorable win-loss statistics boost prosecutors' egos, their esteem, their praise by colleagues, and their prospects for promotion and career advancement. Thus, prosecutors may prefer the certainty of plea bargains, even if the resulting sentence is much lighter than it would have been after trial. The psychology of risk aversion and loss aversion reinforces the structural incentives to ensure good statistics and avoid risking losses. The public also has an interest in certainty of punishment, which plea bargaining will sometimes further. At other times, the public might prefer to gamble on a trial to secure heavier punishment, while the prosecutor's fear of personal embarrassment favors a plea bargain.

Prosecutors. . . . may push strong or high-profile cases to trial to gain reputation and marketable experience. This dynamic is the opposite of what one might expect: strong cases should plead guilty because trial is hopeless, while weak cases have genuine disputes that merit resolution at trial. In other words, the shadows of trials in strong cases are so clear and crisp that the shadow-of-trial model predicts settlement. In weak cases, however, the parties have imperfect information about the cases' weaknesses. Trial shadows in these cases may be fuzzy enough that the parties can disagree in predicting trial outcomes, and as a result, bargaining may break down. The shadow-of-trial model, in short, predicts that most trials should involve weak cases. Self-interest, in contrast, pushes prosecutors toward trying the strongest cases. Prosecutors can discourage defendants in strong cases from pleading guilty by refusing to make any concessions, while they can make irresistible offers in weak cases.

Thus, instead of allowing juries to air and wrestle with the hard, troubling cases, prosecutors may hide them from view. If, for example, prosecutors bargain away most cases involving dubious confessions, they avert public scrutiny of police interrogation tactics. If they buy off credible claims of innocence cheaply, they cover up faulty investigations that mistakenly target innocent suspects. By pressing the easiest cases, prosecutors turn jury trials into rubber stamps or mere formalities. Moreover, easy cases do not cast good or representative shadows. To discern trials' shadows, lawyers need to know the outcomes of hard, disputable cases rather than of slam dunks. Lawyers may thus have difficulty predicting how hard cases would come out if they were to go to trial. . . .

Another reason why plea results diverge from likely trial outcomes is that plea bargaining is hidden from public view. First, plea bargaining is a secret area of law, unlike trials, which have clear rules. In plea bargaining, it is easier for inexperienced lawyers to fall afoul of unwritten norms by pushing too hard, not hard enough, or not in the right way. The paucity of hard legal rules also leaves more room for favoritism, favor-seeking, and connections to operate. Second, prosecutors who are tempted to cut corners find it easier to avoid pursuing every lead and pressing every advantage during plea bargaining. At public trials, in contrast, concern for reputation and for avoiding acquittals checks prosecutors' desires to minimize effort.

2. Defense Attorneys' Pressures and Incentives. Like prosecutors, defense attorneys are not ideal, perfectly selfless, perfectly faithful agents. They too are human and subject to similar failings and temptations. Some defense attorneys are more talented or more industrious than others, and some desire the fame and fortune that come from a high-profile trial. And like prosecutors, defense lawyers prefer to avoid losing cases at trial, which would harm their reputations.

In some ways, defense representation is even more variable and vulnerable to skewing than is the prosecution. One of the main culprits is funding. Many defense lawyers are public defenders, who are paid fixed salaries to represent large numbers of indigent clients. Others are private appointed lawyers, whom courts appoint and pay fixed fees or low hourly rates subject to caps. Still others are privately retained counsel, who may receive flat fees, retainers plus hourly rates, or simply hourly rates. Some clients of private lawyers have modest means and cannot afford to pay more than a certain amount. This financial constraint may operate as a cap on representation unless the client then qualifies for and seeks court-appointed counsel. For other clients, money is no object.

One obvious problem with this patchwork quilt is that it leads to inconsistent incentives. Though not all lawyers are slaves to their pocketbooks, financial incentives influence many to varying degrees. A lawyer who receives a fixed salary or a flat fee per case has no financial incentive to try cases. On the contrary, flat fees create financial incentives to plead cases out quickly in order to handle larger volumes. A lawyer who receives a low hourly rate or an hourly rate subject to a low cap also has little financial incentive to try cases. The desire for a lighter workload and free time may incline that lawyer toward plea bargaining. Involuntarily appointed private lawyers are especially unlikely to push cases to trial, particularly because courts often compensate poorly. To put it bluntly, appointed or flat-fee defense lawyers can make more money with less time and effort by pushing clients to plead. Encouraging pleas out of financial self-interest is part of what Abraham Blumberg famously called "the practice of law as confidence game."

If a lawyer is bent on plea bargaining and does so all the time, he cannot credibly threaten to go to trial. Prosecutors will offer fewer concessions to these lawyers' clients because they do not have to offer more. In other words, financial conflicts of interest slant many defense attorneys toward pleas, which may mean less favorable negotiating results. Even if a particular appointed lawyer resists these financial pressures, clients still believe the adage that you get what you pay for. Defendants trust appointed counsel less and so are less likely to heed their advice. Thus, the psychology of trust exacerbates the structural problem of funding indigent defense. This mistrust may somewhat offset bad advice to plead, but it may also poison perfectly sound legal advice.

In contrast, privately retained lawyers who receive generous hourly rates have incentives to bill more hours and to fight matters out and go to trial if necessary. They spend more time preparing their cases and mount more vigorous defenses. As a result, the client's plea-bargaining posture improves, particularly when the attorney has a strong reputation for trial prowess. Unlike appointed lawyers, retained lawyers have an economic incentive to fight hard enough to obtain good results so as to attract future paying clients. Because these lawyers face less pressure to bargain, prosecutors may have to offer them more generous concessions in order to induce guilty pleas. One would expect the same of defense lawyers who volunteer for court appointments to gain experience. If anything, these inexperienced lawyers will be too unyielding in plea bargaining because they want trial experience. The result may be the rejection of a fair plea offer and a harsher sentence after trial.

Another problem is that many public defenders are overburdened. They handle hundreds of cases per year, far more than privately retained attorneys do.

This volume ordinarily means that pleas become the norm, making trial a less realistic threat in plea bargaining. In addition, overburdened defense attorneys cannot spend enough time to dig up all possible defenses. The result is fewer plea-bargaining chips and less favorable plea bargains. Financial incentives may also lead some private attorneys to take on more cases than they can handle, with similar results.

Public defenders work closely with prosecutors and judges, developing close relationships that can influence plea bargaining. Judges and clerks put pressure on defense counsel (especially public defenders) to be pliable in bargaining. Repeat defense counsel often must yield to this pressure in order to avoid judicial reprisals against clients and perhaps to continue to receive court appointments. Some clients benefit from this relationship of trust, particularly those whom the public defender believes are innocent. Conversely, public defenders must choose their battles wisely, which may require an implicit tradeoff of some clients against others. There are even occasional anecdotes in which a defense lawyer agrees to trade a concession in case A for a harsher sentence in case B. The inequity is particularly troubling when a private defense lawyer cashes in favors that he is owed in order to benefit paying clients but not court-appointed clients.

Defense lawyers vary also in bargaining skills and knowledge. Public defenders and some private attorneys are repeat players who come to know prosecutors and judges. As a result, they develop a feel for cases and can gauge the going rate for particular types of crimes and defendants. Public defenders have a particular institutional advantage, because they can pool information about judges and prosecutors with others in their offices. Similarly, retained counsel who are former prosecutors have not only experience, skill, and knowledge, but also close relationships with prosecutors and judges. . . .

Repeat players understand not only bargaining, but also trials, better than neophytes do. . . . The most experienced, most talented defense lawyers are very marketable. After they have cut their teeth as prosecutors or public defenders, many of the best lawyers earn much more in the private sector by serving well-to-do clients. At the other end of the spectrum, many criminal defense lawyers provide poor representation. Ineptitude, sometimes combined with inexperience, huge caseloads, or sloth, harms many a defendant's case. Needless to say, inept lawyers are disproportionately likely to represent poor defendants, because those with money will be able to hire better counsel. . . .

Another factor that warps plea outcomes is the complexity of modern sentencing law, which puts a premium on lawyers' familiarity with lengthy and intricate rules. Most of the shadow-of-trial literature predates mandatory sentences and sentencing guidelines; scholars have not yet explored how these developments exacerbate discord between plea and trial outcomes. . . . The Federal Sentencing Guidelines have put a huge premium on another plea-bargaining technique: cooperating with the government. This venerable tactic has become much more important in recent years as one of the few ways around sentencing guidelines and mandatory minima. . . .

Finally, a defense lawyer's adversarial stance may reduce the defendant's plea discount. The Federal Sentencing Guidelines significantly discount the sentences of defendants who accept responsibility in a timely manner, typically by pleading guilty. Defendants whose lawyers take extensive discovery or file many motions may suffer retaliation by judges and prosecutors and thus lose some or all of this discount. . . .

E. QUESTIONABLE NEGOTIATION CONDUCT: PUFFING, MISREPRESENTATION, AND LYING

1. Comments and Questions

a. The title of the section reflects the fact that representations can range from totally complete and truthful to entirely untrue. Both the law and common morality have long recognized that people are entitled to considerable "poetic license" in their negotiations with one another. The circumstances of the negotiation, the sophistication of the respective parties, their prior dealings (if any), and many other contextual factors have an impact on the judgment about what behavior is appropriate.

b. Truthful and accurate but incomplete statements can constitute misrepresentation. That this must be so is nicely illustrated by the story of the film critic who saw his review quoted as stating: "by all means see this movie." This phrase did indeed appear in the review, but the full sentence read: "If it's mediocrity you crave, by all means see this movie."

c. Is a separate body of rules needed at all, beyond that provided by contract law? These rules normally only apply to completed transactions, and not to failed attempts at an agreement.

2. Charles B. Craver, *Negotiation Ethics: How to Be Deceptive Without Being Dishonest; How to Be Assertive Without Being Offensive*, 38 S. TEX. L. REV. 713 (1997)

Most attorneys feel some degree of professional discomfort when they negotiate with other lawyers. If they hope to achieve beneficial results for their clients, they must convince their opponents that those parties must offer more generous terms than they must actually offer if agreements are to be generated. To accomplish this objective, lawyers usually employ some deceptive tactics. Take for example two parties bargaining over the purchase/sale of a small business. The Seller is willing to accept $500,000, while the Buyer is willing to pay $575,000. The Seller's attorney initially indicates that the Seller must obtain $600,000, with the Buyer's lawyer suggesting that the Buyer cannot go above $450,000. Once these preliminary offers have been exchanged, the parties are pleased with the successful way in which they have begun their discussions. Yet both have begun with position statements designed to mislead the other side

Have they behaved unethically? Are they obliged to disclose their true bargaining needs and intentions to preserve their professional reputations? May they never reject offers they know their clients will accept?

During their subsequent discussions, the Seller's representative is likely to embellish the value of the business being sold, while the Buyer's advocate undervalues that firm. Must the Seller's attorney admit that the Seller believes that future competition from foreign firms is likely to diminish the economic value of his company? Must the Buyer's lawyer disclose the Buyer's innovative plan to enhance the competitive position and future value of this particular firm? When does the Seller-advocate's embellishment exceed the bounds of bargaining propriety? To what extent may the Buyer's representative disingenuously undervalue the company being discussed? Are the Buyer and Seller representatives ethically obliged to ensure a "fair" price for the business? If the Seller is willing to accept less than the Buyer anticipated or the Buyer is willing to pay more than the Seller imagined, would the lawyer representing the other side be duty bound to disclose this fact and attempt to moderate the other side's "unrealistic" beliefs?

Some advocates may try to advance client interests through tactics that are designed to make their opponents feel uncomfortable. They may be rude or inconsiderate, or may employ overly aggressive bargaining tactics. A few may resort to abrasive or even hostile behavior they hope will disconcert unsuspecting adversaries. To what extent may Buyer or Seller representatives employ highly competitive or adversarial negotiating techniques in an effort to obtain beneficial client results? At what point would such conduct transcend the bounds of appropriate behavior?

I frequently surprise law students and practitioners by telling them that, while I have rarely participated in legal negotiations in which both participants did not use some misstatements to further client interests, I have encountered few dishonest lawyers. I suggest that the fundamental question is not whether legal negotiators may use misrepresentations to further client interests, but when and about what they may permissibly dissemble. Many negotiators initially find it difficult to accept the notion that disingenuous "puffing" and deliberate mendacity do not always constitute reprehensible conduct.

Did the Buyer and Seller representatives mentioned above commit ethical violations when they disingenuously said that the Seller had to obtain $600,000 — while willing to accept $500,000 — and that the Buyer could not go above $450,000 — while willing to pay $575,000? Some lawyers attempt to circumvent this moral dilemma by formulating opening positions that do not directly misstate their actual intentions. For example, the Buyer may indicate that he or she "doesn't wish to pay more than $450,000" or the Seller may say that he or she "would not be inclined to accept less than $600,000." While these preliminary statements may be technically true, the italicized verbal leaks ("wish to" or "inclined to") would inform attentive opponents that these speakers do not really mean what they appear to be communicating. The Seller does not care whether the Buyer wishes to pay more than $450,000, but only whether he or she will do so, just as the Buyer does not care whether the Seller is inclined to accept less than $600,000. If these were true limitations, the speakers would be likely to use more definitive language containing no undermining modifiers, such as "I cannot go above or below X." As a result of these speaker efforts to maintain their personal integrity, careful listeners should easily discern the disingenuous nature of the statements being made by them. The use of these devices to "truthfully" deceive opponents would thus be unavailing.

When students or practicing attorneys are asked whether they expect opposing counsel to candidly disclose their true authorized limits or their actual bottom lines at the beginning of bargaining interactions, most exhibit discernible discomfort. They recall the numerous times they have commenced negotiations with exaggerated or distorted position statements they did not expect their adversaries to take literally, and they begin to understand the dilemma confronted regularly by all legal negotiators.

Some writers criticize the use of deceptive negotiating tactics to further client interests. They maintain that these devices diminish the likelihood of Pareto optimal results, because "deception tends to shift wealth from the risk-averse to the risk-tolerant." While this observation is undoubtedly true, it is unlikely to discourage the pervasive use of ethically permissible tactics that are designed to deceive risk-averse opponents into believing they must accept less beneficial terms than they need actually accept. It is thus unproductive to discuss a utopian negotiation world in which complete disclosure is the norm. The real question concerns the types of deceptive tactics that may ethically be employed to enhance bargaining interests. Attorneys who believe that no prevarication is ever proper during bargaining encounters place themselves and their clients at a distinct disadvantage, since they permit their less candid opponents to obtain settlements that transcend the terms to which they are objectively entitled.

The schizophrenic character of the ethical conundrum encountered by legal negotiators is apparent in the ABA Model Rules of Professional Conduct, which were adopted by the House of Delegates in August of 1983. Rule 4.1(a), which corresponds to EC 7-102(A)(5) under the ABA Code of Professional Responsibility, states that "[A] lawyer shall not knowingly . . . make a false statement of material fact or law to a third person." This seemingly unequivocal principle is intended to apply to both litigation and negotiation settings. An explanatory Comment under this Rule reiterates the fact that "[a] lawyer is required to be truthful when dealing with others on a client's behalf. Nonetheless, Comment Two acknowledges the difficulty of defining "truthfulness" in the unique context of the negotiation process:

> Whether a particular statement should be regarded as one of fact can depend on the circumstances. Under generally accepted conventions in negotiation, certain types of statements ordinarily are not taken as statements of material fact. Estimates of price or value placed on the subject of a transaction and a party's intentions as to an acceptable settlement of a claim are in this category. Even state bars that have not appended this Comment to their version of Rule 4.1 have appropriately recognized the ethical distinctions drawn in that Comment.

Although the ABA Model Rules unambiguously proscribe all lawyer prevarication, they reasonably, but confusingly, exclude mere "puffing" and dissembling regarding one's true minimum objectives. These important exceptions appropriately recognize that disingenuous behavior is indigenous to most legal negotiations and could not realistically be prevented due to the nonpublic nature of bargaining interactions.

If one negotiator lies to another, only by happenstance will the other discover the lie. If the settlement is concluded by negotiation, there will be no trial, no public testimony by conflicting witnesses, and thus no opportunity to examine the truthfulness of assertions made during the negotiation. Consequently, in negotiation, more than in other contexts, ethical norms can probably be violated with greater confidence that there will be no discovery and punishment. One of the inherent conflicts with regard to this area concerns the fact that what people label acceptable "puffing" when they make value-based representations during legal negotiations may be considered improper mendacity when uttered by opposing counsel.

When lawyers negotiate, they must constantly decide whether they are going to divulge relevant legal and/or factual information to opposing counsel. If they decide to disclose some pertinent information, may they do so partially or is complete disclosure required? They must also determine the areas they may permissibly misrepresent and the areas they may not distort.

A. Nondisclosure of Information

Even though Model Rule 4.1(a) states that attorneys must be truthful when they make statements concerning material law or fact, Comment One expressly indicates that lawyers have "no affirmative duty to inform an opposing party of relevant facts." In the absence of special relationships or express contractual or statutory duties, practitioners are normally not obliged to divulge relevant legal or factual information to their adversaries. This doctrine is premised upon the duty of representatives to conduct their own legal research and factual investigations. Under our adversary system, attorneys do not have the right to expect their opponents to assist them in this regard. It is only when cases reach tribunals that Model Rule 3.3(a)(3) imposes an affirmative obligation on advocates "to disclose to the tribunal legal authority in the controlling jurisdiction known to the lawyer to be directly adverse to the position of the client and not disclosed by opposing counsel." No such duty is imposed, however, with respect to pertinent factual circumstances that are not discovered by opposing counsel.

Suppose attorneys representing a severely injured plaintiff learn, during the critical stages of settlement talks, that their client has died due to unrelated factors. Would they be under an ethical duty to disclose this fact to defense counsel who are clearly assuming continuing pain and suffering and future medical care for the plaintiff? Although one court held that "plaintiff's attorney clearly had a duty to disclose the death of his client both to the Court and to opposing counsel prior to negotiating the final [settlement] agreement," this conclusion is not supported by the Comment to Rule 4.1 pertaining to negotiation discussions. Nonetheless, since the death of the plaintiff would presumably have necessitated the substitution of plaintiff's estate executor, plaintiff's counsel may have been under a duty to notify defense attorneys of this development before concluding any agreement that would have affected the estate. A similar issue would arise if plaintiff lawyers learned that their client had miraculously recovered from the serious condition that provides the basis of the current lawsuit. If plaintiff's attorneys in either of these situations had previously answered interrogatories concerning the health of the plaintiff, they would probably be obliged under Federal Rule of Civil Procedure 26(e)(2) to supplement their previous responses. A party is under a duty to seasonably amend a prior response to an interrogatory request for production, or request for admission if the party learns that the previous response is in some material respect incomplete or incorrect and if the additional or corrective information has not otherwise been made known to the other parties during the discovery process or in writing.

Suppose the party possessing the relevant information regarding the plaintiff is not the plaintiff's attorney, but rather defense counsel. This issue was confronted by the Minnesota Supreme Court in *Spaulding v. Zimmerman*. Plaintiff Spaulding was injured in an automobile accident when defendant Ledermann's car, in which the plaintiff was riding, collided with defendant Zimmerman's vehicle. He suffered multiple rib fractures, bilateral fractures of the clavicles, and a severe cerebral concussion. Several doctors who treated the plaintiff concluded that his injuries had completely healed. As the trial date approached, the defense attorneys had Spaulding examined by a neurologist who was expected to provide expert testimony for the defense. That physician agreed that the ribs and clavicles had healed, but discovered a life-threatening aneurysm on Spaulding's aorta. Defense counsel were never asked by plaintiff counsel about the results of this examination, and the defense lawyers did not volunteer any information about it.

A settlement agreement was achieved, which had to be approved by trial court, since Spaulding was a minor. After the case was settled, Spaulding discovered the aneurysm, which was surgically repaired, and he sued to set aside the prior settlement. The trial court vacated the settlement, and this decision was sustained by the Minnesota Supreme Court. Despite the fact that most people would undoubtedly regard an affirmative duty to disclose the crucial information as the morally appropriate approach, the Minnesota Supreme Court correctly determined that the defense attorneys were under no ethical duty to volunteer the new medical information to plaintiff counsel. In fact, without client consent, the confidentiality preservation obligation imposed by Model Rule 1.6 would preclude volitional disclosure by defense counsel under these circumstances. Comment 5 explicitly states that "the confidentiality rule applies not merely to matters communicated in confidence by the client but also to all information relating to the representation, whatever its source."

The *Spaulding* court circumvented the Rule 1.6 prohibition by holding that, as officers of the court, defense counsel had an affirmative duty to disclose the newly discovered medical information to the trial court prior to its approval of the settlement agreement. Had Spaulding not been a minor, the court may have had to enforce the original accord, because of the absence of any trial court involvement in the settlement process. If courts are unwilling to impose affirmative disclosure obligations on advocates who possess such critical information pertaining to opposing clients, they should sustain the resulting settlement agreements despite the lack of disclosure. This would at least permit defense lawyers to divulge the negative information as soon as the settlement terms have been satisfied. By voiding such agreements after plaintiffs learn of the withheld information, courts effectively require defense attorneys to remain silent even after the lawsuits have been finally resolved.

Attorneys can easily avoid these disclosure problems by remembering to ask the appropriate questions concerning uncertain areas before they enter into settlement agreements. Defense lawyers can directly ask if the plaintiff's condition has changed in any way. Plaintiff representatives could not ethically misrepresent the material condition of their client. If they were to use evasive techniques to avoid direct responses, defense lawyers should restate their inquiries and demand specific answers. If plaintiff attorneys know that defense counsel have had the plaintiff examined by a medical expert, they should always ask about the results of that examination. They should also request a copy of the resulting medical report, since they are entitled to that information in exchange for the right of defense counsel to have the plaintiff examined. While defense counsel may merely confirm what plaintiff lawyers already know, it is possible that plaintiff attorneys will obtain new information that will affect settlement discussions.

B. Partial Disclosure of Information

Negotiators regularly use selective disclosures to enhance their positions. They divulge the legal doctrines and factual information beneficial to their claims, while withholding circumstances that are not helpful. In most instances, these selective disclosures are expected by opponents and are considered an inherent aspect of bargaining interactions. When attorneys emphasize their strengths, opposing counsel must attempt to ascertain their undisclosed weaknesses. They should carefully listen for verbal leaks and look for nonverbal signals that may indicate the existence of possible opponent problems. Probing questions may be used to elicit some negative information, and external research may be employed to gather other relevant data. These efforts are particularly important when opponents carefully limit their disclosures to favorable circumstances, since their partial disclosures may cause listeners to make erroneous assumptions.

When I discuss negotiating ethics with legal practitioners, I often ask if lawyers are obliged to disclose information to correct erroneous factual or legal assumptions made by opposing counsel. Most respondents perceive no duty to correct legal or factual misunderstandings generated solely by the carelessness of opposing attorneys. Respondents only hesitate when opponent misperceptions may have resulted from misinterpretations of seemingly honest statements made by them. For example, when a plaintiff attorney embellishes the pain being experienced by a client with a severely sprained ankle, the defense lawyer may indicate how painful broken ankles can be. If the plaintiff representative has said nothing to create this false impression, should he or she be obliged to correct the obvious defense counsel error? Although a respectable minority of respondents believe that an affirmative duty to correct the misperception may exist here — due to the fact plaintiff embellishments may have inadvertently contributed to the misunderstanding — most respondents feel no such obligation. So long as they have not directly generated the erroneous belief, it is not their duty to correct it. They could not, however, include their opponent's misunderstanding in their own statements, since this would cause them to improperly articulate knowing misrepresentations of material fact.

When opponent misperceptions concern legal doctrines, almost no respondents perceive a duty to correct those misconceptions. They indicate that each side is obliged to conduct its own legal research. If opposing counsel make incorrect assumptions or carelessly fail to locate applicable statutes or cases, those advocates do not have the right to expect their adversaries to provide them with legal assistance. The more knowledgeable advocates may even continue to rely on precedents supporting their own claims, so long as they do not distort those decisions or the opinions supporting the other side's positions.

Under some circumstances, partial answers may mislead opposing counsel as effectively as direct misrepresentations. For example, [consider again the Spaulding case.]. . . While defense counsel were probably under no ethical obligation to voluntarily disclose existence of the aneurysm and they could use evasive responses to avoid answering opponent inquiries regarding the plaintiff's condition, they could not overtly misrepresent their physician's findings by stating that the plaintiff was in perfect health. Could defense attorneys respond to plaintiff's counsel questions by indicating that "the ribs and the clavicles have healed nicely?" Would this partial disclosure constitute a deliberate misrepresentation of material fact, because the defendant lawyers realize that plaintiff counsel are interpreting this statement in a more expansive manner? Most practitioners have indicated that they would refuse to provide partial responses that would mislead plaintiff's counsel into believing the plaintiff had completely recovered. While they could decline to answer questions regarding the plaintiff's health, they should not be permitted to provide partial responses they know will deceive plaintiff's counsel. Nonetheless, recipients of answers limited to such specific conditions should become suspicious and ask follow-up inquiries about other problems that may have been discovered.

C. Overt Misrepresentation of Information

Almost all negotiators expect opponents to engage in "puffing" and "embellishment." Advocates who hope to obtain $50,000 settlements may initially insist upon $150,000 or even $200,000. They may also embellish the pain experienced by their client, so long as their exaggerations do not transcend the bounds of expected propriety. Individuals involved in a corporate buyout may initially over-value or under-value the real property, the building and equipment, the inventory, the accounts receivable, the patent rights and trademarks, and the goodwill of the pertinent firm.

It is clear that lawyers may not intentionally misrepresent material facts, but it is not always apparent what facts are "material." The earlier noted Comment to Rule 4.1 explicitly acknowledges that "estimates of price or value placed on the subject of a transaction and a party's intentions as to an acceptable settlement of a claim" do not constitute material facts under that provision. It is thus ethical for legal negotiators to misrepresent the value their client places on particular items. For example, attorneys representing one spouse involved in a marital dissolution may indicate that their client wants joint custody of the children, when in reality he or she does not. Lawyers representing a party attempting to purchase a particular company may understate their client's belief regarding the value of the goodwill associated with the target firm. So long as the statement conveys their side's belief — and does not falsely indicate the view of an outside expert, such as an accountant — no Rule 4.1 violation would occur.

Legal negotiators may also misrepresent client settlement intentions. They may ethically suggest to opposing counsel that an outstanding offer is unacceptable, even though they know the proposed terms would be accepted if no additional concessions could be generated. Nonetheless, it is important to emphasize that this Rule 4.1 exception does not wholly excuse all misstatements regarding client settlement intentions. During the early stages of bargaining interactions, most practitioners do not expect opponents to disclose exact client desires. As negotiators approach final agreements, however, they anticipate a greater degree of candor. If negotiators were to deliberately deceive adversaries about this issue during the closing stage of their interaction, most attorneys would consider them dishonest, even though the Rule 4.1 proscription would remain inapplicable.

The relevant Comments to Rule 4.1 are explicitly restricted to negotiations with opposing counsel. Outside that narrow setting, statements pertaining to client settlement objectives may constitute "material" fact. ABA Commission on Ethics and Professional Responsibility, Formal Opinion 370 indicated that knowing misrepresentations regarding client settlement intentions to judges during pretrial settlement discussions would be impermissible, because the misstatements would not be confined to adversarial bargaining interactions.

When material facts are involved, attorneys may not deliberately misrepresent the actual circumstances. They may employ evasive techniques to avoid answering opponent questions, but they may not provide false or misleading answers. If they decide to respond to inquiries pertaining to material facts, they must do so honestly. They must also be careful not to issue partially correct statements they know will be misinterpreted by their opponents, since such deliberate deception would likely contravene Rule 4.1.

A crucial distinction is drawn between statements of lawyer opinion and statements of material fact. When attorneys merely express their opinions — for example, "I think the defendant had consumed too much alcohol" and "I believe the plaintiff will encounter future medical difficulties" — they are not constrained by Rule 4.1. Opposing counsel know that these recitations only concern the personal views of the speakers. Thus, personal view statements are critically different from lawyer statements indicating that they have witnesses who can testify to these matters. If representations regarding witness information is knowingly false, the misstatements would clearly violate Rule 4.1.

A frequently debated area concerns representations about one's authorized limits. Many attorneys refuse to answer "unfair" questions concerning their authorized limits, because these inquiries pertain to confidential attorney-client communications. If negotiators decide to respond to these queries, must they do so honestly? Some lawyers believe that truthful responses are required, since they concern material facts. Other practitioners assert that responses about client authorizations merely reflect client valuations and settlement intentions and are thus excluded from the scope of Rule 4.1 by the drafter's Comment. For this reason, these practitioners think that attorneys may distort these matters.

Negotiators who know they cannot avoid the impact of questions concerning their authorized limits by labeling them "unfair" and who find it difficult to provide knowingly false responses can employ an alternative approach. If the plaintiff's lawyer who is demanding $120,000 asks the defense attorney who is presently offering $85,000 whether he or she is authorized to provide $100,000, the recipient may treat the $100,000 figure as a new plaintiff proposal. That individual can reply that the $100,000 sum suggested by plaintiff's counsel is more realistic but still exorbitant. The plaintiff's attorney may become preoccupied with the need to clarify the fact that he or she did not intend to suggest any reduction in his or her outstanding $120,000 demand. That person would probably forego further attempts to ascertain the authorized limits possessed by the defense attorney!

3. James J. White, *Machiavelli and the Bar: Ethical Limitations on Lying in Negotiation*, 1980 ABA RES. J. 921

Although it is not necessary to draft such a set of rules, it is probably important to give more than the simple disclaimer about the impossibility of defining the appropriate limits of puffing that the drafters have given in the current Comments. Comment 4.2 states: "The precise contours of the legal duties concerning disclosure, representation, puffery, over-reaching, and other aspects of honesty in negotiations cannot be concisely stated." To test these limits, consider five cases.

Easiest is the question that arises when one misrepresents his true opinion about the meaning of a case or a statute. Presumably, such a misrepresentation is accepted lawyer behavior both in and out of court and is not intended to be precluded by the requirement that the lawyer be "truthful." In writing his briefs, arguing his case, and attempting to persuade the opposing party in negotiation, it is the lawyer's right, and probably his responsibility, to argue for plausible interpretations of cases and statutes which favor his client's interest, even in circumstances where, privately, he has advised his client that those are not his true interpretations of the cases and statutes.

A second form of distortion that the Comments plainly envision as permissible is distortion concerning the value of one's case or of the other subject matter involved in the negotiation. Thus, the Comments make explicit reference to "puffery." Presumably, they are attempting to draw the same line that one draws in commercial law between express warranties and "mere puffing" under section 2-313 of the Uniform Commercial Code. While this line is not easy to draw, it generally means that the seller of a product has the right to make general statements concerning the value of his product without having the law treat those statements as warranties and without having liability if they turn out to be inaccurate estimates of the value. As the statements descend toward greater and greater particularity, as the ignorance of the person receiving the statements increases, the courts are likely to find them to be not puffing, but express warranties. By the same token, a lawyer could make assertions about his case or about the subject matter of his negotiation in general terms, and if those proved to be inaccurate, they would not be a violation of the ethical standards. Presumably, such statements are not violations of the ethical standards, even when they conflict with the lawyer's dispassionate analysis of the value of his case.

A third case is related to puffing but different from it. This is the use of the so-called false demand. It is a standard negotiating technique in collective bargaining negotiation, and in some other multiple issue negotiations, for one side to include a series of demands about which it cares little or not at all. The purpose of including these demands is to increase one's supply of negotiating currency. One hopes to convince the other party that one or more of these false demands is important and, thus, successfully to trade it for some significant concession. The assertion of and argument for a false demand involves the same kind of distortion that is involved in puffing or in arguing the merits of cases or statutes that are not really controlling. The proponent of a false demand implicitly or explicitly states his interest in the demand and his estimation of it. Such behavior is untruthful in the broadest sense; yet, at least in collective bargaining negotiation, its use is a standard part of the process and is not thought to be inappropriate by any experienced bargainer.

Two final examples may be more troublesome. The first involves the response of a lawyer to a question from the other side. Assume that the defendant has instructed his lawyer to accept any settlement offer under $100,000. Having received that instruction, how does the defendant's lawyer respond to the plaintiff's question, "I think $90,000 will settle this case; will your client give $90,000?" Do you see the dilemma that question poses for the defense lawyer? It calls for information that would not have to be disclosed. A truthful answer to it concludes the negotiation and dashes any possibility of negotiating a lower settlement, even in circumstances in which the plaintiff might be willing to accept half of $90,000. Even a moment's hesitation in response to the question may be a nonverbal communication to a clever plaintiff's lawyer that the defendant has given such authority. Yet, a negative response is a lie.

It is no answer that a clever lawyer will answer all such questions about authority by refusing to answer them, nor is it an answer that some lawyers will be clever enough to tell their clients not to grant them authority to accept a given sum until the final stages in negotiation. Most of us are not that careful or that clever. Few will routinely refuse to answer such questions in cases in which the client has granted a much lower limit than that discussed by the other party, for in that case, an honest answer about the absence of authority is a quick and effective method of changing the opponent's settling point, and it is one that few of us will forego when our authority is far below that requested by the other party. Thus, despite the fact that a clever negotiator can avoid having to lie or to reveal his settling point, many lawyers, perhaps most, will sometime be forced by such a question either to lie or to reveal that they have been granted such authority by saying so or by their silence in response to a direct question. Is it fair to lie in such a case?

Before one examines the possible justifications for a lie in that circumstance, consider a final example recently suggested to me by a lawyer . . . who represented three persons who had been charged with shoplifting. Having satisfied himself that there was no significant conflict of interest, the defense lawyer told the prosecutor that two of the three would plead guilty only if the case was dismissed against the third. Previously, those two had told the defense counsel that they would plead guilty irrespective of what the third did, and the third had said that he wished to go to trial unless the charges were dropped. Thus, the defense lawyer lied to the prosecutor by stating that the two would plead only if the third were allowed to go free. Can the lie be justified in this case?

How does one distinguish the cases where truthfulness is not required and those where it is required? Why do the first three cases seem easy? I suggest they are easy cases, because the rules of the game are explicit and well developed in those areas. Everyone expects a lawyer to distort the value of his own case, of his own facts and arguments, and to deprecate those of his opponent. No one is surprised by that, and the system accepts and expects that behavior. To a lesser extent, the same is true of the false demand procedure in labor-management negotiations where the ploy is sufficiently widely used to be explicitly identified in the literature. A layman might say that this behavior falls within the ambit of "exaggeration," a form of behavior that, while not necessarily respected, is not regarded as morally reprehensible in our society.

The last two cases are more difficult. In one, the lawyer lies about his authority; in the other, he lies about the intention of his clients. It would be more difficult to justify the lies in those cases by arguing that the rules of the game explicitly permit that sort of behavior. Some might say that the rules of the game provide for such distortion, but I suspect that many lawyers would say that such lies are out of bounds and are not part of the rules of the game. Can the lie about authority be justified on the ground that the question itself was improper? Put another way, if I have a right to keep certain information to myself, and if any behavior but a lie will reveal that information to the other side, am I justified in lying? I think not. Particularly in the case in which there are other avenues open to the respondent, should we not ask him to take those avenues? That is, the careful negotiator here can turn aside all such questions and, by doing so, avoid any inference from his failure to answer such questions.

What makes the last case a close one? Conceivably, it is the idea that one accused by the state is entitled to greater leeway in making his case. Possibly, one can argue that there is no injury to the state when such a person, particularly an innocent person, goes free. Is it conceivable that the act can be justified on the ground that it is part of the game in this context, that prosecutors as well as defense lawyers routinely misstate what they, their witnesses, and their clients can and will do? None of these arguments seems persuasive. Justice is not served by freeing a guilty person. The system does not necessarily achieve better results by trading two guilty pleas for a dismissal. Perhaps its justification has its roots in the same idea that formerly held that a misrepresentation of one's state of mind was not actionable, for it was not a misrepresentation of fact.

In a sense, rules governing these cases may simply arise from a recognition by the law of its limited power to shape human behavior. By tolerating exaggeration and puffing in the sales transaction, by refusing to make misstatement of one's intention actionable, the law may simply have recognized the bounds of its control over human behavior. Having said that, one is still left with the question: Are the lies permissible in the last two cases? My general conclusion is that they are not, but I am not nearly as comfortable with that conclusion as I am with the conclusion about the first three cases.

Taken together, the five foregoing cases show me that we do not and cannot intend that a negotiator be "truthful" in the broadest sense of that term. At the minimum, we allow him some deviation from truthfulness in asserting his true opinion about cases, statutes, or the value of the subject of the negotiation in other respects. In addition, some of us are likely to allow him to lie in response to certain questions that are regarded as out of bounds, and possibly to lie in circumstances where his interest is great and the injury seems small. It would be unfortunate, therefore, for the rule that requires "fairness" to be interpreted to require that a negotiator be truthful in every respect and in all of his dealings. It should be read to allow at least those kinds of untruthfulness that are implicitly and explicitly recognized as acceptable in his forum, a forum defined both by the subject matter and by the participants.

4. John W. Cooley, *Defining the Ethical Limits of Acceptable Deception in Mediation*, 4 PEPP. DISP. RESOL. L.J. 263 (2004)

This article proceeds from the premise that consensual deception is the essence of caucused mediation. This statement should not come as a shock to the reader when it is considered in the context of the nature and purpose of caucusing. Actually, it is quite rare that caucused mediation, a type of informational game, occurs without the use of deception by the parties, by their lawyers, and/or by the mediator in some form. This is so for several reasons.

First, a basic ground rule of the information system operating in any mediated case in which there is caucusing is that confidential information conveyed to the mediator by any party cannot be disclosed by the mediator to anyone (with narrowly limited exceptions). This means that: (1) each party in mediation rarely, if ever, knows whether another party has disclosed confidential information to the mediator; and (2) if confidential information has been disclosed, the non-disclosing party never knows the specific content of that confidential information and whether and/or to what extent that confidential information has colored or otherwise affected communications coming to the non-disclosing party from the mediator. In this respect, each party in a mediation is an actual or potential victim of constant deception regarding confidential information — granted, agreed deception — but nonetheless deception. This is the central paradox of the caucused mediation process. The parties, and indeed even the mediator, agree to be deceived as a condition of participating in it in order to find a solution that the parties will find "valid" for their purposes.

Second, mediation rarely occurs absent deception, because the parties (and their counsel) are normally engaged in the strategies and tactics of competitive bargaining during all or part of the mediation conference, and the goal of each party is to get the best deal for himself or herself.

These competitive bargaining strategies and tactics are layered and interlaced with the mediator's own strategies and tactics to get the best resolution possible for the parties — or at least a resolution that they can accept. The confluence of these, initially anyway, unaligned strategies, tactics, and goals creates an environment rich in gamesmanship and intrigue, naturally conducive to the use of deceptive behaviors by the parties and their counsel, and yes, even by mediators. Actually, even more so by mediators, because they are the conductors — the orchestrators — of an information system specially designed for each dispute, a system with ambiguously defined or, in some situations, undefined disclosure rules in which the mediator is the Chief Information Officer who has near-absolute control over what non-confidential information, critical or otherwise, is developed, what is withheld, what is disclosed, and when it is disclosed. As mediation pioneer Christopher Moore has noted: "The ability to control, manipulate, suppress, or enhance data, or to initiate entirely new information, gives the mediator an inordinate level of influence over the parties."

Third, the information system manipulated by the mediator in any dispute context is itself imperfect. Parties, rarely, if ever, share with the mediator all the information relevant, or even necessary, to the achievement of the mediator's goal — an agreed resolution of conflict. The parties' deceptive behavior in this regard — jointly understood by the parties and the mediator in any mediation to fall within the agreed "rules of the game" — sometimes causes mediations to fail or prevents optimal solutions from being achieved.

Thus, if agreed deception is a central ingredient in caucused mediation, the question then becomes what types of deception should be considered constructive, within the rules of the mediation game, and ethically acceptable and what types should be considered destructive, beyond the bounds of fair play, and ethically unacceptable. Or, perhaps more simply, in the words of mediator Robert Benjamin, in mediation, what are the characteristics of the "noble lie" — deception "designed to shift and reconfigure the thinking of disputing parties, especially in the conflict and confusion, and to foster and further their cooperation, tolerance, and survival"? Because formal mediation is generally viewed as "nothing more than a three-party or multiple-party negotiation," we can begin to formulate an answer to this question by examining the current limits of acceptable deception as employed by lawyer-negotiators.

III. Acceptable Deception by Lawyer-Negotiators

The launch point for our exploration of the ethical norms governing the extent to which a lawyer must be truthful in negotiations is Rule 4.1 of the ABA Model Rules of Professional Conduct. Rule 4.1 Truthfulness in Statements to Others, provides: "In the course of representing a client a lawyer shall not knowingly: (a) make a false statement of material fact or law to a third person;

or (b) fail to disclose a material fact to a third person when disclosure is necessary to avoid assisting a criminal or fraudulent act by a client, unless disclosure is prohibited by Rule 1.6."

In relation to lawyers representing clients in negotiation, there is a wide chasm dividing expert opinion on the applicable standard of truthfulness. At one extreme on the "truthfulness spectrum," Judge Alvin B. Rubin . . . proposed two "precepts" to guide a lawyer's conduct in negotiations: (1) "The lawyer must act honestly and in good faith," and (2) "The lawyer may not accept a result that is unconscionably unfair to the other party." In 1980, Professor James J. White published an article in which he asserted his belief that misleading the other side is the very "essence of negotiation" and is all part of the game. White observed that truth is a relative concept that depends on the definition one chooses and the circumstances of the negotiator. He further pointed out that lawyers hunt "for the rules of the game as the game is played in the particular circumstance." He identified the paradox of the lawyer's goal in negotiation — how to "be fair but also mislead." In 1981, Yale Law Professor Geoffrey C. Hazard, Jr., principal draftsman of the Model Rules of Professional Conduct, after reviewing Judge Rubin's and Professor White's articles and other pertinent literature of the day, concluded that "legal regulation of trustworthiness cannot go much further than to proscribe fraud." In 1982, Professor Thomas F. Guernsey sought a middle-ground solution. He suggested that conventions regarding truthfulness dilemmas be formulated to guide those lawyers aspiring to be ethical, but that the default standard in all negotiations should be "caveat lawyer." More recently, other commentators have advocated various truthfulness standards for lawyers in negotiation in terms of "total candor"; of avoiding "creating an unreasonable risk of harm"; of forbidding all deception; of "permissible conventions of untruthfulness"; of allowing "advantageous results consistent with honest dealings with others"; of "the golden rule" — reciprocal candor; of defining "what is not a lie and what lies are ethically permissible."

These varying perceptions of what standards of truthfulness should guide lawyers' conduct in representing a client in negotiation offer little by way of identifying the standards that do currently guide them. Under Model Rule 4.1(a), what exactly is a false statement of material fact in negotiation? What is a false statement of law? And, under subparagraph (b) of that rule, when is a lawyer's disclosure of a material fact necessary to avoid a client's fraudulent act in negotiation? . . . The Comments actually complicate the search for answers to the questions presented by the text of Model Rule 4.1, and the formal and informal Recent Ethics Opinions published by the ABA offer little assistance in interpreting Model Rule 4.1's application to a lawyer's permissible conduct in negotiation.

Determining what constitutes unethical conduct is also difficult because of numerous excuses and justification lawyers typically marshal for lying in negotiation and the plethora of well-recognized negotiation strategies and tactics that have developed in recent years. Such strategies and tactics are widely considered to be within the rules of the negotiation game. Lawyers have names for them; law books describe them in detail; law professors teach them to students in law school. Many of these strategies and tactics rely for the effectiveness on

techniques of timed disclosure, partial disclosure, nondisclosure, and over-
stated and understated disclosures of information — all of which involve
degrees of deception. Their effectiveness is also dependent on lawyer's avoidance
techniques and on subtle distinctions between what information consists of
facts as opposed to what is lawyer's opinion. "Puffing" — a type of deception —
is generally thought to be within the permissible limits of a lawyer's ethical conduct in negotiation, yet even with puffing, at some mysterious, undefined point
the line may be crossed and "the lack of competing inferences makes the statement a lie."

Larry Lempert, *In Settlement Talks, Does Telling the Truth Have Its Limits?*
2 INSIDE LITIGATION 1 (1988), poignantly illustrates the differences of opinion and
confusion among the experts regarding truthfulness standards in negotiation.
Using four hypothetical negotiation situations, the author conducted a survey
of fifteen participants, which included eight law professors who had written on
ethics and negotiation, or both; five experienced litigators; a federal circuit
court judge; and a U.S. Magistrate. . . .

Situation 1. Your clients, the defendants, have told you that you are authorized to pay $750,000 to settle the case. In settlement negotiations after your offer
of $650,000, the plaintiffs' attorney asks, "Are you authorized to settle for
$750,000?" Can you say, "No I'm not"?

Yes: Seven; No: Six; Qualified: Two

Situation 2. You represent a plaintiff who claims to have suffered a serious
knee injury. In settlement negotiations, can you say your client is "disabled"
when you know she is out skiing?

Yes: One; No: Fourteen; Qualified: None

Situation 3. You are trying to negotiate a settlement on behalf of a couple who
charge that the bank pulled their loan, ruining their business. Your clients are
quite up-beat and deny suffering particularly severe emotional distress. Can you
tell your opponent, nonetheless, that they did?

Yes: Five; No: Eight; Qualified: Two

Situation 4. In settlement talks over the couple's lender liability case, your
opponent's comments make it clear that he thinks plaintiffs have gone out of
business, although you didn't say that. In fact, the business is continuing and
several important contracts are in the offing. You are on the verge of settlement;
can you settle without correcting your opponent's misimpression?

Yes: Nine; No: Four; Qualified: Two

In the midst of all this confusion and disagreement about the appropriate
truthfulness standard, one could reasonably conclude, as apparently did Professor Hazard, that . . . ethical norms for lawyers do little more than proscribe
fraud in negotiation — or, at most, they proscribe only very serious, harmful misrepresentations of material fact made through a lawyer's false verbal or written statement, affirmation, or silence. Assuming that this is the current
standard of truthfulness for lawyers who are advocates in negotiation, the
question then becomes: does this same standard of truthfulness apply to lawyers

who are advocates in mediation, as opposed to negotiation? To that topic, we now turn.

IV. Acceptable Deception by Mediation Advocates

Very little has been written about the ethical standards for lawyers who represent clients in mediation, much less the standards of truthfulness which should guide them. Nothing in the ABA Model Rules of Professional Conduct for lawyers addresses lawyer truthfulness in mediation. In mediation, of course, the advocate's duty of truthfulness has to be measured not only in relation to "others" but also a special kind of "other" — a neutral who is sometimes a judge or a former judge. Thus, two questions emerge: (1) do the ethical standards for truthfulness in negotiation described in the immediately preceding section also govern the advocate's truthfulness behavior vis-a-vis the opponents in mediation; and (2) do those ethical standards also govern the advocate's truthfulness behavior vis-a-vis a neutral (lawyer, nonlawyer, or judge) in mediation?

First, since the Model Rules are silent on the truthfulness standards for mediation advocates vis-a-vis their opponents, one would seemingly be safe in concluding that the rules regarding truthfulness in negotiation apply. However, one could make a persuasive argument that a heightened standard of truthfulness by advocates in mediation should apply because of the "deception synergy" syndrome resulting from a third-party neutral's involvement. We know from practical experience that the accuracy of communication deteriorates on successive transmissions between and among individuals. Distortions also have a tendency to become magnified on continued transmissions. Also, we know from the available behavioral research concerning mediator strategies and tactics that mediators tend to embellish information, translate it, and sometimes distort it to meet the momentary needs of their efforts to achieve a settlement. To help protect against "deception synergy" perhaps we should require more truthfulness from mediation advocates and commensurately require more truthfulness of mediators. But the practicality of such a proposal is questionable. Can we reasonably expect advocates to behave any differently in mediation than they do in negotiation? Would such truthfulness distinctions be impossible to define and even less possible to enforce? It seems very likely. Thus, it appears that the standards governing advocates' truthfulness in negotiation vis-a-vis each other would also govern their conduct in mediation.

Second, with respect to truthfulness standards for mediation advocates vis-a-vis the mediator, apparently the only available guidance having even a modicum of applicability appears to be Model Rule 3.3, "Candor Toward the Tribunal." It is arguable, of course, that Rule 3.3 applies only to court tribunals which adjudicate matters in a public forum — and not to mediators, special masters, part-time judges, or former judges, and the like, who conduct settlement conferences. If that is the intent of this rule, the Model Rules do not specifically say so. Nowhere do they define "tribunal." It is not even clear whether Rule 3.3 applies to a lawyer's conduct before a private tribunal consisting of an arbitrator or arbitrators, although it reasonably could be. If they do apply in arbitration, would they also apply in hybrid ADR processes, such as med-arb or binding mediation? While it is true that the Comments to the above-quoted Rule 3.3 make no reference to settlement conference or mediation, it is also true that they do not explicitly exclude settlement conferences and/or mediation from its coverage.

Other Model Rules further obfuscate the scope of the coverage of Model Rule 3.3. For example, Comments to Rule 3.9, "Advocate in Nonadjudicative Proceedings," refers to "court" and not "tribunal," except administrative tribunal. So the question becomes: is "court" different in meaning than the unmodified term "tribunal?" Comment (1) to Rule 1.12, "Former Judge or Arbitrator," defines "adjudicative officer" as including such officials as judges pro tempore, referees, special masters, hearing officers and other parajudicial officers, and also lawyers who serve as part-time judges." Is the term "tribunal" then broader than "adjudicative officer?" That is, does the unmodified term "tribunal" include both "adjudicative" and "nonadjudicative" officers? If so, would mediators or settlement officers fall within the scope of "nonadjudicative" officers, thus making Rule 3.3 applicable to mediators? For those readers who believe this analysis is an exercise in tautology, you may be correct. The objective of all this is to make two important points: (1) the current Model Rules are thoroughly deficient in providing guidance to mediation advocates on what their truthfulness behavior should be vis-a-vis mediators (whether or not the mediators are judges, former judges, or court-appointed neutrals); and (2) if Model Rule 3.3 were deemed to apply to mediation advocates, it would significantly enhance the standards of advocates' truthfulness-to-mediator responsibilities, most probably to the point that no advocate would find it sensible to participate in the mediation process. This describes the current state of affairs regarding mediation advocates, but what about mediators?

V. Acceptable Deception by Mediators

Neither the Ethical Standards of Professional Responsibility of the Association for Conflict Resolution (ACR) ("Ethical Standards"), nor the Model Standards of Conduct for Mediators ("Model Standards") prepared by a joint committee of the AAA, ABA, and ACR, addresses the question of how truthful a mediator must be in conducting a mediation. The Ethical Standards merely make a passing reference to a duty they owe to the parties, to the profession, and to themselves and state that mediators "should be honest and unbiased, act in good faith, be diligent, and not seek to advance their own interests at the expense of their parties." The Ethical Standards contain no explanation of what "honest" means.

The Model Standards are similarly void of any specific guidance to the mediator regarding standards for truthfulness. They do, however, provide general guidance to the mediator in handling confidential information. Thus, while the Model Standards come closer than the Ethical Standards toward the topic of mediator truthfulness, the Model Standards fail to address this crucial topic directly, opting, perhaps wisely for the time being, to keep standards regarding the matter vague and ambiguous. Although the Model Standards recognize that the parties and the mediator may have their "own rules" regarding confidentiality and that the mediator should discuss the nature of private sessions and confidentiality with the parties, they do not identify any specific information or types of information that must, at a minimum, be communicated regarding confidentiality rules or the private session procedure in order to be in ethical compliance with the Model Standards. And perhaps just as importantly, the Model Standards, unlike the ABA's Model Rules of Professional Conduct for lawyers, do not identify or define any specific type or types of mediator untruthfulness that is intended to be ethically proscribed. Thus, mediators — lawyers and nonlawyers — currently have no specific formal guidance regarding how truthful they must be in conducting mediations. . . .

Despite this serious lack of guidance, even if lawyer-mediators were to look to the ABA Model Code of Judicial Conduct (August, 1990) to find analogous guidance for themselves as to required standards of truthfulness to guide their specific behavior in conducting mediations, they would be disappointed to find that there are none. Remarkably, no canon or commentary of the ABA's Model Code of Judicial Conduct offers any specific guidance regarding a judge's duty to be truthful to others, although such requirement might be presumed from Canon 1 which states that "a judge shall uphold the integrity and independence of the judiciary." But that requirement is so general as to be of no utility whatsoever to our inquiry here.

VI. Questions . . . Regarding Required Standards of Truthfulness in Mediation

The above discussion of the legal profession's minimal regulation of the use of deception in mediation triggers some very important questions about what standards of truthfulness should be developed to guide mediators and mediation advocates in performing their functions. . . .

1. To what standards of truthfulness should a mediator be held?

2. What types of deception are . . . within the bounds of fair play, and acceptable?

3. What types of deception are . . . outside the bounds of fair play, and unacceptable?

4. Should there be different standards . . . for lawyers and nonlawyers?

5. Should the standards of truthfulness be any different for the lawyer-mediator than the lawyer-advocate in either negotiation or mediation?

6. Should there be different standards of truthfulness for a mediator when parties are unrepresented by legal counsel?

7. To what standards of truth and honesty should a judge who conducts a settlement conference be held? Should the standards be higher than the non-judge mediator?

8. Should a judge who conducts a caucused settlement conference in a case be ethically precluded from deciding a case on the merits?

9. Should mediators be held to a higher level of truth or honesty when they are appointed by a judge to conduct the mediation?

10. Should lawyer-advocates be held to a higher level of truth and honesty when representing a client in a mediation where the mediator is court-appointed?

11. Should mediators (lawyers, nonlawyers, or judges) be required to explain certain "rules of the mediation game" before the mediation begins?

12. If "game rules" should be explained, of what would they consist?

13. Would the "game rules" vary depending on the sophistication of the parties? Would the "game rules" vary depending on whether the parties were represented by counsel?

VII. Some Preliminary Thoughts Regarding the Search for Answers to These Questions

If you set about to define rules of a game, you must take care to ensure that those rule are (1) compatible with the game's nature and its purpose; (2) do not significantly interfere with the means by which the players can accomplish the game's purpose; (3) are comprehensible, reasonable, and fair; and (4) are capable of compliance by all of the game's players in all situations. Otherwise — depending on the degree of inappropriateness of the rules — the game will not be played, the rules will be ignored, they will not be enforced, or their application and enforcement will result in unfair treatment of some of the players. . . .

When designing rules to govern ethical conduct in mediation (and by inclusion, negotiation), one must be careful to balance the rigor of an imposed duty, on the one hand, against the reasonable likelihood of compliance in the context in which the duty is to be fulfilled, on the other. To impose an ethical rule in negotiation and mediation that charges lawyers (and non-lawyers) with a duty antithetical to the nature and purpose of these processes, that is incomprehensible, unreasonable, or unfair, and/or that is incapable of compliance by many of the people it is designed to regulate would be a futile act. People would not comply with it, and if such rule or rules were enforced, people would not play the mediation game. They would litigate in court as much as possible. So, our goal should be to find the described balance as derivable from the rule-making criteria appearing at the outset of this section.

A. Rules must be compatible with the game's nature and purpose. Let's first consider the nature and purpose of mediation. The nature of mediation is an information management process, and its purpose is to resolve conflict. The process is not static; rather, it is dynamic in the sense that, in it, parties continuously develop and share information face-to-face or through the mediator. Infusion of new information may cause the parties to rethink what, at any particular moment, their risks are and what they really desire in the settlement. In some situations, these changes may literally occur minute-to-minute. Truth may likewise change from minute-to-minute. What is true for a party in mediation now, may not be true for a party 15 minutes from now in the same mediation. So, in designing ethical rules, we must keep clearly in mind that truth, in the context of an ongoing mediation session, is also dynamic — not static in nature. A party may start a mediation stating that he will not accept less than

$50,000 to settle the case; yet he walks out happily embracing a $37,500 settlement. Thus, whatever truthfulness standard is adopted for mediators and mediation advocates, it must be able to accommodate the mediation process's integral and unalterable truth-mutating nature, and it must not interfere in any significant way with mediation's conflict resolution purpose.

B. Rules must not significantly interfere with the means by which the players can accomplish the game's purpose. That mediation's purpose is to resolve conflict says nothing of the means that may be used to accomplish resolution. And that brings into focus the second criteria for ethical rule design: the rule should not interfere in any significant way with the means by which the mediator or the mediation advocate can accomplish the purpose of mediation. The question that must be addressed here is: may a good end justify any means? May truth be bent, colored, tinted, veneered, or hidden by a mediator or mediation advocate if the result is achieving a satisfactory resolution, or better yet, a win-win solution without harm to any party? In short, is there such a thing as a noble lie? Our immediate instincts beckon us to answer "no"; but the reality is that many of us lied to our children so long about Santa Claus — with no catastrophic results and no tinge of shame — that deep down we know that something like a "noble lie" exists and it's okay. Thus, whatever truthfulness standard is adopted, it must accommodate, or at least acknowledge, the concept of the "noble lie."

C. Rules must be comprehensible, reasonable, and fair. The third criteria for ethical rule design is that any imposed rule should be comprehensible, and it should be reasonable and fair, both in its content and its application. As to comprehensibility, an ethical rule must be stated clearly and unambiguously. A rule that is capable of various interpretations can produce unfair, unwanted, and even nefarious results.

As to content, this third criterion stimulates inquiry into what types of communication (written, verbal, or nonverbal) or withholding of information should be prescribed or proscribed by the ethical rule; or whether there should be any prescriptions or proscriptions at all. My own personal reaction to this question currently is that it would make much more sense for the rules to proscribe certain specifically defined types of untruthful statements, behavior, conduct, or omissions rather than use vague blanket terms like "false statement of material fact or law." In this regard, a review of some of the literature on development of conventions of truthfulness, untruthfulness, and good faith may be of some help to the designers of the truthfulness standard for mediation.

As to the reasonable and fair application of an ethical rule, the third criterion forces consideration of whether the same standard of truthfulness should apply across the board to all participants in mediation whether they be lawyer or nonlawyer mediators, lawyer-advocates, judges, or former judges. My intuitive response is that the standard of truthfulness should be the same for all, unless some exception can be identified and justified. Conceptually, there should be no separate rules for judge-mediated cases as compared to non-lawyer or lawyer-mediated cases. The key is selecting a truthfulness standard that is capable of both comprehension and compliance, and therefore respect. And this leads us to the discussion of the fourth criteria for ethical rule design — the rules must be capable of compliance by all persons whom they intend to regulate.

D. Rules must be capable of compliance by all of the game's players in all situations. Whatever truthfulness standard is selected, there must be a final check to determine whether all persons that the standard is designed to regulate can reasonably be expected to comply with it in all predictable situations. This requires a type of "troubleshooter" thinking to imagine the variety of ways that the truthfulness standard might come into play. There might be certain types of situations, party configurations, or claims or defense types in which the standard needs to be modified by making it more or less rigorous or by limiting its application in some way. By this process, it may be concluded that certain specific exceptions to the truthfulness standards need to be provided and specifically explained in the text of the rule or its accompanying comments. This criterion also requires the designers to consider whether the mediator, for example, should be required to explain the "rules of the game" and truthfulness expectations at the beginning of the mediation, and if so, what the content of that explanation should be. . . .

5. AMERICAN BAR ASSOCIATION STANDING COMMITTEE ON ETHICS AND PROFESSIONAL RESPONSIBILITY, Formal Opinion 06-347 (2006)

This is the latest, and most official, attempt to determine the parameters of the obligation of a lawyer to speak truthfully on behalf of a client in a negotiation. Unsurprisingly, the Committee did not produce a comprehensive answer to this conundrum. (The Opinion does not address the situation where the client makes representations in negotiation that the attorney knows to be false.) Following the language of Model Rule 4.1, the Committee concluded that while an attorney should not make a "false statement of material fact," this standard does not encompass such matters as negotiation goals, willingness to compromise, and puffing. This much we knew already.

The specific question addressed by Formal Opinion 06-347 was whether a different standard of truthfulness was required of an attorney representing a client in the context of caucused mediation. (The Opinion does not consider the obligations of an attorney who serves as a mediator.) On this question, the Standing Committee provided an unequivocal answer: caucused mediation is governed by the same truthfulness standards as other negotiations. Where representations are made to a "tribunal," which term does not include mediation, Model Rule 3.3 governs the duty of candor. This rule applies when a court official is involved in a negotiation or mediation. *See* Formal Opinion 93-370 (1993) (Judicial Participation in Pretrial Settlement Negotiations). The Committee also stated that Model Rule 8.4(c), which proscribes "conduct involving dishonesty, fraud, deceit, or misrepresentation," is inapplicable to conduct permitted under Rule 4.1.

An argument was made for a higher standard of attorney candor in caucused mediation, because a neutral is involved, and because the quality of information deteriorates with multiple communications (as occurs in the game of "telephone"). Conversely, a lower standard of candor might be employed because the mediator is in charge of the communication process between the parties. The Committee gave short shrift to such arguments, because nothing in the Model Rules of Professional Conduct permits different standards of candor in different negotiation contexts. Although not mentioned by the Standing Committee, multiple standards of required candor in negotiation based on the form of the negotiation, would introduce additional complexity and uncertainty into an area that is difficult enough already.

Part III
MEDIATION

Chapter 7
THE MEDIATION PROCESS

A. INTRODUCTION

Mediation can be defined in as little as two words: "facilitated negotiation." Alternative two word definitions are "assisted negotiation" and "moderated negotiation." Each of these definitions makes it clear that mediation is a special form of negotiation. The usual understanding is that the facilitator is neutral. The goal of this chapter is to introduce the mediation process, recognizing that one of the great strengths of mediation is its flexibility and adaptability to particular circumstances.

A few more elaborate general statements about the nature of mediation provide a useful starting point for our consideration of mediation, so long as one recognizes that any brief description of a complex social process such as mediation is necessarily simplistic and incomplete. These brief statements about mediation are not inconsistent with one another, but you should note how they differ somewhat in tone and emphasis.

CHRISTOPHER W. MOORE, THE MEDIATION PROCESS: PRACTICAL STRATEGIES FOR RESOLVING DISPUTES 8 (1996) states that: "Mediation is the intervention into a dispute or negotiation by an acceptable, impartial and neutral third party who has no authoritative decision-making power to assist disputing parties in voluntarily reaching their own mutually acceptable settlement of issues in dispute." PROFESSOR KIMBERLEE K. KOVACH, MEDIATION: PRINCIPLES AND PRACTICE 27 (2004) offers the following explanation of mediation:

> Mediation is a process by which a third party neutral . . . acts as a facilitator to assist in the resolving of a dispute between two or more parties. It is a non-adversarial approach to conflict resolution where the parties communicate directly. The role of the mediator is to facilitate communication between the parties, assist them on focusing on the real issues of the dispute, and generate options for settlement. The goal of this process is that the parties themselves arrive at a mutually acceptable resolution of the dispute.

The Uniform Mediation Act (UMA), § 2(1), defines mediation as "a process in which a mediator facilitates communication and negotiation between parties to assist them in reaching a voluntary agreement regarding their dispute." [The full text of the UMA is found in the Appendix.] The leading supporters of the "transformative" approach to mediation state that: "Mediation is a social process in which a third party helps people in conflict understand their situation and decide for themselves what, if anything, to do about it. . . ." Dorothy J. Della

Noce, Robert A. Baruch Bush, & Joseph P. Folger, *Clarifying the Theoretical Underpinnings of Mediation: Implications for Practice and Policy*, 3 PEPP. DISP. RESOL. L.J. 39, 39 (2002).

Professor Stulberg believes "that a robust vision of mediation systematically supports the notion that a mediator assists parties to a controversy: (a) develop an improved understanding of their situation, and (b) based on that understanding, (i) collectively develop options to structure their relationship (or its termination) that (ii) each embrace." Joseph B. Stulberg, *The UMA: The Road Not Taken*, 2003 J. DISP. RESOL. 221, 223. A leading construction mediator views mediation functionally: "Mediation facilitates communication; gets the necessary information into the process; gets the right parties to the table; overcomes emotional blockages; puts the negotiation process back on track; focuses the parties on the problems; and helps the parties reassess their legal predictions." James P. Groton, *Getting the Mediation Process Started*, in ALAN E. HARRIS, CHARLES M. SINK & RANDALL W. WULFF, ADR: A PRACTICAL GUIDE TO RESOLVE CONSTRUCTION DISPUTES 77-78 (1994).

Section B offers a theoretical overview of mediation. In Section C, we turn from theory to practice and examine the mechanics of the mediation process in some detail. Section D offers a variety of views on the mediation movement and competing schools of thought about mediation.

B. THE MEDIATION PROCESS: THEORY

1. Comments and Questions

a. The two articles in this section offer a theoretical introduction to mediation. Professor Lon Fuller was one of the great legal scholars of the 20th century. In addition to his work on dispute resolution, he wrote about contracts, labor law, and jurisprudence. His work is briefly examined by William Twining in Chapter One. Dr. Christopher Moore is a leading mediation thinker, teacher, and practitioner. His best known work is THE MEDIATION PROCESS: PRACTICAL STRATEGIES FOR RESOLVING CONFLICT (2d ed. 1996).

b. The most important theoretical question about mediation is: Why does mediation succeed with great frequency in producing more and better settlements than parties can achieve without the assistance of a third party neutral? This success is commonly referred to as "the magic of mediation." What factors promote the success of mediative efforts?

c. One possible explanation is that successful mediation has little to do with the process, but instead reflects the special skills of individual mediators. Perhaps mediation is like activities such as sports or chess; while most people can participate in these activities at some level, a small set of people are dramatically more talented than others. Practice and experience are not irrelevant, but most of us will never be able to dunk a basketball or play chess well enough to compete at even a local tournament level, no matter how much we practice. Can most reasonably intelligent people learn how to become successful mediators? An analogy might be drawn to speaking one's native language — almost everyone can do it reasonably well (although some people are better or more successful than others).

2. Lon L. Fuller, *Mediation — Its Forms and Functions,* 44 S. Cal. Rev. 305 (1970)

I have thought it expedient to preface my analysis by putting mediation in the wider context of some assumptions of methodology that appear to shape our efforts to comprehend social phenomena generally. In every branch of human study that has achieved or aspires to the name of science there seems to repeat itself a fundamental difference in the assumptions men make as to the nature of the thing they are examining: . . . structure versus process, substance versus procedure, statics versus dynamics, and — on a more elevated plane — Being and Becoming. As these terms indicate, this recurring difference is not so much thought of as a quarrel about the most profitable posture of the mind as it is about the essential nature of the thing being studied. . . .

One is tempted to say mediation is all process and no structure. Casual treatments of the subject in the literature of sociology tend to assume that the object of mediation is to make the parties aware of the "social norms" applicable to their relationship and to persuade them to accommodate themselves to the "structure" imposed by these norms. From this point of view the difference between a judge and a mediator is simply that the judge orders the parties to conform themselves to the rules, while the mediator persuades them to do so. But mediation is commonly directed, not toward achieving conformity to norms, but toward the creation of the relevant norms themselves. This is true, for example, in the very common case where the mediator assists the parties in working out the terms of a contract defining their rights and duties toward one another. In such a case there is no pre-existing structure that can guide mediation; it is the mediational process that produces the structure.

It may be suggested that mediation is always . . . directed toward bringing about a more harmonious relationship between the parties, whether this be achieved through explicit agreement, through a reciprocal acceptance of the "social norms" relevant to their relationship, or simply because the parties have been helped to a new and more perceptive understanding of one another's problems. The fact that in ordinary usage the terms "mediation" and "conciliation" are largely interchangeable tends to reinforce this view of the matter.

But at this point we encounter the inconvenient fact that mediation can be directed, not toward cementing a relationship, but toward terminating it. . . . Thus we find that mediation may be directed toward, and result in, discrepant and even diametrically opposed results. This circumstance argues against our being able to derive any general structure of the mediational process from some identifiable goal shared by all mediational efforts. . . . The mere presence of a third person tends to put the parties on their good behavior, that the mediator can direct their verbal exchanges away from recrimination and toward the issues that need to be faced, that by receiving separate and confidential communications from the parties he can gradually bring into the open issues so deep-cutting that the parties themselves had shared a tacit taboo against any discussion of them and that, finally, he can by his management of the interchange demonstrate to the parties that it is possible to discuss divisive issues without either rancor or evasion.

But can we go beyond generalities of this sort? I believe we can, but to accomplish this we shall have to begin by examining in detail the functions mediation can perform in a specific illustrative situation. If this illustrative case is aptly chosen we may then, with appropriate adjustments, extend our conclusions to other situations that vary in specific ways from the model adopted for detailed analysis. The model I propose here is that presented by mediational efforts serving to facilitate the negotiation of a collective bargaining agreement between an employer and a labor union.

I begin, then, by supposing that an employer, a corporation engaged in manufacturing, and a labor union representing its production force are about to enter into negotiations concerning the terms of a collective bargaining agreement. I assume that these negotiations will range over a wide variety of issues, either because a collective bargaining agreement is being entered by the parties for the first time, or because an existing agreement has come open for renegotiation and the issues raised by the parties extend over a wide range of subjects, such as rates of pay, seniority provisions, grievance procedures, and the timing and length of annual paid vacations.

Now among the characteristics of this relationship that are relevant to our purposes, the first lies in the obvious fact that the parties mediated are two in number, they constitute a dyad, not a triad or more numerous group. To be sure, during the mediational effort some differences of opinion within the union and, less commonly, within the company, may come to the surface, but basically the mediator's efforts are directed toward an ordering of the relations between the company and the union, and he will generally be at pains to stay out of quarrels arising within either of the participating groups.

The second characteristic of concern here lies in the circumstance that normally neither of the parties, the employer or the union, has any real choice but to reach an agreement with the other. The two parties are locked in a relationship that is virtually one of "bilateral monopoly"; each is dependent for its very existence on some collaboration with the other. This "tied-in" relationship, it should be noted, extends not only to the union as a collective entity but in some measure to the individual union member as well. If, dissatisfied with what his union has achieved for him, he considers taking a job with another employer, he is likely to be reminded that in his new position he will find himself at the bottom of the seniority ladder and vulnerable to lay-off at the first slackening of production. Furthermore, moving into a new employment may forfeit for him any nontransferable "fringe benefits" his union has obtained for him through collective bargaining, these benefits relating to such things as retirement pay, health benefits, paid vacations proportioned to length of service, and the like. We commonly find, then, between the unionized employer, on the one side, and the labor union and its members, on the other, a relationship that may be called one of heavy interdependence: they simply must find some way of getting along with one another.

The third characteristic of the relationship that is relevant here lies in the obvious fact that the negotiation of the collective bargaining agreement has elements of an economic trade. This is plainly true, of course, where rates of pay are being negotiated. But it is also true where "non-monetary" provisions of the contract come under discussion. For example, a manufacturer might be willing to accept a revision of the grievance procedure proposed by the union, in return for some expansion of the clause removing certain management decisions from arbitrational review. The question, "Will this help or hurt us?" is one the parties constantly put to themselves as they negotiate the contract, sometimes even when the issue is simply where a comma ought to be inserted. Into every aspect of the negotiations, then, there is likely to enter some calculation of relative "payoff."

The fourth characteristic of our illustrative situation stands in some contrast to that just described. The enterprise in which the parties are engaged is not simply one in which each seeks to attain the contractual language that will most favor his immediate interests. The parties are also caught up in the task of drafting a constitution, of putting on paper words by which they can in the future live together successfully. A perception of this aspect of their joint endeavor must temper and often redirect their efforts toward the achievement of their separate goals. A clause with hidden ambiguities that invite endless disputes will carry a heavy price tag for both parties, even though the party securing its adoption may at the time have congratulated himself on having served well his own advantage.

The fact that the actual negotiation of the collective bargaining agreement is conducted, not by principals, but by agents or representatives constitutes a fifth characteristic of the situation we are discussing. The employer is an abstract entity called a corporation; those who represent that entity act in a representative capacity and they are by no means commonly the chief executives of the corporation itself. Likewise, of course, the entire membership of the union does not and cannot participate directly in the negotiations; these are commonly conducted on their behalf by an out-of-town expert from the national union headquarters, assisted by a local committee.

The sixth and final characteristic of the relationship we are examining lies in the fact that one of the parties, the company, occupies toward the membership of the union a dual role. In the negotiation of the collective bargaining agreement the parties meet each other as equals, with neither having any recognized authority over the other; in the day-to-day management of the plant, however, the company is boss. Its foremen and superintendents, not the labor union, direct the manufacturing process. Indeed, experienced labor leaders exercise a canny reserve about invading this prerogative, for the responsibilities that go with it could be quite inconvenient for them, and any sharing of those responsibilities would tend seriously to compromise their role as representatives of the union membership.

These, then, are six characteristics of the collective bargaining situation that have suggested to me it might be useful as a model in analyzing the functions of mediation generally. By way of a recapitulation: the parties concerned (1) being two in number, find themselves (2) in a relationship of heavy interdependence exerting a strong pressure to reach an agreement, an agreement that will (3) combine elements of an economic trade with (4) elements of a written charter or constitution for the governance of their future relations; this agreement is (5) negotiated by agents, not principals; and (6) the employer occupies throughout a dual role, being, on the one hand, director of the enterprise and, on the other, a coequal with the union in the negotiation and administration of the collective bargaining agreement. In what immediately follows I shall attempt an analysis of the ways in which these six characteristics affect the need for, and the functions performed by, a mediator. Following that analysis, I shall attempt to draw some analogies between the situation I have taken as my illustrative model and the uses of mediation in quite different social contexts.

The first question is, then, how the need for a mediator, and the role performed by him, are affected by the fact that the parties whose relations constitute the subject of mediation are two in number. . . . Simmel observes that among groups ranked in terms of the number of their members, the group of two, the dyad, is peculiarly handicapped in resolving problems of internal order. Even the triad confronting internal difficulties can be governed openly or tacitly by the majority principle; this is an expedient from which, of course, the dyad is excluded. Then, too, one member of a triad can often undertake to mediate between the other two, having perhaps preserved a posture of detachment precisely in order to assume this role; A seeing trouble brewing between B and C may initially have been inclined to favor B but decided to remain neutral in order to qualify for the role of mediator. This is obviously another resource denied to the dyad.

The dyadic relationship is, then, one eminently suited to mediation and often dependent on it as the only measure capable of solving its internal problems. Indeed, one may ask whether mediation, in the strict sense, is really possible in ordering the internal affairs of any group larger than two. If A, B and C are all at odds with one another, it is extremely difficult for an outsider, say, X, to undertake a mediative role without becoming a participant in the internal maneuvers of the quarreling members. If X asks A's acquiescence in a proposed solution, A may reply that he will give his assent if X will undertake to persuade B to withdraw a concession B made in favor of C. X may thus end by becoming the manipulated tool of those he sought to guide. In this predicament he may face the alternative of retaining the empty title of mediator or becoming, in effect, a fourth member of the group and a participant in its internal games. If he chooses the latter alternative, his accession to membership may not increase, but rather tend to diminish the chance for achieving a functioning order since it introduces for the first time the possibility of a deadlock of two against two, in other words, it impairs an advantage the triad enjoys over the dyad, the capacity to resolve internal difficulties by something like a majority vote.

There is perhaps one situation in which an outsider may, with skill and good luck, serve usefully as a mediator among three. This would be where three different measures are proposed as the solution for some problem faced by the triad. A favors Solution X, B favors Solution Y, while C favors Solution Z. Here the mediator might discuss with each of the parties the grounds upon which, and the degree of conviction with which, he supports his preference for one solution as against the other two. There are thus opened up, in somewhat embarrassing abundance, six separate entries for the mediator's intervention. Exploring these conscientiously he might discover that A's preference for X over Y was based on a mistake of fact; with this mistake corrected A might then be ready to join with B in supporting Y. Or, the mediator might discover that B's preference for Y over Z was very slight and that he was almost indifferent between the two. The mediator might then persuade B to join with C in supporting Z, thus restoring the triad as a functioning entity. These happy outcomes are certainly possible, but it is obvious that the relationships involved are so complex, and the opportunities for misunderstanding so great, that the mediator may find it extremely difficult to maintain the integrity of his role. . . . Certainly if the mediational process can be said to have a home ground, it is to be found in the dyad.

In my analysis of the characteristics of the collective bargaining situation I noted that it involved not only a dyad, but a dyad the members of which stood toward one another in a relation of "heavy interdependence." Perhaps this observation served only to emphasize a characteristic that must be present before a resolution of the internal problems of the dyad becomes a matter of sufficient concern to justify mediative efforts. It is fairly obvious that mediation has scarcely any role to play in human relationships fluidly organized on what may be broadly described as the market principle. If X finds A, B and C all competing to supply his needs through rival contractual arrangements, he may need the services of an expert adviser, but he will scarcely have occasion to call on those of a mediator. Likewise, in a society where transient and freely terminable sexual alliances took the place of marriage it is hardly likely that there would develop any institutional practice comparable to "marriage therapy." Mediation by its very nature presupposes relationships normally affected by some strong internal pull toward cohesion; this is true whether the mediative efforts in question be directed toward the formation, modification or dissolution of such relationships.

Those whose minds are intent on the "structure of authority," rather than on an analysis of social processes, are apt to ask of the mediator not, "What does he do?" but, "Whence comes his capacity or authority to arrange the affairs of others?" In this mood the inquiry is likely to be whether his power rests on a tacit contract with the affected parties, or derives from some charismatic qualities possessed by the mediator himself, or should be attributed to some role or office assigned to him by tradition or higher authority. Now an inquiry along these lines is certainly not meaningless, but taking it too seriously may lead us to ignore the fact that the mediator's "power" may largely derive from the simple fact that he is there and that his help is badly needed. . . . When there is no apparent focal point for agreement the mediator can create one by his power to make a dramatic suggestion. The bystander who jumps into an intersection and begins to direct traffic at an impromptu traffic jam is conceded the power to discriminate among cars by being able to offer a sufficient increase in efficiency to benefit even the cars most discriminated against; his directions have only the power of suggestion, but coordination requires the common acceptance of some source of suggestion. Similarly, the participants of a square dance may all be thoroughly dissatisfied with the particular dances being called, but as long as the caller has the microphone, nobody can dance anything else. The white line down the center of the road is a mediator, and very likely it can err substantially toward one side or the other before the disadvantaged side finds advantage in denying its authority.

A serious study of mediation can serve, I suggest, to offset the tendency of modern thought to assume that all social order must be imposed by some kind of "authority." When we perceive how a mediator, claiming no "authority," can help the parties give order and coherence to their relationship, we may in the process come to realize that there are circumstances in which the parties can dispense with this aid, and that social order can often arise directly out of the interactions it seems to govern and direct.

The third characteristic I found present in the collective bargaining situation lies in the fact that in reaching agreement each party is constantly calculating the relative advantage or disadvantage to him of any particular proposal. There is, in other words, a pervasive evaluation of "payoffs." This evaluation extends even to provisions of the contract that seem unrelated in any direct way to monetary costs. In terms of the mediator's function, this means that the mediator participates in a bargaining situation where each party seeks to get as much for himself as he can at as small a cost as possible, the "cost" involved being that entailed in some concession to the opposing party.

But if it is relatively easy to see that an apt exchange can yield advantages to both parties, it is much more difficult to discern the actual processes of discussion and negotiation that will maximize these gains of reciprocity. Suppose, for example, that one party reveals, intentionally or inadvertently, that he is desperately eager to secure some particular concession from his opposing number. It happens that granting this concession would visit very little disadvantage on the party from whom it is demanded. Does he at once reveal this fact, or does he hold back his concession as a resource on which to draw when he wants something badly that the other party is reluctant to give? Which course of action will, in fact, serve ultimately to maximize the gains of reciprocity for both parties? In judging this last question, it should be recalled that gratuitous concessions falling outside the frame of normal bargaining are apt to arouse suspicions as to their motivation and may be interpreted as requiring the benefitted party to volunteer some counter-concessions, which may itself be unguided by any accurate understanding of its value to the other party — the "exchange" of Christmas presents is notoriously a poor example of maximizing utilities.

An obvious, but mistaken expedient would be to have both parties at once disclose to each other their internal evaluations of all the items under discussion. There are many difficulties with this: the values may be extremely intangible; there is no yardstick that can convert them into numbers. Furthermore, the items on a negotiating agenda may be interrelated in various complex ways. For example, suppose that one party A, asks for concessions X, Y, and Z. Now it might be that if Y and Z were granted, X would become wholly unnecessary. On the other hand, if the other party were willing to concede both X and Y, this concession might yield a return much higher than the value of X alone, say, roughly its double, although Y taken by itself would produce only a small fraction of the value that a grant of X by itself would yield, etc., etc.

Where the bargaining process proceeds without the aid of a mediator, the usual course pursued by experienced negotiators is something like this: the parties begin by simply talking about the various proposals, explaining in general terms why they want this and why they are opposed to that. During this exploratory or "sounding out" process, which proceeds without any clear-cut offers of settlement, each party conveys — sometimes explicitly, sometimes tacitly, sometimes intentionally, sometimes inadvertently — something about his relative evaluations of the various items under discussion. After these discussions have proceeded for some time, one party is likely to offer a "package deal," proposing in general terms a contract that will settle all the issues under discussion. This offer may be accepted by the other party or be subject to certain stipulated changes.

Now it is obvious that the process just described can often be greatly facilitated through the services of a skillful mediator. His assistance can speed the negotiations, reduce the likelihood of miscalculation, and generally help the parties to reach a sounder agreement, an adjustment of their divergent valuations that will produce something like an optimum yield of the gains of reciprocity. These things the mediator can accomplish by holding separate confidential meetings with the parties, where each party gives the mediator a relatively full and candid account of the internal posture of his own interests. Armed with this information, but without making a premature disclosure of its details, the mediator can then help to shape the negotiations in such a way that they will proceed most directly to their goal, with a minimum of waste and friction.

The fourth characteristic of the collective bargaining situation to be examined here lies in what I have called its "constitution-drafting" aspect. It should be kept in mind that the collective bargaining agreement serves, in effect, as the charter of a miniature government; it assigns functions, establishes procedures for the presentation of claims, and in its provisions relating to arbitration, institutes what amounts to a private judiciary. Drafting such a document is a demanding exercise, not only in the accurate and unambiguous use of language, but in the apt design of institutional arrangements.

When I first mentioned this aspect of the collective bargaining situation, I remarked that it stood in some contrast to what we have just examined at length. When the parties have reached the point where they are ready to express their future relationship in written words, their efforts will generally be directed toward an achievement of shared objectives, rather than toward a workable compromise of divergent aims. However, it is obvious that some elements of trade-off are likely to reappear when the parties undertake to reduce to numbered paragraphs an oral agreement previously reached "in principle." Nuance of thought and a clause overloaded with qualifications may forfeit its meaning as a clear guidepost for human interaction. In the drafting of any complex agreement, there is often an inescapable compromise between what can be simply expressed and what might be abstractly desirable. The mediational process plainly has a place in dealing with such problems.

There is another service that a mediator can render when the parties' efforts toward a formed agreement have reached the drafting stage. The mediator can bring to problems of drafting a third-party perspective; in George Herbert Mead's famous phrase, he can serve as "the generalized other." . . . The negotiators must keep in mind, not only what the words mean to them, but what they may mean to one who was not a participant in their deliberations and tacit adjustments. The mediator can help to supply that perspective.

We reach now the fifth aspect of the collective bargaining situation having some significance for the role of the mediator and the contribution he can make to a successful contract. This aspect lies in the circumstance that the contract is negotiated, not by principals, but by representatives or agents. My first observation here relates to limitations, real or pretended, on the agent's authority. Let us suppose that the representative of one of the parties opens the first bargaining session by stating that he has been instructed by his principal that he may not, under any circumstances, make certain specified concessions. The excluded concessions will naturally relate to matters that might reasonably be expected to fall within the scope of the negotiations; the agent is hardly likely to warn the opposite party that his principal will sign no contract requiring him to commit a capital offense. In the collective bargaining situation, the limitation on the agent's authority might, in the case of the employer, exclude a provision granting any version of the closed shop, or in the case of the union, anything like a "management prerogative" clause.

Obviously, the mediator will usually serve the cause of effective bargaining by freeing the negotiations from shackles imposed before any discussion of issues has begun and in abstraction from what the negotiations may later reveal about the actual posture of the two parties' interests. If the limitations on the agent's authority are feigned, the mediator can more readily and gracefully penetrate the pretense than can the opposing party. If the limitations have in fact been imposed by the principal, the mediator may induce the agent to ask for their removal and assist him in bringing about that result. None of this means, of course, that in the contract finally signed the principal will inevitably concede things he hoped to prevent from becoming subjects of bargaining; it simply means that the issues sought to be excluded will, in fact, enter into the discussions and be considered as possible ingredients in the final settlement, where, if included, they may of course undergo some modification.

The exploitation of feigned incapacities for the purpose of securing a bargaining advantage has been analyzed at some length in "game theory." Long before the device was subjected to any such sophisticated treatment, it was familiar to lawyers and businessmen as the technique of "the wicked partner." A and B are discussing the terms of a contract; B demands some concession of A. A replies, "I wish very much I could let you have this. But my partner, who is in Europe and unfortunately cannot be reached, is dead set against it." In analyzing the implications of this bargaining stratagem, it is important to realize that it becomes a serious problem only in situations I have described as those of "heavy interdependence," where the needs of the parties and the intertwining of their interests creates a strong pressure toward some sort of accommodation between them. It should also be noted that even in such situations it is a device that may miscarry and disserve the interest of the party who attempted to exploit it. When A refuses in advance even to consider making a particular concession, he will realize that he might receive something in return for this concession, but he thinks he has grounds for believing that the counter-concession could not possibly compensate him for what he gave to secure it. This judgment may be misinformed, for it has been reached before the internal structure of the other party's interests has been exposed through an open-ended exploration of the different ways in which the parties' diverse interests can be fitted together.

But even if the party exploiting the wicked-partner technique is correct in his assumption that he will gain by forestalling in advance any granting of the concession, the bargaining process itself is distorted, and it becomes impossible to secure the general and uninhibited exploration of diverse interests essential to a realization of the maximum gains of reciprocity. The scars left by this distortion may affect adversely the future relations between the parties. All of this means that where the agent pleads in advance a lack of power to grant certain concessions, and where the granting of these concessions would normally form an appropriate subject for bargaining between the parties, the mediator, by securing the removal of such restrictions, may make a substantial contribution, not only to the interests of the immediate parties, but to the integrity of the bargaining process. . . .

So much for limitations, real or pretended, on the agent's power. There is a second and quite different implication for the mediator's role deriving from the fact that the parties to the negotiations are represented by agents. This lies in the observation that if there is no mediator, the parties' agents may be forced, in effect, to join together in assuming the mediational role.

The negotiation of a collective bargaining agreement is commonly opened by a general session attended by delegations of persons representing both sides. On behalf of the union, there may appear an attorney, a field representative from national headquarters and a committee of the local. Management may be represented by an attorney, the personnel manager, the treasurer, and perhaps several other officers concerned with labor relations. Plainly, this wide and miscellaneous audience constitutes a very poor human milieu in which to conduct the delicate sounding-out procedures by which the two parties' interests are revealed and gradually fitted together into some workable pattern. Spokesmen for both sides may be deterred, for example, from making anything like definite proposals by the fear of audible or visible dissents coming from their associates in the audience. The result is that the general opening session normally serves only a ceremonial and ritualistic purpose.

What is the next step? If a mediator is available, this is not difficult. Each of the two groups will, in turn, meet alternately with the mediator out of the presence of the other. At these repeated meetings, each side will make, perhaps with some initial hesitancy but by degrees more openly, a relatively candid disclosure of the posture of its interests and preferences. Any differences within the ranks that may come to the surface during these meetings need not be damaging; on the contrary, some insight into these differences may furnish the mediator useful guidance as he works his way toward an accommodation of the parties' interests that will furnish a workable charter for their future relations.

What happens in the absence of a mediator? As I have previously expressed it, what not uncommonly occurs is that the two opposing agents join to take over the mediational function. This means that they meet together privately, explore possible ways of bringing to some workable accommodation the diverse interests of their principals, interrupt their discussions to secure advice from their colleagues, return to their joint sessions, and finally agree on the outlines of a settlement which they will propose for acceptance by their respective principals.

Obviously, this procedure requires a degree of trust and mutual respect between the two negotiating agents. A good agent does not antagonize his opposite number, but is at pains to keep on good terms with him. When a lawyer representing industry has occasion over time to deal repeatedly and in different contexts with the same labor representative, a certain camaraderie will normally and quite usefully develop between them. This intimacy may, however, easily drift into a tacit reciprocity in the granting of favors that may in time become detached from the interests of the particular clients being represented. Thus, if a lawyer representing industry was forced by the intransigence of his client to deal rather harshly with his opposite number in Centerville, the question may arise, should he make up for this when the two representatives next meet in Zenith, where the employer is quite generous toward labor and ready to grant any reasonable concession recommended by his lawyer? . . . The mediator can, by his explicit assumption of the mediational role, help those purporting to act as representatives remain what they offer themselves as being.

It should be noted that the problem here suggested is not a new one; it is by no means a sordid by-product of our complex modern industrial age. [Over two centuries ago], Edmund Burke wrote the following lines: "The world is governed by go-betweens. These go-betweens influence the persons with whom they carry on the intercourse, by stating their own sense to each of them as the sense of the other; and thus they reciprocally master both sides." Burke's remarks contain important implications for the ethos of the mediator's office as well as for that of the agent; indeed, Burke seems to have in mind primarily the man who openly assumes the role of "go-between."

Is it, in fact, a common practice of mediators, in communicating the positions of the parties back and forth, to state "their own sense to each of them as the sense of the other." Certainly, when he receives from one party a statement of his position, the mediator, before conveying it to the other party, will normally strip it of vituperation and recrimination; his duty is to convey the substance of what was said, not its tone or the facial expression that accompanied it. But it is not always easy to effect this separation, especially since the depth with which a party feels about an issue is something that enters into the valuations that shape the final adjustment of diverse interests. . . . Like everyone else concerned with the mediational process, the mediator needs to reflect on his proper role and on the sources of his power.

The sixth and final aspect of the collective bargaining situation requires only brief mention. This aspect lies in the fact that the employer occupies toward the union a dual role, being on the one hand, director of an economic enterprise employing the union membership and, on the other, confronting the union as a coequal in negotiating and administering the collective bargaining agreement. . . .

Elaborate as the analysis just concluded has been, it has dealt only inferentially and indirectly with what may be said to be the central quality of mediation, namely, its capacity to reorient the parties toward each other, not by imposing rules on them, but by helping them to achieve a new and shared perception of their relationship, a perception that will redirect their attitudes and dispositions toward one another. This quality of mediation becomes most visible when the proper function of the mediator turns out to be, not that of inducing the parties to accept formal rules for the governance of their future relations, but that of helping them to free themselves from the encumbrance of rules and of accepting, instead, a relationship of mutual respect, trust and understanding that will enable them to meet shared contingencies without the aid of formal prescriptions laid down in advance. . . .

Because it does not bring this aspect of mediation into relief, the illustrative model to which I have just devoted so many pages may seem inaptly chosen. The negotiation of an elaborate written contract, such as that embodied in a collective bargaining agreement between an employer and a labor union, does indeed present a special set of problems for the mediator. But in defense of the choice of this model, it may be observed that complexity and formality of the processes involved may enable us to discern distinctive aspects of the mediator's task which, though present in more informal contexts, would have been blurred and resistant to separate analysis.

Furthermore, it should be remembered that the primary function of the mediator in the collective bargaining situation is not to propose rules to the parties and to secure their acceptance of them, but to induce the mutual trust and understanding that will enable the parties to work out their own rules. The creation of rules is a process that cannot itself be rule-bound; it must be guided by a sense of shared responsibility and a realization that the adversary aspects of the operation are part of a larger collaborative undertaking. The primary task of the [mediator] is to induce this attitude of mind and spirit, though to be sure, he does this primarily by helping the parties to perceive the concrete ways in which this shared attitude can redound to their mutual benefit. . . .

One might have been inclined to assume that as, in the course of history, the various forms of social ordering and dispute-settlement became separated in practice, they would become the subject of an earnest discussion among scholars as to their distinctive functions and their most appropriate applications. Instead. . . . the tendency is to convert every form of social ordering into an exercise in the authority of the state. . . . Legislation, adjudication, and administrative direction, instead of being perceived as distinctive interactional processes, all are seen as unidirectional exercises of state power. Contract is perceived, not as a source of "law" or social ordering in itself, but as something that derives its whole significance from the fact that the courts of the state stand ready to enforce it. Custom is passed over in virtually complete silence by sociologists and is viewed by legal scholars as becoming worthy of attention only when it has been recognized by the courts and thus been converted into "law." Only mediation seems to resist this tendency to subsume every kind of ordering under the rubric of "power" or "authority." Perhaps the attempt made in this essay . . . to analyze the form and functions of mediation may help in some small measure to stimulate a more general interest in the analysis and comparison of the competing forms of social ordering.

3. CHRISTOPHER W. MOORE, MEDIATION 1-7, 10-16 (U.S. Army Corps of Engineers 1991)

Mediation is a dispute resolution process in which a neutral and impartial third party assists the people in conflict to negotiate an acceptable settlement of contested issues. Mediation is frequently used to avoid or overcome an impasse when parties have been unable to negotiate an agreement on their own. Most disputes are resolved by informal conversations, some form of cooperative problem solving, or negotiation. Involved parties reach an acceptable settlement of their differences through direct unassisted interaction. But not all conflicts can be resolved in this manner.

Some conflicts, which involve strong emotions, significant differences in the ways that data is interpreted, perceived or actual conflicts of interest, or extreme bargaining positions, result in impasse. The parties are deadlocked and are either unable to start negotiations, or where negotiations have been initiated, they are stalled, and no progress is possible. In conflicts characterized by the above conditions, the parties may need the assistance of a third party to reach an acceptable negotiated settlement. Mediation is one of the major procedures which can be used to aid parties in the resolution of intractable disputes.

Mediation involves the intervention of a third person, or mediator, into a dispute or negotiation to assist the parties to voluntarily negotiate a jointly acceptable resolution of issues in conflict. The mediator is neutral in that he or she does not stand to personally benefit from the terms of the settlement, and impartial in that he or she does not have a preconceived bias about how the conflict should be resolved.

The mediator is asked by the disputing parties to assist them to voluntarily reach an agreement. The mediator has no decision-making authority and cannot impose a decision. The parties maintain all control over the substantive outcome of the dispute. However, the mediator does have influence in that he or she may provide procedural assistance or possible settlement options to the parties that can assist them in reaching agreement. Mediation assistance involves working with the parties to improve their bargaining relationship and communications, clarifying or interpreting data, identifying key issues to be discussed, uncovering hidden interests, designing an effective negotiation process, generating possible settlement options, and helping to identify and formulate areas of agreement.

Here Is What a Mediated Assistance In a Negotiation
Or Dispute Looks Like

- Two or more individuals or organizations are involved in a dispute. Negotiations may not have been initiated, or may have started and the parties reached an impasse. Each party believes that the other is badly motivated, is hiding information, isn't communicating, and is making unreasonable demands. There are no good settlement options "on the table." The parties see their positions on the issues as being far apart and perceive little chance of reaching an agreement.

- One or more parties assesses its procedural and substantive alternatives to reaching a negotiated agreement, ignoring the conflict and maintaining the status quo, pursuing a third party settlement or escalating the conflict and decides that a negotiated settlement may be more acceptable than its best alternative procedure or outcome, such as avoidance and stalemate, or a legal suit and judicial decision. The party decides to explore whether mediation assistance might promote successful negotiations.

- One or more parties proposes mediation to the other party, both agree to proceed, and a mediator or mediation organization is contacted to set up a mediation session. If an organization is contacted, the parties may have a choice in the selection of the mediator who will work with them.

- At the beginning of mediation, the mediator will usually meet with each of the disputing parties, either jointly or separately, to explain the mediation process. He or she will clarify the voluntary nature of mediation and describe how the mediator will assist the parties to negotiate more effectively. The mediator may also establish some procedural and behavioral guidelines which will foster more productive negotiations. These include guidelines on who talks, limits of confidentiality, how relevant data will be exchanged, and a description of the mediation process itself.

- At the first joint meeting, the parties will each be asked to outline in an opening statement, the key issues which they wish to discuss and to identify some of the interests which they must have addressed or met to reach an acceptable agreement. This educational process assures that all of the parties and the mediator understand the issues and some of the underlying interests.

- The mediator may propose or will work with the parties to develop an acceptable negotiation agenda, the sequence of issues, and procedures to be used to address each item.

- The mediator may assist the parties to handle strong emotions, misperceptions, stereotypes, or miscommunication by listening and legitimizing (but not necessarily agreeing with) feelings, clarifying communications, summarizing statements, and proposing more effective communication structures.

- The mediator will ask the parties to jointly discuss each of the issues, and to identify the various interests or needs to be satisfied. Mediators will usually reframe or define issues to be addressed in terms of meeting the parties' joint interests.

- Many disputes are caused by the inability of a team or organization to reach internal agreements on a negotiation strategy or acceptable settlement options. Mediators often assist a team or spokesperson to build an internal consensus or approach to negotiations.

- The mediator will assist the parties to back off of extreme or hard line positions, preferred solutions which are advocated by each of the parties; and to generate alternative settlement options. Option generation may occur either in joint meetings or in separate caucuses where the mediator meets in private with each of the parties. Impasse commonly occurs because parties dislike and dismiss options on the negotiation table, but fail to assess the benefits and costs of alternative resolution procedure and potential outcomes that may result from their use. Mediators often help parties to evaluate the merits of settlement by means of negotiations in contrast to non-negotiated alternatives. The mediator helps prepare the parties to make "yesable" proposals that will be more acceptable or readily agreed to by the other party or parties. They do this by assisting parties to make offers which meet both their own and others' interests, and by improving the form or manner in which offers are communicated.

- As parties make offers, the mediator may translate or interpret them to the other side. He or she may do this by "shuttle mediation," where the mediator travels between private meetings with the parties; or directly in a joint session.

- The mediator assists parties to identify and define areas of agreement by "testing" for consensus. The mediator listens for and restates common or overlapping views. Since parties in dispute often talk past each other, the mediators' assistance is often invaluable in identifying areas of agreement.

- As the parties reach agreements, the mediator may act as a scribe who captures the settlement in a Memorandum of Understanding (MOU). This MOU, where appropriate, may later be drafted in the form of a contract or other legal document.

Why Use Mediation? What are the advantages of using mediation over other means of resolving disputes, such as litigation or formal administrative procedures? There are a number of advantages:

- Protection of the Relationship. In a significant number of conflicts, the parties have or will have an ongoing relationship. Adversarial or win/lose forms of dispute resolution often result in damaged relationships which may preclude the parties working together in the future. Mediation generally results in a settlement that both parties can accept and support, promotes better communications between them, and encourages a respectful and cooperative relationship.

- Time Savings. Mediation assistance is generally available on short notice. The speed and schedule of settlement is entirely dependent on the parties' willingness to address and reach agreement on the issues.

- Cost Savings. Mediation involves direct negotiations between the parties. While legal advisors may be present and offer assistance,

key managers are the decision makers and are usually the main
actors. This means that legal costs are generally lower in the mediation process. Also, since the parties share the cost of hiring the
mediator, the expense is kept down.

- Greater Flexibility in Possible Settlements. Traditional litigation or
  administrative procedures are generally constrained as to the range
  of possible settlement options by the law or contract limitations. This
  means that the types of issues which can be raised or addressed by
  the parties is often rather narrow. Structural constraints often force
  parties to address "relationship" or "personality" issues, or issues
  not covered under the contract, indirectly using an unsuitable forum
  or procedure. Mediation, because of its more flexible format and lack
  of structural constraints, allows the parties to address relationship,
  procedural and substantive issues. It allows people to get to the "root
  of the problem" without having to "force-fit" a problem into an inappropriate process. Mediation also allows parties to develop customized
  creative solutions which are tailored to meet specific concerns or
  interests.

- Keeps the Decision-Making Authority in the Hands of the Parties.
  Procedures such as litigation, administrative hearings and binding
  arbitration, rely on third party decision makers to break deadlocks
  and render a decision. These procedures remove decision-making
  authority and responsibility from the parties who often are the most
  informed about the issues and options. Mediation keeps the decision-making authority with the people who best know the problems,
  and it preserves both individual and organizational authority.

Initiating and Participating in Mediation. How do you initiate and plan for
participation in mediation? This section provides guidance on the specifics of
preparing for mediation. The basic steps of initiating and planning for participation in mediation are as follows: 1) Determine whether or not a mediation procedure may assist the parties to resolve a particular dispute. 2) Obtain any
needed management commitments to participate in the process. 3) Approach
other parties and gain their agreement to participate, or approach a mediator
or mediation organization and request that the intermediary discuss with the
other party or parties the option of mediation. 4) Identify the key individuals or
groups that should participate in the mediation process for a settlement to be
reached. 5) Select an acceptable mediator. The parties should identify the
expertise that they want the third party to provide, and then jointly select an
acceptable third party or ask a reputable mediation or referral agency to appoint
one. 6) Prepare for the mediation by clearly identifying facts to be presented,
issues to be discussed, interests that must be met, and potential settlement
options. Parties should also assess their best alternative to a negotiated agreement. 7) Discuss with the mediator and all parties the format, ground rules and
process that will be used in the mediation session or sessions. Agreements
should be reached on the above points before proceeding. 8) Conduct the mediation session or sessions. 9) Document any agreement reached.

When is Mediation Appropriate? The key criteria for the appropriateness of mediation is the parties' willingness to participate in the process. Generally, prior to the initiation of mediation, one or more parties will evaluate internally, or possibly with the other party or parties, to determine if the mediation process is the appropriate means for resolving a conflict. Mediation may be appropriate when:

- Parties have tried to initiate negotiations but have been unable to reach agreement on how to begin discussions. In this instance, the mediator may play a "convening" role and will help the parties design an acceptable negotiation process. In large public disputes, the mediator may also play a role in identifying the potential parties that should be involved in the mediation process.

- Parties are having difficulties negotiating because of lack of process, poor process, the wrong process, or the right process being used in an inefficient manner. The mediator can help by clarifying productive steps for problem solving or by providing a new process for negotiations.

- Parties have engaged in negotiations and have reached an impasse. Mediators are often able to assist parties to break a deadlock by providing procedural assistance, helping to overcome psychological barriers to settlement, suggesting new and creative option generation procedures, or identifying potential trade-offs or packages.

- When there are strong psychological or relationship barriers to negotiating a resolution. Mediators can play an intermediary and conciliatory role between the parties. Mediators are trained to handle emotional barriers to settlement, problems of misperception, or poor communications.

- When parties will not, or are reluctant to, meet face-to-face. Mediators can engage in "shuttle diplomacy" carrying messages between the parties and helping them to build an agreement.

- When a matter of legal principle is not involved, and the parties do not want to create a legal precedent.

- When each of the parties believes that it has some flexibility in its position, and a negotiated settlement with the assistance of a mediator is either more efficient, timely, cost effective, or psychologically satisfying than a third party decision by a judge or administrative tribunal.

- When the preservation of a working relationship is important. Many conflicts develop in the context of an ongoing relationship. A negotiated agreement to a dispute is often preferable to a command decision, because the parties maintain control of the outcome and "own" the decision. The mediation process often repairs or builds new working relationships that are critical to the success of ongoing work. Are there circumstances where mediation is not appropriate? Generally, cases where one or more parties is acting in bad faith, information necessary for a fair and informed settlement is being withheld or distorted, one or more parties want to lay blame on another or want their "day in court," or where a legal precedent is desirable are not appropriate for mediation.

Who Proposes Mediation? Any party involved in a dispute may propose mediation as a means to reach a settlement. One party may contact another and propose the process, or a party may contact a mediator or mediation firm and request that the intermediary act in their behalf and contact the other parties. Several approaches can be used to avoid [being perceived as having a weak position]. First, the initiating party can inform the other side, either directly or through an intermediary, that they would like to attempt one last good-faith effort at negotiating a settlement prior to moving to a more adversarial process. . . . This approach clarifies willingness to use adversarial means and be tough, while keeping the door open to a negotiated settlement.

A second approach is for an individual or agency that normally processes a number of disputes to announce before a particular dispute arises, that they will use mediation as a routine step, after unassisted negotiations, in an institutionalized dispute resolution process. By indicating that these two steps will routinely be used prior to moving to more adversarial means, a party can avoid any appearance of weakness on any single case.

Who Participates in Mediation? Generally, the participants in mediation are people who are well informed about contested issues and have the authority to make a decision. In most cases, these will be key individuals or decision makers in an organization. Frequently, decision makers may be advised by legal counsel or other technical experts, and on occasion, a "side" may be represented by a lawyer or negotiating team. Mediation is a forum where key decision makers can talk directly with each other, without the encumbrance of having to talk through representatives. Face-to-face talks by decision makers often result in productive exchanges and settlements.

How Should a Mediator be Selected? There are four major considerations in selecting a mediator: 1) the kinds of process assistance that are needed, 2) the degree of substantive assistance which is desirable, 3) the mediator's prior experience in cases of similar complexity or content, and 4) the relationship or personal chemistry between the mediator and the parties.

Mediators vary in how directive they are in providing procedural assistance to parties. Some mediators are "orchestrators" in that they make general process suggestions, "chair" meetings and basically back-up competent and skilled negotiators who need a structured forum to negotiate a settlement. Other mediators are "deal makers." They are much more directive regarding the negotiating approaches or procedures parties should use, may control the agendas of the meetings, may do extensive work in caucuses or private meetings between the mediator and each of the parties, and may provide substantive advice. Parties selecting a mediator should clarify in their own minds and with the third party which kind of procedural assistance is desired.

A mediator's substantive expertise or knowledge may be another consideration in selecting a mediator. Some parties want a mediator with some substantive knowledge of issues in dispute so that he or she can advise them on possible settlement options or packages. A mediator with some knowledge of the issues may also be more able to conduct "reality testing" of proposals that are unreasonable or untenable. On the other hand, if a mediator has significant substantive knowledge of contested issues, he or she may also have a strong opinion about how the issue should be settled. This knowledge may encourage the third party to lead the parties to his or her preferred settlement rather than facilitate the parties' development of their own solutions. Substantive knowledge and strong opinions on the part of the mediator may also compromise the parties' perception of the mediator's neutrality and thus make the intervenor ineffective in providing future assistance.

Another school of thought is that the mediator does not have to possess specific substantive knowledge of the issues in dispute to be of assistance to the parties. Parties and intervenors who advocate this approach to mediation argue that the parties themselves have the requisite knowledge to settle the dispute and what is needed from the third party is procedural leadership or relationship building assistance, not specific substantive expertise. The premise to this approach is that the intervenor will learn from the parties any substantive expertise that maybe required to settle a case.

Experience is another criteria in the selection of a mediator. It is advisable that the mediator has experience in handling issues of similar complexity as the ones to be negotiated. Parties considering a mediator should investigate the intervenor's track record, range of experiences and references before contracting for services. Relationship, rapport and "personal chemistry" are rather intangible criteria for the selection of a mediator, but they are often key factors in how effective the intervenor will be. Parties have to trust the intervenor, be able to talk freely with him or her, and believe that the third party is working in good faith to help them develop the best settlement possible, if the third party is to be most effective.

How Can a Party Prepare for Mediation? Mediation is assisted negotiations. The best way to prepare for mediation is to prepare well for negotiations. The first step in preparing for mediation is for each party to clearly identify what interests must be addressed or met for a satisfactory agreement to be reached. This means clearly identifying the substantive, procedural and relationship interests for each of the involved parties. Substantive interests are objective needs such as money, performance or time which a party wants to have satisfied. Procedural interests are needs about the way that a dispute is resolved. They may include such needs as efficiency, timeliness, an opportunity to present one's case, or preference for cooperative rather than adversarial proceedings.

Relationship or psychological interests are needs related to trust and respect, and expectations for how one is treated in the dispute resolution process itself, or in a future relationship. Once a party has identified its own interests, it is advisable for him or her to try and identify the needs of the other party or parties who are involved. If others have been explicit about their interests, this will be an easy task. If not, it may require some speculation. Often, a party's interests can be decoded from a position statement, or a preferred solution that a party has advocated to meet its needs. By examining a position, it is often possible to identify the underlying interests or needs that the party wants to have satisfied. In some cases, it may not be possible to discern what another party's interests are. In this case, the mediation meeting may have to be used to discover them.

Once the interests for each of the parties have been identified, it is always advisable to generate some potential settlement options. In some negotiations, options may have been publicly announced or put on the table in the form of positions. In other cases, where the parties have not begun negotiating, each will have to generate a range of options which would be acceptable to them. This range of options will be used by the mediator and negotiators to craft an agreement which is mutually acceptable to all parties.

Before entering into mediation, it is always wise for the parties to assess what their best alternative to a negotiated agreement, or "BATNA" is. The best alternative refers to both possible settlement options and alternative procedures. Explicitly understanding what non-negotiated alternatives are available provides a party with a basis to compare settlement options developed at the table. This comparison will assist a party in deciding when to settle and when to stop negotiating and pursue another means of dispute resolution.

Finally, before beginning mediation, each party should think about what his/her relationship expectations are both during and after the negotiations. Some of the questions which should be considered include: Do the parties want an adversarial relationship, or would they prefer a more cooperative one? Will the parties have to work together? Will there be future contacts? What impacts will a win/lose settlement have on the relationship? If it is important that the parties settle and maintain some kind of amicable relationship, each party should consider what measures need to be taken to "clear the air" and minimize any unnecessary damage to the relationship in the process of resolving the dispute. The negotiators should decide individually or as a team what they can do to create as positive a negotiation climate as possible. This does not mean sidestepping strong emotions, but it does mean thinking about how feelings of anger or frustration can be expressed without further damaging the relationship.

Each party should meet with the mediator, either in pre-mediation information exchange sessions, or at the beginning of the first joint session, to clarify the role of the mediator and to gain a thorough understanding of the mediation process which will be used. In the mediation session, there are a variety of actions that parties can take which will enhance the possibility of a successful outcome and which will help the mediator work more effectively. Generally, mediators make a series of process suggestions, such as behavioral ground rules or ways to approach a particular issue. It is helpful if the parties work with the mediator and do not fight the process. Also, mediators may want to meet with each of the parties separately to help develop settlement options, evaluate a proposal or do some reality or feasibility testing with a party. It is helpful if the parties work with the mediator in these sessions to develop realistic options or appraise potential settlements. . . .

What Happens in a Mediation Session? Mediation sessions usually begin with introductions if the participating parties have never met face-to-face. The mediator will usually outline the issues that have brought the parties to the session and will gain agreement on the purpose of the meeting. Many mediators may also suggest some procedural ground rules such as a non-interruption agreement, clarification of the limits of confidentiality, an agreement on time limits, and a commitment from the parties to bargain in good faith. Often, a mediator will outline the process for the negotiations, including a description of how issues and interests will be identified, the use of caucuses or private meetings, a description of how possible settlement options will be developed, and what happens when an agreement is reached (or not reached).

At this point, the mediator will usually ask the initiating party to begin with an opening statement that details the issues to be discussed, the interests to be met and possibly a preferred settlement option. The mediator may ask questions during the opening statement to clarify an issue or interest. At the conclusion of the first party's opening statement, the mediator will usually summarize what he or she has heard. It is then the other party's turn to make an opening statement.

With the completion of the opening statements, the mediator will assist the parties to order the issues into a workable agenda. Often, the mediator will look for an easy item to start with, one he believes the parties will be able to settle in a fairly brief period of time. An early settlement of at least one issue creates momentum in the negotiations and demonstrates to the parties that agreements can be reached. The mediator may assist the parties to work through the issues one at a time or may help them to link and trade issues in a package arrangement. Settlement options may be generated by the parties through structured discussion in joint session, or may be developed through conversations with the mediator in caucuses.

How are the Results of the Meeting Documented? Meeting documentation can be accomplished in several ways. The mediator may . . . draft a memorandum of understanding (MOU), that summarizes the results of the meeting. It may detail the agreements and any areas of disagreement which may remain. If appropriate, this document may be referred to each of the parties' legal advisors to be turned into a formal contract or legally binding agreement. An alternative to the above procedure is for the parties to take their own notes and to agree at the conclusion of the meeting as to who will draft the final settlement document. In either of these cases, the parties may need or desire a final meeting to sign a formal document. If parties do not believe that there will need to be any final modifications, the final agreement may be circulated by mail for final signatures.

C. THE MEDIATION PROCESS: PRACTICE

1. Comments and Questions

a. In this section, we focus on the "nuts and bolts" of the mediation process, as successfully conducted on a daily basis by thousands of mediators throughout the United States. The division between theory and practice is clearly artificial, but it is convenient for pedagogical purposes.

b. Eric Galton walks us through the mediation process, step-by-step. As with many a complex process, mediation is considerably more comprehensible when one sees it broken down into its component parts. Galton also provides a wealth of useful observations about mediation and practical tips for being an effective mediator.

c. Mediation works. A mantra for many mediators is: "Trust the Process." This perspective has important practical consequences. When success is expected, heroic measures are not called for, and usually should be avoided. In most instances, mediators are well advised to follow the physicians' core principle: *primum non nocere* — first, do no harm. Tom Arnold discusses mistakes in mediation, and how to avoid them.

d. Apparently useful mediator moves can turn out to be harmful. For example, tension among the parties is a fact of life in mediation, and dissipation of tension is an important goal for a mediator. How can a mediator reduce tension over the course of a mediation? Humor seems an obvious approach, but a seemingly innocuous joke may be offensive to someone else and torpedo a mediation that seemed destined for success. Do not snatch defeat from the jaws of victory. As Eric Galton suggests, be careful with humor. Self-deprecating humor may be the best approach.

2. ERIC GALTON, REPRESENTING CLIENTS IN MEDIATION 25-53, 104-112 (1995)

[Galton addresses his remarks to counsel for the parties in a mediation, but the discussion and advice are useful for anyone interested in mediation.] Mediation . . . is a process. While a skilled and fully trained mediator is essential, the process itself is what makes things work. The following illustration is a linear model of the mediation process. My purpose is not to create or imply a rigid model or form, but rather to provide you with a series of reference points so that you, the advocate for a party in mediation, may understand every facet of this process.

1. Mediator Introduction. Typically, all parties and their counsel will initially assemble in the same room, and the proceedings will commence with the mediator making an introduction. Specifically, the mediator in her introduction is attempting to accomplish the following:

(a) Provide some information on her background, expertise, and credentials. The purpose of this part of the mediator's introduction is to humanize the mediator and to help her establish control of the process.

(b) Explain the role of the mediator. The mediator will emphasize her neutrality, will explain that she is not the judge or jury, will assure the parties that she will not offer absolute opinions, and will describe her role as a facilitator.

(c) Explain fully the confidentiality aspects of the mediation process.

(d) Generally outline the sequence of events that will occur during the day. The mediator will explain the various phases of the mediation process, just as a trial lawyer will tell a jury during [an opening statement] how the trial will unfold. The mediator will also explain the special aspects of the separate caucus during this part of the introduction.

(e) Obtain several commitments from the parties. The mediator will ask the parties if they are willing to allocate whatever time is necessary to permit the process to work, whether they possess the requisite authority to resolve the dispute, and whether they are willing to make a good faith effort to resolve the dispute.

More globally, the mediator's introduction is designed to make the parties and their counsel as familiar and comfortable with the mediation process as is possible. Many lawyers, and most clients, have not been through a mediation. As a result, the mediator must assist the participants in fully understanding what is about to take place and to appreciate that the mediation process is a protected, confidential, and safe environment. The mediator will not be able to have the parties open up and participate if the parties have any doubts or fears about the process itself, confidentiality, or the mediator's neutrality. If the mediator is following good form, her introduction usually takes no more than 15 minutes.

2. Pre-mediation issues. Good mediation practice requires that the mediator and all counsel attempt to resolve several important issues prior to the mediation itself. These issues may be handled by a pre-mediation conference call or an exchange of correspondence. The issues that should be resolved prior to the mediation are [authority to settle and scheduling].

The authority to settle issue must be resolved before the mediation. The issue of who has the authority to settle a case for the party is a thorny one, . . . but to summarize the issue for purposes of this chapter: All parties should confer, agree on who will attend the session, and be comfortable that the persons who will attend the session have authority to resolve the dispute. If the proper parties or representatives are not present, the mediation process likely will not work. The mediation may have to be postponed or rescheduled. Parties or representatives may have had to travel great distances to attend a session. A mediation that breaks down because the necessary parties or representatives are not present may further heighten tensions and animosity. Therefore, the authority issue and who should attend the mediation should be fully discussed before the session itself.

All mediation participants should make realistic travel plans before the session. A mediator never knows how long the mediation process itself will take. Some disputes may be resolved in four hours or less. Most disputes seem to require five to eight hours for the process to run its course. Some complex disputes may even require several days of mediation. . . .

3. Opening Statements by Counsel. The opening statement by counsel is one of the most important facets of the mediation process; yet, in my experience, talented and highly skilled counsel routinely ignore the great opportunity associated with their opening remarks. To be sure, counsel's opening remarks are in part designed either to educate the mediator about the dispute or to educate the mediator further in the event a confidential pre-mediation submission has already been provided. But the second and most important aspect of the opening statement is that it permits each party a direct opportunity to set out for the other party (not the other party's lawyer) how counsel sees the case and the basis for such view. Rarely in the litigation process does counsel ever have an opportunity for such direct contact. . . . In mediation, you are not selling the other side on the correctness of your position. The other side, regardless of your legal abilities or oral skills, will always rule against you. Instead, you are communicating your integrity as a human being, your preparedness, your willingness to listen and understand, your good faith participation in the mediation process, and your interest in a sensible resolution.

4. Initial Collective Session. I rarely hold a collective session immediately after the lawyers' opening statements. For some mediators, the concept of having the parties "vent" and express their thoughts and feelings is a critical element of the mediation process. The thinking, of course, is that with such feelings vented and therefore "out of the way," the parties will be predisposed towards more rational thought regarding resolution of the dispute. I am too nervous to permit such an exchange. I would much prefer to allow such venting to occur in separate caucus outside the presence of the other side. . . . If the feelings need to be expressed to the other side, the mediator is able to deliver the message in a "kinder and gentler" way. Also, putting on my negotiator's hat, I do not believe that invectives put people in the mood to negotiate constructively.

As an experienced trial lawyer, I do not see mediation as ESP, voodoo, or a group therapy session. Anything told to me as a mediator in the privacy of the separate caucus is fine, because only I hear it, and it won't hurt my feelings. Further, despite the confidentiality of mediation, lawyers may be leery that their clients' candid statements in mediation may be used against them if the case does not resolve. For these reasons, I omit the collective session and move into the separate caucus except in the following situations:

   a. When little or no discovery has been done. Mediation should never be transformed into a deposition or an adversarial hearing. However, the collective session may be useful in exchanging otherwise discoverable evidence for purposes of evaluation.

   b. When the parties have a long-standing business relationship or friendship. . . . The parties in such situations have a great need to communicate directly with each other before going into the separate caucus. Sometimes the parties may not be prepared to negotiate until such direct words are exchanged.

   c. It may be appropriate to discuss the procedural posture of the case, what discovery is remaining to get the case ready for trial, the length of the trial, the likelihood of appeal, and the remaining costs. The parties may benefit from a candid discussion of both the time and costs associated with the continuation of the dispute.

   d. When an acknowledgment of the negotiation posture may be appropriate. In some instances, the issue of who made the last offer, the amount of the offer and the like needs to be clarified. A party virtually never will bid against herself. The parties should agree whose court the ball is in.

e. When the party has a real interest in "public shaming" as a precondition to resolution. Of course, mediation is a private, confidential proceeding. But a party with such an interest may view the mediator as a member of the public. The party may have an absolute need. . . . Such situations are explosive. And, fortunately, most claimants may fulfill this need by expressing such feelings to the mediator in separate caucus. But in a small group of cases . . . the party will not be able to begin to resolve the dispute until this public shaming interest is met. The mediator, recognizing such a situation, may engage in some damage control. The mediator . . . should advise all parties that candid expressions, no matter how harsh, are appropriate and better stated under the aura of the confidentiality of a mediation. The mediator may also encourage the parties that such candid expressions should, if at all possible, be stated constructively. The mediator, in essence, is attempting to lessen the degree of rancor expressed or to prepare the other party for what is about to occur.

f. When a party needs to express grief. Some litigants feel that "no one cares" or that the other party does not fully understand the extent of their hurt or loss. A party who feels this way may not be able to consider resolution without having the opportunity to express such feelings directly to the other party.

4. The Separate Caucus. The separate caucus is the essence of mediation. The parties and their counsel are placed in separate quarters, and the mediator goes from room to room meeting privately with each side. Everything said in each separate caucus is confidential, save and except for what a party authorizes the mediator to communicate to a party in another room. The mediator must communicate only authorized information and must take whatever precaution necessary to avoid any unauthorized disclosures. The mediator will separately caucus with each party several times. In complex cases, I may have nine or ten separate caucuses with each party. While every mediation is different, and the mediator may vary protocol in a particular case, the separate caucus usually has three general phases: the initial strength/weakness, objective evaluation caucus; the preliminary negotiation caucus; and the closing/resolution caucus.

The initial separate caucus with each party is typically the most lengthy phase of the mediation process. The mediator usually will visit with each party for at least 30 minutes, and perhaps up to an hour. Because of the mediator's goals in the initial caucus, the mediator may, especially in a difficult case, have to hold two (and sometimes more) strength/weakness caucuses with each party. The mediator has several goals in the initial caucus, and it is indeed a highly critical phase of the process.

a. Bonding with the Parties. A mediator will initially make an effort to obtain the trust and confidence of the party. The party already may have confidence in the mediator, but the party may need to get to know the mediator better (and vice versa) before she is willing to "open up." The party needs to be reminded of the confidentiality of the caucus and the mediator's impartiality. The mediator is also looking for insights into the personality of the party and to identify some of her interests unrelated to the dispute; i.e., children, golf, basketball, travel, music, etc. The purpose of this, of course, is for the mediator to "bond" a bit more with the party. Bonding results in a party feeling more relaxed with the process and more comfortable with the mediator. The mediator bonds with the party not through any tactical plan, but by demonstrating that she has listened, is willing to listen, and is willing to understand (not agree). The mediator bonds with the party by demonstrating preparedness, professionalism, neutrality, and compassion.

b. Venting. Many parties really do need to vent their feelings to the mediator. And most people want to do so right away. Parties feel — correctly — that the dispute belongs to them, and they are often tired of all the "lawyer talk." Good mediators understand that a party wants such an immediate opportunity to speak. A good mediator may walk into the caucus, look at the party, and simply ask, "Mr. Williams, how do you feel about this dispute?" Typically, the question triggers a flood of information, often emotionally charged, and the party begins to feel more a part of the process itself. The party comes to understand quickly that the mediator is listening and not sitting in judgment.

In the separate caucus, venting occurs with no destructive consequences. But venting, beyond the relief it affords the party, also usually identifies many of the party's interests and needs. Often, a venting party repeats important words or thoughts, which is not accidental. Good mediators write down key words or phrases and recognize that while the dispute may be about money, such words are often the emotional matter that fuels the dispute.

Parties in mediation sometimes tell me that no one, including their own lawyers, ever asked them what the case was really about. . . . For the lawyer, regardless of how caring she may be, the client's problem becomes a "case" or a "file." For the client, the problem may be her entire life. Lawyers speak in terms of issues and positions. Beneath the line of issues and positions is the realm of interests. More often than not, the client's motivations are in the realm of interests, and often the keys to resolution are found in this territory as well.

c. Identification of the Decision-Maker. At this critical stage, the mediator is also attempting to identify who the decision-maker or decision-makers are in each room. . . . In most instances, the party and the party's lawyer will make the decision. . . . In some disputes, the party may be the only decision-maker, and in other disputes, the party's lawyer may be the only real decision-maker. In certain disputes, the party and the party's lawyer may have very different views of the dispute and its resolution. Identification of the decision-maker(s) is critical, because it is the decision-maker's negotiating style and interests that need to be identified and met if resolution is to occur. . . . If uncertain, the mediator should ask who is going to make the decision.

d. The Lawyer as Decision-Maker. . . . In the great majority of cases, the lawyer functioning as the decision-maker is no problem. The fact that a lawyer has control over her client is usually a great help in a mediation. But, what happens when a lawyer puts her interests ahead of the client's interest and obstructs the mediation process?. . . [In such instances] the mediator may wish to hold a private meeting with the client's counsel to discuss such issues openly and diplomatically.

e. When the Lawyer and Client are at Odds. A more common, and less troublesome, situation is when the mediator perceives that an attorney and client are at odds with each other. In fact, many lawyers suggest mediation because they have lost control over their clients. In such instances, the client is the decision-maker, but she may not be listening to her counsel and often has unrealistic expectations and goals. Typically, a lawyer will cue in the mediator at the first caucus that such a situation exists, or the dynamics in the room will make the problem strikingly obvious. The mediator's role in such situations is not to dispense legal advice or to play the "second lawyer." Rather, by posing specific and appropriate questions, the mediator should attempt to focus the party on the objective realities of the case so that the party will see both the weaknesses and strengths of her position.

f. Identification of Negotiating Style. Everyone has a different negotiating style. Some negotiators are very aggressive. Other negotiators are very conciliatory. Some negotiators wish to exploit; others fear being exploited. Many negotiators have done little formal study on the negotiation process. Often, a person's negotiation style is reflective of her personality. As such, a mediator rarely can change the negotiating style of a party to a mediation and probably should not even try. But, from the mediation perspective, the negotiating "pace" of the decision-makers [not their negotiating style] is the critical issue. . . . Some parties to a mediation want to get down to business quickly; others may want to settle in a bit before getting into serious negotiations. Certain parties need to be dragged into the negotiations. Fortunately, very, very few people are unwilling to negotiate at all.

Many times the parties' pace is the same — all parties want to get right down to serious discussions or all parties want a slow, deliberate negotiation. But the more challenging situation, which often occurs, is when each party has a different (sometimes radically different) negotiating pace — one party wants to "cut to the chase" and the other party wants to go slow and be deliberate. This stylistic pace clash may damage any chance of resolution, unless it is identified and addressed at the outset. In separate caucus, the mediator should openly discuss with each party these stylistic differences and encourage each party to respect the style of the other and not to become frustrated. If the mediator sews together such an agreement in the first caucus, the parties' stylistic differences will not, in themselves, create a fatal impasse. . . .

g. Strength-Weakness Analysis. Another essential aspect of the initial caucus is a strength/weakness analysis. In this regard, the mediator does not render ultimate opinions, i.e., who will win or lose the lawsuit, whether an absolute limitations defense bars recovery, or whether a witness' credibility is subject to an absolute challenge, etc. Remember, the mediator's job is not to determine the legal issues but to assist the parties in identifying potential weaknesses as well as obvious strengths. Most litigants have little difficulty identifying their strong points. The mediator simply plays the role of devil's advocate by asking "what if," "what about," "do you think," or "why do you believe" questions.

Generally, the mediator is asking open-ended questions designed to permit the party to identify weaknesses on her own. Weaknesses may involve specific issues in the case, such as whether a jury will accept or believe an expert witness' testimony, whether a defendant will be able to attribute negligence fully to a third party, whether a certain piece of evidence will be admissible, etc. Weaknesses may also involve a more global assessment of the case, such as whether the claim has more limited value in the county in which the case will be tried, whether proof problems may be ignored because of the nature of the injuries or sympathy, whether a party may not desire a public trial for personal reasons, etc.

Because of the mediator's neutrality, most parties are willing participants in the strengths and weakness analysis. Most lawyers are eager players in this phase as well, because they are interested in a neutral perspective of their case. Advocates, as we all know, may become too close to a case and lose their objectivity. And, . . . a lawyer may have some weaknesses in a case that he identified to the client, but may need the mediator's help in getting the client to understand them. Also, the opening statements and information exchange prior to the initial caucus may produce new information or evidence that may require a re-evaluation of the case. More often than not, however, the opening statements do not produce significant new evidence; rather, the opening statements produce a more clear, coherent and full understanding of the other party's position. Also, the opening remarks are usually the first time the client has heard a complete characterization of the other side's position. The strength-weakness analysis is, therefore, critical to the negotiations themselves.

Parties come to a mediation with an opening offer that is usually inflated or deflated for negotiating purposes, but that also reflects to some extent their sense of the value of the case. A party does not reassess or change value for no reason. Of course, reasons outside of the [dispute itself] may result in value changing, i.e., unwillingness to accept any risk, a desire to avoid delay, avoidance of litigation expenses, a desire for confidentiality, etc. But beyond such factors that a mediator may identify in her introductory remarks, re-evaluating the case with the mediator's help is how the essential change occurs. Parties often do not fully appreciate risk, the other side's position, or the defects in their case without the direct interaction the process affords. The neutral's strength-weakness questions are accepted and welcomed, because she is a neutral and is not contaminated; that is, the neutral is not the other side.

I would make one final, strong statement regarding the strength-weakness phase of the first caucus. The mediator should never, never, never attempt to impose her view of a facet of the case or the whole case on a party. In fact, a mediator should rarely even suggest her view. A mediator who is skilled in good questioning techniques does not even need to suggest her view of an issue. In countless mediations, I have heard a party respond to my question by saying, "You know, I haven't really thought of this before."

h. Money, Expectations, Hopes, Dreams, and Motivations. As you probably realize by now, the initial caucus is a critical aspect of the mediation process. Consider mediation to be like building a house. The initial caucus is like building a good foundation. Ultimately, most resolutions involve the payment of money. In the initial caucus, the mediator will explore monetary issues and attempt to obtain each party's first monetary proposal. Good mediators will go through the strengths and weaknesses analysis before monetary discussions. And good mediators will attempt to identify the non-monetary interests that are motivating the party and that are affecting the party's monetary values.

We all have expectations in life — some of which are realistic and some of which, regrettably, are not. In the first caucus, a mediator may take the following approach regarding monetary expectations:

1. What are your monetary expectations?

2. Why do you have such monetary expectations?

3. Are these expectations realistic?

4. What are your monetary needs?

5. What do you realistically expect the other side to offer?

Monetary values are in part objective and in part subjective. Value may be claimed in non-monetary ways, but money is often more convenient and is something everyone understands. Ultimately, in any negotiation, the situation boils down to what someone is willing to pay and what someone is willing to accept. The mediator's goal is to have credible monetary negotiations occur as soon as is practical. The five questions listed above, obviously framed a bit differently by each mediator, will be asked in either the initial caucus or the second caucus.

5. Subsequent Caucuses. The strength/weakness analysis, which is part of the initial caucus, occurs continuously, albeit in a more focused form, throughout all caucuses. Typically, one or two issues, out of an initial potpourri of many issues, become the primary focus of subsequent evaluation. A facet of liability, including the issue of causation, may become the essence of subsequent evaluation. More often than not, though, damages become the major focus of the subsequent caucus. Damages, whether liability is virtually conceded or not, relate most particularly to the ongoing monetary proposals or counter-proposals. The mediator in second, third, and fourth caucus rounds is making a determined effort to get the monetary negotiations going, to move the parties off their opening, and to encourage one of the parties to make the first, credible significant move. Needless to say, depending upon the negotiating styles of the parties, this is not an easy process. . . .

The mediator must be especially careful in all caucuses to preserve confidentiality and make only authorized disclosures. . . . If a mediator walks into a second or third caucus with you and states "I know I shouldn't tell you this, but," you should consider terminating the session. If the mediator is divulging the other side's confidences, the mediator is probably divulging your confidences. Good mediators are obsessively meticulous about maintaining confidential information, but mediators are, like everyone else, human beings and on rare occasion capable of mistakenly divulging a piece of confidential information. Should a mediator make such a mistake, she should visit immediately with the party whose confidential information she has inadvertently disseminated and admit the mistake. Most of the time, a party will appreciate such candor, admire the mediator's integrity, and wish to continue with the process. On the other hand, if a party's belief in the process or the mediator is fatally contaminated by the admission, the mediator should consider closing the session. Perhaps another mediator will have a better chance to succeed.

The mediation advocate should feel free to make suggestions like the ones below to the mediator in subsequent caucus rounds. The mediator is the captain of the ship and will make the final call, but she should always be interested in hearing any idea that will increase the chances for a successful resolution. The advocate might suggest that the mediator might get together with the parties without the lawyers present. The advocate might suggest a lawyer caucus to review a point of law with opposing counsel or to discuss a particularly sensitive issue. The advocate might wish to have the mediator present a document or an appellate decision to opposing counsel. The advocate might suggest that a more direct, expedited negotiation would be more helpful.

6. Mediation Advocates' Opinions — What to Tell. Confident mediators, sure of their own skills, may even ask the mediation advocates what they think will work or admit to being a little lost and in need of direction. Such confessions are signs of strength, not weakness. The mediator may be sensing that an unidentified issue or interest is blocking progress, but the only way she will find out is by asking for help. Many mediators have strong intuitive skills. Some mediators have uncanny intuitive skills. But mediators are not psychics and cannot read minds. One of the greatest tools in the mediator's toolbox is the same as the litigator's most important tool — the ability to ask the right question.

7. Lawyer Caucuses. Lawyer caucuses sometimes are called because a resolution is stalled by a legal issue. Of course, the mediator is not the judge and will not rule on a point of law. But the mediator may believe that counsel are not fully understanding each other's legal positions and that additional discussion would be beneficial. Typically, "law talk" sails over clients' heads and sometimes mediation advocates feel they cannot fully discuss points of law in the initial group setting. A lawyer caucus provides a forum for a more expanded discussion of legal issues. Admittedly, a mediation that gets bogged down in extended legal debates may be doomed to failure, but in certain instances, focusing or clarifying the legal issues may be helpful. A lawyer caucus may be useful in breaking a negotiation impasse.

In other circumstances, a mediation advocate may wish to suggest a lawyer caucus in order to have a private meeting with the mediator. Typically, a mediation advocate may make such a request when she wishes to let the mediator know she is having a problem with her client. Mediators . . . must never come between an attorney and her client. But, an attorney may believe her client has an exaggerated or incorrect view of the case and would like the mediator's assistance in helping the client better understand things. Often, mediators are intuitively aware of such situations, but sometimes a mediator may be uncertain and will hold back so as not to interfere with the attorney-client relationship. A private meeting with the mediator permits the mediation advocate to explain fully those areas in which her client may need some additional reality checking. . . . One caveat: Lawyer caucuses should be used sparingly and selectively, and should be brief. The dispute, of course, belongs to the parties. Parties may become apprehensive and concerned if too many lawyer caucuses occur or if such caucuses take too long. The parties will wonder what is going on behind their backs and may begin to feel disenfranchised from the process.

8. Additional Collective Sessions. An inherent advantage of mediation is its flexibility. As the mediation evolves, a mediator must always be thinking of ways to maximize communication and, thereby, increase the chances of a successful resolution. The mediation process, in fact, improves communication and assists parties who had no desire or ability to understand each other's positions in engaging in a meaningful dialogue. Further, the mediation process unearths interests, feelings and motivations that may not have been known or expressed prior to the mediation.

As participants settle into and become comfortable with the mediation process, they may become more willing and able to have a helpful and constructive discussion later in the day. Additionally, a party may indicate to the mediator in caucus a real need to communicate something to the other side. The mediator may assist the party in considering the most constructive way of getting such a message across. Consider the following examples in which such subsequent collective meetings might be useful:

a. A mediator in private caucus learns that the plaintiff's primary motivation in filing a medical malpractice complaint was his feeling that the physician didn't care and never expressed regret. The mediator obtains authorization to tell that to the physician and her counsel. In caucus with the physician, the mediator learns that the physician, while denying liability, wanted to express regret, but did not do so out of fear that such expression would be misconstrued as an admission of liability. The mediator then may wish to reconvene the parties so that the physician, under the safety of mediation, may communicate regret and concern for the family.

b. In a partnership dispute, the mediator in caucus learns that a matter unrelated to the business issues was the real genesis of the current dispute. The mediator also learns that this matter has never been communicated to the other partner, and the other partner has no idea that his former associate was angry about the matter. The mediator may decide to bring the parties back together so that such issue may be directly communicated and discussed.

c. The mediator may feel that both sides are not negotiating in a manner likely to obtain resolution and, therefore, may elect to reassemble all the participants in order to suggest that, if negotiating progress is not made, an impasse will result and no resolution will be reached. In many instances, the participants will elect to continue the negotiations, as opposed to declaring an impasse.

9. Impasse — And What to do About It. You probably would guess that impasse is the bane of most mediators. Although mediators are trained how to avoid impasse, some live their lives dreading it. In my opinion, mediators should learn to live for impasse. After all, ostensible impasse will occur in every medi-ation, often several times, and if the parties could resolve their dispute by themselves, a mediator would not be needed. All declared impasses are not real impasses at all.

"Impasse" has a strong subjective component. Who thinks that an impasse exists? The parties? The lawyers? The mediator? And how and when does one conclude that a "deadlock" has occurred and that all "less than obvious escapes" have been explored? A declaration of impasse by a party may, in fact, be a thinly disguised negotiating strategy. . . . Mediators become used to parties declaring "I will never" or "I will not." Mediators — not disrespectfully — learn to ignore or discount such declarations. The mediator must keep pushing through such barriers — after all, if the mediator does not try to, who will? If they use good form, mediators will push on without being coercive by constantly re-visiting issues and maximizing communication. When everyone else feels they are wasting their time, mediators maintain optimism and encourage the parties to continue on. I cannot tell you how many times I have heard "we are wasting our time" in the seventh hour and had the case resolve in the ninth hour. . . .

Mediators must become skilled at impasse avoidance techniques and must emotionally and mentally look forward to impasse situations. A mediator's art is in part defined by the ability to work parties out of ostensible impasses. . . . Each mediation is different and unique. Each mediation has its own feel, its own players, and its own tempo. Some of the impasse breaking or avoidance tech-niques I have listed below may be perfect for a particular mediation, but wholly inappropriate in a different one. This is an attempt to provide you with an extensive laundry list of options for impasse situations or impasse avoidance.

1. People moving. Mediators are in the people-moving business. Sometimes you may have the wrong people together. Sometimes new and different combi-nations of people produce a better chemistry, which generates intriguing options. The mere physical act of motion suggests progress. New combinations create the perception that a new chapter is being started and renews hope. In his intro-duction, the mediator should preview and explain the possibility of people involved in the mediation being put together in different combinations. As a result, parties will be less intimidated when it happens and perceive such changes as part of the process.

2. Change the scenery. Mediators lose sight of the fact, particularly in the sep-arate caucus phase, that parties may feel stuck or claustrophobic in their room. Sometimes, especially in an impasse situation, I may take one room "for a walk." . . . People get to move their legs, look out the window, and feel more ener-gized. In several mediations, I have taken one room outside and caucused with them on a park bench. Be especially vigilant of this if your caucus rooms don't have windows. Imagine how you would feel after eight hours in such a room.

3. Food. If an impasse occurs at, for example, 4:00 p.m., I often send out for snacks. Food changes moods. Food energizes. Food keeps people going. Food is something new and different. Food implies we are going to continue to work. Many people can't think if they are hungry. Some people, in this non-smoking age, use food to relax. For whatever reason, people become more agreeable when they are eating. As an interesting side note, observe who is eating and who is not eating. You can get a good read on the participants' temperatures through such an observation.

4. Humor — please be careful. Something you think might be terribly funny may be terribly unfunny to the listener or perceived as demeaning. On the other hand, I have used humor to break tense moments, which has served on several occasions to break an impasse. The safest form of humor is self-deprecating humor. If you can demonstrate that you don't take yourself all that seriously and can laugh at yourself, perhaps the listeners may begin not to take themselves so seriously.

5. Lawyer caucus. When things get stuck, I sometimes find it useful to call a lawyer caucus. In my introduction, I advise the parties and their counsel that I may do so.

6. Recess. Most mediators, myself included, believe that progress made in a mediation is cumulative and that momentum towards resolution is created. However, in certain situations, the parties may be too tired to continue or need some time to reflect. A party may also feel pressured. Fatigue or feeling pressured should never become a basis of a fatal impasse. A mediator should consider calling a recess and setting up a time to continue the mediation.

7. Reconvene the group. The impasse may suggest the parties need more direct interaction. A feeling may need to be expressed. The parties may be more inclined to talk later in the day than they were at the beginning of the mediation. Additionally, the mediator is more aware of the interests and feelings at this point and may be in a better position to facilitate the discussion.

8. Confess being stuck. Mediators must be willing to check their egos at the door. At some later phase of the mediation, a mediator may need to advise the parties that he has "run out of ideas" and that, if the matter is to be resolved, the parties should consider providing him with some ideas. Also, in the wake of such a confession, the parties may come up with some excellent ideas.

9. Suggest the possibility of fatal impasse. The mediator's confidence and belief that resolution will happen is critical. If the mediator does not believe in resolution, no one else will. But late in a mediation, the mediator may suggest that unless some progress occurs, a fatal impasse may result. Most parties do not want a fatal impasse and will work to overcome the possibility.

10. Re-review litigation costs. Undoubtedly, the mediator has discussed costs in the group session and initial caucus. But in the heat of a mediation, parties may forget. Review the future costs again, but not in a coercive manner.

11. Re-review risks. Again, the mediator has already discussed risk in the initial caucus. But re-assessing risk late in a mediation may be very effective. As always, re-assessment of risk should not be coercive or heavy-handed.

12. The value of today. Most parties want to achieve closure. In most matters, the trial date (even when set) is uncertain, and the possibility of appeal may exist. The problem may not be resolved for . . . years. The parties have a window of opportunity to resolve their problems today. "Today" has a great deal of value.

13. Retrace the parties' progress. After five or six hours, the parties may have forgotten the progress that has been made. The mediator must remind the parties of where each was at the beginning of the mediation and where they are now.

14. Solicit disagreement by the party's counsel. In a separate caucus, ask the party's counsel whether he seriously disagrees with an identified weakness in the other party's position. The party may need to hear that his lawyer disagrees with him. The mediator, however, must never come between the party and his counsel or humiliate the party's counsel. To do so would be unethical, coercive, and just plain wrong.

15. Review the party's initial goals. During the first caucus, the parties should have identified their goals and interests. But during the mediation, a party may have changed his goals. The mediator should review with the party his initial goals and discuss whether these goals have changed and why.

16. Declare a goal unattainable. While it is not appropriate for the mediator to criticize a party's goals, it may become apparent during the mediation that the other side simply will not meet one of the party's goals — and the mediator may choose to make this declaration. Certainly, such a declaration risks fatal impasse, but much more often, a party may welcome knowing what is not possible.

17. Focus on future relationships. When the parties may have future relationships beyond the particular problem, the mediator should discuss with the parties how the resolution of this problem will affect future relationships or the possibility of future relationships.

18. Acknowledge that everyone is trying. While the mediator must never be coercive, he may occasionally need to be a "cheerleader" for resolution. The parties may need to be reminded that, while a logjam exists, everyone is trying hard to work through it.

19. Have the party's lawyer describe what will happen at trial. Sometimes a party may need to hear what the trial will be like, the nature of cross-examination, and what issues may be covered in cross-examination.

---

10. Memorandum of Agreement. Assuming the mediation results in a resolution of the dispute, a memorandum of agreement should be prepared and signed by all parties and their counsel. Most mediators have standard memorandum of agreement forms. Of course, the memorandum of agreement is not the final release, and dismissal documents will be prepared by counsel after the mediation. The memorandum of agreement, however, should be clear and specific enough to avoid any post-mediation controversy as to what was agreed to at the mediation session. In most cases, the memorandum of agreement will simply set out that the claimant will release any and all claims and dismiss the suit with prejudice in exchange for a specified sum of money. In complex business disputes, the memorandum of agreement will likely include numerous other specific items. . . .

I think it is better practice for the mediator to draft the memorandum of agreement, as opposed to counsel for the parties. A memorandum of agreement drafted by an attorney for one of the parties may be subject to question. If counsel insist upon drafting the memorandum of agreement, all counsel should collaborate on its preparation. After all parties and counsel have executed the agreement, the mediator should provide copies to all participants.

3. Tom Arnold, *Twenty Common Errors in Mediation Advocacy,* ADR TODAY, Spring 1995, at 2

Advocacy in mediation tends to be poor to unsophisticated. Trial lawyers often don't know how they foul their own nest or miss important persuasions. And so I here present a quickie list of twenty common errors in mediation advocacy.

1. Wrong Client in the Room. CEOs settle a strikingly larger percentage of cases than any VP and/or house counsel or other agent. Why? Any lesser agent than the CEO, even with explicit "authority," but who is to some degree concerned about review or criticism back at the office by a constituency which was not a participant in the give and take of the mediation, is not the best "client" to settle the case. That may be the best "client" rep available, but it is not the best that exists. No more so than an aggressive, critical, unforgiving, hot head, bellicosely self-righteous personality. An interesting mix of personality traits, charity towards others and their mistakes, conciliatory attitude, creativity flexibility, and authority with immunity from fear of criticism by a constituency, is the preferred client representative for a mediation. Of course, she should know the subject. But when feasible, be biased against a corporate representative who will inherently be defending her own actions.

2. Wrong Lawyer in the Room. First, some trial lawyers will not prepare themselves or their client for good mediation advocacy. In the small case this is understandable. The process can tolerate a lot of unpreparedness when it must, as in small cases. Second, many of the better trial lawyers are so arrogantly confident that they can persuade a jury of anything, anything at all (after all, they've done it before), and are so militant of personality that they cannot be sensitive to the importance of preserving relationships or the exorbitant costs and emotional drain of litigation. Why no sensitivity? Because they can smell a "win" in the court room, and that is what drives them. On average, it could be that, if reasonable compromise of good faith differences is the business goal, transaction lawyers are on average better mediation counsel than some of the most successful jury trial lawyers. The transaction lawyer's lack of confidence in what they can do in the court room contributes to a willingness to compromise and get a disposal of the dispute quickly and cheaply. At the least, parties should look for a sensitive, understanding personality no matter his job experience. Not a limp, wet rag, lest he give away the store; even so, prefer an intelligent, flexible and understanding personality who will do his homework, over inflexible arrogance.

3. Wrong Mediator in the Room. Some mediators bring nothing to the table but the loan of their conference room. Some arrogantly determine their view of the case and urge the parties to accept that view without exploring likely win-win alternatives. There is a continuum of mediation styles, continuum from the mediator focusing only on narrowly defined issues and those who are totally facilitative, to those whose imagination brings in a broad scope of party interests and those who fully evaluate the case and become directive of the parties rather than merely facilitative. The best mediators move around in the continuum from narrow to broad, from purely facilitative to evaluative and somewhat directive and back again — to fit the mediation to the case and the parties before them. But while mediators who are masters of the process can render valuable service in any subject matter whether they know the subject or not, many cases or the parties involved need an expert's suggestive evaluation, want a directive mediator, need someone experienced in the technology, the finances of the business, or the law that is in issue, need a person to help cast lights and shadows on the merits of the case and alternative settlements. Its tough to know and evaluate a mediator and fit the choice of mediator to your case. It may be impossible. But the wrong mediator may fail to get a settlement another mediator might have effectively contributed to.

4. Wrong Case. Contrary to popular thought, almost every type of case is a likely candidate for mediation — mediation which, unlike arbitration, is an essentially safe procedure costing usually no more than perhaps two or three days of depositions of an expert. But some few cases don't fit the mold. It is not the legal topic which renders mediation inapposite; it is the value that is not on the table. By way of example: a case where the franchisor, for reasons not related to the case at hand, critically needs a legal precedent by way of construction of a clause found in 3,000 franchise contracts, or a binding legal precedent construing some statute her way, is an unlikely case for mediation settlement. Why? Because the major value one party seeks and essentially must have is not on the table in the mediation room. Any case where major value is involved in the precedent generated, should be looked at carefully as a case where mediation likely is inapposite.

5. Omitting the Client Prep. For good mediation, clients need to know and understand a good deal about the mediation process and the particular dispute. Sadly, counsel rarely prepare their clients well for the process. Better preparation produces more and better settlements.

6. Failure to Use Advocacy Tools Effectively. Advocacy includes the proper use of advocacy tools: e.g., exhibits, charts, copies of relevant cases, or contracts with key phrases highlighted. Visiting mindlessly or in generality about the many admissions the adversaries' various witnesses have made in video depositions and documents has none of the impact of a 90 second video clip where witness A makes his admission in living color, followed by witness B making her admission, followed by witness C making his admission, followed by the readable size copy of the February 29 letter with the key admission highlighted. Putting them together effects power. Further, the client and senior lawyer whose juniors took the depositions, on the other side, likely never appreciated that all those admissions had been made, much less evaluated their impact. Prepare your materials for persuasive impact. Use the good tools of advocacy. Too few do in mediations.

7. Opening Statements to the Mediator as to a Judge or Jury, Rather than to the Other Party and Counsel. Most lawyers begin a mediation opening statement addressing the mediator, telling his side of the case in language laced with righteous indignation and as adversarial as though to a jury whose mind the lawyer seeks to poison toward the adversary. The lawyer shows no interest in, much less understanding of, the emotional hurt being inflicted upon the adversary, nor the plight the other party perceives herself to be in and which gave rise to the dispute. In its disrespect for the other people, in its sometimes outright charges of gross impropriety by the adversary, this opening is a terrible poisoning of the well from which the party must drink in order to get his settlement. This is an often tragic abandonment of a marvelous opportunity to persuade and get together with the other party. The "judge or jury" you want to persuade in a mediation is not the mediator, but the adversary. It is the other party you want to persuade to be sympathetic to your cause. So don't hurt him. Adversary parties arrive at a mediation with much distrust of the opposing lawyer, which means they won't hear much of what is said. Turn them even further off with accusations and you copper rivet failure to settle.

In plenary sessions, simply do not address inflammatory issues beyond a neutral statement of facts and how client X feels. Why? Because the mediator can discuss the inflammatory points in his private caucus "reality checks" more effectively and with less "poisoning" effect than the adversary in his opening statements or the like. In plenary sessions, the lawyer/client should rather show their own humanity, respect, warmth, apologies, and sympathy. It continues to surprise me to see the shocking degree that a good sympathetic opening by a well-rehearsed and skillful lawyer (or better yet, by his client) directed to the adversary party rather than the mediator, can so often set the stage for a good settlement. Persuasion addressed to the "jury," which in mediation means the adverse party and his/her counsel, always aids the process of settlement.

8. The Lawyer Instead of the Client at Center of the Process; Show Off a Good Witness. Let any articulate client be the center of the process. Prepare him to speak to and be spoken to by the mediator and the adversary as he explains his plight, and to extend empathy to the other party while explaining why he feels the way he does, or why the responsibility is not his, or why the damages caused by what he did are only peanuts or are great. The lawyer should not try to explain every word the client utters, or to protect the client from herself. The insurance adjuster or defendant's vice president has not attended depositions, does not know the plaintiff. If the plaintiff comes across as an appealing witness, prep her and show her off to the adjuster by having her talk. People pay more to appealing plaintiffs. If the client presents a negative appeal, of course the lawyer should do the talking for the client.

9. Failure to Let a Sympathetic Client Open for Herself. Many lawyers are arrogant, or feel they are not doing their job if they don't "plead" or "argue" the case, or they feel their client expects them to deliver the opening. Hogwash. At least as often as not, letting the properly coached client do most or even all of the opening, telling why she feels the way she does, induces more and better settlements more quickly than the typical adversarial lawyer opening.

10. Time for Mediation; Flexibility in Needed Discovery. Not too early. Get and give the core, critical discovery first. And not too late. Don't spend exorbitant time or sums in discovery and trial prep before seeking mediation. The mediation process can climb over a lot of non-discovery, and can precipitate a limited bit of critically necessary discovery and resumption of mediation, when the counsel and mediator are flexible and alert to the need. . . .

11. Failure to Listen to the Other Side. Many lawyers and clients come in so loaded with their own arguments, they are incapable of giving open minded attention to what is being expressed from across the table. It is sad to lose a settlement out of such stupidity.

12. Perceptions, Motivations. Brainstorm and determine the other party's motivations and perceptions by preparing a chart of how he sees the relevant things. Seek first to understand, only then to be understood. Understanding the other party's perceptions will make you more realistic. If the perceptions make sense, they will make you also more charitable and, hence, will help induce a fair settlement. If they make no sense, they will make you more firm and, hence, help induce you to persevere for a more favorable settlement.

13. Hurt, Humiliate the Adversary, Threaten and Deliver Ultimatums? Of Course Not. Don't poison the well from which you must drink to get a settlement. Rather, humanize yourself to the adversary. You can be firm and strong on your facts, and still a decent human. That means you don't hurt, humiliate or ridicule the other folks. No pejoratives — "maligner," "fraud," "cheat," "liar." Essentially all settlements are based in some degree upon trust, lawyer to lawyer trust, client to client trust, and client to lawyer trust. If you anger them with ridicule or with pejorative terms like "crook" and "stealing," if you seek to extort from them with threats, if you attack their integrity, they won't trust you and anyway they won't settle with you.

Ultimatums destroy the process, destroy credibility. Yes, there is a time in mediation to walk out whether or not with intent to return, but a series of ultimatums, or often even one ultimatum, is tremendously counterproductive. The same can be said for threats, like a threat to get the other lawyer's law license for urging such a frivolous cause as he has here, or for his grossly inaccurate pleadings, or whatever. Threats are not usually conducive to compromise settlements. Rather, let the objective, balanced recitation of facts project any threat you use in a mediation.

14. Close Too Fast to the Bottom Line: "The Dance." If a party opens at $1 million and moves immediately to $500,000, she has telegraphed that there is more give to be obtained. Right or wrong, the other side will believe it and, likely, will never come to a $500,000 offer. By contrast, a move from $1 million to $750,000, to $650,000, to $600,000, to $575,000, to $560,000, to $550,000 telegraphs a different story and is likely to beget a counter offer of $500,000 that then can be accepted. In 80 percent of mediations, "the dance" is a necessary part of communication. Sorry about that, but it usually is true. To skip the dance is to risk losing a settlement that could be obtained. Rather, plan your dance to convey the subliminal messages you want to be understood.

15. The Backwards Step. A party which before the mediation offered to pay $300,000, then at the mediation says it is willing to offer only $200,000, without some clear and dramatic reasons for the reduction in the offer, has injured its own credibility, caused animosity and a feeling of bad faith on the other side, and has otherwise interfered with the progress of the process. It is likely to take the better part of a day to overcome the deleterious effect of such a maneuver. The backwards step is a powerful card to play at the right time, a walk away without yet walking out. But powerful devices are also dangerous devices. The times and circumstances for its productive use are few. Its use should be reserved for the true negotiation experts with vast experience. The general instruction must be, Don't do it.

16. Too Many People. Advisors, people to whom the decision maker must display respect and courtesy, people who feel that since they are there they must put in their two bits worth, all delay a mediation immeasurably while they state and restate the obvious as well as the non-obvious. A caucus that with only one lawyer and VP would take 20 minutes, with five people will take an hour and 20 minutes, or some such. The nominally one-day mediation stretches to two or three, but only if the folks have more patience for the stretch than usually they do. And if it doesn't stretch, an available settlement is lost. Moreover, the advisors by natural instinct all seem to advise through their own rose-colored-glasses view of the issues, feeding resistance to yielding on a perhaps five to one ratio over feeding confidence in a particular yielding. Whereby, five people per side (e.g., VP in charge of, Marketing Manager, Chief Engineer, house counsel, trial counsel) will only rarely settle a typical commercial case that almost any two people per side would certainly have settled.

This is one of the contexts where I use the "one martini lunch" — send out the two adversary principals alone after X hours of mediation, when all the issues are understood by all, to negotiate on their own with no advice from anybody. The percentage of oral settlements in principal occurring within three hours or less would appall most folks. Of course, there often is need for some brush ups on details they overlooked, and there is need for writing up and signing of the deal before the day is over, but usually those finishing touches don't queer the deal the two principals have made.

17. Failure to Truly Close the Deal. It is important to close the agreement before breaking up from the mediation, with a written, signed, enforceable contract. Too often, when left to think overnight and draft tomorrow, new ideas occur that preclude finalizing the agreement as discussed before parties went home. Unless parties have strong reasons to sleep on it, to need a further evaluation of the deal or a further check on what may have been forgotten, enough so to risk loss of the settlement, it is much better to get some sort of enforceable contract written and signed before the parties separate.

18. Confidentiality. Mediation parties have been known unthinkingly, or irresponsibly, to disclose in open court information disclosed only in confidence in a mediation. Where the information is highly sensitive, consider keeping it confidential. Or, if revealed in a mediation where the case did not settle, consider moving before the trial begins for an order in limine with respect to it.

19. Patience; Perseverance. The process takes time. The "dance" takes time. With time, people will change their mind when they will not change it without time. The six most important qualities of good advocacy in mediation, are (1) patience, (2) perseverance, (3) patience, (4) perseverance, (5) patience, and (6) perseverance.

20. What is a dispute? A dispute is a problem to be solved together, not a combat to be won.

4. James J. Alfini, *Trashing, Bashing, and Hashing It Out: Is this the End of "Good Mediation?"* 19 FLA. ST. U. L. REV. 47, 66-73 (1991)

[Most of Professor Alfini's article is devoted to court-annexed mediation in Florida state courts, but his alliterative typology of mediation styles has general applicability.] Our interviews with the circuit mediators and lawyers revealed three distinct styles. These three approaches to the mediation process are characterized as (1) trashing, (2) bashing, and (3) hashing it out.

1. *Trashing.* The mediators who employ a trashing methodology spend much of the time "tearing apart" the cases of the parties. Indeed, one of these mediators suggested the "trasher" characterization: "I trash their cases. By tearing apart and then building their cases back up, I try to get them to a point where they will put realistic settlement figures on the table." To facilitate uninhibited trashing of the parties' cases, the overall strategy employed by these mediators discourages direct party communication. Following the mediator's orientation and short opening statements by each party's attorney, the mediator puts the parties in different rooms. The mediator then normally caucuses with the plaintiff's attorney and her client in an effort to get them to take a hard look at the strengths and weaknesses of their case.

2. *Bashing.* Unlike the trashers, the mediators who use a bashing technique tend to spend little or no time engaging in the kind of case evaluation that is aimed at getting the parties to put "realistic" settlement figures on the table. Rather, they tend to focus initially on the settlement offers that the parties bring to mediation and spend most of the session bashing away at those initial offers in an attempt to get the parties to agree to a figure somewhere in between. Their mediation sessions thus tend to be shorter than those of the trashers, and they tend to prefer a longer initial joint session, permitting direct communication between the parties. Most of the bashers interviewed were retired judges who draw on their judicial experience and use the prestige of their past judicial service to bash out an agreement.

3. *Hashing It Out.* The third circuit mediation style can best be described as one involving a hashing out of a settlement agreement, because it places greater reliance on direct communication between the opposing attorneys and their clients. The hashers tend to take a much more flexible approach to the media-

tion process, varying their styles and using techniques such as caucusing selectively, depending on their assessment of the individual case and the needs and interests of the parties. When asked to describe the mediator's role in one sentence, a hasher responded, "Facilitator, orchestrator, referee, sounding board, scapegoat." The hasher generally adopts a much less directive posture than the trashers and bashers, preferring that the parties speak directly with one another and hash out an agreement. However, if direct communication appears counterproductive, the hasher acts as a communication link. . . . Although hashers prefer to adopt a style that encourages direct party communication to hash out an agreement, they are willing to employ trasher or basher methodologies if they believe it to be appropriate in a particular case.

D. DIFFERENT VIEWS OF MEDIATION: HOW TO DEFINE SUCCESS?

1. Comments and Questions

a. In this section, we switch from an examination of what mediation is, to a discussion of what mediation ought to be. Instead of judging mediation simply by the quality of results achieved, broader criteria are employed. These are nothing less than battles among "insiders" over definition of the process and control of mediation as a movement. In Professor Moffitt's vocabulary, the issue is as fundamental as who gets to describe themselves as mediators, and who are something else — mere "schmediators."

b. Professors Bush and Folger are the leading advocates of mediation as transformation. To them, the key is the process rather than the result. Indeed, they can sometimes be viewed as arguing that it is better for mediation to be conducted properly and fail, than to push the parties into achieving an apparent success — a false consensus. This approach does not ignore results; rather, it focuses on settlements that last. A deal pushed on the parties by a mediator may well fall apart when subsequent events place pressure on the relationship between the disputing parties.

c. Elements of what Bush and Folger call the Oppression Story are considered at several places in this book, usually in the broader context of ADR processes generally. In particular, see the pieces by Judge Edwards in Chapter One, Professors Delgado and Menkel-Meadow in Chapter Five, and by Professor Fiss in Chapter Thirteen.

2. ROBERT BARUCH BUSH & JOSEPH P. FOLGER, THE PROMISE OF MEDIATION: RESPONDING TO CONFLICT THROUGH EMPOWERMENT AND RECOGNITION 15-27 (1994)

The Mediation Movement: Four Diverging Views

While the growth of mediation is remarkable, what is even more striking is the extraordinary divergence of opinion about how to understand that growth and how to characterize the mediation movement itself. This divergence is so marked that there is no one accepted account of how the mediation movement evolved or what it represents. Instead, the literature of the field reveals several very different accounts or "stories" of the movement, told by different authors and stressing different dimensions of the mediation process and its societal impacts. Thus, the movement is portrayed by some as a tool to reduce court congestion and provide "higher-quality" justice in individual cases, by others as a vehicle for organizing people and communities to obtain fairer treatment, and by still others as a covert means of social control and oppression. And some, including ourselves, picture the movement as a way to foster a qualitative transformation of human interaction. Indeed, these are the four main accounts of the mediation movement that run through the literature on mediation. We call them, respectively, the Satisfaction Story of the movement, the Social Justice Story, the Oppression Story, and the Transformation Story.

The fact that there are four distinct and divergent stories of the movement suggests two important points. On one level, it suggests that the mediation movement is not monolithic but pluralistic — that there are in fact different approaches to mediation practice, with varied impacts. The stories represent these different approaches. On a deeper level, the existence of divergent stories suggests that, while everyone sees the mediation movement as a means for achieving important societal goals, people differ over what goal is most important. The stories thus also represent and support different goals, each of which is seen by some people as the most important one for the movement to fulfill. Recounting the different stories of the movement is, therefore, a good way both to illustrate the diversity of mediation practice and also to identify the value choices implicit in varying approaches to practice. The following summary of the four stories presents each one as it might be told by its authors and adherents.

The Satisfaction Story. According to this story: The mediation process is a powerful tool for satisfying the genuine human needs of parties to individual disputes. Because of its flexibility, informality, and consensuality, mediation can open up the full dimensions of the problem facing the parties. Not limited by legal categories or rules, it can help reframe a contentious dispute as a mutual problem. Also, because of mediators' skills in dealing with power imbalances, mediation can reduce strategic maneuvering and overreaching. As a result of these different features, mediation can facilitate collaborative, integrative problem solving rather than adversarial, distributive bargaining. It can thereby produce creative, "win-win" outcomes that reach beyond formal rights to solve problems and satisfy parties' genuine needs in a particular situation. The mediation movement has employed these capabilities of the process to produce superior quality solutions to disputes of all kinds, in terms of satisfaction of parties' self-defined needs, for all sides.

Furthermore, in comparison to more formal or adversarial processes, mediation's informality and mutuality can reduce both the economic and emotional costs of dispute settlement. The use of mediation has thus produced great private savings for disputants, in economic and psychic terms. Also, by providing mediation in many cases that would otherwise have gone to court, the mediation movement has also saved public expense. It has freed up the courts for other disputants who need them, easing the problem of delaying access to justice. In sum, the movement has led to more efficient use of limited private and public dispute resolution resources, which in turn means greater overall satisfaction for individual "consumers" of the justice system.

This holds true for all the various contexts in which mediation has been used. . . . Small-claims mediation has resulted in higher party satisfaction with both process and outcome, and higher rates of compliance than litigation. Environmental and public policy mediation have produced creative and highly praised resolutions, while avoiding the years of delay and enormous expense that court action would have entailed. Moreover, mediation in these areas has reduced court caseloads and backlogs, facilitating speedier disposition of those cases that cannot he resolved without trial in court. In these and other kinds of disputes, mediation has produced more satisfaction for disputing parties than could have been provided otherwise.

The next two interpretations of the mediation movement, the Social Justice Story and the Transformation Story, differ somewhat from the Satisfaction Story. The Satisfaction Story claims to depict what has generally occurred in the use of mediation thus far, while the other two describe something that has admittedly occurred only in part thus far. In effect, these are "minor" stories of the movement, but each is seen by its adherents as representing the movement's most important potential.

The Social Justice Story. According to this story: Mediation offers an effective means of organizing individuals around common interests and thereby building stronger community ties and structures. This is important because unaffiliated individuals are especially subject to exploitation in this society and because more effective community organization can limit such exploitation and create more social justice. Mediation can support community organization in several ways. Because of its capacity for reframing issues and focusing on common interests, mediation can help individuals who think they are adversaries perceive a larger context in which they face a common enemy. As a result, mediation can strengthen the weak by helping establish alliances among them.

In addition, by its capacity to help parties solve problems for themselves, mediation reduces dependency on distant agencies and encourages self-help, including the formation of effective grass-roots community structures. Finally, mediation treats legal rules as only one of a variety of bases by which to frame issues and evaluate possible solutions to disputes. Therefore, mediation can give groups more leverage to argue for their interests than they might have in formal legal processes. The mediation movement has used these capacities of the process, to some extent at least, to facilitate the organization of relatively powerless individuals into communities of interest. As a result, those common interests have been pursued more successfully, helping ensure greater social justice, and the individuals involved have gained a new sense of participation in civic life.

This picture applies to many, if not all, of the contexts in which mediation is used. Interpersonal neighborhood mediation has encouraged co-tenants or block residents, for example, to realize their common adversaries, such as landlords and city agencies, and to take joint action to pursue their common interests.

Environmental mediation has facilitated the assertion of novel (and not strictly legal) claims by groups that have succeeded in redressing imbalances of power favoring land developers. Even mediation of consumer disputes has helped strengthen consumers' confidence in their ability to get complaints addressed, which has led to other forms of consumer self-help and increased consumer power. In short, mediation has helped organize individuals and strengthen communities of interest in many different contexts, and could be used more widely for this purpose.

The Social Justice Story of the mediation movement has been told for a long time, though by a relatively small number of authors, usually people with ties to the tradition of grass-roots community organizing. While the numbers of its adherents are few, this story has been told consistently from the earliest stages of the movement. The third story, the Transformation Story, focuses on some of the same features of the mediation process as the first two. However, it characterizes them, and especially their consequences, in distinct and quite different terms than the other stories.

The Transformation Story. According to this story: The unique promise of mediation lies in its capacity to transform the character of both individual disputants and society as a whole. Because of its informality and consensuality, mediation can allow parties to define problems and goals in their own terms, thus validating the importance of those problems and goals in the parties' lives. Further, mediation can support the parties' exercise of self-determination in deciding how, or even whether, to settle a dispute, and it can help the parties mobilize their own resources to address problems and achieve their goals. The mediation movement has (at least to some extent) employed these capabilities of the process to help disputing parties strengthen their own capacity to handle adverse circumstances of all kinds, not only in the immediate case but in future situations. Participants in mediation have gained a greater sense of self-respect, self-reliance, and self-confidence. This has been called the empowerment dimension of the mediation process.

In addition, the private, nonjudgmental character of mediation can provide disputants a nonthreatening opportunity to explain and humanize themselves to one another. In this setting, and with mediators who are skilled at enhancing interpersonal communication, parties often discover that they can feel and express some degree of understanding and concern for one another despite their disagreement. The movement has (again, to some extent) used this dimension of the process to help individuals strengthen their inherent capacity for relating with concern to the problems of others. Mediation has thus engendered, even between parties who start out as fierce adversaries, acknowledgment and concern for each other as fellow human beings. This has been called the recognition dimension of the mediation process.

While empowerment and recognition have been given only partial attention in the mediation movement thus far, a consistent and wider emphasis on these dimensions would contribute powerfully — incrementally and over time — to the transformation of individuals from fearful, defensive, and self-centered beings into confident, empathetic, and considerate beings, and to the transformation of society from a shaky truce between enemies into a strong network of allies. This picture captures the potential of all branches of the mediation movement, not just certain areas in which human relationships are considered important (implying that elsewhere they are not). Consumer mediation can strengthen and evoke mutual recognition between merchants and consumers, transforming both the individuals involved and the character of commercial transactions and institutions. . . . Personal injury mediation can strengthen and evoke recognition between individuals who work for loss-coverage institutions and individual accident victims, transforming both the persons involved and the character of compensation processes and institutions in our society. In every area, mediation could, with sufficient energy and commitment, help transform both individuals and society. . . .

Here, then, are three very different accounts of the mediation movement. Each of them expresses two different kinds of messages about the movement. On one level, each story is a description, purporting to recount what the mediation movement has actually done and what its actual character is today (in whole or in part). On another level, each story is a prescription, suggesting what the movement should do to fulfill what the story's authors see as the most important societal goal or value that mediation can help achieve. The final story of the movement differs from all the others. The first three all see positive effects or potentials in the movement, although each sees them differently. The fourth, by contrast, sees only negative effects or potentials. It presents not a prescription for the movement but a warning against it. We call it the Oppression Story.

The Oppression Story. According to this story: Even if the movement began with the best of intentions, mediation has turned out to be a dangerous instrument for increasing the power of the strong to take advantage of the weak. Because of the informality and consensuality of the process, and hence, the absence of both procedural and substantive rules, mediation can magnify power imbalances and open the door to coercion and manipulation by the stronger party. Meanwhile, the posture of neutrality excuses the mediator from preventing this. Therefore, in comparison to formal legal processes, mediation has often produced outcomes that are unjust, that is, disproportionately and unjustifiably favorable to stronger parties. Moreover, because of its privacy and informality, mediation gives mediators broad strategic power to control the discussion, giving free rein to mediators' biases. These biases can affect the framing and selection of issues, consideration and ranking of settlement options, and many other elements that influence outcomes. Again, as a result, mediation has often produced unjust outcomes.

Finally, since mediation handles disputes without reference to other, similar cases and without reference to the public interest, it results in the "dis-aggregation" and privatization of class and public interest problems. That is, the mediation movement has helped the strong to "divide and conquer." Weaker parties are unable to make common cause and the public interest is ignored and undermined. In sum, the overall effect of the movement has been to neutralize social justice gains achieved by the civil rights, women's, and consumer's movements, among others, and to help reestablish the privileged position of the stronger classes and perpetuate their oppression of the weaker. This oppressive picture is found in all the movement's manifestations. . . . Landlord-tenant mediation allows landlords to escape their obligations to provide minimally decent housing, which results in substandard living conditions and unjust removals for tenants. Employment discrimination mediation manipulates victims into accepting buy-offs and permits structural racism and sexism to continue unabated in businesses and institutions. Even in commercial disputes between businesses, mediation allows the parties to strike deals behind closed doors that disadvantage consumers and others in ways that will never even come to light. In every area, the mediation movement has been used to consolidate the power of the strong and increase the exploitation and oppression of the weak.

The Oppression Story is clearly a different kind of story than the other three. Rather than offering a description of and prescription for the mediation movement, it sounds a warning against it. This story is almost as widely told as the Satisfaction Story, but by very different authors. In general, many . . . writers and thinkers concerned with equality tend to interpret the mediation movement through the Oppression Story and to see it as a serious threat to disadvantaged groups.

3. Michael L. Moffitt, *Schmediation and the Dimensions of Definition*, 10 HARV. NEGOT. L. REV. 69 (2005)

. . . Compared with the medical profession, the practice of mediation operates with virtually no regulation. One would expect, therefore, to see far more practice variation among mediators, and anyone who has spent much time in the field can confirm that this variation exists. Mediators do a wide range of things, all without ever taking off their "mediator" hats. Indeed, because mediators operate without much risk of sanction for variation, positive law provides no reason for mediators to resort to the gambit of titular re-description. Mediators who want to do things differently from their colleagues need not announce, "I am now a schmediator." They simply engage in whatever practices they want, free to call the enterprise mediation. Without stiff controls, practices like mediation adapt to market demands, to developing theories, and perhaps to practitioners' whims.

As a result, we now see an extraordinary collection of people who self-describe as mediators. A retired judge offers her services as a mediator to parties in a high-stakes litigation. Jimmy Carter offers his services in mediating the settlement of an international crisis. A seventh-grade student trained in peer mediation proudly wears a t-shirt that says "Mediator." A therapist mediates in helping a couple to work through their misunderstandings of each other. These people continue to use the same description of their role, though none would deny that they are engaged in activities that are quite distinct. And each currently can use the "mediator" label without fear that the state will sanction his or her activities, provided they cause no injury.

Because the specter of state sanction does not loom over practitioners, mediators operate without the strict need to consider the definitional boundaries of their practices. Yet many practitioners and scholars have spent considerable time developing definitions, categories, and arguments about the boundaries of mediation. Many in the mediation community care passionately about the boundaries attached to the practice of mediation, and there is very little consensus regarding appropriate limits and definitions. . . . Despite the challenges facing those who seek to craft a definition of mediation, I suggest that two aspects of definition-crafting . . . remain important. Definitions of mediation are either prescriptive or descriptive, and they are either acontextual or contextual.

A. Prescriptive-Acontextual Definitions

Some definitions of mediation are purely prescriptive-acontextual in character. That is, they include components at odds with observable practice and usage. They also include no qualifiers or contextual parameters. The definitions at least appear to apply to all uses of the word equally.

"Evaluative mediation is an oxymoron." The article by this title, written by Lela Love and Kim Kovach, [14 ALTERNATIVES TO HIGH COST LITIG. 31 (March 1996)], has received extraordinary attention — surely some of it due to the article's catchy, definition-suggesting title. The article appeared as part of a broader debate about the propriety of mediators assessing likely court outcomes — so-called "evaluative mediation." Prior to this article, most of the voices on each side of the facilitative-evaluative debate had limited their arguments to why the practice of evaluation was or was not appropriate. The arguments were largely in the nature of trying to define the "best practice" for mediators. The Love and Kovach article, or at least its title, raised the stakes in a sense, by suggesting that evaluation falls outside of the proper definition of mediation. One can almost hear the suggestion embedded in the authors' argument that those who evaluate should be labeled schmediators — or something else.

"Evaluative mediation is an oxymoron" is a component of a prescriptive definition, as opposed to a descriptive one. Love and Kovach were not contending that no practitioners are providing evaluations. Indeed, it was the very fact that some practitioners were evaluating that caused the authors to write their piece. Instead, what troubled the authors was that there were practitioners out there evaluating and calling themselves mediators. This practice, under the name of mediation, offends their normative vision of the proper definition of mediation practice. Hence, their definitional assertion is prescriptive. Their assertion is also acontextual. If one is to trust . . . the authors' rhetoric, evaluation falls outside of the scope of mediation, no matter the context. . . .

A second example of prescriptive-acontextual definitions related to mediation is found in many explorations of mediation ethics. "Mediators are neutral." Some scholars use the term impartial, some use the term neutral. Many, however, include one or the other in even the most basic definition of mediation. Not all of those who call themselves mediators are neutral. This fact alone does not make it prescriptive to define mediators as neutrals. What makes it prescriptive is that this practice variation regarding neutrality is not just a matter of variation-by-error. It is not merely that some people who call themselves mediators mess up and slip out of neutrality. What makes the inclusion of neutrality in a definition of mediation prescriptive is that not all scholars and mediators embrace the underlying idea that mediators should be neutral.

Perhaps the most vivid example of this disagreement over the proper role of neutrality comes from those interested in mediation in the context of international diplomacy. Jimmy Carter was in no way neutral, nor did he view it as integral to his role that he try to be (or even try to pretend to be) neutral. The definition "mediators are neutral" would suggest that Jimmy Carter was not a mediator, a conclusion that is unsatisfying for those who concern themselves with the descriptive aspects of definitions. If one took a poll on the street, asking passers-by to "name a mediator," Jimmy Carter would probably be among the most frequently named. How then, the descriptivists would ask, could we possibly craft an acontextual definition that does not include him?

B. Prescriptive Contextual Definitions

Not all prescriptive definitions are acontextual. Some of those who offer definitions limit the scope of their prescriptive definitional assertions by adding some type of practice parameter. Rather than saying "mediation is. . . ." for all purposes, they say "in this context, mediation means. . . ." or "this kind of mediator does. . . ." Their definitions remain prescriptive, however, because not all of those who practice within the particular context ascribe to the definitional parameters being offered.

One prominent example of prescriptive-contextual definitional work is found in the descriptions and applications of so-called "transformative" mediation. The term "transformative mediation" gained popular attention with the publication of THE PROMISE OF MEDIATION (1994) by Robert A. Baruch Bush and Joseph Folger. At the heart of this vision of mediation is the idea that a mediator's function is limited to two essential tasks: searching for opportunities to empower the disputants to exercise self-determination and self-reliance in solving their own problems (empowerment), and searching for opportunities to help the disputants acknowledge each other as fellow human beings (recognition). The work of Bush and Folger is clearly contextual — the authors are not asserting that this is the only definition of any mediator's tasks. Instead, they create a subcategory of mediators — transformative mediators — and assign the definition to this more limited set of practitioners. What I wish to highlight is that their definition, though contextual, is also prescriptive.

Bush and Folger present the reader with two different prescriptive definitions in their treatment of mediation. First, they offer a prescriptive definition of "transformative." A mediation is transformational, according to their definition, if it helps the parties to achieve a particular form of human moral development. That is the only meaning of "transformative" consistent with the authors' construction. Within their view, therefore, a mediation that enabled a party to resolve an issue and put it behind her would not be properly labeled "transformative." Nor would a mediation be deemed "transformative" if it caused a massive collapse in the relationship between the parties, a marked escalation of rhetoric, or a fundamental shift in the nature of the dispute. An outsider might report that the mediation session was "transformative," in that it transformed the dispute, but Bush and Folger's definition includes a more limited view of the term. It is, therefore, a prescriptive definition.

Second, Bush and Folger appear to attach a procedural definition to an adjective that is facially focused on the outcome. That is, Bush and Folger define a mediation's transformative components by reference to the mediators' actions, rather than by reference to the impacts on the parties. The question that follows is this: can a mediator achieve the goals of transformation — that is, of promoting human moral development in mediation — through some other set of practices? . . . Jeff Seul has argued persuasively that other sets of mediator practice have at least as good a claim of "transforming" disputants. If Seul is correct, as I suspect he is, then Bush and Folger's definition of what is "transformative" is at most prescriptive. They define one path to transformative mediation as the path — a prescriptive definitional move.

The authors' definition of transformative mediation is also prescriptive in its treatment of mediators and their practices. Unlike Love and Kovach, however, Bush and Folger offer a contextual definition. They do not claim that only transformative mediators are mediators. Instead, they assert that all transformative mediators are engaged in a particular practice. And yet, in practice, one sees more variation among even those who profess to be "transformative mediators" than the authors would presumably countenance. Concerned with the prospect of such variation, some program designers have gone so far as to impose relatively rigid structures and practice parameters on their mediators. For example, the United States Postal Service has explicitly adopted the "transformative" model of mediation in its REDRESS program. My anecdotal interviews with REDRESS mediators, however, suggest strongly that actual practices in that program vary considerably from the singular model presented in program trainings. The mediators with whom I spoke varied not only as a matter of mis-step, but of practice. In the words of one, "I don't go strictly by the book, but I still consider myself transformative." This sort of practice variation helps to illustrate why the definitions offered by Bush and Folger are contextually prescriptive, rather than descriptive. Outside of a prescriptive definition of "transformative mediation," no mediator who is otherwise inclined to describe his or her practice as transformative would need to hesitate in adopting the label.

C. Descriptive Definitions

What can those who would prefer not to craft prescriptive definitions offer with respect to defining mediation? Theirs is a more challenging enterprise, in many ways. The variety of things people do while calling themselves mediators is extraordinary. And yet a good descriptivist would search for the essential and common in those practices. Consider the definition, "Mediators are third parties, not otherwise involved in a controversy, who assist disputing parties in their negotiations." SARAH R. COLE ET AL., MEDIATION: LAW, POLICY, PRACTICE § 1:1 (2d ed. 2003). The treatise from which this definition is drawn is almost certainly the most comprehensive, thorough treatment of mediation available today. That the authors of these volumes chose to offer a descriptive definition makes sense, given the breadth of audiences to whom they speak.

This definition has the effect of drawing certain behavioral boundaries. Under this definition, it is not that anything one might do is considered mediating. A mediator's job is to assist the parties with their negotiations — not to design their building, or treat a disease, or fix their car. Intuitively, such behavioral boundaries make sense. And yet, if one examines closely the work of architects, doctors, and mechanics, pieces of their jobs are surely at least related to mediation. No architect practices for long without recognizing the need to help satisfy a range of different interested parties' desires. No doctor practices for long without recognizing the complicated decision making processes at play in families in which one member is seriously ill. And no mechanic goes without seeing disagreements arise within households regarding car repair expenditures and practices. Should they be considered mediators?

Within the notion that mediators are third parties who assist disputing parties in their negotiations," we see a structural component (this is who a mediator is) and a behavioral component (this is what a mediator does). In a dispute between two parties, according to this definition, one of the two parties cannot suddenly claim to be "the mediator." Instead, the mediator is said to be a "third party." Intuitively, this sort of structural limitation makes sense. As one pushes the definition a bit, one quickly sees that there are ways in which this aspect of mediation may be overstated from a descriptive perspective. For example, in a circumstance involving absent clients or constituents, the representative of one side might take on a mediative role, mediating between her constituents and her counterpart — assisting in their negotiations. A manager in an organization may not have an immediate stake in a particular fight, and may step in to help the disputants resolve their issue. The mediating manager is not entirely removed, however, from interest in the outcome or in the process by which the disputants resolve their differences.

Still, the descriptive accuracy of this definition of mediation is relatively high. The vast majority of people out there who are calling themselves mediators are trying to help disputants with their negotiations. And the vast majority of them enter the dispute as a mediator, rather than as an initial disputant. Therefore, if descriptive definitions aim only for accuracy, a definition such as this may hit the mark. To one who is interested in learning more about the term being defined, however, accurate descriptive definitions tend to be relatively less helpful. If all we can say about mediators is that they are third parties who try to help disputants as they negotiate, we have said painfully little.

D. The Ascendancy of Categorization Within Mediation

One response to the difficulties in crafting both prescriptive and descriptive definitions has been the development of intra-mediation categorization. Some scholars and observers of mediation do not concern themselves so much with the question of who is in or out of the circle of mediators. Instead, they look at the world of those who call themselves mediators and then seek to describe ways of categorizing the population they observe. Their aim is not inclusion or exclusion with respect to the broader term "mediation." Instead, it is to craft better descriptive tools with which to improve our understanding of what those who call themselves mediators are and what they do.

Len Riskin's often-cited grids of mediator orientation are an example of an effort to provide categorization — without explicit definition. Leonard L. Riskin, *Decisionmaking in Mediation: The New Old Grid and the New New Grid System*, 79 NOTRE DAME L. REV. 1 (2003). According to Riskin's grids, those who practice mediation have tendencies or orientations with respect to certain questions. And their tendencies may be measured along multiple continua. For example, Riskin suggests that mediators vary in the way they treat problem-definition. Some tend to view problems in narrow terms (Who owes whom how much money? What business issues are at stake here?) and some view them in relatively broader terms (What is the ongoing dynamic between these two? What community interests are at stake in this dispute?). The way a mediator conceives of the problem to be solved influences the rest of the mediator's decisions. Hence, Riskin suggests that both mediators and mediation consumers ought to have an understanding that different mediators fall into different problem-definition categories.

Other efforts to describe the variations among mediators have also stopped short of describing any of the variants as falling outside of the definition of mediation. Shortly after Riskin first published his grid, I described the differences between mediators who adopt transparent and non-transparent approaches to various aspects of mediating. Put simply, the question of transparency asks about the degree to which mediators share their thoughts with the parties. Do they tell disputants what dynamics they observe? Do the mediators share their diagnoses of what is happening between the disputants? Do they describe the processes they intend to follow and the changes in the bargaining dynamic they hope to achieve? Like Riskin, I suggest that mediators and those who work with mediators would be well-served to consider these variations on the mediation theme.

The questions Riskin and I ask, and the categories we suggest, are relevant to mediators regardless of their context. The retired judge will have a problem-definition orientation of one sort or another, under Riskin's grid. Perhaps she will see the dispute as a narrow legal contest. Perhaps she will see it as a larger, ongoing struggle for emotional satisfaction and appreciation between business partners. The same questions face each type of mediator. Is this international mediation about getting food to a particular group of refugees? Or is it about the systems of government in place in this region? Is the schoolyard mediation about a particular name-calling incident or a larger pattern of respect and security? Is the family mediation session about the division of concrete responsibilities, or about an ongoing relationship? Similarly, transparency issues arise for mediators in every context. Should the retired judge share her assessment that the negotiation dynamics are breaking down because of the tactics of one of the lawyers in the room? Should the international diplomat tell the parties what steps she envisions next? Should the schoolyard mediator share her perspective on why the two students can't seem to get along? Should the therapist tell the couple what changes she hopes to see in their interactions?

The move toward categorization is important, because strong categorization may ultimately help us to better understand and advance the field. Without good descriptions, observational research is virtually impossible. One cannot test theories about the efficacy of different approaches unless one has the tools with which to differentiate the approaches. Distinguishing one practice from another is important — not for purposes of honing a definition, but for purposes of learning. . . . Even if we are incapable of delimiting the outer boundaries of practice, we may nonetheless benefit from clearer intra-practice categories. Neither necessarily depends on the other being strictly fixed.

Chapter 8
MAJOR MEDIATION MATTERS

A. INTRODUCTION

This Chapter addresses three important mediation topics. Most of the discussion is equally applicable to other procedures where a third party neutral assists the parties in resolving disputes. The important topic of good faith participation in mediation is examined in Chapter Ten, because that matter arises most commonly in the context of court-connected ADR.

Section B considers the considerable volume of reported cases about mediation. Section C examines confidentiality issues related to mediation and mediators. The norm (default position) is silence with regard to all aspects of mediation, but the nature and extent of exceptions is a vexed subject that continues to generate litigation and heated disputes within the ADR community. The Uniform Mediation Act (UMA) is the most important formal attempt to set forth a comprehensive set of standards for mediation confidentiality. (You should consult the text of the UMA, as well as the Texas ADR Act, both found in the Appendix.) We also consider the leading cases on mediation confidentiality. Taken together, the materials in sections B and C cover most of the law of mediation. The obligation to report child and elder abuse, which is not limited to mediators, is considered in Chapter Fifteen, as is the potential malpractice liability of mediators.

Section D examines mediation advocacy, by or on behalf of participants in mediation. While discussions about the benefits of mediation address the nature of the process and the role of the mediator, mediation advocacy focuses on achieving the best possible outcome for a particular party. (The advocate commonly is an attorney, but not always.) Mediation advocacy is about how to represent a client effectively in the cooperative process of mediation and how that role differs from representation in litigation. With the mediator primarily responsible for finding "win-win" solutions, the advocate can place a greater emphasis on winning than is true in negotiation. Of course, advocacy that is too contentious can undermine the cooperation that is the essence of mediation and the goal of finding solutions that work reasonably well for everyone.

B. MEDIATION IN THE COURTS: THE LAW OF MEDIATION

1. Comments and Questions

a. One way of identifying "major" issues in any context, particularly from the perspective of an attorney, is to focus on those questions which are important enough to generate litigation that results in published opinions. As with most definitions, this one is circular, and litigation is not the only indicia of importance, but certainly the large amount of mediation-related litigation described by Coben & Thompson is worthy of careful consideration. Reported cases are only a small part of the litigation iceberg — for every reported decision, there are probably ten or so unreported cases.

b. Professors Coben and Thompson have created a Mediation Case Law web site that offers a litigation update and other interesting ADR information. *See* www.hamline.edu/law/adr

c. The law of mediation in any particular jurisdiction begins with relevant legislation. The Texas ADR Act is reproduced in the Appendix, as is the Uniform Mediation Act. Other statutes may have an impact on mediation and mediators. A notable example is the power, and sometimes the duty, to breach the general obligation of confidentiality to report child and elder abuse. This topic is discussed in Chapter 15.

2. James R. Coben & Peter N. Thompson, *Disputing Irony: A Systematic Look at Litigation About Mediation*, 11 HARV. NEGOT. L. REV. 43 (2006)

Introduction and Principal Conclusions

First, we did not anticipate the sheer volume of litigation about mediation. We have analyzed all 1223 state and federal court mediation decisions available on the Westlaw databases "allstates" and "allfeds" for the years 1999 through 2003. In this five-year span, when general civil case loads were relatively steady or declining nationwide, mediation litigation increased ninety-five percent, from 172 decisions in 1999 to 335 in 2003.

Second, a major surprise from the database is how frequently courts consider evidence of what transpired in mediations. The concerns about confidentiality, paramount among ADR scholars, appear to be of much lesser importance to practitioners, lawyers and judges in the context of adversarial litigation. There are over 300 opinions . . . in which courts considered mediation evidence without either party raising confidentiality issues. Moreover, mediators offered testimony in sixty-seven cases, with objections raised only twenty-two times, and the evidence was precluded in only nine cases. This rather cavalier approach to disclosure of mediation information is certainly at odds with the conventional wisdom positing that confidentiality is central to the mediation process.

Third, the mediation issues being litigated are quite diverse. We expected, and indeed found, large numbers of opinions about mediation confidentiality (152), enforcement of mediated settlements (568), duty to mediate (279), and sanctions (117). However, we did not anticipate the significant number of decisions addressing mediation fee and cost issues (243), ethics/malpractice (98), the intersection between mediation and arbitration (88), the procedural implications of a mediation request or participation (50), or acts or omissions in mediation as a basis for independent claims (20). Equally surprising was the dearth of cases addressing mediator misconduct, which was asserted as a contract defense only seventeen times in five years. Either the concern about coercive mediators is unwarranted or the litigation process does not provide an appropriate forum to address this issue.

Most of the enforcement cases raised traditional contract defenses. One general conclusion to be drawn from the data set is that, in litigation, existing legal norms force defects in the mediation process to be framed in terms identical to those used to address issues that plague unfacilitated party-bargaining. Thus, when parties attempt to enforce mediation settlements in court, the litigation focuses on typical contract issues, such as claims of unenforceable agreements to agree, failure to have a meeting of the minds, fraud, changed circumstances, and mistake. These traditional contract defenses may not adequately protect the fairness of the mediation process. Rarely has a mediation participant successfully defended against enforcement of a mediated agreement based on a traditional contract defense. These contractual defenses were developed in the context of a free enterprise bargaining process and may not be sufficient to ensure a fair facilitative process and a self-determined agreement.

In light of these trends and others, we make recommendations for statute and rule reform, ranging from the use of "cooling off" periods during which parties are free to exercise a right of rescission of a mediated settlement, to the adoption of special confidentiality rules regarding third party access to mediation evidence. We also offer a number of best practice suggestions for advocates, neutrals and mediation consumers. Some discourage particular behavior, such as over-promising on mediation confidentiality or continuing mediation when decision-makers leave the room; others encourage behavior, such as obtaining a signed agreement to mediate, aggressively investigating and disclosing conflicts of interest, or anticipating that drafting releases may be difficult. The good news is that the misery and expense incurred by the unfortunate parties forced to litigate their mediation mistakes provide valuable lessons for those willing to review them. . . .

II. Confidentiality

The database contains 152 opinions where courts considered a mediation confidentiality issue, including fifteen state supreme court decisions and eight federal circuit court opinions. The number of cases raising confidentiality issues more than doubled between 1999 and 2003, from seventeen to forty-three. In a number of opinions, confidentiality issues were commonly interlinked with other mediation dispute issues: enforcement (46); ethics/malpractice (21); sanctions (21); fees (18); mediation-arbitration (9); and duty to mediate (8).

The majority of the confidentiality opinions (130) considered whether to permit testimony or discovery from mediation participants. Courts upheld statutory or rule limitations on availability of such evidence in fifty-seven opinions (44%), upheld limitations in part in eight cases (6%), and declined to protect confidentiality in sixty opinions (46%). In five cases (4%), the issue was left undecided. The balance of the confidentiality decisions (22) address a range of questions other than admissibility or discovery, most commonly judicial disqualification or consequences for breach of confidentiality agreements.

While these confidentiality disputes certainly merit discussion, the more significant finding is the large volume of opinions in which courts considered detailed evidence of what transpired in mediations without a confidentiality issue being raised — either by the parties, or sua sponte by the court. Indeed, uncontested mediation disclosures occurred in thirty percent of all decisions in the database, cutting across jurisdiction, level of court, underlying subject matter, and litigated mediation issues. Included are forty-five opinions in which mediators offered testimony, sixty-five opinions where others offered evidence about mediators' statements or actions, and 266 opinions where parties or lawyers offered evidence of their own mediation communications and conduct — all without objection or comment. In sum, the walls of the mediation room are remarkably transparent.

III. Enforcement of Mediated Settlement Agreements

The mediation issue most frequently litigated involved the attempt to enforce a mediation agreement. Enforcement issues, raised in 568 opinions (46% of the opinions in the database), include many of the highly publicized mediation cases. For example, *Olam v. Congress Mortgage Co.*, 68 F. Supp. 2d 1110 (N.D. Cal. 1999), an opinion cited in over sixty legal journal articles, involved a mortgage company's attempt to enforce an agreement reached after a lengthy mediation session with a sixty-five-year-old woman in poor health. In *Haghighi v. Russian-American Broadcasting Co.*, 173 F.3d 1086, 1089 (8th Cir. 1999), cited in forty-four articles, the Eighth Circuit refused to enforce a written, signed mediation agreement that did not include specific words required by a Minnesota statute. In *Vernon v. Acton*, 732 N.E.2d 805, 806 (Ind. 2000), cited in forty-eight articles, the Indiana Supreme Court did not enforce an alleged oral mediation agreement because of court rules making oral mediation communications confidential.

Hundreds of less familiar cases detail a wide range of enforcement disputes. Many focus on traditional contract defenses, but others deal with legal technicalities unique to mediation, or the impact of a mediated settlement on third parties. Included in the latter category are nearly three dozen opinions in class action cases in which the judge ruled on whether to approve a settlement that was obtained through mediation. In most of the enforcement cases (362), the courts enforced the alleged mediation agreement in whole or in part. Courts refused to enforce the alleged agreement in ninety-two opinions and remanded the case for further consideration in fifty-three cases. Some cases were resolved on procedural issues, so the court never decided whether to enforce the agreement. Of the ninety-two enforcement cases where the alleged mediation agreement was not enforced, twenty-eight were contract or commercial cases, and twenty-five were family law cases. In only six personal injury cases did a court refuse to enforce an alleged mediated settlement agreement.

Numerous commentators have expressed concern about fairness in the mediation process. If unfair practices are common in the mediation process, however, they are not causing courts to disregard the mediated settlement agreements with any frequency. Several explanations are possible. The most obvious conclusion is that, notwithstanding the commentators' concerns, fundamental unfairness is uncommon in mediation practices. This conclusion is reinforced by numerous studies that find high satisfaction ratings among participants in mediations. A second explanation could be that courts are not carefully scrutinizing the fairness of the mediation process out of self-interest — mediation eliminates numerous cases from the court dockets. It is also possible that confidentiality rules in some jurisdictions may shield potentially unfair mediation processes from judicial review or that the application of traditional contract law does not adequately assure fair mediation processes.

IV. Conduct of Participants

In ninety-nine opinions, courts ruled on issues relating to ethics or malpractice in mediation. Sixty-one of the opinions were published decisions, including twenty-one state supreme court cases and three federal circuit court decisions. The cases break into five general categories, listed in order of frequency: neutral misconduct (34); lawyer malpractice (30); lawyer discipline (19); judicial ethics (11); and lawyer conflict of interest (5). Often, the ethics issue is part of a larger dispute about mediation. Seventeen ethics/malpractice opinions were raised in the context of challenges to enforcement of mediated settlements; twenty-two opinions also addressed confidentiality, and twelve discussed issues at the intersection of arbitration and mediation. . . .

During the five-year period covered by the database, there were only four cases naming mediators as defendants. All four were dismissed on the pleadings or by summary judgment in the mediator's favor. *Goad v. Ervin*, 2003 WL 22753608 (Cal. Ct. App. Nov. 21, 2003) (asserting quasi-judicial immunity to preclude suit against mediator for alleged defamation and filing of a false document); *Jefferson v. William R. Ridgeway Family Courthouse*, 2002 WL 819859 (Cal. Ct. App. May 1, 2002) (relying on statutory litigation privilege to affirm dismissal of claim that alleged that mediator had falsified mediation investigation report prepared in context of child custody proceedings); *Jewell v. Underwood*, 2000 WL 1867565 (Ohio Ct. App. Dec. 22, 2000) (dismissing claim that mediator committed fraud by falsely representing that "she was trained as a mediator and . . . could ably provide mediation services" in family law matter); *Lehrer v. Zwernemann*, 14 S.W.3d 775, 777-78 (Tex. App. 2000) (failure by mediator to affirmatively disclose relationship with opposing counsel could not be basis for [liability] where the complaining party had "constructive knowledge" of the prior relationship between the mediator and opposing counsel and could not articulate any damages from alleged improper behavior). . . .

V. Duty to Mediate/Condition Precedent

Disputes about parties' obligations to participate in mediation are detailed in 279 cases in the database, including 122 opinions coded as condition precedent cases, where mediation could be considered a mandatory pre-condition to litigation or arbitration. There were twenty-one state supreme court decisions and twenty-five federal circuit court decisions. These types of disputes more than tripled in frequency between 1999 and 2003, from twenty-one to seventy-three. Collectively, the 279 opinions support a simple principle: courts are inclined to order mediation on their own initiative, and will generally enforce a pre-existing obligation to participate in mediation, whether the obligation was judicially created, mandated by statute, or stipulated in the parties' pre-dispute contract. . . . The best overview of judicial authority to compel mediation is provided by *In re Atlantic Pipe Corp.*, 304 F.3d 135 (1st Cir. 2002). . . . The decision exhaustively reviews the four sources of court authority to compel mediation: local court rule; applicable statutes; the Federal Rules of Civil Procedure; and the court's inherent power. [The *Atlantic Pipe* decision is reproduced in Chapter Ten]. A small number of courts . . . refuse to compel mediation when convinced the process will be futile. . . .

In *Liang v. Lai*, 78 P.3d 1212 (Mont. 2003), the Montana Supreme Court denied an unopposed motion to dispense with appellate mediation required by local court rule in all actions seeking monetary damages. In the court's view, even though the issue on appeal was a challenge to an order for change of venue, the determining factor for mediation eligibility was the relief sought in the underlying action and not the type of order or judgment being appealed. Any other approach, reasoned the court, would have doomed the appellate mediation program given initial lawyer hostility.

Successful challenges to judicially compelled mediation are rare, if for no other reason than such orders are viewed as interlocutory and unappealable. Courts favor mediation on efficiency grounds and are willing to exercise power to compel the attendance of necessary parties. Requiring non-party participation, however, is another matter.

Judicial power to compel mediation is not unlimited. . . . In *Connolly v. National School Bus Service, Inc.*, 177 F.3d 593 (7th Cir. 1999), the Seventh Circuit Court of Appeals opined that a party has no obligation to mediate before a District Court judge's law clerk, and failure to participate in such mediation was found to be an impermissible basis for an attorney fee award reduction. Sometimes, the limitation is not on the referral to mediate but on the extent of power delegated to the mediator. For example, in *Martin v. Martin*, 734 So. 2d 1133 (Fla. Dist. Ct. App. 1999), the Florida Court of Appeals found that empowering a mediator to establish a visitation schedule was an improper delegation of judicial authority. . . .

VI. Sanctions for Failure to Mediate or Other Inappropriate Acts

Parties must overcome a number of hurdles to obtain relief for another party's alleged non-participation in mediation. First, not everyone has standing to challenge a failure to mediate. Second, ambiguity about the exact nature of the mediation obligation makes courts unwilling to take action. Third, sometimes there are good factual defenses. . . . Once the court determines an obligation exists and was flouted, however, a range of consequences may ensue. . . . Sanctions may be granted, including attorneys' fees, dismissal, and even contempt. . . .

Courts decided mediation-related fee and cost issues in 243 opinions. There were 135 state cases, including five state supreme court decisions. Federal Circuit Courts of Appeals rendered twenty-six decisions, including at least one decision from each circuit. . . . Fee and cost issues considered by courts divided more or less into four categories: mediation participation (76); sanctions, either for failure to mediate or for other inappropriate acts in mediation (65); compensation for actions to enforce mediated settlements (44); or compensation for the case as a whole, whether settled in mediation or not (54). Many of the fee/cost cases simply list mediation expenses without discussion as part of a laundry list of costs that were granted or denied. . . . Numerous opinions confirm taxation of mediation costs despite the lack of clear statutory or rule authority to do so. . . . Attorneys' fees were awarded as a sanction for a variety of offenses, including failure to attend mediation, failure to have persons with settlement authority present at the mediation, breach of an obligation made in mediation to produce wage statements, insertion of new terms in general releases prepared post-mediation that were not included in the original mediated settlement, or filing an unsealed motion to enforce a mediated settlement in violation of the settlement's confidentiality clause. . . .

Mediation participants sought sanctions for the adverse party's or counsel's conduct during mediation in 117 opinions. Courts imposed sanctions in nearly one-half of those cases (53). The litigation over sanctions was spread evenly among the different types of cases. Parties sought sanctions in thirty-one contract/commercial cases, twenty-nine personal injury cases, twenty-three family law cases, and fifteen employment cases. . . . The claim for sanctions was combined with a claim involving a duty to mediate in sixty-six opinions. The typical issues involved . . . no one appearing at the mediation, or the correct party not appearing at the mediation. Usually, the sanctions included a small fine, attorneys' fees, or costs incurred by the adverse party. For example, in *Segui v. Margrill*, 844 So. 2d 820, 821 (Fla. Dist. Ct. App. 2003), the party sent his attorney to the mediation with "full settlement" authority and was available by telephone during the mediation. Nonetheless, the court granted sanctions, holding that the court's order required the presence of the parties. . . .

X. Lessons Learned

While the database as a whole provides no evidence of systematic coercion or duress corrupting the mediation process, there is a steadily increasing number of enforcement disputes. No doubt, such cases frequently are caused by the buyer's remorse that plagues all negotiations, whether facilitated or not. Compounding the problem is the innocent, but often flawed, overconfidence that the mediated "outline" for settlement will be easily formalized into enforceable legal documents at some later point. Add to this mix the presence of a neutral third party who has a vested interest in attaining settlement, and you have the perfect recipe for an early declaration of "victory" when, in reality, no deal is really done. . . .

More than anything else, the project confirms the development of a broad and evolving "common law" of mediation. . . . Hundreds of litigated cases each year, together with efforts like the drafting of the Uniform Mediation Act, inevitably mean that mediation practice is increasingly defined and standardized by courts and legislatures. The full impact of this aspect of institutionalization remains to be seen. For now, mediators, parties and lawyers must swim in a relative sea of ambiguity. They are brought together in a process designed to honor self-determination and promote collaborative approaches to dispute resolution. Yet the success or failure of such efforts, including the propriety of the individual acts and omissions of its participants, are increasingly judged in the purely adversarial world of litigation. Sophisticated players know and can plan for this ambiguity with careful strategies calculated to achieve maximum advantage. This, of course, inevitably skews the evolution of mediation toward a future where it begins to resemble litigation; mediation becomes an alter ego, not an alternative. This "legalization" of mediation is certainly disturbing to mediation proponents. Far more disturbing, in our view, is the impact of ambiguity on the unsophisticated participant, the one-time player, who risks being lulled into the perceived safety of a non-adversarial process not knowing or anticipating the shadow of litigation just beyond. . . .

C. CONFIDENTIALITY

1. Comments and Questions

a. Confidentiality is a matter of central importance throughout the subject of mediation. The discussion is equally applicable, *mutatis mutandis*, to other forms of dispute resolution conducted with the assistance of a third party.

b. The topic of good faith in mediation is considered in Chapter Ten, in a section titled: What Is the Minimum Acceptable Level of Participation in Court-Connected ADR? While the confidentiality of what transpired, or did not transpire, in a dispute resolution process is a central issue in good faith participation in mediation, this topic arises predominantly in the context of court-annexed dispute resolution processes. While a voluntary mediation not associated with litigation could provide the basis for a lack of good faith participation claim, this happens infrequently. In addition, relief would require resort to the judicial process.

c. State statutes commonly override normal confidentiality rules by permitting or requiring certain professionals to report specified conduct, with child abuse being the most common example. This topic is considered at the end of Chapter Fifteen.

d. The Uniform Mediation Act (UMA), which focuses on confidentiality issues, is set forth in the Appendix. Would you recommend that your state enact the UMA? [To answer this question for a particular jurisdiction requires some knowledge about the current state of the law.]

2. Carol L. Izumi & Homer C. La Rue, *Prohibiting "Good Faith" Reports Under the Uniform Mediation Act: Keeping the Adjudication Camel Out of the Mediation Tent*, 2003 J. DISP. RESOL. 67 (2003)

This article examines. . . the prohibition in the Uniform Mediation Act (UMA) on mediator communication to judges about a party's good faith participation or "problem" behavior in mediation. UMA, § 7(a), subject to narrow exceptions, § 7(b). Early drafts of the UMA contemplated exceptions to the mediation privilege, including claims that a party failed to negotiate in good faith.

[G]ood faith requirements strike at the heart of the mediation process by undermining core mediation values of party self-determination, confidentiality, and third party neutrality. Furthermore, allowing or requiring a mediator to disclose specifics about what occurred during mediation elevates legal values over mediation values. When we refer to "legal values," we refer to those qualities of a lawyer and/or legal institutions which most in the profession would find desirable, useful and important to their role as lawyers and/or to the integrity of various legal institutions. These legal values include judicial control, efficiency of the process, a finding of "right" and "wrong", client advocacy, and defining client interests and needs in terms of legal remedies. "Mediation values" refer to those qualities of the process of mediation and/or those characteristics of the third-party which participants in the process find desirable, useful and important to the ongoing viability and integrity of the process. Mediation values include confidentiality, mediator impartiality and party self-determination. . . .

We conclude . . . that the UMA strikes the correct balance by rejecting arguments in favor of mediator reports to judges and others about the actions and statements of parties during the mediation for the purpose of assessing and sanctioning "bad faith" behavior. For the rare and extreme case, the UMA provides a mechanism to address egregious party behavior, such as lying and fraudulent inducements, causing another party to settle.

3. *National Labor Relations Board v. Joseph Macaluso, Inc.*, 618 F.2d 51 (9th Cir. 1980)

WALLACE, Circuit Judge:

The single issue in this National Labor Relations Board (NLRB) enforcement proceeding is whether the NLRB erred in disallowing the testimony of a Federal Mediation and Conciliation Service (FMCS) mediator as to a crucial fact occurring in his presence. We enforce the order.

Retail Store Employees Union Local 1001 (Union) waged a successful campaign to organize the employees of Macaluso, Inc. (Company). The Company and Union commenced negotiating a collective bargaining agreement. Several months of bargaining between Company and Union negotiators failed to produce an agreement, and the parties decided to enlist the assistance of a mediator from the FMCS. Mediator Douglas Hammond consequently attended the three meetings between the Company and Union from which arises the issue before us. To frame that issue, it is necessary first to describe the history of this litigation.

During the unionization campaign, Company engaged in conduct which led the NLRB to charge it with unfair labor practices. Proceedings were held, and the NLRB ruled that the Company had violated the National Labor Relations Act (NLRA) by threatening pro-union employees and by discharging an employee for union activity. At this unfair labor practice proceeding, the NLRB also found that the Company and Union had finalized a collective bargaining agreement at the three meetings with Hammond, and that the Company had violated the NLRA by failing to execute the written contract incorporating the final agreement negotiated with the Union. The NLRB ordered the Company to execute the contract and pay back-compensation with interest, and now seeks enforcement of that order in this court. In response, the Company contends that the parties have never reached agreement, and certainly did not do so at the meetings with Hammond.

The testimony of the Union before the NLRB directly contradicted that of the Company. The two Union negotiators testified that, during the first meeting with Hammond, the parties succeeded in reducing to six the number of disputed issues, and that the second meeting began with Company acceptance of a Union proposal resolving five of those six remaining issues. The Union negotiators further testified that the sixth issue was resolved with the close of the second meeting, and that in response to a Union negotiator's statement "Well, I think that wraps it up," the Company president said, "Yes, I guess it does." The third meeting with Hammond, according to the Union, was held only hours before the Company's employees ratified the agreement, was called solely for the purpose of explaining the agreement to the Company accountant who had not attended the first two meetings, and was an amicable discussion involving no negotiation.

The Company testimony did not dispute that the first meeting reduced the number of unsettled issues to six, but its version of the last two meetings contrasts sharply with the Union's account. The Company representatives testified that the second meeting closed without the parties having reached any semblance of an agreement, and that the third meeting was not only inconclusive but stridently divisive. While the Union representatives testified that the third meeting was an amicable explanatory discussion, the Company negotiators both asserted that their refusal to give in to Union demands caused the Union negotiators to burst into anger, threaten lawsuits, and leave the room at the suggestion of Hammond. According to the Company, Hammond was thereafter unable to bring the parties together, and the Union negotiators left the third meeting in anger.

In an effort to support its version of the facts, the Company requested that the administrative law judge (ALJ) subpoena Hammond and obtain his testimonial description of the last two bargaining sessions. The subpoena was granted, but was later revoked upon motion of the FMCS. Absent Hammond's tie-breaking testimony, the ALJ decided that the Union witnesses were more credible and ruled that an agreement had been reached. The Company's sole contention in response to this request for enforcement of the resulting order to execute the contract is that the ALJ and NLRB erred in revoking the subpoena of Hammond, the one person whose testimony could have resolved the factual dispute. The Company did not challenge the NLRB's finding of unfair labor practices from the threatening and discharge of employees.

Revocation of the subpoena was based upon a long-standing policy that mediators, if they are to maintain the appearance of neutrality essential to successful performance of their task, may not testify about the bargaining sessions they attend. Both the NLRB and the FMCS (as amicus curiae) defend that policy before us. We are thus presented with a question of first impression before our court: can the NLRB revoke the subpoena of a mediator capable of providing information crucial to resolution of a factual dispute solely for the purpose of preserving mediator effectiveness? . . . Stated differently, we must determine whether the reason for revocation is legally sufficient to justify the loss of Hammond's testimony.

The NLRB's revocation of Hammond's subpoena conflicts with the fundamental principle of Anglo-American law that the public is entitled to every person's evidence. . . . The facts before us present a classic illustration of the need for every person's evidence: the trier of fact is faced with directly conflicting testimony from two adverse sources, and a third objective source is capable of presenting evidence that would, in all probability, resolve the dispute by revealing the truth. Under such circumstances, the NLRB's revocation of Hammond's subpoena can be permitted only if denial of his testimony has a public good transcending the normally predominant principle of utilizing all rational means for ascertaining truth. We thus are required to balance two important interests, both critical in their own setting. We conclude that the public interest in maintaining the perceived and actual impartiality of federal mediators outweighs the benefits derivable from Hammond's testimony.

This public interest was clearly stated by Congress when it created the FMCS: "It is the policy of the United States that . . . the settlement of issues between employers and employees through collective bargaining may be advanced by making available full and adequate governmental facilities for conciliation, mediation, and voluntary arbitration to aid and encourage employers and employees to reach and maintain agreements concerning rates of pay, hours, and working conditions, and to make all reasonable efforts to settle their differences by mutual agreement. . . ." 29 U.S.C. § 171(b).

Since Congress made this declaration, federal mediation has become a substantial contributor to industrial peace in the United States. The FMCS, as *amicus curiae*, has informed us that it participated in mediation of 23,450 labor disputes in fiscal year 1977, with approximately 325 federal mediators stationed in 80 field offices around the country. Any activity that would significantly decrease the effectiveness of this mediation service could threaten the industrial stability of the nation. The importance of Hammond's testimony in this case is not so great as to justify such a threat. Moreover, the loss of that testimony did not cripple the fact-finding process. The ALJ resolved the dispute by making a credibility determination, a function routinely entrusted to triers of fact throughout our judicial system.

The FMCS has promulgated regulations which explain why the very appearance of impartiality is essential to the effectiveness of labor mediation. 29 C.F.R. § 1401.2(a), (b):

> Public policy and the successful effectuation of the FMCS's mission require that . . . labor and management or other interested parties participating in mediation efforts must have the assurance and confidence that information disclosed to commissioners and other employees of the Service will not subsequently be divulged, voluntarily or because of compulsion, unless authorized by the Director of the Service. No person officially connected in any capacity with the Service shall, in response to a subpoena or other judicial or administrative order, produce any material contained in the files of the Service, disclose any information acquired as part of the performance of his official duties or because of his official status, or testify on behalf of any party to any matter pending in any judicial, arbitral or administrative proceeding, without the prior approval of the Director.

During oral argument, the suggestion was made that we permit the mediator to testify, but limit his testimony to "objective facts". . . . We do not believe, however, that such a limitation would dispel the perception of partiality created by mediator testimony. In addition to the line-drawing problem of attempting to define what is and is not an "objective fact," a recitation of even the most objective type of facts would impair perceived neutrality, "for the party standing condemned by the thrust of such a statement would or at least might conclude that the (FMCS) was being unfair. Not even the strictest adherence to purely factual matters would prevent the evidence from favoring or seeming to favor one side or the other.

We conclude, therefore, that the complete exclusion of mediator testimony is necessary to the preservation of an effective system of labor mediation, and that labor mediation is essential to continued industrial stability, a public interest sufficiently great to outweigh the interest in obtaining every person's testimony. No party is required to use the FMCS; once having voluntarily agreed to do so, however, that party must be charged with acceptance of the restriction on the subsequent testimonial use of the mediator. We thus answer the question presented by this case in the affirmative: the NLRB can revoke the subpoena of a mediator capable of providing information crucial to resolution of a factual dispute solely for the purpose of preserving mediator effectiveness.

4. *In re Anonymous*, 283 F.3d 627 (4th Cir. 2002)

PER CURIAM:

This attorney discipline action arises out of a dispute over litigation expenses between an attorney (Local Counsel) and his client (Client), which developed following a successful mediation conducted by the Office of the Circuit Mediator for this Court (the OCM). Local Counsel and Client agreed to resolve their "expense dispute" before an arbitral panel sponsored by the Virginia State Bar (the VSB arbitration). In their submissions to the VSB arbitration, Client, Local

Counsel, and a third party (Current Counsel) (collectively, the participants), disclosed information about or relating to the mediation and also sought responses to interrogatories from the Circuit Mediator. Upon being informed of these disclosures and the discovery effort, the Standing Panel on Attorney Discipline ordered each participant to submit briefs and present argument regarding the propriety of their disclosures in light of the confidentiality provisions of our Local Rule 33. Having considered the various submissions and heard argument in this matter, we undertake to resolve the following issues: (1) whether Client, Local Counsel, and/or Current Counsel breached the confidentiality of the mediation required by Rule 33; (2) whether sanctions are warranted for any breach; (3) whether and under what standard the confidentiality of a mediation may be waived for future disclosures; and (4) whether and under what standard the mediator may divulge information relating to the mediation.

The participants do not deny that they each submitted statements to the VSB arbitration revealing information disclosed during the mediation conference. Despite the apparent violations of the plain language of the Rule, the participants maintain, for a variety of reasons, that their disclosures did not violate the confidentiality required by Rule 33.

The participants first argue that their disclosures were not prohibited by Rule 33, because the disclosures did not involve matters central to the mediated dispute. The unambiguous text of Rule 33, however, does not draw the suggested distinction; instead, it prohibits the disclosure of "*all* statements, documents, and discussions." Moreover, because the confidentiality provision, as written, provides clear guidance in the form of a bright line rule, we decline to adopt an exception allowing for the disclosure of matters collaterally related to the mediation.

The participants next argue that, because their submissions were made to a confidential forum, the submissions should not be construed as violating Rule 33. Again, the unambiguous text of Rule 33 does not provide an exception for disclosures made to a confidential forum. Rather, it has at all relevant times restricted disclosures "to any other person outside the mediation program participants."

Current Counsel also asserts that, because he was not acting as counsel during the mediation conference and because he was not a party to the mediated dispute when he attended the mediation conference, his disclosures did not fall within the scope of Rule 33. The term "parties," as used in . . . Rule 33, is not limited to the formal parties of the mediated dispute, as Current Counsel asserts, but instead applies to all participants in the mediation, including attendants at the mediation conference. Moreover, it is significant to us that Current Counsel is a lawyer, who was made aware of Rule 33's confidentiality provision prior to his participation in the mediation conference, and who explicitly agreed to abide thereby. . . .

The participants also argue that due process requires us to conclude that their submissions did not violate Rule 33, in that a contrary conclusion would deny Client and Local Counsel the right to resolve their expense dispute. We disagree. Rule 33, in both its current and previous form, does not deprive participants of a forum for resolution of disputes; rather, it limits the availability and use of information gleaned during the mediation in subsequent proceedings. . . . Courts routinely have recognized the substantial interest of preserving confidentiality in mediation proceedings as justifying restrictions on the use of information obtained during the mediation. *Calka v. Kucker Kraus & Bruh,* 167 F.3d 144, 146 (2d Cir.1999) (holding that Second Circuit's rule protecting the confidentiality of matters disclosed during mediation barred use of statements regarding the mediation in a subsequent state court proceeding). Further, Rule 33 does not and has never precluded requests for consent to disclosures, as is evidenced by Local Counsel's attempt to gain the Circuit Mediator's consent to his disclosures and our prompt adoption of Standing Order 01-01 subsequent to this attempt. . . . Accordingly, we reject the participants' claim that due process renders the confidentiality provision of Rule 33 unenforceable.

Finally, in addition to their disclosures about conversations that took place at the mediation conference, Client and Current Counsel disclosed conversations relating to the mediated dispute that took place as the participants were leaving the mediation conference. Client and Current Counsel claim that these disclosures did not violate Rule 33, because they involved conversations that occurred after the mediation had concluded. Although Rule 33 does not specifically define the duration of "mediation" for purposes of maintaining confidentiality, it is plain that the "mediation" is not limited to the mediation conference, but continues until the mediated dispute has been either dismissed or is otherwise removed from the OCM. This conception of the duration of mediation is a practical necessity of the process itself, in that the mediated dispute is rarely conclusively resolved during the mediation conference. Instead, the parties to the dispute often resume mediation, or refine aspects of the settlement agreement, subsequent to the mediation conference, and many times do so outside the presence of the mediator. These conversations and the information disclosed therein are entitled to the same degree of confidentiality as disclosures made during the mediation conference. Accordingly, until a mediated dispute is dismissed or is otherwise removed from the OCM, all "statements, documents, and discussions" relating to the mediation remain within the bailiwick of the OCM and, therefore, remain confidential.

We next turn to the question of whether the violations of Rule 33 committed by Client, Legal Counsel, and Current Counsel warrant the imposition of sanctions by the Standing Panel. In assessing the sanctions issue, we review the totality of the circumstances, and determine, first, whether sanctions are warranted, and if warranted, the severity of any such sanctions. In so doing, we analyze and weigh the following and other relevant factors: (1) whether the mediator explained the extent of the confidentiality rules, and the clarity of such explanation; (2) whether the parties executed a confidentiality agreement; (3) the extent of willfulness or bad faith involved in the breach of confidentiality Rule; (4) the severity or adverse impact of the disclosure on the parties or the case; and (5) the severity or adverse impact of the disclosure on the mediation program. *See generally* Robert J. Niemic, et al., *Guide to Judicial Management of Cases in ADR* 104 (Federal Judicial Center 2001) (discussing various considerations regarding the propriety of sanctions).

Applying these factors, we note that the participants agree that the mediator clearly explained the confidentiality provision prior to commencement of the mediation conference and that they each agreed to abide by it. Although no one executed a confidentiality agreement at that time, the settlement agreement, which Client and Local Counsel both signed, contained a confidentiality provision that provides for confidentiality as to all of the "terms of the agreement." On the other hand, at the time of these disclosures, we had not previously interpreted the scope of Rule 33, and Current Counsel, as a participant but not a formal party to the mediated dispute, had some basis, however modest, for asserting that his disclosures did not fall within the literal scope of the former Rule's prohibition. Additionally, Local Counsel had some basis to believe that his disclosures did not breach confidentiality, in that the Model Rules of Professional Conduct provide an exception to confidentiality for disclosures of confidential client information where the disclosures are for the purpose of establishing an attorney's entitlement to compensation. Model Rules of Prof'l Conduct R. 1.6(b)(2) & cmt. 18; Restatement (Third) of Law Governing Lawyers § 65 (1998).

Weighing these factors and considering the participants' statements and submissions before the Standing Panel, we are convinced that none of the participants intended to violate Rule 33, and we are unable to conclude that the disclosures were made in bad faith or with malice. Moreover, the disclosures have not had an adverse impact on the mediated dispute, and because the disclosures were made to a non-public, confidential forum, any adverse impact on the mediation program has been slight. Accordingly, considering the totality of the circumstances, we conclude that the violations of Rule 33 are not sufficient to warrant sanctions in this case. . . .

The participants next contend that, pursuant to Rule 33's provision allowing participants to seek the Standing Panel's approval for future disclosures of confidential information, we should grant a limited waiver of confidentiality to permit the VSB arbitration to consider their previously submitted disclosures in resolving the expense dispute. Local Counsel also argues that we should grant consent for the Circuit Mediator to submit written answers to the informal interrogatories posed in his letter dated March 27, 2001. We address each argument in turn, setting forth the standard by which we will determine whether waiver is appropriate in each context.

To determine when the Standing Panel should grant a waiver of confidentiality to the participants, it is necessary to examine the relevant interests protected by non-disclosure. The assurance of confidentiality is essential to the integrity and success of the Court's mediation program, in that confidentiality encourages candor between the parties and on the part of the mediator, and confidentiality serves to protect the mediation program from being used as a discovery tool for creative attorneys. In a program like ours, where participation is mandatory, and the mediation is directed and sanctioned by the Court, the argument for protecting confidential communications may be even stronger, because participants are often assured that all discussions and documents related to the proceeding will be protected from forced disclosure.

On the other hand, we must recognize that, under certain circumstances, non-disclosure may result in an untenable loss of information to the public and the justice system. We believe that the balance between these interests is best resolved by disallowing disclosure, unless the party seeking such disclosure can demonstrate that "manifest injustice" will result from non-disclosure. Application of the manifest injustice standard requires the party seeking disclosure to demonstrate that the harm caused by non-disclosure will be manifestly greater than the harm caused by disclosure.

In evaluating the harm resulting from non-disclosure, we observe that, in most instances, an expense dispute between lawyer and client should easily be resolved without reference to settlement negotiations, primarily because the client is obligated to reimburse advanced litigation expenses as a matter of the state's ethics rules, independent of mediation proceedings. On the other hand, where an attorney seeks to establish his entitlement to reimbursement of expenses, the attorney typically is permitted to disclose confidential client information.

With these general principles in mind, we turn to our application of the manifest injustice standard to Local Counsel's and Client's submissions. Local Counsel and Client agree that disclosure of information related to the mediation proceedings is critical to resolution of their expense dispute. As Local Counsel and Client note, the expense dispute arose during the mediation conference, and resolution of the dispute requires disclosures relating to the context of the dispute's origination. Additionally, portions of information disclosed during the mediation may shed light on their understanding of the expense obligation at that time. Specifically, Client contends that the disbursement of the settlement proceeds between herself and Local Counsel, which is set forth in the settlement agreement, is evidence that her obligation to reimburse legal expenses was incorporated into Local Counsel's share of the settlement proceeds. In response, Local Counsel argues that conversations that took place during the mediation conference are evidence that Client understood that the settlement agreement did not affect Client's obligation to reimburse the litigation expenses in any manner, and he contends that his notes regarding the settlement conference corroborate his assertion that these conversations took place. Insofar as the mediation conference was the genesis of the expense dispute, and information divulged during the conference is critical to resolution of the expense dispute, the harm resulting from non-disclosure might, in the context of the expense dispute, be substantial.

Further, any harm resulting from disclosure would be slight, in that the contemplated disclosures will be made to a non-public, confidential forum, and all of the attendants of the mediation, excluding the Circuit Mediator, have consented to a limited waiver of confidentiality for disclosures relating to the expense dispute. Additionally, it is significant that little mention needs to be made regarding the mediation of the substantive merits of the appeal. In light of these considerations, we conclude that Local Counsel and Client have demonstrated that non-disclosure of limited and relevant information related to the mediation would cause manifestly greater harm than the disclosure of such information. Accordingly, we grant conditional consent for Local Counsel and

Client to disclose the following limited material: (1) conversations that took place during the mediation regarding the expense dispute and their notes, or portions thereof, regarding the settlement negotiations corroborating these conversations; and (2) the settlement agreement and notes regarding the settlement agreement, but only to the extent that these materials explain or relate to the disbursement of the settlement funds. Our consent is conditioned upon Local Counsel and Client securing from the VSB arbitral panel its written agreement to abide by Rule 33's confidentiality provision. We caution Local Counsel and Client to adhere strictly to the parameters of this limited waiver, and we direct that all previous submissions outside the confines of this waiver be withdrawn from the VSB arbitration.

With respect to Current Counsel's disclosures, our analysis is impacted by different considerations. In Current Counsel's submitted statement to the VSB arbitral panel, he has detailed his recollection of conversations that he overheard during and after the mediation conference regarding the expense dispute. This submission allows Current Counsel impermissibly to act as both an advocate and as a witness on behalf of Client in the expense dispute, which is forbidden by the Rules of Professional Conduct. Regardless of the extent to which Current Counsel's statement may be necessary or helpful in resolving the expense dispute, we decline to grant consent for him to violate his ethical obligation to refrain from acting as both an advocate and a material witness on behalf of Client. If, however, Current Counsel withdraws as Client's attorney in the expense dispute, we grant consent for Current Counsel's disclosures, subject to the same conditions and limitations that we have set forth with respect to Local Counsel and Client. Assuming that Current Counsel does not withdraw as Client's advocate, we direct Current Counsel to retract all documents previously submitted to the VSB arbitration in his capacity as a witness of the mediation.

Turning to the question of whether to consent for the Circuit Mediator to divulge information related to the mediation, we observe that allowing disclosures by the mediator in subsequent proceedings implicates concerns well beyond those implicated by disclosures of other participants to a mediation. For example, our granting of consent for the mediator to participate in any manner in a subsequent proceeding would encourage perceptions of bias in future mediation sessions involving comparable parties and issues, and it might encourage creative attorneys to attempt to use our court officers and mediation program as a discovery tool. Thus, we will consent for the Circuit Mediator to disclose confidential information only where such disclosure is mandated by manifest injustice, is indispensable to resolution of an important subsequent dispute, and is not going to damage our mediation program.

Local Counsel has failed to establish that the expense dispute is incapable of resolution absent the Circuit Mediator's involvement. Further, Client objects to the Circuit Mediator's involvement, contending that she will be biased in her responses to Local Counsel's inquiries. And the mediation program may be damaged when a party who has been assured of confidentiality subsequently faces a disclosure of confidential material by a mediator who is perceived, rightly or wrongly, as biased. This perception of bias is the type of damage against which our confidentiality rule, as applied to the Circuit Mediator, is attempting to protect. Accordingly, we decline to consent for the Circuit Mediator to . . . disclose confidential information in the expense dispute.

5. *Goodyear Tire & Rubber Co. v. Chiles Power Supply, Inc.*, 332 F.3d 976 (6th Cir. 2003)

SUHRHEINRICH, Circuit Judge.

Defendant Chiles is a national manufacturer of heating and snowmelt systems. Chiles purchased a significant amount of "Entran II" rubber hose from Goodyear. Chiles subsequently incorporated the hose into a hydronic radiant heating and snowmelt system, which it then sold to Julian and other homeowners in and around Vail, Colorado. Julian and other Colorado homeowners intervened in this action and moved the district court to vacate or modify a confidentiality order. Julian appeals from the district court's denial of his petition to vacate the order which prevents either of the named parties from discussing the contents of settlement negotiations. The issue presented on appeal is whether statements made in furtherance of settlement are privileged and protected from third-party discovery. We affirm the decision of the district court and find that they are. . . .

There exists a strong public interest in favor of secrecy of matters discussed by parties during settlement negotiations. This is true whether settlement negotiations are done under the auspices of the court or informally between the parties. The ability to negotiate and settle a case without trial fosters a more efficient, more cost-effective, and significantly less burdened judicial system. In order for settlement talks to be effective, parties must feel uninhibited in their communications. Parties are unlikely to propose the types of compromises that most effectively lead to settlement, unless they are confident that their proposed solutions cannot be used on cross examination, under the ruse of "impeachment evidence," by some future third party. Parties must be able to abandon their adversarial tendencies to some degree. They must be able to make hypothetical concessions, offer creative *quid pro quos*, and generally make statements that would otherwise belie their litigation efforts. Without a privilege, parties would more often forego negotiations for the relative formality of trial. Then, the entire negotiation process collapses upon itself, and the judicial efficiency it fosters is lost.

Moreover, confidential settlement communications are a tradition in this country. This Court has always recognized the need for, and the constitutionality of, secrecy in settlement proceedings. In *In re the Cincinnati Enquirer*, 94 F.3d 198, 199 (6th Cir. 1996), and *Cincinnati Gas & Elec. Co. v. General Elec. Co.*, 854 F.2d 900, 903-04 (6th Cir. 1988), we denied members of the press access to pretrial settlement procedures, relying on the historical secrecy in settlement talks. Although not recognizing a privilege as such, we stated that the need for privacy in settlement talks outweighed any First Amendment right of access to the proceedings. In each case, we addressed whether there exists a right of access to summary jury trials. In *Cincinnati Enquirer*, we found that summary jury trials are essentially settlement proceedings, and no "tradition of accessibility" because "settlement proceedings are historically closed procedures." In *Cincinnati Gas & Elec.,* we found likewise: "historically settlement techniques are closed procedures rather than open." . . .

Other courts have gone further and recognized the existence of some sort of *formal* settlement privilege. . . . Settlement negotiations are typically punctuated with numerous instances of puffing and posturing, since they are "motivated by a desire for peace rather than from a concession of the merits of the claim." *United States v. Contra Costa County Water Dist.,* 678 F.2d 90, 92 (9th Cir. 1982). What is stated as fact on the record could very well not be the sort of evidence which the parties would otherwise actually contend to be wholly true. That is, the parties may assume disputed facts to be true for the unique purpose of settlement negotiations. The discovery of these sort of "facts" would be highly misleading if allowed to be used for purposes other than settlement. *See Wyatt v. Security Inn Food & Beverage, Inc.,* 819 F.2d 69, 71 (4th Cir. 1987). The public policy favoring secret negotiations, combined with the inherent questionability of the truthfulness of any statements made therein, leads us to conclude that a settlement privilege should exist, and that the district court did not abuse its discretion in refusing to allow discovery. . . .

The fact that Rule 408 provides for exceptions to inadmissibility does not disprove the concept of a settlement privilege. . . . The exceptions have been used only to admit the occurrence of settlement talks or the settlement agreement itself for "another purpose." *See, e.g., Breuer Elec. Mfg. Co. v. Toronado Sys. of Am., Inc.,* 687 F.2d 182, 185 (7th Cir. 1982) (holding existence of settlement negotiations admissible to rebut claim that party had no knowledge of suit); *Prudential Ins. Co. of Am. v. Curt Bullock Builders, Inc.,* 626 F. Supp. 159, 165 (N.D. Ill. 1985) (holding occurrence of settlement talks admissible to establish agency relationship). Thus, as with other privileges, the relationship itself is not privileged, but only the underlying communications.

The settlement privilege is also necessary, because permitting third-party discovery of negotiation communications would lead to other undesirable results. In general, and in this case, there is no transcript of the settlement talks. And it is unlikely that there exist any written notes reflecting Goodyear's alleged attempt to bribe Chiles. Thus, in order to obtain or refute any evidence, the parties would have to depose each of the persons present at the negotiations. . . .

6. *Foxgate Homeowners' Ass'n, Inc. v. Bramalea Cal., Inc.,* 25 P.3d 1117, 1126 (Cal. 2001)

BAXTER, J. (for a unanimous court)

The questions we address here are independent of the issues in the underlying lawsuit. Instead, we face the intersection between court-ordered mediation, the confidentiality of which is mandated by law, Evid.Code, §§ 703.5, 1115-1128, and the power of a court to control proceedings before it and other persons "in any manner connected with a judicial proceeding before it," Code Civ. Proc.,

§ 128(a)(5), by imposing sanctions on a party or the party's attorney for statements or conduct during mediation.

The Court of Appeal held that, notwithstanding § 1119, which governs confidentiality of communications during mediation and § 1121, which limits the content of mediators' reports, the mediator may report to the court a party's failure to comply with an order of the mediator and to participate in good faith in the mediation process. In doing so, the mediator may reveal information necessary to place sanctionable conduct in context, including communications made during mediation. The court concluded, however, that in this case, the report included more information than necessary. It, therefore, reversed a trial court order imposing sanctions on defendants and defendants' attorney.

We granted review to consider whether §§ 1119 and 1121 are subject to any exceptions. We conclude that there are no exceptions to the confidentiality of mediation communications or to the statutory limits on the content of mediator's reports. Neither a mediator nor a party may reveal communications made during mediation. The judicially created exception fashioned by the Court of Appeal is inconsistent with the language and the legislative intent underlying §§ 1119 and 1121. We also conclude that, while a party may do so, a mediator may not report to the court about the conduct of participants in a mediation session. We nonetheless affirm the judgment of the Court of Appeal, as that judgment sets aside the order imposing sanctions.

The underlying litigation is a construction defects action in which the defendants are the developers, Bramalea, and various subcontractors. The plaintiff is a homeowners association made up of the owners of a . . . condominium complex developed and constructed by defendants. In a comprehensive January 22, 1997 case management order (CMO), . . . the superior court appointed Judge Peter Smith, a retired judge, as a special master to act as both mediator and special master for ruling on discovery motions. Judge Smith was given the power to preside over mediation conferences and to make orders governing attendance of the parties and their representatives at those sessions. Defendants were ordered to serve experts' reports on all parties prior to the first scheduled mediation session. The order confirmed that privileges applicable to mediation and settlement communications applied. The parties were ordered to make their best efforts to cooperate in the mediation process.

Bramalea, was (and continues to be) represented by Ivan K. Stevenson. The record reflects that, on the morning of September 16, 1997, the first day of a five-day round of mediation sessions of which the parties had been notified and to which the court's notice said they should bring their experts and claims representatives, plaintiff's attorney and nine experts appeared for the session. Stevenson was late and brought no defense experts. Subsequent mediation sessions were canceled . . . because the mediator concluded they could not proceed without defense experts.

Two days after the aborted mediation session, Judge Smith filed the report that is the object of this dispute with the superior court. . . . The report of the mediator stated: "Mr. Stevenson has spent the vast majority of his time trying to derail the mediations . . . Mr. Stevenson has refused to make demands on the sub-contractor/cross-defendants who were sued by Bramalea defendants. On September 16, 1997, Mr. Stevenson arrived 30 minutes late. Even though the purpose of the mediation session was to have Bramalea's expert witnesses interact with plaintiff's experts on construction defect issues, Mr. Stevenson refused to bring his experts to the mediation. . . ."

Plaintiff filed a motion . . . for the imposition of sanctions of $25,000 on Bramalea and Stevenson (Bramalea/Stevenson) for their failure to cooperate in mediation. The sanctions sought reflected the cost to plaintiff of counsel's preparation for the sessions, the charges of plaintiff's nine experts for preparation and appearance at the mediation session, and the payment to the mediator, which was no longer refundable. Plaintiff's memorandum of points and authorities and declaration of counsel in support of the motion for sanctions recited a series of actions by Bramalea and Stevenson that, plaintiff asserted, reflected a pattern of tactics pursued in bad faith and solely intended to cause unnecessary delay. The actions described included objections to the schedule and attempts to postpone the mediation sessions, and culminated with Stevenson's appearance without experts at the mediation session at which architectural and plumbing issues were to be discussed.

The motion recited that, when asked by plaintiff's counsel if he would have expert consultants present for the future mediation sessions, Stevenson replied that "I can't answer that." When asked why he had arrived without expert consultants, Stevenson replied: "This is your mediation, you can handle it any way you want. I'm here, you can talk to me." In an ensuing conversation, Stevenson said that regardless of settlement between plaintiff and the subcontractors, who had not appeared in the case, Bramalea would not allow the subcontractors to get out of the case and, in a cross-complaint, sought indemnity from them. . . .

Bramalea/Stevenson opposed the motion on numerous grounds, advising that a new mediator had been agreed upon, but in claiming that the motion was improper, did not assert confidentiality of the mediation sessions as a basis for the opposition. They objected to the declaration of plaintiff's counsel regarding events during the mediation session on grounds of hearsay (§ 1200) and on the basis that the declarant offered no foundation for how he was able to recall the statements exactly. They objected to the content of the report of the mediator, but again did not assert the confidentiality of mediation, instead giving their own version of the events during mediation. . . .

The superior court denied this first motion without prejudice. . . . After one mediation session, the new mediator advised the court that further mediation would not be constructive and recommended that the discovery stay be lifted. Bramalea filed a motion seeking return of mediation fees to be paid to Judge Smith, asserting that the mediator was biased and had done nothing during the mediation process to further the mediation, again describing events during the mediation. A new declaration by Judge Smith was offered in support of an opposition to that motion. This declaration stated that Stevenson had aborted the September 1997 mediation session by refusing to participate in good faith.

Plaintiff filed a new motion for sanctions in May 1998, seeking $31,000 based on the same grounds as the first motion and supported by the same declaration of its counsel and the initial report of Judge Smith. In their opposition to this motion, Bramalea/Stevenson asserted the same reasons put forth in the original opposition, adding an objection based on § 1121. . . . Plaintiff's second motion for sanctions was granted by the superior court. Bramalea/Stevenson filed a timely notice of appeal, . . . [contending] that the superior court violated the confidentiality of mediation when the judge considered the report of the mediator in assessing the events and communications that occurred during the September 1997 mediation in imposing sanctions on them. . . .

The Court of Appeal concluded that the rule precluding judicial construction of an unambiguous statute should not apply here. It invoked instead the rule that permits judicial construction of an apparently unambiguous statute where giving literal meaning to the words of the statute would lead to an absurd result or fail to carry out the manifest purpose of the Legislature. With regard to the latter, the court acknowledged that the purpose of the confidentiality mandated by § 1119, which makes evidence of anything said during mediation inadmissible and undiscoverable, is to promote mediation as an alternative to judicial proceedings and that confidentiality is essential to mediation. The Court of Appeal reasoned, however, that it should balance against that policy recognition that, unless the parties and their lawyers participate in good faith in mediation, there is little to protect. It concluded that the Legislature did not intend statutory mandated confidentiality to create an immunity from sanctions that would shield parties who disobey valid orders governing the parties' participation. The Court of Appeal also expressed doubt that § 1121 was intended to preclude a report to the trial court if the parties engaged in improper conduct by attacking or threatening to attack an opposing party. In sum, § 1121 was not intended to shield sanctionable conduct.

Relying on the statement of purpose offered by the California Law Revision Commission at the time the section was proposed, the Court of Appeal concluded that § 1121 served to preserve mediator neutrality and prevent coercion of the parties. The Law Revision Commission Comment on Evidence Code § 1121 . . . states, in pertinent part: "A mediator should not be able to influence the result of a mediation or adjudication by reporting or threatening to report to the decisionmaker on the merits of the dispute or reasons why mediation failed to resolve it. Similarly, a mediator should not have authority to resolve or decide the mediated dispute and should not have any function for the adjudicating tribunal with regard to the dispute, except as a nondecisionmaking neutral." 27 Cal. Law Revision Com. Rep. 595, 602 (1997).

The Court of Appeal acknowledged that it was creating a nonstatutory exception to the confidentiality requirements. The court described the exception as narrow, permitting a mediator or party to report to the court only information that is reasonably necessary to describe sanctionable conduct and place that conduct in context. The report in this case was not so limited. It included extraneous information, recommendations, conclusions, and characterized the conduct and statements reported, all matters for argument by the parties, not a report by a neutral. The Court of Appeal cautioned: "The report should be no more than a strictly neutral account of the conduct and statements being reported along with such other information as required to place those matters in context." The

Court of Appeal directed the trial court to disregard any portions of the report or the declarations submitted by the parties that did not conform to this limitation.

Bramalea/Stevenson claim that any exception that permits reporting to the court and sanctioning a party on the basis of a mediator's report of conduct or statements allegedly undertaken in bad faith during mediation violates the statutes that guaranty confidentiality of mediation. And, notwithstanding the limited scope of the exception the Court of Appeal believed it had created, numerous *amici curiae* with an interest in alternative dispute resolution urge the court to enforce the statutory rule of absolute confidentiality. . . .

The language of §§ 1119 and 1121 is clear and unambiguous, but the Court of Appeal reasoned that the Legislature did not intend these sections to create "an immunity from sanctions, shielding parties to court-ordered mediation who disobey valid orders governing their participation in the mediation process, thereby intentionally thwarting the process to pursue other litigation tactics." The court, therefore, crafted the exception in dispute here. As stated and as applied, the exception created by the Court of Appeal permits reporting to the court not only that a party or attorney has disobeyed a court order governing the mediation process, but also that the mediator or reporting party believes that a party has done so intentionally with the apparent purpose of derailing the court-ordered mediation and the reasons for that belief.

Appellants contend that the legislative policies codified in §§ 1119 and 1121 are absolute, except to the extent that a statutory exception exists. The only such exception they acknowledge is the authority of a mediator to report criminal conduct. They argue that the report of the mediator, which plaintiff submitted to the court with its motion for sanctions and which the court considered, was a form of testimony by a person made incompetent to testify and violated the principle that mediators are to assist parties in reaching their own agreement, but ordinarily may not express an opinion on the merits of the case. In permitting consideration of any part of the report, the Court of Appeal has created a vague and inconsistent exception to the mandate of confidentiality, one that the Legislature did not authorize.

Amici curiae suggest that the trial court and Court of Appeal need not have considered Judge Smith to be acting as a mediator when he submitted his report. Had he been classified as a special master ordered to report to the court, his report would not have been subject to the mediation confidentiality statutes and would be governed by the parties' agreement to the CMO provision for reporting. The superior court CMO states: "Judge Peter Smith . . . is appointed as Special Master pursuant to Code of Civil Procedure § 638 et seq., and shall act as mediator for settlement conferences and as discovery referee. The Special Master shall rule on all discovery disputes, shall assist in the implementation of this Order and *shall preside over mediation conferences* and make any orders governing the attendance of parties and their representatives thereat." (Italics added.)

[Alternatively, it has been suggested] that Judge Smith acted as though he was conducting a settlement conference and asks this court to clarify the differences between a settlement conference at which a court may, on its own motion, sanction a party for not participating, Code Civ. Proc., § 177.5, and mediation. . . . We have no occasion to do so here. It seems clear from the record, and the parties appear to agree, that the proceeding about which Judge Smith reported was a mediation proceeding and the judge was acting as a mediator. . . .

We do not agree with the Court of Appeal that there is any need for judicial construction of §§ 1119 and 1121 or that a judicially crafted exception to the confidentiality of mediation they mandate is necessary either to carry out the purpose for which they were enacted or to avoid an absurd result. The statutes are clear. Section 1119 prohibits any person, mediator and participants alike, from revealing any written or oral communication made during mediation. Section 1121 also prohibits the mediator, but not a party, from advising the court about *conduct* during mediation that might warrant sanctions. It also prohibits the court from considering a report that includes information not expressly permitted to be included in a mediator's report. The submission to the court, and the court's consideration of, the report of Judge Smith violated §§ 1119 and 1121.

The legislative intent underlying the mediation confidentiality provisions of the Evidence Code is clear. As all parties and *amici curiae* recognize, confidentiality is essential to effective mediation, a form of alternative dispute resolution encouraged and, in some cases required, by the Legislature. Implementing alternatives to judicial dispute resolution has been a strong legislative policy since at least 1986. In that year, the Legislature enacted provisions for dispute resolution programs, including but not limited to mediation, conciliation, and arbitration, as alternatives to formal court proceedings which it found to be "unnecessarily costly, time-consuming, and complex" as contrasted with noncoercive dispute resolution. . . . By a 1988 amendment of Evidence Code § 703.5, the Legislature made arbitrators as well as judges incompetent to testify about proceedings over which they presided, and a 1993 amendment added mediators as persons incompetent to testify. In 1993, the Legislature gave further impetus to the policy of encouraging mediation when it enacted Code of Civil Procedure § 1775.10 which created a mandatory arbitration or mediation pilot project for Los Angeles County. Statements made by parties during mediation were expressly made subject to the confidentiality provisions of the Evidence Code.

The Legislature extended the same confidentiality to statements made during mediation in a recently enacted early mediation pilot program. (Code Civ. Proc., §§ 1730, 1738.) Corresponding confidentiality provisions may be found in Business and Professions Code § 6200(h) (attorney fee dispute arbitration); Code of Civil Procedure §1297.371 (conciliation in international commercial disputes); Food and Agricultural Code § 54453(b) (agricultural cooperative bargaining associations); Government Code §§ 11420.10-11420.30 (administrative adjudication), 12984-12985 (conciliation, etc., in housing discrimination complaint), 66032-66033 (land use mediation); Insurance Code § 10089.80 (earthquake claim mediation); and Labor Code § 65 (labor dispute mediation).

Heretofore, the only California case upholding admission, over objection, of statements made during mediation in which no statutory exception to confidentiality applied, was *Rinaker v. Superior Court*, 62 Cal. App. 4th 155, 74 Cal. Rptr. 2d 464 (1998), a case that is clearly distinguishable. There, a juvenile court judge conducting a jurisdictional hearing in a delinquency matter ordered disclosure by a volunteer who had mediated a civil harassment action between the victim and juveniles who had engaged in a rock throwing incident. The minors who were the subject of the hearing claimed that the victim's statements at the mediation session differed from his testimony at the delinquency hearing. The Court of Appeal held that, although a delinquency proceeding is a civil action, and the confidentiality provisions were applicable, that statutory right must yield to the minor's due process rights to put on a defense and confront, cross-examine and impeach the victim witness with his prior inconsistent statements. To maintain confidentiality to the extent possible, however, the Court of Appeal stated that the juvenile court judge should first have held an in-camera hearing to weigh the minors' claim of need to question the mediator against the statutory privilege to determine if the mediator's testimony was sufficiently probative to be necessary

Although criticized, *Rinaker* is consistent with our past recognition and that of the United States Supreme Court that due process entitles juveniles to some of the basic constitutional rights accorded adults, including the right to confrontation and cross-examination. In this matter, however, plaintiffs have no comparable supervening due-process-based right to use evidence of statements and events at the mediation session.

In the only other reported case arising in California in which a mediator's testimony about events during mediation was compelled and admitted, a federal magistrate judge, Wayne Brazil, an expert in mediation law, ruled that the testimony of a mediator could be compelled notwithstanding §§ 703.5 and 1119, which were held to be applicable, because the evidence was necessary to establish whether a defaulting party had been competent to enter into a settlement that another party sought to enforce. *Olam v. Congress Mortgage Company*, 68 F. Supp. 2d 1110 (N.D. Cal. 1999). There, the plaintiff had waived confidentiality, and the defendant had agreed to a limited waiver of confidentiality, and the agreement in question fell within the exception of § 1123 for settlement agreements resulting from mediation if the agreement provided that it was enforceable.

Nonetheless, the magistrate judge was not satisfied that the waivers were an adequate basis on which to compel the mediator's testimony, as the mediator had not waived the mediation privilege. After considering *Rinaker,* in which . . . the mediator had not invoked § 703.5, the magistrate judge concluded that a similar weighing process should be used to determine if the parties' interest in compelling the testimony of the magistrate outweighed the state's interest in maintaining confidentiality of the mediation. After doing so, the magistrate judge concluded that the mediator's testimony was the most reliable and probative evidence on the issue, and there was no likely alternative source, the testimony was crucial if the court was to be able to resolve the dispute and was essential to doing justice in the case before him. That case, too, is distinguishable as Bramalea/Stevenson have not waived confidentiality.

The mediator and the Court of Appeal here were troubled by what they perceived to be a failure of Bramalea to participate in good faith in the mediation process. Nonetheless, the Legislature has weighed and balanced the policy that promotes effective mediation by requiring confidentiality against a policy that might better encourage good faith participation in the process. Whether a mediator in addition to participants should be allowed to report conduct during mediation that the mediator believes is taken in bad faith and therefore might be sanctionable under Code of Civil Procedure §128.5(a), is a policy question to be resolved by the Legislature. Although a party may report obstructive conduct to the court, none of the confidentiality statutes currently makes an exception for reporting bad faith conduct or for imposition of sanctions under that section when doing so would require disclosure of communications or a mediator's assessment of a party's conduct, although the Legislature presumably is aware that Code of Civil Procedure § 128.5 permits imposition of sanctions when similar conduct occurs during trial proceedings.

Therefore, we do not agree with the Court of Appeal that the court may fashion an exception for bad faith in mediation, because failure to authorize reporting of such conduct during mediation may lead to "an absurd result" or fail to carry out the legislative policy of encouraging mediation. The Legislature has decided that the policy of encouraging mediation by ensuring confidentiality is promoted by avoiding the threat that frank expression of viewpoints by the parties during mediation may subject a participant to a motion for imposition of sanctions by another party or the mediator who might assert that those views constitute a bad faith failure to participate in mediation. Therefore, even were the court free to ignore the plain language of the confidentiality statutes, there is no justification for doing so here. . . . The [superior] court violated § 1119(a) when it admitted in evidence at the sanctions hearing "anything said . . . in the course of . . . mediation."

The remedy for violation of the confidentiality of mediation is that stated in section 1128: "Any reference to a mediation during any other subsequent noncriminal proceeding is grounds for vacating or modifying the decision in that proceeding, in whole or in part, and granting a new or further hearing on all or part of the issues, if the reference materially affected the substantial rights of the party requesting relief." Inasmuch as the superior court's sole basis for imposing sanctions on Bramalea/Stevenson was allegations in and the material offered in support of the motion for sanctions, it is clear that reference to the mediation materially affected their rights. . . . If, on remand, plaintiff elects to pursue the motion, the trial court may consider only plaintiff's assertion and evidence offered in support of the assertion that Bramalea engaged in conduct that warrants sanctions. No evidence of communications made during the mediation may be admitted or considered.

7. Comments and Questions

a. In *Rojas v. Superior Court*, 93 P.3d 260 (Cal. 2004), the California Supreme Court relied on *Foxgate* in reaffirming — once again, unanimously — its strong stance in favor of confidentiality of mediation communications. The owner of an apartment building sued the contractor for defective construction. Owner collected considerable information about structural defects and conducting air tests within the building. Subsequently, the court entered a case management order (CMO) that called for mediation and provided for confidentiality of everything related to the process, pursuant to Evidence Code § 1119. Subsequently, the matter was settled in mediation, with the final agreement calling for as much confidentiality as allowed by law.

These developments were mere prologue to the *Rojas* case, in which the apartment tenants sued the owner and the contractor for their losses due to defective construction. As one would expect, the tenant group sought broad discovery regarding the owner-contractor proceeding, and mediation confidentiality was interposed as a defense to disclosure. In rejecting the discovery request of the tenants, even for data collected before suit was filed, the trial judge noted that information important for supporting the tenant's claims could be obtained only from the owner and contractor.

The court of appeals ruled for the tenants, holding that § 1119 did not protect "pure evidence," but only "the substance of mediation, i.e., the negotiations, communications, admissions, and discussions designed to reach a resolution of the dispute at hand." The court relied on § 1120 (a), which provides that "[e]vidence otherwise admissible or subject to discovery outside of a mediation . . . shall not be or become inadmissible or protected from disclosure solely by reason of its introduction or use in a mediation." The California Supreme Court rejected this approach, in an opinion larded with quotations from *Foxgate* and strongly supportive of mediation confidentiality.

b. Sarah Williams, *Confidentiality in Mediation: Is It Encouraging Good Mediation or Bad Conduct?*, 2005 J. OF DIS. RESOL. 209, argues that *Rojas* was wrongly decided, and that a contrary result could easily be squared with *Foxgate*. The various statutory arguments were not determinative, so the matter came down to a policy choice. "Because of the possibility of injustice to a party such as the *Rojas* plaintiffs, and because this injustice should outweigh the importance of encouraging mediation, the Supreme Court should have upheld the appellate court's decision." The *amicus* brief of the Southern California Mediator Association argued for limited disclosure, because otherwise, "the approach taken by defendants would make mediation a tool for burying unfavorable evidence." That, in turn, undermines the integrity of mediation, and discourages the use of mediation, at least prior to discovery, due to a fear that the other party could use mediation to shield evidence.

c. Laura A. Stoll, *"We Decline to Address": Resolving the Unanswered Questions Left by* Rojas v. Superior Court *to Encourage Mediation and Prevent the Improper Shielding of Evidence*, 53 UCLA L. REV. 1549 (2006), supports the *Rojas* decision but expresses concern that the protection of materials "prepared for mediation" could be used to shield potentially damaging evidence. The author proposes that the "prepared for mediation" standard should be taken seriously, and the courts should require proof that material was, in fact, prepared exclusively for mediation, thereby excluding from protection materials created in the litigation context, even if used in mediation. Parties claiming protected status for mediation materials should be prohibited from using it in subsequent litigation.

d. How would you decide the *Rojas* case? Can the trial courts pick out the occasional situation where discovery is truly important, or would the result be a slippery slope that leads to much discovery of mediation communications, and ends up undermining the process. Even if the courts are firm about confidentiality, will permitting exceptions result in expensive satellite litigation and associated delay? (If discovery proceeds, that is expensive; if discovery is stayed, important evidence may be lost.)

e. Based on *Williams v. New Jersey*, how do you think the New Jersey Supreme Court would decide the *Rojas* case? Do you agree with the *Williams* decision? (A sharp dissent is omitted.) What is the precise holding in *Williams* (if there is one)?

8. *State v. Williams*, 877 A.2d 1258 (N.J. 2005) (5-2 decision)

JUSTICE ZAZZALI delivered the opinion of the Court.

In this appeal, we must decide whether a mediator appointed by a court under *Rule* 1:40 may testify in a subsequent criminal proceeding regarding a participant's statements made during mediation. Defendant's brother-in-law phoned defendant and left several taunting messages, leading to a face-to-face argument that quickly escalated into a physical fight. Defendant claims that his brother-in-law hit him in the shoulder with a large construction shovel. The brother-in-law counters that defendant retrieved a machete from the trunk of his car and cut the brother-in-law's wrist and foot. Police later apprehended defendant in his apartment where they found a machete.

After his arrest, defendant filed a municipal court complaint against his brother-in-law, alleging that the phone messages constituted harassment. The municipal court, in accordance with *Rule* 1:40, appointed a mediator in an attempt to resolve the harassment dispute. The mediation was unsuccessful, and the mediator referred the matter back to municipal court.

A grand jury later indicted defendant for aggravated assault and two charges of possession of a weapon. Defendant asserted self-defense as his primary theory and proffered the mediator as a defense witness. Questioned by the court outside of the jury's presence, the mediator indicated that the brother-in-law stated during the mediation session that he had wielded the shovel. The court, however, excluded that testimony under *Rule* 1:40-4(c), which prohibits a mediator from testifying in any subsequent proceeding. Defendant was convicted of assault and a weapons charge. The Appellate Division upheld the trial court's exclusion of the mediator's testimony and affirmed defendant's conviction. For the reasons set forth below, we . . . affirm. . . .

At trial, Renee Oliver, who was testifying for the State, pointed out Hall, the mediator, who was seated in the audience section of the courtroom. At a recess, defense counsel spoke with Hall and then requested permission to call him as a defense witness. With the jury excused, the court interviewed Hall, who confirmed that he was the mediator who conducted the mediation between defendant and Bocoum more than a year earlier. He said that he attended the trial because defendant had stopped by his house and told him that the trial was scheduled to start. Although Hall denied being a "friend" of defendant, he indicated that he lived near defendant's mother, and as a pastor, he was obligated "to be friendly with everybody."

Defendant contends that the mediator's testimony may serve to exculpate him and that the trial court's refusal to allow the mediator to testify deprived him of his right to fully present a defense. Defendant explains that his defense depends on whether he can establish that he acted in self-defense. He maintains that "[t]he relevance and probative value of Pastor Hall's proffered testimony was clear and substantial, as it would have established, from an unbiased witness, that Bocoum indeed wielded a shovel during the fight." Defendant insists that his right to compulsory process was violated when he was unable to proffer the mediator's testimony as substantive evidence that Bocoum had the shovel and to boost defendant's own credibility as a prior consistent statement. Defendant further argues that the trial court's ruling interfered with his ability to impeach the credibility of the State's witnesses regarding their testimony that Bocoum did not charge at defendant with the shovel. Accordingly, defendant urges this Court to relax *Rule* 1:40-4(c) to allow the mediator to testify on remand.

The State opposes relaxation of *Rule* 1:40-4(c). Although the State acknowledges defendant's right to present a complete defense, it argues that that right is not unfettered and that "trial courts may impose reasonable limits upon defense counsel." The State maintains that defendant has not presented compelling reasons for introducing Hall's testimony, and therefore, the trial court's decision was not erroneous. . . .

Rule 1:40-4(c) governs the confidentiality of statements made during mediation: No disclosure made by a party during mediation shall be admitted as evidence against that party in any civil, criminal, or quasi-criminal proceeding. . . . *No mediator may participate in any subsequent hearing or trial of the mediated matter or appear as witness or counsel for any person in the same or any related matter.* (Emphasis added.) In this matter, the mediator's act of testifying constitutes an appearance as a witness. And, although defendant's municipal court proceeding dealt primarily with the allegedly harassing phone messages from Bocoum that precipitated the fight, the municipal action also is a "matter" that is "related" to defendant's "subsequent . . . trial" for assault and weapons charges. Therefore, under a plain reading of *Rule* 1:40-4(c), the trial court correctly prevented the jury from hearing the mediator's testimony.

Defendant asks this Court to relax the *Rule* 1:40-4(c) prohibition of mediator testimony under *Rule* 1:1-2, which provides that court rules "shall be construed to secure a just determination . . . [and] fairness in administration." Unless a rule specifically disallows relaxation, it "may be relaxed or dispensed with by the court in which the action is pending if adherence to it would result in an injustice." The CDR rules allow relaxation or modification if an "injustice or inequity would otherwise result." *Rule* 1:40-10. Justice Clifford's dissent in *Stone v. Township of Old Bridge* captures the spirit that animates *Rule* 1:1-2: "Our Rules of procedure are not simply a minuet scored for lawyers to prance through on pain of losing the dance contest should they trip." 543 A.2d 431 (1988) (Clifford, J., dissenting). Case law and common sense, however, demonstrate that *Rule* 1:1-2 is the exception, rather than the norm.

Determining whether relaxation is appropriate in this appeal requires an examination and balancing of the interests that are at stake. The Fourteenth Amendment guarantees every criminal defendant the right to a fair trial. At its core, that guarantee requires a fair opportunity to defend against the State's accusations. This right is effectuated largely through the several provisions of the Sixth Amendment, which entitles a defendant "to be confronted with the witnesses against him" and "to have compulsory process" to secure testimonial and other evidence. Our State Constitution, containing identical wording, affords those same rights. *N.J. Const.* art. I, ¶ 10.

The confrontation right assures a defendant the opportunity to cross-examine and impeach the State's witnesses. The right to confront and cross-examine accusing witnesses is among the minimum essentials of a fair trial. The right to compulsory process is grounded in similar sentiments: Few rights are more fundamental than that of an accused to present witnesses in his own defense. Together, the rights of confrontation and compulsory process guarantee a meaningful opportunity to present a complete defense. That opportunity would be an empty one if the State were permitted to exclude competent, reliable evidence bearing on . . . credibility . . . when such evidence is central to the defendant's claim of innocence.

But the rights to confront State witnesses and to present favorable witnesses are "not absolute, and may, in appropriate circumstances, bow to competing interests." Generally, courts conducting criminal trials may reject proffers of evidence helpful to the defense, if exclusion serves the interests of fairness and reliability. Because assertions of privilege often undermine the search for truth in the administration of justice, they are accepted only to the extent that they outweigh the public interest in the search for truth.

With that law as a backdrop, we now must determine whether the trial court's exclusion of the mediator's testimony under *Rule* 1:40-4(c) was constitutionally permissible. The recently enacted Uniform Mediation Act (UMA), N.J.S.A. 2A:23C, 1-13, was not in effect when the trial court excluded mediator testimony in this matter. However, two amici, the Committee and the NJSBA, urge this Court to apply the principles expressed in the UMA when determining whether to allow mediator testimony in criminal matters, because the statute "is much more finely tuned and precise than Rule 1:40-4(c)." We agree that the UMA principles are an appropriate analytical framework for the determination whether defendant can overcome the mediator's privilege not to testify.

The UMA protects mediation confidentiality by empowering disputants, mediators, and nonparty participants to "refuse to disclose, and [to] prevent any other person from disclosing, a mediation communication." The privilege yields, however, if a court determines "that the mediation communication is sought or offered in" a criminal proceeding, "that there is a need for the evidence that substantially outweighs the interest in protecting confidentiality," and "that the proponent of the evidence has shown that the evidence is not otherwise available." The burden is on defendant to satisfy these requirements, and he can only prevail if he meets each condition. . . .

The first requirement is clearly satisfied, because defendant is on trial for assault and weapons charges and seeks to introduce evidence of mediation statements into that trial. Therefore, we must assess whether the interest in maintaining mediation confidentiality is outweighed by the defendant's need for the mediator's testimony. Finally, we consider whether the substance of the testimony is available from other sources. Ultimately, we conclude that defendant has not met those requirements and, therefore, cannot defeat the privilege against mediator testimony.

We begin by considering the "interest in protecting confidentiality" and examining the social and legal significance of mediation. An integral part of the increasingly prevalent practice of alternative dispute resolution (ADR), mediation is designed to encourage parties to reach compromise and settlement. The rationale is simple: If settlement offers were to be treated as admissions of liability, many of them might never be made.

Successful mediation, with its emphasis on conciliation, depends on confidentiality, perhaps more than any other form of ADR. *See Foxgate Homeowners' Ass'n, Inc. v. Bramalea Cal., Inc.,* 25 P.3d 1117, 1126 (2001). Confidentiality allows "the parties participating to feel that they may be open and honest among themselves." Without such assurances, disputants may be unwilling to reveal relevant information and may be hesitant to disclose potential accommodations that might appear to compromise the positions they have taken. Indeed, mediation stands in stark contrast to formal adjudication, and even arbitration, in which the avowed goal is to uncover and present evidence of claims and defenses in an adversarial setting. Mediation sessions, on the other hand, "are not conducted under oath, do not follow traditional rules of evidence, and are not limited to developing the facts." Mediation communications, which would not even exist but for the settlement attempt, are made by parties without the expectation that they will later be bound by them. Ultimately, allowing participants to treat mediation as a fact-finding expedition would sabotage its effectiveness.

If mediation confidentiality is important, the appearance of mediator impartiality is imperative. A mediator, although neutral, often takes an active role in promoting candid dialogue by identifying issues and encouraging parties to accommodate each others' interests. To perform that function, a mediator must be able "to instill the trust and confidence of the participants in the mediation process. That confidence is insured if the participants trust that information conveyed to the mediator will remain in confidence. Neutrality is the essence of the mediation process." Thus, courts should be especially wary of mediator testimony, because no matter how carefully presented, it will inevitably be characterized so as to favor one side or the other.

There is a growing body of evidence that mediation is particularly successful at facilitating settlement. A recent study of a court-mandated mediation program in New Jersey found that nearly 40 percent of matters diverted to mediation were resolved at the mediation or within three months afterward, most "with little or no discovery" and the concomitant expense to disputants. *Report of the Committee on Complementary Dispute Resolution on the Evaluation of the Presumptive Mediation Pilot Program 2000-2004,* at 1 (2005) [hereinafter *Pilot Program Report*]. Further, although some litigants who settle an acrimonious lawsuit may feel as though they have achieved nothing more than an "equitable distribution of dissatisfaction," mediation's great strength is that disputants who settle in that forum are generally satisfied with the process and the result, *see Pilot Program Report, supra,* at 1 ("Both mediators' performance and the process itself were rated exceedingly high by both litigants and attorneys responding to post-mediation exit questionnaires.").

Defendant argues that the admission of the mediator's testimony would not "obliterate the whole dispute resolution process" because "the only prejudice posed by Pastor Hall's testimony . . . was inconvenience to the mediator and the municipal court. Such inconvenience was relatively insignificant." According to defendant, mediation participants cannot reasonably expect their assertions to be confidential, because *Rule* 1:40-4(c) allows the admission of statements of a mediation participant if that participant is not a party to the later proceeding where admission is sought. Defendant contends that, as a non-party to this matter, Bocoum has no interest in defendant's prosecution and, therefore, no reason to complain about the manner in which his statements are used.

Defendant's position trivializes the harm that will result if parties are routinely able to obtain compulsory process over mediators. Simply because the mediator does not actually testify *against* the victim (who is, by definition, a non-party to a State criminal prosecution) does not mean that the victim is unaffected by the prospect that his statements, made with assurances of confidentiality, will be used to exculpate the person who victimized him. In such circumstances, the victim could hardly be expected to trust that the mediator was impartial. . . .

Because there is a substantial interest in protecting mediation confidentiality, we must consider defendant's need for the mediator's testimony. To ascertain whether that testimony is "necessary to prove" self-defense, we assess its "nature and quality." The mediator's testimony in this matter does not exhibit the indicia of reliability and trustworthiness demanded of competent evidence. . . . Furthermore, the mediator's testimony does not corroborate defendant's version of what transpired during the fight. . . .

Finally, by asking the mediator to divulge the disputants' statements made during mediation, the defense induced the mediator's breach of confidentiality without first seeking the court's permission. Defendant now seeks to benefit from that breach. Condoning such behavior would encourage all similarly situated defendants to do likewise. As the trial court explained: "[B]ecause someone else has already violated the rule (i.e., defense counsel), that doesn't mean the court should now disregard the rule. That would be solicitation for rules not to be followed." Moreover, the defense failed to comply with evidence rules designed to ensure that only reliable impeachment evidence is put before the jury in a manner that is fair to both parties.

In sum, the mediator's testimony was not sufficiently probative to strengthen defendant's assertion of self-defense. In light of the importance of preserving the role of mediation as a forum for dispute resolution, we conclude that defendant's need for the mediator's testimony does not outweigh the interest in protecting mediation confidentiality. Apart from whether the need for the mediator's testimony outweighed the interest in confidentiality, we also consider whether defendant failed to demonstrate that evidence of Bocoum's use of the shovel was "not otherwise available." Both parties had access to, and presented at trial, substantial evidence from other sources bearing on the issue of self-defense. . . .

We note that defendant's own trial testimony recounted Bocoum's mediation statements about the shovel. Under the UMA, there is a serious question, however, whether defendant should have been allowed to testify at all regarding Bocoum's mediation communications. The UMA's confidentiality provision applies with equal force to a mediation participant, such as defendant, as it does to the mediator. *See N.J.S.A.* 2A:23C-4b. Nonetheless, the parties have not raised that issue before us, and we decline to address it further. . . .

D. MEDIATION ADVOCACY

1. Comments and Questions

a. Is mediation advocacy a separate topic, or merely an integral aspect of the mediation process? After all, people do not cease to be maximizers (optimizers, if you prefer) when they become participants in a mediation — they still prefer "more" to "less," and we should expect that they will advocate for themselves just as in other negotiation situations. These goals may be sought directly, or through agents — often, lawyers.

b. The discussion of mediation advocacy is directed primarily at the mediation advocate. It does not suggest that advocacy will not normally take place in mediation, but rather is addressed to the question of how to advocate effectively in mediation. Mediation advocacy is to mediation as trial advocacy is to trials.

c. The key determination, as Professor Robinson notes, is how to mix competitive and cooperative strategies in a mediation. What to do, and when, depends in important part on the interests and conduct of the mediation parties, and on mediator-related considerations.

2. Peter Robinson, *Contending With Wolves in Sheep's Clothing: A Cautiously Cooperative Approach to Mediation Advocacy*, 50 BAYLOR L. REV. 963 (1998)

The advocate in a mediation faces the dilemma of fighting for a client's best interests within a process designed to conciliate and peacefully resolve conflict. The appropriate resolution of this dilemma is complicated by the uncertainty of the techniques and strategies that will be used by the opposing parties. All parties involved in a mediation are likely to seek settlement terms that are in their respective best interest. However, it is uncertain whether they will seek those terms through cooperative or competitive means. This Article examines both competitive and cooperative advocacy techniques available in mediation and recommends that the use of such techniques must vary depending on the behaviors of the opposing parties and, in some instances, the mediator. . . .

Advocates generally adopt either a competitive or cooperative approach when negotiating. The competitive strategy involves making large demands, providing few concessions, and challenging the opponent's positions and conclusions. Conversely, a cooperative approach focuses on seeking to understand both parties' objectives and finding creative solutions that maximize the outcome for both sides. Both styles are legitimate methods of reaching agreement. Research indicates that competitive negotiators generally achieve better results, but are also more likely to fail to reach agreement. Cooperative negotiators are more likely to reach an agreement, but may not maximize all potential gains for a client in a given negotiation. A survey of attorneys found that a greater percentage of cooperative negotiators were deemed by their peers to be effective. . . .

Advocates in a mediation must negotiate. . . . Since the parties make the decisions in a mediation, each party has the responsibility of participating as a negotiator in the mediation process. The mediation will resolve the dispute only when the parties can agree to terms of resolution. If the participants in a mediation relate to each other as negotiators, then the strategic uses of cooperative and competitive strategies . . . should apply to mediation advocacy. There is a danger that a party to a mediation may enter the process with an excessively cooperative attitude, because most perceive mediation as a mutual effort to accomplish a settlement. The avowed purpose of mediation is to move beyond the "winner and loser" dynamics of litigation and explore mutually acceptable options for parties in conflict. For this reason, parties often presume that their opponents are participating in the mediation in good faith. Clients generally expect that a mediation will be successful in resolving the dispute, rather than generating an unnecessary pre-trial expense. The mediator contributes to this dynamic by encouraging the parties to trust her and the mediation process.

A problem with this trusting approach is that one side may suggest or agree to mediation in order to take advantage of the appearance of a cooperative venue. While the venue may be an opportunity for cooperation, that opportunity is merely an illusion if either participant disguises a competitive strategy with a cooperative style. The effective mediation advocate must guard against these "wolves in sheep's clothing." The cautiously cooperative approach balances an advocate's cooperative behavior, designed to accomplish a mutually beneficial resolution of the dispute, with the necessity to guard against exploitation by a competitive opponent. It allows the advocate to maximize mediation's opportunity to accomplish agreement without becoming unnecessarily vulnerable to an opponent. Additionally, since many mediations occur between parties that have continuing relationships, the cautiously cooperative approach fosters an environment that can maintain the goodwill between the two sides. Competition is a response, rather than a rule, and the party using this approach will not create discord in the ongoing relationship unless provoked.

In addition to negotiating with the opponent, a participant in mediation frequently negotiates with the mediator. The mediator seeks to influence all participants to take steps helpful to reaching an agreement. While a mediator does not have a stake in the specific settlement in a mediation, the mediator does have a stake in finding a settlement. Recognizing this motivation in the mediator is important when evaluating her behavior. The mediator's methods of influencing settlement vary widely. Mediators have no power to order participants to make a concession, make an apology, or admit responsibility. Participation in mediation is voluntary, and a party can remove herself from the process at any time. The mediator/advocate relationship is also a negotiation. The mediation advocate must recognize that he is also negotiating with the mediator and consciously balance cooperation and competition tactics within that relationship.

V. Illustration of the Cautiously Cooperative Mediation Advocacy Strategy

The discussion above proposes a . . . strategy which balances competitive and cooperative mediation advocacy behavior in an effort to maximize a mediation's opportunity to reach a satisfactory settlement while minimizing the likelihood of one of the parties being exploited. This Part will illustrate the application of the cautiously cooperative strategy to a variety of situations in a mediation, . . . [and also provide] practical advice for handling a number of sensitive advocacy dilemmas in a mediation.

A. Arranging for the Mediation. The cautiously cooperative mediation advocacy strategy should first be applied when arranging for a mediation. The advocate considering a mediation has a variety of strategic issues to manage, including who should propose the mediation and how to do so. Additionally, the advocate must also consider what terms and conditions should accompany the agreement to mediate. How these issues should be handled may vary depending upon the degree of acceptance of mediation in a particular geographic area or practice specialty area. For example, in states where mediation is more commonplace, such as Florida, Texas, and California, and in practice areas where mediation is more common, such as construction and employment disputes, it would probably be harmless to simply call one's opponent and inquire whether they are willing to refer the matter to mediation. In contrast, in geographic areas and practice specialty areas where mediation is not commonplace, the appearance of being eager to mediate could be interpreted as a sign of a "lack of confidence" in one's case. Thus, a cautiously cooperative strategy is especially important for advocates in areas where either the geographic area or practice specialty makes an interest in initiating a mediation subject to misinterpretation.

The need to create positive momentum towards settlement causes the cautiously cooperative advocate to be willing to raise the question of whether a particular case should be referred to mediation. Otherwise, cases in which both advocates desire mediation would never be referred, because both advocates would be reluctant to initiate it. While an advocate should be willing to be the first to explore mediation, the cautiously cooperative strategy would suggest that the advocate be intentionally vague about the terms and conditions of the mediation in the event that it becomes necessary to become more competitive. For example, if the initial inquiry about the propriety of mediation for a case is met with a demeaning comment regarding an alleged weakness in the case, the initiating advocate can rehabilitate his credibility by suggesting a mediator who is a highly regarded legal authority on the subject matter of the dispute. This would imply that the initiating advocate is confident as to the legal strength of his case. The initiating advocate is eager for a prominent, qualified legal authority to react to his factual and legal theories and expects the mediator to confirm his evaluation of the case. Note that the terms and conditions of the agreement to mediate need not embrace such bravado should the other advocate assume a more cooperative attitude about the invitation to mediate.

An advocate can use additional measures to reduce the potential for stigma when suggesting mediation. If a client or law firm makes it a matter of policy to explore early settlement through mediation in every dispute, then the exploration about mediation will be seen as part of the standard procedure for that lawyer's handling of cases and would not carry any specific significance for the case at hand. Alternatively, the mediator or mediation organization could contact the other party to determine her interest in mediating. If the other party is skeptical, the advocate can explain that she referred the matter to the mediator as a matter of policy or courtesy, and that she is only marginally interested in mediation herself.

B. First Impressions on the Opposition. In many instances, the mediation will be the first occasion to make an in-person impression on opposing counsel and her client. The dilemma between competition and cooperation is readily apparent in the initial stages of a mediation. A mediation advocate may wish to start competitively in an effort to intimidate the other side or to demonstrate resolve about the matter. In contrast, the cooperative mediation advocate seeks to gain credibility and create momentum for settlement by appearing to be reasonable.

The application of the cautiously cooperative strategy would cause the advocate to err on the side of more cooperative behaviors in the mediation's initial stage. This "cooperative bias" in the initial stage is essential to impress upon the opponent that you are serious about settling the case and are not participating in the mediation in bad faith. Remember that the opponent may suspect your motives and, thus, may be assessing your initial behavior to determine how much effort and energy she is willing to invest in the mediation. By beginning more cooperatively, an advocate will enhance the likelihood of a reciprocal response from the adversary and the likelihood that an agreement will be accomplished at the mediation. Examples of cooperative behaviors in the initial stages of a mediation include:

a)   arriving early;

b)   warmly greeting opposing counsel and opposing counsel's client;

c)   expressing genuine empathy for the difficulties experienced by opposing counsel's client;

d)   expressing apology for the mutual frustration in not being able to reach an agreement and acknowledging that sometimes reasonable people will disagree;

e)   crafting the opening presentation at the mediation to emphasize being a reasonable person and seeking a reasonable outcome for this dispute;

f)   specifically omitting comments that may insult or offend the opponent from what will be the opening statement and closing argument at trial; and

g)   apologizing for those aspects of the presentation that will be difficult for the other side to accept as part of your view of this case.

The more congenial negotiator seeks to use the beginning of the mediation to enhance his credibility and charismatic influence with opposing counsel's client and possibly even opposing counsel herself.

Attorneys sometimes explain to their clients that mediation is necessary, because the opposing counsel is unreasonable and difficult to work with. Thus, an attorney who begins the mediation in a reasonable and amicable manner could cause opposing counsel's client to ask whether it is her attorney who is the one who is unreasonable and difficult to work with. Since it is the opposing client who is the ultimate decision maker, making a good first impression on her could go a long way towards establishing the credibility of your view of the case.

While the cautiously cooperative strategy creates an initial cooperative advocacy bias, it recognizes that such behaviors could be misinterpreted. The cautiously cooperative advocate must gauge the behavior of her adversary and recognize when her adversary is adopting a more competitive strategy.

The competitive response focuses on the reality that the opposing counsel and client will immediately begin "sizing up" the resolve and courtroom capabilities of their mediation opponent. If opposing counsel or her client sense weakness in either category, they will be more confident in their evaluation of the case. The opposition's assessments will be continually evolving, but the competitive mediation advocate seeks to take advantage of the importance of first impressions. The competitive mediation advocate will:

a)   avoid social pleasantries by arriving late or talking on her cellular phone until the mediator begins the session;

b) demean opposing counsel and opposing counsel's client in her greet-ings;

c) express frustration that this mediation would not have been neces-sary had the other side been reasonable;

d) offer gratuitous insults about the abilities and character of oppos-ing counsel and/or opposing counsel's client;

e) describe recent similar cases in which he accomplished an out-standing result; and

f) proceed to deliver a well-prepared combination of trial opening statement and closing argument without regard for how those state-ments may alienate and offend their adversary.

These behaviors will irritate and offend opposing counsel and opposing counsel's client, but the mediation advocate with a competitive strategy believes he has gained a psychological advantage by demonstrating resolve.

The cautiously cooperative strategy encourages the advocate to seek to cre-ate "settlement momentum" by starting cooperatively, but also mandates that the advocate protect his eventual results in a mediation by mirroring his oppo-nent's competitive behavior. The cautiously cooperative mediation advocate should begin with the cooperative behaviors described above, but be prepared to respond in kind if the adversary exhibits the competitive behaviors.

C. Determining the Depth of Disclosure. The approach in competitive negoti-ations is to predict what will happen if the case goes to trial and, thus, discuss a financial settlement in the "shadow of the law." The competitive negotiation is almost always focused around an exclusively monetary settlement. This type of negotiation usually consists of arguing over competing legal theories, admis-sibility of the legally relevant facts associated with those theories, and jury sympathies about the case. A mediation advocate may choose a narrowly focused mediation dialogue if she has an extremely strong legal case or there are rea-sons not to disclose the broader type of information.

In contrast, a mediation advocate may elect to implement the cooperative model of negotiation. The classic cooperative approach to negotiation necessi-tates an open agenda that considers extra-legal concerns in expectation that a broader base of information may suggest a greater array of possible solutions. The ability to structure settlements not based entirely, or at all, on a dollar amount is one of the possible benefits of a more cooperative approach to medi-ation. This approach requires an exploration of information that may be legally inadmissible, such as the client's motives, goals, principles, values, humiliation, and other feelings arising out of the conflict and the relationship. Thus, infor-mation about future dreams and aspirations, how the plaintiff plans to utilize a cash settlement, and the client's emotional attachment or investment in the dispute could become critical information. Anecdotes abound in which significant progress toward settlement occurred at a mediation by letting a client vent, extracting an apology, creating a structured settlement to provide for predictable future expenses, or providing in kind compensation based on this type of broader discussion.

The cautiously cooperative advocate should generally push for a broader conversation resembling the cooperative model. Such an approach will give the advocate more options when bargaining. However, the cautiously cooperative mediation advocate should monitor whether such broad disclosures are beginning to create an imbalance in information. If so, the cautiously cooperative response must insist on an equal sharing of information from the adversary. If a competitive adversary is less than forthcoming, the cautiously cooperative advocate should refuse further broad disclosures.

D. The Degree of Posturing in Opening Offers. When used skillfully, the opening offer can be the most significant opportunity to manage the other side's expectations. The first number on the table is the first point of reference regarding acceptable outcomes. This first point of reference sometimes has a magnetic effect, pulling the other side's opening offer, and range of acceptable solutions, toward the first number on the table.

Mediation advocates wrestle with the tension between the competitive or cooperative approaches when deciding how much to exaggerate the initial demand. The initial offer could be a genuine "bottom line, take-it-or-leave-it" ultimatum. A slightly more competitive approach would be for the initial offer to be a reasonable number, but one which the negotiator is willing to enhance slightly. A more competitive option is a barely credible initial offer that the negotiator expects to significantly improve before a deal is consummated. The most competitive option is an initial offer so extreme that it becomes insulting or offensive.

The cautiously cooperative mediation strategy would suggest that a mediation advocate should seek to be cooperative in the opening offer, but only if the advocate believes that the opposing advocate will reciprocate. This assessment of an opponent's strategy is difficult. The cautiously cooperative advocate can use the mediator to resolve this dilemma by sharing her cooperative opening offer with the mediator in confidence, and instructing the mediator not to reveal that offer unless the opponent's offer falls within a pre-determined range that would also reflect a cooperative strategy. Remember, the "wolves in sheep's clothing" concern requires an advocate to open with a more competitive approach if that technique is employed by an opponent.

E. Making Concessions. The first concession at the mediation can provide a strategic opportunity similar to the opening offer in a negotiation. If the negotiations are originating in the mediation, the "first concession" will consist of making the opening offer. Usually, however, opening offers are exchanged and negotiations conducted prior to the mediation. When the negotiators approach impasse, they agree to seek a resolution through mediation. Even though the mediation continues the same negotiation, there is a sense of beginning a distinctive process. This "second beginning" in the negotiation provides an opportunity to reapply strategies regarding opening offers.

As negotiations begin again in earnest in the context of the mediation, the psychological manipulation strategy in opening offers can apply in making the first concession from the premediation impasse. For example, wrongful termination settlement negotiations may begin with a demand of $200,000 and a response of $20,000. Negotiations prior to the mediation reach impasse at $80,000 and $40,000. The first negotiator to make a $4000 concession at the mediation may psychologically influence his opponent (and the mediator) to think that the resolution at the mediation, if any, will be skewed toward the first negotiator's opening position.

The advocate's competitive or cooperative strategy will be manifest in her view of the sequence and timing of moves in the mediation. Competitive mediation advocates assume that there may be considerable posturing in the early stages of a mediation. They know that rushing the timing and the size of concessions will create a disadvantageous situation; one negotiator's offer may still be significantly postured while the other negotiator's offer is becoming reasonable. This can result in viewing the mediation as a war of wills where the more patient player in the game of "chicken" prevails.

Experienced mediation advocates know that there are usually a series of concessions in a mediation. This series of concessions serves the purpose of convincing the other side that it has acquired the best possible result. In contrast, some people interpret a quick acceptance of an opening, or early offer, as a signal that they could have acquired a better bargain. Therefore, the experienced advocate should consider whether the other party needs a series of concessions at the mediation.

In a sense, many mediation advocates expect a modified law of physics that each and every concession should be matched by an equal and opposite concession. The matching concession may not be dollar for dollar, because the two negotiators may have differing degrees of flexibility. This might be especially true in personal injury litigation where the plaintiff's bar frequently exaggerates its opening offers while many defense lawyers have a modicum of reasonableness in their opening offers for fear of insurance commissioners and claims of bad faith for first party cases. In any event, the cautiously cooperative advocate examines her opponent's concessions to determine whether they are mirroring her efforts to reach a reasonable compromise. If the other side's concessions are determined to be wanting, the cautiously cooperative advocate must become more patient and embrace her opponent's perceived stingy strategy regarding the amount of the next concession.

This phenomenon explains why mediations sometimes turn into marathon sessions lasting into the wee hours of the morning. Overly aggressive mediation advocates hope that they never have to approach their real bottom line; if necessary, they will do so only when there has been a mutual wearing down. If mediation has a defined time parameter, such as three hours, the aggressive mediation advocate continues to position and posture for at least the first two hours and fifty-five minutes.

F. Closing. The final area of potential application of the cautiously cooperative strategy is in the closing stage of a mediation. The closing stage is that period of negotiation after the creative brainstorming and negotiation posturing have been exhausted and the parties must decide whether to embrace a creative solution, make a final gesture to close the difference between final offers, or terminate the mediation without an agreement. The mediator's role as advocate for a resolution frequently becomes accentuated during this stage of the mediation.

Mediators often become more actively involved in the negotiations during the closing stage, pushing the parties towards resolution. The cautiously cooperative advocate will pay extra attention to the mediator in the closing stage. The experienced mediation advocate will anticipate the mediator's final push in the closing stage. The cautiously cooperative strategy requires the mediation advocate to be willing to "do his part" towards closing the final gap or implementing a creative outcome, but only if such a willingness is also evident from the other advocate.

An advocate who is too cooperative runs the risk that, after she "does her part" to accomplish a final agreement, a recalcitrant opponent may demand an additional compromise. In contrast, an overly competitive advocate runs the risk of losing an acceptable potential agreement at a mediation by refusing to "do her part" in the final closing stage. The cautiously cooperative strategy is designed to maximize the likelihood of reaching agreement while minimizing the likelihood of an unpreferred result.

In the closing stage, the cautiously cooperative advocate can condition her final gesture on a reciprocal gesture from her opponent. She could do so openly in a joint session or by authorizing the mediator to disclose a conditional offer, such as "Smith is willing to split the difference if you are." A more cautious technique is to tell the mediator that you are willing to split the difference, but to require the mediator to hold that offer in confidence unless she can extract the same offer from the other side. A variation on this theme is to suggest the mediator propose specific terms (that you would agree to) as a final agreement. If the other side agrees, the cautiously cooperative advocate agrees also to consummate the deal. If the other side refuses, so does the cautiously cooperative advocate, which allows her to preserve her postured bargaining position.

VI. Conclusion

The advocate desiring to settle a case at a mediation faces a dilemma. The likelihood of reaching an agreement will be enhanced if she is more cooperative and reasonable. However, her interest in settling the case is tempered by her determination to accomplish a good result and her concern that the opposing advocate either may not have the same determination to reach an agreement or will seek to take advantage of a perception of excessive eagerness to settle. The reality of bad faith participation at mediation, and the potential for exploitation by such bad faith participants, should be of great concern to mediation advocates. This internal conflict creates complexity and confusion for the mediation advocate. The cautiously cooperative advocacy approach can be an effective way to manage this challenge.

3. James K.L. Lawrence, *Mediation Advocacy: Partnering With the Mediator*, 15 OHIO ST. J. ON DISP. RESOL. 425 (2000)

It is the job of the attorney in the midst of a dispute to manage the conflict and to get the best results as quickly and cost effectively as possible for the client. Mediation is a vehicle to do just that. However, the skills and strategies that are most effective in the courtroom are not effective at the mediation table. It is necessary for the litigator to acquire a new set of "mediation advocacy" skills, because traditional notions of trial advocacy do not ensure success in mediation. . . . This Article melds the seminal conceptual work behind interest-based negotiation and mediation with the practitioner-oriented mediation advocacy literature to create a useful tool for the litigator turned mediation advocate.

This Article focuses on the relationship between the advocate and mediator, and it explores why and how the advocate can partner with the mediator to achieve optimal results. The bottom line is that the advocate, at the mediation table, should let go of adversarial tactics, not because they are morally wrong or "unfair" but because they stand in the way of achieving the best results in mediation. Most often, a mediator is trained in interest-based negotiation and works in the field because she finds creative problem solving superior to adjudication. To a mediator, adversarial tactics are obstructionist and ineffective, and the advocate employing them is considered less than a partner in the mediation process. Moreover, research shows that party satisfaction and compliance with mediated agreements stem largely from how the process works, and two features in particular are responsible: . . . (1) the greater degree of participation in decisionmaking that parties experience in mediation; and (2) the fuller opportunity to express themselves and communicate their views, both to the neutral and to each other. . . .

Mediation requires a change in mind-set from adversarial proceedings, because the objective is different. At trial, the goal is to persuade the judge. In mediation, the goal is to persuade the other party to the dispute. Because the conceptual framework underlying mediation is completely different than litigation, the rules of the game are changed, and lawyers are asked to do different things, to approach each other with different mind-sets, and to seek different outcomes for their disputes. It is important to be cognitive of changing one's mind-set, because the "adversary model" is a powerful heuristic. If lawyers, who have been trained and primarily practice as litigators, are not conscious of its effects, they will operate subconsciously out of the adversary model.

Think of mediation as "enhanced" and "value-added" negotiation. Both the lawyer and the mediator are advocates — the lawyer is an advocate for her client; the mediator is an advocate for a resolution. In addition, keep in mind that "[t]he mediator/advocate relationship is also a negotiation." The mediation advocate must recognize that he is also negotiating with the mediator. By partnering with the mediator and taking advantage of the mediator's training and perspective, the advocate often can achieve results superior to unassisted negotiation.

Client preparation is essential for effective mediation. It is important for the client to take a much more active role in mediation than in adjudication. The client must communicate effectively with the mediator, and she must be comfortable with the process in order to do so. The principal player is the client, because she must be satisfied in order for a settlement to occur. The preparation will depend on the experience and personality of the client. A client with experience in positional or competitive negotiations will need to adopt the same mind-set change discussed above. In addition, an attorney should prepare her client to understand the attorney's role as a mediation advocate. That role includes the following: pressing the client's interest, working with the mediator and the other side sufficiently to forge satisfaction of both sides' interests, and facilitating a settlement.

The preparation requires more than just talking through the elements of a mediation. Books, brochures, videos, and even a rehearsal are appropriate tools. A client who understands the mediation process, has received guidelines for conduct during mediation, and has faced the realities of the dispute, can contribute significantly to achieving resolution. Because the client is the ultimate decisionmaker, it is imperative that she "buys in" to the process.

Ideally, mediation is future-oriented rather than past-oriented. A client who has been intimately involved in the underlying events may need extra prodding to move forward and look for solutions rather than dwelling on assigning blame for the past. However, if the client is the defendant, explain the potential value in allowing or even encouraging the plaintiff to "vent" — to describe her feelings about the conflict. Prepare the client for this opportunity to let the other party get his story out and feel that he has been heard in the mediation room instead of the courtroom.

It is not necessarily advisable for the attorney to be the "lead" negotiator. The attorney certainly is there to reassess the legal strength of the case as more information is developed (because litigation or arbitration is always an alternative) and to provide legal advice on advantages and risks of proposed solutions. However, often, the client is better equipped to do much of the negotiation. An attorney who plays too active a role may add, rather than reduce, barriers to resolving the conflict.

Mediation preparation is critical. One commentator has described this process of preparing for mediation as a "New Beginning." The advocate cannot expect success if she merely goes to the mediation and rehashes legal arguments and entrenched positions. Remember that, in mediation, legally irrelevant arguments may be very persuasive. Identifying interests and developing options for creative solutions is the core of interest-based negotiation and mediation. The bulk of this work should be done with the client before mediation; during the mediation, reassessment can occur. The mediation will be more efficient and effective if the advocate anticipates the information the mediator will ask of her and brings it with her. Whether this information is disclosed to the mediator or to the other side are questions the answers to which are best deferred to timely points during the mediation session.

Some scholars and mediators are of the opinion that the lawyers merely get in the way and obstruct the mediation process. However, it is likely that the real problem is entrenched litigation tactics that do not bend or adjust to the mediation process. It is critical at the outset for the advocate to establish credibility with the mediator and to communicate an intention to "buy into the process" and partner with the mediator to broker a settlement. If — or for the author, because — there is reason to accept a paraphrase of Roger Fisher, "good negotiators mediate their own disputes," a negotiation advocate at a mediation should choose to dance with the person the advocate has accepted as the mediator. That dance strongly suggests that the advocate partners with the mediator in creating productive working relationships without losing sight of getting what the client wants.

As early as the first telephone conference or submission of the premediation statement, an advocate can do potentially irreparable harm to her relationship with the mediator. As one mediator has stated: "Sometimes I am blind sided by the overly-aggressive tenor of an exchanged statement. This tips me off that the lawyer who has taken this approach either (1) has a poor understanding of mediation processes and settlement dynamics, or (2) is a likely obstruction to settlement. In either event, that lawyer loses credibility, and has tipped his mitt with me."

The premediation statement and conference are the opportunities to begin the mediation dialogue and give the mediator the information she will need by way of background to help reach a settlement. The basic information she needs to know consists of the following: the stumbling blocks to unassisted settlement, the negotiation history of the dispute, the client's interests and needs, and creative solutions that may be explored during the mediation. In addition, take the extra step and acknowledge what settlement terms the advocate believes the other party or parties will need to settle the dispute. It also may be helpful to provide the mediator with information regarding the client's unique characteristics, sensitivities, and emotional needs.

To be most effective and efficient, mediators want and need to know what the barriers to settlement are and whether the real sticking point is legal or factual or emotional. Above all, the premediation correspondence should demonstrate an open-mindedness, a reasonableness, and a desire to settle. The client must understand that showing reasonableness, preparedness, and knowledge of the process is not a sign of weakness and will further her cause during the mediation process. . . .

4. Jean R. Sternlight, *Lawyers' Representation of Clients in Mediation: Using Economics and Psychology to Structure Advocacy in a Nonadversarial Setting*, 14 OHIO ST. J. ON DISP. RESOL. 269 (1999)

No single lawyer's role is always best in mediation. Rather, the attorney's appropriate role in mediation should vary depending on which barriers seem to be impeding the appropriate settlement of a particular dispute. That is, while the attorney should remain an advocate for her client at all times, she should adjust the manner in which she attempts to further her client's interest depending upon which barriers are preventing the fair settlement of the dispute. For example, given many of the barriers, the attorney should frequently stop herself from dominating the mediation, instead allowing the client to play an active role in the process. In other situations, however, the attorney must be active and assertive to ensure that her client is not coerced by the opposing party or client. The attorney should not herself determine these relative roles, but rather, should in most circumstances consult with the client regarding this issue. . . . Lawyers need to be particularly vigilant in guarding against their own tendencies to behave in mediation exactly as they would in litigation. Instead, to serve their clients' interests, and in light of the conflicts of interest and perception between lawyers and their own clients, attorneys should often encourage their clients to play an active role in the mediation, allow the discussion to focus on emotional as well as legal concerns, and work toward mutually beneficial, rather than win-or-lose, solutions. Those lawyers who, seeking to advocate strongly on behalf of their clients, take steps to dominate the mediation, focus exclusively on legal issues, and minimize their clients' direct participation, will often ill serve their clients' true needs and interests. Such overly zealous advocates are frequently poor advocates. . . .

III. ADVOCACY CAN BE APPROPRIATE IN MEDIATION

Attorney advocacy, properly defined, is entirely consistent with and supportive of mediation. While many commentators have attacked attorneys' use of advocacy in the mediation process, . . . the problem is not advocacy per se, but rather, certain kinds of advocacy or adversarial behavior employed under particular circumstances. However, some attorney behavior should be proscribed in mediation (as it is in litigation), and some attorneys have a lot to learn regarding how best to advocate for their clients in a mediation.

If advocacy is defined broadly as supporting or pleading the cause of another, there is no inconsistency between advocacy and mediation. Permitting an attorney to act as an advocate for her client simply allows that attorney to speak and make arguments on her client's behalf and to help her client achieve her goals. The purpose of mediation is to reach an agreement which is acceptable to and desired by all parties. To reach such an agreement, both parties may wish to share their views as to their likely success in court, as well as to engage in problem-solving. . . . The problem-solving that works well in mediation does not require sacrifice of one's self-interest, but rather allows parties to search for solutions that are mutually beneficial. . . .

While attorneys may appropriately advocate for their clients in mediation, it is certainly true that those attorneys who attempt to employ traditional "zealous" litigation tools when representing their clients in mediation may frequently (but not always) fail either to fulfill their clients' wishes or to serve their clients' interests. Those who would hoard information, rely solely on legal rather than emotional arguments, or refuse to let their clients speak freely will often have little success in mediation. This is not because attorneys ought not to advocate for their clients, but rather, because attorneys ought not to advocate poorly on behalf of their clients. . . .

The worst mistake one can make in determining the appropriate roles of lawyer and client in a mediation is to refuse to see the issue and simply operate out of habit. Too many lawyers and clients have never thought seriously about how the lawyer-client relationship should work in the context of a mediation. Many lawyers, particularly those with extensive deposition or trial experience, have simply transferred their assumptions and behavior from those areas to the mediation forum without thinking through the differences between a trial or a deposition and a mediation. Such lawyers often instinctively try to do all the talking for the client, tell the client not to volunteer anything, try to stifle emotional outbursts, and focus primarily on establishing the superiority of their clients' legal positions rather than on a problem-solving approach. Adopting this dominating approach as a general rule will prevent the use of mediation to overcome the various barriers to negotiation.

Equally inappropriately, some lawyers (and mediators) assume that mediation is exclusively the clients' process and either fail to attend altogether or do attend but act as the much discussed "potted plant." Such a lawyer may figure that, because comments made in mediation are protected by confidentiality, and because no settlement can be reached without her client's agreement, the lawyer need not worry much, if at all, about protecting her client's interests. Again, while this approach may sometimes be appropriate, adopting it unthinkingly in every case is a mistake which may subject certain clients to coercion and abuse and, ultimately, cause them to accept a settlement which is unfair.

Instead of exclusively taking one approach or the other, lawyers and their clients should divide their responsibilities on a case-by-case basis after taking into account such factors as the nature of the clients and their attorneys, the respective goals of these participants, and the nature of the dispute. Anyone who says they have a simple answer to the question of how lawyers and clients should divide their responsibilities in a mediation must be wrong. Either their answer is not simple, or their answer is not right. The answer is complicated, because the division of responsibilities should vary substantially depending upon who the client is, who the lawyer is, and what factors appear to be blocking a reasonable and fair settlement of the dispute. . . .

5. Harold Abramson, *Problem-Solving Advocacy in Mediations: A Model of Client Representation*, 10 HARV. NEGOT. L. REV. 103 (2005)

Let me start by defining a problem-solving mediation process. In such a process, the mediator's sole purpose is to assist the clients and their attorneys in resolving the dispute. The mediator knows how to structure a process that can provide both sides with an opportunity to fashion enduring, and when at all feasible, inventive solutions that can go beyond what a court might be willing to craft. The mediator serves as a guide by managing a structured discussion that includes gathering specific information; identifying issues, interests, and impediments; and generating, assessing, and selecting options for settlement. . . .

Problem-solving mediations should be distinguished from judicial settlement conferences, because some mediations can resemble settlement conferences. These settlement conference-type mediations, like judicial settlement conferences, can consist of the third party hearing each side's arguments, asking questions, challenging partisan points, assessing arguments and legal positions, and hinting at or urging compromised settlement terms. Such mediations, using dispute resolution nomenclature, are often a directive, evaluative process. . . . In problem-solving mediation, there is no third party decision maker or evaluator, only a third party assistant. The third party assistant usually is not even the primary audience. The primary audience is the other side, who is surely not neutral and can often be quite hostile. In this different representational setting, the adversarial approach is less effective, if not self-defeating. . . .

V. Solution: The Mediation Representation Formula

Mediation Representation presents a five component formula in which attorneys advocate by using (1) a creative problem-solving approach to achieve the two goals of (2) satisfying their client's interests and (3) overcoming any impediments to settlement. During the mediation the attorneys (4) enlist the assistance of the mediator while negotiating with the other side at (5) key junctures in the process. The first three components focus on how to negotiate in the mediation.

A. Negotiation Approach: Creative Problem-Solving. Selecting the negotiation approach was easy. If an advocate views mediation as a problem-solving process, then the attorney should negotiate as a problem-solver. A problem-solving negotiator who is creative does more than just try to settle the dispute. Such a negotiator creatively searches for solutions that go beyond the traditional ones based on rights, obligations, and precedent. Rather than settling for win-lose outcomes, the negotiator searches for solutions that can benefit both sides. To creatively problem solve, the negotiator develops a collaborative relationship with the other side and participates throughout the process in a way that is likely to result in solutions that are enduring as well as inventive. Solutions are likely to be enduring because both sides work together to fashion nuanced solutions that each side fully understands, can live with, and knows how to implement. Solutions are likely to be inventive because both sides advocate for their client's interests instead of legal positions; use suitable techniques for overcoming impediments; search expansively for multiple options; and evaluate and package options imaginatively to meet the various interests of all parties. . . .

B. Goal: Advance Your Client's Interests. For the next step in constructing this model, I . . . sought a goal that would isolate a key trigger for launching a problem-solving process. The obvious goal was to settle the dispute. However, settlement . . . is the goal of most negotiations, whether the parties are adversarial or problem-solving. Also, the goal failed to shape how parties and attorneys negotiate. I needed another goal. . . . After reflecting on a full range of techniques and moves within the self-contained problem-solving approach, one single move stood out because it could instantly shift a negotiator's perspective on a dispute from an adversarial distributive one to a problem-solving mutually beneficial one. This shift can happen when the attorney identifies and advocates his or her client's interests, . . . acquires an understanding of the other side's interests, and then advocates to advance his or her client's interests in a way that sufficiently addresses the other side's interests to move toward an agreement. . . .

There is a second reason for selecting the goal of focusing on a client's interests: to make clear what is not the primary goal of problem-solving. Problem-solving is sometimes misconstrued to mean placing a premium on getting along with the other side at the expense of a client's interests. Correcting this false perception registered high when drafting the new assessment criteria for the ABA Mediation Representation Competition. We had heard numerous competition judges criticize students' advocacy as too cooperative at the expense of their clients' needs. We resolved to send an unmistakable message to students by adding a separate and specific judging criterion entitled "Advocating Client's Interests."

C. Goal: Overcome Impediments. I also identified another primary goal, one that applies to any negotiation regardless of the objective: to overcome any impediments to settlement. This goal entailed a return to a basic premise: parties would not be in mediation unless they were facing an impediment in the negotiation; otherwise, the parties could probably settle the dispute without the assistance of a mediator. Selecting this goal was obvious. Less obvious, however, was identifying an impasse-breaking strategy that comported with a problem-solving approach.

A number of distinguished authors have devised methodologies that demystify the murky world of impasse-breaking. . . . Christopher Moore's approach is built around his critical observation that impasses can be divided into five conflict categories that he labels relationship, data, value, interest, and structural. Under his approach, you first inquire about the cause of the impasse; then you classify the cause into one of the five impasse categories; and finally, you devise a suitable intervention for overcoming the impasse. Let me describe Moore's five impasse categories while leaving for the next section how advocates might use his classification system as a basis for enlisting assistance from the mediator.

1. Relationship Conflict. Relationship conflicts can arise when participants are deeply upset with each other, cling to destructive misperceptions or stereotypes of each other, or suffer from poor communication. These types of conflicts are common in disputes where parties distrust each other and are occupied with hurling threats. These disabling tensions can arise between clients, between attorneys, and between an attorney and his or her client. . . .

2. Data Conflict. Data conflicts can be caused by inadequate, inaccurate, or untrustworthy information. Alternatively, they can be caused by different views of what is relevant information or different interpretations of relevant data. Data conflicts are common in court cases where parties may hold conflicting views of what happened, what might happen in court, or what is an appropriate interpretation of decisive data such as financial statements. . . .

3. Interest Conflict. Interest conflicts can arise when parties' substantive, procedural, or relationship wants conflict with each other. Interest conflicts cover the classically positional conflict inherent in adversarial negotiations. They can be caused by parties wanting the same thing (such as property), wanting different amounts of the same thing (such as time), wanting different things that the other is not prepared to give (such as one party wanting a precedent that the other party opposes), or even wanting something that another is not even aware of (such as an apology). . . .

4. Structural Conflict. Structural conflicts can be the murkiest to identify. The two most common, as well as easiest, structural obstacles to spot, are impasses due to unequal bargaining power or impasses due to conflicting goals of attorneys and their clients, which are known as principal-agent conflicts. Other structural conflicts can be more subtle, such as those caused by no deadline, time constraints facing one side, a missing key party, a party without sufficient settlement authority, geographical or technological limitations that impact one side disproportionately, and unequal control of resources for resolving the conflict. Because the causes of structural conflicts also frequently contribute to relationship conflicts, it can be difficult to decipher the nature of the conflict.

5. Value Conflict. Value conflicts can be the most intractable ones, because they implicate a party's core personal or moral values. This narrow category can embrace matters of principle, ideology, or religion that can not be compromised. A grassroots environmental group, for instance, may have difficulty settling with a housing developer, because to do so might compromise the group's ideology of preserving all large tracts of open space. Value conflicts can be difficult to recognize in court cases, because values can be masked by all too familiar legal categories, arguments, and remedies. When a party wants to win in court, for example, the party may be motivated by the need for a clear victory to preserve a personal value, such as personal integrity. . . .

D. Strategy: Enlist the Assistance of the Mediator. For this next component, I needed to consider the types of assistance that can be offered by the third party in the room, the mediator. The mediator can contribute in three general ways: by the way the mediator implements his or her orientations, uses his or her techniques, and controls the mediation stages. The particular contributions depend on the type of mediation process envisioned. In a problem-solving process in which the advocate does not scheme to manipulate or "game" the mediator, the third party can be enlisted in the various ways described in this section.

Mediators bring a mix of distinct orientations to the mediation process. They can be grouped into four discrete areas: (1) How will the mediator manage the mediation process? Will he or she be primarily problem-solving, evaluative, or transformative? (2) Will the mediator approach the problem narrowly as primarily a legal dispute or more broadly? (3) Will the mediator involve clients actively or restrictively? (4) Will the mediator use caucuses extensively, selectively, or not at all? When an advocate knows the mediator's mix, then he or she knows some of the opportunities for enlisting the mediator for assistance. . . . The mediator's orientation should be especially highlighted, because it can singularly shape an attorney's representation strategy. An attorney's entire approach to interacting with and enlisting assistance from the mediator will be influenced by the mediator's process management — i.e., how problem-solving, transformative, or evaluative the mediator might be.

E. Implement Plan at Key Junctures in the Mediation Process. Finally, these four distinct components of the model had to be woven together. . . . The advocate needed a representation plan that could be used throughout the mediation process. However, simply saying "throughout the process" was too vague, leaving the advocate with little practical guidance. Three of the key junctures arise before the first mediation session, when (1) selecting a mediator, (2) preparing a pre-mediation submission, and (3) participating in a pre-mediation conference. The other three junctures arise in the mediation session when (4) presenting opening statements, (5) participating in joint sessions, and (6) participating in caucuses.

VI. Conclusion

This article described the five components of the mediation representation formula as well as how the formula was derived. This model of client representation that forms the foundation of Mediation Representation offers the advocate an approach to representing clients that takes full advantage of the distinctive opportunities in a problem-solving mediation process. . . . This model of client representation ought to be applied by an advocate for the duration of the representation, starting as soon as the first client interview. . . .

E. GOOD FAITH PARTICIPATION IN MEDIATION

This topic is discussed in Chapter Ten.

Chapter 9
MEDIATION APPLICATIONS

A. INTRODUCTION

Mediation is used in an enormous variety of substantive areas, and we do not purport to provide anything approaching comprehensive coverage. Indeed, we eschew such a goal; rather, we offer an in-depth consideration of a few important uses for mediation. These topics are mediation in the medical context, victim-offender mediation (restorative justice), and business transactions. In addition, the FmHA's Farmer-Lender mediation program is examined in Chapter Twelve.

B. MEDIATION IN THE MEDICAL SETTING

1. Comments and Questions

a. There is voluminous literature on the use of ADR in the medical setting, of which we offer only a small sample. For additional readings, see for example, Kathy L. Cerminara, *Contextualizing ADR in Managed Care: A Proposal Aimed at Easing Tensions and Resolving Conflict*, 33 Loy. U. Chi. L.J. 547 (2002); Glen Cohen, *Negotiating Death: ADR and End of Life Decision-Making*, 9 Harv. Negot. L. Rev. 253 (2004) (presents several detailed case histories); Dale C. Hetzler, Virginia L. Morrison, Debra Gerardi & Lorraine Sanchez Hayes, *Curing Conflict: A Prescription for ADR in Health Care*, 11 Disp. Resol. Mag. 5 (Fall 2004).

b. In view of the incredibly vast sums of money that are expended in the United States on medical expenses, however defined and whoever the payor, it is certain that large numbers of health care disputes will continue to arise and that dispute resolution services will be much in demand.

c. Extensive excerpts from several of the pieces discussed by Professor Bernard appear elsewhere in these materials: Judith Resnik (Chapter One), Richard Delgado (Chapter Five), and Owen Fiss (Chapter Thirteen). The uses of an Ombudsperson are examined in Chapter Eleven.

2. Nancy Neveloff Dubler, *Mediating Disputes in Managed Care: Resolving Conflicts Over Covered Services*, 2002 J. HEALTH CARE L. & P. 479

[M]any "bioethics" dilemmas that arise in the hospital setting are not really bioethics disputes at all. Rather than necessitating appeals to ethical principles such as autonomy, beneficence, non-malfeasance and justice, most clinical conflicts can be resolved by using the techniques of dispute resolution and mediation. It stood to reason, then, that if disputes involving managed care organizations (MCOs) — especially those dealing with medical necessity or the question of benefit coverage — share these characteristics of clinical conflicts, then it might be possible to use a dispute mediation process to address MCOs disputes at an early stage, resolve the disagreement, and support the patient-physician alliance. A major study on resolution of disputes in managed care recently posed the question: Is there a role for ADR in the structure of the MCO grievance and appeals system? And if so, would these techniques be most helpful in the window of opportunity before grievance and appeal are triggered and before the company and patient are divided into opposing camps? This article is one response to these important questions. . . .

The disputes selected for this project had already been resolved, and have been analyzed retrospectively by asking whether mediation might have been helpful if it had been available at an early stage. Not surprisingly, many MCOs contacted for the project refused to discuss case histories of disagreements and disputes. The seven plans that did agree were proud of their relationships with patients and their systems for managing conflicts. The materials they shared did reveal conflicts, but were designed to present their operations in a complimentary light. They were all pleased with the quality of care they provided and were not averse to exposing past conflicts and idiosyncratic solutions. The organizations interviewed for this project, the cases reviewed, and the policies examined indicate that managed care conflicts that are uncovered early . . . share characteristics with bioethics conflicts in the acute care setting and, like those conflicts, may be amenable to mediation if the plan is willing to expend the resources toward this end.

The characteristics shared by bioethics disputes and managed care conflicts include: uncertainty about the most appropriate plan of care for the patient; a multiplicity of voices all claiming to have relevant information and a perspective that should be respected; an urgency to the decision; possible negative consequences for the patient if the correct path of care is not chosen; and, finally, disparate financial consequences that attach to the contrasting choices. There is one major difference between the settings. In the context of bioethics disputes in the acute care setting, there is generally the need to seek the agreement of the patient or the family in the form of an informed consent to treatment. Despite the discrepancies of knowledge, power and authority that separate patients and families from physicians and staff, this ability to provide or withhold permission for patient interventions gives both sides a place at the table. In the managed care context, especially when the benefit coverage is uncertain, the patient or family is less likely to be at the table by right. Interviews with plans indicated that patients and family members were included because of uncertainty about the best plan of care, social commitment, public health outlook, or a fear of negative publicity. . . .

III. The Current State of Dispute Resolution in Managed Care

Elaborate federal regulations and state administrative requirements stipulate the rules governing dispute resolution between the MCOs and patients when disagreements arise about contractually covered benefits and reach the stage of appeal and grievance. At such times, when agreement and consensus are clearly no longer feasible goals, case data are arrayed as weapons in the adversary process where each side presents the facts, and spins the analysis in support of partisan interests. Despite this, few managed care plans and none of those studied had alternative dispute mechanisms in place to address disputes at an early stage of evolution.

A comparison of the literature and news media present diverging pictures of managed care organizations in the consumer dispute arena. While newspaper articles often represent MCOs as uncaring and rapacious, evidence suggests that these cases are the exception rather than the norm. The California Department of Corporations, which tabulates complaints against California health providers, reported fewer than two requests for assistance per 10,000 consumers for 1999, and a study by American Association of Healthcare Plans (AAHP) found 0.7 appeals per 10,000 enrollees. The managed mental health care organization interviewed for the project reported merely one complaint per 10,000 enrolls in the category "Disputes Over Covered Services" and one in the category "Does Not Like Benefits" giving the company a 0.03 complaint rate in those two categories. While these data are not conclusive, they suggest uncertainty about the approach and range of behaviors of managed care organizations. Certain commentators have argued that these numbers understate the problem by ignoring lack of consumer awareness of appeal rights or lack of confidence in the appeal process. However, these reports bring into question the premise that managed care providers systematically and unjustifiably deny care.

One traditional response to the problem of complaints has been the ombudsman, an independent official appointed by an institution to investigate and resolve complaints. More recently, many ombudsman programs include an advocacy component as well. Several states have established various forms of ombudsman programs to help resolve problems with health plans, especially for vulnerable populations. For example, as part of the settlement of the lawsuit brought by the Texas attorney general alleging Aetna misled customers by offering financial incentives to doctors to limit their costs of medical care, Aetna was obligated to hire an ombudsman to handle patient complaints. Although this article focuses on the usefulness of mediation in health plan disputes, consumers may also benefit from the implementation of ombudsman programs. Such programs could be particularly valuable in helping patients (consumers) understand the terms of their contract and their appeal rights.

Physicians, communities of patients and MCOs all have substantial stakes in reaching agreements about disputed matters in the most timely and least ran-

corous fashion. Most disputes address questions of medical necessity and benefit coverage and generally pit the dyad of treating physician and patient
against plan physicians and administrators. These conflicts undermine the
centrality of the doctor-patient relationship, devalue the collaborative decisions reached, and subordinate individual care plans to contractual cost-con-
tainment. Both the process and the result are often experienced by the patient
and the provider as an assault. . . .

V. Findings: Mediation versus Prospective Policy in Acute Care and Managed Care

The acute care setting is largely collaborative and composed of medical professionals as peers. Discussions are open and accessible among involved professionals and documented in a medical chart, the purpose of which is to
communicate the changing medical facts, record consultations, and note agreements and disagreements about the developing care plan. The medical chart documents the progress of the discussion. The consultants' notes and progress
notes from regular medical rounds expose the reasoning and logic of the
providers. And, at least in teaching hospitals, residents question all stages of the
process.

Mediation is useful in the acute care setting, because it intervenes at
moments of uncertainty when there are equally powerful medical and ethical
choices to be made. The process of mediation assists in clarifying positions,
framing the issues, identifying the competing parties and their interests,
expanding and arraying the options for agreement, testing the component parts
of any solution, crafting a consensus and recording the process, and documenting the logic of the choice and the eventual outcome in the chart. The
closer that disputes in managed care approach this paradigm, the more they
provide a platform for mediation.

Managed care disputes are first noted by a staff member at the plan responsible for some sort of response or triage, who records a patient's request and
notes the likely answer. This person may or may not have professional training.
The request may not reach a level of professional scrutiny and may remain hidden within the complex response and record keeping systems of the company.
In some of the cases, the dispute is raised not by the patient but rather by the
community provider directly with the medical professionals in the plan. This
approach leads to collaborative discussion between professionals, which may be
more suited to reaching consensus than patient-plan discourse. This collaborative exploration in pursuit of a care plan does not necessarily need an independent, trained, professional mediator. However, mediation may assist in
developing common understandings of the issues, identifying overlapping interests, reframing the issues, testing those against bioethics principles and legal
rules, and arriving at a "principled resolution" or consensus. In this as in other
arenas, technology may soon provide answers to logistical difficulties.

If disputes in managed care about benefit coverage and medical necessity are
seen as binary decisions, the notion that mediation could assist in resolution
seems far-fetched. But once those decisions are arrayed along a topography of
parties and interests, the utility of mediation becomes evident. First, it creates

a setting in which all parties can listen to the reasoning of the others. It facilitates an evaluation of the emotional tenor of the case and the passion of the patient and family. Lastly, it disaggregates the case into comprehensible components and helps find areas of agreement that could become the basis for a consensus.

Review of the plans interviewed for this study identified common strands of operation and indicated that, at present, the potential for resolving disputes in managed care appears most related to clear policies, available in advance to and known by the patient's regular medical or mental health provider and to the patient. However, the creation and publication of these sorts of policies is difficult, since both internal and government regulations pertaining to the managed care dispute resolution process are often complex and are in a constant state of flux.

The second factor that seems related to managing conflict is a collegial and collaborative working relationship among the professionals who treat patients in the community and the clinically trained professionals in the company who can evaluate patient need in light of company policy. Both of these approaches are currently being taken by many MCOs throughout the country. Practically every health care provider in the country has a website and some managed care providers train their employees in conflict management skills and have systems in place to maintain collegial relationships with community physicians. Collegial relationships support dispute resolution as they reinforce the relevance of the doctor-patient relationship by including the community physician in the decision-making process and enlisting that person in the process of seeking agreement.

VI. Guidelines for Addressing Early Stage Managed Care Disputes

Assuming that like cases will repetitively emerge in practice, negotiated agreements, meeting the needs of all parties, should provide prospective models for resolving similar cases in the future. One of the benefits of good conflict management should be the creation of new, successful, tested pathways for dispute resolution. The natural clash of perspectives between and among patients, families, hospitals and MCOs frames repeated conflicts for which template solutions are useful in "mutualizing" interests as a way of identifying common ground for future agreement.

Whenever patient health is at risk, denials of benefit coverage will be accompanied by conflict, no matter how clear the contract language. Addressing consequences of conflict cannot be ignored by plans that care about their patients and their standing in the civic and medical communities. Thus, ongoing, easily triggered, immediate review of developing disputes seems practically, ethically and medically an appropriate solution. Where there is a heightened awareness of the potential for conflict and an intelligent organizational response, mediation may be the best available intervention. . . . A review of the widely disbursed plans in this study revealed that the MCO policies that support conflict resolution could be described as follows:

- *Participatory*: including non-company personnel — patients, citizens and members of the medical community — in the process of setting policy and guidelines;

- *Scientifically based*: include peer review and/or consultation with outside experts prior to rejecting beneficiary's request for unusual or expensive potentially uncovered benefits;

- *Transparent*: being open and clear about policies and practices;

- *Accessible*: providing information on the web and disseminating copies of policies and procedures;

- *Accepting of challenges*: having an automatic appeal process before denials of benefits in order to protect the company and the patient;

- *Committed to public and community health*: assessing the health needs of its covered lives as the basis for creating a responsive benefit package;

- *Consistent*: treating similarly situated patients the same way (justice and fairness);

- *Communicative*: providing information about its process through use of a regularly updated open access web-site with scholarly and educational materials for physicians and patients; and

- *Organizationally sensitive*: committed to processes to explore the medical, social, financial, and public relations consequence of decisions.

Were these principles to be augmented by mediation, . . . it would link the policy perspectives to instances of individual need. The one company closest to meeting all of these sets of characteristics saw its commitment grounded in the notion that the key to ethical decision-making is not only a fair process of appeal and grievance but also an initially responsive system that adheres to the idea that, "when people buy health insurance, they expect that it will cover them when they are sick."

VII. Conclusion

Mediation, based on a recognition of multi-party interests, provides a simple and appealing process for thinking about the management of conflicts in managed care settings that may be imbued with ethical issues or overtones but are actually disagreements about benefits coverage. In addition to the possible advantages of mediation observed from the cases, it offers several other tangible benefits to the parties in the health care dispute. Statistically, mediation is significantly cheaper and faster than arbitration. In addition, participants have been shown to be more satisfied with the outcome and effect of the process on the parties' relationship than arbitration. Mediation allows for a positive collaboration to remain among the MCO and physician, while preserving the physician-patient relationship. Finally, mediation creates a template for addressing similar conflicts that may arise in the future.

Conflicts in managed care about appropriate benefit coverage care can be distinguished from conflicts in the acute care setting about specific treatment plans. Managed care conflicts are more likely to focus on costs; to involve non-physician and non-medical staff in the first instance; to be related to contract interpretation rather than the notion of patient well-being; to be distant from the open peer review process of the clinical setting; and to be affected by printed policy and contractual exclusions. As these differences from the acute setting become more pronounced, the logistics of mediation become more difficult. However, in many cases there is still value in bringing the parties together to hear one another, to maximize the understanding of the opposing decision, and to undergird the search for an agreed upon solution. Clear policies known to providers and patients in advance and collaborative decision making among plan professionals and community providers combine to offer a basis for good preventive management of conflict. . . . Whether this promise will be realized will depend on the willingness of the MCO to allocate funds for this endeavor.

3. Phyllis E. Bernard, *Mediating with an 800-Pound Gorilla*, 60 WASH. & LEE L. REV. 1417 (2004)

With the infusion of over 200 billion Medicare dollars annually, health care services now constitute one of the largest industries in the country. Medicare serves about forty million elderly and disabled persons annually and pays nearly 1 million hospitals, physicians, and other health care providers. In 2000, the Medicare program represented about 11% of the federal budget. According to colloquial labels for power relationships, Medicare surely qualifies as the 800-pound gorilla that sits wherever it wants.

A skeptical observer might question the marginal role the beneficiary-patient plays in the perennial Medicare debates. Relative to those whose incomes derive from Medicare payments, the beneficiary-patient has only a muted voice. This outcome should not surprise us. It is the logical result of having relegated the recipient of services to the sidelines. In so doing, health care for seniors and the disabled has increasingly veered away from doctor-patient relationships of long duration and substantial trust, and towards high-intensity, invasive tertiary care that increases revenues to providers, but does not increase satisfaction to the patient.

This Article proposes that we reorient Medicare. Medicare should refocus financing in ways designed to sustain a collaborative doctor-patient relationship, emphasizing primary care fitting the level of support the beneficiary and her family prefers. Such a reorientation would shift the direction of Medicare from provider-oriented to beneficiary-centered. The mechanism for effecting this change would be mediation aimed at developing a collaborative medical treatment plan. This plan would establish principles for anticipated hospitalizations and other tertiary care, establishing the balance of services (degree of intensity and invasiveness), and institutionalized versus non-institutionalized long-term care that comports with the patient's preferences. Mediation between the patient, the patient's relevant family member(s), and the medical team would facilitate efficient use of known Medicare (and other) resources.

A third-party neutral trained in the skills of restating and reframing to build consensus can: (1) reveal mistaken assumptions and unrealistic expectations; (2) identify shared values so that services meet underlying needs; and (3) address otherwise unarticulated and poorly managed anxieties. A nonstakeholder can bring confidence in the process itself specifically because this neutral person is not a member of the medical team, nor a designated patient representative (whom the medical team could view as an adversary). The use of trained neutral parties can assure fairness as a matter of system design, not relying primarily upon the right blend of temperaments to achieve optimal communication. . . .

This Article also proposes that all the services Medicare provides pursuant to such a mediated plan would be paid without delay. This offers a substantial, tangible incentive for full participation by the beneficiary and by the practitioner. They both need incentives to undertake a process that HHS's Office of Inspector General (OIG) recognizes as "labor-intensive" and "a burden," which operates under the perpetual cloud that "there is likely to be a perceived imbalance of power between the participants." OIG posited that these factors partially explain the low rates of participation in the five limited pilot mediation projects reviewed as of August 2001. In the OIG study, Peer Review Organizations (PROs) extended offers to mediate complaints fifty-eight times. Only twenty-eight beneficiaries and only eleven providers mediated.

Placing the mediation process at the predispute/pregrievance/precomplaint stage substantially reduces the need to sort through which types of complaints would be appropriate or inappropriate for mediation. Vastly improved communication may largely prevent disputes rising to the level of grievances or complaints. Placing the mediation at the formation stage in the doctor-patient relationship — before the beneficiary's health has deteriorated and before a dispute has raised the emotional stakes — lifts yet another serious burden from the beneficiary. Finally, institutionalizing these mediated dialogues and making payment contingent upon the resulting treatment plan assures follow-up to protect the interests of beneficiaries, as the OIG requested.

The mediated treatment plan, once institutionalized, could substantially reduce the future volume of appeals for denials of claims and coverage. It can offer a mechanism to assure compliance with HHS's treatment guidelines, especially for chronic conditions. It offers an appropriate, compassionate means to address access and end-of-life decisions. This process, however, takes time and deserves compensation. Thus, the mediation time of the medical team should be separately paid as a billable service. By making such mediations standard procedure, the Medicare program could emerge as the salvation of the doctor-patient relationship it has been accused of destroying. . . .

Most importantly, one must ask whether any unrepresented patient can effectively mediate with the gatekeeper who seeks to deny the services the patient perceives as essential to life or to an acceptable quality of life. The medical institutions hold power that dwarfs the power of the vulnerable patient. How can mediation achieve balance and thus fairness in such negotiations? Taking it a step further, how can one structure an equitable mediation in which the patient confronts not only the medical establishment, but the federal government, in the form of the Medicare program? . . .

II. Are Medicare and Mediation Compatible?

A. A Brief Overview of ADR in the Medicare Program. Like most federal agencies designated as the primary interface between the public and the government, the Health Care Financing Administration (HCFA), now known as the Centers for Medicare and Medicaid Services (CMS), has sought to be efficient, fair, and user-friendly. These goals in theory are unquestionable. In practice, however, they prove not only elusive but often contradictory.

The annual volume of Medicare cases that HCFA/CMS faces requires that justice be processed through mass production quite unlike the image of litigated, individualized justice dispensed in the court room. If millions of beneficiaries, providers, and suppliers are to receive some sort of hearing concerning a dispute with the program, fairness requires attention to the mundane, unglamorous features of due process. The chosen system for resolving disputes over payments cannot attempt to replicate the formal Administrative Procedure Act (APA) trial-type proceeding. It would prove too slow, too varied in result, and too costly.

Medicare disputants need a response in a fairly short period of time, especially when the answer makes a fundamental difference in a beneficiary's course of treatment, or in the fiscal viability of a provider institution. Results must be consistent enough to assure the public that their government has not acted in an arbitrary and capricious manner. Actions must be sufficiently predictable that businesspeople can make realistic plans. And, the final prong of the *Mathews v. Eldridge*, 424 U.S. 319 (1976), due process test looms ever larger as the volume of cases also grows. Namely, administrative costs for maintaining an adjudicatory process must be affordable even when multiplied by an extraordinary volume of cases.

Throughout the 1980s and into the 1990s, the Administrative Conference of the United States (ACUS) addressed these considerations to develop thoughtful, neutral studies and recommendations designed to meet the goals of efficiency, fairness, and accessibility for the lay public. In 1986, ACUS determined that the Medicare appeals system was a "patchwork with differing administrative and judicial review requirements" that needed to be rationalized. [Among the options was] a proposal to bring ADR to the Part A adjudications the Provider Reimbursement Review Board (PRRB) handles. ACUS. . . . suggested that the PRRB's adjudicatory functions be reduced or eliminated entirely, replaced by ADR, possibly through the HHS Departmental Appeals Board (DAB). Those who utilized PRRB adjudicatory services, within the government and within the provider community, expressed remarkable willingness to undertake such a change. In 1998, CMS determined that the time for mediation of PRRB cases had arrived and implemented a pilot mediation project. The in-house mediation program has been a major success, from the perspective of both providers and government representatives.

The advent of managed care emphasized negotiation, mediation, and arbitration as preferred methods for resolving disputes between the Medicare program, providers, and beneficiaries. Private sector, private payor managed care organizations had led the way with varied success. Medicaid managed care demonstration projects at the state level experimented with ADR components. These experiments later informed the choices that CMS made. On both the federal and state levels, legislators made ADR provisions boilerplate in almost every managed care statute and other health reform statutes over the past ten years. We must reserve some doubt, however, about the basis for these public affirmations that ADR is appropriate in virtually all managed care settings. Does this stem from a desire to make appeals processes rapid, flexible, and truly user-friendly? Or is it tinged with an unacknowledged desire simply to save administrative costs and shift responsibility?

B. Mediating in Private About Public Matters. The issues for discussion here illustrate in a tangible way the theoretical concerns Professor Owen Fiss raises in his now-classic article, *Against Settlement.* His critique of institutionalized ADR may sound caustic. "Consent is often coerced; . . . although dockets may be trimmed, justice may not be done. Like plea bargaining, settlement is a capitulation to the conditions of mass society and should be neither encouraged nor praised." But it has the ring of truth. For, unless the contending parties stand on roughly equal footing, coercion is built into the very structure of society and the legal system. What happens if both parties do not have access to the same resources?

Fiss explains that disparities in resources between the parties can influence the settlement in three ways. All three reflect the power dynamics of mediations between private parties and the Medicare program. In considering the situation of beneficiaries mediating with health care providers and with Medicare as payor, the influence of such disparities is amplified. The poorer party may be less able to amass and analyze the information needed to predict the outcome of the litigation and, thus, be disadvantaged in the bargaining process. No provider institution, individual provider, or beneficiary has at their disposal the arsenal of data concerning Medicare treatment and payment practices and policies that CMS possesses. Furthermore, the federal government holds immediate and, increasingly, ultimate authority over the outcome by controlling not only the adjudicators, but all principles used for decision-making.

The poorer party may need the damages he seeks immediately and thus be induced to settle as a way of accelerating payment, even though he realizes he would get less now than he might if he awaited judgment. In 1984, Fiss wrote "simply" about the fiscal exigencies pressuring a party who confronts on one side a growing hill of debts (such as medical expenses) already incurred because of the litigated incident, and on the other side, the loss of regular income, again because of the underlying dispute. Today, in the context of Medicare fiscal disputes, both time pressures and time value for their resolution have magnified considerably. Here, by definition, most beneficiaries live on fixed incomes that have little margin for unanticipated, unpaid medical expenses. Even in situations that are not fee-for-service, both the managed care organization and the patient must know promptly whether Medicare will or will not cover a service, or risk impairment of the patient's health by failing to provide the service in a therapeutically efficacious time frame.

The poorer party might be forced to settle because he does not have the resources to finance the litigation, to cover either his own projected expenses, such as his lawyer's time, or the expenses his opponent can impose through the manipulation of procedural mechanisms such as discovery. Most patients lack the financial or emotional resources to support protracted litigation over health care services or payment denials. Furthermore, few advocates (attorney or non-attorney) can undertake such representation on terms affordable for the bulk of the elderly or disabled receiving Medicare benefits. Without a reasonably knowledgeable and dogged advocate, it is unlikely that most Medicare beneficiaries could successfully navigate the confusing world of health care appeals. Yet, such patient advocacy is rare.

How does society rebalance such imbalances of power? Through the courts. Fiss argues eloquently that: "Civil litigation is an institutional arrangement for using state power to bring a recalcitrant reality closer to our chosen ideals." He sees adjudication "American-style" not as a "reflection of our combativeness," but rather as "a tribute to our . . . commitment" to equal justice even when the parties are not economically, socially, or politically equal.

In this paradigm of justice, although recognizing that true equality may be illusory, fairness requires adjudicatory processes so the playing field is tilted less abusively. Legal scholars from perspectives as diverse as Professor Richard Delgado to Professor Judith Resnik have challenged the institutionalization of ADR. Resnik has urged caution in the apparent rush to make ADR the default setting for adjudication. That is to say, when the courts fail to fulfill their promise of justice — due to crowded dockets and high litigation costs — we should think carefully whether the system should divert parties to ADR. This would assure some access to justice, but it may be sub-optimal.

On the other hand, Resnik notes that some parties might prefer ADR over adjudication. For them, ADR would not constitute a mere "default" setting. Rather, they may prefer the informality of ADR as a way to promote candid communication and improved problem-solving. The very absence of procedural and evidentiary rules found in the court room could equate to more, not less, justice. Still, a wide disparity of resources between the parties (as Fiss described) would undermine fairness. And clearly, there is no greater disparity of resources than in a dispute between a private person and the federal government. . . .

Some observers have posited that negotiation and mediation should fit readily into the language of health care professionals, because the transactions of daily work involve so much give-and-take. Whether the issue is developing medical treatment plans, communicating those directives to all patient care staff, or negotiating rates of payment with payors, ADR methods steer health care operations. If this thesis is correct, then it helps illuminate the relatively rapid expansion of mediation at HHS. From the 1992 listing of a potential pilot project in the exploratory stage to use ADR in disputes before the PRRB in the HCFA to implementation, took only six years.

Another series of notices came during this period, erecting a regulatory framework for rapid resolution of disputes among patients, providers, physicians, and managed care organizations over denials or terminations of treatment. These procedural changes sought to ameliorate the overwhelming and unfair pressures of time-sensitive decision-making. . . . The cited issues of power dynamics, unequal resources, and the exigencies of time pressures coalesced in 1993 in the form of a federal class action, *Grijalva v. Shalala*, 946 F. Supp. 747 (D. Ariz. 1996).

In *Grijalva*, Medicare beneficiaries enrolled in risk-based managed care organizations sued to assure that their rights be heard concerning quality of care complaints, medical treatment decisions, and adequacy of information. Four years later, Congress enacted the Balanced Budget Act of 1997, which included in Section 4001 a new Subpart C of the Medicare Program known as the "Medicare+Choice Program" (M+C) embracing managed care plans. This new statutory mandate required M+C organizations to provide "meaningful procedures for hearing and resolving grievances between the organization and enrollees."

In December 2000, the Arizona District Court approved the settlement agreement negotiated to resolve *Grijalva* and to implement the mandates of the Balanced Budget Act. As the Department described in the preamble to its final rule: "A key element of the agreement was that CMS would propose to establish an independent review entity [IRE] to conduct fast-track reviews of appeals of decisions to terminate services." Beneficiaries having a grievance — any other complaint about service — would have a different track. Grievances would go through ADR, with an emphasis on negotiation, conciliation, and mediation. Beneficiary advocacy groups primarily had demanded that CMS assure safeguards would protect neutrality in the ADR intervention. Therefore, CMS designated a neutral party for disputes concerning termination of services by an MCO. In this Article's proposal, the use of a trained third-party neutral mitigates deeply embedded concerns about perceived conflicts of interest and severe imbalances of power.

III. Deconstructing the 800-Pound Gorilla

Most people would look at the Medicare program, with its vast powers of financial and legal coercion, and see overwhelming power over a provider of services and over a beneficiary of services. In the view of most program participants, what Medicare wants, Medicare gets. Providers comply with the Medicare decisions, if only because of the enforcement power of the federal government. . . . This includes the power to impose criminal sanctions. If only for ease of administration, services for other patients, which are covered by other payors, often are structured to be compatible with Medicare's requirements.

Under these circumstances, how can one assert that there is a balance of power sufficient to recommend mediation between the payor and provider concerning a dispute in payment or coverage? Mediation can work when the providers are sophisticated, institutional entities with legal representation present at the negotiations, principles of law are not central to resolving the dispute, perceptions of facts are more important than the law, and personal credibility and trustworthiness are essential to the use of a flexible approach in resolving the dispute. With these factors in place, mediation of Part A disputes has proven successful at the PRRB. But can it work when the mediation involves the beneficiary?

Mediation is ideal for the "people problems" that present themselves disguised as "legal problems." Thus, it can work well or is appropriate when: the parties are not in a gross imbalance of power, such that any agreement could not be considered the product of freely exercised will; there is a prior, existing, or continuing relationship between the parties; or, if there is no prior or likely future relationship, the parties desire a good reputation in the community; there are few legal issues at stake and no precedent that needs to be enunciated; all persons necessary to effect and hold to a successful resolution are present at the table; all participants have available to them whatever is required to make informed choices; the mediation participants are ready and able to speak for themselves, even if they must be assisted by persons the participants have designated in advance; a pragmatic resolution will be acceptable, even if it does not follow the technicalities of the law; and the parties will voluntarily comply with the resolution.

When Medicare mediations are framed in this light, one questions the basic premise entirely. Is mediation of such issues appropriate at all when the parties are not sophisticated institutional providers of care, but instead are unsophisticated, typically unrepresented lay persons confronted by a denial of care, reduction in treatment, refusal of coverage, or an experience of disrespect or discord in the provision of medical care?

Some researchers studying the dynamics of conflicts concerning medical practice have described the psychological context of these conflicts in ways that we should consider with regard to coverage issues. Although the system may see this as a payor-payee or provider-beneficiary matter, for the individual caught in the midst of it all, this is about a doctor-patient relationship that has gone sour. It is about trust that either has been broken or had not been forged from the beginning. To understand the dynamics of the conflicts mediation seeks to resolve or prevent, we must return to the generating circumstances. We must understand the interrelationships of the stakeholders to understand the possibilities for settlement beginning with the mind-set of the patient-beneficiary.

Clearly, when a person is ill enough to go to a doctor, he is experiencing some level of physical discomfort. This physical issue also has psychological and emotional dimensions, even if it is not what society would categorize as a psychosomatic disorder. As one registered nurse and conflict resolution specialist astutely described, the patient typically enters the relationship with a diminished self-image. This is accompanied by a feeling that he is losing control over his life, which may be a reality. Hence, the patient experiences considerable anxiety and insecurity. These stresses may reveal themselves in a heightened desperation to believe the "myth that Western medicine is infallible," such that anything short of a complete cure violates trust. Lack of a perfect outcome, therefore, equals betrayal.

The physician also experiences the therapeutic relationship at a psychological and emotional level. When confronted with the complaint, grievance, or general displeasure of a patient, his attitude evidences defensiveness. The patient's disapproval threatens the physician's self-image as a healer. The sense that his work has not been appreciated feeds an underlying anger, which may or may not be expressed. Undeniably, the doctor becomes increasingly tense. There is much resentment over the "significant amounts of time taken from their practice to respond to what they believe are frivolous claims." And, finally, there is frustration and bewilderment, as he sincerely believes he has met his promises to his patients. It would be appropriate to extend the psychological and emotional context of the physician to include the psychological and emotional context of the provider organization. Although some do not believe that organizations have a psyche or emotions, the expansion should include the MCO's representatives. . . .

Chris Currie offered a useful description of the relational goals a patient seeks when he files a complaint or grievance against his managed care organization or physician. The patient wants: answers to questions he feels the physician or provider institution, or both, have not been willing to answer honestly; recognition from the physician or provider institution, or both, that his condition is serious and his condition has long-term, life-changing consequences; to vent his anger over a poor doctor-patient or MCO-enrollee relationship in which he felt ignored, neglected, or mistreated; and to hold the physician or the MCO, or both, accountable in order to prevent the same situation from recurring with another patient.

The goals described above embody what a transformative approach to mediation describes "empowerment." . . . Empowerment with regard to goals occurs when a party reaches a clearer realization, compared to before, of what matters to her and why, together with a realization that it's important and deserves consideration. The transformative model frames party power in personal terms, as a matter of personal (not necessarily material) power. This can manifest in the ability of parties "to clarify their views — to know what they want and do not want, to stand up for those views, and what resources they have to address the situation." Given this subjective, self-referencing understanding of power, Bush and Folger posit that no one is wholly without power. Everyone has the potential to acknowledge and exercise his or her own personal power in a mediation. Indeed, this becomes one of the most important aspects of a mediation.

A transformative mediation "succeeds" when there is empowerment. This occurs when a party experiences a greater sense of self-worth, security, self-determination, and autonomy. Clearly, the transformative model overlays well with the concept of mediation to heal a troubled doctor-patient relationship. However, one must ask whether these goals are sufficient when the patient or beneficiary confronts institutional power. . . .

It is important that any system for ADR present opportunities for party empowerment. But it is equally important that the parties be fully informed and make knowledgeable choices in the exercise of their autonomy. The physician can serve as the single most valuable information resource for the patient. The challenge is designing reliable, replicable methods to facilitate that sharing of information and power in a nonthreatening way that is sensitive to emotional cues. . . . The overarching goal, particularly in primary care, is for the physician-patient relationship to be "a primary therapeutic tool." This impressive goal could be realized through [empowerment mediation]. . . .

The style will likely parallel the Individuals with Disabilities Education Act (IDEA) mediations used to resolve disputes among parents, teachers, counselors, therapists, and school administrators concerning disabled children mainstreamed into public education. . . . In IDEA cases, a multidisciplinary team develops an individualized education plan (IEP), which is a comprehensive assessment of the child's full range of abilities and disabilities, used to guide educational activities for the student. The IEP attempts to bridge the child's worlds at home and at school to achieve coherence and cooperation among the adults who are vital to the child's well-being. Although the IEP is far from immutable, the exercise of creating an IEP has the capacity to focus the team away from turf issues and towards the best interests of the student. A productive, nonadversarial experience in such problem-solving builds a positive foundation for future interactions between parents and the school.

Typically, a successfully negotiated IEP can establish a baseline of trust capable of sustaining good faith efforts through the inevitable changes and crises that develop over time. When the initial IEP development does not manage to create a productive baseline, or when other issues have destabilized the IEP, the parent can request an IDEA mediation to facilitate problem-solving with the team. Success of such mediations varies, due at least in part to the style of mediation used, and the perceived neutrality of the mediation process. Compliance by schools and school districts often hinges on whether the key administrators recognize that the large investment of time by staff in a mediation is far less than the resources that would be invested in a due process hearing. Otherwise, there can be concerns about the burden placed upon the teachers, counselors, therapists, and school administrators whose time in mediation is not compensated. Under such conditions, mediation itself can be resented. . . .

It is unquestioned that comprehensive . . . assessments and treatment plans developed pursuant to such assessments represent the right therapeutic approach. Nevertheless, it remains a practice in only a minority of hospitals and medical schools. If it is undoubtedly the right thing to do as a matter of medical practice and ethics, then why is it so rare? In a word: money. Under current payment structures, the time of the interdisciplinary team conducting the comprehensive assessment and modifying the plan according to the needs of the patient and caregiver largely goes unpaid. Although the physician's time is recognized, that of others may not be factored in. Time spent in consultation with the patient and caregiver as an integral part of developing and finalizing the plan typically must go unrecognized. Programs that have adopted this approach and have implemented it in full have relied upon outside grant funds to cover these costs. Once such funding ends, the comprehensive model also likely ends.

Medicare could advance its agenda of streamlining and humanizing appeals by investing finances at the front end. Assuring compensation for all providers of services in the comprehensive medical assessment (applicable to both the elderly and to the disabled), coupled with compensation for time spent mediating the medical treatment plan, would guarantee full implementation. Once the plan has been finalized in writing and reviewed generally for coverage, all services rendered pursuant to the plan should be deemed covered and paid promptly. These changes in billing could create a powerful and lasting incentive for providers to make the necessary commitment of resources.

What would the Medicare program receive in return for its investment? The program should see greater rationalization of services, major reductions in disputes over coverage or denial of services, greatly reduced incentives to practice costly, often inefficient "defensive medicine" to stave off malpractice suits, and improved tools to implement continual quality improvement. Moreover, the Medicare program could forge the mechanism whereby the doctor-patient relationship returns to its proper place as the primary therapeutic tool.

4. Nancy Neveloff Dubler & Carol B. Liebman, *Bioethics: Mediating Conflict in the Hospital Environment*, DISP. RESOL. J. May-July 2004 at 32

Bioethics is about people: the lives and deaths of individual patients in the context of family, friends, and care providers — and the personalities, history, attitudes and feelings, including fears and a sense of guilt, and the commitments of each person involved. In recent years, bioethics disputes have become more common. The patients' rights movement, along with the consumer movement, have legitimized the place of the family and the patient in the deliberation regarding medical matters. At the same time, awareness of the potential for conflict has grown as a result of the shifting structure of health care funding and delivery. The growth of managed care and the shift from fee-for-service medicine (with its incentives for overtreatment) to capitated arrangements (with their incentives for under-treatment) have fueled a growing mistrust among patients and their families, who perceive that the integrity of the care provided may be affected by factors external to the best interests of the patient. This shift has also led to increased tension between doctors and nurses, on one hand, and organizational administrators, on the other, who seek to improve the profitability of the health care institution by increasing the productivity of health care providers, reducing admission to hospitals, and shortening the time spent in acute care institutions. . . .

In 1992, the Joint Commission on Accreditation of Healthcare Organizations established a new standard that required all accredited institutions to have the capacity to address ethical issues in medical care and practice. The result of that pronouncement was the creation of a new wave of ethics committees, which sought to develop the capacities to engage in case consultation, education, and policy development. It would be difficult now to find a health care institution of any quality that does not have an ethics committee addressing staff education, policy protocols, and, at the very least, retrospective case consultation or review. . . .

But just how to move forward was a puzzle to many committees and fledgling consultation efforts. Intervening in cases as they evolve, and by intervening perhaps changing the medical plan, brings with it the need for a theory of practice to guide the intervention. Analyzing what has happened in the past has fewer moral consequences than helping to determine what will happen in the future. Should the ethics consultant or committee advise the caregivers? Should they write their opinions in the chart? Should they intervene in the care plan being developed? Should they impose their values and notions of the "right" and the "good" on the care team? And how should the patient's family be involved in these discussions? Consultations often address issues, such as the withdrawal of treatment or the limitation of care, although they may equally well suggest a more aggressive care plan. One cannot and should not be prepared to intervene in this process of decision making without having clear notions of the governing principles and procedural guidelines that will structure and constrain the intervention. . . .

We propose that the best process for identifying, understanding, and resolving conflicts in bioethics consultations is a mediative intervention. Such a process identifies the parties to the conflict; clarifies the medical facts; helps the patient and, if involved, the family to amplify the values and interests of the patient in the complex and intimidating structure of the medical center; and helps the parties determine whether there is space for a shared resolution.

Mediation is now used in a variety of medical settings to deal with disputes between residents and staff in nursing homes, disputes over Medicare reimbursement, quality-of-care complaints involving Medicare and Medicaid, and medical malpractice claims and bioethics disputes, most notably by Montefiore Medical Center in its pioneering program. Bioethics mediation combines the clinical substance and perspective of bioethics consultation with the tools of the mediation process, using the techniques of mediation and dispute resolution in order to:

- identify the parties to the conflict (although disagreements between family and care providers are common, most conflicts have more than two sides);

- understand the stated and latent interests of the participants;

- level the playing field to minimize disparities of power, knowledge, skill, and experience (to the degree possible) that separate medical professional, patient, and family;

- help the parties define their interests;

- help maximize options for a resolution of the conflict;

- search for common ground or areas of consensus;

- ensure that the consensus can be justified as a "principled resolution," compatible with the principles of bioethics and the legal rights of patients and families;

- help to implement the agreement; and

- conduct follow-up.

Bioethics mediation in the acute care setting can serve many ends. It may, under certain circumstances, enhance the autonomy of the patient, support the shared values of patient and family, or make clear and strengthen the agreed-upon principles of health care provision. Sometimes, it results in the implementation of a commonly shared plan. Whatever the end result, the fundamental goal of mediating bioethics disputes is to maximize the likelihood that a principled resolution will be reached in a way that is comfortable for all parties.

A key component of bioethics mediation is the creation of "neutral turf," made possible by the presence of a person who is not a member of the health care team and who has not participated in the interventions that have gone awry or the discussions that have broken down. Unlike the classical mediator, who is assumed to be totally impartial and is not connected to either party, the bioethics mediator will likely be an employee of the hospital that is the site of the dispute. Nonetheless, the bioethics mediator brings a distinct set of concerns and skills to the meetings with providers, patients, and family and must be impartial to the situation at hand. One important reason for a bioethics mediation is to "level the playing field" and give patients and families opportunities to be heard. . . .

What makes bioethics mediation unique? There are several ways in which bioethics mediation differs from other types of mediation.

1. The bioethics mediator is generally employed by the hospital.
2. The bioethics mediator and members of the treatment team are repeat players.
3. The bioethics mediator provides information, enforces norms, and ensures that resolutions fall within medical "best practice" guidelines.
4. Deciding not to reach a resolution is not an option.
5. The playing field is usually uneven for patients and their families.
6. Confidentiality is limited to information not relevant to patient care.
7. Time is of the essence.
8. Bioethics mediations involve life-and-death issues.
9. Facts play a different role.
10. The person with the greatest stake in the dispute, the patient, is often not at the table.
11. There may be a sequence of separate, prior meetings in addition to the group mediation.
12. Bioethics mediations are almost always multiparty events.
13. The parties usually do not sign an agreement to mediate.
14. The physical setting may not be in the mediator's control.
15. Bioethics mediators are often involved in following up on implementation of the agreement.
16. All participants in a bioethics mediation have a common interest in the well-being of the patient.

5. Charity Scott, *Mediating Life and Death: Review of Nancy N. Dubler & Carol Liebman,* BIOETHICS MEDIATION: A GUIDE TO SHAPING SHARED SOLUTIONS (2004), Disp. Resol. Mag., Fall 2004, at 23

Bioethics Consultation Versus Bioethics Mediation. How does bioethics consultation differ from bioethics mediation? Bioethics consultation is analogous to medical consultation, in which generally the consultant (individual, team or committee) reviews a case and gives an expert opinion or recommendation as to how it should be handled. In this book, bioethics mediation is different in at least three key respects. First, usually a single bioethics mediator is involved in mediating a case, rather than several ethics committee members who may form the review body consulting on a case. Second, the primary goal of mediation is for the parties themselves to arrive at consensus as to the appropriate course of action. In a consultation, while consensus would be a desirable outcome if it occurred, the desired end is generally for the consultants to provide recommendations for resolving the conflict, which the parties may or may not accept. Third, in a description that may irk some ethics committees and consultants, the authors declare: "Mediation is more inclusive and empowering, and consultation is more authoritarian and hierarchical." A primary premise of this book, whose authors are both trained as lawyers, is that the best process for analyzing and resolving conflicts in bioethics consultation is a mediative intervention. . . .

A Practical Guide to Bioethics Mediation. Readers who are already familiar with the process of bioethics consultation will recognize many similarities with this book's seven stages of bioethics mediation:

1. Assessment and preparation. After receiving a request to consult on a case, the mediator will undertake a background investigation of the medical facts and nature of the dispute, often interviewing the health care team, patient (if able to communicate) and family members in order to make a preliminary identification of the issues to be resolved, the appropriate decision-makers and the parties who should be at the mediation.

2. Beginning the mediation. Like many bioethics consultations, bioethics mediations begin with introductions and a formal opening statement by the mediator that describes his or her role in helping the parties to find common ground, the process and goals of mediation and confidentiality concerns. Using sample language, the book demonstrates how mediators can set an appropriate tone and begin to build trust from the very outset of a mediation.

3. Presenting and refining the medical facts. A corollary of the adage that hard cases make bad law is that "good ethics begins with good facts." The mediator often faces difficulty in establishing the medical facts, however, since the very concept of a "differential diagnosis" in medicine implies the possibility of multiple explanations for certain conditions.

4. Gathering information. At this stage, the mediator will summarize the discussion in his or her own words and begin to ask questions to identify and explore the relevant issues, interests and feelings of the participants. Sifting important from unimportant information is a complex task for even the most skilled bioethics mediators, since often, the participants are reluctant to discuss matters that are highly sensitive.

5. Problem solving. The mediator will begin to identify and develop the range of options in the case, and will guide the discussion of these options in light of the parties' various interests and shared values. The authors acknowledge that it is unlikely that this stage will proceed in a purely linear manner, since "feelings are facts" which must be acknowledged throughout the discussion.

6. Resolution. If the parties reach agreement on a shared solution, then the mediator should ensure that it is realistic, reflects the parties' interests, and is documented in the patient's chart. The book provides a detailed sample chart note for illustration.

7. Follow-up. The mediator should follow up to ensure that the agreement is implemented, and to ensure that the family and health caregivers are adequately supported during the process of implementation.

This approach seems similar to the one recommended by the American Society for Bioethics and Humanities in its 1998 report entitled "Core Competencies for Health Care Ethics Consultation." The two core features of its recommended "ethics facilitation" approach to ethics consultation are "identifying and analyzing the nature of the value uncertainty [or conflict] and facilitating the building of consensus." Whether mediation and consultation are distinct processes, however, is not as important as how to employ effectively the interpersonal, process and communication skills that this book aptly describes and persuasively promotes. These skills can be adapted not only to formal mediations and consultations, but also to daily interactions to encourage problem solving and conflict management in health care settings before a case rises to the level of needing a formal intervention.

Role for Mediation in Other Health Care Conflicts. Mediation presupposes that there is a conflict or dispute among the parties, but often, the antecedent treatment dilemma is one of uncertainty: When should treatment turn from curative to palliative? What would the patient have wanted under the circumstances? To what extent should health caregivers honor cultural and religious differences in making treatment choices? As the authors observe, often a mediation presents not a true bioethics problem, but a prior communication problem. If the uncertainty that attends modern health care is not adequately communicated and discussed thoughtfully among the health care team, the patient and the family early in the course of treatment, then it can provide a breeding ground for conflict later on. . . . Ethics consultation or mediation can offer a constructive opportunity for other kinds of pre-conflict problem solving, such as clarifying thinking, brainstorming options, and offering supportive feedback to patients, families and health caregivers alike. . . .

6. Marc R. Lebed & John J. McCauley, *Mediation Within the Health Care Industry: Hurdles and Opportunities*, 21 GA. ST. U. L. REV. 911 (2005)

A great deal of money is expended on health care distribution, and today's hospitals are under extreme pressure from budgetary restrictions. Money for outsourcing to ADR, therefore, is very limited, and hospitals continue to rely on traditional risk management-based conflict management, a traditional approach that has limitations and high costs. In addition, such traditional approaches to conflict do not address the growing complexity within health care organizations, necessitating conflict resolution approaches that take into account the multi-layered interests of the various stakeholders. This growing interactive complexity requires processes that are more compatible with the culture of health care than are generally used within health care institutions at the present time. . . .

Among physicians, there is a resistance to relinquishing power to others, thereby losing a sense of autonomy. This has led to frustration and anger, and in our experience, a prevailing attitude that it is up to physicians to handle their own conflicts. The position they take is, "If I can't fix it, it can't be fixed, certainly not by outsiders!" In short, health care professionals, we have found, meet offers to institute dispute resolution programs with one of the following three responses: (1) "This is a great idea, but we don't have those problems"; (2) "We just don't have the resources and personnel"; or (3) "It won't work. If it would work, we would have done it." Or, in the alternative, they recognize the value of the suggested programs, but just never get around to instituting them.

Physicians fear their autonomy is being threatened from many sources, such as hospital administrators, insurance companies, managed care, medical corporations, medical boards, legislative actions, and malpractice carriers. In addition, patients are demanding more collaborative and informed relationships with historically authoritarian physicians. [W]e believe that there is growing relational stress between the growing "corporate-minded" administrations and private medical staff, in which highly positional posturing is becoming more prevalent. However, none of these hurdles appear insurmountable. As long as the right kind of mediators are available, overcoming these challenges should only require greater awareness of their availability and greater familiarity with the processes they use. And that familiarity, in turn, can be fostered by the introduction of educational programs, especially at the medical and nursing school levels.

III. The Additional Barrier Impacting the Special Case of Medical Malpractice Actions

A final important barrier applies uniquely to the one type of dispute that we tend to associate most commonly with health care disputes: medical malpractice. That barrier is the physician's statutory obligation to report settlements of disputes involving quality of care issues to state and federal agencies. The need to report settlements often makes consensual resolution appear, from the physician's viewpoint, to be a "bad bet." What is worse, this obligation creates a barrier which, in contrast to the others discussed, is not easily surmountable.

Consider for a moment the present legislative impediments to settlement from the doctor's perspective. If even one penny is paid to a patient disputant as a result of a negotiated settlement arising out of a written claim or notice of allegations of professional negligence, the physician is reported to the National Practitioner Data Bank (NPDB), regardless of whether the physician is to blame, and even if the disputants agree the physician is not to blame. This information, although not openly available to the public, is available to hospitals, state medical boards, medical associations, and insurers. This can directly or indirectly negatively impact physicians' ability to maintain good standing with their malpractice carriers, providers, peers, and patients, and may even jeopardize their hospital staff privileges and medical board status.

If a negotiated amount exceeds the state's reporting limit, then the physician is reported to the state medical board, again regardless of blame or the degree of adverse outcome associated with the claim. This information is considered by the medical board for physician censuring and disciplinary actions including, but not limited to, licensing restrictions, remedial mandates, and practice restrictions. Such reports made to the state medical board, at least in California, are available to the public for review. This reporting process can have an even greater negative impact than NPDB reporting.

As a result of this potential negative impact, for a broad range of cases, "standing firm" is arguably a tactically sound approach for physicians to take. In polling several nationally-recognized plaintiffs' law firms, it appears that only about 10% of disputes that patients want to litigate are accepted for filing. Although there appears to be little published data citing the attrition rate of claims, the following represent figures most commonly quoted by insurers and major medical malpractice plaintiff law firms: Approximately 75% of disputes that reach the point of being filed are eventually dismissed by the plaintiffs, often because the expected recovery is not worth the cost to litigate the case to conclusion (especially in states with statutory "caps" on damages in medical malpractice cases). Approximately 15% of cases are resolved through negotiated settlements. Of the approximately 10% that go to trial, about 80% of cases end with the physician defendant prevailing. Overall, "only 1.3% of all claims result in a jury award to the plaintiff." Thus, very few claims that are accepted by plaintiffs' attorneys result in financial restitution. Most are either dropped by the plaintiff or the plaintiff's attorney, or terminated by court dismissal or summary judgment grants. When considering the low selection percentage and case attrition rate, the physician who refuses to engage in settlement discussions even after a case has been filed has a very high chance of being spared an adverse judgment. Malpractice insurers and defense attorneys recognize and respond to these statistics. Through our discussions with several malpractice carriers active in California, we find they are generally resistant to mediation proceedings, with the exception of eleventh hour distributive bargaining processes, when the likelihood of the physician defendant prevailing is poor. They are particularly resistant to early mediation proceedings that may "breathe life into dead cases," and are concerned that malpractice claims would skyrocket, with the certainty that the doctor will be reported for any settlement dollars paid. The upshot of this is that only about 15% of cases settle in pre-trial negotiations or mediation, and a full 10% get resolved at trial.

The perverse incentive posed by statutory reporting requirements makes an already bad situation worse. There is already a resistance of health care providers to admit errors, accept responsibility for adverse outcomes, and openly discuss such matters with their patients. Following the 2000 Institute of Medicine report, *To Err is Human*, which claimed that as many as 98,000 patients die in hospitals each year as a result of avoidable errors, patient safety issues have become appropriately prioritized. However, error reporting by physicians has been less than ideal, primarily as a result of deficiencies in the existing reporting systems. With the recent passing of the federal Patient Safety and Quality Improvement Act of 2005, guaranteeing anonymity for error reporting, it is hoped that physicians will be more forthcoming in reporting the errors of themselves and others.

In the current institutional setting, overcoming this attitudinal resistance to settlement will often not be enough. Even if a physician were otherwise prepared to resolve the dispute through facilitated communication or to simply authorize the insurer to proceed to purchase the patient's offered release, that physician would suffer the pain of a generally punitive reporting system. When faced with a choice between resolving a conflict with a non-adversarial process and pursuing litigation and likely prevailing, litigation becomes a matter of professional survival. The impact of being reported is significant to a doctor's ability to practice in a market of highly competitive provider contracts, tightening institutional staff privilege standards, and rapidly escalating malpractice premiums. [T]hese circumstances give insight into the Winston Churchill-inspired "war metaphor" that is now widely applied within the medical profession. The prevailing attitude is: "We are at war, with the very survival of the practitioner and the specialty at stake; under these circumstances, customary rules of engagement can be temporarily suspended." Until the health care industry establishes reporting reforms and some degree of confidentiality for mediated settlements — along with providing education about the nature and benefits of mediation, the market for mediation in malpractice actions is destined to remain quite limited.

IV. Other Available Markets for Mediation Within Health Care

Not all health care disputes are malpractice disputes, and the breadth of those non-malpractice disputes is immense. An overview of a few developing patterns in this $1.6 trillion industry is more telling than the numbers. According to Blue Shield of California, roughly 90% of that distribution goes to about 10% of their insured patients. Further, a large part of that distribution is for care within the last 30 to 90 days of a patient's life, and much of that money is spent on futile care (that is, care administered without chance of survival). Hence, bioethical conflict management and the specter of rationed care conflicts, which may be looming in the near future, are issues of increasing importance.

Roughly 44 million Americans did not have health insurance as of 2002. An increasing percentage of these people are employed, but cannot afford the cost of health care insurance premiums, which continue to climb with percentages of increase in the double digits. In addition, most employers can no longer pay for all or most of their employees' health care costs and are being forced to put more of this burden on the employees themselves. . . .

Financial stresses and the organizational restructuring of medical institutions and medical staff have created new areas of conflict within hospitals and staff. Among the conflicts is a growing adversarial relationship between attending physician staff and hospital administrators. Moreover, "turf wars" between different specialties remain a major source of conflict. . . . Yet another area in need of some form of ADR is professional associations. ADR in this arena would take the shape of conflict resolution and consensus building between professional associations, such as medical associations and hospital associations, and among the constituents of the associations, in conflicts pertaining to such matters as staff privileges and hospital by-law modifications. . . .

These patterns alone suggest several areas of growing social need for ADR, other than resolving malpractice lawsuits. One such area of need is medical education programs. Health care providers and medical students need to be educated in communication skills and conflict prevention and management. Another area of social need for ADR is that of intra-institutional conflict management. ADR in this area would consist of mediation, including consensus building mediation of conflicts within medical institutions pertaining to patient safety, risk management, integrated system management, staff privilege, and quality management. Further, disputes arising from the availability of and unanticipated outcomes of new drugs and new technologies would be well-served to explore mediation as an alternative to litigation. . . .

C. VICTIM OFFENDER MEDIATION (VOM): RESTORATIVE JUSTICE

1. Comments and Questions

a. The self-described Restorative Justice "movement" is broader than just victim-offender mediation (VOM); however, VOM is much the best developed and most commonly used approach. As evidenced by the developments described in the following article by Umbreit and colleagues, the use of VOM and other restorative justice approaches has grown dramatically in the United States, and the rest of the world as well.

b. Umbreit and colleagues are strong supporters of, and active participants in, the restorative justice movement. The article by Jennifer Brown that follows is considerably less sanguine about restorative justice in general, and VOM in particular.

c. Professor Brown suggests that VOM may be the result of a Prisoner's Dilemma (created by the prosecutor). Because their fates turn in part upon the actions of the other party, with whom they cannot communicate or contract in a binding way, the parties may agree to mediation despite their mutual preference for adjudication. In addition to the coercion created by this victim-offender dilemma, prosecutors can use uncertainty and ignorance to secure participation in mediation.

d. A set of questions that is useful for organizing your thinking about restorative justice is found at the end of the Umbreit article.

2. Mark S. Umbreit, Betty Vos, Robert B. Coates & Elizabeth Lightfoot, *Restorative Justice in the Twenty-First Century: A Social Movement Full of Opportunities and Pitfalls*, 89 MARQ. L. REV. 251 (2005)

II. Overview of Restorative Justice

Most contemporary criminal justice systems focus on law violation, the need to hold offenders accountable and punish them, and other state interests. Actual crime victims are quite subsidiary to the process and, generally, have no legal standing in the proceedings. Crime is viewed as having been committed against the state, which essentially owns the conflict and determines how to respond to it. The resulting criminal justice system is almost entirely offender-driven.

Restorative justice offers a very different way of understanding and responding to crime. Instead of viewing the state as the primary victim in criminal acts and placing victims, offenders, and the community in passive roles, restorative justice recognizes crime as being directed against individual people. It is grounded in the belief that those most affected by crime should have the opportunity to become actively involved in resolving the conflict. Repairing harm and restoring losses, allowing offenders to take direct responsibility for their actions, and assisting victims to move beyond vulnerability towards some degree of closure stand in sharp contrast to the values and practices of the conventional criminal justice system with its focus on past criminal behavior through ever-increasing levels of punishment.

Within the English-speaking world, roots of the prevailing focus on harm to the state can be traced back to eleventh-century England. Following the Norman invasion of Britain, a major paradigm shift occurred in which there was a turning away from the well-established understanding of crime as a victim-offender conflict within the context of community. . . . Restorative justice values, principles, and practices hearken back to such earlier paradigms, not only in British and American history, but also in numerous indigenous cultures throughout the world. . . .

In addition, the values of restorative justice are deeply rooted in the ancient principles of Judeo-Christian culture that have always emphasized crime as being a violation against people and families, rather than "the state." Many biblical examples are found in both the Old and New Testaments setting forth the responsibility of offenders to directly repair the harm they caused to individuals, harm that has created a breach in the "Shalom community."

The most succinct definition of restorative justice is offered by Howard Zehr, whom many consider the leading visionary and architect of the restorative justice movement. His seminal book, *Changing Lenses: A New Focus for Crime and Justice* (1990), provided the conceptual framework for the movement and has influenced policy makers and practitioners throughout the world. According to Zehr, "Restorative justice is a process to involve, to the extent possible, those who have a stake in a specific offense and to collectively identify and address harms, needs, and obligations, in order to heal and put things as right as possible."

Instead of focusing upon the weaknesses or deficits of offenders and crime victims, restorative justice attempts to draw upon the strengths of these individuals and their capacity to openly address the need to repair the harm caused. Restorative justice denounces criminal behavior yet emphasizes the need to treat offenders with respect and to reintegrate them into the larger community in ways that can lead to lawful behavior.

From a restorative perspective, the primary stakeholders are understood to be individual victims and their families, victimized communities, and offenders and their families. The state and its legal justice system also clearly have an interest as a stakeholder but are seen as more removed from direct impact. Thus, the needs of those most directly affected by the crime come first. Wherever possible, opportunities for direct engagement in the process of doing justice through various forms of dialogue are central to the practice of restorative justice.

Like many reform movements, in its early years, the restorative justice movement focused on contrasting its values and principles with those of the status quo. The phrase "retributive justice" emerged to describe the conventional criminal justice system approach, particularly regarding its emphasis on offenders getting what they deserved. . . . Zehr has come to a different understanding, stating that such a sharp polarization between retributive and restorative justice is somewhat misleading. The philosopher of law, Conrad Brunk, argues that on a theoretical level, retribution and restoration are not the polar opposites that many assume. He notes that both actually have much in common: a desire to vindicate by some type of reciprocal action and some type of proportional relationship between the criminal act and the response to it.

Retributive theory and restorative theory, however, differ significantly in how to "even the score" — how to make things right. Retributive theory holds that the imposition of some form of pain will vindicate, most frequently deprivation of liberty and even loss of life in some cases. Restorative theory argues that "what truly vindicates is acknowledgment of victims' harms and needs, combined with an active effort to encourage offenders to take responsibility, make right the wrongs, and address the causes of their behavior."

Restorative justice can be contrasted with conventional criminal justice along four key variables: (1) Crime as an offense against the state v. crime as a violation of relationships; (2) Violations as creating guilt v. violations creating obligations; (3) Justice as determination of guilt and imposition of punishment v. justice as involving victims and community members in an effort to put things right; and (4) Focus on punishment v. focus on repairing harm. The conventional criminal justice system focuses upon three questions: (1) What laws have been broken?; (2) Who did it?; and (3) What do they deserve? From a restorative justice perspective, an entirely different set of questions are asked: (1) Who has been hurt?; (2) What are their needs?; and (3) Whose obligations are these? . . .

In its more than a quarter century of development, the restorative justice movement has gone through a number of stages quite similar to other social movements. The mid-1970s marked the birthing phase of what would become known as the restorative justice movement. . . . Through the mid-1980s, in many jurisdictions, restorative justice initiatives remained small in size and number and continued to have little impact on the larger system. Few criminal justice officials viewed such programs as a credible component of the system. From the mid-1980s to the mid-1990s, the movement slowly began to be recognized in many communities as a viable option for interested crime victims and offenders, though still impacting a very small number of participants. England initiated the first state supported Victim Offender Mediation Programs ("VOM") during this period.

In 1994, the American Bar Association ("ABA") endorsed victim-offender mediation. This followed a year-long study and considerable skepticism over the previous years. The ABA recommended the use of victim-offender mediation and dialogue in courts throughout the country and also provided guidelines for its use and development. Specific guidelines emphasized in the ABA endorsement included that participation by both offenders and victims be entirely voluntary, that offenders not incur adverse repercussions, and that statements and information shared be inadmissible in criminal or civil court proceedings.

Victim organizations were initially skeptical about victim-offender dialogue and other restorative justice initiatives, in part, because of the early history of focusing on offenders and their needs. However, in 1995, the National Organization for Victim Assistance ("NOVA") endorsed the principles of restorative justice. . . . As dialogue programs and other restorative initiatives continue to demonstrate a strong commitment to the needs and wishes of crime victims, victim organizations are increasingly supportive.

The movement began to enter the mainstream in some local and state jurisdictions beginning in the mid-1990s. . . . There are individual restorative justice programs in virtually every state of America, and a growing number of states and local jurisdictions are dramatically changing their criminal and juvenile justice systems to adopt the principles and practices of restorative justice. [As of 2006,] twenty-nine states have enacted statutes promoting victim-offender mediation, a hallmark of restorative justice. . . . Restorative justice is also developing in many other parts of the world. . . . The United Nations, the Council of Europe, and the European Union have been addressing restorative justice issues for a number of years. . . . . In 2001, the European Union adopted a policy in support of "penal mediation," otherwise known as victim-offender mediation. In 2002, the United Nations adopted Basic Principles on the Use of Restorative Justice Programs in Criminal Matters.

III. Restorative Justice Dialogue

As a means of providing an in-depth examination of restorative justice in practice, we have elected to turn our close-up lens on restorative justice dialogue. . . . [specifically] VOM and group conferencing. . . . Both have in common the inclusion of victims and offenders in direct dialogue, nearly always face-to-face, about a specific offense or infraction; the presence of at least one additional person who serves as mediator or facilitator; and usually, advance preparation of the parties so they will know what to expect. The focus of the encounter nearly always involves naming what happened, identifying its impact, and coming to some common understanding, often including reaching agreement as to how any resultant harm would be repaired. Use of these processes can take place at any point in the justice process, including pre-arrest, pre-court referral, pre-sentencing, post-sentencing, and even during incarceration.

VOM — also called victim-offender conferencing, victim-offender reconciliation, or victim-offender dialogue — usually involves a victim and an offender in direct mediation facilitated by one or sometimes two mediators or facilitators; occasionally, the dialogue takes place through a third party who carries information back and forth, a process known as shuttle mediation. In face-to-face meetings, support persons (such as parents or friends) for victims or offenders are often present. A 1999 survey of victim-offender mediation programs in the United States found that support persons, including parents in juvenile cases, were present in nearly nine out of ten cases.

Group conferencing . . . routinely involves support persons for both victims and offenders as well as additional participants from the community. Many group conferencing programs rely on a script, though some are more open-ended. The number of support persons present can often range from ten to six to only a few, much like victim-offender mediation. Increasingly over time, distinctions across these categories have begun to blur. . . . The present review attempts to maintain the distinction between VOM and group conferencing, but it seems likely that knowledge building may be better served in the future by collapsing the categories. Doing so would allow for participant responses and outcomes to be analyzed across actual variations in structure and format, rather than according to what the intervention is called.

The present review examines participation rates and reasons, participant satisfaction, participant perception of fairness, restitution and repair of harm, diversion, recidivism, and cost. A total of eighty-five studies were reviewed for the present report, including fifty-three mediation studies, twenty-two group conferencing studies, . . . and three meta-analyses.

1. Participation Rates and Reasons. Inviting victims to meet with the offender that harmed them was first conceived of as a means to help young offenders understand the impact of their crime and possibly decrease the likelihood of their re-offending. In those early days of the restorative justice dialogue movement, no one knew how likely it would be that victims would even want to participate in such a meeting, or whether they would find it helpful. In fact, large numbers of victims who are approached about the possibility of such a meeting elect to participate.

Participation rates for crime victims are addressed in several VOM studies and typically range from 40% to 60%, though rates as high as 90% have been reported. Several studies noted that victim willingness to participate was driven by a desire to receive restitution, to hold the offender accountable, to learn more about the why of the crime, to share their pain with the offender, to avoid court processing, to help the offender change behavior, or to see the offender adequately punished. . . . Among victims who elected not to participate in VOM, reasons included feeling the crime was too trivial to be worth the time, feeling fearful of meeting the offender, and wanting the offender to have a harsher punishment.

Gehm studied 535 eligible VOM cases and found 47% of the victims willing to participate. Victims were more likely to participate if the offender was white (as were the victims), if the offense was a misdemeanor, and if the victim was representing an institution. Wyrick and Costanzo similarly found that property cases were more likely to reach mediation than personal offenses. They further noted an interaction between type of crime and the passage of time: the longer the time lapse between the offense and the mediation opportunity, the less likely property crimes would come to mediation, but the more likely personal crimes would meet. Offender reasons for not participating are less frequently explored. Some offenders have reported being advised by lawyers not to participate, and some simply did not want to be bothered.

In regards to mediated dialogue in severely violent crimes, victims' chief reasons for wishing to meet are to seek information (58%), to show the offender the impact of their actions (43%), and to have some form of human contact with the person responsible for the crime (40%). Offenders who agreed to meet offered the following victim-related reasons: to apologize (38%), to help victims heal (38%), and to do whatever would benefit victims (26%). Offenders also hoped the experience would benefit themselves (74%), including that it would contribute to their own rehabilitation (33%), that it could change how their victims viewed them (21%), and that they had spiritual reasons for wanting to meet with their victim (18%).

2. Participant Satisfaction. The vast majority of studies reviewed reported in some way on satisfaction of victims and offenders with victim-offender mediation and its outcomes. Expression of satisfaction with VOM is consistently high for both victims and offenders across sites, cultures, and seriousness of offenses. Typically, eight or nine out of ten participants report being satisfied with the process and with the resulting agreement. Two studies that utilized shuttle mediation yielded slightly lower satisfaction rates for those participants than for participants who met face-to-face.

Secondary analysis of satisfaction data from a United States study and a Canadian study yielded similar high rates of satisfaction. Using step-wise multiple regression procedures to determine those variables most associated with victim satisfaction, the authors discovered that three variables emerged to explain over 40% of the variance. The key variables associated with victim satisfaction were as follows: (1) the victim felt good about the mediator; (2) the victim perceived the resulting restitution agreement as fair; and (3) the victim, for whatever reason, had a strong initial desire to meet the offender. When asked, typically nine out of ten participants would recommend a VOM program to others. These high levels of satisfaction with VOM also translated into relatively high levels of satisfaction with the criminal justice system. Where comparison groups were studied, those victims and offenders going through mediation indicated being more satisfied with the criminal justice system than those going through traditional court prosecution. Group conferencing also yields fairly high satisfaction responses from participants.

3. Fairness. Many studies of victim-offender mediation asked participants about the fairness of the mediation process and of the resulting agreement. Not surprisingly, given the high levels of satisfaction, the vast majority of VOM participants (typically over 80%) across setting, cultures, and types of offenses reported believing that the process was fair to both sides and that the resulting agreement was fair. Again, these experiences led to feelings that the overall criminal justice system was fair. Where comparison groups were employed, those individuals exposed to mediation came away more likely feeling that they had been treated fairly than those going through the traditional court proceedings. In a study of burglary victims in Minneapolis, Umbreit found that 80% who went through VOM indicated that they experienced the criminal justice system as fair compared with only 38% of burglary victims who did not participate in VOM.

Fairness is also an issue of concern for participants in group conferencing and is often a focus of research. In an Australian study, 80% to 95% of victims and offenders reported that they were treated fairly and had a say in the agreement. Similarly, preliminary data from the Australian Reintegrative Shaming Experiments ("RISE") found that 72% of the offenders felt the outcome of group conferencing was fair, compared with 54% of comparison offenders prosecuted in the traditional courts. Interestingly, the conference offenders were also more likely to feel that they would be caught if they re-offended. In three United States studies, about 95% of victims indicated the process or outcome was fair. Regarding offenders, 89% of the juvenile offenders in a Minnesota-based study indicated that the resulting conference agreement was fair. All seven offenders in another Minnesota group conferencing program felt the process was fair. . . .

4. Restitution and Repayment of Harm. About half the VOM studies addressed the issue of restitution or repair of harm. Of those cases that reached a meeting, typically 90% or more generated agreements. Restitution of some sort was part of the vast majority of these agreements. Looking across the studies reviewed here, it appears that approximately 80% to 90% of the contracts are reported as completed. Results from comparative studies have been somewhat mixed, with some studies reporting higher amounts of restitution or greater completion rates for VOM participants than comparison groups, while another reported no difference. The meta-analysis covering both mediation and group conferencing found that offenders participating in these programs had substantially higher completion rates than offenders processed in other ways. . . .

5. Diversion. Among other reasons, many restorative programs are nominally established to divert offenders from the traditional justice system processes. While such diversion was a goal lauded by many, others expressed concern about the unintended consequence of widening the net — that is, sanctioning offenders who otherwise would not have received sanctions through traditional procedures. . . . Two mediation studies, both in the United Kingdom, have reported a net-widening impact for the intervention. One concluded that at least 60% of the offenders participating in mediation were true diversions from court prosecution, and overall there was a 13% net-widening effect, much less than expected. In the other, fully 43% of the comparison group cases were not prosecuted and received no sanction, a fairly broad net-widening result. . . .

Two United States-based studies found that the mediation programs successfully diverted offenders from court. One North Carolina program apparently reduced court trials by as much as two-thirds. An Indiana-Ohio study compared consequences for seventy-three youth and adults going through VOM programs with those for a matched sample of individuals who were processed in the traditional manner. VOM offenders spent less time incarcerated than did their counterparts, and when incarcerated, they did county jail time rather than state time. . . .

6. Recidivism. The goal of restorative processes is to meet the needs of all parties affected by crime — victims, offenders, and communities. Preventing recidivism is often used as a long-term measure of the "effectiveness" of such programs; such prevention benefits offenders directly, and more broadly, benefits communities. . . . Results from studies examining the impact of mediation on recidivism have been mixed overall. Several studies found lower rates for mediation participants than for offenders processed through traditional means. In addition, five of the six programs examined by Evje and Cushman also found reduced recidivism. Two studies also found that youths who did re-offend tended to incur less serious charges than their counterparts. Others reported little or no difference, as did one of the six programs studied by Evje and Cushman. As with mediation, group conferencing results have been somewhat mixed. . . .

A number of recent studies have begun to attempt to sort out factors that make a difference in the rate of re-offending among conferenced offenders. In 1996, Maxwell and Morris were able to contact 108 young people (67% of their original sample) and 98 parents who had participated in family group conferencing in 1990-91. Several multivariate analyses were conducted to sort out predictors of reconviction and pathways to re-offending. Critical factors that were correlated with lessened re-offending included the following: having a conference that was memorable, not being made to feel a bad person, feeling involved in the conference decision making, agreeing with the outcome, completing the tasks agreed to, feeling sorry for what they had done, meeting the victim and apologizing to him or her, and feeling that they had repaired the damage. As the authors point out, "These factors reflect key restorative values, processes and outcomes." . . .

7. Costs. The relative costs of correctional programs are difficult to assess. . . . In some instances, mediation was less costly than other options and in others more costly. Given the [modest size] . . . of these programs, it remains difficult to evaluate their cost if implemented on a scale large enough to impact overall program administration. Evaluation of a large scale VOM program in California led the authors to conclude that the cost per case was reduced dramatically as the program went from being a fledgling to being a viable option. Cost per case was $250. A Missouri program reported total cost per case that ranged from $232 to $338, but did not provide comparison data.

Public Policy Support for Restorative Justice Dialogue

To illustrate the range and types of legislative changes that emerge as restorative justice moves into the mainstream. . . . we summarize the fairly extensive development of formal public policy at the state level supporting . . . VOM. The review examined the state codes of all fifty states and the District of Columbia, [and is] current as of Spring 2005.

1. Continuum of State Statutory Support for VOM. A growing number of states have passed legislation related to implementation of VOM. Twenty-nine states currently have at least a reference to VOM or VOM-type programs in their state codes. The majority of the states passed legislation since the late 1980s, and new VOM bills are being introduced every year. There is a continuum of statutory authority related to VOM. The states fall loosely into five categories along the continuum, including: "Comprehensive VOM Legislative Framework," "Specific Statutory Provision for VOM," "Basic Statutory Provision for VOM," "Programs that May Include VOM," and "No VOM Statutes."

Seven states, Delaware, Indiana, Kansas, Montana, Nebraska, Oregon, and Tennessee, fall into the "Comprehensive VOM Legislative Framework" category. These states have statutes that detail comprehensive guidelines for VOM programs within their states. The statutes in these seven states are quite varied, but all include a variety of specific requirements for the VOM programs within their states, such as oversight, mediator training requirements, funding, costs, confidentiality, eligibility for participation, and liability. The structure of the statutes themselves varies as well. Some states have one specific statute detailing all the aspects of VOM, while others with a comprehensive legislative framework have the VOM requirements in a variety of sections of their state code. The unifying factor among this category of states is that state agencies have a clear statutory authority for VOM as well as guidance on the operations of such programs.

An additional seven states, Arkansas, Louisiana, Minnesota, Ohio, Oklahoma, Texas, and Virginia, have a "specific statutory provision for VOM." These states have a clear statutory authority for VOM, usually in a specific section of the state code, but fewer detailed requirements than states with a comprehensive VOM legislative framework. These state statutes provide an overarching framework for VOM with one or two specific requirements, but do not detail a broad array of requirements. In these states, while VOM may be mandated and a few operational details are mandated, most of the implementation particulars are left to the state agencies or court system.

Nine states, including Alabama, Arizona, California, Colorado, Iowa, Missouri, North Carolina, Washington, and Wisconsin, have a basic statutory provision for VOM. A basic statutory provision essentially allows VOM as an option for courts to consider, but provides no details or requirements as to any aspect of the auspices of the program. In these nine states, VOM is included as an option among a list of many other options, with no special emphasis on VOM as a preferred or desired approach. . . . Seven states, Alaska, Florida, Illinois,

Maine, New Jersey, New York, and Vermont, have statutes that authorize programs that may include restorative justice dialogues, but they do not specifically discuss VOM within their state code. . . .

Twenty-one states and the District of Columbia do not have any reference to VOM in their state codes or statutes. . . . However, state statutes are not required for states to implement VOM or other restorative justice programs. As noted above, virtually every state in the United States has some sort of restorative justice program. However, state statutes help to promote the legitimacy of VOM and other restorative justice programs, which can be valuable when legal issues arise.

2. Variations in Statutory VOM Provisions. There is no standard model for VOM legislation across the states that have adopted VOM statutes. The thirty state VOM statutes vary in regards to structure of VOM programs and the various requirements for VOM program and program participation. States have adopted several different statutory approaches for implementing VOM. Six states have general referral language; eight states have authorized state VOM programs; eight states have authorized grants to nonprofits to run VOM programs; and four states . . . have authorized county-level VOM programs.

Other key variations among state statutes relate to the program details of VOM. States differ on the eligibility age of offenders for participation in VOM programs. Twelve states authorize VOM solely for juveniles, and seven states authorize VOM solely for adults. Seven states have separate provisions authorizing VOM for juveniles and adults, and four that authorize VOM for juveniles and adults under the same statute. Altogether, twenty-three states authorize VOM for juveniles, and eighteen authorize VOM for adults.

Many of the other VOM requirements are only included in a handful of state statutes. For example, seven states have codified mediator requirements for those providing VOM services. Of these seven, Kansas, Louisiana and Nebraska have detailed requirements for mediators involved in VOM, while Delaware, Minnesota, New York and Tennessee have general requirements that agencies providing services establish minimum training requirements for VOM mediators. Likewise, seven states provide specific statutory immunity to parties involved in VOM, such as mediators, agencies or prosecutors. Virginia and Indiana require victims to sign a waiver of liability, while Illinois, Minnesota, Nebraska, Oklahoma and Tennessee provide general immunity to participants. . . . Another common statutory provision is in regards to confidentiality of VOM provisions. Ten states . . . have mandated VOM proceedings to be confidential. . . .

IV. Continuing Issues

The restorative justice movement is grounded in values that promote both accountability and healing for all affected by crime. It emphasizes positive human development, mutuality, empathy, responsibility, respect, and fairness. Yet, the principles and practices of the restorative justice movement are not inherently benign or incapable of doing harm. In fact, as in so many other movements and interventions grounded in lofty values and good intentions, reports of unintentionally harmful consequences or outcomes surface periodically. In large part, the pitfalls derive from the inherent difficulty of attempting to balance so many valid needs: needs of victims, needs of offenders, needs of the community, and ultimately, the needs of the state. . . .

Despite the wide and increasing international acceptance of restorative justice principles and practices, and despite the many opportunities facing the movement in the twenty-first century, there remain numerous unresolved and often troubling issues. Many of these issues speak to the core integrity of the movement, while others pose questions about fair and effective implementation. . . .

1. Is restorative justice in fact about developing an entirely new paradigm of how our criminal justice systems operate at a systemic level, or is it a set of processes, specific principles, and practices that can operate within our conventional criminal justice systems?

2. How does the restorative justice movement avoid becoming a micro-level intervention serving victims, offenders, and communities? [The movement would then have no macro-level impact on the contributing factors to crime and delinquency in our communities, which are inseparable from the social injustice that permeates our society.]

3. Can restorative justice really be a victim-centered approach when the overwhelming emphasis and resources in the system are so heavily focused upon identifying, apprehending, processing, and punishing or even treating the offender?

4. How big is the tent under which policies and practices are considered to be part of the restorative movement? How can the restorative justice movement avoid the predictable co-opting of its philosophy?

5. The vast majority of crime victims never have their offenders apprehended and processed in the system. These victims are currently largely ignored by the justice system — restorative or conventional. How can restorative justice address the multitude of needs facing victims of crime whose offenders are never caught?

6. Will restorative justice be marginalized through being essentially required to deal with only the most minor types of criminal and delinquent offenses, many of which would self-correct on their own?

7. Will restorative justice as a movement gravitate toward a "one size fits all" approach in which a specific intervention or approach will be viewed as appropriate for nearly all cases, or all cases of a given type?

8. A major pillar of the restorative justice approach is its emphasis upon the involvement of communities and respecting the needs of the community. How will the restorative justice movement deal with the reality that many communities express a wish for policies and practices that are far from being restorative in nature? Will the

movement be able to integrate respect for those positions while still advocating more restorative approaches?

9. How will the restorative justice movement effectively deal with cases involving domestic violence? This is a tremendously controversial area and many different opinions exist in the field already. In theory, restorative justice may have a great deal to offer to the field of domestic violence. In practice, however, it carries a tremendous capacity for doing harm, despite good intentions. How can the dangerous territory of domestic violence be reconciled with the good intent of those involved with the restorative justice movement?

10. Within the United States, the criminal justice system has a vastly disproportionate number of persons of color caught in its policies and practices. How does the restorative justice movement avoid mirroring this same reality? How many restorative justice policies and programs affect communities of color? How many of these programs and policies actively engage persons of color in leadership roles and service delivery roles?

11. How can the informal nature of community-based justice . . . be reconciled with the protection of rights offered by our formal criminal and juvenile justice systems? How can extensive and unfair disparity in sanctions and outcomes be avoided as individual victims and communities are given a wide range of options for holding the offender accountable?

3. Jennifer Gerarda Brown, *The Use of Mediation to Resolve Criminal Cases: A Procedural Critique,* 43 EMORY L.J. 1247 (1994)

In the ancient days of Western legal systems, criminal offenders could settle with victims and their families to avoid prosecution. For some criminal offenders in the United States, privatized criminal law survives: Victim-Offender Mediation ("VOM") allows offenders to avoid public prosecution or punishment by mediating criminal cases with their victims. An offender may be given the opportunity to participate in VOM at various stages in the criminal justice process. VOM may even divert cases from the criminal justice system, with little or no involvement by state officials, unless the mediation fails to resolve the case. Offenders participate in VOM in order to reduce their expected punishment. An offender who participates may be rewarded by dismissal of charges or reduction of penalties. . . . The outcome of the mediation can influence judges, parole boards, and prosecutors as they decide how to charge or punish the offender. And the outcome of the mediation turns in large part upon the victim's satisfaction. Thus, VOM transforms the criminal justice paradigm by placing victims at the center, rather than on the periphery, of the criminal process. In effect, VOM transfers the power to resolve all or part of a criminal case from the state to . . . the victim.

The thesis of this Article is that placing such control in the hands of the victim is inconsistent with the character and purpose of the criminal law as it has evolved since ancient times. As currently structured, VOM's relationship to the criminal justice system disserves the interests of victims, offenders, and the state. VOM disserves the interests of victims by stressing forgiveness and reconciliation before victims have the vindication of a public finding that the offender is guilty. In addition, VOM suppresses victims' outrage and loss by assuming that these negative feelings can be expressed and resolved in the course of a few hours spent meeting with the offender.

VOM disserves offenders in three ways: by using selection criteria that are not clearly related to the goals of the program; by eliminating procedural protections such as the right to counsel or rules of evidence; and by using the leverage of pending criminal process to gain advantages for the victim, a private party. If offenders believe that they will be worse off in the ordinary criminal justice system, should they fail to reach a mediated agreement satisfactory to their victims, the offenders may have an unduly strong incentive to mediate and reach agreement, no matter what the psychological or monetary cost.

VOM characterizes many crimes as private disputes that fracture relationships between individuals; the state's interest in these disputes is minimal. The structure of VOM often belies this assumption, however, because the mediation occurs before a backdrop of state involvement and coercion. Victims of crime negotiate not only with their own individual bargaining strength, but also with the threat of enhanced state punishment should the parties fail to reach agreement. The victim appropriates some of the state's leverage over the offender, because both the victim and the offender know that the offender is more likely to be prosecuted or incarcerated if the victim is not satisfied with the negotiation.

VOM disserves the interests of the state, because it devalues the substantive and procedural norms observed in public processes. Despite proponents' claims that VOM can resolve criminal cases according to the substantive standards of the "community" in which the crime occurred, such a community rarely exists in the United States today apart from the state itself. When centralized rules of criminal law are rejected in the name of a "community" that may not even exist, any standard may fill the vacuum to resolve individual cases. Success is measured by the victim's satisfaction with the outcome, rather than consistency with substantive legal rules. VOM programs ignore procedural norms, because the end (the parties' ability to reach agreement) often justifies the means (lack of counsel for the offender, coercion prior to and during the mediation).

This Article calls for a decoupling of mediation from the criminal justice system: the success or failure of the mediation should have no impact on the offender's prosecution or punishment. The Article suggests several procedural rules to effect such a separation. A "Chinese wall" between VOM and the criminal justice system is necessary to protect the integrity of the system and the integrity of mediation as a fundamentally voluntary process. A Chinese wall would address the dangers of VOM to victims, because it would preserve an independent process and the opportunity for catharsis that a public process could offer. The dangers to offenders would be decreased if a Chinese wall were in place, because the separation would reduce incentives for prosecutors and program administrators to coerce offender participation. The dangers of VOM to the state would be reduced if the process were separated from the criminal justice system, because the Chinese wall would preserve the public forum for public purposes.

These conclusions are subject to an important qualification: If VOM proponents and prosecutors could show that VOM does promote deterrence or rehabilitation, then it might be reintegrated into the criminal justice system. This qualification is consistent with a larger theme: public coercion should only be used to vindicate public interests. To the extent that mediation is shown to further the goals of rehabilitation or specific deterrence, conditioning prosecution on mediation and its results is appropriate. But the standard for proving that VOM promotes the traditional goals of the criminal law should be rigorous. And even if the system incorporates victim-offender mediation to resolve criminal cases, additional process is required to insure that selection criteria are fair, that the process and its outcomes are as noncoercive as possible (within an admittedly coercive system), and that the public is afforded some opportunity to monitor mediation and its results through regular judicial review. This Article suggests various procedural guidelines that might reduce the dangers, including the provision of counsel for indigent offenders who participate in VOM, court monitoring of mediation agreements, and strict enforcement of rules that exclude from trial and sentencing any evidence of failed mediation attempts.

By proposing a separation between mediation and the criminal justice system, I intentionally seek to eliminate one of the stated goals of most VOM programs: to serve as an alternative to incarceration. Allowing offenders to buy their way out of prison with monetary and nonmonetary compensation to victims unacceptably confounds the private goals of mediation and the public goals of criminal law. If a jurisdiction is serious about creating alternatives to incarceration, then the state, rather than crime victims or private administrators of VOM programs, ought to decide whether offenders are entitled to such alternatives. And the state should place these alternatives in the hands of private parties only after they have fully accounted for the "process dangers" of such a change.

Although the state achieved its monopoly in criminal law enforcement centuries ago, in recent years activists have worked to swing the pendulum back toward greater involvement by victims in the criminal process. As one mechanism to increase victims' roles, VOM has been lauded by some activists as a benefit to victims. Other victims' advocates have been skeptical of VOM. A substantial body of literature has grown to document the existence of a rising victims' rights movement. The movement to amend state constitutions to include some provisions for victims' rights began in the early 1980s, when President Reagan's Task Force on Victims of Crime recommended that the Sixth Amendment to the U.S. Constitution be changed to guarantee that "the victim, in every criminal prosecution, shall have the right to be present and to be heard at all critical stages of judicial proceedings." Soon after that, California became the first state to grant constitutional status to a Victims' Bill of Rights. Rhode

Island followed with a constitutional amendment granting victims the right to restitution, to submit victim impact statements at sentencing, and to be treated "with dignity and respect." According to the National Victim Center, thirteen states have enacted constitutional amendments recognizing victims' rights. . . .

D. MEDIATORS AS BUSINESS DEAL MAKERS: AGENCY THEORY REVISITED

1. Comments and Questions

a. Our discussion of negotiation considered reasons why parties sometimes failed to find an available agreement, or reached a sub-optimal deal. These include unwillingness to disclose information, inaccuracy, and agency problems. Then we learned how mediation can address these and other barriers to reaching agreement.

b. Since mediation is such a valuable approach to resolving disputes that parties cannot settle by themselves, one might think that it would be of particular value in the context of major business and commercial transactions. Why not use mediators to assist parties in reaching mutually beneficial agreements? We limit this question to "major" transactions only to focus on ones large enough to warrant the expenditures associated with mediation. In principle, mediation might be employed to facilitate any business transactions.

2. Scott R. Peppet, *Contract Formation in Imperfect Markets: Should We Use Mediators in Deals?*, 19 OHIO ST. J. ON DISP. RESOL. 283 (2004)

This Article asks a simple question: Could third-party mediators be helpful in deals, just as they are in disputes? This Article makes a theoretical argument for such interventions, and also presents preliminary empirical evidence suggesting that transactional mediation may already be taking place. . . . Mediators can help disputing parties overcome information asymmetries, optimize their settlements, manage psychological barriers to negotiation, and cope with emotional and relational issues. In many ways, an impartial mediator is uniquely suited to help parties overcome the various transaction costs that can impede settlement. . . .

This Article argues that many of the same barriers to negotiation that plague litigation settlement exist in commercial transactions, particularly during the closing stage of a deal when lawyers attempt to negotiate terms and conditions. It further argues that a transactional mediator could help lawyers and clients to overcome such barriers. . . . [M]ediators can help litigating parties overcome two types of bargaining failure. First, if the parties behave strategically, they may fail to reach agreement even when doing so would create gains from trade. Second, even if the parties reach a settlement, they may settle for an economically inefficient agreement. . . .

[A]s part of a larger project on fair division procedures, Steven Brams and Alan Taylor note that a mediator should theoretically be able to help merging companies resolve disagreements over "social issues," such as how to name the post-merger corporation, how to resolve status and position questions (e.g., who will be CEO), and where to locate the new company's headquarters. STEVEN J. BRAMS & ALAN D. TAYLOR, THE WIN-WIN SOLUTION: GUARANTEEING FAIR SHARES TO EVERYBODY 125-30 (1999). After reviewing a sample of large mergers that collapsed because of disputes over such issues, they concluded that "these deals highlight the need for effective dispute-resolution techniques in merger negotiations." Their "adjusted winner" procedure is designed to reduce deal failure and optimize the efficiency of trades about these social issues. The parties assign points to the various issues in contention, and a mediator referee then uses their assignments to plumb for the most value-creating solutions to their disagreements.

Howard Raiffa also suggests that a mediator might serve as a "contract embellisher" in transactions. HOWARD RAIFFA, THE ART AND SCIENCE OF NEGOTIATION 100-01 (1982). He suggests that, at the start of bargaining, a mediator could privately interview each party about its needs, priorities, and perceptions. The mediator would lock away that information, and the parties would be left alone to negotiate a deal. At the conclusion of their negotiation, but prior to closing the deal, the intervenor would return. After examining the terms of the parties' agreement, the intervenor would try to use his private information about the parties' interests to craft a superior deal. He would then show his substitute agreement to each party privately. If both sides agreed that the mediator's suggestion was superior to their own contract, the substitution would be made. There would be no haggling about the terms of the mediator's proposal — it would be a take-it-or-leave-it situation. . . .

Like disputes, transactional negotiations are certainly not immune from emotions and attributions. Tempers flare, accusations are made, and relationships sour. Mergers and acquisitions, for example, can give rise to intense emotional disagreements that put great strain on the underlying business relationships. As Robert Kindler, an M&A partner at Cravath, Swaine & Moore has said, "Even transactions that make absolute economic sense do not happen unless the social issues work." Particularly if one party is more accustomed to negotiations than another or more sophisticated with doing deals in a particular context, transacting parties may spend a great deal of time and energy on these relational issues.

Consider the example of recent merger negotiations between SmithKline Beecham and Glaxo Wellcome. In February 1998, a deal was announced that promised to create a pharmaceutical giant with annual sales of $25 billion. The combination was much applauded by industry and Wall Street analysts. Nevertheless, three weeks into the merger negotiations, the companies' CEOs managed to kill the deal. In essence, Sir Richard Sykes, the CEO of Glaxo, put an ultimatum offer to Jan Leschley, the CEO of SmithKline that effectively removed Leschley and SmithKline from the management structure of the new entity. Leschley walked, incensed at Sykes' audacity. The next day, the combined market valuation of the two companies dropped by $19 billion, destroying the significant run-up each had enjoyed as a result of the disclosure of merger negotiations. . . . Despite calls from the investment community to overcome their differences, the Glaxo SmithKline deal remained off the table until September of 1999, when Leschley announced his decision to retire and Jean-Pierre Garnier was named as his successor at SmithKline. Negotiations began again in earnest, and in January 2000, the merger was re-announced. . . . The GlaxoSmithKline example illustrates that negotiation breakdowns occur in transactional bargaining, sometimes to the detriment of both parties. To some extent, agents such as investment bankers and lawyers already serve to mediate emotional conflicts during mergers, acquisitions, and other transactions. . . .

A neutral sometimes has an advantage over an agent in this regard, however. An agent can fall prey to the same attribution errors as her principal. In discussions with a client, a lawyer, real estate agent, or banker may try to mollify the client rather than test the client's perhaps biased story about the other side. In the worst-case scenario, an agent may fan the flames and aggravate a client's emotions. But even without trying to escalate a conflict, an agent may naturally take his client's perspective as given and discount the likelihood that the other side has a valid interpretation of events or more benign intentions than the client understands. A neutral positioned between two parties can often help them to gain such perspective. . . . Given these potential benefits, the most obvious objection to the argument laid out so far is economic and empirical: if mediators could be so helpful in transactions, there should already be a market for their services. Social and economic roles that create value evolve into robust institutions; those that do not fail to thrive. . . .

[M]y own survey of 122 practicing mediators unearthed forty-eight who claimed to have served as a transactional mediator. This survey was designed simply to trawl for mediators in hopes of determining whether dispute mediators were also being hired in the transactional context. The survey asked respondents for information about their education and training, their experience as a dispute mediator, and their experience as a transactional mediator. In the section on transactional work, it asked how often the respondent had engaged in transactional mediation and allowed the respondent to indicate in how many of various types of transactions he or she had intervened. The survey then asked the respondent to describe the largest (in dollars) transaction they had worked on, and to indicate what sorts of functions they fulfilled in that mediation.

I posted the survey on a web site and e-mailed over five hundred mediators, inviting them to fill out the survey on-line. I make no claim that the sample was random or representative of all practicing mediators — lacking any systematic and efficient way to contact large numbers of mediators, I simply searched leading mediation-related Internet sites for email addresses. After reviewing the results, I eliminated any respondents whose responses suggested confusion about the survey or the definition of transactional mediation and contacted some of those who indicated that they had served as a transactional mediator to verify the information provided and clarify that the respondent was indeed reporting the type of mediation I was focused upon. This weeded out false positives.

The survey results are intriguing. Over forty mediators claimed to have been involved in a transactional mediation. They indicated that they had served as mediators in various types of transactions, including residential real estate, commercial real estate, business formation, mergers and acquisitions, joint ventures, and both union and non-union employment agreement negotiations. Examples included assisting with negotiations over the formation of a partnership of practicing physicians, the sale of a motorcycle dealership, the formation of pre-nuptial agreements and domestic partnerships, re-allocation of property rights and governance in a golfing community, the establishment of a joint venture between a small business and a Fortune 500 company, the sale of cable television access rights, formation of a cross-country ski league, the creation of a houseboat community association, the creation of a joint venture to produce software, negotiations over the terms of a real estate brokerage contract, the transfer of control within a closely held software development firm, the formation of a partnership to own an airplane (where the parties needed to work out issues as varied as fees and the placement of stickers on the tail fin), the negotiation of angel funding for a privately held business, and mergers between two or more corporations. These transactions ranged in value from $100,000 to $26 million.

None seemed to make transactional mediation their primary practice. Of the forty-eight respondents who had conducted a transactional mediation, twenty-seven had done ten or fewer such interventions, and of those, twelve had done only one or two. Although only thirty-one respondents (of these forty-eight) provided sufficient information to draw a comparison between how many dispute mediations and how many transactional interventions they had done, of those who did give such information, it seemed clear that transactional work was a small fraction (average 6.14%) of their portfolio of mediations. These thirty-one respondents had each conducted an average of 409 total mediations (maximum 1,500, minimum 50, standard deviation 344), and an average of only 12 transactional mediations (maximum 67, minimum 1, standard deviation 13). These results suggest that mediators do intervene occasionally in transactions pre-closing. Although I place no stock in the fact that such a high percentage of those surveyed had done so (because the sample was not random), I had initially set out merely to find whether any such interventions are occurring. The survey at least indicates that mediators are sometimes asked to facilitate transactions. . . .

3. Mark C. Suchman & Mia L. Cahill, *The Hired Gun as Facilitator: Lawyers and the Suppression of Business Disputes*, 21 LAW & Soc. INQUIRY 679 (1996)

Lay discourse often criticizes the legal profession for generating disputes and for introducing adversarial bias into "naturally cooperative" social relations. Many academic observers, too, suggest that attorneys foster an inflated "rights consciousness" that disrupts more flexible and consensual extralegal relationships. Often, lay discussions and scientific analyses alike move from initial observations regarding lawyers' disputatious impact on bilateral relationships to more speculative assertions regarding lawyers' chilling effects on larger systems of economic activity. The underlying assumption seems to be that self-interested attorneys goad their clients into an excessively punctilious awareness of legal rights and that such an awareness, in turn, drains the reservoir of trust and good faith that would otherwise lubricate the wheels of commerce. . . . As researchers have turned their attentions to the high-priced business attorney, they have had to confront the vexing question of why apparently rational executives would be willing to pay such large sums of money for the services of an unproductive trouble-maker. While one could perhaps explain the demand for legal counsel entirely in terms of corporate self-defense, the empirical evidence suggests that lawyers may be earning their keep as more than simply hired guns.

In this regard, at least two general themes seem to be emerging: First, several researchers have highlighted lawyers' potentially significant contributions to the "engineering" of complex transactions. By designing and implementing innovative legal devices, attorneys assist their clients in minimizing transaction costs, circumventing regulatory constraints, escaping encumbering liabilities, and pursuing various strategic objectives. A second, less well-developed theme in the recent literature addresses the contributions that lawyers make by deploying evocative symbols rather than by providing concrete technical services. In this view, clients face a complex, turbulent, and unpredictable social environment, and they seek legal counsel primarily as a way of fending off cognitive chaos. Thus, lawyers are rewarded for performing rituals that persuasively symbolize certainty and order, even when those rituals produce few material benefits. . . .

The present essay adds to this emerging body of evidence on corporate lawyers' positive contributions to commerce. . . . Our analysis does not dispute the claim that lawyers occasionally inject elements of rights consciousness into arenas previously governed by informal norms of reciprocity and good faith. Nor does it question the assertion that such a transformation, were it to occur, might well disrupt preexisting extralegal business practices. Rather, the following pages advance the more limited contention that neither an elevation of rights consciousness nor a disruption of commercial conviviality are inevitable consequences of an assertive legal profession. The argument, here, takes the form of a detailed empirical counterexample, constructed from qualitative interview data on the role of lawyers and law firms in California's Silicon Valley.

Contrary to the popular image of lawyers as purveyors of discord, Silicon Valley attorneys see themselves (and are seen by others) as key players in an informal apparatus of socialization, coordination, and normalization that serves to avert potential disputes between members of the local business community. This integrative role becomes most notable in interactions between Silicon Valley lawyers and the region's high-technology entrepreneurs and venture capitalists, and it is on this central aspect of Silicon Valley legal practice that the present essay focuses. By virtue of their distinctive location within the Silicon Valley community, lawyers quite literally produce and reproduce the social structures underpinning the local high-risk capital market. Through their relations with both entrepreneurs and investors, they identify, create, transmit, and enforce the emerging norms of the community. In so doing, Silicon Valley lawyers absorb and control some of the central uncertainties of encounters between venture capitalists and entrepreneurs, facilitating what might otherwise be prohibitively costly, complex, and unpredictable transactions. . . .

Silicon Valley's legal practitioners appear to foster market development and to suppress business disputes in three distinct but interrelated ways: First, and most simply, Silicon Valley lawyers often interpose themselves as third-party buffers in particular transactions. While such active intervention may be ethically problematic from the standpoint of the larger legal profession, it allows attorneys to directly absorb transactional uncertainties, facilitating agreements that might otherwise prove unattainable. Second, Silicon Valley lawyers also stabilize the local capital market in general by transmitting community norms to their clients and by embodying those norms within standardized contractual structures and practices. In so doing, attorneys reduce the transaction costs of negotiating agreements, creating a cooperative climate in which the dangers of opportunism and uncertainty fade from view: Tutored in community norms, contracting parties know which demands are (or are not) "legitimate" and "reasonable" — which concessions they may expect of others, and which concessions others may expect of them in return. Third, Silicon Valley lawyers increasingly act to insulate the local community against exogenous regulatory shocks and competitive challenges, by transforming parochial norms into national legal standards. This "double-institutionalization" of local expectations further reduces the uncertainty of high-technology start-up finance, once again facilitating economic expansion.

The uncertainties of high-technology finance persistently threaten to render transactions between entrepreneurs and venture capitalists costly, unstable, and cognitively intractable, even when such exchanges might, in the abstract, seem mutually beneficial. In Silicon Valley (and perhaps in other regions as well), the local legal community shoulders a substantial share of the responsibility for managing such challenges. In contrast to the conventional image of lawyers as sources of disruptive litigiousness, Silicon Valley law firms seem to be active facilitators of local economic development — both through their efforts to absorb some uncertainties and to subject these to collective control, and through their parallel efforts to symbolically downplay other uncertainties and to render these less paralyzing. Indeed, by reducing both perceived and actual levels of cognitive disorder, the local bar may substantially moderate pressures toward disputatiousness in the community as a whole. . . .

Part IV
ADDITIONAL PROCESSES AND APPROACHES

Chapter 10

COURT-CONNECTED ADR PROCESSES

A. INTRODUCTION

This chapter is devoted to court-connected ADR, while the next chapter considers private forms of ADR. Chapter Twelve examines the use of ADR by the executive branch of government. As with other attempts to divide something into two parts — one is reminded of substance and procedure; haves and have-nots; and even being and becoming — the distinction between public and private dispute resolution processes is useful if not pushed too hard. Terms like "court-connected" and "court-annexed" are sufficiently flexible to include any use of ADR in relation to the judicial process. Where ADR is grounded in a statute, a line must be drawn, but a looser approximation is sufficient for our purposes.

Today, ADR is a central part of the judicial process; some observers even think that ADR has been "co-opted" or "high-jacked" by the courts. Whatever one's view about that value judgment, the extensive use of ADR on the road to obtaining a judicial trial is a fact in the federal courts and in most states. In some jurisdictions, going through ADR (most commonly, mediation) is a condition precedent to getting to trial — as much a necessary step as the filing of pleadings and responding to requests for discovery.

Mediation is not discussed in this chapter, even though it is by far the most used form of court-annexed ADR, because Chapters Six through Nine have already examined mediation at great length. We also do not consider settlement procedures conducted within the courts — e.g., judicial settlement conferences. Particularly useful discussions of this topic are Jeffrey A. Parness, *Improving Judicial Settlement Conferences*, 29 U.C. DAVIS L. REV. 1891 (2006); and Wayne D. Brazil, *Effective Lawyering in Judicially Hosted Settlement Conferences*, 1988 J. DISP. RESOL. 1. In addition to formal court procedures for dispute resolution, court personnel often put informal pressure on lawyers to settle cases. These practices vary with time and place, and the predilections of individual judges. The judicial processing of criminal matters is examined at length in Chapter Six.

Section B examines the authority of the courts to require litigants to participate in — and pay for — dispute resolution procedures, even though some or all of the litigants prefer to proceed directly to trial. Common law theories, as well as legislation, support judicially imposed ADR requirements. The most important legislation is the federal Alternative Dispute Resolution Act of 1998. Although court-connected ADR is well established in the federal courts, as well as most state courts, one might still question whether this is a good idea. Section B closes with an article by Judge Wayne Brazil, our leading commentator on, and practitioner of, court-connected ADR that accepts this challenge.

The next three sections of the chapter consider specific forms of court-annexed ADR: early neutral evaluation (ENE); summary jury trial (SJT); and court-annexed (nonbinding) arbitration (CAA). Section F examines the obligation to participate in court-connected settlement activities and what level of participation is sufficient to satisfy that obligation. The chapter concludes with the use of ADR by appellate courts, notably appellate mediation.

B. AUTHORITY OF COURTS TO REQUIRE LITIGANTS TO USE (AND PAY FOR) ADR

1. *In re Atlantic Pipe Corp.*, F.3d 135 (1st Cir. 2002)

SELYA, Circuit Judge.

This mandamus proceeding requires us to resolve an issue of importance to judges and practitioners alike: Does a district court possess the authority to compel an unwilling party to participate in, and share the costs of, non-binding mediation conducted by a private mediator? [The case grew out of problems with a large construction project in Puerto Rico that resulted in a] googol of claims, counterclaims, cross-claims, and third-party complaints. . . . We hold that a court may order mandatory mediation pursuant to an explicit statutory provision or local rule. We further hold that where, as here, no such authorizing medium exists, a court nonetheless may order mandatory mediation through the use of its inherent powers, as long as the case is an appropriate one and the order contains adequate safeguards. Because the mediation order here at issue lacks such safeguards (although it does not fall far short), we vacate it and remand the matter for further proceedings. . . .

There are four potential sources of judicial authority for ordering mandatory non-binding mediation of pending cases, namely, (a) the court's local rules, (b) an applicable statute, (c) the Federal Rules of Civil Procedure, and (d) the court's inherent powers. Because the district court did not identify the basis of its assumed authority, we consider each of these sources.

A. The Local Rules. A district court's local rules may provide an appropriate source of authority for ordering parties to participate in mediation. In Puerto Rico, however, the local rules contain only a single reference to any form of alternative dispute resolution (ADR). . . . Respondents concede that the mediation order in this case falls outside the boundaries of the mediation program. It does so most noticeably, because it involves mediation before a private mediator, not a judicial officer. Seizing upon this discrepancy, APC argues that the local rules limit the district court in this respect, and that the court exceeded its authority thereunder by issuing a non-conforming mediation order (i.e., one that contemplates the intervention of a private mediator). . . . [W]e take judicial notice that there is no formal, ongoing ADR program in the Puerto Rico federal district court. Because that is so, we conclude that the District of Puerto

Rico has no local rule in force that dictates the permissible characteristics of mediation orders. . . .

B. The ADR Act. There is only one potential source of statutory authority for ordering mandatory non-binding mediation here: the Alternative Dispute Resolution Act of 1998 (ADR Act), 28 U.S.C. §§ 651-658. Congress passed the ADR Act to promote the utilization of alternative dispute resolution methods in the federal courts and to set appropriate guidelines for their use. The Act lists mediation as an appropriate ADR process. Moreover, it sanctions the participation of "professional neutrals from the private sector" as mediators. Finally, the Act requires district courts to obtain litigants' consent only when they order [non-binding] arbitration, not when they order the use of other ADR mechanisms (such as mediation).

Despite the broad sweep of these provisions, the Act is quite clear that some form of the ADR procedures it endorses must be adopted in each judicial district by local rule. *See id.* § 651(b) (directing each district court to "devise and implement its own alternative dispute resolution program, by local rule adopted under [28 U.S.C.] section 2071(a), to encourage and promote the use of alternative dispute resolution in its district"). In the absence of such local rules, the ADR Act itself does not authorize any specific court to use a particular ADR mechanism. Because the District of Puerto Rico has not yet complied with the Act's mandate, the mediation order here at issue cannot be justified under the ADR Act.

The respondents essay an end run around this lacuna: they contend (borrowing a phrase from the court below) that the "spirit" of the ADR Act authorizes the mediation order, because the Act was intended to promote experimentation with ADR techniques. We reject this attempt to press the ADR Act into service by indirection. Although the ADR Act was designed to promote the use of ADR techniques, Congress chose a very well-defined path: it granted each judicial district, rather than each individual judge, the authority to craft an appropriate ADR program. In other words, Congress permitted experimentation, but only within the disciplining format of district-wide local rules adopted with notice and a full opportunity for public comment. To say that the Act authorized each district judge to disregard a district-wide ADR plan (or the absence of one) and fashion innovative procedures for use in specific cases is simply too much of a stretch.

We add, however, that although the respondents cannot use the ADR Act as a justification, neither can APC use it as a nullification. Noting that the Act requires the adoption of local rules establishing a formal ADR program, APC equates the absence of such rules with the absence of power to employ an ADR procedure (say, mediation) in a specific case. But that is wishful thinking: if one assumes that district judges possessed the power to require mediation prior to the passage of the ADR Act, there is nothing in the Act that strips them of that power. After all, even the adoption of a federal procedural rule does not implicitly abrogate a district court's inherent power to act merely because the rule touches upon the same subject matter.

Even though Congress may cabin the district courts' inherent powers, its intention to do so must be clear and unmistakable. Not so here: we know of nothing in either the ADR Act or the policies that undergird it that can be said to restrict the district courts' authority to engage in the case-by-case deployment of ADR procedures. Hence, we conclude that where, as here, there are no implementing local rules, the ADR Act neither authorizes nor prohibits the entry of a mandatory mediation order.

C. The Civil Rules. The respondents next argue that the district court possessed the authority to require mediation by virtue of Rule 16 of the Federal Rules of Civil Procedure, which states in pertinent part that "the court may take appropriate action with respect to . . . (9) settlement and the use of special procedures to assist in resolving the dispute when authorized by statute or local rule. . . ." But the words "when authorized by statute or local rule" are a frank limitation on the district courts' authority to order mediation, and we must adhere to that circumscription.

D. Inherent Powers. Even apart from positive law, district courts have substantial inherent power to manage and control their calendars. This inherent power takes many forms. *See* Fed. R. Civ. P. 83(b) (providing that judges may regulate practice in any manner consistent with federal law and applicable rules). By way of illustration, a district court may use its inherent power to compel represented clients to attend pretrial settlement conferences, even though such a practice is not specifically authorized in the Civil Rules. *See Heileman Brewing Co. v. Joseph Oat Corp.,* 871 F.2d 648, 650 (7th Cir.1989) (en banc).

Of course, a district court's inherent powers are not infinite. There are at least four limiting principles. First, inherent powers must be used in a way reasonably suited to the enhancement of the court's processes, including the orderly and expeditious disposition of pending cases. Second, inherent powers cannot be exercised in a manner that contradicts an applicable statute or rule. Third, the use of inherent powers must comport with procedural fairness. And, finally, inherent powers "must be exercised with restraint and discretion."

At one time, the inherent power of judges to compel unwilling parties to participate in ADR procedures was a hot-button issue for legal scholars. Although many federal district courts have forestalled further debate by adopting local rules that authorize specific ADR procedures and outlaw others, the District of Puerto Rico is not among them. Thus, we have no choice but to address the question head-on.

We begin our inquiry by examining the case law. In *Strandell v. Jackson County,* 838 F.2d 884 (7th Cir. 1987), the Seventh Circuit held that a district court does not possess inherent power to compel participation in a summary jury trial. In the court's view, Fed. R. Civ. P. 16 occupied the field and prevented a district court from forcing "an unwilling litigant to be sidetracked from the normal course of litigation." *Id.* at 887. But the group that spearheaded the subsequent revision of Rule 16 explicitly rejected that interpretation. *See* Fed. R. Civ. P. 16, advisory committee's note (1993 Amendment). . . . Thus, we do not find *Strandell* persuasive on this point.

The *Strandell* court also expressed concern that summary jury trials would undermine traditional discovery and privilege rules by requiring certain disclosures prior to an actual trial. We find this concern unwarranted. Because a summary jury trial (like a non-binding mediation) does not require any disclosures beyond what would be required in the ordinary course of discovery, its principal disadvantage to the litigants is that it may prevent them from saving surprises for the time of trial. Since trial by ambush is no longer in vogue, that interest does not deserve protection.

Relying on policy arguments, the Sixth Circuit also has found that district courts do not possess inherent power to compel participation in summary jury trials. *See In re NLO, Inc.*, 5 F.3d 154, 157-58 (6th Cir. 1993). The court thought the value of a summary jury trial questionable when parties do not engage in the process voluntarily, and it worried that "too broad an interpretation of the federal courts' inherent power to regulate their procedure encourages judicial high-handedness. . . ."

The concerns articulated by these two respected courts plainly apply to mandatory mediation orders. When mediation is forced upon unwilling litigants, it stands to reason that the likelihood of settlement is diminished. Requiring parties to invest substantial amounts of time and money in mediation under such circumstances may well be inefficient. *Cf.* Richard A. Posner, *The Summary Jury Trial and Other Methods of Alternative Dispute Resolution: Some Cautionary Observations,* 53 U. Chi. L. Rev. 366, 369-72 (1986) (offering a model to evaluate ADR techniques in terms of their capacity to encourage settlements).

The fact remains, however, that none of these considerations establishes that mandatory mediation is always inappropriate. There may well be specific cases in which such a protocol is likely to conserve judicial resources without significantly burdening the objectors' rights to a full, fair and speedy trial. Much depends on the idiosyncrasies of the particular case and the details of the mediation order. In some cases, a court may be warranted in believing that compulsory mediation could yield significant benefits, even if one or more parties object. After all, a party may resist mediation simply out of unfamiliarity with the process or out of fear that a willingness to submit would be perceived as a lack of confidence in her legal position. In such an instance, the party's initial reservations are likely to evaporate as the mediation progresses, and negotiations could well produce a beneficial outcome, at reduced cost and greater speed than would a trial. While the possibility that parties will fail to reach agreement remains ever present, the boon of settlement can be worth the risk.

This is particularly true in complex cases involving multiple claims and parties. The fair and expeditious resolution of such cases often is helped along by creative solutions — solutions that simply are not available in the binary framework of traditional adversarial litigation. Mediation with the assistance of a skilled facilitator gives parties an opportunity to explore a much wider range of options, including those that go beyond conventional zero-sum resolutions. Mindful of these potential advantages, we hold that it is within a district court's inherent power to order non-consensual mediation in those cases in which that step seems reasonably likely to serve the interests of justice. *Cf. Reilly v. United*

States, 863 F.2d 149, 156-57 (1st Cir. 1988) (finding that district courts have inherent power to appoint technical advisors in especially complex cases).

E. The Mediation Order. Our determination that the district courts have inherent power to refer cases to non-binding mediation is made with a recognition that any such order must be crafted in a manner that preserves procedural fairness and shields objecting parties from undue burdens. We thus turn to the specifics of the mediation order entered in this case. As with any exercise of a district court's inherent powers, we review the . . . order for abuse of discretion.

As an initial matter, we agree with the lower court that the complexity of this case militates in favor of ordering mediation. At last count, the suit involves twelve parties, asserting a welter of claims, counterclaims, cross-claims, and third-party claims predicated on a wide variety of theories. The pendency of nearly parallel litigation in the Puerto Rican courts, which features a slightly different cast of characters and claims that are related to, but not completely congruent with, those asserted here further complicates the matter. Untangling the intricate web of relationships among the parties, along with the difficult and fact-intensive arguments made by each, will be time-consuming and will impose significant costs on the parties and the court. Against this backdrop, mediation holds out the dual prospect of advantaging the litigants and conserving scarce judicial resources. . . .

Next, APC posits that the appointment of a private mediator proposed by one of the parties is per se improper (and, thus, invalidates the order). We do not agree. In the context of non-binding mediation, the mediator does not decide the merits of the case and has no authority to coerce settlement. Thus, in the absence of a contrary statute or rule, it is perfectly acceptable for the district court to appoint a qualified and neutral private party as a mediator. The mere fact that the mediator was proposed by one of the parties is insufficient to establish bias in favor of that party. We hasten to add that the litigants are free to challenge the qualifications or neutrality of any suggested mediator (whether or not nominated by a party to the case).

APC also grouses that it should not be forced to share the costs of an unwanted mediation. We have held, however, that courts have the power under Fed. R. Civ. P. 26(f) to issue pretrial cost-sharing orders in complex litigation. Given the difficulties facing trial courts in cases involving multiple parties and multiple claims, we are hesitant to limit that power to the traditional discovery context. *See id.* This is especially true in complicated cases, where the potential value of mediation lies not only in promoting settlement but also in clarifying the issues remaining for trial.

The short of the matter is that, without default cost-sharing rules, the use of valuable ADR techniques (like mediation) becomes hostage to the parties' ability to agree on the concomitant financial arrangements. This means that the district court's inherent power to order private mediation in appropriate cases would be rendered nugatory absent the corollary power to order the sharing of reasonable mediation costs. To avoid this pitfall, we hold that the district court, in an appropriate case, is empowered to order the sharing of reasonable costs and expenses associated with mandatory non-binding mediation.

The remainder of APC's arguments are not so easily dispatched. Even when generically appropriate, a mediation order must contain procedural and substantive safeguards to ensure fairness to all parties involved. The mediation order in this case does not quite meet that test. In particular, the order does not set limits on the duration of the mediation or the expense associated therewith.

As entered, the order simply requires the parties to mediate; it does not set forth either a timetable for the mediation or a cap on the fees that the mediator may charge. The figures that have been bandied about in the briefs — $900 per hour or $9,000 per mediation day — are quite large and should not be left to the mediator's whim. Relatedly, because the mediator is to be paid an hourly rate, the court should have set an outside limit on the number of hours to be devoted to mediation. Equally as important, it is trite but often true that justice delayed is justice denied. An unsuccessful mediation will postpone the ultimate resolution of the case — indeed, the district court has stayed all discovery pending the completion of the mediation — and, thus, prolong the litigation. For these reasons, the district court should have set a definite time frame for the mediation.

The respondents suggest that the district court did not need to articulate any limitations in its mediation order, because the mediation process will remain under the district court's ultimate supervision; the court retains the ability to curtail any excessive expenditures of time or money; and a dissatisfied party can easily return to the court at any time. While this might be enough of a safeguard in many instances, the instant litigation is sufficiently complicated, and the mediation efforts are likely to be sufficiently expensive that, here, reasonable time limits and fee constraints, set in advance, are appropriate. We do not mean that a mediation order in such a case must be etched in stone. The mediator and the parties remain free, for good cause shown, to ask the district court to extend or modify the original order.

A court intent on ordering non-consensual mediation should take other precautions as well. For example, the court should make it clear (as did the able district court in this case) that participation in mediation will not be taken as a waiver of any litigation position. The important point is that the protections we have mentioned are not intended to comprise an exhaustive list but, rather, to illustrate that when a district court orders a party to participate in mediation, it should take care to assuage legitimate concerns about the possible negative consequences of such an order. . . .

We admire the district court's pragmatic and innovative approach to this massive litigation. Our core holding — that ordering mandatory mediation is a proper exercise of a district court's inherent power, subject, however, to a variety of terms and conditions — validates that approach. We are mindful that this holding is in tension with the opinions of the Sixth and Seventh Circuits in *NLO* and *Strandell,* respectively, but we believe it is justified by the important goal of promoting flexibility and creative problem-solving in the handling of complex litigation.

That said, the need of the district judge in this case to construct his own mediation regime ad hoc underscores the greater need of the district court as an institution to adopt an ADR program and memorialize it in its local rules. In the ADR Act, Congress directed that "[e]ach United States district court shall authorize, by local rule the use of alternative dispute resolution processes in all civil actions. . . ." 28 U.S.C. § 651(b). While Congress did not set a firm deadline for compliance with this directive, the statute was enacted four years ago. This omission having been noted, we are confident that the district court will move expediently to bring the District of Puerto Rico into compliance. . . .

For the reasons set forth above, we vacate the district court's mediation order and remand for further proceedings consistent with this opinion. The district court is free to order mediation, if it continues to believe that such a course is advisable. . . .

2. Caroline Harris Crowne, *The Alternative Dispute Resolution Act of 1998: Implementing a New Paradigm of Justice*, 76 N.Y.U. L. REV. 1768 (2001)

After a decade of tentative experimentation with alternative dispute resolution (ADR) in the federal courts, Congress finally put its stamp of approval on ADR by passing the Alternative Dispute Resolution Act of 1998, 28 U.S.C. §§ 651-658. The Act requires all federal trial courts to implement ADR programs for litigants and allows courts to mandate participation in those programs. In order for court administrators to implement the Act successfully, they must reconcile the new paradigm of justice inherent in ADR with the traditional adjudicative paradigm of justice that currently guides the courts. Furthermore, they must sift through the many varieties of ADR to design programs that are compatible with the court system and that provide benefits to litigants. This Note explores how court administrators, by understanding and respecting differences among ADR processes, and between ADR and adjudication, may integrate ADR into the court system without compromising either justice or the effectiveness of ADR.

Addressing concerns about justice is tricky, because standard notions of justice are tied up inextricably with the principles and processes of traditional adjudication. ADR processes represent a different paradigm of justice. Whereas adjudication is concerned primarily with serving the interests of the public (the "public-service" paradigm), ADR is concerned primarily with serving the interests of disputants (the "customer-service" paradigm). Given that ADR has been embraced because it is different from adjudication, courts and commentators should not demand that ADR conform to traditional notions of justice. Rather, awareness of the ADR paradigm should inform evaluations of the quality and success of court ADR programs, allowing for an effective integration of ADR into the court system.

Furthermore, court administrators should be aware of the differences among various forms of ADR when deciding how to make use of these processes. Facilitative processes, such as mediation, raise different issues and call for different approaches than determinative processes such as arbitration. The desired benefits of ADR, such as speedy and amicable resolution and party control, accrue in varying degrees from different procedures and easily can be forfeited if essential characteristics of a process are altered. The label "ADR" alone does not confer desired benefits, and poorly implemented programs could do more harm than good.

The Act provides no guidance as to the proper role of ADR in the court system and leaves district courts tremendous discretion to design ADR processes. . . . There is a danger that ADR programs could turn into a system of "second-class" justice, with "unimportant" cases being summarily disposed of through ADR, or that ADR could become just another procedural hurdle on the path to trial, contributing nothing of substance to the disputants or society. On the other hand, thoughtful incorporation of ADR into the courts could enrich our justice system and provide substantial benefits. . . .

Since there exists such great flexibility in ADR processes, courts can design their programs in a wide variety of ways. It would be easy, and unfortunate, for court administrators to fall into the familiar habits of adjudicative procedure in designing ADR procedure. Instead, court administrators should understand the unique goals of ADR so that they thoughtfully may design ADR programs that provide unique benefits.

The paradigms of alternative dispute resolution and adjudication are distinctly different. These two paradigms of dispute resolution may be termed the "public-service model" and the "customer-service model." The procedural characteristics of adjudication and ADR demonstrate that they are designed to serve the interests of two different constituencies: the public and the customer, respectively. The hallmarks of adjudication, uniformity and transparency, allow for the imposition of legal standards and appellate review. These characteristics in turn make judges responsive to public interests, by limiting individual discretion and requiring compliance with common norms and public laws. On the other hand, the hallmarks of ADR are flexibility and privacy. These characteristics make neutrals responsive primarily to customers — the disputants.

Various formal procedures help adjudication serve public interests. Court decisions are supposed to be consistent with objective legal standards that are applied consistently to individual cases. Legal standards are announced publicly and reflect social values. Each judge's discretion is limited; decisions that deviate from the law can be appealed and modified. Requirements of public access and publication apply to many aspects of adjudication, from evidentiary hearings to legal decisions. In sum, adjudicative procedures assure public accountability by requiring judges' decisions to conform to public values and by ensuring compliance through public disclosure and rights of appeal.

By comparison, ADR's flexibility and privacy allow it to respond to disputants' varied interests. Disputants can consider a wide variety of ADR processes and choose one that best suits their needs, and an ADR neutral often can modify the process to handle a particular dispute. Outcomes reached through ADR may be tailored to particular circumstances and may be based on personal conceptions of fairness (which frequently are influenced by the law). Occasionally, the parties, or an ADR organization chosen by the parties, may indicate in advance what standards should apply. ADR sessions are conducted in private, and disclosures made during the session, and even the resolution itself, often are confidential. Privacy benefits disputants directly, by making them more comfortable and by protecting sensitive information, which in turn can facilitate frank, exploratory settlement discussions. Privacy also makes flexibility possible, by ensuring that the process is responsive to participants rather than outsiders and allowing for discretionary decisionmaking. Possibilities for judicial review of ADR outcomes are limited. Thus, neutrals in ADR are accountable only to the disputants.

This characterization of ADR as based on customer service, and of adjudication as based on public service, risks oversimplification. While ADR primarily serves disputants' interests, it also benefits society, for example, by channeling conflict in a civil, ordered way; and while adjudication primarily serves public interests, it also benefits litigants, for example, by providing resolution. The public-service paradigm and the customer-service paradigm are compatible, not hostile. Therefore, ADR and adjudication are capable of working in tandem to serve the interests of both the public and disputants. The main point is that ADR and adjudication are designed primarily to be accountable to different groups, and their procedures reflect this distinction. . . .

II The Alternative Dispute Resolution Act of 1998

The Alternative Dispute Resolution Act of 1998 proclaims a permanent role for ADR in the federal courts. The Act was passed in the wake of two earlier pieces of legislation, the Civil Justice Reform Act of 1990 (CJRA) and the Judicial Improvements and Access to Justice Act of 1988. These earlier acts had provided for some experimentation with ADR within the federal courts for the purposes of study and demonstration but were set to expire after a limited time. The Act salvages the ADR reforms authorized under the two previous acts, permitting courts to continue their experiments permanently and requiring courts that had not participated in those experiments to adopt ADR programs of their own. The legislative history of the Act reveals a desire both to alleviate courts' case burdens and to serve disputants better by offering ADR processes that are efficient and that promote amicable resolution.

The nearly uniform approval of the ADR Act and praise for the benefits of court-sponsored ADR may seem surprising in light of commentators' strong criticism of the CJRA and the Judicial Improvements Act, and studies conducted pursuant to those acts that yielded lukewarm results. The studies failed to produce clear evidence of greater efficiency, although they did find high levels of satisfaction among those involved with the ADR programs. These findings, however, may say little about the potential of court ADR programs. Under the CJRA and the Judicial Improvements Act, some courts did not have substantial ADR programs, and some of the programs were rarely used.

Whether the programs under the Act will fulfill its promise depends on whether courts respect the integrity of ADR and its specific forms in implementation. The drafters of the Act spoke of efficient determination and amicable resolution, but failed to acknowledge the different capacities of various forms of ADR for delivering those benefits. Likewise, the Act itself does not provide either meaningful distinctions among different forms of ADR or guidance on the proper role of various forms in the courts. Its broad mandate, however, clears the path for courts to develop ADR programs that provide real benefits to disputants.

The Act calls upon every federal district court to develop an ADR program. Under the Act, courts must require litigants in civil cases to consider ADR, and courts may choose to require litigants to participate in some forms of ADR. The Act defines alternative dispute resolution as "any process or procedure, other than adjudication by a presiding judge, in which a neutral third party participates to assist in the resolution of issues in controversy, through processes such as early neutral evaluation, mediation, mini-trial, and arbitration." There are no requirements as to the structure of these processes, and the Act allows courts to adopt or devise additional forms of ADR.

The Act's arbitration provisions do include some concrete requirements and restrictions. Courts may not mandate participation in arbitration. Furthermore, the Act specifically exempts from arbitration constitutional cases, civil rights cases, and cases with more than $150,000 in controversy. It also restricts the binding effect of arbitrations — either party may request a trial de novo for any reason. Unlike prior legislation, the Act does not allow the imposition of arbitration costs or attorney fees on parties who request a trial de novo. If neither party requests a trial within thirty days of the arbitration, the arbitration award becomes binding as a court judgment and is not appealable. The Act does not state whether parties may waive the right to trial de novo prior to arbitration.

Although the Act sets out some definite procedures with respect to arbitration, it leaves much in the hands of the courts. Courts must determine which ADR procedures are suitable for the court system, how to structure ADR procedures, and whether facilitative forms of ADR should be voluntary or mandatory. The Act also delegates to courts the responsibility to provide for the confidentiality of ADR processes and communications, to determine which cases to exempt from ADR, and to ensure that parties freely consent to arbitration and that parties are not penalized for refusing to submit to arbitration. Courts will need to determine at what point during litigation to refer cases to ADR and whether referral to ADR puts trial preparation on hold. The Act does not provide any substantive requirements as to the training, qualification, or compensation of neutrals. Finally, courts are left on their own to oversee ADR programs and to craft mechanisms for maintaining quality and ensuring that ADR truly benefits disputants.

It may have been wise for Congress to delegate broad implementation power to the courts. Court administrators — both judges and the professional staff of individual courts and the Judicial Conference — are in a better position than legislators to see and understand how ADR operates. Allowing for flexibility by leaving discretion for specific implementation in the hands of local administrators is in keeping with the spirit of ADR. Nonetheless, . . . the lack of guidance in the Act as to the proper role of ADR in the courts leaves room for misdirection and error. Furthermore, several specific provisions of the Act effectively eliminate certain beneficial features of ADR.

Hasty, unguided implementation may jeopardize the potential benefits of the legislation. The provision of poor-quality ADR programs, with uninformed administrators and poorly trained neutrals, could undermine faith both in the courts and in ADR generally. Furthermore, the use of poor-quality programs to dispose quickly of "unimportant" cases could result in a system of second-class justice, with disputants receiving neither justice nor any of the benefits attributed to ADR. On the other hand, a fear that ADR programs will be of poor quality, or cannot do "justice," could lead to the creation of numerous exemptions, denying many disputants the benefits of ADR. Even with sufficient funding, ineffective quality control could result in the unfair treatment of many disputants at the hands of neutrals who ignore their training or abuse their power. Conversely, hasty creation of safeguards, based on the adjudicative model, could interfere with essential attributes of ADR processes, like flexibility and privacy, depriving disputants of the potential benefits of those processes, or at the very least could encumber ADR processes unnecessarily. In this way, disputants could come to see ADR as a waste of time — merely a procedural hurdle on the path to trial.

Not only does the Act leave wide latitude for misdirection, but it also hinders implementation of effective arbitration. First, the Act gives any party to arbitration the right to request a trial de novo, which effectively amputates the one feature of arbitration that promotes speedy determination — its finality. Studies under previous legislation found that nonbinding arbitration (that is, arbitration that is "binding" but also entails the right to trial de novo) does not decrease average cost or time to final disposition. Participants in those programs did say, however, that they found the arbitration award useful as a starting point for negotiations. Facilitative processes such as mediation are designed to aid negotiation and, therefore, would be more effective than arbitration to that end. Arbitration is a determinative process and must be binding to be effective.

The second flawed feature of the Act is the provision on exemptions from arbitration. The Act exempts constitutional cases, civil rights cases, and cases with a lot of money at stake. Unfortunately, the exemption is not expressed with reference to any well-considered rationale about the appropriate roles of adjudication and ADR in the court system. District courts are authorized by the Act to enact additional exemptions from their local ADR programs but are given no guidance on creating principled criteria for choosing what sorts of cases to exempt. One possible rationale for the first two exemptions is that the public interest in cases involving a challenge to government power argues against removing these cases from the public adjudicative process into private processes that are not open or otherwise accountable to the public. This is a reasonable rationale for exempting these cases from arbitration, but it is inconsistent with the fact that settlement through ADR in cases involving the government is permitted, even encouraged. Also, this rationale does not account for the exemption for cases involving large sums of money. A possible rationale for this monetary exemption is that courts will not provide sufficient resources to support arbitration programs capable of handling complex cases. Such an assumption should

not be made in advance, because it prevents courts from developing arbitration programs that can handle such cases. Arbitration in the private sector frequently handles complex commercial cases.

A better approach would be for individual courts to draft exemptions in light of the type of ADR programs they offer. Exempting high-stakes cases could decrease political pressure for quality ADR programs. Another possible rationale for the Act's three exemptions is that arbitration cannot be trusted to resolve "important" cases. Exemptions should not, however, be based on the premise that ADR is only acceptable for "unimportant" cases, because that premise could become a self-fulfilling prophecy and result in a system of second-class justice. If there are problems with using determinative processes like arbitration in the court system, they should be confronted directly and resolved so that no cases are given inferior treatment. Regardless of their merits, these rationales are only surmises. Courts are left without a real framework for crafting further exemptions.

The Act illustrates how fears about the capacity of ADR to deliver justice can lead to limitations that deprive disputants of the benefits of ADR. While it gives courts broad power to develop ADR programs, it provides little guidance and imposes several handicaps. Such responses are bound to increase the probability that ADR programs will be ineffective and of low quality. Courts implementing the Act should strive to treat ADR as a distinct, independently valid means of resolving disputes. Concerns about justice should be addressed by carefully selecting among and further modifying ADR processes to achieve certain goals, by identifying ways of accommodating public interests without interfering with essential characteristics of ADR, and by adopting quality-control mechanisms that are consistent with the purposes and paradigms of ADR.

3. Comments and Questions

a. Crowne makes reference to the settlement of "important" cases. This topic is considered at length in Chapter Thirteen. *See particularly*, Owen M. Fiss, *Against Settlement*, 93 YALE L.J. 1073 (1984); and Jeffrey R. Seul, *Settling Significant Cases*, 79 WASH. L. REV. 881 (2004).

b. Both Crowne and Brazil, in the article that follows, discuss concerns about two-tiered justice, with particular concern about the impact on have-nots. To the extent that their views cannot be reconciled, which position (if either) do you prefer, and why?

c. How do you assess the trade-off between flexibility and consistency? How can the system encourage innovation without also producing mistakes? A major argument for innovation is that sub-optimal approaches will be weeded out in the marketplace of ideas.

d. As demonstrated by Crowne and Judge Selya, the combination of legislation and inherent authority have put to rest any doubts about the general power of the federal courts to require people involved in law suits to engage in, and pay for, (non-binding) ADR prior to trial. The same is generally true at the

state level, subject to variations in local law and practice. *See, e.g.*, The Texas ADR Act, set forth in the Appendix.

e. The fact that court-annexed ADR is authorized does not prove that it is a good idea. In the next article, Wayne Brazil asks whether court-sponsored ADR should survive; his answer is a ringing Yes. Judge Brazil's combination of judicial experience and thoughtful scholarship makes him our leading commentator on the use of ADR by the courts.

4. Wayne D. Brazil, *Should Court-Sponsored ADR Survive?*, 21 OHIO ST. J. ON DISP. RESOL. 241, 242-44, 252-258 (2006)

It is important to make clear, at the outset, the context that shapes my thoughts. . . . In the ADR program that I have supervised for many years [in the U.S. District Court for the Northern District of California], the court offers the services of its neutrals — mediators, evaluators and arbitrators — for free. The parties are permitted to choose among four or five process options, one of which is to retain a neutral of their own choice from the private ADR provider community and to tailor a process that seems to best fit their specific situation. The neutrals . . . are selected and trained by the court. Before admission to the pool of court-provided neutrals, they must meet a set of objective requirements and "pass" the training course. They are volunteers, mostly seasoned lawyers, and are expected to serve without compensation in two or three cases a year.

My answer to the question, should court ADR programs survive, is an emphatic yes. Why? A short set of core propositions informs this view. I start from the premise that to sustain the health of our democracy, it is essential that our public institutions be healthy — that they be truly useful to the people, that they be able to make the necessary adjustments in the way they operate to remain responsive to the people's needs, and that the procedures they follow and the orientation they project encourage the people's respect. I also believe that courts are, fundamentally, service institutions. I contend that courts fail in their fundamental mission if they provide real service to only a small percentage of cases or to only a small percentage of persons with judicially cognizable disputes. Further, I fear that the substantial cost of civil litigation has resulted, for many people, in a demoralizing disproportion between litigation transaction costs and the economic significance or value of their disputes. In large measure because of that disproportion, it is likely that many people feel that they cannot turn to the courts to try to protect their rights or, in the case of defendants, cannot afford to use to defend themselves the tools that the civil litigation system, in theory, offers. For such people, the disproportion between cost and value has the effect of closing the courthouse doors, and making the judicial branch of our government a mirage. Moreover, this same disproportion forces many of those people who try to use the court system to leave it before the judiciary has provided them with any really useful service.

[O]ne of the very few ways a court can be useful to a substantial segment of the population is to offer a free or low-cost ADR program. By offering such a pro-

gram, a court acknowledges the real-world limitations, for many people, of the services it traditionally has offered. As important, the court demonstrates that it understands that its mission is to offer useable and respect-worthy service to as large a percentage of the people who have judicially cognizable disputes as possible. This kind of acknowledgment and demonstration earn a court the gratitude and respect of the people — and gratitude toward and respect for our public institutions is essential to the long-range health of our polity. . . .

III. Does Court ADR Promote a Two-Tiered System of Justice?

The system of justice was two-tiered long before courts began establishing ADR programs — and it will remain two-tiered regardless of whether or not courts continue to offer ADR services. Money separates the two tiers. Those who have it get first tier justice. Those who do not have it, or whose case does not carry a clear promise of generating it, get the second tier version, or none. Court provision of ADR services begins with an acknowledgment of this reality and is intended to be responsive to it. Courts that provide ADR services at no cost, or for below market fees, can reduce the disparity between the level of public service that courts provide to the "haves" and the level of service courts provide to the "have-nots."

Court provision of inexpensive or no-cost ADR services also can increase the percentage of have-nots to whom the courts are accessible in fact, rather than only in theory. For most have-nots, the courthouse doors, as traditionally configured, remain locked. The only have-nots with keys that can open courthouse doors are those whose claims (1) are likely to be perceived by lawyers as strong on the merits (liability appreciably more likely than not), and (2) are likely to generate either a substantial and collectable pot of money or a collectable attorneys' fees award. Have-nots who are not so fortunately situated are much less likely to find representation and much less likely to see any point in filing a lawsuit — at least if they understand how much financial staying-power will be demanded of them before the court will give them a trial or rule on a dispositive motion. But such litigants might be more inclined to try to use the judicial system if they — and their prospective counsel — could see that, relatively early in the pretrial period, the court would provide them, at little or no cost, a meaningful opportunity to address the merits of their dispute directly with the other parties and to try, with the aid of an experienced neutral, to forge a settlement.

There is another perspective from which policymakers might ask whether court provision of ADR services tends to create a two-tiered system of justice. Does court provision of ADR services perpetuate a two-tiered system of justice by taking pressure off legislatures to improve access to and reduce the cost to users of adjudicatory processes? The short answer is no. Given all of the budgetary pressures under which governments at all levels seem destined to labor for the foreseeable future, it seems almost laughable to suggest that legislatures would provide significant additional funding for courts if the courts abandoned their ADR programs. The litigants to whom court ADR services are most important are not likely to have anywhere near the clout with legislatures as their wealthier institutional counterparts — many of whom already have found a substitute for a good public court system in private ADR providers. . . .

Before shifting our focus away from the topic of two-tiered justice, we should highlight an assumption that some critics of court ADR seem to bring to this debate. Some critics assume that the "justice" that is provided, in theory, by traditional adjudication is better — top tier — than "justice" that is accessible by agreement between the parties through an ADR process — bottom tier. Is this assumption well made? There is no easy answer to this question, and no one answer is likely correct for all situations or as measured by all criteria. It does seem important to emphasize, however, that the question is hardly self-answering, and that in some cases, all the parties are likely to feel that the justice that ADR is capable of delivering is superior to the justice that traditional adjudication would yield. . . . [M]ediation permits the parties to decide for themselves which criteria or values should be used to determine what constitutes a "just" disposition in their specific circumstance. So for litigants who ascribe greater weight to some values or considerations than would be ascribed in an adjudication, ADR offers access to a more attractive result.

IV. What Would Happen If the Courts Dropped ADR Programs?

This question is most significant for court programs that offer ADR services for free or at rates well below market. If such courts were to drop their programs, many poor litigants would have little or no access to private or public ADR services. Presumably, the same "no-ADR-service" fate would befall many cases of limited economic value. As the gap between realistic case value and the cost of securing ADR service in the private sector narrows, there probably is a roughly parallel decline in parties' willingness to make an investment in a proceeding that cannot promise to deliver closure. . . . [F]or litigants without significant financial resources or clear access to substantial damages, or attorneys' fees, the only viable alternatives, in a court that does not provide ADR services, are to try to directly negotiate a quick settlement or to give up. Leaving any significant percentage of our population with only these options would represent a major failure of government.

The private ADR provider community and the ADR "movement" also would suffer substantial losses if courts dropped their ADR programs. Court programs have been important sources of enrichment and stimulation in the development of ADR generally. Whole new processes, like early neutral evaluation, have been developed in court programs. Court programs also have been sources of refinement in and learning about other processes, like mediation, that were initially developed in other settings. Courts have deepened thinking in the ADR field about ethical issues — as court policymakers and program administrators have addressed ethical dilemmas their neutrals have encountered during their work for the courts and have developed ethical rules and guidelines to discipline the provision of services in their programs.

Circumstances unique to court programs make them especially rich sources of learning for the field at large. Driven by a sense of institutional responsibility for the character and quality of programs they sponsor and, in some instances, by statutory mandate, courts have been pushed into a "regulator's role" in this field. As they have worked from scratch through the full implementation of their programs, they solicited, researched, and debated various program design options; they have crafted rules for parties and neutrals; they have set up and monitored programs to train neutrals and to educate lawyers and clients; they have fielded questions from their neutrals and helped them shape responses to process challenges and ethical dilemmas; they have hosted in-service seminars of mature neutrals who teach one another, and the court, effective techniques, search for creative solutions to recurring problems, and suggest experience-based modifications to existing rules or process models; they have systematically collected feedback and evaluations from parties, their lawyers, the neutrals, court personnel, and judges; and they have collected and analyzed empirical data about a host of aspects of their programs.

Required to satisfy so many mandates, and fed so much information through so many channels, the people who design and run court ADR programs are uniquely positioned to generate learning that can be valuable for ADR practitioners and policymakers in a wide range of private and public settings. In short, court programs constitute the most instructive laboratories for the entire field of ADR. They may well be the only settings in which controlled experiments involving sizeable samples of participants can be conducted. Furthermore, federal trial courts are required by Congress to evaluate the experiences and data such experiments produce. Such evaluations could help demonstrate the potential benefits of various forms of ADR to broader segments of the population — thus spurring greater demand for ADR services from private providers. In addition, by drawing from systematically collected data and from the experiences and innovations of individual neutrals serving in their programs, courts can help develop or adjust an array of ADR process models and can identify new practice techniques or tips for both neutrals and parties.

There is an additional way that court programs can serve as important sources of learning about the field of ADR — and as important arenas for developing norms for conduct in that field. Good court programs provide mechanisms by which participants in sponsored ADR processes can complain and seek relief when they believe that a party, a lawyer or a neutral has violated one of the program's rules or has failed to meet one of the program's requirements. Such complaints, and the responses to them by other participants, can shed light on dynamics inside the ADR events and can help policymakers develop strategies for preventing, defusing or responding to potential problems.

Moreover, when such complaints mature into contested proceedings, judges are called upon to make rulings and to develop standards that may have widespread applicability. Through these kinds of disputes, judges develop law and policy in a host of subjects, including conflicts of interest, confidentiality, the play between ADR proceedings and the operation of traditional privileges and work product protections, the scope of neutrals' authority and the extent of their immunity or other protections, and the appropriateness of various behaviors by neutrals and other participants in particular kinds of ADR processes. Through opinions and rulings on issues like these that arise in their programs, courts can become sources of legal discipline and ethical guidance for the field at large. If courts dropped their ADR programs, there would be appreciably fewer occasions for learning from this source.

Withdrawing of judicial sponsorship of ADR programs also could hurt the field by undermining the sense of "legitimacy" and "validity" that court endorsement may confer on ADR processes. At least some portion of the population likely would interpret a widespread judicial retreat from this arena as sending some kind of negative message about the wisdom of using means other than the courts to resolve disputes. Thus, even if driven by entirely unrelated motives, court abandonment of ADR might undermine public confidence in the integrity and effectiveness of ADR generally, thereby discouraging new users, if not established customers.

A related consequence of court withdrawal from ADR warrants mention here. Court programs have played a major role in accelerating familiarity with and acceptance of ADR processes. By mandating or encouraging the use of mediation, early neutral evaluation, and non-binding arbitration, courts have extended exposure to and experience with these procedures into a much broader portion of the population. For the most part, these judicially prodded experiences have been positive. As noted earlier, in most surveys of litigants and lawyers, even in mandatory court programs, high percentages of respondents report positive feelings about court referred ADR processes. The discontinuance of court ADR programs would deprive the field of this important source of converts and would slow the spread of familiarity with alternative dispute resolution processes. Less experience means more ignorance — and more ignorance means more fear. Fear of the unknown is a barrier to first use, and the field should not welcome artificial barriers to first use.

Court withdrawal from ADR would be accompanied by one additional negative consequence. After substantial periods of resistance and ambivalence, the executive and legislative branches of the federal government have decided that ADR can be a valuable tool and have endorsed or mandated its use, in one form or another, in a wide variety of settings. If the judiciary were to abandon ADR, it would, in effect, cede to the other two branches of government the power and responsibility to develop and to provide all forms of dispute resolution service other than litigation. For at least two major reasons, such a wholesale surrender would be unwise.

First, among the three branches of the government, the courts have the deepest and richest experience with dispute resolution processes — and it is the courts that have the greatest expertise in working to assure procedural fairness. Because of its experience, the judiciary is the branch of government best positioned to detect, and to assess the magnitude of, different kinds of threats to process integrity. Moreover, this view is likely shared by a substantial percentage of the population. Given the courts' process expertise, and the public's confidence in that expertise, the branch of government under whose wing it makes the most sense to develop and regulate new procedures for resolving disputes is the judiciary. The courts are less likely than the other branches to err in this arena — and their endorsement of new procedures is likely to carry more weight with the people — and thus to be more helpful to the ADR "movement."

Second, ceding the public sector's responsibility for all dispute resolution processes, other than litigation, to the other branches of government would threaten to reduce the role and significance of the third branch. If growing percentages of parties whose rights have been invaded cannot afford to seek protection through adjudication, a substantial share of public dispute resolution work can be expected to gravitate toward another branch of government, especially if that branch offers ADR services. If the judiciary provides no such service, its share of dispute resolution work will decline considerably. Were that to happen, the judicial branch would become less relevant to the people, who, in turn, would be less interested in or concerned about any decline in the judiciary's institutional health — including reductions in jurisdiction and budgetary support. With less support from the people, narrower jurisdiction, and fewer resources, the judiciary's standing as a co-equal branch of government would be jeopardized, potentially compromising its capacity to perform the crucial role assigned to it under our constitutional system. An anemic judiciary might find it difficult to serve as an effective check and balance on the other two branches of government. While this kind of scenario obviously is in no sense imminent, and may appear to be the product of little more than a paranoid third branch imagination, it would be unwise to discount it completely. . . .

C. EARLY NEUTRAL EVALUATION

1. Comments and Questions

a. Early Neutral Evaluation (ENE) is a term that can be, and is, used in several senses. ENE began as a private form of ADR, with the names moderated settlement conference, advisory opinion, and even non-binding arbitration sometimes used to describe similar proceedings. Private ENE consists of an early evaluation of a dispute by a neutral based on a general presentation (usually without live witnesses) by representatives of each side. The neutral(s) then provide an evaluation of the base for the parties.

b. The Rosenberg & Folberg article provides a detailed description and analysis of a court-connected ENE program. Note the problems identified by the authors, and the solutions proposed by them. How did the court-connected context shape the problems that arose in the Northern California ENE pilot project? Are the proposed solutions equally applicable to private ENE?

c. In the wake of the Civil Justice Reform Act of 1990, ENE has become a court-connected process in many federal districts. As such, it is defined with greater specificity in court rules, and is less amenable to being custom designed by disputants. Nevertheless, Rosenberg & Folberg found that the ENE proceedings varied considerably, with the most significant variable being the orientation and approach of the neutral. Do these variations simply reflect the inception of a new process, that will narrow over time, or would you expect them to persist? Is uniformity important for an advisory (as opposed to a binding) dispute resolution process? Is your answer the same for both court-connected and private ENE?

2. Joshua D. Rosenberg & H. Jay Folberg, *Alternative Dispute Resolution: An Empirical Analysis*, 46 STAN. L. REV. 1487 (1994)

This article [reports] on a quantitative and qualitative study of the early neutral evaluation (ENE) program of the United States District Court for the Northern District of California. . . . Our most important findings include the following:

(1) Approximately two-thirds of those who participated in the mandatory ADR program felt satisfied with the process and believed it worthy of the resources devoted to it (dissatisfaction resulted primarily from dissatisfaction with the particular neutral assigned to the case);

(2) while the percentage of parties who reported saving money approximately equaled the percentage who reported that the process resulted in a net financial cost, the net savings were, on average, more than ten times larger than the cost of an ENE session;

(3) approximately half the participants in the program reported that participation decreased the pendency time of their cases;

(4) the majority of parties and attorneys reported learning information in the ENE session that led to a fairer resolution of their case; and

(5) the ENE process varied significantly from case to case and from neutral to neutral, and the most important factor in determining the success of the process in any one case was the individual neutral involved. Consequently, we focused many of our suggestions for improvement on ensuring the quality of the neutrals.

While these findings and suggestions are based on the Northern District's ENE program, we believe that they are likely to be relevant for other court-based ADR.

In 1982, then Chief Judge Robert F. Peckham appointed a task force to develop procedures to reduce pretrial costs and delays for litigants in the Northern District of California. A subcommittee identified the following major sources of pretrial cost and delay: (1) complex and unclear pleading practice that often confuses the real substance of the dispute; (2) lawyers' and parties' failure to assess their case thoroughly and dispassionately at an early stage; (3) clients' and attorneys' unrealistic expectations of success; (4) clients' feelings of alienation from the legal process; (5) poor and indirect communication between the litigation parties; and (6) attorneys' reluctance to raise the possibility of settlement out of fear of being perceived as weak. This subcommittee designed the ENE process to encourage each party to confront and analyze its own situation early in the suit and to enable each litigant and lawyer to hear the other side present its case. The process was also intended to help the parties identify the real areas of agreement and dispute and to help them develop an approach to discovery that would focus immediately on the central issues and disclose the key evidence promptly. In addition, ENE was intended to offer all counsel and litigants a confidential, frank, and thoughtful assessment of the relative strengths of their positions and the overall value of the case. Finally, the committee also hoped that ENE would provide the parties with an early opportunity to try to negotiate a settlement.

The court established a pilot ENE program in 1985. It handled about a dozen cases assigned by Wayne Brazil, the magistrate who administered the program at that time. An early study of the pilot program revealed promising results. In the second phase of the ENE experiment, the court assigned 150 cases in specified subject areas to the program, with sixty-seven actually proceeding through the ENE process. A study of these cases concluded that most ENE participants strongly believed ENE was worthwhile. Based on the apparent success of the experimental program, the court further expanded and refined the ENE program. . . .

Absent a waiver granted by the court, every party in a case assigned to ENE must attend the ENE session, together with the attorney who will be lead counsel should the case go to trial. If a party is a corporation, it must be represented at the session by a person (other than outside counsel) who has authority both to enter stipulations and to bind the party to the terms of a settlement. Prior to the ENE session, each side must submit to the neutral a statement identifying session participants, major disputed issues, and any discovery that would be a necessary prelude to meaningful settlement discussions. The session is expected to last approximately two hours, during which the following events are expected to take place:

1. The evaluator explains the purposes of the program and outlines the procedures.

2. Each side in turn presents a 15-minute opening statement, either by counsel, client, or both, without interruption from the evaluator or the other party. The statement presents the side's case and legal theories and describes the supporting evidence.

3. The evaluator may then ask questions of both sides to clarify issues, arguments, and evidence, to fill in evidentiary gaps, and to probe for strengths and weaknesses.

4. The evaluator identifies the issues on which the parties agree (and encourages them to enter stipulations where appropriate), and also identifies the important issues in dispute.

5. The evaluator [then] prepares a written case evaluation. The evaluation assesses the strengths and weaknesses of each side's case, determines which side is likely to prevail, and establishes the probable range of damages in the event the plaintiff wins.

6. The evaluator . . . announces that she has prepared an informal evaluation of the case, and asks the parties if they would like to explore settlement possibilities before she discloses the evaluation to them. If either party declines the offer to begin settlement discussions, the evaluator promptly discloses her written assessment. If, on

the other hand, both sides are interested in working on settlement, the evaluator facilitates these discussions.

7. If the parties do not hold settlement discussions or if discussions do not produce a settlement, the evaluator helps the parties develop a plan for efficient case management. This aid may include scheduling motions or discovery that would put the case in a position for rapid settlement or disposition.

8. After the ENE session, the parties may agree to a follow-up session or other activity. With the consent of the court, the parties may engage the evaluator for additional sessions on a compensated basis. . . .

III. FINDINGS

This study is based on a review of all cases filed from April 1988 through March 1992 that met the subject matter criteria for automatic referral to ENE. Of these, the even-numbered cases constitute the "experimental" (ENE) group, and the odd-numbered cases make up the "control" group. The review also included all cases that went through ENE by one of the two other potential avenues for entry into the process — stipulation or referral by the judge.

Our study revealed an ADR program strongly influenced by the individual assigned as the neutral for a given case. For example, when the evaluator was skilled in mediation, ENE often resembled mediation. When the evaluator was more familiar with hard-nosed settlement tactics, that approach appeared to dominate the ENE session. When the evaluator was interested primarily in discovery, there was often little settlement discussion. We found that the nature and outcome of ENE sessions depended more on variations among evaluators than on any other factor, despite the relatively clear guidelines given to evaluators about how to conduct the sessions.

The creators of ENE intended for the session to take place within 150 days of filing. The timing of ENE sessions varied substantially, however, and some cases were not referred to the process until they had been pending for well over a year. The ENE process was intended to lie somewhere between mediation, in which a third party with substantial procedural expertise facilitates communication among the parties in the interest of settling some or all of the issues in dispute, and nonbinding arbitration, in which a third party with substantial subject matter expertise reviews the case presented by the litigants and determines an appropriate outcome. As conducted, ENE ran the gamut from one extreme to the other, and sometimes bore little resemblance to any other process. Most evaluators appraised their cases in some respects, but the specificity and directness of these appraisals varied tremendously from actual predictions of jury verdicts to subtle hints about possible weaknesses of a claim or defense.

Despite this variation in the ENE process, about two-thirds of the parties who participated in an ENE session believed that the session was helpful and worth their efforts. Parties and attorneys divided relatively evenly over the questions whether ENE reduced costs and whether it resulted in decreased pendency time. More significant, however, was the fact that those who believed ENE did not make a valuable contribution to their case reported that the process was, at worst, a waste of time with an average cost of about $4,000 (including attorneys' fees, preparation time, and transportation). Those satisfied with the ENE process, however, reported earlier disposition of their cases, increased understanding of their cases, and an average savings of over $40,000 per participant. . . .

After determining that ENE participants on average saved money and time, and were satisfied with the process, we next sought to identify the specific outcomes that produced these results. We found that to a great extent ENE was accomplishing just what its originators had intended: The ENE program organized, streamlined, and generally increased the efficiency of discovery and trial preparation; in many cases, it increased prospects for early settlement; and almost all participants who were satisfied with the ENE process reported gaining a better understanding of both the law and the facts of the case. Moreover, these participants noted that subsequent settlement discussions were informed by, and furthered as a result of, this increased understanding.

Thirty-five percent of the parties and 23 percent of the attorneys reported that their cases settled either in ENE or as a direct result of it. Fifty-four percent of the attorneys and 52 percent of the parties reported that ENE increased the prospects for early settlement of their cases. Fifty-nine percent of the attorneys and 66 percent of the parties reported that ENE resulted in the identification and clarification of issues. Fifty-four percent of the attorneys and 41 percent of the parties who responded to questions regarding ENE's impact on costs reported that ENE decreased discovery and trial-preparation costs by improving communication between the sides. Forty-five percent of the attorneys reported that fees were reduced in part because they obtained specific, discoverable information in the ENE session. In addition, 29 percent of the attorneys and 49 percent of the parties reported that they agreed on future discovery exchanges in the ENE session, and smaller numbers reported cost savings as a direct result of agreeing to stipulations or to specific motion practice at the sessions. Finally, 16 percent of the attorneys reported that ENE allowed them to "back burner" certain unsettled issues that otherwise might have generated substantial discovery costs.

One way that ENE produced the above outcomes is simply by forcing the participants to give earlier attention to their cases. Approximately 42 percent of the attorneys and 37 percent of the parties reported that ENE required their side to focus on the case earlier than they otherwise would have. In addition, 54 percent of the attorneys and 49 percent of the parties believed that ENE forced the other side to focus on the case earlier. Significantly, in cases that did not go through ENE, 59 percent of the attorneys reported that the other side's failure to focus on the case until a later time posed at least a moderate impediment to the commencement of serious settlement discussions.

In addition to requiring participants to focus on their case earlier, ENE also eliminated another significant obstacle to serious settlement discussions — the fear that initiating settlement discussion would give the other side a strategic negotiating advantage. In cases that did not go through ENE, 27 percent of the attorneys reported that earlier settlement discussions were impeded, because neither side wanted to initiate such discussions out of fear of being perceived as weak. By forcing the parties to discuss their case and possible settlement at an early stage, ENE facilitated useful discussions that might never have commenced otherwise.

For many participants, the primary factor improving both settlement prospects and discovery planning was their increased understanding of the case. . . . The greater understanding that attorneys and parties developed in ENE also helped them more realistically evaluate their case. . . . In addition to learning about the law and facts of their cases, ENE participants also gained valuable insights into procedural aspects of the litigation. Fifty-two percent of the parties and 31 percent of the attorneys stated that their development of a more realistic assessment of the costs of continuing litigation through trial improved settlement prospects.

Overall, our data reveal that the ENE program works. Its designers effectively responded to specific problems that tend to result in increased costs, fees, time, and dissatisfaction with the litigation process. . . . The most important factors influencing the success of ENE are the personal skills and abilities of the individual evaluator. In addition to identifying some of the most important ingredients in a successful court-connected ADR program, our research also identified several potential pitfalls. The most important of these was expectations. Participants who expected ENE to be something substantially different from what it actually was were among the most dissatisfied with the process. . . . On several occasions, delays in selecting a qualified neutral prevented a timely ENE session. Selecting neutrals and checking for conflicts of interest were difficult to conduct efficiently through the mail. . . .

D. SUMMARY JURY TRIAL

1. Neil Vidmar & Jeffrey Rice, *Jury Determined Settlements and Summary Jury Trials*, 19 FLA. ST. U. L. REV. 89, 95-103 (1991)

Courts began early to incorporate ADR devices to resolve disputes. . . . Courts are frequently motivated by objectives not primarily designed for the parties' benefit. Specifically, they are often predominantly interested in court-centered efficiency: saving the court time and money. Many of the court-administered procedures have not been successful when judged by other, and perhaps more appropriate, goals. They certainly have not transformed the disputes to foster better quality solutions and nonadversarial results. In addition, they often do not increase disputant-centered process efficiency. . . . What is efficient for the courts is not necessarily efficient for the parties. The end result of many of the courts' attempts at ADR has been processual inefficiencies and injustice such as injection of delay, the obtaining of nondiscoverable evidence, and manipulation of the rules, time or information.

It is not surprising, therefore, that many disputants view these attempts as unwelcome additional steps in the litigation process. It is also not surprising that adversarial attorneys have turned to litigation to protect their clients' interests. But what if court-caused effects are removed? Is adversary legal culture necessarily hostile to the concept of ADR? We now compare the summary jury trial (SJT), a child of the court, and jury-determined settlements, a privately developed and administered voluntary ADR device.

III. THE SUMMARY JURY TRIAL: ITS ASSETS AND LIABILITIES

The SJT, developed by federal judge Thomas Larnbros, is an ADR procedure that aims to achieve settlements without full-length trials. The disputants' lawyers present summaries of their respective evidence and arguments to a jury composed of regular veniremen in a hearing limited to one day or less. The jury then renders a verdict, and the lawyers and their clients are encouraged to talk to the jurors about how they perceived the merits of the two positions. The verdict is not binding on the parties, and they can have a regular trial de novo on an expedited calendar if no settlement is forthcoming. The theory of the SJT is that by presenting their positions quickly and efficiently in the abbreviated hearing, the parties can learn about the "probable" verdict if the case is submitted to a regular jury. They can then negotiate a reasonable settlement in light of the predicted verdict to avoid the higher costs associated with a full scale trial. Not only do the parties presumably benefit if a settlement is reached, but the case is removed from the court's trial docket.

Observe that the SJT preserves important aspects of the traditional legal approach to the resolution of conflict. First, the advisory verdict is couched in terms of winning and losing. The outcome, if the plaintiff wins, is limited to the setting of a quantum of damages. Second, it preserves components of the adversary system. . . . Lawyers describe evidence favorable to their client's side and argue why, under the law, their clients should win. Third, and very significantly, it uses judgments — if only advisory — from a group of lay persons rather than a judge (or arbitrators).

Jury decisions are treated as having greater legitimacy than those rendered by professionals. In our own research with ADR in medical malpractice and other personal injury suits, we have found that plaintiff and defense lawyers alike have resisted arbitration procedures on the grounds that they believe a jury would render a fairer outcome. Their clients sometimes prefer a jury resolution on symbolic or emotional grounds. For example, in one case, the parents involved in a wrongful death suit stated that they wanted a jury rather than an insurance adjuster or lawyer to say what they should be compensated for the life of their daughter. . . . Despite a preference for resolution by jury, parties often do not want to endure the slow, inefficient and costly court system to obtain a jury verdict.

Despite its potential assets, the SJT largely fails. First, it is nonbinding — an imperative, given federal and state constitutional guarantees of jury trials in civil matters. However, the nonbinding nature points up a primary limitation of court-annexed ADR. At minimum, disputants do not get the promise of a termination of their conflict and, thus, must endure an extra step in the resolution process with the added costs of time and money. At worst, it allows the SJT to be used as an adversarial weapon to force a compromise of strategy or resources that will be used at trial.

The second limitation of the SJT is that it is court-instituted and court-controlled. Legal and political constraints on the court result in compromised procedures, and court-centered efficiency concerns ultimately take precedence over disputant-centered interests. The courts put pressure, sometimes explicit and sometimes implicit, on parties to engage in SJTs. Yet consider what the parties get. The SJT is carefully controlled by the court. The hearing is theoretically limited to a half day or, at most, a full day. Generally, the court keeps a tight rein on jury selection, procedural matters, the form of evidence presented to the jury, and even the instructions to the jury. Thus, live witnesses are usually verboten, even though the case may hinge on the credibility of these witnesses. Why is there not more flexibility? The answer, of course, is that court-centered administrative efficiency concerns take priority over disputant-centered processual interests. The court cannot justify devoting more time, space and judicial resources to a procedure that does not promise to remove the case from the docket.

Thus, courts adopt ADR to relieve pressure on caseloads but are limited by legal constraints to nonbinding procedures. The nonbinding nature not only goes against disputant interests in termination of the case, but it causes the courts to devise the procedure so as to serve the courts' efficiency interests over the disputants' interests. The consequence is litigation by adversary lawyers to protect those interests, which adds to court caseloads. The developing "common law" of ADR . . . is not caused by adversariness but, rather, is a result of the process.

This analysis leads us to the conclusion that court-centered ADR frequently will result in compromised procedures that serve neither the interests of the court nor the interests of the disputants. At best, its overall success, measured against either goal, will be marginal. In contrast, the real opportunities for quality justice can be found in the realm of voluntary ADR. Furthermore, we submit that adversarial culture is not necessarily incompatible with ADR when the effects of court-centered interests are removed. Our own research with jury determined settlements helps to illustrate this proposition.

Over the past several years, the authors and our colleagues, in association with the Private Adjudication Center, have experimented with an ADR device that we have labeled a Jury-Determined Settlement (JDS). It was originally developed for medical malpractice cases through Duke Law School's Medical Malpractice Research Project. More recently, however, it has been used in other types of personal injury suits. Like the SJT, the JDS is designed for disputes that are basically binary in nature. JDS is an abbreviated procedure and uses a jury to decide the outcome. It differs, however, from the SJT in some very key aspects. It is voluntary, the parties and their layers retain almost total control over the process, and the jury verdict is binding.

The assumptions underlying the JDS are straightforward. Parties in personal injury disputes often attempt a settlement. They want to settle to decrease transaction costs, avoid the risks of trial, and have a final resolution as early as possible. They may also want to avoid publicity or the emotional trauma of a lengthy trial. The focal point of settlement negotiations involves arguments about how a jury is likely to decide the case. Although both parties may be acting reasonably, impasses occur when there are different interpretations about evidence and jury equities. Often a mindset towards trial overtakes both parties at this point. Additionally, many forms of ADR are viewed as inappropriate to break the deadlock. Mediation is unlikely to change their differing interpretations of how the jury will decide, and arbitration is seen as rendering a less fair result than a jury of laypersons will provide. Even if a court procedure, such as a SJT, is available, the parties may be concerned about compromising key evidence or . . . other legitimate adversary concerns.

The JDS was designed as a process whereby the parties can agree to settle many issues, and agree to disagree on certain issues, but seek to resolve the latter by quasi-traditional means. Specifically, the JDS attempts to satisfy the disputants' interests by providing them with an abbreviated trial decided by a jury which is binding and which allows the exercise of adversarial control over the procedures. The parties also set limits on the range of the jury award through a high-low agreement. In cases in which liability is strongly contested, the low may be set at zero. For cases primarily involving damages, the high is typically determined by the least amount plaintiffs assert they will take to settle the dispute, and the low is determined by the most defendants assert they will give to settle. In this latter instance, plaintiffs are guaranteed the amount specified by the low regardless of the verdict, and defendants are protected from an extreme award by the agreement that they will pay no more than the high, even if the verdict falls outside that limit.

In JDS "trials" conducted to date, the Center has solicited the cooperation of the local court to provide both jurors and a courtroom, though jurors could be obtained in other ways, and the procedure could take place in a private setting. Although the Center provides guidance and advice, the parties negotiate how the rest of the trial will be carried out. Negotiations include: choosing a judge; setting a discovery schedule and trial date; determining length of total proceeding and allocation of time between parties; setting the size of the jury and the length of voir dire; and agreeing on numbers of witnesses and form of testimony, evidentiary rules, and jury instructions. The negotiations over these procedural issues are often intense and adversarial. The end result has been "trials" that lasted as long as two-and-one-half days and included live witnesses who also were cross-examined.

Even though the parties must share the costs of the proceeding, and extensive time is spent in negotiations and preparation for the JDS "trial," the parties and their lawyers have generally expressed great satisfaction with the procedure. Plaintiffs receive a verdict rendered by a jury, are guaranteed at least the money provided for in the low agreement, and receive their damages immediately after the trial rather than after lengthy appeals. Defendants and their insurers have been spared the risk of exposure to large damage awards. In the malpractice cases, physicians are spared the days or weeks away from their office practices that regular trials would consume. In addition, the trial is arranged privately and public exposure is reduced. Our interviews with the parties and their lawyers suggest that the most important key to party and lawyer satisfaction is the extent of processual control that is provided by the JDS procedure. The lawyers are encouraged to negotiate creative solutions to procedural road blocks or other matters rather than have them imposed by a judge. On balance, adversarial interests may be better served by the JDS than by traditional legal proceedings. . . .

Our commentary has involved two main themes. First, we believe more attention needs to be given to assumptions about the mediation and adversary models and about the types of disputes that enter the legal system. Second, by separating court-centered efficiency effects from adversarial approaches to dispute resolution, we conclude that adversarialness is not necessarily incompatible with ADR. Many ADR proponents seem wedded so strongly to the mediation model as the ideal mode of dispute resolution and to the goal of dispute transformation, that they give short shrift to disputes for which resolution along more traditional legal lines is appropriate. The proponents also ignore the social and psychological limits of disputants' desire for control over the resolution process, and they misconceive legal-adversarial approaches to disputes as incompatible with — indeed, hostile to — ADR. . . .

2. Comments and Questions

a. Vidmar and Rice range far beyond SJT. Their article illustrates the value of considering different approaches in designing ADR procedures. Note how JDS could be used as a private or a public process, with only modest adjustment for court participation.

b. SJT proceedings are private settlement meetings, not judicial proceedings. Accordingly, the SJT is not open to the public, notably the press. *See, Cincinnati Gas and Electric Co. v. General Electric Co.*, 854 F.2d 900 (6th Cir. 1988).

c. At one time, the use of SJT generated divided federal court opinions and legal critiques on its mandatory use. *See, e.g., G. Heileman Brewing Co., Inc. v. Joseph Oat Corp.*, 871 F.2d 648 (7th Cir 1989) (en banc), considered at length in the next section. The Judicial Improvements Act of 1990 specifically mentions SJT as a permissible ADR option, 28 USC § 473(a)(6)(B), and the Federal Rules of Civil Procedure were amended accordingly in 1993. These changes have put to rest the court debate over mandatory SJT and other forms of mandatory ADR. *See generally*, Lucille M. Ponte, *Putting Mandatory Summary Jury Trial Back on the Docket: Recommendations on the Exercise of Judicial Authority*, 63 FORDHAM L. REV. 1069 (1995).

d. SJT has been criticized for using jurors without informing them that their verdict is not binding on the parties, but only advisory. Most notably, Judge Posner questioned the ethics of withholding this information:

> not telling the jury worries me. Telling the jurors after they have delivered the summary verdict that the verdict is not legally binding is only a partial anodyne for my concern. The jurors are still being fooled; and

they are learning that juries sometimes make decisions and at other times simply referee fake trials. As word spreads, the conscientious-ness of jurors could decline; it is almost a detail that the utility of the SJT would also decline.

Richard A. Posner, *The Summary Jury Trial and Other Methods of Alternative Dispute Resolution: Some Cautionary Observations*, 53 U. CHI. L. REV. 366, 386-387 (1986)

e. The nondisclosure concern could be easily eliminated by informing jurors in advance about the SJT, and the role of the advisory jurors therein. However, such disclosure comes at a cost: it may limit the effectiveness of the SJT process, because jurors will take the process less seriously, or because the parties think the jurors take the matter less seriously. Attorneys believe that not telling the jurors until after SJT is complete is important to help maintain responsible juror determinations. *See* James J. Alfini, *Summary Jury Trials in State and Federal Courts: A Comparative Analysis of the Perceptions of Participating Lawyers*, 4 OHIO ST. J. ON DISP. RESOL. 213 (1989) (reporting a comparison study of SJT use in Florida state and federal court programs).

f. Your authors have asked a number of attorneys who have participated in SJTs about the attitudes of the "jurors" upon learning that they had participated in a sham trial rather than a real one. None of the jurors were upset at being "fooled" or otherwise used inappropriately. In most instances, it probably never occurred to the jurors that there was anything unusual about their service as jurors. (And, to the extent that SJT was different from the service rendered by most jurors, that made them feel special — a positive, not a negative factor.) Concerns about the "fake trials" aspect of SJT seems to be limited to judges and professors.

The experience of SJT jurors is superior to that of most members of a jury pool, if for no other reason than that most of the people called for jury duty do not have an excellent experience. Many of those called for jury duty do not get selected as jurors at all — after commuting to an urban courthouse, and then sitting around for many hours. Those dismissed from the jury panel are not told why, but commonly leave with the perception that they were deemed to be unworthy. Among those who do get selected onto a jury, some are chosen for lengthy trials, which entails major sacrifices: inconvenience and lost income. Most people who serve on a jury decide in a matter of minor importance — unless the case settles during trial, in which case they do not even get to ren-der a decision. Where a jury does not reach an agreement, most of the partici-pants will find the experience unsatisfactory.

By contrast, the experience of SJT jurors is nearly always positive. The mat-ter at hand is important — SJT is not used for minor matters — yet the pro-ceeding is quickly completed. After rendering their verdict, the SJT jurors get to participate in a discussion of their deliberations, where they are encouraged to explain the basis for their opinions. All the participants are interested in what the SJT jurors think, an exciting and empowering experience. Jurors in regu-lar trials get to say little, if anything, about their conclusions.

E. COURT-ANNEXED (NON-BINDING) ARBITRATION (CAA)

The U.S. and all state constitutions guarantee access to the courts and a trial by jury in most circumstances. (Texas even offers jury trials for traffic offenses.) Accordingly, arbitration ordered by a court is necessarily non-binding. While the use of court-connected ADR has expanded greatly in recent years, the use of CAA has actually diminished. This is doubly surprising because of the vast growth in private arbitration — see discussion in Chapter Eleven.

Ten federal district courts experimented with CAA in the late 1980s, and the initial results seemed positive. *See generally*, BARBARA S. MEIERHOEFER, COURT-ANNEXED ARBITRATION IN TEN DISTRICT COURTS 70-73 (Federal Judicial Center 1990). The respected and influential Judge Brazil was involved in this project and reported favorable results. A study of CAA-users (clients and attorneys) in the Northern District of California, asked respondents which among several deciders they preferred "considering costs, time and fairness." The responses were Arbitrator (54%), Judge (29%), Jury (11%), and Indifferent (7%). Research on all ten of the federal district courts that employed CAA during the late 1980s showed results similarly favorable to CAA. Wayne D. Brazil, *Court ADR 25 Years After Pound: Have We Found a Better Way?*, 18 OHIO ST. J. ON DISP. RESOL. 93, 96-97 (2002).

There were also critics, notably Professor Lisa Bernstein, who concluded that court-mandated CAA was not an efficacious approach and should be abandoned.

> Although the cost and delay involved in civil litigation continue to increase and to impede access to justice, CAA programs will not increase access to justice and may in fact decrease access to justice for poorer and more risk-adverse litigants by either adding an additional layer of costly procedure, or in programs with post-arbitration fee and cost-shifting provisions, by forcing them to take more risk. The analysis presented here suggests that further experimentation with . . . [CAA] is unwarranted, since the programs will produce neither private nor social benefits.

Lisa Bernstein, *Understanding the Limits of Court-Connected ADR: A Critique of Court-Annexed Arbitration Programs*, 141 U. PA. L. REV. 2169, 2253 (1993).

By the time Congress was considering the legislation that became the ADRA, five of the ten experimental CAA programs had abandoned it entirely, or made use of CAA voluntary. Even those districts that retained mandatory CAA used it infrequently. In Congressional hearings, Judge D. Brock Hornsby, Chair of the Federal Judicial Conference Committee on Court Administration and Case Management, testified in favor of authorizing the federal courts to require ADR, but not the use of mandatory court arbitration programs.

At the same time as Congress authorized the use of mandatory ADR in the ADR Act of 1998, 28 U.S.C. §§ 651-658, it expressly rejected mandatory CAA. Accordingly, a federal court cannot refer a case to CAA without the consent of all the parties. The Act makes no provision for any sanctions if a party to a CAA subsequently demands a trial. This approach may say more about the rise of mediation than defects in CAA. While mandatory CAA initially seemed like a promising approach, in a milieu where court-connected ADR was not well established, it subsequently came to be seen as a less attractive option when judicial ADR requirements became common.

CAA continues to be available in some states, but it has been largely eclipsed by mediation and other forms of ADR in selected instances. On the basis of his experience with court-annexed mandatory arbitration (CAMA) in the New Mexico state courts, Judge William Lynch rejects the use of CAMA (although he would permit parties to voluntarily select CAA). After discussing problems with the use of CAMA in New Mexico, he concludes that the process cannot be repaired, and the only solution is termination of the program. William P. Lynch, *Problems With Court-Annexed Mandatory Arbitration: Illustrations From the New Mexico Experience*, 32 N.M. L. REV. 181 (2002).

F. WHAT IS THE MINIMUM ACCEPTABLE LEVEL OF PARTICIPATION IN COURT-CONNECTED ADR?

1. *G. Heileman Brewing Co., Inc. v. Joseph Oat Corp.*, 871 F.2d 648 (7th Cir 1989) (en banc) (the judges split by a 6-5 vote)

KANNE, Circuit Judge.

May a federal district court order litigants — even those represented by counsel — to appear before it in person at a pretrial conference for the purpose of discussing the posture and settlement of the litigants' case? After reviewing the Federal Rules of Civil Procedure and federal district courts' inherent authority to manage and control the litigation before them, we answer this question in the affirmative. . . . A district court may sanction a litigant for failing to comply with such an order.

A federal magistrate ordered Joseph Oat Corporation to send a "corporate representative with authority to settle" to a pretrial conference to discuss disputed factual and legal issues and the possibility of settlement. Although counsel for Oat Corporation appeared, accompanied by another attorney who was authorized to speak on behalf of the principals of the corporation, no principal or corporate representative personally attended the conference. The court determined that the failure of Oat Corporation to send a principal of the corporation to the pretrial conference violated its order. Consequently, the district court imposed a sanction of $5,860 upon Oat Corporation pursuant to Federal Rule of Civil Procedure 16(f). This amount represented the costs and attorneys' fees of the opposing parties attending the conference.

A. *Authority to Order Attendance.* [The court ruled that the district court had inherent authority to order Joseph Oat Corporation to participate in the SJT. In 1990, Congress expressly authorized the use of SJT by federal courts. *See* 28 USC § 473(a)(6)(B).] Inherent authority remains the means by which district judges deal with circumstances not proscribed or specifically addressed by rule or statute, but which must be addressed to promote the just, speedy, and inexpensive determination of every action. Obviously, the district court, in devising means to control cases before it, may not exercise its inherent authority in a manner inconsistent with rule or statute. *See Strandell v. Jackson County,* 838 F.2d 884 (7th Cir.1988). This means that where the rules directly mandate a specific procedure *to the exclusion of others,* inherent authority is proscribed.

B. Exercise of Authority to Order Attendance. Having determined that the district court possessed the power and authority to order the represented litigants to appear at the pretrial settlement conference, we now must examine whether the court abused its discretion to issue such an order. We conclude that the court did not abuse its authority and discretion. . . .

At the outset, it is important to note that a district court cannot coerce settlement. In this case, considerable concern has been generated, because the court ordered "corporate representatives with authority to settle" to attend the conference. In our view, "authority to settle," when used in the context of this case, means that the "corporate representative" attending the pretrial conference was required to hold a position within the corporate entity allowing him to speak definitively and to commit the corporation to a particular position in the litigation. We do not view "authority to settle" as a requirement that corporate representatives must come to court willing to settle on someone else's terms, but only that they come to court in order to consider the possibility of settlement. . . . If this case represented a situation where Oat Corporation had sent a corporate representative and was sanctioned because that person refused to make an offer to pay money — that is, refused to submit to settlement coercion — we would be faced with a decidedly different issue, a situation we would not countenance. . . .

As an alternative position, Oat argues that the court abused its discretion to order corporate representatives of the litigants to attend the pretrial settlement conference. Oat Corporation determined that, because its business was a "going concern," it would be unreasonable for the magistrate to require the president of that corporation to leave his business [in Camden, New Jersey] to travel to Madison, Wisconsin, to participate in a settlement conference. We recognize . . . that circumstances could arise in which requiring a corporate representative (or any litigant) to appear at a pretrial settlement conference would be so onerous, so clearly unproductive, or so expensive in relation to the size, value and complexity of the case that it might be an abuse of discretion. Moreover, "[b]ecause inherent powers are shielded from direct democratic controls, they must be exercised with restraint and discretion." *Roadway Express, Inc. v. Piper,* 447 U.S. 752, 764 (1980). However, the facts and circumstances of this case clearly support the court's actions to require the corporate representatives of the litigants to attend the pretrial conference personally.

This litigation involved a claim for $4 million — a claim which turned upon the resolution of complex factual and legal issues. The litigants expected the trial to last from one to three months, and all parties stood to incur substantial legal fees and trial expenses. This trial also would have preempted a large segment of judicial time — not an insignificant factor. Thus, because the stakes were high, we do not believe that the burden of requiring a corporate representative to attend a pretrial settlement conference was out of proportion to the benefits to be gained, not only by the litigants but also by the court. Additionally, the corporation did send an attorney, Mr. Fitzpatrick, from Philadelphia, Pennsylvania to Madison, Wisconsin to "speak for" the principals of the corporation. It is difficult to see how the expenses involved in sending Mr. Fitzpatrick from Philadelphia to Madison would have greatly exceeded the expenses involved in sending a corporate representative. . . . Consequently, we do not think the expenses and distance to be traveled are unreasonable in this case. . . .

C. Sanctions. Absent an abuse of discretion, we may not disturb a district court's imposition of sanctions for failure of a party to comply with a pretrial order. The issue on review is not whether we would have imposed these costs upon Oat Corporation, but whether the district court abused its discretion in doing so. . . . .

POSNER, Circuit Judge, dissenting.

Rule 16(a) authorizes a district court to "direct the attorneys for the parties and any *unrepresented* parties to appear before it for a [pretrial] conference." The word I have italicized could be thought to carry the negative implication that no *represented* party may be directed to appear — that was the panel's conclusion — but I hesitate to so conclude in a case that can be decided on a narrower ground. . . . We should hesitate to infer inadvertent prohibitions. . . .

The question of the district court's power to summon a represented party to a settlement conference is a difficult one. . . . [T]here are obvious dangers in too broad an interpretation of the federal courts' inherent power to regulate their procedure. One danger is that it encourages judicial high-handedness ("power corrupts"); several years ago, one of the district judges in this circuit ordered Acting Secretary of Labor Brock to appear before him for settlement discussions on the very day Brock was scheduled to appear before the Senate for his confirmation hearing. The broader concern illustrated by the Brock episode is that, in their zeal to settle cases, judges may ignore the value of other people's time. One reason people hire lawyers is to economize on their own investment of time in resolving disputes. It is pertinent to note, in this connection, that Oat is a defendant in this case; it didn't *want* its executives' time occupied with this litigation.

The narrowly "legal" considerations bearing on the question whether district courts have the power asserted by the magistrate in this case are sufficiently equivocal to authorize — indeed compel — us to consider the practical consequences for settlement before deciding what the answer should be. Unfortunately, we have insufficient information about those consequences to be able to give a confident answer, but fortunately, we need not answer the question in *this* case — so clear is it that the magistrate abused his discretion, which is to say, acted unreasonably, in demanding that Oat Corporation send an executive having "full settlement authority" to the pretrial conference. This demand, which is different from a demand that a party who has not closed the door to settlement send an executive to discuss possible terms, would be defensible only if litigants had a duty to bargain in good faith over settlement before resorting to trial, and neither Rule 16 nor any other rule, statute or doctrine imposes such a duty on federal litigants.

There is no federal judicial power to coerce settlement. Oat had made clear that it was not prepared to settle the case on any terms that required it to pay money. That was its prerogative, which once exercised, made the magistrate's continued insistence on Oat's sending an executive to Madison arbitrary, unreasonable, willful, and indeed petulant. This is apart from the fact that, since no one officer of Oat may have had authority to settle the case, compliance with the demand might have required Oat to ship its entire board of directors to Madison. Ultimately, Oat did make a money settlement, but there is no indication that it would have settled sooner if only it had complied with the magistrate's demand for the dispatch of an executive possessing "full settlement authority." . . .

EASTERBROOK, Circuit Judge, dissenting.

Our case has three logically separate issues. First, whether a district court may demand the attendance of someone other than the party's counsel of record. Second, whether the court may insist that this additional person be an employee, rather than an agent selected for the occasion. Third, whether the court may insist that the representative have "full settlement authority" — meaning the authority to agree to pay cash in settlement (maybe authority without cap, although that was not clear). Even if one resolves the first issue as the majority does, it does not follow that district courts have the second or third powers, or that their exercise here was prudent.

The proposition that a magistrate may require a firm to send an employee, rather than a representative, is puzzling. Corporate "employees" are simply agents of the firm. Corporations choose their agents and decide what powers to give them. Which agents have which powers is a matter of internal corporate affairs. Joseph Oat Corp. sent to the conference not only its counsel of record but also John Fitzpatrick, who had authority to speak for Oat. Now Mr. Fitzpatrick is an attorney, which raised the magistrate's hackles, but why should this count against him? Because Fitzpatrick is a part-time rather than a full-time agent of the corporation? Why can't the corporation make its own decision about how much of the agent's time to hire? Is Oat being held in contempt because it is too small to have a cadre of legal employees — because its general counsel practices with a law firm rather than being "in house"?

At all events, the use of outside attorneys as negotiators is common. Many a firm sends its labor lawyer to the bargaining table when a collective bargaining agreement is about to expire, there to dicker with the union (or with labor's lawyer). Each side has a statutory right to choose its representatives. 29 U.S.C. § 158(b)(1)(B). Many a firm sends its corporate counsel to the bargaining table when a merger is under discussion. Oat did the same thing to explore settlement of litigation. A lawyer is no less suited to this task than to negotiating the terms of collective bargaining or merger agreements. Firms prefer to send skilled negotiators to negotiating sessions (lawyers are especially useful when the value of a claim depends on the resolution of legal questions) while reserving the time of executives for business. Oat understandably wanted its management team to conduct its construction business.

As for the third subject, whether the representative must have "settlement authority": the magistrate's only reason for ordering a corporate representative to come was to facilitate settlement then and there. Fitzpatrick was deemed inadequate, only because he was under instructions not to pay money. E.g.: "While Mr. Fitzpatrick claimed authority to speak for Oat, he stated that he had no authority to make a [monetary] offer. *Thus,* no representative of Oat or National having authority to settle the case was present at the conference as the order directed" (magistrate's opinion, emphasis added). On learning that Fitzpatrick did not command Oat's treasury, the magistrate ejected him from the conference and never listened to what he had to say on Oat's behalf, never learned whether Fitzpatrick might be receptive to others' proposals. (We know that Oat ultimately did settle the case for money, after it took part in and "prevailed" at a summary jury trial — participation and payment each demonstrating Oat's willingness to consider settlement.) The magistrate's approach implies that, if the Chairman and CEO of Oat had arrived with instructions from the Board to settle the case without paying cash and to negotiate and bring back for the Board's consideration any financial proposals, Oat still would have been in contempt.

Both magistrate and judge demanded the presence not of a "corporate representative" in the sense of a full-time employee but of a representative with "full authority to settle." Most corporations reserve power to *agree* (as opposed to power to discuss) to senior managers or to their boards of directors — the difference depending on the amounts involved. Heileman wanted $4 million, a sum within the province of the board rather than a single executive even for firms much larger than Oat. Fitzpatrick came with power to *discuss* and *recommend;* he could settle the case on terms other than cash; he lacked only power to sign a check. The magistrate's order, therefore, must have required either (a) changing the allocation of responsibility within the corporation, or (b) sending a quorum of Oat's Board.

Magistrate Groh exercised a power unknown even in labor law, where there is a duty to bargain in good faith. 29 U.S.C. § 158(d). Labor and management commonly negotiate through persons with the authority to discuss but not agree. The negotiators report back to management and the union, each of which reserves power to reject or approve the position of its agent. We know from Fed. R. Civ. P. 16 — and especially from the Advisory Committee's comment to Rule 16(c) that the Rule's reference to"authority" is "not intended to insist upon the ability to settle the litigation" — that the parties cannot be compelled to negotiate "in good faith." A defendant convinced it did no wrong may insist on total vindication. Yet, if parties are not obliged to negotiate in good faith, on what ground can they be obliged to come with authority to settle on the spot — an authority agents need not carry even when the law requires negotiation? The order we affirm today compels persons who have committed no wrong, who pass every requirement of Rules 11 and 68, who want only the opportunity to receive a decision on the merits, to come to court with open checkbooks on pain of being held in contempt.

Settling litigation is valuable, and courts should promote it. Is settlement of litigation more valuable than settlement of labor disputes, so that courts may do what the NLRB may not? The statutory framework — bona fide negotiations required in labor law but not in litigation — suggests the opposite. Does the desirability of settlement imply that rules of state law allocating authority within a corporation must yield?

The majority does not discuss these problems. Its approach implies, however, that trial courts may insist that representatives have greater authority than labor negotiators bring to the table. And to create this greater authority, Oat Corp. might have to rearrange its internal structure — perhaps delegating to an agent a power state law reserves to the board of directors. Problems concerning the reallocation of authority are ubiquitous. For example, only the Assistant Attorney General for the Civil Division has authority to approve settlements of civil cases, and his authority reaches only to $750,000; above that, the Deputy Attorney General must approve. 28 C.F.R. §§ 0.160(a)(2), 0.161. An attorney for the government, like Fitzpatrick, lacks the authority to commit his client but may negotiate and recommend. Does it follow that a magistrate may require the presence of the Assistant or Deputy Attorney General or insist that they redelegate their authority? If such a demand would be improper for the Department of Justice, is it more proper when made of Joseph Oat Corporation?

These issues will not go away. The magistrate's order was to send a representative *with the authority to bind Oat to pay money*. What is the point of insisting on such authority if not to require the making of offers and the acceptance of "reasonable" counteroffers — that is, to require good faith negotiations and agreements on the spot? Fitzpatrick had the authority to report back to Oat on any suggestions; he had the authority to participate in negotiations. The *only* reason Oat was held in contempt of court was his inability to sign Oat Corp.'s check in the magistrate's presence. What the magistrate found unacceptable was that Fitzpatrick might say something like "I'll relay that suggestion to the Board of Directors," which might say no. Oat's CEO could have done no more. We close our eyes to reality in pretending that Oat was required only to be present, while others "voluntarily" discussed settlement.

2. Comments and Questions

a. The Oat majority is acutely aware that travel from Camden, New Jersey to Madison, Wisconsin may present considerable costs. It responds that Oat Corporation sent a lawyer, but it could have sent a senior executive instead for about the same price, so cost is not a factor. What about the opportunity costs of the executive's time, and the harm to the Oat Corporation of having that person not attending to business? The approach suggested by this question reflects the law and economics orientation long championed by Judges Posner and Easterbrook.

b. At the risk of offending some personal friends, your authors have observed that judges (particularly those with lifetime appointments) sometimes have an unduly expansive view about the value of their time, and a more moderate appreciation of the value of other people's time. This point is driven home by the William Brock incident described by Judge Posner.

c. Should it matter that the party objecting to personal attendance at a settlement conference is the defendant, an involuntary participant in litigation? Where venue is available in several places, the plaintiff is likely (other things being equal) to select the geographically most convenient court, which often is the least convenient forum for defendant. This was true in *Heileman Brewing*.

d. Heileman Brewing is a troubling and much discussed case. Professor Sherman appears to support the majority, and he favors allowing flexibility to the courts:

> There should be no fixed rule either way as to party representative attendance; the efficiency and proportionality considerations identified by the majority provide appropriate guidance for case-by-case determinations. . . . Although anti-coercion and litigant-autonomy policies favor honoring the party's choice of a representative, a court should be entitled to determine that the day-in-court and promotion-of-ADR-settlement objectives cannot be served by the sole attendance of an attorney.

Edward F. Sherman, *Court-Mandated Alternative Dispute Resolution: What Form of Participation Should be Required?*, 46 S.M.U. L. Rev. 2079, 2106 (1993).

e. Professor Riskin, a strong proponent of the healing aspects of mediation, would "routinely require attendance of represented clients, and representatives of organizational clients with full settlement authority, in the absence of suitable and suitably presented objection." Leonard L. Riskin, *The Represented Client in a Settlement Conference: The Lessons of* C. Heileman Brewing Co. v. Joseph Oat Corp., 69 Wash. U. L.Q. 1059 (1991). In this article, Riskin recounts the following story of a successful mediation:

> The disputants were two brothers. The legal issue involved partnership. The case settled and the brothers renewed an old friendship, but only after [the mediator] asked them two personal questions: "What was your relationship as children?" and "What would your parents [who were deceased] think if they saw you in court?"

This story wonderfully illustrates the transformative potential of mediation, but what does it have to do with a commercial dispute between two unrelated corporations located half a country apart?

f. Should a court require participation in an SJT proceeding in the following situation, drawn from *Strandell v. Jackson County*, 838 F.2d 884 (7th Cir. 1988)? The parents of Michael Strandell brought a civil rights action against Jackson County, Illinois seeking damages of $500,000, based on the arrest, strip search, imprisonment, and suicide death of their son. During discovery, the plaintiffs had obtained statements from 21 witnesses. After discovery closed, the defendants filed a motion to compel production of the witnesses' statements. The district court denied the motion to compel production, because defendants had failed to establish "substantial need" and "undue hardship," as required by Rule 26(b)(3) of the Federal Rules. Could Strandell participate in good faith in an SJT proceeding without revealing information grounded in the witness statements? If SJT is not appropriate, does any other court-connected ADR approaches make more sense?

g. The implicit model for court-annexed ADR, reflecting the trial process, is an in-person meeting with all participants in the same room. The only communication device other than an in-person conversation mentioned in the materials in this section is the telephone. What about the use of video conferencing and other forms of electronic communication?

h. Much of the discussion of minimum adequate participation in court-connected ADR is framed in terms of "good faith" action. The ensuing article by Professor Lande adopts more specific and less emotively named categories and helps to frame the issues in a more concrete manner.

3. John Lande, *Using Dispute System Design Methods to Promote Good Faith Participation in Court-Connected Mediation Programs*, 50 UCLA L. REV. 69 (2002)

. . . . The controversy over good-faith requirements is part of a larger debate over the purpose and nature of court-connected mediation programs. This debate focuses on competing program goals and ideas about what is needed to ensure the programs' integrity. On one side of the debate, people view mediation programs as mechanisms to dispose of a portion of court dockets. Courts order parties to spend time and money for mediation and want to be sure that the time and money are well-spent. Courts also want to ensure that parties and attorneys comply with their orders and cooperate with the courts' case management systems. From this perspective, a good-faith requirement seems to be the logical way to ensure the integrity of court-connected mediation programs.

On the other side of the debate, people focus on the integrity of the mediation process, defined as an adherence to mediation practice norms. Many mediators are especially concerned that people participate in mediation without coercion, take advantage of opportunities for open discussion and problem-solving, and receive assurance that courts will honor confidentiality protections. From this perspective, good-faith requirements seem to violate mediation norms and, thus, undermine the integrity of court-connected mediation programs. Although this brief summary oversimplifies the debate, it captures a real tension in debates about the future of court-connected mediation programs.

Although the concept of good faith is used in many areas of the law and has become part of the legal vernacular, there is no clear definition of the concept. In the mediation context, statutes, rules and cases do not provide a clear definition of good faith. To remedy that problem, Professor Kimberlee Kovach proposes a statute with an itemized list of behaviors that constitute good-faith conduct in mediation. Kimberlee K. Kovach, *Good Faith in Mediation — Requested, Recommended, or Required? A New Ethic*, 38 S. TEX. L. REV. 575, 622-623 (1997). Professor Maureen Weston endorses Kovach's definition and argues that good faith should be judged under a "totality of the circumstances" standard. Maureen A. Weston, *Checks on Participant Conduct in Compulsory ADR: Reconciling the Tension in the Need for Good-Faith Participation, Autonomy, and Confidentiality*, 76 IND. L.J. 591, 630 (2001).

Proponents argue that a good-faith requirement is necessary, because without the threat of sanctions for bad faith, some participants might use mediation to take advantage of their opponents, and others might merely "go through the motions" of mediating. Although proponents recognize that court enforcement of a good-faith requirement would involve an exception to the general rule providing confidentiality in mediation, they contend that such an exception is necessary and can be limited to issues related to alleged bad faith. Thus, they argue, a good-faith requirement would not undermine parties' faith in the confidentiality of their communications.

Statutes, court rules, mediation referral orders, and the common law establish good-faith requirements in mediation. At least twenty-two states and the territory of Guam have such statutory requirements. At least twenty-one federal district courts and seventeen state courts have local rules requiring good-faith participation. In addition, several courts have relied on Rule 16 of the Federal Rules of Civil Procedure as the basis of a good-faith requirement. Only one of all these statutes and rules includes a definition of good faith; that statute applies only to farmer-lender disputes. Minn. Stat. Ann. § 583.27(1)(a). Many of these statutes and rules are trans-substantive. Others apply to mediations in particular subject areas.

In some of these statutes and rules, the reference to good faith seems incidental, as if the term is innocuous language with no particular consequence. More than a third of these statutes and rules include a good-faith requirement without providing sanctions for noncompliance. Thus, it is unclear if the drafters of those provisions intended to create a litigable issue. Most of the statutes and rules, however, do provide for sanctions or other legal consequences, though many do not specify the sanctions that may be imposed. When sanctions are specified, they frequently involve payment of fees and costs related to the mediation. Other sanctions include holding individuals in contempt and empowering the mediator to suspend or terminate the mediation. . . . In some instances, bad-faith participation may affect the merits of a case. . . . Most of the good-faith statutes and rules do not state whether mediation confidentiality protections would preclude admission of evidence of bad faith or preclude mediators from testifying or making recommendations for sanctions. . . .

Most of the twenty-seven reported cases dealing with bad faith in mediation arise in court-connected mediation. The number of reported cases increased in the 1990s. The growth in the number of bad-faith cases may be a function of courts' increasing reliance on court-ordered mediation and an increasing legalization of mediation. The increasing number of disputes over good faith also may be an indicator of a backlash against court-ordered mediation in some situations. The behaviors alleged to constitute bad faith can be grouped into five categories.

One such allegation is simply that a party has failed to attend. A second allegation involves the failure of an organizational party to send a representative with sufficient settlement authority. A third group of allegations involves activities in preparation for mediation, including failure to produce a pre-mediation memorandum or to bring experts to mediation. A fourth group of allegations involves the sufficiency and sincerity of efforts to resolve the matter, including claims that a party has not made any offer or any suitable offer, has not participated substantively and attempted to resolve the case, has not provided requested documents, has made inconsistent legal arguments, or has unilaterally withdrawn from mediation. Finally, a fifth group consists of miscellaneous allegations such as failure to sign a mediated agreement, failure to release living expenses pending farmer-lender mediation, or engaging in unspecified bad-faith behavior.

The final court decisions in these cases generally have been quite consistent in each category. The courts have found bad faith in all the cases in which a party has failed to attend the mediation or has failed to provide a required pre-mediation memorandum. In cases involving allegations that organizational parties have provided representatives without sufficient settlement authority, the courts have split almost evenly. In virtually all of the other cases in which the courts ruled on the merits of the case, they rejected claims of bad faith. In effect, the courts have interpreted good faith narrowly to require compliance with orders to attend mediation, provide pre-mediation memoranda, and in some cases, produce organizational representatives with sufficient settlement authority.

This apparent clarity in the results masks a pattern in which appellate courts frequently reversed lower court findings of bad faith. In eight of the thirteen reported cases in which findings of bad faith were appealed, the appellate court rejected the lower court's decision on this issue. This pattern of reversals suggests that trial courts become frustrated with one side's refusal to cooperate in mediation and that some trial courts overreach their authority to sanction mediation behavior. By comparison, only five cases were found in which a trial court's rejection of a bad-faith claim was appealed. All those trial court rulings were upheld. . . .

1. Problems Defining and Proving Good Faith. The definition of good faith in mediation is one of the most controversial issues about good-faith requirements. Legal authorities establishing good-faith requirements and commentators' proposals do not give clear guidance about what conduct is prohibited. As a result, mediation participants may feel uncertain about what actions mediators and judges would consider bad faith. This uncertainty could result in inappropriate bad-faith charges as well as a chilling of legitimate mediation conduct.

In practice, the courts have limited their interpretation of good faith in mediation to attendance, submission of pre-mediation memoranda, and in some cases, attendance of organizational representatives with adequate settlement authority. Despite the narrow scope of courts' actual application of good-faith requirements, good-faith language in the legal authorities and commentators' proposals go far beyond these specific matters. Commentators agree that the definition of good faith needs to be clearly and objectively determinable so that everyone can know what conduct is considered bad faith. Commentators disagree, however, about whether the definition of good faith can be clear, objectively determinable, and predictable, and whether good faith is a function of the reasonableness of participants' offers or their state of mind.

Kovach argues that "without an explanation or definition of just what is meant by the term good faith, each party may have in mind something different. It is important that the parties are clear about the term." She maintains that "judg[ing] a party's state of mind is too complex and subjective" to be appropriate in determining good faith in mediation. She also contends that bad faith does not include failure to make an offer or come down "enough," stating that the economic aspects of the negotiations — the offers and responses, in and of themselves — may not create a bad faith claim. Most of the elements of good-faith definitions do not satisfy Kovach's criteria. Virtually all good-faith elements depend on an assessment of a person's state of mind, which is, by definition, subjective. Consider the following definition from *Hunt v. Woods*, 1996 WL 8037 (6th Cir.):

> A party has not "failed to make a good faith effort to settle" under [the statute] if he has (1) fully cooperated in discovery proceedings, (2) rationally evaluated his risks and potential liability, (3) not attempted to unnecessarily delay any of the proceedings, and (4) made a good faith monetary settlement offer or responded in good faith to an offer from the other party. If a party has a good faith, objectively reasonable belief that he has no liability, he need not make a monetary settlement offer.

Good faith under this definition is not objectively determinable, readily predictable, or independent of parties' states of mind or their bargaining positions. To assess their risk evaluations, courts must determine the merits of the case, whether parties' evaluations are objectively reasonable, and whether their negotiation strategies are deemed acceptable by the courts. Courts make these assessments at subsequent hearings in which there is a great temptation to take advantage of hindsight. . . .

Parties rarely begin negotiations by offering the amount that they believe "the case is worth." The timing and amount of offers often depend on the context of prior offers and the conduct of the litigation more generally. Parties vary in negotiation philosophy; some prefer to negotiate early and make apparently reasonable offers, whereas others prefer to engage in hard bargaining, taking extreme positions and deferring concessions as long as possible. Although Kovach argues that hard bargaining is not bad faith, courts applying the Hunt definition could easily interpret it as bad faith. In any event, to determine parties' good faith fairly, courts would need to assess and second-guess the parties' offers and their states of mind. . . .

2. Overbreadth of Bad-Faith Concept. Kovach's and Weston's proposed good-faith requirements are so broad that they effectively would prohibit defensible behaviors in mediation. Under Kovach's proposed statute, if one side claims that the other participated in bad faith, the moving party could use the legal process to investigate whether all participants adequately prepared for the mediation, followed the rules set out by the mediator, engaged in direct communication with the other parties, participated in meaningful discussions with the mediator and all other participants during the mediation, and remained at the mediation until the mediator determined that the process is at an end or excused the parties. Under Weston's proposed "totality of the circumstances" test, this wide-ranging inquiry would be limited only by the court's discretion.

Both proposals raise many problems. . . . Under a duty to engage in direct communication and meaningful discussions, parties could be confused about what information they would be compelled to disclose to the mediator and opposing parties. In sensitive mediations, parties often want to withhold information justifying their bargaining strategies. Although exchanging such information in mediation can be helpful and appropriate, court-connected mediation should not be a substitute for formal discovery. Kovach presumably does not intend her proposed statute to be interpreted as such, but that could be the result.

Relating to Kovach's proposed requirement of remaining at the mediation until the mediator declares an impasse or excuses the parties, she writes that "while the good faith requirement might include remaining at the mediation, the length of time to remain should be reasonable, such as two or three hours rather than overnight." Under Kovach's proposal, mediation participants are effectively in the custody of the mediator for an open-ended period. Even if the text of Kovach's proposed statute included a requirement of reasonableness, participants who believe that continued mediation would be unproductive could legitimately wonder whether mediators or judges would second-guess those judgments.

3. Inclusion of Settlement-Authority Requirement. Although mediations generally work better when organizational parties send representatives with a reasonable measure of settlement authority, courts have difficulty strictly enforcing such a requirement — and regularly doing so can stimulate counterproductive mediation tactics. Slightly more than half of the courts have found bad faith when entities fail to send representatives with sufficient settlement authority. An element of good faith in Kovach's proposed statute is personal attendance at the mediation by all parties who are fully authorized to settle the dispute. Even Sherman, a critic of good-faith requirements, favors requiring attendance by a person with settlement authority. Edward F. Sherman, *Court-Mandated Alternative Dispute Resolution: What Form of Participation Should Be Required?*, 46 S.M.U. L. REV. 2079, 2103-2111 (1993).

Leonard Riskin, *The Represented Client in a Settlement Conference: The Lessons of* G. Heileman Brewing Co. v. Joseph Oat Corp., 69 WASH. U. L.Q. 1059, 1110 (1991), provides a useful framework for analyzing the meaning of full settlement authority. He . . . argues that full settlement authority for organizational representatives should resemble certain attributes of individual litigants. These attributes are (1) authority to make a commitment, (2) sufficient knowledge of the organization's needs, interests, and operations, (3) sufficient influence within the organization that the representative's recommendations likely would affect the organization's decisions, and (4) discretion to negotiate arrangements that are likely to be accepted by the organization. He writes that possessing only two or three of these attributes would be sufficient to constitute full settlement authority, recognizing that organizations sometimes have difficulty finding representatives with all these attributes. He argues that the representative's role as an executive, full-time general counsel, or outside part-time

counsel does not necessarily indicate whether the particular individual has these attributes. Riskin's analysis suggests that to enforce a settlement-authority requirement, courts would need to interrogate witnesses about the extent to which various actual or potential representatives possess the four listed attributes.

G. Heileman Brewing Co. v. Joseph Oat Corp., 871 F.2d 648 (7th Cir. 1989) (en banc), illustrates the difficulties of implementing a requirement of attendance with appropriate settlement authority. Sitting en banc, the U.S. Court of Appeals for the Seventh Circuit, by a six to five vote, affirmed an imposition of sanctions for failure to send a corporate representative with appropriate settlement authority. The Heileman majority ruled that the corporate representative attending the pretrial conference was required to "hold a position within the corporate entity allowing him to speak definitively and to commit the corporation to a particular position in the litigation."

Judge Frank H. Easterbrook's dissent in *Heileman* highlights the problems with settlement-authority requirements. He argues that the majority does not consider realistically the structure of most corporations, and that requiring attendance by a representative with settlement authority would force a party to make an offer it did not want to make. Judge Easterbrook identifies a legitimate concern about courts using a settlement-authority requirement to coerce settlement. . . .

When courts focus heavily on settlement authority, participants may be distracted from various ways that mediation can help litigants achieve goals other than reaching final monetary settlements. Settlement-authority requirements typically focus only on monetary resolutions; mediation can be useful to explore non-monetary aspects of disputes. These requirements also assume that cases should be settled at a single meeting; in some cases, it may be appropriate to meet several times, especially when organizational representatives need to consult officials within the organization based on information learned at mediation. Moreover, settlement-authority requirements do not recognize benefits of exchanging information, identifying issues, and making partial or procedural agreements in mediation.

4. Questionable Deterrent Effect and Potential Abuse of Bad-Faith Sanctions. Sanctions for bad faith in mediation actually may stimulate adversarial and dishonest conduct, contrary to the intent of proponents of a good-faith requirement. Proponents argue that a good-faith requirement would cause people to negotiate sincerely, would deter bad-faith behavior, and when people violate the requirement, would provide appropriate remedies. Although a good-faith requirement presumably would deter and punish some inappropriate conduct, it might also encourage surface bargaining, as well as frivolous claims of bad faith or threats to make such claims. Proponents seem to assume that participants who might act in bad faith but for the requirement would behave properly in fear of legal sanctions. It seems at least as likely that savvy participants who want to take inappropriate advantage of mediation would use surface bargaining techniques so that they can pursue their strategies with little risk of sanction. This would be fairly easy given the vagueness of a good-faith requirement. Participants can readily make "lowball" offers that they know the other

side will reject and generally go through the motions of listening to the other side and explaining the rationale for their positions. Although attorneys often are quite sincere, making arguments with feigned sincerity is a skill taught in law school and honed in practice. Because mediators are not supposed to force people to settle, participants who are determined not to settle can wait until the mediator gives up. This scenario illustrates how a good-faith requirement could ironically induce dishonesty, when providing more honest responses might put participants in jeopardy of being sanctioned.

Similarly, tough mediation participants could use good-faith requirements offensively to intimidate opposing parties and interfere with lawyers' abilities to represent their clients' legitimate interests. Given the vagueness and over-breadth of the concept of bad faith, innocent participants may have legitimate fears about risking sanctions when they face an aggressive opponent and do not know what a mediator would say if called to testify. In the typical conventions of positional negotiation in which each side starts by making an extreme offer, each side may accuse the other of bad faith. Without the threat of bad-faith sanctions, these moves are merely part of the kabuki dance of negotiation. With the prospect of such sanctions, bad-faith claims take on legal significance that can spawn not only satellite litigation, but satellite mediation as well. After a volley of bad-faith charges in a mediation, mediators may need to focus on bad faith as a real issue rather than simply a negotiation gambit. Moreover, the mediator could be a potential witness in court about the purity of each side's faith in the mediation, further warping the mediator's role. . . .

Weston includes a "safe harbor" provision in her proposal that would require notice and a reasonable opportunity to correct the problem before courts imposed sanctions. Such a safe harbor provision might not solve the problem of wasted time and money in sham mediations. If one side charges the other with being unprepared or not having a representative with settlement authority, the "cure" would be to reschedule the mediation, to which the alleged offender could send a fully authorized representative to engage in surface bargaining. The result would be that the innocent party would bear the time and expense of two unpro-ductive mediation sessions rather than only one. Thus, this well-intentioned proposal could easily backfire. Policymakers may have difficulty predicting the extent to which mediation participants would respond to a sanction-based good-faith system by "gaming" the requirements. . . .

5. Weakened Confidentiality of Mediation Communications. Establishing a good-faith requirement undermines the confidentiality of mediation. The mere prospect of adjudicating bad-faith claims by using mediator testimony can dis-tort the mediation process by damaging participants' faith in the confidential-ity of mediation communications and the mediators' impartiality. Proponents of a good-faith requirement cite the need for an exception to rules providing for con-fidentiality of communications in mediation. Weston contends that a good-faith requirement is "essentially meaningless if confidentiality privileges restrict the ability to report violations." Noting the existence of some exceptions to con-fidentiality in mediation, she argues that reports of bad faith should be added to the list of exceptions. Weston and Kovach assert that an exception for bad-faith participation can be clearly and narrowly limited, and that the need for an

exception outweighs the general need to encourage open discussion in mediation through confidentiality protections. . . .

The Uniform Mediation Act's (UMA's) provisions regarding confidentiality of mediation communications are relevant to the admissibility of evidence of bad faith. The main provision establishes an evidentiary privilege for mediation communications. Section 6 includes nine exceptions to the privilege; bad faith in mediation is not one of them. Section 7 generally precludes mediator disclosures, with limited exceptions; again, bad faith is not among them.

Good mediators are likely to feel violated by being compelled to give evidence that could be used against a party with whom they tried to establish a relationship of trust during a mediation. Good mediators are deeply committed to being and remaining neutral and non-judgmental, and to building and preserving relationships with parties. To force them to give evidence that hurts someone from whom they actively solicited trust (during the mediation) rips the fabric of their work and can threaten their sense of the center of their professional integrity. These are not inconsequential matters. The possibility that a mediator might be forced to testify over objection could harm the capacity of mediators in general to create the environment of trust that they feel maximizes the likelihood that constructive communication will occur during the mediation session. . . .

Proposals for a confidentiality exception for reports of bad faith are not justified. The UMA includes model language describing the goals of the statute, the first of which is to "promote candor of parties through confidentiality of the mediation process, subject only to the need for disclosure to accommodate specific and compelling societal interests." The benefits of bad-faith sanctions do not outweigh the need for justified faith in the confidentiality of mediation.

6. Encouragement of Inappropriate Mediator Conduct. A good-faith requirement gives mediators too much authority over participants to direct the outcome in mediation and creates the risk that some mediators would coerce participants by threatening to report alleged bad-faith conduct. Courts can predict abuse of that authority given the settlement-driven culture in court-connected mediation. The mere potential for courts to require mediators' reports can corrupt the mediation process by instilling fear and doubt in the participants.

Proponents of a good-faith requirement apparently assume that mediators will not abuse any good-faith reporting authority to coerce parties into accepting mediators' opinions about appropriate resolutions. The proponents also seem to assume that even if mediators do not abuse their good-faith reporting authority, participants will not fear taking positions at odds with the mediators' apparent views and will not perceive mediators as biased. These assumptions are troubling. . . . Even without the prospect of a later court hearing about good-faith participation, mediation participants sometimes feel pressured to change their positions in response to mediator evaluations and "reality-testing" questions. Under a bad-faith sanctions regime, mediators might apply pressure arising from their authority to testify about bad faith. If local courts hold a sufficient number of bad-faith hearings, participants may reasonably fear the effect of mediators' reports, even if mediators do not threaten to report bad faith. . . .

Conclusion. Given the serious foreseeable problems of a good-faith requirement, the burden should be on the proponents to demonstrate that: (1) there is a serious and recurring problem of clearly defined bad-faith conduct in mediation in a local community, (2) the requirement would be effective in deterring such conduct, (3) the benefits of the requirement would outweigh the problems, and (4) the net benefits of the requirement would exceed the net benefits of alternative policies. Most mediation programs would not satisfy all these conditions, and thus, a good-faith requirement rarely would be justified.

A good-faith requirement in mediation is very troublesome. Although it may deter some inappropriate conduct, it also may stimulate even more. It risks undermining the interests of all the stakeholder groups of court-connected mediation, especially interests in the integrity of the mediation process and the courts. Barring evidence of a substantial number of problems of real bad faith (as opposed to loose litigation talk), the large cost of a bad-faith sanctions regime is not worth the likely small amount of benefit, especially considering the alternative policy options available. Using Riskin's metaphor, a good-faith sanctions regime would "raise a fist" when policymakers first should consider policies that "extend a hand." . . .

4. Comments and Questions

a. Judge Posner's dissenting opinion in the *Heileman Brewing* case states in categorical terms that there is no obligation of good faith bargaining in settlement negotiations. Do you agree? If so, courts can require parties to attend mediation, but not to settle or even to make an offer. "Millions for defense but not one cent for tribute" is an acceptable position for a party to take. To use another common expression, "you can lead a horse to water but you cannot make it drink." *See generally*, Richard D. English, Annotation, *Alternative Dispute Resolution: Sanctions for Failure to Participate in Good Faith, or Comply with Agreement Made in Mediation*, 43 A.L.R.5th 545 (1996); Annette M. Sansone, *Annotation, Imposition of Sanctions by Federal Courts for Failure to Engage in Compromise and Settlement Negotiations*, 104 A.L.R. FED. 461 (1991).

b. It is widely accepted in contract and commercial law that good faith has a negative meaning only — good faith means the absence of bad faith. Put another way, good faith is an "excluder," defined by what is excluded from its ambit. The duty of good faith in bargaining, or in performance of an agreement, is an obligation to avoid bad faith conduct. "Bad faith" is hardly a self-defining term, and it can only be determined in the context of the circumstances of particular parties and their dealings with each other. A focus on bad faith does, however, clarify the task at hand: to prevail, a party must allege and prove that specific conduct took place, and that it constituted bad faith (failed to meet the good faith standard). Both the Restatement Second of Contracts, § 205, and the Uniform Commercial Code, §§ 1-201(19), 1-203, and 2-103(b), impose a general duty of good faith, but they offer little in the way of concrete guidance about what good faith means, or a methodology for applying this general concept to concrete instances.

c. The leading American articles on good faith in contract law are Friedrich Kessler & Edith Fine, *Culpa in Contrahendo, Bargaining in Good Faith, and Freedom of Contract: A Comparative Study*, 77 HARV. L. REV. 401 (1964) (German and U.S. law); Robert S. Summers, *The General Duty of Good Faith — Its Recognition and Conceptualization*, 67 CORNELL L. REV. 810 (1982); Steven J. Burton, *More on Good Faith Performance of a Contract: A Reply to Professor Summers*, 69 IOWA L. REV. 497 (1984). Burton and Summers have both written extensively on aspects of good faith in contract and commercial law; in each instance the citation is to the latest of a series of articles. See also Malcolm Clarke, *The Common Law of Contract in 1993: Is There a General Doctrine of Good Faith*, 23 HONG KONG L.J. 318 (1993) (England and Commonwealth law).

d. In collective bargaining negotiations, a "take it or leave it" strategy is commonly known as "Boulwarism" — named after a General Electric vice-president who formulated the approach of making of a non-negotiable "final and fair offer." This approach was held to constitute bad faith bargaining in *General Elec. Co.*, 150 NLRB 192 (1964), *enforced*, 418 F.2d 736 (2d Cir. 1969), *cert. denied*, 397 U.S. 965 (1970).

e. Professor Riskin favors an expansive role for the duty of good faith in mediation, but he also has the good sense to recognize that attempts to enforce such a duty would probably be harmful to the use of ADR. In the judicial settlement context, where Rule 16(f) establishes an obligation to "participate in good faith," each side should:

> be obliged respectfully to consider, and reconsider, with the other parties or the judicial host, the positions and the interests of both sides, and to think about ways to resolve the dispute. The reader might argue that this is not the sort of a duty that the law can enforce, and the reader would be correct. If, however, we think of the order to attend as an invitation to discuss as much as debate, to converse as much as to convince, to perceive as persuade, we may see more settlements and more "justice" than we expect.

Leonard L. Riskin, *The Represented Client in a Settlement Conference: The Lessons of* G. Heileman Brewing Co. v. Joseph Oat Corp., 69 WASH. U. L.Q. 1059, 1114 (1991).

f. Assuming there is some duty of good faith participation in court-ordered ADR, can the minimum level of compliance be stated in advance with any reasonable degree of specificity? Put another way, can we do better than fall back on Justice Potter Stewart's observation about "hard core" pornography: "I shall not today attempt further to define the kinds of material I understand to be embraced within that shorthand description; and perhaps I could never succeed in intelligibly doing so. But I know it when I see it." *Jacobellis v. Ohio*, 378 U.S. 184, 197 (1964) (concurring opinion).

5. Settlement Authority of Government Representatives

a. *In re Stone*, 986 F.2d 898 (5th Cir. 1993)
PER CURIAM:

In these petitions seeking writs of mandamus, we decide whether a federal district judge has the power, by a standing order, to direct the federal government to send a representative with full settlement authority to settlement conferences and, if so, whether he abused his discretion by so doing in these routine civil lawsuits involving the United States. In addition to requiring counsel to attend these conferences, the court also requires the attendance of a designated representative of each party with full authority to settle the case; that representative must appear in person — availability by telephone is not sufficient. We conclude that, although the district judge possesses the ultimate power to require the attendance at issue, it is a power to be very sparingly used, and here the district judge, albeit with the best of intentions, has abused his discretion.

In each of the petitions before us, the federal government objects to this order as applied to it. By statute, the Attorney General of the United States has the power to conduct all litigation on behalf of the United States, its agencies, and its officers, unless otherwise provided by law. Pursuant to authority given by 28 U.S.C. § 510, the Attorney General has developed a set of regulations delegating settlement authority to various officials. As we read these regulations, United States Attorneys often will be able to settle a case without approval from a higher authority, as the regulations provide that each local United States Attorney has settlement authority up to $500,000. If the client agency disagrees with the United States Attorney over the terms of the settlement, however, an Assistant Attorney General must approve the settlement. In addition, settlements in various classes of important cases always must be approved by the Deputy Attorney General or one of the Assistant Attorneys General. . . .

District courts have the general inherent power to require a party to have a representative with full settlement authority present — or at least reasonably and promptly accessible — at pretrial conferences. This applies to the government as well as private litigants. We find no statute or rule that attempts to regulate the court's use of that inherent power. But a district court must consider the unique position of the government as a litigant in determining whether to exercise its discretion in favor of issuing such an order.

The purpose of the structure established by the Attorney General is to promote centralized decisionmaking on important questions. Centralized decisionmaking promotes three important objectives. First, it allows the government to act consistently in important cases, a value more or less recognized by the Equal Protection Clause. Second, centralized decisionmaking allows the executive branch to pursue policy goals more effectively by placing ultimate authority in the hands of a few officials. Third, by giving authority to high-ranking officials, centralized decisionmaking better promotes political accountability.

Given the reasonable policy justifications for the Justice Department's settlement regulations and the insignificant interference with the operation of the courts, the district court abused its discretion in not respecting those regulations. Where the interference with the courts is slight, courts should not risk becoming "monitors of the wisdom and soundness of Executive action." The order at issue here imposes a major inconvenience on at least one of the parties without the showing of a real and palpable need.

The district court contends that the government is not special and should not be treated differently from private litigants. The government is in a special category in a number of respects, however, in addition to its need for centralized decisionmaking. The Government is a party to a far greater number of cases on a nationwide basis than even the most litigious private entity. Obviously, high-ranking officials of cabinet agencies could never do their jobs if they could be subpoenaed for every case involving their agency. As a result, we have held that such subpoenas are appropriate only in egregious cases. In determining whether to require the government . . . to send a representative to a pretrial conference with full authority to settle, a district court should take a practical approach. The court must be permitted to conduct its business in a reasonably efficient manner; it need not allow the parties or counsel to waste valuable judicial resources unnecessarily. On the other hand, the court should recognize that parties have a host of problems beyond the immediate case that is set for pretrial conference. This is particularly true of the government. . . .

We conclude that the district court abused its discretion in routinely requiring a representative of the government with ultimate settlement authority to be present at all pretrial or settlement conferences. We do not suggest that the district court can never issue such an order, but it should consider less drastic steps before doing so. For example, the court could require the government to declare whether the case can be settled within the authority of the local United States Attorney. If so, the court could issue an order requiring the United States Attorney to either attend the conference personally or be available by telephone to discuss settlement at the time of the conference.

According to the government at argument, most of its routine litigation can be settled within the United States Attorney's authority. Where that is not so, and failure of the government to extend settlement authority is a serious, persistent problem, substantially hampering the operations of the docket, the court could take additional action, such as requiring the government to advise it of the identity of the person or persons who hold such authority and directing those persons to consider settlement in advance of the conference and be fully prepared and available by telephone to discuss settlement at the time of the conference. Finally, if the district court's reasonable efforts to conduct an informed settlement discussion in a particular case are thwarted because the government official with settlement authority will not communicate with government counsel or the court in a timely manner, the court, as a last resort, can require the appropriate officials with full settlement authority to attend a pretrial conference.

The measures we outline above are intended to be exemplary, and we express no ultimate view as to such hypothetical situations except to point out that there are many steps that reasonably can be taken, far short of the standing order at issue here. We include these scenarios to demonstrate that the district court, before issuing an order such as the directive under review here, must give individualized attention to the hardship that order will create. The court must then exercise its discretion in light of the circumstances of that case. We believe that such practical measures will enable the courts to administer their dockets efficiently while allowing the Department of Justice to handle effectively the burdensome volume of litigation thrust upon it.

b. Comments and Questions

a. Settlement authority problems at the state and local level may be more difficult than those presented in the *Stone* case. For example, the settlement authority of the city attorney in Houston (the fourth largest city in America) is limited to $5,000. Any larger amount requires the approval of the City Council — and, supporters of open government will be pleased to know, proposed settlements are considered in public meetings. Would it be crass to suggest that public posturing by the elected members of the council sometimes takes place, and that political factors sometimes play a role?

b. Can a judge, whether state or federal, order the Houston City Council to even consider, let alone approve, a tentative settlement? Suppose the Council disapproves a settlement, or authorizes a settlement amount significantly lower than the tentative settlement? Would your view of the matter change, depending on the source of the $5,000 limitation? Among the possibilities are custom, written Council policy, local ordinance, state statute, and state constitution.

c. Another type of government entity that is a common party to lawsuits is state universities. Large state universities are separate legal entities governed by a board of regents. The regents are state residents, but they live throughout the state. (Indeed, geographic diversity is a common consideration in the appointment of regents.) Regents serve on a part-time basis, and they usually receive no cash compensation (expenses are reimbursed and there are other rewards). Regents typically are successful (and highly compensated) executives or professionals. Placing such persons at the beck and call of judges all over America would be a severe impediment to recruiting highly capable regents. Boards of Regents hold four to eight regular meetings per year, and these normally are scheduled a full year in advance. Special meetings are held for important issues, but commonly some regents participate by telephone or through notational voting.

G. APPELLATE MEDIATION

1. Ignazio J. Ruvolo, *Appellate Mediation — "Settling" The Last Frontier of ADR*, 42 SAN DIEGO L. REV. 177 (2005)

[The Author is an Associate Justice on the California First District Court of Appeal, Division Two, and chair of that court's Appellate Mediation Committee.]

In the closing years of the last century, the American appellate judicial process has remained the last frontier of ADR. Until the last decade or so, only the antediluvian settlement conference was available to help parties settle cases on appeal, and then only in the infrequent instance where the parties voluntarily requested one. Appellate settlements were viewed as an oxymoron: conventional wisdom questioned how someone could expect civil litigants to resolve their legal differences after pursuing formal adjudication so doggedly through the judicial system, and particularly when one party has been declared a winner at the trial level. But perhaps fueled by the heady success of ADR at the trial level, and driven by ponderous appellate backlogs and changing mindsets about the use of courts to resolve all forms of legal disputes, ADR encampments have been erected by appellate judges and practitioners around the country, most in the form of mediation programs. . . .

II. The California Experience, First District

[A lengthy discussion of the origins of appellate mediation in California is omitted.] Like all of the programs examined prior to the commencement of its own program, the First District's four-year experience reveals that tremendous benefits were realized from the program's operations. As of the end of June 2003, 3,079 civil cases have been assessed and 639, or 21%, selected for mediation. Approximately 500 cases have completed their mediations, and 268 have settled, for an overall settlement rate of 55%. Based on the attorney and party evaluations received, it is estimated that mediation program operations have saved the parties an estimated net savings of $136 million.

III. Appellate Mediation in Other Jurisdictions

The following review of appellate mediation programs in other states, and in the federal judicial system, reveals that California is not the only jurisdiction where appellate mediation has taken root and proved successful in helping litigants settle their disputes in a nonadversarial setting. Virtually all of the programs examined make party participation mandatory, and most use selection criteria to choose cases for inclusion in the program. However, other programs have been very successful while relying on in-house mediators exclusively, while others conduct virtually all mediations via teleconference or video.

A. Oregon.

Funding for the first two years came from the State Justice Institute, which enabled the Oregon Court of Appeals to employ a half-time administrator, and a program evaluator. The initial mediator panel consisted of thirty attorney volunteers who received court-sponsored and funded mediation training through the University of Willamette School of Law. To help compare results, the program included cases selected at random, as well as screened cases selected because they appeared to represent good candidates for mediation. During this period, . . . the program achieved a full settlement rate of 43% and an additional partial settlement rate of 5%. Categorically, the highest settlement rates were achieved in workers compensation, family law, and general commercial litigation cases. Significantly, 86% of the cases were settled before the completion of briefing, and one-third involved global settlements.

During this initial phase, the emphasis for case selection shifted from random selection to a more criteria-based process. Litigation involving governmental agency decisions was generally excluded from the program, due, in part, to statutory changes. Selection criteria centered around the willingness of parties to engage in mediation, the assessment by counsel as to the potential of the case for settlement, the extent to which the subject of the litigation involved an industry wide practice, the need to rely on statutory interpretation to resolve the case, and the strength of existing applicable precedent to decide the appeal.

A challenge faced in Oregon, which was shared by many jurisdictions employing a similar mediation model, was how to encourage the involvement of attorney volunteers in a pro bono program that inevitably competed for contributions of scarce non-billable attorney time with a wide array of other pro bono programs. The Oregon Legislature provided a solution that helped alleviate the recruitment dilemma by mandating parties in cases directed into the program to share a flat fee of $500 per case ($300 for workers compensation appeals).

By 1998, the Oregon program had expanded to include a panel of sixty to eighty neutrals, and 240 to 300 civil cases annually were being diverted into mediation. Further, the state legislature provided permanent funding for the program, as well as legislative assistance by enacting a rule of procedure staying for 120 days all appellate deadlines for cases selected for inclusion into the program. More recently, the Oregon program has expanded, and the results it achieved surpassed the program's impressive initial two years of operation. For example, in 2001, Oregon's attorney volunteer mediator panel had swelled to 120 neutrals, who mediated 350 cases, while settling 200 — an impressive rate of 60%. In 2002, 220 cases were mediated, and of this number 151 settled. This computes to a settlement rate of 69% — the highest rate encountered in the research for this Article since the Ninth Circuit's astounding settlement rate of 73% achieved in 1994. By case types, settlement rates, in descending order, were as follows: workers compensation (63%), general civil (54%), family law (50%), and probate (50%). . . .

B. Federal Ninth Circuit

The settlement program of the federal Ninth Circuit Court of Appeals was first implemented in 1984 and is by far the largest appellate ADR program examined. The program, which operated as an independent unit of the Ninth Circuit, was originally staffed by five full-time circuit mediators and three support members in San Francisco, with one mediator and support person in Seattle, Washington. Ten staff mediators are currently employed. Reports of program operations were made to the chief judge of the court by a designated chief mediator. The circuit mediators are employees of the court, and cases are assigned to them on a random basis. They are hired based on their civil litigation experience, as well as prior training and experience as ADR neutrals.

In 1994, circuit mediators screened 2,016 program-eligible cases (2,500 in 1995), and scheduled 773 settlement conferences (1,000 in 1995). Selection was generally made based on information provided by the parties through the submission of a Civil Appeals Docketing Statement (CADS), which were required to be filed in all program-eligible cases. The CADS includes information concerning the nature of the case, including the basis for the court's jurisdiction, result at the trial level, issues on appeal, and whether there are any related matters pending in any federal court, or proceedings pending in any court involving the same subject matter. Where the information in the CADS was insufficient to allow the screening mediator to decide whether to include the case, an initial assessment conference was scheduled with the attorneys of record. Initial assessment conferences occurred in about 25% of the eligible cases. Once selected, participation in the Ninth Circuit program is mandatory. The rules provide that overlooked cases could opt into the program. This occurred in approximately 5% of the cases not selected for participation by the circuit mediator.

Because of the extensive geographic area served by the Ninth Circuit, it was not surprising to learn that 70-75% of the mediation sessions were conducted by telephone, and not in person. Moreover, while it was customary that parties attend the telephonic conferences, such attendance was not required in all instances. In-person mediations were scheduled at the discretion of the circuit mediator at which both counsel and a client representative were required to appear. Telephonic mediation conferences generally lasted one to two hours while in-person mediations were typically four to eight hours in duration.

To ensure confidentiality, program rules prohibited counsel from disclosing the content of any settlement discussions in briefs or arguments. Furthermore, filings and documents pertaining to the selected cases and the program's operations were kept in files inaccessible to other court personnel, including judicial staff. In those rare instances in which a judge participated as a mediator, the judge was precluded from later involvement in the adjudication of the case, but could vote on whether the court should hear the case en banc.

What was completely unexpected was the impressive level of settlements achieved despite the absence of in-person conferences in most cases. In 1994, 598 cases settled, resulting in a jaw-dropping disposition rate of 73%, while the 573 settlements in 1995 represented a settlement rate of 66.5%. But apparently this is no anomaly, because it compares favorably with the Ninth Circuit's results in other years.

C. New Mexico

New Mexico's intermediate appellate court is comprised of ten appellate justices who hear cases predominantly in Albuquerque and Santa Fe. . . . The court processes approximately 1,000 appeals annually of which 500 are civil, 450 criminal, and 50 are interlocutory appeals. . . .

New Mexico's mediation program commenced in the fall of 1998, and since its inception has operated using a single full-time staff mediator who is assisted by a part-time administrative assistant. The mediator was selected by the court from its central staff, and the mediator underwent training in modern mediation technique early in the life of the program. The court considered and rejected the idea of using sitting appellate judges to mediate cases. In making this decision, the court recognized the important differences in skill sets between judging and mediating. Not all judges make the most effective mediators. Second, the court wanted to avoid encumbering judicial resources by eliminating one of the court's jurists from the ability to sit on the appellate panel hearing an unsuccessfully mediated case. Lastly, there was a desire to remove any possible hint that confidential information disclosed in the mediation might affect a later appellate decision on the merits.

The court similarly examined the option of relying on appellate attorney volunteers for mediation services. Positive factors favoring the use of attorneys included the absence of cost (other than party time and the cost of their own counsel) to the parties participating in mediation, the ability of the parties to rely on the specialized substantive knowledge of the volunteers, geographic diversity on a panel of volunteers, and a perceived benefit of fully involving the bar association in the process. The court finally chose to use a court-hired, full-time mediator believing this choice would still allow direct contact between the program and the bar, while affording a more streamlined administration.

Cases screened for inclusion in the program come from the court's regular case docket. Because the matters disposed of through the court's summary disposition calendar were relatively small and uncomplicated, the cases resolved quickly, and with little expenditure of judicial resources, it was concluded that the focus of the program should be on the regular calendar cases. Of course, counsel in any case could request to be included in the mediation program.

Although the program designers looked at other appellate mediation models that used both case screening selection criteria and random selection systems, the New Mexico court decided to use a random system. Once a case is selected, however, participation in mediation is mandatory, although the mediator considers the views of counsel as to whether the case is appropriate for mediation. Mediation conferences are generally conducted before briefing begins, and usually are telephonic. In-person conferences are occasionally held in Santa Fe and Albuquerque. Furthermore, direct participation by clients is encouraged, but is not mandatory in most cases. The program mediator held the view that mandating client participation could alienate the parties and ultimately prove to be counterproductive. Additionally, in some cases, the absence of the clients reduced the risk of attorney posturing, which is an impediment to settlement. Most civil appeals are eligible for mediation, although cases in which the parties are self-represented (pro per), writ proceedings, civil cases brought by incarcerated individuals, or cases involving New Mexico's health and welfare statutes are categorically excluded.

Typically, cases are assigned to the mediation program after the parties are notified that the case has been placed in the court's regular disposition calendar, but before briefing has commenced. Placement in the program does not result in any routine suspension of timelines for preparation of the trial court record or briefs, and some appellants resist any delays in the appellate adjudicative process occasioned by diversion into the mediation program. Nevertheless, the court's mediator is authorized to grant verbal requests for extensions of court rule-mandated deadlines where needed to facilitate the mediation process.

The operations of New Mexico's mediation program are kept separate from the court's adjudicative processes. Court personnel not directly involved in the program have no access to program files or information concerning the progress towards settlement of any one case. Similarly, the program operates under strict rules guarding the confidentiality of matters disclosed by the parties and counsel during the mediation process. Any communications between the mediator and court personnel necessary to carry out a settlement reached in mediation is made only with the express authorization of the parties as to its content.

From commencement of the program until June 2000, a period of almost two years, approximately three hundred cases were sent to mediation, a prodigious number considering the New Mexico court uses a single mediator. Moreover, largely relying on telephonic conferences, eighty-eight cases, or 29%, settled. While perhaps a bit lower, this rate is roughly comparable to disposition rates enjoyed by other programs mentioned in this article, and is indeed laudable, particularly in light of the fact that primary reliance is placed on telephonic conferences, often without clients' presence. . . .

D. Michigan

The mediation program of the Michigan Court of Appeals has been in operation for six years. Its day-to-day functions are directed by a full-time Settlement Director . . . The Michigan court employs a hybrid system of mediator assignments. The majority of the mediations are conducted personally by the court's Settlement Director, although complex cases are assigned to volunteer circuit court judges. Additionally, volunteer mediators are used in domestic relations appeals, and the Director maintains a list of private mediators, if the parties prefer to use such mediators. The Director has undergone formal mediation training at court expense, although mandatory training is not required for the program's volunteer mediators. No matter who mediates the case, the mediator's services are provided to the program on a pro bono basis.

The court utilizes a case screening system to select cases for program inclusion. No random selections are made. Parties may request to be included in the program, if not otherwise selected, and will be accommodated if the program's general case criteria are met. Cases in which the parties are self-represented, administrative mandamus appeals, and domestic relations and dependency proceedings dealing with child custody issues are categorically excluded from the program. Categorically included are appeals arising from negligence actions, automobile no-fault appeals, and appeals from the granting or denial of attorney fees and sanctions. Beginning in 2004, the program started to include all employment actions in which the plaintiff was the prevailing party in the trial court.

Case selection occurs within sixty days from the filing of the appeal, and the mediation usually takes place before briefing is required, in order to minimize expense to the parties for those cases destined to settle (and to serve as an inducement). For those cases scheduled for mediation, there is no routine suspension of the time for briefing or for the preparation of the record. However, there is a procedure available for the parties to request extensions of the time for record preparation and briefing upon a showing of good cause. Settlements typically occur within six months from the filing of the appeal, which compares very favorably with the typical time of eighteen months or more to achieve a disposition by opinion. In its six years of operations, the Michigan program has enjoyed settlement rates ranging from 25-35%. . . .

E. Hawaii

Hawaii's program . . . was born partially in response to an increasing appellate backlog, . . . in March 1995. . . . Once a case is selected, participation is mandatory. Cases not selected can request inclusion into the program. Like other programs, early intervention was viewed as a key component of the Hawaii program, with cases selected for mediation within three weeks after the notice of appeal was filed, and before cost of preparation of the trial record was incurred.

Mediators are selected from the ranks of retired justices and trial judges, as well as retired or semi-retired practitioners, who are then trained in mediation technique. During the first eighteen months, approximately one case per week was mediated in Honolulu, the Center headquarters, and one additional case mediated in either Maui or on the island of Hawaii. Mediators volunteered their time at no cost to the parties, although parties were afforded the option of selecting their own mediator who would be compensated by the parties. During the initial program period of eighteen months, no one opted for their own paid mediator. . . . [F]or geographic reasons, many of the conferences were held at the state's video conference center. . . .

The program has mediated a total of almost 300 cases, approximately 50% of which have settled. In the last reported fiscal year, 53.8% of the mediated cases resulted in complete settlements, and an additional 5.4% were partially settled — the highest settlement rates in the last three years. By case type, settlements were achieved in the following descending order: contract (70%), torts (67%), agency appeals (50%), family (43%), and real property (33%).

IV. Reflections & Conclusions: Programmatic Features That Favor Mediated Settlements

1. Mandatory Participation. Virtually all appellate mediation programs reviewed for this Article now make participation mandatory, once a case has been assigned into the program. . . . Making appellate mediation mandatory breaks down these barriers to acceptance of ADR. While some day soon, appellate ADR will be as common and accepted as trial court ADR, and thus, participation can be made voluntary, we have not yet reached this point. Until then, exploiting the captive market appears to be justified. A further reason mandatory mediation seems superior is that it helps attorneys to overcome client resistance to the idea of settlement without raising a question of the attorney's loyalty to the client in suggesting mediation. . . .

2. Paid, Dedicated Program Administration. It is imperative that any court system contemplating the implementation of an appellate mediation program set aside funds necessary to hire and retain at least a part-time program administrator. The work needed to design, implement, operate, and collect data for an ADR program successfully cannot be minimized. Each established, reputable mediation program incorporates this feature. . . . Furthermore, it is in the best interests of the program to separate mediation processes from the court's adjudicative function. . . . Lastly, having a separate, professional staff dedicated to the program's operations gives the enterprise much needed gravitas within the legal community. It communicates to members of the bar and to their clients alike that the court is making a serious commitment to mediation. . . .

3. Trained, Experienced Mediators. Some courts use their program administrators as the principal mediator, others call upon the pro bono services of retired judges, and still others rely on the good offices of active practitioners to staff mediator panels. Regardless of the source from which the mediator panel is derived, formal training in modern mediation techniques and appellate procedure is desirable. It should be abundantly clear by now that mediation is a far distant relative to the ham-fisted settlement conference of yesterday. Surely, by the time a case reaches the appellate level, badgering or cajoling the parties or counsel is unlikely to be fruitful in bringing about a negotiated resolution. . . . .

Court-funded training helps to attract and maintain high-quality volunteer mediators. Such training can serve as a form of compensation for the volunteers, since quality training is expensive to obtain. It also demonstrates a willingness by the court to invest in its mediator pool. . . . Training also benefits the program and the volunteer mediators by improving the settlement rates over a period of time. High settlement rates enhance the reputation of the program, and encourages attorney volunteers to get involved. They also reflect well on the ability of the mediator. . . .

4. Selection by Criteria vs. Random Selection. The debate continues as to whether selection of cases for appellate mediation should be criteria-based or random. While random selection may appear to be more democratic, sending cases that have little or no chance of success to mediation can be disabling to the program for several reasons. First, forcing the parties and counsel to spend time, and therefore money, mediating a hopeless case will undoubtedly engender resentment towards the court and its program. Such damage to the reputation and prestige of the program can be substantial. Similarly, assigning a hopeless case to a volunteer mediator may undermine the mediator's commitment to the program. . . .

Additionally, the potential for wasting court resources cannot be overlooked. Every appeal with no chance for settlement that is assigned to the program reduces the time the administrator has to devote to more promising cases. The corollary to this is that for every random case placed in the program, one having a statistically better chance of settlement is likely excluded. Thus, random selection raises the risk of missing opportunities to settle cases, contrary to the very raison d'etre for the program's existence. Certainly, using a criteria-based system can still result in some deserving cases not being selected. However, this possibility can be ameliorated by allowing cases to opt into the program, thereby assuaging any concern that criteria-based case selection is anti-democratic.

5. *Relationship Between Mediation Success and Case Type.* Appeals from family law and probate judgments appear to enjoy the highest rates of settlement through mediation. An important reason for this high success rate appears to relate to the fact that both family law and probate cases typically involve disputes over wasting assets. Commercial disputes also appear to be good candidates for mediation. Experience suggests that personal injury cases are good candidates for mediation, at least if the judgment being appealed from was one in favor of the injured party.

The settlement rate in employment cases is lower for several reasons. Like family and probate cases, employment cases carry high emotional content, but without the familial bonds, which sometimes can be used to forecast an eventual end to the litigation. Second, burdened by substantive law which is still developing, the outcome on appeal remains less predictable than in other categories of cases. Third, depending on the issue involved, employers are understandably concerned about the effect settlement may have on the remainder of its workforce.

The low settlement rate in insurance cases may also be suppressed by uncertain substantive law and institutional factors. For example, the insurance industry, a sophisticated, repeat player in California litigation, is far more perspicacious about the precedential value of cases than many other commercial entities. Ready settlements justified, perhaps, by the circumstances of a given case must be tempered by the fear that other policyholders would be emboldened by this apparent capitulation. Moreover, because of the high volume of litigation into which most carriers are thrust, the insurance industry may arguably have a greater ability to weather the financial ebb and flow of adverse judgments than other, less frequent litigants. For this additional reason, insurers may be less risk adverse and, therefore, more likely see an appeal to its conclusion on the merits. . . .

6. *Timing of Mediation.* Appellate court programs dedicated to early mediation have a significant advantage over those that divert cases only after the record has been received and the appellate issues briefed. Certainly, deferring cases until post-briefing ensures that appellate issues have crystallized. This, in turn, may afford greater focus and efficiency during the mediation session. However, any advantage in this regard is more than offset by the loss of financial leverage that early mediation provides. . . . Furthermore, in many cases, appeals are commenced by trial counsel, with appellate counsel being retained, if at all, only later in the proceedings. Conducting mediation early with trial counsel — and before appellate counsel has been retained — may also improve settlement leverage in several ways. Bringing in new counsel undoubtedly carries with it a significant cost just in bringing appellate counsel up to speed. . . .

2. Comments and Questions

a. The most striking, and perhaps most important, aspect of appellate mediation is that it succeeds with some frequency. Why? After all, the parties were unable to settle their dispute prior to trial, and then they were unwilling to abide by the verdict of the trial court. At this juncture, the parties have already incurred the costs, both economic and psychological, associated with preparing for and conducting a trial. In addition, the risks associated with uncertainty about what will transpire at trial have disappeared.

b. Post-mortem analysis by the participants in cases settled through appellate mediation often will lead them to conclude that they should have settled the dispute much earlier. Are there instances where parties might conclude, even in hindsight, that they needed to have a decision by a third party before settlement made sense? If yes, identify categories of examples. Might these disputes be amendable to settlement through a more directive form of ADR than mediation?

c. The first federal appellate ADR program was created in 1974 by the Court of Appeals for the Second Circuit. Irving R. Kaufman, *Must Every Appeal Run the Gamut? The Civil Appeals Management Plan*, 95 YALE L.J. 755 (1986). Today, every federal circuit has some form of appellate ADR program. The Federal Circuit was the last holdout. *See* Thomas Hitter, *What Is So Special About the Federal Circuit? A Recommendation For ADR Use in the Federal Circuit*, 13 FED. CIR. B.J. 441 9 (2004).

d. Thirty-one states currently operate some form of appellate ADR programs. Shawn Davisson, *Privatization and Self-Determination in the Circuits: Utilizing the Private Sector Within the Evolving Framework of Federal Appellate Mediation*, 21 OHIO ST. J. ON DISP. RESOL. 953, 959 (2006). For more on state appellate mediation, see Susan FitzGibbon, *Appellate Settlement Conference Programs: A Case Study*, 1993 J. DISP. RESOL. 57 (Missouri Court of Appeals, Eastern District); *Firelock, Inc. v. District Court*, 776 P.2d 1090 (Colo. 1989) (en banc).

e. For a consideration of the documentary formalities required for enforcement of a purported appellate mediation agreement, see *Bezar East, Inc. v. Mead Corp.*, 412 F.3d 429 (3d Cir. 2005) and the discussion in Chapter Thirteen.

Chapter 11

PRIVATE ADR PROCESSES

A. INTRODUCTION

This chapter examines a variety of private, consensual ADR procedures. The very fact that the process is private means that the process can be custom tailored to address the problem at hand. The discussion here is largely limited to the "standard" version of each process and a few important variations, but bear in mind that each process can be adjusted to meet the needs of the parties. (Once the parties have agreed to a process, however, it can be changed only with their consent.)

Section B considers the mini-trial, an unfortunately named structured settlement process that has nothing to do with litigation. There is a similarity in that a presentation of the case is made, but the audience is composed of senior executives so the format is quite different from a trial.

Section C offers an overview of private, binding arbitration. Non-binding private arbitration is not an oxymoron, but it is uncommon. Court-annexed arbitration must be non-binding, due to the constitutional right to a judicial trial (and, usually, a trial by jury). The law is crystal clear that, absent express federal statutory provision to the contrary, the right to a judicial hearing can be waived by a pre-dispute agreement to arbitrate. Binding arbitration is beyond the scope of this book, which is limited to the resolution of disputes by the parties (often with the assistance of a third party neutral), but the topic is too important not to offer a brief overview.

Section D introduces collaborative law, the newest innovation in the dispute resolution pantheon. Collaborative law is a settlement process, the key feature of which is that the parties and their counsel all agree (in writing) that, in the event the dispute cannot be settled, the lawyers for both sides will not represent the parties at trial. Collaborative law originated in the family law context, and in only a few years it has become widely used in divorce proceedings.

Section E introduces the Ombuds, a dispute resolution official appointed by an organization, public or private, to receive complaints and suggestions from employees or customers of the appointing entity — commonly a corporation or university. It does not make sense to consider private and public ombudspersons in separate chapters, because their functions are similar, so both types of ombudsmen are discussed here. Of course, the reader should look for instances where the fact that the ombuds is a public or a private official makes a difference.

Finally, section F looks at partnering and dispute review boards (DRB), two approaches to addressing potential and actual problems that are commonly used for very large construction and commercial projects. Sometimes the two approaches are used in tandem.

B. MINI-TRIAL

1. Jethro K. Lieberman & James F. Henry, *Lessons From the Alternative Dispute Resolution Movement*, 53 U. Chi. L. Rev. 424, 427-29 (1986)

The mini-trial is not, in fact, a trial at all, but a highly-structured settlement process. Because it is a flexible device that can be tailored to the precise needs of the parties, no single procedural model of the mini-trial has yet prevailed. But in general, the known mini-trials share many of the following characteristics:

1. The parties negotiate a set of procedural ground rules (a protocol) that will govern the nonbinding mini-trial.

2. The time for preparation and the amount of discovery is relatively short.

3. The hearing itself is sharply abbreviated — usually no more than two days.

4. The hearing is often conducted by a third-party neutral . . . advisor.

5. The case is presented to representatives of the parties with authority to settle.

6. The lawyers present their "best" case; they do not have time to delve into side issues.

7. After the hearing, the party representatives meet privately to negotiate a settlement.

8. If the parties cannot reach a settlement, the neutral advisor may render an advisory opinion on how he thinks a judge would rule if the case were to go to court.

9. The proceedings are confidential: the parties generally commit themselves to refrain from disclosing details of the proceedings to any outsider.

Several observations are in order about the trust-building capacity of the mini-trial. First, the very process of negotiating the protocol tends to foster trust. Second, by concentrating on their best possible case, the lawyers usually feel constrained to discuss the central issues. Third, the hint of lawyerly hairsplitting, name calling, and pettifogging that might delight courtroom regulars would leave the business executives to whom mini-trials are presented singularly unamused. Finally, the presence at the hearing of a neutral advisor, to whom both parties have consented, enhances the prospect that they will credit any advisory opinion that he renders.

In a mini-trial held by Texaco and Borden, for example, the parties resolved a breach-of-contract claim and antitrust counterclaim totaling in the hundreds of millions of dollars by renegotiating the entire contract for the supply of natural gas. Both parties claimed a net gain. No court could have ordered the parties to renegotiate; at best, a judge or jury could only have compromised on the amount of damages it awarded the "winner."

2. Lester Edelman, et al., THE MINI-TRIAL 1-6, 9-17 (U.S. ARMY CORPS OF ENGINEERS 1989) (IWR Pamphlet 89-ADR-P-1)

First of all, a mini-trial isn't a trial. There's no judge or lengthy procedures. Decisions are reached quickly and made by managers who have managerial and, often, technical shills, not by third parties such as judges. In fact, the mini-trial is a structured form of negotiated settlement. All parties enter into a mini-trial voluntarily, and any party can drop out when it wants to. A mini-trial is successful when there is a mutual agreement. Here is what a mini-trial might look like:

Two or more organizations involved in a dispute would agree to use a mini-trial as an alternative to going to court, a contract appeals board, or some other judicial body. Each participating organization would designate a senior manager to represent the organization and to make binding commitments on behalf of the organization. Ideally, this manager would not have had any substantial previous involvement in the dispute. The management representatives and their attorneys would then jointly develop a mini-trial agreement. Since the mini-trial is to help them make decisions, they need to define what they want to happen before and during the mini-trial.

Attorneys for the participating organizations would then go about preparing their case, advocating the position of their organizations. One unique thing about these preparations, though, is that the attorneys know that they will have only a few hours, or at most several days, to present their case. Normally, the mini-trial agreement will specify that both parties will prepare short position papers outlining their case. These papers will be exchanged at an agreed-upon time before the mini-trial so that management representatives will be able to read them prior to the mini-trial itself.

At the agreed-upon date, attorneys for the participating organizations will present their cases in front of the management representatives of the organizations. In many mini-trials, the management representatives are assisted by an impartial neutral advisor. This is optional. Following the presentations and any questions, the management representatives would then move to another room, without their staffs, and attempt to resolve the dispute.

The results of the mini-trial are then documented as carefully as any other negotiated settlement which could be subjected to review by whoever has an interest in whether the negotiated settlement is fair. The mini-trial agreement will also include a provision that statements made by participants during the mini-trial can't be used against participants in court if no agreement is reached during the mini-trial. This means that concessions made in the relatively informal mini-trial conference can't be dragged up later on in court.

What are the advantages of a mini-trial over more traditional ways of resolving disputes, such as litigation or formal administrative procedures? There are a number of advantages:

- Puts the Decision Back in the Hands of Managers
- Greater Flexibility in Possible Settlements
- Protect the Relationship
- Time-Savings
- Cost Savings
- Protect Management Time

Every dispute resolution technique has its strengths and weaknesses, and mini-trials are no exception. Some concerns expressed about mini-trials are not, however, well-founded. Here's a list which includes both very real limitations of mini-trials, and concerns expressed by people who have not used the technique:

- Not Appropriate for Some Issues
- Extra Work for Managers
- Cost of Preparation
- Is It the Best Possible Deal?
- Protection Against Lying
- To Offer to Use a Mini-Trial Says We Have a Weak Case
- It's Not Supporting the Field

The senior management people who will represent each organization are normally selected before the mini-trial agreement is developed. This is done so that they can participate in developing the agreement. There are two basic criteria for selection of the senior managers to represent the organizations:

- Not Previously Associated with the Issue
- Able to Bind the Organization

While the mini-trial is a structured negotiation process, there is considerable latitude in how the mini-trial is conducted. The management representatives need to ensure that the procedures described in the agreement will serve their needs.

Although it is not mandatory that a neutral advisor be selected, there are distinct advantages in using a neutral advisor. The advantage of early selection of the neutral advisor is that the neutral advisor may be able to assist in developing the agreement. There may still be some suspicion or even hostility between the parties, and suggestions coming from the neutral advisor may be treated with more openness than those coming from the other side. The neutral advisor can also provide a communication link if communication between the parties becomes difficult. The neutral advisor can encourage the management representatives to take charge of the mini-trial agreement, to make sure it meets their needs. The exact role of the neutral advisor can be agreed upon beforehand, or it can be covered in the mini-trial agreement. The original idea of the neutral advisor was to introduce both an impartial opinion and an element of mediation into the proceedings. The history of mini-trials suggests that the negotiation period can be rocky, and the neutral advisor may be able to keep the negotiations moving. . . .

There are several aspects to the neutral advisor's role. The neutral advisor can act like a technical expert or consultant. The neutral advisor can act like an arbitrator in a non-binding arbitration, suggesting what a reasonable outcome might be, but with no authority to bind the parties. Finally, the neutral advisor can act like a facilitator or mediator, helping to keep communication open, clarifying positions, and seeking out new compromises. Clearly, the role you decide upon will influence your selection of a mini-advisor.

To date, most neutrals have been retired judges, or law professors with special expertise in the issues under discussion. Technical experts have also been used where management representatives primarily wanted advice on technical rather than legal issues. In at least one mini-trial, there was a small panel of neutral advisors, including an attorney and two technical experts. Some organizations have also talked of using a mediator as a neutral advisor, putting the emphasis on helping the negotiation process. . . .

3. Comments and Questions

a. The mini-trial, like other customized dispute resolution processes, is largely limited to high dollar cases. Still, the model is worthy of consideration, and can be streamlined for smaller disputes.

b. Rules of professional conduct prohibit lawyers from engaging in direct communication with a represented party. Where both parties are represented — the norm where the use of a mini-trial (or other specialized ADR procedure) is contemplated — all communications are channeled through counsel. The business clients hear about the case and the positions of the other side, if at all, only though their attorneys. Often, the advocate and the client reaffirm each other about the rightness and justice of their position, a process that produces polarization rather than an understanding of the position of the other party to the dispute.

c. In these circumstances, the opening statements in a mini-trial, as in mediation, should be addressed to the other party (one or more senior officials, usually not legally trained) more than the neutral. There will be ample time later in the process to educate the neutral, beyond what has already been achieved in prior paper submissions. Frequently, the parties understand the views of the other side for the first time.

C. ARBITRATION — PRIVATE AND BINDING

In arbitration, a third party neutral renders a binding decision that resolves a dispute. The basis for private, binding arbitration is contract. This subject is generally beyond the scope of this book, which focuses on consensual dispute resolution by parties (often with the assistance of a third party neutral). Nevertheless, arbitration is a hugely important form of dispute resolution and, therefore, cannot be ignored entirely. Here, we offer no more than an overview of arbitration topics and issues. For an extended treatment of the subject, see STEPHEN K. HUBER & MAUREEN A. WESTON, ARBITRATION: CASES AND MATERIALS (2d ed. 2006).

1. The Place of Arbitration in Modern America

Arbitration is sweeping the American legal landscape, and is now a central feature of our system for the binding resolution of disputes. Simply stated, arbitration is everywhere. Today, arbitration provisions are a standard feature of all manner of contracts that touch the daily lives of everyone. Virtually every business and individual with legal capacity to contract (and some who lack such capacity) has entered into multiple agreements that specify arbitration as the forum for resolving most or all disputes that might arise between the parties. Until the late 20th century, arbitration was largely limited to specialized commercial settings and labor-management grievance proceedings.

The importance of arbitration as the preferred mode of binding dispute resolution has grown dramatically during the last several decades, strongly supported by the Supreme Court, and this trend has not yet run its course. This favorable legal environment has, in turn, prompted business organizations to dramatically expand the use of arbitration provisions in their contracts with both individuals and other businesses. Thus, arbitration continues to be a growth industry.

A few examples of the contexts in which arbitration is commonly used should suffice to demonstrate its importance in the American economy and legal landscape. Everyone with a brokerage account has agreed to arbitrate any and all disputes arising out of or related to that relationship. Credit/debit card issuers and banking organizations commonly require arbitration in their customer agreements. Computer purchase contracts usually require arbitration, as do numerous agreements related to "on-line" transactions. Agreements related to medical services, which includes the paying employers and insurers as well as the actual providers, commonly require arbitration. Even contests sponsored by McDonald's (and other fast food purveyors) call for arbitration of all disputes. *See, e.g., James v. McDonald's Corp.*, 417 F.3d 672 (7th Cir. 2005). None of these consumer transactions were subject to arbitration in 1985. *See, e.g.,* Charles L. Knapp, *Taking Contracts Private: The Quiet Revolution in Contract Law*, 71 FORDHAM L. REV. 761 (2002).

Since the Supreme Court in 1991 ruled that employers may require individual employees to arbitrate statutory rights claims, *Gilmer v. Interstate/John-*

son Lane Corp., 500 U.S. 20 (1991), arbitration has become a common feature of employment contracts. After a period that produced much litigation and "a small Alexandrian library of law review articles," the current state of the law "is relatively stable and clear: employees outside the transportation industry may require employees to arbitrate all employment disputes as a condition of employment so long as certain due process requirements are met." David Sherwyn, *Samuel Estriecher & Michael Heise, Assessing the Case for Employment Arbitration: A New Path for Empirical Research*, 57 STAN. L. REV. 1557, 1558-1559 (2005) (citing leading cases, articles, and reform proposals). Mandatory arbitration is not limited to unsophisticated employees: law firms often require attorneys (including partners) to arbitrate disputes, *see, e.g., Moncharsh v. Heily & Blasie*, 832 P.2d 899 (Cal. 1992), as do major accounting firms. *See, e.g., Hottle v. BDO Seidman, LLP*, 846 A.2d 862 (Conn. 2004) (latest of seven litigated disputes between one-time BDO Seidman partners and the firm).

Franchise agreements commonly call for arbitration of most disputes (a few situations where franchisors prefer access to the courts are excluded). *See, e.g., Southland Corp v. Keating*, 465 U.S. 1 (1984); *Doctors' Associates, Inc. v. Casarotto*, 517 U.S. 681 (1996). At the most sophisticated end of the business spectrum, arbitration terms are standard features of reinsurance contracts (i.e., sharing of risk agreements between insurance companies), and maritime bills of lading. Numerous trade associations have long mandated arbitration of all disputes among their members. *See, e.g.,* Soia Mentschikoff, *Commercial Arbitration*, 61 COLUM. L. REV. 846 (1961).

Arbitration has long been the norm for multinational transactions, because businesses do not relish the prospect of litigation in the courts of another country. The Supreme Court decisions are particularly favorable to arbitration in the international context. The leading cases are discussed in STEPHEN K. HUBER & E. WENDY TRACHTE-HUBER, ENFORCEMENT OF INTERNATIONAL ARBITRATION AGREEMENTS BY AMERICAN COURTS, YEARBOOK ON INTERNATIONAL FINANCIAL AND ECONOMIC LAW 227 (Kluwer 1998).

2. Arbitration Law in Earlier America and England

Once upon a time, American law was hostile to arbitration, treating it as a creature outside the law. People could choose to settle disputes by arbitration, but courts would not enforce agreements to arbitrate or even require people who commenced with arbitration to complete the process. Actual arbitration awards were sometimes enforced, but local practice varied widely from state to state.

This section offers a brief introduction to arbitration in earlier America, and to its English arbitration law antecedents. Justice Storey's *Tobey* opinion is the classic statement of the anti-arbitration animus that prevailed in America before the enactment of the FAA in 1925. Judge Jerome Frank's learned discussion in the *Kulukundis* decision is the official history of arbitration in America. It has been cited in hundreds of judicial opinions, including three times by the Supreme Court. *See Southland Corp. v. Keating*, 465 U.S. 1, 32 (1984); *Mitsubishi Motors Corp. v. Soler Chrysler-Plymouth, Inc.*, 473 U.S. 614, 638 (1984);

and *Rodriguez de Quijas v. Shearson/American Express*, 490 U.S. 477, 480 (1989).

a. *Tobey v. County of Bristol*, 23 Fed. Cas. 1313 (D.Mass. 1845)

STORY, J.

It is certainly the policy of the common law not to compel men to submit their rights and interests to arbitration, or to enforce agreements for such a purpose. Nay, the common law goes much further, and even if a submission has been made to arbitrators . . . with an express stipulation that the submission shall be irrevocable, it still is revocable and countermandable by either party before the award is actually made, although not afterwards.

b. *Kulukundis Shipping Co., S/A v. Amtorg Trading Corp.*, 126 F.2d 978, 982-985 (2d Cir. 1942)

FRANK, Circuit Judge.

. . . . The early English history of enforcement of executory arbitration agreements is not too clear. Arbitration was used by the medieval guilds and in early maritime transactions. Some persons trace an influence back to Roman law, doubtless itself affected by Greek law; others discern the influence of ecclesiastical law. The English courts, while giving full effect to agreements to submit controversies to arbitration after they had ripened into arbitrators' awards, would — over a long period beginning at the end of the 17th century — do little or nothing to prevent or make irksome the breach of such agreements when they were still executory.

Prior to 1687, such a breach could be made costly: a penal bond given to abide the result of an arbitration had a real bite, since a breach of the bond's condition led to a judgment for the amount of the penalty. It was so held in 1609 in Vynoir's Case, 8 CokeRep. 81b. To be sure, Coke there, in a dictum, citing precedents, dilated on the inherent revocability of the authority given to an arbitrator; such a revocation was not too important, however, if it resulted in a stiff judgment on a penal bond. But the Statute of Fines and Penalties (8 & 9 Wm.III c. 11, s. 8), enacted in 1687, provided that, in an action on any bond given for performance of agreements, while judgment would be entered for the penalty, execution should issue only for the damages actually sustained. Coke's dictum as to revocability, uttered seventy-eight years earlier, now took on a new significance, as it was now held that breach of an undertaking to arbitrate the damages was only nominal.

Recognizing the effect of the impact of this statute on executory arbitration agreements, Parliament, eleven years later, enacted a statute, 9 Wm.III c. 15 (1698), designed to remedy the situation by providing that, if an agreement to arbitrate so provided, it could be made a "rule of court" (i.e., a court order), in which event it became irrevocable, and one who revoked it would be subject to punishment for contempt of court; but the submission was revocable until such a rule of court had been obtained. This statute, limited in scope, was narrowly construed and was of little help. The ordinary executory arbitration agreement, thus, lost all real efficacy, since it was not specifically enforceable in equity, and was held not to constitute the basis of a plea in bar in, or a stay of, a suit on the original cause of action. In admiralty, the rulings were much the same.

In 1833, a statute (3 & 4 Wm.IV, c. 42) was passed which was intended to reinforce the 1680 statute, but it still left a submission revocable until an action was brought in connection with an arbitration proceeding. An Act of 1854 (17 & 19 Vict.c. 125) provided that any arbitration agreement could be made the basis of a stay and irrevocable except by leave of court, granted in the exercise of the court's discretion. The Arbitration Act of 1889 (52 & 53 Vict.c. 49) provided that any such agreement, unless a contrary intention is expressed therein, shall be irrevocable, except by leave of court, and shall have the same effect as if it had been made an order of court; it provided adequate court review of questions of law raised in the arbitration hearing.

It has been well said that the legal mind must assign some reason in order to decide anything with spiritual quiet. And so, by way of rationalization, it became fashionable in the middle of the 18th century to say that such agreements were against public policy, because they "oust the jurisdiction" of the courts. But that was a quaint explanation, inasmuch as an award, under an arbitration agreement, enforced both at law and in equity, was no less an ouster; and the same was true of releases and covenants not to sue, which were given full effect. Moreover, the agreement to arbitrate was not illegal, since suit could be maintained for its breach. Here was a clear instance of what Holmes called a "right" to break a contract and to substitute payment of damages for non-performance; as, in this type of case, the damages were only nominal, that "right" was indeed meaningful. Holmes, *The Path of The Law*, 10 HARV. L. REV. 457 (1897).

An effort has been made to justify this judicial hostility to the executory arbitration agreement on the ground that arbitrations, if unsupervised by the courts, are undesirable, and that legislation was needed to make possible such supervision. But if that was the reason for unfriendliness to such executory agreements, then the courts should also have refused to aid arbitrations when they ripened into awards. And what the English courts, especially the equity courts, did in other contexts, shows that, if they had had the will, they could have devised means of protecting parties to arbitrations. Instead, they restrictively interpreted successive statutes intended to give effect to executory arbitrations. No similar hostility was displayed by the Scotch courts.

Lord Campbell explained the English attitude as due to the desire of the judges, at a time when their salaries came largely from fees, to avoid loss of income. There was no disguising the fact that, as formerly, the emoluments of the Judges depended mainly, or almost entirely, upon fees, and as they had no fixed salaries, there was great competition to get as much as possible of litigation into Westminster Hall for the division of the spoil. And they had great jealousy of arbitrations whereby Westminster Hall was robbed of those cases. . . . Therefore, they said that the courts ought not to be ousted of their jurisdiction, and that it was contrary to the policy of the law to do so. Indignation has been voiced at this suggestion; perhaps it is unjustified. Perhaps the true explanation is the hypnotic power of the phrase, "oust the jurisdiction." Give a bad dogma a good name and its bite may become as bad as its bark. . . .

In 1855, in *Scott v. Avery*, 5 H.C.L. 811, the tide seemed to have turned. There it was held that if a policy made an award of damages by arbitrators a condition precedent to a suit on the policy, a failure to submit to arbitration would preclude such a suit, even if the policy left to the arbitrators the consideration of all the elements of liability. But, despite later legislation, the hostility of the English courts to executory arbitrations resumed somewhat after *Scott v. Avery*, and seems never to have been entirely dissipated.

That English attitude was largely taken over in the 19th century by most courts in this country. Indeed, in general, they would not go as far as *Scott v. Avery*, and continued to use the "ouster of jurisdiction" concept: An executory agreement to arbitrate would not be given specific performance or furnish the basis of a stay of proceedings on the original cause of action. Nor would it be given effect as a plea in bar, except in limited instances, i.e., in the case of an agreement expressly or impliedly making it a condition precedent to litigation that there be an award determining some preliminary question of subsidiary fact upon which any liability was to be contingent. In the case of broader executory agreements, no more than nominal dangers would be given for a breach.

Generally speaking, then, the courts of this country were unfriendly to executory arbitration agreements. The lower federal courts, feeling bound to comply with the precedents, nevertheless became critical of this judicial hostility. There were intimations in the Supreme Court that perhaps the old view might be abandoned, but in the cases hinting at that newer attitude, the issue was not raised. Effective state arbitration statutes were enacted beginning with the New York Statute of 1920. The purpose of the FAA . . . was deliberately to alter the judicial atmosphere previously existing. The report of the House Committee stated: 68 Cong., 1st Sess., H.R. Report No. 96.

> Arbitration agreements are purely matters of contract, and the effect of the bill is simply to make the contracting party live up to his agreement. He can no longer refuse to perform his contract when it becomes disadvantageous to him. An arbitration agreement is placed upon the same footing as other contracts, where it belongs. The need for the law arises from an anachronism of our American law. Some centuries ago, because of the jealousy of the English courts for their own jurisdiction, they refused to enforce specific agreements to arbitrate upon the ground that the courts were thereby ousted from their jurisdiction. This jealousy survived for so long a period that the principle became firmly embedded in the English common law and was adopted with it by the American courts. The courts have felt that the precedent was too strongly fixed to be overturned without legislative enactment, although they have frequently criticized the rule and recognized its illogical nature and the injustice which results from it. . . . [S]uch agreements for arbitration shall be enforced, and provides a procedure in the Federal courts for their enforcement. It is particularly appropriate that the action should be taken at this time when there is so much agitation against the cost-

liness and delays of litigation. These matters can be largely eliminated by agreements for arbitration, if arbitration agreements are made valid and enforceable.

In the light of the clear intention of Congress, it is our obligation to shake off the old judicial hostility to arbitration. Accordingly, in a case like this, involving the federal Act, we should not follow English or other decisions which have narrowly construed the terms of arbitration agreements or arbitration statutes. With this new orientation, we approach the problems here presented. . . .

c. Comments and Questions

a. The law school focus on legal rules can cause us to overlook the significance of common practices that are not sanctioned by the formal legal order. Arbitration was in common use for many centuries, particularly by merchants, despite the absence of legislative or judicial backing.

b. Prior to the enactment of the FAA in 1925, arbitration was governed by state law and local practice, which varied considerably from place to place and among different communities. A particularly valuable example is Bruce Mann, *The Formalization of Inform Law: Arbitration Before the American Revolution*, 59 N.Y.U. L. REV. 443 (1984) (focus on Connecticut). John R. Van Winkle, *An Analysis of the Arbitration Rule of the Indiana Rules of Alternative Dispute Resolution*, 27 IND. L. REV. 735 (1994) discusses the history of arbitration in Indiana, which enacted an arbitration statute in 1852.

c. Blackstone, writing in the 18th century, noted the widespread use of arbitration for commercial disputes, writing of "the great use of these peaceable and domestic tribunals, especially in settling matters of account and other mercantile transactions, which are difficult and almost impossible to be adjusted on a trial at law." WILLIAM BLACKSTONE, III COMMENTARIES 17 (1765).

d. Trade associations (and their predecessors, the guilds) have long required arbitration of all disputes among members. Members followed association rules and complied with arbitration awards, because expulsion from the association was a highly effective sanction. *See, e.g.,* Lisa Bernstein, *Opting Out of the Legal System: Extralegal Contractual Relations in the Diamond Industry*, 21 J. LEGAL STUD. 115 (1992).

e. The next selection reminds us that arbitration has long been in common use by merchants. The author, Soia Mentschikoff, was a distinguished commercial law scholar and the associate reporter for the original Uniform Commercial Code.

3. Soia Mentschikoff, *Commercial Arbitration*, 61 COLUM. L. REV. 846 (1961)

Mercantile disputes have been decided by merchants in the Anglo-American world since at least the thirteenth century. In the early period, the decision of mercantile cases was assigned to courts staffed by merchants, such as the piepowder courts or the staple courts, and the town courts, or merchant juries were utilized. The guilds and trading companies had their own tribunals. In the Tudor period, the Privy Council, a major forum for commercial matters, solved its mercantile cases by reference to merchant arbitrators. . . . Chancery referred its mercantile cases to arbitration, while the common law courts seemed to be using merchant juries. The Mayor's Court of London handled merchant cases. The trading companies emerged and had as a common feature provisions for resolution of disputes between members by the organization itself. Following the Restoration, the prerogative courts lost jurisdiction, but the common law courts seem not to have been used extensively by merchants. The guilds and trading companies continued, as did the city and borough courts. In 1697, an arbitration statute was enacted to render the awards of arbitrators "the more effectual in all cases." Forms for arbitration bonds and awards became readily available and legal textbooks on arbitrators were published. Clearly, it was the accepted method of resolving disputes arising out of accounts.

In the colonies, arbitration existed as a form of dispute settlement from the earliest period. In 1768, the New York Chamber of Commerce was founded with one of its purposes being the arbitration of disputes among its members. It was the sole civil tribunal to operate during the British occupation at the time of the revolution. In the nineteenth century, as trade became more specialized, exchanges were organized with arbitration provisions for their members. Later, trade associations come into the picture. Side-by-side with these self-contained trade group arbitrations were individual arrangements, and courts references of matters to arbitration which was sometimes conducted with the aid of local chambers of commerce. Always, however, merchants were involved as deciders, and always there were the two basic institutions — the self-contained trade groups and the forums open to everyone.

The development of arbitration in England and the United States was not completely parallel. The law of arbitration in the United States took a significantly different turn from the one it took in England. In England, the Common Law Procedure Act of 1854 specifically permitted arbitrators to refer matters for decision on the law to the courts by stating the arbitration [as a special case]. The Arbitration Act of 1889 permitted such submission of a special case to the court whenever the arbitrators were empowered to do so by the parties in their original submissions, or whenever the arbitrators felt it desirable. To this day, English arbitrators can and do submit awards in the form of a special case to the courts for final adjudication as to the substantive rules of law.

In the United States, however, if we take the law of New York as the most "progressive" example, it is clear that there was no similar development. The New York Legislature never provided a method by which arbitrators could have the aid of the courts in the disposition of a case on a substantive rule of law. In fact, the first of the so-called modern arbitration statutes, the New York Arbitration Act of 1920, made it clear that errors of law were not grounds for setting aside an arbitration award. This general position that the courts are not available for final determination of the legal issues in an arbitration was reemphasized by the Federal Arbitration Act of 1925 and is supported today by the Uniform Arbitration Act. The effect of this difference in law was that, in England, it was virtually impossible to develop the process that is known as "ad hoc" arbitration — arbitration without any precedential value. On the other hand, in the United States, except for the self-governing trade groups, the formal legal machinery made it difficult for anything other than ad hoc arbitration to develop. The most pressing legal questions concerning the enforceability of an arbitration award in the United States thus became questions of procedure. If the procedure followed by the arbitrators was correct, the award would be enforced. In England, both the procedure and the substance were subject to review.

4. Arbitration Legislation

Arbitration is governed by statutes at both the federal and state level. This means that analysis of any arbitration question must begin by taking account of the applicable legislation. Most arbitration statutes are short and general — like the United States Constitution — so many issues are addressed only in a general manner, if at all. This approach permits flexibility and adjustment to changing circumstances, but it also generates litigation about the meaning and application of the FAA and permits the meaning of the statute to change over time. This has allowed the federal courts, led by the Supreme Court, to dramatically expand the scope and meaning of the FAA in recent decades. For example, the Supreme Court changed its mind about the arbitrability of statutory claims, first denying and then authorizing (indeed, requiring arbitration of such claims). The leading cases involve securities law: *Wilko v. Swan*, 346 U.S. 427 (1963); *Shearson/American Express, Inc. v. McMahon*, 482 U.S. 220 (1987) (Distinguishing Wilko); *Rodriguez de Quijas v. Shearson/American Express, Inc.*, 490 U.S. 477 (1989) (overruling Wilko).

a. The Federal Arbitration Act (FAA)

The story of modern federal arbitration law begins with the enactment of the Federal Arbitration Act (FAA). 43 Stat. 883 (1925), *codified* at 9 U.S.C. §§ 1 *et. seq.* This statute was originally known as the United States Arbitration Act (USAA), but the modern usage of FAA is employed throughout these materials. The FAA was based on arbitration legislation enacted by New York State in 1920. The FAA and the New York statute were enacted due in important part to the active leadership and support of commercial interests.

The FAA has remained largely unchanged to the present day. Provisions for the enforcement of foreign arbitration awards were added to implement the Convention on the Recognition and Enforcement of Foreign Arbitral awards [New York Convention] and the Inter-American Convention on International Commercial Arbitration [Panama Convention].

Although the text of the (domestic) FAA has not changed materially, it has been interpreted expansively by the Supreme Court in recent decades, so that the scope and significance of arbitration has grown dramatically. In a series of decisions starting with *Prima Paint Corp. v. Flood & Conklin Mfg. Co.*, 388 U.S.

395 (1967), the Supreme Court has expanded the ambit of disputes subject to arbitration by upholding arbitration agreements and the subsequent arbitration awards against (almost) all challenges. The Court has read the FAA to largely preempt state law limitations on arbitration. Since 1983, the Supreme Court has decided an average of more than one arbitration decision per year. These decisions form the backbone of current arbitration law.

The response to the expansive judicial reading of the FAA has been just what one would expect: a dramatic rise in the use of arbitration, and a concomitant increase in the number of judicial proceedings that raise arbitration issues. During the last decade, the federal courts of appeals have decided over 150 arbitration cases per year. This figure is particularly impressive, because most cases arising under the FAA are heard by state rather than federal courts. The FAA created substantive federal law but not an independent basis for federal jurisdiction. *Moses H. Cone Memorial Hospital v. Mercury Construction Corp.,* 460 U.S. 1, 24-25 (1983).

b. The Uniform Arbitration Acts

After the enactment of the FAA, the National Conference of Commissioners on State Laws (NCCUSL), which has been drafting model uniform state laws since the 1890s, promptly promulgated a model state arbitration statute. This model act was not a success, being enacted in only six states (Nevada, North Carolina, Pennsylvania, Utah, Wisconsin, and Wyoming). By contrast, the second effort of the NCCUSL, the 1955 Uniform Arbitration Act (UAA), was a huge success. The UAA was promptly endorsed by the House of Delegates of the American Bar Association (ABA), which aided in the widespread adoption of the UAA by state legislatures. The provisions of the UAA closely track those in the FAA, a strategy intentionally (and wisely) chosen to promote widespread enactment of the proposed statute.

The NCCUSL claims the UAA as one of its most successful acts, with thirty-five states having enacted the UAA and another fourteen states having adopted similar statutes. Every state has enacted a general arbitration act, with Vermont in 1987 being the last to join the fold. For background on the enactment of the UAA, with a focus on developments in Minnesota, *see* Peter H. Berge, *The Uniform Arbitration Act: A Retrospective on Its Thirty-Fifth Anniversary*, 14 HAMLINE L. REV. 211 (1990). The state law predecessors of the UAA are discussed in Maynard Pirsig, *Some Comments on Arbitration Legislation and the Uniform Act*, 10 VAND. L. REV. 685 (1957).

The NCCUSL promulgated a Revised Uniform Arbitration Act (RUAA) at its August, 2000 annual meeting, after a five year drafting process that included extensive hearings, an exhaustive examination of issues associated with arbitration, and multiple drafts of the proposed statute. The RUAA includes extensive comments — like the Uniform Commercial Code (UCC), but unlike the UAA. The RUAA does not depart from the basic provisions of the UAA (or the FAA), but it covers a considerable number of topics not covered by the other statutes. These include:

1. Whether court or arbitrator determines arbitrability, and by what criteria;

2. Provisional remedies — court and arbitrator;

3. Initiation of arbitration proceedings;

4. Consolidation of arbitration proceedings;

5. Arbitrator disclosures;

6. Immunity from suit of arbitrators and arbitral organizations;

7. Testimony of arbitrators in other proceedings;

8. Power of arbitrators to manage the arbitration process, including discovery, protective orders, and summary disposition motions;

9. Judicial enforcement of pre-award rulings by arbitrators;

10. Remedial authority of arbitrators, especially attorney's fees and exemplary damages;

11. Award of fees and costs by courts to prevailing party and/or arbitrators; and

12. Specification of which RUAA provisions are waivable by contract.

These topics are clearly important, and a quality arbitration statute should address them. Coverage of these matters, together with the careful deliberative process that preceded the adoption of the RUAA, make the final draft statute "better" than the UAA (or the FAA) — at least, your authors think so. It does not necessarily follow, however, that the RUAA is an improvement over the status quo as measured by the central goal of the NCCUSL — uniform law among the states.

The UAA, whatever its imperfections, achieved the goal of national uniformity. Uniformity has two aspects: one is the adoption of some legislation on a topic, and the other is enactment of the same legislation. Both are required for uniformity, and the UAA has been a magnificent success in that regard. The immediate impact of the RUAA will be to decrease the national uniformity of state arbitration law, even if states limit their choices to retaining the UAA or enacting the RUAA. (One can argue that uniformity of state arbitration legislation is not an important or valuable objective, but doing so challenges the very *raison d'etre* of the NCCUSL.) In addition, the longer and more comprehensive the scope of a proposed statute, the greater is the chance that a state will adopt amendments, thereby rendering the legislation less uniform between states. Because the RUAA differs in material respects from the FAA, it cannot be argued on behalf of the RUAA — as it could on behalf of the UAA — that this proposed legislation is simply doing at the state level what the FAA already does at the federal level, thereby enhancing national uniformity.

As of late 2005, the RUAA had been enacted in 10 states: Alaska, Colorado, Hawaii, Nevada, New Jersey, New Mexico, North Carolina, North Dakota, Oregon, and Utah. Notably absent from these lists are all the major commercial states. For an update on RUAA enactments, see the NCCUSL web site, http://www.nccusl.org. Even if the RUAA is eventually adopted in all or most American jurisdictions — an unlikely scenario — there will be a period of reduced uniformity that will extend well into the 21st century.

c. Labor-Management Arbitration

Labor arbitration refers mainly to grievance arbitration pursuant to a collective bargaining agreement (CBA). Upon rare occasions, the parties agree to authorize an arbitrator to determine the substantive terms and conditions of employment, which is known as "interest arbitration." Arbitration of disputes between employers and employees outside the CBA context is "employment arbitration," and is governed by the FAA.

It is national policy to promote industrial self-government and industrial peace. Much of our present system grew out of the World War II experience, where industrial strife was an unacceptable threat to the success of the war effort. A War Labor Board (WLB) was created, with power to "finally determine" any labor dispute that might interfere with the war effort. The WLB encouraged resort to arbitration, and recognized the awards of arbitral tribunals. Since World War II, express provision for arbitration of grievances has been a standard feature of almost every CBA.

Section 301(a) of the 1947 Taft-Hartley Act amendments to the LMRA, 29 U.S.C. § 185(a), provides the (quite sketchy) statutory basis for labor arbitration, Section 301 states:

> Suits for violation of contracts between an employer and a labor organization representing employees in an industry affecting commerce . . . may be brought in any United States district court . . . having jurisdiction of the parties, without respect to the amount in controversy or . . . the citizenship of the parties.

This short and simple provision, which does not even mention arbitration, is the entire statutory basis for labor arbitration. (The FAA is detailed, by comparison.) Section 301 authorized federal courts to enforce the terms of CBAs, and provided a basis for the creation of substantive federal law — despite contrary state law. In *Textile Workers Union v. Lincoln Mills*, 353 U.S. 448 (1957), the Supreme Court ruled that a CBA provision calling for arbitration of grievances was, like other contract provisions, enforceable by the federal courts.

In 1960, the Supreme Court decided three cases that conclusively validated CBA grievance arbitration and adopted an extremely deferential posture toward such awards that left little place for judicial review. *United Steelworkers v. American Mfg. Co.*, 363 U.S. 564 (1960); *United Steelworkers v. Warrior & Gulf Navigation Co.*, 363 U.S. 574 (1960); and *United Steelworkers v. Enterprise Wheel & Car. Corp.*, 363 U.S. 593 (1960). These decisions, all authored by Justice Douglas and appearing on consecutive pages of the United States Reports, are universally known as "the Steelworkers Trilogy." Simply stated, the Supreme Court adopted the following principles:

1. The courts will enforce contractual promises to arbitrate, and will presume that the parties want the arbitrators to determine whether the parties agreed to arbitrate a type or class of disputes;

2. The courts should order arbitration without inquiring into the merits of the underlying grievance; and

3. The courts should enforce an arbitration award, so long as it can be said to have "drawn its essence" (the "essence" test) from the CBA.

The consequence was that labor arbitration has "passed from an awkward step-child of the courts to their favorite off-spring. With the Supreme Court in the lead, the federal courts lent their considerable support to arbitration agreements, to the arbitration process, and to the enforcement of resulting arbitration awards." LAURA J. COOPER, ET. AL., ADR IN THE WORKPLACE 15 (2005). For an overview of these developments, see two articles by Dennis R. Nolan and Roger I. Abrams, *American Labor Arbitration: The Early Years*, 35 U. FLA. L. REV. 373 (1983) and *American Labor Arbitration: The Maturing Years*, 35 U. FLA. L. REV. 557 (1983).

Labor and commercial arbitration have different histories, different traditions, and are based on different statutes. Even the alternatives to arbitration are fundamentally different: one provides a substitute forum for judicial proceedings, while the other is an alternative to industrial actions (a strike or lockout). Commercial arbitration represents a breakdown of the relationship between the parties, while grievance arbitration is just another skirmish within the framework of an on-going relationship.

5. An Overview of the Arbitration Process

This section considers the arbitration process itself, from the appointment of the arbitrator(s) to the end of the proceeding, including reconsideration of an initial arbitral decision. In some instances, the reconsideration is conducted at the behest of a court, after a challenge to the initial award by one of the parties.

We examine how the commercial arbitration process typically works — and arbitration nearly always does work. The focus of law school on "trouble cases" too easily causes us to lose sight of the fact that arbitration is a social process that is widely and successfully selected by consenting adults to settle disputes. The heavy reliance of teaching materials on appellate case law, while convenient and pedagogically useful, masks the success of contracts generally, and arbitration in particular, in ordering human affairs. Arbitration really does regularly produce rapid, inexpensive, fair, and expert disposition of disputes.

Nearly all the "law" of arbitration is applicable before an arbitration hearing commences or after it is completed, but not during the arbitration proceeding itself. Motions to recuse appointed arbitrators, requests for preliminary relief directed to a court or arbitrator, discovery, and similar matters are all held in abeyance until the arbitration is completed. Any concerns that arise during the arbitration proceeding must be timely objected to, on penalty of waiver.

[This is not so different from judicial proceedings; once a trial commences, interlocutory appeals are hardly ever permitted.]

An arbitration proceeding is like a judicial trial, only less so. To understand how arbitration works, begin by considering a civil jury trial. Then take away the jury. Next, eliminate the applicable rules of civil procedure and the law of evidence. Finally, replace the generalist judge with an arbitrator with subject matter and/or industry expertise. Unlike judges, arbitrators frequently are not lawyers. A useful analogy is found in adjudication conducted by an Administrative Judge under the Administrative Procedure Act (APA), 5 U.S.C. §§ 551, *et. seq.*

There are, of course, important similarities between a trial judge and an arbitrator. Most important, each hears evidence presented by the parties and then renders a (nearly always final) decision that is binding on the parties. [Nonbinding arbitration is an exception that has no judicial analogue, because courts are normally prohibited from issuing advisory opinions.] Both judges and arbitrators are accorded respect by participants, and they are very much in charge of the proceedings. Ex parte contacts are forbidden (with limited exceptions for party arbitrators). Witnesses are sworn. Like in a judicial trial, there is cross-examination after the initial testimony of the witness. The presentation of evidence is more like an APA proceeding than a judicial trial — live testimony is commonly truncated, and far greater reliance is placed on written submissions.

There are also important differences between arbitrators and judges. Arbitrators do not wear costumes — no robes or wigs. Arbitrations take place in whatever location is available: a law office, a hotel conference room, or on business premises — there is not a dedicated location like a court room. Arbitrators are ad hoc deciders, while judges are full-time deciders. Arbitrators are experienced professionals, but often, they are not lawyers. Pre-trial conferences and similar proceedings are used in arbitration, but much less so than in the judicial context. Discovery takes place entirely at the discretion of the arbitrator (unless the contract between the parties includes a provision regarding the availability, vel non, of discovery). Three-member arbitration panels are common, whereas trials are conducted by a single judge.

One major difference between the role of judge and arbitrator remains. The judge fills an office that has a continuous existence and exists independently of the role the incumbent who temporarily fills that office. The arbitrator, by contrast, is appointed to hear a specific dispute, and fills a temporary role. (An individual can be named as the arbitrator for all disputes between two parties — the term "umpire" often is used — but this arrangement is uncommon outside the labor-management context.) The authority of the arbitrator terminates with the issuance of a final opinion in a particular dispute, which fact is the basis for the doctrine of *functus officio*. This structural difference between the position of arbitrator and judge has great practical significance.

Both arbitrators and judges rule on requests to exclude or limit evidence, but this similarity is more apparent than real. Arbitrators rarely exclude any evidence, and repeated requests to that end will only irritate the arbitrators and undermine a client's case. [The one exception is for privileged information.] In arbitration, all questions regarding proffered evidence go to its weight, and none to its admissibility. Among the very few grounds for vacating an arbitration award is that the arbitrators refused to hear "evidence pertinent and material to the controversy. . . ." FAA, § 10(a)(3). Trial court judges can have their decisions reversed for admitting too much or too little evidence. Arbitration awards, by contrast, can be vacated only for the exclusion of material evidence. The response of arbitrators and arbitral organizations is entirely predictable: the exclusionary rules that law students examine at length in the course on Evidence are ignored, and almost everything is admitted into evidence.

6. Judicial Review of Arbitration Awards Is Extremely Limited

The few grounds for judicial review of final arbitration awards are specified in the FAA. The relevant provisions of the UAA (1955) and RUAA (2000) closely track those of the FAA, so the standards of review — albeit not necessarily the judicial interpretation thereof — are usually the same under state and federal law. Two non-statutory grounds for review are widely recognized: manifest disregard of the law and public policy, but the public policy exception is narrow.

Courts rarely vacate arbitration awards; the legal barriers to getting an award overturned are higher than for judicial decisions. Judicial review of arbitration awards is *extremely* limited, and courts vacate arbitration awards infrequently. This approach is reflected not only in legal doctrine, but also in the basic attitude of judges toward challenges of arbitration awards. Even more striking, this approach has been the law in America for over 150 years — long before the courts enforced agreements to arbitrate. Apart from the absence of citations to the FAA, Justice Grier's opinion in *Burchell v. Marsh* might have been written this year instead of 1854. *See, e.g., Moncharsh v. Heily & Blase,* 832 P.2d 899 (Cal. 1992). For some empirical data, see Lawrence R. Mills, J. Lani Bader, Thomas J. Brewer & Peggy J. Williams, *Vacating Arbitration Awards: Study Reveals Real-World Odds of Success,* DISP. RES. J. 23 (2005). These real world odds are long indeed.

a. *Burchell v. Marsh*, 58 U.S. 344 [17 How. 344] (1854)

Mr. Justice GRIER delivered the opinion of the court.

The appellees . . . pray the court to set aside an award made between the parties, as "fraudulent and void." The bill charges that "the award was made either from improper and corrupt motives, with the design of favoring," said Burchell, "or in ignorance of the rights of the parties to said submission, and of the duties and powers of the arbitrators who signed the said award." The answer . . . avers that they acted justly, fairly, and with a due consideration of the rights of the parties. . . .

The general principles upon which courts of equity interfere to set aside [arbitration] awards are too well settled by numerous decisions to admit of doubt. . . . Arbitrators are judges chosen by the parties to decide the matters submitted to them, finally and without appeal. As a mode of settling disputes, it should receive every encouragement from courts of equity. If the award is within the submission, and contains the honest decision of the arbitrators, after a full and fair hearing of the parties, a court of equity will not set it aside for error, either in law or fact. A contrary course would be a substitution of the judgment of the chancellor in place of the judges chosen by the parties, and would make an award the commencement, not the end, of litigation. In order . . . to induce the court to interfere, there must be something more than an error of judgment, such as corruption in the arbitrator, or gross mistake, either apparent on the face of the award, or to be made out by evidence; but in case of mistake, it must be made out to the satisfaction of the arbitrator, and that if it had not happened, he should have made a different award. . . .

Courts should be careful to avoid a wrong use of the word "mistake," and by making it synonymous with mere error of judgment, assume to themselves an arbitrary power over awards. The same result would follow if the court should treat the arbitrators as guilty of corrupt partiality, merely because their award is not such a one as the chancellor would have given. We are all too prone, perhaps, to impute either weakness of intellect or corrupt motives to those who differ with us in opinion.

The submission recites that controversies and disputes had arisen between the firm of March and Freer, and of Freer and Arbuckle, with Burchell. It states the controversies to have arisen from suits brought by said firms against Burchell, to recover certain debts claimed to be due by him to the firms, respectively, and the said Burchell claims to have sustained damages by reason of having been sued by said firms and by reason of the doings of the said firms towards him. On the hearing, the arbitrators received evidence of the debts alleged to be due from Burchell to the two firms, and of the alleged oppressive and ruinous suits brought against him by one Cross, who acted as agent of the firms. The witnesses, in proving these transactions, were permitted to state certain slanderous language used by Cross in speaking to and of Burchell, charging him with dishonesty and perjury.

It has been argued that, because the arbitrators received evidence of the slanderous language used by Cross, they included in their award damages for his slanders, for which his principals would not be liable; and therefore, they had taken into consideration matters not contained in the submission. But the answer to this allegation is that the record shows no admission or proof the arbitrators allowed any damages for the slanders of Cross. Whether the complainants were liable, and how far they were justly answerable for the conduct of their agent, were questions of law and fact submitted to the arbitrators. All these questions were fully argued before them by counsel. Whether their decision on them was erroneous does not appear. The transactions which were testified to, with regard to the suits brought against Burchell, and whether they were oppressive, wrongful, and ruinous to him, was one of the very matters submitted to the arbitrators. The words, as well as the acts, of Cross made part of the *res gestae*, and could not well be severed in giving a history of them.

Every presumption is in favor of the validity of the award. If it had stated an account, by which it appeared that the arbitrators had made a specific allowance of damages for the slanders of Cross, it would have been annulled, to that extent at least, as beyond the submission. But it cannot be inferred that the arbitrators went beyond the submission, merely because they may have admitted illegal evidence about the subject matter of it. We are of opinion, therefore, that there is nothing on the record to show that the arbitrators, in making this award, exceeded their authority, or went beyond the limits of the submission.

The charges of fraud, corruption, or improper conduct in the arbitrators are wholly denied by the answer, which must be assumed to be true, unless facts are admitted from which they are a necessary or legal inference. We can see nothing in the admitted facts of the case from which any such inference can be justly made. The damages allowed for the alleged oppression of Burchell, and the ruin of his business as a merchant may seem large to some, while others may think the sum of four or even five thousand dollars as no extravagant compensation for such injuries. It may be admitted, that, on the facts appearing on the face of the record, this court would not have assessed damages to so large an amount, nor have divided them so arbitrarily between the parties; but we cannot say that the estimate of the arbitrators is so outrageous as of itself to constitute conclusive evidence of fraud or corruption. Damages for injuries of this sort cannot be measured by any rules, nor can the court properly impute corruption to others, because they differ with them in their estimation of a matter which depends on discretion rather than calculation. It is enough that the parties have agreed to trust the discretion and judgment of neighbors acquainted with them, and their relative standing and credit.

The admission of witnesses to prove their estimate of the damages (even if it had been in the face of the objection of counsel, and not by consent) may have been an error in judgment, but it is no cause for setting aside the award; nor can the admission of illegal evidence, or taking the opinion of third persons, be alleged as a misbehavior in the arbitrators which will affect their award. If they have given their honest, incorrupt judgment on the subject matters submitted to them, after a full and fair hearing of the parties, they are bound by it; and a court of chancery has no right to annul their award because it thinks it could have made a better one.

b. *Perini Corp. v. Greate Bay Hotel & Casino, Inc.,* 610 A.2d 364 (N.J. 1992), concurring opinion by Chief Justice Wilenz, adopted as the governing law of New Jersey in *Tretina Printing, Inc. v. Fitzpatrich & Assoc.,* 640 A.2d 788 (N.J. 1994)

People generally choose arbitration for many reasons: speed, economy, and finality. They trust the process, and they trust arbitrators. Whatever the combination of reasons, the bottom line is the same: they choose arbitration, because they do not want litigation. When parties choose arbitration, the role that the judiciary should aim at is to have no role at all. The courts are not the sole repository of justice. The parties too want justice, but they look solely to the arbitrators and to the process of arbitration to achieve it. That is their right, and the courts have no right to take it away from them. Will they achieve better justice from them? That is not for us to decide. That's their decision to make, theirs alone.

7. The Supreme Court Strongly Favors Arbitration

a. Comments and Questions

a. Supreme Court arbitration decisions in recent decades have been strongly supportive of arbitration and decisions by arbitrators. This trend has drawn powerful criticism from some judges and many academic commentators, notably in the context of consumer and employment arbitration.

b. The *Cardegna* decision, the latest word on arbitration from the Supreme Court, is highly supportive of and deferential to the arbitration process. In adopting this approach, the Court continued an almost unbroken trend over the last quarter of a century.

c. In *Cardegna*, the Attorneys-General of 42 jurisdictions (40 states plus the District of Columbia and Puerto Rico) submitted a joint amicus brief asking the Supreme Court not to use the FAA as a club to defeat the application of state consumer protection laws. This extraordinary document — rarely do officials from so many American jurisdictions agree in writing on anything — did not receive so much as a mention from the Supreme Court. The Court's opinion in *Cardegna* is short and dismissive of all challenges to arbitration and the preemptive effect of the FAA.

b. *Buckeye Check Cashing, Inc. v. Cardegna,* 126 S. Ct. 1204 (2006)

Justice SCALIA delivered the opinion of the Court.

We decide whether a court or an arbitrator should consider the claim that a contract containing an arbitration provision is void for illegality. Respondents John Cardegna and Donna Reuter entered into various deferred-payment transactions with petitioner Buckeye Check Cashing (Buckeye), in which they received cash in exchange for a personal check in the amount of the cash plus a finance charge. For each separate transaction, they signed a "Deferred Deposit and Disclosure Agreement" (Agreement), which included [an] arbitration provision. . . .

Respondents brought this putative class action in Florida state court, alleging that Buckeye charged usurious interest rates and that the Agreement violated various Florida lending and consumer protection laws, rendering it criminal on its face. Buckeye moved to compel arbitration. The trial court denied the motion, holding that a court, rather than an arbitrator, should resolve a claim that a contract is illegal and void *ab initio*. [A Florida] Court of Appeal reversed, holding that, because respondents did not challenge the arbitration provision itself, but instead claimed that the entire contract was void, the agreement to arbitrate was enforceable, and the question of the contract's legality should go to the arbitrator. Respondents appealed, and the Florida Supreme Court reversed, reasoning that to enforce an agreement to arbitrate in a contract challenged as unlawful "could breathe life into a contract that not only violates state law, but also is criminal in nature." We granted certiorari.

To overcome judicial resistance to arbitration, Congress enacted the Federal Arbitration Act (FAA), 9 U.S.C. §§ 1-16. Section 2 embodies the national policy favoring arbitration and places arbitration agreements on equal footing with all other contracts:

> A written provision in . . . a contract . . . to settle by arbitration a controversy thereafter arising out of such contract . . . or an agreement in writing to submit to arbitration an existing controversy arising out of such a contract . . . shall be valid, irrevocable, and enforceable, save upon such grounds as exist at law or in equity for the revocation of any contract.

Challenges to the validity of arbitration agreements "upon such grounds as exist at law or in equity for the revocation of any contract" can be divided into two types. One type challenges specifically the validity of the agreement to arbitrate. *See, e.g., Southland Corp. v. Keating,* 465 U.S. 1, 4-5, (1984) (challenging the agreement to arbitrate as void under California law insofar as it purported to cover claims brought under the state Franchise Investment Law). The other challenges the contract as a whole, either on a ground that directly affects the entire agreement (*e.g.,* the agreement was fraudulently induced), or on the ground that the illegality of one of the contract's provisions renders the whole contract invalid. Respondents' claim is of this second type. The crux of the complaint is that the contract as a whole (including its arbitration provision) is rendered invalid by the usurious finance charge.

The issue of the contract's validity is different from the issue of whether any agreement between the alleged obligor and obligee was ever concluded. Our opinion today addresses only the former, and does not speak to the issue decided in the cases cited by respondents . . . which hold that it is for courts to decide whether the alleged obligor ever signed the contract, *Chastain v. Robinson-Humphrey Co.,* 957 F.2d 851 (C.A.11 1992); whether the signor lacked authority to commit the alleged principal, *Sandvik AB v. Advent Int'l Corp.,* 220 F.3d 99 (C.A.3 2000); *Sphere Drake Ins. Ltd. v. All American Ins. Co.,* 256 F.3d 587 (C.A.7 2001); and whether the signor lacked the mental capacity to assent, *Spahr v. Secco,* 330 F.3d 1266 (C.A.10 2003).

In *Prima Paint Corp. v. Flood & Conklin Mfg. Co.,* 388 U.S. 395 (1967), we addressed the question of who — court or arbitrator — decides these two types of challenges. The issue in the case was "whether a claim of fraud in the inducement of the entire contract is to be resolved by the federal court, or whether the matter is to be referred to the arbitrators." We held that "if the claim is fraud in the inducement of the arbitration clause itself — an issue which goes to the making of the agreement to arbitrate — the federal court may proceed to adjudicate it. But the statutory language does not permit the federal court to consider claims of fraud in the inducement of the contract generally." We rejected the view that the question of "severability" was one of state law, so that if state law held the arbitration provision not to be severable, a challenge to the contract as a whole would be decided by the court.

In *Southland Corp.,* we held that the FAA "create[d] a body of federal substantive law," which was "applicable in state and federal court." 465 U.S., at 12. We rejected the view that state law could bar enforcement of § 2, even in the context of state-law claims brought in state court. *See also Allied-Bruce Terminix Cos. v. Dobson,* 513 U.S. 265, 270-273 (1995).

Prima Paint and *Southland* answer the question presented here by establishing three propositions. First, as a matter of substantive federal arbitration law, an arbitration provision is severable from the remainder of the contract. Second, unless the challenge is to the arbitration clause itself, the issue of the contract's validity is considered by the arbitrator in the first instance. Third, this arbitration law applies in state as well as federal courts. The parties have not requested, and we do not undertake, reconsideration of those holdings. Applying them to this case, we conclude that, because respondents challenge the Agreement, but not specifically its arbitration provisions, those provisions are enforceable apart from the remainder of the contract. The challenge should, therefore, be considered by an arbitrator, not a court.

In declining to apply *Prima Paint's* rule of severability, the Florida Supreme Court relied on the distinction between void and voidable contracts. "Florida public policy and contract law," it concluded, permit "no severable, or salvageable, parts of a contract found illegal and void under Florida law." *Prima Paint* makes this conclusion irrelevant. That case rejected application of state severability rules to the arbitration agreement *without discussing* whether the challenge at issue would have rendered the contract void or voidable. Indeed, the opinion expressly disclaimed any need to decide what state-law remedy was available, though Justice Black's dissent *asserted* that state law rendered the contract void. Likewise, in *Southland,* which arose in state court, we did not ask whether the several challenges made there — fraud, misrepresentation, breach of contract, breach of fiduciary duty, and violation of the California Franchise Investment Law — would render the contract void or voidable. We simply rejected the proposition that the enforceability of the arbitration agreement turned on the state legislature's judgment concerning the forum for enforcement of the state-law cause of action. So also here, we cannot accept the Florida Supreme Court's conclusion that enforceability of the arbitration agreement should turn on "Florida public policy and contract law."

Respondents assert that *Prima Paint's* rule of severability does not apply in state court. They argue that *Prima Paint* interpreted only §§ 3 and 4 — two of the FAA's procedural provisions, which appear to apply by their terms only in federal court — but not § 2, the only provision that we have applied in state court. This does not accurately describe *Prima Paint.* Although § 4, in particular, had much to do with *Prima Paint's* understanding of the rule of severability, *see* 388 U.S., at 403-404, this rule ultimately arises out of § 2, the FAA's substantive command that arbitration agreements be treated like all other contracts. The rule of severability establishes how this equal-footing guarantee for "a written [arbitration] provision" is to be implemented. Respondents' reading of *Prima Paint* as establishing nothing more than a federal-court rule of procedure also runs contrary to *Southland*'s understanding of that case. One of the bases for *Southland*'s application of § 2 in state court was precisely *Prima Paint*'s "reli[ance] for [its] holding on Congress' broad power to fashion substantive rules under the Commerce Clause." 465 U.S., at 11, *see also Prima Paint,* at 407 (Black, J., dissenting) ("[t]he Court here holds that the [FAA], as a matter of *federal substantive law . . .*" (emphasis added)). *Southland* itself refused to "believe Congress intended to limit the Arbitration Act to disputes subject only to *federal*-court jurisdiction."

Respondents point to the language of § 2, which renders "valid, irrevocable, and enforceable" a written provision or an agreement in writing to submit to arbitration an existing controversy arising out of a "contract." Since, respondents argue, the only arbitration agreements to which § 2 applies are those involving a "contract," and since an agreement void *ab initio* under state law is not a "contract," there is no "written provision" in or "controversy arising out of" a "contract," to which § 2 can apply. This argument echoes Justice Black's dissent in *Prima Paint:* "Sections 2 and 3 of the Act assume the existence of a valid contract. They merely provide for enforcement where such a valid contract exists." 388 U.S., at 412-413. We do not read "contract" so narrowly. The word appears four times in § 2. Its last appearance is in the final clause, which allows a challenge to an arbitration provision "upon such grounds as exist at law or in equity for the revocation of any *contract*." (Emphasis added.) There can be no doubt that "contract" as used this last time must include contracts that later prove to be void. Otherwise, the grounds for revocation would be limited to those that rendered a contract voidable — which would mean (implausibly) that an arbitration agreement could be challenged as voidable but not as void. Because the sentence's final use of "contract" so obviously includes putative contracts, we will not read the same word earlier in the same sentence to have a more narrow meaning. We note that neither *Prima Paint* nor *Southland* lend support to respondents' reading; as we have discussed, neither case turned on whether the challenge at issue would render the contract voidable or void.

Our more natural reading is confirmed by the use of the word "contract" elsewhere in the United States Code to refer to putative agreements, regardless of whether they are legal. For instance, the Sherman Act states that "[e]very contract, combination. . . , or conspiracy in restraint of trade . . . is hereby declared to be illegal." 15 U.S.C. § 1. Under respondents' reading of "contract," a bewildering circularity would result: A contract illegal because it was in restraint of trade would not be a "contract" at all, and thus, the statutory prohibition would not apply.

It is true, as respondents assert, that the *Prima Paint* rule permits a court to enforce an arbitration agreement in a contract that the arbitrator later finds to be void. But it is equally true that respondents' approach permits a court to deny effect to an arbitration provision in a contract that the court later finds to be perfectly enforceable. *Prima Paint* resolved this conundrum — and resolved it in favor of the separate enforceability of arbitration provisions. We reaffirm today that, regardless of whether the challenge is brought in federal or state court, a challenge to the validity of the contract as a whole, and not specifically to the arbitration clause, must go to the arbitrator.

D. COLLABORATIVE LAW

1. What is Collaborative Law?

Collaborative law (CL) is based on conventional lawyering, with a twist: the lawyers may act as settlement counsel but not as litigation counsel. This is achieved through a collective agreement among counsel and their clients that, if the represented parties do not settle the dispute, then the lawyers must withdraw and different trial counsel be hired. Note that both parties are represented by counsel, and a second set of counsel will be required in the event of trial, so collaborative law does represent a low cost approach to divorce. Collaborative law has arisen largely in the family dissolution context, but the same principles could be applied to many other types of disputes. It remains to be seen whether CL will be adopted with any frequency outside of the family law arena.

Collaborative law can be viewed as a solution to the Prisoner's Dilemma aspect of attempting to settle family disputes short of litigation. While the parties and their counsel can commit to such an approach, the Prisoner's Dilemma suggests that there are rewards for defecting from a promised cooperative posture and, instead, engaging in competitive bargaining. As for counsel, she is obliged to follow the lead of the client. The obligation of counsel to withdraw if the dispute does not settle, largely (but not entirely) eliminates enticements for strategic behavior. The collaborative law process is similar to interest based bargaining, aided by creative problem solving.

Useful recent articles about collaborative law include the following: Gay G. Cox & Robert J. Matlock, *The Case for Collaborative Law*, 11 TEX. WESLEYAN L. REV. 45 (2004); Christopher M. Fairman, *A Proposed Model Rule for Collaborative Law*, 21 OHIO ST. J. ON DISP. RESOL. 73 (2005); David A. Hoffman, *Collaborative Law: A Practitioner's Perspective*, 12 DISP. RESOL. MAG. 25 (Fall 2005); Joshua Issacs, *A New Way to Avoid the Courtroom: The Ethical Implications Surrounding Collaborative Law*, 18 GEO. J. LEGAL ETHICS 833 (2005); John Lande, *Possibilities for Collaborative Law: Ethics and Practice of Lawyer Disqualification and Process Control in a New Model of Lawyering*, 64 OHIO ST. L.J. 1315 (2003); Julie McFarlane, *Experiences of Collaborative Law: Preliminary Result From the Collaborative Lawyering Research Project*, 2004 DISP. RESOL. J. 179 (2004); SCOTT R. PEPPET, LAWYERS' BARGAINING ETHICS, CONTRACT, AND COLLABORATION: THE END OF THE LEGAL PROFESSION AND THE BEGINNING OF PROFESSIONAL PLURALISM 479 (2005); William A. Schwab, *Collaborative Lawyering: A Closer Look at an Emerging Practice*, 4 PEPP. DISP. RESOL. J. 351 (2004); Larry R. Spain, *Collaborative Law: A Critical Reflection on Whether a Collaborative Law Orientation Can be Ethically Incorporated Into the Practice of Law*, 56 BAYLOR L. REV. 141, 158-72 (2004); Elizabeth Z. Strickland, *Putting "Counselor" Back in the Lawyer's Job Description: Why More States Should Adopt Collaborative Law Statutes*, 84 N.C. L. REV. 979 (2006); Pauline H. Tessler, *Collabora-*

tive Family Law, 4 PEPP. DISP. RESOL. L.J. 317 (2004). This far from exclusive list of recent articles about collaborative law, including writings by some of the leading dispute resolution scholars, makes it clear that collaborative law is much more than a passing fancy.

2. A Movement Within the ADR Movement

Collaborative law is a "movement" within the ADR movement, and it has been widely adopted since its inception circa 1990. Professor Fairman reports that, as of 2004, there were more than 4,500 lawyers trained in collaborative law. Eighty-seven distinct collaborative law practice groups exist, and collaborative law is practiced in at least 35 states. It flourishes in certain jurisdictions, including Minnesota, Ohio, Connecticut, Texas, Georgia, and the Canadian provinces. Even cursory Internet searches turn up a bevy of collaborative law websites. Professor Lande reports "more than 150 local CL practice groups, which develop local practice protocols, train practitioners, build demand for CL, and form referral networks." John Lande, *The Promise and Perils of Collaborative Law*, 12 DISP. RESOL. MAG. 29 (Fall 2005). Some lawyers are engaging in collaborative arrangements, but without a provision for mandatory withdrawal in the event of litigation, a process some call "cooperative law."

There is a major empirical research study of collaborative mediation underway in the United States and Canada. For an early report, see Julie McFarlane, *Experiences of Collaborative Law. Preliminary Results From the Collaborative Lawyering Research Project*, 2004 J. DISP. RESOL. 179. Among the many interesting questions that the study seeks to address are:

1. Does CL allow clients and lawyers to escape the Prisoner's Dilemma?

2. Can CL enable open disclosure and the development of sufficient trust to produce less hostile negotiations?

3. Do CL clients enjoy qualitatively better outcomes than from other processes?

3. Mediation and Collaborative Law

Professor McFarlane suggests that part of the impetus behind the collaborative law movement is that the hegemony of lawyers is threatened by expanded resort to mediation.

> CL lawyers are reluctant to acknowledge this. However, a number of CL lawyers do explain their interest in CL as deriving from a disappointment in the earlier promise of mediation, and a desire to actually utilize skills they learned in mediation training programs. ... Generally, however, non-lawyer mediators appear to display a higher level of anxiety over CL than CL lawyers do over mediation. However, this is probably no more than a reflection of the relative professional power between the two groups.

Id. at 215-16. The "sibling rivalry" between collaborative law and mediation needs to be addressed, else there be a schism between two closely related activities that should be supporting one another. Lawyers need to understand that every move toward regulation and professionalization in the ADR arena is seen by other providers of services as an attempt to exclude them. Giving the expansive interpretation and vigorous policing of "unauthorized practice of law" over the decades by state bar associations throughout the nation, such fears are plainly justified.

4. Potential Professional Responsibility Issues Associated With Collaborative Law

Larry Spain discusses no fewer than seven "ethical dilemmas" that are posed by collaborative law. These are (in the order he considers them):

1. Scope of Representation

2. Informed Consent

3. Withdrawal of Counsel

4. Limitations on Zealous Representation

5. Confidentiality

6. Competence of Counsel

7. Conflict of Interest

Christopher M. Fairman, *A Proposed Model Rule for Collaborative Law*, 21 OHIO ST. J. ON DISP. RESOL. 73, 94-96 (2005) discusses four ethical issues associated with collaborative law:

1. Duty of Loyalty (Zealous Advocacy)

2. Duty of Candor and Truthfulness to Others

3. Rules Governing Termination of Representation

4. Duty of Confidentiality

In the end, the writers about the ethical issues agree that collaborative law agreements are not unethical, albeit grudgingly. Fairman concludes that collaborative law "probably can be shoehorned into an ill-fitting pair of ethical shoes." On the merits, Fairman supports collaborative law, finding it to be "squarely in the mainstream of nonadversarial ADR techniques" and its practice "an ethically appropriate representational role for an attorney." (p. 122) Spain, after an extended tour of the ethical issues raised by collaborative law, states that the "complexity of these issues should not deter lawyers" but they should give "careful attention to ethical issues that may arise." (p. 173)

Already in 1984, Professor Riskin pointed out that the behavioral standards for lawyers are based on litigation, and do not take adequate account of lawyers who engage in ADR activities. Leonard L. Riskin, *Toward New Standards for the Neutral Lawyer in Mediation*, 26 ARIZ. L. REV. 329 (1984). It is readily apparent that this problem is particularly acute with collaborative law. Robert C. Bordone, *Fitting the Ethics to the Forum: A Proposal for Process-Enabling Ethical Codes*, 21 OHIO ST. J. ON DISP. RESOL. 1 (2005) calls for different ethical rules for different activities. A similar approach is recommended by Scott R. Peppet, Lawyers' Bargaining Ethics, Contract, and Collaboration: The End of the Legal Profession and the Beginning of Professional Pluralism 479 (2005). As ever in the law, there are costs and benefits to both generality and detail, bright line rules and general standards. What do you think should be done with respect to collaborative law?

5. State Action in Support of Collaborative Law

Three approaches present themselves: legislation, state bar ethics opinions, and an explicit provision in the rules governing the conduct of lawyers. The last two approaches would not govern the conduct of collaborative law participants other than lawyers. State bar opinions have been issued in Kentucky, North Carolina, and Pennsylvania, but each is equivocal. The good news for advocates and practitioners is that none rejected the use of collaborative law as unethical. Ky. Bar Ass'n Eth. Comm., Op. E-425 (2005); N.C. Formal Eth. Op. 1 (2002), 2002 WL 2029469; Pa. Bar Ass'n Comm. Leg. Eth. & Prof. Resp., Informal Op. 2004-24, 2004 WL 2758094. For discussion of the Kentucky opinion, see *Concept of Collaborative Lawyering Receives Qualified Approval in Kentucky*, 21 ABA/BNA LAW. MANUAL ON PROF. CONDUCT 453 (2005).

An apparent solution to the professional conduct concerns would be an express provision in the ABA's Model Rules of Professional Conduct. States could act unilaterally, but the Model Rules approach would allow for uniformity. Since the rules of professional conduct in most states are based on the Model Rules, many states are likely to follow the ABA's lead. Of course, there has not been a proposal from the ABA, and amendments to the Model Rules are neither common nor quickly adopted. As more states take action, and the widespread use of collaborative law in the family law context continues to grow, the likelihood of uniformity becomes ever less likely.

Christopher M. Fairman, *A Proposed Model Rule for Collaborative Law*, 21 OHIO ST. J. ON DISP. RESOL. 73, 117-118 (2005) proposes a model rule titled The Collaborative Lawyer that expressly authorizes lawyers to engage in collaborative law.

(a) A lawyer may serve as a collaborative lawyer. Collaborative law is a procedure in which the parties and their lawyers agree to use their best efforts and participate in good faith to resolve a dispute on an agreed basis without resorting to judicial intervention. An agreement to use collaborative law must be the result of informed consent, confirmed in writing, with terms that can be reasonably understood by the parties, and signed by all parties and their lawyers.

(b) A collaborative lawyer shall be competent by training and experience to engage in collaborative representation.

(c) While all collaborative lawyers engaged in resolving a dispute share a common commitment to the collaborative law process, a collaborative lawyer represents the client who has retained the collaborative lawyer's services.

(d) A collaborative lawyer shall facilitate the resolution of all issues in the dispute using cooperative strategies, instead of adversarial techniques. A collaborative lawyer shall not initiate or threaten to initiate any contested court procedure.

(e) A collaborative lawyer shall make a voluntary, full, honest, and open disclosure of all relevant information that a reasonable decision maker would need to make an informed decision about each issue in the dispute.

(f) All information arising from and relating to a collaborative representation is confidential, including any written or verbal communication or analysis of any third-party experts used in the collaborative law process.

(g) A collaborative lawyer shall withdraw from representation if: (1) either party chooses to litigate; (2) the parties do not reach a settlement. . . ; or (3) either party knowingly withholds or misrepresents information having a material bearing on the case or otherwise acts to undermine the collaborative law process. Following withdrawal, the collaborative lawyer shall assist the clients in selection of new counsel.

The Texas collaborative law legislation is found at the end of Appendix D, with the Texas ADR Act. Note that the Texas statute is part of the Family Code rather than the general ADR Act. By contrast, Professor Fairman's proposed legislation would have general applicability, rather than being limited to family law matters.

E. OMBUDSPERSONS: GOVERNMENT AND CORPORATE

1. Philip J. Harter, *Ombuds: A Voice For the People*, 11 DISP. RESOL. MAG. 5 (Winter 2005)

The modern version of ombuds started 200 years ago in Sweden when the Parliament appointed an overseer — the *Justitieombudsmän* — to ensure that the royal officers obeyed the law. That action followed by a century the King himself appointing someone for the same purpose. Since then, ombuds have sprouted in all sorts of institutions, and they are now a varied lot. A number of them, especially in emerging democracies, are designed to protect civil rights and human dignity.

The Comptroller General of the United States — a de facto ombuds — investigates on behalf of Congress to ensure that the executive branch performs adequately. Government agencies themselves have established similar offices to investigate allegations of wrongdoing or to receive and process complaints over maladministration. Companies, likewise, have created ombuds to field complaints, to work out difficult issues in the workplace, and in this era of corporate scandals, to provide a means by which insiders can call potentially difficult issues to the attention of senior management. Newspapers have ombuds to serve as "watchdogs" on behalf of the public. Other ombuds investigate complaints filed on behalf of vulnerable people, and if the facts merit, these ombuds become advocates for redressing wrongs and securing change. . . .

Given the extraordinary variety of issues ombuds address, two logical questions arise: Just what do these people called ombuds have in common, and how do they function? At bottom, an ombuds is authorized to receive complaints and questions from a defined constituency about issues within the ombuds's jurisdiction. To a very real extent, the foundation of the process is the ombuds's charter that defines the nature of the duties and the people to whom the office responds. For example, the traditional ombuds that is created by a legislature hears complaints from the citizens about the activities of the executive, whereas in a company, it may be that an ombuds would hear only complaints from employees about designated issues or from customers. It is essential to define this jurisdiction — who complains and what is complained about — in advance and in a publicly available document. . . . Unlike a court, the ombuds customarily has discretion . . . to investigate without waiting for someone to complain.

The ombuds then develops sufficient information and takes appropriate action, such as issuing a report (which may or may not be public depending on the circumstances) with recommendations, raising the issue to an appropriate level within the organization, working out an agreement addressing the issue, or providing information so that the complainant can take individual action. An ombuds is not, however, limited to addressing only individual complaints. Because the ombuds is in a position to see trends or patterns, the ombuds frequently will point out systemic or general problems or issues. An ombuds does not have authority to compel action of any sort, however.

An ombuds office must possess three essential characteristics to function effectively and with integrity: (1) It must be independent from control of anyone who may be the subject of a complaint or inquiry. Were it otherwise, the ombuds would not be likely to take strong, appropriate action. (2) The ombuds must conduct investigations or inquiries in an impartial manner, without bias or preconceived orientations. Once the facts are determined, however, the ombuds may become an advocate for securing appropriate change. (3) The ombuds must not voluntarily disclose matters provided in confidence, and the establishing institution needs to assure the ombuds and those using the office that it will not seek anything provided confidentially. Were it otherwise, those who come to the office could be badly hurt. These are characteristics that all ombuds should share, regardless of where they are located, how they function, or which subjects they address. . . .

An ombuds obviously has a complex relationship with the institution in which it works. Often, it is an in-house goad whose job is to make sure that those in authority abide by the rules. In the words of one charter, the ombuds is to investigate abuse or unjustifiable exercise of power or unfair, capricious, discourteous, or other improper conduct or undue delay and to rectify any act or omission by any means that may be expedient in the circumstances. In other instances, the ombuds serves as a mediator who attempts to work out agreements that would rectify the situation. But for this strategy to work, the ombuds must be seen as impartial and effective. That, in turn, means that the ombuds must be fairly autonomous within the institution and must be able to function independently and without interference. In many ways, the same notion that underlies the separation of functions to protect the integrity of administrative law judges in government hearings applies to an ombuds. Another manifestation of the complexity is that an ombuds needs to be careful not to interfere with traditional labor relations by addressing issues that arise under collective bargaining agreements or that are the proper subject for another office, such as an Inspector General.

This autonomy has some interesting and important implications for what happens to information provided to the ombuds in confidence. If the ombuds is, in fact, an autonomous office within the institution and meets the essential characteristics, then there is no way the management of the institution will know of the confidential information unless the ombuds supplies it. Thus, it seems logical that information provided to the ombuds in confidence should not be imputed to the institution for purposes of providing a legally cognizable "notice."

The ombuds may, however, give some of the information to the institution when attempting to solve the difficulty. In that case, the institution may or may not have sufficient information to constitute "notice" depending on the nature of the information provided. In particular, if the ombuds provides factual information about an alleged violation or series of related allegations to management, it makes no sense to argue that the information does not constitute notice to the entity simply because it was the ombuds who provided it. Rather, it is the specificity of the information furnished that is determinative. Were it otherwise, and the ombuds could whisper in the ear of management, the ombuds would legitimately be viewed as an agent of management instead of the independent neutral that befits the office. This perception would, of course, be self-defeating, because the case for imputation of that information to management would be stronger, not weaker, if an ombuds were able to gather information for management.

Concerns about the variety of types and applications of ombuds, and the different perspectives over what they should and should not do involve more than academic speculation. Rather, they go to the heart of the concept and affect the way individuals from all perspectives relate to the office. For example, someone may come to an ombuds for help only to have the ombuds reveal information that the person furnished in confidence to that person's considerable detriment. Or, the complainant may think the ombuds is in a position to provide a legal remedy or at least advice on how to pursue a legal remedy, and yet the time for filing a legal action may expire while the person is working with the ombuds. Or, the ombuds may not have sufficient independence or stature to get anything done, so the office is largely ineffectual. Further, some ombuds assert legal privileges that simply do not exist and, in other cases, contend that normal legal rules do not apply to their actions. Finally, if there is not a common understanding about what an ombuds is and how the office functions, it is likely that some jurisdictions or other institutions that could greatly benefit from an ombuds office will not create one precisely because of the resulting confusion over just what it is, how it works, and why it may be to their advantage to institute one. . . .

2. ABA Standards for the Establishment and Operation of Ombuds Offices (2004)

The ABA's Ombuds Standards, promulgated in 2004, reflect the increasing importance of this approach to dispute resolution. The ABA standards reflect "best practices, and are not binding on anyone, but they are likely to be widely influential." The text of the Standards is concise (about five typed pages) and general. The Standards address the following topics:

1. Establishment and Operation. There should be a publicly available, written document (called a Charter) that clearly explains the role and jurisdiction of the ombuds. The Standards then list, in general terms, the functions that an ombuds should be authorized to undertake.

2. Qualifications. The ombuds should be someone of "recognized knowledge, judgment, objectivity, and integrity." No one could disagree with that statement. In addition, the establishing entity should allow (i.e., pay) for "relevant" education, both initial and continuing.

3. Essential Characteristics: Independence, Impartiality, and Confidentiality. Once again, the level of discussion is general, and no one is likely to disagree with this approach.

4. Limitation on the Ombud's Authority. The ombuds supplements, but does not replace, existing procedures. Simply stated, an ombuds does not have the power to order anyone to do anything. The ombuds' scope of authority, and limitations thereon, are established by the Charter. An ombuds may not undertake activities inconsistent with a collective bargaining agreement.

5. Removal From Office. An ombuds should be removed from office only for "good cause" and based on a fair procedure. The standards do not address the common approach of appointing an ombuds for a fixed term of years (usually with an option of renewal).

6. Notice. This topic encompasses two quite different matters. The ombuds must give notice of various matters to "people who contact the ombuds for help or advice." This is in addition to the public, written notice about the role and jurisdiction of the ombudsperson. Secondly, communications to an ombuds, whether from a person who consults the ombuds or a third party, does not constitute notice to the appointing organization (or anyone else).

7. Special Rules for Four Classes of Ombuds. The ABA Standards conclude with a few provisions applicable only to the following types of ombuds: Legislative, Executive, Organizational, and Advocate. This set of categories lacks currency outside the ABA Standards. People in the field usually speak of two classes of ombudspersons: Organizational and Government. (Ombuds appointed by state universities and parastatal organizations arguably fit in both categories.)

3. Comments and Questions

a. Americans were introduced to the ombuds idea by WALTER GELLHORN, OMBUDSMAN AND OTHERS (1966). For a thoughtful discussion of how an organizational ombuds functions, see Mary B. Rowe, *Options, Functions, and Skills: What an Organizational Ombudsman Might Want to Know*, 11 NEGOT. J. 103 (1995) [the author is Ombuds at Massachusetts Institute of Technology].

b. Ombuds are usually found in large organizations and the executive branch of government, but even courts have ombudspersons. *See Ombudsman For the Eastern District of Michigan*, 85-JUN MICH. B.J. 40 (2006).

c. The ABA Standards have received considerable attention in the ombuds community. *See, e.g.*, Judy Kaleta & John Barkat, *The ABA Ombuds Standards: Advancing An Important Profession*, 11 DISP. RESOL. MAG. 9 (Winter 2005) (summarizes the ABA Standards); Katherine A. Welch, *No Notice is Good News: Notice Under the New Ombuds Standards for the Establishment and Operation of Ombuds Offices*, 2005 J. DISP. RESOL. 193 (approving provision that communications to an ombuds about workplace violations or unlawful practices not notice to employer).

d. Concerns about the ABA Standards reflect style as well as substance. The formal, rules-based approach characteristic of the law is foreign to most ombuds practitioners — particularly the most innovative ones. This theme is developed in the article that follows; the author, Howard Gadlin, is the director of the Office of the Ombudsman at the National Institutes of Health.

4. Howard Gadlin, *New Ombuds Standards Create Tension and Opportunity*, 11 DISP. RESOL. MAG. 15 (Winter 2005)

Until recently, organizational ombuds standards have been asserted . . . as a set of ideals for a role that exists largely outside the realm of regulation. There have been no laws or rules that define necessary credentials for declaring oneself an organizational ombudsman, no training path required to be entitled to use the name, and no criteria for certifying any program as legitimate. Rather, the profession developed as a creative adaptation of the classical legislative ombuds role to the problems and issues of organizations, such as workplaces, government agencies, universities, and colleges. The idea was to provide a confidential, informal place where people could air their concerns, raise issues they might be uncomfortable raising through traditional channels, and learn about their options for addressing those concerns. . . .

At first, there were no concrete guidelines for the role, just abstract principles that the pioneers in the organizational ombuds field translated into practices tailored to the structure, cultural dynamics and missions of particular organizations. These principles included a commitment to impartiality and neutrality, independence and confidentiality, as well as an orientation toward justice. Only after considerable experience and experimentation were organizational ombuds able to create professional associations and to formulate standards of practice. . . .

It took many years before key figures in organizational bureaucracies — top managers, legal counsel and human resources — became familiar and comfortable with the role and were reassured that an organizational ombuds office was not a threat to formal procedures and policies. In time, these informal procedures coalesced into standards approved by what became the leading professional organizations for organizational ombuds, The Ombudsman Association (TOA) and the University and College Ombuds Association (UCOA).

These industry standards of practice reflect an informal consensus among practitioners about preferred interpretations of the role of the organizational ombuds. The standards have met with some success in recent years as organizations seeking to establish an ombudsman program began to require that the office would practice according to the standards of TOA or UCOA. But obviously, an informal consensus among practicing professionals does not answer many of the questions about how the practices of ombuds are to be regarded by the law. And while individual ombuds may have convinced individual lawyers within their organizations about the appropriateness of their standards of practice, it is not the same as convincing the legal profession. . . .

The TOA and UCOA standards did not reflect the interests and concerns of the wide array of competing legal stakeholders, such as the plaintiffs' bar, management lawyers, or even union lawyers. This is not a criticism of the standards that the organizational ombuds themselves had established, but rather reflects the fact that the array of legal stakeholders was not at the table during their formulation, and rightly so. The TOA and UCOA principles were about professional practice standards, and there is a difference between professional practice standards and the legal environment in which they operate. Both, of course, should understand and respect the obligations of the other, and in some respects, that is the heart of the challenge.

The 2004 ABA Standards for The Establishment and Operation of Ombuds Offices . . . marked the first time another profession has critically examined the ombuds role in the light of its own perspectives and interests, and has offered its interpretation of the role. The ABA Standards seek to harmonize standards for all types of ombuds, and are the first comprehensive statement of the legal profession that specifically addresses the organizational ombuds role. The standards got the attention of organizational ombuds in two respects. First, having been reassured by the growing acceptance of its own standards of practice by organizations using ombuds, it was something of a shock to see in the ABA report and recommendations some provisions that interpreted key aspects of the organizational ombuds role differently than had become the norm in the field.

Second, and on the other hand, the ABA report revealed to organizational ombuds how the justifications for some of their own standards of practice have not been articulated with enough specificity to assuage the concerns of those interested in protecting employee rights, clarifying organizational responsibilities vis-à-vis ombuds communications, and delineating the domain of ombuds responsibility within an organization.

The legal profession and the ombuds profession survey the world from very different perches and with very different sensibilities. It makes sense that the legal profession would be wary of a profession that claims for itself the privilege of confidentiality and personal discretion. And it is not surprising that ombuds view some of the inflexible procedures imposed by the ABA Standards as counterproductive to the very flexibility they need to do their jobs. It is only in the arena of ADR that their common goals are revealed — a concern with fairness and justice and recognition of the importance of protecting minority and individual rights.

Clashing Cultures. I suspect that, more than a difference in interests, we have a clash of sensibilities. Although lawyers and ombuds often share the common goal of protecting individual and minority rights, they are trained to achieve this goal in diametrically opposed ways — lawyers by eliminating discretion and ombuds by enhancing it. Lawyers regularly confront circumstances where managers substitute personal discretion for consistently applied procedures, and have responded by curtailing that discretion in hopes of eliminating the opportunity for discrimination. Indeed, laws preventing discrimination and protecting individual rights have been immeasurably important as a counterweight to the arbitrary, capricious and often prejudicial wielding of managerial power.

By contrast, it is in the very nature of ombuds work to confront situations that reveal the limitations of procedures, rules and laws. Procedural safeguards, such as whistleblower statutes, are sometimes mere paper protections. Other times, it is the rules themselves that are part of the problem to be solved. . . . Ombuds have responded by using their discretion and creativity to protect minority rights that are ill served by the very inflexible rules that lawyers seek to create. To enable an individual to come forward safely with a complaint of harm or a report of wrongdoing, for example, almost every whistleblowing or sexual harassment complaint procedure contains formal proscriptions against retaliation. But the social-psychological dynamics of organizations are such that these guarantees are often empty promises. There are just too many subtle means of retaliation, and many sorts of retaliation cannot be reversed, even if, which is not often the case, the retaliator is caught and punished. . . .

Need to Specify Concerns. The ABA Standards represent important progress for the ombuds field in a number of respects. One of the most important features of the ABA Standards is the insistence that every organization with an ombuds should have a charter or establishing document that specifies the functions, roles, limitations, and protections of that ombuds office. By offering specific suggestions regarding each of these, the Standards will encourage the ombuds associations to address more carefully the question of consistency in the practice of organizational ombuds offices. Similarly, their endorsement by the ABA will give comfort to corporate counsel who may continue to have concerns about organizational ombuds.

However, three sections of the report in particular have raised concerns within the organizational ombuds community, either because their implications seem ambiguous or because they appear to constrain or undermine key aspects of the organizational ombuds role. There is not space here for a detailed discussion of the points of difference, but it is useful to identify them so we can contemplate a process whereby differences such as these could be addressed in a spirit consonant with the general sensibility of ADR.

Employment restrictions. The first area of tension deals with the limitations on the authority of ombuds in situations involving unions and employment law. As the ABA Standards rightly recognize, independence is a core value for ombuds, and it is challenged by limitations on the authority of the ombuds. Organizational ombuds understand that the ABA standards are intended to provide important safeguards for the legal rights of employees and employers and they also recognize that an ombuds program supplements, and does not substitute for, the procedures and remedies associated with those rights. But organizational ombuds are concerned that limitations on the ombuds authority, as worded, may be impracticable. Simply put, workplace disputes do not come to the ombuds neatly packaged . . . as "pertaining to employment law," or "covered by a union contract."

Often, people come to the ombuds office trying, in a confidential setting, to make sense of and assess possible options for addressing a multiplex situation, some dimensions of which may be covered by rules or regulations. The organizational ombuds work with those people to help them unpack what might be quite inchoate experiences of workplace situations. Frequently, even when there might be relevant rules or regulations, the person might prefer to explore informal options for addressing matters — strategies for handling a problematic situation on their own, drafting a letter to send to the person with whom they are in conflict, and exploring nonadversarial approaches to addressing a conflict, to name just a few.

Obviously, if there are relevant rules, laws or organizational procedures for addressing some part of the employee's (or manager's) concerns, the organizational ombuds will review those with the employee (or manager). Many times, however, those coming to the ombudsman strongly prefer to address issues without resorting to formal . . . complaint mechanisms and would not go forward . . . if those were the only means for addressing the issue. As currently written, this section does not appear to take into account what is considered one of the most valuable qualities of the organizational ombuds, the ability to offer an effective alternative to pursuing issues through formal channels, which in many instances, are seen as untrustworthy or too debilitating to be worth the effort.

Organizational ombuds, of course, agree that ombuds should defer to union processes for matters covered by a union contract. However, organizational ombuds also believe there are many issues not covered by the contract that union members can and should be able to address with an ombuds. Many personal workplace conflicts between union members place union grievance officers in an awkward position, and I have often had such issues referred to me by the union. In unionized universities, for example, faculty disputes over authorship create serious headaches for the faculty union grievance officers. . . .

528 PRIVATE ADR PROCESSES CH. 11

Notice procedures. The second and third tensions revolve around the notice provision, Section F. . . . This section identifies six things the ABA believes an ombuds should communicate to people who contact the ombuds. In the organizational ombuds world, this has been interpreted as requiring that an ombuds provide a person who contacts the office a "Miranda"-like warning. Ombuds would generally agree that the publicity for the office (brochures, websites, etc.) ought to include such information. However, many are concerned that greeting each visitor to the office with a Miranda-like statement at the outset would violate the informality of the office, as well as the ombuds' ability to tailor interactions to the needs and condition of the person who comes to the ombuds.

Sometimes, a person merely needs a referral to another office or program. At other times, if a person arrives at the office visibly upset and crying or raging, it is important for the ombuds to attend to that person's condition before launching into an explanation of the role and limitations of the office. Here, too, some organizational ombuds question whether the report's language actually serves the intentions of the authors. It is important that ombuds have the latitude to exercise good judgment and timing when they explain the essential features and limitations of the office to those who come to them.

Confidentiality Rules. There is concern, too, about the report wording that would require the ombuds to assert that he or she would not voluntarily disclose to anyone outside the office information provided in confidence, unless necessary to address an imminent risk of serious harm. In practice, ombuds sometimes do report confidential information, but only as part of reporting trends and only in a way that protects the person's confidentiality or identity. For example, if an ombuds learned that an organization was inconsistent in setting salaries for equivalent level positions in different parts of an organization, the ombuds would most likely find a way to bring that to the attention of the organization, while not revealing the identity of the person or people who brought the problem to the ombuds' attention. The ABA Standards appear to preclude this practice.

Although there is a passage in the confidentiality clause that allows the ombuds "discretion to disclose . . . confidential information so long as doing so does not reveal its source," this passage appears to be contradicted by the language of the section on notice, which allows for no exception. While the drafters say they may be read together, it's not clear exactly what that means or that a court would necessarily agree. At minimum, some clarification would be helpful to assist practitioners in the field, especially the many non-lawyers who work in ombuds offices.

Finally, many organizational ombuds are concerned about the relationship between notice and confidentiality. The issue of when a communication from an ombuds to an organization might constitute notice to the organization is one of the most complex and charged issues raised in the ABA report. It has long been an article of faith in the ombuds world that an ombuds is not an agent of the organization for purposes of placing the organization on notice. At the same time, there are important legal questions to be answered about what sort of specificity in a communication from an ombuds would be required for the organization to be on notice. This is an area in which, until recently, ombuds have simply asserted a position without having carefully worked through all the complex organizational and legal issues involved. . . .

More Communication Needed. Between ombuds' substantive concerns about the ABA standards and the natural aversion that any unique profession might feel toward outside regulation, it seems that the ABA standards have created some tension between the ABA and the organizational ombuds communities. I see that as an opportunity for understanding and growth. One cannot reasonably doubt that the ABA and the organizational ombuds community both share the common interest of doing what is best for the field, and that includes working out genuine differences of perspective among good people acting in good faith. That begins with resisting the natural tendency for these professional organizations to be somewhat territorial.

Similarly, it is interesting to note that these professional associations that are so concerned with notions of justice and fairness, and that are otherwise so meticulous about procedural fairness and due process, should rely on such an improvisational approach to addressing major policy issues with important implications for all. Collectively, we lack a process for systematic discussion, communication and resolution of differences between or among different professionals when common interests are at stake, and the leaderships of all relevant organizations should come together to consider how to bridge this gap. Going it alone is always possible, but it is not the path of our field. Our highest values include harnessing the energy of conflict for greater understanding and constructive social process. This is a more difficult path, as we all know, but as we also know, it is generally worth the effort.

F. LARGE CONSTRUCTION PROJECTS: PARTNERING AND DISPUTE REVIEW BOARDS

1. Comments and Questions

a. Partnering serves the dual purpose of proactive management to avoid disputes, while also planning for addressing those problems that do arise. The costs associated with implementing dispute review boards and/or a partnering process limit their use to long term, large dollar projects — notably major construction projects.

b. Professor Stipanowich has written several thoughtful articles about dispute resolution in the construction industry. *See, e.g.,* Thomas J. Stipanowich, *Reconstructing Construction Law: Reality and Reform in a Transactional System,* 1998 WIS. L. REV. 463; Thomas J. Stipanowich, *Contract and Conflict Management,* 2001 WIS. L. REV. 831.

c. The term "construction" typically refers to buildings, roads, dams, and other structures that are permanently attached to land. However, variants on partnering and dispute review boards can be used for large commercial projects, such as building ships and airplanes. Long term commercial relationships based on many smaller contracts, rather than a single large project, also could benefit from the dispute resolution and prevention principles associated with review boards and partnering.

2. DANIEL D. MCMILLAN & ROBERT A. RUBIN, DISPUTE REVIEW BOARDS: KEY ISSUES, RECENT CASE LAW, AND STANDARD AGREEMENTS, 25-SPG Construction Law. 14 (2005)

Due to the ubiquity of disputes on construction projects and the accompanying expense and disruption of litigation, the construction industry has struggled to find an effective and efficient process to resolve such claims. Several means of traditional, alternative dispute resolution (ADR) have been utilized. At present, the standard contracts of the American Institute of Architects (AIA), the most frequently used construction agreements, specify ADR through mediation and binding arbitration under the Construction Industry Arbitration Rules of the American Arbitration Association (AAA). For many practitioners, the preferred type of ADR is whatever was not used during the last construction dispute. However, dispute review boards (DRBs) have been developed specifically for the challenges of large construction projects and have become the ADR of choice on substantial, high-profile work across the country. For example, DRBs have been used to resolve disputes on the Massachusetts Central Artery/Tunnel project, the Los Angeles subway, and the new terminal at John F. Kennedy International Airport.

The increasing use . . . of DRBs heightens the need for construction lawyers to become more familiar with the DRB process. This understanding cannot be gleaned from reading court decisions, because the available case law remains relatively scant. We identified a total of two published decisions and five unpublished trial court opinions. Nonetheless, those rulings serve as an important reminder that DRB agreements, as all construction documents, must be carefully drafted, or else collateral disputes concerning the DRB process itself may become the subject of litigation.

Model DRB provisions have proliferated in the past few years, thus requiring owners, contractors, and their respective counsel to differentiate between the available forms. This article highlights the nature of DRBs, the role of lawyers in drafting DRB agreements and in the operation of DRBs, the sources of available model DRB agreements, other resources regarding DRBs, and recurring issues that should be considered when selecting among the available model agreements.

General Description of DRBs and Their Process. DRBs are a creature of contract. Thus, the agreements creating them may alter various aspects of the DRB and its procedures. For ease of analysis, this section utilizes the most conventional form of DRB, rather than the many variants. The DRB process helps the parties to a construction project avoid and resolve claims without litigation or arbitration. The usual DRB consists of a three-person board of construction industry experts who periodically visit the site, attend project meetings, conduct hearings on disputes between the parties, and issue written recommendations for the disposition of such claims. Typically, the owner appoints one board member (subject to approval by the contractor), the contractor appoints another (subject to approval by the owner), and the first two appoint a third (subject to approval by the owner and the contractor). This last appointee customarily serves as the chairperson. Each of the three members is to be impartial, neutral, and not an advocate for either side. The DRB represents a hybrid form of ADR, which shares some attributes of adjudication, as well as some traits of mediation.

The DRB should be established at the outset of the project. . . . Most boards meet and visit the site each quarter. The board's familiarity with the project enhances its preparedness when disputes arise. During the periodic meetings, owner and contractor representatives update the DRB on the project's status and alert the three members to potential disputes. Either the owner or the contractor may request that the DRB conduct a hearing concerning a dispute. All model DRB provisions require that a party submit a claim to the board before initiating litigation.

The DRB schedules and conducts an informal hearing in which the parties may make written submissions and oral presentations. After the hearing, the board prepares nonbinding recommendations. The parties are expected to use the DRB recommendations in an attempt to settle their dispute, while still being free to accept or reject them. In addition, most model agreements provide that the DRB recommendations are admissible into evidence in the event of subsequent litigation. In theory, the owner and the contractor should be inclined to accept the guidance of the board members, especially when the parties know that the opinions of these respected experts will be prominently featured as evidence in any subsequent lawsuit or arbitration. In reality, acceptance of DRB recommendations and the success of the DRB process depend largely on the owner and the contractor's mutual trust and confidence in the board itself. . . .

Expertise of DRB Members. The technical competence of DRB members enhances the credibility of their recommendations. In litigation, there is no assurance that the judge will have any familiarity with the type of project under construction. A lay jury will be even less equipped to assess technical issues associated with complex construction disputes, plus jurors are prone to information overload or simple boredom. Although arbitration and mediation afford parties the opportunity to utilize industry experts as arbitrator(s) or mediator(s), both lack a number of the other important features inherent in the DRB process.

Project Familiarity. The DRB members, in addition to being construction experts, develop knowledge about the particular project by reviewing the job documents, attending quarterly progress meetings, and making site visits. The DRB members have a frame of reference when a dispute arises, allowing the parties to make more focused presentations. In contrast, the judge, jury, mediator, or arbitrator first learns about the construction process after the claims occur and, therefore, lacks the project familiarity garnered by DRB members.

Real-Time Consideration of Disputes. DRBs normally address disputes as they arise rather than waiting until the end of the project. This feature can minimize the damage to relations between the owner and the contractor, which occurs when claims linger and accumulate. The availability of the DRB and its familiarity with the job enable prompt resolution of disputes, which furthers the goal of preserving cooperative relationships between the contracting parties. Traditional claim resolution takes place long after and far from the events forming the basis of the dispute. Much time and effort must be spent recreating those circumstances for the trier of facts and then sorting out which version to accept. Thus, DRBs combine job familiarity with real-time dispute resolution to allow the parties to concentrate on the technical issues in controversy.

Nonbinding Recommendations. The written recommendations of the DRB do not bind the parties, absent express or tacit acceptance by the owner and the contractor. In contrast, litigation and arbitration result in a judgment or award that, unless set aside through an appeal, resolves the dispute. Participants in those processes do not have the option simply to reject the results. In this respect, DRBs function like a mediation or facilitation. However, unlike traditional mediation, DRBs frequently issue findings much like a judge's statement of decision following a bench trial or an arbitrator's reasoned award. The DRB provides the parties with written opinions reflecting the views of three construction experts. Most DRB agreements provide that those findings are admissible into evidence in subsequent litigation or arbitration. Even if the DRB provisions specify that the recommendations are not admissible, the parties still will review them, and they very well may influence how to settle the dispute. In view of the advisory nature of DRB conclusions, it is important for the board to maintain the confidence of the parties as that trust influences how parties receive and evaluate DRB recommendations and the success of the DRB process itself.

Proliferation of Model DRB Provisions. Construction lawyers need not draft DRB provisions from scratch, because several model documents exist. Indeed, the number of exemplary Three-Party Agreements and specifications has grown and more are emerging. Until 2000, there were three primary sources of model DRB provisions constituting successive generations of the same source documents. In 1989, the American Society of Civil Engineers (ASCE) published an exemplary Three-Party Agreement and DRB specifications (the 1989 ASCE Guide). Two years later, the ASCE issued an updated booklet with a slightly modified model Three-Party Agreement and DRB specifications (the 1991 ASCE Guide). In 1996, many of the same people involved with the development of the 1989 ASCE Guide and the 1991 ASCE Guide published the Construction Dispute Review Board Manual, which again included a revised Three-Party Agreement and DRB specifications (1996 DRB Manual). These three sources . . . have served as the primary forms for Three-Party Agreements and specifications in the United States.

In 1996, the Dispute Resolution Board Foundation (DRBF) was established. Its mission is "to promote use of the [DRB] process, and serve as a technical clearinghouse for owners, contractors, and Board members in order to improve the dispute resolution process." In 2004, the DRBF published a portion of its practices and procedures guide, . . . [as well as] its model Three-Party Agreement and DRB specifications. The DRBF's model DRB provisions are meant to serve as a revision to the model provisions in the 1996 DRB Manual and constitute the fourth generation of documents tracing their lineage to the 1989 ASCE Guide. The DRBF's model provisions contain a number of notable differences as compared to prior model provisions, including the manner in which board members are selected and the standard for their removal.

Since 1996, several other organizations have developed new form DRB specifications and Three-Party Agreements, including the AAA and the International Chamber of Commerce (ICC). In 2004, the ICC published its own "Dispute Board Documents." Its version of the Three-Party Agreement is entitled "Model Dispute Board Member Agreement," and it references a series of rules governing the operation of ICC dispute review boards. Three types of "Dispute Boards" exist under the ICC regime. The first example, called a "Dispute Review Board," employs recommendations that may be rejected. The second type is a "Dispute Adjudication Board" whose "Decisions" ultimately may be disregarded by a party, but the contractor and owner remain bound by the determinations until the dispute is resolved finally by arbitration or litigation. The ICC offers a third approach, known as "Combined Dispute Boards," which (as the name implies) merges features of the ICC's "Dispute Review Boards" and "Dispute Adjudication Boards."

DRB Membership. . . . The importance of investigating the proposed members and rejecting those where bias or the perception of bias is detected cannot be overstated. . . . A growing number of construction counsel have been appointed to and ably served on DRBs. Some observers believe that lawyers should not act as board members, because lawyer involvement can cause the process to become more formal and adversarial. Traditionally, lawyer membership is not encouraged. Still, qualified lawyers continue to be appointed to and successfully serve on boards.

DRB Quarterly Meetings and Hearings. The direct involvement of lawyers in DRB hearings has been discouraged. In practice, attorneys seldom attend DRB sessions, although they are not usually barred from attending. For disputes that involve major points of law, attorneys do occasionally attend. There is some concern that attorneys as advocates (as opposed to advisers) tend to make the process adversarial and unnecessarily formal. Ordinarily, cross-examination of those in attendance by the parties or their representatives is not permitted at a DRB hearing; however, board members frequently ask the parties questions. A transcript or recording is not normally prepared, but parties may request that the DRB permit a court reporter. . . .

Nonbinding Recommendations That Can Become Final. Model DRB provisions generally state that DRB recommendations do not bind the owner or the contractor. Importantly, however, advisory DRB proposals can become binding through inaction — a fact sometimes lost on those inexperienced with the process. A party must respond in writing to DRB opinions within a fixed period of time, typically fourteen days, indicating acceptance or rejection of the recommendations. If the owner or contractor fails to respond, the recommendations are deemed accepted.

Admissibility of DRB Recommendations. A key feature of DRBs is the admissibility of the board's written recommendations in later legal proceedings. Conventional wisdom holds that parties are more likely to accept adverse DRB proposals and, thereby, avert litigation if these recommendations reflect the considered judgment of three industry experts and may be used as evidence in any litigation. . . . [P]arties should consider whether to modify model DRB forms to specify that the board's recommendations shall not be admissible. . . .

Potential "Carve Outs" from the DRB's Jurisdiction. As a general proposition, model DRB provisions broadly direct the board "to assist in the resolution of disputes, claims and other controversies" between the owner and the contractor without any specific limitations on the subject matters. The . . . model agreements do not specify any limitations on the type of disputes between the owner and contractor that may be submitted to the DRB. Such broad authority may come as a surprise to public owners that may believe some claims are inappropriate for DRB consideration. . . . An owner may wish to specifically exclude claims concerning Owner Controlled Insurance Policies or disputes under Project Labor Agreements. Public owners should consider whether a termination for default should be within the jurisdiction of the DRB. Likewise, shutting down the job due to safety concerns or directing replacement of contractor personnel may not be controversies an owner wishes to have submitted to a board. Thought should be given to whether certain types of statutory claims (e.g., direct actions by the public owner under a state false claims act, disputes over prevailing wage issues, and audits) should be expressly withheld from the DRB's jurisdiction.

Subcontractor Claims. The DRB process, as it applies to subcontractor claims, requires special attention for several reasons. Many disputes between owners and contractors on large public works projects involve so-called subcontractor pass-through claims. Indeed, where an owner substantially holds up a project, the resulting claim for delay damages invariably includes losses suffered by subcontractors. Subcontractors sometimes file lawsuits directly against the prime contractor, who then almost always files an indemnification action against the owner. In some cases, subcontractors do not wait for the prime contractor to bring the owner into the litigation; they file direct claims against the owner designed to establish privity of contract or otherwise overcome the usual privity requirement. In each of these circumstances, owners frequently assert claims back against the prime contractor or subcontractor. If DRB provisions do not clearly indicate whether some or all of these actions must be submitted to the board before litigating, expensive and time-consuming uncertainty arises, and the effectiveness of the DRB process can be frustrated. Thus, to fully help the parties avoid litigation, it is important to understand how a board may function with respect to a source of claims as potentially significant as subcontractors.

The existing model DRB provisions and available practice guides focus on disputes between owners and contractors and, with the exception of the DRBF's model provisions, do not specifically address subcontractor claims. Still, if the contractor sponsors the subcontractor's claim and "passes it through" to the owner, DRBs established under the model agreements can address such disputes. Subcontractor "pass-through" claims really are in the nature of disputes between the owner and the prime contractor for the purposes of the traditional DRB process. However, conventional DRBs do not address disputes between the prime contractor and the subcontractor or three-way disputes that also involve the owner. The traditional DRB rightfully should be reluctant to review disagreements under a subcontract. If a DRB addresses a "pass-through" claim, the board ordinarily leaves it to the prime contractor and the subcontractor to sort out the effect of its recommendations. Because most DRB members are not lawyers, confusion may abound if boards are called upon to separate out liability under the subcontract from liability under the prime contract.

Although the traditional DRB was not structured to address disputes purely between a prime contractor and a subcontractor, some owners and contractors have modified model provisions to broaden the scope of issues to be heard by boards in the hope of establishing a one-stop, all-purpose dispute resolution forum. In some instances, owners and contractors now expressly require that subcontractor claims be submitted to the DRB before the subcontractor may commence litigation. To accomplish this, DRB provisions have been incorporated into subcontracts and purchase orders. Altering the process in this fashion injects unpredictability. . . .

3. Kathleen M. J. Harmon, *Construction Conflicts and Dispute Review Boards: Attitudes and Opinions of Construction Industry Members*, 58-JAN DISP. RESOL. J. 66 (2004)

God's creation of the world in seven days is the oldest construction project and a miracle of efficiency. However, construction projects undertaken by mere mortals tell a quite different story. Most cannot be completed without lots of paperwork and the involvement of numerous parties with different agendas and financial restraints. By and large, construction projects are a breeding ground for disputes of all kinds. They result from many factors, including among other things, unfair allocation of risk, multiple prime contracts, unrealistic expectations and schedules, poorly prepared contract documents, financial issues, communication problems, and even the economy.

The construction industry has been on the forefront of the alternative dispute resolution movement. The recent trend is to look for methods of resolving disputes other than traditional processes, which typically begin after the conflict has escalated and the parties' positions have hardened. One of these methods is the dispute review board (DRB). This is a panel, made up of three experienced construction professionals (often engineers), formed at the beginning of a project to hear disputes when they arise and make non-binding recommendations regarding their resolution. Using a DRB is usually a condition precedent to the commencement of binding dispute resolution processes, such as litigation or arbitration.

Although DRBs are generally considered to be highly effective, there is little, if any, empirical evidence to validate that opinion. Moreover, there is also a dearth of data concerning the impact of disputes on the project and the parties' relationship. This study attempts to partially fill that void. . . . The primary issues addressed in the study are: (1) how disputes affect the project; (2) how disputes affect the party's relationship; (3) the impact of a DRB on the project; and (4) the effectiveness of DRBs in resolving disputes.

The DRB is different from other ADR methodologies in that disputes can be addressed during the course of the contract, not at its end. Typically, DRB members make periodic visits to the construction site and become familiar with the parties and the project. This enables the parties to bring conflicts to the board while the project is ongoing. Generally, the DRB panel is established during the pre-construction phase. The owner and contractor each nominate one member to the panel, and each must approve the other's nominee. The two DRB nominees (or the owner and contractor by mutual agreement) select the third member of the DRB. DRB members are compensated by the parties in accordance with a DRB agreement. The contract specifications outline the DRB's role. A DRB only has the authority granted to it by the parties.

[S]ince 1975, 922 projects (nearly all in the United States) have used a DRB. These DRBs heard a total of 1,108 disputes, but only 25 (involving nine projects) were not resolved by the DRB and required litigation. The use of DRBs has been endorsed by a number of construction-related organizations. Since the mid-1990s, the financing documents of the World Bank have provided for DRBs on large construction projects. The construction documents of the Federation Internationale des Inginieurs-Conseils (FIDIC) also provide for DRBs in the General Conditions. Moreover, DRBs are required on certain projects by several public-sector agencies.

This research involved a mix of quantitative and qualitative methodologies (i.e., statistical data from a survey questionnaire and interviews with a group of survey respondents) in an effort to obtain a rounded picture of the views of construction industry professionals about construction disputes and DRBs. For the quantitative research, 703 survey questionnaires containing 76 questions were mailed to individuals in the U.S. construction industry. The mailing was followed by reminder letters, e-mails and telephone calls in an attempt to facilitate the return of outstanding questionnaires. Four hundred and fifty-six questionnaires were returned, an excellent response rate (65%). . . .

Overall, this research indicates that 71% (317 respondents) had a positive attitude toward DRBs (with only 5% or 22 respondents dissenting). An even greater number (88% or 390) agreed that DRBs contribute to the success of a project. We can infer from the data that the success of a project depends in part on the parties' approach to conflict and dispute resolution. An important goal of every construction project should be the early recognition of conflicts and action to resolve them before the parties become polarized in their positions. A conflict resolution process that allows for disputes to be evaluated by professional experts, and to be resolved by the parties themselves while the job is in progress, offers a way to achieve this goal. . . .

3. Lester Edelman, PARTNERING 1-5, 7-10, 17-20 (U.S. ARMY CORPS OF ENGINEERS 1991) (IWR Pamphlet 91-ADR-P-4)

What is Partnering?

How many times have you reached the end of a construction project only to be faced with a number of unresolved conflicts? There is a way to prevent these conflicts during construction by establishing a partnering relationship between the owner and the contractor. Partnering lays the foundation for better working relations on a project including better dispute resolution. By taking steps before construction begins to change the adversarial mindset, to recognize common interests, and to establish an atmosphere of trust and candor in communications, Partnering helps develop a cooperative management team. This team has the ability to appreciate the roles and responsibilities each will have in carrying out the project.

Partnering is the creation of an owner-contractor relationship that promotes achievement of mutually beneficial goals. It involves an agreement in principle to share the risks involved in completing the project, and to establish and promote a nurturing partnership environment. Partnering is not a contractual agreement, however, nor does it create any legally enforceable rights or duties. Rather, Partnering seeks to create a new cooperative attitude in completing government contracts. To create this attitude, each party must seek to understand the goals, objectives, and needs of the other — their "win" situation — and seek ways that these objectives can overlap.

Why Use Partnering?

From the beginning of a typical construction project, the structure of the relationship promotes an adversarial attitude between the parties. There are two distinct management teams, each making independent decisions with the intent of reaching their own goals for the project. These decisions directly affect the path each party chooses to achieve its goals — but they are often made in a vacuum, without regard for the other party's interests and expectations. Communication may be limited, or non-existent. Conflicts are inevitable as paths diverge and expectations are not met. The worst stereotypes of the other side are remembered, and they seem to block the way to our goals. An adversarial management style takes over, and the goals each party had for the project get lost in preparation for litigation. The stage is set for future conflict and, often, litigation. It's as if two people are planning to travel together to a common destination, but each has his own map and refuses to show it to his traveling companion!

The bottom line is clear: The adversarial management relationship jeopardizes the ability of either side to realize its expectations. The result is increased costs for the taxpayer and declining profit margins for the contractor. This is truly a lose-lose outcome for all. Both parties have recognized that there needs to be a better way of doing business. Efficiency and productivity must be increased. Neither the government nor contractors can afford the costly posturing that the present adversarial climate promotes. Partnering offers the chance to change from an adversarial style to a more cooperative, synergistic relationship that takes full advantage of the strengths of all team members. . . . Partnering seemed to offer the opportunity of harnessing the capabilities, talents, and positive energies of both owner and contractor groups and focusing them on mutually agreed-upon goals. It offered the opportunity for all parties to change preconceived attitudes in order for both to win in the long run.

How Does Partnering Work?

Partnering creates a climate for success by building a cooperative management team dedicated to a win-win atmosphere. . . . There are three basic steps involved in establishing the Partnering relationship. Since Partnering is an attitude change aimed at building a new relationship, it is important as a first step to establish the new relationship through personal contact. Success in a Partnering arrangement depends on the personal commitment of the management team. This commitment is built through personal relationships that must be formed early and reinforced throughout the project. The second step in Partnering is crafting a joint statement of goals and establishing common objectives in specific detail for reaching the goals. Achieving these intermediate objectives will lead to success for both the owner and the contractor. Finally, Partnering identifies specific disputes prevention processes designed to head off problems, evaluate performance, and promote cooperation.

Although these basic steps create the Partnering relationship, teamwork is essential to instill the Partnering spirit. Through a series of joint workshops, guided by facilitators, Partnering builds team spirit. The emphasis in the workshops is on identifying shared interests and focusing on cooperative effort. There are other factors to consider in establishing a Partnering relationship. Here's a list of some of the considerations:

- prepare early for Partnering;
- secure top management support and commitment to Partnering;
- identify Partnering "champions";
- choose participants for the Partnering workshop;
- select neutral facilitators for the Partnering workshop;
- conduct the joint workshop;
- create a Partnering Charter;
- arrange regular follow-up sessions; and
- plan combined activities.

Establishing cooperative processes for evaluating progress and solving problems is another feature of successful Partnering. Evaluation mechanisms should be specific in measuring the achievement of the objectives that will make the project a success. A system for problem-solving, which will provide for expedited decisions, should be established. . . .

How Do We Know It's Working?

When Partnering is working, old adversarial patterns change, and a new spirit pervades the working relationship. . . . Look for these signs of successful Partnering.

Sharing: The partners share a common set of goals.

Clear Expectations: Each partner's expectations are clearly stated, up front, and provide the basis for working together.

Trust and Confidence: Partners' actions are consistent and predictable. Trust is earned when one's actions are consistent with one's words. We must "walk the talk."

Commitment: Each partner must make a real commitment to participate in the partnership.

Responsibility: Responsibility is recognizing and accepting the consequences of our choices. Partners should agree up front on measures for mutual accountability.

Courage: Partners have the courage to forthrightly confront and resolve conflict.

Understanding and Respect: Partners understand and respect each other's responsibilities, authorities, expectations, and boundaries, as well as any honest differences between them.

Synergy: The partnership is more than the sum of the individual partners. The relationship is more powerful than any of the partners working alone, because it is based on the collective resources of the partners.

Excellence: Partners expect excellence from each other and give excellence in return.

These are the positive indicators of a successful Partnering effort. If you look closely at the list again, it's clear that most of these indicators are based on the ability of the partners to communicate and solve problems.

What Concerns Are There About Partnering?

Some people have expressed a concern that Partnering may place the owner and the contractor "too close," and that there is a need for distance between the parties to maintain objectivity and proper oversight. Unfortunately, this adversarial attitude leads to some very expensive and counterproductive actions. Not only is the climate of trust and communication hindered, but distance between the parties can allow room for an expensive "wall of paper" to rise between the parties. Documents are exchanged to begin building a case for litigation.

Another concern is the view that contract requirements will be relaxed in the interest of Partnering. This concern, however, is based on a misconception about the nature of Partnering. Partnering does not mean that the public interest takes a back seat to the interests of the parties. All federal procurement laws and regulations must be complied with by the parties. This does not mean that the government and the contractor have to avoid cooperation in effecting compliance. In a Partnering relationship, the contractor should understand and appreciate government regulatory requirements, and the government should understand and appreciate the contractor's expectations.

Some individuals have said that Partnering is all relationships and no substance, that the benefits are intangible and not worth the extra effort and expense. Experience has shown others that there are benefits, both tangible as well as intangible. And the expense, shared by the government and the contractor, is not great — even where a facilitated initial workshop and follow-up sessions are used. Perhaps the most telling comment, however, may be that no matter what the tangible advantages, Partnering represents the fair way of doing business. One Corps manager wrote: "I have field employees who say it's a pleasure to come to work and not be afraid to advise the contractor of any perceived problem and be proud of working on the project as a team member."

Partnering Process

A successful Partnering program starts with an understanding of the important elements of the process and careful planning of each step. Essentially, the important elements are 1) early preparation, 2) management commitment to the concept, 3) a joint workshop, 4) a team charter, and 5) follow-up meetings and evaluation processes. . . .

1. Early Preparation: Introduce the Concept to Bidders. After an internal commitment has been made to use Partnering in a contract, the Corps should state its intent to use the concept in its solicitation for bids. This will introduce the concept to the bidders. The point to be stressed is that Partnering is a voluntary relationship designed to improve cooperation and communications during construction.

2. Management Commitment. Partnering requires a personal commitment between contracting parties to accept a new relationship and a senior management decision to commit resources to the effort. Top management of both the Corps and the contractor must be supportive. Visible top management commitment sends the vital message that Partnering is acceptable and will be supported. Management support, instilling enthusiasm and overcoming obstacles, empowers people to act. Top managers can most visibly show their support by attending the Partnering workshop and introducing the concept in person. A Partnering program can be implemented without a huge commitment of resources. The additional costs (for the workshop and facilitators) are relatively small and are shared by the parties. There is a commitment of management time, and there must be a willingness to "go the extra mile" for the benefit of the team.

Partnering needs "champions" to foster the new relationship. There are two kinds of champions that an effective Partnering program needs: a top management champion who will instill the Partnering ethic within the organization, and a "managing partner" champion who will carry out the nurturing of the Partnering relationship throughout the course of the contract. Top management support is vitally important to provide the favorable environment for Partnering to grow. Operational level champions for Partnering are important in the day-to-day managing of the process by providing administrative and logistical support, encouraging communication, and promoting problem-solving. The Resident Engineer is the natural choice for operational level champion.

3. The Joint Partnering Workshop. A Partnering workshop is the starting point for the new relationship. The participants in the Partnering workshop should be key stakeholders in the success of the project. . . . Partnering depends on developing relationships and committing to cooperation toward common goals. The change in mindset from the adversarial to the cooperative does not come automatically, simply by talking about it. An effective way to develop this new attitude is to use a neutral facilitator to guide the workshop.

A neutral facilitator is a third party who manages the process of the workshop and who can guide the participants to discover for themselves the benefits of cooperative action. Professional facilitators provide expertise in organizational development, communications, group dynamics, and team building. As an outsider, the facilitator can devote attention to guiding the workshop in developing the Partnering structure. Because the facilitator has no association with either party, the impartial status allows the facilitator to be the focus of comments or criticism from one side to the other without the resentment or conflict that may be the result of a direct confrontation. . . .

The Partnering workshop helps participants establish open communications, develop a team spirit, set long range Partnering goals for the project, and gain commitment to the implementation plan. A combination of group activities, lectures, and experiential learning exercises has been effective in helping groups reach these goals in the workshop setting. Suggestions for a successful Partnering workshop include conducting the workshop as soon as possible after contract award; scheduling the workshop for several days, since new working relationships take time to develop; and using a location away from the office or project site to allow participants the chance to get away from their daily duties and concentrate on Partnering.

The Partnering workshop should mold a single-minded joint management team for the project. To build an effective team, the workshop must strengthen the ability of the participants to communicate as a team. Team members must also develop and practice the skills and attitudes required of teamwork. At the workshop, one of the important activities will be to learn from the past and create for the future. This involves an honest evaluation of the strengths and weaknesses of past experiences and the strengths and weaknesses of the project team. The team then makes a group decision about positive strategies.

Since no project can be completed without the need to solve problems and resolve conflicts, conflict management and problem-solving skills should be a part of the workshop as well. The team must develop a problem-solving strategy that enables managers to address problems quickly and efficiently. "No action" on a problem is not an option! Problems that are not addressed sow the seeds of discord and division for the team. Expedited negotiations and ADR techniques offer methods for successful resolution of problems.

4. The Partnering Charter. At the conclusion of the Partnering workshop, the parties need to create a blueprint for their new relationship, which can be summed up in a Charter. The Partnering Charter defines the long-term goals and objectives for the project. This is a win-win charter. It is a collaborative effort written at the workshop by all participants and, therefore, includes the overlapping goals of the project team. Common goals are: a quality project carried out safely, in a timely and cost effective manner. To achieve these goals, the team must transform them into concrete objectives and action items which can be measured at follow-up sessions. If all the goals and objectives are achieved, both contracting parties will win.

The Partnering Charter should include objectives that will provide measurable milestones for success on the project. These objectives should be specific and should be the framework for a Partnering implementation plan. As an example, the following is a list of some project objectives:

- meet the design intent;

- encourage a maximum amount of value engineering savings;

- limit cost growth;

- cause no impact to follow-on projects;

- lose no time due to job-related injuries;

- encourage a fair sharing of contract risks;

- use ADR methods;

- avoid litigation;

- finish ahead of schedule;

- include an implementation plan.

The implementation plan fills out these objectives by including measurable details. For example, the implementation plan can call for a specific number of value engineering submittals or a target dollar amount of savings; a specified cost growth percentage; or a joint safety awareness program. These are just a few examples of how specifics can be added to the objectives to make them part of a viable plan for ensuring project success.

5. Follow-up Meetings and Evaluation. The importance of following up on the initial Partnering workshop cannot be stressed enough. The lessons of Partnering need continued reinforcing so they do not fade with time or under the stress of the job. On-going evaluation of Partnering goals and objectives is essential. The best method is to conduct regularly scheduled follow-up sessions between the key leaders.

To evaluate performance, successful Partnering efforts have included a jointly developed evaluation form. The evaluation form assigns weights to the Partnering objectives relative to the overall project. Ratings are determined for each evaluation period, and then compared to an agreed-upon standard. Corps and contractor leaders jointly rate performance. The result is a numerical score as well as a narrative evaluation. Such an evaluation can be the focus for a team meeting where problems are addressed and the values of partnership are encouraged and reinforced. Evaluation is important for good management of a project and encouragement of Partnering values.

There are other ways to advance the Partnering relationship through combined activities. Follow-up workshops could be scheduled to nurture the lessons and skills of Partnering. Debriefing sessions following significant milestones in the project could be the occasion for review of achievement. Awards ceremonies jointly conducted could recognize and reinforce cooperative effort. Professional development programs such as lectures, workshops, and breakfast seminars could be scheduled to emphasize job skills as well as team work.

5. Colleen A. Libbey, *Working Together While Waltzing in a Mine Field: Successful Government Construction Contract Dispute Resolution with Partnering and Dispute Review Boards*, 15 OHIO ST. J. ON DISP. RESOL. 825 (2000)

[M]any parties think partnering is all the ADR needed on a construction project. Partnering, however, is not a miracle cure, and a significant disadvantage of partnering is that many disputes cannot be resolved during the course of the construction project, because partnering does not provide for an active intermediary or decisionmaker. . . . Government construction projects begin with a design phase that involves planning and preparation. Next, the contractors bid and the government awards the project. Finally, the actual construction begins. Problems occur at multiple points in the construction phase. . . .

The 1978 Contract Disputes Act (CDA), 41 U.S.C. §§ 601-613, was the federal government's first attempt to use ADR in the government contract setting. The purpose of the CDA is to resolve government contract disputes through negotiation rather than litigation. All government contracts are governed by the CDA regulations, but the contracting parties may use other ADR techniques as alternatives to negotiation. Resolving a construction dispute under the CDA begins with the contracting officer. The contracting officer is an agency official whose primary function is to enter into and administer government contracts. Any claim that results from the construction contract must be presented to the contracting officer. The CDA requires the officer to issue a written decision if the dispute is not resolved amicably, and if a contractor is not satisfied with the contracting officer's decision, the claim may be appealed to an agency Board of Contract Appeals (BCA) or the United States Court of Federal Claims. . . .

The U.S. Army Corps of Engineers has adopted policies to further the use of an array of dispute prevention and ADR methods. The highest ranking officer of the Corps expressed the strong commitment of the Corps to ADR: "The U.S. Army Corps of Engineers seeks to accomplish its missions in the most effective and efficient manner possible. . . . The Corps of Engineers is the leader in the Federal Government in using ADR." The Corps' leadership in government ADR is one reason it pioneered the use of partnering and dispute review boards. Although the Corps pioneered the DRB method, the Corps and other members in the private and public construction industry rely on partnering to resolve disputes. However, partnering is not actually a dispute resolution method. There-fore, a dispute resolution method must be available. DRBs are an appropriate dispute resolution method for the federal government to use, for a variety of reasons. . . .

Reasons to Use Partnering with a Dispute Review Board. Overall, partnering and DRBs on their own successfully save costs and time. However, despite the general success of partnering, there are weaknesses of partnering that do not ensure dispute prevention. DRBs successfully complement the weaknesses of partnering.

Partnering has been highly effective in saving costs for all stakeholders in a construction project in many ways. First, open communication and creation of issue resolution strategies such as DRBs reduce litigation exposure. Open communication and cooperation also reduce the risk that the project will run over budget. A report by the Dispute Avoidance and Resolution Task Force of the AAA revealed that use of partnering in several projects involving a total of $492 million averaged seven percent in savings. Partnering was the favored cost-mini-mizing technique among construction industry contractors.

DRBs are also effective at saving costs. These cost savings are a result of the early resolution of disputes. Disputes are resolved early for two reasons. First, parties remedy disputes with specific DRB recommendations. Also, the presence of the DRB creates an incentive for settlement, which reduces other dispute resolution costs. Deferring a dispute for later resolution only increases the expense for attorney fees, documents, or expert witnesses.

Partnering and DRBs are highly effective at completing the project on time. A survey by the Construction Industry Institute showed that, out of thirty partnered construction projects totaling $684 million, eighty-three percent were completed on time or early. Using DRBs to resolve disputes as they occur also increases the likelihood of timely project completion. Resolving disputes as they arise reduces their impact on the project as a whole. DRBs effectively resolve issues that are critical to timely project completion, such as design issues, supply issues, delay issues, and follow-up work issues. Resolving these issues as they arise allows the project to continue uninterrupted. DRBs also promote timely project completion, because the presence of DRBs stimulates set-tlement, even when partnering does not.

Disadvantages of Partnering. The idea of partnering sounds great, but atti-tudes of the parties sometimes destroy the partnering relationship. Partnering is really an attitude and a mindset in which the ultimate goal is the elimination of "us" versus "them." This abstract attitude is difficult to maintain. It is even more difficult to maintain an "us" attitude when parties are self-interested. These selfish interests are perpetuated in government construction contracts as a result of government bureaucracy. Politics and bureaucratic pressure may con-trol an official's attitude and actions. If an "us" attitude is not maintained, communication may not be productive or even friendly. In sum, if the attitudes between the parties fail to foster a cooperative environment, then partnering will not prevent disputes.

Second, partnering may not prevent disputes because of flaws in the partnering process. Failure to create the partnering relationship before the project begins will minimize the dispute prevention potential of the partnered relationship. If the senior management on the project is not involved in the partnering process, then partnering will be ineffective. Failure to involve senior management in the partnering process will provide little incentive for lower management and employees on the project to cooperate. When government contracts are involved, "politics may be so bad on the project that senior management is afraid to override lower management project representatives." In addition, even if senior management has adopted partnering, personnel may not embrace it because it requires more work for them. Finally, the partnering process requires continual cooperation. Failure to exchange information continually and focus on team spirit will render the partnering relationship ineffective at preventing disputes.

The ultimate weakness of partnering is its failure to offer the services of an intermediary or decisionmaker when disputes are not prevented. Because the seeds of a dispute may need more than communication and cooperation to prevent its growth, the goodwill of those attending a partnering session is often not enough to settle problems that may have resulted from decisions or other factors beyond their immediate control. Once the partnering process has failed to prevent disputes, it is difficult for personnel to resolve disputes on their own. Leaving unresolved disputes to litigation or arbitration is not the answer. Employing DRBs is the answer.

Advantages of Using DRBs with Partnering. Even the most enthusiastic partnering advocates believe partnering cannot avoid disputes entirely; therefore, DRBs should be an available safety net for the parties. There are other ADR methods that one could use instead of partnering, such as mediation or summary jury trial, but partnering and DRBs strongly complement each other in a variety of areas. Partnering and DRBs complement one another because each lends itself to complex construction projects. The more complex, lengthy, and large the project, the greater the potential for partnering. Likewise, DRBs have become popular to resolve large, complex construction claims, such as tunnels, highways, and bridges. DRBs have enjoyed an almost 100% success rate on underground and tunneling projects, both considered extremely difficult construction jobs. Because both of these methods are suited to large construction disputes, they will complement each other when used in conjunction on a project.

DRBs complement partnering, because the DRB will not terminate until the project is complete, whereas partnering terminates when the relationship dwindles. There is no dwindling away of the DRB. Once the partnering relationship has deteriorated, the likelihood for disputes increases. Without a dispute resolution procedure available, the project may never be completed. The DRB will not terminate until the project is complete and all disputes are resolved.

Parties involved in construction disputes tend to favor dispute resolution mechanisms like DRBs, because they involve neutral parties. A DRB may be more effective at resolving disputes than partnering, because the DRB members are entirely neutral. In contrast, construction parties in a partnered relationship cannot remain entirely neutral. For instance, in many cases, government managers feel they must distance themselves from a contract to avoid the appearance of any impropriety. In addition, if a dispute is sent to the contracting officer, it creates a dual, potentially conflicting role for the contracting office. The contracting officer is not only to represent the government as a party to the contract, but also is to make decisions on claims. The neutrality of the DRB counterbalances partnering biases of those involved in the partnered relationship, such as managers or contracting officers. Parties are likely to accept DRB recommendations versus a recommendation from nonneutral parties in the partnering relationship, because the DRB recommendation is the product of an impartial, mutually acceptable panel's decisionmaking process. Such a decision is hard to reject in good faith.

Finally, dispute review boards work. DRBs resolve disputes that partnering cannot prevent. In addition, there have been very few court challenges to DRB recommendations. . . . While most people would agree that "the best dispute resolution is dispute prevention," it is difficult to prevent all disputes. Partnering cannot always prevent disputes, and therefore, it becomes critical to use dispute resolution methods concurrently with partnering, specifically DRBs. Despite the acclaim for partnering, there are too many opportunities for a partnered relationship to fail. For this reason, both federal and state agencies should employ DRBs to resolve construction disputes. . . . If both partnering and DRBs are used on government construction contracts, the parties will keep together, work together, and the project will be a success.

Chapter 12

GOVERNMENT USE OF ADR: THE EXECUTIVE BRANCH

A. INTRODUCTION

This Chapter deals with three distinct but related topics: the government as provider *of* ADR services, administrative agencies *as* ADR, and the use of ADR *by* administrative agencies. The discussion is largely limited to federal agencies, and even then only a small part of the administrative dispute resolution landscape is examined. Only specific dispute resolution programs are considered; negotiation, which government does at all levels on a vast scale, is excluded. We considered plea bargaining in Chapter Six. (The courts comprise the judicial branch of government, but prosecution of crimes is an executive function.)

Adjudication under the Administrative Procedure Act (APA), 5 U.S.C. §§ 551 *et. seq.*, might be regarded as ADR, because it replaces judicial hearings. Contested disability determinations by the Social Security Administration and claims for benefits by Veterans provide examples. These agencies decide far more contested claims each year than the entire federal court system. Adjudication is the administrative analogue of a judicial trial, albeit with significant differences: there are no juries, the exclusionary rules of evidence are not used, and the decider of fact is a subject-matter expert. In each of these respects, administrative adjudication is more like an arbitration proceeding than a judicial trial.

Rulemaking is the administrative analogue of legislation, except that the scope of an agency's rulemaking authority is defined (and circumscribed) by Congress. The English employ the illuminating term "subordinate legislation" for what the APA calls a rule. The most important use of ADR in this area is negotiated rulemaking, commonly known as "reg-neg." The authority for reg-neg proceedings is the Negotiated Rulemaking Act of 1990. Section F covers this important topic.

In some instances, federal agencies provide ADR services to the public, notably in the context of emergencies and labor disputes. An assortment of ADR procedures have long been used to settle disputes between government and contractors, notably by the Army Corps of Engineers.

Conversely, the federal government is an important purchaser of ADR services from private providers. For an introduction to this subject, see Dave Alexander, *How to Sell ADR to the U.S. Government*, 59-OCT Disp. Resol. J. 80 (2004).

Although the federal government has long made use of ADR in a wide variety of contexts, express general authority originated with the Administrative Dispute Resolution Act (ADRA) of 1990. Enactment of the ADRA (together with the important 1996 amendments) provided the impetus for a dramatic expansion in the use of ADR by the government, with leadership provided by the Department of Justice (DOJ). Section B introduces the provisions of the ADRA, while Section C discusses implementation of the Act.

The remainder of the Chapter examines several particular instances of ADR use by the federal government. Section D presents two case studies: the settlement process employed by the DOJ for claims made pursuant to the Federal Tort Claims Act (FTCA), and Farmer-Lender mediation. Section E discusses the use of ADR procedures by the Internal Revenue Service (IRS). This topic is important, because the IRS has been using various forms of ADR for decades, and because taxpayers have regular interaction with the IRS. Section F introduces negotiated rulemaking ("reg-neg"), a specialized form of rulemaking used particularly for educational and environmental rules.

B. THE ADMINISTRATIVE DISPUTE RESOLUTION ACTS (ADRA) OF 1990 AND 1996

1. Comments and Questions

a. The use of ADR by agencies of the federal government to settle individual disputes has a lengthy provenance, as illustrated by the settlement procedures of the Internal Revenue Service (IRS), which are discussed below. During the 1980s, the use of ADR processes by the government increased, as happened throughout our society.

b. Congress explicitly authorized and encouraged the use of ADR by administrative agencies in The Administrative Dispute Resolution Act (ADRA) of 1990. The 1996 ADRA Amendments further solidified the place of ADR in the federal government.

c. The Negotiated Rulemaking Act, which provides the statutory basis for Reg-Neg, also was enacted in 1990. Both this legislation and the ADRA amend the Administrative Procedure Act (APA). Legislation promoting the use of ADR by the federal courts is discussed in Chapter Ten.

2. Stephen K. Huber, The Administrative Dispute Resolution Act of *1990* 266 (1996)

The Administrative Dispute Resolution Act (ADRA) of 1990 covers the use of ADR in lieu of adjudication "to resolve issues in conflict including, but not limited to, settlement negotiations, conciliation, facilitation, mediation, factfinding, mini-trials and arbitration, or any combination thereof." [§ 571(d)] Congress sought not simply to clarify the authority of agencies to make use of ADR, but also to promote the use of voluntary alternative means of dispute resolution.

Agencies were given plenary authority to settle disputes through ADR, "if the parties agree to such proceeding." The ADRA directed that agencies "*consider*" not using ADR in several circumstances [§ 572(b), emphasis supplied]:

- authoritative precedent needed;
- uniformity of result important for policy reasons;
- significant impact on third parties;
- full public record important; and
- matters not subject to complete and final disposition.

The ADRA does not prohibit the use of ADR in these circumstances, and the agency decision is not subject to collateral attack by persons not party to the proceeding. Party acquiescence is not a concern, since consent is a condition precedent to the use of ADR pursuant to the ADRA in lieu of agency adjudication.

The decision of an agency to use ADR, *vel non*, or to choose one ADR procedure instead of another, "is committed to the discretion of the agency and shall not be subject to judicial review." [§ 581] Review of arbitration awards is available pursuant to the Federal Arbitration Act (FAA), which is to say only on very limited grounds.

3. Jonathan D. Meister, *The Administrative Dispute Resolution Act of 1996: Will the New Era of ADR in Federal Administrative Agencies Occur at the Expense of Public Accountability?*, 13 OHIO ST. J. ON DISP. RESOL. 167 (1997)

The Administrative Dispute Resolution Act of 1996 provided for permanent reauthorization of the Administrative Dispute Resolution Act of 1990, which sunset on October 1, 1995. While maintaining many of the same provisions of the 1990 Act, the new law enacts two major changes designed to further agency use of ADR in suits with private parties. Section 8 permits the use of binding arbitration, removing the thirty-day "opt-out" provision in the 1990 Act, which allowed agencies to unilaterally vacate an arbitration award if the agency found the arbitrator's decision to be disadvantageous to the government. Section 3 broadens the confidentiality of ADR proceedings by exempting any dispute resolution communication between a party and a neutral from the disclosure requirements of the Freedom of Information Act (FOIA). Together, these provisions greatly enhance the incentives for parties involved in agency adjudications to utilize ADR. While these changes will undoubtedly lead to a new era of ADR use in the federal government, . . . the 1996 Act may have gone too far due to its potentially devastating effects on public accountability.

The 1990 Act resulted in further use of ADR in agency adjudications. Mediation became especially prevalent in the 1990s, particularly in equal employment opportunity claims against the federal government. The use of mediation by the Air Force Civilian Appellate Review Agency resulted in the settlement of more than half of its equal employment opportunity complaints. The Federal Aviation Administration also implemented mediation for use in equal employment opportunity claims. Nonbinding arbitration was also utilized by several agencies, particularly in environmental disputes and in claims faced by the Army Corps of Engineers. These and other success stories convinced Congress, as well as the Bush and Clinton administrations, that permanent statutory reauthorization of ADR mechanisms was essential to the ongoing effort to streamline government.

Despite these achievements, however, there were several perceived shortcomings in the 1990 Act that limited the use of ADR in agency adjudications. The biggest impediment was the nonbinding arbitration clause, which granted agencies thirty days to vacate an arbitrator's decision. This "trap door" provision of the 1990 Act was inserted during the hearing stage in order to allay concerns that the establishment of a binding arbitration award by a private party would raise constitutional issues over the adjudication of public disputes by unelected, unappointed private arbitrators. Under the Bush Administration in 1989, the Department of Justice (DOJ) opined that binding arbitration of agency disputes potentially violated the Constitution in several ways. First, binding arbitration violated Article II under the Appointment Clause, because arbitrators often are not federal employees, and thus are not authorized to make such policy determinations. Moreover, binding arbitration was thought to violate separation of powers, since the Act in effect permitted Congress to legislate the use of private parties in potentially executive roles. DOJ also found binding arbitration to be contrary to Article III in that adjudicative powers were conveyed to persons outside the judicial branch. Finally, DOJ indicated a potential due process problem because of the higher due process protection generally accorded private parties subject to a federal suit brought by the federal government.

In 1995, however, DOJ changed its position concerning the constitutionality of binding arbitration of agency disputes. In its revised opinion, the Department reasoned that binding arbitration by private parties is permissible as long as the parties consent, the arbitration agreement sufficiently details the nature of the remedies available to the arbitrator and preserves the review of constitutional issues, and an Article III court is accorded review of the arbitrator's findings for fraud, misconduct or misrepresentation. This saving interpretation by DOJ permitted Congress to include binding arbitration as part of the 1996 Act.

A second perceived problem with the 1990 Act was the lack of an express FOIA exemption. Under the 1990 Act, ADR communications were not expressly confidential. Instead, a communication was deemed confidential only if it fell within one of the nine disclosure exemptions of FOIA. Among the most notable of these FOIA exemptions are any "inter-agency or intra-agency" communication, and any "trade secrets and commercial or financial information." According to critics of the 1990 Act, the lack of an express exemption from FOIA created a "chilling effect" on the use of ADR in agency adjudications, because private parties and agencies alike were reluctant to use ADR for fear of unwanted public disclosure.

As a result of these shortcomings, the use of ADR has met much resistance and made a limited impact to date on dispute resolution in federal agencies. While the parties have moved beyond the traditional manifest distrust of neutrals, the 1990 Act was largely ineffectual. As a result, many agencies have implemented only cursory ADR programs, and have indicated no intent to implement these programs further. Even the Department of Justice, whose endorsement of the constitutionality of binding arbitration led in part to the expansion of ADR programs under the new Act, has evinced a reluctance to implement widespread ADR programs by utilizing ADR in only three of its divisions since passage of the 1990 Act.

The 1996 Act was, therefore, enacted with far stronger language than its predecessor. The binding arbitration and FOIA exemption provisions are indicative of Congress's desire to overcome this reluctance to use ADR in agency adjudications. Parties to an ADR proceeding may now freely utilize arbitration without fear of an eventual reversal of the decision by the government. Private parties also need no longer fear disclosure of confidential information via the FOIA. Certainly, there appears to be little question that these provisions will lead to increased use of ADR.

C. THE USES OF ADR BY THE FEDERAL GOVERNMENT: JUSTICE DEPARTMENT LEADERSHIP

1. Comments and Questions

a. The Department of Justice is the agency with primary responsibility for implementation of the ADRA by the federal government. It is not self-evident that an agency that litigates on behalf of the government would prove to be a strong supporter of ADR, but that has been the case. During the Clinton administration, Attorney General Janet Reno was a vigorous advocate for ADR. Support for ADR has continued during the Bush II administration, although perhaps not with the vigor that characterized General Reno's leadership.

b. The author of the next article, Jeffrey Senger, has been the leading ADR staff person at the Justice Department in both the Clinton and Bush administrations. For more background on the ADRA and the leadership role of the Justice Department in its implementation by the participants, see Daniel Marcus & Jeffrey Senger, *ADR and the Federal Government: Not Such Strange Bedfellows*, 66 Mo. L. Rev. 709 (2001).

2. Jeffrey M. Senger, *Turning the Ship of State*, 2000 J. Disp. Resol. 79

I. Federal ADR Law and Policy

A. Legislation. The 1990s have clearly been the most productive decade in history for government ADR. The enactment of a number of laws in the past ten years has changed the nature of the way the government handles conflict. It is heartening that this has been a true bipartisan effort, with bills passed by both Democratic and Republican Congresses and signed into law by both Republican and Democratic Presidents. . . .

B. Presidential Orders. Recent U.S. Presidents have also been active in promoting ADR. In 1991, President George Bush issued an executive order calling on government counsel to be trained in dispute resolution techniques, noting that ADR can "contribute to the prompt, fair, and efficient resolution of . . . claims." However, paralleling the uncertainty Congress also showed at the beginning of the decade, Bush said these procedures were not to be used unless unassisted negotiation had failed: "Whenever feasible, claims should be resolved through informal discussions, negotiations, and settlements rather than through utilization of any formal or structured ADR process." In 1996, President Clinton removed this qualification and issued an executive order that endorsed ADR with greater enthusiasm. In particular, it required the following:

> Litigation counsel shall make reasonable attempts to resolve a dispute expeditiously and properly before proceeding to trial. . . .Where the benefits of ADR may be derived, and after consultation with the agency referring the matter, litigation counsel should suggest the use of an appropriate ADR technique to the parties. . . .To facilitate broader and effective use of informal and formal ADR methods, litigation counsel should be trained in ADR techniques.

C. Department of Justice Policies. One of the greatest friends to ADR in the government has been Attorney General Janet Reno. A person who believes strongly in the value of ADR (or "Appropriate Dispute Resolution," as she calls it), the Attorney General has worked tirelessly to ensure the government uses these processes wherever appropriate. When she created the Department's dispute resolution office in 1995, we were hoping she would provide a spark to our efforts. Instead, she has provided a blowtorch.

Reno first issued a Department of Justice order in 1995 to promote the broader use of ADR, ordering training for all civil attorneys and requiring each litigating component to publish an ADR policy statement in the Federal Register. These policy statements are extensive and provide a valuable guide into ADR practices at the Justice Department. They include factors favoring and disfavoring the use of ADR for specific types of cases, descriptions of available ADR techniques, criteria for selecting an appropriate technique, and procedures to be followed in the use of ADR. Each litigating component in the Department published its own individualized guidelines. The Attorney General also published a forcefully worded statement on behalf of the entire Department in the Federal Register:

> Our commitment to make greater use of ADR is long overdue. Clearly, our federal court system is in overload. Delays are all too common, depriving the public of swift, efficient, and just resolution of disputes. The Department of Justice is the biggest user of the federal courts and the nation's most prolific litigator. Therefore, it is incumbent upon those Department attorneys who handle civil litigation from Washington and throughout the country to consider alternatives to litigation.

Critically, the Attorney General backed up this commitment by creating a $1 million fund to pay for mediators. Department of Justice managers around the country have reported that this was the single most effective way to get them to use ADR, as they no longer had to pay mediator fees out of their own office budgets. The Attorney General has also followed through on the commitment to provide training. Over the past four years, we have given ADR training to more than 1,600 DOJ lawyers, both in Washington and in all ninety-four United States Attorneys' Offices around the country. The Department has begun emphasizing dispute resolution skills in its hiring practices as well. . . .

D. The Interagency ADR Working Group. One of the biggest engines for change in federal government dispute resolution recently has been the Interagency ADR Working Group, which the Attorney General agreed to chair in 1998 at the request of the President. The mission of this group is to promote the use of administrative ADR government-wide and to "facilitate, encourage, and provide coordination for agencies. . . . The group is also working with the EEOC, which recently issued regulations requiring every federal agency to implement an ADR program for workplace disputes." 29 C.F.R. § 1614. These new regulations will greatly increase the use of agency ADR, as workplace grievances are among the most common in the government.

E. Research and Evaluation. As we look to the future in this field, additional research and evaluation on the effectiveness of ADR will be essential. Congress and taxpayers insist on documented cost savings in order to provide funding for government programs. . . . At the Justice Department, we have conducted a study of nearly one thousand reporting forms filled out by Assistant United States Attorneys using mediation over the past four years. . . . Almost two-thirds of the cases in this study settled during the mediation. In those cases that did not settle, almost one-half of the time the attorneys reported that there were valuable results of the mediation nonetheless (such as insight into the other side's point of view, informal discovery, or agreement on some issues). Attorneys have estimated substantial savings in time and money from ADR as well.

Other agencies report similar success. The Air Force has used ADR in more than 7,000 workplace disputes between fiscal years 1997 and 1999, with a resolution rate higher than 70%. The Air Force has also found ADR effective in the government contracts area, where they have used it in approximately one hundred contract controversies with a 93% settlement rate. Of particular note is the agency's recent successful use of ADR to resolve two major contract disputes with claims for more than $190 million and $500 million. The Secretary of the Air Force has recognized the success of these programs and codified them in formal agency procedures. It is now official Air Force policy to use ADR "to the maximum extent practicable."

The U.S. Postal Service has another leading ADR program in the workplace area, which helps address the needs of the agency's eight hundred thousand employees (more than any employer except the military and Wal-Mart). The need for ADR is particularly acute at this agency, where employees filed more than 20,000 informal EEO complaints during 1997. Postal Service policy is to conduct a mediation within two weeks after a complainant requests it. The average mediation takes just four hours, and 81% of mediated cases are closed without a formal complaint being filed. Satisfaction is extremely high. Employees participating in mediation report they are twice as satisfied with the amount of control, respect and fairness of the process as they are with the traditional process (88% satisfaction rate versus 44%). Both employees and supervisors are equally satisfied with mediation.

Another benefit of the Postal Service program has been that mediation appears to be creating lasting changes in the behavior of people in the workplace. With the increased communication that mediation provides, employees and supervisors may actually be learning to get along better. In fiscal year 1999, the number of complaints filed dropped by approximately 16%. This translates into thousands of fewer complaints per year, which represents a huge cost savings. EEO complaints are very expensive to process, and cost estimates range from a conservative $5,000 for handling a simple case up to $77,000 for taking a more complicated complaint all the way through to the end of the process. Even using the lower figure, the reduction in complaints is saving millions of dollars each year in processing costs, not to mention the costs in morale and productivity.

II. Barriers to the Use of ADR in the Federal Government

We run into many barriers to ADR in the government, and some are easier to address than others. We have heard many excuses for why ADR should not be used for a particular case or a particular program.

A. The "Litigation Mentality." One of the most common sources of resistance to ADR is the "litigation mentality." Many people perceive ADR to be soft, "touchy-feely," and something more appropriate for people holding hands at a Zen Buddhist retreat than for litigants in a federal lawsuit. Government litigators are no exception. One manager recently told us that he is distressed because his lawyers are "settling too many cases."

Dealing with this element of the legal culture is often an uphill fight. The government, like the country as a whole, has a long tradition glorifying the lawyer as a warrior. I started my career as a trial lawyer at the Justice Department, and there was nothing like the excitement in an office when someone was in trial. Supervisors would provide daily reports of how the trial was going, praising the clever things the lawyer did that day. At the end of the trial, win or lose, we would have a big staff meeting to talk about what happened. A lawyer who lost a trial still received some respect for fighting the good fight. A lawyer who won generally received an award and cash bonus at the end of the year. In contrast, a lawyer who negotiated a settlement received little fanfare. The settlement might only be mentioned in a weekly written report. Even if the result was better than we ever would have received from a jury, there was not much glory in settling a case.

Yet another factor here is that a lawyer who settles a case before trial misses out on courtroom experience. The opportunity to try cases is a key reason some young attorneys come to the Justice Department, sacrificing lucrative salaries in the private sector. Negotiation experience, while it can be at least as important in the long run, is not valued as highly. . . . We have worked internally to address this issue by changing attorney performance evaluations to measure and reward not just trial skills but also settlement skills. We also have created a new department-wide award called the John Marshall Award for use of ADR, which includes a cash bonus and is presented by the Attorney General.

B. Fear of Looking Weak. Some people tell us they are afraid that even offering ADR to the other side is akin to confessing that their case is weak and they are worried about it. They fear that a plaintiff will see the offer of mediation as signaling a blank check on the part of the government. We advise lawyers to say the Attorney General has asked them to consider mediation in all appropriate cases, and that is what they are doing. We also tell them that there is plenty of room to represent a client zealously in a mediation, and participating in mediation is by no means the equivalent of abject submission. This fear should be reduced as ADR becomes . . . institutionalized, and as more organizations and judges require parties to consider it.

C. Perception of ADR as a Passing Fad. Another source of resistance is skepticism based on the view that ADR is the latest "flavor of the month," a fad that will pass by if people merely wait long enough. Government employees get tired of repeatedly being told what to do from headquarters, and in fairness, there are a lot of new directives coming out of Washington each month. . . . Some of these people seem to feel that when we teach them ADR, we are impliedly criticizing the way they have been doing their jobs up to this point. . . .

D. Lack of Experience. Sometimes we face simple inertia based on lack of experience. Lawyers who have been doing their job for twenty years or more sometimes do not want to change or are concerned about what would happen if they did. They are reluctant to try something new that they may not be very good at, or that may not turn out well. Often, the young lawyers fresh out of law school are more accustomed to ADR than the senior managers, which can add to the awkwardness of the situation. . . .

E. Negative Experience. We have also encountered resistance from people who have used mediation once and had a bad experience. . . . Many lawyers are control-oriented, and the prospect of losing control in a mediation is upsetting to them. . . . We seek to counter this perception by reminding lawyers that the greatest loss of control comes not when you mediate, but when you begin your opening statement to the jury. That is when you have truly put your matter into someone else's hands. You can always walk out of a mediation that is not going well, an option you do not have in a trial.

F. Perverse Incentives. Perverse incentives sometimes hinder settlement in corporations, and the government has its share of these as well. Perhaps the most egregious example for the government occurs in employment discrimination cases, which are a big part of the workload of government attorneys. If an agency wants to settle one of these cases at the administrative stage, it must investigate the claim and pay any award out of current operating funds. If, however, an agency refuses to settle and the claimant files in federal court, the case is transferred to the Department of Justice. Justice then supplies its own attorneys and pays the costs of litigation out of its own budget. Even further, the agency does not have to pay any award that comes from litigation, as all damages or settlement proceeds are paid from a government-wide account called the Judgment Fund.

There are many problems with this system. First, cases are often easiest to settle early on, before parties get hardened into their positions. The adversarial process has a way of pushing parties farther apart the longer it goes on, and this is particularly true in emotionally charged cases involving employment discrimination. By the time an agency denies a claim and the case gets to the Justice Department, the best opportunity to settle the claim has often been lost. Second, attorneys' fees grow rapidly as a case progresses, making the case harder and more expensive for the government to settle later on. Third, it can be argued that forcing agencies to pay their own damages would create more appropriate incentives for them to avoid future suits by training and disciplining their employees.

Plaintiffs' attorneys as well have a perverse incentive not to settle early. By statute, attorneys' fees for a Federal Tort Claims Act case that settles at the administrative stage are 20% of the award, while fees for a case settling once a federal court complaint is filed are 25% of the award. This extra 5% can be significant, and it can place counterproductive pressures on attorneys to avoid settlement at the administrative stage.

There are a number of complicated factors that led to the present system and will also make it difficult to change. For example, agencies do not currently have budget resources to start paying for their own damage claims, and considerable financial restructuring would be necessary to institute a reform in the system. There are also advantages to having settlement decisions made in a centralized way at the Justice Department rather than risking inconsistent determinations by dozens of different agencies. Other concerns exist as well. However, we are hopeful that the ADR movement will provide the impetus for improvements in this area.

G. Lack of Funding. In this time of government downsizing, when agencies are repeatedly asked to do more with less, another problem we have faced is inadequate funding. It has often been difficult to find the resources necessary to get ADR programs off the ground. The government ADR program has largely been built by people working on "collateral duty," fitting in their ADR work as best they can. Few agencies have dedicated ADR staffs, which would be important in providing training, coordination, and promotion of mediation in an agency. . . .

H. Lack of Support. Sometimes support for ADR is lacking at one level of an agency even if it exists at another. We have seen this phenomenon in two ways — in some cases upper management is uninterested while middle management and staff want to move forward, and sometimes the situation is reversed. Both levels need to be enthusiastic for the process to take hold. If middle managers and staff don't want to use ADR, they will find many ways to avoid it, no matter how often department heads issue guidance and memoranda. It is most often the staff lawyer on a given case who is going to choose whether or not to use ADR, not the immediate supervisor, and not the Attorney General. On the other hand, if upper management won't dedicate resources, a program will not be successful either. Employees seek recognition and appreciation from their supervisors, and they won't use ADR if it is not rewarded. In a survey we conducted of staff employees asking what the biggest obstacle was to implementing an ADR program in their agency, the highest response was lack of top-and mid-level support (39%).

I. Resistance Based on Type of Case. Many people resist ADR by claiming it only works in certain limited cases. We have heard people say, "Our cases involve only money, and ADR doesn't work in these cases." Interestingly, we've also heard, just about as often, "ADR works in cases that only involve money, but not in our more complicated cases." Frequently, people mention equal employment opportunity ("EEO") cases, as in, "ADR only works in EEO cases" or "We've got ADR covered; we already have an EEO mediation program and don't need anything else." While we do not argue that ADR is appropriate in every case, situations where we recommend against it are rare, such as when the government needs a court ruling for a public sanction or a legal precedent.

Attorneys in government enforcement agencies sometimes argue that ADR is inappropriate in their cases, because it dilutes the message sent to violators. The idea is that the government can't compromise on its enforcement cases, because there is no room to negotiate when the public's interest is at stake. Followed strictly, this approach would mean that a government attorney should make a single, fair settlement offer, and then simply go to court if the other side doesn't take it. However, we have found that very few government attorneys, even in the enforcement area, ultimately follow this approach. Most have learned that opposing parties view negotiation as something of a dance and expect movement from the government. Single-offer negotiation is so rare in the world that few people would believe a government attorney who attempted to try such an approach. Once enforcement attorneys admit they do negotiate their cases, we point out that a mediator can sometimes be helpful. Further, a consensual resolution is often uniquely valuable in an enforcement case. Compliance levels are higher when parties have agreed to settle a case rather than had a judgment imposed on them by a court. Consensual settlements allow parties to craft their own settlements using a wide range of injunctive remedies that would be unavailable to a court.

J. Resistance from Opposing Counsel. The Attorney General recently talked about dispute resolution at an ABA House of Delegates Meeting and then received a telephone call from a very irate person who said, "You are taking cases from lawyers!" Indeed, one mediator notes that private sector lawyers sometimes believe that ADR stands for "Alarming Drop in Revenue." Fortunately, government lawyers do not share this particular perverse incentive. Most are altogether happy to settle cases more quickly in order to spend more time on their other matters. Settlements do not reduce the partnership billing share of anyone in the government. Nonetheless, it can be frustrating to have an opposing counsel who does not seem to share this perspective. . . .

K. Lack of Settlement Authority. One problem that government attorneys have more often than their private sector counterparts is dealing with limited settlement authority. Many mediators want someone at the table with full authority to settle the matter. However, the Justice Department is involved with some 40,000 civil cases each year, and the Attorney General cannot personally attend every one that goes to mediation. We have faced private mediators as well as federal judges who were upset with us on this issue, and we have even filed appeals in certain cases where district judges have required the personal appearance of a high-ranking official.

Generally, the best thing a staff lawyer can do in this situation is to prepare for it as much as possible beforehand. By writing settlement memoranda and having discussions with the appropriate supervisors ahead of time, a lawyer can go into a mediation with reasonable authority to handle whatever is likely to take place. Other times, a supervisor can be available by telephone. Overall, we recognize that this can sometimes make mediation more difficult, but we do the best we can with the limitations of the situation.

L. Concerns About Confidentiality. Still another problem for the implementation of ADR is the fear that some people have that the sky will fall if we do not get immediate and final answers to some difficult questions in the field. Confidentiality is one such issue that people on all sides get upset about. This is a very difficult area to resolve neatly and to everyone's satisfaction, particularly when the government is involved. For example, if government law enforcement agencies seek access to mediation communications, ADR providers understandably become very concerned, because reducing confidentiality could curtail parties' candor and limit the effectiveness of mediation. On the other hand, non-mediators are equally agitated if the government holds that mediation confidentiality automatically prevents public access to evidence of crime. These objections are particularly strong if the evidence is from a taxpayer-funded mediation and involves alleged public fraud, waste, or abuse. Many examples can be imagined in which neither granting confidentiality nor denying it seems entirely satisfactory. Fortunately, we have found that confidentiality problems in mediation are rare. In the thousands of ADR cases at the Justice Department in recent years, problems with confidentiality have occurred only a few times. While confidentiality is a vital issue to resolve correctly, we should remember that, in the vast majority of cases, it never comes up. . . .

3. *Too Little Too Late? Ashcroft Issues Support Letter to Agency ADR Officials*, 22 ALTERNATIVES TO HIGH COST LITIG. 71 (May 2004)

Attorney General John Ashcroft has issued a letter of support to the federal government's top alternative dispute resolution officials, backing their efforts and urging them to grow their conflict resolution practices. Practitioners seem to be relieved to receive Ashcroft's support after more than three years in office. But some Washingtonians familiar with federal ADR complain that the attorney general's support is weak.

In his March 12 letter to the Steering Committee of the Interagency ADR Working Group, a group of executive branch ADR officials (see www.adr.gov), Ashcroft immediately dealt with the appearance of a lower profile of federal government ADR. He explained that the Sept. 11, 2001, terrorist attacks "required us to refocus our resources." Adding that the government "must continue to discharge many other important responsibilities that are essential to the well-being of our country and our citizens," Ashcroft wrote that "[t]he effective and successful use of ADR is making a significant contribution to that effort."

Jeffrey Senger, senior counsel in the Justice Department's Office of Dispute Resolution and a point person for federal ADR efforts including the Interagency ADR Working Group, also welcomes the letter and believes it will boost ADR use. "The attorney general and the Department of Justice are committed to expanding and further developing the government's use of ADR," he says, adding, "With the continued assistance of the Interagency ADR Working Group Steering Committee and agencies throughout the government, we will utilize ADR processes wherever appropriate to resolve disputes more efficiently, more effectively, and more harmoniously."

But not everyone is satisfied. Deborah S. Laufer, executive director of the Federal ADR Network in Silver Spring, Md., which monitors executive branch ADR use and trends and disseminates program information, says that "[w]hile Ashcroft's letter is rightly complimentary to the Steering Committee and to ADR efforts throughout the government, it avoids setting government goals for ADR, . . . and does little to position the Steering Committee toward thoughtful leadership of government-wide ADR implementation.". . . Jeff Senger of the DOJ's Office of Dispute Resolution counters that the department "has used ADR in about 10,000 cases nationwide since 2001, including some of the most important litigation in the government, such as the Microsoft case."

For his part, Attorney General Ashcroft has indicated support for ADR principles and processes since he was sworn into office in early February 2001. "Disputes are inevitable, but litigation is not," said Ashcroft in commencement remarks two years ago at the University of Missouri-Columbia School of Law, which is home to one of the nation's top dispute resolution programs. He said that the Justice Department's use of ADR to settle matters had climbed to 3,000 annually in 2002, at the time of the speech, from 550 in 1995. And also two years ago, the Bush administration instituted awards for creative uses of ADR in procurement. . . .

D. TWO GOVERNMENT ADR CASE STUDIES: TORT CLAIMS AND FARMER-LENDER MEDIATION

1. Daniel Shane Read, *The Courts' Difficult Balancing Act to be Fair to Both Plaintiff and Government Under the FTCA's Administrative Claims Process*, 57 BAYLOR L. REV. 785 (2005)

When an employee of the federal government is negligent in a tort, the wronged individual may sue in federal court under the Federal Tort Claims Act (FTCA) only after filing a claim for damages with the federal agency whose employee was negligent. Such procedure was set up to encourage settlements before incurring the costs and resources of attorneys (both plaintiff and Government), federal agencies, and judges in federal court litigation. This Article examines the administrative claims process. . . .

Prior to the enactment of the FTCA in 1946, a plaintiff had very few avenues for relief if he suffered from a tort caused by the Government. The reason was a long standing legal precedent, existing since the founding of the United States, that a suit could not be brought against the Government without its consent. This precedent is known as the doctrine of sovereign immunity. . . . Before the FTCA, it was well-settled that the Government was not liable for the negligence of its employees and that the sole relief for an injured person was to request damages from Congress. Thus, an injured individual had a very difficult and unappealing choice. First, one could sue the government employee in his individual capacity, spend time and money trying to get a favorable judgment, and then hope that the individual defendant could afford to pay the judgment. Or, a plaintiff could petition Congress for relief. The former was risky unless the government employee was wealthy, and the latter was burdensome and time-consuming.

As decades passed, the process of private citizens petitioning Congress for legislation for relief from wrongs done by federal employees proved unworkable. The number of claims taxed Congress's time and Congress was ill-suited for the task of administering justice. President Franklin Roosevelt commented in 1942 that during the last three Congresses, almost 6,300 private claim bills were introduced, less than twenty percent of which became law, and that of all the Presidential vetoes during those Congresses, one-third were made up of private claim bills. The President also noted that the existing Congressional procedure for tort relief was "slow, expensive, and unfair both to the Congress and to the claimant." . . .

The FTCA was enacted in 1946 and provided American citizens with a cause of action against federal agencies when employees of the agency — acting within the scope of their federal employment — committed negligent acts such that if the United States were a private person, it would be liable under the law of the particular state in which the incident took place. It was designed to give injured persons an avenue of recovery "as a matter of right." When the FTCA was enacted, there was no requirement — as there later would be — that a plaintiff first present a claim for damages to the federal agency allegedly responsible for the tort before filing a lawsuit. Thus, a plaintiff could immediately file his lawsuit in federal court after the injury in question. . . . Although the government was trying to be fairer to plaintiffs by providing a streamlined process for justice in contrast to the cumbersome process of seeking private relief bills from Congress, the results were not completely satisfactory. The new flood of lawsuits created a burden on the courts and government agencies defending the lawsuits. . . . After twenty years, Congress addressed this undesirable situation with passage of a mandatory administrative claim requirement.

In 1966, Congress enacted an administrative claim requirement to address concerns arising from the passage of the FTCA. Congress added this additional step pursuant to the well-settled doctrine that a sovereign may define the conditions under which it may be sued. The 1966 Amendment had two goals: to ease court congestion and provide fairness to plaintiffs by aiding the Government in its attempts to settle meritorious cases. . . . The legislators hoped that passage of the amendment would permit federal agencies to settle substantial numbers of tort claims, thus enabling the Department of Justice's Civil Division to give greater attention to those cases that involved difficult legal and damage questions in such areas as medical malpractice, drug and other products liability, and aviation accidents. . . .

A. Procedures for Filing Administrative Claim. If a person is injured by the negligence of a government employee, he must make a claim in writing. Although not required, this claim is often submitted to the federal agency on the government's Standard Form 95, either by the plaintiff or the plaintiff's attorney. The Form 95 is a one page document that requires very little information from the plaintiff. Other than the obvious fact that personal information is requested, the form has only a few other boxes: one for the date and time of the accident; a box that has room for approximately four sentences to describe the "basis of claim" including the location and those people involved; a small box for a description of injury; and a box for the amount of claim in dollars.

B. Requirements of Claim. Whether the claim is submitted on a Form 95 or in a letter, the requirements of a proper claim are that (1) the claim must provide the federal agency with sufficient notice and details of the occurrence in question to allow the federal agency to conduct its own investigation, (2) the claim must assert a sum certain of damages, and (3) the claim must be presented to the agency within two years after the claim accrues. The submission of a claim to the agency is paramount, because a plaintiff cannot file a lawsuit in federal court until the agency has denied the claim in writing and notified the plaintiff by certified or registered mail. However, the failure of an agency to make a final decision on the claim within six months after the claim is filed may be deemed a final agency denial at the plaintiff's option for purposes of beginning litigation in federal court. In any event, a plaintiff must file his lawsuit in federal court within six months of the agency's denial of his claim.

Form 95 gives scant information for the agency to act on other than the date, time, location, amount of damages claimed, and a few sentences about the nature of the injury and witnesses. Thus, Form 95 and its request for damages is simply a starting point for the settlement process. For example, if there is a medical malpractice claim occurring at an agency's hospital (such as a Veteran's Administration Hospital), the agency will need medical documentation from the claimant regarding injuries, and bills and pertinent information from any other hospital the claimant may have visited.

C. Federal Regulations Regarding Settlement. . . . The regulations provide that, in personal injury cases, a plaintiff may be required by the agency to submit (1) information about employment and salary; (2) an itemized bill for medical expenses; (3) a detailed statement from a physician specifying injuries, duration of pain and suffering, degree of temporary or permanent disability, the prognosis, period of hospitalization, and any diminished earning capacity; and (4) the plaintiff may be required to submit to a physical and mental examination. In a death case, the plaintiff may be required to provide additional information such as a death certificate, names of relatives who were dependent on decedent for financial support, and decedent's physical and mental condition prior to death. Finally, as a catch-all category, the agency may require a detailed statement from a treating physician, medical bills, and any other evidence having a "bearing on either the responsibility of the United States for the death or the damages claimed."

D. Government Argues Regulations Require Mandatory Compliance. The government advanced the position that, if a plaintiff did not comply with the regulations during the administrative process, he would later be barred from filing a lawsuit. The rationale of the government made sense. Because the administrative claim was now mandatory, and accompanying regulations authorized federal agencies to request documents in connection with those claims, it follows that a plaintiff's failure to abide by the regulations would undermine the administrative claims process, and thus, a plaintiff should be barred from later filing suit in federal court.

In contrast, § 2675(a) does not suggest that a settlement is mandatory but simply indicates that a plaintiff must file an administrative claim before filing a lawsuit. Why, then, should there be the additional burden for the plaintiff to take the time and effort to submit documents to the agency during this process? This line of reasoning continues with the proposition that a failed settlement and possible lawsuit were taken into account by Congress, since it provided that formal litigation was an avenue to pursue after a claim had been denied by the federal agency.

E. Current Interpretation of Settlement Requirements. . . . In *Adams v. United States*, 615 F.2d 284, 285 (5th Cir. 1980), parents brought a claim on their son's behalf for negligent prenatal care at a government hospital. In accordance [with the statute and regulations], the parents submitted an administrative claim. The agency claims officer requested, under the authority of the regulations, written reports of attending physicians who were not government employees, itemized bills and expenses, and other documents. The plaintiffs' attorney responded:

> In my opinion, you have at your disposal all the necessary records to properly evaluate this claim. We will fully develop this claim with respect to the private physicians and the necessary future expenses, and when you have had an opportunity to fully investigate everything at your disposal, we will be more than happy to exchange information in full.

The agency claims officer responded that the agency could not evaluate the claim without all the facts and that the plaintiffs' failure to provide information as stated in the regulations could "result in a denial of your claim on that basis and prejudice your rights to proceed in federal court." After more than six months had passed without a settlement of the claim, the plaintiffs filed suit in federal court.

The Government argued that the Adams' refusal to comply with the agency claim representative's demands pursuant to 28 C.F.R. § 14 was a failure to comply with the jurisdictional requirements of § 2675 to present an administrative claim before filing a lawsuit. However, the Fifth Circuit held that the filing of a claim and its settlement are distinct procedures. The court reasoned that the requirements [set forth in the regulations went] far beyond the notice requirement of § 2675. "Equating these two very different sets of requirements leads to the erroneous conclusion that claimants must settle with the relevant federal agency, if the agency so desires, and must provide that agency with any and all information requested in order to preserve their right to sue." The court. . . . declared that an "agency's demand for anything more than a written and signed statement setting out the manner in which the injury was received, enough details to enable the agency to begin its own investigation and a claim for money damages is unwarranted and unauthorized." Although a claimant has an obligation to give notice of a claim under § 2675, he or she does not have an obligation to provide further information to assist settlement of the matter.

2. Comments and Questions

a. The *Adams* rationale has been adopted by other federal circuits. *See, e.g., Tidd v. United States,* 786 F.2d 1565, 1567 (11th Cir. 1986); *Warren v. Dept. of Interior,* 724 F.2d 776, 778 (9th Cir. 1984); *Tucker v. U.S. Postal Serv.,* 676 F.2d 954, 957-60 (3d Cir. 1982).

b. Note the parallel between the "good faith participation" arguments here and the similar arguments in the context of court-connected mediation. See the extended discussion in Chapter Eleven.

c. Professor Riskin's article on Farmer-Lender mediation illustrates the interaction of state and federal government in the regulatory sphere. Financial intermediaries are chartered and closely regulated by the federal government (and sometimes at the state level as well).

3. Leonard L. Riskin, *Two Concepts of Mediation in the FmHA's Farmer-Lender Mediation Program,* 45 ADMIN. L. REV. 21 (1993)

This article concerns just one mediation program conducted by one federal agency, but it has, I hope, significant implications for mediation efforts in other contexts. In 1988, the Farmers Home Administration (FmHA) launched a massive effort, mandated by Title V of the Agricultural Credit Act of 1987, to mediate between farmers and their creditors over delinquent loans. The effort's most striking aspect is that it embraced two radically different forms of mediation. . . .

[T]his program was large and diverse, including thousands of mediations conducted by hundreds of mediators in at least thirty states. Seventeen of these states created mediation programs for which the FmHA provided matching funds. In more than a dozen other states, the FmHA arranged for mediation services through contracts. In some states, FmHA used its own employees to conduct "voluntary meetings of creditors." The circumstances facing mediation participants varied not only state-to-state but also by region within state and by time periods. Every farm family had its unique set of personalities and circumstances — legal, economic, social, psychological, and interpersonal — and so did every mediator and every lender. Moreover, the mediations often were set in an elaborately complex system of loans and loan servicing options. . . .

I. Background

The FmHA is the successor to the Resettlement Administration, which was created in 1935, and the Farm Security Administration. Its . . . mission statement directs it to "serve as a temporary source of supervised credit and technical support for rural Americans for improving their farming enterprises, housing conditions, community facilities, and other business endeavors until they are able to qualify for private sector resources." The Agency's 11,558 full-time employees operate numerous loan programs through forty-six state offices, 264 district offices, and 1,904 county offices. The Agency often is called a "lender of last resort," because it generally makes loans to persons who can secure no other financing.

The farm sector enjoyed a boom in the 1970s. . . . [and] farm income rose greatly. Because of the widespread expectation that income would continue to climb, the price of farmland increased dramatically. As a result, many farmers borrowed to purchase machinery and to develop their land, a practice that was highly profitable during boom times. In the early 1980s, however, a rise in interest rates was accompanied by a precipitous decline in the prices of land and machinery. Consequently, many farmers were unable to service their debt, and delinquencies on loans to major farm lenders — principally banks, the Farm Credit System, life insurance companies, and the FmHA — grew substantially. Because the FmHA is a lender of last resort, large numbers of farmers who were denied credit assistance by other sources turned to the FmHA for help, and the FmHA responded by increasing its portfolio. In the first six months of 1985, FmHA made $763 million in new loans to over 7,000 farmers who were technically insolvent. It also made new loans to over 12,000 farmers who had extreme financial difficulties. Because FmHA borrowers tend to be greater risks than other borrowers, FmHA's delinquencies peaked earlier than those of the other major sources of farm lending. The FmHA was slower than other lenders to liquidate, because it is a public entity with a quasi-social function. During each of the years 1980, 1981, and 1982 the FmHA charged off less than $50 million, but the charge off figures were $1 billion in 1983 and 1984, $3 billion in 1985, and $4 billion in 1986. All four major sources of loans experienced heavy losses.

In the economic downturn afflicting the agricultural sector, FmHA borrowers were hit particularly hard. FmHA, in turn, began to exercise frequently its right to accelerate loans and foreclose on property securing those loans. Borrowers filed numerous lawsuits challenging the FmHA's procedures, with some success. And a widely seen motion picture, "Country," starring Jessica Lange and Sam Shepard, dramatized the plight of a family treated roughly by the FmHA. Accompanying the economic decline in the farm sector was a deterioration in family structures and the social fabric in many rural areas, especially in the Midwest. Rates of divorce, child abuse, depression, suicide, and drug abuse escalated, and many rural communities suffered community-wide depression marked by a feeling of hopelessness, exacerbated by a shortage and lack of coordination of social services. . . .

Iowa and Minnesota responded early to these conditions. The cornerstone of the efforts in both states was successful mediation programs that have greatly affected the development of farmer-lender mediation efforts in other states. Although these two programs were created in very different ways and have very different structures, they share, and have promoted, a common philosophical approach to farmer-lender mediation.

The Minnesota program grew from the work of a task force that was initiated by the Minnesota Department of Agriculture in 1984 and included both public and private agencies that provided services to farmers. It subsequently added bankers, farm advocates, church groups, educators, economists, and farmers. As the crisis deepened, some farm advocates pressed for a one-year moratorium on foreclosures. In November 1985, bankers agreed — at the Governor's request — to a voluntary ninety-day moratorium on foreclosures on agricultural property and the creation of a farmer-lender mediation program under which the University of Minnesota Extension Service offered farmer-lender mediation to parties who requested it. In short order, the Service located and trained over 300 mediators, and by December 1985 they began to conduct mediations. . . .

In May 1986, the Minnesota legislature, "in a remarkable bipartisan effort," enacted a statute to address the farm crisis. Among other things, the statute established a farmer-lender mediation program that was "mandatory" in the sense that it prohibited persons from moving to enforce interests in farm property securing debts of more than $5,000 without first serving the debtor with a notice of the availability of mediation. The statute also provided that the creditor may not move against the property until ninety days after the debtor files a mediation request, and it required the Agricultural Extension Service to train and provide mediators, as well as credit analysts (to help the farmer prepare for mediation). The Agricultural Extension Service moved quickly to provide mediation along with credit analysis services. During the first six months, the service handled over 2,000 cases. . . . In the first eighteen months of the program, it put 645 volunteers through an intensive two-day training program. The group includes retired and active farmers, retired bankers, teachers, ministers, and farm financial consultants.

By its terms, the Minnesota statute applies to the FmHA as a creditor. But the FmHA refused to participate in mediations or to restructure loans. . . . FmHA representatives were available, however, to meet with FmHA borrowers who were in mediation with other lenders. As a result of the FmHA's refusal to participate, many mediations in both Minnesota and Iowa were frustrated, and according to one commentator, "farmers began filing for bankruptcy because then FmHA would be forced to participate in bankruptcy proceedings."

The Iowa program also began with voluntary mediation, which legislation turned into a program that required farm lenders to participate in mediation requested by borrowers before proceeding against farm property. A broad-based working committee under the leadership of Lieutenant Governor Bob Anderson, with help from the Conflict Clinic, Inc., held forums to discuss mediation. This group rejected the notions of locating the mediation service in a government agency, as had been done in Minnesota, or in a private organization, out of a concern that the providers would appear biased. It decided to create a nonprofit corporation that "represented farmers, creditors, mediators, attorneys, educators and business executives" to operate the Iowa Farmer-Creditor Mediation Service. The principal goal of the program was to build commitment to the mediation process, rather than seek specific outcomes, such as keeping farmers on the land. . . .

In response to these and related events, Congress passed the Agricultural Credit Act of 1987, 101 Stat. 1568 (1988), a massive attempt to deal with problems in the agricultural credit realm. Title V propelled the Department of Agriculture into mediation by requiring the Secretary to certify and provide matching grants to state mediation programs that met certain criteria; to participate in state mediation programs; and to make "a reasonable effort" to contact and encourage creditors to take part in a restructuring plan. To fulfill this last requirement, the FmHA included in its rules on restructuring a requirement that delinquent borrowers be offered a chance to participate in mediation or a voluntary meeting of creditors; in addition, it began a program to contract for mediation services in some states that lacked certified mediation programs. Title V required the Secretary to provide states that have "qualified" mediation programs with matching funds, limited to 50 percent of the cost of each program and to $500,000 per year for each state. . . . The statute also directed the Farm Credit Administration (FCA), an independent regulatory agency of the executive branch charged with regulating the Farm Credit System, to . . . cooperate in good faith with requests for information or analysis of information made in the course of mediation . . . and to present and explore debt restructuring proposals advanced in the course of such mediation. . . .

The Act included significant changes in the functioning of the FCA as well as the FmHA. The most important of these, for present purposes, were requirements that these lenders restructure loans where restructuring is in the government's financial interests and would help keep the farmer on the farm. The FmHA was required to modify delinquent farmer program loans to the maximum extent possible; . . . [however,] the loan, if restructured, must result in a net recovery to the Federal Government, during the term of the loan as restructured, that would be more than or equal to the net recovery to the Federal Government from an involuntary liquidation or foreclosure on the property securing the loan. . . . The statute also provided an option for some borrowers who do not meet the above criteria to buy out their FmHA loan for its net recovery value. . . .

II. FmHA Implementation

As the FmHA began to implement this program in January 1988, it faced a daunting situation: 85,000 delinquent Farmer Program borrowers and another 33,000 in an "inactive" status, such as bankruptcy or foreclosure. The loan portfolio of delinquent FmHA farmer program borrowers totaled $11.4 billion (out of the total FmHA farm loan portfolio of $26 billion, which represented fifteen percent of total farm debt); $9.6 billion of the $11.4 billion in payments were overdue. In addition, and to make matters more difficult for the FmHA, it was operating under both federal court injunctions forbidding it to take further adverse actions until it revised the forms used to advise delinquent borrowers of servicing options and appeal rights, and Agricultural Credit Act requirements to revise substantially its procedures for dealing with delinquent borrowers.

The statute not only called for the Department of Agriculture to certify state mediation programs and to participate in those programs that it certified, but also required that it make "a reasonable effort" to contact and encourage creditors to take part in a plan of restructuring. This led the FmHA both to encourage FmHA offices in states that lacked certified mediation programs ("noncertified states") to contract for mediation services and to provide, in its rules, that delinquent borrowers in such states would have a chance to request mediation or a "voluntary meeting of creditors."

The final rule establishing the certification process provided that the FmHA will participate in mediations conducted under a State agricultural loan mediation program "under the same terms and conditions applicable to agricultural creditors generally, and will cooperate in good faith in such mediations by complying with requests for information and analysis, and in presenting and exploring debt restructuring proposals, wherever feasible, when that State is . . . a qualifying State."

In setting out the requirements for certification of state programs, the rule imposed standards identical to those set forth in the statute. The FmHA rejected suggestions that the certification requirements be made more restrictive. Some comments on the proposed rule had urged that the FmHA impose minimum numbers of hours for training of mediators and detailed provisions as to "brochures, broadcast announcements, and notification of the mediators' names, addresses and phone numbers on foreclosure notices." The FmHA rejected these proposals that it "micro-manage," stating that such provisions were not contemplated by the statute, and that varying local conditions could call for different activities in the states. These decisions to defer to the state programs in the details of their activities seem not only consistent with the statute but also quite sensible. . . .

The rule also establishes mediation, or something approaching mediation, in states that do not have certified programs. It requires the state director to "provide the means of conducting a voluntary meeting of creditors, either with a mediator or a designated FmHA representative," encourages the state directors to "contract for qualified mediators within their jurisdictional areas," and states that the "National Office will provide the State a list of qualified mediators for contracting purposes." . . . The rule also provides that when a mediator is not available, the State Director will designate an FmHA employee "to conduct a meeting of creditors and attempt to develop a plan with borrowers and their creditors that will assist the borrowers to resolve their financial difficulty." This FmHA representative must not have been previously connected with the borrower's account and must "have demonstrated good human relations skills and ability to resolve problems and settle disputes." The State Directors are to provide the training needed. . . .

There are two basic kinds of loan servicing actions: primary loan servicing and preservation loan servicing. Primary loan servicing includes: consolidation; rescheduling and/or reamortization; deferral of principal and interest payments; reducing the interest rate; writing down (reducing) amount of the debt; or a combination of these. Preservation loan servicing may be available to borrowers who are ineligible for primary loan servicing. Preservation loan servicing includes: leaseback/buyback and homestead protection.

The farmer who wishes to apply for servicing must complete numerous forms, the most important of which is the "farm-home plan," on which the farmer is to set forth all information relevant to his cash flow situation. Once this is done, the FmHA will determine whether the farmer is eligible for any of the primary loan servicing options. The farmer will be considered eligible for a servicing option if he is unable to pay his debts to the FmHA for reasons beyond his control; has acted in good faith; and has a feasible plan. A "feasible plan" means that the farm-home plan shows a cash flow that allows the farmer to: pay necessary family living and farm operating expenses; pay all debts, including the restructured debt to FmHA; and pay FmHA an amount worth more than the "net recovery value" of the loan.

Such criteria demand very complex computations. To aid its county offices in making the determination of eligibility for primary loan servicing, the FmHA has developed DALR$, the Debt and Loan Restructuring System, a computer program operated on the FmHA County Office computer systems. The program assists the FmHA loan officer in making a decision "about whether any combination of primary loan servicing options will make it possible for the borrower to develop a feasible plan and thus stay on the farm and avoid loss to the government." DALR$ considers the primary loan servicing options in the order listed above, that is, from the least to the most extreme. The borrower is not eligible for debt write off if he is eligible for any of the less drastic options.

The county supervisor makes decisions as to the input, based on the farm-home plan submitted by the borrower and other factors, and the DALR$ program then . . . provides a printout for the FmHA and the borrower. If the DALR$ program shows that the borrower has a feasible plan, the FmHA will offer the primary loan servicing option for which the farmer is eligible. If, however, the DALR$ program shows that the borrower is ineligible for primary loan servicing, the FmHA will send a notice, along with a printout of the DALR$ program. This notice advises the farmer of the FmHA's conclusion that the farmer has been unable to develop a feasible plan because of debts to lenders other than FmHA.

The mediation programs were started in many different ways and are organized differently. The Minnesota Program is operated by the University of Minnesota Extension, and the Iowa program by a non-profit corporation created for this purpose. The Nebraska program is conducted jointly by the Nebraska Legal Aid Society and the Interchurch Ministries of Nebraska under contract with the Nebraska Department of Agriculture. In Texas, the program is conducted by Texas Tech University. In Kansas, the program was originally operated by a non-profit corporation and then transferred to the State Board of Agriculture. The Oklahoma Department of Agriculture contracted with the Oklahoma Conference of Churches to operate its certified program. Several programs, including those in Alabama, North Dakota, South Dakota and Utah, are conducted directly out of state offices. There is great variety in the manner in which the mediators were selected and compensated. Notwithstanding these differences, these programs have something in common besides federal matching funds: They share a philosophy of mediation that differs from that which informs the mediation practitioners in some noncertified states. . . .

This program also fostered the development in 1989 of an important organization, the Coalition of Agricultural Mediation Programs (CAMP). It "provides a framework for people to work together on: (1) common legislative goals; (2) expansion of USDA's use of mediation beyond FmHA farm debt restructuring; and (3) representing and promoting rural/agricultural mediation." Extending mediation services to rural matters other than farm credit is an explicit goal of CAMP. At CAMP meetings, the conventional wisdom is that both CAMP and FmHA should address not only the crisis in the farm sector, but also a chronic condition in rural America marked by a deterioration in the social fabric in many rural communities. . . . In some states, farm-credit mediation programs have begun to mediate other kinds of matters connected to rural communities. . . . These developments exemplify mediation's potential for promoting more collaborative ways of planning and of resolving disputes in rural America.

Numerous FmHA offices in states without certified programs [at least twelve states] awarded contracts for mediation services to private individuals or organizations. . . . In 1989, the FmHA contracted with the Federal Mediation and Conciliation Service (FMCS) to provide pilot mediation services in Georgia, Maine and New York. In some states, the FmHA arranged for its own employees to preside at "voluntary meetings of creditors." The FmHA sponsored numerous mediation training programs for FmHA representatives or contractors in noncertified states. . . .

III. Two Concepts of Mediation

The farmer-lender mediation effort is infused with a tension between two different conceptions — which I will call "broad" and "narrow" — of the goals, purposes and, perhaps, very nature of mediation. The broad approach assumes that the goal of farmer-lender mediation is to reach a wise agreement that deals with the underlying interests of the parties. The mediator might help a farmer consider, or reconsider, whether to make additional changes in the farm operation or in off-farm employment, which could change the farm-home plan. It also means, of course, that a mediation could deal with barriers to negotiation, such as: (1) emotional problems within the family (which could be addressed directly or through referral); (2) communication problems between borrower and lenders; and (3) disputes between lenders. There are any number of possible outcomes, and the process is open to discussion of whatever seems to be relevant. . . .

Under a narrow view of the purposes of farmer-lender mediation, the principal, and sometimes the exclusive, issue is whether the creditors will adjust their debts so that a rerun of the DALR$ program would show a feasible plan. A feasible plan would allow the FmHA to provide primary loan servicing so that the borrowers could continue farming, and owning, the land. A number of directors of certified state mediation programs have indicated that some of the FmHA representatives in their states held this narrow view so strongly that it severely limited FmHA's participation in mediations. In some noncertified programs, this narrow view of mediation . . . also controlled the outlook of the mediators. The mediations under these programs tended to be much shorter and more formulaic than under certified state programs. . . .

3. *Effects of the Divergence in Approaches to Mediation.* The divergence in views on the proper approach to mediation has manifested itself in several ways. First, as already indicated, the mediations typically conducted under certified programs differ greatly from those conducted in at least some contract mediation programs. Second, in some certified states, at some times, while mediators yearned or pushed for a broad approach, FmHA representatives at mediations clung to the narrow view, believing or maintaining that they had no authority to discuss options other than primary loan servicing, and that the DALR$ program was the only avenue toward that approach. At CAMP meetings, directors of state certified mediation programs have reported difficulties resulting from such restricted participation by FmHA, including resentment by other creditors of FmHA's inflexibility. They stressed that the mediation process could be improved if more discretion were vested in FmHA representatives. However, some of these state program directors also reported that many FmHA representatives were willing, sometimes "with some nudging," to interpret their mandates generously. Third, in noncertified states, some contractors who were imbued with a broad mediation vision may have spent much more time as mediators — in preparing, conducting, and following up — than they or the FmHA anticipated. . . .

4. *Advantages and Disadvantages of Each Approach.* Each approach to farmer-lender mediation has its own internal logic and advantages and disadvantages. The narrow approach accepts the definition of the problem that is implicit in FmHA rules: will non-FmHA creditors adjust their debts sufficiently to allow primary loan servicing? The broad approach seeks out underlying interests and works with the parties to define the problems and identify options as broadly as they wish. Thus, the narrow approach is more predictable and, in a sense, efficient. The objective is clear, the types of outcomes limited. It demands less involvement of the participants. All concerned spend less time, so the costs to the government and to participants should be lower. . . . If the burdens of participation are lower in narrow mediations, perhaps some borrowers and lenders would find participation more appealing. On the other hand, the narrow approach may cause all concerned to miss opportunities to develop solutions that will meet the needs of the parties and to improve relationships and communications. It can provide a convenient myopia for an FmHA representative who has decided against primary loan servicing.

The broad approach offers the opportunity to develop a diverse array of problem-solving solutions that better meet the parties' actual needs. Where this is effective, it produces superior results. In such cases, the broad approach has a bigger payoff than the narrow. It also has an important educational function and can lead to problem-solving approaches to community-wide problems. Potential disadvantages of the broad approach are that it can demand more of the time and energy of all concerned and may call for some interpersonal skills in the mediation that are less necessary in the narrow approach.

5. Why The Two Concepts Developed. It is easy to see why broad mediation developed more readily in certified state mediation programs than in some of the mediation programs that were created in noncertified states through contracts with FmHA state offices. The two kinds of programs were created and developed quite differently. Many of the certified programs were launched before FmHA began participating in farm credit mediation in 1988. Creditors with whom the programs dealt did not have the kind of rigid requirements for adjusting loans that govern the FmHA. The programs often grew out of efforts that had strong community and high level political support. Many of the people who became mediators in such programs did so on a semi-volunteer basis, i.e., for small fees, and had strong connections to the agricultural sector and to rural communities.

Thus, many of the leaders of these programs began with concerns not just to keep farmers on the land, but also to help farmers and rural communities cope with economic and social deterioration. These concerns, as well as the mediation philosophies of the leaders of these groups, helped shape a broad concept of mediation. The Iowa and Minnesota mediation programs, the first and probably the largest, became prototypes for most of the other certified programs, though all of the certified programs differed from them in significant ways. Thus, the certified programs developed their own concepts of mediation in response to concerns, such as those listed above, and the Agricultural Credit Act of 1987 directed the FmHA to participate in those programs.

In contrast, in the noncertified states, the FmHA set the terms for mediation. And in doing so, the FmHA has shown a deep and understandable ambivalence. Recall that the Agricultural Credit Act requires the FmHA to participate only in the mediations offered by certified state programs. It does not direct FmHA to offer or participate in mediation in other states. The statutory basis for the contract mediation program is a requirement that the FmHA make "a reasonable effort" to contact and encourage creditors to take part in a restructuring plan. In addition, implementation of a broad form of mediation is more time consuming and expensive, and the certified programs generally were better funded.

One reason why a narrow concept of mediation evolved in some FmHA offices is the place assigned to mediation in the FmHA's procedures for reviewing the status of delinquent borrowers. Under the FmHA's rules, the delinquent borrower is officially notified of the mediation option only after the FmHA has determined, normally through the DALR$ program, that the farmer is ineligible for primary loan servicing. Many FmHA officials apparently feel that, at this stage, their only option is to attempt to arrange for other creditors to adjust their debts, and to do this through a mediation or a voluntary meeting of creditors, both of which they see as limited to such narrow purposes. . . . The narrow vision is reinforced by several official FmHA pronouncements, including the notice sent to the farmer, which suggests just one purpose for the mediation, an attempt to persuade other creditors to adjust the farmer's debts.

In one sense, the FmHA has tried to make the contract mediation services comparable to the mediation services provided by certified programs. The brochures describing the two programs would give no hint of a substantive difference. But the FmHA has given certified programs great leeway in the conduct of mediations and, deliberately or not, may have imposed limits on the way in which contract mediators defined their tasks. The contracting process also may have encouraged the development of narrow mediations. In this process, the FmHA generally spoke the language of broad mediation in seeking contractors, but frequently wound up with narrowly focused mediations

6. Addressing the Dichotomy. How should the Department of Agriculture and FmHA react to the problems created by the existence of these two alternative views of farmer-lender mediation? . . . I believe that the broad approach is generally preferable — that it is more congenial and usually produces superior outcomes. But I have no empirical data to back up that conclusion, either from this program or another, and so I am relying on my own experience and discussions with others, both of which are filtered through my own values. [Professor Riskin goes on to recommend widespread adoption of the broad approach.] . . .

Moving toward broad mediation will not be simple. Each model of mediation has its own values and internal logic. Yet in practice, it may sometimes be difficult to distinguish one approach from the other. Good mediators are sensitive to the participants' needs. Accordingly, sometimes a mediator who starts with a narrow approach will broaden it, and one who starts with a broad approach will narrow it in response to developments in the mediation. . . .

The narrow model of mediation has the virtue of simplicity, whereas the broad model may call upon FmHA personnel to exercise judgment and to develop new and innovative solutions. Some government officials might fear that this sort of endeavor, requiring the exercise of greater discretion, could jeopardize their careers. Moreover, the FmHA's farm lending programs are very large and require hundreds of people in their administration. Therefore, the need for efficiency, fairness, uniformity, and order makes understandable the allure of a narrow approach to mediation, sometimes with exclusive reliance on the DALR$ program. For all these reasons, there may be a great deal of internal resistance to change in the direction I am proposing. . . .

FmHA could consider a number of activities, however, that would enhance the likelihood of success in moving toward a broad mediation approach, such as modifying the rules of loan restructuring so that mediation takes place earlier, or otherwise giving more discretion to FmHA representatives than some believe they currently have. For example, the FmHA could take appropriate measures to reduce the tendency of the DALR$ program to limit the purposes of mediation, such as encouraging the FmHA county offices to initiate mediation proceedings at an earlier stage in the processing of delinquent loans. . . .

E. RESOLUTION OF TAXPAYER DISPUTES BY THE INTERNAL REVENUE SERVICE

1. Comments and Questions

a. The Internal Revenue Service (IRS) has been using ADR to settle claims related to tax obligations for over 75 years. Most taxpayer disputes with the IRS are settled by informal negotiation (letters and telephone calls) prior to resort to the more formal dispute resolution processes that are discussed in this section.

b. For more on the use of ADR by the IRS, see Amy S. Wei, *Can Mediation Be the Answer to Taxpayers' Woes?: An Examination of the Internal Revenue Service's Mediation Program*, 15 OHIO ST. J. ON DISP. RESOL. 549 (2003).

c. Do you agree with Mathews that the IRS should move to far greater reliance on mediation? What other alterations to the present system for addressing disputes with taxpayers might be helpful? Are your answers the same for large dollar and small dollar disputes? How might the system be adjusted to protect the interests of ordinary taxpayers (modest dollar amount at issue, lack of sophistication about tax matters) who represent themselves?

d. How does an agency whose mission is to collect money balance the goals of fairness to all taxpayers with its (arguably conflicting) financial objectives? Similar pressures are faced by public prosecutors in the charging and sentencing of persons accused of crimes. See the discussion of plea bargaining in Chapter Six.

2. Gregory P. Mathews, *Using Negotiation, Mediation and Arbitration to Resolve IRS-Taxpayer Disputes*, 19 OHIO ST. J. ON DISP. RESOL. 709 (2004)

Disputes between the Internal Revenue Service (IRS or Service) and taxpayers arise when a taxpayer fails to agree with an IRS finding, refuses to file a tax return, or refuses to comply with an IRS request for information. The stated mission of the IRS is to "provide America's taxpayers top quality service by helping them understand and meet their tax responsibilities and by applying the tax law with integrity and fairness to all." This emphasis on service is seen not only in taxpayer understanding of the law, but also in the Service's dispute resolution process. The IRS aims at resolving taxpayer disputes at the earliest possible point in the resolution process. In pursuit of this goal, the IRS has an Appeals Office (Appeals), which has a longstanding record of settling taxpayer disputes outside of a courtroom. In recent years, the IRS has developed other, more formal and narrowly focused, alternative dispute resolution (ADR) programs designed to add to the efficient resolution of disputes. These programs include forms of negotiation, mediation, and arbitration and are aimed at both dispute prevention and resolution. Additionally, mediation and arbitration are available even after a case reaches the United States Tax Court. . . .

Prior to examining the methods of resolving disputes, a cursory view of the conflict process is helpful. Conflicts generally begin through the audit process. If an audit is not followed by an agreement between the taxpayer and the IRS agent concerning the amount of tax owed, the taxpayer may file a protest letter with Appeals or pursue his claim legally (i.e., in court). If the taxpayer chooses not to submit his case to Appeals, or if resolution is unsuccessful after the Appeals process has run its course, he may sue the IRS.

A. *The Appeals Office: Negotiation.* With the establishment of the Appeals Office in 1927, the IRS first embraced the value of resolving taxpayer disputes without litigation. The Appeals Office operates independently from the local IRS office with which the taxpayer has interacted; however, a case that goes to Appeals remains under the jurisdiction of the IRS. An appeal to the Appeals Office represents an administrative option to contest a claim of the IRS, and it is designed to be an impartial forum in which a taxpayer can try to settle the dispute. A taxpayer can initiate the Appeals process by filing a protest letter. An Appeals officer then considers the merits of the case and the time and cost of litigation to arrive at a settlement figure. An Appeals conference is then scheduled so that the Appeals officer and the taxpayer can attempt to negotiate a mutually acceptable settlement.

Appeals process is designed to be neutral and has the purpose of effecting decisions regarding the settlement of taxpayer disputes. After reviewing the facts and evidence, and upon considering the hazards of litigation, the Appeals officer determines a fair position for the IRS. The IRS model is designed so that the Appeals officer enters the settlement negotiations with a "quasi-judicial" attitude embodying an "open mind and [with] genuine interest in working out a mutually acceptable agreement." The primary focus of the Appeals process is negotiation. That is, the taxpayer and Appeals officer try to settle the dispute "through persuasion regarding the merits of their respective positions." The taxpayer has the right to have representation at an Appeals conference, but according to the IRS, representation is not necessary.

The use of negotiation by Appeals represents a system designed to cover a broad range of disputes and has shown great success statistically. In fact, between eighty-five and ninety percent of the cases that reach Appeals result in settlement. However, in 1996, Congress mandated that all government agencies begin to implement ADR into their administrative dispute resolution processes. Additionally, the IRS Restructuring and Reform Act of 1998 has led the IRS to develop more formal ADR policies and procedures. This congressional action, along with a desire for greater efficiency, has brought about the development of mediation and arbitration programs designed to supplement the existing Appeals process.

B. *Formal ADR Initiatives: Mediation and Arbitration.* As a result of congressional mandate, and as part of its efforts to make substantial gains in improving its image and service, the IRS has developed formal dispute resolution mechanisms for tax cases. With the historically high settlement rate experienced by Appeals, the IRS initially designed its more formal ADR programs to supplement, rather than replace, the existing system. That is, new initiatives tend to have a more narrow focus, as compared to Appeals.

1. Mediation. Mediation is available throughout the dispute resolution process: first while the case is under the jurisdiction of the IRS, and second when the case is in the Tax Court's jurisdiction. The IRS has made significant efforts to expand the availability of mediation as another tool to effect agreement. Mediation has seen less success in Tax Court, however, due in large part to the fact that formal procedures have yet to be developed. . . .

The mentality within the IRS is that the use of mediation can supplement the success of Appeals. In fact, . . . is generally available only at the conclusion of the traditional Appeals process. The Service's first experiment with mediation came in 1995, with limited scope and availability. Three years later, Congress required the development of procedures for the availability of mediation in the Appeals process. In 2002, the mediation program became a permanent part of the Appeals process, and even greater expansions in availability were made, with the removal of many of the eligibility requirements. In fact, the IRS completely abolished the amount in controversy requirement, making mediation available to a much wider taxpayer audience than previously was the case. Additionally, mediation is no longer limited to the resolution of factual issues. This change makes mediation available for any qualifying issues that are already in the Appeals administrative process. The progressive increase in the popularity of mediation is the result of success of the various trial programs since 1995, and it demonstrates an effort by the Service to ensure that even more cases avoid litigation. One significant limitation remains for the availability of mediation in Appeals: mediation is available only after taxpayer-Appeals officer negotiations have failed.

2. Arbitration. Arbitration is also available for the resolution of tax disputes. Theoretically, arbitration is available both while a case is under the jurisdiction of the IRS and after it has gone to Tax Court. If both negotiation and mediation have failed in Appeals, the taxpayer may request arbitration for the issue. However, the use of arbitration has been largely limited to cases that are in Tax Court. This is due, in large part, to the fact that the IRS has only recently extended the availability of arbitration in Appeals.

II. Analysis of the Implementation of ADR in Resolving IRS-Taxpayer Disputes

Recent history has certainly evidenced movement toward broader use of ADR in the resolution of tax disputes. Both Congress and the IRS have recognized the potential value ADR is capable of providing for taxpayers and government alike. . . . While the success of existing ADR mechanisms cannot be doubted, they may be open to even greater improvements in efficiency and quality. Particularly, the current Appeals structure, which relies predominantly on taxpayer-Appeals officer negotiation, presents problems as to very large or very small tax disputes. Ultimately, the IRS and taxpayers would be well served were Appeals to shift its focus from a negotiation-based system to one that relies predominantly upon mediation. . . .

A. The Appeals Office — A Good Foundation. The longevity of, and the Service's commitment to, the Appeals process rests largely on the fact that it has successfully produced resolution in most cases. Appeals allows taxpayers to pursue settlement in a personal conference with the IRS and represents an advantageous alternative to litigation in many cases. However, in spite of its impressive eighty-five to ninety percent settlement rate, Appeals is not the best alternative when two distinct groups of taxpayers are involved: first, those with relatively few resources pursuing relatively small claims, and second, those with a great deal of resources pursuing relatively large claims.

Appeals does not necessarily provide complete fairness for taxpayers defending small claims. As a matter of economics, a small claim will not justify hiring professional counsel. If the amount in controversy is not above a certain level, a taxpayer will probably choose not to pay for representation. Taxpayers may be disadvantaged, however, if they elect not to acquire professional representation. According to the IRS, "there is no need for . . . representation at an Appeals conference." However, taxpayers that forego representation will sit across the table from Appeals officers, who — no matter how impartial and judicious — possess a degree of expertise as IRS employees. Based on this disparity in expertise between an average taxpayer and an IRS Appeals officer, the current structure of Appeals presents the possibility that small tax disputes will be resolved inequitably, casting significant doubt on the ultimate efficacy of Appeals's seemingly impressive settlement rate.

An additional deficiency for small claimants in the Appeals system lies in the fact that the fear of "the burdens of litigation, primarily time and expense, often overwhelm the taxpayer," and may lead to a possibly inequitable settlement. Especially for relatively small claims, it may make little economic sense for a taxpayer to invest much time and money in a vigorous attempt to win a dispute, causing the taxpayer to cut his losses and accept the existing IRS offer. Yet, even in the case of relatively small claims, this mentality may deprive taxpayers of plenary justice — a result that runs in the face of the Service's mission. Ultimately, a taxpayer with limited financial resources may not be able to fully realize the strength of his claim, and that fact may lead to hastened and unfair settlement. By restructuring Appeals so that almost every case immediately enters mediation, these problems could be mitigated. Specifically, in mediation, an unrepresented taxpayer will not be disadvantaged by his lack of expertise, because a neutral third party is involved who will fairly assess the merits of each side's claim.

The current Appeals system is equally deficient as to disputes over large monetary sums. The problem here is that the method employed by Appeals, negotiation, is not optimally suited for the most efficient resolution of large tax disputes. The opportunity for face-to-face discussions will suffice to produce agreement in some cases, but many cases are destined for litigation, because the amount in controversy is so high that zealous representation is warranted. Where the respective proposals of the taxpayer and the IRS are separated by hundreds of thousands of dollars, each side is much more likely to remain steadfast, justifying mounting costs, and the prospective costs of litigation, with the thought of how much will be won in the end. The current structure of Appeals relies on negotiation to bring the taxpayer and IRS Appeals officer to an agreement. In fact, every case that enters Appeals must go through the negotiation process. The potential of the current system is ultimately limited in cases where parties are unwilling or unable to gain a realistic view of the merits of their claims. Negotiation facilitates stalemate in these situations. This means that certain cases will never be resolved through the negation process. Mediation can help remedy this problem. Mediation is successful largely because it allows a neutral third party to take a fresh look at the case, evaluating the merits of each side's claim.

By requiring each case to go through the negotiation process, Appeals may cause one of two problematic results for large taxpayers. First, after spending over a year in the Appeals system, a taxpayer may become dissatisfied with the progress of the available administrative remedies and decide to forgo mediation. Alternatively, a taxpayer may spend a significant amount of time in negotiation, only to eventually settle through mediation. In either scenario, time and money are wasted. Mediation is more optimally suited for the resolution of large tax disputes, and by directing most cases to mediation immediately (and not requiring traditional negotiation to run its course), both taxpayers and the IRS would stand to save resources.

Ultimately, the impressive settlement rate demonstrated by Appeals must be questioned in two respects. First, of those cases that are settled, are the outcomes fair from the perspective of most taxpayers? In light of the probable lack of representation of many taxpayers and of a general fear of the cost and uncertainty of litigation, that question should probably be answered in the negative. And second, could an even more impressive settlement rate result from a process that forces the parties to reevaluate their proposals? A consideration of basic economics in decisionmaking demonstrates that this question should be answered in the affirmative. Therefore, a reconsideration of the effectiveness of Appeals, and a move toward a mediation-based system, may help lead to an increase in both the quality and quantity of tax dispute settlements within the IRS.

B. Mediation — Realizing a Problem-Solving Mentality. The Service's use of mediation is a promising development that should result in an increase in the number of cases resolved before litigation, and an improvement in the fairness of final settlement agreements. The promotion of mediation is a means by which the IRS can work toward greater efficiency and fairness, and it may be a significant tool that could persuade the taxpaying public to rethink its preconceptions about what the IRS is all about. Mediation is optimally suited for the resolution of many tax disputes, particularly those involving very large and very small claims. Specifically, through mediation, small claims may find more equitable settlement, and large claims may be settled more frequently, because mediation forces parties to focus on the strengths and weaknesses of their case. The words of a high-ranking IRS director convey the potential mediation possesses toward those ends:

> Mediation gives you a chance to take another shot, a chance possibly to recruit an ally who may agree with your position and tell the Appeals Officer, "I think the taxpayer has a good argument." At the same time if there is a hole in your argument, you may find out in advance of litigation, and it gives you a chance to step back and settle.

Along with the intrinsic benefits of its methodology (i.e., informality, flexibility, and forcing parties to reexamine the strength of their claims), mediation offers tremendous economic benefits. The parties involved, both the taxpayer and the IRS, stand to save time and money when mediation is successful and litigation is avoided.

Confidentiality and impartiality are two characteristics that are essential to successful mediation. The confidentiality of mediation communications may vary according to whether the mediation is in Appeals or in a federal court. In Appeals, the mediation process is confidential. Accordingly, the communication that takes place in the mediation session should not be subject to discovery in later judicial proceedings. The confidentiality of mediation proceedings in federal court, however, is less certain. While particular rules of evidence may protect mediation communications, there is no federal evidentiary rule that explicitly protects confidential mediation communications. A rule of evidence explicitly protecting mediation communications from discovery and admissibility in a subsequent judicial proceeding should be promulgated, so as to encourage open communication in the mediation process. . . .

The Service's mediation programs, however promising, contain room for improvement regarding mediator impartiality. Deficiencies in this area could potentially lead to serious inequities for taxpayers and compromise the ultimate effectiveness of mediation. One of the key characteristics of successful mediation is the impartiality and independence of the mediator. In its pilot programs, the IRS had given taxpayers a choice in selecting a mediator. The taxpayer could select an independent mediator or elect to use an Appeals officer who was trained as a mediator. The IRS clearly favored the use of its own personnel, and reserved the right to not mediate if the taxpayer chose a non-IRS employee. Proponents of the use of an in-house mediator argue that using a mediator familiar with tax issues is vital to the efficiency of the system. Based on the success of similar programs in other government agencies, it is believed that bias in favor of the IRS position is not a significant problem. In fact, the IRS is so confident that an in-house mediator will not compromise the program, that its newest initiative eliminates the taxpayer's choice altogether. Under the new plan, the mediator will be an employee of the IRS. The mediator may even be a member of the same office in which the taxpayer's case is assigned.

There are apparent advantages to using in-house personnel for mediation. For example, an Appeals mediator presumably possesses expertise regarding tax issues and will be able to fully understand a taxpayer's claim. This may not be the case with a truly independent mediator who may lack tax expertise. Second, an Appeals mediator will be able to offer considerably more practical experience in tax dispute settlements than most private mediators. Finally, being a part of the IRS, an Appeals mediator is likely to possess an "institutional incentive" to have the case result in settlement. However, even if Appeals mediators can in fact be neutral, and even if they possess advantages over non-expertised mediators, the perception of a lack of impartiality among taxpayers may limit the number of taxpayers who are willing to pursue mediation, thereby limiting the overall effectiveness of the program. Therefore, the IRS should modify its mediator selection procedures to at least give taxpayers the option of having a non-IRS mediator.

C. Arbitration — Still A Good Alternative to Litigation. Like the other forms of ADR utilized in resolving tax disputes, arbitration offers significant advantages over litigation. First, arbitration creates a much more favorable atmosphere for taxpayers, especially those with small claims, that do not have legal representation. Tax Court presents two significant factors that disadvantage non-expertised taxpayers. The most obvious is that the taxpayer presents his case against a trained lawyer who is knowledgeable of tax law. The taxpayer is further handicapped by the court's strict rules of evidence. The use of arbitration can mitigate these inequities. The taxpayer's lack of legal knowledge is aided by the fact that an increased level of informal interaction is permitted with the arbitration panel as compared to what degree of interaction the taxpayer would experience with a Tax Court judge. Additionally, arbitration is characterized by less formal rules of evidence, allowing the taxpayer to make a more effective statement of his case. So, especially for those taxpayers who have chosen not to have, or who simply cannot afford, legal representation, arbitration offers meaningful advantages over litigation. . . .

Arbitration, however, offers few advantages over mediation. The advantages arbitration presents to pro se taxpayers are only amplified in mediation. Compared to arbitration, mediation presents even fewer obstacles for an untrained, non-expertised taxpayer. For this reason, the IRS should focus more on the development of its mediation programs than arbitration. Additionally, the Tax Court should consider making mediation more of a priority for docketed cases.

IV. Bringing About Even Greater Efficiency in Tax Dispute Resolution

The IRS Appeals Office truly does operate as an alternative dispute resolution forum. That is, through the Appeals process, eighty-five to ninety percent of all tax disputes are resolved outside of a courtroom. However, the current Appeals system is not optimally suited to the most efficient and fair resolution of tax disputes. Taxpayer-Appeals officer negotiations may lead to inequitable settlements in small tax disputes, and many large tax disputes may go unresolved after the Appeals process has run its course. In light of the fact that the current Appeals structure displays areas that warrant improvement, the IRS should pursue a major restructuring of its dispute resolution process. That restructuring should entail a commitment to mediation, rather than negotiation.

The IRS should restructure its Appeals Office so that mediation is the default method of dispute resolution. Mediation should not just be pursued in the event that negotiation fails to bring about settlement; instead, taxpayers and the Appeals officers should sit down with a third party neutral from the outset so that a greater number of and higher quality resolutions can be effected. The IRS does make mediation available before a case even reaches Appeals through its fast track mediation program, but that alternative is inadequate because of the restraints placed on IRS agents at that level. . . .

The implementation of a mediation-focused Appeals Office would require two initial determinations. First, Appeals would need to determine which cases would qualify. Second, Appeals would need to determine for which cases, if any, mediation would be mandatory. The first issue may easily be answered: all cases within the jurisdiction of Appeals qualify. Any tax dispute that has reached Appeals can be submitted to mediation; negotiation sessions do not have to prove ineffective before mediation is available. This then leads to the second determination. Initially, it is important to point out that not every tax dispute finds its way to Appeals. A taxpayer has the right to forego the Appeals system altogether and immediately sue the IRS. But of those cases that are pursued within Appeals, most should be handled through mediation. As a practical matter, in some cases, the respective positions of the taxpayer and the Service are close enough so that the dispute can be resolved with minimal time and effort by either party. With that in mind, cases should not be immediately directed to mediation. Instead, only if the dispute is not resolved through an initial phone conversation or meeting, should mediation be mandatory. Mediation, then, should be the second step in the Appeals process.

Additionally, important changes should be made in the Service's mediation procedure. Using Appeals officers as mediators presents serious inequities for taxpayers and may contribute to a perception among taxpayers that they cannot get a fair deal. In order to eliminate a lack of real or potential impartiality, taxpayers should have three options regarding mediator selection. The first two options involve just one mediator, while the third would involve two persons acting as co-mediators. First, a taxpayer should have the right to request that a non-IRS mediator be the sole mediator. Second, a taxpayer could agree to use an IRS employee mediator. This option should be paralleled by the creation of a mediator division within the IRS so that Appeals officers do not perform the role of IRS advocate one day and act as neutral mediators another. This mediator division would be wholly separate from Appeals, and its mediators would perform just one function — that of mediator. A third option for taxpayers would be to use both an IRS and non-IRS mediator. . . .

Mediation will ensure that small claims are settled fairly for taxpayers and will lead to a greater number of settlements in large disputes. Additionally, the IRS will benefit from an increase in time and cost savings. The development of ADR demonstrates recent efforts to improve the service, efficiency, and perception of the IRS. Unfortunately, decades of apparent success with the Appeals Office has lulled the IRS into believing that new forms of ADR should only supplement the traditional use of negotiation techniques. However, to achieve optimum service, efficiency, and goodwill, the IRS should pursue mediation more fully. . . .

3. Thomas Carter Louthan, *Building a User-Friendly Internal Revenue Service: ADR Programs Are Set for Taxpayer Use*, 18 ALTERNATIVES TO HIGH COST LITIG. 1 (Jan. 2000)

Under the IRS Restructuring and Reform Act of 1998, referred to in this article as RRA 98, the role of Appeals is cast in a new light. Section 1001 requires the IRS Commissioner to ensure an independent appeals function within the IRS, and prohibit ex parte communications between appeals officers and other IRS employees to the extent that such communications appear to compromise the independence of the appeals officers. As the IRS shifts toward becoming a more customer-oriented agency, the Internal Revenue Service's commitment to the Appeals administrative dispute resolution process is reaffirmed by the following principles in the recently published Policy Statement P-8-1:

(1) Taxpayers are generally entitled to appeal disputes arising under the Internal Revenue Code, regulations and procedures. They also are entitled to an explanation of the Appeals process, and to have a timely conference and resolution of their dispute.

(2) Local Appeals offices are separate from and independent of the IRS office that proposed the adjustment in question. Issues should be fully developed by compliance functions before an administrative appeal.

(3) The Appeals Office is the only level of appeal within the IRS, and generally is the principal administrative function that exercises settlement authority to resolve tax disputes for cases that are not docketed in the U.S. Tax Court. The National Director of Appeals, as the administrative dispute resolution specialist in tax matters for the IRS commissioner, has authority over the Appeals field operations throughout the country.

(4) The IRS supports the development and use of alternative dispute resolution techniques by Appeals to create an administrative forum, independent of compliance functions, to efficiently prevent or resolve disputes. . . . .

In response to growing taxpayer interest, Appeals has established a number of ADR procedures intended to resolve tax disputes more effectively and efficiently. These procedures primarily are designed to identify particular issues in a case which, if resolved, could serve to bring the entire case to an expeditious conclusion. . . .

If the taxpayer and Appeals agree in principle to mediate one or more issues, the parties will prepare a concise, written agreement to mediate. Usually, the parties negotiate the agreement and select the mediators within two weeks. Announcement 98-99 contains a model agreement to mediate, with exhibits that can be used in the process. The IRS's experience is that the entire mediation process can be completed within 90 to 120 days. Appeals and the taxpayer share the cost of the mediator's expenses, but if the parties select a mediator from Appeals, the National Office Appeals will assume all of the mediator's expenses. The taxpayer and Appeals can use any local or national organization that provides a roster of neutrals in selecting a mediator. Most mediation sessions are concluded in one day, and the parties can schedule two additional mediation sessions to follow the initial session, if needed.

Early Referral. Section 7123 of the Internal Revenue Code provides that the Secretary of the Treasury shall provide procedures by which any taxpayer may request early referral of one or more issues from a tax examination or the Collection Division to National Office Appeals. Consequently, the early referral procedure has been expanded to allow for additional cases to be eligible for early referral. Early referral is no longer limited to the largest cases in the

IRS's Coordinated Examination Program. The early referral procedures allow taxpayers whose returns are under examination, to request the transfer of a developed, open issue to Appeals while the other issues in the case continue to be developed in the district. The purpose of early referral is to resolve cases more quickly. The early resolution of a key issue may encourage taxpayers and the IRS to agree on other issues in the case. Early referral may save time, because Appeals and the district are working simultaneously.

The district will advise the taxpayer of its decision to approve or deny the early referral request within 14 days of the date the request is received from the taxpayer. A taxpayer's early referral request no longer requires the concurrence of Appeals. Taxpayers can request an informal conference with the supervisor of the case or a group manager to discuss the district's denial of an early referral request. Regular Appeals procedures apply, including taxpayer conferences. . . .

F. NEGOTIATED RULEMAKING [REG-NEG] AND RULEMAKING SETTLEMENTS

1. Comments and Questions

a. The origin of negotiated rulemaking (reg-neg) was a law review article that suggested an alternative that addressed perceived shortcomings of notice and comment rulemaking under the Administrative Procedure Act (APA), 5 U.S.C. §§ 561 *et. seq. See* Philip J. Harter, *Negotiated Regulations: A Cure for the Malaise*, 71 GEO. L.J. 1 (1981). The idea was favorably reviewed and fleshed out by the Administrative Conference. *See Procedures for Negotiating Proposed Regulations*, 47 FED. REG. 10,708 (1982). Congress enacted the Negotiated Rulemaking Act in 1990, as an amendment to the APA. 5 U.S.C. §§ 561-570. In addition, Congress has mandated the use of a reg-neg proceeding in a number of statutes. The *Riley* decision discusses one such instance, and the orthotics legislation discussed by Sylvester and Lobel provides another example.

b. Reg-neg seeks to overcome the basic concern that the public and adversarial notice and comment rulemaking process is ill-suited for interactive participation between, and compromise among, competing interests. Quite apart from less effective regulations, the rulemaking process frequently was merely a way station to a high stakes court of appeals proceeding (frequently in the D.C. Circuit), with all parties and interests attacking aspects of the rule adopted by the agency. The courts returned rules to the agencies for consideration of additional issues and further hearings often enough that parties unhappy with an agency rule commonly challenged final rules. Agencies responded by becoming defensive in their rulemaking, and proceedings took ever longer to complete.

Reg-neg permits — even encourages — an agency that wants to promulgate a rule to convene a group that is representative of all the interests in the rulemaking topic, and try to find common ground. No one can be forced to agree, so everyone effectively has a veto. The desired payoff is better rules adopted more quickly (i.e., accepted by the parties without judicial challenge). Of course, a failure by any party or group of interests to compromise may result in an agency-proposed rule that is less favorable to that party or interest, as the *Riley* decision demonstrates.

c. Daniel P. Selmi, *The Promise and Limits of Negotiated Rulemaking: Evaluating the Negotiation of a Regional Air Quality Rule*, 35 ENVT'L L. 415 (2005) (rule limiting emissions of chromic acid from metal plating facilities) suggests the use of seven factors to evaluate a regulatory negotiation proceeding. These are: "(1) the role of information, (2) the expansion of the universe of outcomes, (3) the effect of public agency institutional arrangements, (4) the scale of the negotiation, (5) the role of civility and trust, (6) the threat of a unilateral alternative, and (7) the tractability of the dispute." Keep these factors in mind as you consider the materials in this section.

d. The Sylvester & Lobel article closely examines an unsuccessful reg-neg proceeding. The authors were the neutral facilitators and, thus, have a particular insight into why the process did not produce a consensus. As with mediations that do not produce a settlement, the process can still have the salutary effect of clarifying and narrowing the issues at stake and the interests of the parties. The responsible agency is then in a position to better determine the contents of a proposed rule. If the agency wants a compromise, it understands the positions of interested parties. If the agency wants to take a more controversial approach, it will know what to expect by way of opposition.

e. Note the disputation among different orthotics service providers, described by Sylvester & Lobel. Might something similar happen with the credentialing of mediators? The topic of mediator credentialing is discussed in Chapter Fifteen.

2. Lynn Sylvester & Ira B. Lobel, *The Perfect Storm: Anatomy of a Failed Regulatory Negotiation*, 59-JUL DISP. RESOL. J. 44 (2004)

In the film the "Perfect Storm," the actor George Clooney takes a reluctant crew out to sea to catch swordfish. They find themselves in the middle of the convergence of two furious storms. In the film, there were no survivors. In October 2002, we participated in a regulatory negotiation ("reg-neg") that felt much like being in a perfect storm. [The proceeding was conducted at the behest of the Center for Medical Services (CMS), a part of the Department of Health and Human Services.] After 19 days of meetings, the negotiations concluded without an agreement.

We are both experienced mediators and facilitators. Our approaches to mediation are different but complimentary, one emphasizing process and strategy, the other focusing on the end product. These differences can become strengths as we found out during this reg-neg. However, no amount of experience as a mediator or facilitator can guarantee that an agreement will be reached. Since this is one of the few reg-negs that was not successful, we write this article with the luxury of 20/20 hindsight, to analyze what made the negotiation so stormy and what, if anything, could have been done to change the outcome.

What Is a Regulatory Negotiation? A regulatory negotiation is a multiparty negotiation in which a sponsoring regulatory agency convenes a group of representatives from diverse interest groups concerned about a proposed regulation of a particular subject matter. The explicit goal of the negotiation is to reach a consensus on a proposed regulation that will be published in a Notice of Proposed Rulemaking. For all the reg-negs that we are aware of, the participants agree to support the regulation during the regulatory process, if consensus is reached. This can dramatically reduce attacks on a proposed rule during the rulemaking process. Since the participants in regulatory negotiations represent not only their own specific interests, but are supposed to represent similarly situated organizations, they should be in communication with these groups during the reg-neg process to insure that the proposed rule is acceptable to all concerned.

In this way, key participants in the affected industry have the chance to discuss issues of common concern and get to know the regulators. They also can see how difficult it is to write a rule that would be acceptable to a variety of interests. Another intangible benefit is that the regulators can become better acquainted with the industry they regulate and understand its issues and concerns. Reg-negs can help create a productive working relationship between industry participants and regulators that can extend into the future. In theory, they can also produce better regulations that are less subject to attack during the notice and comment process.

Reg-negs usually operate on the basis of a consensus. For the purpose of a reg-neg, consensus is usually defined as a solution that is acceptable to all members of the reg-neg committee. One objector is enough to prevent a consensus from being reached. When that occurs, the agency can issue a Notice of Proposed Rulemaking (NPRM) that reflects its view of the rule, and the participants can file adverse comments to the NPRM or file a lawsuit to prevent implementation of the rule. The advantage of the reg-neg is that participants know the exact rule that will be published. It is often advantageous for industry representatives to compromise to obtain this certainty; likewise, the regulating agency may compromise to reduce the potential for attack on the proposed regulation.

It is common for a regulatory agency to retain an outside convenor-facilitator to help them decide whether negotiated rule making should proceed, and if so, who should participate on the reg-neg committee, and the potential issues to be decided. Using an independent, outside convenor-facilitator not only helps obtain professional experience in this area, but also may allay suspicions that the agency is trying to determine the outcome of the negotiations.

Orthotic Regulation under Medicare. Under current Medicare practice, any provider who has a Medicare supplier number can bill Medicare for fitting and dispensing an orthotic. There are few federal standards under which these providers must operate. While there are orthotists in every state, fewer than 10 states have any licensing requirements. Professional qualifications are largely governed by two national organizations: the American Board for Certification of Orthotics and Prosthetics (ABC) and the Board for Orthotist/Prosthetist Certification (BOC). These two organizations have slightly different philosophies.

ABC is mostly geared to formal education and residency requirements; BOC relies heavily on experience in lieu of formal education. Both organizations test prospective certified orthotists and prothetists.

An October 1997 report published by the Inspector General concluded that a significant number of custom orthotics paid for by Medicare were medically unnecessary and that professional orthotists were less likely to supply questionable orthotics than durable medical equipment companies. In 2000, Congress passed the Benefit Improvement and Protection Act (BIPA), which included a provision regulating orthotics. Section 427 states in pertinent part:

> no [Medicare] payment shall be made for an item of custom fabricated orthotics . . . unless such an item is (1) furnished by a qualified practitioner and (2) fabricated by a qualified practitioner or qualified supplier at a facility that meets such criteria as the Secretary of Health and Human Services, which is responsible for the Center for Medicare Services (CMS, formerly the Health Care Financing Administration) determines appropriate.

The statute went on to provide that "custom fabricated orthotics" must be included in a list to be established by the Secretary "in consultation with appropriate experts in orthotics (including national organizations representing manufacturers of orthotics)." Importantly, it also stated: "No item shall be included in such list unless the item is individually fabricated for the patient over a positive model of the patient." In addition, the legislation directed the Secretary to use the negotiated rulemaking process before developing regulations implementing Section 427 of the statute.

In addition to setting these requirements, BIPA changed the landscape with respect to certification. It dictated that CMS recognize certification from ABC, BOC or any state that licenses orthotists. Many people in the orthotic industry believed that this requirement would help prevent orthotic devices from being fitted by "the guy who operates out of the backseat of his car."

Forming the Reg-Neg Committee. After we were appointed by CMS to act as convenor-facilitators, our task was to form a reg-neg committee to negotiate a regulation under BIPA Section 427. The challenge was to form a group that was not too large and had a cross section of interested parties, without over-representation by one group or interest. There was intense competition to participate on the committee. We interviewed about 40 interested groups.

The fact that the reg-neg was mandated by law may have had a subtle but important impact on the formation of the committee. Those in competition to join the committee may have been less than candid with us about the potential for reaching a consensus, because they did not have to consider whether it would be productive to have a reg-neg. We also suspect that some people may have been more apt to say that a compromise could be reached on the issues even if they believed otherwise.

Upon our recommendation, CMS ultimately invited 21 groups to participate on the committee. These organizations included ABC; BOC; the American Academy for Orthotists and Prosthetists (AAOP); the American Orthotic and Pros-

thetic Association (AOPA); the International Association of Orthotics and Pros-
thestics (IAOP); the National Association for the Advancement of Orthotics
and Prosthetics (NAAOP); the American Physical Therapists Association
(APTA); the American Occupational Therapists Association (AOTA); the American Academy of Orthopedic Surgeons (AAOS); the American Academy of Physical Medicine and Rehabilitation (AAPMR); the National Orthotic and
Manufacturers Association (NOMA); the National Commission on Orthotic and
Prosthetic Education (NCOPE); representatives of orthotic shop owners and
operators; representatives of states with orthotic licensing statutes (Coalition
of State Boards); and three "consumer" organizations: the Amputee Information
Exchange, the Paralyzed Veterans of America and the Barr Foundation. We
believed that these groups had knowledge that would be helpful in promulgat-
ing a workable regulation.

When we did the convening, it appeared that the orthotics organizations represented different areas of the industry: licensing, education and member-
ship/lobbying/trade. However, once the meetings began, it quickly became
apparent that many of these orthotic organizations were affiliated with each
other and had members who sat on each other's boards. Concern about these
myriad affiliations led one participant to suggest creating a spreadsheet showing these interrelationships. In retrospect, there were too many affiliates and too
many groups representing the orthotic community. Unfortunately, due to their
large numbers, the orthotic community representatives mostly kept to themselves, which tended to reinforce their own positions and biases and made them
more unwilling to compromise. Those who wanted to seek common ground with
other interest groups were subtly pressured not to do so. In terms of group
dynamics, this quickly led to an "us against them" mentality.

We have previously worked with a committee of this size, but in that case,
there was no one interest group representing more than 20% of the committee.
Usually, representatives from the different interest groups ate and conversed
together during breaks and lunch sessions, and formed new coalitions during the
course of the negotiations and worked cooperatively together. We could have proposed limiting participation on the reg-neg to the groups mentioned in BIPA.
However, given the competition to get on the reg-neg, CMS probably would not
have accepted this suggestion.

We are not suggesting that a reg-neg necessarily will fail simply because
there is a dominant group. Dominance can be tempered when committee members know and trust each other and recognize shared interests. For example,
firefighters made up approximately one third of a committee (albeit a smaller
committee than in the orthotic case) formed to negotiate a regulation governing
ambulance fee schedules. Their dominance was unavoidable, because emergency medical services in this country are largely provided by the fire department. However, despite their dominance, the firefighters did not impede the
negotiation, perhaps because they were open to hearing other groups' interests. This could not be said of the members of the relatively new orthotic profession, which is starting to struggle with concepts such as licensing and
educational requirements. Professional recognition vis-a-vis these issues was not
on a par with other recognized medical professions and tended to make them

more insecure. Further, there appeared to be very limited interaction professionally and socially between the orthotists, physicians, occupational therapists (OTs), and physical therapists (PTs), making them incapable of seeing that they had anything in common.

First Meeting. At the first meeting in October 2002, we emphasized the need for compromise and open-mindedness. We let the committee members introduce themselves and announce their goals for the reg-neg. All said they wanted to do what was best for the patient. All acknowledged that Section 427 contemplated that customized orthotics would be provided by qualified professionals. All agreed that some orthotic providers were not qualified and manipulated the system to their economic benefit. All agreed that a principal aim of Section 427 was to eliminate "fly by night" practitioners who over-bill Medicare and provide substandard care. This was a good start. However, after that, there was little agreement.

As the talks continued, it became obvious that orthotic services were delivered in a variety of ways. Most custom orthotics are prescribed by physicians. Once prescribed, physicians may produce the orthotics themselves. However, they rarely have the skill or inclination to do so. Usually, physicians delegate the responsibility for orthotic work to persons who work under their supervision or to a professional who specializes in orthotics.

Depending on their needs, some patients were referred to an OT or PT, who performed orthotic services. In most cases, however, the patient took the prescription to an orthotist, who would make the casts, perform fittings, evaluate the device on the patient, and instruct the patient how to use them. (Fittings can also be performed by less qualified individuals, such as an orthotic fitter, a technician working in a doctor's office, or a salesperson working in conjunction with a physician.) Some orthotists make orthotics themselves while others send them to a centralized fabricating laboratory. Thus, there appeared to be no uniformity of care making orthotics. How customized orthotics were delivered varied with the location, available professionals, type of product required, and the desires of the patient and the treating professionals.

Second Meeting. At the second meeting, the OTs and PTs (i.e., AOTA and APTA) made a presentation on the delivery of care and the educational backgrounds of their members, followed by representatives of the orthotic licensing and education groups (ABC, BOC and NCOPE). Each group claimed to be uniquely qualified to provide a wide spectrum of orthotic care. An outsider listening to the presentation probably would have thought that only the presenter's group was able to provide customized orthotics.

The discussions heated up when the AOTA and APTA representatives stated that their members could "legally" provide the "full scope" of orthotic care. The orthotic community reacted angrily, since they viewed this statement as an assault on their livelihood. They failed to appreciate that AOTA and APTA were not threatening to take work away from orthotists. Rather, they meant that they have legal authority under BIPA to bill Medicare for custom orthotics, while at the same time, they have a legal responsibility to perform only those tasks for which they are properly trained. This usually does not include the "full scope" of orthotic care.

NCOPE's representative, when asked the extent to which an ABC or BOC certified orthotist could engage in the full scope of orthotic care made almost the same pronouncement about certified orthotists: that they could provide the full spectrum of care if they believed they had the education and training to do the required task. For example, the orthotist representatives acknowledged that certain specialized tasks should be done only by an orthotist with special training to perform such tasks. Unfortunately, the OT and PT representatives did not use this point of similarity to show that they all shared the same view of professionalism. It may have focused the conversation on assuring that all practitioners maintain this professionalism rather than on a turf battle about who can do certain work. Indeed, there was no question that all physicians, including dermatologists, could legally perform orthotic services under BIPA. But there was no concern that dermatologists would actually perform such services because doing so was out of their area of expertise and could subject them to malpractice claims and jeopardize their license.

This issue grew in importance. The different groups were unable to agree on a basic principle: that all BIPA-authorized professionals and practitioners (physicians, OTs, PTs and certified orthotists) should act professionally and perform only those tasks for which they are qualified. Consequently, instead of considering a regulation that would prevent persons from performing orthotic services, the orthotic group representatives sought to impose special training requirements only on the OTs and PTs. This was surprising, because during the convening process (i.e., when the groups were interviewed, prior to their invitation to join the committee), the issue of OT and PT qualifications never came up.

Role of Congress. It was unfair of Congress to saddle CMS with a contradictory and poorly drafted statute and then require a reg-neg process to sort it out, particularly in a new area of regulation for the agency. Given CMS's institutional inexperience in regulating orthotics, a difficult goal was rendered impossible to achieve. We are not suggesting that Congressionally mandated reg-negs are inherently bad, since we have both led Congressionally mandated reg-negs with good outcomes. However, we think that Congress should take more care in selecting the matters it sends to the negotiated rulemaking process. In the future, we think that it should consider to what degree a reg-neg committee will be presented with a precedent-setting question, the clarity of the statutory mandate and the agency experience in the regulated area, all considerations that should be assessed in determining whether or not to use negotiated rulemaking.

We have been told that Congress thought this reg-neg would be good for the industry, because it would give industry participants an opportunity to work cooperatively with the government. But what actually happened is that the reg-neg turned into a forum where industry groups staked out institutional claims before the regulating body. Unfortunately, many participants failed to see any value in working with the regulators. This is one of our greatest disappointments. Perhaps because other groups we have dealt with on other reg-negs appreciated that it was in their interest to cooperate with the agency in drafting regulations, we did not give this point enough emphasis.

Role of CMS. For a reg-neg to be effective, the sponsoring agency's representative must, at some time, lay out the agency's vision for the final rule. The agency representative, despite having only one vote on the committee, is the first among equals. Committee members tend to give great deference to those views, so having them expressed helps give the committee direction, even if others on the committee don't agree with them.

Although orthotic care was a new area of regulation for CMS, its staff performed admirably. They absorbed the intricacies of the new subject and understood many of its nuances. However, CMS's working group, made up of between 10-20 people, never reached a real consensus itself about where it wanted to end up. CMS was also handicapped by the fact that its physician/staff member most knowledgeable about coding orthotics was unable to participate in the negotiations due to other commitments. However, when this individual was available to the committee, her insights were invaluable and seemed to have credibility with the rest of the reg-neg committee.

Before the negotiations began, CMS's representative asked us if he should submit a formal proposal to the committee as a starting point in the negotiations. We both recommended against doing so, because we believe it is important for the agency to at least appear to be open-minded in the first few meetings and listen to the view of the committee members. However, we told him that CMS should develop a preliminary idea of the shape the regulation should take so that he can give the committee some direction. Knowing what an agency might do in the absence of consensus can help a reg-neg committee, especially one that has groups with strong opposing interests. It serves as a reality check that can guide the choices committee members make. Accordingly, our view was that CMS should make a proposal, not at the outset but later in the negotiations.

The agency representative did not take a leadership role, and he left the agency toward the end of the negotiations without ever giving the committee a clear view of the agency's position. He was replaced by a representative who took a more assertive role, worked hard to understand the participants' different interests and tried to forge a consensus by making specific suggestions for compromise. But his efforts came too late. Because the agency did not earlier share its interpretation of BIPA, the groups represented on the reg-neg committee acted as if they could prevail in their positions.

In retrospect, we should have advised the first CMS representative to press the agency to take a position on its statutory interpretation and present its conception of an ideal regulation to the committee soon after the first or second meeting. The risk of doing so, of course, was that CMS could become enamored of its position and become inflexible. However, it would have given the rest of the committee some direction in terms of what would and would not have been possible from a regulatory standpoint.

A technique we have used in the past involves meeting with agency officials the evening before a reg-neg meeting to develop a coordinated plan for the negotiations. This technique can be particularly useful when the agency does not have a clear direction. However, it may be less effective when the number of involved agency officials is large, as was the case in this reg-neg. Another logistical problem is arranging prior meetings with officials when the reg-neg committee meets on Mondays, as it did in this case.

Role of the Parties. Ultimately, in any negotiation, the role that individual negotiators play is critical to the outcome. Negotiations are about people, and there is no overcoming that fact. Facilitators have a limited ability to overcome the impact of individual actions on negotiation. Facilitators can create an environment conducive to negotiation, but at the end of the day, it is the negotiators themselves who make a negotiation successful.

In selecting representatives and alternates, participating groups should appoint representatives who have both substantive or technical knowledge and good negotiation and leadership skills. This can be a challenge. The fact is that many representatives are selected because of the positions they hold within the group or association they represent. Notwithstanding an individual's talents, representatives are beholden to the political will of the group that sent them to the table. There is no under-estimating the political pressure under which these representatives operate.

In most reg-negs, interest groups are represented by a primary and an alternate member. In general, both attend the meetings, along with technical advisors, attorneys and sometimes other supporters. In the orthotic reg-neg, the primary representatives sat at the table while the alternate and advisors sat behind them. Many reg-neg ground rules usually provide that the facilitator recognize each speaker. Alternates do not participate except when their primary representative is not present, or they ask to be recognized, or the facilitator invites their participation.

In this reg-neg, we encouraged the alternates to participate when the subject matter required their expertise. At various times, they moved up to the table to discuss technical matters and often stayed there. To our surprise, their participation became an issue, because it sometimes seemed that some groups had more than one member on their team (even though each group got only one vote for consensus decisions). This is the first time in our experience that alternate participation became a problem. In hindsight, because of the uneasy feelings committee members had about each other, it might have been prudent to strictly enforce the "primary at the table rule."

Obnoxious Members. It seems that every committee has an obnoxious member. This committee had a large number of members who behaved unprofessionally. At one point, bad behavior took the place of rational discussion and argument. It was not uncommon for members to make insulting remarks about another committee member or question the integrity of other groups. We were both concerned that these individuals might make inflammatory comments at the wrong time. We did our best to curb this behavior; we met privately with these individuals to urge their forbearance. At times, . . . we took a blunt, in-your-face approach. Unfortunately, not much helped, because the participating groups never took responsibility for the bad behavior of their members.

What this reg-neg committee lacked was a person whom all participants respected and recognized as a leader. The importance of having such a person on a negotiation committee cannot be minimized. Often, such a person emerges after a couple of meetings; it was bad luck that this reg-neg had no such person. Fortunately, every committee also has two or three people who try to keep the discussion on track. The consumer and state representatives on the committee played that role here. They were the moral minds of the committee, and we sought their help near the end of the negotiations in reminding their colleagues that their primary talk was to agree on a rule they could live with that would protect the public. This reminder was particularly critical on the last day, but it came too late.

Role of Attorneys. Several members of the reg-neg committee were lawyers. This became an unspoken issue for some unrepresented committee members who felt "out-gunned," especially when it came to interpreting BIPA or other legal requirements. The attorneys aggressively represented their client's interests. As a result, they did not gain the trust of the non-attorneys, even on legal issues. There were many instances when represented groups would have been better served by a low key approach. This is not intended to be an indictment of attorneys (we are both attorneys). However, it can be less threatening when a legal statement is made by an interested industry person, rather than by an attorney. On many occasions, we privately asked a represented group to have a non-attorney make a particular presentation. This technique should have been used more often. However, raising this issue could raise sensitivities, because the parties decide who represents their interests, and they may resent the facilitator's interference.

The Failure of Group Development. Many experienced facilitators will tell you that successful groups go through four phases of group development: forming, storming, norming, and performing. There are several things a facilitator can do to assist a group in its development. The first is to sponsor a social hour (also known as an attitude adjustment hour) after the first day of meetings. These informal gatherings allow people to renew old acquaintances and make new ones. This is essential if the negotiations are to be effective. We sponsored a social hour in the orthotic reg-neg, hoping that it would start building new relationships. However, that never happened. The orthotic community stuck together like glue. Moreover, each group had a number of alternates and supporters attending the main sessions, further hampering intermingling. In retrospect, although we were meeting these people for the first time, we should have seen this dynamic earlier. It would have enabled us to make introductions and encourage mingling.

The Divisive Issue. The key issue in this reg-neg was who was qualified to fit and fabricate customized orthotics. The therapist organizations, APTA and OPTA, concluded that the word "qualified" (as in "qualified physical therapist" and "qualified occupational therapist") meant licensed. There is precedent for this view elsewhere in the Medicare statute. Accordingly, they believed that licensed OTs and PTs were qualified to provide orthotic services, but they did not see that the therapists, like the physicians, had a professional responsibility on which their licenses were dependent, to act in a medically appropriate manner and provide only those services for which they had the skill and training. The OTs and PTs feared any regulations limiting their scope of practice for two reasons: (1) it was not appropriate and (2) it would set a bad precedent for the future.

The orthotic community, on the other hand, feared that the OTs and PTs could appropriate their work. Wanting to eliminate them as competitors, the orthotist representatives argued that the term "qualified" did not mean "licensed"; thus, the OTs and PTs should be required to have additional training. Before this reg-neg, this concern had never risen to the degree that it would overshadow the success of the reg-neg. It appeared that each group, in their specific locales, worked out their professional turf. While there were turf battles being fought in the field by some of these groups, by and large it appeared that the professions had carved out appropriate niches for themselves. In the reg-neg, however, in the global view, everyone had a "worst case" scenario in mind.

The fact that this issue was not targeted as a bedrock issue at the beginning was a missed opportunity. Moreover, when the issue surfaced at the second meeting, the CMS representative said he saw value in both arguments, which did not help to bring the parties together. It was not a good strategy to keep the hopes of both sides alive in this way. Had CMS's representative introduced doubt and indicated which side he was leaning toward, the other side may have been inclined to accept his position in order to obtain concessions in other areas.

Conclusion. We succeeded in keeping the discussions going for 19 meetings. Although the reg-neg failed, many of the participants were dedicated, knowledgeable professionals who felt passionately about the orthotic industry. It is unfortunate that the members of the reg-neg committee were never able to reach consensus on the core issue that divided them. We can only speculate on some of the possible causes: the lack of balance in the representation on the committee, an insufficient amount of direction from the agency, and the late identification of the main divisive issue.

We also believe that the youth of the orthotic industry worked against reaching consensus. Compared to the medical and therapy professions, which are regulated in all 50 states and are subject to stringent educational and licensing requirements, this industry is in its infancy regarding these types of issues. It does not yet have a secure place in the health care delivery system, and it has far to go in terms of state regulation, licensing, educational requirements, and training.

In each reg-neg, the facilitator decides on the appropriate approach, using his or her best judgment of the situation at the time. A facilitator cannot take a group where it does not want to go. While it is not clear to us that we would have made any fundamental changes in our approach to this reg-neg, there are things we could have done differently. But whether that would have made the process more productive is pure speculation. The purpose of this exercise is to enlighten. We hope this discussion will be helpful to other facilitators and students of the process.

3. *USA Group Loan Services, Inc. v. Riley*, 82 F.3d 708 (7th Cir. 1996)

POSNER, Chief Judge.

The federal government has an enormous program, administered by the Department of Education, of subsidizing student loans. The loans are made by banks but are guaranteed by state and private agencies that have reinsurance contracts with the Department, making it the indirect guarantor of the loans and thus inducing banks to make what would otherwise be risky loans. The proceeds of the loans are used to pay tuition and other expenses; so the colleges and other schools whose students are receiving these loans are also involved in the federal program. Like so many government programs, the student loan program places heavy administrative burdens on the entities involved in it — the lenders, the guarantors, and the institutions. A whole industry of "servicers" has arisen to relieve these entities of some of the administrative burdens. As agents of the educational institutions, the servicers maintain records of the institution's student loans. As agents of the banks, they collect the loans from the students as the loans come due and dun the students when they are slow in paying. As agents of the guarantors, the servicers keep track of defaults and make sure that the banks comply with the various conditions for triggering the guarantees. In any of these roles, a servicer who makes a mistake can end up costing the federal government money. If the servicer remits loan moneys to a school for the tuition of a student not eligible for a loan, or fails to pursue a defaulting student, or honors an invalid claim by a bank for reimbursement from a guarantor, federal money is disbursed in violation of the regulations governing the student loan program.

Mistakes and outright fraud by servicers, some resulting in large losses of federal money, led Congress in 1992 to amend Title IV of the Higher Education Act to authorize the Secretary of Education to "prescribe . . . regulations applicable to third party servicers (including regulations concerning financial responsibility standards for, and the assessment of liabilities for program violations against, such servicers) to establish minimum standards with respect to sound management and accountability." 20 U.S.C. § 1082(a)(1). The Secretary has done this, and the servicers have brought this suit to invalidate portions of the regulations on substantive and procedural grounds. The district court rejected the challenge, and the servicers appeal.

The challenged provisions make servicers jointly and severally liable with their customers (lenders, guarantors, and institutions) for violations of the statutes, regulations, or contracts governing the student loan program. To be liable, the servicer must itself have violated a statute, regulation, or contract. But it is not a defense that the violation was inadvertent or even that it could not have been avoided at reasonable cost, though given the complexity of the rules and regulations governing the program, and the volume of transactions, mistakes are inevitable even if all due care is used. Although liability is thus strict, as the servicers complain, the regulations use the term "joint and several liability" in a special sense. The usual meaning is that if two or more tortfeasors produce a single injury, the victim can sue any of the tortfeasors for the full amount of his damages and collect that amount from the tortfeasor he has sued. That tortfeasor may or may not have a right to obtain contribution or indemnification — a right to a sharing or shifting of the cost of liability — from the other tortfeasors. But under the challenged regulation, the Department may go against a servicer only if unable to collect the overpayment from the servicer's customer. The servicer's liability is thus a back-up liability. . . .

The [challengers argue] . . . that the Secretary adopted the challenged regulation in violation of the conditions of "negotiated rulemaking," a novelty in the administrative process. . . . The servicers argue that the Department negotiated in bad faith with them. Neither the 1992 amendment nor the Negotiated Rulemaking Act specifies a remedy for such a case, and the latter act strongly implies there is none. 5 U.S.C. § 570. But even if a regulation could be invalidated because the agency had failed to negotiate in good faith, this would not carry the day for the servicers.

During the negotiations, an official of the Department of Education promised the servicers that the Department would abide by any consensus reached by them unless there were compelling reasons to depart. The propriety of such a promise may be questioned. It sounds like an abdication of regulatory authority to the regulated, the full burgeoning of the interest-group state, and the final confirmation of the "capture" theory of administrative regulation. At all events, although the servicers reached a firm consensus that they should not be liable for their mistakes, the Department refused to abide by its official's promise. What is more, the draft regulations that the Department submitted to the negotiating process capped the servicers' liability at the amount of the fees they received from their customers, yet when it came time to propose a regulation as the basis for the notice and comment rulemaking, the Department abandoned the cap. The breach of the promise to abide by consensus in the absence of compelling reasons not here suggested, and the unexplained withdrawal of the Department's proposal to cap the servicers' liability, form the basis for the claim that the Department negotiated in bad faith.

We have doubts about the propriety of the official's promise to abide by a consensus of the regulated industry, but we have no doubt that the Act did not make the promise enforceable. *Natural Resources Defense Council, Inc. v. EPA*, 859 F.2d 156, 194 (D.C. Cir. 1988). The practical effect of enforcing it would be to make the Act extinguish notice and comment rulemaking in all cases in which it was preceded by negotiated rulemaking; the comments would be irrelevant if the agency were already bound by promises that it had made to the industry. There is no textual or other clue that the Act meant to do this. Unlike collective bargaining negotiations, to which the servicers compare negotiated rulemaking, the Act does not envisage that the negotiations will end in a binding contract. The Act simply creates a consultative process in advance of the more formal arms' length procedure of notice and comment rulemaking. *See* 5 U.S.C. § 566(f).

The complaint about the Secretary's refusal to adhere to the proposal to cap the servicers' liability misconceives the nature of negotiation. The Secretary proposed the cap in an effort to be accommodating and deflect the industry's wrath. The industry, in retrospect, improvidently rejected the proposal, holding out for no liability. So, naturally, the Secretary withdrew the proposal. A rule that a rejected offer places a ceiling on the offeror's demands would destroy negotiation. Neither party would dare make an offer, as the other party would be certain to reject it in order to limit the future demands that his opponent could make. This concern lies behind the principle that settlement offers are not admissible in litigation if the settlement effort breaks down. Fed.R.Evid. 408. By the same token, the negotiating position of the parties in negotiated rulemaking ought not be admissible in a challenge to the rule eventually promulgated when the negotiation failed.

The servicers argue that they should be allowed to conduct discovery to uncover the full perfidy of the Department's conduct in the negotiations. Discovery is rarely proper in the judicial review of administrative action. The court is supposed to make its decision on the basis of the administrative record, not create its own record. There are exceptions, and the main one has some potential applicability here: discovery is proper when it is necessary to create a record without which the challenge to the agency's action cannot be evaluated. *Citizens to Preserve Overton Park, Inc. v. Volpe*, 401 U.S. 402, 420 (1971). Negotiated rulemaking does not usually produce a comprehensive administrative record, such as notice and comment rulemaking, or a cease and desist order proceeding, or a licensing proceeding would do, any more than a settlement conference will usually produce a full record. Some discovery was conducted in the district court in order to present a picture of what went on at the negotiations between the servicers and the Department. The servicers argue that if only they could get access to the notes of certain participants in the negotiating sessions they could demonstrate additional instances of bad faith on the part of the Department.

Their conception of "bad faith" reflects, as we have noted, a misconception of the negotiation process. It is not bad faith to withdraw an offer after the other side has rejected it. If, as we doubt, the Negotiated Rulemaking Act creates a remedy as well as a right, we suppose that a refusal to negotiate that really was in bad faith, because the agency was determined to stonewall, might invalidate the rule eventually adopted by the agency. But we do not think that the Act was intended to open the door wide to discovery in judicial proceedings challenging regulations issued after the notice and comment proceeding that followed the negotiations. If, as in this case, the public record discloses no evidence of bad faith on the part of the agency, that should be the end of the inquiry. A contrary conclusion would stretch out such judicial proceedings unconscionably. The Act's purpose — to reduce judicial challenges to regulations by encouraging the parties to narrow their differences in advance of the formal rulemaking proceedings — would be poorly served if the negotiations became a source and focus of litigation. Affirmed.

4. Comments and Questions

a. A participant in the HEA reg-neg proceeding had offered his views on why the process failed. Mark Pelish, *Regulations Under the Higher Education Amendments of 1992: A Case Study in Negotiated Rulemaking*, 57 LAW & CONTEMP. PROBS. 151 (1994). Pelish thinks the conditions were right for resort to a negotiated rulemaking, specifically:

1. Discrete and well-defined set of issues;

2. Right parties and representatives at the table;

3. Knowledgeable parties with ample information;

4. A statutory deadline to prompt action; and

5. Experienced and capable neutral facilitator.

Pelish offers three reasons why the HEA reg-neg did not succeed, two structural and one related to scheduling. Most important, the negotiators lacked the authority to bind the organizations they represented — a fundamental problem for any negotiation. The Department of Education also was not committed to implementing the outcome of a successful reg-neg. While the Government cannot legally bind itself to promulgate a regulation proposed by private parties, it can strongly indicate its inclination to adopt any plausible consensus proposal. As for scheduling, the reg-neg consisted of two long meetings, an approach that did not allow parties time to consider options and alternatives, and to consult with their principals. More frequent and shorter meetings would have increased the chances of reaching a consensus proposal.

b. Whether or to what extent reg-neg has been a success is a matter of contention. *See, e.g.,* Cary Coglianese, *Assessing Consensus: The Promise and Performance of Negotiated Rulemaking,* 46 DUKE L.J. 1255 (1997) (negative); Philip J. Harter, *Assessing the Assessors: The Actual Performance of Negotiated Rulemaking,* 9 N.Y.U. ENV. L.J. 32 (2000) (positive).

c. Recall the discussion by Tom Melling, in Chapter Six, of the legislative negotiation regarding the Central Utah Project. Compare and contrast that process with reg-neg proceedings.

5. Jim Rossi, *Bargaining in the Shadow of Administrative Procedure: The Public Interest in Rulemaking Settlement,* 51 DUKE L.J. 1015 (2001)

In recent years, a new account of administrative law, favoring private ordering over state-imposed solutions, has bolstered the acceptability of negotiated approaches to regulatory problems. Consistent with this account, administrative law has seen a growing trend toward flexible, consensual mechanisms for regulation, emphasizing less rigid, cooperative approaches over prolonged adversarial disputes. Procedural innovations, such as negotiated regulation (known less formally as "reg neg"), have proliferated as alternatives to more traditional administrative procedures, such as notice and comment rulemaking. Reformers' embrace of such solutions for their promise in promoting private consensus over public mandate has engendered much discussion in the literature.

This Essay addresses the type of private ordering relating to the settlement of lawsuits challenging administrative rules or final agency actions, also known as "rulemaking settlements." Hardly a procedural innovation, the prospect of settlement is a traditional component of any strategy to influence agency decisionmaking. Rulemaking settlement is not only a private strategy, but also may serve as an important vehicle for an agency to implement its policy decisions. . . . Settlement is certainly more common than negotiated regulation, but unlike negotiated regulation, it has received scant attention in the administrative law literature. . . .

I. Rulemaking Settlement

Agencies routinely enter into settlements limiting the scope of their regulatory discretion. To a degree, rulemaking settlement fits into a broader trend toward collaborative governance in the administrative state. However, the analogy between rulemaking settlement and other collaborative governance techniques, such as negotiated regulation, is limited. At the fore are concerns about the potential for abuse of settlements by private stakeholders and the more general implications for administrative legitimacy. Because settlement is most controversial when it reflects a compromise on substantive issues of interpretation or policy, this Essay focuses its discussion on these types of settlements rather than on less controversial — but perhaps more common — settlements in which the government merely agrees to a schedule or process for rule consideration. Conceptually, rulemaking settlement may be more likely than negotiated regulation to present a principal-agent gap, because agency negotiators, in an appellate posture, face incentives for skirting important stakeholder perspectives — including those that may be most concerned with safeguarding the public interest.

A. Settlement as a Type of Collaborative Governance. . . . For several years, regulators have embraced settlements and other alternative dispute resolution techniques as fundamental components of the administrative process. Unlike traditional litigation, alternative dispute resolution provides an opportunity to deflect the adversarial nature of many administrative proceedings, while also empowering private stakeholders. Such techniques are touted . . . for their flexibility, efficiency, and legitimacy over more traditional administrative procedures. For example, it is now commonplace for an agency to offer the opportunity for mediation and settlement to parties to an adjudication, such as an enforcement proceeding. Such techniques can assist an agency in securing compliance with its regulations while also offering private parties the opportunity to avoid protracted litigation. Settlement raises little potential for controversy where it is bilateral and between two private parties, as may be the case in a license contest proceeding. In a sense, the government is not a party to such proceedings, although an agency may play an important role as referee in ensuring that the settlement outcome between private parties reflects the public interest. The greater the public interest issues raised in an agency proceeding, the more controversial settlement may become. . . .

If for example, an agency brings an enforcement action against a private party, the dispute between the agency and the private party is often bilateral, but the nature of the interests at stake differs in a fundamental way from a bilateral settlement between private negotiators. The position of a regulated party in challenging the agency's action and entering into negotiated solutions may be motivated by private interests, but the agency is constrained (and hopefully motivated) by the public interest, including institutional and procedural checks designed to ensure that this public interest is not sacrificed. Matters become substantially more complex when private stakeholders with divergent interests must reach consensus and negotiated solutions to complex, multipolar private conflicts in addition to accommodating the public interest.

This last scenario is perhaps most common in the context of agency rulemaking. The APA sets out the basic framework . . . that agencies use to make law and policy. In the typical notice and comment procedure, an agency will publish a notice of proposed rulemaking, allow a period for public comment, consider comments submitted to it, and then approve and publish a final rule. Judicial review of the agency's process and regulation is separate from, but inextricably linked to, this process. Courts review agency regulations adopted through the rulemaking process to determine whether they are "arbitrary, capricious, an abuse of discretion, or otherwise not in accordance with the law." Since the 1970s, more expansive definitions of standing have increased the number, and broadened the range, of parties allowed to participate meaningfully in the judicial appeals process. Doctrinal developments also have created more opportunities to challenge rules, not just in as-applied enforcement proceedings but also prior to their enforcement. The result is a system of "adversarial legalism," characterized by the breathtaking frequency and length of judicial appeals of agency rules.

Settlement of appeals is a common way for an agency to dispose of an ongoing adversarial dispute. As a category, rulemaking settlement includes pure bilateral settlements, in which private entities and an agency agree on a course of action, but courts play little or no enforcement role, as well as consent decrees, in which a court's judicial imprimatur has preemption and enforcement effects far beyond purely consensual contractual settlement. Like negotiated regulation, settlement of appellate litigation has much to commend it, including the promotion of flexibility, efficiency in litigation and agency enforcement, expediency on the part of both government and private litigants, and legitimacy — to the extent settlement reflects the shared consensus of stakeholders.

Not surprisingly, the legality of rulemaking settlements is sometimes called into question. Once an agency enters into an otherwise valid settlement, modification of the terms of the settlement through interpretation by that agency can give rise to considerable confusion and undermine private stakeholder incentives for participating in settlements with the government. Similarly, if settlements are not capable of enforcement, private stakeholders will face little incentive to participate. On the other hand, always allowing settlement to bind agencies can thwart flexibility and undermine the public interest values promoted by administrative process.

B. Problems with Rulemaking Settlement: A Principal-Agent Gap. Although rulemaking settlements may overlap with collaborative governance mechanisms such as negotiated regulation, they also differ in fundamental and important ways. In the course of briefly discussing the key differences between rulemaking settlement and negotiated regulation, I sketch a simple principal-agent account of administrative procedure to illustrate the particular deficiencies unique to rulemaking settlement as compared to other collaborative governance techniques, such as negotiated regulation. These differences illustrate how settlement may fall short of the goals of collaborative governance techniques. The principal-agent model posits an agent, here an administrative agency, as influenced by institutional principals, here Congress, the president, and private stakeholders, who are routinely key participants in the decision-making process under the APA. . . . The incentives an agency faces to settle an appeal may increase monitoring costs for these principals, thus contributing to a principal-agent gap.

The differences between rulemaking settlement and other collaborative governance techniques can be traced in large part to the unique incentives that private litigants and agencies face when settling appeals of agency rules. My analysis of the structural architecture of rulemaking settlement draws on the common tripartite focus on "exit," "voice," and "loyalty" as ways to influence institutional behavior. ALBERT O. HIRSCHMAN, EXIT, VOICE, AND LOYALTY: RESPONSES TO DECLINE IN FIRMS, ORGANIZATIONS, AND STATES (1970). In the settlement context, the threat of exit — in the form of expected private stakeholder litigation and the ensuing costs to the agency — is the predominant incentive influencing agency litigants. By threatening continued litigation against an agency, private stakeholders in the appellate posture may be in a position to extract concessions that an agency refused to make in the notice and comment process. This is the primary incentive that private stakeholder exit presents to agency litigants. The incentives that private exit poses for agency negotiators to settle appeals, coupled with high expected litigation costs to the agency as a consequence of such exit, contribute to the principal-agent gap in the appellate context. That is, private incentives for exit coupled with high expected litigation costs for the government may lead agency negotiators to make concessions in settlement that are not necessarily in the public interest, widening the disparity between the agency's actions and those institutions and participants to which the agency is accountable. . . . [A]ttention to voice and loyalty might help to minimize the principal-agent gap created by the threat of exit. . . .

The principal-agent gap in the context of rulemaking settlement is more problematic than in other contexts. . . . Because the notice and comment process runs its course prior to appeal of a final regulation, rulemaking settlement does not provide the same benefit of discouraging litigious behavior. Rulemaking settlement becomes a useful strategy only once negotiated regulation has failed to prevent litigation. It should be noted, however, that rulemaking settlement in the context of appellate litigation also may jump-start a new negotiated regulation process before the agency. Although rulemaking settlement can provide a range of benefits, including providing a forum for negotiating outside the litigation process altogether, it does not provide the same forward-looking opportunity to avert adversarialism that negotiated regulation does. To the extent an adversarial mindset already has set in, and perhaps solidified, among parties to an appeal by the time that settlement negotiations commence, the prospect for strategic behavior on the part of participants is stronger in the context of rulemaking settlement than in other collaborative governance contexts. Such strategic behavior has consequences for how the agency and private parties participate in settlement negotiations.

A second difference is that rulemaking settlement frequently involves a more limited number of parties than negotiated regulation. In rulemaking settlement, the stakeholders participating in the settlement are not necessarily inclusive of all those who might have been interested in a regulation from initiation of the notice and comment process, but instead is limited to parties present on appeal. If the incentives for private exit are particularly strong, and expected litigation costs are high, agencies may find it advantageous to limit the parties to an appeal and enter into negotiations.

For example, consider the settlement that grew from OSHA's 1989 lockout/tagout rule. . . . OSHA published a final regulation that required employers to place locks and tags, such as circuit breakers, on machines and power supplies to prevent industrial accidents. Six industry groups and two labor unions filed for judicial review. The parties could not agree to a settlement. However, one of the industry appellants, American Petroleum Institute, entered into a compromise with OSHA. Pursuant to this compromise, OSHA agreed to insert nonmandatory guidelines into its enforcement manual. OSHA also made an official "correction" to the rule, clarifying that "work permits or comparable means" could substitute for group lockouts in certain situations. By adopting guidelines outside of the notice and comment process — as permitted under the interpretive rule or policy statement exceptions to notice and comment rulemaking — OSHA was able to make concessions to private stakeholders on appeal without undergoing the full notice and comment process.

Although the lockout/tagout settlement seems like a pragmatic effort on behalf of an agency to manage its scarce resources on appeal, the difference from traditional negotiated regulation should raise concerns. Union groups challenged the interpretation reached during the settlement, but the District of Columbia Circuit upheld the agency's new interpretation, because it was "consistent with the record evidence and would have constituted a logical outgrowth of the proposed rules if originally promulgated as corrected." At a minimum, the lockout/tagout settlement is suspect to the extent that it excluded the concerns of third parties that were central to the acceptability of the agency's action under almost any account of agency legitimacy. The fact that the settlement agreement did not include the labor union heightens the potential for interest group capture of the agency decisionmaking process, rendering the agency's interpretation suspect. . . .

A third reason that rulemaking settlement raises heightened principal-agent gap problems is the secretive nature of the process. Settlement procedures, unlike negotiated regulations, are often closed to the public. Settlement often results from confidential mediation in which the parties may not only be few, but also free from public scrutiny. Rules governing ex parte contacts, for example, do not apply once a final rule has been issued. Confidential mediation is valued as a negotiation tool to the extent that it encourages all parties to air their concerns openly and honestly. At the same time, confidential settlement processes may lead agencies to adopt positions that later raise opposition from affected stakeholders. The results of a settlement may be rendered even more suspect if an agency makes concessions outside of the notice and comment process and fails to publish them in the Federal Register. Where the incentives for private exit are strong and where expected litigation costs are high, agencies may even be the party to seek to ensure confidentiality in the settlement process.

The effects of confidentiality, coupled with the limited range of stakeholder participants, pose a monitoring cost problem in the context of rulemaking settlement. In an appellate posture, an agency and its lawyers have incentives to settle to avoid litigation costs and more quickly implement enforcement of a rule. Settlement may be preferable in such a context, but it is not always socially desirable simply because of litigation savings. Sometimes the stakeholders agreeing to a settlement may not accurately reflect the full complexities of the principal-agent relationship surrounding an agency's decisionmaking process. In particular, the interests of principals such as Congress or stakeholders not actively participating in the judicial appeal may be given short shrift. Compare this process with the ordinary negotiated regulation process, where these principals are more likely to be included in the agent's negotiations, because notice and comment rulemaking has yet to run its course. In other words, a principal-agent gap may create a bias of sorts in the appeals settlement process that does not necessarily apply in other collaborative governance contexts.

A fourth and final contrast between rulemaking settlement and negotiated regulation relates to the role of the courts. While negotiated regulation occurs prior to appeal and, thus, operates largely outside the pale of judicial scrutiny, the involvement of appellate courts in rulemaking settlement has both adverse and beneficial implications. In the literature on civil settlements, commentators treat settlements with skepticism on the grounds that they impede the generation of precedents on important matters of public policy, or that they enable settling parties to act strategically to cause the creation of favorable precedents while avoiding the generation of unfavorable ones. To the extent that courts play a significant role in creating precedents that protect the public interest, settlement of rule appeals would seem to present the same concerns about stifling case law development and manipulation of precedent that plague settlements more broadly.

Of more potential benefit, however, is the role that courts have an opportunity to play in evaluating rulemaking settlements by approving dismissal of a case, approving consent decrees, or staying an adopted rule pending implementation of a settlement. Whether judicial involvement in a rulemaking settlement promotes or impairs the public interest will depend on the terms of the settlement, as well as the standards the courts apply in approving it. On the one hand, courts' willingness to approve settlements based on the consensus of a narrow range of stakeholders provides private stakeholders the opportunity to hold an agency hostage to a consensus that runs counter to the public interest. On the other hand, notwithstanding the District of Columbia Circuit's deferential approach in the OSHA lockout/tagout rulemaking settlement, judicial involvement holds promise to police the public interest aspects of rulemaking settlements. To serve this function, courts must fashion an appropriate set of evaluative standards for approving settlements. In addition, once settlement is reached, courts continue to play a monitoring role: if an agency reneges on the terms of a settlement, other parties to the agreement might seek judicial enforcement. In contrast to their role in rulemaking settlement, courts serve little or no role in monitoring negotiated regulation, and no role whatsoever in enforcing agency departures from the terms of negotiated regulation.

In its ideal form, negotiated regulation may be a measuring stick against which rulemaking settlements can be evaluated, and perhaps even an ideal toward which settlement should strive. It cannot be assumed, however, that rulemaking settlements automatically adhere to the collaborative governance ideals proponents of negotiated regulation embrace simply because they reflect private ordering. Rulemaking settlement raises a potential principal-agent gap for an agency's policy choices that negotiated regulation does not always raise. The gap is due in part to the more strategic mindset of private litigants, in part to strong incentives for exit coupled with litigation cost consequences for the agency, and in part to the increased role of the courts and the potential for the manipulation of precedent. The involvement of courts in the settlement process may hold promise as a way of mitigating this gap, increasing the accountability of the settlement process and its regulatory results.

III. Closing the Principal-Agent Gap in Rulemaking Settlement

Agency concession on substantive policy issues in the course of an appellate settlement raises serious legitimacy concerns, especially when it occurs in the context of presidential transitions. In the context of rulemaking settlements, there is a potential that negotiations will be limited to a small number of parties who are not carefully selected for inclusion. Since settlement can occur outside the realm of procedural protections afforded by the APA, an agency can readily make concessions that run contrary to the views of excluded stakeholders. To the extent that an agency uses settlement to commit itself to a substantive policy position, there is no guarantee that this position will be consistent with an agency position developed earlier under APA procedures. If courts merely rubber-stamp settlements, they will contribute to the principal-agent gap in monitoring the accountability of agency rulemaking.

Yet, under existing doctrine, the exact role that courts should play in evaluating settlements and their implementation is unclear, leaving much to judicial discretion. In terms of mood, courts can take a deferential approach and treat settlements as any other contract, or may decide to invoke more rigorous, arbitrary and capricious review in evaluating the merits of settlements. A deferential approach places a strong emphasis on exit interests as a monitoring device. My argument is that, although protecting participatory rights of exit (in the form of a party's right to object to a settlement) is necessary, a focus on voice and loyalty concerns over exit interests also will serve an important function in enhancing the accountability of rulemaking settlement. Courts should not rely on exit incentives alone to protect the public interest during rulemaking settlement. They also must play a role in striking a balance between voice and loyalty as distinct ways of holding the agency's policy choices to account. . . .

Since private stakeholder bargaining in rulemaking settlements often takes place outside of the formal legal protections of administrative process, an agency may find it expedient to give short shrift to the public interest in order to settle lawsuits. Courts and litigants should not treat settlement of substantive challenges to rules as mere private contracts. Nor should strong deference to agency interpretations necessarily be the norm. Such a judicial approach heavily favors exit interests over other concerns such as voice and loyalty. Exit, voice, and loyalty interests each must play a part in the evaluation of settlements. Voice and loyalty interests, in particular, may be in tension at times, but this is the same tension with which courts struggle elsewhere in defining participation for administrative law.

Due to a principal-agent gap that fails to protect the public interest in administrative agency concessions during settlement, some ex ante judicial role in policing the public interest is appropriate. Simultaneously, courts must evaluate carefully participation in such settlements, allowing broad collateral opportunities for challenge to ensure that key stakeholder perspectives are not omitted. With a balanced approach to monitoring participation and reviewing the merits of settlements, courts can help avoid the potential for undermining the public interest while also preserving incentives for private stakeholder participation in settlements of rule appeals.

Chapter 13

SETTLEMENT: LAW AND POLICY

A. INTRODUCTION

At first blush, it might seem strange to find a chapter titled Settlement late in a book devoted to the subject of resolving disputes short of litigation, particularly since we have already considered specific types of dispute resolution processes and devoted considerable attention to issues associated with the settlement of disputes. Settlement of disputes generally, and of lawsuits in particular, has long been much the most common form of dispute termination. To borrow the title of the article by Galanter & Cahill, "most cases settle."

The first, and central topic examined in this chapter is "The Great Settlement Debate" that followed upon the publication of Owen Fiss's justly famous article, *Against Settlement.* It is a measure of the success of the ADR movement that a distinguished legal scholar was moved to write an article *Against Settlement,* that cautions against the settlement of too many disputes/cases. Fiss's arguments against settlement have generated a lively debate in the legal literature, that has not yet run its course.

After this philosophical, even religious, consideration of settlement, the remainder of the chapter is devoted to more mundane issues regarding settlement law and practice. Section C provides an overview of the settlement of civil law suits, a topic about which surprisingly little is known. The settlement of criminal cases, commonly known as plea bargaining, is discussed in Chapter Six. Section D considers the law of settlement, and the enforcement of (alleged) settlement agreements. The related topic of mediation confidentiality is discussed in Chapter Eight.

B. THE GREAT SETTLEMENT DEBATE

1. Owen M. Fiss, *Against Settlement*, 93 YALE L.J. 1073 (1984)

In a recent report to the Harvard Overseers, President [and former law professor] Derek Bok called for a new direction in legal education. He decried "the familiar tilt in the law curriculum toward preparing students for legal combat," and asked instead that law schools train their students "for the gentler arts of reconciliation and accommodation." He sought to turn our attention from the courts to "new voluntary mechanisms" for resolving disputes. In doing so, Bok echoed themes that have long been associated with the Chief Justice [Warren

Burger], and that have become a rallying point for the organized bar and the source of a new movement in the law. This movement . . . has even received its own acronym — ADR (Alternative Dispute Resolution).

The movement promises to reduce the amount of litigation initiated, and accordingly the bulk of its proposals are devoted to negotiation and mediation prior to suit. But the interest in the so-called "gentler arts" has not been so confined. It extends to ongoing litigation as well, and the advocates of ADR have sought new ways to facilitate and perhaps even pressure parties into settling pending cases. . . . Rule 16 of the Federal Rules of Civil Procedure was amended to strengthen the hand of the trial judge in brokering settlements: The "facilitation of settlement" became an explicit purpose of pre-trial conferences, and participants were judicially invited, if that is the proper word, to consider "the possibility of settlement or the use of extrajudicial procedures to resolve the dispute."

The advocates of ADR are led to . . . exalt the idea of settlement . . . because they view adjudication as a process to resolve disputes. They act as though courts arose to resolve quarrels between neighbors who had reached an impasse and turned to a stranger for help. Courts are seen as an institutionalization of the stranger and adjudication is viewed as the process by which the stranger exercises power. The very fact that the neighbors have turned to someone else to resolve their dispute signifies a breakdown in their social relations; the advocates of ADR acknowledge this, but nonetheless hope that the neighbors will be able to reach agreement before the stranger renders judgment. Settlement is that agreement. It is a truce more than a true reconciliation, but it seems preferable to judgment because it rests on the consent of both parties and avoids the cost of a trial.

In my view, however, this account of adjudication and the case for settlement rest on questionable premises. I do not believe that settlement as a generic practice is preferable to judgment or should be institutionalized on a wholesale and indiscriminate basis. It should be treated instead as a highly problematic technique for streamlining dockets. Settlement is for me the civil analogue of plea bargaining: Consent is often coerced; the bargain may be struck by someone without authority; the absence of a trial and judgment renders subsequent judicial involvement troublesome; and although dockets are trimmed, justice may not be done. Like plea bargaining, settlement is a capitulation to the conditions of mass society and should be neither encouraged nor praised.

By viewing the lawsuit as a quarrel between two neighbors, the dispute resolution story that underlies ADR implicitly asks us to assume a rough equality between the contending parties. It treats settlement as the anticipation of the outcome of trial and assumes that the terms of settlement are simply a product of the parties' predictions of that outcome. In truth, however, settlement is also a function of the resources available to each party to finance the litigation, and those resources are frequently distributed unequally. Many lawsuits do not involve a property dispute between two neighbors, or between AT&T and the government, . . . but rather concern a struggle between a member of a racial minority and a municipal police department over alleged brutality, or a claim by a worker against a large corporation over work-related injuries. In these cases, the distribution of financial resources, or the ability of one party to pass along its costs, will invariably infect the bargaining process, and the settlement will be at odds with a conception of justice that seeks to make the wealth of the parties irrelevant.

The disparities in resources between the parties can influence the settlement in three ways. First, the poorer party may be less able to amass and analyze the information needed to predict the outcome of the litigation, and thus be disadvantaged in the bargaining process. Second, he may need the damages he seeks immediately and thus be induced to settle as a way of accelerating payment, even though he realizes he would get less now than he might if he awaited judgment. All plaintiffs want their damages immediately, but an indigent plaintiff may be exploited by a rich defendant because his need is so great that the defendant can force him to accept a sum that is less than the ordinary present value of the judgment. Third, the poorer party might be forced to settle because he does not have the resources to finance the litigation, to cover either his own projected expenses, such as his lawyer's time, or the expenses his opponent can impose through the manipulation of procedural mechanisms such as discovery. It might seem that settlement benefits the plaintiff by allowing him to avoid the costs of litigation, but this is not so. The defendant can anticipate the plaintiffs costs if the case were to be tried fully and decrease his offer by that amount. The indigent plaintiff is a victim of the costs of litigation even if he settles.

There are exceptions. Seemingly rich defendants may sometimes be subject to financial pressures that make them as ardent to settle as indigent plaintiffs. But I doubt that these circumstances occur with any great frequency. I also doubt that institutional arrangements such as contingent fees or the provision of legal services to the poor will in fact equalize resources between contending parties. The contingent fee does not equalize resources; it only makes an indigent plaintiff vulnerable to the willingness of the private bar to invest in his case. In effect, the ability to exploit the plaintiff's lack of resources has been transferred from rich defendants to lawyers who insist upon a hefty slice of the plaintiff's recovery as their fee. These lawyers, moreover, will only work for contingent fees in certain kinds of cases, such as personal-injury suits. And the contingent fee is of no avail when the defendant is the disadvantaged party. Governmental subsidies for legal services have a broader potential, but in the civil domain the battle for these subsidies was hard-fought, and they are in fact extremely limited, especially when it comes to cases that seek systemic reform of government practices.

Of course, imbalances of power can distort judgment as well: Resources influence the quality of presentation, which in turn has an important bearing on who wins and the terms of victory. We count, however, on the guiding presence of the judge, who can employ a number of measures to lessen the impact of distributional inequalities. He can, for example, supplement the parties' presentations by asking questions, calling his own witnesses, and inviting other persons and institutions to participate as amici. These measures are likely to make only a small contribution toward moderating the influence of distributional inequalities, but should not be ignored for that reason. Not even these small steps are possible with settlement. There is, moreover, a critical difference between a process like settlement, which is based on bargaining and accepts inequalities of wealth as an integral and legitimate component of the process, and a process like judgment, which knowingly struggles against those inequalities. Judgment aspires to an autonomy from distributional inequalities, and it gathers much of its appeal from this aspiration.

The argument for settlement presupposes that the contestants are individuals. These individuals speak for themselves and should be bound by the rules they generate. In many situations, however, individuals are ensnared in contractual relationships that impair their autonomy. . . . But a deeper and more intractable problem arises from the fact that many parties are not individuals but rather organizations or groups. We do not know who is entitled to speak for these entities and to give the consent upon which so much of the appeal of settlement depends.

Some organizations, such as corporations or unions, have formal procedures for identifying the persons who are authorized to speak for them. But these procedures are imperfect: They are designed to facilitate transactions between the organization and outsiders, rather than to insure that the members of the organization in fact agree with a particular decision. Nor do they eliminate conflicts of interests. The chief executive officer of a corporation may settle a suit to prevent embarrassing disclosures about his managerial policies, but such disclosures might well be in the interest of the shareholders. The president of a union may agree to a settlement as a way of preserving his power within the organization; for that very reason, he may not risk the dangers entailed in consulting the rank and file or in subjecting the settlement to ratification by the membership. Moreover, the representational procedures found in corporations, unions, or other private formal organizations are not universal. Much contemporary litigation, especially in the federal courts, involves governmental agencies, and the procedures in those organizations for generating authoritative consent are far cruder than those in the corporate context. . . .

These problems become even more pronounced when we turn from organizations and consider the fact that much contemporary litigation involves even more nebulous social entities, namely, groups. Some of these groups, such as ethnic or racial minorities, inmates of prisons, or residents of institutions for mentally retarded people, may have an identity or existence that transcends the lawsuit, but they do not have any formal organizational structure and therefore lack any procedures for generating authoritative consent. The absence of such a procedure is even more pronounced in cases involving a group, such as the purchasers of Cuisinarts between 1972 and 1982, which is constructed solely in order to create funds large enough to make it financially attractive for lawyers to handle the case. . . .

The dispute resolution story trivializes the remedial dimensions of lawsuits and mistakenly assumes judgment to be the end of the process. It supposes that the judge's duty is to declare which neighbor is right and which wrong, and that this declaration will end the judge's involvement (save in that most exceptional situation where it is also necessary for him to issue a writ directing the sheriff to execute the declaration). Under these assumptions, settlement appears as an almost perfect substitute for judgment, for it too can declare the parties' rights. Often, however, judgment is not the end of a lawsuit but only the beginning. The involvement of the court may continue almost indefinitely. In these cases, settlement cannot provide an adequate basis for that necessary continuing involvement, and thus is no substitute for judgment.

The parties may sometimes be locked in combat with one another and view the lawsuit as only one phase in a long continuing struggle. The entry of judgment will then not end the struggle, but rather change its terms and the balance of power. One of the parties will invariably return to the court and again ask for its assistance, not so much because conditions have changed, but because the conditions that preceded the lawsuit have unfortunately not changed. . . . The structural reform cases that play such a prominent role on the federal docket provide another occasion for continuing judicial involvement. In these cases, courts seek to safeguard public values by restructuring large-scale bureaucratic organizations. The task is enormous, and our knowledge of how to restructure on-going bureaucratic organizations is limited. As a consequence, courts must oversee and manage the remedial process for a long time. . . . This, I fear, is true of most school desegregation cases, some of which have been pending for twenty or thirty years. It is also true of antitrust cases that seek divestiture or reorganization of an industry.

The drive for settlement knows no bounds and can result in a consent decree even in the kinds of cases I have just mentioned, that is, even when a court finds itself embroiled in a continuing struggle between the parties or must reform a bureaucratic organization. The parties may be ignorant of the difficulties ahead or optimistic about the future, or they may simply believe that they can get more favorable terms through a bargained-for agreement. Soon, however, the inevitable happens: One party returns to court and asks the judge to modify the decree, either to make it more effective or less stringent. But the judge is at a loss: He has no basis for assessing the request. He cannot, to use Cardozo's somewhat melodramatic formula, easily decide whether the "dangers, once substantial, have become attenuated to a shadow" because, by definition, he never knew the dangers.

The dispute-resolution story makes settlement appear as a perfect substitute for judgment by trivializing the remedial dimensions of a lawsuit, and also by reducing the social function of the lawsuit to one of resolving private disputes: In that story, settlement appears to achieve exactly the same purpose as judgment — peace between the parties — but at considerably less expense to society. The two quarreling neighbors turn to a court in order to resolve their dispute, and society makes courts available because it wants to aid in the achievement of their private ends or to secure the peace.

In my view. however, the purpose of adjudication should be understood in broader terms. Adjudication uses public resources, and employs not strangers chosen by the parties but public officials chosen by a process in which the public participates. These officials, like members of the legislative and executive branches, possess a power that has been defined and conferred by public law; not by private agreement. Their job is not to maximize the ends of private parties, nor simply to secure the peace, but to explicate and give force to the values embodied in authoritative texts such as the Constitution and statutes: to interpret those values and to bring reality into accord with them. This duty is not discharged when the parties settle,

In our political system, courts are reactive institutions. They do not search out interpretive occasions, but instead wait for others to bring matters to their attention. They also rely for the most part on others to investigate and present the law and facts. A settlement will thereby deprive a court of the occasion, and perhaps even the ability, to render an interpretation. A court cannot proceed (or not proceed very far) in the face of a settlement. To be against settlement is not to urge that parties be "forced" to litigate, since that would interfere with their autonomy and distort the adjudicative process; the parties will be inclined to make the court believe that their bargain is justice. To be against settlement is only to suggest that when the parties settle, society gets less than what appears, and for a price it does not know it is paying. Parties might settle while leaving justice undone. The settlement of a school suit might secure the peace, but not racial equality. Although the parties are prepared to live under the terms they bargained for, and although such peaceful coexistence may be a necessary precondition of justice, and itself a state of affairs to be valued, it is not justice itself. To settle for something means to accept less than some ideal.

I recognize that judges often announce settlements not with a sense of frustration or disappointment, as my account of adjudication might suggest, but with a sigh of relief. But this sigh should be seen for precisely what it is: It is not a recognition that a job is done, nor an acknowledgment that a job need not be done because justice has been secured. It is instead based on another sentiment altogether, namely, that another case has been "moved along," which is true whether or not justice has been done or even needs to be done. Or the sigh might be based on the fact that the agony of judgment has been avoided.

There is, of course, sometimes a value to avoidance, not just to the judge, who is thereby relieved of the need to make or enforce a hard decision, but also to society which sometimes thrives by masking its basic contradictions. But will settlement result in avoidance when it is most appropriate? Other familiar avoidance devices, such as certiorari, at least promise a devotion to public ends, but settlement is controlled by the litigants, and is subject to their private motivations and all the vagaries of the bargaining process. There are also dangers to avoidance, and these may well outweigh any imagined benefits. . . . Someone has to confront the betrayal of our deepest ideals and be prepared to turn the world upside down to bring those ideals to fruition.

To all this, one can readily imagine a simple response by way of confession and avoidance: We are not talking about those lawsuits. Advocates of ADR might insist that my account of adjudication, in contrast to the one implied by the dispute-resolution story, focuses on a rather narrow category of lawsuits. They could argue that while settlement may have only the most limited appeal with respect to those cases, I have not spoken to the "typical" case. My response is twofold.

First, even as a purely quantitative matter, I doubt that the number of cases I am referring to is trivial. My universe includes those cases in which there are significant distributional inequalities; those in which it is difficult to generate authoritative consent because organizations or social groups are parties or because the power to settle is vested in autonomous agents; those in which the court must continue to supervise the parties after judgment; and those in which justice needs to be done, or to put it more modestly, where there is a genuine social need for an authoritative interpretation of law. I imagine that the number of cases that satisfy one of these four criteria is considerable; in contrast to the kind of case portrayed in the dispute resolution story they probably dominate the docket of a modern court system.

Second, it demands a certain kind of myopia to be concerned only with the number of cases, as though all cases are equal simply because the clerk of the court assigns each a single docket number. All cases are not equal. The Los Angeles desegregation case, to take one example, is not equal to the allegedly more typical suit involving a property dispute or an auto accident. The desegregation suit consumes more resources, affects more people, and provokes far greater challenges to the judicial power. The settlement movement must introduce a qualitative perspective; it must speak to these more "significant" cases, and demonstrate the propriety of settling them. Otherwise it will soon be seen as an irrelevance, dealing with trivia rather than responding to the very conditions that give the movement its greatest sway and saliency.

Nor would sorting cases into "two tracks," one for settlement, and another for judgment, avoid my objections. Settling automobile cases and leaving discrimination or antitrust cases for judgment might remove a large number of cases from the dockets but the dockets will nevertheless remain burdened with the cases that consume the most judicial resources and represent the most controversial exercises of the judicial power. A "two track" strategy would drain the argument for settlement of much of its appeal. I also doubt whether the "two track" strategy can be sensibly implemented. It is impossible to formulate adequate criteria for prospectively sorting cases. The problems of settlement are not tied to the subject matter of the suit, but instead stem from factors that are harder to identify, such as the wealth of the parties, the likely post-judgment history of the suit, or the need for an authoritative interpretation of law.

The authors of the amendment to Rule 68 make a gesture toward a "two track" strategy by exempting class actions and shareholder derivative suits, and by allowing the judge to refrain from awarding attorneys fees when it is "unjustified under all of the circumstances." But these gestures are cramped and ill-conceived, and are likely to increase the workload of the courts by giving rise to yet another set of issues to litigate. It is, moreover, hard to see how these problems can be avoided. Many of the factors that lead a society to bring social relationships that otherwise seem wholly private (e.g., marriage) within the jurisdiction of a court, such as imbalances of power or the interests of third parties, are also likely to make settlement problematic. Settlement is a poor substitute for judgement; it is an even poorer substitute for the withdrawal of jurisdiction.

For these reasons, I remain highly skeptical of a "two track" strategy and would resist it. Most ADR advocates make no effort to distinguish between different types of cases or to suggest that "the gentler arts of reconciliation and accommodation" might be particularly appropriate for one type of case but not for another. They lump all cases together. This suggests that what divides me from the partisans of ADR is not that we are concerned with different universes of cases, that Derek Bok, for example, focuses on boundary quarrels while I see only desegregation suits. I suspect instead that what divides us is much deeper and stems from our understanding of the purpose of the civil law suit and its place in society. It is a difference in outlook.

Someone like Bok sees adjudication in essentially private terms: The purpose of lawsuits and the civil courts is to resolve disputes, and the amount of litigation we encounter is evidence of the needlessly combative and quarrelsome character of Americans. Or as Bok put it, using a more diplomatic idiom: "At bottom, ours is a society built on individualism, competition, and success." I, on the other hand, see adjudication in more public terms: Civil litigation is an institutional arrangement for using state power to bring a recalcitrant reality closer to our chosen ideals. We turn to the courts because we need to, not because of some quirk in our personalities. We train our students in the tougher arts so that they may help secure all that the law promises, not because we want them to become gladiators or because we take a special pleasure in combat.

2. Comments and Questions

a. *Against Settlement* is widely cited and much admired, even by those who disagree with Professor Fiss. Of course, Professor Fiss is not against all private dispute resolution; he just does not want settlement "institutionalized on a wholesale and indiscriminate basis." Conversely not even the fiercest advocates of ADR propose the elimination of courts.

b. An important aspect of the sentiment favoring settlement is the view that disputing is bad, and the less we have of it the better. A classic statement of this view was made by Professor Grant Gilmore, in closing his 1974 Storrs Lectures:

> Law reflects but in no sense determines the moral worth of a society. The values of a reasonably just society will reflect themselves in a reasonably just law. The better the society the less law there will be. In Heaven there will be no law, and the lion will lie down with the lamb. The worse the society, the more law there will be. In hell there will be nothing but law, and due process will be meticulously observed.

GRANT GILMORE, THE AGES OF AMERICAN LAW 111 (1977). How might Fiss respond to his former Yale Law School colleague?

c. Fiss points out that officials of organizations may settle disputes in a manner that favors personal over organizational interests. This certainly happens, and this is another example of the principal-agent problem. In the corporate context, is the solution to limit settlements, or are the best solutions likely to be found in the context of corporate governance — fewer "inside" directors, or a litigation committee dominated by outside directors?

d. Government officials, including judges, also are subject to principal-agent problems. They may promote their own objectives, which are not identical to the public interest. This is one of the central insights of public choice theory. *See generally*, DANIEL A. FARBER & PHILIP P. FRICKEY, LAW AND PUBLIC CHOICE (1991); GLEN O. ROBINSON, AMERICAN BUREAUCRACY: PUBLIC CHOICE AND PUBLIC LAW (1991).

e. Judicial decisions gain legitimacy because judges are, as Fiss states, "public officials chosen by a process in which the public participates." Is it unfair to suggest that public participation in the selection of the U.S. district court is severely attenuated? We resist the temptation to delve into the political and financial aspects of how state judges are appointed. Should Fiss favor the election of judges, in the name of increased public participation? Public choice theory suggests that the prospect of future election campaigns will undermine judicial autonomy.

f. Why does Fiss oppose the idea of a "two track" strategy for channeling disputes? After all, as Fiss tells us, the quality of justice already depends on wealth. A multi-track system operated by the courts would no doubt be imperfect, but should not Fiss's approach lead him to prefer a system where the channeling is done by "public officials chosen by a process in which the public participates" rather than by private parties in settlements? See also the view of Judge Wayne Brazil, set forth in Chapter Ten, on two-track channeling of disputes.

g. If some persons are coerced into settlement by inability to finance litigation, isn't the solution to reform litigation? To blame settlement seems akin to shooting the messenger who delivers the bad news. The faith placed by Professor Fiss in the judicial system to redress imbalances of wealth and power is doubted by many. The best article on point still is Marc Galanter, *Why the "Haves" Come Out Ahead: Speculation on the Limits of Social Change*, 9 LAW & SOC'Y REV. 95 (1974). See the discussion by Professor Menkel-Meadow in Chapter Five.

3. Andrew W. McThenia & Thomas L. Shaffer, *For Reconciliation*, 94 YALE L.J. 1660 (1985)

Professor Owen Fiss, in his recent comment, Against Settlement, weighs in against the Alternative Dispute Resolution (ADR) movement. . . . Fiss attacks a straw man. His understanding that the plea of ADR advocates is based on efficiency reduces the entire question to one of procedures. Fiss's argument rests on the faith that justice — and he uses the word — is usually something people get from the government. He comes close to arguing that the branch of government that resolves disputes, the courts, is the principal source of justice in fragmented modern American society.

Fiss's view that the claims of ADR advocates arise from a popular dissatisfaction with law reduces the issue to one of order. As his first stated understanding reduces justice to statism, this understanding reduces justice (or, if you like, peace) to a tolerably minimum level of violence in the community. In our view, an appropriate engagement of the Fiss attack on ADR must go all the way back to these two characterizations in his argument against ADR and in favor of court-dominated dispute resolution. We are not willing to let him frame the issue.

Certain themes recur in the ADR literature. Many advocates of ADR make efficiency-based claims. And a plea for ending the so-called litigation explosion, and for returning to law and order, runs through the rules-of-procedure branch of the ADR literature. But the movement, if it is even appropriate to call it a single movement, is too varied for Fiss's description. Rather than focusing on the substance of claims made for ADR, Fiss has created a view of the function of courts that he can comfortably oppose. . . .

The soundest and deepest part of the ADR movement does not rest on Fiss' two-neighbors model. It rests on values — of religion, community, and work place — that are more vigorous than Fiss thinks. In many, in fact most, of the cultural traditions that argue for ADR, settlement is neither an avoidance mechanism nor a truce. Settlement is a process of reconciliation in which the anger of broken relationships is to be confronted rather than avoided, and in which healing demands not a truce but confrontation. Instead of "trivializing the remedial process," settlement exalts that process. Instead of "reducing the social function . . . to one of resolving private disputes," settlement calls on substantive community values. Settlement is sometimes a beginning, and is sometimes a postscript, but it is not the essence of the enterprise of dispute resolution.

The "real divide" between us and Fiss may not be our differing views of the sorts of cases that now wind their way into American courts, but, more fundamentally, it maybe our different view's of justice. Fiss comes close to equating justice with law. He includes among the cases unsuited for settlement "those in which justice needs to be done, or to put it more modestly, where there is a genuine social need for an authoritative interpretation of law." We do not believe that law and justice are synonymous. We see the deepest and soundest of ADR arguments as in agreement with us: Justice is not usually something people get from the government. And courts . . . are not the only or even the most important places that dispense justice.

Many advocates of ADR can well be taken to have asked about the law's response to disputes, and alternatives to that response, not in order to reform the law but in order to locate alternative views of what a dispute is. Such alternatives would likely advance or assume understandings of justice (or, if you like, peace) that are also radically different from justice as something lawyers administer, or peace as the absence of violence. They assume not that justice is something people get from the government but that it is something people give to one another. These advocates seek an understanding of justice in the way Socrates and Thrasymachus did in the Republic: Justice is not the will of the stronger; it is not efficiency in government; it is not the reduction of violence: Justice is what we discover — you and I, Socrates said — when we walk together, listen together, and even love one another, in our curiosity about what justice is and where justice comes from.

Most of us who have gone to college know something about Socrates. Many more of us who grew up in the United States know something about Moses and Jesus. It is from Torah and Gospel, more than from Plato, that we are most likely to be able to sketch out radical alternatives to the law's response to disputes. As a matter of fact, our religious culture contains both a theoretical basis for these alternatives and a way to apply theory to disputes.

Professor Miler S. Ball, who discussed this comment with us, suggested that Fiss is not arguing so much against religious or community-based ADR as against DR (deregulation). Fiss may, Ball suggests, be asking us to consider whether an overly enthusiastic support of settlement is not another form of the deregulation movement, one that permits private actors with powerful economic interests to pursue self-interest free of community norms. We may, Ball suggests, be reacting to Fiss's overly inclusive statements about ADR; he may have over-stated, and we may have over-reacted. Thus, we may have more common ground than we think. Ball's suggestion is one we will enjoy pursuing. When we do, we will want to tell Ball that the powerful economic interests are as much members of the fragmented but also reconciling community as the oppressed are. And we will want to tell Fiss that it may make a general and important difference that, in almost any kind of ADR, (a) the parties talk to one another, rather than to the government; and that (b) the third party, if there is one present, comes not as a resolver of disputes but as a neighbor.

In the Hebraic tradition (as in the Islamic), scripture is normative. Judaism, for example, does not merely seek to follow Torah; it loves Torah, it finds life in Torah, it celebrates Torah as one might celebrate the presence of a lover or of a loving parent, or of a community that nourishes peace — commitment to common well being, and even a feeling of being well. (Salvation is not too strong a word for it.) Justice is the way one defines a righteous life; justice does involve according other persons their due but, more radically, in the Hebraic view; it involves loving them. Such a justice is the product of piety, to be sure, but not piety alone; it is the product of study, of reason, and of attending to the wise and learning from them how to be virtuous.

The Christian side of the Hebraic tradition has, or should have, all of this. It also has a unique procedure established in St. Matthew's Gospel — a system backed up by stern condemnation of Christians who turn from the Gospel and seek instead the law's response to disputes. In this system, as well as in Judaism, religious community claims authority to resolve dispute and even to coerce obedience. The procedure involves, first, conversation; if that fails, it involves mediation; if mediation fails, it involves airing the dispute before representatives of the community. If the dispute goes so far as judgment, the system, as is also the case in Judaism, permits pressure: "If he refuses to listen to the community, treat him like a pagan or a tax collector. I tell you solemnly, whatever you bind on earth shall be considered bound in heaven; whatever you loose on earth shall be considered loosed in heaven." Matthew 18: 17-18.

Thus, the procedure gives priority to restoring the relationship. Hebraic theology puts primary emphasis on relationships, a priority that is political and even ontological, as well as ethical, and therefore legal. And so, most radically, the religious tradition seeks not resolution (which connotes the sort of doctrinal integrity in the law that seems to us to be Fiss's highest priority) but reconciliation of brother to brother, sister to sister, sister to brother, child to parent, neighbor to neighbor, buyer to seller, defendant to plaintiff and judge to both. (The Judge is also an I and a Thou.) This view of what a dispute is, and of what third parties seek when they intervene in disputes between others, provides an existing, traditional, common alternative to the law's response. . . . This alternative has both a vigorous modem history and a suitable contemporary vitality. . . .

Contemporary manifestations of the Hebraic tradition claim adherence to a moral authority that is more important than the government. The Torah is the wisdom of God; the Gospel is the good news that promises a peace the world cannot give. From one perspective, theology makes such religious views of dispute and resolution seem peripheral. That impression is deceptive, though: In the aggregate these views of what a dispute is are consistent with one another and, as such, consistent with the moral commitments of most people in America. The numbers of people in this country who might find them so is not declining; it is increasing. "In the aggregate" is an appropriate consideration, as one assays radical alternatives to the law's response to disputes, because there is substantial commonality among the practitioners of this radical, Hebraic alternative. Religious systems of reconciliation rest on a substantively common theology and on a substantively common argument that, contrary to the implications of Fiss's view of justice, the government is not as important as it thinks it is.

Professor David Trubek ends a recent and pessimistic essay on alternative dispute resolution, *Turning Away From Law?*, 82 MICH. L. REV. 824 (1984), with a paradox: "No one," he says, "really seems to believe in law any more." The "elites" who complain of a litigation explosion — Chief Justice Warren Burger and others who champion alternatives — question the law's efficacy. But so do those who criticize the law as political and oppressive, most notably scholars in the Critical Legal Studies movement. The elites exalt an informalism they don't believe in, Trubek says, and the radicals exalt a formalism they distrust. Apparently the legal process school — or at least one of its eloquent spokesmen, Owen Fiss — still believes in law. Fiss's writing on structural reform is powerful. It may not reflect the way the world actually is, but it is a statement of hope. And that is important in an age of nihilism. But we suspect those who believe in law and in nothing else; we hope Fiss is not among them. Informalism of the Chief Justice's formulation may deserve distrust. But informalism has some contemporary manifestations — many of them resting on the most ancient and deepest of our traditions — that deserve trust and even celebration. These manifestations too are statements of hope. Suggestions for alternatives to litigation need to be critically examined — no doubt many of them are hollow. What they do not need, and what the legal community does not need, is an argument that reduces these alternatives to a caricature.

4. Owen M. Fiss, *Out of Eden,* 94 YALE L.J. 1669 (1985)

Religion can inspire. It can also distort, and this is precisely what it does for Professors McThenia and Shaffer. It leads them to mistake the periphery for the center. In my earlier article I tried to come to terms with a movement that seeks alternatives to litigation. . . . Professors McThenia and Shaffer now lend their voices to [the ADR] movement, but in an unusual way. They add a religious dimension. They emphasize reconciliation rather than settlement, and appear to be moved by a conception of social organization that takes the insular religious community as its model: "Justice is what we discover — you and I, Socrates said — when we walk together, listen together, and even love one another, in our curiosity about what justice is and where justice comes from." McThenia and Shaffer speak out on behalf of social mechanisms that might restore or preserve loving relationships and, not surprisingly, they find the judicial judgment a rather inept instrument for that purpose.

I have no special interest in countering their plea: I am as much for love as the next person. What McThenia and Shaffer say is not wrong, just beside the point: Their reasons for seeking alternatives to litigation are not those of the movement. Chief Justice Burger is not moved by love, or by a desire to find new ways to restore or preserve loving relationships, but rather by concerns of efficiency and politics. He seeks alternatives to litigation in order to reduce the caseload of the judiciary or, even more plausibly, to insulate the status quo from reform by the judiciary. Of course, McThenia and Shaffer are entitled to their own reasons for supporting a social and political movement, but they should not delude themselves that they have given a general account of ADR or explained its saliency and sway within the bar today.

McThenia and Shaffer should also understand that their plea for reconciliation does not respond to the primary social situation to which ADR is addressed. In their search for alternatives to litigation, the advocates of ADR focus on social situations in which interpersonal relationships have been so thoroughly disrupted that there is no chance of reconciliation: People turn to courts when they are at the end of the road. That is why I focused my attention on settlement rather than reconciliation. . . . To be against settlement is not to be against reconciliation but to address another social situation altogether.

Of course, it would be nice if the blacks of Chicago, to take one example, did not have to go to court in order to obtain all that the Constitution promises, and instead were able to work things out with the school board by walking, and talking, and loving. But once they have turned to the courts, it strikes me as absurd for the legal system to create incentives or pressures that force them to settle. It is costly to litigate, as they well know, but it also is costly to settle. To ignore these costs and to disfavor litigation because you hope that social relations between the parties can be restored is like ignoring the dangers of plea bargaining and favoring it over trial because you wish the crime that gave rise to the prosecution had not occurred.

In defending their variant of ADR, Professors McThenia and Shaffer might contest my factual premise about the divided character of our communities. They might argue that the blacks of Chicago who turn to the courts are mistaken in their belief that they cannot get justice on their own. Or McThenia and Shaffer might insist that no matter how improbable, reconciliation is always a possibility, at least as a logical or formal matter, and that one should not be allowed into court unless one first has attempted reconciliation — a miracle is always possible. On this account, ADR emerges as an exhaustion requirement, and at one point McThenia and Shaffer draw on the experience of the ancient Hebrews and Christians to proffer such an idea: "The [preferred] procedure involves, first, conversation; if that fails, it involves mediation; if mediation fails, it involves airing the dispute before representatives of the community." Only if the claimant refuses to heed the advice of the community elders will he or she be allowed to turn to the courts, and then only at the greatest risk: Whatever you lose on earth should be considered lost in heaven.

I am sure that there is much to be learned from the ancient Hebrews and Christians. I am sure that there is much force to the plea for reconciliation when it is addressed to the insular religious communities that still dot the American landscape. But I think Professors McThenia and Shaffer are fundamentally misguided in their effort to model law and the legal system of modem America on these religious communities. Such exercises result in a marvelous display of learning, and one cannot help being moved by the underlying religious commitments. But I must also admit that I am left with the firm impression that such efforts misunderstand the character of our social life and the role that the state and its courts must play in our search for justice today.

From the perspective of an insular religious community, distinguished by its cohesiveness and the devotion of its members to a set of shared values, there may be reason to doubt the claim of those who turn to the courts that reconciliation is not possible. There may even be reason to force the claimant to try those mechanisms that might restore the relationship, for what is at stake is not just a claim of right, but the totality of relationships known as the community. But once we stop thinking about the Anabaptists and start thinking about Chicago, once we stop thinking about the ancient Hebrews and Christians and turn to modern America, we can see that there is no reason in the world to engage such assumptions. There is no reason to assume either that the despair of blacks over getting justice on their own is unwarranted, or that they sue because they want some high class counseling. The more reasonable assumption is that they turn to the courts because they have to.

Moreover, once we change our perspective and consider the modem American community, whether it be a Chicago, an Evanston, or a Gary, we can understand why an exhaustion requirement of the type Professors McThenia and Shaffer propose is likely only to compound the costs of justice. Society will come to have two (or more) processes where it now has one, because the claimant is not likely to be satisfied with conversation, mediation, or a lecture by the representatives of the community, and thus will eventually turn to the courts. The McThenia-Shaffer proposal is likely to obstruct access to the courts without increasing the chance that the fabric of the community will be restored.

Milner Ball, referred to in the McThenia and Shaffer essay, is a scholar whose work is infused with a religious perspective, and yet he gets the point. He understands that my critique was not aimed at this religion-based strand of

ADR, which plays a slight and trivial role in the professional debates of the day. He also understands the more general ADR version for what it is: not a vindication of community, religious or otherwise, but just another assault upon the activist state, "another form of the deregulation movement, one that permits private actors with powerful economic interests to pursue self-interest free of community norms." The force of Bali's observation is not lost on McThenia and Shaffer. They seem genuinely reluctant to defend this more general form of ADR, and specifically disassociate themselves from what they call the "informalism of the Chief Justice's formulation." They do, however, have something in common with the Chief Justice, namely his distrust of the state, and its courts. McThenia and Shaffer are antistatists: "Justice is not usually something people get from the government." Apparently people get it from talking and listening to one another.

I believe that people should talk and listen to one another. But sometimes that is not possible, because their relationships have disintegrated, or because the community is fractionated, or because those who have power are not interested in either talking or listening to the weak and disadvantaged. Moreover, even when people are prepared to talk and listen to one another, they might not understand the norms of the community, or, as Professor Ball suggests, they might not be prepared to abide by them. Adjudication is but a response to this predicament. It is a social process that uses the power of the state to require the reluctant to talk and to listen, not just to each other, but also to a judge (and sometimes juries) who must in turn listen and talk to the parties. These public officials are the trustees of the community. They are given the power to decide who is right and who is wrong and, if need be, to bring the conduct of the parties into conformity with the norms of the community. The underlying hope is that if all goes well, justice will be done.

I realize that all might not go well and that adjudication might fail. Justice is not reducible to the law or to the particular decisions of any court: It is an aspiration. The truth of the matter, however, is that all institutions — not just those of the state — stand in jeopardy of failing in this aspiration. And there is no reason whatsoever for believing that adjudication suffers this risk more than any other institution. In fact, given the inequalities and divisions that so pervade our society, and given the need for a power as great as that of the state to close the gap between our ideals and the actual conditions of our social life, adjudication is more likely to succeed in this aspiration. Adjudication is more likely to do justice than conversation, mediation, arbitration, settlement, rent-a-judge, mini-trials, community moots or any other contrivance of ADR, precisely because it vests the power of the state in officials who act as trustees for the public, who are highly visible, and who are committed to reason. What we need at the moment is not another assault on this form of public power, whether from the periphery or the center, or whether inspired by religion or politics, but a renewed appreciation of all that it promises.

5. Jethro K. Lieberman & James F. Henry, *Lessons From the Alternative Dispute Resolution Movement*, 53 U. Chi. L. Rev. 424, 432-35 (1986)

Proponents of ADR suggest that its value lies in reducing the burden on courts and disputants. Alarmed at the ever-increasing numbers of cases filed, the Chief Justice and others see arbitration and other practices as ways of removing large numbers of individual cases and even large classes of cases from the courts, thus removing a burden from the shoulders of judges (while shifting it to someone else). To the delight of their critics, they have occasionally forgotten that whether this change is beneficial depends on the relative justice and expense of dispositions through formal in-court adjudication and through less formal out-of-court methods of dispute resolution.

Critics of ADR, like Owen Fiss, suggest that ADR proponents mistake the function of courts as "mere" dispute resolvers." By diverting cases from courts, society loses the benefit of court sanctioned judgments. . . . Fiss also argues that advocates of ADR have an unstated political agenda: to keep the activist state from meddling with powerful private economic interests. Finally, Fiss suggests that settlements lacks the legitimacy of cases fully adjudicated to judgment.

Four responses to this critique are in order. One short answer to Fiss is that most ADR proponents make no claim for shunting all, or even most, litigation into alternative forums. The ADR movement . . . does not suppose that every legal dispute has a non-judicial solution. Indeed, the ADR literature recognizes that some types of cases are not suited to resolution outside the courtroom, including particularly cases in which the plaintiff seeks a declaration of law by the court. Fiss overlooks this accepted limitation of ADR. . . . Automobile accidents, divorces, breaches of contract, and other common types of suits do not cry out to be memorialized in the official reports, and, in any event, most are settled far short of trial.

A second response to Fiss's critique is that his "conspiracy theory" of ADR is dubious. Many people who seek to use ADR are scarcely "powerful" economic interests — ADR is not limited to adoption by Fortune 500 companies. Moreover, ADR does not dispense with community norms. All dispute resolution takes place with an eye toward existing alternatives — including litigation. Finally, the choice to employ ADR is made by parties who have determined that the injustice resulting from delay and the prohibitive costs of pursuing a case through the courts (direct expenditures for lawyers and expenses, as well as significant indirect expenditures, like lost opportunity costs) far outweigh any putative injustice stemming from the decision to forgo judgment by the court.

A third response to Fiss is that not all questions need to be answered. An open society needs the tension of open questions; parties who settle do not thereby foreclose answers at some later time when matters of principle are truly at stake and the issues cannot be compromised. Fiss agrees that avoidance has a value to society, "which sometimes thrives by masking its basic contradictions." He questions, however, whether settlement will result in too much avoidance. But we know of no way to measure the appropriateness of avoidance. Furthermore, Fiss's concern is one-sided. We should be equally concerned to prevent courts from rendering judgment when settlement is more appropriate.

Finally, Fiss's position is seriously weakened by his failure to offer proof that court judgments are more just. He says, for example, that adjudication is more likely to do justice than . . . ADR, "precisely because it vests the power of the state in officials who act as trustees for the public, who are highly visible, and who are committed to reason." Does ADR reach a just result or merely an expedient one? How can one measure the justice of a private settlement? The question is important, but it has not been well discussed in the ADR literature — no doubt because it is so difficult a proposition to test. Whatever the answer, it seems fair to ask the same questions of courts. In theory, courts are committed to reason, but in practice much stands in their way. . . . Moreover, the maneuvering of partisan lawyers alone is often enough to ensure that justice will not be done.

A perhaps more controversial response to Fiss's argument about the quality of outcomes is that in certain important classes of cases — cases involving public institutions like schools, hospitals, and prisons (the very cases that particularly interest Fiss) — courts themselves invoke processes that are firmly lodged in the ADR arsenal. Stories that describe litigation over unconstitutional prison conditions, inhumane mental hospital conditions, and segregated schools frequently depict the judge acting as mediator, helping the parties to negotiate the remedy the court will impose by consent decree. If the courts themselves find these processes useful or even necessary chances are good that the same processes can be as beneficial when invoked outside the courts. . . .

6. Jeffrey R. Seul, *Settling Significant Cases*, 79 WASH. L. REV. 881 (2004)

Relatively few litigants attempt to obtain a hearing before the United States Supreme Court. Parties engaged in run-of-the-mill litigation may feel they have been wronged and that justice must be done, but most cases settle without a hearing on the merits. Legal disputes that have the potential to create new law on important public policy matters — one class of what Owen Fiss dubbed "significant cases" in his oft-cited polemic Against Settlement — are, however, different. When a dispute is about abortion, affirmative action, religion, use or preservation of the natural environment, gun control, controversial medical technologies like stem cell research, or other issues involving deep value differences, settlement is rare, and talk about the possibility of settlement may seem naive or even reckless to some. . . .

Litigation of a dispute involving deep moral disagreement has costs as well as benefits, from the perspectives of both the parties and the public. Negotiation also has costs and benefits. Even in the realm of significant cases, litigation's ultimate value — to the parties and to society as a whole — can be assessed only by comparing litigation to other available means of responding to the dispute. The comparative costs and benefits of litigation versus settlement have been explored extensively with respect to the everyday types of disputes that crowd court dockets. Legal scholars have said less about the relative benefits of litigation and negotiation with respect to significant cases.

In Part I of this Article, I examine some key differences between ordinary and significant cases — differences that may make settlement of significant cases seem inappropriate or implausible to some. In Part II, I discuss two ironies that are little acknowledged and discussed, but are implicit in resistance to the idea of settling significant cases. In Part III, I respond to claims that it is impossible to settle significant cases because of the intractable nature of disputes involving deeply held values. In Part IV, I consider what litigants and the public stand to gain, and lose, when cases that present significant public policy questions are settled. I explore the relationship between settlement and deliberative democratic theory in Part V, arguing that settlement processes that invite collective moral deliberation can be an important form of democratic participation. In Part VI, I anticipate and respond to claims that my perspective represents a form of moral relativism. I also present a set of principles for designing consensual dispute resolution processes geared toward resolving disputes involving deep value differences. Fidelity to these principles, I argue, increases the likelihood that the outcomes of such processes will be morally sound, socially desirable, and durable.

I. DIFFERENCES BETWEEN ORDINARY AND SIGNIFICANT CASES

The types of cases I refer to as "ordinary cases" typically involve disputes that occur against a background of relatively well-settled legal norms that the parties accept as legitimate. For example, in a typical contract action, the parties do not question whether the plaintiff is entitled to damages if the defendant breached a contract with the plaintiff. They disagree about whether the defendant breached and, if the judge or jury concludes that it did, the amount of damages to which the plaintiff is entitled. Similarly, in the typical tort action, the parties dispute whether the defendant caused the plaintiff's injuries and, if so, how much compensation is appropriate. They do not question whether a party responsible for another's injuries is liable to the injured party.

Significant cases are different. They involve contested social norms, and the competing norms defended by the parties often are foundational to their respective world views. Fiss identifies four types of significant cases: cases in which there are significant distributional inequalities; those in which it is difficult to generate authoritative consent because organizations or social groups are parties or because the power to settle is vested in autonomous agents; those in which the court must continue to supervise the parties after judgment; and those in which justice needs to be done, or to put it more modestly, where there is a genuine social need for an authoritative interpretation of law.

I give some attention to cases that exhibit the first three of these characteristics, but I focus on the final type of case for two reasons. First, I believe cases likely to produce an authoritative interpretation of law often also fall into one or more of the other categories. For instance, the early school desegregation and busing cases exhibited all four characteristics to some degree, but the fourth characteristic arguably is what made them most socially, politically, legally, and morally significant. Second, I consider Fiss's and others' objections to settlement to be most compelling with respect to the fourth type of case, and less has been offered by way of rebuttal to these objections.

Significant cases either present novel legal issues or, much to the contrary, arise against a well-settled background of legal norms that a segment of the population considers to be out-of-step with contemporary (or at least their preferred) social norms. In the first instance, background legal norms are extremely thin or nonexistent. Because the parties are not "bargaining in the shadow of the law" in any meaningful sense, it would be very difficult for them to resolve their dispute consensually based upon convergent expectations about how a court would resolve it. The most reliable type of information — a prior decision that addresses the disputed issues — is simply unavailable. A notable example of the second type of case — one where existing law was challenged and unsettled as a result of a shift in prevailing social norms — is *Brown v. Board of Education*. Brown I upended segregationist legal norms established, legitimated and protected by *Plessy v. Ferguson* and a series of prior U.S. Supreme Court decisions. In this second type of significant case, a prior decision addressing the disputed issues exists, but one party opposes it and is hopeful that it can persuade the Court to alter or reverse the decision. . . . [S]ignificant cases are difficult to resolve through the type of rational argumentation and decision-making that occurs when fundamental principles are not at stake and generally accepted legal norms make the outcome of litigation more predictable.

[M]ost difficult legal problems involve not only complicated empirical problems, but also problematic judgments concerning questions of moral value, and (often as a direct consequence of these other difficulties) various conceptually incommensurable definitions of what sorts of facts are said to constitute legal meaning. These latter types of disputes will tend not to be amenable to resolution through the procurement of more evidence via the workings of the dispute processing system, either because they involve conceptual disagreements about what should even count as evidence, or because they can't usefully be thought of as involving evidentiary questions at all. One might say that ordinary cases involve questions of justice with a small "j," whereas significant cases involve questions of Justice writ large. . . .

II. TWO IRONIES OF LITIGATION

The ardor with which significant cases are litigated is understandable in light of the depth of the litigants' respective commitments to the values they seek to advance or defend, but two characteristics of adjudication as a process for achieving one's objectives also make it somewhat ironic. Litigation is a lottery in which the substantive values a party seeks to defend, and which it claims are absolute, may be wholly or partially discredited by the court. Furthermore, litigation merely shifts the burden of negotiation to judges. In both of these ways, litigation, like negotiation, entails compromise. . . .

The fact that people litigate over their most deeply held values calls into question their claims that those values are absolute. . . . The parties' competing values may be incommensurable in the abstract, but their actual disputing behavior seems to demonstrate that they are willing to compromise their values to some extent because they wish to inhabit a social system that is capable of containing and processing their dispute in a reasonably pacific manner. Litigation also plays a significant role in the construction and maintenance of individual and group identities. As a form of social activism, litigation has the advantage of seemingly saving disputants from making accommodative exchanges on matters they consider sacred and incommensurable, thereby sparing competing individuals and groups from the uncomfortable process of identity reconstruction that might be occasioned by a consensual resolution of the dispute. Public defense of one's values through litigation sends powerful signals to one's cohorts. It rallies others around the same cause, making social groups to which one belongs, and which contribute to one's self sense, more cohesive and distinct. Litigating a case . . . is a relatively public and taxing way to demonstrate the genuineness and strength of one's convictions. An activist who attempts to advance his or her cause incrementally, through forms of political engagement that require others' acquiescence or active support, may be perceived as making taboo trade-offs. Negotiation may seriously undermine one's social identity or standing in the eyes of others. For some, litigation may seem to be the only means to defend values one considers non-negotiable without undermining one's sense of self and risking sanction by one's peers. . . .

III. IS SETTLEMENT POSSIBLE?

There is understandable skepticism about the possibility of settling the types of disputes that give rise to significant cases. As Fiss contends, "[w]e turn to the courts because we need to, not because of some quirk in our personalities." Before considering what the disputants and the public might gain through efforts to settle the types of disputes that give rise to significant cases, it is worth considering whether settlement is possible in the first place. . . .

Despite the many barriers to settlement of the types of disputes that give rise to significant cases, two types of settlements, though rare, can and do occur. One type can be thought of as strategic settlement. Strategic settlement occurs when at least one of the parties is motivated primarily by a desire to avoid the risk of an adverse decision. This party hopes that progress can be made politically, without the burden of a recently affirmed, adverse legal norm. Perhaps this party also hopes to bring "better facts" before the court at a later date. The other type of settlement results from some degree of true perspective change that produces an informal understanding or a formal agreement regarding . . . matters of common concern. . . .

IV. POTENTIAL COSTS AND BENEFITS OF
SETTLING SIGNIFICANT CASES

One may advocate litigation of significant cases because one believes settlement is not possible or because it is better for the parties and society in very practical ways, but I find it difficult to regard the U.S. Supreme Court as an institution peculiarly capable of making moral judgments. Given that the Court often compromises through a stylized blend of the same decision-making processes used by other political institutions and social groups (i.e., negotiation and voting), it is difficult to view the Court as a body uniquely capable of dispensing justice and of articulating "our chosen ideals." Indeed, each word in this brief quote from Fiss's Against Settlement — our, chosen, ideals — is questionable. As others have argued extensively, the judiciary is in many senses the least democratic of the three branches of government because it is unelected and does not consult the full spectrum of its constituents before acting, so a Supreme Court decision arguably expresses "our" ideals in a very thin sense, if one grants that it expresses them at all. . . .

Adjudication is but one process for managing social conflict; the judiciary is but one institution among many that assist in social coordination and the development of social norms. Accordingly, we must consider what the parties and society gain and lose by turning to the courts to settle not only ordinary cases, but also the types of disputes that give rise to significant cases. Even in the realm of significant cases, litigation's ultimate value can be assessed only by comparison to other available means for managing the dispute.

Too little sustained attention has been given to the comparative costs and benefits of litigation versus settlement of significant cases, because . . . almost all of the literature on legal negotiation, and most of the literature on negotiation generally, focuses on ordinary disputes. The negotiation literature, in a sense, conveniently sidesteps the problem of values by focusing on trade-offs of interests among parties who are already in agreement on the basic nature of the dispute. Settlement of a significant case, or of a dispute that could give rise to one, involves both costs and benefits for the parties and the public, and the costs and benefits differ depending upon whether settlement occurs for strategic reasons or results from changed perspectives about the dispute. . . .

I am not suggesting that we should actively promote coarse bargaining over litigation of significant cases, but I believe we should not be surprised, or consider it an abomination, when a strategically motivated settlement does occur. . . . While I acknowledge the limitations and potential costs of such deliberative processes, I argue that, unlike coarse bargaining, we should actively promote deliberative processes as a method for helping parties explore whether their respective values, needs and preferences, as well as the public interest, might be better served through settlement than through continued litigation. . . . [T]he relative costs and benefits of settlement take on a different character, depending upon whether they are being assessed in the context of a strategic settlement or a settlement resulting from genuine moral deliberation. . . .

VI. THE MORAL LEGITIMACY OF SETTLING SIGNIFICANT CASES

Some argue that "peace" by whatever name — for example, "participatory politics," "social capacity to deal with tough problems," or "consensus" — should not come at the expense of "justice" or moral rightness. From this perspective, a compromise reached by parties to a value-laden dispute is indicative of weakness of character and moral relativism. . . . Greater public participation and greater social capacity to manage strong disagreement may be important benefits of deliberative forms of democratic practice, but are the decisions they produce morally unsound? Is peace achieved at the expense of justice? . . .

In this Part, I present . . . a set of principles for designing consensual dispute resolution processes geared toward resolving disputes involving deep value differences. Fidelity to these principles, I argue, increases the likelihood that the outcomes of such processes will be morally sound (as well as socially desirable and durable). We should not be satisfied with the increased public participation and greater social capacity to manage strong disagreement that may result from deliberative forms of democratic practice unless we also believe that such practices are capable of producing agreements that are morally sound. . . .

Fiss and others are too quick to associate firmness of principle with morality, and compromise with expedience and moral weakness. Settlements reached through truly deliberative processes are not sell-outs. We do not succumb to moral relativism merely by challenging ourselves to understand, and, when we glimpse something of their logic and legitimacy, accommodate, others' values through agreements that also acknowledge our own. Settlements resulting from moral deliberation are evidence that the parties recognize the moral and social costs of effectively outlawing one perspective or the other, and have concluded that justice may find a fuller expression under the circumstances in some arrangement that attempts to confront the full complexity of the situation. We can compromise asserted claims and favored policies without sacrificing the moral principles on which they are based.

Who determines whether the basic rights of those affected by a settlement are adequately protected? In the United States, the decision about whether to settle, and on what terms, typically is wholly within the discretion of the parties themselves. . . . Fiss and other critics of settlement of significant cases would not, of course, deprive parties of the right to settle their dispute on terms of their own choosing. They simply do not recognize settlements as morally legitimate to the extent they reflect an apparent compromise of the parties' moral convictions. This perspective is ironic, given that many judicial decisions often are careful "balancing acts" that try to accommodate features of competing moral views. . . .

If the structure of a deliberative process cannot ensure the moral integrity of the outcome it produces, sound design and administration of the process according to the principles of deliberative democratic theory can at least help promote the just, consensual resolution of disputes involving deep moral disagreement. Deliberative democratic theory provides meta-principles that dispute resolution practitioners can use to structure and manage dialogues intended to contribute to the resolution of disputes involving divisive moral issues. These principles are distinct from the many micro choices and moves that neutrals make, but they can serve as touchstones that guide their process choices. The foundational principles of deliberative democracy are concerned with its goals, its procedural features, and the ideal disposition of the participants in deliberative processes. . . . To the extent these principles do not encompass other, more familiar principles that are widely considered to be cornerstones of mediation and consensus-building processes — such as facilitator neutrality, informed consent, and party self-determination — they are intended to complement, rather than displace, them.

Principles for Deliberative Dispute Resolution Process Design

A. Goals

1. *Reasoned Agreement.* Consensus based on reasons that all parties recognize as being grounded in legitimate moral visions which are sincerely held and advocated in good faith.

2. *Protection*. All parties believe the agreement adequately protects basic of basic liberties and opportunities.

3. *Public Influence*. To the extent practicable, the process and/or its output are formally or informally linked to official political processes or otherwise designed to influence the developmentof social norms regarding the subject matter of the dispute.

B. Procedure

4. *Inclusiveness*. The process is broadly inclusive of those potentially affected by its outcome or representatives who are accountable to them, all of whom have an equal opportunity to be heard.

5. *Publicity*. The process and its outcome are made as public as they can be without compromising the physical or psychological security of the participants or the sustainability of the process itself.

6. *Open Agenda*. Participants are free to make any assertion and to introduce any issue that could be addressed effectively through an agreement or could influence its terms.

7. *Open Exchange*. Participants exchange and critically evaluate perspectives, information, proposals, and reasons.

C. Participant Disposition

8. *Reciprocity*. Participants regard one another as free and equal persons and treat each other respectfully, keeping strategic motivations and coercive behavior in check, speaking to make oneself understood, and listening and inquiring in a sincere effort to understand.

9. *Reflection*. Participants are willing and able to express and jointly reflect upon the needs, attitudes and assumptions that underlie their own and others' ideals, interests, and preferences.

10. *Openness to Influence*. Participants attempt to suspend attachments to pre-existing positions and established norms at least enough to remain open to others' perspectives and proposals.

Needless to say, complete fidelity to these deliberative principles will be difficult or impossible to achieve, both for neutrals and for those well-intended participants who strive to maintain the proper disposition throughout the settlement process. The closer the ideal they represent is approximated, however, the more integrity the outcome of a deliberative settlement process is likely to have from a moral perspective. The principles can operate as regulative ideals that practitioners and parties attempt to approach without expecting to fully realize them. . . .

Some principles of deliberation will be harder to remain faithful to than others in the context of settlement discussions among parties to a significant case. The principle of inclusiveness will be difficult to honor in many two-party disputes — particularly those among private parties, but even in those where the public is nominally represented through a government official or agency. . . . The principle of publicity potentially is compromised if parties want the process to remain private, though the principle should acknowledge exceptions where secrecy is necessary to protect the security of the participants or the sustainability of the process. The less the outcome of the process will affect non-participants, however, the less concerned we should be about lack of inclusiveness and the secrecy of the process (as opposed to its outcome, which we should hope will be made public, so that it influences others' perspectives and actions).

C. SETTLEMENT PRACTICES IN THE AMERICAN LEGAL SYSTEM

1. Comments and Questions

a. As Galanter and Cahill tell us, we know little about law suits that are settled. We know even less about the far larger number of disputes that are settled prior to any formal proceeding — whether judicial, administrative, or ADR. To mention just one important example, consider the resolution of disputes between insurers and insureds about the dollar value of covered claims.

b. Variables such as time, place, and public attitudes have an impact on the outcomes of law suits. Readers should also bear in mind that the vast majority (far over 90 percent) of cases are decided in state rather than federal courts, so variations from state-to-state are to be expected.

c. In addition to the materials here, public policy considerations relating to settlement were considered in the context of plea bargaining in Chapter Five, and rulemaking settlements at the end of Chapter Twelve.

2. Marc Galanter & Mia Cahill, *"Most Cases Settle": Judicial Promotion and Regulation of Settlement,* 46 STAN. L. REV. 1339 (1994)

V. CONCLUSION

What have we learned . . . [about] the benefits of judicial promotion of settlement? We began by observing that most litigation results in settlement and that the portion of cases settled is increasing. Both the overall context that frames legal disputes and the characteristics of individual disputes make it seem highly unlikely that the portion of disputes ending in settlement will decrease in the near future. Demand for adjudication-backed remedies is increasing faster than the supply of facilities for full-blown adjudication. Much of this remedy-seeking is suffused by a scarcely concealed readiness to compromise, commended by normative and strategic considerations that are more intense in some settings and less in others.

The enlargement of the legal world enhances the opportunities for compromise. As society gets richer, the stakes in disputes become higher, and more organizations and individuals can make greater investments in litigation. Expenditures on one side produce costs on the other. Again, as the law becomes more voluminous, more complex, and more uncertain, costs increase. Virtually every "improvement" in adjudication increases the need and opportunity for greater expenditures. Refinements of due process require more submissions, hearings, and findings; elaborations of the law require research, investigation, and evidence. As transaction barriers (time, resources, uncertainty about recovery and its amount) rise, there is a greater chance of overlap in the bargaining positions of the parties. There is more of a "settlement range" in which both parties are better off than if they had run through the full course of adjudication.

This increase in settlements is largely independent of self-conscious efforts to promote them. Indeed, these promotion efforts are at least as much the result as the cause of settlement activity. As settlement ranges are extended, actors face the problem of how to reach agreement within the settlement range. The recent proliferation of settlement brokers (e.g., private judges, mediators, and special masters) and devices (minitrials and summary jury trials) testifies to the increasing demand for signals to identify points of convergence within the broad settlement ranges created by higher transaction costs.

Settlement is not intrinsically good or bad, any more than adjudication is good or bad. Settlements do not share any generic traits that commend us to avoid them per se or to promote them. This does not mean that some settlements are not preferable to some adjudications — and to other settlements. . . . [T]here is, we would suppose, great variation in the quality of settlements from one disputing arena to another and within such arenas.

When we think about trials, we are concerned that they be of high quality, meeting standards of fair procedure, accurate decision, and beneficial outcome. The occurrence of a settlement is in itself no more an assurance of a quality result than is the occurrence of a trial. (Indeed, it provides somewhat less assurance, since trials are constrained to conform publicly to tested procedural standards and to apply norms that are widely shared and publicly endorsed.) To produce settlements of high quality is not simply a matter of embracing whatever seems to produce more settlements. It is a challenge not only for those who negotiate settlements, but also for those judges and mediators who intervene in them and for those who formulate policy that affects the settlement process.

The task for policy is not promoting settlements or discouraging them, but regulating them. How do we encourage settlements that display desirable qualities? This requires that we have a sense of which qualities we consider important in a particular settlement arena — full disclosure of relevant facts, adequate compensation, fair sharing of the exchange surplus, encouraging future relations between the parties, providing guidelines for future negotiators, or any of the many other features by which we might judge a settlement. When we are evaluating the efficacy of policies to promote settlement, we have to assess their net contribution to the occurrence of desirable (and undesirable) features.

What do we know of the effects of judicial intervention on the number or the quality of settlements? As to number, the available studies provide no basis for thinking judicial promotion leads to a number of settlements that is sufficiently higher than would otherwise occur to compensate for the opportunity costs of the judicial attention diverted from adjudication. Some very effective programs may be hidden among the dismal aggregates, waiting to be revealed by more discriminating research. As to the effects of judicial promotion on the quality of settlements, we simply do not know. Again, there may be some splendid results out there, but so far they have remained unobserved by research. Are settlements arranged by judges less variable, more principled, more reflective of the merits? No one knows.

Developing reliable knowledge of the quality of settlements is fraught with difficulties. The difficulty of assessing this judicial activity is compounded when we enlarge the inquiry to include general effects. We simply don't know about the wider effects of judicial settlement promotion. Are judicially promoted settlements accompanied by more deterrence, by more reinforcement of legal norms, and by other desirable effects on wider audiences than bilateral settlements? (Or, if we have reason to think that a settlement would not have occurred without judicial intervention, than adjudication?) There is some reason to believe that settlement may entail substantial costs in information loss, but it is not clear how much of this loss can be attributed to judicial intervention. Beyond these effects of single instances of judicial intervention, we may ask about the effects of the overall pattern. Does judicial participation affect the style of lawyers in conducting bilateral negotiations? Does it affect the styles of judges when they are trying cases, ruling on motions, and so forth? Once again, we must confess ignorance.

Although there is a lot we don't know about settlement, existing knowledge supplies both useful ideas about things worth trying and valuable cautions against the snares of policy fashion. As we noted earlier, settlement is not an "alternative" process, separate from adjudication, but is intimately and inseparably entwined with it. They are two faces of a single process of strategic maneuvering and bargaining in the (actual or threatened) presence of the adjudicative forum. Because settlement is bound intimately to litigation, settlement outcomes reflect in some measure the potential results and costs of litigation. Substantive and procedural rules, and the practices of courts and lawyers, confer bargaining endowments upon the parties in settlement negotiations. Power to achieve an attractive settlement may be dependent on having adjudication as a viable alternative. Even those who emphasize the power of principle in negotiation recognize that the relative negotiating power of two parties depends primarily upon how attractive to each is the option of not reaching agreement. So the promotion of quality settlements implies at the least a continuing production of adjudicated outcomes needed to equip deserving parties to achieve such settlements. But the bargaining endowments produced by the legal rules are not self-implementing. They are translated into outcomes by the features of the particular bargaining arena. Many features of the arena offer possibilities for policy intervention: the skills and styles of the negotiators; the ethical constraints under which they operate; the presence of mediators or other settlement facilitators; the review of negotiation results by third parties (as, for example, in judicial hearings to determine the fairness of settlements in class action lawsuits and in cases involving minors); and requirements about publicity and disclosure.

How do alterations in these features affect the costs of the settlement process? How do they affect the distribution of the "savings" produced by the settlement? How do they affect the "general effects" or "public goods" produced by the settlement? Are settlements in a particular arena improved by detaching them from adjudication — for example, by removing them into different institutions or setting up cost barriers against recourse to de novo adjudication? Or is it better to couple them more closely with adjudication, for example by summary jury trials before the fact or fairness hearings afterward?

Even though we don't know the answers to these questions, the fact that we ask them reflects a change in our understanding of the relation of the courts to civil justice that has profound implications for policy. Once, courts were envisioned as dedicated exclusively to adjudication, so that settlement was seen as the product of a consensual private departure from the public forum. The results were an accidental byproduct for which the court was not accountable. The only instances in which courts had a responsibility for the quality of settlements were in cases involving minors and class actions, where there was a danger of divergent interests between a party and its representative. But now it is common knowledge that most remedy seeking in the vicinity of courts is going to eventuate in settlement. We share an inescapable awareness that courts do more than adjudicate. They preside over a cluster of dispute processes. They project models, sanctions, bargaining chips, categories, and doctrine that support processes of negotiation, mediation, and arbitration, some within the precincts of the courts and some at a distance. Once we see settlements not as a stray byproduct of the judicial process, but as part of the essential core, the responsibilities of courts can no longer be defined as coextensive with adjudication. Once we apprehend the multiplex connection between court and settlement, ensuring the quality of these processes and the settlements they produce is a central task of the administration of justice.

The Civil Justice Reform Act's enlargement of judicial concern to include the promotion of settlements and the fostering of "alternative" devices for resolving cases reflects an important, but still incomplete, reformulation of the responsibilities of courts. Once we recognize that all components of the intricate ecology of disputing are linked in complex and sometimes paradoxical ways to what courts do, it is manifest that the obligation of seeing that justice is done is not discharged by uncritical celebration of settlement (or uncritical condemnation of it). It requires a discriminating appreciation of the complex dynamics of the various species of settlements in different bargaining arenas and an appreciation of the limited capacity of the devices for regulating them. Settlement is not the answer; it is the question.

More generally, ADR, so ardently embraced as a solution, quickly decomposes into a whole new set of questions that courts must address if they are to deliver justice. To answer them requires a body of knowledge of which only scattered patches presently exist. Having abandoned the exclusive focus on adjudication to embrace the whole dispute process, the courts have launched themselves on a voyage over seas that can be charted only with instruments still to be fashioned.

D. THE LAW OF SETTLEMENT

1. Comments and Questions

a. There is a good bit of law surrounding settlement. Important topics include confidentiality of settlement negotiations, authority of agents to settle on behalf of their principals, and the formal requirements for a binding settlement.

b. What happens when one party to a dispute claims that the parties have reached a settlement, and the other party (a) denies that a settlement was reached, or (b) seeks to disavow an admitted agreement? A closely related scenario is where the parties have agreed on some issues, and one party claims the agreement to be binding while the other party responds that there was no final agreement until all outstanding issues were settled.

c. Should the finality accorded a claimed settlement depend on whether it was the result of a direct negotiation between the parties, or obtained with the assistance of a mediator? What if the settlement resulted from one of the other processes discussed in this course? Should the type of process, or the extent of court-connectedness thereof, make a difference in the treatment of an admitted or purported settlement?

2. *Goodyear Tire & Rubber Co. v. Chiles Power Supply, Inc.*, 332 F.3d 976 (6th Cir. 2003)

SUHRHEINRICH, Circuit Judge.

Defendant Chiles is a national manufacturer of heating and snowmelt systems. Chiles purchased a significant amount of "Entran II" rubber hose from Goodyear. Chiles subsequently incorporated the hose into a hydronic radiant heating and snowmelt system, which it then sold to Julian and other homeowners in and around Vail, Colorado. Julian . . . intervened in this action and moved the district court to vacate or modify a confidentiality order. Julian appeals from the district court's denial of his petition to vacate the order which prevents either of the named parties from discussing the contents of settlement negotiations. The issue presented on appeal is whether statements made in furtherance of settlement are privileged and protected from third-party discovery. We affirm the decision of the district court and find that they are. . . .

There exists a strong public interest in favor of secrecy of matters discussed by parties during settlement negotiations. This is true whether settlement negotiations are done under the auspices of the court or informally between the parties. The ability to negotiate and settle a case without trial fosters a more efficient, more cost-effective, and significantly less burdened judicial system. In order for settlement talks to be effective, parties must feel uninhibited in their communications. Parties are unlikely to propose the types of compromises that most effectively lead to settlement unless they are confident that their proposed solutions cannot be used on cross examination, under the ruse of "impeachment evidence," by some future third party. Parties must be able to abandon their adversarial tendencies to some degree. They must be able to make hypothetical concessions, offer creative *quid pro quos,* and generally make statements that would otherwise belie their litigation efforts. Without a privilege, parties would more often forego negotiations for the relative formality of trial. Then, the entire negotiation process collapses upon itself, and the judicial efficiency it fosters is lost.

Moreover, confidential settlement communications are a tradition in this country. This Court has always recognized the need for, and the constitutionality of, secrecy in settlement proceedings. In *In re the Cincinnati Enquirer,* 94 F.3d 198, 199 (6th Cir.1996), and *Cincinnati Gas & Elec. Co. v. General Elec. Co.,* 854 F.2d 900, 903-04 (6th Cir.1988), we denied members of the press access to pretrial settlement procedures, relying on the historical secrecy in settlement talks. Although not recognizing a privilege as such, we stated that the need for privacy in settlement talks outweighed any First Amendment right of access to the proceedings. In each case, we addressed whether there exists a right of access to summary jury trials. In *Cincinnati Enquirer,* we found that summary jury trials are essentially settlement proceedings, and that no "tradition of accessibility" because "settlement proceedings are historically closed procedures." In *Cincinnati Gas & Elec.,* we found likewise: "historically settlement techniques are closed procedures rather than open." . . .

Other courts have gone further and recognized the existence of some sort of *formal* settlement privilege. . . . Settlement negotiations are typically punctuated with numerous instances of puffing and posturing since they are "motivated by a desire for peace rather than from a concession of the merits of the claim." *United States v. Contra Costa County Water Dist.,* 678 F.2d 90, 92 (9th Cir.1982). What is stated as fact on the record could very well not be the sort of evidence which the parties would otherwise actually contend to be wholly true. That is, the parties may assume disputed facts to be true for the unique purpose of settlement negotiations. The discovery of these sort of "facts" would be highly misleading if allowed to be used for purposes other than settlement. *See Wyatt v. Security Inn Food & Beverage, Inc.,* 819 F.2d 69, 71 (4th Cir.1987). The public policy favoring secret negotiations, combined with the inherent questionability of the truthfulness of any statements made therein, leads us to conclude that a settlement privilege should exist, and that the district court did not abuse its discretion in refusing to allow discovery. . . .

The fact that Rule 408 provides for exceptions to inadmissibility does not disprove the concept of a settlement privilege. . . . The exceptions have been used only to admit the occurrence of settlement talks or the settlement agreement itself for "another purpose." *See, e.g., Breuer Elec. Mfg. Co. v. Toronado Sys. of Am., Inc.,* 687 F.2d 182, 185 (7th Cir.1982) (holding existence of settlement negotiations admissible to rebut claim that party had no knowledge of suit); *Prudential Ins. Co. of Am. v. Curt Bullock Builders, Inc.,* 626 F.Supp. 159, 165 (N.D.Ill.1985) (holding occurrence of settlement talks admissible to establish agency relationship). Thus, as with other privileges, the relationship itself is not privileged, but only the underlying communications.

The settlement privilege is also necessary because permitting third-party discovery of negotiation communications would lead to other undesirable results. In general, and in this case, there is no transcript of the settlement talks. And it is unlikely that there exist any written notes reflecting Goodyear's alleged attempt to bribe Chiles. Thus, in order to obtain or refute any evidence, the parties would have to depose each of the persons present at the negotiations. . . .

3. *Sarkes Tarzian, Inc. v. U.S. Trust Department of Florida Savings Bank*, 397 F.3d 577 (7th Cir. 2005)

WILLIAMS, Circuit Judge.

Sarkes Tarzian, Incorporated ("STI") brought this suit for breach of an oral contract for the sale of non-publicly traded shares of STI stock against U.S. Trust Company of Florida Savings Bank ("U.S.Trust"). A jury found that U.S. Trust breached its contract entered into by James Pressly, who was acting on U.S. Trust's behalf, and awarded STI $4 million in damages. . . . For the reasons discussed, we find that STI presented no evidence at trial showing that Mr. Pressly had actual authority to bind U.S. Trust in a contract. We reverse . . . and remand for entry of judgment for U.S. Trust. We also find that the jury instructions that the district court gave to the jury were sufficient to apprise the jury correctly of the applicable law of agency under New York law. As such, the district court did not err by refusing to instruct the jury on apparent authority. . . .

STI is a closely-held Indiana corporation. STI, which owns and operates four radio and two television stations, was founded by Sarkes Tarzian and his wife, Mary Tarzian. Mary Tarzian's will stated that upon her death, her shares in STI were to be transferred by her estate (the "Estate") to the Tarzian Family Trust ("the Family Trust"). Mary Tarzian hired James Pressly, a Florida trust and estates lawyer, to revise her will and trust documents, instructing him to modify these documents so that within nine months after her death, the Family Trust's trustees could disclaim, or legally detach themselves from, the 301,119 shares of $4 par value STI stock that Ms. Tarzian owned. One way for the trustees to disclaim themselves of the stock was to sell it. After the trustees disclaimed this stock, the shares would pass to the Mary Tarzian Charitable Foundation. This action would enable the Estate to avoid paying death taxes. . . . After Mary Tarzian died in 1998, U.S. Trust retained Mr. Pressly as counsel for the Estate. Through Mr. Pressly, U.S. Trust retained a broker to find a purchaser for the shares.

U.S. Trust had some difficulty finding a buyer for the shares because Tom Tarzian, a beneficiary of the trust, was unwilling to sell his controlling interest in STI. With the nine-month deadline fast approaching and no willing buyer for the shares identified, Mr. Pressly, on behalf of U.S. Trust, held a meeting with representatives of STI on January 25, 1999 in New York City. The purpose of the meeting was to negotiate a sale of the shares. Present at the meeting were Tom Tarzian and two STI attorneys, Herbert Camp, and Valerie Carney; Mr. Pressly, as the Estate's legal counsel; and periodically by telephone, lawyers who represented Patricia Tarzian, co-trustee of the Family Trust and beneficiary of the Estate and Trust. However, no principal of U.S. Trust attended this meeting.

There is little dispute about what the parties said at the meeting. Mr. Pressly started the meeting by telling the STI representatives not to be concerned about the fact that no one from U.S. Trust was present. Reading from his prepared notes, Mr. Pressly stated, "U.S. Trust is standing by, is fully briefed, and is prepared to sign a definitive purchase and sale contract today if we can negotiate one." . . . Mr. Pressly also stated during the meeting that, "If there is a way to cut the Gordian knot, we're here at your invitation to decisively make a deal today." STI offered to purchase the shares for $4 million cash and a $2 million promissory note. The promissory note had a six-year term at a 7% interest rate. Mr. Pressly conferred with Patricia Tarzian's counsel and then stated, "This is not what we had hoped for and I can't say we're happy with it, but we'll take it." Tom Tarzian asked Mr. Pressly if they had a deal. Mr. Pressly replied, "Yes, we have a deal." After Mr. Pressly made that statement, the parties shook hands.

Mr. Pressly was then told that STI's general counsel, Valerie Carney, was marking up a sale agreement. Supposedly, Ms. Carney was using as a template the contract for an earlier sale of Patricia Tarzian's STI shares to STI. Ms. Carney faxed the document to Mr. Pressly that night. After leaving the meeting and on his way to the airport, Mr. Pressly received a message from Gray Communications, Inc. offering to pay U.S. Trust $10 million in cash for the shares. On January 28, 1999, U.S. Trust sold the shares to Gray's affiliate, Bull Run, for that price. That same day, Mr. Pressly informed STI of the Bull Run transaction. On February 2, 1999, STI wrote to U.S. Trust asserting that it had a binding contract and demanded return of the shares.

Ten days later, STI sued . . . the Estate, naming U.S. Trust as the Estate's personal representative. STI claimed that the Estate breached an oral contract to sell its shares to STI for $4 million in cash and a $2 million promissory note. STI had two theories about how the oral contract was made: (1) that the parties had agreed to all material terms and had agreed to negotiate a written document in good faith (referred to under New York law as a "Type I" agreement); or (2) that the parties had agreed to certain important terms and had agreed to negotiate the remaining terms in good faith (referred to under New York law as a "Type II" agreement). STI sought specific performance of the oral contract or damages resulting from the breach.

With motions for summary judgment on both Type I and Type II agreements denied, the case went to trial. The jury found that the Estate had entered into a binding Type I agreement, and awarded STI $4 million in damages. This amount represented the difference between the STI contract price (total of $6 million) and that of Bull Run ($10 million). Per the district court's jury instructions, the jury made no finding on the alleged Type II agreement.

[W]e must decide as a threshold matter whether the district court properly denied U.S. Trust's motion for judgment as a matter of law. U.S. Trust's central argument in support of its motion is that no binding contract of any type was created between U.S. Trust and STI. U.S. Trust asserts that Mr. Pressly, the attorney representing the U.S. Trust, did not have the authority necessary to bind U.S. Trust in a stock purchase and sale agreement. As a result, U.S. Trust contends . . . the district court's judgment should have been for the Estate as a matter of law. Consequently, U.S. Trust argues that STI can claim no damages for U.S. Trust's sale of the STI shares to Bull Run.

Oral contracts for the sale of stock are enforceable under New York law, N.Y. U.C.C. § 8-113(a). We therefore direct our attention to the question of whether there was sufficient evidence presented at trial to demonstrate that Mr. Pressly had the authority to bind U.S. Trust in the oral contract with STI. The party asserting that an attorney had authority to enter into a contract on behalf of the attorney's client (in this case, STI) bears the burden of proving it. Without authority for the agent to bind its principal in a contract with a third party, or without the principal's subsequent ratification, the contract must be set aside under New York law.

A party's mere retention of an attorney, and its assignment to that attorney the responsibility to negotiate on behalf of the client does not create authority in the attorney to bind the principal in a contract. With this rule in mind, the question before this court is what kind of authority is sufficient under New York law? Is actual authority sufficient, or does a party need actual and apparent authority? The New York Court of Appeals, has explicitly recognized that "without a grant of authority from the client, an attorney cannot compromise or settle a claim." *Hallock v. State*, 474 N.E.2d 1178, 1181 (1984). While this language suggests that only actual authority will do, as U.S. Trust contends, closer study reveals that apparent authority can also suffice. *See Hallock*, 474 N.E.2d at 1181-82 (principal had cloaked attorney in apparent authority and therefore was bound by a settlement agreement into which attorney had entered client in open court).

U.S. Trust cites Restatement (Third) of Law Governing Lawyers § 22(1) and comment (e) to that section to support its contention that an attorney must have actual authority from the client to bind the client in a significant contract. However, the parties have not pointed us to, nor has our own research yielded any cases demonstrating the New York Court of Appeals's adoption of these particular provisions. . . . Therefore, we rely on the actual pronouncements of the New York Court of Appeals on the law of its state on this issue [in Hallock and other cases]. . . .

A principal confers actual authority on his agent when he objectively manifests to the agent consent to the agency. As for apparent authority, it is created by "words or conduct of the principal, communicated to a third party, that give rise to the appearance and belief that the agent possesses authority to enter into a transaction." *Hallock*, 474 N.E.2d at 1181. New York explicitly rejects the idea that an agent can confer apparent authority on him or herself. Rather, the existence of "apparent authority" depends upon a factual showing that the third party relied upon the misrepresentation of the agent because of some misleading conduct on the part of the principal — not the agent." . . . A third party may rely on an appearance of authority . . . only to the extent that such reliance is reasonable. Finally, the New York Court of Appeals has held that "[o]ne who deals with an agent does so at his peril, and must make the necessary effort to discover the actual scope of authority." With these principles in mind, we turn to the facts of this case to discern whether there was sufficient evidence presented to support a finding that Mr. Pressly had actual or apparent authority to bind U.S. Trust in a contract with STI.

A. Actual Authority

Because there was no writing between U.S. Trust and Mr. Pressly outlining the scope of Mr. Pressly's authority, only testimonial evidence was available to determine whether Mr. Pressly had actual authority. In its appellate brief, STI highlights the testimony of U.S. Trust Chief Executive Officer Callaway as the strongest affirmative evidence from which the jury could infer actual authority. When asked, "was Mr. Pressly authorized to go to New York to negotiate the deal?", Callaway responded, "He was authorized to go to New York to negotiate a deal, yes." . . .

U.S. Trust directs our attention to the following evidence in the record as supporting its contention that Mr. Pressly did not have actual authority. First, it is undisputed that no one from STI had any communication with U.S. Trust concerning that scope of Mr. Pressly's authority other than with Mr. Pressly himself. Second, U.S. Trust Senior Vice President Cavanaugh testified that Mr. Pressly was authorized "to negotiate a possible deal," but his authority was limited. Specifically, Mr. Pressly "was not authorized to actually execute a contract." U.S. Trust CEO Callaway testified to the specific instructions he gave Mr. Pressly: he was to go out and try to find a buyer for the Sarkes Tarzian stock and he was given the authority to negotiate terms . . . with the people that he actually found, if any, and was specifically instructed, and there was no argument at all, that he would come back to us with those terms, and present them to us for review, analysis, and a final decision as to whether they were something that we should move forward with. . . .

[A]fter the negotiation session concluded, . . . Mr. Pressly called U.S. Trust CEO Callaway, who was standing by all day long, and stated that there would not be an agreement signed that day. Furthermore, Mr. Pressly told Mr. Callaway that he was released from standing by. In addition, U.S. Trust argues that the signature blocks on the unsigned written agreements STI prepared after the negotiation meeting were for U.S. Trust's signature, not that of Mr. Pressly. This assertion is consistent with the other record evidence that only U.S. Trust signed agreements on behalf of the Mary Tarzian estate.

U.S. Trust wanted Mr. Pressly to testify concerning the scope of his authority to corroborate Mr. Callaway's testimony. However, the district court prohibited Mr. Pressly from testifying on this issue and U.S. Trust challenges this evidentiary decision on appeal. Apparently concerned about gamesmanship, the district court did not permit Mr. Pressly to testify as to whether he had actual authority to bind his principal in a contract with STI. The district court made this ruling because Mr. Pressly refused to answer STI's question on this point in his deposition. Mr. Pressly claimed attorney-client privilege. The day after Mr. Pressly's deposition, U.S. Trust implicitly waived its attorney-client privilege when Ms. Cavanaugh responded fully to the same questions STI asked Mr. Pressly the day before. The court regarded Mr. Pressly's desire to change his position taken at his deposition as "not playing right." . . .

In any case, whether it was reversible error for the district court to deny Mr. Pressly's testimony on the scope of his authority does not matter here. This is because our review of the record demonstrates that there was no evidence presented at trial showing that Mr. Pressly had actual authority to bind U.S. Trust in a contract. Mr. Callaway and Ms. Cavanaugh's testimony — that they allowed Mr. Pressly to negotiate a deal but not to enter into it without first consulting with U.S. Trust and getting its approval — stood unrebutted. In other words, STI did not discharge its burden of showing that Mr. Pressly had actual authority. Nor did STI discharge its duty under New York law to ascertain the scope of Mr. Pressly's authority. Mr. Pressly told the STI representatives at the negotiation meeting that U.S. Trust was "standing by" all day "to sign" an agreement, if the parties could reach one. STI did not reach out to or call U.S. Trust's principals. Doing nothing cannot be construed as making "the necessary effort to discover the actual scope of the agent's authority. . . .

STI cites *Carter v. Chicago Police Officers*, 165 F.3d 1071 (7th Cir.1998) for support. In that case, we maintained that "Given the inconsistencies among the evidence and testimony presented to the jury, it was certainly within the province of the jury to parse the facts, to weigh the credibility of each witness and to disregard the testimony of witnesses it found to be less credible or not worthy of credence." *Id.* at 1081. In other words, STI suggests that the jury could have disbelieved Mr. Callaway and Ms. Cavanaugh and set aside their testimony. However, Carter, as the text quoted above indicates, involved a situation in which the parties had two distinct and inconsistent stories about the events that triggered the lawsuit. Here, even viewed in the light most favorable to STI, the evidence STI points to is not inconsistent with Mr. Callaway and Ms. Cavanaugh's testimony about the scope of Mr. Pressly's authority, namely that Mr. Pressly was authorized to negotiate a deal but not to sign a contract or otherwise bind U.S. Trust without consulting it first. On these facts, Carter is not helpful to STI. . . .

B. Apparent Authority

We agree with the district court's decision not to submit an apparent authority instruction to the jury. Under New York law, apparent authority is created by "words or conduct of the principal, communicated to a third party, that give rise to the appearance and belief that the agent possesses authority to enter into a transaction." *Hallock*, 474 N.E.2d at 1181. New York explicitly rejects the idea that an agent can confer apparent authority on him or herself. Rather, the existence of "apparent authority" depends upon a factual showing that the third party relied upon the misrepresentation of the agent because of some misleading conduct on the part of the principal — not the agent." The district court was correct in concluding that STI did not produce any evidence demonstrating that STI had any direct interaction with U.S. Trust principals before or during the negotiations for the sale of the shares. Nor did STI observe any actions by U.S. Trust that would indicate that U.S. Trust had cloaked Mr. Pressly in apparent authority. . . .

STI also cites *National Labor Relations Board v. G & T Terminal Packaging Co., Inc.*, 246 F.3d 103, 115 (2d Cir.2001) to support its contention that apparent authority arose from Mr. Pressly's statements. However, we find that *G &*

T Terminal does not apply in this situation. In *G & T Terminal*, the court found there was substantial evidence to support the Administrative Law Judge's conclusion that the attorney had apparent authority to bind the client. In *G & T Terminal*, the client company's president had attended an earlier negotiating session at which time he agreed to all of the contract terms except an arbitration clause. The attorney stated at the meeting, "she was there to enter into an agreement." By contrast, in this case, U.S. Trust's CEO Callaway did not speak to Mr. Pressly the entire day. Nor was he was ever present at the negotiation meeting. In essence, there were no actions or words of CEO Callaway which STI could construe as cloaking Mr. Pressly with authority to bind U.S. Trust. Further, unlike the president in *G & T Terminal*, Mr. Callaway was unaware of any of the terms Mr. Pressly had discussed with STI. Finally, unlike the attorney in *G & T Terminal* who said she (as opposed to her client) was there to "enter into an agreement," Mr. Pressly made no such statement. Rather, Mr. Pressly stated only that he was there to negotiate an agreement which U.S. Trust, the principal, was standing by to sign. . . .

4. *Padilla v. LaFrance*, 907 S.W.2d 454 (Tex. 1995)

PHILLIPS, Chief Justice, delivered the opinion of the Court.

The primary issue presented is whether a series of letters between the parties' representatives constituted a written settlement agreement enforceable under Texas Rule of Civil Procedure 11, even though plaintiffs withdrew their consent to the settlement before the letters were filed with the court and before judgment was rendered on the agreement. The court of appeals held that any agreement was unenforceable under Rule 11 because plaintiffs revoked consent before the letters were filed with the court. Because we hold that the letters constituted an enforceable Rule 11 agreement, we reverse the judgment of the court of appeals and remand to the trial court with instructions to enforce the parties' settlement agreement.

One member of the LaFrance family was killed and two others were seriously injured when their vehicle collided with that driven by Enrique Padilla. After the LaFrances sued Padilla, his insurer, State Farm Mutual Automobile Insurance Company, assumed defense of the claims. The parties subsequently engaged in settlement negotiations. . . .

On April 10, 1991, Jeffrey Steidley, the LaFrances' attorney, mailed a settlement demand to Brian Chandler, Padilla's attorney, providing in pertinent part as follows: Dear Mr. Chandler: You are quite familiar with the facts and circumstances surrounding the above referenced matter. At this time we make demand for policy limits of $40,000 for full and final settlement of this case against the insured that you represent. Payment of this sum should be made on or before Tuesday, April 23, 1991 at 5:00 p.m., by delivery of checks in the appropriate amount to the offices of the undersigned made payable in the following amounts and to the following payees: One check in the amount of $20,000 to Madeleine LaFrance As Next Friend of Michelle LaFrance and Olivier & Steidley. One check in the amount of $20,000.00 made payable to Ernest J. LaFrance, Marlene Luther, Marilyn Koenig, Madeleine LaFrance and Olivier & Steidley, their attorneys of record. Please be advised that although I will be more than happy to discuss this case with you or any of your representatives, no oral discussion that we may have will serve to alter the time limits expressed in the correspondence. I look forward to receipt of the checks on or before date specified, failing which this offer to settle will be withdrawn and my clients will proceed to perfect their rights under Texas law. . . .

Chandler forwarded this letter to Phil Bradshaw, the State Farm adjuster handling the claim, who telephoned Steidley's office on April 15 and spoke with Sherea Carry. Bradshaw informed Carry of an outstanding $1,600 medical lien for treatment to Michelle LaFrance that needed to be cleared up in connection with the settlement. Carry responded that she would have Steidley call Bradshaw to discuss the lien. When Bradshaw did not hear back from Steidley, he called Steidley's office on April 18 and again on the morning of April 23 to discuss the lien. Each time he was able to speak only with Carry, who informed Bradshaw that the lien had not yet been resolved.

When Bradshaw still had not heard from Steidley by the afternoon of April 23, the settlement deadline, he faxed this handwritten letter to Steidley: Dear Mr. Steidley, This will confirm our settlement agreement hereby State Farm agreed to meet the policy limit demands set out in your letter of 4/10/91. The only thing holding up resolution of this is the hospital lien re: Michelle. I await word from you regarding the lien so I know to whom to make drafts payable. . . . Steidley responded before 5:00 p.m. the same day, by fax and regular mail, with this letter: Dear Mr. Bradshaw: This letter will confirm that the above referenced matter has been settled for all applicable policy limits, which have been represented to us to be $40,000. Please forward settlement checks in the above referenced matter. This office will take care of the lien filed by Medical Center Hospital out of the settlement funds forwarded by your office. Your attention to this matter is greatly appreciated. . . . Approximately one week later, Chandler tendered two settlement checks for $20,000 each to Steidley, along with a formal settlement agreement. Steidley, however, refused to accept the checks or sign the agreement, contending that Padilla had not timely accepted the April 10 settlement offer.

Padilla subsequently filed Steidley's April 23 letter with the court, describing it as "an acceptance of a settlement." Padilla then filed a counterclaim in the pending suit, seeking enforcement of the alleged settlement agreement. . . . Padilla argued that the letters between the parties' representatives constituted a written settlement agreement. Although acknowledging that the court could not render a consent judgment incorporating the terms of the settlement, as the LaFrances had revoked consent, he nonetheless contended that the court could enforce the settlement by summary judgment. The LaFrances countered that the parties did not have an enforceable agreement under Texas Rule of Civil Procedure 11, which requires agreements regarding pending suits to "be in writing, signed and filed with the papers as part of the record." The LaFrances further argued that, even if an otherwise valid Rule 11 agreement existed, it could not be enforced since the LaFrances had revoked consent prior to any judgment being rendered on the agreement. . . .

Texas Rule of Civil Procedure 11 provides as follows: Unless otherwise provided in these rules, no agreement between attorneys or parties touching any suit pending will be enforced unless it be in writing, signed and filed with the papers as part of the record, or unless it be made in open court and entered of record. This rule has existed since 1840 and has contained the filing requirement since 1877. The rationale for the rule is straight forward: Agreements of counsel, respecting the disposition of causes, which are merely verbal, are very liable to be misconstrued or forgotten, and to beget misunderstandings and controversies. There is great propriety in the rule which requires that all agreements of counsel respecting their causes shall be in writing, and if not, the court will not enforce them. They all then speak for themselves, and the court can judge of their import, and proceed to act upon them with safety. The rule is a salutary one, and ought to be adhered to whenever counsel disagree as to what has transpired between them. A settlement agreement must comply with Rule 11 to be enforceable. . . .

The LaFrances argue that 1) the writings in this case do not evidence a binding agreement, 2) even if there was an agreement, it did not comply with Rule 11 because the LaFrances withdrew their consent before the writings were filed with the court, and 3) any agreement was further unenforceable because the LaFrances withdrew their consent before judgment was rendered on the agreement. We consider each of these arguments in turn.

Rule 11 requires settlement agreements to be "in writing." Although we have never articulated what is necessary to satisfy this "in writing" requirement, we may analogize to the statute of frauds, which requires certain contracts to be in writing. To satisfy the statute of frauds, there must be a written memorandum which is complete within itself in every material detail, and which contains all of the essential elements of the agreement, so that the contract can be ascertained from the writings without resorting to oral testimony. The written memorandum, however, need not be contained in one document. These principles apply equally to Rule 11 agreements. Applying them here, we hold that the series of letters between Steidley, Bradshaw and Chandler are sufficient to constitute an agreement in writing satisfying Rule 11. . . .

Rule 11 requires settlement agreements to be filed "with the papers as part of the record." Padilla did not file any of the settlement letters until after the LaFrances had refused to accept the settlement checks tendered by Padilla. . . . Although Rule 11 requires the writing to be filed in the court record, it does not say when it must be filed, The purpose of the rule — to avoid disputes over the terms of oral settlement agreements — is not furthered by requiring the writing to be filed before consent is withdrawn. "To require the parties to immediately rush to the courthouse with a signed document in order to quickly comply with the requirements of Rule 11 before the other party reneges on his agreement goes against the grain of the policy in Texas jurisprudence which favors the settlement of lawsuits." The purpose of the filing requirement . . . is to put the agreement before the court so that "the court can judge of [its] import, and proceed to act upon [it] with safety." This purpose is satisfied so long as the agreement is filed before it is sought to be enforced. Padilla met that requirement here by filing each of the settlement letters with his motion for summary judgment on the counterclaim.

Finally, the LaFrances argue that the settlement is unenforceable because they withdrew consent before judgment was rendered on the agreement. The LaFrances rely on *Kennedy v. Hyde*, 682 S.W.2d 525, 526 (Tex. 1984), where we held that "notwithstanding a valid Rule 11 agreement, consent must exist at the time an agreed judgment is rendered." The LaFrances, however, confuse the requirements for an agreed judgment with those for an enforceable settlement agreement. Although a court cannot render a valid agreed judgment absent consent at the time it is rendered, this does not preclude the court, after proper notice and hearing, from enforcing a settlement agreement complying with Rule 11 even though one side no longer consents to the settlement. The judgment in the latter case is not an agreed judgment, but rather is a judgment enforcing a binding contract.

In *Quintero v. Jim Walter Homes, Inc.*, 654 S.W2d 442 (Tex. 1983), we held that the trial court erred by rendering an agreed judgment of dismissal based on a release signed by plaintiff because plaintiff did not consent to the judgment at the time it was rendered. We noted, however, that "our reversal of the judgment of dismissal is without prejudice to the rights of the Jim Walter Homes in its attempt to plead and prove an enforceable settlement agreement under the release." An action to enforce a settlement agreement, where consent is withdrawn, must be based on proper pleading and proof. In this case, for example. Padilla filed a counterclaim seeking enforcement of the parties' agreement, and both sides moved for summary judgment on that claim. The summary judgment evidence established an enforceable settlement agreement as a matter of law. The trial court therefore should have granted Padilla's motion for summary judgment and enforced the agreement.

5. Comments and Questions

a. In *Padilla*, Chief Justice Phillips proceeds to find a settlement agreement by examining the communications between the parties in the same manner as with any other contract, by looking for offer, acceptance, and consideration. Should courts look for settlement agreements in the same manner as any other contractual undertaking, or should they require something closer to a single document that is labeled "Settlement Agreement"? While the facts in *Padilla* are not close to the limiting case, the court did have to construe several documents to find a settlement agreement.

b. The Uniform Commercial Code, section 2-201, and the case law in most states, require dramatically less detail in a writing in order to satisfy the statute of frauds than does the opinion by Chief Justice Phillips. Section 2-201, comment one, states:

> The required writing need not contain all the material terms of the contract and such material terms as are stated need not be stated precisely. All that is required is that the writing afford a basis for believing that the offered oral testimony rests on a real transaction. The only

term which must appear is the quantity term. . . . The price, time and place of payment or delivery, the general quality of the goods, or any particular warranties all may be omitted.

Texas has adopted the UCC, so in a case similar to *Padilla*, except that the claim being settled was for the sale of goods instead of a tort, the analysis might be quite different. Few if any other states would apply the statute of frauds as strictly as suggested by Chief Justice Phillips. Should less complete writings be sufficient to establish a settlement agreement?

c. The consequence of finding a binding agreement is not trivial — the unhappy party is denied access to the courts, and the jury trial guaranteed by the U.S. and every state Constitution. Texas regards jury trials so highly that they are available even in traffic ticket cases.

d. In 1995, the Texas Legislature amended the Family Code § 153.0071 by adding the following language regarding mediated settlements:

> (d) A MEDIATED settlement agreement is binding on the parties if the agreement:
>
>   (1) provides in a separate paragraph an underlined statement that the agreement is not subject to revocation;
>
>   (2) is signed by each party to the agreement; and
>
>   (3) is signed by the party's attorney, if any, who is present at the time the agreement is signed.
>
> (e) If a MEDIATED settlement agreement meets the requirements of Subsection (d), a party is entitled to judgment on the MEDIATED settlement agreement notwithstanding Rule 11, Texas Rules of Civil Procedure, or any other rule of law.

e. Does it make sense to have one body of rules for mediated settlement agreements and another for other settlements? Does it make sense to have a separate body of rules for mediated settlement agreements in the family law context? Does it make sense to have separate provisions for mediated and for unmediated divorce or separation agreements?

f. How should state law treat purported settlements by the parties to a dispute? Should it matter if a law suit has been filed? Should it matter if the parties were represented by counsel when the agreement was reached?

g. Based on the materials that you have just read, write a short essay addressed to Texas lawyers that summarizes settlement law in Texas.

h. Assume that you are a state legislator eager to avoid the uncertainties that have arisen in Texas. What policy recommendations would you make?

i. The story told in the *Padilla* case is common and fairly simple: an automobile accident that causes serious personal injury, followed by a settlement for the insured's policy limits. In the real world, settlements take place over time, there is miscommunication between parties, people are not in their office and neglect to return phone calls (or e-mails). The moral of the *Padilla* mess is that rational maximizers mess things up on many occasions.

j. *The Beazar East* decision required a writing in the context of appellate mediation. This decision is based on local rules, and governs appellate mediation only. Should these principles be equally applicable to all mediated settlements?

6. *Beazer East Inc. v. Mead Corporation*, 412 F.3d 429 (3d Cir. 2005)

ROTH, Circuit Judge.

Beazer's motion to specifically enforce the alleged oral settlement reached at the appellate mediation and to dismiss this appeal with prejudice must be rejected. Both Local Appellate Rule (LAR) 33.5 and sound judicial policy compel the conclusion that parties to an appellate mediation session are not bound by anything short of a written settlement. Any other rule would seriously undermine the efficacy of the Appellate Mediation Program by compromising the confidentiality of settlement negotiations.

Beazer requests enforcement of the alleged oral settlement but admits that there are genuine factual disputes regarding whether the parties actually reached an agreement. Mead correctly argues that we cannot resolve these disputes without violating the confidentiality rule, LAR 33.5(c). With exceptions not relevant here, Rule 33.5(c) provides that no one at the mediation session-neither mediator, counsel, nor party-may disclose "statements made or information developed during the mediation process." The provision further provides that "the parties are prohibited from using *any* information obtained as a result of the mediation process as a basis for *any* motion or argument to *any* court." LAR 33.5(c) (emphases added). Beazer cannot prove the existence or terms of the disputed oral settlement without violating this provision's broadly stated prohibitions. . . .

Beazer concedes that it may not use information obtained at the conference in any argument going to the *merits* of the appeal, but contends that it must be able to use that information for the limited purposes of proving the existence and terms of a settlement. This argument is unpersuasive. First, the rule is stated in the broadest possible language and does not contemplate any such exception. Second, Beazer's proposed exception would effectively undermine the rule and would compromise the effectiveness of the Appellate Mediation Program. A confidentiality provision permits and encourages counsel to discuss matters in an uninhibited fashion often leading to settlement. If counsel know beforehand that the proceedings may be laid bare on the claim that an oral settlement occurred at the conference, they will "of necessity . . . feel constrained to conduct themselves in a cautious, tight-lipped, non-committal manner more suitable to poker players in a high-stakes game than to adversaries attempting to arrive at a just resolution of a civil dispute." Third, Beazer's proposed exception would require appellate courts to receive evidence and resolve factual disputes, tasks more properly suited to the district courts.

We must also consider LAR 33.5(d), which provides that "[n]o party shall be bound by statements or actions at a mediation session unless a settlement is reached." The rule further provides that "if a settlement is reached, the agreement shall be reduced to writing and shall be binding upon all parties to the agreement." Mead argues that the most "straightforward" reading of this rule is that no agreement is binding until it is written. Mead's reading is serial: 1) if the parties reach an agreement, 2) then that agreement shall be written down, and 3) then, and only then, the agreement shall be binding. However, the grammatical structure of the rule is consistent with a parallel construction: 1) if the parties reach an agreement, 2)a) then it shall be reduced to writing, and, 2)b) then it shall be binding. Under this reading, the agreement is binding because it has been reached, not because it has been written down.

The "parallel" construction of Rule 33.5(d) — which would make oral settlement agreements binding on the parties — is irreconcilable with Rule 33.5(c), because . . . there is no way to prove the existence or terms of a disputed oral settlement without violating the confidentiality provision. Therefore, we adopt Mead's "serial" reading of Rule 33.5(d), according to which an agreement is not binding unless it is reduced to writing. The Ninth Circuit adopted a serial interpretation of similar language in *Barnett v. Sea Land Serv., Inc.*, 875 F.2d 741, 743-44 (9th Cir.1989).

Further, Judge Easterbrook's opinion in Herrnreiter v. Chicago Housing Authority, 281 F.3d 634 (7th Cir. 2002), provides persuasive policy justifications for requiring written settlements. In Herrnreiter the parties admitted that they had reached an oral settlement at a voluntary appellate mediation session but they did not agree on the terms. The court denied the defendant's motion to implement the oral settlement. The court noted that there is no transcript of appellate mediation sessions and that settlement conference attorneys presiding over such sessions promise both sides that nothing that transpires at the conference will be revealed to the judges; the court finally observed that appellate courts are not well-positioned to conduct fact-finding missions. Accordingly, the court concluded that nothing short of a mutually satisfactory written settlement agreement could terminate an appeal. "Any other approach would compromise the confidentiality of the negotiations, require the settlement attorneys to become witnesses in appellate factfinding proceedings, and substantially complicate the disposition of litigation." All of these concerns are equally present in this case. In fact, the argument for preserving confidentiality of proceedings is even stronger in this case, where participation in the appellate mediation program is mandatory and the mediation is directed by a court-employed mediator or a judicial officer. *See In re Anonymous,* 283 F.3d 627 (4th Cir. 2002).

Beazer complains that if Mead's interpretation of Rules 33.5(c) and (d) is accepted then parties will be able to enter into oral agreements at settlement conferences and simply back out on a whim, significantly deterring the federal policy of encouraging settlements. Beazer also relies on our oft-repeated position that a written agreement is not necessary to render a settlement enforceable. Mead's first argument is simply incorrect: if parties know beforehand that only a written settlement agreement is binding, they will be sure to memorialize their agreement in writing at the end of the mediation session. Its second argument is based on basic common law contract principles, and has no application where specific court rules provide otherwise.

For all these reasons, Beazer's motion to enforce the alleged oral settlement agreement and dismiss the appeal is denied. . . .

Chapter 14
DISPUTE RESOLUTION AND
THE COMMUNICATIONS REVOLUTION

A. INTRODUCTION

Perhaps the place to begin is with a confession: both of your authors are over 40, and neither of us is a technology expert. The nature and impact of the continuing communications revolution is a topic about which we, like many other teachers, know less about than some/many/most of our students. The topics discussed in this chapter are a moving target, because one of the few certainties about the communications revolution is that it continues, and that the pace of change is increasing. An important matter for readers to consider is how technology, both new and old, will change dispute resolution processes and proceedings over the next decade, and beyond.

The field of "on-line" dispute resolution is sufficiently new that there is not yet an agreed upon way of writing the term: "on-line, " "online," and "on line" are all in use. Apparently, everyone agrees that the proper abbreviation is ODR. An alternative term is technology-mediated dispute resolution (TMDR), which allows us to consider on everything except in-person, face-to-face, dispute processes. The "in-person" qualifier is necessary because inexpensive cameras allow people to see each other while meeting remotely.

Is ODR something fundamentally new and different, or simply a different and faster way of doing things that people have done for a long time? Of course, there is not a single answer to this question, but the various possible answers are worth careful consideration. As suggested in the article by Professor Larson, fully understanding on-line communications requires that it be understood in terms of itself and not in terms of what came before. Learning a foreign language offers a helpful analogy. Real knowledge of a language requires thinking in that language, rather than translating into or drawing analogies to one's native tongue.

Culture offers another helpful perspective, with modern forms of communication considered as a form of unique culture. Think of on-line communications as a sub-culture with some special features and characteristics different from what some (mostly older) people are used to. (Bankers commonly observe that their youngest customers prefer to use ATMs, while their elderly customers prefer to interact with live tellers.) What are the likely characteristics of the early adopters of technologically-mediated dispute resolution?

Alternatively, consider ODR/TMDR as primarily a new approach to addressing dispute resolution (including planning for and avoiding disputes). Negotiation has been technologically-mediated for as long as writing has been in common use. Recall the "mailbox rules," the "battle of the forms," and the parol evidence rule (if a principle with so many exceptions can properly be called a "rule") from your Contracts course. The enforcement of purported agreements to settle disputes was examined in Chapter Thirteen. How will ODR alter the settlement process, and the disposition of challenges to agreements purporting to be final and binding?

Many of the topics that are problems for ODR/TMDR are also issues for "conventional" dispute resolution, and the ODR/TMDR response should provide a basis for rethinking how these issues are addressed in ADR processes that are not technology-mediated. Concerns about the building and repairing of trust in on-line communications is valuable not just for thinking about ODR, but also for reflecting about how similar issues are dealt with in face-to-face dispute resolution. Conversely, as you read these materials consider the strengths and weaknesses of ODR, and to what extent ODR could be used to overcome problems encountered in "ordinary" ADR.

The materials in this chapter consider "pure" forms of ODR/TMDR, and the latest forms of these processes. Modern technology plays an increasing role in conventional dispute resolution, even where the final process is a judicial trial or ADR process. For example, electronic exchange of documents is so well established that even late adopters like courts commonly provide for electronic submission of pleadings, motions, and other documents. In many instances, ADR proceedings are preceded by extensive preparation and formal exchange of reports and position papers.

Modern technology allows for "face-to-face" meetings from remote locations. Again, even the courts have made use of this approach. Video habeas corpus proceedings in federal courts provide a striking example. The need to bring prisoners from distant prisons to court houses in the midst of cities involves significant costs, not to mention security concerns. Several years ago, one of your authors witnessed an argument before the Second Circuit Court of Appeals in New York City, where counsel for one side was in the courtroom while counsel for the other party was "live" from Syracuse on a large monitor. The three judges were all in the courtroom, but judges too could participate from one or more remote locations.

ODR is particularly effective in overcoming barriers of distance and cost. ODR could be particularly effective for consumers in their dealings with businesses (B2C) and government (G2C). Think about how one might design such a system that is fair, fast, and inexpensive. Consider in this regard product servicing offered by computer manufacturers and sellers. The solution could (and should) take place at several levels, beginning with clear instructions about how to begin use of the product, a "frequently asked questions" (FAQ) location (both written and on-line), a "help" program on the computer, a virtual hot line for purchasers to submit questions, a telephone service for answering questions, and only lastly a dispute resolution mechanism. Think about how the form of communication affects the interaction between parties.

The communications revolution has changed almost everything, even including the lives of soldiers at war. *See* Lizette Alvarez, *An Internet Lifeline for
Troops in Iraq and Loved Ones at Home*, NEW YORK TIMES, July 8, 2006. (The online version does not provide page numbers.) Alvarez reports that many active
duty troops are able to communicate with their families (and friends) in America on a regular, often daily, basis. "Military deployments have a way of chew-
ing up marriages, turning daily life upside down and making strangers out of
husbands and wives. But for this generation of soldiers, the Internet, which is
now widely available on bases, has softened the blow of long separations, helping loved ones stay in daily touch. . . ." Web cameras allow for visual communication. There can be a downside, however, for both the families and the military.
Learning about problems at home — a child is ill, or just got a tattoo — can be
distracting to a soldier. On balance, however, it seems clear that this is a beneficial development overall, improving military morale and the subsequent
adjustment back to civilian life.

The materials in this chapter are not as neatly organized as the table of contents might suggest, because we are dealing with a fairly new field whose
parameters have not yet been clearly developed or extensively studied. Section
B introduces the new developments in the provision of dispute resolution services in business, outside the commercial context, and government-to-citizen
ODR. Section C shifts the focus to the theory of developing ODR and the issues
associated with the use of ODR, while also providing many points of comparison between on-line and in-person dispute resolution activities.

Section D shifts the focus to providers of ODR. Susan Raines offers up the
possibility of being a dispute resolution provider from home — "mediating in
your pajamas." And, no sooner do we have a new way of delivering dispute resolution services than accreditation of providers is suggested. Credentialing of
ADR providers is examined at length in Chapter Fifteen — the Taylor & Bornstein article provides a bridge to that topic.

B. THE BRAVE NEW WORLD OF THE INTERNET AND ON-LINE DISPUTE RESOLUTION

1. Comments and Questions

a. Professor Hadfield examines and explains existing forms of ODR in the
commercial sphere. Professor Braeutigan looks outside the commercial sphere.
What are the new developments since these articles were written, and how
have the processes described been improved?

b. What experiences have you and your friends had with ODR? What about
your parents or others of their generation? How might ODR systems be
improved?

c. Professor Ramasastry's consideration of G-2-C dispute resolution examines
the Executive branch of government, which implements and enforces law. While
not discussed here, the legislative branch also uses electronic communication in
its dispute resolution work — commonly called "constituent work." Every Con-

gressional office employs staff persons who spend much of their time assisting constituents in their interaction with government agencies. The trend to expanded use of ODR by all parts of government — at the state and local as well as the federal level — is certain to accelerate; the only question is how and how fast.

2. Gillian K. Hadfield, *Delivering Legality on the Internet: Developing Principles For the Private Provision of Commercial Law*, 6 AM. L. & ECON. REV. 154 (2004)

The story of commercial law begins not with the state but with private legal regimes. The history of the long-distance trade that opened up the modern world is the history of efforts by traders to develop rules and regimes to overcome the most basic challenges of commercial relationships: verifying identity, coordinating activities, securing commitments. Without an effective public law of contract that traveled across local boundaries, the early traders in Europe and the Mediterranean developed their own legal codes — applicable to those who wished to trade with them — and set up their own methods of adjudicating the claims and promises on which long-distance trading and thus economic growth was built. Backed by the threat of exclusion and sometimes the agreement of a ruler to use sovereign power to enforce the decisions of the merchants' private legal regimes, these regimes were the product of the same entrepreneurial and competitive process that underlay trade itself. They were essentially private legal regimes. . . .

Unlike the commercial revolution, the digital revolution is taking place in a world saturated with publicly provided law. Yet, like the medieval world before the rise of nation-states, the world of cyberspace is still largely a legal vacuum. The law of off-line trade simply does not reach so much of what takes place there: What is identity when identity can be changed with the click of a mouse? How does one trust an entity that may lack any physical location or reside outside the jurisdiction of local law enforcement to protect credit card numbers, or deliver quality goods or services? But, although the questions posed by cyberspace may be new, the needs of trade in this new world are the same as they were in the middle ages: securing commitment and coordination and communication to facilitate transactions. And, like the commercial revolution before it, the absence of state-generated legal rules to govern the digital revolution is generating private regimes to deliver legality: authoritative structures supplying the ordering and commitment that facilitate trade. . . .

Delivering Legality on the Internet: The Market for
"Trust" and "Assurance" Services

I survey here some of the emerging regimes for delivering legality on the Internet, noting in particular how law is combined with other devices to secure the basic requirements of commitment, coordination, and communication for trade. Private regimes to deliver legality on the Internet are emerging in two distinct ways: through formally established private law-making bodies, such as the Internet Corporation for Assigned Names and Numbers (ICANN), which is responsible for the development and implementation of domain-name dispute resolution rules, and through the spontaneous, market-driven provision of "trust" and "assurance" services in the forms of packages of encryption, codes of conduct, and dispute resolution mechanisms coordinated through digital certificates and seal programs, such as BBBonline.

Transactions on the Internet face the basic challenges of all commercial transactions: How can individuals and entities doing business together trust that their trading partners will do as they say? In the Internet setting this means, how can consumers and businesses be sure that the information they transmit online will remain confidential and used only for the purposes to which they have consented? How can they ensure that charges will be made against a credit card only as authorized, that goods and services will be delivered as ordered? How can they ensure that the entity they are dealing with is in fact the one they think it is?

Solutions to these challenges are rapidly emerging online. Most are coordinated through digital certificates, digital seal programs, or both. Digital certificates are electronic documents issued, managed, and stored by a third party verifying an online entity's identity, compliance with required standards, or both. Digital seals are identifiable trademarks owned by an organization that grants participants in its "program" the right to display the seal, subject to meeting the requirements of the program. Seals are used in the offline world — such as the Good Housekeeping Seal of Approval — to denote certification of practices or status by a third-party "watchdog" organization. On the Internet, however, there is the technological capacity to use "clickable" seals on a web site to initiate direct contact between a viewer of the seal (a consumer at a web site, for example) and the verification agency. This establishes a virtually costless means of verifying the authenticity of a seal and disabling a seal's functionality in the event that a program participant violates the requirements of the seal program. This technology means that cyber-seals can perform a much more extensive role in regulating commercial relationships on the Internet than traditional seals do in the offline world.

Digital certificates and seal programs represent the use of a variety of techniques to regulate and support commercial transactions online. What gives them the character of a privately provided "legal" regime is the fact that the administrator of the certificate or seal program establishes the rules under which the certificate or seal can be obtained and used, monitors compliance, resolves disputes, and imposes consequences for failure to adhere to the program's rules: disabling the certificate or seal, publishing information about the transgressor, implementing remedies as ordered by a private dispute resolution provider, and so on.

A. Encryption. One of the most widespread uses of digital certificate and seal programs on the Internet is to solve the fundamental problem of identity verification and the exclusion of others from access to information. Encryption ensures that information sent over the Internet cannot be "seen" by anyone who does not have access to the "key" to the encryption. Encryption coordinated through a digital certificate or seal program takes this a step further to solve the problems of verifying the identity of trading partners and the integrity of encryption efforts by trading partners.

Encryption technology is currently evolving as a "public key infrastructure." This process rests on a pair of codes or "keys" — inversely related mathematical algorithms. One is distributed as the public key; the other is retained by its owner as the private key. This infrastructure provides a method of achieving both identity verification and secured transmission. Identity verification is achieved when a message is encrypted with the private key, to be read with the public key: only the holder of the private key can send such a message. Secured transmission is achieved when a message is encrypted with the public key: it can then be read by only the holder of the private key.

Encryption technology alone does not provide assurance that trading partners are who they say they are and that information will be protected from unauthorized users. If I receive a message to which is attached the public key allowing me to read the message, how do I know that it was sent by the entity that purports to own the corresponding private key? When I respond with a message encrypted with the public key, how do I know that the only entity that has access to the private key is the one that I intend to read the message? The solution that is emerging on the Internet to this piece of the puzzle is the provision of identification-certification services by private firms. An online entity that wishes to be able to positively identify itself to its customers or business partners applies for a digital certificate from a third-party known as a certification authority. A recipient that wishes to confirm the identity of a sender that has obtained a certificate contacts the certification authority, essentially to ask, is this a valid certificate and did you grant it to the entity that presented it to me?

The revolution of the Internet is that these verification steps, which sound cumbersome and unfeasible in real space, are instantaneous and virtually costless in cyberspace. VeriSign is a leading provider of encryption technology and public key infrastructure. VeriSign has established the VeriSign Trust Network (VTN), a hierarchy of "certification authorities," with the root certification process performed by VeriSign. An online entity can purchase from VeriSign a package that includes the public key infrastructure technology, a digital certificate (maintained by a certification authority in the VTN on its secure server) verifying that messages encoded with a particular private key are sent by the entity to whom VeriSign (or a certification authority within the VTN) distributed that key, an audit service that monitors the entity's use of and continued security of its private key, and a "legal" authority to revoke or suspend a certificate in the event that an entity does not comply with the requirements (for truthful identification and disclosure, for maintaining security of the private key, etc.) established by VeriSign. Among other things, this structure facilitates digital signatures for electronic transactions and secures data flows within and between organizations, controlling, for example, access to company servers or transmissions. The public key infrastructure also underlies the secure server environment for online credit card or other confidential transactions.

Within an organization or between business partners, the implementation of VeriSign encryption technology and practices may be sufficient to encourage the reliance necessary to a transaction. For Internet transactions more generally, this structure can be supplemented with the VeriSign seal: a "trustmark" that the purchaser of the VeriSign product posts on its web site. Clicking on the seal takes the web site user to the certification authority's repository on its secure server, displaying the current information and status of the digital certificate for that web site. The seal signifies that the web site uses VeriSign encryption technology and is in compliance with VeriSign requirements: if not, the digital certificate is revoked, and the user will not be taken to a valid digital certificate when clicking the seal. This digital structure allows both the identity of the web site (checked by the certification authority that issued the digital certificate) and the validity of the seal to be verified at the click.

By participating in the VTN (and becoming customers of VeriSign, making use of VeriSign digital certificates and the VeriSign seal), subscribers commit themselves to VeriSign's privately provided "legal" regime: they agree to be bound by the practices and requirements set out and administered by VeriSign. VeriSign has established through its "Certificate Policies" document the standards and contractual terms that must be included in the relationships that make up the branches of the VTN. The authority of a certification authority to manage the use of the technology and certification procedures is governed by its Certification Practice Statement, which sets out the requirements and procedures for certification, ongoing auditing, certificate revocation, and dispute resolution.

B. Codes of Conduct. VeriSign's privately provided legal regime for solving the problems of online identity and secured transmission of data ultimately requires yet another commitment challenge to be met. VeriSign's system relies on its ability to assure its customers that it, in fact, follows the procedures it sets out in its Certificate Policies, Certification Practices Statement, and so forth. Participants in this regime need to trust, for example, that VeriSign is conducting regular audits of the entities it certifies to monitor the security of private keys. VeriSign acts as the root certification authority, but who oversees the integrity of the root?

In VeriSign's case the answer is, WebTrust. WebTrust is a family of seal programs administered by the American Institute of Chartered Public Accountants and the Canadian Institute of Chartered Accountants. AICPA/CICA have established procedures to license CPAs and CAs to audit the business practices of an online firm with respect to a variety of criteria. WebTrust operates a specific program for auditing certification authorities such as VeriSign; the accountant hired to provide the WebTrust services assesses the business practices and audits the compliance of the certification authority with procedures meeting the requirements of the WebTrust program. For other online entities WebTrust offers to provide "assurance" services for any of six principles for which the entity wants to submit to the requirements of the WebTrust program: "Privacy," "Security," "Availability," "Business Practices & Transaction Integrity," "Confidentiality," and "Non-Repudiation." The confidentiality principle, for example, certifies that "the entity discloses its confidentiality practices, complies with such confidentiality practices and maintains effective controls to provide reasonable assurance that access to information obtained as a result of electronic commerce and designated as confidential is restricted to authorized individuals, groups of individuals, or entities in conformity with its disclosed confidentiality practices." The business-practices-and-transaction-integrity principle certifies that "the entity discloses its business practices for electronic commerce, executes transactions in conformity with such practices, and maintains effective controls to provide reasonable assurance that electronic commerce transactions are processed completely, accurately, and in conformity with its disclosed business practices."

For each of these principles, the WebTrust program specifies criteria that must be met in order for an entity to receive certification that the principle has been satisfied. These criteria take the form of a code of practices, similar in form to what one could find in publicly provided law. For example, the criteria for the business practices and transaction integrity principle specify that:

- The entity discloses the terms and conditions by which it conducts its electronic commerce transactions,

- The employees responsible for transaction integrity are aware of and follow the entity's policies related to transaction integrity and relevant security matters,

- Accountability for the entity's policies related to transaction integrity and relevant security matters has been assigned,

- The entity uses encryption or other equivalent security procedures to protect transmissions of user authentication and verification information over the Internet, and

- Positive acknowledgment is received from the customer before the transaction is processed.

An online entity that receives an unqualified report attesting to compliance with a particular principle from the accountant providing the WebTrust service receives an enrollment identification (EID). Using the EID, the entity can then apply for certification with a seal manager (such as VeriSign) that has agreed to manage the WebTrust seal. The manager will then issue a digital certificate that links to the WebTrust seal placed on the online firm's web site. Clicking on the seal will take the user to the certificate and the accounting practitioner's report on the seal manager's secure server, and to verification that the seal is authentic and valid. Periodic audits, the frequency of which is determined by the practitioner who issued the initial unqualified report, are then conducted by the accounting professional to ensure ongoing compliance with the WebTrust principles and criteria.

The WebTrust program spans the full range of online commercial transactions, from retail business-to-consumer (B2C), sales to complex business-to-business (B2B) relationships. Other developments focused more exclusively on the B2B segment of Internet transactions include the GeoTrust and TruSecure alliance announced in January 2001. GeoTrust conducts due diligence reviews of companies to create a "True Credentials" profile with a summary of business practices, credit worthiness, and past performance. TruSecure administers a seal verifying that the company has technology and processes to maintain confidentiality of company data. As expressed by the alliance, "the combination of GeoTrust's True Credentials and TruSecure's Enterprise solution provides reliable and almost instantaneous online security and background checks on a company — a process that can take days or weeks to complete in the offline world."

Targeted programs for consumer transactions are provided by entities such as the Better Business Bureau (BBB). The BBBonline Reliability seal appears on over 15,000 Internet sites. Posting of the seal — the authenticity of which can be checked by clicking on the seal — attests that the web site operator is a member of the Better Business Bureau and has complied with the BBBonline reliability requirements (and has paid the required license fee to BBBonline). These requirements include providing company identification that can be verified by the BBB by a visit to the company's physical location, demonstrating at least one year of operation with a satisfactory complaint-handling record, and agreement to abide by BBB advertising guidelines and the BBB Code of Online Business Practices and to participate in dispute resolution that meets the standards set by the BBB. These latter requirements, in particular, give the BBBonline seal program its "legal" quality. The BBB Code of Online Business Practices, for example, consists of five general principles: "truthful and accurate communications," "disclosure," "information practices and security," "customer satisfaction," and "protecting children." These principles are then spelled out in detail with examples in the code. . . . When an online merchant seeks to display the BBBonline seal, it thus commits itself to a set of rules and standards developed by the BBB and adjudicated by them. Failure to comply results in the BBBonline seal's being disabled.

BBBonline also offers a privacy seal program. The most visible privacy seal program, however, is that offered by TRUSTe, a nonprofit corporation founded by CommerceNet (a business development network dedicated to fostering the growth of e-commerce), the Electronic Frontier Foundation, a nonprofit public interest group promoting freedom of expression on the Internet, and the Boston Consulting Group. TRUSTe seals appear on more than 1,200 web sites; clicking on the seal takes the user to the web site's privacy policy, where a "click-to-verify" seal, linked to TRUSTe's secure server, appears. To post the seal, participants must pay an annual license fee (ranging from $400 for a single-brand company with annual revenues under $500,000 to $25,000 for a multibrand company), comply with TRUSTe's privacy principles, and agree to ongoing oversight and dispute resolution through TRUSTe. The privacy principles include adoption and implementation of a privacy policy; notice and disclosure of information collection and use practices; choice and consent, giving users the opportunity to exercise control over their information; and data security, quality, and access measures to help protect the security and accuracy of personally identifiable information.

TRUSTe monitors compliance with the web site's privacy policy and the TRUSTe principles through a variety of initial and periodic reviews, seeding (whereby TRUSTe submits personal user information to a site to verify that it is following its stated privacy principles), compliance reviews by professional accounting firms, and feedback and complaints from users. Users can file "watchdog" complaints with TRUSTe. In the event of violations of the requirements of the program, TRUSTe can revoke the license to use the TRUSTe seal, launch breach of contract or trademark proceedings, and refer the violation to law enforcement (in the event, for example, of violation of the federal Children's Online Privacy Protection Act, 15 U.S.C. §§ 6501-6505). . . .

Finally, even individuals seeking to promote their participation in the relatively freewheeling world of online auctions can make use of emerging seal programs. SquareTrade offers a seal program for sellers on eBay. For a monthly fee of $7.50, sellers can submit to the review process conducted by SquareTrade — verifying their identity and contact information and checking their history of feedback on prior trades on eBay and their participation in dispute resolution. To qualify for the seal sellers must commit to SquareTrade's code of selling practices: responding to disputes filed against them, participating in a timely manner and abiding by agreements made under the Square Trade Dispute Resolution process; describing their goods and services, prices and service and shipping policies in a clear and accurate manner on their listings or web site; offering products for sale that comply with eBay's guidelines; disclosing contact information (sufficient to ensure customers can contact the seal member offline); and defining a privacy policy if they collect personally identifiable information and use the information for marketing purposes.

SquareTrade monitors selling history and investigates complaints against seal members for violation of these standards; it retains the discretion to suspend participation in the seal program if a member is found to "consistently violate these Standards and/or fail to act in a fair and ethical manner." In the event of suspension the SquareTrade seal goes blank on the eBay listing; SquareTrade's direct access to the eBay site thus serves as the mechanism proving the validity of the seal. According to SquareTrade, within less than a year of operation, the SquareTrade seal was posted on 300,000 listings a day (4% of total eBay listings); seal members receive on average 20% more bids than non-seal members on their items and enjoy sale prices that are on average 413% higher than starting prices, compared with 143% for non-seal member listings.

C. Dispute Resolution. The "legality" delivered by digital certification and seal programs is contained in the codes established by WebTrust, VeriSign, BBBonline, TRUSTe, and SquareTrade; these codes constitute in large part the "trust" services delivered by these market entities. All of these services, however, also appear to come bundled with explicit requirements establishing rules and procedures for dispute resolution, of varying degrees of differentiation and independence from the public courts. This is a further attribute identifying these services as a privately provided legal regime.

VeriSign, for example, requires that subscriber and relying-party agreements along the branches of the VTN contain dispute resolution clauses requiring an initial negotiation period of 60 days before formal legal action. If initial negotiation does not succeed, litigation is required to take place in Santa Clara County, California (the county in which VeriSign headquarters resides), in the case of claimants who are United States residents and in an arbitration administered by the International Chamber of Commerce under ICC Rules of Conciliation and Arbitration in the case of all other claimants. This represents minimal independence from the public courts.

WebTrust's business-practices-and-transaction-integrity principle requires disclosure of procedures for customer recourse for complaints that are not resolved by the entity and specifies that this resolution process should include a commitment by management to use a specified third-party dispute resolution process, together with a commitment from the third party to handle these unresolved complaints. This moves dispute resolution requirements slightly further beyond the public courts, but does not involve WebTrust in design or oversight of the dispute resolution process.

BBBonline, by way of comparison, includes dispute resolution design and oversight in its service. BBBonline requires participants in its BBBonline Reliability seal program to commit to participating in binding arbitration administered by the BBB or another dispute resolution provider that meets BBB criteria. These criteria include provision of documentation to the BBB to permit auditing of the process by BBB, case administration conducted by someone who is insulated from all parties, and costs (including travel costs) that must be reasonable in light of the amount of money in dispute.

TRUSTe also includes dispute resolution provision and oversight in its service. Participation in TRUSTe's WatchDog Dispute Resolution process is mandatory for participants in its seal program. Under this dispute resolution process a consumer may, at no cost, file a privacy-related complaint online. . . . The complaint triggers an electronic negotiation conducted by TRUSTe between the consumer and the seal program participant against which the complaint was lodged. TRUSTe determines when this mediated negotiation process has closed the case and issues a case report stating the resolution of the complaint. This resolution can require that the seal program participant correct, modify, or delete information; change its stated privacy policy or privacy practices; or commission a third-party auditing firm to review the company's practices to ensure the validity of its claims and that a working solution has been implemented.

Either party can appeal the resolution to the TRUSTe Appeal Board, which consists of a TRUSTe board of directors representative designated by its chairman, a privacy expert from the academic-university community, and a representative chosen by a consumer or privacy advocacy group designated by TRUSTe's president and chief executive officer. The TRUSTe board of directors selects the chair of the Appeal Board. Objections to Appeal Board members may be filed, and these objections are decided by the chair of the Appeal Board. Results of the Appeal Board are by majority vote; the outcome at the appeal stage is either to decide that the original resolution is satisfactory or to direct TRUSTe to reevaluate its resolution. The outcome is not binding on the consumer, in the sense of altering any rights the consumer might have to pursue legal action in the courts, but failure by the seal program participant to comply with the resolution results in revocation of the seal; it may also result in TRUSTe's suing the seal participant for breach of contract or trademark violations, or in referral to law enforcement. Reports on the outcome of the Watch-Dog Dispute Resolution process are posted on the TRUSTe web site. TRUSTe resolved an approximate average of 130 privacy-related complaints per month from October 2000 to October 2002. The vast majority of complaints were handled with no changes required in either the web site's privacy statement or its practices. The WatchDog reports indicate that there were occasions, however, on which changes in privacy statements or practices were required. On two occasions during this period audits of practices were required; one of these audits was of Microsoft's Hotmail service. Eight sites have been included in advisories, and two sites have been sued for trademark violations.

Finally, the SquareTrade product is fundamentally a dispute resolution service. SquareTrade has developed an online dispute resolution process available for any dispute, not just those arising under its eBay seal program. Participants in the eBay seal program, however, are required to participate in a professional manner and in good faith in the process in the event of a complaint against them, and they are required to implement the mediated solution. The Square-Trade process involves use of an online "direct negotiation" tool — an automated communications process — on a password-protected secure case page on the SquareTrade web site. In the event direct negotiation does not result in a solution (SquareTrade claims that 85% of cases are settled during direct negotiation), a SquareTrade mediator can be requested by either party (the requesting party pays the filing fee, currently $20 for a dispute involving an eBay auction). The mediator communicates with both parties via the case page on the SquareTrade Web site, but the parties no longer see each other's messages on the case page once a mediator becomes involved. SquareTrade's mediators are drawn from a panel of independent mediators, including a business panel of mediators with substantial expertise in commercial mediation . . . who agree to abide by the SquareTrade Standards of Practice. These standards of practice for mediators are supplemented by the commitments SquareTrade makes itself, to engage only in contractual relationships that promote and maintain mediator and arbitrator neutrality, for example, and to maintain a secure and available system. . . .

The Internet is a tremendously low-cost means of communicating and coordinating potential exchanges. For online commercial relationships to develop, however, potential trading partners need more than to find each other and have at their disposal a virtually costless means of communicating and coordinating a cooperative activity. Each needs assurance that the other entity is the one it claims to be. Each needs assurance that the other will perform its part of the arrangement. Cooperative arrangements create vulnerabilities: one party acts before the other; valuable information is shared; access and control over assets is granted. A commitment mechanism gives cooperating entities a rational basis for believing that any vulnerability they expose through cooperation will not be exploited.

In some relationships commitment comes from the social and ethical norms and practices of the community in which the relationship is embedded: altruism, benevolence, trust. Online, however, these communities are largely absent. The developments on the Internet are a direct market response to the fundamental need for commitment mechanisms as commercial relationships move beyond personal, local, or established communities in this "new world." Entrepreneurs have recognized that there is value in providing "assurance" or "trust" services, and their use of these terms is an overt recognition of the importance of commitment as an input for commercial activity. . . .

Commitment is an economic service that can be provided by reputational, technological, and organizational, as well as legal, means. The innovations in cyberspace demonstrate not only that commitment services are an input for economic transactions that can be supplied through markets; they also demonstrate that commitment services can be provided by a multitude of mechanisms. Legal rules are only one such mechanism, and they are often a component of a combined mechanism rather than the exclusive means of producing commitment. . . .

3. Andrea Braeutigam, *Fusses that Fit Online: Online Mediation in Non-Commercial Contexts,* 5 APPALACHIAN L.J. 275 (2006)

As the field of dispute resolution has grown, practitioners and disputants alike have become increasingly adept at choosing whether their matter is well suited to litigation, arbitration, mediation, or negotiation. . . . Mediation has attained status as a forum of choice for a wide variety of fusses. Then along came the Internet. The Internet has significantly impacted the field of dispute resolution. The burgeoning online marketplace opened the door for online disputes, which gave rise to a new forum for mediation. Initially, online dispute resolution (ODR) focused on dispute resolution systems for handling disputes that arose in e-commerce. Despite early criticisms of online mediation, several types of disputes traditionally handled in face-to-face mediation are handled in the text-based online world. It is now clear that ODR is no longer an experiment, nor is its use limited to disputes of online origin. . . .

All of the processes available under the alternative dispute resolution (ADR) umbrella . . . are offered online. Consequently, the growth of online dispute resolution raises important forum selection issues for mediators, lawyers, and disputants alike: Is cyberspace a good forum for this dispute? Might a disputant fare better online than off? What characteristics of the dispute and the disputants should be considered? Should a practitioner offer services online? I have chosen to focus particularly on online mediation for two reasons. First, there is resistance to it within the ADR profession due to untested assumptions about mediating without face-to-face contact, along with basic unfamiliarity with the medium. Second, raising the awareness of mediation practitioners, lawyers involved in dispute resolution, and disputants about online mediation, will help them to make more informed choices about what disputes are better suited to the online forum.

There are advantages and disadvantages to online mediation over face-to-face mediation. These considerations should be taken into account when deciding on a forum for dispute resolution. The decision depends upon the nature of the parties and the type of dispute involved. . . . Online mediation began as a forum generally reserved for commercial disputes where parties are geographically separated. However, there are attributes unique to the online forum that render it a preferred forum in non-commercial contexts. Specifically, cyberspace is superior to face-to-face mediation for parties of unequal negotiating power. . . .

ODR is an outgrowth of the broader ADR movement that we have seen in recent decades. The same search for convenient, cost-effective, efficient ways of resolving disputes that supported the growth of ADR also supported the development of ODR. Since the wide adoption of the Internet as a mode of communication in the mid-1990s, ODR began to develop as a response to conflicts generated by the new medium. The driving force behind ODR was the growth of commercial activity on the Internet. As commercial activity grew, so did disputes between commercial actors and trading partners. The move to bring ADR processes online was influenced by two factors: (1) the potential of the online medium to provide more effective ADR methods for both online and offline disputes; and (2) the difficulty of using traditional ADR methods in low-value, cross-border online disputes. Developments can be divided into three time periods:

1. Pre-1995: individual online communities used informal dispute resolution, but no organized institutions for ODR existed;

2. 1995-1998: experimental projects funded by organized institutions, universities and foundations attempted to address online disputes;

3. 1998-Present: emergence of for-profit online dispute resolution sites, with significant entrepreneurial activity and support for ODR by high level governmental and corporate bodies.

Now, ODR is entering a fourth phase of development that is characterized by increasing integration of ODR technologies in private and government ventures. Commensurate with the historical growth rooted in the search for efficient, cost-effective, and innovative ways of handling disputes, emerging trends in our time are:

1. ongoing growth in simpler contexts;

2. adoption in disputes traditionally handled offline;

3. experimentation and use in more complex disputes.

There is little doubt that ODR will continue to impact the field of dispute resolution; the future is now. Thus, practitioners and disputants should be aware of the range of ODR options. . . .

ODR has adapted traditional ADR processes for use online. At its basic level, ODR is the use of technology to assist people with the resolution of their dispute out of court. Colin Rule, a pioneer of the field, states that, "Any use of technology to complement, support, or administer a dispute resolution process falls into the world of ODR." The main ODR processes include arbitration, automated negotiation and negotiation support systems, and mediation. . . .

Online Mediation. The online mediation process mirrors many aspects of the traditional offline process. The process starts with opening statements by the mediator to all parties to explain the process. Then, the parties are invited to give their story. Interests and concerns are explored in a series of discussions and options are discussed. The mediator may address the parties jointly and in private caucus. If the mediation is successful, the parties will agree on a solution and an agreement is posted for review and acceptance.

Online mediation also offers many of the same process advantages as traditional face-to-face mediation as compared to litigation; it is an efficient, cost-effective method for resolving disputes in a manner that gives parties a say in the ultimate outcome. There are other significant advantages of the online forum related to its unmatched accessibility and the convenience it affords the parties. ODR processes, mediation or otherwise, are easy to schedule and cost-effective to convene. Parties do not need to coordinate schedules or take time from work to attend or travel to the sessions. Instead, the mediation takes place at the click of a mouse. Even when conducted synchronously, parties can access their case at any time, from different time zones, and from the comfort of their home or office. It also reduces losses due to time off from work and other responsibilities.

In addition, the online forum is especially appealing where parties are not able to meet face-to-face. If a dispute arises between people of different countries, the online forum eliminates the expense of travel. Of greater significance is that it brings a possibility for redress to those who would not otherwise seek it. In e-commerce, for example, jurisdictional issues may make it impossible to pursue a claim, and the low-dollar value of most claims makes it financially infeasible to do so. Thus, in many ways, ODR processes are the only processes that can successfully bridge the distance between parties.

The basics of the technological platforms commonly used are as follows: Online mediation is conducted on the Internet via digital communication. Early sites tended to rely mainly on email to exchange messages, while current platforms use threaded discussion technology, or "bulletin boards," that archive the messages on a secure page. This allows parties and the mediator to access one site in order to send, receive, and read messages. Some platforms are set so that parties cannot see each other's messages to the mediator, and they cannot "cross talk" between themselves. Other platforms enable the mediator to edit or delete party postings from a universally viewable posting space. Secure Discussion™ is a new program that may prove to be particularly useful to the private practitioner. It provides secure message space, caucusing, calendaring, and case management options that the user can customize and replicate. It is possible to conduct the session in real time using chat technology. However, in most online mediation platforms, the communication is asynchronous, which means there is a time delay. While this has advantages that are discussed in greater detail below, the asynchronous format means that mediators and parties must be prepared to work at maintaining consistent contact.

In addition, the fact that the communications take place over the Internet creates an opportunity for increased efficiency and greater trust when mediators use private meetings, or caucuses, with the parties. Caucusing is a basic feature of many offline mediation processes that is particularly effective in the online forum. The online mediator can caucus with participants concurrently, throughout the process, and without the other's knowledge of when it is happening. Offline caucuses interrupt the flow of discussions and create delays while the mediator meets with each side. This can give rise to frustration or suspicion as participants wait and wonder what is being discussed with the other side. These problems are eliminated in online asynchronous mediations, since the online mediator can strategically and seamlessly use caucuses to get a better under-standing of issues and concerns without disrupting the process or frustrating the waiting party. Thus, online caucusing is superior to offline caucusing.

The most significant differences between online and traditional mediation is that online communication is textual and the participants are not in the phys-ical presence of one another. Some services supplement the textual communi-cations with videoconferencing; however, there are bandwidth issues for broadcast-quality videoconferencing that affect its utility. Consequently, online mediators and participants cannot rely on the non-verbal cues of body lan-guage and facial expressions, nor the verbal intonations that supply important cues in face-to-face mediation. Further, text is often interpreted differently than words spoken in the shared context of face-to-face communication. For example, a calming remark might come across as patronizing when typed or a joke might turn into an insult because the reader did not catch the intentionally sarcastic tone. Without tone of voice, it can be difficult to capture and convey the emotional content of words. For example, it may be difficult for the partici-pants to catch a sincere and empathetic remark, or they may not feel the medi-ator has understood the degree of anger and frustration they are experiencing.

Friendly banter, a common technique used to establish and build rapport, may also be rare in the online environment, and many communicators tend towards a businesslike tone. Consequently, even a friendly, gregarious person can come across in text as cold or callous. There is no doubt that these are significant dif-ferences; one cannot fully replicate the dynamics of synchronous face-to-face interaction online. The key issue is how these differences affect the mediation process. Nonetheless, online mediation has some obvious convenience-related advantages: the parties and the mediator do not have to be in the same location, city, or time-zone; the mediation can occur outside of traditional business hours; and the parties can participate from their own home or office.

IV. Unique Attributes of the Online Forum

The online forum has several obvious advantages: speed, twenty-four hour access, ability to handle and process data, and ability to span the globe. There are, however, a number of unique features of the online environment attribut-able to the nature of online communication itself. . . . Potential users should con-sider these advantages when choosing among dispute resolution forums: the online forum promotes clearer, more focused communication; is less hostile; and enables disputants to express anger, or "vent," without impacting the progress of the mediation. Further, the online forum may actually resolve power imbalances and provide a better forum for disputants who are at a disadvantage in a traditional face-to-face mediation due to race, gender, ethnicity, socio-eco-nomic factors, and differences in negotiating behaviors. Consider the following attributes:

A. Freedom from Body Language. One advantage of mediating in the online forum is the freedom from the effects of body language. Body language can be misinterpreted, or worse, can be negative. If, for example, a person has crossed arms, they may be perceived as angry, closed off, or simply cold. When a party perceives negative behavior, whether or not it is a misinterpretation, they tend to focus on negative content and will react to it, increasing the likelihood of retaliatory behavior and impasse. Hostile behaviors like yelling, using threatening gestures, or otherwise signaling harm or ill-intent can escalate conflict to the point of impasse or cause the complete withdrawal by one or both parties. In a text-based environment, it is impossible for people to observe negative behavior or to misinterpret each other on the basis of non-verbal cues. When the distractions of non-verbal cues are eliminated, parties are better able to focus on the substantive issues, rather than the negative emotional content conveyed by the visual or auditory cues that are present in face-to-face encounters. By filtering out communication cues, the online forum actually assists parties in focusing on the issues, and fosters a less-confrontational engagement. The effect of freedom from body language and other linguistic cues when communicating online suggests that the online forum is a good fit where parties are known to one another and have a history of negative verbal or non-verbal behavior patterns.

B. Distance. Distance is another advantage to mediating online. The online disputing environment is less hostile for the disputant who finds face-to-face confrontation unsettling. Conflict can make people uncomfortable and nervous, especially when faced with the prospect of engaging with someone face-to-face. These participants tend to be conflict-avoidant and are, therefore, in a disadvantageous position when negotiating towards agreement: they may make concessions or wholly give in to the demands of the more assertive (or aggressive) participant simply to end the mediation as soon as possible. Parties who are anxious about face-to-face confrontation are more likely to be at ease when physically separated, and therefore able to more fully engage in the search for mutually acceptable solutions, rather than avoid the conflict or fall into the pattern of concession.

Similarly, the experience of being online, i.e., being out of sight, but connected at the same time, is disinhibiting for people. People will adapt their personalities and take on behaviors they otherwise would not face-to-face. For example, individuals who are shy, reserved, or nervous in social interactions become assertive and straightforward online. Many disputants will project their "best self." Empowered, disputants negotiate from a position of strength and communicate more directly. In disputes between higher status and lower status individuals, the lower status individual is at a disadvantage. A common dynamic in small groups is that persons of lesser status, a worker, for example, will show deference to those of higher status, such as an executive. As a result, such individuals end up dominating discussions. There is a tendency on the part of the lower-status person to make concessions that are in line with the thinking of the dominant group. This clearly works to the disadvantage regarding equitable settlement of the issues to be decided in an ADR session. Online, however, the dynamics of power shift because the lower status individual, an employee, for example, will tend to adopt a more assertive persona and therefore will be less deferential. Thus, the disinhibiting factor of online communication compensates for the power differences that are inherent in hierarchical relationships.

As with the freedom from body language, the effects of physical separation suggest that the online forum is a good fit where disputants are uncomfortable or unwilling to meet face-to-face. It is a good fit for those who tend to be conflict-avoidant because the environment is less confrontational and they can participate without undermining their bargaining position. Lower status disputants are less inhibited, and even empowered; they act assertively, without passively buying-in to the thinking of the dominant group, thereby mitigating the effects of power imbalances. Therefore, it is a good fit where parties are of unequal status.

C. Asynchronous, Textual Communication. The asynchronous, textual nature of online communication impacts the dynamics of mediation as well. Synchronous interactions can easily escalate a conflict because a person's first response might not be his best or most reasonable. It is not uncommon for disputants to be sarcastic, angry, or insulting in heated moments. Conversely, the asynchronous nature of ODR creates "cooling distance," which is essentially a built-in cooling-off period. Asynchrony allows disputants to take time for reflection before responding. Consequently, disputants can craft stronger responses and process emotional concerns before responding, or can process those concerns with the mediator without risking making a statement to the other party that may derail the process. As a result, the communication is more focused and less likely to be inflammatory. Even where emotions run high, potentially damaging statements may never be made because disputants have taken the time to reflect on the situation before responding. Of course, the time lag does not prevent parties from being emotional or insulting in online communication, but it does give them the time to make considered contributions instead.

Asynchrony benefits the neutral as well. The temporal distance provides them time to reflect upon the parties' needs and how best to assist them. Online neutrals have more time to craft thoughtful responses, put any biases in check, or process their own emotional responses. With a clear head and direction in mind, the mediator is better able to promote understanding between the parties. Asynchronous communication and textual communication are complementary. Evidence shows that typing and the resulting time lag causes disputants to focus their attention on the content of their communications. Responses are more direct and understandable, and therefore less likely to be misinterpreted. This helps lessen the emotional stress of conflict resolution.

Further, asynchronous, textual communication actually improves communication dynamics between the parties. One of the challenges that mediators face is keeping parties from interrupting one another. Part of a mediator's job, after all, is helping disputants listen to and hear what the other person is saying. Disputants often develop frustrating and destructive communication patterns, like interrupting one another and "tuning out" to what the other person is saying. So, mediators work to change the pattern or minimize the damage using a variety of techniques, like reminding parties of ground rules. Online, however, disputants end up interacting in entirely different ways and will adopt new patterns of communicating. This is due at least in part to the nature of asynchronous, textual communication. First, it is impossible to interrupt some-one online. Second, people tend to take greater care and pay more attention to the content of written messages. Online communication is not conducive to "tuning out." Rather, disputants are actively, mutually involved in getting their messages across by typing, reading, and reviewing them. They must focus on their thoughts and refine them in order to communicate them clearly in writing. Research shows that "two-thirds of email users take about the same care com-posing email as they do with memos and letters." Thus, the online environ-ment is conducive to changing and thereby improving communication patterns because interruptions and inattentiveness are not readily accomplished online.

To reiterate, asynchronous, textual communication buys parties time to reflect and cool down. Communication is clearer, and counterproductive hostility is minimized. The online environment fosters new patterns of interaction and increases understanding between people in conflict. Therefore, the online envi-ronment is generally an appropriate forum for mediation. Online mediation is a good fit for disputes where communication is frustrated by the tendency to interrupt, and for disputes that are emotionally charged.

D. Anonymity. The online forum blinds us to one another's age, social status, gender, and race. Without these cues, we are free of preconceived notions about one another: we are anonymous. This unique feature of the online environ-ment benefits disputants who are traditionally disadvantaged in mediation due to socio-economic factors. In the non-commercial context, the parties have usually seen each other at some point in their relationship. But, where the mediator has never met the parties, the mediator will not know their identity. This is an important feature of online mediation because it counteracts the possibility of mediator bias. The concept of mediator bias rises out of studies in traditional mediation that found that women and minorities experience less unfavorable outcomes in mediation because mediators are negatively influ-enced by the race and gender of the parties. Race and gender were believed to influence the conduct of the parties themselves, and also the conduct of medi-ators. This bias, they theorized, lead to consistently less favorable outcomes for minorities. The anonymity of Cyberspace by its nature limits the information given to a mediator about a disputant's ethnicity or gender. This characteristic of online mediation may reduce disadvantaging of minorities, women, and oth-ers, by excluding information about race or gender. Therefore, disadvantaged disputants may experience more favorable outcomes online than those that may be achieved in a face-to-face mediation environment.

These principles apply where parties are not known to one another. In today's world, we have seen the growth of multinational organizations, virtual work-places, and online consumer transactions. Government agencies provide serv-ices to people whom they may never have had contact with, in licensing, permits, and benefits, for instance. Insurance companies may be involved with their customers regarding property settlement claims without ever having met. So, disputes certainly exist in these environments, between people who have never met and who are therefore anonymous to one another. Online mediation can pro-vide protection from socio-economic disadvantage in these matters as well. Thus, anonymity is an advantage of the online forum that suggests online mediation is a good fit for parties who are disadvantaged on the basis of socio-economic factors.

4. Anita Ramasastry, *Government-to-Citizen Online Dispute Resolution: A Preliminary Inquiry,* 79 WASH. L. REV. 159 (2004)

This Article . . . suggests that a new and innovative use for ODR may be for public sector dispute resolution — between governments and citizens. The use of technology for public dispute resolution may promote access to justice in the administrative context. ODR is simply about the use of new information management and communication tools for dispute resolution It is essentially an offspring of ADR; ODR deploys information technology and distance communication in the context of traditional ADR processes. Like ADR, it can provide some of the same potential advantages over litigation: greater efficiency, greater party control, and lower costs. In fact, the introduction of online technology appears to increase these advantages of ADR over litigation in terms of cost, efficiency, and convenience.

Remote disputing parties can use ODR to "meet" one another online and use a web portal, e-mail, or other forms of interactive communication (e.g., web conferencing) to resolve their disputes without having to go to court and choose a forum that may be geographically inconvenient for one or both parties. Third-party neutrals (often referred to as ODR Providers) may or may not be involved in an ODR process. In other words, parties may resolve their disputes independent of a third-party mediator or arbitrator, or may choose to have a neutral party facilitate the proceedings. ODR has been portrayed as particularly convenient and efficient where the parties are geographically distant because it obviates the need for traveling. In principle, ODR can be used both for disputes arising from online interactions or transactions and for disputes arising offline. . . . The presumption that ODR is convenient and efficient pertains especially to disputes over transactions that are of the "high-volume, low-cost" type. . . .

III. THE PROMISE OF ODR: PUBLIC SECTOR DISPUTE RESOLUTION

Could technology-assisted dispute resolution be useful in other contexts, outside of the e-commerce arena? The answer is yes — with respect to resolving government-to-citizen (G2C) disputes. To date, there has been little focus on the promise of ODR in the public sector. Many reasons for the lack of ODR deployment in the private sector may be eliminated when ODR is deployed in the public sector. When ODR is employed as a public good rather than as a private commodity, the economics of running a successful business become less of a concern. The government could assess the cost of deploying technology in order to offer dispute resolution mechanisms for its citizens and decide whether to offer such a service in light of competing priorities within the justice system.

What would make ODR attractive to government entities? At present, it may be premature to advocate full-blown court-based adjudication that is conducted solely in cyberspace. Although there have been some moves to create online courts (at least in the civil context), there are much greater considerations at stake with respect to transferring litigation proceedings, which involve complex issues relating to documentary evidence, witnesses, and the role of counsel, for example, into the online context.

Where might ODR play a role in government-based adjudication? At present, a starting point might be situations in which the government is already engaged in high-volume administrative proceedings that are currently adjudicated remotely. If the state has already provided a mechanism for citizens to appeal or contest government actions remotely, by mail for example, it may streamline the process by offering similar functionality with the assistance of technology.

Citizens routinely have administrative appeals and other types of disputes with government entities at the local, municipal, state, and federal levels. Disputes arise in multiple contexts. For example, citizens appeal parking tickets or participate in mitigation hearings for such citations, as well as for tax assessments, zoning permits, etc. In many instances, governments have an administrative system in place to deal with citizen appeals and to adjudicate them either by mail or in a person-to-person context. Citizens can, for example, often appeal the issuance of a parking ticket or a moving violation in a court or administrative hearing. Alternatively, they can often choose to have a hearing by mail. By expanding the methods by which citizens can have claims involving the government adjudicated through the use of ODR, one may ultimately expand access to justice by creating greater opportunities for citizens to interact with the state and to have their grievances resolved in a timely fashion. Similarly, this may allow for the state to deal with a larger number of cases because technology can be deployed to speed up a traditionally paper-based process.

Another instance where ODR may be useful is for citizens who have problems arising from online transactions that they conduct with government entities. Many government services, such as renewing car licenses, requesting vital records, and paying taxes, are available online. Errors are bound to arise with such transactions. An online or "electronic" ombudsman could serve as an intermediary for resolving problems that arise with G2C electronic transactions.

Have governments deployed ODR for public sector dispute resolution? To date, the general answer appears to be no. In the United States, the Internal Revenue Service recently announced that it would launch a new service to resolve tax disputes online. If this occurs, it would be the first such federal government initiative in the United States. At the municipal level, New York City offers "Parking Violation Hearings by Web" as a counterpart to its hearings by mail program for parking infractions. In developing or transition economies, governments are exploring the use of ODR for public dispute resolution. In Hungary, for example, the federal telecommunications ministry may engage in an ODR pilot program to resolve consumer complaints with respect to telecommunications service providers.

The European Union is also exploring ways to facilitate public sector dispute resolution. The Information Society Directorate within the European Commission is exploring the potential use of ODR in the e-government sector for disputes that arise relating to data protection, copyright infringements, and domain name. It has established a European Extra-Judicial Network (EEJ-NET) that links together many dispute resolution services offered by member states within the European Union. European countries have a tradition of publicly-funded and privately-operated ombudsman and other ADR providers who resolve consumer disputes with businesses in the private sector. Many of these existing offline dispute resolution services are beginning to consider offering ODR components. EEJ-NET, as a government clearinghouse, could help to facilitate consumers' ability to access ODR services. The European Union has also funded a pilot program for private sector dispute resolution known as ECODIR (Electronic Consumer Dispute Resolution). ECODIR, which is currently offered free of charge, allows businesses and consumers to use this ODR service to resolve e-commerce disputes. While this is not G2C ODR, it provides a model for government-subsidized and implemented ODR. . . .

IV. G2C ODR AND ACCESS TO JUSTICE CONSIDERATIONS

One of the main focuses when looking at access to justice and technology is to examine the types of commitments that a government should make when it deploys technology as part of the legal system. If deployed with proper safeguards, ODR does facilitate access to justice. How would one ensure due process within the context of G2C ODR? First, such ODR would be regulated — not unregulated. Thus, just as current hearings by mail are regulated through statutes and rules, ODR would be likewise regulated. Additionally, to the extent that administrative procedures are similar to state or federal administrative procedure laws, there would be additional safeguards in place with respect to a citizen's right to be heard.

In addition, in devising new public sector ODR, one could adapt principles that have been developed in the private sector ODR context and apply them to the public sector process. There are a series of guidelines and principles for B2C ODR that government bodies, nongovernmental organizations, and industry have developed as a way of articulating best practices for private ODR. In many senses, these principles are meant to embody principles of access to justice, fairness, and due process that replicate principles derived from the traditional legal system. Thus, they embody principles that are highly relevant for public sector ODR. Some of the principles that appear in statements of ODR best practices include: Transparency; Independence; Impartiality; Effectiveness; Fairness and Integrity; Accessibility; Flexibility; and Affordability. For these principles, one could substitute "government" for "business" to achieve a similar list of principles for G2C ODR. Given the "legal" and possibly binding nature of G2C ODR, self-regulatory principles or best practices would not be enough. One would still need formal rules and procedures.

In a broader sense, G2C ODR would involve public magistrates or officials, it has the potential to instill greater confidence and trust in the proceedings than ODR in the private sector, where the problem of unilateral fees being paid by the industry creates perceptions of bias or partiality in the process. To the extent that citizens feel confident in remote adjudicatory processes to date, ODR may enhance trust and confidence by allowing citizens to interact more directly with the adjudicator and the state — using e-mail or online real time communication.

Of course, the concept of ODR raises other concerns that must be considered. First, not everyone will have the means to access technology to engage in ODR processes in the administrative context. Creative use of public sector kiosks and terminals, perhaps even in government buildings or courthouses, might ensure greater access to ODR than would be feasible if individuals were required to deploy their own technology as a precursor to benefitting from ODR. Second, as with private sector ODR, issues of computer literacy, culture, language, and other factors will certainly come into play with respect to ODR in the public sector. This suggests at least initially that ODR cannot supplant in-person hearings or remote hearings by mail; ODR becomes an alternative or supplement rather than an end in itself. . . .

C. DISPUTE RESOLUTION IN A TECHNOLOGY-MEDIATED ENVIRONMENT

1. Comments and Questions

a. The materials in this section shift the emphasis from what is being done (substance) to how it is being done (procedure). As ever, the line between the two is neither consistent nor bright. David Larson tells us about how the disputants of tomorrow are using communications technology today, which will determine their style of communication in disputes and disputing. Your authors, who did not use computers or cell phones as children, are painfully aware that they probably need the wisdom offered by Professor Larson more than do our readers.

b. Lodder and Zeleznikow offer a theoretical model of negotiation that allows parties to negotiate in an optimal manner without the assistance of a third party. As with game theory, very abstract and mathematical models can teach us much about bargaining behavior. By contrast, Janice Nadler addresses down-to-earth issues like the impact of small talk on improving ODR. Much of what we learned about "conventional" dispute resolution is useful in thinking about ODR.

c. What's new? Use your modern technology skills to find out.

2. David Allen Larson, *Technology Mediated Dispute Resolution (TMDR): A New Paradigm for ADR*, 21 OHIO ST. J. ON DISP. RESOL. 629, (2006)

One cannot say that dispute resolution practitioners and academics are ignoring technology. Attention tends to focus, however, on two questions. First, how can one use technology to enhance existing dispute resolution processes? And second, how can an environment of trust be established in cyberspace so that "we," meaning adults, will feel comfortable transacting business and resolving disputes online? But those questions may not be the critical ones for the near future. The children who soon will become adults will want dispute resolution processes that take advantage of the technologies they already have mastered. They will approach the interplay of dispute resolution and technology in reverse, at least as compared to current dispute resolvers. The next generation will not be asking how technology can enhance existing dispute resolution practices and models. Because they will be comfortable using technology to communicate, they instead will want to know what dispute resolution processes they can use in the virtual spaces where they live. They will be searching for dispute resolution processes to complement their technology, not technology to complement their dispute resolution models and practices. . . .

II. Mediated Communication

The term "computer mediated communication" (CMC) often is used to describe online communications. It may be more appropriate, however, to use a new terminology and frame the discussion in terms of technology mediated communication (TMC). Wireless cellular telephones and satellite support systems now supplement Internet communications with audio, text, and video capabilities. Individuals can be connected to the world essentially everywhere and anytime.

But much still can be learned by examining CMC in isolation because, at least until recently, CMC offered a relatively pure opportunity for studying language and communication. Researchers observed that individuals who use e-mail, instant messaging, chat rooms, and bulletin boards relied almost completely on language and did not introduce physical appearance, vocal pitch, body orientation, and other cues that exist in other types of communication. With the introduction of more sophisticated graphics, avatars, and the improving ability to send one's image along with one's voice, however, many of those cues can be reintroduced through technology mediated communication. Yet we should not ignore the possibility that there may be something uniquely valuable about text-based communications. The fact that computer-integrated video cameras . . . are not being widely adopted, suggests that the anonymous and asynchronous capabilities of text-only messaging are important for certain types of communication.

Research examining computer mediated communication has emphasized either the capacity to perform certain tasks (the "task-oriented model") or the ability to communicate emotions (the "social-emotional-oriented model"). . . . Social Presence, Media Richness, and Social Context Cues theories, on the one hand, take the view that because computer mediated communication lacks the nonverbal clues available in face-to-face meetings; CMC is best suited to performing discrete tasks. This viewpoint is commonly referred to as "cues filtered out." The social-emotional-oriented model asserts that individuals can establish social identities, create relationships, and maintain relationships through online communications. Because communicators have undeniable needs for affinity and uncertainty reduction, they will adapt technology mediated communication to satisfy those needs. . . . This article incorporates research conclusions from . . . both models.

Many alternative dispute resolution academicians and practitioners accept that ADR practice already is becoming a hybrid of offline and online activities.

It is doubtful, however, whether many believe that virtual spaces may become the primary venue for dispute resolution or whether many recognize how quickly this change may occur. Regardless of what you and I think about the optimum environment for dispute resolution, our children will resolve disputes relying heavily on technology. The next generation will demand dispute resolution processes designed specifically not only for the online environment, but also for the wireless environment. . . .

V. Technology Mediated Communication Can Create Intimacy and Maintain Relationships

It may seem impossible to resolve at least some types of disputes using technology. For instance, how can one ever find the high level of trust necessary to reveal his or her most intimate interests and vulnerabilities? How can we trust someone when we cannot scrutinize his or her face, when we cannot search for the slightest flinch and cannot see whether another's eyes are averted?

As surprising as it may seem, it is possible to create a trustworthy environment through technology mediated communication. Consider e-mail: e-mail messages can be saved and forwarded, for example. If one is inclined towards prevarication, then he or she should be reminded that messages can be saved and forwarded to the sender's friends, families, colleagues and employer. College students' conversations conducted by telephone, face-to-face, and by e-mail/Instant Messaging reveal that the students lied most frequently during telephone conversations, which are synchronous, do not leave a record, and occur when the parties are not in the same place. Face-to-face conversations, which also are synchronous, recordless, and do engage the parties in the same location, produced the second most lies. E-mail, which is asynchronous, does create a record, and does not place the parties in the same location, resulted in the least deception. Although the Social Distance Hypothesis asserts that deceivers will use less-rich media when lying because that medium reduces discomfort, there is some evidence to the contrary. If the objective is to reduce deception during interactions, then perhaps one should actually seek an asynchronous and recordable communication medium.

Researchers have questioned whether information technology allows users to offer signs of availability and affection that are necessary to affective relationships. But developments like buddy lists and away messaging illustrate that technology is being used to indicate availability and attention. Technological accessibility literally may change what it means to be close to another person. A study was undertaken to determine the degree to which online communications can reveal emotions instructed participants to express greater or less affinity in both face-to-face and synchronous online chats. The goal was to compare the level of affect achieved online and offline as well as the specific behaviors responsible. In the introduction to the study, two dominant schools of thought are identified. One viewpoint argues that online communications are less social, relational, understandable, and ultimately effective because nonverbal vocal and physical cues are lacking. The other position maintains that individuals adapt to different mediums and can glean information about another person by inserting and interpreting stylistic and contextual cues.

A "cues filtered out" approach concludes that because nonverbal cues that transmit relational information, such as voice quality, vocal inflections, facial expressions, physical appearance, and physical movements, are not available in CMC. CMC users are limited in their ability to exchange impressions and emotions. But research supports the view that individuals can adapt to environments that do not provide nonverbal cues, which the 2005 study identified above presents as social information processing theory (SIP). SIP rejects the view that CMC is inherently impersonal and instead argues that the verbal characteristics of CMC can be used to convey relational information that otherwise would be communicated through nonverbal cues.

One particular cue that has attracted attention is "immediacy." Immediacy is defined as a combination of involvement, affection and warmth: the emotional expression of one individual towards another. Nonverbal cues such as proximity, smiling, eye contact, body orientation, and postural lean have been studied as to their relation to immediacy. Equilibrium theory suggests that communicators dynamically adjust these behaviors and that one person's action will prompt a response to maintain, increase, or decrease the intimacy level. Early research about teleconferencing suggested that language can compensate for missing nonverbal cues, observing that statements like "I agree" can be substituted for the nod of one's head. . . .

Researchers readily acknowledge that measurement is difficult. For instance, when one describes a sibling to a friend, any measure of verbal immediacy may reflect feelings about the sibling rather than feelings about the friend. In contrast, nonverbal immediacy expressed through actions such as touching and posture is more indicative of the speaker's feelings toward the person with whom he or she is speaking.

Strategies for validating and invalidating one's sense of worth were identified. In total, the study codes 125 separate variables for the expression of affinity. The results indicate that the amount of subjectively experienced affinity, measured in terms of immediacy and affectionate communication, does not vary significantly depending upon whether communication is CMC or face-to- face. On the specific subject of affinity, the study concludes that affinity issues may be translatable among cue systems. Whether communication is by phone, text, or face-to-face is not determinative. Even minimally motivated individuals can effectively adapt their affective intentions into text. This conclusion is not universally accepted. But the declaration is a powerful one. If individuals can effectively communicate their emotions through different mediums, then this opens up tremendous opportunities for technology mediated dispute resolution

One must always be cognizant of potential problems, however. Society is moving from spatially proximate to more dispersed and less tightly knit communities. Although technology mediated communication can assist in bridging those distances, there are dangers. The speed at which individuals can interact, combined with an ignorance of, or unwillingness to acknowledge, the cues that are available may lead to regrettable messages being exchanged.

Yet one still can make a strong case that interpersonal relationships can be created through text that are as intimate and trusting as those created face-to-face. Relying on the nonverbal cues that are available online, certain individuals may feel more secure and confident communicating through text. Some people may feel more comfortable relying on typographic and chronemic cues, for example, as well as content and linguistic strategies. Intimacy can be achieved on the Internet. Online communications may, in fact, be more intimate than offline exchanges. Computer-mediated communications can even be "hyperpersonal." Even though impressions may not be as wide reaching, those impressions may be particularly intense.

One way intimacy can be achieved online is through the use of uncertainty reduction strategies. If one asks direct questions and volunteers information (which encourages reciprocal disclosures) more frequently than would be typical in a face-to-face conversation, then an online conversation may become very personal and revealing. The visual anonymity that exists online and the feeling that individuals are communicating in a protected, private space (which may or may not be warranted), can lead to disclosures that exceed those that would occur in a face-to-face meeting.

Instant Messaging, e-mail, and other telecommunication strategies are increasingly being utilized to maintain relationships over significant distances. For instance, when a student graduates from high school and leaves home to study at college, it is not unusual for the friendships formed in high school to weaken and perhaps even end. . . . According to a recent study that followed one thousand high school students accepted to Carnegie Mellon University in 2000 and 2001, telephones, e-mail and instant messaging can help to maintain relationships when students leave their homes to attend college. These communication technologies, however, are not equally effective. . . .

E-mailing and instant messaging slowed the predictable decline in closeness between friends, even when face-to-face and telephone communications did not. Contrary to expectations, the relative media richness and sense of physical presence that telephone communications can provide did not result in telephone conversations being the most effective way to preserve relationships. Why are e-mail and instant messaging more effective at preserving relationships than telephone communications? One possibility is that it costs much less to connect with far away friends via e-mail and instant messaging than by using the telephone. A comparatively low cost communication medium can be used frequently without hesitation. In fact, the researchers cited above conclude that the key to preserving relationships is not the ability to create a sense of closeness with any communication, but instead the key is the frequency of the communication. In other words, communication frequency, rather than quality, preserves relationships. . . .

Dispute resolvers must consider not only how our children are relying on technology mediated communication to interact and resolve disputes, but also how other cultures are using that technology. Regardless of the nature or size of a dispute, parties may be located anywhere on the planet. Those parties may expect dispute resolvers to understand how, and perhaps why, the parties rely upon technology mediated communication. . . . We are moving from a "command and control" model to a "collaborate and connect" model. We can source any product or any service from anywhere on the planet. Dispute resolvers and problem solvers need to understand and use the same technology that is making trade and communication increasingly global. One reason we need to develop our technology mediated communication skills is that if we do not, someone else in the world who already is comfortable with communication technology can step in and take our place in any virtual space. . . .

For some individuals, the Internet is not the most suitable venue for initiating problem solving or a simple conversation. Yet even for those individuals, the Internet still may offer the best "space" for continuing and building upon the momentum created through an initial face-to-face meeting. If nothing else, the ability to communicate quickly, easily, and asynchronously means that communication channels can remain open. And for some individuals, the online environment provides the sense of distance and protection they need for an intimate conversation. Quite simply, the Internet may provide a more productive environment for continuing a conversation than a series of face-to-face meetings would provide.

Dispute resolvers understand that it is essential to recognize cultural differences. One of the great challenges is to identify and respect those differences and to create an accommodating environment. Although e-mail messaging can utilize verbal cues and appropriate language choice is a critical consideration, body language and appearance are not at issue. E-mail and short text messaging can make it easier to communicate cross-culturally, keeping in mind that presentation, tone, and word choice still have cultural significance. . . .

3. Arno R. Lodder & John Zeleznikow, *Developing am Online Dispute Resolution Environment: Dialogue Tools and Negotiation Support Systems in a Three-Step Model*, 10 HARV. NEGOT. L. REV. 287 (2005)

ADR has moved dispute resolution away from litigation and the courts. Online dispute resolution extends this trend even further. While ADR represents a move from a fixed and formal process to a more flexible one, ODR — by designating cyberspace as a location for dispute resolution — extends this process even further by moving ADR from a physical to a virtual place. . . . While, originally, ADR took the resolution of disputes outside of the courtroom, the Internet has brought ADR directly to each individual's personal computer. . . . Before outlining our proposal for an integrated ODR environment, it is helpful to give some examples of existing ODR services. We will . . . limit ourselves to describing a few relevant ODR sites.

Many of the existing ODR tools have been developed primarily to resolve e-commerce disputes or other Internet-related issues. The major reasons for the popularity of handling e-commerce or Internet-related disputes online are that 1) access to the Internet is not a problem because the parties concerned already had online contact before the dispute arose, and 2) the information crucial to their dispute will usually be available electronically.

One very popular, and probably the most successful, ODR site to date is SquareTrade, which primarily handles conflicts between traders of the online auction site eBay. By 2004, SquareTrade had already dealt with over one million disputes. SmartSettle, an ODR system that assists parties in overcoming the challenges of conventional negotiation through a range of analytical tools, is designed to clarify interests, identify trade-offs, recognize party satisfaction, and generate optimal solutions. The aim is to better prepare parties for negotiation and support them during the negotiation process.

Under the auspices of the Internet Corporation for Assigned Names and Numbers (ICANN), the Uniform Domain-Name Dispute Resolution Policy (UDRP) was developed as an online procedure to fight domain-name grabbers. An online dispute resolution procedure is offered by several providers appointed by the ICANN, including the World Intellectual Property Organization's (WIPO) Arbitration and Mediation Center, which has handled more than six thousand domain-name disputes over the past five years.

The European Union-funded Electronic Consumer Dispute Resolution (ECODIR) project provides a mechanism similar to SquareTrade where many types of consumer disputes can be filed. In early 2004, a new European Union initiative, CCform, was launched. CCform facilitates the online resolution of standard consumer complaints in all of the official languages of the European Union. These EU-funded projects have not been very successful in attracting consumers and businesses to their services, however. A complicating factor that underlies these EU projects is the difficulty of presenting information in all of the official EU languages. This need for translation probably also has contributed to the lack of success of the European Extra-Judicial Network for cross-border dispute resolution (EEJ-NET), an ADR/ODR general clearing house, and its financial counterpart FIN-NET, which deals with financial disputes.

Although ODR sites have primarily been used for Internet-related disputes, ODR can also facilitate resolution of disputes that have not originated online. For instance, many blind-bidding sites that exist can be used to solve financial disputes, such as insurance claims, that are not necessarily related to e-commerce. There is no reason why offline disputes could not be resolved online. In addition, if we consider the ease with which the younger generation uses online tools, we expect that in the next decade ODR will become a central method of dispute resolution.

II. Essentials of Our Online Dispute Resolution Environment

A. Assumptions

Our ODR environment should be envisioned as a virtual space in which disputants have a variety of dispute resolution tools at their disposal. Participants can select any tool they consider appropriate for the resolution of their conflict and use the tools in any order or manner they desire, or they can be guided through the process. Our proposed three-step model is based on a fixed order.

1. The Three Steps. In considering the principles and theory underlying our integrated ODR environment, we first evaluated the order in which online disputes are best resolved. The system that we propose conforms to the following sequencing, which in our opinion produces the most effective ODR environment:

1) The negotiation support tool should provide feedback on the likely outcome(s) of the dispute if the negotiation were to fail - i.e., the BATNA.

2) The tool should attempt to resolve any existing conflicts using dialogue techniques.

3) For those issues not resolved in step two, the tool should employ compensation/trade-off strategies in order to facilitate resolution of the dispute.

4) If the result from step three is not acceptable to the parties, the tool should allow the parties to return to step two and repeat the process recursively until either the dispute is resolved or a stalemate occurs.

2. Information Technology and Communication. E-mediation, and ODR more generally, may denote three different concepts: 1) mediation/ODR conducted exclusively online (in cyberspace), or 2) mediation/ODR of e-commerce or technology disputes, or 3) mediation with the use of electronic media, such as video conferencing and e-mail.

We are interested in dispute resolution performed entirely online, whereby, in principle, all information is exchanged electronically. We realize that for purposes of proof, however, some procedures may require confirmation in paper format. Our ODR application does not require any paper-based exchange of information, except where information is not available in an electronic format and cannot be reproduced electronically by scanning or other means. A dispute regarding a purchased item that is not delivered or was damaged on arrival is an example where not all information is available electronically. That said, in the latter case electronic evidence, such as a digital picture of the damaged product, might still be of help.

Various means can be used for information exchange, including e-mail, SMS messaging, web-based forms, and special dispute environments created for the very purpose of ODR. We aim to create the last, an environment specifically designed for ODR. The exchange of information in an ODR environment can be real-time or asynchronous. Our environment supports both types of exchange, leaving it up to the parties to decide whether they desire to be online simultaneously.

Many commentators argue that the most important aspect of ADR is face-to-face communication. There are many circumstances, however, where face-to-face communication is either not feasible or undesirable. Examples include, but are not limited to: Parties who have a history of violent conflict; Parties for whom the costs of being in the same room are exorbitant; Parties who are in different time zones; or Parties who cannot agree upon a joint meeting time.

ODR's lack of in-person interaction can actually be an advantage for disputes in which the emotional involvement of the parties is so high that it is preferable that they do not see each other. In addition to providing potential logistical and emotional benefits, ODR also helps parties to be better able to distinguish between the person and the conflict (as is suggested in principled negotiation). In combination, these advantages may outweigh any disadvantages created by a lack of face-to-face contact. . . .

B. The Argument Tool

1. Introduction. When initiating a two-party dispute, one of the parties introduces her grievances and the remedies she requires. Her opponent responds with counterarguments and her own proposed remedies. Our argument support tool makes explicit how the statements of the parties support their arguments. The argument support tool makes explicit to the disputants the support relations between the statements put forward by them by representing the entered statements in a graphical, layered manner, whereby each lower layer indicates support for the layer directly above. The tool forces the parties to enter statements in a sequence that reflects the support relations.

The argument tool used in our proposed ODR environment is based on AI & Law research about dialogical models of legal reasoning, in particular on DiaLaw, a dialogical model of justification. In the AI & Law field, scholars have created a number of models that concentrate on various characteristics of legal reasoning. For example, the Pleadings Game was developed to identify what issues, both legal and factual, exist between disputing parties. The HELIC-II system attempts to represent a unified model of legal reasoning; its creators also provide a portable software tool based on such a model.

2. Lodder's Approach to Negotiation and Argumentation. DiaLaw, developed by Lodder, is a two-player dialogue game designed to establish justified statements. It is a procedural model in which logic and rhetoric are combined. Logic is used to force, under certain circumstances, an opponent to accept a statement. The rhetoric element is represented in that the model defines as justified any statement on which the parties agree.

A dialogue in DiaLaw starts when a player introduces a statement she wants to justify. The dialogue ends if the opponent accepts the statement (justified) or if the statement is withdrawn (not justified). The rules of the game are rigid and the language used in the game is formal. This rigidity and formality help in presenting a clear picture of the relevant arguments. Due to its formal language and the fact that it was not designed to be used in practice in its prototypical form, DiaLaw is not an easy game to play. That said, the ideas underlying DiaLaw make it well-suited for supporting a natural language exchange.

Lodder and Paul Huygen have been creating an ODR tool they call eADR, based on the principles behind the construction of DiaLaw. Through a careful structuring of the information entered, the tool aims, in particular, to support parties engaged in an arbitration procedure. Nonetheless, Lodder and Huygen claim that the tool could also be used for other types of online dispute resolution, such as negotiation and mediation.

The argument tool used in the ODR environment proposed by the authors of this article operates as follows. "Statements" are natural language sentences. A party using the argument tool can enter one of . . . three types of statements.

1) Issue: A statement that initiates a discussion. At the moment of introduction, this statement is not connected to any other statement. 2) Supporting statement: Each statement entered by a party that supports statements of the same party. 3) Responding statement: Each statement entered by a party that responds to statements of the other party. . . .

The tool presented in this article differs from the tool constructed by Lodder and Huygen in that it is no longer a game in which parties take turns. Rather, parties can add statements at any given moment, and even simultaneously. We believe that for negotiation/mediation, this is a more natural way of exchanging information, especially in an online environment. . . .

C. The Negotiation Support System Approach

1. Introduction. We often know what criteria are important in making a decision but are unsure how best to evaluate these criteria. . . . In such situations, using a multi-criteria decision support tool could help highlight possible best alternatives.

Zeleznikow and others have previously used the multi-criteria decision-making approach. The most typical approach requires the user to directly assign values to each alternative for a given criterion. Under an alternative approach known as the Analytical Hierarchy Process, the user responds to a series of pair-wise comparisons: given two alternatives, the user is asked to express her preference for one over the other. . . . Upon reaching the lowest level in the hierarchy (as specified by the disputants), the system mathematically calculates the value of each sub-issue or item with respect to the relative super-issues or items. It does so for each party. Once completed, the system calculates which party is allocated particular sub-issues or items through pair-wise comparisons over the derived values from both parties.

Although there is an argument that one should assume bounded rationality and the presence of incomplete information in developing real-world negotiation support systems, our model of legal negotiation assumes that all actors behave rationally. The model is predicated on economic bases, that is, it assumes that the protagonists act in their own economic best interests. While much human negotiation is not necessarily based upon rational economic behavior, the goal of negotiation support systems is to provide rational advice. The environment that we are developing therefore assumes the existence of rational actors.

Traditionally, negotiation support systems have been template-based, with little attention given to the role the system itself should play in negotiations and decision-making support. Two template-based software systems that are available to help lawyers negotiate are "Negotiator Pro" and "The Art of Negotiating." Other template-based negotiation support systems include INSPIRE, which used utility functions to graph offers, and DEUS, in which the goals of the parties (and their offers) were set on screen side by side. The primary role of these systems has been to demonstrate to users how close (or far) they are from a negotiated settlement. The systems do not specifically suggest solutions to users. However, by informing users of the issues in dispute and a measure of the level of the disagreement, they provide some decision support.

The earliest negotiation support system that used artificial intelligence in order to provide decision-making support was LDS, which assisted legal experts in settling product liability cases. Another early system, SAL, helped insurance claims adjusters evaluate claims related to asbestos exposure. These two systems represented the first steps in recognizing the virtue of settlement-oriented decision support systems. Other examples of negotiation support systems include MEDIATOR, PERSUADER, NEGOPLAN, and GENIE.

There has been much recent research on building web-based negotiation support systems. For instance, Zeleznikow and others are modeling arbitration in the United Kingdom construction industry. Modeling legal reasoning derived from existing case law and unreported decisions, they are creating a software tool to support the adjudication process and to assist all of its stakeholders. Such a web-based decision support system will advise users/adjudicators as to likely outcomes of the dispute. A project in Victoria, Australia . . . is developing an online plea bargaining system to allow prosecutors and defense barristers to negotiate pleas and sentences with regard to criminal offenses. A model of sentencing has been developed using knowledge discovery from database techniques.

2. Zeleznikow's Approach to Building Negotiation Support Systems. Influenced by John Nash's significant research on game theory and Raiffa's work on using game theory for negotiation support, Zeleznikow wished to integrate artificial intelligence and game theory techniques to develop intelligent negotiation support systems. . . . He saw that an important way in which mediators encouraged disputants to resolve their conflicts was through the use of compromise and trade-offs. Once the trade-offs have been identified, other decision-making mechanisms must be employed to resolve the dispute. From efforts to build negotiation support systems, he noted that while it appears counterintuitive: the more issues and sub-issues in dispute, the easier it is to form trade-offs and hence reach a negotiated agreement, and we choose as the first issue to resolve the one on which the disputants are furthest apart — one party wants it greatly, the other considerably less so. . . .

The trade-offs pertaining to a disputant are graphically displayed through a series of trade-off "maps." Their incorporation into the system enables disputants to visually understand trade-off opportunities relevant to their side of the dispute. A trade-off is formed after the system conducts a comparison between the ratings of two issues. The value of a trade-off relationship is determined by analyzing the differences between the parties. . . . The amount of any compensation resulting from the triggering of a trade-off has been empirically determined from an analysis of data.

In order to use [this approach] we must assume that: 1) The dispute can be modeled using "principled negotiation"; 2) Weights can be assigned to each of the issues in dispute; and 3) Sufficient issues are in contention to allow each side to be compensated for losing an issue. The algorithms implemented in the system support the process of negotiation by introducing importance values that indicate the degree to which each party desires to be awarded each issue. The system assumes that the importance value of an issue corresponds directly to how much the disputant wants the issue to be awarded to her. The system also uses this information to form trade-off rules. . . .

D. How the Argument Tool and Negotiation Support System Work Together

In our three-step model we suggest that the parties commence with the argument tool. If the parties do not reach agreement on all issues through use of the argument tool, they can then use the negotiation support system. If the proposal suggested by the negotiation support system is not acceptable, then the argument tool can be used again to provide additional support or a response. In fact, the parties can at any point go back to the argument tool in order to discuss further issues introduced during use of the negotiation support system.

We could have recommended that the parties begin with the negotiation support system phase, moving to the argument tool to discuss one or more sub-issues if the negotiation support system failed to suggest an acceptable proposal. If agreement was not reached on one or more issues, the parties could further consult the negotiation support system.

We recommend commencing with the use of the argument tool because the use of a negotiation support tool first might discourage the parties from conducting a dialogue. It is important that the parties discuss the issues in dispute and become aware of the opposing side's arguments prior to trade-offs being suggested. An important task of a mediator is to have the parties communicate with each other. This task is hindered if a decision support system automatically suggests trade-offs before any attempt at communication or conciliation occurs.

Another problem with beginning with the negotiation support system as opposed to the argument tool is that the parties would then need to assign values to the issues before discussing them. Following a dialogue, the disputants might realize they wish to reallocate points — perhaps because their opponent was awarded an issue which, on reflection, they realize they greatly desired. . . . By beginning with the dialogue, the parties are more likely to consider why they desire particular outcomes before they assign values to such outcomes. In addition, we believe that it is best to assign points only after the dialogue has been concluded, as such a sequence makes inequities less likely to occur. . . .

Notwithstanding the concerns we have raised, should parties choose to begin with the negotiation support system, we believe that the above examples of potential problems are exceptional cases. Generally, the combination of the negotiation support system and the dialogue tool will lead to satisfactory results. Parties simply will not cede issues that are very important to them. . . . Consensus remains the leading principle of our ODR environment. No party will be confronted with an undesired outcome. . . . We imagine that ultimately both the negotiation support system and the argument tool will be offered in the online environment, and the parties will be left to decide in which order to use them. . . .

E. Negotiation and Justice

We would be remiss in not raising a serious shortcoming of the ODR approach and, indeed, of any proposed negotiation support system. A fundamental issue arises whenever anyone builds a negotiation support system for use in legal domains: is the system being developed concerned with supporting mediation or providing justice? When issues of justice are not reflected in the outcome of the mediation process, bargaining theory has its limitations. . . . One safeguard for use of ODR in fields such as family law may be required certification of the result by a legal professional. . . .

ODR combines the effectiveness of ADR with the comfort of the Internet. We believe our proposed online dispute resolution environment delivers both ease and effectiveness, and that the participants will consider the outcomes fair. It is likely that in the not-too-far future, online environments will surpass offline dispute resolution, even if face-to-face communication is not supported. As long as the humans remain in control, the supporting power of technology is infinite.

4. Janice Nadler, *Rapport in Legal Negotiation: How Small Talk Can Facilitate E-Mail Dealmaking,* 9 HARV. NEGOT. L. REV. 223 (2004)

This Article reports findings from an empirical study that addressed the question of whether the use of e-mail can hinder negotiators' abilities to craft mutually-beneficial negotiated agreements. [T]he absence of social cues in e-mail communication can lead to unwarranted suspicion, blame, and ultimately, negotiation impasse. Does this mean that lawyers should avoid e-mail at all costs when engaging in negotiations? [T]here is a simple way to avert the escalation of negative emotion, miscommunication, and eventual impasse that can characterize e-mail negotiations. Indeed, the study discussed here confirms what every Persian rug merchant knows when he insists that his customer sit down for a cup of tea prior to talking business: engaging in small talk prior to negotiating can set the stage for an atmosphere of trust and communication that can ultimately create value for both parties in the negotiation. . . .

The benefits of e-mail . . . are especially evident in negotiation. Whereas in the past lawyers were forced to arrange a series of face-to-face meetings with opposing counsel to conduct settlement discussions or to discuss the terms of a deal, the availability of communication technology such as e-mail allows lawyers to negotiate "on the fly" without the need to set aside special days and times to talk with other lawyers involved in the deal or dispute. Because many negotiations . . . take place over a period of days, weeks, or months, e-mail affords the advantage of allowing each negotiator to reply to proposals at his or her own convenience, rather than coordinating availability with the counterpart.

Beyond convenience, e-mail affords certain strategic advantages. The lag time inherent in e-mail enables negotiators to take time to plan their next negotiating move, and to carefully craft their communications before sending them. E-mail also has the capacity to transmit complex, precise, quantitative information, which can be crucial in complex negotiations. One study of electronically mediated negotiations reports that e-mail discussions generate more complex, integrative proposals compared to face-to-face negotiations.

To create an agreement that efficiently captures value for both parties, there must be sufficient exchange of information to identify potential tradeoffs among the available issues. Exchanging offers involving many issues has proven to be a more effective method for generating integrative agreements than resolving issues one-by-one. The ability to transmit complex offers and integrative proposals is especially important in the context of transactional negotiations, in which the issues often are numerous and intricate. Despite the importance of discussing issues simultaneously, face-to-face negotiations tend to progress on an issue-by-issue basis due to the limited "baud rate" of face-to-face conversation and conversational norms of brevity. In contrast, e-mail negotiators can and do make complex offers involving packages with multiple issues. E-mail communications also offer negotiators a chance to convey complex messages without the threat of being interrupted or the need to squeeze one's message into the cadence of the conversation.

At the same time, however, e-mail can be a hazardous form of communication. Statements made in e-mails often come across as abrasive or negative simply because they are not embedded in the shared context that face-to-face communicators experience. Face-to-face contact contributes to smooth communications because, although seldom consciously recognized, people rely heavily on nonverbal signals to help them conduct social interactions. Important behavioral, cognitive, and emotional processes are set into motion when people interact in person. Face-to-face negotiation allows people to develop rapport — the feeling of being "in sync" or "on the same wavelength" with another person.

In negotiation, rapport is a powerful determinant of whether people develop the trust necessary to engage in the kind of information exchange needed to reach integrative agreements. Nonverbal (body orientation, gestures, eye contact, head nodding) and paraverbal (speech fluency, the use of "uh-huhs," etc.) behaviors are key to building rapport. When the person with whom we are negotiating sits at a greater distance, with an indirect body orientation, backward lean, crossed arms, and little eye contact, we feel less rapport than when the same person sits with a forward lean, an open body posture, and maintains steady eye contact. Without realizing it, people involved in face-to-face interaction tend to mirror one another in posture, facial expression, tone of voice, and mannerisms. This phenomenon, known as social contagion, is the basis for the development of rapport between people. On the surface, it might seem that mimicking would be extremely annoying — almost like a form of mockery. The type of mimicry that is involved in everyday social encounters, however, is quite subtle — people do not usually recognize when it is happening. At the same time, the effects of social contagion are very powerful. When two people are mirroring one another, their movements become a choreographed dance. To the extent that our behaviors are synchronized with those of others, we feel more rapport, and this increases our trust in those with whom we communicate.

As a communication mode, e-mail effectively silences the music that drives the social contagion dance. E-mail negotiators are deprived of cues from the other person's body language (e.g., "She is frowning, so I know she doesn't like my offer"), as well as cues from the other person's voice (e.g., "He is laughing so that remark was clearly meant sarcastically"). Other social cues that we routinely use in face-to-face communication but are missing from e-mail communication include tone of voice, facial expression, head nodding, and mimicry of facial, vocal and postural movements. In a bargaining context, the impoverished nature of the e-mail medium makes it difficult to establish a feeling of interpersonal connection with the other person, which in turn can lead to misunderstandings, sinister attributions, and ultimately, negotiation impasse. . . .

To test the idea that in legal e-mail negotiations, substantial rapport can be built through a quick, simple chat, resulting in positive economic and social benefits, I designed and conducted an experiment [in which] law students who were strangers to one another engaged in a negotiation exercise via e-mail involving the purchase of a new car. Members of half of the negotiation dyads engaged in small talk via telephone prior to beginning negotiations via e-mail. The remaining participants communicated entirely via e-mail. Because of the absence of non-verbal and paraverbal cues in e-mail communication, rapport is difficult to establish and maintain in the absence of an intervention. I hypothesized that the telephone small talk intervention introduced in this experiment would encourage negotiators to establish a small degree of rapport at the outset, and to encourage the reciprocity necessary for information exchange and a higher likelihood of negotiated agreement.

"Small Talk" negotiators who had a brief "getting-to-know-you" telephone conversation prior to negotiating via e-mail reached superior economic outcomes and markedly better social outcomes than negotiators who did not talk on the phone. "Small Talk" negotiators were over four times as likely to reach an agreement as "No Small Talk" negotiators. Only three out of thirty-five "Small Talk" pairs (less than 9%) failed to reach an agreement, whereas fourteen out of thirty-seven "No Small Talk" pairs (nearly 40%) failed to reach agreement. The high percentage of "No Small Talk" pairs that were unable to reach agreement is especially noteworthy in light of the fact that a positive bargaining zone existed, making it economically desirable for each party to reach a negotiated agreement. Interestingly, the value of the outcome (measured both in terms of joint outcome and individual outcome) for the pairs that did reach agreement appears to be unaffected by small talk. . . .

The success of "Small Talk" negotiators cannot be explained by differences in motivation and ambition. Talking to the other negotiator on the telephone did not result in "Small Talk" negotiators setting higher reservation prices or more ambitious aspirations for themselves as measured prior to the negotiation, compared to negotiators who did not engage in small talk. The striking superiority of negotiation outcomes where negotiators chatted briefly about personal matters on the telephone prior to talking business via e-mail must be attributable to other mechanisms. . . .

What accounts for the huge differences between the "Small Talk" and "No Small Talk" negotiators in their propensity to reach a mutually beneficial agreement? Prior to negotiating (but after the phone call, if there was one) negotiators indicated on a scale from one to seven (1 = Not at all; 7 = Quite a bit) how "competitive" they were feeling toward their counterpart as they entered into the negotiation. They also indicated how "cooperative" they were feeling toward their counterpart. Negotiators who did not engage in small talk with their counterpart prior to negotiating reported feeling more competitive and less cooperative toward their counterpart than negotiators who did engage in small talk.

Why would negotiators who adopt more cooperative, less competitive attitudes toward the negotiation achieve greater success economically than negotiators who adopt the opposite attitudes?. . . Negotiators who established initial rapport with a brief telephone chat felt more cooperative in the negotiation and trusted the other negotiator enough to share the kind of information necessary to reach an efficient solution. In addition to offering more freely their own information about relative priorities, information sharing was reciprocated more often for negotiators in the "Small Talk" condition than for negotiators in the "No Small Talk" condition. . . . Negotiators who engaged in small talk expected more strongly to cooperate, did cooperate by sharing more relevant multiple-issue information, and received more cooperation in return from their counterpart. . . .

The negotiation transcripts were also analyzed to examine whether negotiators provided information that related to one's own alternative, because such a reference can be akin to a threat to walk away from the table (e.g., "I can buy a similarly equipped car much more cheaply at another dealership"). Compared to negotiators whose initial contact was strictly business-like, negotiators who engaged in small talk before negotiating were less likely to reference their own alternative. Thus, in the absence of an initial getting-to-know-you telephone conversation, negotiators assumed a competitive mental model and behaved competitively during the negotiation by making subtle (or not so subtle) threats to walk away from the table. . . .

Negotiators who did not chat beforehand ended the negotiation with a substantially different attitude toward both the process and their counterpart than the negotiators who did chat initially. Negotiators who did not chat found the process of e-mail communication more difficult. They ended up feeling significantly more angry, annoyed, and cold toward their opponent, as well as less friendly and pleasant, compared to negotiators who had the opportunity to chat with their opponent. These feelings are consistent with the competitive mindset and inferior economic outcomes of negotiators in the "No Small Talk" condition. The increased cooperation and trust that the telephone chat engendered led to smoother interactions and a friendlier attitude toward the opponent after the negotiation concluded. This attitude was also associated with respect — negotiators who engaged in small talk formed an impression of their counterpart as significantly more accomplished, skilled, effective, and perceptive than the impression formed by negotiators who did not engage in small talk.

Finally, this experiment also measured the extent to which negotiators came away trusting their counterparts. One of the many ways to define trust is the expectation that the other person will cooperate with you when you are in a vulnerable position. In legal communities, lawyers who face each other in one negotiation often can expect to cross paths again in the future. If trust is eroded during negotiation in one matter, this is likely to affect the way the lawyers approach the negotiation in the next matter when they meet again. To explore the question of whether engaging in small talk prior to negotiating would increase trust, negotiators in this experiment answered two questions relating to trust. First, they were asked to suppose that they and their counterparts were in the position of working together on a future project and to rate how smoothly such a project would go (1 = Not at all; 7 = Very much so). Second, negotiators were asked to imagine that sometime in the future, they were in a vulnerable position in a dispute with their counterpart's firm. Would they prefer to negotiate with the same counterpart, or some other unknown attorney (1 = Prefer unknown; 7 = Prefer same)? Responses on these two items were highly correlated and were averaged to form a summary variable called Working Trust. Negotiators who had an initial chat with their opponents left the negotiation with significantly more trust in their counterparts than did negotiators who did not chat initially. . . .

[There is a striking] similarity between the results of this study and a phenomenon identified by decision theorists and social psychologists called the "self-others discrepancy." In general, when we are asked to make predictions about the abilities or preferences of others, our predictions are strongly influenced by the extent to which we feel a personal connection with those others. For example, if I am asked to judge how dependable, intelligent, considerate, etc. I am compared to others, my answer is likely to depend on the abstractness of the others. If the other is "the average person" then my comparison tends to be more favorable toward myself than if the other is an individual stranger sitting next to me. In other words, the less abstract the other person about whom I make a judgment, the more likely I am to judge that person as more similar to me. In addition to the abstractness of the other person, the degree of personal contact also encourages feelings of similarity: I judge myself more favorably in reference to a stranger on a videotape than I do in reference to a stranger who is in the same room.

The "self-others discrepancy" extends to other judgments besides estimating personality traits. For example, people estimate that "an average person" making a decision will choose a riskier option than themselves, but the stranger sitting next to them will choose a similar option to the one chosen themselves. In Milgram's famous experiments in which the experimenter instructs a "teacher" to administer painful electric shocks to a "learner," the "teacher" is more likely to refuse to do so if the "learner" is visible and in the same room as the "teacher," compared to when the "learner" is not visible and in an adjoining room. STANLEY MILGRAM, OBEDIENCE TO AUTHORITY 35 (1974).

The "self-others discrepancy" has important implications for negotiating via e-mail. It suggests that conceptualizing one's negotiation counterpart as a concrete, identifiable individual person reduces the perceived difference between the counterpart and oneself. The anonymous character of e-mail leaves negotiators imagining a vague and abstract opponent whom they have never seen or met, making it more likely that negotiators will succumb to the self-others bias. Yet, the simple act of making personal telephone contact with the opponent prior to negotiating via e-mail enabled negotiators to substitute perceptions of an invisible, abstract opponent with a concrete human being who shares one's own characteristics. As a result, negotiators who engaged in small talk prior to negotiating via e-mail were more successful at exchanging the right kind of information necessary to reach agreement, and at recognizing a beneficial agreement when the opportunity for such an agreement presented itself. . . .

D. PRACTITIONERS OF ON-LINE DISPUTE RESOLUTION

1. Comments and Questions

a. In this section, we shift our perspective from the dispute resolution process to the dispute resolution professionals who make the processes operate effectively. As with other dispute resolution formats, knowledge and experience matter

b. Susan Raines suggests the attractive option for ODR practitioners of working at times and in places that suit their lifestyle and other responsibilities. Quite apart from personal style, this option has great economic value. Work that can be performed when the opportunity costs are low is more valuable than work that must be performed at a time (and place) certain.

c. Strikingly, there has already been a call for government oversight of ODR providers. The Taylor & Bornstein article addresses this topic. *See also*, Orna Rabinovitch-Einy, *Technology's Impact: The Quest For a New Paradigm for Accountability in Mediation*, 11 HARV. NEGOT. L. REV. 253 (2006), and the articles cited therein.

d. Once again, a central question is, what's new in the provision of ODR services? How are dispute resolution providers adjusting to the brave new world of TMDR? What issues are largely the same as old style dispute resolution, and what things are new or different?

2. Susan R. Raines, *Mediating in Your Pajamas: The Benefits and Challenges for ODR Practitioners*, 23 CONFLICT RESOL. Q. 359 (2006)

Millions of disputants are seeking and receiving assistance with the resolution of their disputes on-line through mediation, arbitration, facilitated dialogues, teleconferences, video-conferences, and hybrids that integrate on-line technologies into traditional ADR processes. As with all processes and forums, the goal is to fit the forum to the fuss. Just as mediation is not the right process for all disputes, ODR will not be appropriate in every case. ODR cases are typically similar to off-line ADR cases: they involve real people seeking redress or resolution to a problem with the help of a third-party neutral, at a reasonable cost, within a reasonable time frame. Disputants often choose the ODR format to overcome problems posed by multiple jurisdictions or geographic distance, or purely for convenience.

This essay will discuss some of the ways in which the "human factor" (that is, emotions and cognitive limitations) influence the mediation process on-line, possible methods by which ODR neutrals may address human needs, and some of the challenges and rewards experienced by ODR practitioners as they use technology to deliver traditional ADR services. In the end, you are likely to find that ODR is simply another way of supplying ADR services, with neutrals required to use *generally* the same skill set, with the added twist of doing so via the medium of technology.

While there has been more research on ODR in recent years, very little work has yet to examine the practice of ODR. This article represents an attempt to begin the process of raising questions about what it is like to be an ODR practitioner. It does this by sharing the author's personal experiences as an ODR practitioner with more than five years of experience on more than eight thousand cases, as well as through sharing the experiences of a number of other ODR practitioners. . . . The majority of these ODR practitioners worked for Squaretrade.com, while others had independent ODR practices or worked through other organizations.

The Human Factor in ODR: Dealing with Anger and Frustration On-line. Neutrals who practice both on-line and off-line tend to agree that on-line disputants often express higher levels of anger during their opening statements (typically typed, not spoken) and in the initial communications that follow the commencement of mediation. Because these communications are not occurring in a face-to-face environment, disputants are less inhibited and more likely to engage in escalatory behavior, such as name calling, blaming, accusations of negative intentions and dispositions, and other highly negative attributions. Societal norms concerning communication etiquette seem to be less influential in restraining expressions of anger and hostility in on-line communication than in face-to-face or telephone communication. The anonymity of the on-line medium makes people feel safer expressing strong emotions than they do in the face-to-face environment. It is also likely, however, that because body language is absent in the on-line environment, communicators feel a need to use strong language to communicate explicitly emotion that in-person would be implicitly conveyed through eye contact, sighs, cold stares, and so on. . . .

Neutrals need to recognize and validate the emotions of on-line disputants repeatedly and explicitly as an important step in the mediation process. If disputants come to know that the mediator has registered their emotion, they may feel less need to keep conveying it over and over again. For example, just as off-line neutrals might do, ODR neutrals commonly begin their communications with statements such as, "I can tell this has been really frustrating for you," or "I know it is hard to be patient in a case like this, and I really appreciate your efforts to work this out cooperatively in mediation." Expressions of recognition and empathy allow disputants to feel that the mediator has heard them and that their emotions have been understood.

As in off-line mediation, refusing to acknowledge the expression of emotions can lead to feelings of alienation from the neutral and a sense that the mediator simply is not concerned or does not "get it." Many of these disputants may be tempted to drop out of mediation in protest, as a way to express their anger or out of frustration with the dispute itself While more research needs to be done, anecdotal accounts from on-line mediators suggests that it is more common for disputants to "walk out" on an on-line mediation session than it is for them to leave a face-to-face process. When frustration with the process gets high or when disputants feel that impasse is likely, they may quit responding to messages from the neutral or the other parties. This is the on-line equivalent of walking away from the table in a traditional mediation process, but doing so is easier, with fewer concerns about losing face, in an on-line format.

To reduce this possibility, neutrals can educate and remind disputants about the empowering elements of the mediation process itself. As is the case in off-line mediation, this acknowledgment and validation need not be confused with a loss of impartiality. Anger, which often stems from fear, is heightened by a feeling of powerlessness and a lack of control. Reminding disputants of their power and influence in the mediation process can help mediators to diffuse the disputants' anger and get them focused on problem solving.

Because some asynchronous processes take place over days or even weeks, it is also important for the mediator to use many summary statements to remind parties of where they are in the process, of what they have achieved so far, and about the issues left to be resolved. Asynchronous mediation formats allow mediators and parties to write draft comments and responses, giving them time to reflect more deeply on how best to communicate their needs and ideas. This is one important benefit of ODR over face-to-face processes.

Feedback from on-line neutrals also indicates the important role that mediators can play in refraining angry language into more neutral language before sharing it with the other party or parties. This is most frequently possible when the on-line mediation takes place in the "shuttle diplomacy" format, in which disputants send their messages only to the mediator and the mediator then shares the concerns of disputant A with disputant B. This is similar to an off-line mediation done solely through a caucus format, except that the ODR format gives the neutral more time to digest what was said and then craft an effective response.

[S]ometimes angry disputants do not channel their anger toward the other party but instead direct it toward the mediator. One on-line neutral noted that for this reason ODR practitioners need to have a "thick skin." Any social distance or sense of respect toward the mediator commonly shown in face-to-face processes is sometimes absent or reduced in on-line processes. On-line disputants may make a statement such as the following to their mediator or other neutral: "Any intelligent person could tell that the other person is a liar." Attacking the mediator occasionally occurs in off-line processes, but it appears to be more common on-line. When communication is occurring in an asynchronous environment (meaning that communication is not occurring simultaneously between the disputants and mediator, as in a chat room, but instead through a series of e-mails or other messages separated by time), the mediator can take the necessary time to calm down, reflect, and make a cool response instead of a hot response. . . .

Trust Building and Repair. Trust building and trust repair are frequently important in off-line ADR processes, but trust-related problems can pose even larger barriers to resolution for disputants who have had all of their interactions on-line and have never met face to face. When individuals buy from or sell to people they have not met personally, they cannot benefit from face-to-face communication, eye contact, handshakes, and other forms of incoming nonverbal information. In the absence of this information, individuals are more likely to be wary of their transaction partner and to think the worst of him or her if problems arise. Ongoing relationships, whether professional or personal, help to ensure that transaction partners will behave in cooperative and appropriate ways yet many business relationships developed in cyberspace are "one-shot" interactions. On-line disputants often state that they are hesitant to reach an agreement because they have little faith that the other party will live up to the mediated agreement or abide by the arbitrator's decision. This lack of trust can keep resolution from occurring even when it is clear that both disputants would be better off by reaching a resolution through ODR. It is therefore imperative for ODR practitioners to be well versed in how to handle issues of trust building and repair.

When it is clear to an on-line neutral that lack of trust is hampering the process of dispute resolution, the neutral needs to decide how best to build trust between the parties. Spending time to build a positive relationship is one way this can happen. This is a good idea when the parties may have future interactions (such as a recurring buyer-seller relationship) or when either party has exhibited dehumanizing behavior toward the other (for example, voicing a belief that the other person is worthless, a "scammer;" and the like). There are two basic kinds of trust: identification-based trust (IBT) and calculus-based trust (CBT). The former depends on the existence of a good relationship and empathy between the parties. When the parties care about each other and can understand the other side's perspective, IBT may suffice. ODR practitioners may encourage parties to look into each other's reputations in order to build this kind of trust (for example, is the other party a member of the Better Business Bureau? What is the party's "feedback rating" if he or she is an eBay seller? and other documentable traits). They may also encourage the parties to introduce themselves by sharing brief biographies and pictures.

Anything that helps to rehumanize the parties to each other and to build a sense of understanding between them may help address issues of distrust. This may be done best by phone, if adequate ground rules apply and the parties agree to remain civil. Likewise, if the disputants seem wary of using a mediator they have never met in person, the neutral may want to spend some time introducing him- or herself, summarizing his or her experience and qualifications, addressing the disputants' concerns, and building rapport with and between the disputants. On-line disputants often appear to have a heightened sense of skepticism of the other party (or parties) and of the mediator.

The joint creation of shared ground rules may be one way to further this process and build trust in both the process and the parties, but the ground rules for on-line dispute resolution may be substantially different from traditional ground rules. For example, ODR neutrals may wish to have explicit discussions about when and how communication will take place via the chosen technology (for example, through the mediator only; parties check messages and respond within twenty-four hours; no e-shouting).

When building relationships is either inappropriate or not desired by the disputants, neutrals may instead try to focus on the use of increasing calculus-based trust. In CBT, individuals do what they promise to do or what is clearly expected of them out of a desire to avoid unpleasant penalties, rather than out of a sense of obligation or empathy. This has also been called deterrence-based trust. On-line neutrals can work with the parties to craft agreements that have incentives to increase the chances of smooth implementation. For example, the agreement might state that party A will pay party B a specified amount of money by date X. If the money is not received by then, there will be a 10 percent penalty or some other appropriate penalty will apply. For the deterrence to be effective, the punishment for noncooperation must be higher than the reward for noncooperation and the likelihood that punishment will occur must be high. Agreements reached through ODR can generally be enforced through the courts, just as private mediation agreements are enforced. The "agreement to mediate" may need to spell out which jurisdiction any enforcement disputes will use.

From speaking with ODR practitioners, it seems that building trust and repairing trust after norm violations is an important and challenging part of working in an on-line environment. While many family mediators also deal with these issues on a daily basis, the situations are somewhat different: divorcing or divorced couples often lack trust in each other on the basis of a history of trust violations in the presence of a deep personal relationship. In this case, CBT approaches (that is, building trust through self- enforcing, binding agreements) are more likely to work than are IBT approaches (that is, building trust by building relationships and empathy between the parties). In contrast, many disputants using ODR have never met one another face to face, yet they are likely to be cynical about the other's trustworthiness even when no clear history of norm violation exists. In these instances, building relationships and empathy may be as effective as using CBT approaches. ODR practitioners often spend time rehumanizing the parties to one another by playing "devil's advocate" or asking them to place themselves in the other's position (that is, "perspective taking").

Challenges and Benefits of ODR Practice. . . . Who goes into on-line dispute resolution? Just like traditional ADR practitioners, ODR practitioners come from all walks of life and include both attorneys and non-attorneys. Many ODR neutrals also work with court-connected ADR programs where they mediate civil, domestic, juvenile, or small claims cases in off-line formats. Like many ADR providers, many ODR neutrals have primary careers as attorneys, human resources professionals, teachers, ombudsmen, conflict resolution trainers, and counselors, and they practice ODR in addition to these other responsibilities.

Due to the convenience factor, it is likely that a slightly higher percentage of ODR neutrals include retirees, stay-at-home parents, or others for whom a full-time, traditional practice is either impractical or undesirable. Some ODR practitioners begin offering ADR services through on-line formats as a way to expand their traditional practice or they offer these services after requests from their existing clients. Some practitioners integrate ADR and ODR, choosing to manage some of the dispute resolution process through e-mail, conference calls, or other technologies, while keeping some face-to-face meetings as well. This integration of ODR and ADR is increasingly common and can be used to maximize the efficiency of the dispute resolution processes by saving face-to-face meetings for those issues that cannot easily be dealt with on-line. For some disputes of low economic value, or when the parties live in differing legal jurisdictions on-line dispute resolution simply makes economic and jurisdictional sense, as it may be less costly and more practical than other formats.

Rewards of ODR Practice. ODR practitioners were asked to summarize the rewards and challenges of ODR practice. In general, their responses were strikingly similar to what we would expect from off-line practitioners, with only a few exceptions. One of the clearest exceptions comes from "the convenience factor." On-line neutrals can generally work from homes or offices, rather than traveling to courthouses or other places where ADR services are traditionally offered. This not only is convenient, but also cuts down on the hours for which clients are billed for travel time. One respondent noted that ODR can be done from anywhere and that this has many advantages: "When I travel internationally for business or pleasure, I usually have to put my traditional ADR cases on hold until I get back. But with my ODR cases, I can take them wherever I go. . . . As long as I can find an Internet café or other place to connect, I can take my work with me." This convenience was also noted by two semi retired practitioners and one stay-at-home parent who had temporarily withdrawn from her other work in order to be home with her young children.

In addition to the convenience factor, ODR neutrals found their work very rewarding in other ways. They enjoyed the expressions of appreciation that sometimes come from the disputants at the end of a difficult case. While this also occurs in face-to-face processes, some disputants using ODR stated a belief that they would have lacked an outlet for resolution entirely if ODR had not been made available to them. Going to court simply is not an option for many of these disputants. Doing so might cost them more than the economic value of the case, especially if the disputants are geographically separated. A number of ODR neutrals stated they felt good about being able to help people who might otherwise not have adequate access to either ADR or justice processes.

ODR neutrals . . . also noted that the on-line format had a "laboratory" element to it that allowed mediators to try different techniques in different cases and to learn from trial and error in order to improve their skills. While this is certainly true of traditional ADR processes, an asynchronous on-line format perhaps allows more time for reflection and conscious application of various skills and techniques. Additionally, ODR formats generally produce written records of the interactions that may allow for deeper reflection and study.

Challenges of ODR Practice. Some ODR practitioners noted that it can be difficult for disputants to overcome the barriers posed by communicating solely through the written word. "On both sides, the meaning behind the words in print is often lost or misconstrued, both between myself and a party and between the parties themselves, previous to beginning mediation. However, this is often the area that is easiest to 'fix' once I enter the picture and can help the parties to see the true meanings behind each other's words." It appears that ODR neutrals and other frequent on-line communicators are increasingly finding ways to express nonverbal emotions on-line. For example, writing in all capital letters is the on-line equivalent to shouting. The use of smiley faces or other symbols is also increasing, with shared meanings existing at least within national or cultural groups. On the whole, ODR neutrals felt that communication barriers posed by technological problems, computer illiteracy or poor writing skills were insurmountable barriers in only a relatively small minority of cases. However, there was agreement that these problems are serious obstacles in some cases and that ODR neutrals need to be vigilant in addressing these problems proactively whenever possible and in admitting defeat when they become impossible to overcome. It is better to have a case end in an impasse than to have a resolution that is not clearly understood by all parties.

Advice for New ODR Practitioners. Be patient with yourself and with the parties, as there will be a learning curve with new technologies and formats. Practice on your own before launching your skills with real disputants. The work can leave you feeling somewhat isolated. You "talk" to disputants all day via computer, but it is not the same. Make sure you get involved in civic or professional organizations, or form some sort of support group with other mediators so you can meet your social and professional networking needs outside the online environment. ODR is sometimes too convenient. You can find yourself mediating at 2 A.M. or in the middle of a family reunion. As work and home merge, make sure you establish and maintain good boundaries so you do both well.

3. Melissa Conley Taylor & Jackie Bornstein, *Accreditation of On-Line Dispute Resolution Professionals*, 23 CONFLICT RESOL. Q. 383 (2006)

There has been a long history of debate within the conflict resolution community regarding standards and accreditation of practitioners. ADR practitioners can be subject to two types of standards to ensure the quality and effectiveness of their services: requirements for recognition or approval as a precondition to practice ("accreditation"), and standards for conduct (such as codes of practice). Accreditation involves a practitioner meeting certain levels of education, training, or performance in order to practice ADR. Accreditation can be imposed by ADR service providers or by government and can follow a central or localized approach. . . . There is currently no single recognized standard or criteria for accreditation across the ADR field, and ODR is no exception. . . .

In line with the development of accreditation standards for ADR, a number of standards for ODR have been developed. Most ODR sites have formal policies and procedures, including dispute management protocols, standards of conduct, codes of practice, and explicit policies on privacy. Typically, ODR standards of practice have evolved as an adaptation of standards of practice for traditional ADR. However, new accreditation practices for ODR have also evolved, including:

1. Federal Mediation and Conciliation Service, a U.S. government service that brings mobile technology to the workplace to help conciliate labor-management disputes.

2. Hong Kong International Arbitration Centre, a China-based company offering arbitration for domain name disputes.

3. Mediate.com, a portal that provides an on-line referral process to ODR practitioners, mainly in the United States.

4. Nova Forum (The Electronic Courthouse), a Canadian membership-based provider of on-line mediation and arbitration for consumer and business disputes.

5. On-line Resolution, a U.S.-based provider of on-line mediation and arbitration services.

6. SquareTrade, a U.S. service that offers negotiation and mediation of mainly on-line disputes, such as for eBay, Google, Yahoo!, and others.

What is common among the systems is the stress placed on the importance of practitioners acquiring practical skills, especially through a structured process. [These include:]

Providing opportunity for practitioners to take part in ODR simulations before they tackle actual cases on-line

- The mentoring of novice ODR practitioners by more-experienced ODR practitioners

- Encouraging practitioners to discuss difficult ethical and practical issues related to ODR with other on-line practitioners

- Encouraging practitioners to share the language they are using (such as opening statements and ground rules) so that practitioners can provide each other with feedback. . . .

Criteria for Accreditation in ODR. ODR will require ADR practitioners to make changes to their knowledge and skills that will need to be reflected in the criteria for accreditation in ODR. Current ADR standards regarding practitioner skills, knowledge, and ethics should serve as a useful reference for the development of ODR practitioner accreditation.

Practitioner Knowledge. To provide ODR services, ADR practitioners must possess a minimum level of knowledge and familiarity with the computer system and ODR software being used. They need to be comfortable with navigating the program interface, whether it is text or video based. The technological competence to handle the software and platform used are a prerequisite for successfully managing ODR. If a neutral doesn't know how to manage the platform she is using to work with the parties, or if she can't effectively multitask between multiple caucus spaces and the joint discussion, or if she doesn't get online and respond to the parties enough, it doesn't matter how well she can engage in face-to-face active listening. . . . Given the rapid development of ODR, initial training in ODR should be followed by ongoing training to ensure that skills keep pace with technological innovations.

Practitioner Skills. ODR has grown directly out of the history of off-line ADR, and many of the skills used there can be easily translated to the new technology. For this reason, some experience or knowledge of ADR processes can be built into or assumed as a required ODR skill. The lessons learnt in ADR over the years about the importance of impartiality; how to effectively move parties towards resolution, about the importance of listening and transparency; and the challenges of managing power imbalances all are central to effective ODR practice.

Some skills are relatively easily translated; for example, practitioners can reframe by cutting and pasting sentences to reflect and give priority to certain issues. However, on-line practitioners also need to develop new skills. Specific things practitioners need to learn include:

1. Maintaining communication with parties where communication is delayed and may extend over time;

2. Controlling information flow through quick and active intervention — particularly important because on-line communication can encourage greater expression of emotion;

3. Creating on-line "rituals" and "ceremonial moments;" and

4. "Active reading" between the lines.

Some knowledge of how on-line communication differs from verbal communication could be part of the accreditation process. This could be tested through on-line role-play observation or transcript analysis. Continuing good practice could be maintained through practitioner performance assessments or skills audits and the submission of on-line sessions for assessment and discussion.

Options for Accreditation of ODR. The potential for ODR use to increase has significant implications for the ADR profession, including internationalization of ADR markets and increased competition, and thus pressure for accreditation. If ADR providers are to keep up with the trend, they will need to consider their current accreditation practices in light of the ODR context.

There are four broad options for accreditation of ODR practitioners: Incorporation of ODR into current practitioner accreditation systems; Independent accreditation of ODR practitioners; Accreditation of specialist ODR skills; and Accrediting agencies to provide ODR. The strengths and weaknesses of each option will be considered in the following discussion.

Incorporation of ODR into Current Practitioner Accreditation Systems. This option involves incorporating ODR skills into current ADR practitioner accreditation systems. In most cases, ADR agencies would find it easy to add ODR to initial practitioner training, and implementing this option would be relatively low cost. This option would mean that all practitioners accredited by these agencies would have skills in ODR.

Independent Accreditation of ODR Practitioners. This option involves establishing a separate accreditation system for ODR practitioners. This could be administered by a central or independent body or by one ADR agency on behalf of other ADR agencies. Practitioners would be accredited as ODR practitioners and their skills would be recognized across agencies.

Accreditation of Specialist ODR Skills. This option involves offering additional accreditation of ODR skills to currently accredited practitioners. This would mean that not all ADR practitioners would need to develop on-line skills, but accreditation in ODR would be available as a "specialty" for those who are interested. The specialist accreditation could be provided either by the agency that provided initial ADR accreditation or by a central or independent body that administers accreditation of ODR.

Accrediting Agencies in ODR. Finally, it is possible to accredit agencies, rather than individual practitioners, in ODR. These approved agencies could then accredit ODR practitioners. Agencies could be accredited by an independent accreditation body to offer ODR if that agency has developed and implemented standards for its practitioners.

Preferred Option. The decision between these four options for each ADR agency will depend on the context of the dispute resolution provider involved. For example, issues such as whether or not a national or local accreditation system is already in place, the maturity of the ADR industry and specific characteristics of the agency or ADR service involved will all influence the decision on how to deal with accreditation of ODR practitioners. However, some guidance can be offered. First, where an agency offers both ADR and ODR, it makes little sense to have separate accreditation processes. Given the great overlap between the two sets of skills, knowledge, and attitudes required, there are two better options. If it is likely that many or most practitioners will be called on to use on-line technology in their role, it makes sense to incorporate ODR into the overall accreditation system for all practitioners. Even if individuals are not called on to use these skills immediately, they will gain understanding of their colleagues' work and of the potential of on-line communication. If ODR is likely to be conducted only by a smaller group, at least initially, then ODR should be seen as an additional specialization within ADR. This would mean that accredited ADR practitioners would have the opportunity to gain an extra "qualification" or specialty in ODR. In the longer term, if consumer protection or confidence require it, there is an argument for establishing a system of accrediting agencies in ODR rather than individual practitioners. This will depend on wider debates about accreditation in each jurisdiction.

Trust has been identified as one of the keys to promoting ODR services. Just as ADR went through a period of building trust, including through systems of accreditation, ODR will be faced with the need to create perceptions of reliability through practitioner credentialing. New ODR service providers and existing ADR agencies incorporating ODR into their services will face a choice of how to ensure and communicate the quality of their services. An understanding of the different models for accreditation based on the combination of hurdle and maintenance criteria chosen will help agencies with this choice.

PART V
DISPUTE RESOLUTION PROFESSIONALS

Chapter 15

PROFESSIONAL QUALIFICATIONS, PROFESSIONAL LIABILITY

A. INTRODUCTION

This Chapter focuses on two closely related topics: (minimum) professional qualifications, and the standards for professional liability of persons and organizations that provide dispute resolution services. These two topics are closely related because they are both aspects of what it means to be a professional. One consequence of being a recognized professional with special skills is a higher duty of care toward clients, and a greater potential of legal liability for breach of that duty.

While much of the chapter focuses on actual or proposed qualifications, and asks the reader to evaluate them on their merits, the consideration of qualifications begins with the source of authority, and whether government should mandate qualifications. There is a vast difference between government established minimum qualifications, and a private organization (e.g., AAA, ACR) requiring adherence by its members to an identical standard. Government regulation of ADR providers is already well established, either directly or because so many ADR providers are also members of licensed professions.

The primary basis for liability of professionals, including persons involved in dispute resolution, is malpractice, an amalgam of tort and contract law theories. The ADR professional who works in the context of a court-related proceeding may be the beneficiary of (absolute) quasi-judicial immunity or at least qualified immunity. In addition to protection for individual ADR professionals, the availability of immunity lends prestige to dispute resolution activities.

Government regulation of occupations is a topic that has been widely studied by economists, political scientists, sociologists, and others. It is commonly observed by outsiders that the primary beneficiaries of such regulation are the groups being regulated rather than the public, for whose benefit and protection the regulation is supposedly undertaken. In section B, a typology of government regulation of occupations is followed by an article by Walter Gellhorn that discusses abuses of occupational licensure. After this outsider's perspective on professional standards, we turn to the insider perspective — presented by people associated with (and true believers in) the ADR Movement.

Mediators and other dispute resolution professionals argue vigorously for regulation of the profession, by means of credentialing of mediators and standards of conduct. These two topics are the subject of Sections C and D, respectively. The open promotion of professional regulation for ADR professionals is a quite recent development — note that not a single one of the readings in these two sections predates 2005. Section E examines the expanded liability that accompanies the status of being associated with a legally recognized profession. As explained by Professor Moffitt, however, liability for dispute resolution providers is largely a theoretical concern.

Finally, in section F, we examine statutory or common law exceptions to the obligation of dispute resolution professionals to maintain confidentiality of anything learned in a professional capacity or context. The standard example is child abuse; some states have adopted similar statutes for elder abuse. The obligation to report abuse in specified circumstances extends far beyond the ADR arena, and these laws also cover attorneys and members of the helping professions. While the topic of confidentiality is considered at length in the mediation context in Chapter Eight, we address the abuse exception here because it is *sui generis*, and usually created by state statute.

B. REGULATION OF SKILLED CRAFTSMEN AND "PROFESSIONALS"

1. Typology of Approaches to Professional Regulation

The licensure or other government regulation of dispute resolution professionals is just one instance of the general category of professional regulation. In order to think sensibly about professional qualifications it is useful to adopt a widely accepted set of labels. Moving from the least to the most restrictive, these are registration, certification, and licensure. The discussion omits the often important revenue raising aspects of professional regulation.

a. Registration. Under a registration system, anyone who fits within a certain category must notify the state, and provide relevant individual and activity information. Often, identifying information must be publicly displayed. Examples from the professions are difficult to find, because demonstrated competence and licensure are among the hallmarks of a profession. Taxi drivers commonly are required to have a registration, with a picture and identifying number, prominently displayed at a specified place in the taxi. Owners of automobiles are required to register them with the state, and to display an identifying plate supplied (sold) by the state. Firms without a permanent place of business might be required to register with the state, and provide information about who the owners are and where they can be found. In each instance, the basis for registration is to promote the general welfare by facilitating the recovery of lost property, preventing fraud, and identifying wrongful activity.

b. Certification. Under a certification system, the government certifies that people have specified skills, but identical activities may be performed by uncertified persons. (This definition excludes non-government assertions of quality such as a "best buy" rating from Consumers Report, Newsweek's ranking of professional schools, or membership in exclusive professional organizations that admit only people with specified qualifications.) Anyone may engage in the business of helping people with the design of a house, but in most states the title of "architect" is reserved for individuals who have met state certification standards. As with accountants and appraisers, this example is not a pure one because in each instance some work — typically the most complex, prestigious, and remunerative work—is open only to licensed professionals.

c. Licensure. Under a licensing scheme, the practice of activities ranging from law and medicine to barbering and cosmetology is limited to persons who have met the standards for licensure established by state law. While there may be questions at the margin about what constitutes the practice of law or barbering, it is clear that encroachment on core activities by the unlicensed constitutes the unauthorized practice of law or barbering. The explosion of professional licensure in America, mostly at the state level, is detailed in the following article by Walter Gellhorn.

In many states, there is a system for lawyers to become specialists, which typically requires experience, passing a test, and then continuing education to maintain specialist status. Attorneys who meet these specialist standards may so identify themselves to the public, but other attorneys are not precluded from undertaking the same work as recognized specialists. The person who meets the state's standards for specialists is often said to be a "licensed" specialist, but that usage in inaccurate under the definitions used here. Such a specialist is *licensed* to be an attorney, an exclusionary category, but is *certified* as a specialist, because other attorneys are not excluded from doing the same work as the specialists.

2. Walter Gellhorn, *The Abuse of Occupational Licensure*, 44 U. CHI. L. REV. 6 (1976)

[L]iterally hundreds of occupations are subject to licensing laws in one or more states. Possibly the founding fathers knew of restrictions in some of the new American states on the practices of law and medicine. They would, however, have been aghast to learn that in many parts of this country today aspiring bee keepers, embalmers, lightning rod salesmen, septic tank cleaners, taxidermists, and tree surgeons must obtain official approval before seeking the public's patronage. After examining the roster of those who must receive official permission to function, a cynic might conclude that virtually the only people who remain unlicensed in at least one of the United States are clergymen and university professors, presumably because they are nowhere taken seriously.

A consideration of the proliferation of occupational license requirements is especially timely because it may help in evaluating two contemporary currents of public policy. First, prominent politicians and public officials assert that too much economic activity is subject to regulation; they urge "regulatory reform," a code phrase meaning the reduction of regulation. Second, within the legal profession demand is mounting for some formal means of identifying "specialists" among lawyers.

In recent decades occupational licensing has grown explosively. One consequence has been a debilitation of the concept of a "profession" and a distortion of the idea that licensing should serve primarily as an instrument of social control to protect the public against unfit or unscrupulous practitioners. If occupational licensing resulted simply in downgrading the word "profession" or in enlarging the ranks of the "learned," one would have small cause for alarm. After all, the complexities of modem life have created new demands for special training and perceptions. As long ago as 1956, a former Surgeon General of the United States noted that nurses and other health aides are called on to "master a body of knowledge greater in extent and usefulness for the care of the sick than all of the medical knowledge of a century ago. . . .

Licensing has done far more than simply gratify the understandable status-longing of semi-skilled or specialized workers who, in Professor Merton's words, "want to acquire at least the outer appearance and preferably the inner substance of professional standards, values and education." It has also badly eroded the right to work, one of man's most precious liberties.

Licensing has only infrequently been imposed upon an occupation against its wishes. Unwelcomed licensure has indeed occurred, as when stockbrokers were brought under federal regulation in response to the financial scandals of 1929. In many more instances, however, licensing has been eagerly sought — always on the purported ground that licensure protects the uninformed public against incompetence or dishonesty but invariably with the consequence that members of the licensed group become protected against competition from newcomers. That restricting access is the real purpose, and not merely a side effect, of many if not most successful campaigns to institute licensing schemes can scarcely be doubted. Licensing, imposed ostensibly to protect the public, almost always impedes only those who desire to enter the occupation or "profession"; those already in practice remain entrenched without a demonstration of fitness or probity. The self-interested proponents of a new licensing law generally constitute a more effective political force than the citizens who, if aware of the matter at all, have no special interest which moves them to organize in opposition.

The restrictive consequence of licensure is achieved in large part by making entry into the regulated occupation expensive in time or money or both. In Iowa, for example, a person who aspires to ease the pains of those who suffer from bunions and corns must have graduated from "a school of podiatry approved by the board of podiatry examiners" and must then be examined, according to the statute, "in the subjects of anatomy, chemistry, dermatology, diagnosis, pharmacy and materia medica, pathology, physiology, histology, bacteriology, neurology, foot orthopedics, and others, as prescribed by the board." This does indeed sound imposing. One suspects, however, that the verbiage is of more benefit to bunion removers than to bunion sufferers.

In California a license to cut hair can be won only after the completion of a long apprenticeship, graduation from a barber college, and success in an examination that in past years has demanded knowledge of such esoteric things as the chemical composition of the bones and the name of the muscle that is inserted in the hyoid bone. Illinois purportedly tests a would-be barber's knowledge of, among other things, physiology, electricity, anatomy, and barber history. Fifty years ago not a single American state required a barber to attend a tuition-demanding "college" for the equivalent of an academic year. Now most of the states insist that new recruits to the hair-cutting profession receive institutionalized instruction in bacteriology; histology of the hair, skin, nails, muscles, and nerves; diseases of the skin, hair, glands, and nails; and other matters about which one may venture to guess few barbers are consulted. . . . The costly and time-consuming acquisition of artificial learning in a pseudo profession nevertheless blocks an occupational choice that might otherwise be available to the impecunious.

Barbering has been used as a horrible example, but irrelevancies are by no means confined to any one of the new "professions." Years ago a Wisconsin legislator, after examining some of that state's occupational requirements, exclaimed sadly that as a practical matter, her child could no longer aspire to become a watchmaker, but fortunately could still qualify to seek the presidency of the United States. In some states virtually the only "profession" open to a once-convicted felon is that of burglar; he is barred from other activities because he is presumed to be a person of bad moral character, regardless of the nature of the felony or its relevance to his intended occupation. Until the courts finally called a halt, becoming a master plumber in Illinois took just a bit longer than becoming a Fellow of the American College of Surgeons.

Some restrictions on occupational choice are blatant absurdities. For example, Georgia insists that those who seek to be commercial photographers must pass with flying colors a Wasserman test for syphilis. At one time the Indiana Athletic Commission insisted that boxers and wrestlers take a loyalty oath before being allowed to enter the ring. Silliness like this is probably not motivated by anything so rational as a desire to discourage competition.

More often, however, the statutory constraints have had truly exclusionary intent and effect. These constraints include requirements that licensees be citizens or residents of a locality. Some states insist that only an American citizen can qualify to become, for instance, a pharmacist, chiropodist, tree surgeon, embalmer, bill collector, or osteopath. Other laws provide that, regardless of national citizenship, a licensee must have been a resident of the license-issuing state for a substantial period of time — although the relationship between prior residence and occupational qualifications may be undiscoverable, as in the case of optometrists, accountants, masseurs, and dentists. One would suppose that lenses are ground and teeth are cleaned in essentially the same manner in different states, but the statutes pretend that one must have lived within the license-issuing state in order to understand its citizenry's needs. Occupational licenses have also been conditioned upon residency in political subdivisions smaller than a state. Twenty-eight states provide for the licensing of plumbers, but in most of these states the plumbers have managed to prevent licensing on a statewide basis. Instead, licenses are issued by the cities, which impose municipal residence requirements aimed at excluding "outsiders" from the local job market.

If men were angels, as has been remarked, external controls over their conduct would be superfluous. Since the most recent census fails to disclose a significant increase in the angelic population, I do not join those who advocate ending occupational licensing altogether. Painful economic experiences might ultimately lead consumers of services to locate the most efficient, most trustworthy suppliers. Meanwhile, however, many persons would suffer avoidable wounds to person or purse. The anonymity of a largely urbanized American society prevents the kind of informed choice which may have been possible when clients, patients, and customers could rely with reasonable confidence upon neighbors' opinions of professionals and tradesmen. For that reason I accept the view that in some occupations some kind of quality control may be needed to protect the uninformed against blatant incompetents, wily charlatans, and persons whose past delinquencies suggest the probability of future corrupt conduct.

Everything is, however, a matter of degree. I am comforted by the thought that surgeons and structural engineers must pass scrutiny by somebody more knowledgeable than I am or am likely to become about their qualifications. On the other hand, I think it absurd to set up elaborate mechanisms as precautions against my being dissatisfied with the way my hair has been cut, my toenails trimmed, my muscles kneaded, my hearing aid fitted, or my drains unclogged. Only the credulous can conclude that licensure is in the main intended to protect the public rather than those who have been licensed or, perhaps in some instances, those who do the licensing.

To say that licensing has been abused and overused is not to say that prophylactic administration should be abandoned. I do not advocate reviving the doctrine of caveat emptor, nor do I suppose for a minute that customers and clients who have been ill served can be made whole by lawsuits against their miscreant servitors. Litigation is too unwieldy to meet the needs of those who have suffered minor injuries. What are needed are measures that will provide protection against those demonstrably deficient in capability or integrity without in the process creating artificial limitations upon career choices, work opportunities, and stimuli to provide superior service at lesser cost. Among these protective measures are permissive certification and mandatory registration.

Permissive certification may be suitable when a program of prior training or a demonstration of an objectively measurable degree of skill can be regarded as a genuine precondition of a person's claiming an occupational status. For example, some state laws provide that before a person identifies himself as an "architect" he must have been certified as one who deserves that title because he has given proof of his education and capability. These laws do not, however, bar others from engaging in the work architects do; those who are uncertified may not call themselves "architects," but they may do work of an architectural nature without risking prosecution for engaging in the "unauthorized practice" of a licensed occupation. Certification of this kind permits pertinently defined expectations, so that the consuming public can differentiate between a self-styled expert and a person whose qualifications have been passed on by a state authority. Yet, unlike licensure, this control mechanism does not wholly withdraw occupational opportunity from persons who, though unable to meet all the requirements of certification (for example, formal education), may be competent.

A far more comprehensive regulatory device is the simple registration of anyone who desires to receive a particular occupational license, with the automatic issuance of the license upon registration. Engaging in the occupation without a license, or obtaining it by misrepresentation, would be made a serious offense, in order to stimulate prompt and accurate registration. An appropriate state agency, not linked with an occupational group, would be created to receive complaints against licensees, investigate them, and, if objectionable conduct is found, initiate proceedings looking toward revocation, suspension, or other appropriate discipline by a court or a special tribunal.

A plan of this nature would, I believe, end the present abuse of licensure that serves selfish interests by constricting occupational freedom. It would recapture the public power now delegated to multiple licensing boards whose members are drawn from and owe allegiance to the occupations they supposedly regulate in the public interest. It would require that licensees be subject to stern discipline, but only after carefully formulated charges, fair hearings, and impartial determinations, untainted by suspicion that the determiners' self-interest has influenced their judgment. It would take away the eligibility of those whose occupational unworthiness could be demonstrated, but would not, as so many licensing laws now do, place artificial roadblocks in the path of work opportunities or squelch career aspirations by treating predictive opinions as final judgments.

3. Comments and Questions

a. Walter Gellhorn was perhaps the leading administrative law teacher and scholar in America over the last seventy-five years — i.e., from the inception of modern administrative law. He clearly was not reflexively opposed to government regulation or intervention in economic activity.

b. A common criticism of professional licensure is that the real beneficiaries are not the public but the profession, because it limits entry and thus results in higher prices. Licensure also provides a form of group organization, what in other contexts might be called a trade union, which also helps to raise the income of the profession and the costs to the public that is supposedly being protected.

c. None of these ideas are new. Over 200 years ago, Adam Smith observed: "People of the same occupation seldom meet together, even for merriment and diversion, but the conversation ends in a conspiracy against the public, or in some contrivance to raise prices."

d. Occupational licensure is not simply a matter of economic policy, but also a fundamental limitation on individual freedom. As Milton Friedman, himself an economist, noted:

> The overthrow of the medieval guild system was an indispensable early step in the rise of freedom in the Western world. It was a sign of the triumph of liberal ideas, and widely recognized as such. . . . [B]y the mid-nineteenth century . . . [individuals] could pursue whatever trade or occupation they wished without the by-your-leave of any governmental or quasi-governmental authority.

MILTON FRIEDMAN, CAPITALISM AND FREEDOM 137 (1962).

e. Do you favor government regulation of mediation? If so, what form should that regulation take? Should the federal government establish minimum standards for mediators that it hires, either as employees or consultants? If so, to what extent should these standards be uniform, and to what extent should they be determined at the agency level?

f. Serious professional standards require a bureaucracy to test for initial competence, monitor continuing competence, and enforce professional standards. Preventing unauthorized practice is another common undertaking of professional regulation. Is the primary beneficiary the public or the profession? Typically the state agency created for professional regulation is controlled by persons who are members of the regulated profession. Is this an example of what the public administration and administrative law literature calls "the capture thesis?" (The hypothesis is that agencies are to an important extent "captured" by the interests they were supposedly created to regulate.)

g. As you consider the recommendations for various forms of credentialing, note what is said (if anything) about the associated costs. Does the absence of a discussion of costs, and who pays evidence a lack of seriousness? Do the authors need a stiff dose of "reality testing"?

C. CREDENTIALING OF MEDIATORS AND OTHER DISPUTE RESOLUTION PRACTITIONERS

1. Paula M. Young, *Take It or Leave It, Lump It or Grieve It: Designing Mediator Complaint Systems That Protect Mediators, Unhappy Parties, Attorneys, Courts, The Process, and the Field*, 21 OHIO ST. J. ON DISP. RESOL. 721, 731-41 (2006)

A comprehensive regulatory system typically consists of several components. First, the regulatory system creates barriers of entry to the field consisting of several possible components: (a) training requirements that vary depending on the type of mediations the mediator intends to conduct, (b) ethics training, (c) moral character reviews, (d) minimum degree or professional license requirements, (e) written tests, and (f) performance-based testing or evaluation. The system may also grant official recognition that the mediator has passed these barriers to entry by certifying, registering, or rostering the mediator. The regulatory system may regulate or approve mediation training programs. The system may also require mediators who have successfully passed the barriers of entry to prove at a later date — through a recertification or re-registration process — that they are committed to the mediation field and to their skill development. The system may require continuing mediation education, including additional ethics training, or proof that the mediator has completed a specified number of mediations in a specified time period. The regulatory system may also support mediators by providing ethics information, encouraging compliance with aspirational ethics guidelines, creating a mandatory ethics code, and issuing ethics advisory opinions. The regulatory system may further provide rules or guidelines for interacting in the legal world on issues of mediation confidentiality, the unauthorized practice of law (UPL), and mediator immunity. It should offer public oversight through well-designed grievance systems.

Finally, a comprehensively designed regulatory system will grant the state supreme court or its ADR administrator the power to sanction mediators for ethical violations or other misconduct. Those sanctions would at least include the ability to remove mediators from court-approved mediator rosters. . . .

Only [a few] states have implemented most or all of these components of a comprehensive mediator regulatory system. Florida's more mature system reflects its 30 year experience with court-connected mediation. Virginia modeled its system on Florida's system, and Georgia in turn modeled its system on Virginia's system. Minnesota designed its grievance rules the same year Virginia adopted its grievance system. Maine, the most recently designed regulatory system, has the least formal grievance process. . . .

2. Charles Pou, Jr., *Assuring Excellence or Merely Reassuring? Policy and Practice in Promoting Mediator Quality*, 2005 J. DISP. RESOL. 303

Drawing on program and literature reviews, and interviews with experienced administrators, practitioners, and academics, this article tries to map the ways in which the dispute resolution field has sought to define and assure mediator competence. This article suggests, among other things, that the historical focus on credentialing efforts has been largely misguided — putting excessive attention on certification measures and "evidence of competence" (such as law degrees or substantive knowledge) that have less to do with real mediation ability than with ease of administration, and courts' and other programs' desire to "reassure" clients.

Describing several of the more innovative or high-profile quality assurance (QA) efforts over the past decade, this article categorizes mediator quality assurance systems by employing a two-dimensional grid: one dimension reflects the nature and height of "hurdles" a mediator must meet at the outset to engage in practice, and the other corresponds to the amount of "maintenance," or continuing educational activities and other support, expected by program administrators. Based on this grid, the article describes and assesses five prototypical approaches to mediator QA — High hurdle/Low maintenance, High hurdle/High maintenance, Low hurdle/Low maintenance, Low hurdle/High maintenance, and No hurdle/No maintenance. It offers examples of each, discusses potential implications of employing any given one, and offers policy and implementation advice.

Based on this inquiry, the article suggests that whatever the psychological or other benefits of approaches that certify some as "competent" mediators and exclude others, the risks inherent in such methods — including exclusivity, overvaluation of marginal skills, and reduced innovation, diversity, and collegiality — can well outweigh the advantages. It advocates a system that — either instead of or in addition to — provides encouragement, incentives, and a support structure that allows mediators (using performance-based approaches and user feedback, among other things) to target developmental needs, work collaboratively on continually improving process skills, give systematic attention to "reflective practice," and deal with shortcomings. Such an approach, the piece concludes, will do far more than an approach placing primary emphasis on credentialing to advance the field's overall competence and enhance its credibility over the long haul. . . .

The growing use of ADR processes has led some to argue that standards related to competence and the selection of mediators are needed to protect consumers and the integrity of dispute resolution processes. The topic has been controversial for years, in part because the competence a mediator needs may vary from one context to another. Moreover, nearly all agree, measuring competence cannot be done based on paper credentials alone. Several professional membership organizations and others have developed policies, principles, or qualification standards regarding who can serve in various settings. . . .

V. What's Happening? Some Quality Assurance Initiatives

While professionals and researchers have tried over the past fifteen years or so to define "what mediators do" and better understand "how to do it well," ADR programs, roster administrators, and parties seeking neutrals have had to deal with day-to-day choices. Moreover, mediators and "wannabes" often use their training, continuing education, roster listings, court "certifications," or credentials to practice another profession as indicators of claimed competence to mediate. Ways to qualify mediators are being developed in literally thousands of different programs. These range from professional organizations creating membership categories to judges, court administrators, and agencies establishing rosters or other means of "vouching for" their mediators. This section describes some of the more interesting, innovative, or timely of these activities.

1. Association for Conflict Resolution. ACR is involved in several quality assurance initiatives. These include participation on the Joint Committee on Model Standards of Conduct for Mediators, now considering revisions in these ethical standards; its Ethics Initiative, described below; and the Advanced Practitioner Workgroup. The most significant of ACR's recent QA initiatives is its Mediator Certification Task Force, which has developed recommendations regarding a certification process. The Task Force concluded that the field has developed to the point of needing certification that documents and acknowledges that a mediator has completed a minimum level of training and experience. Among its stated goals is a process that is accessible to a broad range of practitioners and allows for diversity of practice and people. After considering a variety of options, the Task Force recommended that ACR establish a certification program with the following elements:

- Presentation of a "portfolio" of experience and training.
- Successful completion of a written knowledge assessment.
- Periodic re-certification.
- A process for requesting a waiver of some of the requirements
- Potential de-certification for violation of ethical and professional standards.
- Appeals of decisions at various stages in the certifying process.

The intent of the Mediator Certification Program is that the program to be "purely voluntary and open to both members and non-members of ACR." . . . ACR and the ABA Section of Dispute Resolution are beginning to work together to create an independent entity that will provide a voluntary certification process.

2. ABA Section of Dispute Resolution. The Section established the Task Force on Credentialing in 2001. The goals of the Task Force were to inform the Section about past and current dispute resolution professional credentialing practices and policies; to consider the direction the field is moving related to credentialing and to make recommendations to the Section for policy and action; and to assure networking with professional membership organizations and others engaged in credentialing policy and program development. The ABA Task Force's 2003 Report on Mediator Credentialing and Quality Assurance discusses past and current mediator credentialing practices, analyzes the relation of credentialing to quality practice, and puts forth some recommendations on policy actions. The recommendations were approved by the Section's Council in early 2003 — these included a statement favoring mediator credentialing, a policy to support mediator competency and growth (quality assurance) over paper credentials, and development of model standards for mediator preparation programs.

Since approval of the ABA Task Force's report, members of the group have begun informal consultation with representatives of ACR and other national and state mediation organizations and is joining ACR in commissioning a feasibility-marketing survey by an independent expert. The Section of Dispute Resolution's Council does not envision the ABA or the Section serving as a credentialing body, but rather to support the field in the development of quality practice and credentialing. The Task Force will also develop model standards for mediator preparation programs and outline one or more model systems of mediator credentialing to recommend to states or to the field, focusing initially on the accreditation of mediator preparation programs. . . .

3. National Association for Community Mediation. The NAFCM Quality Assurance Committee recently completed an initiative that has produced a Community Mediation Center Self Assessment Manual, a non-prescriptive assessment tool that will help community mediation centers focus on improving general management for non-profits, case administration, and training, development, nurturing, and handling of volunteers. For each of these areas, the NAFCM document addresses practical service delivery considerations for centers and sets forth some potentially useful approaches to dealing with them. Consonant with most community programs' emphasis on some regimen of basic and advanced training, mentoring, co-mediation, observation, and continuing education — as opposed to credentialing individual mediators, which NAFCM officials describe as inherently exclusive — the initiative describes aspirational standards, poses questions to consider regarding how to reach these goals, and offers examples of how some centers have dealt with these issues. . . .

4. Texas. Two recent, and considerably different, quality assurance initiatives are worth noting. An advisory committee to the supreme court submitted a proposal in 2001 for creating a registry of state court mediators (attorneys and non-attorneys). Advisory committee members gathered extensive data on other jurisdictions' approaches during their deliberations, drawing especially from Tennessee and Georgia. The Texas Supreme Court did not act on the report, which contained recommendations concerning minimum qualifications for mediators, a recommendation for a Commission on Training, and Rules of Ethics for Mediators.

The advisory committee did not make a recommendation on "credentialing" for a variety of reasons, but it did recommend minimum qualifications for court mediators. In addition to the required training courses, the committee proposed requiring continuing education for court mediators. The committee also recommended having judges select from the list of mediators possessing minimum qualifications, while allowing a judge to go outside the list if she provides a written explanation for doing so. In addition, the advisory committee would have required that mediators adhere to the Texas Rules of Ethics for Mediations and Mediators as promulgated by the Texas Supreme Court. As to enforcement, the committee recommended that the court in which the action is pending, or the local administrative judge of the county, district or region, enforce the ethics rules in any manner provided by law, or by submitting the matter to mediation.

While the supreme court advisory committee's efforts have not produced concrete results, a second Texas initiative, the Texas Mediator Credentialing Association (TMCA), has recently been incorporated as a not-for-profit entity to serve as a voluntary credentialer for mediators and mediation trainers in all fields. The Association's ten-member board includes representatives from Texas' major mediator and trainer groups, the bar, consumers, education institutions, and the judiciary. The Board set credentialing and training standards, and set up an administration system and a grievance process, and has begun to accept applications. TMCA's model entails a four-tiered approach, in essence a seniority system with basic certification and advanced levels of credentialing based on training and experience. TMCA's collaborative effort to promote quality in a judge and lawyer-centric system has built a broader understanding and acceptance among diverse groups of mediators in the state. In April 2003, its Board joined to oppose unanimously several entities that wanted the supreme court to revive its activities leading to credentialing of court mediators. . . .

5. *Florida.* Florida was among the first states to credential court mediators, and probably has the largest such program. In order to receive referrals directly from the courts, a mediator must be certified by the Florida Supreme Court. The qualifications are established in the Florida Rules for Certified and Court-Appointed Mediators. In addition, parties to mediation are free to select a certified or non-certified mediator who is otherwise qualified by training or experience to mediate all or some of the issues in the particular case. The selection of a non-certified mediator is subject to review by the presiding judge.

"County Court Mediators" in Florida must be certified as a circuit court or family mediator or complete a minimum of twenty hours in a training program certified by the supreme court; observe a minimum of four county court mediation conferences conducted by a court-certified mediator and conduct four county court mediation conferences under the supervision and observation of a court-certified mediator; and be of good moral character. "Circuit Court Mediators" must complete a minimum of forty hours in a circuit court mediation training program certified by the supreme court; be a member in good standing of the Florida Bar with at least five years of Florida practice and be an active member of the Florida Bar within one year of application for certification; . . . observe two circuit court mediations conducted by a certified circuit mediator and conduct two circuit mediations under the supervision and observation of a certified circuit court mediator; and be of good moral character.

"Family Mediators" must complete a minimum of forty hours in a family mediation training program certified by the supreme court; have a master's degree or doctorate in social work, mental health, or behavioral or social sciences; be a physician certified to practice adult or child psychiatry; or be an attorney or a certified public accountant licensed to practice in any United States jurisdiction; and have at least four years practical experience in one of the aforementioned fields or have eight years family mediation experience with a minimum of ten mediations per year; observe two family mediations conducted by a certified family mediator and conduct two family mediations under the supervision and observation of a certified family mediator; and be of good moral character.

6. United States Postal Service. The United States Postal Service (USPS) trained a number of trainers to offer several thousand experienced mediators a two-day session on using a transformative approach to postal workplace mediation. Rather than evaluating trainees at that point, USPS then required those wishing to obtain paid referrals to submit to observation in an initial pro bono case. USPS also sought to train its mediation program administrators to assess neutrals on an ongoing basis, and provided listed mediators an opportunity to participate in periodic "mini-conferences" to discuss real-world problems and research findings. This approach has resulted in USPS paring its mediator list considerably, based largely on observations. Program managers expressed the view that QA is a continuing process, rather than a one-time assessment, and emphasized the importance of defining quality in connection with the program's goals [in this instance, transformative mediation only] rather than generically.

7. Department of the Navy. The Navy's workplace mediation program relies almost entirely on several dozen employee-mediators who, after being nominated by their "commands," have received training and mentoring before being certified to mediate Navy workplace cases part-time. The Navy's four-step process seeks to assure competence, and involves a basic twenty hour mediation course, a supplemental twenty hour course emphasizing role-plays, a screening based on observation of how the trainee handles a one and one half hour role-play, advanced training on ethics and other issues, and three co-mediations and extended debriefs with experienced contractor-mediators or internal mentors. After completing these steps, a Navy mediator can apply for certification. The Department of the Navy has developed several instruments to aid this program (e.g., observer's checklist, co-mediator evaluation form), and provide occasional refresher sessions. The program's director expressed intent to develop a recertification process, based on the notion that approval is not "for life."

8. Federal Deposit Insurance Corporation. In the early 1990s, the FDIC sought the advice of a "Blue Ribbon Panel" of experts to develop a set of criteria for private mediators wishing to be listed on the agency's nationwide roster of neutrals who could be used to resolve agency cases. In brief, these experience-based criteria were total hours spent as a neutral, number of cases, diversity of substance and process, dollar amount involved, multi-party experience, and complexity of cases. The panel considered and rejected several factors, including education, training, prior certifications, and professional association memberships. An initial decision to award points for women or minority status was later reversed in light of recent federal court decisions. . . .

IX. Assistance Instead of Assurance: Learning To Accept Ambiguity

The growth of ADR has led many courts and mediation programs to develop credentialing and other approaches that seek to assure high quality, ethical practice. Local political and professional factors; persistent, strong divisions as to how to define and promote "good" mediation; and a variety of practical difficulties have led courts and other programs to take very diverse — and sometimes dubious — paths in trying to assure quality. Chris Honeyman has set forth some of these approaches and described their pitfalls:

> More and more, we can expect the heavily-trumpeted legal and "substantive knowledge" skills to be used to fill the gap. The logical result makes mediation an adjunct function within each of several occupations which are really about something else. At the same time, on the professional side of the field, we are in effect helping to promote in the marketplace mediators whose key skills overlap the core skill set of mediation only to a degree, at the expense of those whose balance of skills is closest to mediation itself. Over a period of time, we should logically expect this to lower the public's reasonable expectations of what mediation should be able to accomplish.

Given what we do know about mediators' behavior, clients' needs, and the political realities involved, addressing mediator quality assurance will never be a simple or straightforward matter. . . .

High-quality mediators come from a variety of backgrounds, and many good ones have learned on the job or developed skills in ways other than standard ones. Any approach to quality assurance that is exclusive, as opposed to inclusive, runs a risk of eliminating some potentially excellent mediators. Similarly, those who believe that reliance on a single test, a research-based questionnaire, or credentials based on background or experience will succeed in denoting or predicting good practice are doomed to disappointment. None of the five QA strategies is so superior that all should adopt it. . . . A strategy that would, among other things, encourage, or even require, regular exposure to other mediators, styles, and experiences to promote "reflective practice" will be both more stringent than laissez faire and less rigid than regulation involving the "certainty" of prescriptive edicts as to "who can mediate." Those implementing a QA strategy should consider these general recommendations:

- The definition of "quality mediation" may not be the same in every context.

- Substantive knowledge can be important in some mediation settings but is not generally determinative of a mediator's abilities or long-term potential.

- Voluntary approaches . . . are preferable to mandatory credentialing or "elitism."

- Hurdles should be kept modest, and incentives and encouragement to participate in long-term improvement programs should serve as a middle way between mandatory certification and market-based approaches.

- While . . . some percentage of trainees and experienced mediators will never be able to master necessary skills, a great majority possess either basic skills or the ability to acquire them with some sustained effort.

- All mediators have something to learn about good mediation, and benefit from exposure to a variety of sources and styles.

- Performance-based testing activities should be developed that serve to permit identification of areas where skills could stand improvement and remedial education plans be developed.

- Ongoing outreach, education, and related interactions that involve users and providers of mediation services will be important. They should explore what to look for in an ADR process and in a neutral, as well as the limits of particular credentialing approaches.

QA processes and decisions that emphasize approaches that assist mediators to improve — not those that purport to "assure" competence pursuant to readily measurable criteria of questionable significance — are likely to produce clear advantages for courts, provider organizations, and other mediation users. Ideally, these groups will begin to value such a "quality assistance" philosophy, both as a vehicle for mediators' growth and as an indicator of their skill.

3. Sarah Rudolph Cole, *Mediator Certification: Has the Time Come?*, 11-3 DISP. RESOL. MAG. 7 (Spring 2005)

The widespread adoption of certification standards for mediators appears to be on the horizon. The American Bar Association (ABA) and the Association for Conflict Resolution (ACR), a major dispute resolution organization, have joined forces to study the feasibility of developing a national mediator certification program. At the same time, ACR is planning to put into place its first voluntary mediator certification program. In addition, Florida has proposed a revised certification program for court mediators. The Federal Mediation and Conciliation Service (FMCS) also proposed a new certification system, although it was forced to shelve it due to financial considerations.

To assess whether this movement toward certification is cause for commendation or for concern, we must first consider the stated goals of certification, along with the related questions of whether, and to whom, those goals are important. Second, if the goals are worthwhile, we should consider the efficacy of the various certification approaches in achieving the goals. This article explores both of these topics, and suggests potential areas of concern regarding each. It ultimately concludes that the organizations should make greater efforts to ensure that there is buy-in regarding the appropriate goals. It further concludes that the certification proposals now on the table may, in fact, be counterproductive, even for achieving the currently stated goals.

The goals of mediator certification include: (1) protecting consumers from the effect of "bad" mediators, (2) reducing court congestion (assuming that more cases will settle if high quality mediators handle them), and (3) promoting mediation by, among other things, improving mediator credibility through an external indication of quality. The ACR Task Force on Mediator Certification stated that a voluntary certification process would also: (1) provide uniform verification of a basic level of training, (2) create among mediators a "more solid foundation of competency and professionalism," (3) assist consumers in selecting a mediator, and (4) enable certified mediators to influence the development of the mediation field.

As a general matter, these goals all seem directed at three interrelated and symbiotic objectives: protecting and assisting consumers, improving overall mediator quality, and enhancing the credibility of "good" mediators in the marketplace. The first question, then, is whether these are necessary, or even worthwhile, goals to pursue. Do consumers need greater protection from bad mediators or more help in selecting qualified mediators? Do "good" mediators need or want to enhance their market credibility through certification? In the mediation circles, anecdotal tales of bad mediators are common. But is there a consensus on what constitutes a bad mediator, or, conversely, on what characteristics "good" mediators share?

The last question is perhaps the most elusive. For some time, the mediation community has believed that a key component of a good mediation is a quality mediator. But the necessary attributes of a quality mediator are often described in subjective terms that may not easily lend themselves to paper-file-based certification programs. For example, some have suggested that quality mediators must listen actively; identify issues; frame issues so that mediation parties understand them; use clear, neutral language; deal ably with complex factual scenarios; show respect for parties; earn the trust of parties; and separate their own values from the issues before them. Magistrate Judge Wayne Brazil has offered additional characteristics: moral integrity, honesty, sensitivity, sustainable energy and positive spirit, commitment to procedural fairness, and the ability to refrain from forming premature opinions.

All of these characteristics sound good — it is hard to argue against moral integrity and honesty — yet sources for concern remain as we consider certification designed to achieve or promote "quality" mediators. . . . If the goal of certification programs is "separating the wheat from the chaff," more work should be done to determine how to differentiate the two. Until there is a shared consensus on which attributes we should be looking for, it is difficult at best to discuss the specifics of certification programs for assessing whether those attributes are present.

Nor is it clear that consensus within the mediation community as to what constitutes mediator quality is the final answer on that issue. If a goal of mediator certification is to enhance the market credibility (and thus, perhaps, the market value) of "good" mediators, perhaps we should be looking to mediation consumers to ascertain what they think constitutes mediator quality. . . . Under this approach, market surveys would determine what customers want, and then certification could act as a "seal of approval" that the listed mediators possess those consumer-selected attributes. . . .

To date, remarkably little empirical work has been done that demonstrates a strong link between training or education, on the one hand, and mediator quality on the other. I am aware of only one study that has looked at the issue, and that study concluded that the only relevant variable for predicting mediator quality was experience. In addition to the lack of any empirical evidence supporting a link between training or education and mediator quality, there are also reasons to think that such requirements may in fact be counterproductive. A brief examination of ACR and Florida's proposed mediator certification plans shows how such plans might, in some ways, undermine an effort to ensure mediator quality.

To obtain ACR's proposed certification, an applicant submits a portfolio of experience, training and education. ACR evaluates the portfolio and then requires that the applicant take a written test to become eligible for placement on the ACR roster. A successful applicant for ACR's roster must have 100 hours of training, 80 of which must be training in mediation process skills. A mediator may satisfy up to 20 of the 100 hours as a trainer or teacher.

Applicants must also demonstrate that they have 100 total hours of mediation or co-mediation within the last five years or 500 hours over a lifetime. Successful applicants will also be subject to periodic recertification and decertification for ethical and professional standards violations. In addition, applicants denied placement on the roster are entitled to appeal ACR's decision. Applicants must obtain professional liability insurance, disclose criminal convictions, and provide letters of reference in order to gain and maintain placement on the roster.

Florida's Supreme Court Committee on Alternative Dispute Resolution Rules and Policy is planning to recommend a major change to existing mediator certification requirements. The proposed plan would quantify experience somewhat differently than does ACR. Rather than directly examining hours of training and experience and educational degrees obtained, Florida would utilize a point system for credentialing mediators. To obtain certification, a prospective applicant would have to have a combination of education, training and experience. For example, a circuit court mediator would need to complete Florida's mediation training, obtain a combined 25 points for general education (a mediator would receive points for the highest level of education obtained; for example, 20 points for a college degree) and experience (one point for each year that a mediator mediates 15 cases of any type). Florida mediators would also be required to show that they had participated in a mentorship program. Mentorship means observation of pre-suit or court mediations or co-mediations within the court system for which the applicant wishes certification. Applicants would also have to demonstrate that they had taken a certified Florida Supreme Court mediation training. . . . Unfortunately, such systems tend to reward those who have sufficient funds to pay for mediation training and advanced degrees.

Recommendations

While certification, correctly structured, could provide benefits to the mediation field by protecting the public, promoting mediation, increasing the likelihood that some mediators may have more productive careers and reducing court congestion, providing certification through points accumulation and written testing is problematic. Moreover, even though the current certification plans are voluntary, the ACR-ABA plan is to explore creation of a national mediator certification program. If certification becomes widespread, it seems likely that certification will be viewed as an essential characteristic of a mediator and that mediators who choose not to pursue certification or who do not meet the proposed standards will not be able to maintain a viable practice.

In an effort to preserve diversity within the mediation field and to avoid precluding qualified mediators from obtaining certification, the national mediator certification effort should add a holistic review to the certification process for mediator applicants whose background strongly suggests that they could be quality mediators. Advocates of national mediator certification should also consider certifying mediator preparation programs. These efforts would be more consistent with the various articulated organizational goals and would be more equitable to existing and future mediators. At the same time, this refocusing might provide a more useful credential for mediators as well as helpful information to consumers that they might utilize when selecting a mediator.

4. Craig McEwen, *Giving Meaning to Mediator Professionalism*, 11-3 DISP. RESOL. MAG. 3 (Spring 2005)

Swirling around the current debate about certifying mediators is an interest in promoting mediator "professionalism," but this aspiration often lies below the surface of discussion because its meaning has not been clearly articulated. Sarah Cole's thoughtful critique of proposals for certification raises challenging questions focused on the contribution that such a process would make to promoting high quality mediation. A recent report by the Association for Conflict Resolution (ACR), however, argues that another goal for certification is to "create a more solid foundation of competency and professionalism." Indeed, the preamble to the report asserts the central value of promoting "the continuing development of a vital and distinct conflict management profession."

This article brings the discussion of professionalism to the surface, shows the significant confusion and ambivalence about the meaning of the concept and makes a case for viewing professionalism as collegial control. It then examines how certification and other activities of local, state and national dispute resolution organizations might promote collegial control and, ideally, high quality mediation by supporting the development of active communities of practice among mediators.

Although the Report of the ACR Task Force on Mediator Certification argues that certification will advance both competency and professionalism, it also reveals some confusion and ambivalence about this aspiration. The report notes that one of its guiding concerns is "that the certification process is intended to encourage professionalism and the professional development of conflict management practice. It is not meant to professionalize the field, but rather to add a degree of quality assurance to it." This effort to offer professionalism without professionalization suggests the multiple meanings of these concepts as well as some concerns about their negative connotations. Sorting through those meanings and the baggage attached to them helps set the stage for a sharper understanding of what professionalism might mean and of the challenges of translating that aspiration to practice.

By several common definitions, mediation would not qualify as a profession, given that paid and unpaid individuals, many of whom have 100 or fewer hours of training, engage in practicing it. In one such view, professions are those occupations — such as law, medicine and architecture — that are based on a substantial body of formal knowledge and lengthy, formal training. Dictionary definitions of profession range from the exclusive group of four traditional professions (law, medicine, clergy, military) to almost any paid work (professional as compared to amateur). And in common idiom, professional can refer as easily to a standard of attire ("professional dress expected") as to the nature of particular work. Such widely varied usage makes it problematic to use the rhetoric of professionalism as a guide to collective action by organizations such as ACR.

The histories of aspiring groups help explain the ambivalence about professionalization that appears in the ACR Task Force report. The stories of optometrists, nurses, accountants, psychologists and midwives, for example, represent efforts to win respect in the world at large and in relation to more established professional peers. They also reflect the eagerness of rising occupations to make a claim on some share of business, income, authority and prestige — often against the resistance of entrenched professions such as law, medicine and psychiatry. Such struggles are primarily for control of the occupation: for the right to define the standards of entry, to control that entry through certification of programs of study, to oversee the administration of tests for licensing practitioners and to define the boundaries of practice in relation to competing and collaborating professionals. In this historical context, professionalization can appear self-interested and self-protective.

Those perceptions are only reinforced by critiques of established professions that note their monopoly power, high barriers to entering practice and resulting ability to command high fees. They also highlight the mixed record of professions in policing incompetence, problematic or self-serving conduct and laziness by professional peers. These patterns of established and aspiring professions further confuse our understanding of what professionalism means and create uncertainty about its desirability.

ELIOT FREIDSON, PROFESSIONALISM REBORN: THEORY, PROPHECY AND POLICY 173 (1994), helps us work our way through this conceptual confusion and moral uncertainty by identifying the central principle of professionalism: "that the members of a specialized occupation control their own work." In LYNN MATHER, CRAIG MCEWEN & RICHARD MAIMAN, DIVORCE LAWYERS AT WORK: VARIETIES OF PROFESSIONALISM IN PRACTICE (2001), my coauthors and I develop the concept of collegial control and contrast it with three other forms of control over work:

- Control by organizations: bureaucratic control involving hierarchy, supervision, rules and accountability to superiors in relation to an organization's goals;

- Market control: workers producing what customers or clients demand and pay for, letting the market — and consumers — dictate the character and quality of work; and

- Control by government and legal rules: regulation by agencies of government, perhaps with licensing, inspection and competency examinations.

The impulse to establish a professional identity often arises as a way to resist or preclude alternative forms of control over the work of practitioners. In the case of mediation, those might come from statute or, as the ACR Task Force made explicit, from "any other existing profession."

How practitioners deal with the many discretionary decisions that must be made in day-to-day practice distinguishes collegial from other forms of control over work. For you as a mediator, these everyday choices might include whether or not to reveal skepticism of a party's claims in a caucus, shut down emotional expressions of parties or conclude a mediation with a resolution you view as unfair. In the context of collegial control, these choices are made not by asking a bureaucratic superior, by bowing to anticipated client wishes or by looking to government regulations. They are made by referring to best practices of a field, perhaps by imagining how respected peers might handle the situation or by talking with colleagues about how they would respond.

To make collegial control effective requires strong identity with and connection among colleagues within a field. It means encouraging practitioners to know and pay attention to agreed standards of practice and codes of ethics. But because such rules and standards must be general and pose "often-competing priorities," they cannot provide sufficient guidance for dealing with the daily demands of practice. Thus, although practitioners must always problem-solve on their own, they also need to interact with experienced colleagues through conversation, electronic bulletin boards, reading, observing and shared continuing education. Much of this occurs in "communities of practice" — groups of practitioners finding regular means of communication with one another and sharing common conceptions about how to deal with everyday decisions.

The idea of collegial control does not capture all of the varied meanings associated with the idea of professionalism. Through a more narrow focus, however, it defines both an aspiration and an obligation for professional organizations seeking to promote professionalism. This clarity, however, does not ease the challenges of translating collegial control into practice.

One might aspire to collegial control not only to escape other forms of control, but also because of the ideal that it offers. According to Freidson, it is "based on the democratic notion that people are capable of controlling themselves by cooperative, collective means and that in the case of complex work, those who perform it are in the best position to make sure that it is done well." Accompanying this affirmative vision of a democratic and cooperative enterprise is a substantial responsibility. If a collegially controlled occupation is to avoid charges of self-aggrandizement, it must be effective at providing the public with a high quality service and at identifying, weeding out or transforming "the incompetent, the venal and the negligent" practitioners. The challenges of building and sustaining meaningful collegial control thus go far beyond creating boundaries to entering the field and writing standards of practice. To date, dispute resolution organizations have not explicitly articulated a strategy for building collegial control and have tended to emulate the models provided by established professions while at times pushing creatively beyond them. Indeed, certification is one of the next possible steps beyond the current accomplishments.

Many crucial steps toward collegial control have already been taken. Strong national organizations have developed and work collaboratively — including the American Arbitration Association, the ABA's Section on Dispute Resolution and ACR. Consolidation and cooperation among professional organizations are themselves substantial achievements. The organizations together provide a general voice for mediators and articulate standards and expectations for practice while also connecting individual practitioners with their colleagues through meetings, Web sites and newsletters, training and other crucial forms of ingroup communication. The expression of expectations for fair and ethical practice serves to reflect and shape collegial norms. These formulations include AAA/ABA/ACR Model Standards of Conduct for Mediators. . . .

Several organizations have moved creatively beyond the usual means of supporting aspiring and experienced practitioners through continuing education and training programs. These initiatives create collegial networks to assist both individuals and mediation programs in improving their practices. ACR's One-to-One Mentoring Program is available to members at no cost. The ABA's Section on Dispute Resolution assists court programs through the Court ADR Program Advisors (CAPA) Project. Such initiatives provide models for state and local organizations that may be even better situated to strengthen local communities of practice among mediators.

Proposals for certifying mediators need to be thought of in the context of a wide range of strategies for building collegial control in the mediation field. As Cole argues, setting entry barriers through certification is not likely by itself to markedly affect quality of practice. But certification — perhaps somewhat refocused — could serve as one important aspect of a strategy to strengthen collegial control in mediation and through it, the quality of practice. That larger strategy must take account of the enormous challenge of actively engaging thousands of mediation practitioners — some part time and others full time, some volunteer and others paid — who work in very different forms of practice.

The capacity to create sharp boundaries between practitioners and non-practitioners lies at the heart of traditional notions of professions. Such boundaries establish clear definitions of insider groups and a lever for disciplining members, but there is little evidence from other fields that entry tests accurately predict performance in the profession. The central challenge for mediation is to find plausible, acceptable and appropriately inclusive ways to identify insiders to a collegial community while also precluding regulation by outsider groups. The boundaries to mediation practice, however, can never be as sharp as those in law and medicine because mediation activities occur in such a wide variety of settings and institutions, and are undertaken by elementary school children as well as paid practitioners with professional degrees. It is difficult to imagine clear enough boundaries that might lead to complaints of "unauthorized mediation practice." At the same time, it is possible to imagine voluntary certification by ACR becoming the statutory standard for including mediators on rosters and in publicly funded programs. That prospect of the government co-opting collegial rules as well as the boundary problem must shape the form that certification proposals ultimately take.

Hopes to assure quality of practice through certification might well be focused on promoting future engagement in collegial communities of mediation practice rather than on past performance, test scores or training. That is, certification could encourage active mediators to identify and engage with other practitioners. The key to certification thus might well be ongoing requirements to participate in conferences, training programs or networking activities — including those using electronic media that enable practitioners in remote locations to be involved. Setting expectations for engagement will encourage mediators to continue to learn from one another and require attentiveness to the shared goals, values and unresolved challenges of the enterprise. Such ongoing engagement arguably is the most promising support for quality of practice in the long term.

Certifying training programs. Any move to certify individual mediators must be accompanied by a system for certifying mediation training programs. If past and future training is required for certification, that training should meet the expectations of the mediation community and be directed at least in part toward building collegial engagement. Such programs, especially local ones and those focused on specialty areas, will be important vehicles for building collegial contact and communities of practice.

Building local organizations and identity. National organizations have been instrumental in providing leadership for collegial control, but they cannot effectively connect to widely dispersed individual practitioners. For collegial control to be meaningful, broad identities with the mediation community must be complemented by personal contacts that reinforce professional standards and expectations and help practitioners with problem-solving, reflection and professional growth. Local, regional and state organizations are especially important for establishing and sustaining accessible communities of practice.

Standards for mediation programs. The relationships, expectations, cultures, training, incentives and rewards within organized mediation programs provide the immediate collegial context for much dispute resolution practice. A particularly important step toward enhancing collegial support and control is for professional organizations to establish standards for mediation programs — variable by type of program — and to create mechanisms for their periodic review and certification in relation to those standards. The process of accreditation for law schools and colleges provides an analog for such a review process. A program certification process should encourage programs to develop their own communities of practice and collegial controls consistent with those of the larger mediation field.

Formal and informal control. If general codes of professional responsibility and practice have limited utility in guiding practitioners in some of the most difficult day-to-day decisions, then there may be some room for more rules after all — but largely as tools for the reflection, discussion, and problem-solving. . . . More particularized codes of conduct or best practices that capture the challenges of diverse practices serve as vital complements to generic codes. . . .

Specific standards are the starting rather than the ending point, however. Their utility comes from the problems that they pose and the exchanges they stimulate among mediators in relation to problems of practice. Thus, we should take seriously Pou's suggestion that online discussions of ethics and practice supplement periodic face-to-face discussions among mediators gathering locally, regionally and nationally. Professional organizations at all levels have the responsibility to engage practitioners in such discussions and could make such participation a criterion for any certification. These activities will all be stronger if they attend to the variability of mediation practices and help make collegial control sensitive and relevant to the everyday dilemmas and challenges of mediators.

Local practice interventions. Formal complaint systems run by organizations such as ACR are unlikely to touch many of the issues of quality of practice in mediation. Complaints are likely to be infrequent and will not reach nonmembers over whom the organization has no jurisdiction. The existence of such a complaint process is important symbolically, but will only give the illusion of a complete system of discipline and peer control. Such a system cannot substitute for strong informal peer controls and intervention. Achieving informal peer controls poses enormous challenges. We know that colleagues find it hard to confront peers whose conduct they feel falls short of a collective standard. Local, state and national professional groups must take up the task of supporting and structuring informal intervention by peers to talk to and work with colleagues whose conduct raises concerns.

Control and quality of practice. Despite the lack of clarity about the meaning of professionalization, leading organizations in the mediation field have followed a path of development that is focused less on self-promotion and more on establishing collegial control to support high quality practice. Certification is one possible further step in that direction, although one fraught with difficulties and of limited promise on its own. By embracing collegial control as a goal, organizations such as the ACR, the Section on Dispute Resolution, and the AAA have the opportunity to work collaboratively in designing a strategy for strengthening communities of practice among mediators as the best hope for building both professionalism and quality.

5. Melissa Conley Tyler & Jackie Bornstein, *Accreditation of On-line Dispute Resolution Practitioners*, 23 CONFLICT RESOL. Q. 383 (2006)

This article is excerpted in Chapter Fourteen.

D. STANDARDS OF CONDUCT FOR ADR PROVIDERS

1. Comments and Questions

a. Codes of conduct are a common feature of professional organizations, whether or not the group is subject to state regulation. Monetary compensation for violation of codes of conduct is rare. For that, resort to the courts is necessary — but rarely successful. Legal liability for misconduct by ADR providers is the topic of Section E, below.

b. The most important code of conduct in the ADR field is that AAA/ABA/ACR Model Standards (2005), the text of which is found in the Appendix. Such documents do not make for light reading, and connections between various provisions and concepts may not be obvious. So, Paula Young will guide us through the 2005 AAA/ABA/ACR standards. Pay particular attentions to changes from the previous (1994) Standards.

c. ADR providers who are also members of other professions may be subject to multiple codes of conduct, some aspirational and some with the force of law. Professions that spring immediately to mind are social workers, psychologists, and attorneys. Organizations that maintain rosters of dispute resolution professionals commonly have extensive rules of conduct that cover everything from important principles of disclosure and integrity to minutae of doing business such as the types of records required to support expense statements.

2. Paula M. Young, *Rejoice! Rejoice!, Rejoice, Give Thanks and Sing: ABA, ACR, and AAA Adopt Revised Model Standards of Conduct for Mediators*, 5 J. L. 195 (2006)

This article discusses the nine standards of the 2005 Model Standards in a conceptual framework that I hope will prove more useful to mediators who must resolve ethical dilemmas quickly as they arise in mediation. My experience as a mediation trainer tells me that mediators often have difficulty transferring ethical guidelines set out in the typically drafted framework into principles they can use in the moment. The 2005 Model Standards, for instance, provide guidelines that affect neutrality in six separate standards, without showing how they relate to each other and without always showing the aspects of impartiality they affect. Similarly, guidelines affecting party-self-determination appear in two standards. The 2005 Model Standards also discuss the core value of confidentiality in two standards. In addition, they discuss mediator competence in two standards. Finally, this article considers whether the 2005 Model Standards meet the goals set by the Joint Committee and respond to criticisms of the 1994 version. It concludes that the values expressed in the 1994 Model Standards have proved very durable. While the 2005 Model Standards continue to provide only general guidelines on many difficult ethical issues, they provide a healthy framework for discussing and resolving the ethical dilemmas mediators face. To the extent the field needs ethical guidance in specific situations, state ethics advisory boards could (and do) provide that guidance through advisory opinions. In addition, party complaints against mediators provide additional ethical information to practicing mediators when the regulatory body publishes the dispositions of the complaints. However, these bodies still need a set of ethics standards to interpret or enforce. . . .

III. Discussion of The 2005 Model Standards: A Different Conceptual Framework

A. Preamble. The 2005 Model Standards immediately acknowledge that mediators provide services in many different contexts. The standards define mediation as "a process in which an impartial third party facilitates communication and negotiation and promotes voluntary decision making by the parties to the dispute." The Reporter's Notes emphasize that the revised definition is not intended to exclude any mediation style or approach consistent with Standard I's commitment to support and respect the parties' decision-making roles in the process. The Reporter's Notes identify the more limited role the standards would play in a more pluralistic mediation world: "The Standards . . . retain their original function of serving as fundamental, basic ethical guidelines for persons mediating in all practice contexts while simultaneously recognizing that mediation practice in selected contexts may require additional standards in order to ensure process integrity."

The preamble also expressly states the five purposes of mediation: "Providing the opportunity for parties to define and clarify issues, understand different perspectives, identify interests, explore and assess possible solutions, and reach mutually satisfactory agreements, when desired." As a general matter, the Joint Committee determined that the standards would only direct mediator behavior. Accordingly, several provisions in the 1994 Standards that related to the responsibilities of program directors do not appear in the 2005 Model Standards.

B. Note of Construction. The Note of Construction [is designed to]. . . . provide clarity to the interpretation and application of the Standards. It first notes that the Joint Committee tried to shape the 2005 Model Standards so they would provide mediators guidance when one or more standards provided conflicting rules. It sought to achieve that goal by providing that persons referring to the standards read and construe them "in their entirety" to promote consistency with other standards. Moreover, the sequence of the nine standards does not show any intent to prioritize them.

The standards also contemplate that they may clash with state or federal laws, regulations, court rules, other professional codes, and agreements made by the parties. The Joint Committee instructs mediators to nonetheless comport with the spirit and intent of the standards when resolving these conflicts among legal and contractual authority. Mediators, in any event, must comply with the remaining standards that are not in conflict with other legal or contractual authority. . . .

C. Mediator Impartiality and Neutrality. Mediator impartiality, one of the core values of mediation, gets a lot of attention in the 2005 Model Standards, for good reason. Conduct that makes a party believe that the mediator has lost his or her impartiality is the most frequently cited reason for filing a complaint against a mediator in Virginia and Maine. It appears as the second most frequently raised allegation in Florida, Georgia, and Minnesota. Not surprisingly, the 2005 Model Standards address the issue of impartiality in six standards. However, the organization of the standards makes it difficult to understand the underlying conceptual framework of conflicts of interest, conduct bias, bias in favor of a specific outcome, and lapses of impartiality that undermine party self-determination.

Greg Firestone, a Florida mediator, . . . [has] suggested that the field think about these issues along two dimensions that create four quadrants on a grid. On one side of the grid are the terms "parties" and "outcome." On the other side of the grid are the terms "relationship" and "conduct." The resulting four quadrants are the following: "relationship-parties," "conduct-parties," "relationship-outcome," and "conduct-outcome."

Quadrant 1: Impartiality in the Mediator's Relationships With the Parties. The mediator's impartiality towards the parties is often discussed in terms of conflict of interests. Firestone suggests that parties should consider the following issues when choosing a mediator. A party should learn if the mediator has any current or prior relationships with the other parties to the mediation or their counsel. Has the mediator represented a party in a legal matter previously? Has she provided one of the lawyers therapeutic counseling? Does she play golf with one of the lawyers? Does the mediator attend the same church as one of the parties? Do their children play on the same soccer team? Does the mediator get most of his or her business from one company or firm? Can she remain impartial to the party who is not the repeat player in the referral system? Mediators should error on the side of over-disclosure of conflicts of interest or potential conflicts of interest. They should check for conflicts with the same care imposed on lawyers by legal ethics rules. Mediators must also avoid creating any conflicts of interest during the course of the mediation — for instance, by buying stock in the company owned by one of the parties. Finally, mediators should avoid creating an appearance of impropriety by representing parties in the future in the same or similar matter.

The 2005 Model Standards deal in Standard III (A) with conflicts of interests in relationships with the parties. It requires mediators to avoid conflicts of interest or any appearance of a conflict of interest during or after the mediation. The standards define a conflict of interest by saying that it may arise "from involvement by a mediator with the subject matter of the dispute or from any relationship between a mediator and any mediation participant." The relationship giving rise to a conflict can be "past or present, personal or professional" so long as it raises a question about the mediator's impartiality. The standards rely heavily on full disclosure and discussion of any conflicts of interest "reasonably known" to the mediator.

The standards require the mediator to conduct a reasonable conflicts check. Depending on the context of the mediation, that process may resemble the traditional conflicts check conducted by lawyers in multi- lawyer firms. However, mediators working in court-connected or community based programs, who receive cases without sufficient time to conduct a more formal conflicts check, should instead explore with the parties any relationships that might create a conflict of interest or the appearance of a conflict of interest. . . . The mediator has an on-going duty to disclose conflicts that may arise during the mediation.

The parties, nonetheless, can agree to use a mediator even if he or she has disclosed a conflict of interest. A mediator must then independently make the decision whether it is wise to continue as the mediator under circumstances that may affect the appearance of impartiality. Firestone notes that depending on the outcome of the mediation session, the parties' perceptions and concerns about the mediator's conflicts of interest may change. A conflict that did not concern a party at the start of the mediation may seem highly relevant if the party perceives the process as procedurally unfair at the end of the mediation. The 2005 Model Standards acknowledge this problem by requiring the mediator to withdraw from the mediation if he or she believes the conflict of interest "might reasonably be viewed as undermining the integrity of the mediation, even if the parties have agreed to continue despite the existence of the conflict."

Finally, the mediator has a duty to avoid future relationships with any mediation participant that would "raise questions about the integrity of the mediation" if viewed retrospectively. However, the standards suggest that the mediator may create later relationships with participants, but must first consider the "time elapsed following the mediation, the nature of the relationships established, and services offered."

Quadrant 2: Neutrality of the Mediator's Conduct Toward the Parties. Next, Firestone urges mediation parties to consider whether the mediator can maintain, through his or her conduct, neutrality towards the parties. Will the mediator become frustrated, disrespectful, or heavy-handed if he or she believes a party or his or her client is uncooperative? Does the mediator hold any racial or cultural biases? Can he work with people that express racial bias? Does she think in traditional ways that may impose gender biases or reinforce gender-role expectations in the mediation? Does anger make the mediator uncomfortable in a way that he may cut off a party's expression of it? Does crying make the mediator uncomfortable in a way that he may suppress the expression of sadness, fear, vulnerability, regret, and other emotions expressed in this way or other ways? Can she work with borderlines, narcissists, sociopaths, and other high conflict personalities without those parties pushing her buttons or manipulating her?

Does she accept referral fees from lawyers who regularly use her in mediation, therefore consciously or unconsciously creating a bias in favor of the referring attorneys and their clients? Is one party paying the full cost of the mediation so that the mediator may show bias in favor of that party? Is the party a repeat player? Can the mediator remain even-handed knowing that she may be dependent on one party for her next referral? The standard governing solicitation of business also weighs in on this issue. It prohibits a mediator from soliciting business in a "manner that gives an appearance of partiality for or against a party or otherwise undermines the integrity of the process."

The 2005 Model Standards discuss these aspects of conduct neutrality in Standard II. That standard requires a mediator to "decline a mediation if the mediator cannot conduct it in an impartial manner." It defines impartiality as "freedom from favoritism, bias or prejudice." It requires the mediator to conduct the mediation in "an impartial manner and avoid conduct that gives the appearance of partiality." A mediator may not be partial or prejudiced in favor or against any participant based on "personal characteristics, background, values and beliefs, or performance at a mediation, or any other reason."

The 2005 Model Standards recognize the corrosive role fees may play in undermining mediator impartiality or neutrality. It requires full disclosure, typically in writing, to the parties of fees, expenses, and charges. Standard VII (B) states: "A mediator shall not charge fees in a manner that impairs a mediator's impartiality. While a mediator may accept unequal fee payments from the parties, a mediator should not allow such a fee arrangement to adversely impact the mediator's ability to conduct a mediation in an impartial manner." The Reporter's Notes explain that disclosure of the unequal fee arrangements may eliminate the perception of partiality. And the standards also require the mediator to remain "attentive to how that practice, even when acceptable to all parties, impacts the integrity of the process. . . ."

Another standard precludes a mediator from accepting a "gift, favor, loan, or other item of value that raises a question as to the mediator's actual or perceived impartiality." This provision, however, does not preclude the mediator from accepting de minimis gifts, items, or services, especially if culturally expected. The mediator may also allow one of the attorneys to pay for lunch during the mediation session. But the mediator must still prevent any actual or perceived impartiality.

Quadrant 3: Impartiality in the Mediator's Relationship to the Outcome. In an ideal setting, a mediator will defer to the high-quality decision making of the parties to settle (or not) and on what terms. Firestone suggests that parties, however, should consider the following situations because they change a mediator's relationship to the outcome of the mediation. Does the mediator brag about a high settlement rate? Does the court-connected program director refer cases to mediators with high settlement rates? Should a party, therefore, be concerned that the mediator views the case as the next notch on his belt? Will he work hard for his settlement rate even if it requires coercive interventions that disfavor one party? Does he have a vested interest in the outcome because his fee is based on a percentage of the agreed settlement? Does she unduly prolong the mediation session to earn a larger fee? Does he act in a way to ensure future referrals from the repeat player? Does she believe that all civil rights-related mediations must result in an agreement consistent with Title VII law? Can he mediate with impartiality as to the outcome in an air pollution case if his son suffers from severe asthma? . . .

The 2005 Model Standards address these aspects of impartiality in the standard dealing with party self-determination. This treatment shows how the fundamental values of party self-determination, mediator impartiality, and confidentiality often overlap or create tension between values. Standard I provides: "A mediator shall not undermine party self-determination . . . for reasons such as higher settlement rates, egos, increased fees, or outside pressures from court personnel, program administrators, provider organizations, the media or others." The Reporter's Notes state: "[A] mediator must not coerce parties to settle; the language of the Model Standards has been sharpened to eliminate any ambiguity regarding that duty."

The April 2005 draft of the Model Standards did not preclude contingency fees. The Joint Committee expressed concern that a flat prohibition against certain types of fees potentially raised anti-trust issues. It therefore removed the language appearing in the 1994 Model Standards and adopted the more general language appearing in Standard VIII of the draft. The ABA House of Delegates, in adopting the 2005 Model Standards, added a provision discouraging the use of contingency fees by mediators. Language drafted by the Administrative Law and Anti-Trust Sections of the ABA assuaged delegates' anti-trust concerns. The ABA sections explained that the provisions found in ethics guidelines were "defensible and justifiable" and so appropriate to include.

Finally, under the 2005 Model Standards, the mediator may not show bias or impartiality towards the outcome based on a party's values or beliefs. The mediator must also disclose any conflict of interest that may arise "from involvement by a mediator with the subject matter" and the mediator must "determine whether there are any facts that a reasonable individual would consider likely to create a potential or actual conflict of interest."

4. Quadrant 4: Neutrality of the Mediator's Conduct Towards the Outcome. Firestone also suggests parties should consider whether the prospective mediator can maintain neutral conduct towards the outcome. This article interprets that concern as conduct that undermines party-self determination intentionally or unintentionally. Conduct towards the outcome may reflect a mediator's belief that he knows more than the parties about the law, their dispute, or other factors and so he should play a role in its substantive resolution. Conduct towards the outcome may also reflect a lack of mediation skill or an over-reliance on the skills the mediator has developed in his profession of origin. For instance, does the mediator use coercion, intimidation, or other heavy-handed tactics? Does she fall back on her lawyerly problem-solving skills of giving legal advice because she lacks the skills to adopt a less coercive approach? Does he or she truly respect party-self determination? Does the mediator engage in interventions or processes inconsistent with the definition of mediation? Does she add terms to the settlement agreement on which the parties have not agreed?

The 2005 Model Standards require the mediator to protect party self-determination as to mediator selection, process design, participation in or withdrawal from the process, as well as to outcome. The standards define self-determination as "the act of coming to a voluntary, uncoerced decision in which each party makes free and informed choices." The standards also make the mediator the guardian of the quality of the process by requiring him or her to conduct the mediation in a manner that promotes "party participation, procedural fairness, party competency and mutual respect among all participants."

The 2005 Model Standards, unlike some codes of conduct, do not preclude certain types of professional behaviors. For instance, they do not expressly permit a mediator from giving legal advice, legal information, or case evaluations. Nor do they preclude this conduct. Instead, the 2005 Model Standards acknowledge that "[t]he role of a mediator differs substantially from other professional roles. Mixing the role of a mediator and the role of another profession is problematic and thus, a mediator should distinguish between the roles." It continues: "A mediator may provide information that the mediator is qualified by training or experience to provide, only if the mediator can do so consistent with these Standards."

The 2005 Model Standards also suggest that a mediator must clearly indicate when he is assuming another dispute resolution role. Apparently, he may not make the shift to a more evaluative or adjudicatory role without consent of the parties. He must also inform the parties of the implications of shifting to another role. The standards also suggest a mediator "should make the parties aware of the importance of consulting other professionals to help them make informed decisions." Taken together, these provisions limit the control of the mediator over the outcome or allow greater control only with the permission of the parties.

Finally, the 2005 Model Standards do not directly address the situation when a mediator becomes more than the scrivener of the parties' agreement, but instead adds provisions he or she thinks appropriate. The standards address the issue in the context of party self-determination. Other guidelines existing outside the model standards deal with this situation, which is often characterized as the practice of law.

As catchall provisions, the 2005 Model Standards require in several places that the mediator withdraw if he or she can not conduct the mediation with impartiality or if someone could view a conflict of interest as undermining the integrity of the process. The Joint Committee rejected the suggested language ensuring that the mediator would withdraw "without harming any party's interests." Members of the Joint Committee questioned whether that result was ever possible. They concluded that the concern about the effect of withdrawal was a matter of best practice beyond the scope of the standards. They also concluded that the suggested language was inconsistent with a broader policy approach that did not require mediators to insure particular outcomes.

D. Party Self-Determination, High-Quality Decision Making, and the Quality of the Process. Professor John Lande, *How Will Lawyering and Mediation Practices Transform Each Other?* 24 FLA. ST. U. L. REV. 839, 854-57 (1997), invites us to think about party self-determination and mediator interventions that may undermine it, by thinking of the parties' opportunity to exercise high-quality decision making. The idea captures the concepts of individual-level party empowerment and party decision making responsibility. He defines high-quality decision making "as a condition in which a principal has exercised his or her responsibility for making decisions in a dispute by considering the situation sufficiently and without excessive pressure." He identifies seven factors affecting the quality of decision making: (1) explicit identification of the principal's goals and interests, (2) explicit identification of plausible options for satisfying these interests, (3) the principal's explicit selection of options for evaluation, (4) careful consideration of these options, (5) mediators' restraint in pressuring principals to accept particular substantive options, (6) limitation on use of time pressure, and (7) confirmation of principals' consent to selected options. . . .

The 2005 Model Standards support a party's high-quality decision making in more ways than a reader might first appreciate. Parties need these protections. Interference with a party's self-determination, by offering legal advice; by giving legal opinions; by recommending settlement; or by engaging in more overt acts of coercion, formed the most frequent allegation against mediators in grievance complaints filed by unhappy mediation parties in Florida and Georgia. Interference with party self-determination was the second most frequent allegation in complaints filed against Virginia mediators.

E. Confidentiality in Mediation. The Joint Committee has not tried to duplicate the work leading to the creation of the Uniform Mediation Act (UMA) in 2003. Instead, the Joint Committee chose to outline the most basic principles of confidentiality in mediation. Provisions governing confidentiality in mediation should consider the following questions: Who is the holder of the privilege? Who may prevent the disclosure of confidential information? Against whom can confidentiality be enforced? In what subsequent proceedings will confidentiality prevail? What is confidential? How absolute or comprehensive is the grant of confidentiality?

The 2005 Model Standards answer some of these questions by requiring the mediator to maintain confidentiality of "all information obtained by the mediator in mediation." The mediator may disclose to the court, if required, "whether parties appeared at a scheduled mediation and whether or not the parties reached a resolution." He or she may not reveal, however, whether a party acted in good faith, unless required by other law. The parties may also agree that the mediator may make additional disclosures of information. And, of particular interest to those of us who teach or train mediators, or engage in mediation research or evaluation, we may disclose information about the mediation under the new Model Standards if we take care to protect the anonymity of the parties and "their reasonable expectations regarding confidentiality."

The mediator must also pay attention to the expectations of the parties because they may vary in connection with mediation confidentiality and because the parties can craft their own rules about confidentiality. A mediator's "accepted practice" or the practice of an institution can also shape party expectations about confidentiality. In addition, the Model Standards require the mediator to promote the parties' understanding of the role they play in preserving the confidentiality of information. Thus, the Model Standards encourage a conversation about the scope of confidentiality and how party expectations may fit with the mediator's practice, their own responsibilities for preserving confidentiality, [and] . . . court rules or statutes governing mediation confidentiality. . . .

F. Competence and the Mediator's Representations About It. Standard IV reflects the "lively debate" over who is competent to mediate. The Reporter's Notes reinforce earlier statements that the Joint Committee recognized that mediators operate in many contexts. Accordingly, they bring diverse backgrounds and competencies to their practices. . . . The 2005 Model Standards retain the 1994 Model Standard's commitment not to create "artificial or arbitrary barriers to serve the public as a mediator." They side-step most of the credentialing issues. . . .

The standards explicitly support, for the first time, the need for mediators to keep "sharpen[ing] the saw." They provide: "A mediator should attend educational programs and related activities to maintain and enhance the mediator's knowledge and skills related to mediation." In addition, the mediator may only accept cases in which the mediator has the competence needed to satisfy the reasonable expectations of the parties. If the mediator learns, during the course of the mediation, that he or she cannot conduct the mediation competently, the mediator must discuss the situation with the parties and take appropriate actions. Based on the results of the discussions with the parties, the mediator may need to withdraw or seek appropriate assistance. . . .

To help the parties exercise informed decision making in the choice of mediator, a mediator "should have available for the parties' information relevant to the mediator's training, education, experience, and approach to conducting a mediation." However, the standard governing advertising and solicitation would require the mediator to communicate only truthful information. In an obscure paragraph that requires a reader to consult the Reporter's Notes, it also limits when a mediator may represent that he or she is "certified," "approved," "registered," "rostered," or "licensed." He or she may advertise these designations only if a government entity, court, administrative agency, or private sector organization has a developed, publicized procedure for obtaining the "certified" or other identified status. A mediator cannot advertise himself as "certified" if he has simply gotten a certificate showing successful completion of a course. Finally, a mediator may not exaggerate his or her skills by promising any outcome in his or her advertising or solicitation communications.

G. Advancement of Mediation Practice. The 1994 version of the standard acknowledged the mediator's obligation to educate the public, to make mediation accessible, to "correct abuses," and to improve his or her skills. The 2005 Model Standards elaborate on these requirements (1) by requiring mediators to participate in "outreach and education efforts" designed to develop public "understanding of, and appreciation for, mediation"; (2) by inviting mediators to provide pro bono or reduced fee services; (3) by expecting mediators to foster diversity and demonstrate respect for differing points of view within the field; (4) by asking mediators to participate in research; (5) by urging mediators to assist newer mediators through training, mentoring, and networking; (6) and by prodding mediators to learn from each other, to work together to improve the profession, and to better serve people in conflict. Noticeably missing from the new version of the standards is the obligation of mediators "to correct abuses." The Reporter's Notes do not explain its omission.

H. Miscellaneous Provisions Preventing Abuse of the Process. Two provisions
of Standard VI, Quality of the Process, do not fit in the organizational framework I have created in this article. The first provision prevents a mediator
from conducting a dispute resolution process other than mediation, but calling
it mediation to trigger rules, statutes, or other governing law that may protect
some aspects of the process, like confidentiality protections. The second provision prevents participants from using the process to further criminal conduct.
The Joint Committee, however, rejected suggestions that the standards impose
an affirmative duty on the mediator to report possible criminal activity.

E. LIABILITY OF MEDIATORS AND OTHERS

1. Comments and Questions

a. Michael Moffitt explains the law regarding suits against mediators. *See
also* James R. Coben & Peter N. Thompson, *Disputing Irony: A Systematic Look
at Litigation About Mediation*, 11 HARV. NEGOT. L. REV. 43 (2006), excerpted in
Chapter Eight. *Wagshal* is the leading case in the context of court-connected
ADR.

b. After reading the Moffitt article and the *Wagshal* opinion, summarize the
legal principles that govern suits against mediators (and other ADR providers)
in one short paragraph. What would you say to a person who wants to retain you
(and has the money to pay your fees) to sue a mediator? Under what circumstances would you take such a case on a contingent fee basis?

c. Providers of ADR services may have internal review policies; party complaints may result in the dispute professional being dropped from the provider's
roster (but not monetary damages). Indeed, organizations seek such input, so as
to avoid unhappy present or future customers. The very fact of asking evidences this concern, and is likely to increase customer satisfaction.

2. Michael Moffitt, *Suing Mediators*, 83 B.U. L. REV. 147 (2003)

As the use of mediation explodes in popularity, assuring the quality of mediation services has become an increasingly visible challenge. Most occupations
and professions have credentialing or other barriers to entry into practice,
statutory or regulatory restrictions on practice methods, and oversight of some
sort. In addition to these structural methods of assuring quality services, most
service providers operate under the potential threat of private legal actions
brought by dissatisfied clients. In contrast, mediation operates with few, if any,
formal structures for assuring the quality of mediation services.

In the absence of formal quality control mechanisms, private lawsuits offer
a theoretical vehicle for controlling mediators' practices. In reality, however, it
is extraordinarily difficult to sue a mediator successfully for her mediation conduct. As an empirical matter, few former clients have sued mediators for injuries
stemming from mediation-specific conduct, and none of those suits has resulted
in an enforced legal judgment for the former client. A number of factors may con-

tribute to the infrequency with which parties resort to lawsuits against mediators. The most significant barrier . . . stems from the current legal theories applicable to mediators' practices. . . .

Several unique aspects of mediation suggest that mediators' exposure to liability should be crafted differently from that of other service providers. Because mediation parties have extraordinary insight into mediation practices, they are the best judges of mediator conduct. Mediation parties also have the ability to terminate mediation services they deem inadequate. An appropriate liability regime would consider each of these factors. Furthermore, the fluid nature of mediation practice — both at the individual level and in the broader field of mediators generally — demands that a responsible liability system distinguish between accusations that a mediator breached a customary duty of care, and accusations that a mediator breached a duty articulated beyond custom.

I. Suing a Mediator Successfully is Difficult

Mediators make decisions about a host of issues during the course of a mediation. Who should be in the room? How should sessions be structured? What questions should be explored? In what order? What ideas, opinions, or advice should be given? By whom? What deadlines should apply? Mediators face these and many other issues as they work. As a result, one can with little imagination construct an array of mediator behaviors that could raise legitimate concerns. A mediator in a private caucus gives the parties fabricated, conflicting information, inducing a settlement. Part-way through a mediation, a mediator secretly buys stock in the defendant's corporation. A mediator adopts an untested, and ultimately unsuccessful, agenda management technique and refuses to adapt her approach to the needs of the parties. A mediator discloses a party's confidential information to the media. A mediator drifts into a lengthy catnap as a party attempts to recount the circumstances underlying the dispute. A mediator berates and humiliates one party in front of the other parties. In theory, a mediator who makes bad decisions during the mediation creates the grounds upon which the injured parties may sue. In practice, however, very few mediator behaviors create exposure to liability.

A. *Few Mediators Have Been Sued for Their Mediation Conduct.* As an empirical matter, mediators have enjoyed almost absolute freedom from lawsuits alleging injury stemming from mediation conduct. Reported cases in U.S. federal courts, in U.S. state courts, and in the court systems of Canada, Britain, Australia and New Zealand include only one case in which a mediator was found liable to a party for mediation conduct. In the Missouri case of *Lange v. Marshall*, 622 S.W.2d 237, 239 (Mo. Ct. App. 1981), the defendant mediator successfully appealed the jury award, and the judgment was reversed. . . . No cases exist in the official reporters in which a mediator ultimately paid a former client for injuries the mediator caused during a mediation. Official reporters, of course, capture only a fraction of lawsuits, and it is possible that there have been instances of unreported, successful cases against mediators. However, mediation association newsletters, academic journals, and on-line resources reveal no such cases. Even malpractice insurers, who do an apparently healthy business providing insurance to mediators annually, report very few claims against those policies. In a series of telephone interviews, mediator liability insurance providers reported no more than a handful of claims in any year. . . .

B. Liability is Hard to Establish. The most significant contributing factor to the lack of lawsuits against mediators is the difficulty of succeeding on such claims. Malpractice, professional negligence, and virtually all other tort claims are available only in extraordinary circumstances. Mediation contracts provide few explicit bases for claims, and none of the bases likely to be implied effectively covers mediator behavior. Fiduciary obligations, like other theories of liability drawn from relationships beyond mediation, have never attached to mediators. The immunity and confidentiality shields that protect a significant number of mediators further complicate the establishment of liability.

1. Malpractice and Professional Negligence Standards are Difficult to Meet. In theory, a mediator's conduct may give rise to a claim of malpractice or professional negligence. However, like any other tort claim based fundamentally in negligence, maintaining a malpractice or professional negligence action requires, among other things, that a plaintiff demonstrate both that the mediator had a duty to conform to certain standards of conduct and that the mediator engaged in conduct that breached those standards. Neither of these elements can be satisfied easily in the context of mediator conduct. . . .

Disputants' needs drive mediator practices, making mediator practices difficult to pin down with any certainty. Many experienced, thoughtful mediators would be hard pressed to name any approach they would always or never adopt. The same mediator may even vary her practices in mid-stream, apparently jumping from one "school" to another, during a mediation. Efforts to categorize mediators into clear, consistent practices has yielded little consensus. Given the lack of clear standards of practice and the difficulty of proving any mediator behavior substandard, it would be exceptional if a plaintiff were able to use a malpractice or professional negligence claim to establish liability.

2. Other Tort-Based Actions Pose Similar Challenges. Beyond malpractice or simple negligence, a dissatisfied party could theoretically bring a number of tort claims against a mediator. Intentional infliction of emotional distress, false imprisonment, tortious interference with contractual relations and invasion of privacy each provide a possible basis for recovery from a mediator. In practice, however, none of these exposes most practicing mediators to sweeping liability. . . .

3. Contracts Provide Little Basis for a Claim. Contractual obligations may theoretically bind mediators in a way that would provide legal recourse to injured parties. In order to bring a successful contract action against a mediator, however, a party would need to demonstrate a breach of either an express term or an implied term in the mediation contract. As a practical matter, neither of these is easy to do. In the rare instance when the mediator has ex ante detailed contractually all of the services she will provide, an action for breach of contract would be relatively easy to maintain. . . . Most of the detailed, express promises contained in mediation agreements, however, do not address the question of what the mediator will actually do during the mediation. Instead, most mediation contracts, to the extent they make any express promises, address mediators' behaviors in advance of the mediation (for example, disclosures of conflicts of interest), or after the completion of the mediation (for example, maintaining confidentiality of mediation communications). . . .

The few express contractual provisions addressing a mediator's conduct during the mediation tend overwhelmingly to be statements of broad principle or purpose, rather than specific promises. Some mediation contracts will spell out relatively insignificant aspects of the mediation in great detail. . . . Even when a mediation contract expressly incorporates externally created standards of conduct, there are few specific promises on which to base a contract claim. The standards of conduct created by mediation associations and referral services are often replete with generalized, aspirational calls for mediators to do things like "remain impartial," "recognize . . . the principle of self-determination," or "help [the parties] make informed decisions." The lack of specificity in these standards not only provides little guidance to practicing mediators, but also makes it extraordinarily difficult for a party to demonstrate a mediator's breach. . . .

4. Fiduciary Duties Do Not Regularly Attach to Mediators. As a theoretical matter, an injured mediation party could assert that the mediator's behavior constituted a breach of fiduciary obligations. Fiduciary theories of liability for mediators are premised on the idea that certain mediation circumstances may trigger trust-based fiduciary obligations for mediators. . . . Fiduciary obligations could extend into the realm of mediation, however, only with a degree of judicial adaptation unlikely to be forthcoming. . . .

In practice, a litigant arguing the presence of fiduciary obligations would face considerable obstacles in establishing that mediation obligations are sufficiently fixed to permit the application of fiduciary obligations. Furthermore, a prospective plaintiff would need to overcome the structural difficulty of asserting that the mediator owes simultaneous fiduciary obligations to parties with opposing interests in the matter at hand. Fiduciary obligations cannot be structured responsibly in a way that would damn the mediator no matter what she did, yet holding a fiduciary obligation simultaneously to opposing parties risks exactly that. Finally, a plaintiff seeking to establish a fiduciary obligation on the part of a mediator would be challenged to demonstrate that the mediator occupied a position not only of "influence," but also of "superiority" sufficient to warrant fiduciary status. . . .

7. Immunity Sometimes Extends to Mediators. Even if a complaining party could overcome the obstacles listed above and establish liability, civil immunity attaches to shield certain mediator actions or inactions from the scrutiny of litigation. Immunity does not extend to all functions of all mediators in all contexts. Common law and statutory immunity, however, preclude successful lawsuits against a significant subset of mediators.

Quasi-judicial immunity is one form of protection potentially available to mediators. In order to protect the independence of judicial functions, the common law doctrine of judicial immunity serves as absolute protection for a judge's jurisdictionally sound, discretionary decisions. The Supreme Court has extended this form of immunity to certain actors outside of the judiciary when the functions in question are essentially judicial in nature. . . . When such immunity is extended to non-judicial actors, it is termed quasi-judicial immunity.

The principal case suggesting that quasi-judicial immunity may extend to mediators is *Wagshal v. Foster*, 28 F.3d 1249 (D.C. Cir. 1994) (holding that the mediator was protected by quasi-judicial immunity). . . . In upholding the trial court's extension of quasi-judicial immunity to Foster, the D.C. Court of Appeals determined that the case evaluator's functions were sufficiently judicial and that there was sufficient risk of harassment by dissatisfied litigants to merit quasi-judicial immunity. Although Foster served in this dispute as a case evaluator, a function distinct from mediation, the court's language treated the two terms interchangeably. Because quasi-judicial immunity "flows not from rank or title or location within the Government but from the nature of the responsibilities of the individual official," the Wagshal determination does not stand as an absolute extension of immunity to all court-appointed mediators. Instead, common law quasi-judicial immunity demands a fact-specific inquiry into the functions of the official in question. Wagshal supports but does not resolve the suggestion that mediators affiliated with a court may enjoy quasi-judicial immunity.

Some jurisdictions statutorily supplement or replace quasi-judicial immunity . . . with statutorily defined "qualified immunity." Some states reserve qualified immunity to mediators associated with the court system, while others extend qualified immunity even to purely private mediation service providers. Qualified immunity is more limited in scope than quasi-judicial immunity, often excluding coverage in cases involving bad faith or intentional misconduct. . . . As a practical matter, where it is held to apply, qualified immunity is broad enough to shield mediators from lawsuits in all but the most egregious of cases. . . .

C. Damages Are Often Difficult to Demonstrate. Mediator misconduct could create four different kinds of injuries. First, a mediator's behavior might inappropriately cause the mediation to result in no settlement. Second, a mediator's inappropriate behavior might produce a settlement, with terms injuriously unfavorable to one party. Third, a mediated agreement might injure the interests of a party absent from the mediation, whose interests the mediator was obliged to protect. Fourth, a mediator might injure a party in ways not reflected in the outcome of the mediation. For the reasons listed below, a party alleging any of these injuries faces significant difficulties in establishing damages.

1. Non-Settlement as Injury. If a mediation produces no agreement, the mediator's conduct may be to blame. . . . Even if a party could demonstrate that a settlement would have been reached but for the mediator's actions, the parties' opportunity to mitigate the injury generally would limit the damages from the failure to settle. In almost all circumstances, nothing prevents parties from settling cases outside of the auspices of a mediator. . . . With mediation expenses comparatively low, and damages unavailable beyond the mediation itself, an unhappy mediation party is unlikely to incur the costs of bringing a suit against a mediator merely [to recover] mediation-related expenses.

In an extreme case, a party might assert that the mediator's failure to facilitate an agreement where one was possible caused more significant injury than simple waste of time. For example, a party could claim that the failure of the mediation caused a change in the settlement dynamics such that what was once capable of settlement became incapable of settlement. The proof problems in such an assertion, of course, would be tremendous. A party able to overcome the difficulty of demonstrating that the case proceeded to trial because of the mediator's ineptitude could, theoretically, make a claim for the larger costs associated with trial. The party might even assert that his injuries included the difference between the theoretical settlement point the mediator failed to produce, and the trial outcome and costs. Such a claim, however, lapses quickly into so extraordinary a level of speculation that a court would be unlikely to entertain the assertion. . . .

If, after the fact, parties determine (assuming that such a determination were possible) that a settlement had been possible, they might claim that the no-settlement mediation decreased their ability to identify agreement opportunities. Essentially, the parties would argue: "We didn't settle afterwards because the mediator's performance in the mediation made us hate each other too much even to see that there were grounds upon which to agree." If an unhappy disputant were able to prove such an effect, it might address the mitigation problem mentioned above. Again, however, these claims of injury are so extraordinarily speculative that it is not surprising that no mediation parties have been successful in suing for non-settlement injuries.

2. Unfavorable Settlement Terms as Injury. In some cases, a party will revisit with remorse an agreement he struck as part of a mediation. If a party were sufficiently unhappy with the arrangement upon further examination, the party might seek to have the mediator provide compensation for the injuries caused by the unfavorable agreement. Essentially, a plaintiff in such a case would allege: "The mediator's actions inappropriately caused me to settle for X, when I could have, and should have, received Y." Each part of this assertion creates significant, if not insurmountable legal difficulty. It is no surprise, then, that such claims are almost unheard of. . . .

3. Settlement Terms Injuring Non-Parties. Some mediation outcomes will affect parties who are absent from the mediation process. If a mediation creates a negative impact on a non-party, that non-party could theoretically seek damages from the mediator who facilitated the agreement. Such a claim, however, would demand extraordinary legal creativity in demonstrating the existence of a mediator duty to non-parties, a breach of that duty and injury stemming from that breach. As a result, the prospects of claims by nonparties against mediators are severely limited. . . .

4. Injuries not Reflected in the Mediation Outcome. In certain circumstances, a mediation party could claim that a mediator's inappropriate actions caused an injury that is not reflected in the substantive outcome of the mediation. An example of such a claim is a party who claims to have suffered emotional damage stemming from intentional and tortious mediator behaviors. . . . [T]he plaintiff would need to engage in the often-difficult process of establishing injury from outrageous conduct. Because the injury is often highly speculative and because proving causation is difficult in light of the parties' opportunity simply to leave the mediation session, mediation parties are unlikely frequently to assert damages lying outside of the substantive mediated outcome. . . .

Conclusion

[In an omitted section, Professor Moffitt argues in favor of mediator liability.] The fact that there have been no successful lawsuits against mediators for their mediation conduct should not be mistaken as evidence that mediators are not making mistakes during their service. Instead, the lack of post-mediation legal activity is principally a product of the extraordinary legal obstacles facing any prospective plaintiff. . . . No traditional basis of recovery is readily available to unhappy mediation consumers and, as a result, lawsuits against mediators are rare.

The uncertainty and rarity of lawsuits against mediators is, in some ways, costly. Victims of substandard mediation practices remain uncompensated for their injuries. Mediators who adopt offensive or harmful approaches to mediation may never be educated about, much less deterred from, those practices. Furthermore, the public — including prospective mediation consumers, potential regulators, and other practitioners — may never learn about the current state of mediation practice in any meaningful way.

The solution to the lack of lawsuits, however, is not a wholesale broadening of liability exposure for all mediators. Instead, appropriate liability treatment demands recognition of some of the unique aspects of mediation practice. Mediation has very few, if any, practices so universally embraced that they would be considered customary. As a result, mediators should face significant exposure only to suits alleging a breach of a duty articulated or established by something other than customary practice. This would shield mediators from excessive second-guessing of those mediation decisions that are fundamentally discretionary judgments. At the same time, shielding mediators from liability in cases in which they breach a duty articulated outside of customary practice serves no persuasive policy. A mediator who engages in egregious behavior, violates contractual or statutory obligations, or breaches separately articulated duties should enjoy no legal or de facto immunity from lawsuits. Simultaneously, courts should favor lawsuits from parties who exercised their judgment in terminating an inadequate mediation. Wise policy and respect for autonomy demand deference both to mediators' subjective judgments and to parties' decisions regarding their continued participation in mediations.

3. *Wagshal v. Foster*, 28 F.3d 1249 (D.C. Cir. 1994)

STEPHEN F. WILLIAMS, Circuit Judge:

This case presents the issue of whether a court-appointed mediator or neutral case evaluator, performing tasks within the scope of his official duties, is entitled to absolute immunity from damages in a suit brought by a disappointed litigant. The district court found such immunity and we agree.

Wagshal filed suit against Sheetz, the manager of real property owned by Wagshal. Judge Richard A. Levie, referred the case to alternative dispute resolution pursuant to Superior Court Rule 16 and the Court's alternative dispute resolution ("ADR") program. While the program does not bind the parties, participation is mandatory. Judge Levie chose "neutral case evaluation" from among the available ADR options, and appointed Foster as case evaluator. We use the terms "case evaluator" and "mediator" interchangeably in this opinion. Each acts as a neutral third party assisting the parties to a dispute in exploring the possibility of settlement, the principal difference being that implicit in the name: the case evaluator focuses on helping the parties assess their cases, while the mediator acts more directly to explore settlement possibilities.

The parties signed a "statement of understanding" providing (among other things) that the proceedings would be confidential and privileged, and that the evaluator would serve as a "neutral party." Moreover, the parties were not allowed to subpoena the evaluator or any documents submitted in the course of evaluation, and "in no event could the mediator or evaluator voluntarily testify on behalf of a party." Wagshal signed in January 1992 (under protest, he alleges).

After Foster held his first session with the parties, Wagshal questioned his neutrality. [After some consideration], Foster wrote to Judge Levie, with copies to counsel, recusing himself. The letter also reported on his efforts in the case, and recommended continuation of ADR proceedings. In particular, Foster said that the case was one "that can and should be settled if the parties are willing to act reasonably," and urged the court to order Wagshal, "as a pre-condition to any further proceedings in his case, to engage in a good faith attempt at mediation." He also urged Judge Levie to "consider who should bear the defendant's costs in participating" in the mediation to date."

Judge Levie then conducted a telephone conference call hearing in which he excused Foster. Wagshal's counsel voiced the claim that underlies this suit — that he thought Foster's withdrawal letter "indicates that he had certain feelings about the case. Now, I'm not familiar with the mediation process but as I understood, the mediator is not supposed to say, give his opinion as to where the merits are." On that subject, Judge Levie said, "I don't know what his opinions are and I'm not going to ask him because that's part of the confidentiality of the process." Neither Wagshal nor his counsel made any objection or motion for Judge Levie's own recusal.

Judge Levie soon after appointed another case evaluator, and Wagshal and the other parties settled the *Sheetz* case in June 1992. In September 1992, however, Wagshal sued Foster in federal district court, claiming that Foster's behavior as mediator had violated his rights to due process and to a jury trial under the Fifth and Seventh Amendments, and seeking injunctive relief and damages under 42 U.S.C. § 1983. Besides the federal claims, he threw in a variety of local law theories such as defamation, invasion of privacy, and intentional infliction of emotional distress. His theory is that Foster's conduct as case evaluator forced him to settle the case against his will, resulting in a far lower recovery than if he had pursued the claim.

Foster's first line of defense against the damages claim was the assertion of quasi-judicial immunity. The immunity will block the suit if it extends to case evaluators and mediators, so long as Foster's alleged actions were taken within the scope of his duties as a case evaluator. Courts have extended absolute immunity to a wide range of persons playing a role in the judicial process. These have included prosecutors, law clerks, probation officers, a court-appointed committee monitoring the unauthorized practice of law, a psychiatrist who interviewed a criminal defendant to assist a trial judge, persons performing binding arbitration, and a psychologist performing dispute resolution services in connection with a lawsuit over custody and visitation rights. On the other hand, the Supreme Court has rejected absolute immunity for judges acting in an administrative capacity, court reporters charged with creating a verbatim transcript of trial proceedings, and prosecutors in relation to legal advice they may give state police. The official claiming the immunity bears the burden of showing that such immunity is justified for the function in question.

We have distilled the Supreme Court's approach to quasi-judicial immunity into a consideration of three main factors: (1) whether the functions of the official in question are comparable to those of a judge; (2) whether the nature of the controversy is intense enough that future harassment or intimidation by litigants is a realistic prospect; and (3) whether the system contains safeguards which are adequate to justify dispensing with private damage suits to control unconstitutional conduct.

In certain respects it seems plain that a case evaluator in the Superior Court's system performs judicial functions. Foster's assigned tasks included identifying factual and legal issues, scheduling discovery and motions with the parties, and coordinating settlement efforts. These obviously involve substantial discretion, a key feature of the tasks sheltered by judicial immunity and the one whose absence was fatal to the court reporter's assertion of immunity. Further, viewed as mental activities, the tasks appear precisely the same as those judges perform going about the business of adjudication and case management.

Wagshal protests, however, that mediation is altogether different from authoritative adjudication, citing observations to that effect in radically dissimilar contexts. However true his point may be as an abstract matter, the general process of encouraging settlement is a natural, almost inevitable, concomitant of adjudication. Rule 16 of the Federal Rules of Civil Procedure, for example, institutionalizes the relation, designating as subjects for pre-trial conferences a series of issues that appear to encompass all the tasks of a case evaluator in the Superior Court system: "formulation and simplification of the issues", "the possibility of obtaining admissions of fact and of documents", "the control and scheduling of discovery", and a catch-all, "such other matters as facilitate the just, speedy, and inexpensive disposition of the action." Fed.R.Civ.P. 16(c). Wagshal points to nothing in Foster's role that a Superior Court judge might not have performed under Superior Court Rule 16(c), which substantially tracks the federal model. . . .

Wagshal does not assert that a case evaluator is performing a purely administrative task, such as personnel decisions — e.g., demotion and discharge of a probation officer. Because the sort of pre-trial tasks performed by a case evaluator are so integrally related to adjudication proper, we do not think that their somewhat managerial character renders them administrative for these purposes. Conduct of pre-trial case evaluation and mediation also seems likely to inspire efforts by disappointed litigants to recoup their losses, or at any rate harass the mediator, in a second forum. Although a mediator or case evaluator makes no final adjudication, he must often be the bearer of unpleasant news — that a claim or defense may be far weaker than the party supposed. Especially as the losing party will be blocked by judicial immunity from suing the judge, there may be great temptation to sue the messenger whose words foreshadowed the final loss.

The third of the Supreme Court's criteria, the existence of adequate safeguards to control unconstitutional conduct where absolute immunity is granted, is also present. Here, Wagshal was free to seek relief from any misconduct by Foster by applying to Judge Levie. Alternatively, if he thought Foster's communications might prejudice Judge Levie, he could have sought Levie's recusal. The avenues of relief institutionalized in the ADR program and its judicial context provide adequate safeguards.

Wagshal claims that even if mediators may be generally entitled to absolute immunity, Foster may not invoke the immunity because his action was not taken in a judicial capacity. Wagshal's argument that the acts for which he has sued Foster are not judicial rests simply on his claim that Foster's letter to Judge Levie, stating that he felt he "must recuse" himself and giving his thoughts on possible further mediation efforts and allocation of costs, breached Foster's obligations of neutrality and confidentiality. We assume such a breach for purposes of analysis. But "if judicial immunity means anything, it means that a judge will not be deprived of immunity because the action he took was in error or was in excess of his authority Accordingly we look to the particular act's relation to a general function normally performed by a judge. Applying the same principle to case evaluators, we have no doubt that Foster's announcing his recusal, reporting in a general way on the past course of mediation, and making suggestions for future mediation were the sort of things that case evaluators would properly do.

Wagshal finally argues that Foster cannot be immune for the statements in his letter made after he stated that he "must recuse" himself. This is frivolous. Even if the letter alone effected a recusal (which is doubtful — Judge Levie clearly saw himself as later excusing Foster from service), the simultaneous delivery of an account of his work was the type of act a case evaluator could properly perform on the way out. In fact, we doubt very much if a modest gap in time between effective recusal and recounting of the events would take the latter out of the immunity. . . .

F. EXCEPTIONS TO CONFIDENTIALITY: DUTIES TO WARN OR REPORT

1. Comments and Questions

a. The obligation of mediators to maintain confidences, and the relevant UMA provisions, are discussed at length in Chapter Eight. Here we consider the circumstances under which public policy, usually in the form of legislation, trumps a confidentiality agreement.

b. The leading case on the duty to warn is *Tarasoff v. Regents of University of California*, 551 P.2d 334, 345-47 (Cal. 1976). The California Supreme Court ruled that there was a duty to warn, and liability for the breach of that duty. In the much more recent *Thapar* decision, which follows, the Texas Supreme Court determined there was no duty to warn.

c. Should there be a duty to warn, and if so under what circumstances? Do you prefer the California or the Texas approach, and why? Even if you prefer a duty to warn in the absence of relevant state legislation, are you nevertheless persuaded by the "bowing to the legislature" rationale used by the Texas Supreme Court?

d. Should the rules applicable to psychiatrists be equally applicable to mediators (and other helping professionals)? If different treatment is warranted, what difference and why?

e. To what threats should a duty of disclosure attach — death, severe bodily harm, any physical harm, psychological injury, other threats? How specific must the threat be? What if a person says he dreamed of killing/injuring another person? What if action is taken, such as the purchase of a weapon, but no threatening statement is made?

f. If professionals are subject to a *Tarasoff*-type duty to disclose, is there a risk of numerous false positives — disclosures where the alleged threat did not turn into action. Would it be a problem if persons subject to a duty to disclose adopted a philosophy of "when in doubt, disclose"? This is precisely the recommended approach for disclosures by dispute resolution professionals who are asked to serve as third party neutrals.

g. Assume you are mediating a case in a jurisdiction that follows *Tarasoff*. What, if anything, would you say about the duty of disclosure in your opening statement?

2. *Thapar v. Zezulka*, 994 S.W.2d 635 (Tex. 1999)

Justice ENOCH delivered the opinion for a unanimous court.

The primary issue in this case is whether a mental-health professional can be liable in negligence for failing to warn the appropriate third parties when a patient makes specific threats of harm toward a readily identifiable person. In reversing the trial court's summary judgment, the court of appeals recognized such a cause of action. Because the Legislature has established a policy against such a common-law cause of action, we refrain from imposing on mental-health professionals a duty to warn third parties of a patient's threats. . . .

Because this is an appeal from summary judgment, we take as true evidence favorable to Lyndall Zezulka, the nonmovant. Freddy Ray Lilly had a history of mental-health problems and psychiatric treatment. Dr. Renu K. Thapar, a psychiatrist, first treated Lilly in 1985, when Lilly was brought to Southwest Memorial Hospital's emergency room. Thapar diagnosed Lilly as suffering from moderate to severe post-traumatic stress disorder, alcohol abuse, and paranoid and delusional beliefs concerning his stepfather, Henry Zezulka, and people of certain ethnic backgrounds. Thapar treated Lilly with a combination of psychotherapy and drug therapy over the next three years.

For the majority of their relationship, Thapar treated Lilly on an outpatient basis. But on at least six occasions Lilly was admitted to Southwest Memorial Hospital, or another facility, in response to urgent treatment needs. Often the urgency involved Lilly's problems in maintaining amicable relationships with those with whom he lived. Lilly was also admitted on one occasion after threatening to kill himself. In August 1988, Lilly agreed to be admitted to Southwest Memorial Hospital. Thapar's notes from August 23, 1988, state that Lilly "feels like killing" Henry Zezulka. These records also state, however, that Lilly "has decided not to do it but that is how he feels." After hospitalization and treatment for seven days, Lilly was discharged. Within a month Lilly shot and killed Henry Zezulka. Despite the fact that Lilly's treatment records indicate that he sometimes felt homicidal, Thapar never warned any family member or any law enforcement agency of Lilly's threats against his stepfather. Nor did Thapar inform any family member or any law enforcement agency of Lilly's discharge from Southwest Memorial Hospital.

Lyndall Zezulka, Henry's wife and Lilly's mother, sued Thapar for negligence resulting in her husband's wrongful death. Zezulka alleged that Thapar was negligent in diagnosing and treating Lilly and negligent in failing to warn of Lilly's threats toward Henry Zezulka. It is undisputed that Thapar had no physician-patient relationship with either Lyndall or Henry Zezulka. Based on this fact, Thapar moved for summary judgment on the ground that Zezulka had not stated a claim for medical negligence because Thapar owed no duty to Zezulka in the absence of a doctor-patient relationship.

To decide this case we must determine the duties a mental-health professional owes to a nonpatient third party. Zezulka stated her claims against Thapar in negligence. Liability in negligence is premised on duty, a breach of which proximately causes injuries, and damages resulting from that breach. Whether a legal duty exists is a threshold question of law for the court to decide from the facts surrounding the occurrence in question. If there is no duty, there cannot be negligence liability. Zezulka lists seventeen particulars by which she alleges Thapar was negligent. But each allegation is based on one of two proposed underlying duties: (1) a duty to not negligently diagnose or treat a patient that runs from a psychiatrist to nonpatient third parties; or (2) a duty to warn third parties of a patient's threats. In her motion for summary judgment Thapar asserted that she owed Zezulka no duty. Thus, we must determine if Thapar owed Zezulka either of these proposed duties.

First, we consider Zezulka's allegations that Thapar was negligent in her diagnosis and treatment of Lilly's psychiatric problems. . . . The underlying duty question here is whether the absence of a doctor-patient relationship precludes Zezulka from maintaining medical negligence claims against Thapar based on her diagnosis and treatment of Lilly. In *Bird v. W.C.W.*, 868 S.W.2d 767, 769-770 (Tex. 1994), we held that no duty runs from a psychologist to a third party to not negligently misdiagnose a patient's condition. Since *Bird,* we have had occasion to consider several permutations of this same duty question. Bird and our post-*Bird* writings answer definitively the first duty question presented by the facts before us: Thapar owes no duty to Zezulka, a third party nonpatient, for negligent misdiagnosis or negligent treatment of Lilly. Accordingly, Thapar was entitled to summary judgment on all of the claims premised on Zezulka's first duty theory.

Second, we consider Zezulka's allegations that Thapar was negligent for failing to warn either the Zezulkas or law enforcement personnel of Lilly's threats. . . . The California Supreme Court first recognized a mental-health professional's duty to warn third parties of a patient's threats in the seminal case *of Tarasoff v. Regents of University of California*, 551 P.2d 334, 345-47 (Cal. 1976). The court of appeals here cited *Tarasoff* in recognizing a cause of action for Thapar's failure to warn of her patient's threats. But we have never recognized the only underlying duty upon which such a cause of action could be based-a mental-health professional's duty to warn third parties of a patient's threats. Without considering the effect of differences in the development of California and Texas jurisprudence on the outcome of this issue, we decline to adopt a duty to warn now because the confidentiality statute governing mental-health professionals in Texas makes it unwise to recognize such common-law duty.

The Legislature has chosen to closely guard a patient's communications with a mental health professional. In 1979, three years after *Tarasoff* issued, the Legislature enacted a statute governing the disclosure of communications during the course of mental health treatment. The statute classifies communications between mental health professionals and their patients/clients as confidential and prohibits mental-health professionals from disclosing them to third parties unless an exception applies. Zezulka complains that Thapar was negligent in not warning members of the Zezulka family about Lilly's threats. But a disclosure by Thapar to one of the Zezulkas would have violated the confidentiality statute because no exception in the statute provides for disclosure to third parties threatened by the patient. . . .

Zezulka also complains that Thapar was negligent in not disclosing Lilly's threats to any law enforcement agency. There is an exception in the confidentiality statute that provides for disclosure to law enforcement personnel in certain circumstances. The statute, however, *permits* these disclosures but does not *require* them. See § 4(b), 1979 Tex. Gen. Laws at 514 (emphasis added):

(b) Exceptions to the privilege of confidentiality, in other than court proceedings, *allowing* disclosure of confidential information by a professional, exist only to the following: . . .

> (2) to medical or law enforcement personnel where the professional determines that there is a probability of imminent physical injury by the patient/client to himself or to others, or where there is a probability of immediate mental or emotional injury to the patient/client. . . .

The term "allowing" in section 4(b) makes clear that disclosure of confidential information under any of the statute's exceptions is permissive but not mandatory. Imposing a legal duty to warn third parties of patient's threats would conflict with the scheme adopted by the Legislature by making disclosure of such threats mandatory.

We consider legislative enactments that evidence the adoption of a particular public policy significant in determining whether to recognize a new common-law duty. For example, in recognizing the existence of a common-law duty to guard children from sexual abuse, we found persuasive the Legislature's strongly avowed policy to protect children from abuse. The statute expressing this policy, however, makes the reporting of sexual abuse mandatory and makes failure to report child abuse a crime. Further, under the statute, those who report child abuse in good faith are immune from civil and criminal liability. Thus, imposing a common law duty to report was consistent with the legislative scheme governing child abuse.

The same is not true here. The confidentiality statute here does not make disclosure of threats mandatory nor does it penalize mental-health professionals for not disclosing threats. And, perhaps most significantly, the statute does not shield mental-health professionals from civil liability for disclosing threats in good faith. On the contrary, mental-health professionals make disclosures at their peril. Thus, if a common-law duty to warn is imposed, mental-health professionals face a Catch-22. They either disclose a confidential communication that later proves to be an idle threat and incur liability to the patient, or they fail to disclose a confidential communication that later proves to be a truthful threat and incur liability to the victim and the victim's family.

The confidentiality statute here evidences an intent to leave the decision of whether to disclose confidential information in the hands of the mental-health professional. In the past, we have declined to impose a common-law duty to disclose when disclosing confidential information by a physician has been made permissible by statute but not mandatory. We have also declined to impose a common-law duty after determining that such a duty would conflict with the Legislature's policy and enactments concerning the employment-at-will doctrine. Our analysis today is consistent with the approach in those cases. Because of the Legislature's stated policy, we decline to impose a common law duty on mental-health professionals to warn third parties of their patient's threats. Accordingly, we conclude that Thapar was entitled to summary judgment because she owed no duty to Zezulka, a third-party nonpatient.

3. Child and Elder Abuse

The *Thapar* and *Tarasoff* decisions considered the nature and extent of an obligation to inform a third party or government of threatened activity. The basis for an obligation to report apparent abuse of a person with limited capacity, such as a child or elderly person to a unit of government is state law — statute or administrative regulations. The relevant law will differ from state to state. It is important for a dispute resolution professional to know the relevant legal standards, and the unit of government to which a report should be addressed.

Chapter 16

PLANNING FOR AND AVOIDING DISPUTES: SYSTEMS DESIGN

A. INTRODUCTION

The second best thing to do about disputes is to settle them in an amicable manner that allows relationships to continue. The best thing to do about disputes is to prevent them from happening. This basic truth is easily stated, but maintaining reasonable (let alone excellent) relations with other individuals and organizations often proves to be an elusive goal. System design is planning for disputes, both to prevent disputes and to ameliorate their impact when disputes do occur.

The chapter begins with an examination of factors and approaches to be considered in the design of systems for the avoidance and resolution of disputes. An important and related approach to achieving organizational success is total quality management (TQM). We then move from the general to the specific, and examine dispute resolution systems in particular contexts. The main topic is worker-management relations. Because the employer-employee relationship is highly important, and often long-term, it makes sense for all concerned to invest in win-win approaches to workplace endeavors. The presence or absence of a labor union that represents workers is a major variable in workplace governance, but in either event the structural situation makes system design a useful investment for both workers and management. We close the chapter with three case studies about the design of dispute resolution systems in different contexts: bid protests in government contracting; the Coast Guard; and the delivery of health care services.

Before turning to these topics, something needs to be said about contract planning for the use of ADR in the event that disputes do occur. This is an easy matter — just do it. No imagination or drafting skill is required. Indeed, the temptation to use "home-made" dispute resolution provisions probably should be avoided, because widely used form contract language is easily available. Just let your fingers do the walking — to the web sites of the AAA, CPR, or other organizations. These form provisions commonly can be accessed and used without charge, although some services are reserved for members. Sometimes standardized dispute resolution provisions are found in trade association form contracts. A notable example is the American Institute of Architects (AIA), whose series of form construction contracts have been in use throughout the United States for a century.

The message of this chapter is to plan ahead, but doing so effectively can be difficult. Consider in this regard the cautionary tale of *Aluminum Company of*

747

America, Inc. v. Essex Group, Inc., 499 F. Supp. 53 (W.D. Pa. 1980). Alcoa and Essex entered a long-term contract whereby Alcoa agreed to smelt alumina supplied by Essex, and to return it as aluminum. The amount to be paid by Essex was determined by a complex formula based on three factors (national construction costs, local labor costs at the particular Alcoa facility, and wholesale prices for industrial commodities). This contract was performed for some years, to the apparent satisfaction of both parties. Unfortunately for Alcoa non-labor costs, notably the price of energy (vast amounts of which is consumed in the smelting process), rose considerably more than the wholesale price for industrial commodities, an index that was suggested by Alcoa because its expenses for smelting alumina at its plants closely tracked the fluctuations of this index. Alcoa sued for excuse from performance, or reformation of the contract.

The most striking aspect of this situation is that Alcoa had gone to considerable trouble and expense to assess the possible risks associated with the Essex agreement, and to design a pricing formula that would protect it from major cost increases. As part of that process it hired an expert economic consultant, one Dr. Alan Greenspan — the same Alan Greenspan who served for 18 years as Chairman of the Federal Reserve System Board of Governors. The moral is not that Greenspan was insufficiently clairvoyant, or that his firm provided poor quality analysis, but that the injunction to engage in careful planning is far easier to state than to execute.

B. THE MAIN ELEMENTS OF AN ADR SYSTEM DESIGN

1. E. WENDY TRACHTE-HUBER, ADR SYSTEM DESIGN: THE PRE-LITIGATION OPTION (1993)

All organizations experience conflict of some sort. Often this conflict is handled in inefficient or outdated ways. In an effort to assist organizations in resolving their conflicts, experts are being called on to develop "systems designs." A common premise of dispute systems design is that shifting from a power or rights-based system to an interests-based dispute resolution system is desirable. This paper will provide an overview of the systems design process and will examine some current trends in systems design.

ADR Systems Design involves the use of an ADR professional to develop a comprehensive plan for the resolution of conflict, both internal and external, in an organization. This systematic and institutionalized approach is more desirable than ad hoc efforts for several reasons:

1. A coordinated and systematic approach is the most efficient and cost effective;

2. The systems design approach will generally increase the range of dispute resolution available to an organization; and

3. The coordinated approach allows for an evaluation process which can be fed back to the organization in order to continually evaluate the efficacy of the newly implemented system.

The System Design process generally involves four basic phases: assessment, development, implementation and evaluation.

1. Assessment. During this phase, the organization is examined and inspected for current methods of conflict resolution. The dispute resolution professional gathers data on the organization and meets with key decision makers within the organization. Techniques used in assessment include individual interviews, questionnaires, and personal observation. Working teams are developed to assist in the development of a comprehensive conflict resolution system for the organization.

2. Development. During this phase, the dispute resolution professional and members of the working teams develop a plan to resolve conflicts within the organization. The dispute resolution professional provides expertise in alternative methods of conflict resolution, and the working teams provide expertise on the organization itself. Procedures are developed for the implementation of the conflict resolution system.

3. Implementation. During this phase, the newly-created system is put into operation within the organization. Often there are policy changes which must be implemented, as well as key players who must be trained and educated on the use of the system. The persons who will be affected by the new system, the target population, are educated and trained where necessary. For instance, if peer mediation is to be a component of the conflict resolution system, a mediation training program is provided.

4. Evaluation. After the system has been implemented, some mechanism must be provided for quality control. Often ongoing training is necessary, and changes in the original design may be required. The conflict resolution system design is dynamic rather than static, and may need to change due to shifts in the type of disputes or shifts in the disputants. As with any new process, experience often results in useful suggestions for improvements.

A well-designed conflict resolution system should provide for continual monitoring of the output (the conflicts that pass through the system) to see how it is working. By including a mechanism for feedback, the system can be fine tuned to exactly meet the needs of the users. It is important to avoid the temptation to consider the newly designed and implemented system a finished and unchangeable product. By providing methods in the initial design by which a continual flow of information can be directed to the designers and implementers of the system, the feedback needs will be met, and continuing adjustment and improvement of the system is possible.

Attorneys often take a reactive rather than a proactive approach towards problems. It is a shift in this attitude which will allow attorneys the vision to assist clients with ADR systems design. Rather than react to the actions of others, an attorney may assist a client in developing methods to deal with conflict when it arises, and to prevent it from arising. This proactive approach will ultimately save the client time and money.

One type of consultant is a person from outside the organization. Outside consultants bring a fresh perspective to the organization. As outside consultants, attorneys may work with existing clients in the development of ADR Systems Designs. The working team approach, with the attorney as a member of the team, will allow the attorney an opportunity to advise his or her long-term clients about methods to resolve conflict.

In-house counsel may also act as a consultant if they have the necessary expertise in systems design. This strategy will allow for a comprehensive, systematic approach to handling disputes in-house. Many corporations are moving to an in-house approach to systems design. Methods being used include implementing ADR Committees to develop contract clauses, as well as methods to evaluate cases for ADR techniques. Of course, the in-house and outside approaches can be combined, with the outsider taking the lead in the design stage, and the insider taking the lead during implementation. At least part of the evaluation phase should be conducted by someone not associated with the design and implementation of the System, in order to avoid bias. An independent evaluator also can provide valuable advice about improving the current System.

2. Cathy A. Constantino & Christina Sickles Merchant, Designing Conflict Management Systems — A Guide to Creating Productive and Healthy Organizations 19-32, 117-33 (1995)

The design or improvement of conflict management systems derives many of its practices and principles from well-established organization development (OD) concepts and techniques. We suggest that OD can be thought of as the who, what, and why of organizational action and change, addressing how organizations, their leaders, and their members seek and sustain change: considering, planning, managing, and measuring. These core tasks are also essential to the effective design or improvement of conflict management systems. In general terms, OD is about discovering the need for change, is planned and intentional in nature, and is as durable as possible over time. We suggest that conflict management systems designers need to pursue similar goals in order to achieve a measure of effectiveness in their efforts, and that many OD principles are relevant when exploring conflict management as a system.

Conflict management design extends and applies many OD concepts to the specific area of organizational conflict — the whether and how of dealing with systemic conflict in organizations. Conflict management design draws from the full range of OD theory and practice, particularly systems thinking, change intervention design, search processes, relationship building, strategic redesign and implementation, and action learning for improved conflict management systems development. Moreover, the core values associated with organization development — openness, tolerance of diversity, learning, involvement, appreciation of and management of differences, generation of valid data, and the search for feedback — are particularly critical for successful work with conflict itself and for the systemic management of it in any organization. We examine several of these OD principles, practices, and values here in more detail as they relate particularly to the design of organizational conflict management systems.

When the principles of OD (the who, what, and why) are combined with the principles of conflict management design (the whether and how), a more complete and holistic approach to effective organizational conflict management emerges. OD encourages recognition and understanding of the crucial components of organizations: purpose, structure, leadership, culture, and relationships with internal and external environments. Perhaps one of the reasons that there has been increased dissatisfaction with many of the traditional methods of resolving disputes is their frequent failure to take into account organizational dynamics: how organizations function, how they learn, how they know whether they are performing well, how they adjust to new information and the need for any change, and how they go about the business of changing. We believe that with a grounding in OD values, principles, and processes, practitioners and managers can be more effective in assisting organizations to move away from case-by-case dispute resolution programs and toward more comprehensive, even "global," identification and management of conflict in their systems. . . .

Whole and Open Systems Thinking

Organizations are commonly viewed as open systems: arrangements of parts dynamically interrelated with each other and with the influences in their environment. Anyone who works with or within organizations is well aware of the following prevailing practice: organizations are structured into functional components such as production operations, sales divisions, customer service offices, human resources departments, legal departments, and the like. Each component has its distinctive purpose, population, role, and culture, and each relies to a greater or lesser extent on the other components to achieve overall organizational performance.

Further, each component of the organization is related to the whole system in a broader sense, with the need to move across or span the functional boxes or boundaries of offices, departments, and divisions in order to accomplish organizational purposes. Thus, each structural and functional component of the organization contributes to and adopts organization-wide characteristics with respect to many subsystems. Examples of such subsystems include the human system (how and which individuals are recruited, selected, mentored, and retained), the work system (how the primary mission of the organization is actually accomplished), the reward system (how the organization rewards and recognizes service and accomplishment of objectives), the financial management system (how the organization allocates and accounts for resource use), and the information system (how data is collected, managed, and disseminated within and outside the organization). What we propose is that conflict management also be viewed as a subsystem within a larger system.

A systems approach to working with organizations encourages the identification of those subsystems that make up the whole and the examination of how well they collectively interact in order to discover how to improve them. Improving the systemic functioning of organizations requires focusing attention on the social systems by which organizational members interact to produce results and on the technical systems that advance output and productivity in the workplace. . . . These "socio-technical" aspects of the workplace and its improvement need to be examined and improved collectively rather than segmentally, for when systems interact dynamically with each other within the core of the whole of the organization, it is difficult to identify which is cause and which is effect.

Conflict Management as a System

As one of the many "systems" in organizations, conflict management has been one of the last to be directly recognized and developed. It seems obvious that any organization must have system, consciously or otherwise, by which it exposes and resolves dissatisfaction, yet this concept of conflict as a system has only recently come into focus. Even more interesting is the relatively new notion that the adequacy and effectiveness of the conflict management system has an effect on the successful operation of other systems within the organization and of the organization as a whole. Perhaps these concepts have not been recognized because organizational conflict management systems have usually been housed in discrete components (legal and human resource departments) that have the responsibility to provide conflict management services to the rest of the organization. Characteristically, these departments' specialized knowledge about the rules, processes, and techniques for handling conflict becomes a matter of job security and, as a result, is tightly held onto in order to increase the department's value to the rest of the organization. In a broader sense, the topic of conflict often makes people uneasy, and individuals, groups, and organizations will therefore conspire to avoid facing it directly.

Traditionally, dispute resolution functions have been housed in two locations within an organization: the legal department (dealing primarily with external disputes) and the human resources and/or personnel department (dealing primarily with internal disputes). Typically, separation of these functions is amplified and strengthened by mission, structure, staff qualifications, and reporting relationships separate and apart from the service, sales, or production components (the technical core) of the organization. In practice, it is often the case that the legal and human resource departments of many organizations are viewed as a necessary evil that must be tolerated to handle the conflicts that others neither like nor believe they are equipped to handle.

Looking at conflict management as but one of many systems within the larger organizational constellation permits an enhanced understanding of conflict as it arises and a sharpened recognition of the opportunities for action in managing such conflict. In this way, the OD systemic perspective aids in the process of observing how organizational units interact and produce to achieve organizational goals, including the collateral and ever-present generation and management of conflict and its costs. The adoption of OD's "helicopter perspective" allows one to metaphorically hover in the air and take a look at what is happening on the ground with respect to conflict management and how it affects other systems. The development of the ability to gain a whole systems perspective of the existing causes, costs, and resolutions of conflict is a crucial link and the common ground between OD and conflict management systems design.

Characteristics of Conflict Management Systems

Like other systems within an organization, conflict management systems have certain characteristics:

Boundaries. These borders, some tangible and some intangible, separate one system from another. In the case of the conflict management system, its internal management boundaries are often clearly defined as the human resource and legal components of any organization. It is in these components that disputes arising from within or outside the organization's overall boundaries are received, processed, and resolved.

Purpose. All systems have a goal or mission that is their reason for being. As long as it meets the expectations and requirements of the external environment regarding products and services, the system can continue to operate in pursuit of its purpose or goal. In the case of the conflict management system, its purpose is the resolution of various types of disputes between the organization and internal or external claimants. Explicitly or implicitly, its purpose within the larger organizational context is to reflect the dominant view of preferred responses to conflict and its resolution (for example, fight or flight).

Inputs. Systems absorb multiple resources in anticipation of fulfilling their purpose: they take in ideas, people, dollars, and raw materials. The conflict management system does this as well by staffing and otherwise funding and supporting organizational components intended to perform the multitude of conflict resolution tasks; the raw materials of the system are the disputes to be resolved.

Transformation. The staff, funding, and other inputs taken into the organization from the external environment are transformed or changed in some manner by the people and technology of the system. This happens at the technical core of the organization, whether by transforming raw' materials into saleable products or by providing services to clients. Typically, these core basic processes, which fulfill the system's overall purpose, are accomplished by individuals, in roles, organized into groups with a defined function. Such is the case in the organizational conflict management system where staff work to transform disputes into resolutions and impasse into results through processes such as dispute and case intake, information gathering, investigation and fact finding, meetings, oral and written arguments, negotiations, litigation, and court appearances.

Outputs. A system's products or services are then exported to the external environment, which, ideally, finds them useful and acceptable. The outputs of the conflict management system, which are provided internally to the organization or externally to the environment, are the "ending" of disputes, such as withdrawals of cases, decisions, agreements, and settlements.

Feedback. Determining whether a system has fulfilled its purpose is accomplished through feedback. The external environment expects that the system will use feedback either to improve the products or services delivered or to revise goals and objectives in order to bring them into line with expectations. The environment, external to the subsystem (but still within the organization) or external to the organization as a whole, is thus critical to the continued viability of any open system, for it not only supplies the input of people, material, and energy, but also receives and evaluates the output. Organizational conflict management systems receive feedback from their customers, constituents, and employees regarding the adequacy, quality, cost, and perception of fairness about dispute resolutions and results.

We find that thinking of conflict management as an open system operating within a larger organizational system and within an external environment provides a useful framework for approaching conflict management system design and intervention. . . . Operating from an open systems perspective in managing organizational conflict leads to at least two significant results: (1) identification of key areas for inquiry regarding potential change (that is, within the input, transformation, and/or output processes of the organization's current conflict management system) and (2) uncovering dissonance, dysfunction, and dissatisfaction. The conflict management system gathers this information through assessment, feedback, and other participative methods. Those who need to participate in such processes are most easily identified as internal and external "customers" and stakeholders of the organization's dispute resolution program. The assessment is done by looking at the way the organization currently deals with disputes, since that is actually its current conflict management system. . . .

Conflict Management as a Change Intervention

OD intervenors seek to develop open, empowering, and collaborative relationships with the client systems they serve. Most OD intervenors are aware of and use the "self as instrument" perspective during all aspects of the change intervention process Self-knowledge about bias, blind spots, vulnerability to certain influences, and sensitivity to conflict is of critical importance to anyone seeking to influence others and to guide change in organizational systems dealing with conflict. . . .

Design Architecture: Constructing Conflict Management Models

In contrast to organizational assessment, which looks at the big picture and the "macro" aspects of the design effort, architectural construction focuses on disputes themselves and methods of resolution, which is the "micro" part of managing conflict. Organizational assessment is concerned with the why, what, and who of the current dispute resolution system; design architecture looks at the whether, when, and how of any new conflict management system.

In exploring design architecture, we focus on ADR as one possible enrichment of an organization's capacity to manage conflict in its system. More specifically, we look at architectural considerations: whether, when, and how to use ADR. In exploring each of these issues, we offer six key principles to guide the design architecture process. The first two principles address "whether," the next two focus on "when," and the last two concern "how."

The first question of design architecture is whether to use ADR at all. Perhaps it is not better, cheaper, faster, more durable. Perhaps the current methods of dispute resolution are working just fine, and there is no need for change. Here, the design architects, the organization and its stakeholders ask the following questions in determining whether to use ADR:

- What, if anything, is missing in these disputes?

- Do stakeholders express dissatisfaction and frustration with all or only part of existing dispute resolution processes?

- How do stakeholders express this dissatisfaction?

- Is an ADR process a possible and appropriate way to address the concerns expressed?

- If so, what type(s) of ADR is/are appropriate?

- Would such ADR steps or processes be a good "fit" with the goals of the organization (mission) and the technology of doing its work (culture)?

If it is decided that ADR is appropriate, the next inquiry for the design team, the organization, and the stakeholders is when to use ADR:

- At what stage of the dispute is there a gap or complaint?

- Can an interest-based process be introduced at that point in the existing procedure?

- Would such an addition address the concern expressed?

- If an ADR step is introduced at that time, what is the likely effect on subsequent stages of the existing dispute resolution system?

- Would ADR enhance or diminish the possibility of satisfactory resolution?

- Have preventive forms of ADR been attempted with regard to these disputes?

- For both prevention and new ADR steps, will disputants have the necessary skills and knowledge to use ADR effectively to resolve the disputes at that stage?

The how stage of design architecture is then a blend of the answers to the above questions (whether and when) with the spectrum of ADR options, a continuum from preventive to imposed methods.

Six Principles

The whether, when, how paradigm for design architecture can be translated into practical guiding principles that can help frame any design architecture effort:

1. Develop guidelines for whether ADR is appropriate.

2. Tailor the ADR process to the particular problem.

3. Build in preventive methods of ADR.

4. Make sure disputants have the knowledge and skill to choose and use ADR.

5. Create ADR systems that are simple to use and easy to access and that resolve disputes early, at the lowest organizational level, with the least bureaucracy.

6. Allow disputants to retain maximum control over choice of ADR method and selection of neutral wherever possible.

1. Develop guidelines for whether ADR is appropriate. Although ADR is an acronym for alternative dispute resolution, many practitioners engaging in design architecture find it useful to think of ADR as "appropriate" dispute resolution: is ADR appropriate for this type of conflict, and if so, what type of ADR? This involves helping the organization choose the dispute resolution mechanism that is most tailored to the particular stage or category of dispute — the least costly, most timely, most satisfactory and most durable methods to employ in seeking resolution. ADR is not an off-the-shelf, one-size-fits-all product. . . .

Organizations are made up of people, culture, technology, and mission, and it is important to ensure that the ADR design is congruent with all of these. Based on an organizational assessment, design architects (as a team or as individuals) critically evaluate whether ADR is understood and viewed as useful by employees and disputants, whether it could further the organization's mission, and whether it fits with the organization's culture. For example, an organization that has a "warrior" culture — a preference for adversarial methods of resolution — may be more likely to accept and use imposed methods of ADR (binding arbitration) than to relinquish disputes to facilitated methods (mediation). The same may be true of organizations whose mission is to enforce some regulatory scheme or ensure compliance with a particular set of standards. Conversely, an organization whose mission is to foster international or community relations may be more prone to use facilitated methods of ADR, such as negotiation and consensus building.

In some cases, however, ADR may not be appropriate at all. Where an organization wants to establish a rights-based precedent that can be used in other cases, the court system, rather than ADR, may be the most appropriate forum for resolution. Similarly, if the government has a significant policy that it wants to test, it may be inappropriate to use ADR. In fact, the Administrative Dispute Resolution Act provides that an agency should consider not using ADR if one of the following six factors is present: the need to establish precedent; a question of significant public policy that requires additional procedures before a final resolution can be made; the desire to create an established body of policy and decision; the necessity for a public record, which cannot be provided by ADR; the need to maintain ongoing supervision or jurisdiction for compliance, and ADR would interfere with that requirement; or the matter significantly affects absent persons or organizations who are not parties to the ADR process. The considerations for determining whether ADR is appropriate are applicable to the private and nonprofit sectors as well. For example, a company may decide that it wants to push the edge of the law in a particular area, such as patent infringement or the use of non-compete clauses. A nonprofit organization bringing a class action suit on behalf of disabled students may decide that it needs ongoing court supervision to monitor and enforce any consent decree. Even here, it may still be possible to reach a resolution through some form of ADR, such as mediation, if the parties can petition the court at a later date to enforce the settlement or appoint a master.

2. Tailor the ADR process to the particular problem. Aside from the organizational fit, there should also be a process fit: the ADR process should be appropriate for the particular problem at hand. Choosing mediation as the ADR process when in fact the nuances of a particular case and the interests of the disputants indicate that neutral expert fact finding would be more appropriate (and possibly more successful) can lead to a conclusion by disputants and organizational leadership that ADR does not make sense. For example, in a dispute involving technical or quantitative issues — the value of a real estate parcel, the amount of soil to fill a hole, or the average life expectancy of certain insureds — fact finding or advisory methods may in some instances be more useful than facilitative methods. In a dispute involving how certain franchisee disputes will be resolved, it may be more appropriate to use a form of joint problem solving, which improves the ongoing business relationship, as opposed to a more imposed method of resolution such as arbitration, which may have a chilling effect on the ongoing relationship, reducing it to a matter of winners and losers.

Are there really dangers inherent in selecting an "inappropriate" ADR method? If it fails to work, why not just go back and pick a different method and hope to get it right the second time? The danger in constructing a design built on inappropriate ADR methods is that unsuccessful ADR experiences lead to the impression on the part of managers, resource allocators, disputants, and critics that all forms of ADR are unsuccessful or meaningless exercises: "ADR didn't work here, so why should it work somewhere else?"

3. Build in preventive methods of ADR. It may be useful to think of developing a range of preventive methods of ADR that are applicable in a variety of contexts, such as the individual, group, organization, community, and global environments. . . . For example, methods of prevention at the individual level may include increasing one's tolerance for and acceptance of conflict or improving interpersonal communication and active listening skills; prevention methods at the level of the group may involve practicing consensus decision making, engaging in team building, and generating problem resolution options through brainstorming; prevention methods at the level of the organization could entail circulating ongoing employee feedback surveys, developing strategic visions collectively (search conferences), and involving constituents in change processes on an ongoing basis; prevention methods at the level of the community might include creating multicultural educational programs and forums, as well as conducting search conferences to establish a community vision and direction; prevention methods at the level of nations could include offering assistance, training, and support to emerging nations in the development of institutional dispute resolution processes as well as in training dispute resolvers.

To date, not much attention has been focused on preventive methods of ADR. As organizations continue to adopt "best practices" in their day-to-day operations and relationships — to compete, to control costs, and to maximize resources — dispute prevention becomes increasingly important. Furthermore, organizations will come to expect design architects to be familiar with ADR methods of prevention and to include them in their recommendations for the furtherance of the systemic management of conflict.

4. Make sure that disputants have the necessary knowledge and skills to choose and use ADR. Determining when to use ADR depends in large measure on whether the affected disputants have the necessary knowledge to choose ADR and the skills to use it once they have chosen it. People are unlikely to choose a procedure about which they know nothing. Thus, labor and management need to know how to engage in interest-identification processes, brainstorming, and consensus decision making in order to use interest-based negotiation. A dissatisfied customer needs to know what mediation is and how to participate in it before she can choose it and participate as an informed ADR user. An unhappy claimant needs to know what nonbinding arbitration is before he can decide to submit his claim to such a process. Whether and when ADR is used is often determined by the ADR knowledge and skill levels of those choosing the method.

Practitioners know that disputants, more often than not, are only ready to resolve disputes in their own time. Disputants have to be assured that they have standing and that their complaint has been heard. Further they need information about their dispute before they can consider possible choices for resolution, especially the more unfamiliar forms of ADR. For example, it may be difficult for claimants to choose early neutral evaluation or a mini-trial if they have not assessed their case or they do not have a basic understanding of the facts to be presented to a neutral. It would be hard for claimants to use the services of an ombudsperson without first identifying the issue or being able to articulate the particular grievance. Some practitioners have seen ADR fail because disputants were unfamiliar or uncomfortable with the facts of their case or had not yet assessed their options; they were thus not only unable to commit to a solution but also unable to commit to a process. Conversely, sometimes practitioners see disputants and organizations delay ADR use to the point where the dollars and time already expended in overdeveloping the facts require them to justify such use of resources to the point of litigation. In this way, the optimal time for the use of ADR in a particular dispute is intimately tied to the organization's culture of dispute development and its tolerance of conflict and risk.

5. Create ADR systems that are simple to use and easy to access and that resolve disputes early, at the lowest organizational level, with the least bureaucracy. Effective design architects embrace the KISS principle ("keep it simple, stupid"). They make ADR simple to use, easy to access, and readily available, with a minimum of delay. In order for disputants to actually choose ADR, it must be easier to use than the current dispute resolution system. In most instances, resolving disputes as early as possible decreases costs and increases satisfaction. [E]arly resolution may be impeded by the disputants' own understanding and knowledge (or the lack thereof) of their case. More often, early resolution is impeded by organizational constraints, such as cultural attitudes toward conflict or risk, the need for lengthy review and approval processes, or the failure to make ADR simple to use and easy to access.

Many organizations require the use of multiple levels of the bureaucracy to study, dissect, and review the merits of a dispute before it can be resolved. Thus, although the disputants may want to resolve the dispute as quickly and as early as possible, organizational practices and procedures may constrain them. This is where the principle of "subsidiarity" arises: designing conflict management systems that resolve disputes at the lowest organizational level possible. As an architectural design principle, subsidiarity is often difficult to implement in highly stratified, vertically organized institutions that take pride in their review and approval procedures. Some organizations bifurcate the review and approval processes: they require review and approval through several chains of command to engage in ADR and then a second review and approval (often through the same chain of command) to commit to a resolution reached through ADR. . . . However, some practitioners have found it helpful to work with such an organization's leadership to point out the benefit and wisdom of designing more streamlined approval procedures for particular divisions, offices, or clusters of cases.

6. Allow disputants to retain maximum control over choice of ADR method and selection of neutral wherever possible. Not surprisingly, practitioners have found that disputants are likely to be more resistant to an ADR process if they are not involved in selecting it and even more resistant if they have little or no voice in determining who the neutral will be. Consistently attempting to build on the values of participation, openness, and feedback requires that selection of ADR methods be derived rather than imposed.

3. Comments and Questions

a. What are the key considerations for an organization in determining the optimum approach to implementing a dispute prevention and resolution system?

b. How does an organization develop the expertise to undertake a system design, and the "in-house" training of employees? The basic options are to hire someone, to send some employees for training, or to hire an outside organization to design and implement the process. (All sorts of hybrids are possible, that combine elements of the three basic alternatives.) Assume that a firm has chosen to adopt an "out house" approach to system design. What are the key factors in selecting a system design provider?

c. Is it appropriate for the provider organization subsequently to mediate or otherwise to participate in the resolution of specific disputes?

d. Valuable additional readings on system design include: John P. Conbere, *Theory Building for Conflict Management System Design*, 19 CONFLICT RESOL. Q. 215 (2001); Jennifer Lynch, *Integrated Conflict Management*, 17 NEGOT. J. 213 (2001); Christopher Moore, *Dispute Systems Design: A Pragmatic Approach for the Development of Procedures and Structures to Manage Ethnic and Political Conflicts*. 6 PACIFICA REV. 43 (1994); KARL A. SLEIKAU & RALPH H. HASSON,

CONTROLLING THE COSTS OF CONFLICT: HOW TO DESIGN A SYSTEM FOR YOUR ORGA-
NIZATION (1998); SOCIETY FOR PROFESSIONALS IN DISPUTE RESOLUTION, GUIDE-
LINES FOR THE DESIGN OF INTEGRATED CONFLICT MANAGEMENT SYSTEMS WITHIN
ORGANIZATIONS (2000); William L. Ury, *Conflict Resolution Among the Bush-
men: Lessons in Dispute Systems Design*, 11 NEGOT. J. 379 (1995).

C. TOTAL QUALITY MANAGEMENT (TQM)

1. Comments and Questions

a. This section provides a brief overview of total quality management (TQM),
a well-established approach to management. The leading practitioner, W.
Edward Deming, was honored in Japan long before his work was recognized in
the United States. Deming's ideas helped to drive the post-World War II Japanese economic miracle. Prevention of disputes, and minimizing the impact of
those disputes that do occur, is an important feature of TQM.

b. There are a vast array of differently named quality improvement ideas and
programs, many accompanied by a formidable special vocabulary. Many of the
suggestions of the TQM movement, and workplace improvement programs,
strike outsiders as glorified common sense. Success depends not on intellectual
knowledge, or internalization of a set of catch-phrases, but a strong commitment
to effective implementation and continuous improvement.

2. E. WENDY TRACHTE-HUBER, ADR SYSTEM DESIGN: THE PRE-LITIGATION OPTION — THE ATTORNEY AS CONSULTANT (1993)

The Total Quality Management Movement

The business community has known about total quality management (TQM)
for many years, but the legal community has embraced TQM only recently. The
TQM approach emphasizes customer service and employee teamwork to improve
products and service to customers. TQM has found a new application in the
design of conflict management systems.

W. Edwards Deming, management consultant and leader of the TQM movement, has distilled the core principles underlying TQM into his Fourteen Points,
These are:

1. Create constancy of purpose for improvement of product and service;

2. Adopt a new philosophy;

3. Cease dependence on mass inspection;

4. End the practice of awarding business on price tag alone;

5. Improve constantly and forever the system of production and service;

6. Institute training;

7. Institute leadership;

8. Drive out fear;

9. Break down barriers between staff areas;

10. Eliminate slogans, exhortations, and targets for the work force;

11. Eliminate numerical quotas;

12. Remove barriers to pride of workmanship;

13. Institute a vigorous program of education and retraining; and

14. Take action to accomplish the transformation.

A fifteenth principle could well be, "Develop and implement a dynamic dispute resolution system." Many of these points reflect the importance of a comprehensive, systematic approach to conflict resolution within an organization. It is important to recognize that even though Deming directs his remarks to the business community, attorneys may also benefit from the recognition that clients are customers. Providing a full range of services to clients should be the main objective of the legal profession. ADR systems design provides another important client service to add to the armory of the full service law firm or an in-house legal department.

D. PRODUCTIVE WORKPLACES: PLANNING FOR EMPLOYMENT DISPUTES

1. Comments and Questions

a. The workplace provides an ideal setting for systems work because the interaction among employees is multiplex, and the relationship is both highly important and long-term. It makes sense for employers to devote considerable effort (and money) to creating and maintaining a workplace environment that prevents dispute from occurring, and minimizes the impact of those disputes that do arise by addressing them quickly and effectively.

b. Organizations, both public and private, have their own unique history and culture that must be considered in designing a workplace disputing system. This, of course, is easier said than done, as is evidenced by the many problems associated with most corporate mergers.

c. Several major variables will have a central impact on any workplace system that addresses disputes and disputing. Is the employer a private entity or a unit of government? Is the workforce unionized, in whole or in part? (If so, the union will be a key player in the process, and many of the issues may be the subject of collective bargaining.) Are the concerns being addressed common to many or most employees, or are they unique to individuals (discrimination, grievances)?

d. Note that the workplace is a pervasively regulated environment, even where the employer is a private entity. Examples of topics that are the subject of government oversight include health and safety, wages and hours, environmental quality, use of hazardous materials, immigration status of workers, equal employment opportunity, etc. Thus governments (federal, state and local) are a major player in any workplace environment, and must be considered in the system design.

e. The first reading in this section examines Partnership Councils — an approach used to promote effective labor-management relations for large, high dollar construction projects. While the use of Partnership Councils has traditionally been confined to major construction projects, note that the concept could easily be used in other contexts.

2. U.S. Army Corps of Engineers, PARTNERSHIP COUNCILS: BUILDING SUCCESSFUL LABOR-MANAGEMENT RELATIONSHIPS (IWR Working Paper 94-ADR-WP-5) (1994)

A. Introduction

To establish a successful Partnership Council within an organization requires considerable preparation and careful planning. Although the task may seem formidable, it does not have to be. This pamphlet provides a practical approach to accomplish it. By forming a Partnership Design Team and using a development workshop, a foundation for success can be built for the Partnership Council.

In most organizations, the establishment of a Partnership Council institutes a dramatic change from a traditional adversarial culture to a new cooperative relationship. The quality of this new relationship will stem from mutual trust, honest communications, and teamwork. The effort the partners put into the relationship will be reflected in the lasting results achieved. Building an effective relationship takes understanding and time, but most of all it takes commitment to the mutual goals and vision of the partnership. . . . Creating a successful Partnership Council is a collaborative endeavor that involves labor and management focusing on their common interests. This pamphlet is a blueprint for all partners to use in establishing a new labor-management partnership for their organization.

Acting on the National Performance Review (NPR) partnership recommendation, President Clinton issued Executive Order 12,871 on October 1, 1993. The order states that the involvement of federal employees and their union representatives in a partnership is essential to achieving the NPR's reform objectives. As partners in the design and implementation of comprehensive change, federal employees will transform agencies "into organizations capable of delivering the highest quality services to the American people." To do this, agencies are directed to do the following: create labor-management partnerships by forming councils; involve employees and their union representatives as full partners with management; provide training in consensual methods of dispute resolution and interest-based bargaining; negotiate over the subjects in 5 U.S.C. § 7106 (b)(1); and evaluate progress in organizational performance. [Section 7106 is titled Management Rights, but subsection (b)(1) authorizes agencies to negotiate about "the numbers, types, and grades of employees or positions assigned to any organizational subdivisions, work project, tour of duty, or on the technological methods, and means of performing work."]

1. Why a Partnership? The simple answer to the question is that it is necessary to comply with the National Performance Review and Executive Order 12,871. But beyond meeting these requirements, creating a labor-management partnership makes good business sense, It is logical to involve all parties in reshaping the organizational culture, finding better ways to prevent and resolve differences, and establishing a relationship to meet the needs of the partners and the American people.

2. What Is a Partnership Council? A Partnership Council is an internal group composed of labor and management officials and reflecting a new relationship among the partners. In an organization that has several bargaining units, the organization may have more than one Partnership Council or a single Partnership Council with several bargaining unit members. Regardless of how many Partnership Councils are established, the partners decide the way that an individual partnership develops and the final form that it takes. Each partnership will be different and should be tailored to meet the needs of the partners and satisfy their common interests. Specific details such as the number of members, the level of membership, and the formality of the meetings will depend on the partners.

B. Preparation for Success

1. Make It a Joint Design. The Partnership Council should be collaboratively designed by labor and management. When the partnership is being established, there should be no one-sided objectives or hidden agendas. The partners need to work together to create a Partnership Council to better serve the organization and its employees and to meet the organization's mission.

2. Form the Partnership Design Team. One way to create a Partnership Council is to begin by forming a design team that consists of representatives from labor and management. Full participation by each partner on the design team will significantly increase the chances of success for the Partnership Council since the partners will share ownership in the new relationship that results from their joint endeavor. The members of the design team may be the same individuals who will initially serve on the Partnership Council and may include union members and officers, senior managers, human resources officials, and an attorney. The level of representation for management will depend on the extent of bargaining unit representation in the activity.

3. Consider Partnership Characteristics. The Partnership Design Team should incorporate the following characteristics of successful partnerships when designing the Partnership Council:

    a. *Attitude* — Each partner adopts a positive attitude that reflects the change in attitude from confrontational to cooperative.

b. *Commitment* — Each partner pledges to act and fulfill all duties necessary to make the partnership successful.

c. *Respect* — The partners recognize and acknowledge that individual personalities and organizational structures can differ, yet are entitled to respect.

d. *Communications* — The partners dedicate themselves to open and honest communications that involve speaking freely and frankly and listening actively.

e. *Sharing* — Each partner is willing to share necessary information voluntarily without engaging in positional bargaining.

f. *Trust* — Trust is earned by the partners' actions being consistent with their words.

g. *Goals* — Mutual goals are jointly established by the partnership, which also sets objectives to reach those goals.

h. *Consensus* — Solutions to issues are jointly developed by all partners, are acceptable to all partners, and are supported by all partners.

i. *Responsibility* — All partners accept responsibility for the change in the relationship, feel responsible for the success or failure of the partnership, and act accordingly.

j. *Synergy* — All partners work together to achieve a synergistic partnership in which the totality is greater than the sum of the individual parts.

C. Working for Success

The Partnership Design Team can use a facilitated workshop to develop the partnership. The development workshop should establish open communications, create a team spirit, and enhance commitment to the partnership. To ensure success at the development workshop, the Partnership Design Team should meet for several days soon after the team is formed in order to design the development workshop. During the workshop, the following steps can be useful.

1. Assess Current Relationship. An important activity for the design team is learning from the past. The team should recognize positive and negative aspects of their existing relationship. Specifically, they should identify sources of past conflict that caused disputes and created barriers between the partners, as well as sources of agreement that fostered better relationships. This assessment requires an honest evaluation of the relationship.

2. Discuss Partner Expectations. The partners need to put their expectations for the Partnership Council on the table. Expectations need to be discussed in order to set realistic limits and avoid disappointment and frustration.

3. Identify Common Interests. The workshop can help the partners identify their common interests in a partnership. These interests are often expressed in simple statements such as "reducing tension," "building better communications," "creating a safer workplace," or "improving relationships." By taking the time at the beginning of the workshop to identify common interests, the partners will establish the foundation for a successful Partnership Council.

4. Establish Partnership Functions. The partners need to clarify what they want the Partnership Council to accomplish. The general functions can be to share information, prevent disputes, build consensus, and identify training opportunities.

5. Commit to Bargain Over Discretionary Items. These negotiations should be well-planned and use interest-based bargaining principles.

6. Designate Action Teams. Identify action items that can assist in preventing or resolving problems and designate joint Action Teams to solve those problems. Action items may include traditional subjects such as collective bargaining negotiations, or new areas such as training opportunities, and workplace partnership activities. Action Teams that focus on these subjects should consist of subgroups of the Partnership Council.

7. Develop Future Vision. The partnership should have a joint vision that articulates what the organization will be like in the future as a result of the Partnership Council positive relationship.

8. Set Mutual Goals. Setting mutual goals establishes what the partners want to accomplish within their vision for the partnership. To achieve these goals, the partners also need to establish performance measures to indicate progress that can be reviewed at future Partnership Council meetings.

9. Fix Meeting Procedures. The Partnership Council should have simple, fair, and efficient procedures. Establishing procedures early during the process prevents later disputes over process. Procedures can cover subjects such as: establishing membership on the Partnership Council, selecting meeting locations, setting schedules, establishing the agenda format, and recording meeting minutes.

10. Create Partnership Charter. At the conclusion of the development workshop, the design team needs to create a charter to guide the partnership throughout its relationship. The charter is not a contractual agreement between labor and management, nor does it affect or change any collective bargaining agreements. Rather, the charter expresses the intent of the Partnership Council to work together in a cooperative relationship. The charter should be a concise written document that consists of the partnership vision and a list of jointly developed goals. Typically, the charter comprises one or two pages, and is signed by all members of the design team as an expression of their commitment to the partnership.

D. Maintaining Success

After the design team has conducted the development workshop, signed a charter, and formed the Partnership Council, it is time to initiate the follow-up program. This program consists of regularly scheduled meetings of the Partnership Council and special meetings of the Action Teams. Additionally, partnership training should be part of the program.

1. Partnership Council Meetings. Partnership Council meetings are essential to sustaining a cooperative relationship. Meetings should be held as needed, but at the beginning of the partnership they should probably be held frequently, perhaps monthly at first and later quarterly. The matter of scheduling is an item for the partners to decide. The meetings should be flexible and encourage full participation by the partners. At the meetings, the partners can introduce new members, share information, discuss training needs, review Action Team reports, identify new problems, and evaluate the relationship.

2. Agenda Items. Introducing a new member to the partnership can be done easily. In addition to a simple introduction at the meeting, the new member needs to be provided a copy of the charter and the opportunity to sign it. Sharing information is the responsibility of all partners. Management needs to share information that can impact bargaining unit employees. Similarly, labor must share the attitudes of bargaining unit members on issues. Discussing training needs is necessary to provide the partners with the tools required to build the relationship. Reviewing Action Team reports ensures that problems are being addressed in a timely manner. The partners can review what has been done and offer suggestions on plans for resolution.

Identifying new problems is a responsibility of all partners. Recognizing that the identification of issues is a joint responsibility brings problems into the open, permits statements to be made on interests, and allows the partners to form Action Teams if necessary. Evaluating the relationship may be the most important function of the Partnership Council meetings. The evaluation process can be expedited by developing a checklist of partnership characteristics for each partner to rate.

3. Meeting Minutes. Since the Partnership Council will be involved in a number of diverse activities, minutes of the meetings will be valuable to record what happened and also to set the agenda for the next meeting. The responsibility for recording the minutes can be rotated among the partners.

4. Action Team Meetings. Action Team meetings are separate meetings for the members of the Action Team and others that the team decides to include. The meetings provide the members with the opportunity to focus their full attention on a particular issue. The Action Team will normally engage in a fact-finding process and then make recommendations in a report to the Partnership Council. The frequency and length of the meetings depend upon the difficulty of the problem and the desires of the members.

5. Training. In most Partnership Councils, the partners will need training. The partners should actively participate in these joint exercises. The main training areas will probably concern relationships and consensual methods of dispute resolution. Relationship training may include instruction in communication skills and team building. Training in consensual methods of dispute resolution should center on interest-based bargaining and the techniques of alternative dispute resolution (ADR). After the Partnership Council decides that training is needed, the activity training officer should be contacted to assist in finding training resources.

3. Peter Robinson, Arthur Pearlstein & Bernard Mayer, *DyADS: Encouraging "Dynamic Adaptive Dispute Systems" in the Organized Workplace*, 10 HARV. NEGOT. L. REV. 339, 340-41, 352-75 (2005)

In early 2002, the Federal Mediation and Conciliation Service ("FMCS") embarked on an effort to examine and advance the state of the art in dispute systems design and to determine an appropriate role for FMCS in helping its clients apply best practices in the development of dispute systems for the workplace. This initiative was based on observations that:

(a) a growing proportion of workplace disputes, even in the unionized sector, involve individual conflict [e.g., Equal Employment Opportunity (EEO) disputes, clashes of personality and style, etc.] rather than collective conflict [e.g., disputes over wages, benefits, and other matters collectively bargained for]; and

(b) organizations in the unionized sector have generally not moved toward developing dispute systems for such individual conflict to nearly the same extent as have companies in the non-unionized sector.

FMCS undertook this dispute systems design project by sponsoring a cooperative agreement with the Straus Institute for Dispute Resolution at Pepperdine University School of Law. Together, the Straus Institute and FMCS studied the literature, assembled a group of experts in dispute systems design to share ideas, and held numerous informal discussions with labor and management leaders. The result was a report that set forth a . . . recommended protocol through which FMCS could assist its clients to design and develop workplace dispute systems.

The report proposed an approach to be known as Dynamic Adaptive Dispute Systems (DyADS) through which labor and management stakeholders in an organization could collaboratively design a unique workplace dispute system that would evolve with the organization. Based on the report, FMCS is launching a set of pilot projects around the country aimed at refining the concept and determining the feasibility of offering DyADS to all of its clients.

While the movement to establish workplace dispute systems is not new, the DyADS initiative represents a new stage in the progression of the dispute systems design concept in at least two ways. First, DyADS applies lessons from complexity theory to approach dispute systems from the "bottom up," evolving through broad vision and minimum specifications. This contrasts with the more traditional approach of applying a mechanical model from the "top down" to impose a system by attempting to plan every small detail. Second, DyADS involves labor and management in a joint, creative effort to develop dispute systems that would complement collective bargaining. . . .

[T]he goal of a DyADS is not simply to establish a more efficient and collaborative method for solving disputes, but also to contribute to a more open, cooperative, and congenial workplace. Fundamental to DyADS is appreciating that differences are not a problem to be avoided but a source of strength and creativity to be accepted and understood, and that people can work together cooperatively and effectively even during times of stress and conflict. To achieve this goal, DyADS should reflect the following minimum set of characteristics. . . .

A. *Inclusive.* In creating its own DyADS, an organization should employ an inclusive process involving key users from both labor and management in defining dispute resolution needs, goals and options. The primary goal for DyADS is to create a dispute resolution system that is in keeping with the spirit and specifics of the collective bargaining agreement and will also encourage better individual and intergroup relationships, more creative problem-solving, and more efficient and less costly ways of settling disputes. A secondary goal is to help promote a more productive and cooperative workplace environment. As such, participant involvement in the planning process is key because these goals would all be undercut by the imposition of a dispute resolution system from the outside or the creation of a system that does not involve all participants . . . from the beginning. . . .

While outside consultants can provide experience, perspective, and insight, they can never replace the wisdom and understanding of those who spend their working lives within an organization. Without the very active involvement of workers and management in designing the system, it simply will not be as effective as it might otherwise be. . . . In designing procedures for each workplace, special consideration should be given to how to solicit the participation of people in geographically dispersed workplace settings from different shifts, different job categories, or different cultural groups within the workplace. . . .

B. *Incremental.* Rather than beginning with massive system overhaul, an organization should engage in an incremental, experimental, reflective process consistent with the organization's goals and needs, and building on existing strengths. The "systems" part of this process involves focus on effective connections between elements and prioritized development of organization-wide practices and support structures.

Change in complex systems does not normally occur through a straightforward process of rational planning or in one massive effort but rather through an ongoing process of adaptation and system reorganization around incremental inputs. In addition, change in the culture of disputing within organizations can normally occur only from within the existing culture. To ensure that a redesign effort is likely to succeed and result in its intended benefit, several factors must be present:

(a) an understanding of how an existing system works, its strengths and weaknesses, and the forces that promote and hinder change in the system;

(b) clarity about the goals of change;

(c) focus placed on one or two key changes that can be catalysts or focal points around which the overall system can reorganize;

(d) a built-in process for ongoing reflection, adaptation, revision, and evaluation;

(e) continual involvement of key players and groups in this reflection process;

(f) modesty about the ability to control how a new system will adapt to new inputs; and

(g) attention to how parts of a system interact process.

DyADS integrates these success factors and takes a dynamic, adaptive, systemic approach and helps bring about major change by focusing on smaller rather than larger reforms. . . .

Because the goal of a DyADS is to bring a new spirit and approach to how problems are dealt with in an organization, implementing DyADS requires the commitment of considerable time and energy. The motivation for people to commit to this effort is the desire to implement a different vision for an organization. Therefore, the DyADS process requires a broad vision. At the same time, the actual steps taken need to be strategic, specific, and focused.

C. Interest-Based. As much as possible, a DyADS should allow and encourage parties in conflict to make decisions and resolve conflicts on the basis of needs and interests. Three kinds of interests are generally present in workplace disputes — substantive, procedural, and psychological. There is a greater likelihood that all three kinds of interests can be addressed by creating approaches that encourage direct decision-making by participants and that also promote a focus on the interests of the parties rather than on a simple analysis of rights and obligations. A key challenge for a DyADS system is to develop mechanisms that balance respect for the overall needs of an organization and its internal groups with an appropriate focus on the needs of the specific individuals involved in workplace conflicts. Furthermore, it is important to ensure that individuals are not isolated from the support systems that provide them with protection and reassurance. . . .

D. Multiple Options. A DyADS should include more than one process option and more than one easy-to-access route to accommodate the different needs of disputants. A critical component of an effective DyADS is that it encourages people to deal with their workplace disputes sooner rather than later and directly rather than indirectly. Choice of approach and ease of access are two important factors in encouraging people to deal with the issues they have in a straightforward and constructive way. First, the more clearly workable choices of resolving a dispute people have, the more likely they are to take advantage of a DyADS. Choice itself is usually encouraging to people in conflict but, more to the point, different people will be able to find different mechanisms more in keeping with their needs in conflict. . . .

People in conflict want choices: both whether to deal with a conflict and how to deal with it. A DyADS should not take a "one size fits all" approach to dispute resolution. Instead, a DyADS should be flexible and provide for several different approaches that disputants can choose from and should ensure that each of these approaches is easily understandable and accessible. Some parties may prefer direct, face-to-face, unassisted processes, while others may prefer minimum direct contact or maximum third-party assistance. In the case neither party agrees to the same approach, a DyADS will have to develop mechanisms for helping parties choose which approach to start with. . . .

E. Robust Communication. A DyADS should emphasize frequent and robust communications within the workplace and create an environment for full exploration of differing opinions and ideas. The organization should expressly prohibit any form of reprisal or retaliation for participation in any DyADS process. Effective dispute resolution is closely connected to the culture of communication and problem-solving in an organization. For a system to be truly dynamic and adaptive, ongoing inter-group communication is essential. If an organization's culture is characterized by openness, security, optimism, and creativity, then the differences that develop will be much more easily dealt with, regardless of the dispute resolution system. A DyADS can be an impetus for creating a culture of communication and problem-solving, thus reinforcing the most positive elements of organizational communication.

Participation in any dispute resolution process should be free from retaliation (or even perceived retaliation). No one's sense of personal or professional security should in any way be threatened by participating in a DyADS. It takes just one instance of retaliation (or even perceived retaliation) to undercut a whole system. If someone is less likely to receive a promotion, raise, or desired job assignment because of their involvement in a DyADS, then the system is not going to work as a mechanism for encouraging people to raise their concerns and air their conflicts. . . .

F. Internal Neutral. To build systemic support and structures, labor and management should jointly develop an internal neutral function — performed by a single person, an office or group of offices, or a committee within the organization — to help develop, implement, coordinate and/or evaluate DyADS options, champion core concepts of the DyADS throughout the organization, and perform other related tasks as the organization may determine. Best practice includes an ombuds-type function, but there are a variety of potential arrangements that could be examined.

DyADS are about changing the way people relate to conflicts, communication, and problem-solving in an organization. Unless this system is managed by people who are provided the time and independence to focus on this agenda, it is unlikely that the potential of DyADS to impact decision-making and dispute resolution can be realized. Someone with independence and accountability must champion this system and take responsibility for its overall functioning. Furthermore, both union and management have to buy into the overall concept and into the individuals selected to fulfill the role of an internal neutral party. While the individuals playing this role may or may not act as mediators, factfinders, or facilitators, they need to have an adequate understanding of these and other aspects of a dispute resolution system in order to help people understand their choices, evaluate how well different components of the system are operating, and understand key issues of linkage among dispute resolution processes. Finally, individuals championing the DyADS program need to believe in the value and potential of DyADS along with a commitment to defining and using constructive approaches to dispute resolution. . . . . .

An internal neutral party will have some insulation and protection from immediate, day-to-day pressures or accountability to either labor or management, while his or her longer-term accountability is to both. He or she will devote enough time to this role to allow for all the necessary responsibilities to be fulfilled in a timely and consistent manner and will have a good understanding and appropriate training in relevant conflict resolution approaches. The people fulfilling this role will work to ensure that the principles of an effective DyADS are maintained and will promote the appropriate use of DyADS throughout the organization. They will also have the responsibility for making recommendations about modifying the system. . . .

G. Continual Refinement. An organization should commit to create, review, and refine its DyADS over time in a way that applies organizational learning. A DyADS benefits from and can contribute to an environment characterized by organizational learning. A learning organization is one committed to systemically promoting the processes and atmosphere of organizational self-examination, staff development, and dissemination of important knowledge and insights throughout the organization. When such an atmosphere exists, it will be natural and practical to apply it to the implementation, review, and refinement of a DyADS. The result is long-term effectiveness and durability of the DyADS program.

Too many potentially valuable initiatives fail because they are neither customized nor adjusted to the needs and culture of a particular organization. One cause of an inadequately crafted or tailored program is that it is initiated too quickly and does not have built-in mechanisms for ongoing review and revision. The best model or program will only work if it is created and modified using the experience and knowledge of the organization. Where an organization has not fully developed its capacity to be a learning organization, DyADS can become a catalyst or force for change toward becoming a learning organization. . . .

H. Respect for Collective Bargaining Agreement. DyADS must not be allowed to undermine any aspect of an existing collective bargaining agreement or any other workplace rights created by the Constitution or statute. When workplace rights are institutionalized, cooperative working relations are enhanced, and from this platform, effective dispute resolution systems can be created. Nothing in this or any other program should be about substituting conflict resolution procedures for well formulated and protected workplace rights frameworks. Instead, the entire construction and implementation of a DyADS is carried out with respect and appreciation for the importance of the collective bargaining relationship.

The whole intention of DyADS is to enhance the ability of employees and management to work out, in a constructive manner, the issues that arise. A fundamental underlying assumption is that this must be done with full respect for collective bargaining agreements and all other frameworks that allocate rights in the workplace. The strength of these frameworks, which have evolved over so many years, is exactly what makes an effective DyADS possible. Without these frameworks, any attempt to create a dispute resolution system could very easily become a mechanism for undercutting efforts to create a strong rights-based framework governing workplace relations. Therefore, the structure of DyADS and the means by which it is created, implemented, evaluated, modified, and monitored must be consistent with collective bargaining agreements and must be supportive of those agreements. Hopefully, an effective DyADS can even strengthen these agreements by encouraging a constructive overall working relationship among all participants in an organization. An effective DyADS system should provide a way to quickly address a concern that the DyADS is inappropriately impacting workplace rights or collective bargaining agreements. Ultimately, DyADS will require the full support of both labor and management to be effective in changing how workplace disputes are handled. . . .

4. WILLIAM L. BEDMAN, ADR: THE HALLIBURTON EXPERIENCE, available at Mediate.com (2002)

As Halliburton's in-house labor counsel for the last 24 years, I have had the benefit of experiencing many changes in the workplace and in employment law. Halliburton is an energy services company which serves primarily the petrochemical industry on a global basis. In addition to the most comprehensive array of oilfield services, its operations include engineering, project management, construction, and logistical services for diverse customers ranging from the British Royal Navy to the meat packing industry. Accordingly, our employees and their employment relationships with the Company are the organization's most important assets.

Beginning in 1992, it became clear to me that there was something inherently wrong with the litigation process as it was applied to employment cases. Like most major companies, Halliburton won most of the employment cases filed against it or settled the claims for modest amounts. The amounts we spent on outside lawyers exceeded several times what we paid out in settlements. However, the money Halliburton spent for the privilege of winning most of its cases had little tangible impact on the Company or its employees. Most of the cases were litigated years after the events giving rise to the cases occurred. By that time, the terminated employee was usually working somewhere else, many of the managers and co-employees were gone and there was little institutional value in the events that transpired in the litigation.

What brought about the real need for change in the process was a sexual harassment and tort claim trial which took place in 1992. The facts arose from the Brown & Root business group of Halliburton (now Kellogg-Brown & Root). The case had been around as an EEOC charge or lawsuit for almost five years by the time it reached trial. The Company obtained favorable verdicts for the sexual harassment and state tort claims. However, the case cost almost $450,000 in legal fees, and permanently altered the careers of several employees and former employees including the plaintiff. Apparently, she believed she would be hitting the lottery right up until the time the jury came back and gave her nothing. The financial and human cost associated with that kind of litigation was so high that we began a concerted effort to examine alternatives to the litigation system for resolving employment matters.

At that time, we did have some prior ADR experience; in 1990 we had implemented a binding arbitration program for some of our ERISA benefit plans which was also tied to a more formalized appeals process. One thing that was observed after we adopted this arbitration program, was that the incidence of litigation dropped close to zero. More matters were actually being brought to and resolved in the internal administrative process than previously, largely because the employees were now aware that there was a more formal structure in place for their complaints.

Building on this experience, in the summer of 1992, a series of task forces were established to study and evaluate existing systems within one Brown & Root group for handling employment problems. These task forces were given the responsibility of reviewing options and concepts which ranged from no change to radical change. The task forces included senior operations management, representatives of the Legal and Employee Relations Departments, outside legal experts, outside consultants in conflict management design, and experts in employee relations communications. As part of the development process, about three hundred Halliburton employees from all levels of the Company were interviewed individually and in focus groups to determine their opinions and impressions of the existing company attitude on conflict in the workplace. Additionally, their reaction to different design concepts were catalogued.

The final approval of the Program occurred in 1993. The program is a comprehensive employment dispute resolution program for all employees in the United States from the Brown & Root chief executive officer to the entry level employee. The key features of the Dispute Resolution Program (DRP) are:

- The DRP was designed with input from employees at all levels, from field employees to senior management.

- The DRP is a four-option program: it provides multiple processes, both inside and outside the company, for resolving disputes.

- In keeping with employee input and expert opinion, the DRP encourages collaborative approaches to dispute resolution by offering multiple channels for direct talk, or negotiation, and for both informal and formal mediation.

- The DRP promotes the resolution of disputes at the lowest possible level through in-house options. This is in keeping with the views of those we surveyed. Most disputes are resolved within a month through in-house options.

- The DRP provides some options that offer very high standards of confidentiality, and prohibits retaliation for use of the system.

- As an employee benefit designed to ensure fairness, the DRP offers to each employee access to legal counsel of the employee's choosing.

- To ensure its independence, the DRP reports to a Dispute Resolution Policy Committee composed of senior executives, rather than to a department or a single individual.

- The DRP routinely collects and analyzes data in order to evaluate utilization, cost benefit and employee satisfaction.

THE LITIGATION-BASED SYSTEM FOR EMPLOYMENT DISPUTE RESOLUTION

In the process of developing the Dispute Resolution Program, we spent some time trying to understand how the present system evolved and what are the main factors causing its inefficiency and negative effects when it is applied to employment matters. The present heavy dependence on the judicial system to resolve employment disputes is probably the result of convergence of a number of factors. These factors include the civil rights movement and the expansion of tort law. Before World War One, the principal use of the legal system in employment matters seems to have been the trial of personal injury actions related to the workplace. Then, as now, a consensus developed that the costs, delays and inefficiencies of the judicial system made it unsuitable for employment matters. With the widespread adoption of workers' compensation systems in the early decades of this century, this practice died out.

The period between the two World Wars, particularly the New Deal period, was characterized by active distaste for the judicial system in employment matters. The Norris-LaGuardia Act of 1932 went perhaps as far as constitutionally permissible in withdrawing federal court jurisdiction over "labor disputes". The National Labor Relations Act of 1935 created an administrative body, the National Labor Relations Board, to resolve the most significant labor issues of the time. Even the Fair Labor Standards Act of 1938, which does provide for private enforcement through the court system, delegated significant enforcement powers to the Department of Labor.

Finally, growing labor organizations increasingly pressed for private, nonjudicial dispute resolution as an alternative to contract litigation. Labor organizations had split over support for the Federal Arbitration Act of 1925. However, by the 1950s, organized labor heavily promoted nonjudicial remedies. This effort culminated in the Supreme Court's "Steelworkers Trilogy" of 1960, in which the Court ceded widespread authority to labor arbitrators. *Steelworkers v. American Mfg. Co.*, 363 U.S. 564 (1960), *Steelworkers v. Warrior & Gulf Navigation Co.*, 363 U.S. 574 (1960), and *Steelworkers v. Enterprise Wheel & Car Corp.*, 363 U.S. 593 (1960).

On the other hand, beginning in the 1940s, the civil rights movement pioneered the use of the federal courts to overcome discriminatory practices. This effort was increasingly successful during the 1950s and early 1960s. Thus, when the Civil Rights Act of 1964 was adopted, it seemed natural to turn to the federal courts for enforcement of these individual employment rights. This use of the courts was enormously productive. . . .

Because of the success of the 1964 Act, with its emphasis on individually litigated employment rights, subsequent labor legislation adopted the same model. That is, federal labor policy began to be implemented in terms of individual rights against "discrimination", designed to be enforced primarily by individual plaintiffs in federal court. Examples include the Age Discrimination in Employment Act and the Americans With Disabilities Act. Not surprisingly, state employment legislation since the 1970s has followed the federal model.

It is widely believed that the designers of the 1964 Civil Rights Act feared that the legislation would be undone by hostile local juries. Accordingly, litigation under the Act was designed to be tried without a jury. This feature limited the damages recoverable to traditional equitable remedies. In the meantime, however, tort law and tort damages were expanding rapidly in state courts. These cases were tried to state court juries which, by the 1980s, could no longer be perceived as being hostile to discrimination claims. Thus, employees increasingly began to bring cases under state law, using tort concepts to avoid federal limits. The Civil Rights Act of 1991 reflected the shift to this paradigm of employment dispute resolution, expanding the remedial options to include tort-like damages and introducing trial by jury.

DISADVANTAGES OF THE CURRENT EMPHASIS ON LITIGATION

What the preceding discussion demonstrates is that the present reliance on tort-like litigation to resolve individual employment disputes is not a matter of logical necessity. Rather, it is the result of legal and historical forces which developed outside the employment context. However, American employees, lawyers and managers have become so used to this mechanism that we seldom appreciate that this is a fundamental design characteristic, one that separates American practice from most other national systems of employment regulation.

Most of the world manages employment by direct government regulation of management, direct political involvement of trade unions as political parties, and specialized, quasi-political labor tribunals. In this model, resolution of employment disputes is part of the political and legislative process. By contrast, the American model requires individuals to vindicate broad, rights-based policies through litigation, usually in independent courts of general jurisdiction. American labor regulation is thus made part of the judicial process and, more specifically, the tort law aspect of that process.

Recent statutes, such as the Americans with Disabilities Act and the Family and Medical Leave Act operate in a similar fashion. Not only does such legislation suit our history and national character; it is undeniably inexpensive for the government to impose. Rather than creating expensive bureaucratic controls paid for in tax dollars, the system places the cost of regulation on employers and employees. Further, these costs are imposed by a court system with little political accountability to the legislature. This system does, however, have the virtue of allowing thorough investigation and individualized determinations.

The problem is that the labor litigation system and federal agencies set up to assist in the investigation and adjudication of labor matters are becoming unmanageably slow, expensive and cumbersome. The Equal Employment Opportunity Commission (EEOC) now has the highest backlog it has had in many years. The creation of new rights and the passage of federal legislation has done nothing to ease this burden. A simple employment dispute, involving no more than $5,000 in lost wages and benefits, can easily cost several times this much to resolve — no matter who prevails. Furthermore, administrative investigation and litigation may take years to complete. By the time of trial, the perceptions of the parties and witnesses have been irreversibly colored and polarized by years of conflict. Relatively cost-free remedies, such as reinstatement, have often become impossible. Emotional and economic damages which did not exist at the time of the dispute have accumulated, compounded, and assumed an importance far out of proportion to the nature of the dispute.

To a significant degree, these economic and emotional costs are products of the system itself. An employee who has recently been terminated may be shocked and depressed. These conditions are directly related to the termination. However, these difficulties are normally neither devastating nor permanent. But, a former employee who has spent several years in the litigation system is in an altogether different position. This individual has spent years building mistrust and suspicion, locked in conflict and absorbing the financial and emotional impacts of litigation. Quite often, because of the long-term alienation from former co-workers, he or she has lost an important part of the network of acquaintances that support any career. Further, he or she may become strongly focused on past wrongs, at the expense of present and future career. Naturally, the larger the potential damage award, the more this is likely to occur. Inevitably, earning capacity and employment skills suffer.

Such economic losses are not a natural result of the wrong suffered. They are a natural result of a litigation-based dispute resolution system. What converts this from a highly arbitrary tax on employers to an economic tragedy is that employees do not obtain substantial recoveries with any great frequency. Reliable statistics are not readily available, but practical experience shows that, in the great majority of cases, the employees lose or must settle for far less than what they think they are entitled to receive. Actual large recoveries are quite rare. This is not a defect in law or procedure. It simply reflects a fact of life: the judicial system does not provide ordinary employees who must work for a living any real hope of obtaining significant economic relief in any time period that is realistic from the employee's standpoint. In short, litigation, as a system of employment dispute resolution, is highly inefficient, both economically and morally. It wastes time, money and careers. This is true even if, as assumed here, the end result is always correct. To the extent that the results through litigation are wrong, the social loss can only be greater.

These observations do not prove that contractually resolved disputes are better decided, or even that contractual dispute resolution is more efficient. However, this discussion should dispel any illusion that private litigation has any automatic claim to historical, legal, moral or economic merit.

Before turning to existing alternatives in detail, including Halliburton's experience, the following two sections discuss the state of the law with regard to the enforceability of arbitration agreements in the employment context and the policy framework for other types of dispute resolution.

POLICY IMPLICATIONS OF NONLITIGATION ADR PROCEDURES

The Federal Arbitration Act ("FAA") has carved out a relatively litigation-free zone around arbitration that has, particularly in recent years, allowed arbitration to develop and flourish. The "halo effect" of the FAA has also tended to protect other forms of dispute resolution, which are probably not "arbitration" under the FAA. This trend has been hastened by recent, strong state legislative and judicial initiatives toward alternative dispute resolution of litigated matters. The United States Supreme Court has also weighed in on the desirability of arbitration agreements in the employment context, most recently in *Circuit City Stores, Inc. v. Adams*, 121 S. Ct. 1302 (2001). In Circuit City, the Supreme Court noted that arbitration of employment disputes reduces litigation costs for both parties, which is particularly beneficial because of the smaller damages at issue in employment litigation. The post-Circuit City commentary confirms that the case likely has encouraged many of the nation's employers to consider implementing arbitration programs.

The trend toward arbitration has also been reinforced by experience with the EEOC and analogous state agencies, whose principal function has been to attempt to "conciliate" (mediate) employment disputes. Indeed, this is one of the ironies of the resistance to employer-initiated dispute resolution procedures. If the case is litigated, one of the first steps the court or agency is likely to take is to pressure the parties to undertake an alternative means of resolution. This procedure, typically mediation, is likely to be less well adapted to the particular employment environment than the system the employer would have adopted if left to its own devices.

This versatility is one of the principal advantages of a private dispute resolution mechanism. The particular method adopted can be adapted to fit each individual corporate structure. Indeed, Halliburton's DRP looks unlike other systems, although many of them share common features. In addition to avoiding the one-size fits all approach typical of litigation (and perhaps required by Due Process), private mechanisms avoid most of the other inherent problems with the litigation system. Even the most complex private dispute resolution systems are usually substantially faster than litigation, and are almost always cheaper, at least for the employee. Because the principal social costs of litigation derive from its delay and expense, private systems offer a greater advantage.

Litigation is, or at least is assumed to be, extremely good at finding the truth. However, important as this function may be to resolving disputes, it is also a weakness. Litigation's single-minded search for complete disclosure and legal correctness short-changes other, equally valid goals of a dispute resolution system. One of these objectives is reconciliation, which is best achieved by early mediation where each party retains some level of credibility with the other. Another is the opportunity to "tell one's story" to an outside decision-maker. Many social scientists believe that this is an important act of catharsis, even if the teller loses. In litigation, the opportunity comes only years later and is hemmed in by elaborate and expensive trial procedures. The litigation process is also largely inscrutable to the average citizen. Americans have always felt that even a confessed criminal is entitled to understand what is happening to him and why he is being punished. Yet, litigated employment matters are governed by procedural and substantive rules which are rarely understood by the parties, other than the most sophisticated employers and litigants. Arbitration cannot completely avoid substantive complexity, but it can radically simplify the procedural rules of the road.

Despite these advantages, arbitration and other dispute resolution mechanisms are sometimes criticized for denying employees important substantive rights. We believe these criticisms to be unfounded as applied to a properly designed and managed dispute resolution system which preserves the substantive employment rights of the employees, while providing increased procedural benefits through expedited resolution and cost efficiency. This allows the parties to reach closure on the matter while the events are fresh and the employee can still pursue his career. By a properly designed and managed system, we mean one that includes such features as the key characteristics of our system listed above. It is critical to note that under a system with such characteristics, few disputes reach adjudicatory mechanisms such as arbitration or the courts; the vast majority are resolved by the mutual agreement of the parties, achieved through collaborative processes.

Ultimately, the greatest beneficiary of a private employment dispute resolution system, if it is allowed to flourish, may be the court system itself. Many federal courts are today awash in paper generated by relatively small cases. The Southern Districts of New York, Florida, Texas and California are cases in point. The greatest contributors to the problem are federal drug cases and prisoner habeas petitions. However, federal employment cases probably run a close third. The courts have responded to this crisis by restricting and formalizing discovery, pressuring settlements, placing arbitrary limits on trial time, and developing ever more rigid and complex procedures designed to increase paper flow and decrease the time judges (but not lawyers) spend on each case.

In short, the court system, with regard to employment cases, is being stifled by overload. Its primary virtue, careful and deliberate reconstruction of the past, is becoming a casualty of the pressing need for judicial efficiency. Yet, unlike private dispute resolution, the sacrifice is not offset by any substantial progress toward other legitimate objectives of the litigants, for example, reconciliation, catharsis, closure or comprehension. Certainly there are more settlements of litigated cases than in times past. But these settlements are not driven by reconciliation. They are, as often as not, driven by the litigants' dawning realization that one's day in court may be too long in coming, too short to tell the story, too expensive to afford, and too hard to understand.

HALLIBURTON'S EXPERIENCE UNDER ITS FOUR-OPTION SYSTEM

The Halliburton DRP provides the employee four options for the resolution of a dispute. These options may be employed, or bypassed for another option, at the employee's discretion. The options are:

A. *The Company's Open Door Policy.* Under this option, the employee may speak to his or her immediate supervisor or to a higher level manager in the chain of command.

B. *A Conference.* Under this option, the employee meets with a company representative from the DRP office to talk about their dispute and to choose a method for resolving it. One method available is an internal, informal mediation. . . .

C. *Formal Mediation*. This option involves the use of a neutral third party, usually an AAA mediator.

D. *Formal Arbitration*. This option involves the use of the AAA's arbitration program.

One of the most utilized and cost-effective parts of the Halliburton's DRP is the Ombudsman Program. The program is generally structured to provide a confidential outlet for current and former employees who have employment-related problems, primarily through informal mediation. The actual task the ombudsmen perform varies greatly from one case to the other. They may act as mediators, as fact-finders, or both, or may practice collaborative techniques — all in an effort to obtain resolution at the earliest phase of the dispute. In some cases they may give advice to the employee as to what avenues may be opened within the organization to assist them. They never serve as an advocate for the employee [or the company].

Along with the Ombudsman Program, the DRP places a heavy emphasis on mediation. In the first four years, the resolution rate of mediated disputes exceeded 75%. Resolutions reached in the mediations ranged from a simple apology to reinstatement and substantial monetary damages. The mediators' common link is confidentiality, consistent with the expectations of the parties. Furthermore, the resolutions come very rapidly when compared to either litigated determinations, or even mediated resolutions after matters go to litigation. The timely resolution of the disputed matter is one of the most powerful attributes of the advisor and mediation functions of the Halliburton Dispute Resolution Program.

In its first seven years, over 4,000 employees utilized some aspect of the DRP Program. Of these 4,000 matters, over 75% were resolved within 8 weeks of the employee's initial contact. The vast majority were resolved within the Company. The overwhelming majority of these cases were resolved through collaborative, in-house processes such as informal or formal mediation. About 400 have gone to mediation, both internal and external, and about 100 have gone to final outside arbitration. While the Company has not prevailed in all the arbitrations, its win/loss record is similar to its previous experience in the litigation forum with similar cases.

Even with an employee benefit plan which compensates employees for their legal expenses, fewer than 400 employees have requested the assistance of counsel over the first five years. In many of the arbitrations which have occurred, the employees have elected to proceed without the use of legal counsel. . . . It is clear that the annual expense for this type of Program is substantially less than what a large, litigated employment case can cost both the company and the employee in legal expenses, while doing a much better job of delivering justice in the workplace to the average employee.

CONCLUSION

The Halliburton Program . . . remains somewhat unique because of its comprehensive scope in applying to virtually all employment disputes (except workers' compensation and unemployment claims), and binding all employees from senior executives to entry level employees. We have also developed several training programs for supervisors which provide them with conflict management skills to try to handle employment problems at the lowest possible level. We believe that the equitable and uniform nature of our Program, together with reinforcement of its conflict management purpose through comprehensive and consistent management training are keys to the long term success and viability of any dispute resolution program. Additionally, the DRP Program was developed largely by employees of the company with appropriate external help, but the principle focus was to integrate a new system into the existing processes while maintaining organizational cultural values and norms. By most measurement parameters, the Program has succeeded in both bringing quicker resolution to problems and substantially reducing the Company's transaction expenses and legal fees while preserving employment relationships. These must be basic and fundamental goals of any dispute resolution program.

E. SYSTEMS DESIGN IN CONTEXT: THREE CASE STUDIES

1. Comments and Questions

a. General principles for the design of a dispute resolution system are far easier to state in the abstract, than to apply in particular circumstances. Accordingly, we offer three examples of system design from ADR subject areas examined earlier: government (procurement disputes and the Coast Guard), and the delivery of health care services. In each instance, ask yourself what "cultural" factors affect the design of a workable dispute resolution system that will satisfy the interests and needs of the participants?

b. What progress has the Coast Guard made in its quest to design and implement a dispute resolution system? What problems have arisen? Has the Coast Guard proceeded with its own system, or has the Department of Homeland Security moved to a department-wide approach? An Internet search should quickly yield relevant information about these questions.

c. How will the availability of technology-mediated dispute resolution impact the design of systems for addressing and avoiding disputes, particularly in the context of health services disputes? Reconsider the materials presented in Chapter Fourteen.

2. Daniel I. Gordon, *Constructing a Bid Protest Process: The Choices that Every Procurement Challenge System Must Make*, 35 PUB. CONT. L.J. 427 (2006)

[M]any public procurement systems . . . have established systems for allowing vendors to challenge the conduct of procurement processes. . . . This article discusses the goals of these bid protest systems, and then presents key choices that must be made in crafting such a system. The goal of this article is not to describe an ideal bid protest system, but rather to present the decisions that need to be made when constructing a bid protest system.

What distinguishes a protest from other complaints about the procurement process is who is complaining and when in the procurement process the complaint arises: a protest is a complaint by a would-be contractor regarding the formation stage of the procurement process. A protest may relate to the conduct of the procurement prior to the selection of a winner — in which case it typically alleges that the ground rules of the procurement are unfair to the complainant — or it may relate to the selection of the winner. A typical "pre-award" protest might argue that some aspect of a solicitation will unfairly disadvantage the protesting company in the competition for a contract — for example, the solicitation for laser printers sets a minimum number of pages per minute that the complaining vendor's printers cannot meet. A typical award challenge alleges that the Government's nonselection of the protesting vendor was improper: either the ground rules for the competition were allegedly not followed or the Government otherwise acted improperly or unreasonably. Technically, of course, those protests are almost always "post-award," in the sense that they are filed after the contract is awarded. Those award challenges are properly viewed as protests — indeed, protests of awards are more common than protests challenging the ground rules of a procurement.

Complaints that arise after contract award are not protests. However, where the complainant is the vendor that won the contract and the complaint concerns some aspect of performance of the contract: . . . that disagreement is a performance dispute, not a protest. A protest is always between the Government and a vendor that wants, but does not have, a contract (a "disappointed bidder").

It is worth highlighting the differences between a protest system and the other methods for policing a procurement system: audits, investigations, and criminal prosecutions. Because the key feature of protests is that they are raised by disappointed bidders, those bidders serve as "private attorneys general," in that they "direct" the Government to investigate certain procurements (and certain aspects of those procurements) through their protests. The contrast with the alternatives is stark: where a system relies on audits, or inspectors general, or criminal prosecution, government officials are the ones deciding which procurements to review, and what aspects of those procurements. While it may seem wasteful to let private sector vendors decide where the Government should spend its investigative resources, that approach has advantages. There are so many procurements, large and small, and each procurement has so many aspects, that deciding which aspects of which procurements to review may be a major task, with a significant risk of spending resources on unnecessary investigations. Of course, there remains a role for nonprotest investigations, . . . since even nonprotested procurements may be tainted — indeed, where collusion is widespread, no bidder may have an interest in protesting. Yet where vendors are willing to protest, letting them decide which procurements to investigate may reassure potential bidders, the press, the business community, and the public that the Government is really committed to hearing, and to fairly considering, complaints, and to policing the integrity of the system.

II. COMPETING GOALS OF EVERY PROCUREMENT SYSTEM

Any protest system serves multiple purposes, and there is inevitably conflict among them. These competing goals, like the competing objectives or "desiderata" of a procurement system overall, lead to trade-offs, since one or more goals can be met only at the expense of others. In a protest system, the overarching tension can be viewed as the tension between the desire to exhaustively investigate any complaint, on the one hand, and the need to let the procurement process move forward, on the other. This tension can be viewed as tension between support for the right to protest and opposition to that right, although the opposition may be couched as concern about limiting the disruption caused by the protest process.

The support for allowing disappointed bidders to protest comes from multiple sources, serving multiple — and not necessarily consistent — goals. From the point of view of the disappointed bidders, a protest system provides a forum for them to air their complaints and to obtain relief. Supporters of this goal will focus on what the disappointed bidders may view as "due process" rights: do they have the opportunity to see the procurement file? Do they have the right to a hearing? Do they have a realistic chance of obtaining meaningful relief?

From the point of view of those focused on good government, a protest system serves to enhance the accountability of procurement officials and government agencies. . . . Supporters of this goal may focus on the number of protests filed, and the thoroughness of the investigative aspects of the protest system, and the issue of whether government funds have been wisely spent through the challenged procurement decisions may be a key one. Publishing protest decisions, while it may be of little interest to the individual protesters, is important to those concerned about good government, including the press.

Closely related to the promotion of good government is the goal of protecting the integrity of the procurement system. Those focused on this goal also may be trying to increase competition by encouraging companies to sell to the Government. They want to reduce the barrier to entry that the perception of corruption and a lack of integrity and transparency creates. The presence of a robust protest system can serve as a deterrent to improper conduct. Those who value that aspect of a protest system will underscore the need for transparency in the process, so that contracting personnel and the private sector can have confidence in the robustness of the system. Rules that limit access to the protest system (such as timeliness and standing rules) will often be viewed as detrimental and overly rigid. Those seeking to further this goal will tend to focus on the fight against corruption, so that bid rigging, misrepresentation, and other impropriety on the part of bidders may be just as significant a concern as the actions of government officials.

All of these goals tend to lead to a more lengthy and costly protest process. . . . Weighing against these goals is the competing goal of having the procurement system efficiently and promptly complete its core role, the acquisition of goods or services that the Government needs. Those focusing on this goal will be concerned about avoiding unnecessary costs to the Government and limiting the delay and disruption of procurements during the protest process. They will argue for narrowing standing and setting strict time limits for filing protests and for deciding them. They will argue that frivolous protesters should have to pay fines and the Government's cost of defending against the protest, and that the filing of a protest should not force the Government to suspend the procurement while the protest is resolved. There will always be tension between the first cluster of goals and the goal of avoiding undue disruption to the procurement system. . . .

III. CHALLENGES THAT EVERY PROTEST SYSTEM FACES

There are certain challenges that every protest system faces, whether at the national or local level, and it is important to keep these in mind in crafting the system. A cluster of important challenges pertains to the cooperation that will (or will not) be forthcoming from the contracting agencies when their procurement actions are criticized in protests. In particular, the contracting agencies may not be willing to explain their procurement actions, or they may not want to turn over relevant documents (not even to the protest forum, and certainly not to the protester). . . . Further, there is the question of the protest forum's authority to direct compliance with its decisions.

A completely different cluster of challenges revolves around the conduct of potential and actual protesters. One that often captures the attention of government officials is the concern that companies will abuse the protest system to file frivolous protests, either simply out of malice or for tactical reasons. The risk of abuse can be cited as a reason to charge high filing fees, to punish vendors that file frivolous protests, or to compel unsuccessful protesters to reimburse the Government for the cost of defending against the protests. The reverse concern also arises, and in many contexts it may be more significant: that is, the possibility that dissatisfied bidders will not protest out of concern that they would be wasting their time and money by protesting, because the protest will not be fairly considered or, even if it is found to be justified, the protester will not be awarded the contract. . . . Disappointed bidders also are deterred from protesting by fear that the contracting agency will retaliate against protesting vendors in competitions for future contracts.

IV. KEY DECISIONS REGARDING A PROTEST FORUM

Eight key questions regarding a protest forum can be set out, the answers to which will shape the protest system. . . . There is no right or wrong response to any of these decision points, and there are often advantages and disadvantages to alternative responses. Of particular interest may be the impact of a system's decision regarding one issue on possible decisions in other areas. Some of these decisions can be made by the protest forum itself; others, by their nature, will be made at a higher level of the Government.

A. *Where in the Government Is the Protest Forum Located?* A protest forum cannot itself decide where it will be located in the Government; instead, that decision will be made for it by others. Broadly, it can be said that there are three places in the governmental structure that a protest forum can be located: in the contracting agency itself; in an independent administrative entity, and in a court.

Having the contracting agency whose procurement is being protested [serve as the first place where a protest is filed] . . . has the advantage of efficiency: because the information about the procurement resides within the contracting agency; and, the agency can decide the protest faster and at lower expense than either an independent body or a court. The disadvantage of protests going to the contracting agency is the appearance (and perhaps the reality) of a lack of independence and impartiality, a significant problem for a function that is essentially quasi-judicial. Protesting vendors may fear that the contracting agency will not be willing to admit that the procurement was not handled properly.

Two refinements are used in some systems to address the latter concerns. First, protests can be directed to some person or group within the contracting agency outside (and possibly above) the office that handled the procurement. A second variant, which addresses the bureaucratic sensitivity of the contracting agency, is to require that protests first be filed with that agency, but to allow vendors that are dissatisfied with the result of that review to then pursue their protest at either an independent administrative forum or a court. . . .

Setting up an independent administrative entity to resolve protests appears to be the current trend. Turkey, Norway, and Tanzania are among the countries that have recently established such entities. Quasi-judicial administrative entities have the great advantage of an appearance of independence, which can be reassuring to vendors thinking of filing protests. If the administrative entity is "dedicated" to procurement, in the sense that it has no responsibilities other than for procurement matters, it may bring expertise to protest resolution that allows it to be efficient and respected. Administrative entities, however, add to the cost of government (and of the procurement system) if they are created solely to hear protests.

A court . . . [has] the advantage . . . of being a forum that is both independent and able to enforce its decisions. Court procedures, however, can be slow and expensive. Also, a court of general jurisdiction may have little expertise in procurement matters, which may impair or slow up its resolution of protests, in addition to burdening a docket already full of civil and/or criminal cases.

If the system contains more than one forum for hearing protests, rules need to be established regarding multiple protests. An "exhaustion" requirement would require a bidder to first protest to the agency before a protest to the independent forum or court would be permitted. In crafting these rules, the system will make a series of trade-offs: allowing sequential protests increases accountability and "due process," but also increases the cost and time spent resolving the challenge. Also, if multiple, sequential protests are permitted, the system will need rules on whether interim relief continues throughout what may be a lengthy protest process.

B. How Broad Is the Forum's Jurisdiction? The scope of the forum's jurisdiction can be measured in two different dimensions. Viewed vertically, protest jurisdiction may cover all, or fewer than all, of the levels of Government. Viewed horizontally, the jurisdiction may reach all, or fewer than all, agencies on one level of Government, and all, or fewer than all, the procurements of the agencies that are within the forum's reach.

There are reasons that weigh in favor of restricting the forum's jurisdiction. First, as to "vertical" jurisdiction, it may be impractical in some systems to bring all procurement at multiple levels of Government within one body's jurisdiction. For example, the different levels of Government may have different procurement law systems (as the individual states do in the United States), so that it would be hard for one protest forum to serve multiple levels of Government. In terms of "horizontal" jurisdiction, certain agencies may be so different from the others, or so resistant to outside influence, that putting their procurements within the jurisdiction of an "external" agency may not be feasible. Quasi-public entities may be examples of the former; the ministry of defense, at least in some countries, would be an example of the latter. Limiting the forum's jurisdiction to formation disputes (that is, protests), and leaving performance disputes to another forum, may represent a sensible division of labor with concomitant development of specialized knowledge. Also, for practical or policy reasons (usually attributed to a desire to increase efficiency), a system may decide to prohibit protests for small purchases, or for procurements where competition is limited to multiple contractors holding framework agreements or what in the United States are called task or delivery orders under multiple-award indefinite-delivery, indefinite-quantity (ID/IQ) contracts.

Nonetheless, there are several advantages in having a forum with jurisdiction that reaches both "deep" and "wide." The forum can develop both expertise and a reputation for expertise, so that it is more likely to be respected if it is the government-wide forum for resolving procurement disputes (this would support including performance disputes within the forum's jurisdiction). Moreover, having the forum hear protests of all public procurements may facilitate uniformity in the system's procurement, and ensure that the transparency that a protest system can bring reaches all of the system's procurements. Giving one forum broad jurisdiction creates uniformity of process for vendors wishing to protest, and that uniformity itself facilitates the process. . . .

C. Who Has Standing to Protest? Standing is a key question, because it determines who has the right to call on the forum for investigation and relief. Separate from the question of standing to initiate a protest, protest systems need to decide whether any competitor other than the protesting vendor should be allowed to take part in the protest proceedings — for example, by submitting written arguments to the protest forum. The most important of those other competitors is the "awardee," the vendor that actually won the competition and received the contract (if a winner has been selected). That vendor has an obvious interest in defending the Government's decision to award it a contract, and, if concerns of due process can justify allowing vendors to protest and have their complaints heard, similar concerns weigh in favor of letting the awardee defend its interests. There is even logic in requiring the awardee to take part in the protest, since as to some issues, at least, it may be the party with the most information. Nonetheless, allowing (or requiring) the awardee to "intervene" . . . risks making the protest process more adversarial and potentially more complicated and lengthy.

D. What Are the Time Limits at the Forum? Promptness is a virtue in life, but in the world of bid protests, rules requiring promptness constrict different parties, and their impact on the system overall varies as well. The two key time limits are the window for filing protests and the time that the forum has to resolve them. A third, less important issue relates to the amount of time that the contracting agency has to explain its challenged actions. . . .

E. What Evidence Does the Forum Have Before It in Reaching Its Decisions? When a forum receives a protest, it must gather enough evidence to decide whether the protester's complaint is well founded and, if so, what steps should be taken. [C]reating adequate mechanisms for the forum to obtain evidence can be critical to capacity building within the forum. If the forum lacks the ability to gather evidence so that it can learn what happened in the challenged procurement, it cannot provide meaningful review.

The key source of evidence in virtually every protest will be the contracting agency. Since its procurement action is being criticized by the protester, and the forum is acting in an oversight capacity, the contracting agency may be disinclined to furnish documents or to let its employees provide information orally, which would make it well nigh impossible for the forum to fulfill its mission. The question thus becomes: who will persuade or compel the contracting agency to give documents or individuals' oral statements to the reviewing forum? If the forum is a court with the power to compel the contracting agency to furnish documents and oral statements, the problem may be easy to solve. If the forum lacks that kind of power over the contracting agency, the challenge may be insurmountable. . . .

F. Is the Procurement Put "On Hold" During the Protest? One of the most important decisions that needs to be made with regard to any protest system is the availability of what is often called interim relief. This refers to the procurement being put "on hold," or suspended, while the protest is pending before the forum. Deciding whether interim relief is ever available is typically not a decision the forum itself makes. Instead, that decision is usually made above the level of the forum, whether in statute, regulation, or directive.

If the decision is to never make interim relief available — that is, procurements will go forward regardless of protests pending before the forum — protests may cause minimal disruption to the procurement system. There is, however, a real risk that, by the time the forum resolves the protest, it will be too late to provide any relief at all to the protester, even if the forum concludes that the protester is correct in its claim that the procurement was improperly conducted: either the procurement will be complete (if it involves a simple acquisition of supplies, for example) or it may be so far along that reversing course would be prohibitively expensive (if construction of a building is at issue, for example). In that context, the system will be faced with a choice between offering the successful protester no relief; offering only monetary relief, such as bid preparation costs or lost profits; and causing substantial disruption to the procurement (either re-opening the competition or shifting the contract to the protester). All three options are problematic and risk causing a high level of dissatisfaction on the part of the protester (under the first option), or the contracting agency (under the third option), or both (potentially the case under the second option).

An alternative course is to make interim relief on a case-by-case basis. Under that approach, the protester will presumably need to persuade the forum that the procurement should be suspended while the protest is pending. In court systems, the protester will be seeking to obtain some version of a temporary restraining order or preliminary injunction. A key factor in the decision about granting interim relief may be the forum's judgment about whether the protester is likely to ultimately prevail in the protest. Because public procurements are at issue, another criterion may be the urgency of the Government's need for the goods or services being procured, and the availability (or absence) of alternative ways for the Government to procure them.

A third approach is to make interim relief automatic. This approach avoids the need for litigation of whether to grant interim relief on a case-by-case basis, but that comes at the cost of disruption in every procurement that is protested. This approach is probably too burdensome for any procurement system, unless there is a way for the contracting agency to end the suspension and move forward with the procurement — typically through a process of having a high-level official confirm that this is necessary. The automatic granting of interim relief invites abuse by a protester that knows that it will be asked to provide the needed goods or services, if a suspension is put in place. This situation is most likely to occur where the vendor that has been providing services loses the competition for the follow-on contract, and hopes to be asked to continue providing the services during consideration of the protest, if the contracting agency is barred by interim relief from having the winner of the new contract begin performance.

There are connections, both in logic and in practice, between the availability of interim relief and the length of time that the forum takes to resolve the protest. Where a forum decides protests very quickly (for example, in under fifteen calendar days), the granting of automatic interim relief may be viewed as not imposing too heavy a burden on the procurement system; where the forum takes much longer, automatic interim relief . . . may be viewed as intolerably disruptive to the procurement system. In such a system, balancing elements will probably be needed to limit this disruption.

G. How Difficult Is It for a Protester to Win? Protesters may not have strong views on where within the Government the protest forum should be located and how the protest process should be structured, but they will certainly care about two final questions: how difficult is it for a protester to win and does winning a protest bring any meaningful relief to the protester? . . . Legal formulations regarding the level of deference shown may be less meaningful than a review of statistics. If a forum were to sustain 80 percent of protests, it would suggest a very low degree of deference to agencies. Conversely, if a forum were to only rarely ever sustain a protest, it would suggest a very high level of deference. . . .

H. What Power Does the Forum Have to Provide Meaningful Relief, if It Finds That the Protest Is Justified? While the preceding section addresses the ability of the protesting vendor to win the protest, even more important for most protesting companies is whether the forum will provide meaningful relief, when it does rule in favor of the protester. Otherwise, a decision stating that the protester was correct in contending that the agency had acted unlawfully is of little value to the protester. In some legal systems, the forum may have authority to issue binding orders to the contracting agencies; in others, the forum may be able to do no more than recommend action — in which case the question of the forum's political environment may be critical in terms of whether the recommendations are usually followed.

In terms of the nature of the relief ordered or recommended, the protester's preference would presumably be to receive the contested contract; less desirable might be receipt of the lost profits that were anticipated; and less desirable still, although presumably of some value, would be another opportunity to compete for the contract. In many legal systems, once the contract has been entered into, it is too late for a reviewing forum to order its recompetition; in those systems, the availability of meaningful relief therefore may turn on whether the protest was filed before the contract was entered into and whether interim relief prevented that from occurring after the protest was filed. A separate issue is associated with the considerable money that the protester may have spent litigating the protest . . . so that a protester who succeeds in proving to the forum that the contracting agency acted improperly will want to know if the forum can direct the . . . Government to reimburse the protester's costs incurred in litigating. . . .

3. Ronald J. Bald & Evette E. Ungar, *An Alternative Dispute Resolution Systems Design for the United States Coast Guard*, 3 J. AM. ARB. 111 (2004)

On March 1, 2003, the United States Coast Guard (USCG) officially became an agency of the Department of Homeland Security (DHS), thus adding another chapter to a long history of service to the citizens of the United States of America. The move to DHS required the agency to sever many of its ties to the Department of Transportation (DOT) which served as the USCG's cabinet secretary for over thirty-five years. Among the many relationships that ended between the USCG and DOT was the Coast Guard's membership on the DOT Dispute Resolution Council, and the agency's ability to use established DOT procedures and standards for alternative dispute resolution (ADR). As the USCG has several stand-alone ADR programs that it operates with other agencies but does not have a complete ADR system design, the agency has an excellent opportunity to utilize its "new" position in the federal government to develop, establish, and implement such a system design.

In order to determine the ADR processes that best fit the USCG, it is essential to understand the daily missions and deliverables of the agency. A short discussion of the organization's history may assist in understanding the performance and strategic goals set forth by Coast Guard leadership. In October 1789, Secretary of the Treasury Alexander Hamilton gathered information from the collectors of customs that showed the need for boats to protect and ensure revenue collection. Congress authorized Hamilton to create a maritime service to enforce customs laws. This service was placed under the control of the Treasury Department. The country had no armed federal vessels at this point because the Continental Navy had been disestablished after the Revolution and would not be in existence again until 1799. In 1797, Congress authorized the President to increase the strength of the several Revenue Cutters to defend the sea coast to repel any hostility. Over the next forty years, the Revenue Cutter Service obtained other missions including the preservation of life by rescuing the shipwrecked, promoting safe transportation by supporting lighthouse establishment, conducting inspections and investigations regarding federal steamboat vessel safety standards, licensing and documenting persons and vessels used in marine transportation, and ensuring the security of the nation's ports. In the latter half of the 19th century, the agency was given responsibility for search and rescue at sea. The service received its present name as the United States Coast Guard in 1915 when the Life-Saving Service merged with the Revenue Cutter Service. The USCG began maintaining the country's vast amount of aids to maritime navigation including the operation of lighthouses with the merger of the Lighthouse Service in 1939. Seven years later, the U.S. Congress permanently transferred the Bureau of Marine Inspection and Navigation to the Coast Guard giving the service responsibility for merchant marine licensing and merchant vessel safety.

Today, the USCG is a multi-mission, military, maritime service committed to protecting America. The agency has over 40,000 active duty personnel, 9,000 reservists, 6,000 civilian employees, and 32,000 auxiliarists that provide services over 3.4 million square miles of United States Exclusive Economic Zones. Those services are defined in ten Coast Guard mission areas consisting of: Search and Rescue; Marine Safety; Marine Environmental Protection; Fisheries and Marine Sanctuaries; Enforcement of Laws and Treaties (primarily for drugs and migrants); Enforcement of Laws and Treaties for foreign fishing vessels; Ports, Waterways, and Coastal Security; Defense Readiness; Aids to Navigation; and Ice Operations. Each of these mission areas presents opportunities for conflicts and disputes to occur between the USCG and its internal and external customers. These customers include the Coast Guard's military and civilian employees and anyone who uses, seeks to use, or has an interest in the nation's waterways up to 200 miles off the United States coast. All told, that could essentially be anyone in the world. . . .

V. USING ADR IN CONJUNCTION WITH U.S. COAST GUARD MISSIONS

A. The Federal ADR Program Manager's Resource Manual. The unequivocal bible for ADR system design in the federal workforce is the Federal ADR Program Manager's Resource Manual. As ADR programs were introduced into the federal workplace due to the Administrative Dispute Resolution Act (ADRA) and amendments to EEOC Regulation 1614, there was an essential need for consistency and guidance in ADR systems. The resource manual was developed by ADR specialists from a number of federal agencies and organizations to serve as a general guide as each federal organization operates under its own rules and unique structure. The editors of the manual have specifically stated that there is no one way to design an ADR program that would be suitable for all situations, but that the most effective programs are those that integrate into existing operations causing minimal alteration of the current processes.

The Federal ADR Program Manager's Resource Manual recommends a four step process in designing an ADR system. These broad steps, which encompass multiple sub-parts are a needs assessment, the development of the system design, implementation of the plan, and timely evaluation of the program's effectiveness and its administration.

B. Coast Guard Offices and Organizational Leadership. Every one of the USCG missions can create disputes between the agency and some external or internal customer. The Coast Guard is divided into directorates that oversee various mission areas. Among these directorates are operations, marine safety, workforce personnel, and legal. Within the USCG, multiple persons will be involved in the design, approval, and implementation of an ADR program. The head of the agency is the Commandant of the Coast Guard whose office is designated as (G-C). The Commandant is a four-star Admiral who is nominated by the Secretary of Homeland Security, approved by the President of the United States, and confirmed by the United States Senate. Any agency-wide program or initiative will require the approval and consent of the Commandant. This will normally be accomplished through the office of the Commandant's Chief of Staff (G-CCS). This three-star Vice Admiral is responsible for internal agency policies and procedures and reports and answers directly to the Commandant. Without question, these individuals and their staffs will be among the most important to obtain buy-in from and commitment for the agency's ADR program. The marketing campaign will need to focus a great deal of attention in these offices.

The ADR program, as a legal tool, will be overseen by the Chief Counsel of the Coast Guard (G-L). This rear admiral is responsible for the legal services provided by nearly two hundred attorneys and ninety-five paralegal, administrative, and clerical personnel located at Coast Guard Headquarters offices in Washington, D.C., as well as over thirty field offices throughout the country. G-L is also responsible for Coast Guard law specialists that serve on the staffs of several joint armed forces commands and in other governmental agencies such as the Departments of Transportation, Justice, Defense, and State. A senior executive service civilian employee attorney who serves as the Deputy Chief Counsel supports the Chief Counsel. Any funding or personnel distributions from the legal program will require the approval or authorization of these individuals. Therefore, they are also key figures for the marketing and training programs and must be directly accounted for in the needs assessment, design, and feedback portions of the program.

The USCG has a very broad area of legal practice covering ten specific major areas of law. Each of these areas has at least some potential for using ADR. As one of the five armed forces, the military members of the USCG are subject to the Uniform Code of Military Justice (UCMJ). In the support of Military Criminal Law, USCG law specialists serve a variety of functions including defense counsel and prosecutors for military courts-martial. In the appellate realm of Military Law, these attorneys often brief and argue cases before the Coast Guard Court of Criminal Appeals and the Court of Appeals for the Armed Forces. On rare occasions, the service could find itself before the Supreme

Court of the United States. This program falls under the Office of Military Justice (G-LMJ).

The USCG is also vested with powers for domestic law enforcement. Every day, the agency is involved in enforcing federal laws regarding the interdiction of illegal drugs and illegal immigrants, marine safety and environmental protection, fisheries, and all other general federal laws applicable at sea. Within this area of Operations Law, the USCG attorneys are involved with the development of agency policy and provide real-time advice to the operational commanders on scene. This part of the USCG legal services is gaining increasing awareness, importance, and visibility with the shift to DHS and additional defense related missions.

With an actual budget of $5.6 billion in FY 2002 and a requested budget of $6.7 billion for FY 2004, the agency must pay special attention to all matters of contracting and procurement. The Office of Procurement Law (G-LPL) provides legal advice to management, technical, and contracting officials at every level of the agency. This occurs at an entire range of contract related functions from small purchases to the acquisition of major capital assets and runs from the planning stages through contract administration and subsequent litigation. The USCG is actively involved in a wide variety of criminal and civil litigation ranging from claims made under the Federal Torts Claim Act (FTCA) and other federal statutes. This will also include attempting to collect monies for costs incurred in the damage to USCG property such as vessels and aids to navigation. This extensive Civil Advocacy, Claims, and Litigation practice is directed by the Office of Claims and Litigation.

C. Historical Use, Attempts, and Procedures of ADR by the USCG. [The Coast Guard has used ADR in three areas:] 1. Equal Employment Opportunity/Equal Opportunity; 2. Procurement Matters; and 3. Environmental Matters. [Discussion omitted.]

4. General Feedback Regarding U.S. Coast Guard Use of ADR. The main barrier the USCG faces regarding using ADR is the lack of awareness of the various ADR processes and the applicability and practicality of the programs. In 2000, informal ADR was attempted in a situation involving the sinking of a dredge booster barge, where damages amounted to $54,000 and were raised in an affirmative OPA claim. Mediation was utilized and, unfortunately, found to have no effect on the outcome. . . . Overall, there appears to be a general apathy towards ADR in the USCG coupled with an organizational paradigm that "ADR presumes a 'D' — there has to be a dispute."

Each year the DOT Dispute Resolution Council requests information from member agencies regarding their use of ADR. The USCG had each legal office provide answers to the four-page survey for FY 2002 that consisted of twenty-seven questions. Several offices simply provided a negative response offering that they had not employed any ADR during the year. Of the offices that did provide information, the results were varied. The Office of the Administrative Law Judge (ALJ) reported that out of 865 civil enforcement cases in FY 2002, 600 were settled using an ALJ-assisted settlement procedure and that the sheer volume of settlements and consent orders resulting from ALJ assisted settlements is indicative of the success of the program. The response from the Office of Claims and Litigation provided little useful information, however, and did not provide an answer for many of the questions, demonstrated a lack of knowledge in the number of instances ADR was used, that no funds were provided or associated with ADR, and that the office had no success stories or lessons learned. One of the most interesting answers, though, was that no response was given to the question of "How does your top management encourage ADR?" This shows the need for more buy-in from USCG leadership and a large need for marketing. The agency's statement that there must be a dispute fails to take into account and recognize certain procedures that it undertakes. Results of the solicitation ombudsman program are not tracked in a manner that allows resolution by telephone to be counted as an ADR success. Instead, the efforts go unnoticed where they could be used as a strong measure of effectiveness.

The "dispute requirement" is also inconsistent with internal and DOT beliefs. The Coast Guard has touted its partnering agreement with Integrated Coast Guard Systems on the Deepwater contracting project as a huge achievement in ADR. The partnering arrangement itself, however, is proactive and was not created in response to a specific dispute. Even further, the protocol for the parties' calls for multiple attempts at resolution without a third-party neutral in an effort to prevent disagreements from spiraling into full blown adversarial disputes was ineffective. According to the DOT's ADR Specialist, in order for ADR to be used, "there has to be an issue in controversy" and not necessarily a dispute. DOT looks at the use of ADR as a very broad area, not a narrow one. An expansion of the USCG's view on ADR would serve to shift its paradigm and promote the use of ADR across all program areas.

VI. RECOMMENDED SYSTEM DESIGN FOR THE U.S. COAST GUARD

A. *The Need for A Formal System Design.* The necessity of a formal system design for the USCG is obvious. . . . The 1996 ADRA proclaims that each agency shall adopt a policy that addresses the use of alternative means of dispute resolution and case management. Additionally, in developing such a policy, each agency shall examine alternative means of resolving disputes in connection with formal and informal adjudications, rulemakings, enforcement actions, issuing and revoking licenses or permits, contract administration, litigation brought by or against the agency, and other agency actions. This congressional mandate has been endorsed and encouraged by the executive branch in a 1998 presidential memorandum. According to that document, each federal agency must take steps to promote greater use of mediation, arbitration, early neutral evaluation, agency ombuds, and other alternative dispute resolution techniques, and promote greater use of negotiated rulemaking.

B. *Lessons Learned.* The DOT Dispute Resolution Counsel created a survey, as a follow-up to the Department of Justice inquiry into the use of ADR in federal agencies. The Dispute Resolution Counsel asked that respondents only cover ADR activities performed by the various Federal agencies during FY 2000 or 2001. At the time of this evaluation the Coast Guard declared that they "use ADR in procurement, workplace, civil enforcement, environmental and ad hoc dispute matters." The USCG indicated in the procurement realm they use outcome prediction and independent neutrals in the informal Ombudsman program, and in the formal Ombudsman program the USCG uses expert neutral evaluation. In procurement disputes, all ADR services are collateral duty for employees of the Coast Guard. In FY 2000 the USCG reportedly resolved eight procurement cases using ADR processes and, in FY 2001, the Coast Guard reported twelve procurement cases as being resolved using ADR.

In connection with workplace issues, USCG's National Vessel Documentation Center (NVDC) is using interest-based bargaining (IBB) to negotiate its collective bargaining agreement. The IBB process is being assisted by the use of FAA facilitators. In connection with workplace ADR uses, one contract negotiation session has occurred using IBB at NVDC, as of the calendar year 2001. The Office of Personnel claims to continue monitoring the impact IBB has on the contract and outcome. The Coast Guard's NVDC does not indicate in their report an understanding of what IBB is, nor do they provide proof that IBB has occurred at all.

In the area of civil enforcement the DOT Evaluation disclosed that there is no funding set aside for ADR programs. Any neutral resources that are provided are generally free of charge. If and when ADR is deemed appropriate in this field it is managed via collateral duty. There are no full time employees designated to oversee ADR programs and procedures. No records were kept for FY 2000 and, in FY 2001, the Civil Enforcement Program allegedly used ADR in two instances but was unable to document what process was used to resolve the dispute or even identify the subject matter of the dispute.

In all the areas of ADR use in the Coast Guard over one fiscal year the total reported uses of ADR processes in resolving disputes total less than twenty. The extremely small number of reported uses of ADR in one fiscal year are indicative that USCG employees are: (1) not diligently reporting ADR uses; (2) unclear as to what ADR is and what constitutes use of an ADR process; or (3) unaware that ADR is an option to resolve disputes thus explaining why so few uses of ADR were reported. The above statistics also support the contention that the Coast Guard has a very narrow view of what ADR is and when it should be applied.

The Coast Guard has taken at least one very positive step to utilizing ADR. The Integrated Deepwater System is clearly an exception to the Coast Guard's historically narrow view and approach to ADR. The partnering arrangement itself is proactive and was not created in response to a specific dispute. The Coast Guard should be commended for broadening its application and scope in the intricately designed Deep Water System. It should be noted, however, that the USCG is once again jumping into a system-wide design without doing a needs assessment or attempting to implement a pilot program before applying the program to the entire system.

The Pilot Mediation Program was founded when funding to implement a system-wide mediation program and marketing campaign along with ONE DOT Sharing Neutrals Program was pulled. The system-wide project was terminated and the District Eight Pilot Mediation Program was born. This program was not conceived after a thorough needs assessment; it was jumped into head first. This is not to say that the pilot program was a bad idea, in fact it was a very positive move for the USCG. However, any future programs will greatly benefit from doing a needs assessment and determining the best way to sell the need for the ADR system to key stakeholders and develop an in-depth marketing and training plan before beginning.

The USCG was scheduled to review the results of the pilot program in September 2001. No results were visibly posted on any USCG website or other medium. Thus, is safe to assume that the Coast Guard is still reviewing the District Eight Mediation Program results. The review included examining all aspects of establishing an ADR Program as well as identifying a Most Efficient Organization (MEO). The DOT Program Evaluation recommended that the USCG compare its mediation pilot program to the ONE DOT Sharing Neutrals Program and conduct a needs assessment before implementing a service-wide plan for workplace disputes. . . .

C. *Looking at the U.S. Coast Guard as a Corporation.* The Coast Guard under DHS needs to develop an Integrated Conflict Management System (ICMS). This is especially true in the USCG's management and handling of personnel and interactions between USCG personnel, as well as disputes that arise between USCG employees and external sources. An ICMS can only be created when organizations go beyond ad hoc, case-by-case dispute resolution and turn their focus to systematically integrating all of these approaches into their day-to-day business, plus add processes that turn their conflict culture towards prevention. The difference between a case-by-case approach and a system can be found in the focus of each method. A case-by-case approach to a conflict is a reactive means of addressing a dispute. A system contains processes and techniques to resolve disputes that occur, but also focuses on the prevention of conflicts and a management plan for conflicts if one does occur. Thus, an ICMS lays the foundation for addressing the cause of the conflict, rather than just the dispute.

The first step the Coast Guard needs to take to enable them to create an effective and efficient ICMS, which integrates ADR processes within it, is perform a needs assessment throughout the Coast Guard. The USCG has a very limited history of documented uses of ADR throughout its agency. The documentation the USCG does have regarding use of ADR in various areas indicates that Coast Guard personnel do not understand what practices are defined as ADR. Additionally, Coast Guard personnel do not understand what the agency considers to be using ADR while performing various forms of dispute resolution. The first contention, that Coast Guard employees do not understand what is considered ADR, was verified in a footnote of the DOT Program Evaluation when reporting the number of times Ombudsmen was used during the calendar year of 2001. The footnote stated that the figure in the procurement section "does not capture all the actions handled by the Ombudsman because of the informality of the Ombudsman program: much of the Ombudsman's work was handled via telephone and through other informal means that did not warrant the filing of paperwork."

D. *Further Use of ADR by the U.S. Coast Guard under the Department of Homeland Security.* The USCG is starting a new relationship with her brand new parent department at an extremely challenging time. DHS is still in its infancy and the USCG has only been a member of the department since March 1, 2003. During this short period, the department has been involved with the preparations for, commencement of, and results from the conclusion of the second war with Iraq. As DHS continues to be busy evaluating terror threats, organizing all the components of an executive department, determining funding levels and such, there has not been a priority assigned to establishing a department wide ADR program. Additionally, the Coast Guard has ceased being a member of the DOT Dispute Resolution Council and it would be extremely unusual for an agency which is not a member of the department to attend and participate in those meetings. Therefore, the USCG should expect a period of time where there is little, if any, departmental oversight of their ADR program. Accordingly, this provides an excellent opportunity to improve and expand its use of different ADR methods and processes without having to ask permission from or justify the use to the department.

The first step in analyzing the USCG's use of ADR to establish a system design is to recognize that the design should incorporate current practices and not seek to disturb them unless it is necessary. The current ADR processes in place should be allowed to continue.

E. *Moving Forward from the Present State.* Once the Coast Guard performs a needs assessment and is ready to embark on a system-wide ADR design, the next step the USCG should undertake is to look to already successfully implemented ADR programs within the federal government. This will enable the Coast Guard to copy an existing program if one exists to meet its needs and avoid reinventing the wheel. One federal program that the USCG may want to consider is the Federal Motor Carrier Safety Administration's (FMCSA) use of "night baseball" binding arbitration. Under FMCSA's plan, binding arbitration only would be used after a commercial carrier has acknowledged that a civil penalty is appropriate and the only issue left for resolution is the amount of the penalty and the time frame given to satisfy the award. This program has the flexibility needed by the ever-evolving Coast Guard built into its structure. The FMCSA's plan provides criteria for selecting an arbitrator, but leaves the actual selection of an arbitrator to the discretion of the parties. The outcome of "night baseball" arbitration is binding to the parties involved and is considered a final decision.

Additionally, the Coast Guard may want to consider using mini-trials in the environmental arena. For environmental issues, cognizant programs have also noted that USCG often has a small role in environmental litigation and therefore it should not be up to them to decide whether ADR should be attempted. Mini-trials, however, may be the solution in that the process brings all interested parties leadership together to address the problem. The U.S. Air Force has successfully used mini-trials and should be looked to as a resource for the Coast Guard if the decision is made to utilize mini-trials in its ADR plan.

While the Military Justice System cuts beyond the USCG, and affects every other armed service, there is a tremendous potential for the use of third-party neutrals in this area. The non-judicial punishment system associated with Article 15 of the Manual for Courts Martial allows for commanding officers to administer non-judicial punishment that has wide-ranging effects including liberty restriction and monetary damage assessments. No requirements for compliance with evidence rules currently exist, however, and a finding of guilt necessary for the awarding of punishment is not necessary. Third-party neutrals could serve as a means to resolve disputes between commands and persons who commit minor infractions of the Uniform Code of Military Justice. Such a use may eliminate criticisms of this arcane and one-sided procedure. . . .

4. Debra Girardi, *The Culture of Health Care: How Professional and Organizational Cultures Impact Conflict Management*, 21 GA. ST. U. L. REV. 857, 884-90 (2005)

There is much opportunity for integrating the principles of dispute resolution into the delivery of health services. Given the environment's complexity and the impact of professional culture, the ADR community will need to consider how to modify itself to meet this unique industry's needs. A beginning point would be to reconsider the concept of ADR as currently packaged. Non-litigation alternatives include a mix of power-based and interest-based processes. Power-based processes may settle terms of a dispute but will not address the causes leading to the conflict or lead to stable behavior changes. In addition, the professional culture of those providing arbitration or heavily evaluative processes may be in direct conflict with the professional culture of those experiencing the conflict. Legal professionals have their own cultural assumptions and values that may not mesh with those of the health care sector.

Interest-based processes are more amenable to addressing culture issues than power-based processes, but for health care conflicts, as currently designed, they may be too time intensive or too far removed from where they can do the most good, such as in the clinical setting. Additionally, approaches that only address more superficial interests without taking into consideration cultural assumptions or interactions between organizational and professional cultures may be ineffective and could worsen conflicts or leave the participants even more frustrated. Finding effective ways for integrating the best of interest-based conflict resolution with additional techniques for uncovering cultural and identity needs may help move health care organizations toward more collaborative cultures and may improve the work environment for thousands of health professionals. The following subsections introduce some things to consider in redesigning conflict management services for health care organizations.

A. Time Considerations. The health care environment operates around the clock, allowing very little time for meeting together. Due to the over-commitment of health care workers, scheduling challenges are tremendous and take much attention and many resources. Techniques for working within professionals' time constraints are essential. Mediators who need to schedule frequent facilitated meetings, may need to schedule them for shorter periods of time, and may need to hold them very early in the morning, in the middle of the night, or on weekends. Additionally, those working in health care tend to focus on solutions immediately and frequently exhibit "process intolerance," creating a need for process structures that balance the time constraints with the assessment steps necessary before the group can consider any solutions.

B. Power Imbalances. Power imbalances intertwined within health care disputes depend on professional group membership, level of experience, gender, positional power, market power, union affiliation, and many other variables. Dispute resolution processes must recognize these imbalances and consider ways to foster open communication without jeopardizing individuals who may make themselves vulnerable to retaliation or scapegoating due to the shared information. Subtle methods of retaliation are common within health care culture and fear of this retaliation inhibits health care professionals from addressing conflicts themselves. Examples of these actions include: discontinuance of patient referrals, inappropriate assignments of patients, failure to provide backup for heavy workloads, and exclusion from committees and other political forums.

C. Language. Health care organizations, like any specialized industry, have their own language. Within the organizations, there are further language challenges in communicating with clinicians whose livelihood and professional affiliation rest on their knowledge of the special language of medicine. With the time constraints mentioned, it is difficult for those doing dispute resolution to become proficient in medical jargon, common practices, and technical nuances within the process itself. Stopping the process frequently for clarification on common medical terms may give health care professionals the impression of a lack of competence given the strong tie between competence and clinical expertise. For clinical conflict management, process modification may entail integration of clinical expertise into the dispute resolution team in order to improve comprehension and time management and in order to overcome initial credibility barriers set by participants in the process.

D. Interdependencies. With the complexity of health care organizations, it will be a rare conflict that does not involve multiple groups, departments, or facilities. Communication structures across these entities are not well-developed, and identifying effective ways to limit the scope of the conflict management intervention without omitting key stakeholders is a challenge.

E. Money. The focus on cost containment in health care is alive and strong. Often, organizational leaders will forego dispute resolution interventions in the early stages of a dispute, leading to more expensive interventions once the parties have formed stronger positions. Additionally, the risk of having only a limited amount of time with the participants due to budget constraints limits the effectiveness of any process and may require ethical decisions by consultants as to whether it is appropriate to begin an intervention at all or to take an intervention in a direction that may open old wounds and risk discontinuing before addressing the deeper issues. Additionally, different professional groups have different levels of access to funds; nursing groups and social workers have less money available than physicians for hiring consultants but may have a greater understanding of the benefits of a collaborative process. Adjusting reimbursement expectations to the realities of resource availability can improve access and increase the likelihood that more complete interventions may be available.

F. Autonomy. Interest-based processes such as mediation strongly promote the principle of participant autonomy. This is congruent with some health care professionals' desire for autonomy. Despite this congruence, many health care professionals look to leaders to make decisions as to who is right or wrong in conflict situations and may be uncomfortable with the personal responsibility built in to facilitative processes. Managing expectations as to mediation benefits and the decision-making process is essential when working with health care groups, and a facilitator may need to repeat these expectations throughout the process.

G. Reputation and Identity. Conflict management processes must respect the need for maintaining reputation within the organization while addressing dysfunctional behaviors that may be contributing to the conflict. Reputation correlates to status in health care and can be difficult to regain once damaged. Health care professionals have strong identity ties to their profession, and facilitators' suggestions to acknowledge the value of other professional groups' contributions may meet with strong resistance, suggesting identity conflicts wherein acceptance of the value of "other" appears to diminish the value of self. Techniques designed to address identity conflicts may be helpful in facilitating inter-professional disputes.

H. Patients. Behind most clinical conflicts lies a patient who has faced or faces potential harm. This is always in the minds of those working in health care and can be a strong basis for finding initial common ground. It can also heighten clinicians' fears that their license is at risk, that they will face lawsuits, or that they will cause harm when team functioning breaks down. The high levels of emotion that accompany these fears make health care disputes emotionally charged and make addressing these fears an inherent part of the process. Additionally, health care organizations are just beginning to incorporate patients into interest-based processes involving quality of care. Patients and families' lack of access to the process because of liability fears is a serious barrier to effective resolution of disputes involving this important group of stakeholders. National organizations are just now putting forward recommendations for liability system improvements to increase access to broader alternatives for resolving quality of care disputes.

I. Data. Health care professionals, particularly physicians, are very data-driven, and finding ways to collect data on best practices, improved outcomes, and cost savings associated with conflict management interventions will enhance dispute resolution professionals' ability to market services to health care clients. This data will also provide information to the dispute resolution industry as to what works well. Making use of pilot projects, data collection within mediation programs, and participant surveys can provide some initial foundation for developing the field and improving the receptiveness of health professionals.

J. Skills. Until very recently, communication and conflict resolution skills were not a part of clinicians and health care administrators' professional training. Organizations need to modify their training and professional curricula to address the barrier caused by the lack of ability to address conflicts directly. Recent mandates by the Accreditation Council for Graduate Medical Education, the Commission on Accreditation of Health Care Management Education, and the American Nurses Association indicate that these competencies will be compulsory for future students; however, given the strong reliance on modeling and mimicry common in health care training, it will be important to expand access to training to those who are already working and training others.

K. Expanding the Tool Box. Typically, ADR professionals limit the process tools they provide — arbitration, mediation, facilitation, and training. Expansion of services to include other process tools — such as appreciative inquiry, dialogue, world café (i.e., a network of small conversations in large group settings to facilitate discussion), transformational interviewing, and narrative inquiry — can enhance flexibility and provide access to methods for uncovering underlying assumptions that are motivating behaviors. Additionally, utilizing tools designed to assess culture — such as "cultural consensus analysis," "competing values framework," and "culture inventories" as part of conflict assessments — may provide better information for consultants and participants. Redefining and modifying the offered services to meet the needs of the health care industry can expand the usefulness of ADR and improve access to a much-needed service for those struggling within health care organizations. . . .

Appendix
STATUTES, MODEL LAWS, AND RULES

A. NCCUSL, UNIFORM MEDIATION ACT (Promulgated August, 2003)

PREFATORY NOTE

During the last thirty years the use of mediation has expanded beyond its century-long home in collective bargaining to become an integral and growing part of the processes of dispute resolution in the courts, public agencies, community dispute resolution programs, and the commercial and business communities, as well as among private parties engaged in conflict. Public policy strongly supports this development. Mediation fosters the early resolution of disputes. The mediator assists the parties in negotiating a settlement that is specifically tailored to their needs and interests. The parties' participation in the process and control over the result contributes to greater satisfaction on their part. Increased use of mediation also diminishes the unnecessary expenditure of personal and institutional resources for conflict resolution, and promotes a more civil society. For this reason, hundreds of state statutes establish mediation programs in a wide variety of contexts and encourage their use.

These laws play a limited but important role in encouraging the effective use of mediation and maintaining its integrity, as well as the appropriate relationship of mediation with the justice system. In particular, the law has the unique capacity to assure that the reasonable expectations of participants regarding the confidentiality of the mediation process are met, rather than frustrated. For this reason, a central thrust of the Act is to provide a privilege that assures confidentiality in legal proceedings (Sections 4-6). Because the privilege makes it more difficult to offer evidence to challenge the settlement agreement, the Drafters viewed the issue of confidentiality as tied to provisions that will help increase the likelihood that the mediation process will be fair. Fairness is enhanced if it will be conducted with integrity and the parties' knowing consent will be preserved. The Act protects integrity and knowing consent through provisions that provide exceptions to the privilege (Section 6), limit disclosures by the mediator to judges and others who may rule on the case (Section 7), require mediators to disclose conflicts of interest (Section 9), and assure that parties may bring a lawyer or other support person to the mediation session (Section 10). In some limited ways, the law can also encourage the use of mediation as part of the policy to promote the private resolution of disputes through informed self-determination (Section 2).

A uniform act that promotes predictability and simplicity may encourage greater use of mediation. At the same time, it is important to avoid laws that

diminish the creative and diverse use of mediation. The Act promotes the autonomy of the parties by leaving to them those matters that can be set by agreement and need not be set inflexibly by statute. In addition, some provisions in
the Act may be varied by party agreement, as specified in the comments to the
sections. This may be viewed as a core Act which can be amended with type specific provisions not in conflict with the Uniform Mediation Act.

The provisions in this Act reflect the intent of the Drafters to further these
public policies. The Drafters intend for the Act to be applied and construed in
a way to promote uniformity, as stated in Section 13, and also in such manner
as to:

1. promote candor of parties through confidentiality of the mediation
   process, subject only to the need for disclosure to accommodate specific and compelling societal interests;

2. encourage the policy of fostering prompt, economical, and amicable
   resolution of disputes in accordance with principles of integrity of
   the mediation process, active party involvement, and informed self-
   determination by the parties; and

3. advance the policy that the decision-making authority in the mediation process rests with the parties.

Although the Conference does not recommend "purpose" clauses, States that
permit these clauses may consider adapting these principles to serve that function.

UNIFORM MEDIATION ACT

SECTION 1. TITLE. This [Act] may be cited as the Uniform Mediation Act.

SECTION 2. DEFINITIONS. In this [Act]:

(1) "Mediation" means a process in which a mediator facilitates com-
    munication and negotiation between parties to assist them in reach-
    ing a voluntary agreement regarding their dispute.

(2) "Mediation communication" means a statement, whether oral or in
    a record or verbal or nonverbal, that occurs during a mediation or is
    made for purposes of considering, conducting, participating in, ini-
    tiating, continuing, or reconvening a mediation or retaining a medi-
    ator.

(3) "Mediator" means an individual who conducts a mediation.

(4) "Nonparty participant" means a person, other than a party or medi-
    ator, that participates in a mediation.

(5) "Mediation party" means a person that participates in a mediation
    and whose agreement is necessary to resolve the dispute.

(6) "Person" means an individual, corporation, business trust, estate,
    trust, partnership, limited liability company, association, joint ven-
    ture, government; governmental subdivision, agency, or instru-

mentality; public corporation, or any other legal or commercial entity.

(7) "Proceeding" means:

    (A) a judicial, administrative, arbitral, or other adjudicative process, including related pre-hearing and post-hearing motions, conferences, and discovery; or

    (B) a legislative hearing or similar process.

(8) "Record" means information that is inscribed on a tangible medium or that is stored in an electronic or other medium and is retrievable in perceivable form.

(9) "Sign" means:

    (A) to execute or adopt a tangible symbol with the present intent to authenticate a record; or

    (B) to attach or logically associate an electronic symbol, sound, or process to or with a record with the present intent to authenticate a record.

SECTION 3. SCOPE.

(a) Except as otherwise provided in subsection (b) or (c), this [Act] applies to a mediation in which:

    (1) the mediation parties are required to mediate by statute or court or administrative agency rule or referred to mediation by a court, administrative agency, or arbitrator;

    (2) the mediation parties and the mediator agree to mediate in a record that demonstrates an expectation that mediation communications will be privileged against disclosure; or

    (3) the mediation parties use as a mediator an individual who holds himself or herself out as a mediator or the mediation is provided by a person that holds itself out as providing mediation.

(b) The [Act] does not apply to a mediation:

    (1) relating to the establishment, negotiation, administration, or termination of a collective bargaining relationship;

    (2) relating to a dispute that is pending under or is part of the processes established by a collective bargaining agreement, except that the [Act] applies to a mediation arising out of a dispute that has been filed with an administrative agency or court;

    (3) conducted by a judge who might make a ruling on the case; or

    (4) conducted under the auspices of: a primary or secondary school if all the parties are students or a correctional institution for youths if all the parties are residents of that institution.

(c) If the parties agree in advance in a signed record, or a record of proceeding reflects agreement by the parties, that all or part of a mediation is not privileged, the privileges under Sections 4 through 6 do not apply to the mediation or part agreed upon. However, Sections 4 through 6 apply to a mediation communication made by a person that has not received actual notice of the agreement before the communication is made.

SECTION 4. PRIVILEGE AGAINST DISCLOSURE; ADMISSIBILITY; DISCOVERY.

(a) Except as otherwise provided in Section 6, a mediation communication is privileged as provided in subsection (b) and is not subject to discovery or admissible in evidence in a proceeding unless waived or precluded as provided by Section 5.

(b) In a proceeding, the following privileges apply:

   (1) A mediation party may refuse to disclose, and may prevent any other person from disclosing, a mediation communication.

   (2) A mediator may refuse to disclose a mediation communication, and may prevent any other person from disclosing a mediation communication of the mediator.

   (3) A nonparty participant may refuse to disclose, and may prevent any other person from disclosing, a mediation communication of the nonparty participant.

(c) Evidence or information that is otherwise admissible or subject to discovery does not become inadmissible or protected from discovery solely by reason of its disclosure or use in a mediation.

Legislative Note: The Act does not supersede existing state statutes that make mediators incompetent to testify, or that provide for costs and attorney fees to mediators who are wrongfully subpoenaed.

SECTION 5. WAIVER AND PRECLUSION OF PRIVILEGE.

(a) A privilege under Section 4 may be waived in a record or orally during a proceeding if it is expressly waived by all parties to the mediation and:

   (1) in the case of the privilege of a mediator, it is expressly waived by the mediator; and

   (2) in the case of the privilege of a nonparty participant, it is expressly waived by the nonparty participant.

(b) A person that discloses or makes a representation about a mediation communication which prejudices another person in a proceeding is precluded from asserting a privilege under Section 4, but only to the extent necessary for the person prejudiced to respond to the representation or disclosure.

(c) A person that intentionally uses a mediation to plan, attempt to commit or commit a crime, or to conceal an ongoing crime or ongoing criminal activity is precluded from asserting a privilege under Section 4.

SECTION 6. EXCEPTIONS TO PRIVILEGE.

(a) There is no privilege under Section 4 for a mediation communication that is:

    (1) in an agreement evidenced by a record signed by all parties to the agreement;

    (2) available to the public under [insert statutory reference to open records act] or made during a session of a mediation which is open, or is required by law to be open, to the public;

    (3) a threat or statement of a plan to inflict bodily injury or commit a crime of violence;

    (4) intentionally used to plan a crime, attempt to commit or commit a crime, or to conceal an ongoing crime or ongoing criminal activity;

    (5) sought or offered to prove or disprove a claim or complaint of professional misconduct or malpractice filed against a mediator;

    (6) except as otherwise provided in subsection (c), sought or offered to prove or disprove a claim or complaint of professional misconduct or malpractice filed against a mediation party, nonparty participant, or representative of a party based on conduct occurring during a mediation; or

    (7) sought or offered to prove or disprove abuse, neglect, abandonment, or exploitation in a proceeding in which a child or adult protective services agency is a party, unless the agency participates in the mediation.

(b) There is no privilege under Section 4 if a court, administrative agency, or arbitrator finds, after a hearing in camera, that the party seeking discovery or the proponent of the evidence has shown that the evidence is not otherwise available, that there is a need for the evidence that substantially outweighs the interest in protecting confidentiality, and that the mediation communication is sought or offered in:

    (1) a court proceeding involving a felony [or misdemeanor]; or

    (2) except as otherwise provided in subsection (c), a proceeding to prove a claim to rescind or reform or a defense to avoid liability on a contract arising out of the mediation.

(c) A mediator may not be compelled to provide evidence of a mediation communication referred to in subsection (a)(6) or (b)(2).

(d) If a mediation communication is not privileged under subsection (a) or (b), only the portion of the communication necessary for the application of the exception from nondisclosure may be admitted. Admission of evidence under subsection (a) or (b) does not render the evidence, or any other mediation communication, discoverable or admissible for any other purpose.

SECTION 7. PROHIBITED MEDIATOR REPORTS.

(a) Except as required in subsection (b), a mediator may not make a report, assessment, evaluation, recommendation, finding, or other communication regarding a mediation to a court, administrative agency, or other authority that may make a ruling on the dispute that is the subject of the mediation.

(b) A mediator may disclose:

    (1) whether the mediation occurred or has terminated, whether a settlement was reached, and attendance;

    (2) a mediation communication as permitted under Section 6; or

    (3) a mediation communication evidencing abuse, neglect, abandonment, or exploitation of an individual to a public agency responsible for protecting individuals against such mistreatment.

(c) A communication made in violation of subsection (a) may not be considered by a court, administrative agency, or arbitrator.

SECTION 8. CONFIDENTIALITY. Unless subject to the [insert statutory references to open meetings act and open records act], mediation communications are confidential to the extent agreed by the parties or provided by other law or rule of this State.

SECTION 9. MEDIATOR'S DISCLOSURE OF CONFLICTS OF INTEREST; BACKGROUND.

(a) Before accepting a mediation, an individual who is requested to serve as a mediator shall:

    (1) make an inquiry that is reasonable under the circumstances to determine whether there are any known facts that a reasonable individual would consider likely to affect the impartiality of the mediator, including a financial or personal interest in the outcome of the mediation and an existing or past relationship with a mediation party or foreseeable participant in the mediation; and

    (2) disclose any such known fact to the mediation parties as soon as is practical before accepting a mediation.

(b) If a mediator learns any fact described in subsection (a)(1) after accepting a mediation, the mediator shall disclose it as soon as is practicable.

(c) At the request of a mediation party, an individual who is requested to serve as a mediator shall disclose the mediator's qualifications to mediate a dispute.

(d) A person that violates subsection [(a) or (b)][(a), (b), or (g)] is precluded by the violation from asserting a privilege under Section 4.

(e) Subsections (a), (b), [and] (c), [and] [(g)] do not apply to an individual acting as a judge.

(f) This [Act] does not require that a mediator have a special qualification by background or profession.

[(g) A mediator must be impartial, unless after disclosure of the facts required in subsections (a) and (b) to be disclosed, the parties agree otherwise.]

SECTION 10. PARTICIPATION IN MEDIATION.

An attorney or other individual designated by a party may accompany the party to and participate in a mediation. A waiver of participation given before the mediation may be rescinded.

SECTION 11. INTERNATIONAL COMMERCIAL MEDIATION.

(a) In this section, "Model Law" means the Model Law on International Commercial Conciliation adopted by the United Nations Commission on International Trade Law on 28 June 2002 and recommended by the United Nations General Assembly in a resolution (A/RES/57/18) dated 19 November 2002, and "international commercial mediation" means an international commercial conciliation as defined in Article 1 of the Model Law.

(b) Except as otherwise provided in subsections (c) and (d), if a mediation is an international commercial mediation, the mediation is governed by the Model Law.

(c) Unless the parties agree in accordance with Section 3(c) of this [Act] that all or part of an international commercial mediation is not privileged, Sections 4, 5, and 6 and any applicable definitions in Section 2 of this [Act] also apply to the mediation and nothing in Article 10 of the Model Law derogates from Sections 4, 5, and 6.

(d) If the parties to an international commercial mediation agree under Article 1, subsection (7), of the Model Law that the Model Law does not apply, this [Act] applies.

SECTION 12. RELATION TO ELECTRONIC SIGNATURES IN GLOBAL AND NATIONAL COMMERCE ACT.

This [Act] modifies, limits, or supersedes the federal Electronic Signatures in Global and National Commerce Act [E-Sign], 15 U.S.C. Section 7001 et seq., but this [Act] does not modify, limit, or supersede Section 101(c) of that Act or authorize electronic delivery of any of the notices described in Section 103(b) of that Act.

[This Section adopts standard language approved by the Uniform Law Conference that is intended to conform Uniform Acts with the Uniform Electronic Transactions Act (UETA) and E-Sign. The effect of this provision is to reaffirm state authority over matters of contract by making clear that UETA is the controlling law if there is a conflict between this Act and the federal E-sign law, except for E-sign's consumer consent provisions (Section 101(c) and its notice provisions (Section 103(b) (which have no substantive impact on this Act).]

SECTION 13. UNIFORMITY OF APPLICATION AND CONSTRUCTION.

In applying and construing this [Act], consideration should be given to the need to promote uniformity of the law with respect to its subject matter among States that enact it.

SECTION 14. SEVERABILITY CLAUSE.

If any provision of this [Act] or its application to any person or circumstance is held invalid, the invalidity does not affect other provisions or applications of this [Act] which can be given effect without the invalid provision or application, and to this end the provisions of this [Act] are severable.

SECTION 15. EFFECTIVE DATE.

This [Act] takes effect ....

SECTION 16. REPEALS.

The following acts and parts of acts are hereby repealed:

SECTION 17. APPLICATION TO EXISTING AGREEMENTS OR REFERRALS.

(a) This [Act] governs a mediation pursuant to a referral or an agreement to mediate made on or after [the effective date of this [Act]].

(b) On or after [a delayed date], this [Act] governs an agreement to mediate whenever made.

B. AAA/ABA/ACR, THE MODEL STANDARDS OF CONDUCT FOR MEDIATORS (2005)

Preamble

Mediation is used to resolve a broad range of conflicts within a variety of settings. These Standards are designed to serve as fundamental ethical guidelines for persons mediating in all practice contexts. They serve three primary goals: to guide the conduct of mediators; to inform the mediating parties; and to promote public confidence in mediation as a process for resolving disputes.

Mediation is a process in which an impartial third party facilitates communication and negotiation and promotes voluntary decision making by the parties to the dispute. Mediation serves various purposes, including providing the opportunity for parties to define and clarify issues, understand different perspectives, identify interests, explore and assess possible solutions, and reach mutually satisfactory agreements, when desired.

Note on Construction: These Standards are to be read and construed in their entirety. There is no priority significance attached to the sequence in which the Standards appear. The use of the term "shall" in a Standard indicates that the mediator must follow the practice described. The use of the term "should" indicates that the practice described in the standard is highly desirable, but not required, and is to be departed from only for very strong reasons and requires careful use of judgment and discretion.

The use of the term "mediator" is understood to be inclusive so that it applies to co-mediator models. These Standards do not include specific temporal parameters when referencing a mediation, and therefore, do not define the exact beginning or ending of a mediation.

Various aspects of a mediation, including some matters covered by these Standards, may also be affected by applicable law, court rules, regulations, other applicable professional rules, mediation rules to which the parties have agreed and other agreements of the parties. These sources may create conflicts with, and may take precedence over, these Standards. However, a mediator should make every effort to comply with the spirit and intent of these Standards in resolving such conflicts. This effort should include honoring all remaining Standards not in conflict with these other sources.

These Standards, unless and until adopted by a court or other regulatory authority do not have the force of law. Nonetheless, the fact that these Standards have been adopted by the respective sponsoring entities, should alert mediators to the fact that the Standards might be viewed as establishing a standard of care for mediators.

STANDARD I. SELF-DETERMINATION

A. A mediator shall conduct a mediation based on the principle of party self-determination. Self-determination is the act of coming to a voluntary, unco-erced decision in which each party makes free and informed choices as to process and outcome. Parties may exercise self-determination at any stage of a mediation, including mediator selection, process design, participation in or withdrawal from the process, and outcomes.

  1. Although party self-determination for process design is a fundamental principle of mediation practice, a mediator may need to balance such party self-determination with a mediator's duty to conduct a quality process in accordance with these Standards.

  2. A mediator cannot personally ensure that each party has made free and informed choices to reach particular decisions, but, where appropriate, a mediator should make the parties aware of the importance of consulting other professionals to help them make informed choices.

B. A mediator shall not undermine party self-determination by any party for reasons such as higher settlement rates, egos, increased fees, or outside pressures from court personnel, program administrators, provider organizations, the media or others.

STANDARD II. IMPARTIALITY

A. A mediator shall decline a mediation if the mediator cannot conduct it in an impartial manner. Impartiality means freedom from favoritism, bias or prejudice.

B. A mediator shall conduct a mediation in an impartial manner and avoid conduct that gives the appearance of partiality.

  1. A mediator should not act with partiality or prejudice based on any participant's personal characteristics, background, values and beliefs, or performance at a mediation, or any other reason.

2. A mediator should neither give nor accept a gift, favor, loan or other item of value that raises a question as to the mediator's actual or perceived impartiality.

3. A mediator may accept or give de minimis gifts or incidental items or services that are provided to facilitate a mediation or respect cultural norms so long as such practices do not raise questions as to a mediator's actual or perceived impartiality.

C. If at any time a mediator is unable to conduct a mediation in an impartial manner, the mediator shall withdraw.

STANDARD III. CONFLICTS OF INTEREST

A. A mediator shall avoid a conflict of interest or the appearance of a conflict of interest during and after a mediation. A conflict of interest can arise from involvement by a mediator with the subject matter of the dispute or from any relationship between a mediator and any mediation participant, whether past or present, personal or professional, that reasonably raises a question of a mediator's impartiality.

B. A mediator shall make a reasonable inquiry to determine whether there are any facts that a reasonable individual would consider likely to create a potential or actual conflict of interest for a mediator. A mediator's actions necessary to accomplish a reasonable inquiry into potential conflicts of interest may vary based on practice context.

C. A mediator shall disclose, as soon as practicable, all actual and potential conflicts of interest that are reasonably known to the mediator and could reasonably be seen as raising a question about the mediator's impartiality. After disclosure, if all parties agree, the mediator may proceed with the mediation.

D. If a mediator learns any fact after accepting a mediation that raises a question with respect to that mediator's service creating a potential or actual conflict of interest, the mediator shall disclose it as quickly as practicable. After disclosure, if all parties agree, the mediator may proceed with the mediation.

E. If a mediator's conflict of interest might reasonably be viewed as undermining the integrity of the mediation, a mediator shall withdraw from or decline to proceed with the mediation regardless of the expressed desire or agreement of the parties to the contrary.

F. Subsequent to a mediation, a mediator shall not establish another relationship with any of the participants in any matter that would raise questions about the integrity of the mediation. When a mediator develops personal or professional relationships with parties, other individuals or organizations following a mediation in which they were involved, the mediator should consider factors such as time elapsed following the mediation, the nature of the relationships established, and services offered when determining whether the relationships might create a perceived or actual conflict of interest.

STANDARD IV. COMPETENCE

A. A mediator shall mediate only when the mediator has the necessary competence to satisfy the reasonable expectations of the parties.

1. Any person may be selected as a mediator, provided that the parties are satisfied with the mediator's competence and qualifications. Training, experience in mediation, skills, cultural understandings and other qualities are often necessary for mediator competence. A person who offers to serve as a mediator creates the expectation that the person is competent to mediate effectively.

2. A mediator should attend educational programs and related activities to maintain and enhance the mediator's knowledge and skills related to mediation.

3. A mediator should have available for the parties' information relevant to the mediator's training, education, experience and approach to conducting a mediation.

B. If a mediator, during the course of a mediation determines that the mediator cannot conduct the mediation competently, the mediator shall discuss that determination with the parties as soon as is practicable and take appropriate steps to address the situation, including, but not limited to, withdrawing or requesting appropriate assistance.

C. If a mediator's ability to conduct a mediation is impaired by drugs, alcohol, medication or otherwise, the mediator shall not conduct the mediation.

STANDARD V. CONFIDENTIALITY

A. A mediator shall maintain the confidentiality of all information obtained by the mediator in mediation, unless otherwise agreed to by the parties or required by applicable law.

1. If the parties to a mediation agree that the mediator may disclose information obtained during the mediation, the mediator may do so.

2. A mediator should not communicate to any non-participant information about how the parties acted in the mediation. A mediator may report, if required, whether parties appeared at a scheduled mediation and whether or not the parties reached a resolution.

3. If a mediator participates in teaching, research or evaluation of mediation, the mediator should protect the anonymity of the parties and abide by their reasonable expectations regarding confidentiality.

B. A mediator who meets with any persons in private session during a mediation shall not convey directly or indirectly to any other person, any information that was obtained during that private session without the consent of the disclosing person.

C. A mediator shall promote understanding among the parties of the extent to which the parties will maintain confidentiality of information they obtain in a mediation.

D. Depending on the circumstance of a mediation, the parties may have varying expectations regarding confidentiality that a mediator should address. The parties may make their own rules with respect to confidentiality, or the accepted practice of an individual mediator or institution may dictate a particular set of expectations.

STANDARD VI. QUALITY OF THE PROCESS

A. A mediator shall conduct a mediation in accordance with these Standards and in a manner that promotes diligence, timeliness, safety, presence of the appropriate participants, party participation, procedural fairness, party competency and mutual respect among all participants.

    1. A mediator should agree to mediate only when the mediator is prepared to commit the attention essential to an effective mediation.

    2. A mediator should only accept cases when the mediator can satisfy the reasonable expectation of the parties concerning the timing of a mediation.

    3. The presence or absence of persons at a mediation depends on the agreement of the parties and the mediator. The parties and mediator may agree that others may be excluded from particular sessions or from all sessions.

    4. A mediator should promote honesty and candor between and among all participants, and a mediator shall not knowingly misrepresent any material fact or circumstance in the course of a mediation.

    5. The role of a mediator differs substantially from other professional roles. Mixing the role of a mediator and the role of another profession is problematic and thus, a mediator should distinguish between the roles. A mediator may provide information that the mediator is qualified by training or experience to provide, only if the mediator can do so consistent with these Standards.

    6. A mediator shall not conduct a dispute resolution procedure other than mediation but label it mediation in an effort to gain the protection of rules, statutes, or other governing authorities pertaining to mediation.

    7. A mediator may recommend, when appropriate, that parties consider resolving their dispute through arbitration, counseling, neutral evaluation or other processes.

    8. A mediator shall not undertake an additional dispute resolution role in the same matter without the consent of the parties. Before providing such service, a mediator shall inform the parties of the implications of the change in process and obtain their consent to the change. A mediator who undertakes such role assumes different duties and responsibilities that may be governed by other standards.

    9. If a mediation is being used to further criminal conduct, a mediator should take appropriate steps including, if necessary, postponing, withdrawing from or terminating the mediation.

10. If a party appears to have difficulty comprehending the process, issues, or settlement options, or difficulty participating in a mediation, the mediator should explore the circumstances and potential accommodations, modifications or adjustments that would make possible the party's capacity to comprehend, participate and exercise self-determination.

B. If a mediator is made aware of domestic abuse or violence among the parties, the mediator shall take appropriate steps including, if necessary, postponing, withdrawing from or terminating the mediation.

C. If a mediator believes that participant conduct, including that of the mediator, jeopardizes conducting a mediation consistent with these Standards, a mediator shall take appropriate steps including, if necessary, postponing, withdrawing from or terminating the mediation.

STANDARD VII. ADVERTISING AND SOLICITATION

A. A mediator shall be truthful and not misleading when advertising, soliciting or otherwise communicating the mediator's qualifications, experience, services and fees.

1. A mediator should not include any promises as to outcome in communications, including business cards, stationery, or computer-based communications.

2. A mediator should only claim to meet the mediator qualifications of a governmental entity or private organization if that entity or organization has a recognized procedure for qualifying mediators and it grants such status to the mediator.

B. A mediator shall not solicit in a manner that gives an appearance of partiality for or against a party or otherwise undermines the integrity of the process.

C. A mediator shall not communicate to others, in promotional materials or through other forms of communication, the names of persons served without their permission.

STANDARD VIII. FEES AND OTHER CHARGES

A. A mediator shall provide each party or each party's representative true and complete information about mediation fees, expenses and any other actual or potential charges that may be incurred in connection with a mediation.

1. If a mediator charges fees, the mediator should develop them in light of all relevant factors, including the type and complexity of the matter, the qualifications of the mediator, the time required and the rates customary for such mediation services.

2. A mediator's fee arrangement should be in writing unless the parties request otherwise.

B. A mediator shall not charge fees in a manner that impairs a mediator's impartiality. While a mediator may accept unequal fee payments from the parties, a mediator should not use fee arrangements that adversely impact the mediator's ability to conduct a mediation in an impartial manner.

STANDARD IX. ADVANCEMENT OF MEDIATION PRACTICE

A. A mediator should act in a manner that advances the practice of mediation. A mediator promotes this Standard by engaging in some or all of the following:

1. Fostering diversity within the field of mediation.

2. Striving to make mediation accessible to those who elect to use it, including providing services at a reduced rate or on a pro bono basis as appropriate.

3. Participating in research when given the opportunity, including obtaining participant feedback when appropriate.

4. Participating in outreach and education efforts to assist the public in developing an improved understanding of, and appreciation for, mediation.

5. Assisting newer mediators through training, mentoring and networking.

B. A mediator should demonstrate respect for differing points of view within the field, seek to learn from other mediators and work together with other mediators to improve the profession and better serve people in conflict.

C. AAA, COMMERCIAL MEDIATION PROCEDURES (2005)

M-1. Agreement of Parties

Whenever, by stipulation or in their contract, the parties have provided for mediation or conciliation of existing or future disputes under the auspices of the American Arbitration Association (AAA) or under these procedures, they shall be deemed to have made these procedures, as amended and in effect as of the date of the submission of the dispute, a part of their agreement.

M-2. Initiation of Mediation

Any party or parties to a dispute may initiate mediation by filing with the AAA a submission to mediation or a written request for mediation pursuant to these procedures, together with the $325 nonrefundable case set-up fee. Where there is no submission to mediation or contract providing for mediation, a party may request the AAA to invite another party to join in a submission to mediation. Upon receipt of such a request, the AAA will contact the other parties involved in the dispute and attempt to obtain a submission to mediation.

M-3. Requests for Mediation

A request for mediation shall contain a brief statement of the nature of the dispute and the names, addresses, and telephone numbers of all parties to the dispute and those who will represent them, if any, in the mediation. The initiating party shall simultaneously file two copies of the request with the AAA and one copy with every other party to the dispute.

M-4. Appointment of the Mediator

Upon receipt of a request for mediation, the AAA will appoint a qualified mediator to serve. Normally, a single mediator will be appointed unless the parties agree otherwise or the AAA determines otherwise. If the agreement of the parties names a mediator or specifies a method of appointing a mediator, that designation or method shall be followed.

M-5. Qualifications of the Mediator

No person shall serve as a mediator in any dispute in which that person has any financial or personal interest in the result of the mediation, except by the written consent of all parties. Prior to accepting an appointment, the prospective mediator shall disclose any circumstance likely to create a presumption of bias or prevent a prompt meeting with the parties. Upon receipt of such information, the AAA shall either replace the mediator or immediately communicate the information to the parties for their comments. In the event that the parties disagree as to whether the mediator shall serve, the AAA will appoint another mediator. The AAA is authorized to appoint another mediator if the appointed mediator is unable to serve promptly.

M-6. Vacancies

If any mediator shall become unwilling or unable to serve, the AAA will appoint another mediator, unless the parties agree otherwise.

M-7. Representation

Any party may be represented by persons of the party's choice. The names and addresses of such persons shall be communicated in writing to all parties and to the AAA.

M-8. Date, Time, and Place of Mediation

The mediator shall fix the date and the time of each mediation session. The mediation shall be held at the appropriate regional office of the AAA, or at any other convenient location agreeable to the mediator and the parties, as the mediator shall determine.

M-9. Identification of Matters in Dispute

At least ten days prior to the first scheduled mediation session, each party shall provide the mediator with a brief memorandum setting forth its position with regard to the issues that need to be resolved. At the discretion of the mediator, such memoranda may be mutually exchanged by the parties.

At the first session, the parties will be expected to produce all information reasonably required for the mediator to understand the issues presented. The mediator may require any party to supplement such information.

M-10. Authority of the Mediator

The mediator does not have the authority to impose a settlement on the parties but will attempt to help them reach a satisfactory resolution of their dispute. The mediator is authorized to conduct joint and separate meetings with the parties and to make oral and written recommendations for settlement.

Whenever necessary, the mediator may also obtain expert advice concerning technical aspects of the dispute, provided that the parties agree and assume the expenses of obtaining such advice. Arrangements for obtaining such advice shall be made by the mediator or the parties, as the mediator shall determine.

The mediator is authorized to end the mediation whenever, in the judgment of the mediator, further efforts at mediation would not contribute to a resolution of the dispute between the parties.

M-11. Privacy

Mediation sessions are private. The parties and their representatives may attend mediation sessions. Other persons may attend only with the permission of the parties and . . . the mediator.

M-12. Confidentiality

Confidential information disclosed to a mediator by the parties or by witnesses in the course of the mediation shall not be divulged by the mediator. All records, reports, or other documents received by a mediator while serving in that capacity shall be confidential. The mediator shall not be compelled to divulge such records or to testify in regard to the mediation in any adversary proceeding or judicial forum. The parties shall maintain the confidentiality of the mediation and shall not rely on, or introduce as evidence in any arbitral, judicial, or other proceeding:

(a) views expressed or suggestions made by another party with respect to a possible settlement of the dispute;

(b) admissions made by another party in the course of the mediation proceedings;

(c) proposals made or views expressed by the mediator; or

(d) the fact that another party had or had not indicated willingness to accept a proposal for settlement made by the mediator.

M-13. No Stenographic Record

There shall be no stenographic record of the mediation process.

M-14. Termination of Mediation

The mediation shall be terminated: (a) by the execution of a settlement agreement by the parties; (b) by a written declaration of the mediator to the effect that further efforts at mediation are no longer worthwhile; or (c) by a written declaration of a party or parties to the effect that the mediation proceedings are terminated.

M-15. Exclusion of Liability

Neither the AAA nor any mediator is a necessary party in judicial proceedings relating to the mediation. Neither the AAA nor any mediator shall be liable to any party for any act or omission in connection with any mediation conducted under these procedures.

M-16. Interpretation and Application of Procedures

The mediator shall interpret and apply these procedures insofar as they relate to the mediator's duties and responsibilities. All other procedures shall be interpreted and applied by the AAA.

M-17. Expenses and Fees

The expenses of witnesses for either side shall be paid by the party producing such witnesses. All other expenses of the mediation, including required traveling and other expenses of the mediator and representatives of the AAA, . . . shall be borne equally by the parties unless they agree otherwise.

D. TEXAS CIVIL PRACTICE AND REMEDIES CODE, CH. 154

§ 154.001. Definitions

In this Chapter:

(1) "Court" includes an appellate court, district court, constitutional county court, statutory county court, family law court, probate court, municipal court, or justice of the peace court.

(2) "Dispute resolution organization" means a private profit or non-profit corporation, political subdivision, or public corporation, or a combination of these, that offers alternative dispute resolution services to the public.

§ 154.002. Policy

It is the policy of this state to encourage the peaceable resolution of disputes, with special consideration given to disputes involving the parent-child relationship, including the mediation of issues involving conservatorship, possession, and support of children, and the early settlement of pending litigation through voluntary settlement procedures.

§ 154.003. Responsibility of Courts and Court Administrators

It is the responsibility of all trial and appellate courts and their court administrators to carry out the policy under Section 154.002.

§ 154.021. Referral of Pending Disputes for Alternative Dispute Resolution Procedure

(a) A court may, on its own motion or the motion of a party, refer a pending dispute for resolution by an alternative dispute resolution procedure including:

(1) an alternative dispute resolution system established under Article 2372aa;

(2) a dispute resolution organization; or

(3) a nonjudicial and informally conducted forum for the voluntary set-tlement of citizens' disputes through the intervention of an impar-tial third party, including those alternative dispute resolution procedures described under this subchapter.

(b) The court shall confer with the parties in the determination of the most appropriate alternative dispute resolution procedure.

§ 154.022. Notification and Objection

(a) If a court determines that a pending dispute is appropriate for referral under Section 154.021, the court shall notify the parties of its determination.

(b) Any party may, within 10 days after receiving the notice under Subsection (a), file a written objection to the referral.

(c) If the court finds that there is a reasonable basis for an objection filed under Subsection (b), the court may not refer the dispute under Section 154.021.

§ 154.023. Mediation

(a) Mediation is a forum in which an impartial person, the mediator, facili-tates communication between parties to promote reconciliation, settlement, or understanding among them.

(b) A mediator may not impose his own judgment on the issues for that of the parties.

(c) Mediation includes victim-offender mediation by the Texas Department of Criminal Justice described in Article 56.13, Code of Criminal Procedure.

§ 154.024. Mini-Trial

(a) A mini-trial is conducted under an agreement of the parties.

(b) Each party and counsel for the party present the position of the party, either before selected representatives for each party or before an impartial third party, to define the issues and develop a basis for realistic settlement negotiations.

(c) The impartial third party may issue an advisory opinion regarding the mer-its of the case.

(d) The advisory opinion is not binding on the parties unless the parties agree that it is binding and enter into a written settlement agreement.

§ 154.025. Moderated Settlement Conference

(a) A moderated settlement conference is a forum for case evaluation and real-istic settlement negotiations.

(b) Each party and counsel for the party present the position of the party before a panel of impartial third parties.

(c) The panel may issue an advisory opinion regarding the liability or damages of the parties or both.

(d) The advisory opinion is not binding on the parties.

§ 154.026. Summary Jury Trial

(a) A summary jury trial is a forum for early case evaluation and development of realistic settlement negotiations.

(b) Each party and counsel for the party present the position of the party before a panel of jurors.

(c) The number of jurors on the panel is six unless the parties agree otherwise.

(d) The panel may issue an advisory opinion regarding the liability or damages of the parties or both.

(e) The advisory opinion is not binding on the parties.

§ 154.027. Arbitration

(a) Nonbinding arbitration is a forum in which each party and counsel for the party present the position of the party before an impartial third party, who renders a specific award.

(b) If the parties stipulate in advance, the award is binding and is enforceable in the same manner as any contract obligation. If the parties do not stipulate in advance that the award is binding, the award is not binding and serves only as a basis for the parties' further settlement negotiations.

§ 154.051. Appointment of Impartial Third Parties

(a) If a court refers a pending dispute for resolution by an alternative dispute resolution procedure under Section 154.021, the court may appoint an impartial third party to facilitate the procedure.

(b) The court may appoint a third party who is agreed on by the parties if the person qualifies for appointment under this subchapter.

(c) The court may appoint more than one third party under this section.

§ 154.052. Qualifications of Impartial Third Party

(a) Except as provided by Subsections (b) and (c), to qualify for an appointment as an impartial third party under this subchapter a person must have completed a minimum of 40 classroom hours of training in dispute resolution techniques in a course conducted by an alternative dispute resolution system or other dispute resolution organization approved by the court making the appointment.

(b) To qualify for an appointment as an impartial third party under this subchapter in a dispute relating to the parent-child relationship, a person must complete the training required by Subsection (a) and an additional 24 hours of training in the fields of family dynamics, child development, and family law.

(c) In appropriate circumstances, a court may in its discretion appoint a person as an impartial third party who does not qualify under Subsection (a) or (b) if the court bases its appointment on legal or other professional training or experience in particular dispute resolution processes.

§ 154.053. Standards and Duties of Impartial Third Parties

(a) A person appointed to facilitate an alternative dispute resolution procedure under this subchapter shall encourage and assist the parties in reaching a settlement of their dispute but may not compel or coerce the parties to enter into a settlement agreement.

(b) Unless expressly authorized by the disclosing party, the impartial third party may not disclose to either party information given in confidence by the other and shall at all times maintain confidentiality with respect to communications relating to the subject matter of the dispute.

(c) Unless the parties agree otherwise, all matters, including the conduct and demeanor of the parties and their counsel during the settlement process, are confidential and may never be disclosed to anyone, including the appointing court.

(d) Each participant, including the impartial third party, to an alternative dispute resolution procedure is subject to the requirements of Subchapter B, Chapter 261, Family Code, and Subchapter C, Chapter 48, Human Resources Code.

§ 154.054. Compensation of Impartial Third Parties

(a) The court may set a reasonable fee for the services of an impartial third party appointed under this subchapter.

(b) Unless the parties agree to a method of payment, the court shall tax the fee for the services of an impartial third party as other costs of suit.

§ 154.055. Qualified Immunity of Impartial Third Parties

(a) A person appointed to facilitate an alternative dispute resolution procedure under this subchapter or under Chapter 152 relating to an alternative dispute resolution system established by counties, or appointed by the parties whether before or after the institution of formal judicial proceedings, who is a volunteer and who does not act with wanton and wilful disregard of the rights, safety, or property of another, is immune from civil liability for any act or omission within the course and scope of his or her duties or functions as an impartial third party. For purposes of this section, a volunteer impartial third party is a person who does not receive compensation in excess of reimbursement for expenses incurred or a stipend intended as reimbursement for expenses incurred.

(b) This section neither applies to nor is it intended to enlarge or diminish any rights or immunities enjoyed by an arbitrator participating in a binding arbitration pursuant to any applicable statute or treaty.

§ 154.071. Effect of Written Settlement Agreement

(a) If the parties reach a settlement and execute a written agreement disposing of the dispute, the agreement is enforceable in the same manner as any other written contract.

(b) The court in its discretion may incorporate the terms of the agreement in the court's final decree disposing of the case.

(c) A settlement agreement does not affect an outstanding court order unless the terms of the agreement are incorporated into a subsequent decree.

§ 154.072. Statistical Information on Disputes Referred

The Texas Supreme Court shall determine the need and method for statistical reporting of disputes referred by the courts to alternative dispute resolution procedures.

§ 154.073. Confidentiality of Certain Records And Communications

(a) Except as provided by Subsections (c), (d), (e), and (f), a communication relating to the subject matter of any civil or criminal dispute made by a participant in an alternative dispute resolution procedure, whether before or after the institution of formal judicial proceedings, is confidential, is not subject to disclosure, and may not be used as evidence against the participant in any judicial or administrative proceeding.

(b) Any record made at an alternative dispute resolution procedure is confidential, and the participants or the third party facilitating the procedure may not be required to testify in any proceedings relating to or arising out of the matter in dispute or be subject to process requiring disclosure of confidential information or data relating to or arising out of the matter in dispute.

(c) An oral communication or written material used in or made a part of an alternative dispute resolution procedure is admissible or discoverable if it is admissible or discoverable independent of the procedure.

(d) A final written agreement to which a governmental body is a signatory that is reached as a result of a dispute resolution procedure conducted under this chapter is subject to or excepted from required disclosure in accordance with Chapter 552, Government Code.

(e) If this section conflicts with other legal requirements for disclosure of communications, records, or materials, the issue of confidentiality may be presented to the court having jurisdiction of the proceedings to determine, in camera, whether the facts, circumstances, and context of the communications or materials sought to be disclosed warrant a protective order of the court or whether the communications or materials are subject to disclosure.

(f) This section does not affect the duty to report abuse or neglect under Chapter 261, Family Code, and abuse, exploitation, or neglect under Subchapter C, Chapter 48, Human Resources Code.

(g) This section applies to a victim-offender mediation by the Texas Department of Criminal Justice as described in Article 56.13, Code of Criminal Procedure.

Family Code § 153.0072. Collaborative Law [Child Custody]

(a) On a written agreement of the parties and their attorneys, a suit affecting the parent-child relationship may be conducted under collaborative law procedures.

(b) Collaborative law is a procedure in which the parties and their counsel agree in writing to use their best efforts and make a good faith attempt to resolve the suit affecting the parent-child relationship on an agreed basis without resorting to judicial intervention except to have the court approve the settlement agreement, make the legal pronouncements, and sign the orders required by law to effectuate the agreement of the parties as the court determines appropriate. The parties' counsel may not serve as litigation counsel except to ask the court to approve the settlement agreement.

(c) A collaborative law agreement must include provisions for:

   (1) full and candid exchange of information between the parties and their attorneys as necessary to make a proper evaluation of the case;

   (2) suspending court intervention in the dispute while the parties are using collaborative law procedures;

   (3) hiring experts, as jointly agreed, to be used in the procedure;

   (4) withdrawal of all counsel involved in the collaborative law procedure if the collaborative law procedure does not result in settlement of the dispute; and

   (5) other provisions as agreed to by the parties consistent with a good faith effort to collaboratively settle the matter.

(d) Notwithstanding Rule 11, Texas Rules of Civil Procedure, or another rule or law, a party is entitled to judgment on a collaborative law settlement agreement if the agreement: (1) provides, in a prominently displayed statement that is boldfaced, capitalized, or under-lined, that the agreement is not subject to revocation; and

   (2) is signed by each party to the agreement and the attorney of each party.

(e) Subject to Subsection (g), a court that is notified 30 days before trial that the parties are using collaborative law procedures to attempt to settle a dispute may not, until a party notifies the court that the collaborative law procedures did not result in a settlement:

   (1) set a hearing or trial in the case;

   (2) impose discovery deadlines;

   (3) require compliance with scheduling orders; or

   (4) dismiss the case.

(f) The parties shall notify the court if the collaborative law procedures result in a settlement. If they do not, the parties shall file:

(1) a status report with the court not later than the 180th day after the date of the written agreement to use the procedures; and

(2) a status report on or before the first anniversary of the date of the written agreement to use the procedures, accompanied by a motion for continuance that the court shall grant if the status report indicates the desire of the parties to continue to use collaborative law procedures.

(g) If the collaborative law procedures do not result in a settlement on or before the second anniversary of the date that the suit was filed, the court may (1) set the suit for trial on the regular docket; or (2) dismiss the suit without prejudice.

(h) The provisions for confidentiality of alternative dispute resolution procedures as provided in Chapter 154 apply equally to collaborative law procedures under this section.

Identical Provision in Family Code § 6.603. Collaborative Law [Dissolution of Marriage]

Local Government Code § 143.135. Mediation

(a) In this section, "mediation" has the meaning assigned by Section 154.023, Civil Practice and Remedies Code.

(b) The head of the police department may develop and implement an alternative dispute resolution program to refer certain disputes regarding police officers to mediation.

(c) If a dispute is referred to mediation under this section, the time limitations and deadlines under [enumerated sections] are tolled until the earliest of:

(1) the date the parties reach a settlement and execute a written agreement disposing of the dispute;

(2) the date the mediator refers the dispute to another appeals or grievance procedure under this subchapter; or

(3) the 60th day after the date the dispute was referred to mediation.

(d) The conduct and demeanor of the mediator and the parties to the dispute during the course of the mediation are confidential. A letter, memorandum, document, note, or other oral or written communication that is relevant to the dispute and made between the mediator and the parties to the dispute or between the parties to the dispute during the course of the mediation procedure:

(1) is confidential and may not be disclosed unless all of the parties to the mediation agree to the disclosure in writing; and

(2) is admissible and discoverable in a separate proceeding only if the letter, memorandum, document, note, or other communication is admissible and discoverable independent of the mediation.

(e) A mediator may not be required to testify in a proceeding concerning information relating to or arising out of the mediation.

(f) Subsection (d) does not apply to a final written agreement to which the police department or municipality is a signatory that is reached as a result of a mediation procedure conducted under this section. Information in the final written agreement is subject to required disclosure, is excepted from required disclosure, or is confidential [under] Chapter 552, Government Code, and other law.

(g) If this section conflicts with other legal requirements for disclosure of communications or materials, the issue of confidentiality may be presented to a district court for a judicial district in which the majority of the territory of the municipality is located to determine, in camera, whether the facts, circumstances, and context of the communications or materials sought to be disclosed warrant a protective order of the court or whether the communications or materials are subject to disclosure.

(h) Except to the extent of any conflict with this section, Chapter 154, Civil Practice and Remedies Code, and police department rules apply to a mediation conducted under this section.

(i) Except to the extent of any conflict with this section, Section 2009.054, Government Code, applies to the communications, records, conduct, and demeanor of the mediator and the parties.

(j) Section 143.1014 does not apply to a meeting or hearing conducted under this section.

Government Code § 2009.051. Development and Use of Procedures

(a) Each governmental body may develop and use alternative dispute resolution procedures. Alternative dispute resolution procedures developed and used by a governmental body must be consistent with Chapter 154, Civil Practice and Remedies Code.

(b) Alternative dispute resolution procedures developed and used by a state agency also must be consistent with the administrative procedure law, Chapter 2001. The State Office of Administrative Hearings may issue model guidelines for the use of alternative dispute resolution procedures by state agencies.

(c) If a state agency that is subject to Chapter 2001 adopts an alternative dispute resolution procedure, it may do so by rule.

INDEX

[References are page numbers.]

A

ADMINISTRATIVE DISPUTE RESOLU-TION ACTS
Executive branch use of ADR . . . 548

AGENCY THEORY
Generally . . . 99
Mediators as business deal makers . . . 422

ALCOHOL
Negotiations, effects of alcohol on . . . 170

AMERICAN ARBITRATION ASSOCIA-TION
Commercial Mediation Procedures, text of . . . A-14
Mediator standards of conduct . . . 722
Model Standards of Conduct for Mediators, text of . . . A-8

AMERICAN BAR ASSOCIATION
Ethics Opinion 06-347 . . . 276
Mediator standards of conduct . . . 722
Model Standards of Conduct for Mediators, text of . . . A-8
Ombuds offices, standards for . . . 523

ARBITRATION
Generally . . . 496
American Arbitration Association (See AMERI-CAN ARBITRATION ASSOCIATION)
Awards, judicial review of . . . 509
Commercial arbitration . . . 501
Court connected arbitration, non-binding . . . 460
Federal Arbitration Act . . . 503
Judicial review of awards . . . 509
Labor-Management Arbitration Act . . . 506
Mediation (See MEDIATION)
Negotiation (See NEGOTIATION)
Process overview . . . 507
Supreme Court view of arbitration . . . 512
Taxpayer disputes . . . 573
Uniform Arbitration Acts . . . 504

ASSOCIATION OF CONFLICT RESOLU-TION
Mediator standards of conduct . . . 722
Model Standards of Conduct for Mediators, text of . . . A-8

ATTORNEYS
American Bar Association (See AMERICAN BAR ASSOCIATION)
Collaborative law, professional responsibilities issues associated with . . . 518

ATTORNEYS—Cont.
Communications with clients, effective . . . 48
Consultants in conflict management . . 760
Cooperation and conflict between attorneys . . . 100
Mediation advocacy
    Generally . . . 303; 367
    Common errors . . . 316
Plea bargaining . . . 238
Professional responsibilities issues associated with collaborative law . . . 518

AVOIDING DISPUTES (See CONFLICT MANAGEMENT)

B

BARGAINING (See NEGOTIATION)

BID PROTEST SYSTEMS
Conflict management . . . 780

BIOETHICS
Mediation . . . 385

C

CHEYENNE WAY, THE
Excerpt . . . 118

CHILD ABUSE
Mediator duty to report . . . 745

COAST GUARD
Conflict management system . . . 788

COGNITIVE DISSONANCE THEORY
Generally . . . 93

COLLABORATIVE LAW
Generally . . . 112; 516
Professional responsibility issues . . . 518

COLLECTIONS
Negotiation application . . . 222

COMMERCIAL MEDIATION PROCE-DURES, AMERICAN ARBITRATION ASSOCIATION
Text . . . A-14

COMMERCIAL TRANSACTIONS
Arbitration . . . 501
Construction industry
    Dispute review boards . . . 529
    Partnering . . . 529
Negotiation application . . . 222

I–1

[References are page numbers.]

EXECUTIVE BRANCH

Generally . . . 547

Administrative Dispute Resolution Acts . . . 548

Bid protest processes . . . 780

Coast Guard ADR system . . . 788

Farmer-lender mediation program . . . 563

Federal Tort Claims Act, administrative claims under . . . 559

Internal Revenue Service resolution of taxpayer disputes . . . 573

Justice Department use of ADR . . . 551

Procurement systems . . . 780

Rulemaking . . . 582

F

FARMER-LENDER MEDIATION PROGRAM

Generally . . . 563

FEDERAL ARBITRATION ACT

Generally . . . 503

FEDERAL TORT CLAIMS ACT

Administrative claims process . . . 559

G

GENDER

Negotiation differences between genders, research on . . . 69

Women as negotiators . . . 67

GEORGIA-PACIFIC

ADR program, review of . . . 25

GOOD FAITH

Mediation, good faith participation in 384

Uniform Mediation Act, reports under 343

H

HEALTH CARE

Conflict management . . . 796

Mediation . . . 385

I

INTERNAL REVENUE SERVICE

Resolution of taxpayer disputes . . . 573

INTERNATIONAL PERSPECTIVES (See TRANS-NATIONAL PERSPECTIVES)

J

JAPAN

Negotiating in Japan . . . 205

JUSTICE DEPARTMENT

Use of ADR . . . 551

K

KOREA

Comparison of American and Korean mediation processes . . . 197

L

LABOR-MANAGEMENT ARBITRATION ACT

Generally . . . 506

LEGISLATIVE BODIES

Negotiation application . . . 231

M

MEDIATION

Generally . . . 281; 335; 385

Appellate mediation . . . 481

Arbitration (See ARBITRATION)

Attorney advocacy

    Generally . . . 303; 367

    Common errors . . . 316

Bioethics . . . 385

Collaborative law . . . 112; 516

Commercial Mediation Procedures, text of American Arbitration Association . . A-14

Confidentiality issues . . . 342

Differing views . . . 322

Ethical considerations . . . 256; 385

Farmer-Lender Mediation Program . . . 563

Good faith

    Participation . . . 384

    Uniform Mediation Act, reports under . . . 343

Health care . . . 385

Korean processes compared with American processes . . . 197

Litigation regarding mediation . . . 336

Mediators (See MEDIATORS AND OTHER ADR PRACTITIONERS)

Medical disputes . . . 385

Negotiation (See NEGOTIATION)

Online dispute resolution (See ONLINE DISPUTE RESOLUTION)

Practice . . . 302

Process for dispute resolution . . . 4

Restorative justice . . . 408

Taxpayer disputes . . . 573

[References are page numbers.]

[References are page numbers.]